KOREA

ITS LAND, PEOPLE AND CULTURE OF ALL AGES

KOREA

ITS LAND, PEOPLE AND CULTURE OF ALL AGES

To Faculty & student of Pennsylvania Military College with my best wishes many many Compliments

From Louise Yim

HAKWON-SA, LTD.
SEOUL, KOREA

May 21, 1965

COPYRIGHT, 1960
BY
HAKWON-SA LTD.

PRINTED IN KOREA

Preface

"Korea, Its Land, People and Culture of All Ages," is an attempt to fill what we believe to be an urgently needed gap in foreign understanding for our country.

Numerous books have been written about Korea since the nineteenth century only to disappear quickly into the realms of obscurity. That was only to be expected for the subject, Korea, lends itself to obscurity and the result is that, apart from the particular scholar, the general foreign reader remains very poorly informed.

Yet the need for understanding Korea is universally felt for the country has always stood at the crossroads in the destinies of her neighbors who today are worldwide. Quite emphatically, the issue of war or peace for them has often hinged on Korea. Its importance is inversely proportional to its neglect.

It is in the hopes of contributing, however meagerly, to a reversal of this proportion that we offer this book. For layman or scholar alike, this attempt to present a complete picture of Korea in a single tome should prove both useful and convenient.

Finally, we would like to express our deepest gratitude to all the qualified and authoritative scholars who so kindly supported our project. We must also thank the many translators without whose cooperation the project would have been impossible. Our debt is also acknowledged to the many friends and supporters who gave us the benefit of their help and advice.

March 1960

Introduction;
Towards True Understanding of Korea

Understanding Korean culture may best be realized through appropriate comprehension of Korean society, its people, and their cultural heritage. The Korean people's sphere of activities is presently confined to a small peninsula on the Asiatic continent south of the Yalu and Tumen Rivers. Considered in terms of the entire history of the Korean people, however, it has been but a recent latter-day affair. As far as our present knowledge goes pending further study, the Korean people's sphere of activities once covered Shantung and Shansi Provinces in China and almost the entire territory of Manchuria. By the time of the Three Kingdoms period, the stage was extended to the Chekang Province in China and the Japanese islands. Since the unification of the country into a single state by Silla, however, the Korean people have been more or less confined to the Korean peninsula. This later led to limitations in the mentality of the Korean people and their society.

While they were scattered over the Shantung and Shansi Provinces of China and Manchuria during the ancient times, the Korean people consolidated themselves into the Three Kingdoms of Koguryo, Paekche and Silla by the dawn of the first century. During that time, the highly developed culture of China was embraced.

In the meantime, Korean culture had come to incorporate within itself the cultures not only of China and various tribes of northeast Asia but also of many other tribes living west of the Chinese mainland. The Buddhist culture had been incorporated into the Korean mostly through China via the Mahayana or Northern Buddhism, true as it is that the Theravada or Southern Buddhism was also transmitted by a few Buddhist monks of the Paekche and Silla kingdoms through direct contacts with India. Thus the philosophy of Buddhism presented itself as an entirely new world of thoughts to the Korean people, mostly through Chinese characters. By the end of the Silla period, therefore, Chinese Buddhist culture became stamped in Korea, so much so that it come to be identified as the whole of Korean culture. Nevertheless, there remained the unique, traditional Korean culture of a primitive Altaic origin. Thus the ancient culture of Korea during the Three Kingdoms period as we know it today is a harmonious synthesis of the two. The eminent Buddhist monk, Wonhyo, of the Silla kingdom, for instance, is notable for the nuances of this thought, exhibiting an overall harmony between the traditional Korean, on the one hand, and the philosophies of Buddhism and Confucianism on the other.

Such a fully-developed culture lent itself readily to the national conscience during the Koryo period. True most of the time and energy of Koryo was spent to repulse alien invaders from the north. But the people succeeded in developing a Buddhist world of their own, as evidenced by the publication of the mammoth *Tripitaka Koreana* and exposition of a unique form of Buddhism in the establishment of the Chontae Sect.

However, by the time this cultural heritage was transmitted to the Yi dynasty the national integrity, it became distorted beyond recognition by the neo-Confucian scholars, whose thinking was geared to the Chinese in complete disregard of the national conscience of their own country. Such a trend gained further force during the late Yi dynastic period among certain segments of the leading class and conservatives, but it was by no means a universal phenomenon. In fact, poignant criticism was directed against such negation of national integrity by some other segment of the people. It is indeed they who transmitted down to present-day Korea the unique, cultural heritage of Korea.

Such being the case, it is essential, if Korean culture is to be properly understood, to cleanse oneself of the superficial view that it is but a part of Chinese culture. Such a false conception has been developed partly by some Koreans themselves and partly by the Japanese since the middle of the 19th century for political motives. The time has come even for foreigners to revise such a misleading conception about Korea.

As one of the Altaic tribes the Korean people have a recorded history of their own dating back to more than 2,000 years, with the unwritten history going back still further as advanced by the language and composition of society.

Starting from the world of mythology, the Korean people first embraced Buddhism, then Confucianism and later Christianity with all cultural attributes of each religion. Since the second half of the 19th century, Protestantism has also been accepted. While Korea was struggling to adopt the Western capitalistic civilization at the close of the last century, it fell prey to Japan. Having been subject to the relentless pressure and exploitation of Japanese capitalism as a colony, Korea, then, had to go through a period of stagnation during the first half of the 20th century. Deprived of all liberties by the Japanese, the Korean people, during the period, had to stand still, retaining feudal conservatism. Nevertheless, the traditional spirit of the Korean people — the spirit of resistance, *esprit de corps*, the power of assimilating what is alien into their own reality and tradition — provided a solid ground for future development of the Korean culture.

Comprehension and exposition of contemporary Korean culture has to begin with studies made since August 15, 1945, when Korea shook off the shackles of Japanese imperialism. The tempo and magnitude of this has been unprecedented, but much still remains to be done so that past studies may come into full light, and the distortions therein corrected.

Lucid light is certain to shine upon Korea as she has been and is when — only when — Korean culture is studied as an independent subject, instead of viewing it as a subordinate part of other cultures. Also important for a proper understanding of Korea is correct comprehension of her past history with all of the conditions the historical realities have imposed upon the people.

As economic conditions improve, the full story of Korea — of her people, culture and society — will surely present itself to the world in its true light.

This book, then, is an attempt to present Korean culture in its true form as the first step of its kind ever undertaken.

Explanatory Guide

1. Romanizations are based on the McCune-Reisschauer system. Diacritical and other marks provided under the system to differentiate the Korean pronunciation of identical letters have been dispensed with.
2. Exceptions are:
    a) Chosun, Seoul, spelled contrary to the system by reason for precedents we may consider as absolutely established.
    b) Personal names wherever personal preference has come to our attention or established usage compels observance: viz—Syngman Rhee or Chough Pyongok in the first case; Chung Ilkwon or Lee Ki-poong in the second.
    c) Institutional names wherever an established form has been brought to our attention: Yonsei University, Sukmyong University.
3. Credits are to be found listed on the following five pages.
4. The foreign reader should note that whenever an individual's age is mentioned, it has been computed on the basis of one year upon birth with subsequent additions every New Year's Day rather than on the individual's birthday as in the West. He should also remember that given dates in the historical period, i.e. before the 20th century, follow the lunar calendar.
5. As an independent project, contents of this book do not necessarily reflect the views of the government of the Republic of Korea.

CONTRIBUTORS TO "KOREA" MANUSCRIPTS

Articles	Contributors	Positions
Geography		
General preview	Yi Chiho	Associate Professor, College of Education, S.N.U.*
Rural communities and urban cities		
Topography, Climate, Soil	Kang Soko	Professor, Ehwa Women's University
Geographical distribution of plants and animals	Kang Yongson	Professor, College of Liberal Arts, S.N.U.
History		
Preface	Hong Isop	Professor, Yonsei University
Primitive culture and the beginning of the tribal states	Kim Choljun	Assistant Professor, Yonsei University
The Three Kingdoms: Their formation, development and culture		
Culture of Unified Silla		
Koryo dynasty	Pyon Taesop	Assistant Professor, College of Education, S.N.U.
Yi Chosun—before Hideyoshi	Kim Yongdok	Assistant Professor, Chungang University
Yi Chosun—after Hideyoshi		
Opening of Yi Chosun	Cho Chawho	Professor, Tongguk University
The modern period	Hong Isop	Professor, Yonsei University

*Seoul National University

Articles	Contributors	Positions
People, Language		
People	Kim Kisu	Associate Professor, Kukhak College
Language	Kim Hyonggyu	Professor, Collge of Education, S.N.U.
Politics, Laws		
Politics	Sin Hyongyong	Chief Librarian, Library of National Assembly
Laws	Hwang Sandok	Professor, College of Law, S.N.U.
International Relations and Diplomacy		
An outline of Korean diplomacy	Sin Kisok	Professor, Kyonghui University
Foreign relations of the Republic of Korea.		
United Nations and Korea		
Overseas Korean residents		
Cultural exchanges	Hong Isop	Professor, Yonsei University
Study of Korea by Westerners		
National Defence		
Background	Kim Songgyun	Associate Professor, Kyonghui University
Army	Kim Pyongyul	Colonel, Director of Public Information, ROK Army Headquarters
Navy	Kim Chonggi	Captain, Staff of Information, ROK Navy
Marine Corps	Kim Tukchu	Commandar, Staff of Public Information, ROK Marine Corps
Air Force	So Sangyong	Colonel, Staff of Public Information, ROK Air Force
Finance, Economy		
Outline of Korean finance	Kim Myongyun	Assistant Professor, Korea University
National public finance	Mun Pyongjip	Associate Professor, Chungang University
Local public finance		
Tax system	Kim Yonggap	Assistant Professor, College of Commerce, S.N.U.
An outline of Korean economy under Japanese rule	Choe Hojin	Professor, Chungang University
Financial status	Yi Chonghwan	Professor, Yonsei University
Foreign trade		
Securities exchange	Choe Ilhwan	Assistant Professor, Chungang University
Commodity prices	Yi Chongjae	Assistant Professor, Chungang University
National income		
Foreign Aid	Yi Sanggu	Associate Professor, College of Commerce, S.N.U.

Articles	Contributors	Positions
Public enterprises	Tak Huijun	Associate Professor, Chungang University
Industries		
Outline of Korean industry	So Chindok	Associate Professor, Chungang University
Utilization of Land		
Agriculture		
Manufacturing industries		
Mining industry		
Government Monopoly		
Forestry	Kim Tongsop	Professor, Tongguk University
Fishery	Song Chongguk	Professor, Chungang University
Transportation and Communications		
Transportation	Choe Songsil	Secretary-General, Ministry of Transportation
Communications	Cho Ungchon	Vice Minister of Communications
Social Problem	Tak Huijun	Associate Professor, Chungang University
Health Problems	Song Hyongnae	Secretary-General, Taehan Public Health Association
	No Tonghui	Associate Professor, Tongyang Chinese Herb Medicine College
Thoughts and Religions		
General remarks on Korean thought	Hong Isop	Professor, Yonsei University
Modern Korean thought		
Confucianism in Korea	Kim Chongguk	Professor, Songgyungwan University
Korean Buddhism	Cho Myonggi	Professor, Tongguk University
Christianity in Korea	Yi Mungun	Father, Chongyon Catholic Church
	Pyon Honggyu	Pastor, Namsan Methodist Church
The Tonghak movement	O Ikche	Secretary-General, Head Office of Chondogyo
Taejonggyo	Hyon Sidong	Secretary-General, Head Office of Taejonggyo
Shamanism and Aberrations	Yi Sangbaek	Professor, College of Liberal Arts, S.N.U.
Education	Im Hanyong	Professor, Yonsei University
Mass Communications, Publication and Printing		
Newspapers and the press	Choe Chun	Associate Professor, Hongik College
Broadcasting service	Pyon Simin	Director, Bureau of Culture, Ministry of Education
Printing and publication in ancient Korea	Yu Hongyol	Professor, College of Liberal Arts, S.N.U.
Book publication	Kim Changjip	Former Chairman, Korean Publishers' Association

Articles	Contributors	Positions
Magazines	Kim Myongyop	President, Yowon-sa, Ltd., Monthly Magazine for women
Printing industry of Korea	An Huirim	Chief editor, Munhwa Printing Industry Review, weekly
Social Science		
Outline, Economics	Choe Hojin	Professor, Chungang University
Philosophy Logic	Pak Chonghong	Professor, College of Liberal Arts, S.N.U.
Ethics	Choe Chehui	Professor, College of Liberal Arts, S.N.U.
Sociology	Yi Sangbaek	Professor, College of Liberal Arts, S.N.U.
Psychology	Yi Chinsuk	Professor, College of Leberal Arts, S.N.U.
History	Chon Haejong	Associate Professor, College of Liberal Arts, S.N.U.
Archaeology	Kim Wonyong	Chief, Research Section, National Museum
Folklore	Im Tonggwon	Associate Professor, Sorabol Art College
Geography	Yuk Chisu	Professor, College of Liberal Arts, S.N.U.
Education	Im Hanyong	Professor, Yonsei University
Legal science	Hwang Sandok	Professor, College of Law, S.N.U.
Political science	Sin Tosong	Former Professor, College of Law, S.N.U.
Linguistics	Yi Sungnyong	Professor, College of Liberal Arts, S.N.U.
Korean linguistics and literature	Yi Pyongju	Associate Professor, College of Education, S.N.U.
Foreign literature	Yi Hayun	Professor, College of Education, S.N.U.
Natural Science		
Preface	Hong Isop	Professor, Yonsei University
Mathematics	Choe Yunsik	Professor, College of Liberal Arts, S.N.U.
Physics	Kwon Yongdae	Professor, College of Liberal Arts, S.N.U.
Chemistry	Hong Munhwa	Associate Professor, College of Pharmacology, S.N.U.
Dietetics	Ho Ryong	Director, Chemical Laboratory Center
Western medicine	Ku Kukhoe	Professor, Sudo Medical College
Chinese herb medicine	No Tonghui	Associate Professor, Tongyang Chinese Herb Medical College
Pharmacology	Ha Kudong	Professor, College of Pharmacology, S.N.U.

Articles	Contributors	Positions
Astronomy	Yi Wonchol	Director, National Observatory Center
Meteorology	Kim Songsam	Chief, Statistical Research Section, National Observatory Center
Geology	Son Chimu	Associate Professor, College of Liberal Arts, S.N.U.
Agronomy	Hong Kichang	Professor, Korea University
Fishery	Chong Mungi	Director, Central Marine Product Laboratory, Office of Marine Affairs
Literature		
An Outline of Korean literature, its heritage, Modern literature: Poetry	Yi Hyongu	Professor, Ehwa Women's University
Classic Literature	Cho Yunje / Yi Myonggu	Professor, Songgyungwan University / Professor, Songgyungwan University
The history of modern Korean literature	Paek Chol	Professor, Chungang University
Modern literature: The novel	Cho Yonhyon	Lecturer, Tongguk University
Literary criticism		
The essay	Yun Wonho	Associate Professor, Ehwa Women's University
Stage play	Kim Chinsu	Professor, Kyonghui University
Screen play		
Literature for children	Yun Sokchung	Chairman, Saessak (sprout) Society
Fine Arts		
General introduction to Korean art	Kim Wonyong	Chief, Research Section, National Museum
Korean painting	Yi Kyongsong	Assistant Professor, Ehwa Women's University
Handicrafts	Choe Sunu	Chief, Supply Section, National Museum
Sculpture		
Architecture	Yun Mubyong	Secretary of Art and Science, National Museum
Calligraphy	Pae Kilgi	Professor Tongguk University
Photography	Im Ungsik	Lecturer, College of Arts, S.N.U.
Dance, Music		
Dance	Cho Tonghwa	Dance Critic
Music	Yi Hyegu	Professor, College of Music, S.N.U.
Drama, Motion picture		
Drama	Kim Okkyong / Choe Sangsu	Lecturer, Sukmyong Women's University / Chairman, Korean Folklore Association
Motion picture	Kim Sodong	Chairman, Korean Film Directors' Association

9

Articles	Contributors	Positions
Historical Remains	Kim Wonnyong	Chief, Research Section, National Museum
	Yun Mubyong	Secretary of Art and Science, National Museum
	Hwang Suyong	Member, Committee of Preservation for National Treasures, Historical Remains, and Natural Monuments, Ministry of Education
Manners and Customs 　Outline 　Food 　Home and social life 　Name and the calendar 　Annuals observances and holidays 　Riddles, Folksongs 　Myths, legends, and folktales	Im Tonggwon	Associate Professor, Sorabol Art College
Clothing and costumes	Kim Tonguk	Assistant Professor, Chungang University
Dwelling	Chu Won	Acting Chairman, Economic Development Council
Marriage and funerals	Yu Chongyol	Lecturer, Kukhak College
Proverbs	Kim Sayop	Professor, Kyongbuk National University
Fortune-tellng 　Shamanism 　Shamans, gods, and evil spirits	Chang Chugun	Member, Korean Culture and Anthropology Society
Sports	Yi Pyongui	Professor, College of Education, S.N.U.
Games and Recreation 　Preface	Cho Pungyon	Member of Planning Committee, "Hanguk Ilbo" daily
Traditional games in Korea	Yi Pyongui	Professor, College of Education, S.N.U.
	Im Tonggwon	Associate Professor, Sorabol Art College
Korean games in modern days	So Sangdok	Member of Editorial Staff, Tonghwa News Agency
Tourism	Kim Sejun	Chief, Tourist Section, Ministry of Transportation
	Kum Chol	Managing Director, Korea Tourist Bureau

Photos and other illustrations in this work should be credited, on one hand, to Mr. Chong Toson, the photographer, and, on the other, to the various cultural organizations contacted by the Hakwon-sa.

CONTENTS

Preface
Introduction; Towards True Understanding of Korea III
Explanatory Guide.. V
Contents XI

I Geography 1
   General Preview 1
      Dimensions 1
      Description.. 1
   Topography 2
      Mountains 2
      Plains 4
      Coast lines and islands.. 5
      Rivers and streams 7
   Climate 9
      Geographical factors and climate 9
      Climate and seasons.. 9
      Rainfall.. 9
      Climatic zones 10
   Soil.. 11
      Character of soil 11
      Soil and climate 11
      Type of soil 11
   Rural Communities and Urban Cities 12
      Villages.. 12
      Cities.. 13
   Geographical Distribution of Plants and Animals.. 15
      Distribution of plants 15
      Plants specially designated for protection.. 15
      Distribution of animals.. 15
      Animals specially designated for protection 16

II History.. 17
   Preface.. 17
      Ancient outlook 17
      Modern outlook 18
   Primitive Culture and the Beginning of the Tribal States 20
      Neolithic culture.. 20
      Metal culture 21
      Lolang and the tribal states 22
   The Three Kingdoms: Their Formation,
      Development and Culture.. 23
      From conflicts to unity.. 23
      Social structure 24
      Cultures.. 25

Culture of Unified Silla	26
Silla and Pohai	26
Decline of Silla	27
Koryo Dynasty	28
Characteristics of the Koryo dynasty	28
Establishment of the Koryo kingdom	29
Rise of the aristocracy	31
Buddhism comes to its own	32
Koryo's foreign relations	33
The military revolt	35
After the revolt	36
The Mongol invasion	36
Mongol domination	37
Decline of Koryo	38
Yi Chosun—Before Hideyoshi	40
Significance of the Yi emergence	40
Institutions of early Chosun	43
Strengthening the centralized state	45
Relations with foreign nations	46
Power struggle and party strife	46
The Hideyoshi invasions	48
Yi Chosun—After Hideyoshi	51
Effects of the Hideyoshi Wars	51
The Manchu invasions	51
Intensification of the factional strifes	53
Corruption, decline of power classes	54
The Yongjo-Chongjo era (1775-1801)	56
Growth of Silhak	60
Catholic conversions and state oppression	63
Despotic rule and peasant uprisings	65
Taewongun's regency and Western challenge	69
Opening of Yi Chosun (1875-1910)	72
Opening of Chosun	72
An army revolt and political changes	74
Western entries and Japanese expansion	76
The Tonghak rebellion	77
Sino-Japanese War, Kabo reforms	79
After the Sino-Japanese War	80
Russo-Japanese War	82
Japanese moves and Korean resistance	84
The Modern Period (1910-1945)	90
Definitions	90
The stage	90
Resistances	91
Suppressions	92
Land exploitation	92
The Samil movement	93
Farmers' plight	94
Japanese capital	95

	War on culture	96
	Japanese research	96
	Resistances of '29	97
	Closing years	98
	The Post-Liberation Period (1945-1959)	99
	A cardinal point	99
	Background	99
	Divergent courses	100
	War and truce	101
	Trend of politics	101
	Land reform	102
	Industries	102
	Foreign aid	102
	Basic problem	103
III	People, Language	104
	People	104
	Introduction	104
	Distribution and density of population	104
	Physical characteristics of the Korean race	105
	Further pursuit of Korean origins	106
	Formation of the Korean race	107
	Original natives on the Korean peninsula	109
	Primitive culture of ancient Koreans	110
	Agricultural life of primitive Koreans	111
	Traditions of Korean culture	112
	Language	114
	Introduction	114
	History	114
	Southern ancestry	116
	Origin	117
	Characteristics	118
	The Hangul alphabet	119
	History of Hangul	120
	Attributes	121
	Morphology	122
	Conclusion	123
VI	Politics, Laws	125
	History of Political Institutions	125
	Consultative Organs	125
	Judiciary organs	126
	Government organization	127
	Police system	128
	Fire-fighting	129
	Political Parties in Korea	130
	1945-1948	130
	Constituent Assembly	131
	Second-term National Assembly	131

  Third-term Assembly 132
  Present 133
 Election 133
  Presidential election 133
  Assembly elections 134
  Summary of present election laws 135
 Legislature 137
  Development of modern parliamentary system in Korea 137
  Constitutional amendments 137
  Summary of present parliamentary system 138
 Judicial Organization 140
  General introduction 140
  Organization of court 140
  Justices and judges 141
  Right of court to review law 142
 Government Organization 142
  Central Government organization 142
  Local Government organization 143
  Local autonomous organs 144
 Police and Fire-Fighting 144
 Decorations 145
  Orders 145
  Medals for merit 146
  Service medals 146
 Brief History of Korean Laws 146
  Unwritten 146
  Written 147
  Yi dynastic laws 148
  Japanese laws 149
  Current laws 150

V International Relations and Diplomacy 151
 An Outline of Korean Diplomacy 151
  Diplomacy before opening of the country 151
  Opening of the country 152
  Diplomacy after opening of the country 155
 Foreign Relations of the Republic of Korea 160
  Relations with the United States 160
  Relations with Britain 164
  Relations with France 165
  Relations with West Germany 165
  Relations with Italy 166
  Relations with Vietnam 166
  Relations with Philippines 166
  Relations with Nationalist China 167
  Relations with Turkey 168
  Relations with Japan 168
  Relations with Thailand, other Southeast Asian countries 173
  Relations with Australia and New Zealand 173

	Relations with other countries	174
	Korean missions abroad	176
	The United Nations and Korea	177
	Elections in the south	177
	War from the north	178
	Red China's entry	179
	Armistice negotiations, problem of unity	180
	Geneva political conference	182
	Efforts for U.N. membership	184
	Membership in U.N. agencies	185
	Overseas Korean Residents	187
	Majority in Japan	187
	Repatriation problem	188
	Cultural Exchanges	188
	Introduction—Formation of Korean culture	188
	Contacts with Chinese culture	189
	Pre-Modernization contacts with Japan	189
	Contacts with Western culture	190
	Contacts with Protestants	190
	Contacts with modern Western culture	190
	After World War II	191
	Study of Korea by Westerners	191
	Early studies	191
	Recent studies	193
	Contemporary studies	196
VI	National Defence	197
	Background	197
	Three Kingdoms period (37 B.C. to A.D. 668)	197
	Unified Silla (669-935)	197
	Koryo (936-1391)	197
	Yi dynasty (1392-1910)	198
	Seapower	199
	Army	199
	Before the war	199
	War	201
	After the war	203
	Navy	203
	The fledgling navy	203
	War	204
	After the armistice	204
	Marine Corps	205
	Air Force	206
	The early days	206
	War	207
	Post-war period	207
VII	Finance, Economy	208
	Outline of Korean Finance	208

15

Summary	208
Characteristics of Korean finance	209
National Public Finance	210
Summary	210
F.Y. 1950	211
F.Y. 1951	212
F.Y. 1952	212
F.Y. 1953	213
F.Y. 1954	213
F.Y. 1955	213
F.Y. 1956	213
F.Y. 1957	214
F.Y. 1958	214
Local Public Finance	214
Introduction	214
Tax System	215
Introduction	215
Kind of taxes	215
Tax structure	216
Local share of taxes	217
An Outline of Korean Economy under Japanese Rule	218
Exploitation before the Samil	218
Exploitation after the Samil	219
Korea and the Japanese war effort	219
Financial Status	220
Outline of financial status	220
Revision of fiscal year	221
Recent financial status in Korea	221
Securities Exchange	223
Establishment of Korea securities exchange	223
First year's achievements (April 1956 - March 1957)	223
Second year's achievements (April 1957 - March 1958)	223
Third year's achievements (April 1958 - March 1959)	224
Fourth year's achievements (April 1959-)	224
Commodity Prices	226
Commodity price index in Korea	226
Commodity price trends	226
Commodity price trends since attainment of economic stabilization	226
Economic trends following June 15th measures	227
Foreign Trade	227
Resume of foreign trade in Korea	227
Foreign trade policy	228
Foreign Aid	229
Summary of foreign aid	229
Utilization of American economic aid	229
Utilization of U.N. economic aid	231
Results of foreign economic aid	231
Public Enterprises	231

	Introduction	231
	Monopoly enterprises	231
	Korea coal corporation	232
	Electric enterprises	232
	National Income	233
	Estimates of national income	233
	Changes in national income	233
	Analysis of national income	234
VIII	Industries	237
	Outline of Korean Industry	237
	Quality replacing quantity	237
	Trend in industries	238
	Utilization of Land	239
	Farm land	239
	Pasture	239
	Forests	240
	Natural Resources	241
	Coal	241
	Other underground resources	241
	Electric power	242
	Agriculture	243
	Farm households	243
	Improvement of farm land and land reform programs	244
	Fertilizers and farm implements	245
	Agricultural products	246
	Agricultural financing and farmers' cooperatives	248
	Forestry	248
	Outline	248
	Supply and requirements	249
	Forestration	249
	Erosion control	249
	Forest association	250
	Research and education	250
	Unique forest products	250
	Manufacturing Industries	250
	Trend of manufacturing industries	250
	Government policy for manufacturing industries	251
	Conditions in each manufacturing industry	251
	Mining Industry	254
	Mining production	254
	Government policy toward the mining industry	258
	Fishery	258
	Outline	258
	Fishery products processing industry	259
	Exports of fishery products	259
	Facilities of the fishery industry	259
	Production of fishery	260
	Finance and foreign aid	261

	Problems of Korea's fishery	261
	Government Monopoly	262
	Tobacco	262
	Salt	263
	Korean ginseng	263
IX	Transportation and Communications	264
	Transportation	264
	General survey	264
	Railroad transportation	265
	Railroads at work	266
	Construction project	267
	Highway transportation	268
	Sea transportation	269
	Air transportation	271
	Communications	271
	Telecommunication service	271
	Mail service	274
	Conclusion	276
X	Social Problems	277
	General View	277
	Study in contrasts	277
	The urgent problems	278
	Social Security	280
	For urbanites	280
	Population	280
	Abnormal rates	280
	Back to normalcy	281
	Labor Problem	283
	Characteristics	283
	Wages, etc.	284
	Trade unions	285
	Labor acts	287
	Accidents	287
	Rates and curves	289
	Unemployment Problem	289
	Characteristics	289
	Statistical review	290
	An incomplete problem	291
	Measures	292
	The Woman's Question	292
	Law and tradition	292
	Labor conditions	293
	Juvenile Problem	295
	Child labor	295
	Protection of war orphans and vagrant juveniles	296
	Problem of mixed blood children	296
	Housing Problem	297

	Acute shortages		297
	Housing construction with foreign aids		298
	Korean Family		299
	Chongbop family system		299
	Aftermath of war		301
	Public Welfare		302
	Natural Calamities		304
	Natural disasters and accidents		304
XI	Health Problems		306
	General Preview		306
	Before Western science		306
	Western medicine		308
	Present and Future		310
	Necessary measures		310
	Medical profession		312
	Herb-doctors		313
	Future in hygiene		314
	Herb contribution		314
XII	Thoughts and Religions		316
	General Remarks on Korean Thought		316
	Introduction		316
	Primitive thought and religion		316
	The Three Kingdoms and Unified Silla		316
	Silla		317
	Koryo		318
	Yi dynasty		319
	Modern era		322
	Confucianism in Korea		323
	Introduction		323
	The moulding element		324
	Path of career		325
	Way of life		326
	Korean Buddhism		329
	Introduction		329
	Koguryo		331
	Paekche		331
	Silla		331
	Unified Silla		332
	Koryo		333
	Yi Chosun		335
	Present situation		336
	Christianity of Korea		337
	Catholicism		337
	Protestantism		340
	The Tonghak Movement		342
	The founding		342
	Development		344

Present situation 346
Chondogyo doctrines 346
Chodogyo rituals.. 348
Taejonggyo 348
Preamble 348
Way of life 349
The canons 350
Customs and culture 350
Brief history 350
Present status 351
Shamanism and Aberrations.. 351
Modern Korean Thought 354
Introduction 354
The search for a capitalistic outlet 355
National consciousness 356
A new logic 357
Literary heritage.. 358
Differing generations 359

XIII Education 360
Introduction 360
Aims.. 360
Stages 360
History of Education 362
Part 1 (From Puyo to Unified Silla) 362
Part 2 (Koryo Educaton) 363
Part 3 (Growth of Yi schools) 365
Part 4 (Modern education) 366
Education System 370
Administrative systems.. 370
School system.. 372
Education at Various Levels 374
Kindergarten 374
Compulsory education 374
Secondary education.. 375
Teachers' training 376
Colleges.. 377
Technical institutes at college level 378
Civic schools 378
Special education.. 379
Curriculum and Textbooks 379
Curriculum 379
College curricula.. 381
Text-books 381
Financial Management and Facilities.. 382
Government finance in education 382
School facilities 384
Private foundations 386
Teachers' Training and Group Activities of Teachers 387

20

Teachers' training	387
Teacher licenses	388
Group activities of teachers	389
Extra-Curricular Activities	391
Student movements before the Liberation	391
Extra-curricular activities after the Liberation	392
Education of General Public	393
Adult education	393
Preservation and utilization of cultural heritages	394
Sciences and arts	395
Libraries	395
Museums	395
UNESCO Korean Committee	396
Problems in using the national language	396
Students Abroad	397
Number of Students	397
Government assists	398

XIV	Mass Communications, Publication and Printing	399
	Newspapers and the Press	399
	Brief history	399
	Newspapers in Seoul	401
	Provincial newspapers	403
	Student papers	403
	Press services	403
	Broadcasting Service	405
	Introduction	405
	Round-up	406
	Printing and Publication in Ancient Korea	407
	Before Koryo	407
	The Koryo dynasty	408
	The Yi dynasty	409
	Book Publication	411
	Suppressions and "boom"	411
	Post-armistice squeeze	412
	Magazines	413
	Popular, if not profitable	413
	Medium for nationalism	414
	Printing Industry of Korea	414
	Introduction of Western printing methods	414
	Development of printing industry	415
	After the Liberation	416

XV	Social Sciences	417
	Outline	417
	The classical heritage	417
	Philosophy	418
	Birth of a light	418
	Ethics	420

21

	Logic	421
	Sociology	422
	Psychology	423
	The recent spurt	423
	History	424
	Archaeology	425
	Development	425
	Scope	427
	Folklore	428
	Religious rites of ancient times	428
	Shamanism	428
	Geomancy and fortune-telling	428
	Folklore literature	429
	Present conditions	429
	Geography	430
	A rich heritage	430
	Economics	431
	Under the Japanese	431
	Liberation fever	432
	Education	433
	Legal Science	434
	A short history	434
	Political Science	436
	Linguistics	436
	Korean Linguistics and Literature	438
	Japanese Excesses	438
	Foreign Literature	439
XVI	Natural Sciences	441
	Preface	441
	Mathematics	443
	Physics	446
	Chemistry	447
	Historical summary of chemical studies	447
	Present state of chemical studies	448
	Medical Science	449
	Western medicine	449
	Chinese herb medicine	450
	Pharmacology	453
	Dietetics	455
	Outline of background	455
	Produces and imports	456
	Astronomy	457
	The ancient days of astronomy and astrology	457
	The Three Kingdoms period	458
	The Koryo kingdom period	458
	The Yi dynasty	459
	Western astronomy of modern times	460
	Meteorology	460

22

	The ancient periods	460
	Meteorology during the Yi dynasty	461
	Contemporary meteorology	461
	Geology	462
	Summary history of geological studies	462
	Contributors to geological studies in Korea	463
	Present state of geological studies in Korea	463
	Agronomy	464
	Fishery	466
XVII	Literature	468
	An Outline of Korean Literature, Its Heritage	468
	Geological, seasonal and social background	468
	The characteristics of Korean literature	469
	The birth of modern literature	470
	Classic Literature: Poetry	470
	Poetry	470
	Classic Literature: The Novel	474
	The age of mythology	474
	The early classic novels	476
	Growth of the classic novel	476
	The golden age of the classic novel	477
	The fall of the classic novel	477
	Short outlines of the classic novels	478
	The History of Modern Korean Literature	480
	The era of enlightenment	480
	The era of "new" novels	480
	Rise of songs	480
	The changing literary scene	480
	Young writers of the "Creation" circle	481
	The growth of "The Ruins"	481
	Romanticism of the "White Tide"	482
	The "New Trend" group	483
	The "Proletarian" literature	483
	The new turn in literature	485
	The "dark" age	486
	New writers of the "dark" age	488
	The post-Liberation turmoil	489
	The post-Korean war period	490
	Modern Literature: The Novel	491
	Emergence of the "New Novels"	491
	Early stages of the modern novel	492
	The era of literary group magazines	493
	Some other novelists of the '20's	494
	Late masters of the '20's	494
	The golden era of the '30's	494
	Writers during the second half of the '30's	495
	The post-World War II period	496
	Modern Literature: Poetry	497

	The pioneers of the "new" poetry	497
	Decadent nihilism of the "golden" '20's	497
	Poetry of anxiety in the '30's	498
	Liberated poetry	499
	Renewed growth after the Korean war	500
	The essay	500
	The two pioneers	500
	Recent years	501
	Stage Play	501
	Pioneer days	501
	Modern drama	502
	Japanese oppression	503
	After the Liberation	503
	Screen Play	504
	Literature for Children	505
	Patriotic motive	505
	Contests	507
	Literary Criticism	507
	A new theory of literature	507
	Novelists vs. critics	508
	Nationalism vs. socialism	508
	The rise of professional critics	509
	Communism vs. democracy	510
	Presently active critics	510
XVIII	Fine Arts	511
	General Introduction to Korean Art	511
	History of Korean art	511
	Trends in Korean art	512
	Korean Painting	514
	Paintings of Three Kingdoms period	514
	Paintings of Unified Silla	516
	Paintings of Koryo	516
	Paintings of the Yi dynasty	517
	Modern paintings	518
	Sculpture	525
	Buddhist images of Three Kingdoms period	525
	Sculpture of Unified Silla	527
	Koryo sculpture	527
	Yi dynasty sculpture	528
	Modern Korean sculpture	528
	Architecture	530
	General survey	530
	Historical survey	531
	Modern Korean architecture	534
	Handicrafts	536
	Three-Kingdom period	536
	Unified Silla period	536
	Koryo dynasty	537

	Yi dynasty period	539
	Modern handicrafts	540
	Calligraphy	542
	Three-Kingdom period	542
	Unified Silla period	542
	Koryo dynasty	544
	Yi dynasty	544
	Modern Korean calligraphy	546
	Photography	546
XIX	Dance, Music	549
	Dance	549
	Essential nature of the Korean dance	549
	History of the Korean dance	550
	Court dance	551
	Folk dance	551
	Farm dance	551
	Sword dance	551
	Priest dance	552
	Drum dance	552
	Difference of Korean dance from ballet	553
	Modern dance	553
	Present conditions	555
	Korean Traditional Music	556
	Ancient instruments	556
	Yi music	557
	Trends in music	559
	Classification of Korean music	561
	Korean musical instruments	562
	Western Music	565
	Introduction	565
	Church music	565
	Musical education	566
	Broadcasting system, phonograph records, etc.	566
	Solos and chamber music	567
	Orchestra	568
	Opera	569
	Creative music	571
	Popular music	572
XX	Drama, Motion Picture	573
	Definition of the Korean Drama	573
	Music and dancing prevalent themes	573
	Western tides	574
	Marionette	574
	Three survivals	574
	The Kkoktugaksi	574
	The props	575
	Masque	576

   Four catagories 576
   A typical example 577
  Modern drama 578
   Trends 578
   Importance of the student drama 579
   The music drama.. 580
   Training courses 580
   Theater 580
  Thorny Paths of Modern Motion Picture Industry 581
   Dominating medium in popular appeal 581
   Before the Liberation 581
   Liberation and war 584
  Postwar Boom of Motion Picture Industry 584
   Tax Exemption makes movies a major industry 584
   Production 585
   Theaters 587
   Foreign films 588
   Scenario writers and critics 588
   Actors and actresses 589
   Directors 589
   Technicians 589
   Set shooting stages and laboratories 590
   International relations 590
   Awards 590
   Education and training institutions 591

XXI Historical Remains.. 592
  Of Tombs and Temples 592
   Introduction 592
   Ancient tombs.. 592
   Sites of Buddhist temples 594
   Castle and mountain fortresses 596
   Sites of kilns 597
   Conclusion 598

XXII Manners and Customs 599
  Outline.. 599
  Food and Dwelling.. 602
   The main and side dishes 602
   The table, food containers, and table-manners 603
   Confections.. 604
   Beverages 605
   Cookery.. 606
   Three dominant types of houses and the ondol.. .. 606
   Traditional house 607
   Houses of the Yi dynasty 608
   From the cave to the ondol 608
   Interior decoration and gardens 609
   Contemporary and future dwellings 609

Furniture	610
Clothing and Costumes	610
Traditional Korean costumes	611
Present costumes	612
Professional costumes	613
Western clothes	614
Hair-dressing	614
Headwear	615
Ornaments on the head	615
Make-up	616
Footwears	616
Bedding	617
Marriage and Funerals	617
Roles of parents in marriage	617
Fortune-telling on proposed matrimony	618
Engagement	618
Wedding ceremony	619
Funeral service	620
Home and Social Life	622
Home life	622
Inheritance	623
Social life	624
Social intercourse	625
Name and the Calendar	627
Names of persons	627
Seal	629
Name of places	630
Kinds of calendars in use	632
24 days of the season	632
Measuring and telling time	632
Standard time and daylight saving time	634
The year	634
Annuals Observances and Holidays	634
Traditional holidays	635
National holidays of recent origin	641
Myths, Legends, and Folktales	642
Introduction	642
Myths	643
Legends	647
Folktales	651
Proverbs	659
Riddles	661
Folksongs	662
Fortune-Telling	664
Theory of the five elements	664
Physiognomy	665
Palmistry	665
Divination through mediums	666
Prophets and books of prophecy	666

Interpretation of omens	667
Interpretation of Dreams	668
Fortunes of games and sports	668
Geomancy	668
Origin and theory	669
Applications of the theory	669
Classification of sites	671
Shamanism	671
Origin of Shamanism	672
Motives and processes for becoming a Shaman	673
The Shaman rites	674
Books of incantations and articles for rites	676
Shaman incantations	676
Shamans, Gods, and Evil Spirits	678
The basic ideas of the Shaman divinity	678
The nature of various gods	679
Exorcism of evil gods	681
XXIII Sports	682
Outline	682
Virtual necessity	682
Traditional Sports	683
Judo	683
Archery	684
Archery on horseback	684
Stone-throwing	684
Kicking the ball	684
Hitting the ball	684
Wrestling	685
Sledge-riding	685
Rope-pulling, or tug-o'-war	685
Vase-throwing	685
Shooting the ball	685
Horsemanship	686
Other sports	686
Modern Sports	686
Track-and-field	686
Soccer	688
Baseball	688
Basketball	689
Volleyball	690
Tennis	690
Table tennis	690
Rugby	691
Handball	691
Gymnastics	691
Weightlifting	691
Swimming	692

XXIV	Games and Recreation	693
	Preface	693
	Traditional Games in Korea	694
	Jumping-seesaw	694
	Swinging	694
	Kite-flying	694
	Yut	694
	Hawking	695
	Tuho	695
	Sunggyongdo	695
	Ssangyuk	696
	Kolpae	696
	Flower-cards	696
	Tonchigi (Coin Games)	696
	Chegi	696
	Korean Games in Modern Days	697
	Paduk	697
	Changgi (Korean Chess)	697
	Mahjongg	698
	Angling	698
	Billiards	699
	Hunting	699
	Dancing	700
	Golf	700
	Flower arrangement	701
	Birds and fish	701
XXV	Tourism	702
	Preface	702
	Tourism a "Natural"	702
	Conveniences provided	702
	Tourist Areas	703
	Temples	703
	Palaces and gardens	705
	Beaches	706
	Hot springs	706
	Recommended tourist areas	707
	Tourists' Guide	708
	Cultural resources	708
	Recreation	708
	Calendar of events	709
	Means of communication	711
	Tourist accommodations	711
	Appendix	
	Conversion table of weights and measures	714
	Chronology chart of Korean history compared with world history	715
	Map	

I GEOGRAPHY

General Preview

Dimensions

The Taehan Minguk, frequently called Hanguk for the sake of brevity, and officially designated the "Republic of Korea" in English, has long been known as Chosun – "The Land of the Morning Calm." Its capital is Seoul. It consists of the Korean peninsula stretching from the north to the south in Northeast Asia and comprising some 3,300 islands roundabout.

The national territory lies between 124.11 and 131.55 degrees east longitude and between 33.7 and 43.1 degrees south latitude. The standard time is based on the meridian passing through the center of the peninsula along 127.3 degrees east longitude. The difference with Washington is ten hours and thirty minutes, and with London, eight hours and thirty minutes.

The Korean peninsula separates the Yellow Sea from the Eastern Sea, generally known as the Sea of Japan, and neighbors with Japan to the south through a narrow strait, called the Taehan Strait in Korean and the Tsushima Strait on the international maps. The boundaries on the mainland are the Yalu River, the Tumen River and Mount Paektu. Due to its geographical location forming a land bridge connecting the islands to the south and the land-mass to the north, Korea has long been a communication route. In fact, Korea in ancient ages was long a sort of relaying station, transmitting to Japan the brilliant cultures of China.

At the same time, however, pinched as the country was between the big nations to the north and an aggressive island country in the south, Korea has, throughout its long history, often been a victim of aggressive intents and the power struggles of the neighboring big powers.

The area is 220,845 square kilometers, of which the main peninsula comprises 96.6% with the island rest making up 3.4%. The part of the country north of the military demarcation line, commonly known as north Korea, is 125,608 kilometers and that in the south, the territory of the Republic of Korea, 95,232 square kilometers. Korea can be compared with the British Isles, Rumania, and New Zealand in size; the southern part is almost equal to Jordan, Hungary, Poland or Guatemala. It ranks among the smaller nations of the world.

Description

The major portion of the country is mountainous and only 20% of the country is flat land. Korea is counted as one of the rare mountainous countries in the world. The total population of north and south

Korea exceeds 30 million and ranks 13th among the independent nations of the world in population. The Korean population is equal to those of Mexico, Spain or Poland.

The population of south Korea alone is about 22 million and is comparable with those of the Philippines, Turkey and Argentina. The density of population throughout the country stands at 145 persons per square kilometer and, in the south, exceeds 230 persons per spuare kilometer. South Korea ranks fourth in the world in population density, following the Netherlands, Belgium and Japan, and followed by Britain. Distribution of the population is closely linked with the distribution of arable lands in the country.

Originally there were eight administrative divisions or Provinces, Hamgyong-do, Pyongan-do, Hwanghae-do, Kyonggi-do, Kangwon-do, Chungchong-do, Cholla-do and Kyongsang-do. However, in 1896, in the 33rd year of King Kojong, Hamgyong-do, Pyongan-do, Chungchong-do, Cholla-do and Kyongsang-do were each divided into northern (Pukto) and southern (Namdo) provinces. Following the liberation of the nation in 1945, Seoul was separated from the provincial administration of Kyonggi-do while the island of Cheju was separated from Cholla Namdo as an independent province. Thus, there are at present 14 provinces and the Special City of Seoul for a total 15 administrative units, nine in south Korea.

Geographically, the country is commonly divided into two areas along the boundary connecting Seoul and Wonsan, the so-called Chugaryong Rift. However, it is sometimes divided into three sectors: the northern sector composed of Hamgyong Pukto, Hamgyong Namdo, Pyongang Pukto, Pyongan Namdo, and Hwanghae-do, the central sector consisting of Kyonggi-do, Kangwon-do, Chungchong Pukto and Chungchong Namdo, and the southern sector embracing Cholla Pukto, Cholla Namdo, Kyongsang Pukto, Kyongsang Namdo, and Cheju-do.

Topography

Mountains

The major portion of the crust of Korean land is composed of paleozoic and neozoic layers with the sea layer confined to only a small part of land. There have been no major adjustments in crust formations since the Jurassic and Tertiary Periods, save for some volcanic activities during the Tertiary and Quaternary. Therefore, the features of the land are characterized by flat hills without any notable undulations. Though the eastern part of the country is still in its prime due to its exposure to erosion for many years, the rest of the land is quite worn off.

Korean hills lack vertical carriage and, for the most part, are spread out horizontally. The crests are mostly shaped like plateaux and their peaks constitute monadnocks created as a result of long years of erosion. There is no peak in the land that exceeds 3,000 meters in height. The average for the Kaema, highest plateau in the country, is only 1,500 meters. Mount Paektu, the highest peak, is only 2,744 meters high — the average peak for the country as a whole is only 482 meters high.

From the standpoint of the geographical features, Korea is a chain of hills stretching out from the Asian Continent. Between these hills run winding rivers and meandering streams making for beautiful sceneries throughout the land. Many strangely shaped rocks, mostly granite, protrude from these hills as a result of long weathering and erosive processes. They but enhance the beauty.

Direction of Mountains

As early as 200 years ago, Yi Chunghwan, one of the greatest geographers Korea has ever produced, made an attempt to analyze the direction of Korean mountains in a famous work entitled, *Palyokchi* (Record of the Eight Areas i.e. provinces). The theories he espoused are still being cited by modern geographers to explain the ranges of the country. In general, they take three directions upon which all the characteristic features of the land are determined.

Firstly, there is the Taebaek Range from the north-north-west to the south-south-east close to the east coast. This constitutes the backbone of the country. As its direction corresponds with that of the peninsula, it is sometimes called the "Korea Way."

Secondly, in the northeastern corner of the land, three ranges run east-north-east to west-south-west; the Kangnam, Chokyu and Myohyang. Since these run in the same direction as Liaotung, the once considerable Liao Kingdom in Manchuria, that part of Korea is commonly referred to as the "Liaotung Way."

Thirdly, in the southwestern sector of the land, the Tongnyong and Noryang Ranges run north-west to south-west. As the two ranges run in the same direction as the folded mountain ranges of China's Fukien Province, that area is called the "China Way." These "Ways" constitute most of the important factors that have contributed to determination of the geographical features of the land.

Chugaryong Rift

From the standpoint of topography, Korea can be divided into northern and southern zones, as distinguished by the railroad connecting Seoul and Wonsan. The first is called Chugaryong Rift Zone, which occupies the narrow strip of land cutting through the central part of the peninsula from the northeast to the southwest, between Namdae River running from the north to the east and Imjin River which runs from the south to the west. This part of the land was created as a result of dislocation that occurred during the Tertiary Period of the geological ages. The rocks in this area are mostly gneisses and granites, but few granites are exposed today while the gneisses abound. This is so because gneisses can endure against erosion while granites are very vulnerable to both erosive and weathering processes.

The northern zone can again be subdivided into two regions, one north of the line connecting Hamhung and the mouth of Chongchon River, the Kaema Region; the other, south of this line, sometimes called the Intermediate Region.

Kaema Region

This region is bounded with the eastern part of Manchuria by the Yalu and Tumen Rivers and is surrounded by the Myohyang, Puchon and Hamgyong Ranges. The rivers, Chungman, Tongno, Changjin and Hochon are the tributaries of the Yalu; the Sodu and Yonmyon rivers flow from River Tumen. The people of the region mostly live on the flat lands along these rivers. However, since the region is very mountainous, it is a sparsely populated area. The Nangnim Ranges running in a south-north direction in the center of the region constitute the backbone of the country, along with the Taebaek Ranges. Its average height is 1,500 meters.

The region again is subdivided into two parts, one east of the Nangnim Range which is called the East Kaema region, and the other west of the Range, the West Kaema. The East Kaema region has the highest plateau in the land with an average peak height of 1,000 meters. It is, therefore, commonly called the Kaema Plateau.

In the Neozoic Period an enormous amount of basalts gushed out in this region to form a lava plateau. Today, a dense forest is growing on the plateau. Mount Paektu (2,744 meters) is a conical volcano composed of alkali trachytes. The foot of the mountain is laden with thick forests while the crest is covered with white pumice stones, from which the name of the peak, Paektu, which means white head, is derived. There is a big crater filled with water on the crest of the mountain. The lake is 12 kilometers in circumference, 49 square kilometers in area, 310 meters deep and 2,267 meters above sea level.

The east side of the plateau facing the

Eastern or Japan Sea consists of precipitous cliffs more than 1,000 meters in height. Because of their steepness, the cliffs constitute an obstacle for water transportation along the east coast. However, they serve as ideal terrain for hydroelectricity and large power stations have been constructed along the Puchon, Changjin and Hochon rivers.

The Hamgyong Range embraces many high peaks exceeding 2,000 meters in height, including Mount Kwanmo, the second highest peak in the country. For this reason, it is familiarly called the "Alps of Korea." On the other hand, the mountain range running in a south-south-easterly direction along the boundary between the two Hamgyong-do province is called the Machon Range. This is a chain of volcanos, containing many precious mineral resources.

There is another chain of mountains called the Chilbo, east of the Hamgyong Range. These mountains are formed of basalts and alkali trachytes. The foremost, Mount Chilbo, situated in the center of the range, is 906 meters high.

Intermediate Region

The narrow strip running between the Kaema Mountains and Chugaryong Rift is commonly called the Intermediate Mountainous Region. Geographically, the region plays a mediator's role between the northern and southern areas.

Historically, the region has constituted a contact point where the early cultures of the continental north and the peninsular south met.

The Nangnim Range running through the center of the region constitutes a boundary dividing it into two sectors. The flat land spreading out east of the Nangnim Range along the east coast is called the Hamnam Plain. The western part of the region constitutes an intermediate area connecting the mountains in the northeastern area which run along the "Liaotung Way" and those to the southwest running along the "China Way." This sector of the region generally comprises low hills of not more than 300 meters in height. The main heights are the Myorak Mountains, the northern slopes of which abound with mineral resources. Besides, there are the Chamo and Kuwol Mountains running in a northwesterly direction, and the Masingnyong Mountains to the south.

The eastern part of the region mostly comprises low hills, but the western half is flat land. There is a sort of peneplain south of Taedong River. Here many historical remains of the Nangnim era are to be found. This part of the sector is rich in sedimentary rocks and contains a large quantity of anthracites. Many limestone caves, especially, are to be found in the hills between the plains in the west and the low mountains in the central part of the sector. Of these caves, the Tongnyong Cave in Yongbyon is the biggest and oldest in the world.

Southern Region

The Taebaek Range, which extends southward about 500 meters from the southern tip of Yonghung Bay as far down as the Naktong River, constitutes the backbone of the Korean peninsula along with the Nangnim Range. There are many noted peaks soaring up from this range, such as Mount Kumgang (Diamond Mountain—1.638 meters), Mount Odae (1,663 meters), Mount Sorak (1,708 meters), and Mount Taebaek. Kumgang and Odae, in particular, abound with peculiar rocks, mostly granites. The former, famous for its "Twelve Thousand Rocks," was a major attraction for Far Eastern tourists before the thirty-eighth parallel placed it north.

There are many mineral resources in the area between Mounts Kumgang and Taebaek. From the western slope of the Taebaek extend the Kwangju, Chaeryong and Sobaek Ranges. The Noryong Mountains branch off from the Sobaek. Between these mountains flow the major rivers in the central part of Korea, the Han, Kum and Yongsan Rivers.

Plains

Though much of Korean terrain is senescent, no vast plains are to be found anywhere, most of what plains there are being narrow strips of land surrounded by mountains. Situated in most cases between pared hills and along the lower reaches of rivers, they are shaped like the branches of a tree. There are small alluvial plains which are created as a result of the "accumulative process" of rivers in hollow places. Most plains, however, were created as a result of weathering and erosive processes.

Since most of the mountains are situated in the eastern and northern sectors of the land, the majority of the plains in the country are found in the southern and western parts. The Hamnam Plain is the only large one in the eastern area. It is one of the major plains in the country and yields abundant agricultural products.

Meanwhile, in the western part of the land, there are many extensive plains. In the north, there is a delta along the lower part of the Yalu River. The Anju Plain along the southern part of the Taedong River and the Pyongyang and Hwangju Plains constitute model plains that have been created as a result of erosion. They are the largest among the peneplains in the western part of Korea.

The plains extending along the Chaeryong, Yesong and Imjin Rivers are alluvial, producing rice of the best quality in the country. The plains south of the Chaeryong Mountains that run along the lower part of the Kum River, the Honam Plain in Cholla Pukto, and the plain extending along the Yongsan River, are counted as major plains in the country.

Along the middle part of the Naktong River runs a narrow plain known as the Taegu Basin. Other plains are to be found extending along the southern reaches of the Naktong, the Nam and Milyang Rivers. These plains, together with those in the western sector of the country, constitute the major plains of the country. Together, they constitute a veritable "breadbasket" for Korea is an agricultural land and relies upon these plains for virtually all her essential food supplies.

Coast Lines and Islands

The total coast line of Korea is more than 17,371 kilometers long, and that of the main peninsula 8,600 kilometers. The coast line in the eastern part of the country is generally steep and monotonous, but the southern coast is long and intricate. The total length of the coast line is eight times as long as a straight line between the two extreme points.

The west coast, on the other hand, is not so intricate as the south coast. The entire length here is seven times as long as the crow flies.

Length of coast lines

Coast	Straight Line (km)	Coast Line (km)	Coast Line of Main Land (km)
East	809	1,823	1,700
South	255	6,588	4,700
West	650	8,950	2,200
Total	1,174	17,361	8,600

East Coast

The bulging coast on the east is studded with many bays and as fine ports as may be found along the other coast lines. The major part of the coast line is generally rocky, with beautiful sandy coasts in many places.

The rocky coast line along the eastern coast can be classified into two types: one resulting from coastal dislocations, the other created as a result of the erosion of the sea. The former has developed along the coast line in the vicinity of Mounts Kumgang, Songjin and Chilbo. The coast line along the Kumgang and Songjin constitutes the most beautiful spots along the east coast. The green pines grown on the sandy shores make for sharp contrast with the clean water of the sea, presenting a sight beautiful beyond description. The major ports along the east coast are Unggi, Chongjin, Wonsan, Mukho and Pohang.

Unggi, the northernmost port in the country, is on Chosan Bay. It was opened in 1921 and, linked with Manchuria through a railroad running along the Tumen River, has acted as a door to Manchuria. Chongjin, the best port in the northeastern part of the country, was opened in 1908 and has also served as a door to Manchuria following the building of a railroad in 1929. Songjin was originally opened in 1899 as a base for exploring inland plateaux and has been one of the busiest ports in the country with the coming of rails. Wonsan, opened in 1880, was the best port in the northeastern part of the country until it was linked by rails with the newer and better port of Chongjin. Since then, it has served mainly as a base for fishery and naval activities. Mukho is situated halfway between Wonsan and Pusan. It was originally opened as a base for exploring coal mines in the Samchok area. Pohang is one of the best ports on the east coast and is used as an intermediate station for ships on the Eastern Sea.

The east coast does not have many islands and they are all small. The only one of appreciable size that lies close to the land is the Island of Mayang, forty-nine square kilometers, in north Korea. Out in the sea, some hundred and forty kilometers away, there is a volcanic island, Ullung, and southeast of Ullung is Tokto Island. The population on Ullung is about 10,000, subsisting mostly on farming and fishing.

Tokto has gained some post-Liberation notoriety as a disputed territory between Korea and Japan. Historically part of Korea, the rock island was annexed to Japan under a Korea-Japan Agreement of 1904 and the Japanese immediately integrated it as part of their Shimane Prefecture. Among the surrender terms laid upon Japan by the Allied Powers in World War II was renunciation by that country to all rights on Korean territory. The Republic of Korea Government, as a matter of course, declared the 1904 Agreement on Tokto to be null and void and a Presidential Declaration was issued in 1952, formally restoring the island to Korea proper. The Japanese Government, however, continues to claim it as part of Shimane Prefecture. In 1954, the Korean Government constructed a lighthouse on the island. Its main advantage is that it serves as an outpost for protecting maritime resources of the sea.

West Coast

Contrary to the east coast, there are many zigzags and meanderings on the west coast. Again unlike the east coast, many islands are to be found scattered here. While the coast on the east is rocky and sandy in most cases, that on the west generally falls down into the sea in a gentle slope. The major ports are Tasado, Nampo, Inchon and Kunsan.

Tasado is a trading port and is connected with Sinuiju by a railroad. Nampo, situated at the mouth of the Taedong River, was opened in 1897. Due to its location, it has been the center of trade with China. Inchon is a port protruding from the Inchon Peninsula. The port is deep and wide. Protected by small islands off the shore, it is usually free from strong winds. Traditionally, Inchon was the busiest port in Korea, but following the rapid development of Pusan to the south, it became the second port city of the country. It is important as a corridor to Seoul, the capital. Kunsan is located at the mouth of the Kum River. It flourished as a busy port city during the Japanese occupation because the Japanese used it for shipping Korean rice to Japan. However, since the liberation of the country, most of the trade has been conducted through Inchon and Pusan, and Kunsan has accordingly become a lesser port.

The biggest island along the west coast is Kanghwa. Originally, a group of six hills stood there, isolated from the shore. The dirt, washed away from Imjin, Yesong and Han Rivers, combined to form the big island of today. The island is, therefore, characterized by agriculture flourishing on its extensive farmlands, unlike the case with most islands which are rugged and rocky.

South Coast

The south coast is even more zigzagged and meandering. In fact, it is considered to be one of the rarest coast lines in the world and has been nicknamed the "Korean Coast". Chinhae Bay, Kosong Peninsula and Koje Island are to be found to the east. Along the middle part of the coast line are Namhae Island, Yosu Peninsula, Sunchon Bay, Kohung Peninsula, and Posong Bay. The minor islands of Haegak and Chindo and the major island of the country, Cheju, are located off the western part of the coast line.

The major ports along the coast are, from east to west, Pusan, Chinhae, Masan, Yosu and Mokpo. Pusan started its career as a port city in 1883 along with Inchon and Wonsan and, since the construction of a railroad connecting the southern and northern tips of the Korean peninsula, rapidly developed as the biggest port city in the country. Today, approximately 80% of the trade in the country is transacted through Pusan.

The port has mountains at its back and a land-mass protruding on its east flank, with an island, Yongdo, providing protection from the sea winds in front. Besides the natural conditions for being a good port, it has good modern facilities. Chinhae is the port where the ROK Navy has its base. Surrounded by mountains to the north, east and west, it was always ideal for the military. Masan cuts deep into the land. It is deep and calm and protected by many small islands off the shore. Therefore, big ships can freely move in and out of the port. However, overshadowed by the rapid development of neighboring Pusan Port, it now relies on fishery and industry for its existence. Yosu is a relaying station for ships sailing to and fro between Pusan, Mokpo and Cheju. Mokpo sits on the southwestern tip of the peninsula. It was first opened in 1897. Since the railroad connecting Taejon and Mokpo was constructed, the city rapidly developed into an industrial as well as port city.

The biggest of the islands off the coast is Cheju, 88 miles south of Mokpo. Its area is 1,862 square kilometers, and its population, 300,000. Mostly consisting of trachytes and basalts, it is a volcanic island, with a high mountain soaring up at the center, Halla (1,950 meters). The slopes of this mountain have long been used as pasture grounds for raising cattle and horses. Recently, the Government has established a big pasture field there in an effort to encourage cattle-raising on the island. The capital of the island is Cheju City to the south.

Rivers and Streams
Characteristics

Since the northern and eastern parts of the land are steep and mountainous while the western and southern parts mostly consist of flat lands and low hills, the majority of the big rivers flow along the southern and western areas. Rivers exceeding 400 kilometers in length are the Yalu and Tumen Rivers which flow along the boundary with Manchuria, the Taedong, Han and Kum Rivers in the western sector of the country, and the Naktong River in the southern sector. These constitute the six major rivers of Korea. Since the currents of the rivers are mostly slow, they are conveniently used for water transportation. The rivers flow abundantly in summer when there is much rain and shrink in winter when rain is scarce. In other words, the volume of water varies greatly according to seasonal changes.

Utility of Rivers

Rivers have had close bearing on the lives of the Korean people since olden times. They have been used as a means of transportation and for the farmlands. Thus, Korean civilizations developed along such river banks as the Taedong and Naktong.

Recently, however, due to the development of motor transportation on land, the usefulness of rivers as a means of transportation has been reduced rapidly. But they are still valuable sources of water supply for the nation's agricultural health. The farmlands depend on them for over 70% of their water supply. Moreover, the modern age has also made rivers a source of power more important than coal.

Major Rivers

River	Area of Plain Drained (Sq. km)	Total Length (km)	Navigable Length (km)
Yalu	3.3	790	698
Tumen	1.1	520	85
Han	2.6	514	330
Naktong	2.4	525	334
Taedong	1.7	438	260
Kum	1.0	401	130
Imjin	0.8	254	124
Chongchon	0.9	198	152
Somjin	0.5	212	39
Yesong	0.4	174	65

Rivers such as the Yalu, Chongchon, Taedong, Yesong, Han, Kum and Yongsan flow directly into the Yellow Sea, and are under the direct influence of the tides. The lower reaches of these rivers are navigable.

Many of the cities and villages have developed along the lower parts of these rivers. Modern demands, on the other hand, have led to the construction of many hydroelectric power stations on the upper reaches. The Yalu River has its headspring at the foot of Mount Paektu and runs westward into the Yellow Sea. As its total meandering length is only twice as long as the crow flies, most of the banks consist of steep cliffs save for the delta area at the mouth. Hence, the area for plains is more limited than the length of the river might suggest. Big ships can ply as high and far as Sinuiju at high tide and small boats as far as Hesanjin though recent developments in motor and railroad transportations have considerably diminished the importance of the river as a means of travel. The lower part of the river is conveniently used for supplying water for the farmlands nearby and its upper part for hydroelectric power stations. Presently, four power stations are located along the Yalu: one along the main river, the other three along its tributaries.

Chongchon River flows the "Liaotung Way" in an almost straight line, that part of the river between the mouth and Sinanju being navigable. River Taedong absorbs all the water flowing from its tributaries along the way to widen in the vicinity of Pyongyang. A total 260 kilometer length of Taedong is available for navigation in the lower reaches. Particularly, since the depth of the water at the mouth of the river is deep, big boats of 2,000 or 5,000 tons can sail as far as 63 kilometers up. Big cities like Nampo, Songjin and Pyongyang have developed along the Taedong.

The Yesong River flowing south of Taedong flows out to Kanghwa Bay. Along the lower reaches of the river extends a plain called the Yonbaek.

The Han River is often divided into two parts: the northern half is called the North Han River and the southern half the South Han River. The latter constitutes the main stream while the former is a mere tributary of the river as a whole. The South Han River starts from the southern part of Kangwon-do Province, passes through the northern part of Kangwon-do to absorb the water flowing from the North Han River, and flows into Kanghwa Bay. The Han ranks only fourth in length among the rivers of the country, but the plains extending from its banks are the largest. The currents in the middle and lower parts of the river are slow and abundant. Lower Han, especially, is utilized for hydroelectric power, irrigation and navigation purposes.

The Kum River starts from the northeastern part of Cholla-do Province and passes through Taejon Basin to flow into the Yellow Sea in the vicinity of Kunsan. The plains along the river are wide and low, 25% of them tilled as farmlands. As the river is both deep and wide, big ships can sail up to Puyo. It was an important inland route for Kunsan before the development of modern land transportation.

Of the rivers flowing into the archipelago off the southern coast, only two may be considered major, the Naktong and Somjin Rivers. The Naktong is the longest in the southern sector of the land. Widening at Andong and Hamchang where the waters from the tributaries merge, it proceeds southward to plunge into the sea west of Pusan.

The currents on the river are slow and many big plains fork out from it, in particular, a big delta around Kimhae along the lower part of the river.

The Somjin River flows by the mountains in the Sobaek Range. Since the currents are rapid, it is not fit for navigation. There is no noteworthy plain along the river. On the other hand, the swift currents make it readily available for hydroelectricity. Several power stations, accordingly, are to be found along the Somjin.

Climate

Geographical Factors and Climate

The climate is determined mainly by such factors as monsoon, latitudinal position, terrain and currents washed on the coastlines. The country spans 9 degrees latitude and the level of terrain is higher in the north than in the south. Due to these geographical factors, the nearer the northern frontier, the lower the fall in average temperature. The average throughout the year is 13° (C) along the southern coast while it drops as low as 10° (C) and 8° (C) over the midland and northern zones of climate respectively. The west coast is open to continental Asia and is vulnerable to the influence of the cool monsoons in any season of the year. The east coast, on the other hand, is separated from the west by the steep Chungnyang mountains that keep it from the monsoons of the northwest and moderate the winds from the same direction; it is further affected by the warm currents of the Eastern or Japan Sea. Thus, it is about 2° (C) warmer in the east than in the west.

Climate and Seasons

Differences in temperature are least conspicuous during summer. The average temperature in August in the lower area of the east coast, which is affected by the warm currents, is about 25° (C) while it falls down to about 21° (C) in the northern part of the northeastern coast and the Kaema Plateau. The average maximum temperature throughout the whole land is generally over 35° (C) and the cities of Wonsan and Taegu have respectively registered the record-high temperatures of 39° 6′ (C) and 40° (C). The hottest period of the year lasts about one month, starting from early August. The temperature then is close to the tropical zone and much hotter in the midland and the areas below than in the rest of the country. The area around Taegu is the hottest region in Korea.

The outstanding feature of winter is the clear temperatural difference between north and south. The lowest temperature along the southern coast, in the midland and on the Kaema Plateau up in the north is respectively $-15°$ (C), $-20°$ (C) and $-30°$ (C) or more. The northern frontier town of Chunggangjin once claimed the lowest temperature of $-43° 6′$ (C). The town and its vicinity is known to be the coldest spot in Korea. In winter, the mountains and fields are snow-clad and rivers are frozen. The winter lasts for six months in the northernmost areas while it lasts for only three months in the southern provinces. The undoubted cold of the Korean winter, however, is not so unbearable because three days of successive cold are invariably followed by four successive warmer days as the high atmospheric pressures of the continent alternate in a well-nigh regular pattern of progression and retrogression.

Rainfall

The average annual precipitation of rain in Korea is 500–1,500 mm. More than half of the land registers an annual average precipitation of 800-1,000-mm, two times that of the neighboring mainland of China and half the amount usually registered in Japan. The six months from October to March is the dry period; April-September is the wet period. The rainfall during the wet period corresponds to the total annual precipitation, while the wet season of June-August draws almost 50 to 60% of the total. More rain falls in the western part of the land than in the eastern. Among the areas that draw most rain are the southern part of Kyongsang Namdo, the eastern part of Cholla Pukto, the basins of Han and Kuryong Rivers. All of them register more than 1,300-mm. The area of the Somjin River estuary is known as the wettest spot with 1,500-mm of rainfall. Extreme northwestern or northeastern areas draw very little rain, registering only 700-900-mm a year, while the areas in the upper reaches of River Tumen register the scantiest rainfall with 500-mm.

Climatic Zones

There are eight different climatic zones in Korea. The factors that determine the division of zones are temperature, precipitation, humidity and terrain. The eight zones are:

1) Archipelago Zone (Provinces of Kyongsang Namdo, Cholla Namdo, and Cheju-do). Temperature 1-2° (C)((4° (C) in Cheju-do)) in winter and 22-26° (C)((23° (C) in Cheju-do)) in summer. Precipitation: 1,100-1,400 mm.

2) Eastern Sea Zone (Provinces of the eastern coast south of Mount Kumgang (Diamond), Kyongsang Pukto and Kyongsang Namdo). Temperature: 1.5°-2° (C) in winter and 24°-26° (C) in summer. Precipitation: 950-1250 mm. (Ullung, being under oceanic climatic conditions, registers exceptionally high precipitation of 1,600-mm).

3) Eastern Korea Bay Zone (Southern part of Hamgyong Namdo and the eastern coast north of Mount Kumgang). Temperature: 4-5° (C) in winter and 22-24° (C) in summer. Precipitation: 900-1,300 mm.

4) Southwest Provinces Zone (Cholla Pukto and southern half of Chungchong Namdo sandwiched between Chungnyong and Noryong mountains). Temperature. 2-4° (C) in winter and 26° (C) in summer. Precipitation: 1100-1,300 mm.

5) Central Zone (Kyonggi-do western part of Kangwon-do, Chungchong Pukto, Hwanghaedo and northern half of Chungchong Namdo). Temperature: 8-12° (C) in winter and 25-26° (C) in summer. Precipitation: 800-1,200 mm

Climate of Korea

Cities	Average Temp. (°C) Jan.	July	Annual	H. & L. High	Low	Precipitation Annual	July	Aug.	July & Aug. (%)	Wet days
Songjin	-5.8	22.1	8.1	37.5	-24.6	703	103	163	37.8	105
Chungkangjin	-2.1	21.6	3.7	38.6	-43.1	818	176	183	31.7	131
Sinuiju	-9.8	24.1	8.7	36.9	-27.7	818	176	183	31.7	100
Wonsan	-3.8	23.8	10.3	39.6	-21.9	1,328	270	320	44.6	117
Pyongyang	-8.2	24.4	9.3	37.2	-28.5	941	243	232	50.5	108
Seoul	-4.9	25.5	11.0	38.2	-23.1	1,246	366	250	49.5	112
Inchon	-3.9	25.0	10.8	38.9	-21.0	1,043	286	206	45.9	105
Taegu	-1.7	26.0	12.5	40.0	-20.2	970	299	157	37.7	90
Chonju	-2.0	26.0	12.2	38.2	-17.8	1,233	299	249	44.4	125
Kwangju	-1.1	25.4	13.9	37.6	-19.4	1,243	261	219	38.6	128
Pusan	-1.9	25.6	13.6	36.0	-14.0	1.399	279	179	32.7	101
Mokpo	0.9	26.1	13.2	37.0	-14.0	1,065	197	166	34.1	128
Cheju	4.6	25.9	13.3	87.5	-50.7	1,382	206	216	30.7	141

I GEOGRAPHY

6) Hwangpyong Provinces Zone (Northern part of Hwanghae-do and southern part of Pyongan Namdo south of Taedong River). Temperature: 8-11° (C) in winter and 23-24° (C) in summer. Precipitation: 800-1,200 mm.

7) Pyongan Provinces Zone (Pyongan Pukto and Pyongan Namdo north of Taedong River). Temperature: 7-15° (C) in winter and 22-24° (C) in summer. Precipitation: 1,000-1,300 mm.

8) Kaema Plateau Zone (Northeastern provinces, excluding southern part of Hamgyong Namdo). Temperature: 9-20° (C) in winter and 17-19° (C) in summer. Precipitation: 700-800 mm.

Soil

Character of Soil

Korean soil is characteristic in that the proportion of displaced alluvia composed of soil carried away from base rocks by such external forces as rain, streams and winds is greater than that of stationary alluvia composed of soil that is not carried away by such forces. The most common rocks in Korea are granite (27%) and gneiss (36%). Also abundant are such igneous rocks as basalt and porphyry and sedimentary rocks like limestone, argillite and sandstone. The greater part of Korean soil is, therefore, made up of granite and gneiss. Such soil is generally sandy and contains only 12.5-37.5% of clay.

The southern part of Hamgyong Namdo and Kangwon-do is the limestone belt of Korea. The soil there is known as terra rossa and is of reddish brown color. The proportion of clay contained in the arable soil of Korea diminishes to the north.

Soil and Climate

Korean soil is affected by the climate to a great extent. The climate is characterized by the fact that the year has its spells of dry and wet seasons and that most of the rain falls during the three months of June, July and August. Furthermore, slopes in Korea are generally gentle and the weathered surface of soil is apt to be washed away by torrential rainfalls during the rainy season. This is responsible for the fact that Korean soil has little chance of being settled in its original place and affected by the climate. Little affected, as it is by weather and permanency, the Korean soil tends to maintain the character of the rocks from which it was, to a great extent, derived. Generally speaking, black soil is fertile (though not always) while yellow, yellowish brown, and reddish soil is sterile for lack of organic substances. There are two major factors, social and natural, that count for the fact that Korean soil generally contains little organic substance. Socially, since the end of the Yi dynasty, farmers who had to pay high rates of tenant fees, used primitive fertilizers which were much cheaper to procure. Naturally, organic substances on the surface of the soil would be washed away by the torrential rainfalls of summer to be dissolved under the high temperatural conditions of a continental character, thus losing their chemical functions. Organic fertilizers, then, are amply needed to manage Korean farms.

Type of Soil

The type of soil is determined more by climatic factors, particularly by the rainfall and temperature, than by the character of the original rocks from which it was developed. Because the land is narrow and the climate dull, there are not very many types of soil. Generally speaking, the Kaema Plateau is exposed to cold weather and dense humidity. Under these natural circumstances, the organic substances of the soil are comparatively very well preserved and much podsolized soil is to be found in the area. The small areas around the estuaries both of the Yalu and Tumen Rivers at the Manchurian border are abundant in black soil while terra rossa is to be found largely in the provinces of Pyongan Namdo, Hwanghae-do and the southern part of Kangwon-do. As a whole, the soil of the southern coast is red while that over the better part of the country is brown.

Rural Communities and Urban Cities

Villages

Geographical Conditions of Korean Villages

Villages in Korea are, almost without exception, so settled as to face the plains and turn the back to the mountains. In other words, typical Korean villages shoulder mountains and face streams. The pattern was shaped mainly under the influence of the divination theories that have been prevalent in Korea from the remote ages. The pattern still offers various practical advantages to the inhabitants in many ways.

Mountains rising north of the villages provide effective shields against the cold northwest winds in winter. The gentle slopes that the villages face to the south are extended to the plains before to absorb greater beams and heat from the sun during the day, thus making for evening warmth. Mountains, as it were, bar chilly winds and preserve solar heat.

Plains skirting the villages to the south serve as farmlands, and irrigation of rice paddies is relatively easy because few villages are without streams running nearby. Because of streams, the villages are also spared the problem of water shortage in dry seasons; because of mountains, winter fuel is easily procurable. Smooth drainage is possible as are abundant crops and a variety of natural products.

Functions and Forms of Korean Villages

Korea is an agricultural country and all the villages in the country are farming villages. As a peninsula, Korea also ranks among the nations blessed with rich maritime resources. She has a small number of fishing villages, some strictly so but most relying on both fishing and farming for their existence.

Korea may be a mountainous country but few mountain villages are found because the forests are denuded. Only a limited number of mountain-farm villages are to be found scattered over the mountainous area, presenting a singular picture.

One of the characteristic of Korean villages is that the majority of them are heavily crowded with houses in narrow spaces. Such "concentrated villages" were originally formed mainly to protect the villagers against possible enemy attacks or such natural calamities as floods. Of course, conveniences, such as common use of water, and the sheer grouping instinct of the human also played their dominant parts. But in times of disturbances and insecurity, it was more vital to live closely together and protect the constituents' lives or properties against their common enemies. It was for the same reason that, in the medieval ages, many of the Mediterranean cities or villages in Europe were built on hills or uplands instead of on flat lands or coasts and that the majority of the ancient cities of Korea were surrounded by walls.

Rice farming, for which irrigation is essential, constitutes the major part of agriculture in the monsoon areas of Southeast Asia, and Korea is no exception. The irrigation projects for rice paddies require great 'abor on the part of the beneficiaries, the villagers. Transplantation and harvest of rice require exchange of labor among the villagers. Thus, one of the major reasons for the formation of "concentrated villages" stems from agricultural needs.

Except in summer, most of the year is dry, but few villages suffer from shortage of drinking water because Korean villages hardly fail to shoulder mountains as a backdrop and the mountains serve as a reservoir that supplies drinking water to the wells that are dug in villages. Usually, a well is dug for common use by several households, and one of the most familiar sights of the Korean countryside is the housewife carrying a water jug on her head from the communal well to her home early in the morning. A village has several such common wells and, usually, 10 or more families depend on one each for their potable water.

Since most of the forests are sparse, the mountains bald and temperature differences marked, the people are strongly affected by the climate. Big floods are not an uncommon disaster. In order to counter the floods, banks were constructed along rivers and the embankments, in turn, required heavy labor and cooperation among villagers. This was also one of the factors that necessitated the formation of "concentrated villages".

It is to be noted that the distribution of family villages becomes rarer the deeper north. The largest number of family village units appeared between 300 to 500 years ago, presumably in the wake of the Hideyoshi invasion. It is conceivable that the people, fleeing before the muskets of the foreign invader from the south, formed villages wherever they happened to settle down in groups with the same blood-tie.

If the villages in Korea are to be classified on the basis of population, there are 150 embracing more than 150 families, 251 for 100 to 150 families, 498 for 60 to 100, 595 for 30 to 60, and 191 for 30. Those embracing 30 to 100 families constitute about 65% of the total. The big villages with more than 100 families are dominant in the Cholla-do and Kyongsang-do Provinces. The steady decline of such villages, however, has become inevitable under the impact of industrialization, expansion of urban areas, development in traffic facilities, etc.

Contrary to the case of the concentrated villages, the so-called "scattered villages" in which houses are somewhat separated, have had little chance of growing in Korea. This was only natural in an agricultural country producing rice as the chief crop. Today, most of the scattered villages are to be found over the Kaema Plateau and Taebaek Mountains.

The mountain-farm is the issue of what might be described as plunder farming. Mountain-farm villages have been developed chiefly by those who, losing out in the struggle for existence, escaped deep into the mountains to burn the woods and cultivate untrodden hills. The mountain-farmers usually cultivate acreages a multiple number of times larger than those of the ordinary farmers. It is under such conditions that the mountain villages became scattered.

Cities

Development of Cities

The ancient capital cities of Korea, such as Kyongju of the Silla Kingdom, Puyo of Paekche, and Pyongyang of Koguryo, were described in historical records as having grown into big cities with populations of more than a million at the height of their prosperity. The expansion of capitals, however, was exceptional for most of the other cities were left in poor state. Even capitals that once flourished became deserted villages once the government transferred.

As Korea is an agricultural country, it was difficult to have centralized populations in urban areas. For this reason, the nation has lagged far behind the other countries in the formation and development of modern cities. Until the beginning of this century, farmers constituted about 90% of the total population of the country. On the other hand, the urban population was only 3.4% in 1920, rising to less than 4.4% in 1930. It increased to 7% in 1935 and 11.9% in 1940.

Construction of a hydroelectric plant along the Pujon River and a nitrogenous manure plant in Hungnam in the 1930's marked the beginning of the industrialization of Korea. The development of electricity, exploitation of underground resources and construction of modern industrial installations accelerated the expansion of the urban areas and the emergence of new cities, accompanied by rapid growth of population. In the northern part of the country, the process was faster than elsewhere in the country.

The population of Seoul, the capital city of Korea, rose to about 1,100,000 in 1943 from about 200,000 in 1920. Other major cities, including Pyongyang, Pusan, Chongjin, and Inchon also registered equally great increases in population during the period. Small villages such as Najin, Hungnam or Agoji emerged as important commercial and industrial centers.

The number of cities also rapidly increased. In 1920, there were only 12 cities, in 1944, there were 22. Particularly, the populations of the cities in the southern part have rapidly increased after the liberation of the country from Japanese colonial rule, though urban industries were crippled by the territorial division and the subsequent war. The rapid increase in the population of the southern cities is attributable to the fact that a great number of people returned from abroad following the Liberation and other millions of refugees fleeing either Communist oppression or the havocs of war settled down in urban areas of the south.

There were 12 cities in the south when the country was liberated from Japanese rule. In 1949, there were 19 as Suwon, Chunchon, Iri, Sunchon, Yosu, Kimchon and Pohang were newly promoted to the status of city. This figure was further increased to 25 in 1955, when Cheju, Kyongju, Chungmu, Chinhae, Wonju and Kangnung also entered the city fold. Since 1955, two more cities, Chungju and Samchonpo, emerged to boost the total to 27.

The population of Seoul was inflated to 1,570,000 from 1,450,000 in the same six-year period. The rapid population growth was also noted in all other major cities, including Pusan, Taegu, Kwangju, Taejon, and Masan during the same period. But such small cities as Mokpo, Kunsan, Chinju and Pohang shrunk in population as compared with the major cities.

Functions and Forms of Cities

As administrative centers, most Korean cities consume rather than produce. Although the industries of the nation have now been developed to some extent, industrial cities are still limited in number.

Korea has few resort cities or cities that are centers of religious or academic life.

Following is a classification of cities on the basis of function:

1) Political or Administrative Centers: Seoul, Chongju, Chonju, Kwangju, Kangnung, Taegu, Chunchon, Cheju, Haeju, Hamhung, etc.

2) Commercial Centers: Pusan, Masan, Mokpo, Kunsan, Inchon, Kimchon, Kangnung, Najin, Wonsan, Chinnampo, etc.

3) Industrial Centers: Hungnam, Songjin, Chongjin, Sinuiju, Pyongyang, etc.

4) Mining Centers: Pukchin, Musan, etc.

5) Fishery Centers: Sinpo, Sokcho, Pohang, Chungmu, Samchonpo, Yosu, etc.

6) Agricultural Centers: Iri, Suwon, Sariwon.

7) Transportation Centers: Taejon, Chonan, Seoul, Pyongyang, Iri, etc.

8) Sight-seeing Centers: Kyongju, Seoul, Pyongyang, Kaesong, etc.

9) Military Centers: Chinhae, Wonju, Kwangju, etc.

In a strict sense, however, these classifications do not describe the exact character and functions of the cities, because there are only few cities that are dedicated to any one function.

As Korean cities were founded in the

remote ages and built wihout any planning, their streets are generally narrow and irregular. In particular, Seoul, the capital city, and several other old cities are characterized by complicated, maze-like streets. In general, traces of city planning can be found only in the commercial or industrial cities that have emerged in recent times. The appearance of a street serves as a criterion for judging whether the city to which the street belongs is old or new. Many cities with irregular streets have been readjusted through postwar reconstruction efforts.

Unlike in the United States or European countries where downtown areas are rich in skyscrapers, Korean cities have seen little vertical expansions. For this reason, Korean cities are sometimes called "giant villages" rather than cities. Even in Seoul, the major portion of its downtown areas is occupied by flat, single-storeyed buildings. Residential quarters of the cities are also filled with flat buildings and there are few multi-storeyed apartment buildings.

Geographical Distribution of Plants and Animals

Distribution of Plants

The peninsula is usually divided into three botanical zones according to varied climates in the northern, central and southern areas. Distribution of plants in each area is mainly determined by different temperatures and other climatic factors.

The northern zone occupies the area between the northern frontier and the line which connects Wonsan Bay in the Eastern Sea (Sea of Japan) and Cape Changsan stretching out into the Yellow Sea. Plants peculiar to this zone grow in Hamgyong Pukto, Hamgyong Namdo, Pyongan Pukto and Pyongan Namdo especially on Mount Paektu and the Kaema Plateau.

The southern zone, relatively warm, occupies the area south of the line connecting Yongil Bay in the Eastren Sea and the Taean Peninsula and numerous small islands in the South Sea. In some southern islands, there are rue-family plants such as the *pocirus trifoliate* which is very rare on the mainland.

The intermediate area between the two zones above constitutes the central zone. Plants growing in Kumgang and Sroak Mountains are peculiar to this zone. Cheju-do Province, an island 60 miles off the southern tip of the mainland, and the Ulnung Island, 20 miles off the east coast, have rather different botanical distributions respectively. In the Halla Mountains on Cheju Island, plants of Japanese origin are intermingled with those of native origin. The Ulnung Island is well known for its *fagus nultinervis* which has been fossilized in the mainland and Japan since the last stage of the diluvial epoch, offering interesting data for botanical research.

Plants Specially Designated for Protection

The Government has designated the following plants for special preservation:

256 red pines (*Pinus Bungeana*) distributed throughout the land: 158 *Pinus Tumbergu* growing in the southern zone and coastal area: a selected number of oaks (*Biota orien talis var nepalensis*): 11 willows (*Salix Koreansis*): 9 paulownias (*Paulownia Koreana*): 1 datetree (*Zizyphus jujuba*) growing in Chungchong Namdo: 57 acorns (*Quercus acuttissima*): 72 *Hemipteraia Davidii* distributed in the central and northern zones.

The number of plants under government protection amounts to more than 5,000.

Distribution of Animals

The country generally belongs to the northern zone from geographical and climatic viewpoints and is divided into two regions, sub-Siberian and sub-Chinese. The sub-Siberian region occupies the area embracing Kaema Plateau north of Myohyang and Pujon Ranges. This mountainous region is on high latitude, and its climate is similar to that of the Amur region. Therefore, Arctic animals are peculiar to this area. The sub-Chinese region occupies the rest of the land including western, central and southern areas. The region is relatively on low latitude, warm and inhabited by animals of the temperate zone.

Birds and beasts inhabiting this country are mostly common to those of other regions of the Asian Continent, because the peninsula is connected geographically to the Continent, and the number of animals indigenous to the country is relatively small. Out of 90 kinds of terrestrial mammals found in Korea, only 35 kinds are indigenous and others are common to those of other regions of the Continent. The remarkable fact is that many kinds of wild beasts, rapacious birds and giant animals are still to be found in the country. Tigers (*Felis tigris coreensis*), pards (*Felis pardus orientalis*), Lynxes (*Lynx cervaris*), leopards (*Canis lpus langer*), and bears (*Ursus thibetanus, ussuricus,* and *Ursus cavifrons*) are typical kinds of the wild beasts. In comparison with this, in Japan, 24 kinds of terrestrial mammals are all indigenous and there is no animal common to those on the Continent.

Animals Specially Designated for Protection

The Government has designated several kinds of animals for special preservation on the basis of scientific research. Among them, *Dryocopus rıchardsi tristram*, a kind of woodpecker inhabiting the Kwangnung area, Kyonggi-do, is very famous. Kwangnung is the only place in the world where this kind of pecker, which is diminishing in number, still survives, presenting important data for scientific research.

Chindo dogs, which are indigenous to Chindo Island, Cholla Namdo preserves features of the palaeolithic canine animal. *Collipogon relicpus semonov*. An invertebrate and the biggest beetle found in the country, is also protected. The fact that the same kind of beetle is distributed in Manchuria and Central America, provides a valuable ground for the hypothesis that the Asian and American Continents were once connected.

Some migratory birds of the *Griodae* family which migrate to Siberia after wintering in the country, are also protected.

↑ Autumn landscape of Korea
Blue sky and clear breeze; persimmons in the foreground. A typical scene in the central parts of Korea.

↑ Rock of Demon Face, Mount Kumgang (Diamond Mountains)
   One of the best scenes of Old Manmulsang (Reflection of All Nature) in Mount Kumgang embracing the most typical and magnificent beauty of Nature in its various shaped rocks of oddity and peculiarity.

↑ Mount Halla in Cheju Island
  The snow which covers the mountain is a dear sight for people living at the foot of the mountain where snowfall can hardly be seen all the year round.

↑ Mild Contour Lines of Korean Mountains
  Most mountain peaks constitute monadnocks like this, created as a result of long years of erosion.

↑ Chonji, or Lake Heaven, on the Crest of Mount Paektu
   Calmly rippling clear water filled in the big crater on the crest of this conical volcano seems to have something mystical.

↑ Kaema Plateau
   About 2,000-meter high lava field, the highest and largest plateau in Korea, mostly covered by dense forests now.

↑ Snow Clad Mountains
Ready and waiting for skiers.

↑ A Distant View of Mount Halla
 Showing the complete whole figure towering 1,950 meters at the center of the volcanic island, Cheju-do.

↑ Songsan and Songsanpo
 A fishing port in Cheju Island, with gigantic rocky mountain, Songsan, in the background.

↑ Ipsoktae (Standing Stones) of Mount Mudung
　One of the best scenes in Cholla Namdo. Pillarlike huge rocks standing in crowds on the 1,187-meter high mountain.

↑ Taegwanryong
　A 865-meter high mountain in the Taebaek Range. Once a key point for transportation to cross the Range, now the best resort for skiers in wintertime among the few ski areas of Korea.

↑ Mount Namhan, Kwangju, Kyonggi-do
   Noted as the site of an ancient fortress as well as for its scenic beauty.

↑ A Dead Tree on a High Mountain Range
   A scene on the Sochongbong Peak of Mount Sorak (1,708 ms), Kangwon-do.

↑   Hwachon Dam in the Middle of the North Han River
   The fifth of the hydro-electric power plant dams in Korea. The Hwachon water-power plant near this dam can generate 87,000 Kws of electricity chiefly furnishing the Seoul and Inchon areas.

↑ The Han River (514 kms)
Starting from the Taebaek Range in the middle of Korea, flows west through the three provinces of Kangwon-do, Chungchong Pukto and Kyonggi-do into the Yellow Sea. It is divided into two parts of the South Han, the main stream, and the North Han, the tributary. This picture shows its lower reaches flowing through the city of Seoul.

↑ Lake Anap in Kyongju City, Kyongsang Pukto
   Once the sumptuous palace of Silla dynasty, now dried up and deserted.

↑ Lake Kyongpo
   Kyongpodae Arbor at the lakeside is one of the Most Beautiful Eight Sceneries in Kangwon-do
7 kilometers northeast of Kangnung City, Kangwon-do.

↑ Railway-Bridge over the Taedong River
  The Taedong River flows a total 438 kilometers in length starting from the northeastern tip of Pyongan Namdo, through Pyongyang City, into the Yellow Sea. Some 260 kilometers of the river is navigable.

The South Han River and Tangumdae Arbor
  One of two large tributaries of the Han River flowing nearby Chungju city, Chungchong Pukto.
↓ An arbor called Tangumdae on its side is a famous scenic spot.

←
Tokto Island
A deserted island in the Eastern Sea far off the Korean coast, 49 miles southeast of Ullungdo Island.

Rock of Candlestick →
A peculiarly shaped standing rock at the coast of Ullungdo Island, a center of fishery in the Eastern Sea.

←
The Eastern Sea (Sea of Japan)
Because of alternating warm and cold currents the limpid and tranquil Eastern Sea is abundant in various fishes to make it the treasury of Korean fishery.

↑ Sunset on a Sea-Coast
   Gulls are flying into the port of Soguipo, Cheju Island, with the setting sun in the background.

↑ Hanryo Channel
   The channel between Yosu city, Cholla Namdo, and Hansando island, Kyongsang Namdo, is one of the beautiful sceneries on the southern coast.

↑ Usuyong in Haenam, Cholla Namdo
   Naval base in ancient days, but now noted for its picturesque scenery.

↑ Oryukto Islands
  Islands scattered on the sea off the southern coast of Kyongsang Namdo. At night a blinking light can be seen from the lighthouse on one of these islands.

  Chongsokchong in Tongchon, Kangwon-do
  This arbor, built on stone pillars 4~21 meter in height, soars on the eastern coast of Korea
↓ making the landscape around it more beautiful.

↑ Tabodo Island off Taechon, Chungchong Namdo
  Around this island and Taechon beach is the most prosperous bathing resort on the west coast.

↑ Paeknyongdo Island
  Located on the Yellow Sea off the coast of Hwanghae-do. One of the beautiful sceneries in the west coast.

↑
Harvesting
 Diligent farmers thresh their products as soon as they are gathered in.

→
Rice-Paddy on Sloping Land
 As Korean farming is intensive, every inch of field is to be tilled, if the land is inclined, making for stems as shown in this picture.

←
Neatly Trimed Farm-Field
 All painstaking carings are over, and rice is just beginning to grow now.

↑ Korea's Granary
  Rice, staple food of the Korean people is produced all over the country In autumn, scarecrows are to be found here and there in golden waves of rice paddies.

↑ An Oxcart
One of the most important means of transportation for farmers. They get up early, carry things on carts to town and often have to engage in a lot of business before their meal

↑ Desolate Country Road
  More lonely in wintertime At rare intervals, a farmer appears on his way to sell an ox.

Seoul City

With a population of 1,850,000, the largest city of Korea is the center of politics, business, arts, education, and transportation in Korea.

↑ A Night View of the Capital City, Seoul
Seen from the southern bank of the Han River. The Han Bridge in the foreground.

← City Hall of Seoul

Sejongno Street
　On of th most beautiful streets in Seoul
↓

↑ Chongno Street
　The "Broadway" of Seoul embracing various kinds of shops, department stores, and business firms crowded together to serve as the commercial center of all Korea as well as of Seoul.

Myongdong Street
↓　The most prosperous entertainment section in Seoul.

Yaknyong-si (Chinese drugs market)

  With many Chinese-drugs stores, Taegu is the most famous city in Korea. For trade, many merchants gather twice every year.
↓

↑ City Hall of Taegu

Taegu City

  No. 3 city in south Korea. A distributing center of agricultural products in Kyongsang Pukto Provinces. Population 609,000.
↓

← City Hall of Pusan

Yongdo Bridge →
This is a mobile bascule bridge between main section of Pusan and Yongdo Island.

Harbor at Pusan City
Having 1,019,000 of population, Pusan is No. 2 city in Korea, but it has the largest harbor ↓ in Korea as a center of all foreign trade.

II HISTORY

Preface

Until assuming its modern form, the history of Korea has been a long process of complications and diversities. By this is meant not that the history itself was complicated but rather that the viewpoints and methods of treatment on the part of historians have been diverse and that these diversities led to complications.

Ancient Outlook

The first Korean historians appeared during the era of the Three Kingdoms, Yi Munjin of Koguryo who compiled a five-volume work called the "*Sinjip*", or "New Edition," Ko Hung who wrote a history of his Paekche kingdom, and Kochilbu, editor of the "*Kuksa*," a national history of his country, Silla. None of these works are extant today. We can only assume that they were conscious of the destinies of the kingdoms of which they were citizen and that, in all likelihood, their form of history-writing followed the ancient Chinese method of treatment. Since our only information from other records on these books is about their existence and not about their contents, it is impractical to make further comments thereupon. At least, we learn that history-writing began in the Three Kingdoms.

On the other hand, a number of materials are available from the period that gives us some idea of ancient Korean life. Such are the eighth century work, the "*Hwarang Segi*, (Hwarang Records)*" by one, Kim Taemun, and the "*Samdaemok*," a collection of ballads compiled by the Buddhist priest, Taegu, in the ninth century. It is also possible to a certain extent to peer into the structure of the ancient Korean society through the works of other Silla priests, most notably, the works of the outstanding Buddhist monk, Wonhyo, although their records were not intended to serve as latter-day sources of historical perspectives.

History becomes less ambiguous in the Koryo period which produced the two works on which almost all our information rests about the history of the Three Kingdoms. The first of these, the "*Samguk Sagi*," or "Annals of the Three Kingdoms," was a 50-volume compilation by Kim Pusik, official twelfth century historian of the Confucian school. The sole official record available to understand the Three Kingdoms, the method of treatment was hardly scientific and has been much criticized on that score by modern scholars. There are inconsistencies in the presentation of some historical facts and the style of writing was based on the Chinese. On the other hand, the 5-volume "*Samguk Yusa*," or "Reminiscences of the Three Kingdoms," by an unofficial thirteenth century Buddhist historiographer, was virtually a history of Bud-

II HISTORY

dhism and Buddhist priests of the Three-Kingdom era. Underlying the concept of Korean unity in the separate kingdoms, it is more a history of national ideals and tradition than of objective history.

The perspective becomes clearer in the Yi dynasty with the work of the fifteenth century scholar, So Kojong. In his "*Tongguk Tonggam* (Comprehensive Survey of Tongguk, i.e. Korea)", the writer offers his interpretations of the contents of the "*Samguk Sagi*" and "*Samguk Yusa*" and includes other materials in an attempt to clarify the social structures of all the Three Kingdoms. He also comes down to the history of the recent Koryo past. Much material is, of course, readily available here since Koryo left her writings behind but the succeeding Yi Kingdom was hardly objective in tackling them. The new dynasty had to justify itself. Thus, there had to be a revision of the "*Koryo Sillok*," the detailed official record of the preceding dynasty, and the result was such slanted compilations as the "*Koryosa* (History of Koryo)" which made Koryo social structure out to be nothing but decadent, corrupt, unhealthy. There was an element of truth in this prejudice, especially with regard to descriptions of the later stage of Koryo which, indeed, was in a decaying state. Latter-day historians may gain a realistic insight into the feudal structure of Koryo from the "*Koryosa*" but they must, of course, be aware that the more progressive phases of Koryo history have been overlooked. The Yi kingdom itself retained many Koryo institutions and incorporated these into their own programs of social reform.

The Yi monarchs kept meticulous records of their achievements that serve as good source materials for the study of Yi history. Such are the "*Sungjongwon Ilgi* (Journal of the Royal Secretariat)", "*Yijo Sillok* (True Records of the Yi Dynasty)", *Pibyonsa Tungnok* (Records of the Military Office)", "*Ilsongnok* (Record of Government Administration)", etc. The "*Tongsa Kangmok* (a History of Korea)" and the "*Yonnyosil Kisul* (Record of the Yi Dynasty from Taejo to Hyonjong)", written after the Chinese school of history in the seventeenth century, are original in that the writers, An Chongbok and Yi Kungik respectively, intended to give objective accounts of historical developments aside from state-compiled histories as had hitherto been the case. There were other departures. Thus the "*Haedong Yoksa* (History: from Tangun to Koryo)" by Han Chiyun was an example of writing Korean history from foreign viewpoints, the historian drawing his materials from foreign historical records. Prior to Han, there were such historians as Yu Hyongwon, Yi Ik and Chong Yakyong, who dealt severally with the political, economic or legal aspects of Korean history. Then there was Yi Kyehwan who, in his "*Taengniji* (Records of the Provinces)", approached the social, economic and political histories of the country from a geographical viewpoint.

Modern Outlook

The Korean Scholar

With the coming of modern currents from Japan toward the end of the Yi dynasty, a whole new approach to history was required. Thus, the royal government undertook to compile the "*Tongguk Saryak*" which was a text-book form of history. The late Choe Namson, one of the most prominent of modern Korean historians, wrote a history of Korea called the "*Chosun Yoksa* (History of Korea)" which had the effect of interesting the general public in the subject. Other text-book histories were forthcoming from the pens of such historians as Kwon Tokkyu, Chang Tobin and Hwang Uidon. Sin Chaeho wrote the "*Chosun Sanggosa* (Ancient History of Korea)" and "*Chosun Munhwasa* (History of Korean Culture)" with a view to rediscovering the national consciousness. The "*Chosunsa Yonggu* (A Study of Korean History)" by Chong Inbo was an expanded version of Sin's works as was the "*Chosun Sanggo Sagam* (Review of Korean Ancient History)", by An Chaehong, the moderate political figure of the post-Liberation era.

Other phases of Korean life were also considered.

Such was the "*Chosun Munhak Wollyu* (Origins of Korean Literature)" by Chong Inbo and the works of An Hwak. These historians were followed by a train of Japanese-educated colleagues, Kim Taejun ("History of the Korean Novel"), Kim Chaechol ("History of the Korean Drama"), Cho Yunjae ("A Brief History of Korean Poems"), and many others.

The consolidation of modern approaches yielded many other important works well into the twentieth century. In history, there were a "Study of the Koryo Period" by Yi Pyongdo, "History of Confucianism in Korea" by Hyon Sangyun, "History of Cultural Relations in the East" by Kim Sanggi and "Study of Korean Culture" by Yi Sangbaek. In the field of political history, great strides were made over the pioneering efforts of An Hwak who dealt mainly with political systems. Such was Ko Kwonsam's "Political History of Korea." Socio-economic history was explored extensively by Marxist-minded historians in the years before and after the Liberation year of 1945. Works by Paek Namwun, Choe Ikhan, Pak Sihyong, Pak Kukchae, Kim Sokhyong, Kim Hanju, Pak Mungyu, Chon Soktam, Yi Pukman and Yi Chongwon contributed new landmarks to the economic history of Korea. More recently, the economic theorist, Choe Hojin, completed an "Economic History of Modern Korea" as based on the theories and principles of Karl Wittvogel. This work, together with the "Industrial History of Korea" by Ko Sungje, must be considered in any serious study of contemporary Korean problems in modernization. On the other hand, Chon Kwanu's "Study of Yu Hyongwon" is a significant effort at exploring the feudalistic structure of Yi society. Religious trends in Korean history may be gathered from such works as Yi Nunghwa's "Records of the Ancient Religions of Korea," a collection of classical data; "History of Buddhism in Korea" by the same author, and the English-language "History of Protestant Missions in Korea—1862-1910" by George L. Paek, American-educated President of the Yonsei University. The names, Ko Yusop and Kim Yongjun, are well known for their pioneering research into the history of Korean artistic trends. As yet, no significant historical contribution has been made to trace the origins and spiritual beliefs of the Korean race. The possibility of uncovering enough facts to fill this gap suggests the possibility of a fresh, new approach to Korean history in general at some future date.

The Japanese Scholar

The seeds of modern Japan's imperialism were laid toward the end of the last century to cope successfully with an age of Great Power colonialisms. Her path lay in the direction of the Asian continent and to conflicts with China and Russia. Korea was the corridor through which her ambitions marched. Through Korea her armies marched to victories in the wars against China and Russia and in Korea they stayed to found a colony and consolidate an empire which overreached itself many years after at Pearl Harbor. The peninsula was annexed in 1910.

The corollary to this imperialistic drive was the need to acquire as much knowledge as possible about Korea. The Japanese spearheaded the Great Power efforts to modernize the peninsula and conduct research work after the opening of the "Hermit Kingdom" in the latter part of the nineteenth century. With the Annexation, the Japanese had a free hand and, modernizer or research worker, they were here as conquerors, contributing to the colonization and exploitation of the land. The Government-General for Korea established a Committee for Research into Korean Customs and Mores, commissioned museums to publish reports on archeological findings, and instructed the Keijo Imperial University in Seoul to collect ancient Korean books as well as conduct researches into the history, language and literature of Korea. The Government-General also initiated a Committee for Compilation of Korean History which completed the collection and classification of Korean historical data in 1930. In 1928, preliminary work in cataloguing and indexing these data was completed in 35 volumes and, based on this, a final manuscript prepared. Considerable knowledge of Korean history was brought to light by the work of the Japanese scholars involved.

For all their merits, these works should be carefully evaluated and objectively approached for a true insight into Korean history. One cannot consider the individual works or studies of scholars subjected to colonial policy to be sufficiently objective or truly disinterested. This volume bears that in mind. Prepared by several historians, each dealing with a specific period, the work may lack uniformity in style or continuity from one period to another. It is, however, an attempt to be exact within the specific limitations. Only in this way will the trend of Korean history be better understood with the passage of time.

Primitive Culture and the Beginning of the Tribal States

Neolithic Culture

The most probable theory about the origin of the Korean race was the settlement of the Tungusic branch among the Ural-Altaic tribes in regions of the Shantung Peninsula of northern China, southern Manchuria and the Korean Peninsula, forming one cultural zone in lands around the Yellow Sea with the center at the Gulf of Chihli. Some four to five thousand years ago, the Tungus were moving down the Korean Peninsula to settle in the Taedong River basin before the pressure of population in northern China. No remains of the palaeolithic age have been uncovered in Korea and only few in Manchuria.

Therefore, there is no way of knowing where and how the first ancestors of the Korean people lived. We must come down to the neolithic age before archaeology reveals something.

Neolithic remains show that there were two distinctive kinds of people living in Korea. One group may be called the "comb-ceramic" people after the discoveries of comb-ceramics along coastal regions and river basins. These are similar to the earthenware often found with stone implements of the micralithic age in the river basins of Central Asia, Siberia and Mongolia. Some were red-tinted with iron oxide contents, suggesting the influence of Chinese color-tinted ceramics. The "comb-ceramic" people were a primitive hunting and farming tribe.

The second group left far more to posterity. Tools used by this group included axes, spears, hoes, knives and grain-polishing plates. Mostly they were made by rubbing but often enough they were pounded. There were also such things as bone needles, stone rings, crescent jades, earthenware spinning wheels. Shell-mounds have also been found in the Unggi region of Hamgyong Pukto and the Hoeryong region at the northeastern corner of the peninsula, and some of the pits in these mounds reveal a heating system similar to the *ondol*, the traditional floor heating system of Korean homes to this day. These findings indicate considerable settlements and the position of the mounds with the body laid to face south and the head pointing east betray religious influence.

In the history of Wi written ages later, it is said that each tribe of the Ye community had their boundaries marked by mountains. The tribes were prohibited to hunt, fish or till the land across these high borders in the territory of another. Indogamy was also barred among all the tribes. They knew something of sericulture and astrology but as yet, the tribal chieftains were not powerful.

Metal Culture

Korea did not enter the metal age until the fifth century B.C. For geographical reasons, the Taedong River basin was the first to be acquainted with the next stage in prehistoric civilization. The bronze culture of China and Siberia was first introduced there. In China, itself, bronze was already being replaced by iron. It is interesting to note, in this connection, that traits of both cultures often appear in the archaeological findings of this age.

The bronze culture of the northern tribes have unique features of its own although it derived from the Chinese. It was the culture that predominated in Korea until the establishment of Chinese garrisons in the land and even after this event, which heralded the new iron age, bronze continued to flourish in the southern parts of the peninsula. This bronze culture stems from the Scythian.

The main archaeological findings of the age consist of the Mingtaochien coins which were used by the northern Chinese kingdoms of Yen, Chi and Chao. In China, such coins have been found in Luanping and Fushun in the Mukden province of southern Manchuria. In Korea, they have turned up in Wiwon, Kanggye and Yongbyon of Pyongan Pukto, and in the Yongwon area of Pyongan Namdo. The coins suggest the route taken by the bronze culture.

The legends of Tangun and Kija, rulers of Korea before Wi, have been treated lightly by the Japanese sholars who devoted themselves mainly to the spurious characteristics of the legends without trying to understand or evaluate their historical import. The fact is that the Tangun legend received the influences of Buddhism and Taoism as it was handed down through the ages finally to become a myth of national foundation with Tangun as the founder. From a study of the original structure and scope of the legend, however, we learn that it was the property of just one tribal state in the beginning, specifically, the state that occupied the Taedong River basin. The primitive theocracy was ended with the advent of the bronze culture. Accordingly, it became necessary to revise the tale. It was probably out of this necessity that the beginning of a new legend was born in the person of one, Chi-tzu, of the Chinese state of Yin.

According to this legend, Chi-tzu, or Kija in Korean, was banished from China and he settled in the Taedong River basin to found a country. His subjects called themselves the people of Han and they were the most powerful tribe of the times until Wiman came to power.

About three or four centuries before Christ, the Han were at war with the Yen. The Han lost Liaotung and retreated south across the Yalu. Other tribes of the bronze culture gradually followed suit to integrate with the Han race in the Korean peninsula. In 195 B.C., there were other Yen exiles. Lu-wan settled among the Huns to the north, Wei-man, or Wiman in Korean, went farther east where he soon dominated a group of wandering tribes and eventually overthrew the Han ruler to become master of the Taedong River basin. Thus, the state of Wi was founded by consolidation of the Han race, the wandering tribes, and exiles from northern China. Wi prospered by trading with the Han dynasty of the Central Kingdom thus rising to a position of leadership over the peninsula. But the other tribes did not sit idle. Seeing the advantages of trade with the Han kingdom, they soon sought channels to China without going through Wi land.

The result was running competition with Wi and friction between Wi and Han China whose merchants were tempted to deal directly with all the various peoples of Korea and ran into misunderstandings with Wi which wanted monopoly.

In 109 B.C., Han invaded Wi and established the four colonies of Lolang, Chenfan, Hsuntu and Lintun.

Lolang and the Tribal States

Wiman destroyed Han Chosun to establish Wi Chosun and Han China destroyed Wi Chosun to establish the four Chinese colonies and prevent any union of ancient Chosun with the Huns in northern China. The Han kingdom on the China mainland now had strong defenses to the north and an easternmost base in Lolang which enabled them to extend their trade with all the tribal states in Korea and even with Japan. On the other hand, the tribal states in the peninsula lost whatever potential power they had to unite and solidify their strength. The formation of strong enough tribal states was held back three to four centuries. Also, Japanese power now entered Kaya, a country on the southern tip of the peninsula, in order better to facilitate their Lolang trade.

For four centuries, Lolang lorded it over the Taedong River basin as a Chinese colony bringing the advanced culture of the mainland to the peninsula. Agriculture became a major industry, thanks to the new iron-made farming implements. The Chinese political system was also introduced. Judging from the archaeological remains in Lolang tombs, their living standards were very high compared to that of the tribal states. Their economics was too much for the indigenous society that had not yet developed the concept of private property.

To maintain order, the primitive Korean law had to be expanded from eight provisions, sixty articles. With economic exploitation of the colonizers, a traditional way of life was impaired and slavery came for the first time to the lives of these primitive Koreans.

Eventually, however, China relinquished direct control. For one thing, Yen had its hands full with the conquest of Liaotung. Some Korean tribes were able, more or less, to preserve their own traditions. Such were the five Puyo tribes inhabiting the Manchurian region of Nungan. Part of these tribes drove the Hsuantu out of their settlements along the River Yalu and established the tribal state of Koguryo. Another branch moved down the northeastern coast of the peninsula to form the community of East Ye. While Puyo proper and East Ye remained peaceful, Koguryo developed frictions with Liaotung and Lolang, attacking, Han settlements and cutting off Han routes to Korea.

While the struggle for supremacy was going on in the north through the periods of ancient Chosun and Lolang, many tribes had to move south of the River Han to find new land. Defeated though they were in the north, they rose to power in the south where the tribes they encountered were still in the neolithic age and unable to cope with the new bronze arms and farming tools carried by the newcomers. Native and invader united and soon formed new tribal states, such as Mahan, Chinhan and Pyonhan. As they did not possess enough bronze weapons, they substituted stone swords for burial with their dead. But their chieftains called themselves "kings from heaven" and conquered inferior neighbors. They also had a religious head apart from the tribal chieftain and there were *sodo,* or sacred places, where the tribal chieftain could not trespass. Anybody taking asylum in a *sodo* was immune from his power.

With increased introduction of bronze culture, the southern tribes built irrigations and started paddy-rice farming. With development of agriculture, their economic strength grew.

This, in turn, led to increased cultural exchange among the various tribes and improvement in living standards. Although they were still at the neolithic stage, it is not difficult to assume that their stone dwellings improved considerably; in some cases, perhaps, tiled roofs appeared.

As tribal chieftains throughout the peninsula gained more power, the form of tombs changed from dolmens, cairns, cists or jar-tombs to tombs of the Han pattern.

The dolmen, moreover, gave way to huge

monuments. Koguryo dolmens gradually gave way to the stone-room structure of Lolang and later passed this on to Silla in the south.

The Three Kingdoms: Their Formation, Development and Culture

From Conflicts to Unity

Koguryo was the first of the ancient states to found a kingdom. Its center was located along the Yalu. Next came the Kingdom of Paekche in the valley of the River Han. The third and last was Silla in the Kyongju plain. Koguryo successfully cut off China's invasion route to the east and thereafter expanded vigorously. Its growth may be traced in three stages. First, it wrested Hwando from the Chinese and from there started out on a slow road of subjugating other tribes. The conquest of East Ye a century later enabled them to form a strong alliance among the tribes living generally in the northeastern sector of the peninsula. Meanwhile, the loss of Hwando compelled the Chinese to use the western coastal route to Lolang. The second stage of Koguryo expansion came when they cut this route off and consolidated the tribes along it into the kingdom. A further squeeze was put on the Central Kingdom when the 11th king of Koguryo, Tongchon, established diplomatic relations with the Wu dynasty in southern China. With the fall of Soanpyong, Lolang became completely isolated and, in 313 A.D. fell to Koguryo after more than 420 years of existence. With its national strength thus boosted, Koguryo now turned west to compete with the Wi and Chien Yen Kingdoms of China for supremacy on the Liaotung Peninsula. The third stage begins with the reign of the 19th King, Kwanggaeto. To the west, Koguryo penetrated Liao; to the south, it occupied the entire Han River valley and made Silla a tributary state. In the 15th year of the reign of the twentieth King, Changsu, the capital was moved down to the capital of ancient Chosun, Pyongyang.

While Koguryo rose from the Yalu valley to challenge the Chinese supremacy and finally succeeded in establishing a state, it was, incidentally, defending the rest of the peninsula from further northern encroachments. Thus, with pressure from Lolang relaxed, Paekche in the Han River basin was able to rise. During the reign of its 13th King, Kunchogo (347-374A.D.), the southern Kingdom clashed with Koguryo. Defeated by Kwanggaeto and Changsu, Paekche had to move the seat of its capital from Kwangju on the River Han to Kongju on the River Kum and then again to Puyo farther south.

In the southeastern part of the peninsula, Silla, too, was growing, thanks mainly to its absorption of refugees from the northern arenas of fighting. It was then the least developed of the three kingdoms, beset by Japanese pirates who harassed its coastal areas. In the reign of its seventeenth King, Naemul (356-401), Silla managed to drive these pirates out for good with Koguryo's help and establish a patriarchal monarchy.

It is necessary to pause briefly here to explain the pattern of power in the Oriental world during this period. The Orient was divided into two power blocs, a northern bloc consisting of Chien Chin in North China, Koguryo over wide areas of Manchuria and the northern part of Korea, and Silla in the southeastern corner of the peninsula, and a southern bloc which embraced South China, Paekche in the southwestern part of Korea, and Japan across the seas. Militarily and culturally, then, Silla was aided and supported by Koguryo.

As it grew strong enough, however, it turned against its ally, Koguryo, in alliance with the other peninsular power of the rival southern bloc, Paekche, and, in the reigns of its 20th and 21st rulers between the years 458 and 499, managed to defeat the powerful northern kingdom. The victory gave Silla control of the Han basin and, from the mouth of this river, an open sea route to the China mainland. On the mainland, meantime, the period of the Northern and Southern dynasties was brought to an end as the new power of Sui arose to unite the divided peoples. Confronted with this new power, Koguryo was unable to punish Silla for its impunity. Sui engaged Koguryo in 612 and met a humiliating defeat that resulted in the downfall of the dynasty itself. Its successor, the Tang dynasty, picked up the cudgel in 645 but again Koguryo was victorious. Tang needed help to cope with the Koguryo power and that was where Silla found its advantage. The southeastern kingdom entered into a military alliance with the mainland power and the joint allied forces of Silla and Tang defeated, first Paekche in 661, then Koguryo in 668. Thus Silla was able to unify the entire Korean Peninsula but no more. The vast Manchurian territory beyond the Yalu which had been part of the Koguryo kingdom went out of Korean control.

Social Structure

The introduction of bronze culture meant the dissolution of the tribal communities of ancient Korea. Under Lolang's influence, the tribes formed a new social structure on the foundation of their former community systems. In other words, the tribal chieftains united for the common good of their various communities.

Out of such unities arose a more powerful patriarchal type of leader. The patriarch was called *utchi*, meaning elder, in Koguryo, *kan* or *naema* in Silla. Paekche had no patriarch for its case differed at the outset from the others. To create a state, tribal solidarity came first. The need was met in Koguryo by a "federation of the five tribes" and in Silla by a "league of the six tribes".

But the tribal communities of Paekche were completely dissolved by Lolang before they had a chance to salvage what unity they could and it was a Lolang representative and no native who ruled. Naturally, this resulted in more Chinese cultural influence in Paekche than in the other two states. Paekche land was divided into five different administrative units as was their capital. Koguryo had three cities and a number of districts and counties. Silla had two cities and five districts which, in turn, were subdivided into counties. In both Koguryo and Silla, the structure of the tribal federation was strong enough to ensure the hegemony of the leading classes until the last days of their respective kingdoms.

As regards government, each administrative division had chiefs. In Koguryo, they were called *sohyong*, *taehyong* and *taedaehyong*; in Silla, *saji* and *taesaji*. In both cases they meant the same thing; i.e. they were different ranks: junior chief, senior chief and superior chief respectively. In Paekche, to the contrary, the administrative chiefs were given rank and position after the Chinese model: *chwapyong*, *talsol*, *unsol*, *toksol*; *changdok*, *sidok*, *kodok*, *mundok*, *mudok*, and so forth.

The social classes of Koguryo and Paekche are not known. In Silla, there were four classes; namely, the *sadupum* of minor patriarchs, the *odupum* of major patriarchs, the *yukdupum* of the lower nobility and the *chingol* of upper nobility and royalty. Men of the lower stratum had to obey those of the higher but within the same class, everyone was regarded as equal and any resolution at a meeting required unanimous consent. In each echelon, at least, dictatorial tendencies were checked.

Meanwhile, there was an elite class whose duty was the training of youth. Young men were trained in the military arts and the Chinese classics to qualify themselves for this elite. These students were called the *hwarang*, later to become the backbone of the kingdom in its wars of Korean unification.

Not much material is available to determine the economic system of this period. Certainly, crop farming was the major occupation; cattle raising and fishing came next. The revenue was based on per capita taxation and tributes. The noble classes owned slaves, farms and land. They also practised usury in grains and clothing materials. Those who could not meet taxes or pay off their debts became slaves. Prisoners-of-war and captives from enemy land also became slaves. In this way, a system of slavery gradually came into existence.

Handicraft industry was developed almost exclusively for the benefit of the royal family and nobility. Hemp weaving, however, spread widely and products were exported to China. New knowledge in architecture and arms manufacture came from China. All industries, however, were supervised by the patriarchs for home consumption and were not meant for commercial trade. Mintage was as yet unknown.

Cultures

The bronze age was the beginning of culture in the three kingdoms, the iron age meant agricultural efficiency and increased production. With adaptation of the Chinese political system, governments were instituted, and with Confucianism and Buddhism, spiritual life began. Militarily, Koguryo held out against a series of Chinese invasions, subjected Lolang to its control, and inherited its culture. It further imported the cultures of India and North China.

Of the three kingdoms, Paekche received most from Lolang. The kingdom later added the influence of China's Southern dynasty to develop a most sophisticated culture. Silla was a latecomer in the field, absorbing the cultures of Koguryo and Paekche at a time when these two kingdoms were already long influenced from abroad.

Buddhism reformed the spiritual life of the early Koreans and stimulated their national consciousness. It reached Koguryo first through Chien Chin in the year, 327 A.D., and from Koguryo, went to Silla. Paekche, on the other hand, received Buddhism from Tung Chin and transmitted it to Japan. At times, Buddhism clashed with Shamanism and other native religions but toward the end of the Three-Kingdom era, the monk, Wonhyo, placed it on a firm foundation in all the underdeveloped communities of the country.

With the overall growth of culture, the Chinese Classics became a popular subject for study. In Koguryo, schools were established to teach these Classics. Paekche, the most advanced in this learning, eventually introduced it to Japan. All three kingdoms also began to compile their histories. These are not extant today but from the records of the Koryo period, it may be assumed that they dealt mainly with problems of royal authority and national spirit. Koguryo called its royal family, "Children of the Sun," indicating a native tradition rather than the new foreign influences. Silla evidently had less of a pre-Buddhistic culture judging from what it called royalty. Between the opening of the sixth century and the middle of the seventh, the ruler was called Kshatriya; King Chinbyong was named after the Gautama's father, Suddhodana, and his queen was Maya, Buddha's mother. It follows that virtually all of Silla history was written with Buddhism in mind. Paekche may have been the most advanced as regards the absorption of Chinese culture but it was the least successful in developing a tradition of its own. It would appear that this kingdom had little of the characteristics that made Silla and Koguryo strong.

In art, Koguryo tombs betray a style that was Koguryo's own. The paintings on the walls indicate an aggressive people. Paekche, on the other hand, was far more refined as may be gathered from the fresco paintings and stone stupas it has left behind. Before the period when it controlled all Korea, Silla's appreciation of beauty was but little advanced from the primitive stage, judging from its extant gold crowns and other ornaments.

In music, Koguryo imbibed Indian, Western and Chinese influences and was instrumental in the development of Paekche and Silla music. As for poetry, the only thing we know about it today is Silla ballads.

Culture of Unified Silla

Silla and Pohai

In the Period of the Three Kingdoms, Silla was the least developed and the most constantly oppressed by the other two. The weakening of Koguryo power in the war against Sui and Tang was Silla's opportunity for unity. This opportunity was taken and Silla was on the road that finally brought the Korean Peninsula under its control. But a new state soon arose on the plains of Manchuria.

This was Pohai which took over the social and cultural heritage of Koguryo and served as a dam warding off Tang pressure from the new kingdom of Unified Silla.

With peninsular domination, Unified Silla felt the need to reform its governmental system. It absorbed the erstwhile offiicials of Koguryo and Paekche into its political system, established a "hostages system" for the local clan community chiefs, and expanded local administration. A new criminal law, containing sixty odd provisions, was also legislated and an office of government inspectors created to supervise local officials.

Administrative divisions were reorganized into nine provinces and five cities, three provinces each in the original Silla, Koguryo and Paekche territories, respectively.

With the capital at Kyongju, cities were built at Wonju, Chungju, Chongju, Namwon and Kimhae, roughly skirting the Kyongju perimeter along the Sobaek chain of mountains. The provinces were further subdivided for an aggregate total of 117 counties and 294 districts. In the 16th year of King Kyongdok's reign (757), area units were renamed in accordance with the Chinese system. Military strength was maintained from the preunified stage, troops being stationed at strategic points.

The noble classes of the former kingdoms of Koguryo and Paekche retained considerable power and privileges during the early days of Unified Silla, gradually to decline during the most prosperous period between 654-779 from pressures intended to strengthen the royal hand. To rationalize this policy, the Government espoused the political principles of Confucianism and, in 682, established state schools to teach Confucian doctrine.

Officials from the noble classes originally received their rewards in land from which they collected their own taxes. Now, however, the Government carried out a land reform program depriving them of land and establishing a new system of salaries in order to curb their power among the people. Some of the farmlands were also placed outside the jurisdiction of the local community chiefs for the same reason. The arrangement soon proved unfeasible and the Government had to revert to the original scheme of things. This meant the beginning of autocratic decline.

At any rate, culture flourished during the period on the social and cultural groundwork of Koguryo and Paekche to which was added imported Tang influences. Kyongju became one of the four cultural centers of Asia, the other three being Changan in Tang, Shangking in Pohai and Nara in Japan. The noblemen of Kyongju began to acquire a refined taste for beauty. The representations of Silla art that survive today as Korea's ancient boast are largely drawn from this period: the Sakyamuni Buddha statue of the Sokkuram Cave Temple, the gigantic bronze bell of Temple Pongdoksa and the outstanding temple buildings called the Pulguksa.

Many monks and scholars also travelled to China and India, bringing back many new sciences. Among the brilliant priests were Wonhyo, Wisang, Wonchuk and Hyecho. Kangsu, Solchong and Kimsaeng are among the renowned Confucian scholars. In the reign of King Songdok, the famous scholar, Kim Taemun, wrote his great works, the "*Hwarang Segi*," "*Kerim Chapjon*," "*Hansangi*" and a "Biography of the Great Monks". Nobles read Taoism and Lao Tze, already introduced to bygone Koguryo and Paekche.

While Unified Silla was thus flourishing, the descendents of Koguryo were maintaining the new state of Pohai to the north. When Koguryo fell, one of its generals, Taejoyong, fled with his followers to Yingchou in the Manchurian province of Jehol. At this time, Khitai was growing in power and one of its chiefs, Li Chin-chung, attacked Yingchou in a revolt against Tang (696). Seeing in this pressure on the Central Kingdom an opportunity to increase his power, Taejoyong crossed into Liao and realigned the Koguryo people of the Tungmou mountains in Kirin Province. He united with a people called the Malgals or Niuchens thus to establish a new state in the year, 699. This state was later called Pohai (Palhae in Korean). Its territory embraced Manchuria, the areas around the sea of Okhotsk in Siberia and Korean areas north of the Taedong. Unlike Koguryo, Pohai had practically no trade with Silla, only with Japan and Tang. During the reign of Mu, Taejoyong's son, the Kingdom clashed with Tang at Tengchou, Shantung Province, in 732 in retaliation against the Central Kingdoms' interference in Pohai's earlier bid to absorb the Niuchens. At this time, Tang formerly extended recognition to former Koguryo areas south of the Taedong as Silla territory in a move to present a second front against Pohai. However, in the reign of its next ruler, Pohai exchanged friendly emissaries with the Tang Kingdom and, with cultural exchanges, much of the Tang culture streamed in, influencing the political system of a state which needed something new in order to rule a complex society made up, on one hand, of Koguryo people who were developed but had lost their country, and, on the other, of the Niuchens who were less developed. Copying the Tang structure, it created three departments and six ministries for Loyalty (state affairs), Benevolence (finance), Righteousness (protocol and ceremonials), Propriety (justice), Wisdom (defense) and Sincerity (industry). Its latter-day capital, Shangking in Kirin Province, was a planned city copied after the Tang capital of Changan.

The influence of Buddhist culture produced high artistic and handicraft standards which made Pohai the civilizing force of eastern Manchuria. However, it had adverse conditions, such as the climate and the less-developed segment of the Malgal population. Overall cultural advances were, therefore, proceeding at a very slow pace. Finally, Pohai was destroyed by the rising new nation of Khitai and the Koguryo branch of the state, which constituted the leading class, returned to Korea as refugees as they had once fled from it. By that time, there was a new kingdom in the peninsula, the Koryo dynasty.

Decline of Silla

Although the despotic power of the rulers was strong, so was the power of the noble classes and local chiefs and the strength of the latter became uncontrollable in the middle stage of Unified Silla. The nobles had feudal domains, private troops, slaves. Under the clan system, their power grew to such proportions that there were frequent clashes among them that could easily lead to civil war and even a general revolt against the monarch. During the reign of Hyegong alone (765-779), ninety-six clan chieftains fought one another, and in the latter part of the dynasty (780-925), no less than twenty rulers succeeded to the throne, an average of eight years per ruler. King and noblemen became the victims of one conspiratorial revolt after another.

On the spiritual side of life, the Zen school of Buddhism was newly introduced toward the end of the dynasty to clash with the Buddhist sects already established. The Zen sect, in turn, split into nine different groups later on and fought one another. On the other hand, the nobles continued to read Taoism and Lao Tze, reinforcing spiritual solidarity on another plane.

Out of all the chaos, two trends of power grew to threaten the foundations of the state. One comprised gangs of poverty-stricken people in inland areas who looted taxed grains and other commodities that were enroute to the capital. The other were pirates of the coastal areas who seized control of the Korean waters. They were led by men who are as well known to the general public as Jesse James and Captain Kidd. Conditions were ripe to challenge the existing state of affairs and, in 892, a local chief, Chin Hwon, staged a revolt in the Kum River valley to create a new state called Hu-Paekche (literally, Later Paekche). Another chief, Kungye, went further by leading a direct revolt against the king. Kungye was ousted in 918 by yet another rebellious chief, one, Wanggon. Wanggon made himself King of a new state, Koryo. He then turned against Chin's Hu-Paekche. By 935, he finally succeeded in stamping out the last resistances of both Hu-Paekche and Silla and, with a strong economic background of his clan and control of the seas which he seized from the pirates, established his Koryo kingdom as the kingdom for all Korea. Songdo, or Kaesong as it is now known, was the new capital. It was the home of Wanggon's clan. Wanggon, of course, was the first king of Koryo. His royal name was Taejo, literally "Great Original Ancestor."

Koryo Dynasty

Characteristics of the Koryo Dynasty

With the submission of Silla in 935, order was brought to the chaotic conditions prevailing in the last days of the dynasty. With the surrender of Hu-Paekche in 936, Taejo's new kingdom of Koryo in and around the city of Songdo was able to establish itself as the new dynasty for all Korea. The new dynasty ruled over the Korean peninsula for 475 years. Altogether, there were 34 kings.

Koryo was a dynamic dynasty and, as such, linked the preceding Silla with the succeeding Yi. The new government extended favorable treatment to the ex-nobility of Silla and patterned itself after the governmental structure of the latter in carrying out its task of peninsula-wide reorganization. In essense, however, the kingdom was different from Silla. Whereas the socio-political structure of the latter was based on a patriarchal system that transformed the clanships of the latter years into a successive wave of revolts from the slaves and the uncontrollable growth of local patriarchal powers, Koryo started out with a feudalistic structure of society. It was only natural then that the old patriarchal system should give way gradually with the natural tide of changing social conditions to a rising feudal one.

In Koryo, therefore, the aristocracy and not patriarchs became the core of the state. Pedigree was the decisive factor in determining the political and social status of the individual. On the spiritual plane, Buddhism enjoyed a golden age during the Koryo dynasty, playing a most important role not only in the spiritual but also in the political and economic life of the Korean people.

Koryo was the most energetic of all Korean kingdoms in developing diplomatic relations with foreign countries. Necessity impelled this for throughout its domination, there was never a period when foreign invasion did not cease. In succession, the kingdom had to fight off invaders from Liao, Tartar, Chin and Yuan to the north. In fact, the history of Koryo is a history of recurrent wars against the foreigner. It was from this dynasty that the Occidental world derived its name for Korea.

Establishment of the Koryo Kingdom

Centralization of Power

While Taejo was busy subjecting the peninsula to his control, his sovereign power was yet to be firmly established. In the capital, military leaders commanded their own private foot-soldiers and, in the countryside, powerful families enjoyed a semi-independent status. To consolidate centralized power, then, Taejo had to follow the old Silla system and espouse generous policies. This he generally did, avoiding overall reforms. He recognized the nobilities of Silla and Hu-Paekche and appointed the heads of powerful local familiies to community leadership with self-governing authority and no supervisory officials from the central government. Taejo also wrote a number of books on political science intended to serve as guide for consolidation of the kingdom. While he lived, his educational zeal was effective. As soon as his son, Hyejong, succeeded to the throne, however, squabbles arose among the more powerful of the nobles who saw in the succession a chance to replace the sovereign head. But the urge for centralization was strong in the new state and the aberrations were soon brought under control.

Credit for an effective centralized system of government goes to the fourth King, Kwangjong. On one hand, he mercilessly dismissed many nobles; on the other, he released some slaves to decrease the power of the nobility. He also adopted a new examination system for governmental posts which again proved effective in suppressing the noble classes. Kwangjong was succeeded by Kyongjong who devised a land reform that provided an important source of state revenue. These first series of reforms were completed in the reign of the sixth monarch, Songjong (981-997), and further reforms initiated in the reigns of the next five kings. By the middle of the eleventh century, the kingdom was so firmly saddled that local families of power lost all their self-governing rights to administrators appointed by Songdo. Thereafter, these families became only minor officials under central supervision. Private foot-soldiers, whether of military or noble classes, were gradually disbanded and reorganized into the armed forces of the state. The first effective action in this respect was taken by Songjong who ordered the confiscation of arms from the districts and countries. This paved the way for centralized military forces under the command of his successor, Mukchong.

The central government consisted of two departments. One was the privy council, highest organ of the kingdom, that assisted the king; the other was an executive department divided into six ministries for local administration, finance, protocol-foreign affairs-education, defense, justice and industry. There were also special bodies, such as an office of inspection, an office of audit, etc. Finally, a state council, composed of high-ranking departmental officials.

In Songjong's reign, an administrator was sent to each of the twelve districts. Later, the country was divided into ten provinces which, in turn, were subdivided into districts, sub-districts, counties and sub-counties. However, in the reign of the eighth King, Hyonjong, the provincial pattern was reorganized, providing for the six provinces of Kyonggi, Yanggwang, Kyongsang, Cholla, Kyoju, Sohae, and two border zones, Eastern Boundary and Northern Boundary, the governors of the last two vested with both civil authority and military command. The central government was also wont to send administrators to more than five hundred sub-divisions under these major administrative units. Such administrators were officials of the lowest ranks but their responsibilities were great for they collected taxes and handled legal matters. Naturally, the high-ranking officials were drawn from the Koryo nobility in the capital. They were too lofty to be appointed to offices in lower echelons.

The leaders of once-powerful families in the provinces were now subsidiary officials to the local administrators appointed by Songdo. They had the task of actually collecting the taxes and tributes as well as of mobilizing labor forces for state projects. Humbled though they were, these officials were agents of government and this fact, together with their family backgrounds, yet gave them tremendous authority within their own communities. To check such growth, the central government appointed inspectors from among the noble class and established a hostage system under which the subsidiary officials were obliged to send their sons to Songdo. A unique feature was the special administrative divisions called the *hyang, so* and *pugok*. Carried over from Silla, these divisions existed for the benefit of the lowest stratum of Korean society. They were discriminated from the status of the county or sub-county although the areas involved were sometime much larger. The divisions were governed not by centrally-appointed officials but powerful clan leaders in the locality.

The military system perfected under Mukchong was composed of two field armies, each with six corps. Each corps was commanded by a general officer who was assisted by another lower-ranking general officer. Under the six corps was a total of 45 divisions, each made up of approximately 1,000 soldiers. Thus the regular strength was about forty to fifty thousands. Men between the ages of 20 and 60 were conscripted to serve alternate periods of rotation. The commanding generals of both field armies and corps formed a supreme committee for military affairs It was from this committee that the nucleus of power was born, leading later to the revolt of the military leaders against the political affairs of state and the replacement of civil officials by the military.

Land and Education

In the reign of the fifth ruler, Kyongjong, work began on a new system for the land. The work was completed in the reign of the eleventh King, Munjong (1046–1083), after revisions in Mukchong's time. Under the system, called *Chonjigwa* (Rules for Land and Fuel Resources), all land was nationalized and private ownership denied. Farm and forest lands were allocated to officials in proportion to their 18 grades. When an official died, his allotted land was returned to the government. Apart from the *Chonjigwa*, there was also a special allocation that was hereditary for meritorious services rendered by retainers and high-ranking officials. Other special acreages were also set aside for governmental agencies, Buddhist temples and the royal family.

Land allocations did not mean the transfer of ownership but only the right of the recipient to collect tax on the land as income. Such lands were called *sajon* (literally, private land) as opposed to the *kongjon* (public land) which yielded taxes to the state. Regardless of whether the land was *sajon* or *kongjon*, the cultivators were, of course, farmers. The farming class had only the right to cultivate, never to receive "allocations." The farmer belonged to the land, the land was always reallocated. In other words, only the tax collector changed. On both *kongjon* and *sajon* land, the tax rate was 10 percent on the crops plus a little surtax charge. By the middle of the dynastic era, however, the rate on *sajon* land soared as high as 50 percent and the land recipients, in turn, had to pay the Government about 1.5 percent of what they collected. The grain tribute, another form of taxation, was first stored in the local government warehouse, then shipped by water to the state treasury of the capital. This constituted the revenue that went to the upkeeping of the military forces and the salaries of minor officials.

Nobility's highest aspiration, accordingly, was to become a government official that he might receive a land allocation and all the other privileges that went with the post. To become an official, one had to pass the state examinations and, to pass these, one had to receive an education at school. The sole purpose of education, then, was to serve as a means to office. The government official was required to be well versed in Confucianism, the Master being a political instrument. Naturally, Confucianism was the subject of the state examinations and the schools taught the principles of Confucius. The result was that nobility became interested only in doctrinaire studies. Technological approaches were ignored.

There were schools already established in Pyongyang and Songdo or Kaesong at the time of the founder's reign. The sixth King Songjong (981-997) expanded the University body in the capital by establishing four departments, *kukchahak, taehak, samunhak* and *chaphak*. The *kukchahak* was for children of Grade I-III officials, the *taehak* for children of officials (Grades IV and V), the *samunhak* for children of officials (Grades VI and VII), and the *chaphak* for the children of other ranks of officials, and commoners. The first three departments specialized in Confucian doctrine; the *chaphak* taught accounting and other subjects of a practical or technical nature.

Graduates of these institutes were eligible to sit as candidates for the state examinations that opened the doors to government posts. The examination system was established by the fourth ruler, Kwangjong (950 -975). It was successful in eliminating from the political scene the powerful military leaders whose arms had helped found the kingdom. Instead, the political offices were filled by civil servants and a bureaucracy came into being. Diverse subjects were introduced between the reigns of Kwangjong and Songjong, there were specializations in Literature, the Confucian Scriptures, and such minor subjects as Accounting, Medicine, Geography, etc. For the priests, there was a separate subject for Buddhism. But no subjects on military sciences. The military leaders, not unnaturally, complained about this omission which denied them the opportunity of acquiring enviable privileges of civil servants. Not until the reign of the 16th King, Yongjong, was a department of military science introduced and even then it was abolished with the very next king as the civil leaders put up strong opposition.

Rise of the Aristocracy

With increasing stability, the aristocracy became firmly consolidated. Aristocracy was developed out of the process of ennobling the government officials who came from the leading class in the early period of the dynasty. Such were the Kim family of Ansan, the Yi family of Kyongwon, the Kim of Kyongju, the Choe of Haeju, the Yun of Papyong, the Pak of Pyongsan, and many others. The descendents of Wanggon's associates who had helped him found the kingdom were also, of course, of the aristocracy, but for the most part, the ranks were filled by government officials of former Silla nobility who had passed the state examinations. The aristocrats intermarried with the royal family. The most successful families in this connecton were the Kim of Ansan and the Yi of Kyongwon. The House of Kim married off three daughters to the eighth monarch, Hyonjong (1010-1031), and through three successive accessions to the throne, maintained close matrimonial ties with royal blood. The House of Yi, already related to the Kim, sent three daughters to Munjong, the eleventh King, and maintained this lead through to the seventeenth ruler. Intermarriage with royalty was important in raising the family status so the various aristocratic Houses competed vigorously to send their daughters to the palace. Political power went to the king's left-handed relatives as a matter of course. Merely by being nobility, they held down important offices regardless of individual abilities, enjoying the economic and social privileges that came with their titles. With competition for better privileges came growing frictions among the aristocrats. Plots and conspiracies developed with increasing intensity, and the culminating point was reached in 1126 when Yi Chakyom of the House of the Kyongwon Yi, blood-relative to the monarch, revolted in a bid for the throne. The would-be king failed and later was assassinated by one of his subordinates. All members of the House were removed from government offices and banished from the capital. The Yi ambition was the beginning of the end for aristocracy. Thereafter, it declined but not before a series of other conspiracies, the most serious of which was the Myochong undertaking. Myochong was an aristocrat who held strong power in Pyongyang, the second most important city of the kingdom. He and his followers attempted to effect a reform by moving the capital from Kaesong to Pyongyang. To do this, it was necessary to suppress the Kaesong aristocrats but the latter naturally would have none of this. Whereupon Myochong embarked on military operations in 1135 only to be crushed by the forces of Kim Pusik, one of the most typical aristocrats in Songdo.

To sum up; the Koryo kingdom was founded on the basis of aristocracy. At the height of aristocratic power, the dynasty enjoyed a golden age. Great political strides were made and culture flourished during this age which lasted about 150 years between the reigns of Chongjong, the 10th King, and Injong, the 17th. At the same time, however, the aristocrats were laying the seeds of their own decay by heedlessly pursuing their own selfish interests. Aristocratic monopoly of governmental posts and increased rights on the farmlands led to the rise of strong economic and political factions with a proportionate decline in state finance. The nobles who depended on the government for their power destroyed themselves by weakening that Government.

Buddhism Comes to Its Own

The Koryo aristocrats were not only masters of politics but patrons of arts and sciences. The cultural developments of the dynasty were the work of aristocracy.

In the first of his ten commandments, King Taejo declared that the Koryo kingdom had been founded with the help and guidance of the Buddha and that his successors should worship him and defend his name. Accordingly, his successors devoted themselves to the Gautama's teachings. Buddhism was made the state religion and played an important role in the culture, ideology and way of life of Korea throughout the dynastic reign. It even controlled the political and economic life of the nation.

As a religion, Koryo Buddhism was a practical medium for carrying out state policy rather than an outlet for individual worship. For example in directing the monumental task of compiling and printing the Tripitaka Koreana, King Hyonjong (1010-1031) was motivated by the thought of giving his people a basis for spiritual unity against the Mongol conqueror. Naturally, the religion prospered under state support. Numerous temples were built throughout the country with state funds and the individual wealth of the aristocrats. Kaesong alone had more than three hundred temples. The temple was not merely a center of spiritual life; it wielded vast economic power, possessing large farmland holdings and tempting the tax-exempted monks to engage in usury and brewery business. Throughout the era, the monks held very high positions as advisors to the state. Kings deferred to them and many members of the royal family became monks themselves. There were also many accomplished scholars, studying not only Buddhism but Confucianism as well. Buddhist festivals were at their colorful peak and the whole nation turned out to enjoy them.

Buddhism and Confucianism were not incompatible at this time because the latter did not challenge the former as a religion but was merely a means to the attainment of government appointment. Consequently, Confucianism was developed by the Koryo aristocracy very much as Buddhism. As mentioned, the state examinations centered on Confucian studies and the many private educational institutes established during this period were centers of the most authoritative knowledge about Confucianism.

Koryo art was developed to meet the needs of the temple and the aristocratic taste. Most representative is the celadon, well-known to all connoisseurs. Influenced by Sung ceramics, celadons and their inlaid ceramics attest to the talent and creativeness of the Koryo artisans as well as to the high degrees of living standards achieved by the aristocracy. The Buddhist influence went mostly to temple buildings, stupas and sculptures. Today, only a few wooden monuments remain but enough to attest to the development of architecture. Such are the well-known halls, the Muryangsujon and Chosadang, in the Pusoksa temple of Yongju, the main building in the Sudoksa temple compounds, and the Ungjinjon of Sogwangsa temple in Anbyon. The Muryangsujon is the oldest wooden architectural monument that is extant in Korea today. It shows all the characteristics of Koryo architecture and, as such, is important to the scholars. Stupas, on the other hand, were mostly made of stone so a considerable number of them are still to be found. The most impressive stupas are the seven-storey one of Hyonhwasa temple in Kaesong, the nine-storey one of Woljongsa temple on Mount Odae, and the 13-storey one of Kyongchonsa temple. Statues also abound, the best-known being the stone statue at Unjin and the wooden Amitabha Buddha in Muryangsujon, the one for its size, the other for its grace and beauty.

Koryo's Foreign Relations

Foreign Policy

As a peninsula projecting from the northeastern corner of the Asian landmass, Korea was subject to the direct influence of the continent. Whatever happened on the continent immediately affected the peninsula; big or small, continental changes brought immediate changes in Korea's domestic politics. That was one aspect of the tied-in fate. The other was the fact that the initiative was always with the continent, it could never arise on the peninsula. The continent was the active agent and the peninsula always responded passively. The peninsula, in other words, was the passive- and instant- reagent. It had to find an overall foreign policy that could cope with events to which it could not otherwise rise to the occasion. Short of such a policy, events, instead, would have the overall effect of working against Korean interests. That policy was to hold fast to one ally, the strongest and stablest—the Central Kingdom; to put all the eggs in China's basket, so to speak. Hence arose the traditional and unquestioned policy of subservience to the Sun Emperor. It was one sure way of maintaining sovereignty.

This meant that so long as the Chinese power was strong enough to hold other nations down, Korea enjoyed peaceful relations with the continent, but when other nations gathered enough power to stand up against China, the peace was broken. Then, too, Korea, by tradition again, had always looked up to the Chinese power as teacher and down upon nations that challenged China as barbarians irrespective of their relative strengths. In other words, Korean security rested too heavily on the Sun Emperor and ignored the shaping of other forces. Because of this, Korea always suffered when the "barbarians" toppled the Sun Emperor and seized his power.

Unfortunately for the Koryo kings, they were ruling at a time when the Chinese were weak and the other races on her borders powerful. These races made their power felt on the peninsula throughout the Koryo era. Fortunately, the peninsula had a new dynasty which proved to be one of the most aggressive in all Korean history. Indeed, it had to be if it were to maintain itself against the "barbaric" pressures upon its borders. In succession, the Khitai, the Niuchen and the Mongol races rose to the north and fell upon Koryo. The history of the Koryo dynasty may well be said to have been a history of warding off these encroachments, in battle or by diplomacy. By and large, it did well. Only the Mongol power conquered and even so, the dynasty survived. A policy of subservience was worked out and Koryo sovereignty remained intact, in name if not in fact.

The Khitais and Niuchens

In the first half century or so of Koryo's establishment, China was a united land under the Sung dynasty, so Koryo's relations with the continent were peaceful. But the Khitai power soon reared its head and developed conflicts with Sung. As a prelude to the invasion of the Central Kingdom, the Khitais decided first to attack Koryo, the tributary state.

Three invasions were launched. The first came in the year 993. This was met by the astute diplomat-soldier, So Hui, who proved so persuasive in a face-to-face meeting with the commander of the invading forces that the invaders withdrew back across the Yalu. The gist of the Khitai's *casus belli* for the invasion was that Koryo had succeeded only to Silla's mantle and was, therefore, an aggressor on Koguryo land. To which So Hui replied that Koryo was the successor of Koguryo as well, as testified by the name of the state and, as such, was master of all areas south of the Yalu. The fact was that large areas south of the Yalu had been a sort of no-man's land and this fact apparently had tempted the Khitais. At any rate, the invaders withdrew and Koryo, geared to the emergency, physically occupied this no-man's land. In 1010, the Khitais mounted a more serious, large-scale attack. An army of 200,000 under the Khitai monarch himself swept down the peninsula to capture the capital city of Songdo itself. This invasion was met by the renowned general, Yang Kyu, who followed a scorched-earth policy of strategic retreat, sucked the invaders in, and then retaliated with a decisive victory that drove them all the way back across the Yalu and beyond. Eight years later they tried again only to be defeated at the decisive battle of Kuju by a fully prepared army under the supreme commander, General Kang Kamchan. Thereafter, Koryo and Khitai agreed on peace.

The Khitais had hardly left when the Niuchens came. This race has already been mentioned. Originally inhabiting areas near the northern boundary of Korea, they were subjects of the Pohai state that had been established by the Koguryo exiles who fled when Koguryo fell to Silla. An underdeveloped tribal group, the Niuchens had always looked up to Korea. They called Koryo their "motherland" and paid tributes to Songdo. But they, too, had grown powerful in the meantime and now decided to invade the "motherland." The defending Koryo forces were swept back in the first wave of the attack. Only Yun Kwan, another outstanding general appointed supreme commander to meet the emergency, managed to retaliate to the east, dislodging the invaders from the Hamhung area which Koryo immediately fortified with nine garrisons. But the Niuchen tide was too irresistible and under the pressure of incessant raids demanding the return of the territory, Koryo yielded and the garrisons were withdrawn.

That the Niuchens were out to create a stir was evident in the year 1115 when their leader, Akuta, called his nation Chin and crowned himself Emperor. Ten years later, the Emperor of Chin destroyed Liao (Khitai's nation) in alliance with Sung and followed this up by turning against the ally. The Niuchens drove the Sung Emperor south and occupied North China. Overnight they had grown all-powerful and exerted so much pressure upon Koryo that the latter deemed it wise to resort to the policy hitherto reserved only for the Chinese—the policy of subservience. The tributary status was reversed between the Niuchen and Korean peoples and peace maintained.

On the other hand, Koryo did not drop Sung because the Sun Emperor had been driven from his capital in Peking. Songdo continued to maintain diplomatic relations with the Chinese dynasty in the south. Unlike past experiences, the relationship with Hangchow, the new Sung capital, was more significant in terms of trade and culture than in politics. It was an age of lively international trade and the port of Pyongnando received not only the prosperous merchants of Sung but also Japanese dealers and even Arabian traders. Koryo imported silk, books, medicines and tea among other things from Sung; in return, it exported gold, silver, ginseng, etc. Sung and Arabic fineries found great favor with a Koryo aristocracy that had developed a high taste for luxuries. Koryo was very much part of the brisk trading that was going on in the world.

The Military Revolt

In 1170 occurred what is known as the "Revolt of the Military Leaders." The result was the complete overthrow of aristocratic rule and the assumption of power by army officers and a puppet role for the Koryo throne.

The indirect causes of the aristocratic downfall have been indicated in our previous outline of its decline. Basically, the aristocrats had laid the seeds of its own decline within itself during the hundred and fifty years of the "golden age." Just as the local patriarchs had grown too strong at the expense of centralized control in the patriarchal state of Unified Silla, so had the growing power of the Koryo feudal lords weakened the center and the feudalistic social order. The direct cause was the discrimination of military officers by the civil officials of the state. As mentioned, the state examinations system paved the path to state offices only for civil servants and these had created a bureaucracy that blocked the path of government career for the military. More specifically, both the military and civil servants of the state belonged to the upper classes, the *yangban*. *Yangban* is the Korean equivalent of nobility as distinguished from the *ssangnom*, commoner. Literally, it means "both classes", i.e. the two noble classes. The civil branch of government service belonged to the *tongban* or eastern class and the military to the *soban* or western class. In theory, the *yangban* system was a Dual Class aristocracy of civil and military servants of the state, but in fact, the civil components were the trunk and the military a branch. Ostensibly, they enjoyed equal status but actually, the *soban* was less highly regarded. The *tongban* received a Confucian education, took Confucian state examinations and entered into government service. They attracted the more promising of young noble sons. Only the uneducated and economically underprivileged would subscribe to a military career. No matter how promising, the top-ranking *soban* general could rise no higher than Grade III in government service, a fact which, among other things, affected his economic status. It was a frustrating cycle and the military chafed under the discrimination.

The first breach of the civil monopoly was made in 1014 when two army officers led a military revolt against the civil-dominated government of King Hyonjong and seized control. It was only a temporary reversal for the civil servants soon retaliated and regained control. Such, however, was the temper of the military a hundred and fifty years before the successful revolt—before the "golden age."

The ruler in the eventful year of 1170 was Uijong, the 18th ruler. He was a dissolute monarch who built pleasure-houses and pavilions all over the kingdom and played with his coterie of pleasure-seeking civil servants while entrusting the matter of national defense and royal bodyguards to the impoverished segment of the nobility. It was on one of those riotous events at a place called Pohyonwon that the military, led by Chong Chungbu and Yi Uibang, staged their successful coup d'etat.

After the Revolt

The army vengeance was swift and merciless. All important civil servants were killed in a general massacre. The king was forced to abdicate his throne to Myongjong (1171-1197), a maternal uncle to Uijong, whom the rebels chose and a military regime was imposed on the nation. The next quarter of a century was a period of utter chaos. In the provinces, the remnants of the civil class continued to resist the military regime; in the capital, the army officers fought fiercely among themselves for control of the central government, each with his own troops to protect his person. In the third year of the new monarch's reign, the loyalist, Kim Podang, precipitated another crisis with a counter-revolt against the military leaders. He was crushed but not before many more civil servants were killed in another wave of massacres. The very next year after Kim's bid for power, another loyalist, Cho Wichong, staged a large-scale armed rebellion in the provinces. It took the regime three years to put that one down. Within the military clique, Chong Chungbu assassinated his co-conspirator of the coup d'etat, Yi Uibang, and was in turn murdered by a young general, Kyong Taesung. Kyong was allowed to die peacefully but he was hardly in his death-bed before a General Yi Uimin took over the government and died by the familiar hand of the assassin. The name of his assassin was Choe Chunghon with whom the vicious cycle came to rest. Altogether, Myongjong, the handpicked monarch, had sat on the throne for twenty-six years while the military swirled around him. The swirls subsiding, he was put aside.

As the final victor in the grim power struggle of the army clique, Choe Chunghon succeeded in imposing a strong military regime. He did not hesitate to remove all those who dared to oppose him. Two kings stepped down from the throne and four kings asscended it on his authority. With everything under control, the General laid the cornerstone for a 60-year domination of the Choe warlords with the king as mere puppet.

As the death-knell of the aristocratic Dual Class system, the "Revolt of the Military Leaders" was another great landmark in the overall change of Korea's social structure. Men of humble origins became Cabinet Ministers and slaves rose to generalship. The disruption of social order produced waves upon waves of riots and revolts from farmers and other classes that had suffered oppression. The farmers rose mostly in the northern province of Pyongan-do and the southern province of Kyongsang-do, undoubtedly because the burden of oppression was felt most heavily the farther from the center. The farmers revolted against the military leaders and the slaves rose against the farmers. The system of state land ownership was buried and the rising military leaders had to acquire land by force in order to claim it. The land was then leased to tenants but the only effect of the tenant system was to weaken the sources of state revenue and reduce the farmers to yet lower depths of poverty.

The Mongol Invasion

Koryo had managed to ward off the Kitai and the Niuchen or Chin. With the Mongol, it was a different story. The Mongols, united under the world conqueror, Genghis Khan, had already destroyed the Chin power in Manchuria and occupied North China when they decided to launch another war against that ill-treated Central Kingdom, the Sung dynasty in the south. True to the pattern of Central Asian eruptions, to engage the Central Kingdom was to pressure the Korean peninsula. Confronted by a stubborn Choe regime with a strong foreign policy, the Mongols decided upon the physical occupation of Korea.

In 1231, the invading armies crossed the Yalu and pressed hard upon the capital. Koryo surrendered and concluded a peace treaty with the Mongols. The surrender was an expediency in order to gain breathing time for retrenching defences for a comeback. The Mongols had strong ground forces but no sea power.

Therefore, the Koryo government moved itself to the island of Kanghwa off the west coast the very next year following conclusion of the peace treaty. Here, they bided their time for "Der Tag." The Mongols, suspicious of this move, returned in force but was unable to take the small island just off the coast; they never did. Thus, government successfully defied the Mongol wrath which fell, instead, with shattering impact upon the mainland. The invading soldiery looted and killed at will and vast numbers of the population were left without home or food for a long time.

As hardships mounted to an extreme and complaints grew, division arose on Kanghwa over a policy that was tightening the Mongol grip at the expense of the vast majority of the people. Certain leaders of the government began to urge modification of the anti-Mongol attitude. Instead, the Choe regime embarked on the project, known as the Koreana Tripitaka. The idea was to unite the people under the Mongol heels by offering them a spiritual basis for unity in Buddhism. The Tripitaka was an attempt to compile all Buddhistic data in one large series of volumes. It was an arduous undertaking completed after many years. The defiance could not hold out for long, however, and in 1258, the Choe warlord was overthrown by the moderate party which negotiated a second surrender. Under the terms of the agreement which made Koryo a suzerain state of the Mongols, the government returned to Songdo. Independence-minded military leaders who remained on Kanghwa, opposed to this humility, turned against the returning government only to be met by the overwhelming forces of the government, backed by the Mongols. The die-hard rebels retreated to Cheju Island off the southern coast and here they held out for four more desperate years.

Mongol Domination

With the Mongol suzerainty, Koryo was stripped of every vestige of its political freedom. Kings had to marry Mongol princesses in keeping with the foreign policy of the Mongol Empire and the governmental system had to be modified along Mongol lines. Mongol officials were stationed in Koryo to supervise the activities of the Koryo government and the provinces of Hamgyong and Pyongan came under the direct rule of Karakorum. Pyongan-do was shortly returned but Hamgyong-do was retained for almost a hundred years and renounced only by force of arms applied with the weakening of the Mongol Empire. By that time, Koryo itself was disintegrating.

Finally, Koryo had to supply the ships and food for the Mongol armies which twice attempted the invasion of Japan. The demands caused tremendous economic hardships.

On the other hand, the Mongol domination opened the cultural windows of the peninsula to a wide world. Cultural exchanges between the Mongols and Koreans were frequent as officials, scholars and merchants visited one another. The Mongols did not have any distinctive culture of their own, having just emerged from the steppes, but their capital city of Karakorum was the center of a vast empire bringing together the various cultures from all four corners of the world. Here, Koryo was brought in contact with the astronomy, medicine, mathematics, arts and other cultures of the West. Here, too, the scholar, An Yu, introduced the new Confucian school of Chu Hsi which was to dominate the philosophy of the Yi kingdom. The language, dresses, hair-styles and other customs of the Mongols came to the court and upper classes of Koryo. Korean culture, too, streamed to the steppes, carried by the many travellers and emigrants who went there. Koryo exported gold, silver, ginseng and other things to the Mongols and the artistic merits of Koryo pottery and other crafts were first brought to the world's attention at Karakorum.

Decline of Koryo
Land Corruption

Even before the "Revolt of the Military Leaders," the increased personal domination of the farmlands had made the aristocratic class stronger than the government. We have referred to the hereditary land allocations made for meritorious services in an earlier chapter describing the land redistribution of the new Koryo state. In time, the pressure of growing generations among the hereditary nobles had permitted increases in the acreage of land holdings under the system. Moreover, the powerful were able illegally to qualify themselves for such "hereditary status" and became huge landlords. These private landholdings made the center of power a mere skeleton when the military revolt broke out. Seizing the power at the center, the military leaders, representing the discriminated branch of the *yangban* (Dual Class) system, asserted themselves by appropriating the state-owned lands as their own. It was their turn to be big landowners and their private land holdings multiplied rapidly, especially during the period of Mongol domination. The more powerful of the private aristocrats were able to take the blow to the center and a period of corrupt practices was ushered in with the military leaders, the powerful aristocrats and Buddhist temples reaching out for more and more under a state of nationwide disorganization. In fact, they became large-scale landlords with fields cultivated by tenants who were nothing more than agricultural slaves. Land became not only the economic but the political foundation of power as well.

With the increase in private land ownership, state-owned land decreased proportionately and, correspondingly, the national revenue dwindled to the point where, at last, the Government did not have sufficient resources to maintain itself. At the other extreme, numerous farmers became deprived of their tenant rights and either sold themselves to slavery or drifted helplessly. The monopolization of state-owned lands by a small number of military officers became the target of growing complaints among a new rising generation of civil servants who were being paid miserably on account of scarce national revenue. The civil servants finally came out with a strong demand for land redistribution but the king's power was too weak—and the power of the few aristocrats and military leaders too great—to effect such reform. Some monarchs tried it, each time to meet with strong united opposition.

This decline in the land system became the direct cause for the downfall of the Koryo dynasty. Toward the end, a reform was, indeed, carried out but this was done not by the king but under the weight of a growing upstart class, the civil servants and the less privileged among the military when they generated sufficient power. Naturally, the "reform" was for the benefit of the "reformers" and by no means of king, state or people. The result, therefore, was exactly the opposite of rehabilitating the kingdom. The dynasty fell and, with it, the aristocratic and militaristic classes which had caused the downfall by their all-out greed for personal gains.

Anti-Mongol Trend

Parallel with the economic and social cancers eating away at the corrupted kingdom, a fatal blow was dealt by the change in the international climate as if to speed a downfall that was only a matter of time. The main change that was occurring outside the Koryo borders was the fall of the Mongol Empire which had only recently ruled the better part of the known world. So far as Korea was concerned, the most important development was the revolt of the Chinese against their Mongol overlords whose control over that vast continent had gradually weakened. The Chinese finally succeeded in driving the Mongol power out and the ancient race of Han reasserted themselves under the Ming dynasty.

The Ming supremacy affected Koryo at once. A change in the foreign policy was in order and the kingdom discarded its tributary status with the Mongols and attempted to reinstate its own independence. King Kongmin (1352-1374) started an active anti-Mongol movement in the country. He killed off influential pro-Mongol Koreans, ended the Mongol system of government and drove the Mongol officials out of the country. It was this Kongmin who recovered the Hamgyong territory on which the Mongols had been sitting so long.

Kongmin's example, however, was by no means a decisive pattern. The Ming dynasty was still new and had not yet firmly established itself while, to the north, the Mongol Empire was still huge and powerful. The continental change had affected Koryo overnight and the political pendulum was oscillating like a compass needle. The kingdom was split right down the line, between the pro-Mongol power group which wanted to swing it back and the anti-Mongols who saw in the Ming reassertion the opportunity to throw off the foreign yoke—and more. Leading the pro-Mongols were two members of age-old, powerful families, Choe Hyong and Yi Inim. Two outstanding men of the rising new class of nobles, Yi Songgye and Chong Mongju, united with the Confucian scholars to lead the pro-Ming faction.

The pro-Mongols still held the balance of power and they began using it in blind disregard of the potentialities behind the sharp pro-Ming edge. First, they used their control of government to adopt a strong pro-Mongol policy; then, and heedless of the strong opposition put up by the pro-Ming elements, Choe Hyong led an all-out expeditionary force to invade the Ming Kingdom from its eastern flank—Liaotung. This was in 1388. One of the two field commanders dispatched on this expeditionary force of 40,000-strong was Yi Songgye of the pro-Ming faction that had objected so strongly to the overseas venture. When General Yi reached the Yalu which, at that time, was the Korean-Liaotung boundary, he gave a counter-order to his men. Instead of crossing the river border to engage the Ming kingdom in Manchuria, his army turned and headed straight back into a defenceless capital. He overthrew the King, cracked down hard upon the pro-Mongol power, and set his own chosen monarch on the throne. The foreign policy of the kingdom was reversed overnight.

Transition

The new power group consisted of the rising class of officials we have described as complaining increasingly against the power of reckless aristocrats and military leaders in the throes of nationwide confusion. The first thing they did, therefore, was to wipe out the landowners. Because they shared their dissatisfaction with the Confucian scholars, they encouraged Confucianism and discouraged Buddhism, the state religion. In this, in reforming the land system, in establishing a pro-Ming foreign policy, in short, in every conceivable way, they forced His Majesty's Government to espouse policies which went against the grain of the kingdom. In fact, they were busy nailing the lid on the coffin of a Koryo dynasty which had virtually gasped its last even before General Yi's turnabout. They were clearing the ground for a new dynasty.

With the remnants of the old power still putting up strong opposition to the proposed new land reforms emanating from the capital in the King's name, it was imperative for the new power to push their programs through rapidly to prevent any resurgence at the expense of the new economic foundation they wanted to lay. All land registration records were burned and all landlords deprived of their ownerships outright, irrespective of whether they had come by it legally or illegally. Their land was restored to the state and redistributed to the government officials of the new power group. It was the same kind of reform initiated by Koryo when they started out, a reform that provided a new power group the foundation upon which to establish a successor dynasty. With the redistribution of farmlands, the last nail was clamped on the Koryo kingdom.

A change was also in order on the religious plane and the Confucian scholars were there to effect this. To recapitulate: Koryo's religious tradition had been based entirely on Buddhism. It was the core not only of religious life, affecting the ideology, customs and morals of the nation, but also of the political and economic life of the state. The Buddhist monks enjoyed positions of high prestige and were able to influence politics so greatly that they came to wield both political and economic power. Corruption sank and, toward the end of the dynasty, many monks did not even pretend to be monks in any real sense. Its spiritual significance was lost and it was necessary to find a new center for faith. That faith was available. Confucianism had always been with Koryo and had even flourished but only as an instrument of government, not as a philosophy or ideology serving as the core of a nation's faith. But the declining years of the Koryo dynasty and Buddhism brought new life to the ancient teachings of the Master. This was the Chu Hsi school, introduced to Korea as an ideology. Confucianism and Buddhism now came into conflict and, with the latter badly discredited, the only alternative was the former. The Confucian scholars gave their fullest support to the new power group, thereby coming into their own. It was a historical change for what had been rejected was a deep-rooted religion.

Finis

The old power group lingered for a few more years, unable to summon will or strength to offset the reforms of the new, how much they might have wished to resurrect the "good old days." Not all of the reformers were in favor of scrapping kingdom and tradition. Thus, Chong Mongju, who with Yi Songgye had championed the pro-Ming cause from the start, believed in loyalty to king and state. A great Confucian scholar himself, Chong, defended the last of the Koryo kings to the last to be slain by a son of Yi Songgye while crossing a bridge. The mark on that bridge in Kaesong (former Songdo) today is supposed to be his bloodstain.

With Chong out of the way, there was nothing left to do but proclaim a new dynasty which, indeed, was the only alternative. The day came in July of 1392, four years after General Yi Songgye's coup d'etat, the General himself ascending the throne. Thus, the curtains were quietly drawn down on the 475-year reign of Koryo and a new Chosun era ushered in—the Yi dynasty.

Yi Chosun – Before Hideyoshi

Significance of the Yi Emergence
Emergence of a Bureaucratic State

The redistribution of farmlands and the supremacy of Confucianism at the expense of Buddhism were the two cardinal policies of the new Yi dynasty. At the helm was a general who had proved to be ever-victorious by his successful repulsions of both the Liao invaders to the north and Japanese pirates who had harassed the west coastal regions in the declining years of the Koryo dynasty. Yi Songgye also proved himself an able politician and ruler. Everything he undertook was as firm and decisive as the border turnabout with which he had taken the Koryo kingdom by surprise to speed the collapse of the collapsible. His first steps were to open close and friendly relations with the Ming dynasty and eliminate the pro-Yuan forces at home. That done, he bent his efforts on overall reforms of the economic and social institutions of the country with major emphasis on land redistribution.

As the first measure of a policy aimed at nationalization of all farmlands, his regime confiscated the lands owned by the former landlords and redistributed them to those government officials who had rendered meritorious services in the establishment of the new dynasty. In carrying out this policy even while the last Koryo King was still on his throne, the general defied the rigid opposition of the old aristocratic class. In fact, however, many of the old landlords were allowed to retain their hereditary estates because, while the new land reform prohibited the transfer of land ownership by heredity, it granted certain exceptions to the rule. This was apparently a major concession of the new regime to the old aristocracy. On the other hand, the landowners were asked (and this was a novelty) to pay taxes to the state for their possession of land. Although it was true that the land reform was not totally successful as it failed to do away with hereditary landownerships entirely, the imposition of taxes helped establish the effective control of the state over the farmlands.

Parallel with this distribution of land in general on a more equitable, rational basis, two kinds of other lands were specially set aside in order to strengthen the state machinery. Under the new laws of the state, military personnel were not allowed to own land so the armies were maintained with food raised from farmlands designated for that purpose. This, of course, helped tighten state control over the armed forces as well. The second "land preserves" went toward maintaining the expenses for running the various government offices which, indeed, largely depended upon them.

Generally speaking, the land reform programs brought about many favorable changes upon agricultural production, effectively protecting the farmers as they did from limitless exploitation by landlords. Thus, it marked a significant forward step in the historical pattern of the nation's agricultural systems.

Two years after establishing the new regime, Yi Songgye, changed the name of the country from Koryo to the ancient one of Chosun. In doing so, he first secured the approval of the Ming dynasty. Like the Koryo founder, he also assumed the kingly name, Taejo (Great Original Ancestor), and transferred the capital from Songdo (present-day Kaesong) to Hanyang (present-day Seoul). In the new capital, a large palace, the "*Kyongbokkung*", was built as was a long wall to surround the whole city.

The Yi dynasty rejected Buddhism because its teachings clashed with the needs of a new, rising power to establish a stronger and more prosperous state out of hand labor. Buddhism despised labor and so was detested in turn by the Chosun leaders, most of whom had been eager students of Confucianism and had learned to resent a system of government which gave the advantages of Confucian learning nothing but literary and rhetorical promotions without the opportunity to get into the heart of state affairs where they saw only corrupted or indolent monks. The most noted of these Confucian scholars playing a major role in bringing the new regime to existence was Chong Tojon. Chong not only proved his outstanding abilities as a politician and Confucian theoretician. He was also the author of the famous historical work, the "*Chosun Kyonggukjon*," which was made the basic guide for the rulers of the new kingdom.

Of the various Confucian theories that replaced the long-entrenched body of Buddhist codes on manners, formalities and etiquettes, Chu Hsi, the important Sung innovator of the Master's teachings, was accorded the highest respect and recognition. Confucianist principles were made the basis of the state's policies, and academic institutes created (the *Songgyungwan* and *Obuhaktang* in the capital that provided college-level education, and a system of common schools called the *Hyanggo* in the rural areas) to encourage Confucian studies throughout the country. In 1403, a type-foundry and printing office was established and many books published to spread the Confucian teachings.

For some time after the introduction of the land reform, the Buddhist temples were permitted to retain their slaves and lands. This enabled them to raise the expenditures necessary to maintain themselves and enjoy the support of many enthusiastic Buddhists still to be found within the ruling, privileged classes. It was, of course, a stay of grace extended primarily to give the new dynasty time to consolidate its bureaucratic system. Once such a system was established, the kingdom did not hesitate to adopt all sorts of measures designed to curb the temples. They were deprived of many privileges, including tax-exemptions, and nobody could become a monk without obtaining government permission. The pressure became heavier from the outset of the reign of Taejo's successor, Taejong, whose drastic restrictions led to the confiscation of virtually all their lands. Thus, within ten years, the number of Buddhist temples in the land was reduced to less than one-fifth that of the Koryo era.

Development of the Bureaucratic State

With the kingdom placed on a firm, unshakable foundation, Taejo set about the task of government. A supreme council was formed as the highest collegiate government organ to manage all administrative affairs for the king. This was called the *Topyonguisasa* (General Council of Administrative Offices). Made up of two civic leaders and two military with the king presiding, all decisions taken by the *Topyonguisasa* were referred to a cabinet body, the *Munhabu* (Junior Department) for implementation. The *Munhabu* consisted of six bureaus, handling personnel, population, protocol, military, judicial and technical affairs respectively, In 1400, the *Topyonguisasa* was abolished and replaced by a supreme administrative organ composed only of civic officials, the *Uijongbu* (Office for Management of All Political Affairs). All private armed forces were integrated into the state army placed under the exclusive command of the *Samgunbu*, (Department of the Three Armies), a newly-created military organ. With the *Samgunbu*, military personnel became divorced from politics and civil administration. In 1414, the authority and power of the supreme body, the *Uijongbu*, were again reduced and partially transferred to the six administrative bureaus and these, in turn, were thereafter given virtually exclusive authority to dispose of all matters under their jurisdiction. These rang the major changes in an experimental system leading to the consolidation of a bureaucratic state.

The local administrative units, too, were reformed and reorganized. In 1413, the whole country was divided into eight provinces. The provinces were subdivided into various *mok, pu, kun* and *hyon* units in that order, and a great part of the lower class communities of slaves, butchers or blacksmiths, carried over from Koryo, abolished to strengthen the power of the remotest countryside.

These sweeping reforms that affected almost all walks of national life, however, left the positions of the slave and servant classes intact. Slaves and servants continued to be employed not only for government service but also in the private households of the civic officials.

Meanwhile, to the north, a rejuvenated Korean kingdom drove off the various "barbaric" tribes which had descended from the plains of Manchuria to spell so much trouble in the border areas. The Yi forces successfully restored all Korean territories that had been occupied and pacified the unsettled areas long subject to constant raids and invasions. The boundary-line became stabilized definitely at the Yalu and Tumen borders with Manchuria, and the kingdom began to place special emphasis on the development of the remote areas, especially in the northernmost parts, to effect substantial increases in agricultural production.

Successive kings, in fact, maintained great interest in agricultural development and devoted their fullest attention to the problems of increasing farm outputs. This was particularly true of the fourth monarch, Sejong, who had the government publish many books aimed at acquainting the farmers with new and advanced methods of farming.

Development of Culture

While the reforms of the new dynasty boosted the national wealth, remarkable strides were also being made in the field of culture. A great many of the cultural works that were to prove of great historical import were produced during the first seventy years of Yi Chosun. Of these, the most invaluable were the "*Koryosa* (History of the Koryo Kingdom)", "*Yongbi-ochonga*," the first *hangul* publication, and a couple of medical books that revealed the vigor of Yi researches into herb medicine. The man most responsible for the brilliant age of culture, known as Korea's "Golden Age," was King Sejong (1419-1450), the most scholarly-minded ruler of the dynasty. He established on academic circle, known as the *Chiphyonjon* (literally, Hall for Assembly of the Wise) to which he invited the auhoritative scholars of Confucianist philosophy and technologies to enable them to study and develop ways of promoting the national culture. His encouragement and personal interest led to many new scientific and technological inventions, of which metal-type printing was, perhaps, the most laudable. Above all, he gave the Korean people an alphabet.

In simplifying the written word, Korea released herself from the restrictive bounds of Chinese ideographic mastery and went ahead of the Japanese who stopped at syllabic forms of writing. The task of devising the *hangul*, as the alpahabet was called, was by no means obviously easy for the development of Chinese writing had undergone a long historical process at the expense of the native language. Rather, it was arduous for the proposition was to make a clean break with tradition and that encouraged the ideal of perfection involving numerous complications both for reasons of practicality and ingrained scholarly prejudices.

The king worked personally for decades with a body of outstanding scholars. The result, at last, was a set of a few simple letters based upon plain, scientific principles that makes the Korean alphabet the world's most remarkable one for its degree of near-perfection. Even so, it was to be hundreds of more years before it was to gain any foothold against the scholarly prejudices for Chinese writing. It is still not fully utilized.

Institutions of Early Chosun

Bureaucratic Systems

With consolidation of its bureaucratic systems, the kingdom was ready to establish a basic code for government throughout the country. This was the *Kyongguk Taejon* which brought together the codified customary laws and decrees established since the founding of the new dynasty. The code stipulated the government organizations, central or local. Under the *Uijongbu*, the supreme policy-making body, and the *Yukcho*, a cabinet consisting of six departments, as stipulated by the code, there were three key organs with real power called the *Samsa*, and a secretariat for the King. Besides these, there were the *Uigumbu* and *Podochong* that wielded strong power as security and police headquarters respectively, the former dealing with treason and other serious crimes that might be committed by individuals of the *yangban* nobility. The officials of the *Samsa* enjoyed many privileges, and their status was completely guaranteed. They were authorized even to discuss the faults of the king and present remonstrances to him. They were also given the power to veto any governmental act, including enactment of laws or decrees, or reject the appointment or dismissal of any member of the government services.

The capital city was guarded by five special units of the government army, placed under the command of the *Owidochongbu*. The provincial armies were controlled by military commanders called the *pyongsa* (General) or *susa* (Admiral). The governor of each province, called the *kwanchalsa*, was vested with the power to deal with both the military and civil administrations. In that sense, he held currently the position of a military commander. The governors who exercised such mighty power, covering as it did almost all the branches of local administration, not excluding the military and judicial aspects, were picked almost exclusively from among those belonging to the privileged *yangban* class. The major job given to them was to collect taxes and tributes and mobilize labor power on behalf of the central government. But they were replaced so frequently that, in general, they lacked interest in carrying on effective and efficient administration any the less promote the welfare of the rural populace. In practice, therefore, administration was carried out by low-ranking officials who succeeded to their positions by heredity and these, because they were asked to serve the government without pay, were encouraged to raise wealth for themselves by systematic exploitation of the rural people. Inevitably, local administrations became completely ridden by corruption.

Higher State Service Examinations

To select government officials, there was an examination system called the "*kwago*" that was divided into two branches, one for civil service, and the other for military service. In principle, the examinations were held every three years but special examinations were also given from time to time. Qualifications to apply for the civil service examination were strictly restricted and only the *yangban* were able to sit for it. The restrictions were far less severe for the military service where it was opened widely to people of almost all classes. The engineering officials were also selected through special state examinations for which there were hardly any restrictions on the qualification of applicants. However, owing to the fact that the subjects were confined solely to interpretation of Confucianist theories, it contributed little to promote official efficiency or improve administration. To the contrary, it brought in many evil practices that compounded the tasks of personnel administration because it became one of the many political instruments for factional strife among the government officials.

Taxation

Efforts to rationalize the system of tax impositions upon the people were made. As a result, in 1444, the basis for taxation and the assessment of rates were officially fixed to put an end to unprincipled and unfair tax policies. To that end, a countrywide survey was conducted into the status of farmland and, based on the findings of this survey, the farmlands were classified into six categories, depending on their fertility, in order to determine the capability of the people to bear taxes. The annual productions of the farmlands were also taken into account to set the tax rates. One could well regard the system of Chosun taxation as being well-nigh perfect, but it was so complicated that it soon became merely nominal.

Tributes

A peculiar system of taxation was developed by feudal Yi when it began to collect tributes as a kind of land-tax. The tributes which were made one of the major sources of the government's revenues to meet state expenses included almost all kinds of goods, ranging from handiworks to tigerskins. The burden imposed upon the people by this tribute system was much heavier than was the case with regular taxes. People were often asked to deliver goods which they could neither produce nor acquire and, failing to meet the impossible demands, were compelled to purchase the requested goods at high prices. Eventually, the system had to be modified under the threat of popular restlessness. Instead of a multiple variety of goods that invited deviously unscrupulous practices, a uniform system of grain tributes was enforced.

Transportation and Communications

There were about 500 transit stations throughout the country. These stations, set at main traffic points for the convenience of travellers, especially those of higher classes, provided hostelries, foods, and other travelling or transportation facilities. They were manned mainly by lower class people. As for communications, signal-light stations, easily visible from afar, were built, mostly on mountain-tops. Both transit and signal-light stations existed from ancient days, but they were properly systematized for the first time during the Chosun era.

Social Conditions

During the reign of King Taejong, laws were made that discriminated against illegitimate offsprings in almost all walks of social life. Bastards were kept strictly away from any government service and absolutely denied the right to apply for higher civil service examinations. The purpose was to limit the size of the privileged classes to a small, restricted number. At the bottom of the social ladder were the butchers who were not allowed to mingle with other ordinary people, not to mention the *yangban*. Lower class people other than the privileged were also discriminated in choice of dwelling, clothes, occupation, marriages, etc. Of course, they were strictly prevented from entering any government service. They could not even smoke in the presence of a *yangban*. And they could not bring suit against a privileged *yangban* for any reason whatsoever, not even if they had suffered severe damage.

Strengthening the Centralized State

Taejong and Sejo

The third and seventh monarchs of the Chosun kingdom, Taejong and Sejo, were the two ablest rulers of the dynasty. Both kings ruled the country admirably, although each came to power unscrupulously. Taejong, who was the third son of the founder, figured prominently in the establishment of his father's kingdom. He was extremely disappointed when Taejo chose one of his two half-brothers to succed him and took the first opportunity to stage a successful coup to forcibly seize the throne.

Once king, however, he devoted himself whole-heartedly to the tasks of improving the political, social and economic conditions of the country. It was during his reign (1401-1418) that the capital of the kingdom was transferred. He had the government set up a printing office and let the people bring complaints against government officials directly to him. All they had to do was to beat a big drum in front of the king's palace.

Sejo became king by usurping the throne from his 12-year old nephew, Tanjong. He exterminated all the followers of the former boy king who refused to transfer their loyalties and established a powerful dictatorship. As a means of tightening his control over his subjects, he had the government issue identification certificates which everybody had to carry with them, regardless of their social status or position.

On the other hand, however, he left many brilliant achievements behind. It was Sejo who was largely responsible for driving off the Manchurian tribes and stabilizing the borders. He also eased up on the policy of suppressing Buddhism, among other things, allowing a big new temple to be built in Seoul, and many Buddhist scriptures to be published. He, too, devoted great attention to academic studies and cultural development.

Efforts were stepped up to nationalize as much farmlands as possible after Sejo came to the throne. The seventh king, Sejo (1456-1468) abolished the land reform system of his Yi predecessors and absorbed the private farmlands, granted to individual deserving officials of the founding state into the government fold. The lands thus nationalized were cultivated mainly by serfs.

Relations with Foreign Nations
Ming China

Although the Yi dynasty officially came under the protection of the Ming kingdom, the protectorate status was only a nominal one. All it meant was adoption of the same Ming era on the calendar and exchange of envoys several times a year. The so-called annual tribute was a form of official trade between the royal families of the two nations. Politically, the power of the Yi kings was assured the protection of a big powerful state. The active Ming trade was unfavorable for Korea both ways. On one hand, many handmade articles that could have been produced in the country were imported with the result that domestic industries collapsed. On the other, because Ming pressed Korea to export gold and silver in large quantities, the government closed all gold and silver resources. This was the reason why gold and silver mining remained stagnant for a long time.

Japan

From the start of the dynasty, the government made special efforts to ensure strong defensive measures against a possible invasion from Japan. The government also sent special envoys to Japan to talk the Japanese government into taking measures to stop the plundering activities of Japanese pirates. However, when the Japanese pirates invaded the country again in 1419, the first year of King Sejong, the government sent troops to Tsushima Island where the Japanese pirates had their bases. The people on this island were hard pressed due to the severance of trade relations with Korea and they begged the Korean government to reopen the trade. Whereupon, the government opened three ports, Naeipo (between Chinhae and Masan), Pusanpo and Ulsan. It also gave official titles to some of the Japanese governors there. These governors paid tributes to the government annually in exchange for licences permitting them to trade with Korea.

In 1443, the 25th year of Sejong, the government signed a treaty with the government of Tsushima. Under the treaty, the number of ships the traders of the island sent to Korea for trading purposes was limited to 50; on the other hand, rice which the government had been sending to the island every year was also limited to 200 sok.

Liaotung

The government tried to establish friendly relations with Liaotung. The attitude was conciliatory, and the government even gave leaders of the Liaotung people official titles, authorizing them to engage in trade with Korea. Since poverty spurred the Liao tribes to make frequent incursions upon the border areas, the government established trade centers in Kyongsong and Kyongwon. All trade transactions were carried out through these centers, the Liao traders usually bringing horses and wools in exchange for salt, cotton, farm instruments, tablewares, rice, bean, etc.

Power Struggle and Party Strife
An Age of Coups

As time elapsed, friction began to develop among the government officials. It became intensified during the reign of King Songjong, when the dynasty reached its highest peak of prosperity. Those who had served the nation well during the reign of King Sejo had assumed high positions in the government. For all that, administration became stagnant and corruption set in.

The opposition which was developing as a result was led by the Chuja school, so called because its adherents were versed in the Confucian theories of Chu Hsi, Chuja being the Korean rendition of the Chinese name. Songjong brought Kim Chongjik and his followers to power in an attempt to renovate the administration, Academically, Kim Chongjik belonged to the Kiljae school.

Since Kim hailed from Yongnam district, present-day Kyongsang Pukto and Kyongsang Namdo Provinces, many young Yongnam scholars took important positions in the government following his assumption of power.

These scholars launched a vigorous campaign against the corrupt elements in the government in an attempt to renovate the administration in line with the wishes of the king. Those already in power lacked any theoretical grounds for opposing this new campaign, so they started, instead, to realign themselves on the pretext that they had to protect the king against "evil elements" in government. For about 50 years thereafter, a bloody battle raged between the Chuja School and men united in the common wish to maintain their positions. It was a period of coups, the *Muo* coup in which the men in power seized upon a "subversive" Chuja text to crack down upon Chuja adherents, and the *Kapcha* coup in which a debauched monarch, Yonsan, rid himself of loyal official-scholars.

King Chungjong, who took over the throne following King Yonsan, undertook to renovate the national administration through one, Cho Kwangjo. Cho Kwangjo was a disciple of Kim Kwangpil, a disciple of Kim Chongjik. He immediately established an office which opened the doors for employing wise men whenever they could be found without going through the complicated procedures of examinations. However, Cho Kwangjo was over-enthusiastic in his drive for renovations. He went too far in everything he did with the result that his conduct of administration tended to be too idealistic and, sometimes, dogmatic. At length, he aroused the opposition of the conservative elements in the government. His attempts to slice down the size of land distributions proved too much for the conservatives and he was ousted from power. This was in the fourteenth year of King Chungjong, 1519.

The *Ulsa* coup was started from a quarrel among relatives of the queen. The queen's relatives went out of their way to meddle in almost every field of national administration, thus coming into conflict with power-hungry government officials, ever zealous to ride the tides of the time.

The Sowon

During this turbulent period, scholars were constantly persecuted. However, they were steadfast in their determination to improve the administration and, at the same time, never gave up their zeal for learning. Many scholars began to establish private institutes to teach Chu Hsi, and many others, losing hopes of realizing their ideals through government, retired into deep mountain regions to devote themselves to Confucianist studies. Many famous scholars, such as Yi Toege, Yi Yulgok, and So Kyongdok, were products of this period. In fact, it was a golden age for Confucianism in Korea.

The Confucian scholars were not satisfied with rhetorics based on learnings of the past, but undertook to study, develop and propagate Chu Hsi theories. The private institutes they established in various parts of the country provided favorite places for the Chuja adherents to gather and discuss their academic findings.

Kings who were afraid of the ever increasing powers of existing goverment officials, began to employ many young disciples of the *Sowon* as the institutes were known, to check any arbitrary tendencies on their part. Thus, in the early days of King Sonjo, many *Sowon* members were picked for important government positions. As these young scholars solidified their grounds within the government, they acquired lands and established many newer *Sowon*. Finally the private *Sowon* institues were officialized and a system of public *Sowon* institutes, the *Saaek Sowon*, named by the King and managed by the government, was estabilshed.

Rise of Factions

It is true that during the reign of King Sonjo, the Chuja scholars acquired important positions in the government but there were not enough positions for all. Scholars of lesser influence continued to be confined to their *Sowon* without benefiting from what was a general trend to power. Thus, two distinctly different factions developed among the scholars, one consisting of those in power, the other of those without. While government positions were limited in number, the aspirants were overcrowded. Selections, therefore, were determined variously by blood ties, localities, and patronage.

Factional strife began in the quarrel of two powerful officials named Kim Hyowon and Sim Uigyom, for a government post called the *Chongnang*. The *Chongnang* was only fifth in the ladder of government grades but as the man empowered to select government officials, he was, in practical power, comparable to, or even stronger than the Prime Minister or other Ministers. Moreover, he was, by tradition, head of the young government officials and, naturally, became the target for their aspirations. In fact, the position was originally created with the object of checking dictatorial tendencies on the part of the king or government ministers. Thus, the fight for the *Chongnang* position smacked of party strife from the outset.

Two distinctly opposed political camps emerged from this fight, the *Tongin* (East Men) and the *Soin* (West Men), supporters of Kim Hyowon and Sim Uigyom respectively. The ensuing years saw these two groups fight each other so incessantly that the history of this period may be said, without exaggeration, to have been dominated by episodes of party strife.

At an early stage, the *Tongin* were superior to the *Soin* in numerical strength. Later, new factions branched out from both parties, and party strifes were intensified all the more by the intra-party struggles within each. This deplorable state continued to dominate the national political scene until the famous Hideyoshi invasions from Japan.

The Hideyoshi Invasions
Situation before the Invasion

During the reign of King Chungjong, three ports were opened to Japanese traders and the Japanese were authorized to maintain a Resident-General in the country in the fifth year of his reign (1510). However, when the government intensified its watch over the Japanese residents following a series of violent troubles from these residents, the disgruntled Japanese launched a riot in Pusan port. The government promptly put down the revolt and closed two of the three ports as a punitive measure. Subsequently, the Japanese launched a number of attacks but nothing came of these intermittent attempts. The Japanese had their own troubles at home.

In the early years of King Sonjo, an outstanding Japanese General, Toyotomi Hideyoshi, succeeded in putting down all revolts which had been raging throughout Japan. In an attempt to seek an outlet for the unified strength of the warlike Japanese, and urged by the desire for territorial expansion, Hideyoshi contemplated an attack on foreign nations. Korea, having no effective shield against foreign invasions, provided an excellent target. Gleaning tidings of what was brewing, the Korean government sent two envoys to Japan in order to ascertain the true intentions of the Japanese. The envoys, Hwang Yungil and Kim Songil, however, sent contradictory reports home. Intensive arguments followed over measures for preparing the country against a possible Japanese attack, but no conclusions were drawn. Thus, the nation had to face the tragic invasion of the Japanese without any preparations whatsoever.

The First Invasion

In April 1592, in the 25th year of King Sonjo, two generals of Hideyoshi, Kato Kiyomasa and Konishi Yukinaga, led an invasion force of 150,000 against Korea. The Japanese took only 15 days to capture Seoul since landing on Pusan. They were excellently trained through long years of internal revolts. Moreover, they had a new Western weapon, the shot-gun. The Korean forces, ill-equipped and ill-trained, collapsed easily before the onrushing Japanese army.

The invaders under Kato's command advanced along the east coast of the country to reach the present-day Hamgyong-do provinces; those under the command of Konishi Yukinaga, marched through the central part of the country and easily captured Pyongyang.

The King retreated to Uiju, and there appealed to Ming China for help, while belatedly urging the people to rise up against the all-out conquerors.

Command of the Seas, A Great Admiral

With the very existence of Korea thus at stake, there emerged a great figure, Yi Sunsin. Yi, who was then holding the post of Commanding Admiral for the Cholla Fleet, was the only person who had realized Korea's vulnerable position beforehand, and prepared a bulwark against the Japanese — the famous Turtle ships. First, he sailed against the Japanese fleets and destroyed them at Okpo (present-day Chinhae); next he exterminated an enemy fleet reinforcement off Hansan Isle. His triumphs completely frustrated the enemy strategy which was to make parallel advances both on land and sea.

More, the overall Japanese position was threatened for Admiral Yi was now able to command the sea, ban the enemy's supply of munitions and secure the safety of Cholla-do province, an important source of food and manpower. By virtue of his lheroism, integrity and genius, Admiral Yi became one of the greatest heroes in all Korean history. His famous invention, the Turtle ship, so-called from its shape, was something new on the sea.

The first ironplated battleship in history, mounted with many guns pointing out in various directions, it was both fast and powerful. Without doubt, it was the most highly developed warship of the time.

Ming Aid and Volunteers

Upon Korea's request for aid, the Ming kingdom immediately dispatched a large army. The Japanese had clearly announced that their invasion of Korea was but the prelude to the ultimate conquest of China so, in rallying to Korea's help, Ming was also defending itself. The Ming forces restored Pyongyang and the main Japanese forces had to fall back upon Seoul.

The Ming intervention raised the morale of the Korean troops and encouraged the formation of armed volunteer units all over the country. The *yangban* assumed the lead in recruiting such volunteers and farm and school buildings were utilized as bases of operation. The volunteer ranks included all classes, *yangban*, common folks, Buddhist priests, even slaves.

The volunteers raided and threatened enemy supply channels, posing a great and constant menace to Japanese occupation authorities. Such names as Kwak Chaewu, Chong Munbu and Kim Tongnyong figure prominently as outstanding commanders of these volunteer units. Eventually the government was able to resume normal functions following a temporary lull in fighting, and the volunteer troops then came under the command of the Royal Army.

Discouraged by the Chinese military intervention, the Japanese gradually gathered all their forces in Seoul. Here, they were attacked by a Korean army of 20,000 led by the Governor of Cholla-do, Kwon Yul, who had concentrated this strong force on a mountain fortress, Haengju Sansong, for just such a major engagement. The victory Kwon's troops scored against a full counter-attack from the Japanese was the greatest one won by Korean arms on land.

With Japanese dreams of a quick conquest frustrated and every prospect of a dragged-out war in the offing, truce talks were held between General Konishi, representing the Japanese forces, and General Shen Weiching, a tactician of the Ming armed forces. As a result, a yearlong warfare was terminated and the Japanese troops began to withdraw back to their homeland. The Korean troops immediately recoverd Seoul and pressed hard upon the retreating Japanese. Enroute home, the Japanese besieged Chinju, a stronghold of the Korean army, at the southwestern extremity of the peninsula. The Japanese had once suffered a major defeat here and Hideyoshi's order was that this southern city was to be taken at all costs. For eight days, a most desperate battle was fought for this castle of sixty thousand residents. In the end, the defending garrison had to surrender to the superior enemy.

The Second Invasion

The main developments from the truce talks between the Ming and Japanese armed forces were, on one hand, withdrawal of the main body of Japanese troops from the Korean peninsula, and, on the other, restoration of the Korean capital city of Seoul to the Korean government. In this connection, it should be added that whatever the results, the Koreans were persistently opposed to any idea of a truce on the contention that any agreement with the Japanese was unreliable.

And, indeed, there was a fundamental disagreement between the truce-makers from the outset although Shen Wei-ching and Konishi attempted to present a successful front by either distorting or concealing the real phases through which their negotiations were proceeding.

The Japanese side conducted themselves like victors while the Chinese considered the Japanese as "barbarians" and wanted to arrange a traditional relationship between the Central Kingdom and the "barbarian" state. Thus, the condescending Chinese were "willing" to recognize Hideyoshi as King of Japan and allow him to pay tribute to the Ming kingdom.

The incompatible talks finally broke up and, in 1597, the Japanese renewed their invasion of Korea with a force of 140,000 men. By now, however, the Korean defenses were comparatively strong and the invaders could march no farther than Chiksan, Chungchong-do. The following year, a 150,000-man Ming army retaliated in a general offensive against the Japanese throughout the southern parts of Korea. The latter was in serious predicament. On the sea, however, the Japanese were superior. Admiral Yi at this time was imprisoned, the victim of a factional strife which centered its petty jealousies upon his head. A second Battle of Hansan Isle, where Admiral Yi had scored a brilliant victory over the Japanese, ended this time in the complete rout of the Korean fleet. The victorious Japanese headed for the southern coast of the Cholla-do province in order to control the western sea.

Shocked by the crushing defeat of Hansan, the Korean government hastily released Admiral Yi and restored him to his naval command. The Admiral went into action immediately with a remnant fleet of 12 ships to win an unprecedented battle over overwhelmingly superior numbers in what was nothing short of a miracle off the Myongyang Straits. For the Japanese, it was a fatal blow. It restored command of the sea to the Korean navy and cut the Japanese armies in Korea from their main sources of supply. The Japanese had to live off the land.

The Chinese forces, too, were not faring too well. At Namwon, Wolsan, Sachon, Sunchon and every other battle site, the only certainty in the engagement of the foreign armies was the ruin of the civilian populace. Neither side had much appetite left to carry on the fruitless struggle. With Hideyoshi's death in 1598, the Japanese policy weakened and their troops began to withdraw back home. Admiral Yi won his last battle against the retreating Japanese amassed in a fleet of two hundred boats off Namhae Island. Here, at the height of his glory, Korea's greatest hero was struck down by a Japanese bullet.

With the Japanese withdrawals, the Ming forces gradually followed suit and the seven-year war was brought to an end.

Yi Chosun — After Hideyoshi

Effects of the Hideyoshi War

The seven-year war wrecked untold hardships throughout the peninsula. Both the Japanese enemy and the Ming ally had served to compound the devastations. Urban and rural areas alike lost vast numbers in human lives and property. Peasants, deprived of every means, were unable to resume farming with the result that famine broke loose, countless numbers died of starvation and thieves were rampant. All documents pertaining to census registration and land-books had been burned and taxes were impossible. The disorders were well-nigh complete and recovery seemingly impossible.

For the Japanese, the war, at least, proved immeasurably beneficial in the realms of culture. Chu Hsi books and printing types, plundered by the Japanese soldiery in Korea, were introduced to Japanese culture for the first time. The Korean ceramists carried off by the conquerors were responsible for developing Japanese pottery. In the words of a latter-day Japanese historian; "the Hideyoshi invasion meant overseas study for the Japanese—abnormally." With the ascendency of the Tokugawa Shogunate to power, Japan requested the restoration of friendly relations with Korea and normal ties were at last resumed in 1607.

The strain for the Ming kingdom also proved to be severe. The Korean war had not only drained the treasury to create serious fiscal problems at home; it had also drained the garrison troops in Manchuria to leave important outlying defences quite neglected. The results of the Korean war were the cause of Niuchen revolts that led to the overthrow of the Chinese master and the establishment of a new Manchu dynasty in China.

The Manchu Invasions
Prince Kwanghae

The death of King Sonjo brought the various factions into head-on clashes, each with its royal claimant for the throne. The winning faction was the *Taebuk,* a splinter party within a splinter party. This brought the *Taebuk* claimant, Prince Kwanghae, one of the late Sonjo's three sons, to the throne. The assertion was precarious, to say the least, and the *Taebuk* faction could not rest easy until all its opponents were purged. Both of Kwanghae's brothers and his widowed mother, Inmok, lost their lives.

The prince who thus came to power by unsavory means was, however, a wise politician. He was particularly well-informed about the Liao tribes and, realizing the growing power on the Manchurian plains, remained carefully neutral in the developing frictions between the Ming and Manchu nations.

In 1616, Nurhachi, one of the leaders of the Niuchen tribes, unified the Manchus and established a new kingdom independent of China. Ming decided to send a punitive force against Hu-Chin as the Manchu kingdom was christened and called on Korea to participate. As Korea was a dependency, Prince Kwanghae had to oblige. He dispatched a 13,000-man force but clearly wanted to remain neutral. The Ming expeditionary forces were defeated at the Battle of Sarho and the surrendering Korean contingent was quick to explain to the victors that their participation in the battle on the side of Ming had been unavoidable. It is said that the prince had secretly ordered the troops to disavow Ming loyalty.

The Manchus continued to win one victory after another and the retreating Chinese finally fell back on Korea where they took up a defensive position at Kado, Pyongan-do province, and called on Korea for munitions supplies in order to launch a counter-attack and recover the lost peninsula of Liaotung. The Korean position was more embarrassing than ever before for the militant Manchus were victorious everywhere and pressing upon the Korean borders. The last thing Kwanghae wanted was to bring their wrath down upon the peninsula. It required the closest analyses of the Hu-Chin developments to provide them with no pretexts whatsoever for finding a *casus belli* while manning the border defenses with able generals against any unexpected emergency. In other words, Kwanghae was more concerned about the security of his state than obligations to the Ming kingdom. So long as he was in power, the borders were quiet. But divisions were growing within the government for among his staff members were those who remained loyal to Ming and opposed his neutralist policies. The *Soin* faction took advantage of this friction to revolt against the prince. In 1623, they managed to dethrone him and crown Injo king.

Invasions and Subjection

Having put their king on the throne, the *Soin*, or West Men, fell out over the problem of distributing rewards. For a time, they seemed lost when a certain Yi Kwal suddenly precipitated a revolt and seized control of the capital. Yi Kwal's victory however, was short-lived and he had to flee to the Manchus. The Injo government could pursue its pro-Ming, anti-Hu-Chin policy unopposed. The consequence was a Hu-Chin invasion.

In 1627, during the fifth year of Injo's reign, the Manchus invaded Korea with a force of 30,000 and marched as far south as Hwanghae-do. The government sued for peace and a "Brotherhood Compact" was concluded. But the Manchus had only started out on the road to expansion. They subdued Inner Mongolia, proclaimed a Ching dynasty, and demanded that the "Brotherhood Compact" be altered to a "Protectorate Treaty." In other words, the high-spirited Manchus wanted Korea to be completely subordinated to the Ching kingdom and to help them in their attack against Ming. While the pro-Ming jingoists advocated war against Ching, the impatient Ching monarch marched an army of 100,000 down the peninsula to the vicinity of Seoul. Injo hastily took refuge in a mountain fortress, leaving behind an army of 13,000, paralyzed by the arguments which still raged between the pro-Ming jingoists and their opponents. The king eventually had to surrender and the Ching troops withdrew on conditions that Yi Chosun break off relations with Ming, subordinate itself completely to Ching, and offer a number of important hostages, including one prince, as an assurance of good faith. Seven years after the subjugation of Korea, the Manchus invaded Peking and brought most of the China mainland under the control of their Ching dynasty.

The Manchu invasions were the outcome of short-sighted views on the part of those who were inclined to be too submissive before a higher authority. Had there been more backbone in the kingdom, the tragedies could certainly have been avoided. Yet, despite the bitter and humiliating defeats, many continued to revere Ming and despise Ching. The Ching dynasty was officially proclaimed in 1644 but, for some time, the Ming adherents, both in China and Korea, refused to acknowledge the Manchu supremacy. To them, the Manchus were "barbarians." With Injo's death, Prince Pongnim, the prince held hostage by Ching, returned home to succeed to the throne as King Hyojong. Hyojong attempted to lead a northward expedition but in vain. After that, the Ching supremacy was acknowledged for good and when the Ching kingdom requested Korean help against a Russian encroachment, Hyojong sent a contingent of Korean gunners who fought side by side with the Ching forces in a successful repulsion of the Russians.

Intensification of the Factional Strifes

As we have seen, factionalism originated in the quarrel of two officials for the influential post of the *Chongnang* in the government. Two rival factions stemmed from that quarrel, the *Tongin*, or East Men, and the *Soin*, or West Men. Other branch factions developed thereafter, the *Tongin* weakened and the *Soin* increased their power. On the eve of the Hideyoshi invasions, three factions were well developed, the *Soin*, the *Namin*, or South Men, and the *Pugin*, or North Men. The *Namin* were in power but immediately after the outbreak of the Japanese troubles, Yu Songnyong, the *Namin* leader, was ousted from power and the government was taken over by the *Pugin*. Once in power, the *Pugin* split further into the *Taebuk* or Big North, and *Sobuk* or Small North. The various factions waged an intensive fight over the question of Sonjo's succession. As we have seen, the *Taebuk* faction won out and their champion, Kwanghae, came to the throne although without ever being officially crowned.

The ensuing fifty years saw bloody fighting between the *Taebuk* and *Sobuk* factions. The quarrel revolved around the issue of the Queen Mother's mourning clothes following the death of King Hyojong in 1660. The question was whether she should wear mourning for a period of one year or two years. The *Soin* came in from the bleaches to exploit the *Taebuk-Sobuk* differences and gain the premiership for its leader, Song Siyol. As soon as they had done that, they split in two, *Noron* or Old School, and *Soron* or Young School, due primarily to Song's short tempers and his inadequate management of the party. This revived the issue of the Queen Mother's mourning wear, this time for Hyojong's widowed queen. The *Namin* came in and Song Siyol was banished but the South Men's power was short-lived and the *Soin* brought Song back to lead a bloody purge of political opponents. Finally, at the age of 82, Song was killed in this vicious round of factional purges.

With Song dead, the *Soin* faction was completely removed from power. Party struggles from then on were characterized by what is known as the "four-color pattern," the colors being *Noron*, Old School, *Soron*, Young School, *Namin* and *Sobuk*. The political scene was dominated by the first two factions who, of course, were at loggerheads with each other. The question before them was the physical condition of the heir-apparent, Prince Kyongjong. The prince had been born physically weak and the *Noron* made this the pretext for claiming a brother of the reigning monarch as the proper successor to the throne. The *Soron* strongly rejected this claim and branded its upholders traitors. Four *Noron* ministers were killed in a successful coup and the *Soron* came to power.

So intensive was the nature of these struggles that almost everybody belonging to the *yangban* classes was drawn into them. Not merely were they affiliated with one or other of the various contending factions but they even refused to marry across factional lines. Many able individuals who could have rendered great service to the nation were victims of this power struggle. Amidst the disorders and cruelties provoked, national administration became corrupted beyond description and every official was preoccupied with his own personal interests at the expense of all.

Causes of Factionalism

Factionalism, without a shadow of a doubt, was the dominant trait in the latter years of the Yi dynasty. What were the causes of such intensive factional struggles? Was there some definite defect in the Korean people themselves? Hardly likely. Is it the geophysical position of the country? That and the peculiar social institutions born to it would appear to be the causes.

Whatever the fine sentiments in the slogans and principles espoused, they were, in effect, pretexts for power and the power was sought by fighting for government posts.

On one hand, the number of posts was limited; on the other, aspirants multiplied with the annual increase in the number of *yangban*. Moreover, the government had acquired the habit of choosing officials without proper regard for their qualifications. The result was that posts were filled by partisan favorites and only less than one-fifth of candidates who had passed the state examinations were actually employed by government. Both qualitative and quantitative determinants were easily undermined.

The political position of the country was responsible for the intensified nature of the power struggle. As we have noted in our account of Koryo's foreign relations, it was only by putting all the eggs in China's basket that the peninsula could feel secure. Since the Yi king and government were dependent on China, nobody dared risk a quarrel with the big Chinese power by attempting to bring down the king, the loyal subject of the Central Kingdom. Political quarrels for power, therefore, tended to revolve around the king with contestants trying to get as near to him as possible. Under the circumstances, political struggles became a seesaw affair aimed at getting the favor of the king. Then there was the orthodox nature of the Confucian teachings as based on Chu Hsi. For the better part of the Yi dynasty, Chu Hsi's theories constituted the dominating subject for studies. The very nature of these theories permitted no room for conciliation with any other school of thought, non-Chu Hsi Confucianism included. The outcome was extreme dogmatism, both in the theory and practice of Confucian virtues, and this served to intensify the factional strifes.

The fact that too much power was concentrated on the position of the *Chongnang* was another cause. It made the post a target of aspirations by too many in high government office. The *Sowon* institutes were another factor for the good-for-nothing scholars who congregated there were wont to complain against personnel administration in the government. The *Sowon* were fertile ground for enlisting complaining members and expanding factional strife into rural areas.

Finally, since no significant changes had taken place, politically or socially, for many years, the learned men of the state had nothing to do but wrangle over affairs of no vital interest to the state. The personal grudges and emotional enmities were carried down from one generation to the next. Confucianism which emphasized obligations to the family line did nothing to ameliorate this; rather, it taught that sons and grandsons should share in the quarrels of their forefathers and avenge their wrongs.

Morals and ethics went hand in hand with greed and corruption to narrow the circles of partisan warfare.

Corruption, Decline of Power Classes

The Taedongbop:

With the Manchu invasions following so shortly upon the Japanese, the fortunes of the Yi dynasty began to decline. The weakening power of the kingdom was partly reflected in the considerable decrease of nationalized farmlands. Unlike the initial stage of the dynastic rule when the government administrative system was strengthened through furthering combinations of private and semi-nationalized farmlands into state nationalizations, the total acreage of nationalized farmlands in the reign of Prince Kwanghae was no less than 540,000 *kyol* (*1 kyol*=approx. 1.47 acres), a one-third decrease compared to the total 1,700,000 *kyol* before the Japanese invasions. The drop was attributable to the devastations of war, death of farmers, and increases in the amount of unregistered land holdings that was the result of malpractices of the government officials and landlords. These unregistered land holdings, of course, were encouraged by the loss of land-books during the Japanese wars.

To restore the state on a sound financial foundation, land surveys were contemplated in later years. The one conducted in the second year of King Yongjo (1729 A.D.) revealed that farmlands from which taxes were collected amounted only to some 830,000 *kyol*, a clear evidence that the nation had not fully recovered from the war devastations. With such considerable decrease in the principal sources of national revenue, the government looked for a new source of income. The existing tribute system, it was found, had a number of demerits for both government and taxpayers in terms of assessments and transportation. Accordingly, the government adopted the *pangnap*, a system of taxation whereby businessmen were designated by the government to pay tributes on a contractual basis in lieu of taxpayers, and were authorized to collect later from the taxpayers at rates equivalent to the tributes they had paid. The *pangnap*, however, proved unsatisfactory in time as it became a business, involving the familiar power struggles at the expense of the common classes. With ever-increasing financial difficulties, the government put into effect a system of rice payments in lieu of tributes, at first in Kyonggi-do only, and later, throughout the land. Under this system, the farmer had to pay 12 *mal* (2 *mal*=approx. 1 bushel) of rice to every *kyol* of land or the equivalent amount in either cloth or cash. This law was called the *Taedongbop*, and the rice collected under the system, *taedongmi*. The *taedongbop* proved beneficial to the peasant class by eliminating the many shortcomings of the old tax system. It was, therefore, wholeheartedly welcomed by the farmers and spurned by the malpracticing officials and landlords. The new tax system, however, was not without its defects. The government procured the required supplies through a government contractor called the *kongin*. After the *taedongbop* was adopted, the government turned the *taedongmi* thus collected over to the *kongin*, who, in turn, dealt with other dealers to exchange this rice for whatever materials were required by the government. Through years of experience and practice in the same business, the *kongin* learned to taken full advantage of the new tax system in order to line their own purses.

Kunpo

The foreign invasions meant big changes in civil duties. The most important of the three basic duties imposed upon the people, was military service. During the reign of King Sonjo, farmers between the ages of 16 and 60 were conscripted for the peasant army while youths under the age limitation were sent to Seoul to undergo a certain period of regular military training. On completion of active military service, the peasant-soldiers were required to pay a military tax for the duration of their eligibility; i.e. until they were over 60. The Japanese wars proved the peasant army to be totally ineffectual in actual combat. Accordingly, a prolonged study was made of the shortcomings in the existing conscription system by military experts, and a Training Command finally formed in the 27th year of King Sonjo. This command was responsible for training career soldiers in three fields—swordsmanship, archery, and rifle artillery. The standing troops soon reached more than 10,000, and the government had to solve the financial problem of maintaining such a large command. A law was, therefore, enacted to collect a military tax of 2.2 *mal* to every *kyol* from the nationalized farmland.

In addition, the general public was required to pay 2 *pil* (1 *pil*=approx. 40 yds.) of cloth as substitute for actual military service. This tax was called the *kunpo*, and the job of *kunpo* collections was known as *kunjong*. The *kunjong* resulted in numerous malpractices of the most extreme and even indescribable nature on the part of officialdom, dragging the common classes down to new depths of poverty and despair. The reason was that the officials collected more than ten times the normal amount of *kunpo* and even several times tenfold. For all the sufferings of the common classes, the government officials and the power classes, on the other hand, evaded the *kunpo* by taking every advantages of their privileges. They struck off the names of family members or lists of farmlands from the census registry and land records. The number of evaders thus reached more than two-thirds of the entire population. Besides the peasant class, the destitutes were also victims of the *kunpo*, for the government tried to fill the shortages from the *kunpo* returns, created by the evasive practices of the power class, by sacrificing the destitute class. The more corrupted government organization, the far more exploited the destitute and peasant classes. The degree of exploitation reached such an extent that the *kunpo* records of army eligibles not only embraced old men and infants but reached beyond the graves to the dead and beyond infancy to babies yet unborn.

A Tax Reform

The land taxation of the Yi dynasty, as assessed on the basis of 6 grade fields and 9 grade harvests, was a most advanced and reasonable system. But it did not work in practice because of the lack of a fixed standard to determine the grades of farmland or harvest. Unscrupulous officials could take advantage of this and the farmers were exploited just the same. To make matters worse, the tax rate itself was unusually high and the people subjected to various kinds of assessment. To alleviate the shortcoming, the government set a uniform land tax rate in the 4th year of King Hyojong (1653 A.D.). This rate was applicable regardless of what the year's harvest had been like; it assessed 4 *mal* of rice to every *kyol* for all. The rate was fixed on the basis of a bad crop estimate.

Vigorous attempts were also made to improve techniques in land measuring.

The Kungbangjon and Tonjon

The *kungbangjon* was a system of providing for the living necessities of the royal families, created after the foreign invasions when private land holdings had vanished and the semi-private holdings were in doubt. Privileged with exemption from the land tax, the royal families increased their properties, day in and day out under the *kungbangjon*. Eager to expand their farmlands they utilized every means available to this end, reclamations, purchases, confiscations and outright annexations.

The *tonjon* was the system for providing the needs of the noble and military classes. On one hand, public slaves cultivated land for the "get-rich-quick" schemes of the noble; on the other, land was set aside for military personnel whose "on-the-spot" appetites were whetted after the Hideyoshi wars. The *tonjon* was encouraged to remain in force through many successive years although it was supposed to be a temporaty alleviation. The increases in the amount of farmlands exempted from land tax led to the gradual deterioration of the centralized administrative system. Along with the steady increases in the number of private or unregistered land holdings, the national income decreased year by year. This, in turn, only encouraged increased exploitation of the common class. Every new year was worse than the passing year.

The Yongjo-Chongjo Eras (1775-1081)

The Tangpyongchaek

King Yongjo who reigned in the early years of the 18th century was fully aware of the tragedies caused by factionalism and wanted to do something about it. He made strenuous efforts to bring partisan warfares to an end and to assure fairness in the appointment of government officials. The movement to rectify the ills of factionalism is called the *tangpyongchaek*, a policy to prevent the development of one-sided powers. Among the other measures the King undertook to eliminate the causes of factional frictions were moves to render the *Chongnang* post ineffective and bring the private *Sowon* institutes under strict state control. He was personally on the look-out to prevent the growth of any single faction to proportions that might threaten arbitrary power.

Yongjo's era saw great literary advances, particularly as they pertained to legal works. The *kyunyokpop* was enacted during his time. This was law initiated with a view to applying a fair assessment of the grossly misabused *kunpo* military service tax upon all citizens irrespective of class or position. Under the *kyunyokpop*, the cloth tax in lieu of military service was dropped from 2 to 1 *pil* and the fishing-grounds, salt-fields and ships of the landlords and other privileged classes, hitherto tax-exempted, were assessed new tax rates.

This helped alleviate the plight of the poor somewhat and weigh the rich down with added burdens. But the benefits for the common class were only slight for parallel with the enactment of the *kyunyokpop*, the land-tax was increased by 2 *mal* per *kyol*. At any rate, while the vigorous reforms carried out during Songjo's fifty years of reign produced remarkable social and cultural developments, the drastic measures the government adopted to prevent further crisis from factional strifes led to discouraging tendencies in ensuing years, such as restrictions on freedom of speech.

The Kyujanggak

Yongjo's successor, Chongjo, was also intent on decisive social reforms. Young and intelligent, he established a royal academy called the *kyujanggak* as soon as he mounted the throne. With the *kyujanggak* as headquarters for pursuing affairs of state, he encouraged learnings by opening public offices to talented men. Many literary works were produced, notably the *Taejon Hoetong* (Legal Codes of the Yi Dynasty) and the *Kyujang Chonun*, which was a collection of poems as compiled by the academy.

To all appearances, the *kyujanggak* was only an academic body preserving the handwritings of successive monarchs and collecting all manner of books published within or without the country. Actually, it was a new form of governmental organization emerging out of a corrupted society with a view to insuring better social and living conditions for the general public.

Yongjong Culture

The reigns of Kings Yongjo and Chongjo, known as the Yongjong* era, were characterized in the field of culture by the birth of the *Silhak* or True Learning movement and the growth of low-class literature. Signs of energetic literary activities among unknown scholars of lowly birth began to be noticed. The two best known commoners were Kim Chontaek whose *"Chonggu Yongon,"* a treasury of Chinese poems, became the basis of traditional Korean songs, and Kim Sujang, who also compiled Chinese poems under the title, *"Haedong Kayo,* (Songs of Korea)". Interest in the *hangul* script, Sejong's alphabet that had been disdained down the years by the nobility, was revived with such works as Sin Kyongjun's *Hunmin Chongum Tohae* (Illustrations of the Korean Alphabet) and Yu Hui's *Onmunji* (The Korean Letters. A notable feature was the appearance of the novel, another despised medium. The despised novels, written in the despised *hangul* alphabet, received an unusually warm response from the general public and many unknown writers devoted themselves to novel-writing. It was during this period that *"Chunhyangjon* (Tale of Chunhyang)" was born. Written against the background of a deteriorating class system and high class corruption, it is a love story bringing together the son of a well-born and a commoner's daughter in defiance of class lines and triumphing over the evil practices of a corrupted governor. *Chunhyang* is not merely Korea's undying love story but a lasting product of low-class literature.

The artists of the Yongjong era inherited a rich legacy from the dynasty, the famous landscape paintings of An Kyon, Yi Sangjwa, and Chong Son during the reigns of Sejong, and Sukchong. The outstanding Yongjong painters were Kim Hongdo (literary penname Tanwon) and Sin Yunbok (literary

*Abbreviation of Yongjo and Chongjo

penname Hewon). Tanwon displayed a brilliant talent in paintings about fairyland and native customs; Hewon, on the other hand, has left us a number of masterpieces which give a vivid picture of low-class society in his times. Calligraphy was pronounced in the reigns of Chongjong and Sonjo. There was Yang Saon, famous for his cursive style, Han Ho (literary penname-Sokpong) equally famous for his Wang style, and Kim Chonghui, whose pioneering work on a *Chusa* style has remained down the years as a unique expression of the naive taste of the ancient Korean artist.

Excellent industrial works of art, made of wood, bamboo, metals, mother-of-pearls and potter's clay also appeared. There were not very many pieces but whatever was turned out proved to be of excellent quality for the fullness of natural tastes was brought to objects designed for practical daily use. The influence of Ming and Confucianism was evident in pottery with the prevalence of white porcelains painted with delicate lines of hills and streams. A government-operated kiln in Kwangju, Kyonggi-do, was fully utilized to improve the shapes, colors, paintings and durability of pottery works.

Yi Society

The teachings of Confucius upon which the Yi kingdom had been founded, yielded unimpeachably sound qualities, on one hand, and succumbed to adverse effects, on the other. On the credit side of the balance, the high moral precepts Confucianism taught captured the minds of the people so comletely that such virtues as filial piety, respect for the old and obedience of the young became daily practices in the lives of innumerable individuals.

In the balance, however, the debit side ran higher for these same moral principles created a strong class instinct which led to unfair human relationships and gross social injustices. Thus, concubines' sons had no chance to get along in life, however talented they might be; widows could not remarry, and chances for public office were opened only to individuals with good family backgrounds. The freedom and most elementary human rights of the lowly were ignored if not mercilessly trodded upon. Too many rituals, too much emphasis on formalities, gorgeous, expensive weddings and costly funeral ceremonies all strained the national economy. The self-righteousness of masters encouraged flunkeyism below and the over-emphasis on family considerations weakened one's concern of, and responsibility to, the community to which one belonged. The privileged classes, intent solely on higher government positions, held the artisans in contempt, thus contributing to the shrinkage of the nation's productive powers.

The increase in the numbers of private academic institutes also brought many social and political problems in its wake. The institutes developed direct connections with every faction in existence, serving as footholds for each and every one of them in the rural areas. The institutes, moreover, not only pulled the unsavory climate of partisan warfare to the countryside; they also became haunts for privileged and leisured folks living out their lives in sheer idleness. Above all, the continued existence of such institutes meant great losses to the government for they were tax-exempted and too many had carved out large slices of land under state support.

The Yi period was also marked by the development of a mutual trust system called *kye*. Emergency expenditures tended to be too heavy for the individual in the Confucianistic feudal Yi society so he entered the *kye* system in which the various members pooled their monetary resources to help one another out on emergency occasions. A variety of *kye* developed, each for a different purpose. Thus, there were *kye* for education, tax payment, memorial services for ancestors, wedding ceremonies, the sixty-first birthday, industry, agriculture, the fostering of friendly relations among relatives, etc. The more helpless the members of a village community felt under unstable conditions, the more they tended to bind themselves in *kye* media to help each other out from under. Generally, *kye* organizations considered blood ties, similar vocations or trustworthy partnerships.

The network of close inter-relationships developed through the *kye* media resulted in a feature unique to Korean society, the rise of clan communities organized solely by and for individuals with the same family name. There were 14,672 clan villages throughout the country.

Large-scale constructive projects were also developed through the *Cheonsa*, a governmental agency created in the reign of King Yongjo. Many reservoirs were newly built as part of the agency's river improvement plans and nationwide reforestations initiated against flood damages. Farmers and their primitive tools were mobilized for these vast projects.

Handicraft Industry, Mining and Commerce

The handicraft industry was planned and controlled directly by the government. It was generally developed in the cities, and the manufacturers, who were either public slaves or commoners, were subjected to strict supervision. Of all handicraft lines, the greatest improvement was made in the production of clothing materials. The cotton fabric industry, especially, was well popularized and many good quality products turned out to meet the demands of both domestic and foreign markets. Thus, there were annual exports to Japan of 30,000 to 50,000 *pil* of cotton fabrics.

During the Ming era in China, Korea's mining industry remained sluggish due, as we have seen, to the fact that the balance of trade between the two countries all worked against the tender Korean industries and weak Korean markets. After Ming's fall, gold and silver mines began seriously to be developed but the mining methods were so primitive that little or no headway could be made. Even refinery methods for copper were so crude and expensive that copper had to be imported from Japan although many copper mines were available in the country.

Business, too, was generally sluggish. Besides the *Yugijon*, the store for members of the royal household and government officials, there were some 90 shops in Seoul dealing in such provisions as tobacco, rice, fish, furniture, silver and other metal wares. The markets were crowded with many wholesale dealers and business go-betweens. Local towns had market-days, usually once every five days, and there were a total of 1,054 local towns with their own market-days by Yongjo's reign. Two individuals were indispensable on these occasions. One was the *posang*, more likely a peddler who carried clothing and other miscellaneous materials on his back and travelled from one market to another. The other was the *pusang*, a retailer who wandered from one market to the next carrying such goods as chinaware, salt, dried-horse meat, straw shoes etc., on his back. These itinerant dealers were strongly united in a sort of business association under rules and regulations bringing them under firm control to enable them to render the maximum mutual help among their fellow-colleagues. The towns of Hoeryong and Kyongwon along the Tumen River became trade centers with the Chinese where cows, farming tools, salt, rice and beans were exchanged for Chinese furs and leathers in the presence of responsible officials from both countries. Trade with the Japanese was carried on via ships from Tsushima and the Japanese residents in Pusan, cotton fabrics, rice, beans, and ginseng being the usual commodities in exchange for Japanese copper and spices. The Japanese trade, however, was not carried on for business purposes but as a conciliatory measure. Along the Yalu, the border towns of Uiju and Chunggang, thrived side by side as the official trade center and smuggling point respectively. Later, in the reign of King Sukchong, the smuggling center was closed and the Korean merchants there moved all the way up to the Manchurian town of Chamen to continue their flourishing business with the Manchus. Silver and ginseng were the Korean commodities most highly favored by the Manchus; Chinese books and clothing materials were among the principal demands of the Koreans. On the other hand, the official merchants of Uiju sometimes went as far as Peking to import the needed goods.

Growth of Silhak

Significance of Silhak

The significant feature of Korean culture during the Yongjong era was the growth of the *Silhak* school of learning. This school reached its peak of development during the reigns of Yongjo, Chongjo and Sunjo. What was *Silhak*?

Literally True Learning, the mission of the *Silhak* scholar was to make persistent attempts to transform an almost completely degenerated and corrupted society into a healthy and stable one. He pursued studies into historical research by taking into the fullest consideration the realistic conditions of present-day society to the end of setting forth all-out plans of land reformation, a sound state economy, and an orderly state structure with sound administrative and military set-ups. In other words, the *Silhak* school of learning was a pragmatic approach to overall fields in politics, economics, history, literature and natural sciences. Two foreign influences were involved, the *Kojunghak* and *Sohak*. The *Kojunghak* (literally, Consideration Evidence Learning) was the Ching school of Chinese learning which insisted that concrete facts had to be digested before problems were thought out. The *Kojunghak* scholar not only conducted research work of a most intensively comparative and critical nature into historical and literary records extant, but brought both realistic and erudite methods of study to the subject with especial emphasis on problems of practical administration and the fostering of race consciousness. The *Sohak*, which means Western Learning, introduced the completely new concepts of European knowledge, particularly, Catholic doctrines and natural sciences. Specifically, the *Silhak* school of pragmatic learning adopted *Kojunghak* methods of study subject to *Sohak* influences.

Admittedly, it is difficult to get a clear idea of *Silhak* learning from such a vague, involved picture. According to the concepts set forth, almost any branch of study may be called *Silhak* if only some influence of Western learning were added to it. Both the teachings of Chong Tojon, a scholar in the latter part of the Koryo dynasty when Korea first heard about the West, and Yi Yulgok, prominent Yi politician, may be said to belong to the *Silhak* school if only because of Western influences. How, then, do we get a right definition of *Silhak*? What is the right conception of this school of learning? What do we understand by it?

Since the Liberation, many historians have sought an answer to these questions. In brief, the conclusion was that *Silhak* meant learning not for the sake of a vocation but to foster practical administration for a better society so to assure the welfare of the people who live in that society. *Silhak* was then found to be relative to the particular time and place. Thus, Confucianism was *Silhak* learning during the period of the Spring and Autumn wars in China's ancient history, the Chu Hsi school of Confucian philosophy was *Silhak* during the Sung dynasty, the dogmas of Wang Yangming was *Silhak* during the Ming dynasty, and the *Kojunghak* was equally so under Ching.

In short, *Silhak* was neither new nor exclusive to the Yi dynasty. It was a trans-historical phase of learning with a universal truth that has appeared persistently under varied aspects in different ages and environments. Through all stages, the main idea of *Silhak* learning—truth and practical administration for a better society—never changed. The *Silhak* school of the Yi dynasty was properly initiated during the latter part of the Koryo dynasty by the prominent Koryo scholar of the Chu Hsi chools,

Chong Tojon.

Elements in the Rise of Silhak

The Korean school of *Silhak*, then, prevailed with the introduction of two influential foreign concepts of learning, the *Kojunghak* and the *Sohak*. What elements do we find underlying the rise of this movement?

First of all, the introduction of Western civilization to the East meant striking changes in one's conception of the world. Many Koreans began to doubt the conviction so deeply ingrained in the Korean mind that China was the birthplace of world civilization and that everything Chinese was the best of all possible ways. Korean eyes if not minds were wide-opened to evidences of advanced Western sciences and geography. Indeed, the rise of *Silhak* was quite impossible without the premise of Western civilization.

The Christian missionaries, who landed on China in the last part of the Ming dynasty, brought Catholic dogmas and many books of natural science that were later introduced to the Yi dynasty through the Korean envoys who frequently went back and forth to China. It was these envoys, then, who opened the way to the Western civilization. Yi Sugwang was the first envoy to introduce Western civilization into Korea by bringing with him a world map and Catholic dogmas in the reign of King Sonjo. In the ninth year of King Injo (1631 A. D.), To Tuwon brought a *hwapo* (rifle), *chonnigyong* (telescope), *chamyongjong* (alarm clock), and *sohyangguk pungsokki* (A Record of Customs of the Western Nations). In the fourth year of King Hyojong (1635 A. D.), a more accurate calendar system was enacted by remodelling it after the Gregorian system as a result of suggestions presented by Kim Yuk. In that same year, thirty-eight Hollanders were cast adrift on Cheju shores following a shipwreck. The presence of these provided a rare opportunity for interested intellectuals and academic circles to add to their store of knowledge about the Catholic creed and Western technology. Of all circles, the greatest interest was evinced among the scholars and politicians of the *Namin* faction. As we have seen, the *Namin* was one of the "four colors" in the factional struggles of the latter half of the seventeenth century. It was the fading color. The reign of King Sukchong shattered their power and its members were hardly able to fill a single government post since then. They were reduced to aimless studies about human nature and the principles of the universe that was the legacy of the orthodox Chu Hsi education they had acquired. In the political pastures, such studies failed to arouse any interest whatsoever. Chu Hsi philosophy was meaningful only if one had opportunities to serve the state and the last hope in that direction was denied the men of the *Namin* because they could not sit for the Higher Civil Service Examinations. Their opponents laid too many obstacles in their path. Under such severe handicaps, it was only natural for them to search elsewhere for intellectual employment. They came closer to the reality of the hardships and miserable conditions under which the people were living and approached their studies from practical angles in order to pinpoint their descriptions of social realities and levy sharp criticism against negligent government. Their search led them to the *Sohak* school of learning and the more they probed into it, the more fascinated they became. The practical approaches of the West taught them to look at facts as facts and to set out upon vigorous reforms of the existing, corrupted, contradictory system of government at a time when destiny and history were shaping forces on their side. Mounting unrests and contradictions of society resulted in increased pursuit of *Silhak* studies, not only among well-born intellectuals but also among the lowly and common classes whose access to books was only surpassed by their interest. Further, the Ching dynasty also gave China the *Kojunghak* school of realistic learning and this, introduced to Korea by the same traditional routes of Chinese culture, was an added incentive to the *Silhak* trend. The abstract methods of Chu Hsi studies gave way to the practical *Kojunghak* methods and the trend swept across the nation to such an extent that the saying went: "Learning that does not help the people is no learning". The *Silhak* school of realistic studies produced many fruits in the fields of politics, economics, agcriulture, history, geography, languages, mineralogy, and mapmaking.

Realistic Scholars and Their Works

The realistic scholar was developed from two trends of opposition, the pro-Ching, anti-Ming movement during the Manchu invasions when Yi Chosun was clearly outdated in adhering to a Ming loyalty that was without form or content, and the *Silhak* school which was actually an outcome of the former opposition and which, as we have noted, was spearheaded by the *Namin* protests against a discredited government. The list of realistic scholars, therefore, goes back to the period of the Manchu invasions which bankrupted the rigid pro-Ming tendencies without giving the pro-Ching, anti-Ming movement the chance to flower and avoid the catastrophe.

We may start with Yu Hyongwon who wrote his famous book, "*Pangye Surok* (Collection of Pangye: Pangye being the author's penname)", during the reign of King Hyojong. The work was a systematic analysis of government functions with primary emphasis on the land system and the writer's own views and recommendations on the practical problems to which he called the attention of "conscientious governors." At about the same time, Pak Sedang wrote the "*Saekkyong*" which concentrates on the land question. Perhaps, the most prominent of the early *Namin* scholars of the *Silhak* school was Yi Ik. better known by his penname, Songho, Admired by the people for his vast store of knowledge on a wide range of subjects, Yi Ik turned out a number of books which were to serve as inspiration for later scholars of the realistic school. His best known work is entitled the "*Songho Sasol* (Songho's Essays)" in which he probed into every social problem of his times. An Chongbok, an Yi Ik disciple, devoted himself to history and produced one of the best historical works of this period, the "*Tongsa Kangmok*" (Classification of Korea's History). The "*Palyokchi* (Commentaries on the Eight Areas, i. e. Provinces)", a geographical work basically so sound that even modern Korean geographers profit from its approach, was written by Yi Chunghwan who for thirty years travelled to every nook and corner of the peninsula after being forced to retire from political life. In the reign of King Chongjo when *Silhak* learning had attained maturity, Pak Chega, in his "*Pukhagui*," emphasized that the merits of the new Ching dynastic civilization should be taken into consideration to improve the governmental and economic systems of Chosun. He also declared that foreign trade should be encouraged and called on members of the idle and privileged class to pitch themselves into industrial work. Pak Chiwon, in his "*Yolha Ilgi* (Diary of Yolha)," sharply criticized the contradictions inherent in high class society with a brush noted for its extraordinarily beautiful lines. A point of passing interest is that both Pak Chega and Pak Chiwon belong to a new faction called the *Pukhak* (North Learning). Among the other outstanding writers of the *Pukhak* were Hong Yangho, Hong Taeyong, Yi Tongmo, Yu Tukkong and So Yugu, each of whom contributed new dimensions to a valuable library, especially So Yugu who undertook a voluminous encyclopaedic work and Hong Taeyong who was a great scholar of mathematics and astronomy. The outstanding contributions to history were Han Chiyun's "*Haedong Yoksa* (History of Haedong, or Korea)" and "*Yonnyosil Kisul* (A work comprising all phases of the dynasty from Taejo, the founder, to Hyonjong, such as royal court affairs, geography, literature, astronomy, etc.)" by Yi Kungik. The great scholar of King Sunjo's times was Chong Yakyong (penname: Tasan), whose prodigious out-

II HISTORY

put, "*Yoyudang Chonso* (Collection of Economic, Political and other Data of Yi Society)" consisted of 500 volumes. This thoroughgoing reformist soul is the subject of a paper written by Gregory Henderson, a U.S. Foreign Service officer, for the May 1957 issue of the Journal of Asian Studies. Kim Chonghui, who lived during the reigns of Sunjo and Hyonjong, was the outstanding scholar on epigraphy and Chinese classics. The geographer, Kim Chongho, who, like his earlier colleague, Yi Chunghwan, had visited every nook and corner of Korea, produced a map of the country, called "*Taedong Yojido*", which was remarkable for its high degree of accuracy. It was too accurate for the government that imprisoned and finally executed him. The grounds were that such a map was an expose to foreign nations and, as such, could be used against Korean interests. Yi Kyugyong's ponderous title, *Oju Yonmun Changjon Kyogo*, a voluminous, encyclopaedic compilation of the *Silhak* movement, fittingly rounds off this list of vigorous *Silhak* scholars.

Catholic Conversions and State Oppression

From Silhak to Catholicism

As we have seen, Catholicism came to Korea with other Western sciences in what was called the *Sohak* or Western Learning. The *Silhak* scholars, who saw in the rudiments of Western civilization the basis for rebuilding Korea's static society, in general, acquired depths of knowledge and understanding of the Catholic creed. In the end, their high respect and aspiration for scientific superiority of *Sohak* learning won them over to the religious appeal.

From Learning to Conversion

During the reign of King Chongjo in the latter part of the eighteenth century, the doctrines of the Roman Church were beginning to be accepted by the interested Korean scholars not as a mere subject for study but also as a religion. Young *Namin* scholars established an academic institute which devoted itself fully to the pursuit of Catholic studies in order to probe the religious significance of the creed. A son of a Korean ambassador to Peking, Yi Sunghun, was baptized by a European priest in China and brought back a number of Christian books upon his return to Korea. Yi Sunghun was, thus, Korea's first convert to the Roman Church. One of his intimate friends, Yi Pyok, though unbaptized, became so zealous a champion that every young scholar who came in touch with him was infected by his enthusiasm: Yi Kahwan, Yi Chonchang, the brothers Kwon; Ilsin and Cholsin, and the brothers Chong; Yakchong, Yakchon and Yakyong. Not all progressives were in favor of this trend. An Chongbok, one of the leading *Namin* scholars, wrote such books as "*Chonhak Mundap*" and "*Chonhakko*" in which he tried to reject Catholicism as a religion and consider it only as a school of learning. An's point was that forward—looking scholars should be strictly orientated to the realities of the internal social conditions and that Western Learning, the religion included, should be approached only secularly. Notwithstanding, Catholicism made steady strides and the number of converts increased rapidly. This rapid rise of Christianity in Korea well prior to the coming of the European missionary has often been remarked as a "miracle" in the history of Christian evangelizations.

The Problem of Worship

The principal, perhaps the only, reason why Catholicism came to be regarded as heretic and cast from Korean society by the state lay in the problem of ancestral worship which Confucian morality demanded. Confucianism and Catholicism were incompatible at the core and, from the beginning, were never expected to fuse into one. The Catholic missionaries, during their initial stages of proselytization in China, tried to adapt their religion to the native traditions and customs in order to facilitate their mission. According to Matteo Ricci—since

Confucian rites of ancestral worships received formal state recognition in China, it was only natural that Chinese Catholics should be allowed to observe such ceremonies. The Dominican and other schools of missionaries who came later, however, proscribed such practices on the grounds that they were contrary to the basic teachings of the Church. The Pope himself pronounced them superstitious. From Peking then, the Portuguese priest, Msg. Alexandre de Gouvea, baptizer of Yi Sunghun, sent official word to Korean Catholics proscribing them from ancestral worships.

In the fifteenth year of King Chongjo, a certain *Namin* well-born of Chinsan in Cholla-do province, Yun Chijung, refused to mourn his mother's passing by observing a required ceremony. For this, he was accused of violating one of the three basic moral codes, and executed. Yun was thus the first Korean martyr to Christianity. He was but the first of many other martyrs who died because they had broken with tradition in faithful adherence to the Church's ruling.

While executing all those who had bypassed ritual observances in the name of a foreign religion, the government also took stern measures to prevent any further violations of age-long traditions, particularly this custom of ancestral worship. The foreign religion was the cause of the infection, so the government burned up all Catholic books, barred the importation of further such literature from Peking, and, in every way, pursued an isolationist policy. But the state, for all its power, was unable to kill off the germs completely. Catholics were driven underground and, with the arrival of a Chinese priest, Shou Wen-mou, who smuggled into the country secretly, Catholicism was revived with renewed force and the number of converts increased again.

The Sinyu Massacre

King Chongjo died in 1800 and his successor, Sunjo, was still in his infancy. Accordingly, the Queen Dowager became regent for the boy-king. The change was opportunity for the *Noron* faction which, with the *Namin*, had become the dominating currents in the factional strife. Under the regency, the *Noron* rose rapidly to power, filled all the high government posts, and began a deliberate campaign to oust all their rivals of the *Namin* faction who had dominated the government of former King Chongjo. They found a good excuse in the fact that so many of the *Namin* leaders and their relatives were Catholics or, at least, Catholic sympathizers. They forced the *Namin* men to choose between death and denial of the "Catholic heresy." The *Namin* were stubborn and a host of outstanding leaders of the faction who were Catholic, Chong Yakchong, Yi Kahwan, Kwon Cholsin, Yi Sunghun, and others, were executed. The Chinese priest, Shou Wen-mou, emerged from his underground hide-out to give himself up to the authorities and immediately followed the same fate. The year in which all these executions took place, which was the first year of the boy-king Sunjo's reign and also the first year of the new nineteenth century, was the *Sinyu* year under the Oriental sixty-year cycle of the full human life. The executions, therefore, are known in the history of Korean Catholicism as the *Sinyu* massacre.

The *Sinyu* massacre was only the begining. Oil was poured on the fire by what is known as the incident of Hwang Sayong's petition. Shortly after the *Sinyu* persecutions, a *Namin* Catholic, Hwang Sayong, in a petition addressed to the foreign missionary in Peking, suggested the dispatching of a foreign fleet to force the Yi government to allow freedom of Catholic worship. This document fell into the hands of the government with consequences which may be imagined. A fresh wave of massacres broke out in which practically all of the leading *Namin* circles were killed off and the Catholic adherents among the masses scattered. Over the years, these lowly Catholics were to lead miserable, wandering lives, narrowly escaping death many times but ever keeping their

↑ A Northern-Style Dolmen
 Unyul-gun, Hwanghae-do. One of Neolithic tombs scattered all over the peninsula except the northernmost province of Hamgyong Pukto and the southernmost Cheju Island.

↑ A Southern-Style Dolmen
 Chongup-gun, Cholla Pukto. There are two styles of dolmens; one is the Northern, as shown in above picture, consisting of a plate-stone and several support-stones making a table-like form, and the other is the Southern, as shown in this picture, a plate-stone lying direct on the surface of the earth.

↑ A Northern-Style Dolmen
   Chaeryong-gun, Hwanghae-do. The dolmens standing here along the Hung River have support-stones arranged to open through west to east.

A Northern-Style Dolmen
   Sinchon-gun, Hwanghae-do. Those huge stone monuments have been well preserved since people feared them as mystical ones. The result was the discovery of so many various remains of Stone Age and early Metal Age from those
↓ ancient tombs.

Stone Coffins →
Discovered under a shellmound in Kimhae, Kyongsang Namdo. Comparatively well preserved the original forms.

Prehistoric Remains
Stone-arrowhead, stone-spearhead, and fragments of earthenwares used by the residents in Korean peninsula about 4,000 years ago.
↓

← **Bone and Horn Tools**
Another prehistoric remains made of bone and horn.

↓ **Stone-Swords**

The Base Structure of a Dolmen
Found in Taegu, Kyongsang Pukto. At such places, often excavated many ancient remains.
↓

← An Earthenware
  Discovered in Taedong-gun, Pyongan Namdo. Lolang relic.

↑ A Jar
  Another Lolang remains discovered in Taedong-gun, Pyongan Namdo.

↑ A Pottery
  An Imna relic discovered in an ancient tomb around Mount Chusan, Koryong-gun, Kyongsang Pukto.

Potteries
↓ Also Imna, discovered in a tomb around Chinju, Kyongsang Namdo.

Face of Chomson Monument
A Lolang remain. 1.6 ms in height and 1m in width. The Chinese characters were written in Ye-style. One of the oldest stone monuments in Korea, it was the shrine monument of Chomson county, Lolang Province. ↓

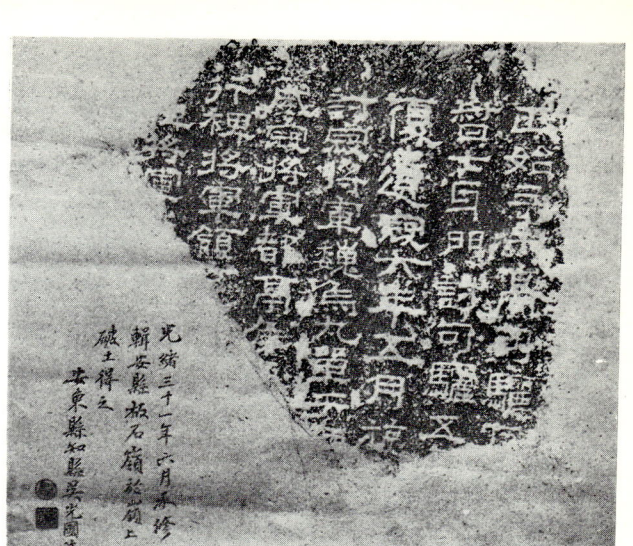

↑ **An Epigraphic Copy of a Fragment of Moku-gomnuk's Monument**
A Koguryo relic discovered in Tsian Province, Manchuria.

Ancient Charcoal Range →
One of the burial objects discovered in an ancient Lolang tomb in Taedong-gun, Pyong-an Namdo.

An Ancient Stone Coffin →
A Ye-period's stone coffin excavated at Kangnung, Kangwon-do.

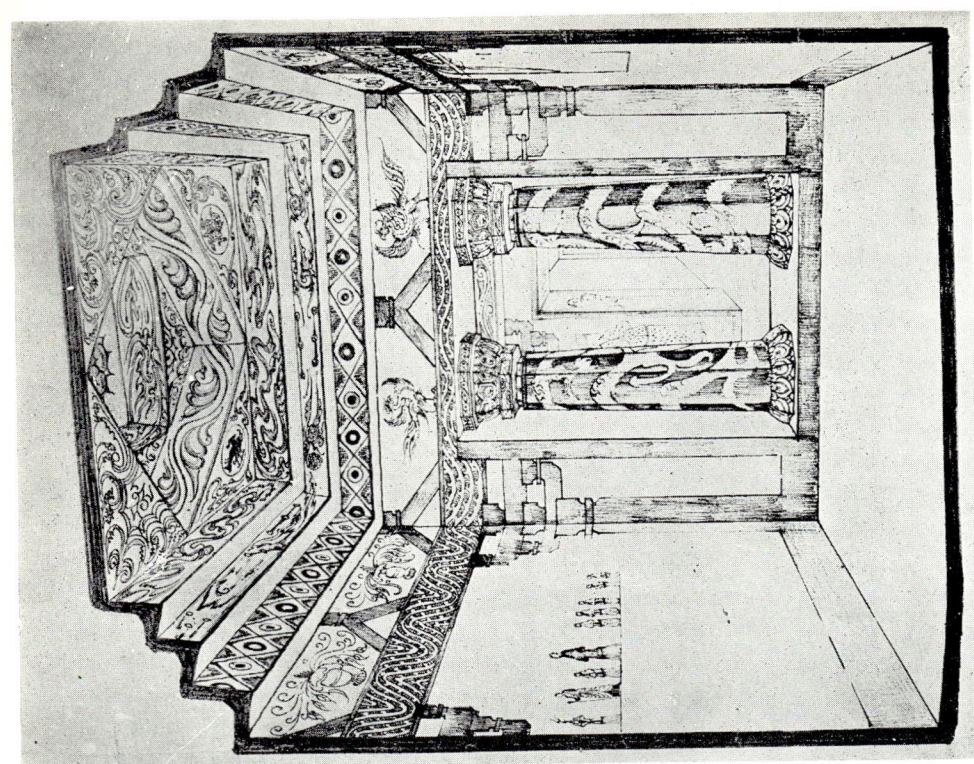

↑ A Sketch of the Front Chamber of Two Pillars Tomb

↓ Ceiling of the Chamber of Two Pillars Tomb

↑ Ssangyongchong (Two Pillars Tomb)
Located in Yonggang-gun, Pyongan Namdo. Of Koguryo period, contains many famous frescoes.

↑ **Front View of the Great Tomb at Uhyonni**
Kangso-gun, Pyongan Namdo. Fine artistic works of frescoes are extant in this tomb. Koguryo tomb.

→ **Ceiling of the Chamber of Great Tomb at Uhyonni**

↑ **Front View of the Middle Tomb at Uhyonni**
Kangso-gun, Pyongan Namdo. This tomb contains many priceless art works of Koguryo frescoes.

→ **A Sketch of Kamsin Tomb Front Chamber**
Another Koguryo tomb located in Yonggang-gun, Pyongan Namdo.

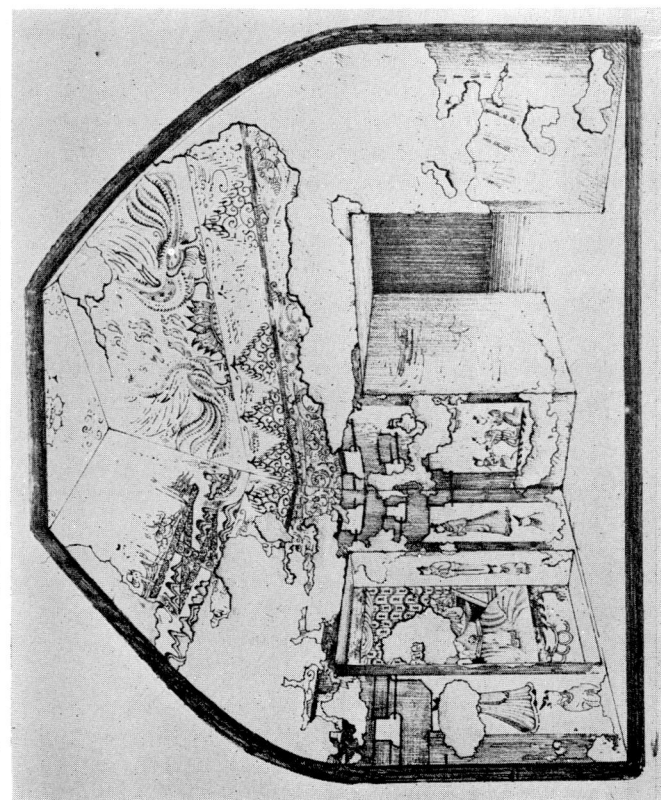

↑ Tombstone of King Hotae
  Tsian Province, Manchuria. Gravestone of Koguryo's 19th king Hotae(392～412).

↑ Inscription of the King Hotae's Tombstone
  One of the oldest and finest calligraphic works in Korea.

Changgunchong(Tomb of General)
↓ Mausoleum of King Hotae. The most complete one among the numerous Koguryo tombs remained now.

Laquerware Fragments
Fragments peeled off from laquerwares discovered in Chungha Tomb of Paekche kingdom around Puyo, Chungchong Namdo

↑ Stone Pagodas of Paekche Period
Around Puyo, Paekche capital, Chungchong Namdo.

↓ White Porcelain of Paekche Period

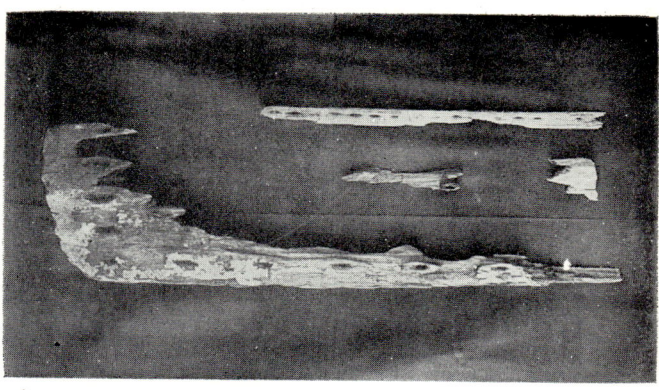

↑ Fragments of a Wooden Coffin of Paekche Period
Discovered in chamber of Chungsangchong, a Paekche king's tomb, near Puyo, Chungchong Namdo.

Grain Charcoal
At 660 A.D. when Paekche kingdom fell, attacked on both sides by allied forces of Silla and Tang, military supply warehouses on the Mount Puso said to have been burnt for few weeks. The grains which had burnt in the warehouses now remain their mountain sites, not as grains but as charcoals—grain charcoals.

←
Pukhansan Monument
 One of four extant hunting monuments of Silla King Chinhung. Located in suburban Seoul.

Changnyong Monument, Changnyong-Gun, Kyongsang Namdo
 Another one of King Chinhung's hunting monuments.
↓

Najong Spring, Kyorgju
 According to a history book, Pak Hyokkose, the founder of Silla kingdom, was born from an egg which had been found by this well.
↓

→
Hamyongnu, a Pavillion of Pulguk-sa Temple
 The most beautiful Buddhist temple in Korea, showing the advanced architectural techniques of Silla dynasty.

Pagodas of Silla Period →
The Tabo-Tower, Sokka-Tower, both of which are within the Pulguk-sa Temple, are real matchless masterpieces

↑ **Chomsongdae**
The first astronomical observatory in Far East. In Kyongju, Silla Capital.

Ruins of Imhaejon Palace →
About 2,000 years ago, here was a luxrious palace of Silla. Only base stones now remain.

←
Posokchong
An entertainment place where king and subjects alike enjoyed themselves during the flourishing Silla dynasty.

↑ Talisman
  A Buddhist talisman issued by a Buddhist temple
  Written in both Chinese Characters and Sanscrit
  A Buddha image is printed on the right side

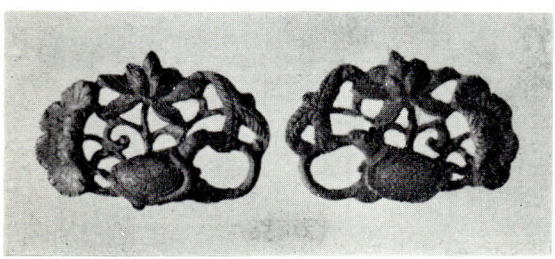

← Gilt-Bronze Ornaments of Koryo Period

Sungyang Sowon (school)
Kaesong, Kyonggi-do. School and private house of Chong Mongju(1337-1392), the scholar~politician and famous patriot at the end of Koryo kingdom.

Sonjukkyo Bridge
A stone bridge in Kaesong, Koryo capital. A legend says the bridge was blood-stained when Koryo's patriot, Chong Mongju was assassinated here. The house to the right contains two stone monuments written about Chong.

↑ An Interior View of Taeungjon of Simwon-sa Temple
  Hwangju, Hwanghea-do. One of few northern Chinese-influenced buildings in Koryo period when the Sung (southern China) architecture dominated this country.

↑ Patrol Lamp
    Used by patrolmen during Yi period.

The Poem, Wolinchongang
    Composed by King Sejong for his deceased consort, Queen Sohon, in 1447. ↓

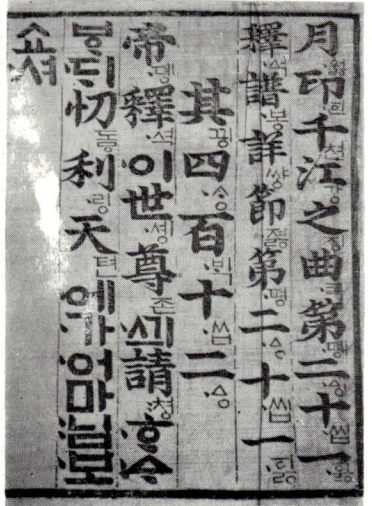

↑ Mapae (Horse Medal)
    An identification mark of a central government official when he goes down to local areas. He shows this medal to station-master to get new relay horses. Made of copper.

↑ Portrait of Admiral Yi Sunsin
    The hero of the Hideyoshi wars.

Royal Tablet Shrine, Seoul
    Built in 1421. There are tablets of all the Yi kings and queens, and some of honorable subjects, too. ↓

Taewongun →
His name was Yi Haung (1820-1898). Taewongun means the king's father. He was the famous regent who adopt the "closed door" policy when the attentions of Western colonizers were centered upon the Far East.

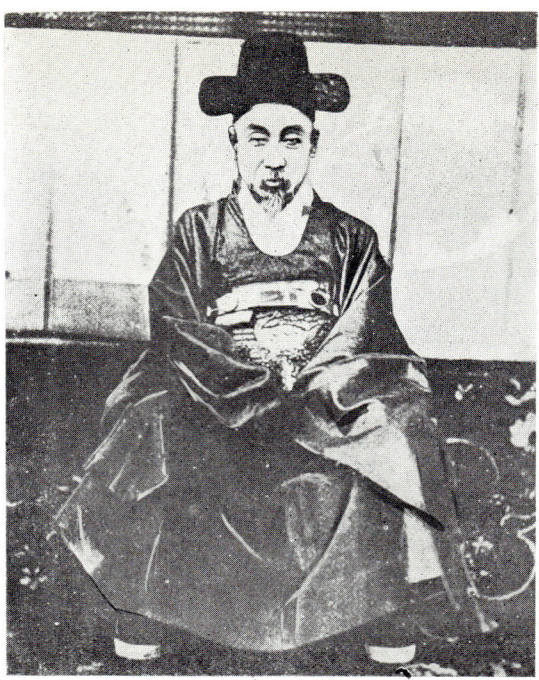

↑ Uiam Rock
In the Nam River, Chinju, Kyongsang Namdo. This is where the kisaeng, Nonge, pulled the enemy commander with her into the water during the Hideyoshi Invasion.

Portrait of Yi Yulgok (1536—1586)
Yi dynasty's most prominent scholar and ↓ statesman, together with Yi Toegye.

←
Tortoise-ships
An old battle-ship invented by Admiral Yi Sunsin prior to the Hideyoshi Invasion. Japanese fleets were almost completely destroyed by these ships.

A Scene of the Samil Independence Movement

On March 1st(Samil), 1919, the Korean people inspired by U.S. President Wilson's declaration of racial self-determination, declared their independence and rose in revolt against Japanse imperialism. This picture shows Japanese police massacring Koreans during the movement.

Emperor Kojong's Secret Letter to International Peace Conference

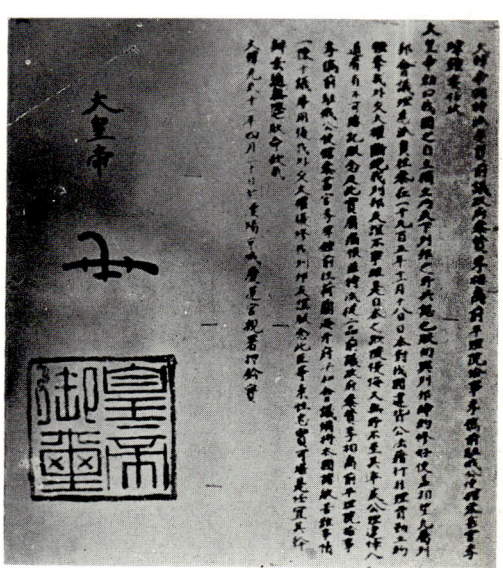

↑ Monument to Kwangju Students' Independence Movement
  Kwangju City, Cholla Namdo.

Monument of General Kim Chwajin(1889～1929)

During the Japanese domination of Korea, General Kim organized an Independence Army to resist the Japanese.

Liberation
The Japanese surrender to the Allied Powers in August, 1945 meant the end of the most disastrous world war for people everything. To the Korean people, it meant even more: liberation from 36 long years of a tyrannical Japanese rule, a liberation of land, people and history.

The End of the Japanese Rule
The Japanese sign the surender terms on Sep. 9, 1945.

Homecoming of the Prominent Men in ROK Shanghai Provisional Goverment

new-found religion of hope alive in their breasts. In 1831, the first church was established on Korean soil and six years later, three French priests of a Paris missionary group, appointed for Korea, slipped into the country in disguise to proselytize. The number of Catholic converts had now reached 9,000.

The Kihae Massacre

Word that European missionaries were in Korea spread from mouth to mouth and finally reached the ears of government. In the *Kihae* year, which was the fifth year of Honjong's reign (1839), a long drought set in and it was suggested that Catholics be hunted down to allay the restlessness among the starving populace. The *Kihae* massacre which followed claimed the lives of the three French priests, arrived just two years ago, among its victims.

The tension between authority and a persistent faith continued down the years, neither side giving an inch. The outstanding Korean Catholic after the *Kihae* massacre was one, Kim Taegon, himself the son of a martyr. Kim was the first Korean to go abroad to study theology. Upon graduating from the Macao Seminary, he was ordained a priest and returned to Korea via Shanghai where he was accompanied back home by a foreign priest. For some years, Bishop Kim was able to carry on an energetic mission only to be executed for his pains in the end. He was only 25.

But the hardships which the people continued to suffer could no longer be laid at the Catholic doors for the reign of King Choljong saw desperate outbreaks of rioting that tied down government hands. What was more, the capture of Peking by an expeditionary allied force of Anglo-French troops in Choljong's 11th year, warned the Yi government against the persecution of Catholicism. Squeezed between internal riots that threatened to get out of hand and the threat of imminent foreign invasion against loss of missionary lives, the government relaxed. The last years of Choljong saw the number of Catholics increase steadily to some 13,000. There were also a dozen French missionaries by then.

Catholicism vs. Yi Feudalism

To sum up: Catholicism contained the seeds of certain necessary reforms that could hardly be fused into one with an outdated feudal structure that was Yi society. The ultimate allegiance of a God in Heaven that Catholicism demanded was directly opposed to the ultimate Confucian allegiance to a king on earth. Above all, the Catholic teaching that all men were brothers under a single Father in heaven, whatever the social status, threatened the rigid class system by heady appeals to the masses. Finally, Catholic appeals over the head of the state to a foreign authority, such as in the Hwang Sayong petition for a foreign fleet, constituted nothing less than denial of the Yi authority. More specifically, the new religion spearheaded the challenge against the existing order by drawing together the scholarly elite of a discredited faction and the rank-and-file of the common people. The kingdom met this challenge by taking unprecedentedly drastic measures without in the slightest altering its indifferent attitude to the contradictions that were dividing society so glaringly between outright corruptions and utter despair and that were the real cause of the Catholic appeal. The sharp lines of conflict drawn between the oppressed who found their consolation in Catholicism and the oppressors who would maintain Confucianism by extreme force were bound up inseparably in the process of the Yi decline in a century of eventful changes.

Despotic Rule and Peasant Uprisings

Sedo

Sedo means the dictatorial exercise of government power by a man or a family with a mandate from the king. The power with which the *sedo* tyrant is vested ranges from supreme policy-making decisions through personnel and financial affairs to national defense. It is not necessary for the tyrant to be a high official. Under *sedo* rule, all reasonable restraints of the political system are paralyzed and corrupt practices dominate.

The *sedo* system was initiated by an official called Hong Kugyong during the reign of King Chongjo in the latter part of the eighteenth century. Hong was appointed by the king to the post of Chief Royal Secretary and, concurrently, as commanding general of the Royal Guard. The king found himself forced to vest such powers in his able servant because of the ceaseless pressure from his maternal relatives who sought every pin-pricking opportunity to discredit him while plotting one conspiracy after another for his overthrow. The king gave Hong a free hand to eliminate his political enemies and take the reins of state administration. With such powers in his hands, it was natural that Hong should work out a despotic form of government.

Hong, however, was dismissed once he had stabilized the political situation but the system he had devised was passed on into the hands of the father-in-law of the next monarch, the boy-king, Sunjo. This man, Kim Chosun, of the Andong House of Kim, arrogated *sedo* power to himself and made it a family instrument for the next sixty years with but one short period of interruption during Honjong's reign when the tyranny passed to another.

Under the despotic rule of the Kim family, government degenerated into a state of utmost disorder while the sufferings of the people reached their peak. Briberies were rampant, offices sold like market wares and the Kim family took over all the posts of provincial governor and county chief, exacting taxes and indulging in outright extortions that were bare-faced robbery in order to scoop up fortunes that might enable them to lead the rest of their lives in luxurious comfort or bribe their way to higher positions as suited their various tastes and fancies. In vain did the monarch try to check all this. It was usual for the king to dispatch a royal inspector incognito to areas where word of the governor's misdeeds reached the royal ear. Such an inspector was usually no higher than sixth grade but he was given the king's complete confidence to find out the actual conditions of the people and often vested with the right to dismiss or execute the official wrongdoers on the spot. The king kept sending inspectors out but not a Kim hair was touched.

With the last shred of dignity cast aside by corrupted officialdom, the productive vitalities of the people were sapped and only thieves thrived. Mounted bandits armed themselves with muskets, pirates appeared along every coast and river, and there were beggar raids upon Seoul stores. With irrigation works neglected, floods and droughts drove starving people to wandering all over the country. The chronicles of this period of *sedo* despotism by one family are full of records about disasters, natural and manmade: droughts, floods, pests, epidemics, hunger, deaths, thieves, extortions, fires, and peasant uprisings.

Financial Chaos

As we may gather from what has been said about taxation, there were three kinds of revenue incomes: land, military and grains.

The Farm Tax comprised taxes on the land itself, on certain farm products, for maintenance of firearm units in the name of internal security, and other various forms of taxation connected with land. In time, the functions of the government organs responsible for these taxations became paralyzed and the terriers left untended. The neglect gave rural officials enough scope to engage in corrupt practices, such as tax evasions by setting good lands aside from the registered terriers, tax committments on wastelands, and various schemes of intermediary exploitation. Inevitably, the tax rates increased to make up for the diminution in national income that was caused by the increases in tax-exempted areas and intermediary exploitations. Inevitably, too, peasants, unable to meet exorbitant taxes, left their farms to drift. An added aggravation was the position of the tax-collector himself. Due to the confusions in farm tax administration, the tax-collectors were not on the regular payroll so they had to fend for themselves with illicit incomes, embezzlements and misappropriation of state funds.

The Military Tax was met in the form of tribute. A certain length of cloth was required in payment as substitute for actual military service. The course of time made the Army Register for cloth collections little more than mere formality for powerful families in the countryside conspired with corrupted officials to evade the tax. Instead, the burden fell totally on the poorer people who were assessed taxes on eligible draftees who, as we have noted, were children, old men, dead, unborn. Anybody who was slightly better off than a relative or a neighbor arranged to have the tax shifted on the other fellow's shoulders.

Taxation in kind, that is to say, in grains, included a system of Loan Grains that was originally meant to relieve the peasants. Under this system, the government loaned seedlings to the peasants in spring for transplantation and the latter returned the loan in grains after the autumn harvest. This system of government "generosity" to the helpless farmer was relief only when properly applied. As the proverb went: "the merits or demerits of a law depend upon its application." In due course of time, the officials responsible for maintaining the system misapplied it outrageously. As Chong Yakyong, one of the *Namin* scholars we have mentioned, indignantly observed: farmers going to the warehouse in spring returned empty-handed while the officials setting forth in autumn returned to stockpile the warehouse. The system, in short, had degraded into a nationwide usury practice, an agency to extort from the farmers through every possible means.

The countryside was ruined through the financial derangements of government. It was a dark world in which the poor, the ignorant, and the superstitious were molested at will and endlessly robbed by the corrupt, the powerful, and the tax-collectors.

Hong Kyongnae, *The First Rebel*

Complaints and resistances inevitably mounted in rural areas under the accumulating injustices. It was only a matter of time before someone would come along to organize the discontented and lead a rebellion. That man was Hong Kyongnae.

Hong was a native of Yonggang in Pyongan Pukto province where the people were especially a discontented lot. Seoul discriminated heavily against the north with the result that no native of Pyongan-do ever saw high office in government. The resentments of this province were well embodied in the person of Hong Kyongnae who was a brilliant scholar and a favorite son of his birthplace. He went to Seoul to sit for the civil service examinations in a period when such a test proved nothing but one's birth, power and money. Hong failed to pass although he had been highly confident of placing first. Bitterly disappointed, this ambitious young northerner of a scholar journeyed all over the country with resentment in his heart. These wanderings brought him in touch with the mounting complaints and resistances of the people and made him aware how weak and corrupted the government really was. He began to conspire against the state with such trusted comrades as U Kunchuk and Kim Changsi. Soon he had many backers among rich nobles, wealthy merchants and local officials. He made preparations for an uprising in a particular district of a particular town in Pyongan-do province and bided his day.

Just about this time, the northwestern regions of the country were visited by the severest famine in a hundred years and whole communities roamed foodless. This was Hong's cue. On the pretext of mining some gold, he managed to assemble the discontented together and sparked off a well-organized rebellion. This was in December in the 11th year of Sunjo (1881). Within a matter of days, the rebel forces occupied Chongju, Kwaksan, Sonchon and five other towns north of the river, Chongchon. They were busy preparing for a raid on Anju when they were attacked by well-trained, well-equiped government army regulars. The rebels were badly defeated at the battle of Songnim and Hong had to retreat to Chongju, trailed by a rabble of hungry peasants.

In the meantime, General Pak Kipung was dispatched from the capital and his forces recovered seven of the eight rebel-held towns and laid siege to the last, Chongju.

The rebel forces, isolated within the fort, valiantly stood siege for more than a hundred days against 9,000 strong and various armaments. They ran out of provisions and made several desperate attempts to break through the government lines without success. The breakthrough, instead, was finally made by the government forces who demolished the walls of the fort and the rebel leader who had displayed such brilliant leadership fell before a stray bullet. He was 33.

In revolting against the government, Hong Kyongnae had proclaimed that he would fight to abolish the unjust discriminations against the people of Pyongan-do province and end the despotic rule of the Andong Kim family to relieve the entire Korean people of their hardships. Whenever a town fell before his forces, the government granary was opened and rice distributed to the starving.

Hong's rebellion, undoubtedly, was an organized conspiracy with other disgruntled men to seize the reins of power. It made the utmost of the peasants' sufferings and encouraged their open defiance by agitation. If the rebellion was so widespread, it was because it bore the character of a genuine peasant uprising through which the people could express their long pent-up resentments and anger against the despotic tyranny of the Kim family.

Waves of Revolts

Although Hong Kyongnae's revolt was suppressed, other peasant uprisings broke out one after another, more and more frequently during the latter part of Choljong's reign when the extravagances and splendors of the Kim despots reached their peak. Resentments were out in the open everywhere and people, congested before the mansion of Kim Pyonggi, the tyrant, in marketlike scenes of confusion, jeered at the provincial governors and officials coming to the capital to seek his favor.

It was in the southern town of Chinju that the next great outbreak occurred. The target of hatred here was Paek Naksin, commander of that fortified army post. The peasants broke into the fort with headbands and bamboo spears, drove the commander away, and plundered the rich. Chinju ignited the sparks of discontent everywhere and the whole south was soon aflame with waves upon waves of revolts.

Clearly the existing order was doomed. It but remained to give expression to these revolts in a framework of purpose and direction. That expression was forthcoming with the birth of a religious movement known as the *Tonghak*, or Eastern Learning.

The Tonghak School

The *Tonghak* school of learning was the first native religion incorporating the first set of systematic dogmas as Korea's original. It was founded by a *yangban*, Choe Cheu, in the 11th year of Choljong (1860). The birthplace was the old Silla capital, Kyongju.

Choe was among the more conscientious *yangban* nobles who were suffering hardships because they could not fit into the degenerated order of their class. He was both a social reformer and a strong traditionalist. On one hand, therefore, he lamented the plight of the people and the sorry state of the world; on the other, he was concerned about the tendencies of the *Sohak* appeal which, he feared, might lead to an influx of Western ways at the expense of the Oriental heritage.

In the true spirit of the missionary, Choe Cheu decided that it was his mission to save the world from its disturbing trends. Thus, he founded the *Tonghak* school which, he proclaimed, constituted the true concept of Oriental learning by reviving its religious inspiration. Within that concept, he combined the essences of Confucianism, Buddhism, Taoism and the native Korean faith in supernatural beings.

This school of Eastern Learning clearly embodied nationalistic ideals inasmuch as it was consciously founded as the modern alternative to Western Learning. In fact, though, it was itself greatly influenced by Western Learning and actually contained elements of Catholic teachings in its dogma. The Catholic elements shared room with such age-long superstitions of primitive origin as Shamanism and the geomantic belief in mystic prophecies known as *Chonggamnok*.

The characteristic feature of this dogma, however, lay in the fact that it offered no theories about the future of man or his after-life. It was wholly concerned about the Present with a capital P. Peace and heaven, it stressed, would be realized on earth by rehabilitating the minds of the people and eliminating evils and corruptions from the society of today. The T*onghak*, its followers propagated, was the "way to save the people and preserve the nation."

The movement was eagerly sought and joined by numbers of suffering commoners all too ready to embrace the helping hand of a supernatural power. Its development was vigorous and rapid and its influence spread sufficiently far enough to cause serious concern and anxiety in the government. Choe Cheu was arrested and executed on the charge of "disturbing the world and deceiving the people." The *Tonghak* movement was banned.

Taewongun's Regency and Western Challenges

Taewongun's Reforms

King Choljong died in 1863 without leaving any male issue. The son of Prince Hungson, great-great grandson of Yongjo, was, therefore, chosen to succeed him as Kojong. King Kojong was only 12 years old when he came to the throne so his father became Regent as Taewongun. This was the common princely title bestowed upon the Father-Regent of a selected boy-monarch. In Korean history, however, the title is identified solely with Prince Hungson, not so much for its unprecedency than for the personality of the man who came to it.

Taewongun was an unusually strong-willed man with the stamp of decision in every move he made. He brought this will to bear upon his attempts to correct the corrupted administration. As the first step, he expelled the entire clique of the Kim family kit-and-caboodle from government service and employed talents regardless of birth, district and faction. At the same time, he cracked down so directly upon the rotten world of *Sowon* institutes that their numbers shrank from 600 to 40. He meted out severe punishments to corrupted officials and sternly prohibited every kind of luxury. He abolished offices that had long outlived their proper functions, restored the *Uijongbu* supreme council and gave standing orders to the *Samgunbu* military command to prepare itself for any emergency.

These were administrative reforms at their courageous best and, as such, the first decisive examples in 500 years. They pulled government officials out of the quagmire of long stagnation and injected vitality in its stead. It appeared that with a strong, right-orientated man at the helm at last, prospects would all be bright for the future of the country.

Such alas, was not to be for Taewongun also brought his strong hand down upon projects which could not in any sense be construed as healthy reforms. The prime example was his insistence on reconstructing the Kyongbok palace which had been devastated in the seven-year Japanese wars of the closing sixteenth century. Apparently, he wanted to display the dignity and authority of royalty. It was an expensive pride for, in order to expedite the reconstruction and meet the expenses entailed, he exacted heavy manpower labor from the people of

Kyonggi-do province, devised a new kind of land tax, forced the people to contribute to a "voluntary" fund, and cast and circulated coins at one hundredth below par value.

The Policy of Isolationism

The foreign policy of the Regent was as stubborn as his domestic policies were coercive. Domestically, he could press inexorably but in his foreign policy, Taewongun was flinging defiances in the teeth of strong, sweeping forces of a changing international world. It was an age of headlong Western encroachments upon the Orient. China had to swallow her pride after the Opium War of 1842 with the humiliating Port Treaties; Japan was visited by Commodore Perry's gunboats and also opened up in 1854. Korea remained closed, dreaming the sweet dream of isolation which neither China nor Japan was able to maintain.

It was inevitable that Korea should be affected by what was happening to her neighbors. Yet Taewongun stubbornly clung to his policy of strict isolation. He wanted to maintain the dignity and very existence of the ancient dynasty and to preserve a declining state of affairs against the forceful workings of international politics. All sorts of problems were bound to arise from an opening of the country as had been amply demonstrated in China. Catholicism would expand to threaten the foundations of the state and foreign goods would flood the Korean markets to destroy Korean self-sufficiency. In short, the imperialistic drives of the Western powers posed a very real threat to the Yi kingdom.

Persecution Renewed

The Catholic Church was fated to suffer fresh waves of persecution under Taewongun's hand. In this, the straight-minded Regent was provoked by the oblique approach of the Catholics to the dilemmas of his isolationist policy.

In 1856, a Russian fleet sailed into Wonsan harbor and called on the Korean government to open trade with the Tsarist Empire. The government cast about for an adequate counter-measure to this foreign threat. The Catholics proposed one. A delegation led by Nam Chongsam and including a secretary to the king himself approached the Regent and suggested an alliance with England and France to check Russia. As go-between in such an alliance, they suggested the French priests who were propagating the faith underground in the country. Thus they betrayed the existence of foreign missionary activities and boldly revealed themselves Catholic, all of which was against the law. It was their bid to secure their freedom of worship not to speak of the opportunities provided for Catholic expansions by the long arm of the Western Powers.

Taewongun, as may be imagined, was not exactly pleased with this amazing frankness which, to him, must have seemed an affront to his foreign policy. To him, Russians and Anglo-French were one; Russia was the immediate problem and, instead of a solution there, the delegation, announcing themselves unlawful Catholics, proposed to substitute one immediate threat for another. The Russian fleet solved the problem for him by leaving without exacting an answer to its query, and anti-Catholic, anti-Western waves broke loose, adding numerous more names to the long list of Catholic martyrs, among them Nam Chongsam and nine French priests. This was the *Pyongin* massacre, in the third year of King Kojong or 1866.

Gunboat Diplomacy

One French priest, a Father Ridel, managed to escape arrest and fled to China where he told an Admiral Roze of the French fleet, stationed in China waters, about the *Pyongin* massacre. Whereupon, in August of the same year, Admiral Roze sailed for Korean waters with three warships. He approached past Kanghwa island, reconnoitered the coastal areas of the Han river delta, and returned a month later with seven warships to inquire into the slaying of the French priests, occupying Kwanghwa and burning the warehouse of historical records on the island. Taewongun's reply was 500 riflemen who inflicted some 80 casualties on the French forces. The French were compelled to withdraw after a 40-day occupation of Kanghwa.

Two years later, a German named Oppert, in concert with a Father Feron, another French priest who had survived the *Pyongin* massacre, attempted to excavate the Toksan tomb of Taewongun's father in reprisal for the Regent's high-handedness. Government and people were extremely offended by this behavior and the mass resentments resulted in the harshest persecution of Catholicism to date. Some 30,000 believers lost their lives or suffered injuries.

Also in the summer of 1866, the year of the *Pyongin* massacre, an armed American merchantman, the USS General Sherman, sailed up the River Taedong to Pyongyang and made the familiar trade request. The Americans resorted to violence when ordered by the local authorities to withdraw. The tempers of both the people and officials of Pyongyang were exploded by the white man's arrogance and all the Americans were killed and their ship burned.

Five years later, the United States government sent Admiral Rodgers of the Pacific fleet command to Inchon with nine warships with the double purpose of inquiring into the General Sherman incident and concluding a treaty of commerce. The Korean coastal artillery fired upon the fleet as it was reconnoitering the coast. Whereupon the Americans landed on the same island of Kanghwa where the French had suffered defeat in the same year the General Sherman had been sunk, and attacked the heavily guarded fort of Kwangson. Again, the foreigner failed.

Highly elated by his successful repulsion of two foreign invasions, Taewongun set up a number of stone monuments with an inscription that read: "There are only two choices when the Western Barbarians invade—fight or surrender. Those who favor friendly relations with them are betrayers of their own country. I hereby warn our descendents thus unto ten thousand generations."

However satisfying to the national pride, the fact remains that these successful repulsions, temporary though they were, proved long enough to delay Korea's approach to the new necessary civilization at a critical time in modern history. The successes themselves were due to accidental lapses in the worldwide expansion of Western imperialisms. The two foreign nations at the receiving end of Korean victories were preoccupied elsewhere, the French in Indo-China and the United States with the pioneering West following the Civil War. Their reprisals against the "Hermit Kingdom" were only of a temporary nature because they did not particularly care to spare either the time or the effort to send sufficiently strong reinforcements to back up their will.

While Taewongun was thus enforcing his strong isolation policy outwardly, the power of the Queen's faction, her House of Min, grew from within. The King had now reached full age and the Regent, for all the national pride he might feed, was unpopular, what with his Kyongbok projects and Catholic persecutions which, while responded by the mobs when the Catholics invited their resentment, palled when he pursued them to extreme degrees. Pressures for his removal mounted, scholars expressed their outright opposition in a petition to the king, and, in 1873, his ten-year regency was ended and political power turned over to the despotic *sedo* rule of the Min House with Queen Min herself as its clever and able leader. Queen Min was born of a good *yangban* family related to Taewongun's wife. This fact, added to the loss of both her parents in childhood, was what prompted the Regent to select her as the royal authority through whom to end *sedo* power. She had no one close to her. But she had brains with which to form a powerful party and turn against her father-in-law.

Opening of Yi Chosun (1875 – 1910)

Opening of Chosun

Taewongun Resigns

The regency of Taewongun was an eventful decade. Under his determined will, nobles were suppressed, the Kyongbok Palace re-erected, a policy of isolation strictly pursued lest foreign capital infiltrate the feudalitic structure of Yi society. To his credit, he strengthened his control over the state to rid it of its evils. Yet, his reforms did not contribute to the elimination of the long-accumulated social malpractices. To the contrary, the net effect of his overall policies was to drive both *yangban* and *ssangnom* into a common resistance. As a result, opposition developed against his strong-man rule. An isolationist outwardly, Taewongun gradually isolated himself by his own policies. The Queen's House of Min and the Andong House of Kim united to plot his overthrow, and when the king reached his 21st birthday, the Min encouraged the outstanding Confucian scholar, Choe Ikhyon, to draft an impeachment of the Regent. The impeachment found ready support in open public criticisms. Realizing that the tides were against him, Taewongun gave up the regency in November of 1873, and retired to Yangju. This brought Min Sungho, Min Kyomho and Min Taeho, the Queen's kinfolks, to power. At first, like the Regent, the Min were not interested in opening Korea to the world. Eventually though, they had to yield to the mounting pressures of the modern powers. The spearhead was Japan.

Treaty with Japan

The neighbor island power had just completed the processes of the Meiji Restoration, overthrowing its version of *sedo* despotism, the Tokugawa Shogunate, restoring the ancient imperial system, and rapidly importing the modern civilization of the West. The foreign policy of the Meiji government was an amalgamation of modernism, anti-foreignism and imperialism. To develop capitalistic society, Japan advocated national wealth through military power which, accordingly, became the core of Japan's policies within and without. Japan's expansionist policy soon began to seek target areas in Asia in competition with the Western Powers. Its first step was the invasion of Korea not only as a market for Japanese goods but also as a bridgehead for further penetration of the Asian mainland. An emissary, Moriyama Shigeru, was sent to Korea in 1874 to negotiate the opening of Korean ports. Formal negotiation took place between Moriyama and Pak Chesil, the Korean delegate appointed by the Min in power. However, the negotiations did not get very far because there were still many government leaders who were opposed to the opening of Korea.

Whereupon, Japan decided to use military strength to force the opening. In a provocative move, a Japanese naval vessel sailed into the mouth of the Han to demand water supply in September 1875. The guns of Kanghwa opened fire. This agitated Japanese public opinion against Korea, and the Tokyo government exploited the advantage by sending a fleet. The threat was accompanied by demands that the Korean government render official apology, open the port of Chinhae and points around Kanghwa to Japanese vessels, and conclude a trade treaty with Japan as the peaceful solution to the Kanghwa Incident. The Japanese delegates, Kuroda Kiyodaka and Inouye Kaoru, then came to Korea to negotiate said treaty. In turn, public opinion in Korea reverted to stronger isolationism and anti-foreignism. Taewongun and his followers took advantage of this sign and swiftly moved to blame the Min. Many government leaders joined him. Shocked by these developments, the government called innumerable cabinet meetings which drifted along without decision. At last, however, Prime Minister Pak Kyusu and Interpreter O Kyongsok insisted on concluding a treaty and this finally materialized on February 26, 1876, with the signing of the treaty of friendship at Kanghwa.

Nature of Treaty

The Japanese treaty consisted of twelve articles. In the preamble, Korea was recognized to be an independent sovereign nation enjoying equal rights with Japan. In this proviso for Korean independence, what Japan actually wanted was to remove the strong influence of China from the Korean government so as to make future Japanese moves in Korea easier. Other articles stipulated that Korea would, within twenty months, open Pusan and three other ports to Japan and grant rights of residence and trade to Japanese nationals; that Korea would authorize the Japanese government to conduct topographical surveys of Korean coasts and islands and to make charts and maps, that the Japanese government would establish consulate offices in the aforementioned ports, and that criminal cases of Japanese residents in these ports would be tried by the Japanese consulates.

In fact, this was not a reciprocal treaty. The Japanese government had no responsibility whatsoever to the Korean government as to the conduct of its nationals in these open ports. They had the right to make free surveys of Korean coasts and ports but no vice versas. Consular officers were sent only one way with consular jurisdiction. It was a replica of the submissive and unequal treaties Japan had signed with Western Powers. Japan had changed the tables and was now forcing one on Korea.

In any case, this was the first of the modern international treaties Korea concluded, backed though it was by military threat and plainly unequal. With it, the self-supporting economic system of feudalistic Korea rapidly crumbled in the process of becoming a semi-colony.

The "Hermit Kingdom" was opened by Japanese guns and naval vessels. The importance of this development was that the independent sovereign rights of Korea were emphasized in order to drive out Chinese influence. Japan wanted to move in at a time when the Central Kingdom was being invaded by Western expansionists and had little time to concern itself about its traditionally tributary state. This created friction between China and Japan that finally led to the Sino-Japanese War of 1894 with its decisive change upon the Korean political climate. In the meanwhile, Korea opened Pusan in 1876, Wonsan, in 1880, and Inchon, in 1883, to Japanese vessels. Japanese nationals began to move into these ports from Kyushu, Chukoku, and Tsushima, carrying their merchandise in with them. Cotton goods, especially, dominated the Korean market. Korea, still non-industrialized, was mainly dependent upon primitive agricultural modes of production. She was, therefore, able only to export rice and some other crops, thus becoming the breadbasket of Japan.

Modern Innovation

Once their country was opened, Koreans began to see this modern civilization of the West first-hand and wanted to import it. In 1880, a Korean diplomatic mission to Japan led by Kim Kwangjip observed the modern development of Japan in military, educational, and industrial fields. Upon their return, they advocated that Korea should learn from the example of the Meiji Restoration to introduce the Occidental civilization. Accordingly, the Korean government sent a largescale inspection party to Japan in May, 1881. This inspection group, composed of Pak Chongyang, Om Seyong, Kang Munhyong, Cho Byongjik, Min Chongmuk, Sim Sanghak, O Yunjung, Hong Yongsik, etc., toured Japan for more than seventy days, observing modern military facilities, educational establishments, industrial plants, and the administrative systems of Japan,

In October of the same year, the government ordered Kim Yunsik to head a group of sixty Korean students to Tientsin, China, where they studied manufacturing as well as maneuvering techniques of new weapons. With this advent of modern civilization, administrative and military organizations and systems were reorganized. Those garrison commanders who had held actual power since the Hideyoshi wars had been placed under the control of the cabinet as soon as Taewongun became Regent. With military matters and international relations far more complicated than in the very recent Taewongun decade, the Korean court needed a new supreme agency which could carry out effective management. In March 1881, therefore, a ministry of state was newly established and headed by a Prime Minister who was assisted by twelve ministers of finance, foreign affairs, home affairs, trade, etc. The six former garrisons were reorganized into two field armies. In addition, a special army of modern military equipments was newly organized. The government invited a Japanese army officer, Horimoto Reizo, to train cadets. Those cadets were selected from among the sons of nobility. However, the conservative Confucian scholars were discontented with the introduction of new ideas and the influence of foreign powers that were brought about by the opening of the country. It is ironical that these Conservatives, who had forced Taewongun to give up the regency, now came out in support of him, for his isolationist and anti-foreign biases. Taewongun was quick to see in this his golden opportunity to regain his power from the Min.

The antagonism between the Liberal and Conservative schools of thought and the power struggle between the Min House and Taewongun were to revolve around each other with interesting results in the next fifteen years of fast-changing events beyond any Korean control. In the end, it was to make incompatible bedfellows of the reactionary ex-regent and the Liberals, while reconciling the Conservative scholars and the House of Min divided at this stage by the opening of the country.

An Army Revolt and Political Changes

Chinese Reassertion

As the protectorate power, the Ching dynasty of China had played a leading role in Korean affairs since the 17th century. The Japanese moved in while China was busy mending her own fences against the Western expansions. As soon as she had regained some semblance of stability in international and domestic affairs, China sought to revive her former authority over Korea. Chinese merchandise began to compete with Japanese products and Peking advised the Korean court to open her ports to Western Powers as well to offset dominant Japanese influences. Specifically, China attempted to regain her ancient hegemony by acting as go-between of Korea and the Western Powers in international affairs. The outbreak of a military revolt at this time provided China her chance for a comeback on the Korean stage.

As stated before, a reorganization of military forces took place with the advent of Occidental civilization. Now, this was precisely what the officers and men of the old army did not like to see for two reasons. First, they knew they would eventually be replaced by the modern troops. Second, these modern-trained and equipped troops, called the "special army," were given better treatment, whereas the salaries of the old army personnel were delayed. The old army saw their opportunity in the possibility of Taewongun's comeback which would mean the overthrow of the Min House.

In July 1882, soldiers of the old army were finally paid grain rations that had been delayed for thirteen months. However, the amount was short and the quality poor, the grains being mixed with sand. The angry soldiers refused to accept the rations, whereupon Min Kyomho ordered the masterminders of the strike, Yu Pokman and Kim Chunyong, chained in prison. More enraged than ever, the soldiers marched out into the streets for open demonstrations to be joined by those who had complaints about the Min. The masses broke into an armory, took up weapons, and attacked the government, killing Min Kyomho who was in charge of the treasury, and Kim Pohyon, magistrate of Kyonggi-do. At the same time, they appealed to Taewongun for support. The rebels also looked for Queen Min but she had already taken flight to Chungju. They killed the Japanese army officer, Horimoto Reizo, and attacked the Japanese Legation, the Japanese Minister, Hanabusa Yoshitada, and his staff of 28, retreating to Inchon and back to Japan. The king delegated his authority to Taewongun and had him handle the situation. Thus, after nine years of retirement, the strong-man was back in power. But not for long for the Min had instructed the Korean emisary in Tientsin, Kim Yunsik, to request China's assistance against Taewongun and the Chinese court took advantage of this opportunity to reassert their authority in Korea. They sent a fleet of 4,500 troops led by Wu Chang-ching and Ting Ju-chang to Korea in August of the same year. Taewongun was arrested as the mastermind of the military revolt and sent to Paoting in the Chihli province of China, where he was kept under house arrest. Later, Yuan Shih-kai came to Korea and suppressed the military revolt. Li Hung-chang followed Yuan to handle Korean affairs. Thus, China reestablished her control over Korea.

On the other hand, Japanese Minister Hanabusa returned to Inchon with Japanese warships and demands for due Korean apologies. Yi Yuwon and Kim Hongjip, on behalf of the Korean government, and Hanabusa, signed a treaty at Inchon, on August 30, 1882. Under this Chemulpo Treaty, the Korean government promised to punish the leaders of the military revolt, pay an indemnity, make an official apology for the loss to Japanese lives and property, allow the Japanese Legation to station troops within the Legation compounds for their own protection, and open another port to Japanese vessels. In compliance with these treaty provisions, the Korean government sent Pak Yonghyo and Kim Okkyun to Japan as Korean envoys for the official apology. It is said that this was the first occasion that Korea used her national flag.

As shown in the above, the Military Revolt provided China with a chance to reenter Korea. The Min who requested the military assistance of China to put Taewongun down gave up Korean sovereignty as the price. They were solely interested in reestablishing their personal position with the help of the suzerain power. China made full use of her interventional opportunities. The Ambassador Extraordinary and Plenipotentiary, Li Hung-chang, recommended the Europeans, P. G. von Mollendorf and Robert Hart, as advisors to the Korean court. Responsibility for the maintenance of public order in the capital city was left entirely in the hands of Wu Chang-ching and his 3,000 Chinese troops. Control of military affairs was transferred to General Yuan Shih-kai. Thus, Korea came under China's sway. In 1882, Korea entered into a trade treaty with China, reclarifying the age-long Sino-Korean relationship. China also led Korea into concluding treaties with Western Powers to prevent Japan from gaining any exclusive position in the country. Accordingly, Korea entered into treaty relations with the United States (1882) and France (1886).

Abortive Reform

The Military Revolt was clearly a big blow to Japan. With China's reassertion in Korea, antagonism between China and Japan steadily increased. Officials of the Korean court were also divided. Young reformist leaders such as Kim Okkyun, Pak Yonghyo, Hong Yongsik, So Chaepil and So Kwangbom, who had visited Japan, wanted to drive out Chinese influence with the help of Japan and follow the pattern of the Meiji Restoration. Antagonism bred between this reformist group and the conservative Min Party and their followers, such as Min Yongik, Min Sungho, Kim Hongjip, Kim Yunsik, Kim Mansik and O Yunjung, who favored China.

In 1884, when news of China's defeat by the French in Indo-China reached Korea, the reformists secretly conferred with the new Japanese Minister, Takezoye Shingichiro, and plotted a coup d'etat with the help of Japanese troops stationed in Seoul. On December 4, 1884, the coup d'etat was staged according to plans and the plotters killed several Conservative leaders while they were attending the completion ceremony of a new office building, abducted the King, placed him under armed Japanese guard, and organized a reformist cabinet. The reformists proclaimed their goals to be enhancement of national prestige, end of subservience to the stronger, establishment of diplomatic relations on equal bases, end to despotic rule by factional clans, employment of talented men in office, and development of industries. It seemed as if a five-century old autocratic rule was being renovated into a modern political system. However, revolution by a few pioneering leaders was destined to fail without the support of the general public. Public support was difficult to expect especially when the reforms were coming under the support of a foreign power. Unexpectedly, China was quick to move her troops against the reformists and Yuan Shih-kai's 2,000-man force drove the Japanese soldiers out of the palaces. Takezoye and his staff had to take the same retreat route home via Inchon followed by his predecessor. Some of the reformist leaders were killed, others exiled to Japan. The modern government had lasted only three days.

Returned to power, the Conservatives became even more subservient to China. Meanwhile, Japan, which was not blameless for the abortive failure of the reformist movement, sent an envoy, Inouye Kaoru, accompanied by two infantry battalions, to demand Korean liabilities for the attack on the Japanese Legation and the massacre of Japanese residents. As a result, another treaty (Hansong Treaty) was signed between Inouye and Kim Hongjip on January 9, 1885. In this treaty, the Korean court promised to make an official apology to Japan, severely punish those who had assaulted the Japanese residents in Korea, pay indemnity, contribute land for a Japanese Legation site, and build a legation building for Japan. This treaty restored Korean-Japanese relations. But the relationship between China and Japan was still left unsolved.

Through the good offices of the British Minister to the Chinese Court, Harris Parkes, a treaty was signed at Tientsin between Li Hung-chang of China and Ito Hirobumi of Japan, on April 18, 1885. In this treaty, the governments of China and Japan both agreed to withdraw their military forces from Korea within four months, and to notify the other party in advance should one party find it necessary to send its troops back. This Tientsin Treaty drove out Chinese influence and provided reciprocal opportunities to China and Japan alike relative to Korean problems. But though both countries withdrew their forces from Korea, China continued to intervene in Korean domestic affairs.

Western Entries and Japanese Expansion

Anglo-Russian Friction

As noted, China pursuaded Korea to open up to Western Powers to offset exclusive Japanese expansion. The Western Treaties, however, weakened China's own position in Korea. Of the various Western Powers, the most actively interested parties were Russia and Great Britain. With the conclusion of the Peking Treaty in 1860, Russia had acquired the Siberian frontier of Primorskaya from China, thus marching her borders with Korean territory. In 1884, Russia sent Karl Waeber, former secretary of the Russian Legation in Korea, to the Korean Court as an envoy, and concluded a trade treaty in July of the same year. Waeber stayed in Korea as the Russian Minister to the Korean Court and won the confidence of King Kojong. At this time, there were government leaders who were unhappy about China's intervention in the domestic affairs of Korea. Those elements began to advocate a pro-Russian policy in order to lower the curve of Chinese intervention. Taking advantage of this development, Waeber succeeded in concluding an overland trade treaty with Korea that promised to open Kyonghung to the Russians for trade over the common Russo-Korean border. China grew impatient at the increasing pro-Russian trend. In 1885, China released Taewongun from house-arrest in China, and sent him back to Korea to build up a pro-Chinese faction against a House of Min which was switching its foreign favorites. The party most concerned about the Russian advancement into Korea, however, was not China but Great Britain which was competing with Russia, especially in the Middle East. The southward movement of Russia in this part of the world became a threat to England's Far Eastern schemes. In 1885, therefore, the British sent its Far Eastern Fleet to the island of Komun off the southern coast of Korea, built barracks and gun emplacements there in order to cut off a possibly important sea route for the Russian fleet in Oriental waters. Quite upset by this move, Russia, somewhat agitatedly, urged China to disapprove of the Komun occupation, warning that Russia would also occupy a part of Korea, if Britain meant to stay on the island. At the same time, Russia requested the Korean government to lodge a protest with the British government. In 1887, Li Hungchang of China succeeded in securing the assurance of Russia that it would not invade Korea provided that Great Britain withdrew its naval fleet from Komun.

Economic Drives

With the abortive failure of the reformist movement, Japan lost political ground in Korea. Instead, Tokyo attempted to make up for this economically. Though Korea's ports were opened to the world, trade was mainly carried on with China and Japan until the 1890's. Between 1877 and 1881, Korea enjoyed a sudden trade boom for an eightfold increase in imports. Between 1885 and 1891, exports soared sevenfold, chiefly in rice, soy beans, and other agricultural products. The main import item, cotton goods, came from both China and Japan. But China was either reselling British-made cloth or offering poor quality from a native cottage industry, while Japan was gradually producing her goods with modern machinery. Most of the Korean grains were shipped to Osaka where it controlled grain prices in the Japanese market. Japanese industry, required an adequate food supply and Korea was the source. For this reason, the Japanese economic penetration of Korea was more active than China's efforts. For all the economic efforts, Japan had to expand politically as well if her capitalistic system was to develop. Behind her economic drives, then, Japan was seeking the opportunity to regain the political ground lost by the reformist abortion.

The Tonghak Rebellion

Appeal to China

After the opening of Korea, farmers suffered severe plights due to mounting exploitations by feudalistic power groups and the invasion of foreign capital. Plutocracy flourished in the corrupted government; state expenditures increased tremendously because of the need to import modern military equipment, dispatch diplomatic delegations abroad, and pay foreign indemnities. The expenditures had to be borne by the farmers because nonindustrialized Korea depended almost exclusively on agriculture for its revenue incomes. On the other hand, the ancient economic system of self-sufficiency rapidly crumbled under excessive imports, turning Korea into a quasi-colonial state in economic terms. Japanese merchandise, especially, flooded the markets everywhere, cotton goods, kitchen utensils, agricultural implements, silk, hemp, petroleum, dyes, etc. Farmers had to sell their grains to buy these products and they also had to pay more taxes to satisfy the officials' increased tastes for luxury. Moreover, by taking advantage of the ancient proprietary rights system in the country, Japanese bought farmlands from Koreans at cheap prices or acquired farms by cunning usurious practices. The government leaders, who were merely hanging on to power with the help of foreign powers, could neither retaliate against any foreign invasion or undergo drastic reforms. The farmers, oppressed by helpless nobility, saw that they would have to retaliate against the foreign Powers themselve to achieve social reform. This aspiration led to the *Tonghak* rebellion which was comparable to the Taiping rebellion of China. The *Tonghak*, as we have seen, was banned. Twenty of its leaders were executed, but this native religion, intensely nationalistic in nature, denying classes and preaching the equality of all mankind, proved to be a powerful appeal to the peasant class. In 1892, several thousands of *Tonghak* worshippers gathered at Poun in Chungchong-do province and passed a resolution requesting the release of the founder who had then as yet to be executed. In March of the following year, *Tonghak* adherents from all over the country came up to Seoul and a 40-man representation sat on the grounds in front of Kyongbok Palace with a petition to the king calling for suspension of Choe's death sentence. The king was sympathetic so they peacefully returned home. But though without incident, this sitdown strike of farmers jolted the political climate of Seoul. The foreigners, especially, were shocked for the *Tonghak* petition also demanded an antiforeign policy. Finding no action, *Tonghak* followers returned to Poun once more. This time, they reportedly numbered over twenty thousand and there were ominous political overtones in what was supposed to be a religious rally. The observer heard ideals about liberation from foreign domination and feudalistic oppressions. The last years of the Yi dynasty were filled with rebel warcries. The year 1894, especially, saw one revolt after another, in Chonju, Iksan and Kobu, the last driving the opening wedge into which thousands upon thousands joined all over the southern areas of Korea. The magistrate of Kobu, Cho Pyonggap, was a classic example of corruption. He mobilized farmers for repair work on the Mansok Irrigation reservoir. When the repair work was completed, he levied taxes on the water that the farmers used on their rice paddies. Enraged at this embezzlement, the farmers gathered on the south side of the reservoir. They broke down the dam they had just repaired, stormed into Kobu, chased out the magistrate, occupied the town. The rebels advocated reforms, overthrowing corrupted aristocracy, driving off foreign capital, and promoting the welfare of the people. The ideals swelled their ranks.

The government sent military forces to suppress these rebels only to suffer a crushing defeat at the battle of Hwangtohyon. The rebel forces now marched into the city of Chonju and occupied it without a single battle. Astonished at this result, the central government requested China to send military help. Receiving word that Chinese forces were coming, the *Tonghak* surrendered Chonju and retreated. In June 1894, a Chinese army of 1,500 was at the Gulf of Asan with eight field guns. At the same time, a Japanese army of 5,000 also came to Seoul. This armed confrontation melted the Tientsin Treaty in war over Korean soil. The modernized Japanese army easily defeated the antiquated Chinese forces and, in November of the same year, crushed the *Tonghak* rebel forces at Kongju. The rebel leader, Chon Pongjun, was captured and put to death in March of the following year. A one-year rebellion was ended

II HISTORY

and, at the same time, Japan's economic invasion speedily transformed itself beyond political maneuvers to outright military pressures.

Import of Revolt

The *Tonghak* rebellion was, indeed, at the forefront of Korea's long history of revolutionary grievances against social injustices. Its intention was both to prevent Korea from becoming a colony of slaves to foreign capitalistic expansion and reform the government by throwing off the yoke of a corrupt feudal order altogether. True, the rebels were unorganized farmers and failed for lack of good central leadership, but in any event, they have undoubtedly influenced the course of latter-day history. Internally, for example, the sharp challenge they posed stimulated a government awakening that immediately produced the *Kabo* Reforms; externally, they brought about the armed confrontation of China and Japan that led to immediate war.

Sino-Japanese War, Kabo Reforms

Cause of War

The reason for China's armed intervention to suppress the *Tonghak* movement is not far to seek. Peking wanted a new government that would follow an absolute pro-Chinese policy rather than the Min who were tending to ignore China for Russia. Their chance came with the government appeal for military help against the *Tonghak*. In the meantime, Japan, too had been waiting to recover the lost grounds of the military revolt and the reformist abortion. Japan was not asked but she sent troops on the basis of the Tientsin Treaty which, from Tokyo's viewpoint, justified intervention because China had intervened. China and Japan sharply clashed in Korea. At the core of the antagonism was the struggle for control of the Korean market. On the eve of the war, the two were nearly equal in developing their respective Korean markets but the Japanese determination to monopolize the peninsular trade was far stronger than China's. It was the Japanese determinant, then, that was the fundamental cause of the war.

Japanese Victory

The Chinese armed force was under the command of General Sha Chih-chao; it was delighted to oblige the government. The Japanese army was under the command of Otori Keisuke; it justified its arrival on the basis of the Tientsin Treaty and to protect the Japanese nationals in the country. The presence of these foreign troops badly undermined the position of the *Tonghak* rebels who were, to all practical purposes, now out of the picture. Once in the country, both foreign forces were hesitant to withdraw. But Japan was the more ambitious party. She wanted to drive out not only the Chinese force but also the Chinese influence which had brought that force in. First, the Japanese abducted Taewongun, now the Chinese favorite against the House of Min. Next, the Japanese Minister and pro-Japanese Koreans stormed the palace gates to overthrow the Min. Finally, a pro-Japanese reformist cabinet was formed.

Alarmed by these developments, China hurriedly prepared for war, sending an additional army of 4,000 strong at the request of the general, Nieh Sieh-cheng. The Chinese navy, carrying this reinforcement, landed the troops at the vicinity of Pungdo Island in the Gulf of Asan. Here the Chinese clashed with Japanese forces at dawn on July 25. On August 1, Japan formally declared war on China who accepted the challenge the same day. Japan wrangled a mutual defense pact from the new Korean government and then proceeded to trounce the opposing Chinese forces everywhere they met in Korea, at Asan, Songhwan, Pyongyang, etc. The Japanese also carried the war to China Proper, occupying the Chinese naval bases of Lushun and Weihaiwei and threatening to invade Peking itself. By February of the following year, the Chinese sued for peace and Li Hung-chang met Ito Hirobumi at Shimonoseki, Japan to conclude a peace treaty. Under the terms, China renounced Liaotung, Penghu and Formosa to Japan, promised to open Yangtze ports to Japanese traders, and recognized Korea to be an independent, sovereign state.

Japanese Control

The war proved Japan's military preparedness and driving territorial expansions. The demand that China recognize Korean independence was exacted to drive Chinese influence out of Korea and clear the field for a mainland base of Empire from which to conquer Manchuria.

As for Korea, the Conservative group was pushed out of power under Japanese pressure and the Japanese-backed reformists were firmly in the saddle with Taewongun as the figurehead and Kim Hongjip as Prime Minister. Taewongun was no reformist but he was, as ever, against the House of Min and so had joined the reformist forces to regain the political initiative they had taken from him. An Office of Military State Affairs was established with Otori, now Japanese Minister, as advisor to devise reform plans. Since everything had to be approved by Otori, actual control of the Government was in Japanese hands. The office drew up 208 plans for reforms in political, social, economic, and educational fields.

Nature of Reforms

The reorganized Government had two departments; Department of Royal Household and Department of State Affairs, the latter consisting of ministries for Home Affairs, Foreign Affairs, Finance, Military Affairs, Justice, Education, Industry, and Agriculture-Trade. The eight provinces were reorganized into thirteen. The new regime denied the ancient social classes, liberated slaves, prohibited early marriages, permitted widows to remarry and ended discrimination against the illegitimate born. It separated civil servants from the military caste and ended the practice of extending criminal punishment to kins. Taxes had to be paid in cash instead of in kind, a silver standard was adopted, a new measurement established, banks and business corporations organized. These changes are known as the *Kabo* Reform of 1894, after the sixty-year cycle of the Chinese calendar.

These sudden and radical reforms, however, were not welcomed by the people. Taewongun, especially, was strongly against them and resisted until he was forced out of power by the Japanese who charged him with plotting the *Tonghak* rebellion. The pro-Japanese Pak Yonghyo and Soh Kwangbom, exiled in Japan since the military revolt of 1882, were brought back to form a new cabinet. The *Kabo* Reform laid the foundation for modernization of the Korean social structure. It was not the work of Koreans but forced by the Japanese for the benefit of Japan. For that reason, it was not effective and were it so, it would have resulted only in unnatural efficiency. The fact that the drastic changes were all drummed through during the Sino-Japanese war is significant. Historically, it was the exigencies of the power struggle between neighbors that determined the birth of Korean modernity.

After the Sino-Japanese War
Russian Influence

Japan was not to enjoy the fruits of her victory over China unmolested from the Western Powers for long. The Powers most interested in curbing Japan's expansion into the Chinese continent were Russia, France and Germany, especially Russia whose paths of ambitions from the north were crossing Japan's from the south. Russia successfully pursuaded the two other Powers, interested in Far Eastern expansions, to join her in lodging a strong protest against Japan. They demanded that the Japanese cede Liaotung Peninsula back to the Chinese or else Japan would have to answer to Moscow,

Paris and Berlin. Unable to defy the triple Western threat at one time, Japan agreed to restore the territory in exchange for an indemnity. The Japanese did not forget this humiliation; it provided fuel for her nationalistic appeals to the Japanese public when she soon fought Russia, the masterminder of the maneuver.

In Korea, this sign of Japanese weakness before the West had the immediate effect of undermining the position of the pro-Japanese cabinet which found itself assailed for permitting gross Japanese interferences in the internal affairs of the kingdom. The return of the Russian Minister, Karl Waeber, for a second tour of duty, helped further to lessen Japanese influences. Waeber, as we have noted, enjoyed the confidence of the Yi court and he made full use of this trust to undermine the Japanese position. The result was a cleavage between a pro-Russian court and a pro-Japanese government. The latter plotted to depose Queen Min, the real master in the court, but the plot was uncovered and the strong queen, instead, had the Cabinet dissolved and the ringleader, Pak Yonghyo, exiled to Japan. In July 1895, a new pro-Russian Cabinet was formed.

This turn of events which decisively altered the balance of power within Korean political circles in Russia's favor enraged the Japanese. Japanese troops and *samurai* attacked the royal palace, murdered the queen, burned her body and buried it on a hill behind the palace. The Japanese then forced the king to dissolve the pro-Russian cabinet and organize a pro-Japanese one, the fourth cabinet change in two years. The new regime began to pursue the Kabo Reforms where they had been left off, reorganizing the military system, making smallpox vaccination compulsory, opening modern postal services, and prohibiting the top-knot. Again, the modernizations could not be carried out effectively because the Japanese were leaving a sour after-taste. People in the provinces rose in armed defiance of Japanese power in their anger against the brutal killing of their queen and the government had to dispatch the better part of its troops to suppress them.

Western Concessions

The significance of these anti-Japanese uprisings was not lost on the ever-resourceful Waeber. First, he arranged the arrival of one hundred Russian soldiers in Seoul ostensibly to protect the Russian Legation, then arranged to have the king take refuge in the Legation. These were astute moves which put the Japanese on the spot. The Japanese could not make any moves except through the king and they could not get to him without risking war with Russia. Korean opinion was impressed by this show of Russian strength and Japanese weakness that was certain so long as the king was under Russian protection and he was in the Legation one full year. Pro-Russian officials and anti-Japanese rebels made full use of this period. The rebels killed three of the pro-Japanese cabinet ministers, while the pro-Russians formed a new cabinet and other pro-Japanese fled to Japan. The new government abolished many of the radical laws introduced by their predecessors. Russia, of course, took full advantage of the considerable control she could exercise over the Korean government as the protector of the royal body. She acquired rights to lumbering along the southern bank of the Yalu as well as on the distant island of Ullung, to mine the mineral resources of Kyongwon and Chongsong regions, to supervise the military training of Korea's armed forces and handle the finances of the Korean government.

Other Powers, however, did not sit idle while everything was seemingly going Russia's way. They descended upon the government with demands for equal opportunities. Thus, the United States obtained rights to a railroad between Seoul and Inchon, mine gold resources at Wonsan, and establish a street-car line in Seoul; Japan to build a Seoul-Pusan railroad and mine gold resources at Chiksan, Britain to mine for Unsan gold,

Germany for Kumsong gold, and France for the Seoul-to-Sinuiju railway line. Between 1896 and 1900, then, Korea became a theater for expansionist powers competing for interests and concessions.

King Kojong returned to his palace in February 1897 with plans to make a completely new start for Korea as an independent, sovereign state. In August, he renamed the country Taehan and, on August 12, crowned himself Emperor. He proclaimed a new education law that established primary schools, high schools and normal schools and effected some changes in the administrative system that seemed to have no purpose other than to underline the fact that the name of the country was changed. Taehan, like Chosun, went back to the earliest of known names for the land and people, the three Han states of prehistoric Korea. In fact, however, Emperor and government were both controlled by Russia.

Independence Society

Meanwhile, many intellectuals were growing increasingly disturbed at the government's lack of independence and foreign exploitation of the nation's resources. This was especially true of those men who had studied in the United States and returned home with eager ideas about Jeffersonian democracy. Such U.S.-educated men as So Chaepil, Yun Tchiho, Yi Sangjae, Namgung Ok and Syngman Rhee, therefore, began movements aimed at the reassertion of Korean independence. Their instrument was the Independence Society, organized in 1896, and their symbol the Independence Gate, erected soon after over the site of a former reception gate for Chinese envoys, Yongun-mun. They also gave Korea her first modern newspaper, Independence News. Printed in both English and Korea, this tabloid-sized paper with So Chaepil as editor emphasized the spirit of freedom, civil rights, and national independence, on one hand; criticized the government, on the other, for selling out Korean interests with foreign concessions. If they favored any foreign power, it was probably China because China was the least ambitious in this matter of concessions which the others were so eager to wring from the Korean government. At any rate, Chinese were the only foreigners to attend the inauguration of the Independence Gate.

The government became alarmed by the popularity of this group of "hot-headed" radicals and organized a Hwangguk Society to counter the effects of the Independence Society. Whereupon, on October 30, the Independence Society called a public rally on Chongno square and adopted a sweeping resolution that demanded the government to 1) withdraw all foreign concessions, 2) give an account of public finances, 3) guarantee freedom of speech, 4) guarantee freedom of the press, and 5) hold public trials for criminals. This rally was broken up by the Hwangguk Society which mobilized thousands of merchants for the break-up. But the Independence Society continued to hold public rallies, promising to keep it up until their demands were met. The two Societies clashed twice more, on November 21 and 22. Finally, on November 26, the Emperor himself appeared before the palace gates to publicly promise that the demands of the Independence Society would be granted and the rallies were ended. The Society was forced to disband soon after but it had done its work as the first organization to speak the language of democracy before the general public. Many of its leaders became political exiles in the United States, notably So Chaepil and Syngman Rhee, with Japanese domination. So became a naturalized American citizen and practised medicine there under the Anglicized name of Philip Jaisohn. Rhee returned to Korea only after the Liberation and the end to Japanese colonization of his country.

Russo-Japanese War

Russo-Japanese Tensions

Russia secured a strong hold over Korea but Japan's ambitions over the peninsula were stronger than the Tsarist Empire's just as they had been when China's influence was paramount. Japan was a newly modernized country, seeking her place under the sun as a colonizing power in an age of Big Power colonizations. Unlike the other Big Powers, she was bending her imperialistic schemes on just one country, neighbor Korea, limited as she was by geopolitics and economic means. Korea was the narrow corridor to a bigger empire tomorrow. It meant that today she could pursue the imperialistic pattern undistracted unlike the case with most of the other Powers. Frustrated Japanese ambitions met Russia's imperialistic advantages in Korea and the friction was developed that led to war.

But Japan was not ready for war, not yet. Instead, she opened negotiations with Russia over the "Korean question." There were three meetings, once every year between 1896 and 1898, the upshot of which was that Russia agreed that neither would intervene in Korean domestic affairs and that Russia would not prevent Japanese commercial or industrial expansions in Korea. This, however, did not mean that Russian ambitions were lessened. Russia's field was wider but her imperialistic urges were no less. Already, she had acquired Lushun and Talien from China as her "reward" for making Japan restore Liaotung to the Chinese and she was busy turning these ports into bases for her outlet to the wide open seas of the Eastern Pacific. In 1899, she furthered her maritime schemes in Korea, on one hand, by obtaining rights to Ulsan and Changjin as whaling bases; on the other, to Masanpo and Mokpo as naval bases for an Oriental fleet. In turn, Japan acquired rights to Masan, Kunsan and Songjin as open ports and bought Masanpo off the Russians. Russia released Masanpo only to acquire Yulgumi south of Masanpo from the Korean government. Clearly, tension was mounting. So far, it was a two-power antagonism confined to Korea.

Now events were to broaden that raised other eyebrows.

At the turn of the century occurred the famous "Boxer Rebellion" in China which brought all the Big Powers down upon that country. Russia took this opportunity to send her armies into Manchuria on the pretext of protecting the Trans-Siberian Railroad. Once there, she did not move even when the "Boxer" trouble had been suppressed and there was no more reason for her to be there. To the contrary, she increased both army and naval power and set up a Government-General. All this caused concern to Great Britain which, as usual, opposed undue Russian expansions. Here was Japan's opportunity to strengthen her hand against Russia—by enlisting the sponsorship, if not the partnership, of Britain against the common dread. England, for her part, preferred to have the Big Power vacuum in Korea filled by Japan which was penetrating up the northern Far East rather than Russia which was expanding southward and out into the Pacific. The result was the Anglo-Japanese Alliance of 1902. The Russian reply was a French alliance the following year and the dispatching of troops to Yongampo at the mouth of the Yalu. In a strongly-worded protest, Japan called on Russia to withdraw her armies from Manchuria and recognize her paramount interest in Korea. Russia refused the first. Regards the second, she suggested a demarcation line at the 39th parallel to divide their respective spheres of interest, the northern zone for Russian expansion, the southern for Japanese. The Japanese refused and the boiling point was reached.

Russia's Defeat

In February 1904, Japan broke off diplomatic relations with Russia and then, without a formal declaration of war, the Japanese navy attacked Lushun and sank a Russian warship off Inchon. The Russo-Japanese war was on. The Korean government immediately declared itself neutral in this war of foreign nations but Japan ignored this nicety and landed her troops on Korean soil. She forced the Korean government to sign the Korean-Japanese Protocol that gave Japan the right to intervene in Korean political affairs, use Korean soil freely for her military purposes, and bar Korea from concluding treaties with any foreign power without Japan's consent. Next, there was a Korean-Japanese Pact, under which Japan sent Higada Tanetaro, chief of the taxation bureau of the Japanese Finance Ministry, and an American employee of the Japanese Finance Ministry, a certain Stevens, to Korea. Higada was named Treasury Advisor to the Korean government and Stevens Foreign Relations Advisor to the Korean court in moves to control Korea's financial and foreign affairs. In the meantime, too, Japan had acquired rights to railroad lines linking Seoul to Wonsan and to Sinuiju respectively. She also obtained some other interests. The more victorious her arms were against Russia, the tighter her screws on Korea.

From the Lushun defeat, the war went badly for Russia. The frontlines were far and a corrupted Tsardom had its hands full with political crises at home. In autumn 1905, therefore, Russia agreed to surrender through the good offices of U.S. President Theodore Roosevelt and a peace threaty was signed September 1905 at Portsmouth, N.H. Under this treaty, Russia recognized Japan's political, military and economic prerogatives in Korea, ceded the southern half of Sakhalin to Japan, and transferred her rights to Lushun and Talien to Japan. Both countries also agreed to withdraw their military forces from Manchuria and to respect one another's interests there. The Manchurian railroads were also divided into respective spheres of interest.

Thus the way was cleared for Japan to exercise a free hand on the Korean peninsula.

Japanese Moves and Korean Resistance

One-Power Control

If Korea had maintained a harried semblance of independence among the appetites of the Big Powers, she had a hard time merely keeping up even the pretence of one under the clutches of a single Power. With Britain and the United States by reasons of expediency, and Russia and China through military defeats, no longer disputing the peninsular kingdom's fate as a Japanese "sphere of influence," Korea did not have a chance in this world. Japan's ambitions were fully realized in the country and she meant to establish a firm foundation on this foothold of the Asian mainland for her imperialistic status of equality with the other major colonial Powers. The stage was set to drag Korea fully into the Tokyo orbit as a protectorate state.

Protectorate Treaty

During the war, the Japanese, as we have seen, pushed through a Korean-Japanese Pact that delivered Korea's financial and foreign affairs into Japanese hands. That was called the First Korean-Japanese Pact. Some members of the pro-Japanese cabinet were opposed to the proposed pact so it was necessary to impress the objectors. Armed Japanese troops surrounded the palace and lined the streets of Seoul, and Ito was accompanied by the Japanese army commander, General Hasegawa Yoshimichi, along with a bodyguard of gendarmes. The Emperor was indisposed and the cabinet members were interviewed individually by Ito with demands for a definite "yes" or "no" answer to the pact. Two members were resistant enough to give negative replies, the Prime Minister, Han Kyusol, and Finance Minister Min Yonggi. The rest were cowed by the military threat and meekly acquiesced. The premier, indignant at this majority concurrence, immediately went to see the Emperor and recommend his denial but enroute, it would appear, was taken by a stroke. At any rate, the Korean-Japanese talks went on without his presence and the pact was finally accepted with slight modifications.

De Facto End

The Second Korean-Japanese Pact stipulated that all Korean diplomatic relations would be handled through the Japanese Ministry of Foreign Affairs in Tokyo, that overseas Koreans and their interests would be protected by Japanese diplomatic and consular missions, that Japan would assume responsibility for carrying out all the provisions of treaties and agreements existing between Korea and foreign states at the date of signing of the treaty, that Korea would not enter into any agreement with foreign states without going through the Japanese Foreign Ministry, that Japan would install a Resident-General under the Korean Emperor to act as the supreme authority in Korean foreign affairs, that the Resident-General would have the right to confer with the Emperor at any time he chose, that the Commissioner of the Residence-General would exercise all the authority formerly invested in the Japanese consular offices of Korea as well as control all authority pertaining to enforcement of the provisions of this Protectorate Treaty, that all the provisions of treaties and agreements previously entered into between Korea and Japan would remain valid unless they were found to be contradictory to the provisions of the Protectorate Treaty, and that the Japanese government would guarantee the safety and dignity of the Korean imperial family.

With this treaty, the Taehan Empire had virtually ceased to exist. A new cabinet was formed with Pak Chesun, who had signed the Treaty for Korea, replacing Han Kyusol, who had boycotted, as Prime Minister. Most of the other Ministers were allowed to remain in their posts, including the Finance Minister who had also cast a negative vote with Han.

Resistances

The Residence-General was established the following year in accordance with the provisions of the Protectorate Treaty with the Japanese signer, Ito Hirobumi, as the first Resident-General. His office had the power to direct the Korean government according to Japan's policies not only in international relations as provided for but actually in every field of Korean governmental activities. Thus, it was not much different from its post-Annexation successor, the Government-General. As Korea's international relations were now entirely in Japan's keeping, all Korean overseas missions were closed as of March 1906, whereupon the Ministers of Britain, the U.S., China, Germany, France and Belgium also closed their Legations in Seoul and returned home. With this, the era of Japan's "Protectorate" rule opened.

The signing of the Protectorate Treaty was kept a secret from the Korean people who first learned about it when the patriot, Chang Chiyon, revealed the facts in his Hwangsong News. The news, as may be expected, came as a shock. All kinds of resistance cropped up in one sweeping pattern of a fierce nationwide resistance, involving the Korean people as one, from court officials to farmers. Many court officials, helpless before the *fait accompli* presented the Emperor, committed suicide before the palace gates, among them, Min Yonghwan, the Emperor's faithful aide-de-camp. In February 1907, Yi Kuntaek, one of the signers of the infamous treaty, was attacked by an unknown individual; in March the same year, Kwon Chunghyon, another signer, was shot and wounded; an enraged mob set fire to the new Prime Minister's home, and all stores in Seoul closed their doors in protest.

All these were sporadic outbursts which did not particularly worry the Japanese. Where the protests were registered by suicides, notably among the impotent but patriotic-minded nobles, the Japanese actually welcomed it for nothing could suit their purposes better than the self-destruction of patriotic convictions. But there was also armed defiance to be reckoned with, especially among the farmers who felt the hand of ruthless colonial exploitation on their lands. In 1906, a former government official, Min Chongsik, staged the first organized rebellion against the Japanese and their puppet cabinet. Styling himself "General Justice," Min recruited the nucleus of his volunteers in Chungchong Pukto province. The people responded enthusiastically to his call to arms and very soon he had a volunteer army of 500 men with 75 guns, assembled in the walled-city of Hongju in Chungchong Namdo. The revolt was speedily put down by two companies of Japanese infantrymen and one cavalry squad dispatched from Seoul. Other former prominent scholars or officials also led similar uprisings, Choe Ikhyon in Cholla Namdo, Chon U in Kyongsang Pukto, Yu Insok in Kangwondo, etc. There were other innumerable revolts on a minor scale, led by unknown leaders, throughout the country. It was, seemingly, an endless business of armed defiances and blood-letting.

Modern Movements

Parallel with these temperamental outbursts, there was a stream of intellectual movements, carried in the main by those who had had some contact with the currents of modern Western civilization and emphasized the spirit of freedom and democracy. They called for reassertion of the national dignity by driving out foreign influences, an end to feudalistic practices, and the establishment of a national, independent state based on democratic principles. A succession of social organizations followed: the Association for Constitutional Research which advocated civil rights expansion in May 1905, the Taehan Club later on in the year, the Association for the Strengthening of Taehan in April 1906 with such prominent patriots as Yun Tchiho, Chang Chiyon and Sim Uisong as the organizers, the *Kongjinhoe* or Association for Public Progress and the People's Representatives' Association in 1907, culminating in the formation of a political organization, the Taehan Society in November 1907. Founded by Chang Chiyon, this organization embraced a large membership that included all the modern-minded patriots of the day. The platform was as yet immature but it was a commendable political venture as an anti-Japanese movement of the Korean people.

These club-forming intellectuals devoted themselves in this dark period of Korean history to long-range tasks of instilling patriotic enlightenment in the hearts of the general public. They published books on Korean history and geography and offered a range of other selected materials well calculated to plant the seeds of enlightened patriotism, a biography of Admiral Yi Sunsin, the outstanding Korean hero of the Hideyoshi wars; a history of the French revolution, a history of Poland and causes for her decline, and so on. They also organized cultural movements, set up schools, and printed newspapers and magazines. Such papers as the Hwangsong Sinmun, Cheguk Sinmun, Maeil Sinbo, Mansebo, Kyonghyang Sinmun and many others were united as one in writing anti-Japanese editorials and columns and castigating the puppet Korean cabinet.

Foreign Sympathizers

Various educational institutes were formed and private schools appeared all over the country offering modern curricular courses. Such outstanding schools today as the Paejae, Kyongsin, Posong, Yangjong, Huimun, Chinmyong and Sungmyong in Seoul, Taesong in Pyongyang and Pochang in Kangwha were founded at this time. The Korean language was also being approached by modern research methods, the most distinguished scholar being Chu Sigyong whose Korean grammar became the cornerstone for future studies. Sin Chaeho and Chang Chiyon contributed many works on Korean history, and the novelist-playwright, Yi Injik, introduced colloquial Korean in his writings to introduce the style for modern literature. Since all these cultural modernization movements were directed at popular enlightenment, it was only natural that they should reflect anti-Japanese sentiments. The *Tonghak* school of learning, which had played such a prominent role as a popular "grassroots" movement, was split by a pro-Japanese wedge in 1906. Naturally, the *Chondogyo*, formed as the answer to the pro-Japanese betrayal, was more popular than the *Sichongyo*, the pro-Japanese counter-reply to the *Chondogyo* walk-out. In that same year, another religious body was formed, the *Taejonggyo*, a revival of mythical Tangun worship.

The world had turned a deaf ear to Korea's lonely plight but individual foreign nationals in the country heard her cries with the greatest of sympathy and vigorously championed her cause. One of the most effective of newspapers was run by a Britisher, Ernest T. Bethell. His Taehan Maeil Sinbo (Korean Dialy News) was published in both Korean and English as opposition to the Seoul Sinmun, published by a Japanese national, Kashiramoto Sadakazu, as the pro-Japanese daily in the country. The Taehan Maeil Sinbo emphasized the injustices that were being perpetrated on Korea. The American missionary, Homer B. Hulbert, was no less vigorous in attacking Japanese ambitions in his "Corea Review." The other American missionaries who had started to arrive in the crucial last years of the nineteenth century as Protestant pioneers, also lifted Korean hearts with their reminders of Korea's natural rights to freedom and liberty. The missionaries, like the modern Korean intellectuals, also had the long-range interests of the country at mind. Patiently and tirelessly, they established schools, hospitals and other welfare organizations to make a solid contribution to the development of modern Korea.

A Mission to the Hague

Meanwhile, the Japanese Residence-General was not satisfied with the way its puppet cabinet was functioning. In May 1907, they effected the resignation of Pak Chaeson as Premier and called on Yi Wanyong to form a new Cabinet. Yi Wanyong who, like the Vicar of Bray, had served loyally in both pro-Russian and pro-Japanese Cabinets, had been among the first supporters of the Protectorate Treaty and had thus remained in his office of Education Minister. Emperor Kojong was strongly opposed to Yi as Prime Minister but was forced to nominate him by the Resident-General. His Cabinet consisted of pro-Japanese ministers right down the line, Yim Sonjun (Internal Affairs), Ko Yongga (Finance), Yi Sungmu (Military Affairs) Yi Chongung (Justice), Yi Chaegon (Education) and Song Pyongjun (Agriculture and Industry). But the bullied Emperor, lonely at the center of his government, was not through yet. In June, the Second International Peace Conference was scheduled to be held at the Hague. Thither he sent three secret emissaries, Yi Chun, Yi Sangsol and Yi Wijong, to plead Korea's cause. The envoys presented the Emperor's credentials to the Conference and appealed to the world body for removal of Japanese oppression in the name of international peace and justice. The Conference, however, explained that the delegation was not qualified to attend the gathering in any official capacity inasmuch as Korea was a Japanese protectorate. Whereupon, the envoys paced the corridors to plead Korea's case in vain with individual national delegates and newsmen. One of the heartbroken delegates, Yi Chun, fell ill and died at the Hague (rumors have persisted that he committed suicide before the world delegates). Whatever the manner of his death, it provoked the Resident-General when he heard the news. That familiar tactic, a ring of Japanese troops around the palace, reappeared as Ito went to take the Emperor to task for sending a secret mission. The Emperor's initiative in "foreign relations" may have been thoroughly naive and impractical from the international point of view but not to the Japanese. On July 19, 1907, they forced his abdication and put his second son on the throne. This was Yunghui, the second Emperor of the Taehan Empire and the last monarch of the 500-year Yi dynasty.

Angered by this move, the Association for the Strengthening of Taehan, the *Ton-*

guhoi and the Y.M.C.A., jointly sponsored a public rally at the Chongno square one day before the formal announcement of the abdication. Some two thousand participants broke loose in a street demonstration. A pro-Japanese newspaper office was raided, Prime Minister Yi Wanyong's house set on fire, slogans shouted before the main entrance to the Emperor's palace, opposing the abdication. When the abdication was announced the following day, the demonstrators crashed the palace gates and tangled with the Japanese police in the streets. Soldiers broke out of a Seoul army barracks to join them and return the police fire.

Ito's answer, however, was another Korean-Japanese accord. On Jnly 24, five days after Kojong stepped down, the Japanese Resident-General handed a draft of this new agreement to Yi Wanyong who immediately called a cabinet meeting that promptly resolved to accept all the provisions therein without the slightest revision. The agreement was then approved by the new Emperor without much loss of time, Yi was appointed plenipotentiary, and the signatures effected at Ito's residence, all in a day's work.

Further Resistances

The seven articles of this agreement stipulated that 1) the Korean government would receive instructions from the Resident-General in matters pertaining to administrative reforms; 2) that legislation of all laws and administrative execution of important matters were subject to approval by the Resident-General; 3) that the judiciary would be divorced from all other operations of government administration; 4) that appointments of high-ranking Korean officials were subject to the consent of the Resident-General; 5) that the Korean government would employ Japanese nationals selected by the Resident-General for Korean offices; 6) that the Korean government would not invite foreign advisors without the consent of the Resident-General, and 7) that Article I of the Korean-Japanese Agreement of August 22, 1904 would be rescinded. On October 29, 1907, Ito and Yi Wanyong signed some papers reestablishing police administration and, from January 1909 onwards, Japanese nationals were appointed to vice-ministerial offices in the Korean government. Japan was virtually in complete control of Korea's foreign relations, internal affairs, military and police powers.

On August 1, 1907, the Korean armed forces were ordered to be dissolved. Instead, Pak Songhwan, commander of the First Battalion of the First Imperial Guard Regiment, shot himself. When the Korean troops stationed in the Seoul area heard this news, they took up arms against the Japanese army. Other military units throughout the country followed suit; the Wonju base on August 6, Kanghwa on August 9, Yangju in December, etc. Civilians joined their brothers-in-arms and overseas Koreans took up cries for Korean freedom. That American national, Stevens, whom the Japanese had appointed as foreign advisor to the Korean government, was slain by two Koreans, Chon Myongun and Chang Inhwan, in San Francisco for defending Japan's course in Korea. On October 26, 1909, Ito Hirobumi, who, in the meantime, had resigned as Resident-General, was also assassinated by the Korean patriot, An Chunggun, at the Harbin railroad station while on an official mission for his government. A youth, Yi Chaemyong, attacked Yi Wanyong but only succeeded in wounding him. These assasins were arrested and executed but, at least, Yi Wanyong had to resign from the premiership to recover from his wounds. Pak Chaesun resumed the post.

While the Korean people were bitterly and desperately fighting Japanese oppression as one, the pro-Japanese officials of the cabinet were as busy currying favors from their alien masters. The puppet leaders actually split into two factions. One was composed of the ousted Yi Wanyong and his followers. The other constituted a political organization called the *Iljinhoi* (Japan Friendship Society). Led by the ardent pro-Japanese official, Song Pyongjun, the *Iljinhoi* was such a hated target that the Japanese deemed it wise to seek elsewhere for Korean support. It was this policy which led to the appointment of Pak Chaesun, rather than Song Pyongjun, for the premiership.

But even the sensitivenesses of Japanese officials on-the-spot to Korean reactions were speedily found to be unworkable in the face of the policy directions from Tokyo. Down the years, the Japanese government was trying to work out the annexation of Korea. Their sole problem was to make the move look like an expression of popular Korean will. This was necessary in order to deceive the world whose good opinion Japan could not yet afford to flaunt.

It was, however clear that the only Korean instrument that could cooperate effectively was the *Iljinhoi*. Sone Arasuke, Ito's successor as Resident-General, was found incapable of pulling off such a delicate and, at the same time, blunt mission. In May of 1910, therefore, he was replaced by Terauchi Masataka whose express mission was the annexation.

Terauchi's first steps were to reinforce the Japanese military and police forces.

On July 29, 1910, he reinstalled Yi Wanyong as Prime Minister when that worthy gentleman had recovered from his wounds. In the meantime, Japanese gendarmes and policemen had been placed at strategic points all over the country. On August 22, the streets of Seoul were lined with Japanese sentries at intervals of every thirty yards. In this armed camp, the Treaty of Annexation was signed that brought the Yi dynasty to an end. Conclusion of the treaty was officially announced the following day. On that date—August 29, 1910—Korea became a Japanese colony and was to remain tightly so until Japanese imperialism had pushed through the narrow peninsula corridor, expanded over the vast Manchurian plains, down the vaster China mainland, hit Pearl Harbor, sprawled over the Pacific islands, and bowed to the atomic era on August 15, 1945.

The Annexation

The Annexation deprived Koreans of freedom not merely in the political field but in every aspect of Korean life. The currency was changed; the transportation and communication systems were controlled by the Japanese government; Korean farmlands became the possession of the Japanese Oriental Development Company. The land exploitation bears detailed mention because it was at the bottom a most complete deprivation of the resources of a nation, predominantly agricultural.

The Japanese government started out by conducting a survey of farmlands throughout the length and breadth of Korea. On the basis of this survey, a modern concept of land ownership was established. In fact, Korea's modern history evolved around this survey program. The most significant characteristic of the program was that the Japanese replaced the ancient system of land ownership with a new capitalistic concept but retained the ancient feudalistic system of land-tenantry. With the application of this new modern concept of ownership, farmlands, the ownerships of which were not clearly defined under the survey, were confiscated by the Japanese government. Thus, numerous farmers lost their lands. The Japanese were taking advantage of the ancient state system of land ownership and had deviced this cunning means to acquire Korean farms for nothing.

The modernization of Korea was not for Koreans but for Japanese and only the Japanese at the cost of Koreans, for all forms of modern institutional developments, political, economic and social, constituted the sum total of the tool that Japan used, backed by military power, to strip the uninformed people of Korea of everything they possessed.

The masses of the Korean people had been cruelly oppressed by their ancient feudalistic rulers but nothing to compare with the scale of this new and greater and incomparably more efficient exploitation by a foreign power.

Guerrilla Resistances

Despite the most complete subjugation, anti-Japanese resistances never ceased. Armed uprisings were most frequent in the provinces of Kyonggi-do, Kangwon-do, Hwanghae-do and the two Hamgyong-do. For example, in March 1910, armed rebels led by Yi Chinyong destroyed the Yongjong railroad and in April, about fifty people attacked the Japanese gendarmerie at the Kangwon county of Kumsong. Kang Tupil and Chae Ungon organized an anti-Japanese force and launched guerrilla warfare in Hamgyong Namdo province, Hwanghaedo and Kangwondo, while Yi Chinyong, Han Chongman and Kim Chongan organized other guerrilla units in Hwanghaedo and Kim Sangtae and Chong Kyongtae waged similar operations in Kyongsang Pukto. As Japanese pressures increased, these guerrillas moved to the mountainous regions of southeastern Manchuria where they established bases from which to attack Japanese military and police establishments across the border in their own country. Innumerable smaller-scale fightings went on all over the country.

In the meantime, the Japanese Residence-General had been replaced by a Goverment-General. The Governor-General was always appointed from among the general officers of the Japanese Imperial armed forces and was directly responsible to the Japanese Emperor. The Governor-General was vested with powers to control the administrative, legislative and military affairs of Korea. Terauchi was the first Governor-General of Korea. It was he who initiated the rule of the bayonet and sought to destroy every vestige of anti-Japanese resistance by outright military force. **The stern militaristic reign continued until March 1, 1919,** when the wilful Japanese **aggression** was countered by a spontaneous **nationwide** movement of the Korean people of which later.

The Modern Period (1910–1945)

Definitions

The period of Japanese colonial domination from August 29, 1910 to August 15, 1945 constitutes the nucleus of Korea's modern history. This period has been variously described as the "critical stage of the Korean people," the "period of Korean cultural erasures," the "Dark Age of Korea," etc. All such generalizations, put together, can hardly begin to convey a proper understanding of the period — to the Korean people themselves let alone foreigners. One point can certainly be made: its effects remain fifteen years after the Liberation suddenly ended it and are likely to linger on into the foreseeable future.

If we must have any single phrase to describe the period, the most suitable one is to call it the "period of resistance" on the part of one victimized state against the crime of another to the end of restoring the lost national heritage. It is difficult to convey to the foreign reader the extent of the ruthless pressures exerted upon both the economic and spiritual resources of the Korean people. The basic thing to understand is how the people struggled for sheer survival under the heels of Japanese despotism and came out from under, their national identity and culture preserved intact.

The Stage

In the latter decades of the nineteenth century, Japan had been steadily consolidating her ground for the invasion of Korea. In 1904, she finally succeeded in taking the first big step by manipulating the Korean government at will in the enforcement of the First Korean-Japanese Treaty. This resulted in what has been called the "Counsellors' Period." During this period, a group of Japanese officials and foreign personnel under the employ of the Japanese government worked for the Korea Residence-General in advisory capacities for the Korean Government.

Less than three years later, in 1907, the Japanese pushed through the Second Korean-Japanese Treaty. The years between 1907 and 1910 were the "Protectorate Period." As a result of Japanese "Protection," Emperor Kojong was dethroned and Japan tightened her grip on all the sovereign rights and economic interests of Korea to set the stage for the third and final period, the 35-year period of the Annexation.

In order to transform a traditional Korean industry so that it might serve as the basis for Japanese economic growth, Japanese capital pounced upon all native capital resources. Those segments of the industry that could contribute to Japanese economic growths were actively promoted by Japanese capitals; other areas that were not likely to serve this end were stifled. From the middle of the nineteenth century on, successive farmer resistances were overcome, armed forces disbanded, other foreign capitals challenged, wars undertaken. Finally, on August 29, 1910, Japan was able to force a powerless Korea to yield the ghost of national sovereignty.

Before the Annexation, Japan had manipulated her international diplomatic relations in such a manner as to secure the tacit approval of foreign Powers to this eventful step. Britain, allied with Japan, had already recognized Korea as Japan's sphere of influence upon the worldwide stage of imperialistic Powers. The United States followed Britain's lead. Thus William Woodville Rockhill, State Department advisor on Far Eastern Affairs, went on record to the effect that the Annexation would bring beneficial results to both the people of Korea and the cause of Far Eastern peace. U.S. Secretary of the Army William Howard Taft gave his government's official sanction to the Japanese move in an exchange memoranda with the Japanese Premier, Katsura Taro, in June 1905.

With the world's two greatest Powers behind her, Japan was able to carry out her long-dreamt policy of exploiting Korea without any foreign interferences. For their part, the Korean people, however hopeless the results, appealed to the world without, resisted within.

The Resistances

Hostility to Japan's policy on Korea was first roused in 1876 when the neighbor country forced an unequal treaty upon Korea. The hostile sentiments erupted into the armed resistance of 1895 when Japanese soldiers forced their way into the royal court and murdered Queen Min to eliminate the seat of anti-Japanese opposition. Scattered armed resistances continued through ensuing periods and after the Annexation. Thus, the commander-in-chief of the Japanese Imperial forces in Korea published a list of the numerous instances in which resistance had broken out throughout the country in less than a year's period following the Annexation. "In four towns of the Kyongsangdo provinces," the report said, "the people have revolted in the wake of the Annexation while, in Hwanghaedo, several armed units under the unified command of Yi Chinyong have exchanged fire with His Imperial Majesty's armed forces in the period November 1910 – March 1911." The relatively prolonged period of resistance in Hwanghaedo was possible because the farmers, the *yangban* and the Confucian institutes all rallied behind the armed fighters. Since 1907, former Korean military personnel had made this northern province the most active area of anti-Japanese resistance.

The resistance was also carried overseas by exiled patriots who established active anti-Japanese centers in Manchuria, Siberia, China, Hawaii and the U.S. mainland. The resistance fighters in Manchuria, who were closest to the motherland, crossed the Tumen river in frequent surprise sorties upon Japanese military and police establishments in their country from 1908 to 1911.

Suppressions

With the displacement of the Korean government by the Japanese Government-General in 1910, Japan stepped up its policy of erasing every vestige of nationalistic sentiments among the Korean people. The first to suffer were the nation's educational and press institutions.

The first restriction was imposed in 1907 when the Residence-General proclaimed a Security Act that promised to "restrict, prohibit or disperse assemblies and/or movements that are either undertaken over a period of days or mass undue crowds."The Newspaper Act that same year was issued to suppress the dissemination of free opinions. Imported foreign papers were stopped and privately-owned domestic papers incapacitated, if not by transferring ownership to Japanese hands, then by clamping suspensions. Publication of books by Koreans or other non-Japanese aliens was also curbed under the Publications Act of 1909 under which all publishers had to receive the prior permission of the Residence-General before publishing anything. The Act was applied repeatedly in order to ban or penalize the works of patriotic Koreans and sympathizing foreigners.

The control of Korean education was equally strict. Interference in this field began in 1895 when the Japanese undertook to reorganize the public school system along Japanese lines. Against this, Korean educationists established numerous private schools. Such schools threatened the foundations which the Japanese were attempting to lay in Korea, especially since too many books were likely to encourage "dangerous thoughts." The danger was removed with proclamation of the Korean Education Ordinance in August 1911. To carry out the educational purpose of training "loyal subjects" of the Japanese Emperor, as set forth in the Ordinance, strict controls were placed both on textbooks for private school use in the country and Korean students studying in Japan. The Educational Ordinance also required all schools to teach and use the Japanese language.

On the other hand, Confucian ideals and institutes, including the numerous village *Sowon*, were accorded unexpected protection and encouragement by the Japanese. Confucianism was supported because its feudal concepts of loyalty and patriotism were considered to be advantageous to the pursuit of the Japanese colonial policy of imperial obedience.

Land Exploitation

The frankest and, therefore, most outrageous area of economic exploitation came in land management. The initial step was taken in 1906 when the Japanese carried out a program of land rearrangements. From the following year, Japanese nationals were authorized to own farmlands in Korea. Subsequently, the Oriental Development Company, the Japanese version of the East India Company of Britain, was established, in 1908, with a ten-year plan of bringing all Korean lands under its control. By the Annexation, almost 76,935 *chongbo* of Korean farmlands were in the hands of a total 8,436 Japanese nationals.

To expand this real estate still further, a land survey program was carried out after the Annexation in order to determine modern land ownerships. All landowners were requested to register their ownerships with the Land Survey Bureau of the Government-General within a specified period of time; all owners, tenants and custodians of land were required to erect poles with designated markings at the four corners of their land, again within a certain specified time; all land disputes were to be settled either in court or under the judgment of the Land Survey Bureau.

This program, when carried out in force, was found to be most discriminating against the majority of the farmers who were generally unfamiliar with the newly-devised red tapes, and most advantageous to *yangban* nobles who conspired with the enforcement agents, the Japanese military police, to manipulate the lands into their own hands. When the survey was over and all disputes settled, more than 331,748 farmers found themselves working on somebody else's farms instead of tilling soil which they believed had been inherited from their ancestors generation after generation.

Land acquired by driving out Korean farmers was either turned over to Japanese peasant immigrants or the several Japanese companies in the country, Fuji, Kogyo, Katakura, Higashiyama, and Fujii, which hired cheap Korean tenant farmers. The giant Japanese interest, the Oriental Development Company, increased its real estate holdings to 104,000 *chongbo* by 1916.

The Samil Movement

The pent-up Korean resistance to unrelenting pressures of Japanese imperialism finally exploded in the tremendous outbreak of the nationwide movement known as the Samil Independence Movement after the date in which it broke out in the year 1919, March 1. It was a spontaneous force of passive resistance calling on Japan for a voluntary withdrawal from her imperialistic course in Korea and was countered by the most thorough means of suppression at the Governor-General's disposal.

March 1 was the day set for the funeral of the Emperor, Kojong. The last but one monarch of the Yi kingdom who had vainly tried to turn the tides against Korean independence to be ousted from the throne had been poisoned a few days before by the Japanese. In Europe, on the other hand, the First World War had just ended and U.S. President Woodrow Wilson had enunciated his principle of the "self-determination of weak nations" at the Paris Peace Conference. As soon as news of the President's principle reached the ears of Korean students studying in Tokyo, they published a statement demanding Korea's independence from Japan. This was in February 1919.

In Korea itself, secret plans were drafted and detailed instructions sent out to all the towns and villages via the swift underground grapevine to seize upon the inspired moment. The stir created by preparations for the forthcoming state funeral service of the late Emperor provided the screen that caught the Japanese fully unaware of the word that passed from mouth to mouth in all the market-places. At the core of the movement was a group of 33 patriots, composed of 16 Christians, 15 *Chondongyo* believers and 2 Buddhists, — and financial expenses were borne by *Chondogyo*. On the fateful day, the 33 men gathered before a crowd at the Pagoda Park in downtown Seoul and read Korea's "Declaration of Independence."

This document refrained from looking back upon the past but called on Japan to look forward to the long-distant future when her course of imperialistic aggression would inevitably lead, beyond Korean enmity, to the enmity of China. It emphasized that it was not too late for the Japanese to alter this course of incurring Asian enmities and embark, instead, on her true mission as the outstanding modern example for Asia. It saw the prospects of Korean independence in a new era of peace and prosperity ushered throughout the world from the devastations of World War I.

This eloquent Declaration moved the crowds which went out into the streets from the park to stage a demonstration for national independence. The ancient system of message-relays by beacon-fires from the peaks of Korea's innumerable hills and mountains carried the event throughout the country with the result that the remotest villages joined in the spontaneous movement within one or two days. The exiled patriots of Manchuria, Siberia, Shanghai and the United States acted in concert with all-out appeals to the governments of their host countries to help Korea in her efforts to recover her lost sovereignty.

Brute Repressions

The Japanese police, caught totally unawares by this unexpected movement, was at first too stunned to do anything. Once they had recovered their senses, however, they moved swiftly and mercilessly to crack down upon the demonstrators with loaded guns and fixed bayonets. The scale of these Japanese suppressions of a passive resistance have been described by an exiled patriot, Kim Pyongjo, in a book, entitled "A Brief History of the Korean Independence Movement" which was published 1921 in Shanghai. According to Kim's book, a total of 1,363,878 individuals participated in the demonstrations. Of these, more than 6,670 were killed, 14,611 wounded and 52,770 arrested by the police.

The efficient manner in which the Japanese police and gendarmes "quelled the riots" in the interests of "preserving peace and public order" was well demonstrated in the atrocities that swept the County of Suwon, some twenty-five miles south of Seoul, for three days beginning March 15. On that day, a Japanese gendarme unit carried a *"banzai"* charge with resounding success into a group of villagers assembled to read the Declaration of Independence. The following night, the villagers retaliated with a "Mansei" charge to set fire to a Japanese gendarme station.

On March 17, the gendarmes drove 30 hand-picked villagers into a church building, locked the gates from without, set the building on fire and mowed down the screaming men, women and children who tried to escape from the burning church with a volley of fire. This was done in open daylight before the full view of the village population and some foreign observers on the scene. Similar "police actions" spread to 15 neighboring villages, the gendarmes burning, ravaging and murdering at will. The news of these terrible atrocities was spread by foreign eye-witness accounts to the world not to speak of the nearby capital. Several Seoul schoolgirls hastened to the scene of the tragedy in order to render whatever aid and comfort they could to the wounded but they had no sooner reached the town of Suwon when the Japanese gendarmes plunged bayonets into their ranks, killing several on-the-spot.

This ended the independence movement, leaving deep scars both upon the Korean people and their Japanese masters. It also brought Korea's plight to world attention for the first time to any appreciable degree, manifesting to anybody who would hear the determined will of an entire people to win national independence.

Farmers' Plight

The lot of the Korean peasantry deteriorated rapidly after the Annexation Act. In 1916, a total of 530,195 farm households were tilling their own lands; ten years later, the number was 525,747, an expropriation of some five thousand families.

On the other hand, the number of tenant households was increased from 971,208 to 1,287,098 during the same period. These parallel decreases in the number of the farmers tilling their own land and increases in the numbers of those hiring out their services reflect the acute nature of land deterioration. A total 278,339 expropriated farmers migrated to Manchuria in the 15-year period between 1910 and 1925; another 126,000 drifted to Japan in search of manual employment as unskilled laborers, in the period between 1915 and 1925.

The successful manner in which the Japanese carried out their land policy measures combined with the inability of the Korean farmers to adapt themselves to modern agricultural methods to undermine their economic status. After the land survey, the Governor-General placed all commercial transactions in agricultural products under tight control through Financial Associations set up throughout the land. The Financial Associations, acting as agents of the Governor-General, loaned funds to land-owning farmers against their real estate and drew most of the debts thus incurred from mortgages. Deliberately high taxes and ridiculously low prices for their hand-made products squeezed Korean farmers both ways and forced many to abandon farms they had inherited from their ancestors.

Despite the sad reality of the Korean farmers' plight, the annual budget figures published by the Government-General pictured the overall Korean economy as having achieved remarkable progress since the Annexation. The total revenue of the Korean government amounted to 52,284,000 won in 1911 from 7,987,000 in the pre-Annexation year of 1906, while expenditures were increased from 7,567,000 to 46,172,000 during the same period. Such enormously increased expenditures, needless to say, fell upon the shoulders of the Korean people.

The annual expenditures kept skyrocketing—from 52,285,000 won in 1911 to 62,722,000 in 1915 and still up to 125,803,000 won in 1919. To meet the accelerating increases, tax rates were raised and new kinds of taxes added, driving the already hardpressed farmers into abject poverty. This was so because the burden of such taxes had to be shouldered by the tenant farmers, most of whom were working for the Oriental Development Company and other Japanese landlords.

As a result of these depressive conditions, the peasant class which made up 73.6 percent of the total population were producing only 46.4 percent of the gross national production in 1938. Every year, thirty to fifty percent starved. Under the circumstances, educational or cultural developments were out of the question. The literacy rate was so low that a "utopian" village, specifically designated by the Governor-General, had only 14 individuals who could read or write. Of the 14, 13 had but attended elementary school; only one went beyond the primary level.

Japanese Capital

After acquiring nearly half of the total land acreage, Japanese capital began to promote the increased production of rice for export to Japan. The main feature of the policy to supplement the food shortage in Japan was a plan prepared by the Government-General in 1920. For many years, the Government-General failed to implement the plan successfully without creating a drastic shortage in Korea itself. Only after the Manchurian invasion was it executed in full force.

Production of Rice and Volume of Export
1912–1940

unit in 1,000 *sok*

Year	Annual Production quantity	%	Annual Exports to Japan quantity	%
1912–1916 average	12.303	100	1.056	100
1922–1926 average	14.501	118	4.342	411
1927–1931 average	15.798	128	6.607	626
1938	26.796	218	10.702	11.32
1940	24.138	196	6.051	573

The table shows the rate of export increases for outstripping the gradual rate of increased production since 1927. The gap, created by this trend at the expense of the Korean belly, was filled by importing coarse grains from Manchuria. Superior Korean rice had to be shared between the Japanese and Korean populations; inferior Manchurian grains were shared between Korea and Manchuria.

The rich mineral resources of Korea were another object of exploitation. Enormous quantities of gold, graphite, tungsten, iron, copper, anthracite coal and other valuable minerals were mined at increasingly rapid rates by Japanese capital utilizing cheap labor forces that were abundantly available under the land expropriations. So many farmers had been driven out of farms to the underground pits that the total number of miners was increased from 37,893 in 1930 to 500,000 in 1942.

While Korea shipped practically all minerals and a substantial quantity of rice to Japan, Japanese industrial finished goods were, in turn, brought to Korea. The Korean markets for Japanese merchandises were so successfully expanded that Japanese exports jumped from 25,348,000 yen in 1910 to 315,325,000 yen in 1929, and 1,229,417,000 yen in 1939. Korea accounted for about one-third of the total volume of Japanese industrial goods exports.

Japanese capital investments, meanwhile, amounted to 1,627 million yen in 1930. Against such an enormous layout, native capital remained at less than 0.5 percent the Japanese level. With war in Asia, the Japanese investments were stepped up still more rapidly since 1930.

Thus practically all fields of Korean industry were placed under the control of Japanese capital. According to estimates, nearly 1.5 billion yen were squeezed out of the land in profits.

War on Culture

From the very day of the Annexation, Japan carried out a policy intended both to isolate Korea from the rest of the world and to stifle every nationalistic sentiment among the Korean people. The more advances in exploitative policies, the stiffer the Korean resistance and the more rapid the pace of efforts to exterminate both national and cultural heritages. The results were tighter grips on the press and what the Japanese themselves called modern education. The people of Korea learned practically nothing of outside developments.

During the late nineteenth century, considerable efforts had been made to streamline Korean education to adapt it to the new civilization of the West. The early schools taught courses in Korean language, Korean history, Korean geography, foreign languages and sciences considered essential for modern life. From 1884 on, the Protestant missions were building a number of schools to bring modern education in line with their missionary work. The foreign missionaries were not merely transmitting the Gospels but enlightening the Korean people to modern conditions.

In contrast with Korean nationalist and foreign missionary efforts to meet the needs of modern society, Japanese education, more and more predominant since 1910, was bent on complete subjugation of the Korean people to the dictates of their Japanese masters. This necessitated the cleansing out of every nationalist thought from the head of the Korean student. The modern aspects of education Japan provided were geared to the harness-wheels of a mythical belief in the origins and foundations of an alien race.

Japanese Research

The Japanese zeal to rule the Korean people as effectively as possible inspired them to undertake research work on Korean history and archaeology. Considerable findings were made in the form of reports on ancient relics and the extensive collections and systematizations of old literature resulted in a 37-volume bibliography on Korean history. The Japanese historians treated Korean history as part of the Japanese and presented it in such a way as to impress the reader with Korean backwardnesses which only Japan could correct.

To equip themselves with basic knowledge of the Korean people, the industrious Japanese also undertook to study the traditional manners and customs of the people they had conquered. The various reports thus produced covered wide fields, the relationship between tenant and landlord, origins of native worship and religions, modes of living, socio-economic conditions, etc. Much of the better researches were carried out by commissioned faculty members of the Keijo Imperial University (present Seoul National University). The extensive studies they made of Korean social, economic and legal institutions were undoubtedly scientific in method and, seemingly, in the interests of pure academic research. It is important to remember, however, that these "academicians" were, at all times, wolves in sheep's clothing. Western methods were copied and experimented in every conceivable way by these scientists to enable their commissioning rulers to dominate the Korean colony more effectively. The Governor-General himself thought so highly of European colonial practices that every time he was about to effect a new measure, he sought the advice of a German advisor to the South Manchurian Railway Co., Ltd. in Tokyo. Every aspect of Japan's cultural policy in Korea, then, had its precedent in advanced European countries.

Much of the cultural legacy the Japanese left behind are still being utilized uncritically because they are the only bases on which modern precedents have been applied. The most critical evaluations must still be brought to these legacies that were primarily motivated to prove an "inevitable" relationship between a subjugated Korean people and a ruling Japanese race which, in turn, was the deliberate bias of the imperialistic policy applied for thirty-five full years of the twentieth century.

Korean Literature

Korean intellectuals were not merely handicapped in every way by the one-way stream of modern sciences; they suffered deep spiritual torments because these sciences rested on a distorted basis. Their approach, necessarily, was to put all the emphasis on correcting this distortion. This could mean only one thing, national independence, and to emphasize that was to run up against the currents of the imperialistic policy, backed readily by armed might. Nevertheless, they resisted and the result was the nationwide Samil movement which forced even the Governor-General to adopt what they called a "cultural policy." Two Korean language dailies, the Tonga Ilbo and Chosun Ilbo, were permitted to be operated by Koreans, albeit under the sharp eyes of Japanese censors who read every word between the lines. A considerable number of other papers and magazines also came off the Korean presses, likewise subject to censorship scrutinies.

Quite apart from the obstacle of the censor, most of the Korean publications could make no headway whatsoever for lack of sufficient capitals and paid subcriptions. The overall economic poverty of the nation compelled their disappearance from newsstands and bookstores after a half-hearted issue or two.

The abject poverty, on the other hand, produced a proletarian literature which proved to be popular. Such literature grew as one of the major means of resistance and, at the same time, endeavored to elevate itself to world standards. A proper appraisal of proletarian literature, however, must await the completion of a history of contemporary Korean literature, a task yet to be accomplished.

The most definite success, however, was to be found in the movement to preserve and systematize the Korean language. Korean literature throughout history had been expressed through the medium of Chinese characters at the expense of the native tongue. The efforts of linguistic scholars to provide the Korean people with their own Hangul script on sound, rational principles was a positive contribution on both cultural and spiritual levels. The core of the movement was the Korean Linguistics Society; its key members were Yi Yunjae, Choe Hyonbae, Kim Yungyong, Chang Chiyong and Chong Insong.

Resistances of '29

The year, 1929, was one of the most memorable of the Japanese period for the people found a set of new and better means than ever to counter the effects of Japanese imperialism.

In that year, factory workers in the city of Wonsan staged a general strike. The strike was significantly different from similar troubles elsewhere in the world because it was prompted solely as an expression of national resistance rather than on any labor demands for higher wages. It was a strike against Japanese capital as such. The labor cause was carried from factory to factory and then to the farms in 1930 when the tenant-farmers of Hamgyong Pukto province rose against their Japanese landlords.

In that same year occurred what is known as the "Students' Incident" in the city of Kwangju, one that was to leave a lasting mark on the history of Korean resistances. According to a report appearing in the Tonga Ilbo in its November 6 issue of the year:".........on (November) 3, about 300 Korean students of the Kwangju high school and a similar number of Japanese students of the Japanese high school in that city clashed in a fierce encounter near the railroad station with both sides suffering numerous casualties. After the fight, the Korean students, each armed with a stick carried on the shoulder like a rifle, marched around the streets in a demonstration. The city police and the police department of Cholla Namdo province immediately alerted the entire police force to guard against possible future developments........."

The developments were not long in coming. Wave after wave of student bodies staged "sympathy strikes" for their Kwangju colleagues throughout the country. The jails swelled with teen-agers. The reports show a total 78 cases in 1929, 107 in 1930, and 103 in 1931. Altogether, 54,000 students took part in the strikes of 1929-30. The verdicts were 583 expulsions from school and 2,330 suspensions for indefinite periods of time. Those expelled received various kinds of harsh sentences from "courts of justice" that twisted the provisions of the criminal code to meet an emergency unprovided for by the Government-General.

The laborers and students of '29 kindled an ever brighter reminder of the unquenchable spirit of national resistance.

Closing Years

The tightest and the most drawn-out period of Japanese domination was yet to come. This began when Japan embarked upon war in Manchuria in 1931 and the effects of that spreading war were intensified upon Korea in the rapid changes that were to suck the country more and more into the war effort.

The change was officially heralded when the "movement of self-rehabilitation," advocated by the peacetime Governor-General, Ugaki Kazushige, was replaced by "a policy of assimilation" which was seriously intended to assimilate the Korean people to the Japanese under the "benevolent fold of Tenno (the Japanese Emperor)." The policy was effected as soon as Ugaki's wartime successor, Minami Jiro, took over.

The totalitarian measures necessitated by the application of this unassimilable policy were enforced all the more recklessly when Japan invaded North China. By that time, the powerful financial combines, commonly referred to as the *zaibatsu,* had won complete monopolistic control of Korean industries. Such powerful concerns as the Mitsui, Mitsubishi, Sumitomo, Noguchi and other lesser Japanese enterprises were all in Korea, controlling every phase of the Korean industry.

As the China war progressed, the Governor-General's policy of exterminating Korean nationalism took on ominous tones. Korean language newspapers and magazines were condemned to extinction, the Korean language barred from schools and discouraged at home, Korean names Japanized. The Korean Linguistics Society ceased to exist after the police rounded up its staff members down to clerks. The key members of the Socetiy received prison terms and most of them were to remain incarcerated until the Liberation. Two outstanding linguists, Yi Yunjae and Han Ching, died in their prison cells.

Overseas, meanwhile, the more the Japanese involved themselves in a world war, the more overjoyed the Korean exiles. In the United States, men like Syngman Rhee and Chong Hangyong lost no opportunity to press Korea's case before any Allied representative who would hear them. In Manchuria and on theina ЧƆ mainland, porary Commission's presence in the northern zone.

In December 1948, the U.N. General Assembly recognized the Republic of Korea government as "the only legal government in Korea." Subsequently, on June 30, 1949, the U.S. armed forces withdrew from south Korea, leaving behind a 500-man Korean Military Advisory Group attached to the Korean army and navy. A mutual defense treaty was signed between the Republic of Korea and the U.S. in January 1950. On June 25, 1950, the Communist forces launched their surprise attack on the south.

War and Truce

The Korean War was far more tragic than any war between two nations because it was fought by two politically split camps of one and the same people. A powerful Communist army broke the 38th parallel in the early hours of Sunday, June 25, 1950 to send chancelleries throughout the world reverberating with fears of war. The capital city of Seoul fell on June 28, and the Communist forces marched on swiftly to occupy more than half of the territory south of the 38th parallel line. They were brought short by the Naktong defense perimeter and the amphibious landing of the U. N. forces on Inchon, the gateway to Seoul, on September 15, 1950, turned the tides, that restored Seoul on September 28. The back of the enemy's will was broken and the ROK and U. N. forces pursued him across the 38th parallel deep into the north, as far as the borders of the Yalu. Here, Communist China came to the aid of its northern ally by pouring in a large army that returned the tides and send the U.N. and south Korean forces back as far south as Wonju. Once again, the Allies pushed north and recrossed the 38th parallel when Malik made his approach for truce talks.

The U.N. General Assembly, adopted a resolution to set up the Korean Armistice Commission on December 14, 1950, and armistice negotiations began at Panmunjom in November 1951. While the prolonged negotiations went on, fierce battles continued to be raged, and, on the eve of a settlement, on June 28, 1952, the ROK government released anti-Communist prisoners-of-war in defiance of the armistice negotiators. Finally, on July 27, 1952, an "uneasy" truce was signed between the U.N. and Communist forces, establishing a military demarcation line with slight modifications from the prewar 38th parallel in accordance with the fortunes of war.

In the seven ensuing years, there have been numerous but fruitless conferences between the armistice commissions of both sides in vain attempts to bring about a settlement of the Korean issue.

Trend of Politics

As soon as the Japanese surrender was announced, a Preparatory Commission for the Foundation of the State (of Korea) was organized on August 17, 1945. The Commission proclaimed the establishment of a Korean People's Republic. The U.S. Military Government which arrived subsequently, however, disbanded this early "People's Republic." Many political parties now sprang up one after another, including the Korean Communist Party, Korean Democratic Party, and the Nationalist Party.

The two foremost exiles, Syngman Rhee and Kim Koo, returned home to form powerful political forces although neither belonged to any political party.

The cleft between Nationalist and Communist elements widened and became clear-cut when the news about the proposed trusteeship of Korea reached the country, the Nationalists violently opposing and the Communists supporting it whole-heartedly.

Repeated attempts were made by the more moderate of Korea's politicians, right or left, to effect national unity by negotiations. All failed. With the establishment of the Republic of Korea government in 1948, a new phase was brought into Korean politics and accentuated by the war.

In 1951, President Rhee organized the Liberal Party. On the other hand, the Korean Democratic Party, reorganized in 1949 as the Democratic Nationalist Party, renamed itself the Democratic Party to emerge as the most powerful opposition party in 1955. As the two parties engaged each other in a bitter power struggle, other lesser parties gradually disappeared, leaving two powerful parties to dominate the scene as the basis for party politics.

Land Reform

A land reform program was effected in June 1949 to redistribute farmlands covering 470,022 *chongbo* or 22.7 percent of the total arable lands among 1,546,379 farmers.

However, the failure to realize increased productivity as well as the devastations wrought by the war have driven the farmers to extreme economic plight. As a result, absentee landlords began to amass farmlands again, while the number of tenants and small-scale farmers have increased at alarming rates. The deterioration of the agricultural economy was reflected on the gross national production: the farmers' share in this fell from 47.8 percent in 1952 to 46.9 percent in 1953 and still further down to 42.2 percent in 1954. The government announced a few years ago that debts incurred by some 2,230,000 poverty-stricken farmers amounted to 20 billion hwan.

Nevertheless, agricultural production has increased year after year since 1945, and the present annual output of grains stands at 16.6 million *sok*. Several measures to improve the agricultural economy have also been taken, including the establishment of an Agricultural Bank and Agricultural Cooperative Associations in 1957. Five-year plans for increased production have been carried out twice since 1945.

Extremely important as it is to overcome the "agricultural crisis," the division of the land, economically as well as politically, renders the task doubly difficult.

Industries

Electric power has posed the basic problem for industries since 1948 when the north Korean regime cut off the power supply which the north, as the area of abundant power resources, has always provided the south. Ever since, prior emphasis has been placed on development of electric power. Presently 190,000 KW's are generated, a figure still far short of the needs.

The production of anthracite coal, on the other hand, has increased to 3,850,000 tons a year, furnishing power to more than 13,000 industrial plants throughout the country. Other mineral products are mostly exported, accounting for about 40 percent of the country's total exports. This is inevitable under the present conditions of industries, underdeveloped after years of an imperialistic policy deliberately designed to keep them subjugated to the Japanese industry. Along other lines, too, industries rely entirely on imports of raw materials. Fishery, also a one-time Japanese monopoly, still remains a primitive occupation in most fishing areas. Annual production, however, has increased to 400,000 tons, and presently earns 20 million dollars through exports. Fishery, however, has yet to await the growth of the shipbuilding industry; the poverty of the little fisherman is another difficult problem.

It is foreign economic assistance which has supported Korean industries throughout the post-Liberation era; even at this moment of writing, aid programs are responsible for the construction of modern facilities that produce such essential goods as cement, fertilizer, plate-glasses and textile goods.

Foreign Aid

Foreign economic assistance amounted to more than 1,400 million dollars from 1945 to the prewar months of 1950. The war devastated the country's economy to such an extent that the initial efforts of E.C.A. and other foreign aid programs had to be started

II HISTORY

all over again after the armistice.

The United Nations Korean Reconstrustion Agency was established in October 1950 to furnish aids amounting to 431.6 million dollars up to 1951. In that year, the International Cooperation Administration (I.C.A.) joined UNKRA to promote rehabilitation programs. As a result, the combined assistance of the two organizations amounted to 154 million dollars in 1954; 236.7 million dollars in 1955; 326.7 million dollars in 1956; 382.9 million dollars in 1957; and 321.3 million dollars in 1958.

The enormous amount in economic aid, especially from the U.S. which has borne most of the expenses, is not likely to continue. The aid is expected to be curtailed from 1959 following the recently announced changes in U.S. policy on foreign aid programs. An early establishment of a self-sufficient economy is, therefore, the most urgent problem facing the country.

Basic Problem

History has taught the people of Korea the bitter lesson that the fate of Korea has been sealed all too often by foreign powers in complete disregard of Korean wishes. The same fate may be awaiting them in the future. Standing at a crossroads of the two Big Powers, we must yet reach the conclusion that it is entirely up to us to decide our destiny.

Recent history teaches us that reliance upon foreign powers for a solution of our own problems invites one tragedy after another. When Japan was invading Korea during the late nineteenth century, our desperate pleas to foreign powers fell on deaf ears. So did the nationwide independence movement of March 1919 carried out in response to U.S. President Wilson's "principle of self-determination by weaker nations."

How to unify the land which has been divided so long under two entirely opposed forces is the decisive issue to be resolved by the people of Korea today and in the foreseeable future.

III PEOPLE, LANGUAGE

People

Introduction

Geographically speaking, the Korean race is considered to be a branch of the Tungus in Manchuria; more specifically, a sub-brachycephalic type of the Mongoloid races. It was the result of waves upon waves of migrations settling down upon the Korean peninsula and forming the first community lives at a neolithic stage of culture at least four thousand years ago. This makes Koreans one of the oldest civilized races in the world. As a people bound by a tight common fate within the confines of a narrow peninsula of a vast Asian mainland, Koreans have developed into a very homogeneous race with distinctive traits of their own. Anthropological studies on Korea in any language are still at a very premature stage and, apart from obscure journals, may be considered non-existent for English readers. As such, any study of the Korean race at the present level of scholarship, especially a scholarship accessible to the Korean, must be sharply limited. For the most part, it can only be dealt as an independent subject.

As an independent subject of cognition, the Korean race is discussed in this chapter from the constitutional, cultural and various other traits of Korean life as are more obviously determinable. The inter-related characteristics between these constitutional and cultural aspects are best studied by whatever observations we are in a position to make about the anthropological and ethnological backgrounds of the race. The formation, derivation and constitution of the race, distribution and density of population, stone age culture and cultural traditions can be dealt with quite satisfactorily in technical fashion as natural science and cultural history. The sub-cultures that are peculiar to any race, language, folklore, customs and so forth, are more difficult to be linked with the sweeping generalizations inevitable in this attempt to describe a "history of the Korean people" from scanty source materials.

The most convenient way to present the overall characteristics of the Korean race, I believe then, are to treat the technical and generalizing aspects of available scholarship as though they were two independent subjects for study. Only then can any basis be laid for inter-relating them for the future scholar who is armed with better source information. The two aspects, therefore, shall be discussed alternatively in the next few pages.

Distribution and Density of Population

According to the census data, the population of Korea was approximately twenty-five million as of October 1, 1940. Considering the natural increase, it is today estimated at more than thirty million. The average density is 100 persons per square kilometer. As for the distribution, about 80 percent are to be found on the farms, indicating a concentration in low altitude areas where tillable lands are to be found as against the infertile regions of high altitude. This puts the majority of the people in western areas where cultivable land is found rather than in the eastern which is made up of high

relatively high. The natural increase in population has been estimated at 30,000-40,000 a year. Structurally, the size of the juvenile population was found to be relatively bigger, indicating the potentiality of yet furthur increases.

These figures, it must be remembered, are based on the afore-mentioned census data for October 1, 1940. Wars, liberations and separations since then have shifted distributions and accelerated the increase.

According to the statistics compiled for the year, 1958, by the Office of Court Admin-

Province	Area in square kilometers	Population	Density per sq. km.
Hamgyong Pukto	20,347	1,124,000	55
Hamgyong Namdo	31,978	2,014,000	63
Pyongan Pukto	28,445	1,881,000	66
Pyongan Namdo	14,944	1,827,000	122
Hwanghae-do	16,733	2,013,000	120
Special City of Seoul	134	901,000	6,724
Kyonggi-do	12,687	2,189,000	173
Kangwon-do	26,263	1,857,000	71
Chungchong Pukto	7,146	980,000	132
Chungchong Namdo	8,106	1,673,000	206
Cholla Pukto	8,554	1,673,000	195
Cholla Namdo	12,025	2,545,000	215
Cheju-do (Island)	1,862	213,000	114
Kyongsang Pukto	18,950	2,604,000	137
Kyongsang Namdo	12,305	2,416,000	196

mountain ridges running down the backbone of the peninsula. Drawing a straight line between Uiju in the northernmost province of Pyongan Pukto to Yongil Bay off the east coast in Kyongsang Pukto (the eastern front of the Allied-held Naktong River perimeter during the crucial war phase of the Communist bid for unification), the greater density to the west makes Korean land there the most populated area in the world with an average 150-200 persons per square kilometer.

As seen from the table on this page, the northern regions are less densely populated than the central or southern parts of the country, mainly due to the fact that the area there is more mountainous with a colder climate, making for less farmlands.

Regards the rate of population increase, the infant mortality and birth rates are both

istration as reported in the Korea Times, an average five babies were born every three minutes against one death in that same period of time for a natural increase rate of slightly over three percent, thus making Korea, the southern part at least, one of the most population explosive forces in the world.

Physical Characteristics of the Korean Race

Regards morphology, I shall attempt to deal only with the property of outward features, such as height, the cephalic index, face, skin, hair and eyes that are more readily observable to the naked eye. By no means should the following be considered satisfactory in the absence of research work to any sufficient degree.

The height of the average Korean male is

1.61 to 1.69 meters, a better-than-average for the world male population. The cephalix index is 83.6 to 85. Faces are a little longish and somewhat egg-shaped although they often tend to be flat and square. Many Western observers have described Koreans as a handsome people. The skin is generally yellowish-brown or pale yellow but there are also many Koreans with a yellowish-white skin. The color of the hair is usually black or brownish-black save for a minority who have reddish-brown hair. The texture of the hair is slick and straight with faint curls for the majority; a minority grow rather curly hair. The tips of the Korean eyes point slightly upward; in other words, we possess the oblique characteristic common to all the Mongoloid peoples. The iris is usually dark and the size comparatively small. The Korean has a narrow-hawked nose with the tip usually pointing down slightly. The root is rather narrow while the nostrils are neither flat nor bulging; the bridge is rather long, the holes horizontally elliptical. In short, the Korean nose is medium. So too is the thickness of the Korean lips.

We shall skip over the ears, hands, feet and other limbs to consider the Korean constitution. When we consider this subject in terms of the stout or lean types, we find the average Korean to be intermediate with statures that are both slim and well-balanced enough to be called graceful.

The Korean woman bears almost identical physical traits as her male counterpart. The height is a little shorter and the breasts usually hemispheric. She is on the average slightly taller in the north than in the south, a fact which has given rise to an old proverb to the effect that the south is the home of stout men and the north of beautiful women.

Further Pursuit of Korean Origins

Anthropologists regard the Korean people as descended from the Mongolian race and linguists as a member of the Ural-Altaic family of the Mongoloid. It is generally believed by scholars, foreign or Korean, that they can be pinned down yet more specifically to the Tungusic branch on the Altaic side of the Turanian, another name for the Ural-Altaic. The Tungus were a people who thrived in the northern areas of Manchuria and adjacent Siberian and other regions. The Tungusic descent from a Mongolian origin is a matter of scholarly certainty. Where then did the Mongolians, the first ancestors of the Korean race in all probability, themselves originate? This is an outstanding problem for controversy among all international scholars who lack indisputable proofs to sustain any one theory. Here, I shall skip over the two major theories existing about the Mongoloid race to determine anthropoid derivations: Direct Ancestry and Collateral Relations. Lengthy arguments exist over these theories which I am in no position to weigh.

Most scholars, however, are agreed that *homo pekiniensis*, more commonly known as the Peking-man, was the first probable ancestor of the Mongoloid. The Chinese anthropologist, Pei Wen-chung, is of the opinion that this "Missing Link" between man and ape lived all over the northeastern areas of Asia about a million years ago. Whether this ape-man is the true ancestor of the Mongol, Siberian and Chinese races, which this theory supports, remains to be proved by further archaeological studies.

From the fact that crude tombs of stone called Dolmens and remains of houses dug partly underground are to be found scattered about the Korean peninsula, it is certain that man was living here during the neolithic age. There are other remains that might have belonged to yet an earlier type of man but speculations about these are uncertain.

From Korea, let us turn to the northern parts of Manchuria and Siberia where several hundreds of thousands of Tungus are still living. Some scholars consider these living folks, the most probably nearest ancestor to the Korean, to be descended from the Tungi races. Physical comparisons between these Tungus and Koreans show that both have about the same height, the same color of skin, eyes and hair, and a skull shape which experts call the Korean--Manchurian type. The word, Tungus, comes from the Chinese word, Tunghou or Tungi, meaning Eastern Barbarian, and derived its Western version in the seventeenth century when the Russians first introduced it to Europe. Before the Chin dynasty of China, the Tungus people lived in Hopeh, Liaoning and Jehol Provinces. The Wuhuan and Hsienpei of the Han dynasty are branches of the Tungusic family, as are the Kitais of the Tang dynasty and the Joujans of the Wei, this last an ancient tribe destroyed by Turks. The Tungus, then, have had a long and varied fortune over wide areas of Northeast Asia but for a long time, Manchuria was their homeland and, after the establishment of the Ching dynasty, they became virtually assimilated into the ancient Chinese race. The Tungusic history was a civilized one and many tribes of this family created dynasties, Pewei, Liao, Pohai, Chin and Ching dynasty and, of course, the Korean kingdom if we can establish the Tungusic kinship as a certainty on the ground of a widely accepted assumption.

Taking this relationship for granted, we may believe that thousands of years of intermingling over the length and breadth of Northeast Asia resulted finally in the formation of two different races, the Chinese and the Korean. In other words, a common Tungusic ancestor was assimilated partly into the Chinese, others developed into Koreans, and a residue has survived to this day. The common ancestry of the Chinese and the Korean, provided by this picture, was, however, a very old story. Subsequently, the Chinese became potent forces in Korean life but despite the persistent threat of assimilation into the Han fold, the people of Korea, bound by the geopolitical logics of the peninsula, managed to preserve their distinctive racial and cultural traditions through four thousand years to grow into the thirty million population of today. For all that, the Korean race underwent the greatest transformation in its physical and cultural attributes over a history of many centuries.

Formation of the Korean Race

According to legend, Hwanung, son of God, wanted to live on earth and breathed his will into the union of a tiger and a bear from which the man, Tangun, was conceived. This Tangun was acknowledged as the leader of nine clans and led them forward to the unification of three thousand tribes to form the first primitive Korean community. The Tangun tale, of course, cannot be confirmed but archaeological studies based on neolithic remains show that the Korean race was, indeed, formed out of such a beginning, shorn off the miraculous concept. In other words, there were three thousand tribes and a tribal leader of nine clans who united them. Farther than that, it is impossible to gauge for palaeolithic discoveries in the country are still far from sufficient. On the basis of outside discoveries, however, international scholars are able to trace many evidences of the Korean origin to the Tungusic branch of the Mongoloid races.

Tangun, or whatever the actual name of the Korean tribal leader, established the capital of his united state at a place called Chonpyong at the foot of Paektusan or White Head Mountains on the Yalu border. With expansion of his state, the capital was moved south to Pyongyang and elsewhere. This made Tangun the ruler of a united land from the Amur River in the north to the Chungchon region in the central part of Korea. This is known as the *Paedal* Age, or the Age of Discovery, so called because the tribes called themselves men of *Paedal*. According to tradition, the Tangun era lasted 1,200 years followed by the Kija Age of about 900 years, bringing us down almost to the time of Christ. With Kija, a Chinese refugee, began the introduction of Chinese civilization.

Old Chosun, as prehistoric Korea was called, later split into various communities. To the south were the three Han States, to the north was Puyo from which tribal chiefs moved to the northeastern part of the country to rule Ye. The first historical kingdoms, Silla and Koguryo, were founded in the land of Cholbon Puyo while Paekche was founded in the area known as South Puyo. Koguryo's territory was the largest. It included Liao or what is now known as Manchuria, and various tribes, the Suksin, the Okcho and the Euplu, were naturalized as Koguryo citizens. Paekche controlled the area from the River Taedong in the north to River Imjin in the southwest and east of the Naktong River basin. All three historical kingdoms were founded as a result of tribal confederations, Silla in 57 B.C., Koguryo in 37 B.C. and Paekche in 18 B.C. First one, then the other, swayed, but eventually, in A.D. 735, both Koguryo and Paekche fell before Silla and all the different tribes in all parts of the peninsula began to form one unit of the Korean race.

Archaeological findings show that neolithic Koreans of the different tribes led a simple life with hand-made tools. With increases in population came the development of clan communities leading finally to territorial states and the limitation of free accessibility to resources provided by nature for the hunting. In the north, the communities of Puyo, Koguryo, Okcho, Euplu and Yemaek grew stronger and at last formed clan tribal states. In the south, the three Han communities consolidated their various neighbors into a single similar state under Mahan. Eventually, Koguryo proved to be the strongest primitive power in the north and used her power to unify the various northern communities into a kingdom. In the south, the kingdoms of Paekche and Silla emerged from the various tribal states there and absorbed them all under their respective folds. Thus the historical period, beginning with the establishment of these three kingdoms, began in Korea just before the time of Christ. Koreans then were in the Metal Age, making tools out of iron and bronze and improving upon the efficiency of their daily work.

The kingdom of Koguryo was founded by an alliance of five tribal states at a time when they were being invaded by Chinese and barbarians, Paekche was formed from an alliance of nine clan tribes and Silla as a result of a resolution made at a conference of six tribal chiefs. Thus, the Three Kingdoms embarked on history with absolute patrimonial rulers in the beginning. Gradually, they were to develop into autocratic states.

Koguryo founded its power mainly in the upstream regions of the Yalu River where the Cholbon Puyo tribe had originally settled. From there, it gradually expanded into the Manchurian plains. Since its territory was mostly mountainous, the livelihood of the people of Koguryo was made up of hunting. Therefore, it was natural that they should be militant. It was a militant people, then, who came to dominate large areas of Liaotung or Manchuria by conquering one tribe after another, North Okcho, Euplu, etc. They also carried on frequent border wars with the Chinese. To gain the edge in these wars over the powerful Han race of the Central Kingdom, they quickly brought all smaller tribes on the borders under their wings, built ten fortresses in Liaohsi and two more in Hsuantu and Liaotung. The occupation of 67 villages making up the Euplu tribe cemented Koguryo as a strong militant kingdom.

Paekche was a kingdom founded by the descendents of the Cholbon Puyo who had moved down the peninsula south of the River Han. They united with the Paekche tribe that dwelt near the mouth of this central river and destroyed Lolang, the powerful Chinese colony. This brought Koguryo and Paekche, hitherto separated by the Chinese power, to conflict and there were constant wars between them. The third kingdom, Silla, took advantage of these struggles for power between the only two powerful neighbors in the country to conquer minor tribes around and develop itself. Paekche, as we can see, was quite a strong state at the beginning of the historical period. It even had garrisons east of the Luan Ho and west of the Liao Ho in China. It was Silla, however, which grew the most steadily and, by a play of power politics, first allying itself with Koguryo against Paekche, then with Paekche against Koguryo, and finally, by an alliance with the Tang kingdom of China, succeeded in destroying its two rivals on the Korean peninsula.

With Korean unity under Silla, the menace of Japanese pirates in the south was lifted, cultural exchanges opened with China, and the racial solidarity of the Korean people consummated. Unlike the cases with the European, Negro or Indian races, the solidarity of the Korean race was from the first a homogeneous one. With this racial solidarity came the gradual development of an autocratic society. The military first came to power during the subsequent Koryo era which had to fight many border wars. Internally, the Koryo kingdom laid the seeds of anti-alienism, slavery and corruption in Korean life. With the military fighting for government power, there was little time to heed the interests of the country with the result that Kitai, Niuchen and Mongol invaded from the north. In the meantime, land reforms led to the establishment of firm control by noble over farmer.

Finally, as Koryo culture had been highly developed and military power strongly established, many foreigners, such as the Pohai nobility, the fifteen clan tribes of the East Niuchen, the tribesmen of the West Niuchen, and others, submitted to Koryo rule and became naturalized Koreans. These, together with naturalizations of the Chin, royal marriages with the Mongols, and Japanese invasions, all led to cross-breedings in the Korean blood.

In the succeeding dynasty, the Yi kings generally followed the systems established by Koryo, the main departures being the adoption of a new military system after the Chinese pattern and the replacement of Confucianism with Buddhism as the state religion. The Yi kingdom sustained severe shocks from foreign invasions, first from the Japanese in 1592-1598, then from the Manchus in 1636-1637. Toward the end of the dynastic era in the nineteenth century, France, Russia, Britain, Germany, the United States and Japan all advanced on Korea to force the opening of a "Hermit Kingdom" to the world. With the turn of the century, Korea was thrown into the turmoil of cataclysmic changes, political, economic, cultural, religious, social, ideological. Korean traditions, not only those general to the Oriental world but also the peculiar native features, confronted world cultures and civilizations.

With the high tides in international imperialistic drives and expansionistic urges, Korea became the first victim of Japan and suffered Japanese domination for almost half a century as the foothold to her attempted conquest of Asia. Thus, Korean adjustment to the modern scheme of the world was retarded at a very crucial period of international currents and the peninsula emerged into the liberated era in 1945 as much in the turmoil of the changes in all walks of modern life encountered by the 19th century Yi kingdom.

Through all these insuperable difficulties, the people of Korea retained their traditional family system, fine arts, language, culture and customs, thanks to their invariable homogeneity.

Original Natives on the Korean Peninsula

No extensive scientific studies have been made regards the original natives of the Korean peninsula. In the Unggi region in Hamgyong Pukto, archaeological remains of the Stone Age, however, were found that indicate the existence of some original Koreans before the Puyo tribes of the Tungusic family migrated into the country. Researches likewise have yet to be made to construct the constitutional characteristics of the original inhabitants, but the distribution of the locations where neolithic remains have been uncovered in Unggi and elsewhere and the types of implements used are enough to show that they came from the northwest, gradually to move down southward. Ancient records also state that some strange remains of primitive folks peculiar to the tropical south were found along the southern coasts of Korea, suggesting the existence of some other original inhabitants in that part of the country. Western scholars have, in this connection, speculated on Dravidian origins from a southern Korean life that led to the establishment of Silla.

There are other theories, too. One study reveals the geographical distribution of the Ottenberg, Indo-Manchurian and Korean-Manchurian types in the western and northern sectors of Korea, Manchuria and North China. Many Westerners have remarked on certain Occidental features in the overall Oriental appearance of the Korean people and find in this evidence of a Proto-Caucasian origin besides the Mongoloid. Another theory refers to the close communications the southern part of the land had with the people on the mainland of Asia, especially the Han race, to explain the Oriental features as a result of a gradual intermixture of Chinese and Korean blood in that part of the land. Generally speaking, it might be said that the Chinese skin appears more readily in the south and the harder Mongoloid skin in the north. Koreans are taller than the Japanese and more robust than the Chinese and may be said to come between the two, combining the best or the worst traits of the two major Oriental races on either side. There is reason to believe that primitive Koreans were taller and more robust than their civilized descendents of today.

In any case, the distribution of the dolmens and the farming techniques, such as the raising of livestock, rice and other crops, in the ages before the period of the shell-mounds of Kimhae, as determined from the ancient records, provide abundant materials for further scientific studies before the presentation of any definite conclusion about the constitutional make-up of Korean forefathers. Suffice to limit ourselves to the most typical of all theories, viz. that some derivation of the Tungus moved gradually from the cold northern regions of Central Asia into Korea and settled down before the Puyo moved in. This theory is supported by the linguistic studies that have been made on the Korean language.

It has been estimated that such migrations took place no less than 5,000 years ago and no more than 10,000, the general time dimensions for the appearance of the neolithic culture upon the world stage. From the primitive stone tools uncovered, it is assumed that the Old Stone men in Korea lived in simple mud huts, used fire, clad themselves in animal hides and the barks of trees, ate meat, fish, wild grass, fruit and potatoes. Excavations further reveal that they had earthenware baked by solar heat and that there was a religious life made up of worshipping stone-axes, stone-knives, stone chopsticks and other stone necessities.

We have already noted the names of these various tribe, Puyo, Koguryo, Okcho, Euplu, Ye, Maek in the north, the Han (Mahan, Chinhan and Pyonhan) in the south. We have also noted the naturalizations of some other foreign tribes, the Yen, Chin, and Uiman among others. By the time the peninsula was united under Silla, all these tribesmen were intermixed and led a settled life to form a distinctive race.

Primitive Culture of Ancient Koreans

Enough about the Stone Age culture can be described from the excavation of numerous articles of archaeological, ethnical and other scientific import. For a brief round-up:

The stone-axes found in the Tumen basin and the northern province of Hamgyong Pukto bordering on that river are T-shaped, counterpoised or shaped like clamshells. Burstone was used mainly besides volcanic glass, augite, andesite, ophite, granite, and firestone soap stone. Whatever the stone, it was first beaten to the pertinent shape; the blade was then sharpened by polishing. In other parts of the country, flat chisel-shaped axes were excavated in the vicinity of Kyongju, the Taedong River basin, the Yangyang region in Kangwon-do, the county of Anak in Hwanghae-do, the vicinity of Puyo in Chungchong

Namdo and near Miryang in Kyongsang Namdo. These were made by polishing the stone with a hole drilled to contain a wooden handle. Those found in the vicinity of Kyongju were made of limestone and argillite while the others were of granite and sandstone. The decorative designs which appear on these early implements vary according to the use to which they were put—for industrial or war purposes. The shell-mounds of Kimhae also revealed wooden sticks used to build fire by friction, indicating that wooden tools were also used at that time, including bowls for rice. In the Kyongju area, too, there were limestone and argillite in burial mounds, sandstone for industrial tools and war weapons, wood rounded for bowls and planked for housing constructions, both stone and metals for hunting and fishing equipment.

Among all these implements were such things as chisels, knives, hammers, spears and many other familiar objects for use in farming and cooking. They all indicate an extensive development and improvement in the lives of Korean neolithic ancestors.

The geographical distribution of the sites of excavations reveals a cross-peninsular pattern in tool-making, from the shell-mounds of Unggi in the north, Sosura, Songjin, Tongganjin, Pyongsongmyon, Hoeryong, to Yonchonmyon in Kyonggi-do, and farther down to Kyongsang Namdo in the south. Bow-and-arrow was used to hunt wild boars, deer, wild oxen, horses, rabbits, wolves, tigers and other beasts then stalking the land. Horns were used to serve as daily utensils, hides for clothing and meat for food. They also ate fish, including shell varieties. Rough mats were made out of weeds for fishing-nets while the shells, after the contents were eaten, became spoons and kitchen knives. The earthenwares betray characteristics that suggest the influence of the polished stone tool culture of northern China. Among these were spinning wheels which appear in the Kimhae shell-mounds. The spinning wheels found elsewhere along with other evidences show that weaving and mat-making were known all over the country.

Agricultural Life of Primitive Koreans

Although the exact year is not known, it is at least certain that primitive Koreans knew about upland and paddy-rice farming before the erection of the Kimhae shell-mounds. Rice and other crops are believed to have been introduced via China. On the other hand, it might have been brought into Korea directly from India by sea. Ancient records as well as legends reveal that there were seafarers from Southeast Asia who had been shipwrecked and washed ashore on the Island of Cheju. In the Pali dialect of India, chicken is called *kukkuta;* the standard Korean noun for the creature is *tak* but it is familiarly called *kuku.* Such possible etymology suggests some ancient form of communication between the Korean peninsula in the Northeastern area of the Pacific and lands in the Southeastern. The chicken itself might then have been introduced from its habitat of Southeast Asia.

The Kimhae shell-mounds (very important as the reader may have guessed from our constant reference) revealed that rice was eaten at the time, that food was cooked, and sericulture known. The last is often mentioned in the historical records of the Three Kingdoms. Rice-farming seems to have been encouraged by the ancient rulers as a state policy; such, at least, was recorded as a case for the year, A.D. 30, in the Chapter on Paekche of Volume XXIII of "The History of the Three Kingdoms." By that time, agricultural techniques had advanced considerably not only in the south but in the northern areas where hunting went on after the development of southern agriculture. The people of Koguryo, Eastern Okcho and Euplu tamed cows and horses in order to till the land. Since the north was not much suitable for paddy-farming and the uplands were not so fertile, they depended partially on dryfield farming and livestock raising. In the south, on the other hand, the people were more settled to a farming life as revealed by

Kimhae and other ancient records. Farming techniques, therefore, were the most developed there and, with the growth of agricultural production, came expansion of economic power. History reveals that Paekche had a system of taxation, thus suggesting an advance of the ancient Korean economy from the primitive stage. This tax was paid in kind: grains, silks, threads, etc.

In Silla, the land tax was paid in rice and the household tax in thread. In Koguryo, it was levied on a per capita basis and paid in cloth and grains while the nomadic segments of the population were taxed only once every three years. In order to increase revenue sources, the ancient rulers all encouraged agriculture so that it became extensively developed and advanced. By the period of Unified Silla, a centralized autocratic system resulted in state ownership of land to deny the right of nobility to private landholdings. With the Koryo dynasty, however, King Songjong completed a program of land reformation between the years 982 and 997 that established a new taxation law and cut grain taxes by one-half. Subsequent Koryo monarchs thereby renewed encouragement of farming and attempted to get those, still leading a more or less nomadic life, to settle down to the plough. In harvest seasons, a special decree was issued to stop the use of manpower for purposes other than tillage. Weapons were then converted into farming tools. In case of poor harvest as a result of some natural calamity, taxes were waived or reduced, depending on the extent of the damage. In each country, warehouses were built to store grains for use in case of such disasters.

Toward the end of the dynastic era, especially following the reign of King Kongmin (1352-1374), the economic system of the kingdom was greatly hampered by the wars against foreign invasions. With corruption in official life, the land system crumbled.

State-owned land was restored by the succeeding Yi dynasty but, as with Koryo, the Yi reform also succumbed due to the overgrowth of feudal power that subjugated tenants to agricultural slavery, thus to decrease the efficiency of agricultural production and lead to the economic degeneration of the state. A small number of the nobility became huge landlords while the rural population in the southern part of the country was practically reduced to tenantcy.

An estimated 80-90 percent of farmers in the central parts belonged to that status, over 70 percent in Hwanghae-do, 60-70 percent in Pyongan-do, and more than 60 percent in Hamgyong-do, to the north. The tenant-slave population was exploited not only by their powerful landlords but also by the agents of the latter who collected the rentals. This exploitation continued with increased severity up to the modern era when the lands were turned over to Japanese colonial exploitation at the turn of the current century.

Thus, through a good part of the Yi dynasty and throughout the Japanese era, the Korean farmer was largely a tenant subjected to increased exploitation up to the date of Liberation on August 15, 1945. With the establishment of the Republic of Korea government in 1948, a land reform program was carried out along modern lines. Farm credits, commercial fertilizers and improved implements have been made available to Korean farmers since then. The modern development of the Korean rural economy is, therefore, a matter of a decade against a background of centuries' old exploitation.

Traditions of Korean Culture

Throughout her unspeakable difficulties, Korea has maintained the core of its culture and tradition as tested and refined against the background of a four thousand year history. In many respects, the civilization of Korea surpassed that of China. Although the cultures of the Han (Chinese) and Japanese races reached higher standards in the overall course of history, the stages of development in the peninsula's neighboring countries have been shortlived and limited. Certainly, it has

A Typical Korean House. →

Bleaching Cotton Cloth
  Korean housewives always
↓ refine clothes for themselves

          Seesaw   →
  It is also for grown-up women.

← A Folk Dance
  Girls in boys'
  garbs.

↑ A Ferry Boat.

↑ Jars for Food Storage
Every home prepares such various earthenware jars for storing food such as soy-bean-sauce, doenjang (soy-bean-paste), kochujang (pepper-sause) and kimchi.

↑ Hair-do Style
A traditional hair-do style of the Korean woman.

← Old Folks
They never change old-time clothing and accessories such as white clothes, black hat, and long smoking pipes.

Korean Housewives
Sewing and washing are two major chores of the Korean women.

A Modernized Drawing Room
In cities and towns, houses tend to follow the western style.

A Traditional Korean Concert

← Children sunning themselves.

A Woman Divers of Cheju
↓ Island

← A paintress practicing oriental painting

↓ Before Her House

↓ Grapes and a Girl

↑ A-Frame
An A-styled wooden frame that can mount unbelievably heavy and bulky objects. It is called "Chige" in Korean.

↑ A Thatch-Roofed House
Most of farm houses in Korea are roofed with rice straw

Carrying Water →
In Cheju Island, women carry potable water on their back from a distant well to their homes

Sleds and Boys
Sled is almost the only winter sport for most of poor Korean youngsters who can't afford to enjoy skating or
↓ skiing.

↓ Mother and Daughter.

← Owls

→ A white crane with a red crest and black neck and tail.

↓ A short-eared owl

← A hawk

↓ A pheasant

→ A kite

↓ Goat and kid

↑ Chickens

↓ A sow and her litter

↑ Mother dog and her puppies

↓ Cows in a ranch

↑ A wild boar

↓ A deer

← A wild cat

↓ A badger

↓ A bear

↑ A Rose

↑ Lotus-flowers

→
Korean National Flower
(Roses of Sharon)

↓ Magnolia

↓ Tree peony

↑ **A Tree of Mandarin Orange**
  Grows only on Cheju Island southern-most point of Korea

↑ **Pine Mushrooms**
  Since they are one of precious cooking materials, they are artificially cultivated now.

Cultivating Hops
  Hops, used for giving a bitter flavor to beer, also are cultivated in Korea. ↓

↑ **Korancho** Named after Koransa Temple in Puyo, Chungchong Namdo, where it grows naturally on the faces of rocks.

↓ **Tropical Plants** Some tropical plants grow on Cheju Island.

↑ Chestnut tree and the burs

↑ Persimmons

↑ Sunflowers

↑ Scrubbing-brush gourd

↑ Hangul (Korean Alphabet)
This is one of the primitive styles of Yi dynasty, when it was used mostly by women to write letters as shown in this picture.

Chungyong Onhae
An interpretation of Chungyong, one of Chinese classics, in hangul
↓

↑ The preface of the Hunmin Chongum.
A prospectus explaining the hangul when it was first promulgated by King Sejong, in 1446.

Korean Text-Book for Middle Schools
Written horizontally instead of vertically as formerly.
↓

↑ Hangul Typewriter
Based on the American typewriters, it was designed by Dr. Kong Pyongu. There are serveral kinds of typewriters for the hangul alphabet today.

not been as lasting or consistent as the over-all Korean culture.

This consistency has created cultural traits in the Korean people that are not to be found either on the mainland or the island country. They are to be found in the fine arts, the political systems, the economic systems, customs and mores of the peninsula. Repeatedly, foreign powers have attempted to dominate Korea but none ever succeeded in destroying the age-old tradition. This fact was all the more accentuated by the Japanese experience of the twentieth century which saw the foreign conqueror attempt the erasure of the Korean national identity.

In short, the people of Korea still live amidst surroundings of shell-mounds, dolmens and stone tools as old as Cheops. They live with things that were the property of their neolithic ancestors, earthenwares, woodenwares, ceramic, sculptural and architectural styles, all peculiarly Korean. They speak the same language throughout the peninsula, the dialects posing no non-understandable barriers as in China and Japan. They wear the same costumes, eat the same kind of food, live in the same kind of houses, and retain the same constitutional characteristics. Such homogeneity is perhaps unequalled in any other nation of the world.

It is still difficult to give any adequate description of Korean traditional features in words, although some may be visually obvious. To tell a long story short and describe a complex matter in simple terms, we take the example of Korean villages.

Throughout the peninsula, the village community consists of 30 to 40 thatched roofs amidst a peaceful setting. The villagers invariably worship the spirits and keep the burial mounds of their ancestors; they are clad in white clothing of the traditional style and designs; the men work in the fields while the women are entrusted with the responsibilities of house-keeping and educating the children at home. The cooperative labor system for rice-transplantation, weeding, and harvesting; the use of oxen for ploughing and transportation purposes, the farmer's bands and traditional forms of dancing; witch-doctor practices and Shamanistic forms of worship, all these and much more are characteristic scenes of the Korean tradition still extant everywhere in the Korean countryside.

Korea has long been known as the "Eastern Land of Civility" (*Tongbang Yejiguk*). In fact, Buddhism was more developed in Korea than in its home country of India; so was Confucianism than in its home country of China. The developments of these outstanding religious or philosophical ways of life contributed to the fostering of the native sense of activity, in turn, enhancing both 'isms. Other examples of Korean ingenuity are the Koryo celadons, architecture, sculptural works and the publication of the Buddhist sutra. Unlike Sung ceramics, Korean ceramics have delicate lines and subtle colors that evoke warm feelings in the observer. During the period of the Three Kingdoms, Chinese culture began to be introduced into Korea to undergo further refinement and adaptations to Korean life, in turn, to be transmitted to Japan where it became known as the culture of the Asuka period. Chinese culture and civilization were steeped in the age-long traditions of Korea without ever affecting anything vital or basic to the Korean individual. The Korean scholar may have swallowed Chu Hsi's teachings but he never wore the Chinese pigtail; the Korean woman may have bound herself to Confucius' place for her but she never bound her feet. The Japanese applied all sorts of pressure which the Korean people as one met with spontaneous resistances, open or under-currented, bore up with humor and endlessly baffled the rulers with an unyielding nationalistic strength that emerged with ever more dynamic force after the Liberation.

Most of all, any careful study of Korean qualities will show that, as a people, Koreans have always acted in the strict name of justice, professing it, adhering to it and appealing to it even in the face of foreign aggression.

Language

Introduction

The Korean language is the common medium of the inhabitants of the Korean peninsula who number an estimated thirty million. The language is also used by the substantial Korean communities that are to be found in Manchuria and Japan. Inasmuch as Korea has never dominated other lands, the Korean language is strictly the mother tongue of the people born to the Korean national identity. True, the ancient kingdom of Koguryo embraced large areas of Manchuria with the northern part of Korea and when the southern kingdom of Silla pushed north to unite the peninsula under a single Korean domain, powerful remnants of fallen Koguryo fled across the Yalu to establish the Pohai state among the foreign tribes of the Manchurian plains. Koguryo may have been a Korean state with its capital in Pyongyang but as a kingdom striding the Yalu, its people probably had affinities with the Manchurian tribes that were as close or even closer than those they enjoyed with the Koreans of the Han or Naktong River basins of the south, and their language was probably Tungusic rather than Korean.

Far from dominating others, Korea has throughout her long history been subjected to the influence and conquests of powerful foreign countries. Chinese, Mongols, Niuchens, Japanese, Manchus, Russians and other Western countries have all affected Korea sharply. Foreign languages, therefore, have had no little effect upon Korean.

The influence of China, of course, was paramount. Korean, like English, is a hybrid language with a dual strain of Chinese and the original native language running through its vocabulary as Latin and Anglo-Saxon runs through the latter. Unlike English, the written and cultural tradition of the Chinese language remained the "superior" strain as against an "inferior" Korean tongue with the result that a sharp cleavage developed between the written and spoken languages and evolution of Korean undermined up to the eve of the modern era in the closing years of the nineteenth century. On the threshhold of the twentieth century, short-lived modern reforms were suppressed by the total domination of a Japan bent on replacing in as few years as possible the historic role of China as the center of Korean reorientation. The result was two generations of bilingual Koreans and an all-out "war" to displace the "inferior" Korean with the "superior" Japanese altogether. The Japanese period, of course, ended when Japan overreached herself at Pearl Harbor and the Liberation of Korea immediately centered on the country the effects of the Russo-American "cold war." The separation of the country as a result has meant that for fourteen long years, there have been separate processes in the development of the Korean language with no foreseeable day of a merger in sight.

In short, the history of the Korean language has been a history of obstacles to growth and development. On the other hand, the pressures, within and without, have served to make the language a resilient one with a uniformity that is the uniformity of the Korean race and national destiny. The distinctive features of the language remain distinctive north and south, and however long the incompatible political separation, the people will surely emerge from it with one tongue.

History

Foreign Influences

Glimpses of the ancient Korean language may be gathered from scanty recorded literature of old Korea. Although transcribed in Chinese characters, we are able to derive some clues about the language spoken by the Korean people's ancestors, especially from the "Songs of Silla Dynasty." These records, moreover, give us bare hints that some kind of writing was known in ancient Korea before the introduction of Chinese ideography. They tell of writing in the shapes of a bird's foot, of characters carved upon the barks of a tree, and of a certain author, named Sinji, who lived during the prehistoric Tangun era.

The Chinese system of writing was first used after the fourth century of the Christian era. To be sure, it was known from the third or second century before the Christian era in the series of Chinese invasions leading to the establishment of Chinese colonies, notably Lolang in 108 B.C. But in the absence of any evidences to the contrary, we can only assume that writing was the occupation only of the Chinese colonists and that the Korean had no hand in it.

It is not clear which of the Three Kingdoms of the historical period first employed written Chinese. The first known record is a stele monument erected in A.D. 414 to a Koguryo monarch. Writing as a systematic practice, however, seems to have first developed in Silla.

Through subsequent dynasties, the superiority of the Chinese language was maintained by the *yangban* nobility and scholars at the expense of the Korean. The difficulty of mastering this system of ideographic writing heightened the division between the common classes which could not begin to undertake the time-consuming efforts required and the scholarly class which had all the leisure to pursue them. By the Yi dynasty, the educational and cultural traditions were steeped in Chinese and the administrative system of the state and social life depended upon it.

Two systems of writing were derived from the Chinese ideography, the *idu* and the *ibgvod*. The former system is believed to have been developed in the first 40 years since the introduction of Buddhism to Silla in 528. The latter took longer to develop; it was started in the seventh century and completed only in latter-day Koryo of the fourteenth century.

Both systems continued to be used until the end of the Yi dynasty. Generally speaking, the *idu* and *ibgvod* were efforts to weld the fundamentally different Korean grammar to the structure of the Chinese language and to serve as Korean grammatical particles.

In the middle of the fifteenth century, there was a stroke of inspiration. A complete departure was made from the Chinese system of writing and an alphabet, suited to the native language itself, devised. This was the *hangul*, promulgated in the year 1446 after three years of hard labor by the foremost scholars of the age. In proclaiming it, the enlightened king, Sejong, declared that it was his wish to extend the blessings of the written word to the common people by offering them a convenient system of writing easily mastered by any individual.

But this liberating instrument of the *hangul* could not budge the entrenched position of Chinese. The scholarly class, ever mindful of their authority and prestige derived from the Chinese Classics, resisted it. *Hangul* experiments failed after a sporadic start and became despised as a medium for womenfolk. It was to remain utterly neglected and forgotten until the advent of the modern era brought by the stream of Western culture and the opening of the "Hermit Kingdom" in the closing years of the nineteenth century. Western culture meant, among other things, a scientific approach to the Korean language and Korean linguists adopted Western methodologies to revive *hangul* interest and popularize it.

But the age of cultural inspirations from the West was also an age of Western-style imperialism. Japan, nearest to Korea and latest in Empire-building, annexed Korea and ushered in forty years of a policy designed to force the conversion of Koreans to Japanese ways of thought and civilization. Efforts to kill the Korean language led to bans and suppressions of books, magazines and newspapers, to the outlawry of the language in school, to its discouragement at home, to the jailing of Korean language authorities, and to compulsory Japanese everywhere. Only

Japanese education was available and the bilingual Korean became stronger in his knowledge of Japanese than Korean.

The Liberation revived *hangul* learning with a vengeance. Overnight, there were movements to replace the Japanese vocabulary, to coin new Korean words for the Chinese vocabulary, to take the next logical step with the *hangul* and liberate it in a horizontal system of writing. Much of this ardent reforming zeal succumbed to the political tensions of the time, but eventually a pattern of go-slow corrections has emerged. Newspapers generally retain Chinese characters on the political or economic pages while giving social news or stories of human interest in *hangul*, school text-books are all in *hangul* but "One Thousand Characters" are also taught, writers are concentrating on *hangul* as much as possible and Chinese characters have quite literally disappeared from street signs. English is the most important foreign language, Japanese is forbidden and untaught and Chinese is far less popular than French or German.

Southern Ancestor

The Korean language was certainly developed in the southern part of the peninsula. Primitive Korean society on the agricultural flatlands there consisted of three tribal communities, Chinhan, Pyonhan and Mahan. We know that the tribes of these "Three Han States," as they are called, were related by blood. That being so, they must have used the same language. Theirs was the language of the subsequent formations of the historic kingdoms, Silla and Paekche, and, as such, the precursors of modern Korean speech.

The third of the historic Three Kingdoms, Koguryo, was formed from the merging of the various tribes in the north. These were hunting rather than agricultural people and, in all probability, spoke various Tungusic dialects. It follows that the citizens of Koguryo must have spoken Tungusic. Thus, there were two quite distinctive languages when Korea entered the historical stage.

Korean and Tungusic most probably belonged to the same Ural-Altaic or Turanian family of languages that originated somewhere on the steppes of Central Asia. Korean was developed by the first migrators from the steppes into the peninsula who settled down in the warmer river basins to the south to advance to a neolithic stage of culture. Tungusic was the language of later migrators who had to be content with the sparer north to subsist on meat or fish and live in caves. Centuries — and Chinese colonial masters (Lolang) — separated these people of a common ancestry in their new habitats of warmer life in Korea and Manchuria. It is, therefore, safe to assume that a once-common language underwent enough changes to make the language of the first settlers distinctly different from that of the latecomers. Korean was certainly more uniform than Tungusic.

As mentioned above, the Korean language of their early ancestors can be studied through the songs recorded in Chinese during the southern Silla dynasty. This kingdom eventually unified the Korean peninsula and was succeeded, in turn, by the Koryo dynasty in the tenth century. Koryo moved the seat of government - and the center of the Korean language - from Kyongju, the Silla capital in the south, to Kaesong in the center. The Korean language was becoming the dominating medium in the country but, inevitably, it, in turn, was being influenced by the Tungusic tongues which an aggressive Koguryo had previously carried down to mid-Korea on the borders of Paekche and Silla. Koguryo, meanwhile, was also being affected by other Manchurian languages, especially the kindred Tungusic of the Niuchens who had extended their hunting-grounds into the Hamgyong-do province of Korea.

A Korean language, comparatively uniform to the whole peninsula, became clear by the time King Sejong promulgated his *hangul* alphabet. As yet, it was a highly standardized language of the aristocratic class only. Aristocracy north or south mingled and shaped a common Korean language influenced by admixtures with Tungusic. The commoners continued to use their primitive speeches,

Tungusic in the north, Korean in the south. These stratifications were first broken by the impact of the Hideyoshi invasions from Japan in the closing years of the sixteenth century. Aristocracy was toppled and the Korean language streamed into the lower ranks of society. Thenceforward, Korean became no longer a common medium for aristocracy but also for the people. It was no longer an aristocrat's but a commoner's language. Since 1894, when Western culture first began to be introduced, it has increasingly become a language of the people and the many changes brought to bear upon it by the sweeping Kabo Reforms affected the speech of the common people as never before.

From this outline of the history of the Korean language, we may classify the stages of its development as follows:

1) From the primitive three Han states in the south of the pre-Christian era to the end of Silla over a united land in the tenth century during which the structure of the Korean language was shaped.

2) The Koryo kingdom of the next four hundred years during which the Korean language became influenced by the Tungusic dialects of the north.

3) The Medieval Period from the founding of the Yi dynasty to the eve of the Hideyoshi invasions (1592-1599) when the aristocratic class was forming the Korean language by applying Chinese culture and letters to Korean ways of thought.

4) The Recent Period from the Hideyoshi to the Kabo Reforms of 1894 when the language was becoming popularized.

5) The Modern Period during which Western culture was introduced, vocabularies were becoming enriched, and linguistic studies began.

Origin

To which family of languages does the Korean language belong?

This question has been debated for a long time. Korean and Japanese are two of the main world languages that have never had their origins clearly defined outside themselves. Even Korean and Japanese, believed by most international scholars to be akin, have never had their kinship established as a certainty. At this stage of linguistic scholarship, it is only possible to base the origin of Korean on probabilities from the migrations of the Korean race and shrewd guesses from the structure of the language. The keys to this answer are to be found somewhere in the vast steppes of Central Asia. These are steppes which have bred numerous races of nomadic migrators east and west.

Many foreign scholars believe it probable that Korean belongs to the Altaic family of languages. This supposition finds wide credence among their Korean colleagues who, in general, claim this origin outright. The scholars further maintain that the Altaic stock is closely connected with the Ural. That would make Korean a relative of such European languages as Finnish and Magyar. The basis for this belief lies in the fact that both the Ural and Altaic groups are agglutinative languages and that both trace their ancestry to Central Asia. Here, we shall confine ourselves to the assumption that Korean is a member of the Altaic family.

The Altaic family is sub-divided into three branches, Turkic, Mongolian and Tungusic. The Turkic branch embraces the most numerous languages and extends over a wide area from Asia Minor to the Japan Sea. The Mongolian branch may be further sub-divided into Chalcha, Kalmuks and Buryad and its once powerful but now dwindling speakers live in the Mongolias and across the steppes of Central Asia where Genghis Khan left the various warriors of his "Golden Horde." It is to the third branch, the Tungusic, that Korean is believed to belong.

The Tungusic language is spoken by various tribes in Siberia but the most numerous people who speak it call Manchuria their home. For this reason, it is often called the Tungus-Manchu language. The Tungus were large in numbers at one time or another in their history and sufficiently civilized to develop their own letters.

We have already noted the presence of Tungusic-speaking peoples in north Korea and pointed to the differentiation of Korean to the south by the historical period which brought the two in contact again. The only language with which Korean shares a marked similarity in the agglutinative structure of its grammar is the Japanese. One branch of the Japanese race also probably stemmed from the Tungusic waves of migrations before the Korean to cross over to Japan and mix with the other races already there, especially the Ainus. Certain Chinese records of the Wei kingdom refer to a land embracing the southern coasts of Korea and the coasts of Kyushu and suggest that the people who plied a sea trade to and fro were one. A few basic vocabularies of modern Japanese and Korean trace their root-words to a common ancestry. Of this order are the morphomes, *mi* for insects, *chi* for fish and *po* for persons.

The first scientific approach to the study of the Korean language was made by Western missionaries, Catholic and Protestant. They spent their entire lives to apply extensive and systematic studies upon the language, publishing books on Korean grammar, spoken Korean and Korean dictionaries. Much of their works have proved to be faulty but what few have endured the test of time remain today among the classics on the Korean language. Overall, their contribution has been significant to the studies of modern Korean linguistic scholars.

Characteristics

Western, Japanese or Korean efforts notwithstanding, Korean language studies are still far from satisfactory. Future linguists will undoubtedly be able to uncover broader characteristics as more archaeological and other evidences come to light. Thus far, we can confidently offer only the following as characteristics of our national language:

Vowels

Korean vowels are divided into three groups and vowel combinations tend to be made within the same groups only. Such vowel harmony is a common characteristic of the Ural-Altaic languages. The three groups are:
A) Hard vowels ㅏ [a], ㅗ [o], ㅐ [ae], ㅚ [oe]
B) Soft vowels ㅓ [ŏ], ㅜ [u], ㅡ [ŭ], ㅔ [e]
C) Medium vowel ㅣ [i]

The vowels of groups A and B tend to combine within themselves but resist combinations across each other; in other words, A and B are kept apart. The single ㅣ [i] vowel of group C combines with the vowels of either A or B.

Consonants

a) Unlike Indo-European languages, Korean words never begin with more than one consonant. That means English words like *strike* or *break* are impossible. In this, it shares a common characteristic with all Altaic languages.

b) In Korean, words do not begin with liquid consonants, such as the *r* or *l* in English, departing in this case from other Ural-Altaic languages, including Japanese, to which this is common. Where the liquid consonant comes into the language through the acceptance of the Chinese vocabulary, it is reflected by *n*. It is as if the English words, *lamp* and *running*, were actually pronounced *namp* and *nunning*. The sole exception is a Chinese *l* accompanied by ㅣ [i], as in the surname, 李. In Chinese, this is Li; in Korean, Yi.

c) There are no *f*'s or *v*'s in Korean. Korean renditions of English words with these consonants usually employ ㅂ (p or b). Other major Western consonants lacking in Korean are the English *z*, the French *j*, and the Russian ш (*sh*).

Grammatical Structure

The most important distinction of the Ural-Altaic family of languages from either the Chinese or Indo-European is its agglutinative structure of grammar. The Chinese family has an isolated structure in which words denoting ideas are fixed and the order of fixed words constitutes grammar if it may

III PEOPLE, LANGUAGE

be called that. The Indo-European languages have various degrees of inflections; that is to say, words denoting ideas are not fixed but modified by cases, numbers and tenses. In the Ural-Altac languages, words denoting ideas are fixed as in Chinese. Unlike Chinese, in which the functional grammar plays a severely restricted and largely suggested role, the Ural-Altaic languages have cases and tenses as flexible as in any Indo-European language. The functional grammar is determined by separate parts of speech "glued" to the fixed word. Such is the case with the Korean which is a language particularly well balanced between fixed words and grammatical particles.

The Hangul Alphabet

Vowels

The vowels of the *hangul* alphabet, as promulgated by King Sejong, were classified in two categories: simple and compound.

Simple: ㅏ[a], ㅑ[ya], ㅓ[ŏ], ㅕ[yŏ], ㅗ[o], ㅛ[yo], ㅜ[u], ㅠ[yu], ㅡ[ŭ], ㅣ[i]

Compound: ㅐ[ae], ㅒ[yae], ㅔ[e], ㅖ[ye], ㅚ[oe], ㅟ[wi], ㅢ[ui], ㅘ[wa], ㅝ[wo], ㅙ[wae], ㅞ[we]

(Romanizations in parentheses follow the McCune-Reisschauer system. The vowels, *a, i, e, o, u* are pronounced as in Italian; *o* as the *o* in *not*, *u* as the French *eu*, *ae* as the *a* in *at*, *oe* is almost like the German umlaut for *o*, and *ui* suggests the Russian ы.)

As enumerated, there are 21 vowels, 10 simple and 11 compound. They are, as we say, based on the original classifications. Modern grammarians, however, prefer to classify them differently into simple and dipthong vowels, We then get the following orders:

Simple: ㅏ, ㅓ, ㅗ, ㅜ, ㅡ, ㅣ, ㅐ, ㅔ and ㅚ.

Dipthong: ㅑ, ㅕ, ㅛ, ㅠ, ㅒ, ㅖ, ㅢ, ㅟ, ㅘ, ㅝ, ㅙ, and ㅞ.

This distribution is explained on the basis of the following triangular chart for the simple vowels.

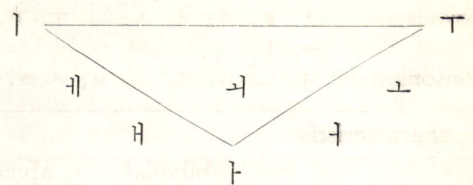

(The dipthongs are formed by the principle of combinations as follows:

ㅑ = ㅣ + ㅏ, ㅕ = ㅣ + ㅓ, ㅛ = ㅣ + ㅗ
ㅠ = ㅣ + ㅜ, ㅒ = ㅣ + ㅐ, ㅖ = ㅣ + ㅔ
ㅝ = ㅜ + ㅣ, ㅢ = ㅡ + ㅣ, ㅘ = ㅗ + ㅏ
ㅝ = ㅜ + ㅓ, ㅙ = ㅗ + ㅐ, ㅞ = ㅜ + ㅔ

(This rule for diphthongs can also apply to the simple vowels: ㅐ, ㅔ and ㅚ. Thus, ㅐ = ㅏ + ㅣ, ㅔ = ㅓ + ㅣ and ㅚ = ㅗ + ㅣ. The chart for simple vowels is based not on Sejong's strokes but on the values of the vowel-sound or phonemes.)

Consonants

a, Simple consonants

ㄱ[k or g], ㄴ[n], ㄷ[t or d], ㄹ[r or l], ㅁ[m], ㅂ[p or b], ㅅ[s], ㅇ[silent or ng], ㅈ[ch or j], ㅊ[ch'], ㅋ[k'], ㅌ[t'], ㅍ[p'], ㅎ[h].

b, Double consonants

ㄲ[kk], ㄸ[tt], ㅃ[pp], ㅆ[ss], ㅉ[tch].

(The alternatives in the parentheses for ㄱ, ㄴ, ㄷ, ㄹ, ㅇ, and ㅈ by no means exhaust the plurality of Romanizations provided for each Korean consonant under the McCune-Reisschauer system. The system takes into consideration the influence of euphonic changes depending on where the consonant comes in the word in relation to other letters. Here, we shall assume that the reader is generally familiar with these Romanizations. Suffice to say that ch', k', and p' are aspirated plosives, suggested more by g, d an j uttered without voicing.)

These consonants are also classified according to the traditional scholars.

There are then 21 vowels and 19 consonants provided under the structure of the *hangul* alphabet of 24 letters, 14 consonants

and 10 vowels, as follows:
vowels: ㅏ, ㅑ, ㅓ, ㅕ, ㅗ, ㅛ, ㅜ, ㅠ, ㅡ, ㅣ.
consonants: ㄱ, ㄴ, ㄷ, ㄹ, ㅁ, ㅂ, ㅅ, ㅇ,

characteristic		Articulation			
	bilabial	alveolar	palatal	velar	glottal
explosive	ㅂ, ㅍ, ㅃ	ㄷ, ㅌ, ㄸ	—	ㄱ, ㅋ, ㄲ	—
africate	—	—	ㅈ, ㅊ, ㅉ,	—	—
fricative	—	—	ㅅ, ㅆ,	—	ㅎ
nasal	ㅁ	ㄴ	—	ㅇ[ŋ]	
liquid trilled	—	ㄹ(r)	—	—	—
liquid lateral	—	ㄹ(l)	—	—	—

ㅈ, ㅊ, ㅋ, ㅌ, ㅍ, ㅎ.
Following is a chart of the characteristics of Korean consonants according to the articulating organs used in each.

History of Hangul

The *hangul* was the product of Korea's "Golden Age of Culture" ushered in with the reign of the fourth Yi king, Sejong, in the fifteenth century. Sejong was the first ruler to realize that the true purpose of writing was to make it accessible to the common people. To that end, he decided to devise an alphabetical system of writing to replace the Chinese ideography and brought several outstanding scholars together to work it out.

Both in Japan and Korea, the need was felt to overcome the barriers to wider learning imposed by the Chinese heritage. In Japan, due to the crude nature of the language with its limited vowels and consonants, syllabic systems were worked out from elementary strokes of the Chinese character. Korean with its richer vowels and consonants permitted an alphabet. Unlike the European alphabets which were the results of unconscious accumulations of earlier alphabetical forms of the Mediterranean Basin, the *hangul* was a conscious one from the outset. The European alphabets are haphazard things; the *hangul* was to be perfectly regular and logical.

The demands for perfection made the task an extremely difficult one and it required many years of hard work to determine the phonetic values of Korean to fit perfection. Some modern linguists believe that the *hangul* scholars were inspired by Sanskrit although others would have it a purely native invention. Western works exist which trace individual consonants to Sanskrit and beyond Sanskrit to the Syric and other alphabets of the Mediterranean Basin, A comparison of letter-shapes can well sustain these views. On the other hand, the claim of the "jingoist" scholars that letters were suggested from the shapes of mouth, teeth and tongue. is also not without ground. Whatever the originality, or lack of it, of the consonants, the vowels appear, by general consensus of opinion, to be native-born.

The alphabet was finally completed and proclaimed by the king as the *"Hunmin Chongum"* (literally, People Instructing Regular Sounds). The book consisted of three parts, preamble, values of sounds, and rules of application. The preamble read: "Due to the fact that the language of this land is different from China's, there is no basis for communication of the written word among the ignorant masses; they are very often unable in the long run to express all that they wish. Greatly concerned as I am by this handicap, I have devised 28 letters for the convenience of every individual who should be able easily to master them." The values of sounds were given by examples as in elementary school education: *C* as in Cat, *D* as in Dog, and so forth. The rules of application explained the combination of the letters into syllabic forms. By popular abbreviation, the *"Hunmin Chongum"* came to

III PEOPLE, LANGUAGE

be called *"hangul"* which means, simply, Korean writing.

From the preamble, we note there were originally 28 letters. Four were eventually dropped because they represented Chinese rather then Korean values of sounds and it was decided that they might as well be absorbed into other letters. Thus ㆆ which is a guttural *h* as in the Chinese word for 'good', *hao,* was discarded and words with that consonant, including *ho* (Korean version of the Chinese 'good'), were represented, instead, by ㅎ (*h* - normal). The same thing happened to ㆍ, ㆁ and ㅿ, represented respectively in the Wade Romanization of Chinese as *e* as in Mao Tze-tung, *j* as in *jih pao* (newspaper) and *hs* as in *hsieh hsiao* (school). The short vowel, ㆍ, appearing in such words as 하ᄂᆞ님 (God) or 며ᄂᆞ리 (daughter-in-law) are now rendered as 하나님 and 며누리 respectively. The consonant ㆁ has disappeared, mostly into the silent ㅇ or vowels. ㅿ is interesting. In the capital, it has disappeared completely as a vowel while in the provinces, the *s* suggestion has been retained. Thus, the old Korean word for village, 마ᅀᆞᆯ (ma-hsŭl) is now 마을 (maŭl) in Seoul but 마슬 (masŭl) in rural areas. Similarly, words for mirror, scissors, etc.

That perfection had not been achieved in devising the *hangul* is born out by the fact that the test of time and usage led to the discarding of these Chinese values of sounds. Other imperfections were also noted in time, particularly the illogical spellifications entailed by a system that had not taken into adequate consideration the phonetic transformation of certain Korean words followed by postpositions. All in all, however, it must be considered one of the truly most remarkable alphabets in the world. It is systematic, economical and comprehensive.

Attributes

The *hangul* is an alphabet but it is not used like the alphabets of the West. The Western alphabets are used to build up separate words, the *hangul* to build up separate syllables. It may be called a halfway house between the alphabetical and syllabic systems of writing; in letters, an alphabet, in word-formations, a syllabary.

The reason is not far to seek. The Chinese form of vertical writing still applies. Chinese characters are essentially a matter of writing within "boxes." The *hangul,* accordingly, is "boxed" in separate syllabic combinations of letters and written vertically. It is as if London and Lancaster were to be written $\boxed{\begin{matrix}LO\\N\end{matrix}}\boxed{\begin{matrix}DO\\N\end{matrix}}$ and $\boxed{\begin{matrix}LA\\N\end{matrix}}\boxed{\begin{matrix}CA\\S\end{matrix}}\boxed{\begin{matrix}TE\\R\end{matrix}}$ respectively. Linguistic reformers in the first flush of the Liberation attempted to take the next logical step and liberate the alphabet into a horizontal form of writing, thus to permit the grouping of full words. One such system was actually publicized. But the attempts were short-lived. The difficulty is the existence of too many homonyms in the Korean vocabulary as a result of the Chinese literary heritage. Such homonyms are instantly recognized as Chinese characters but in *hangul,* they are not apparent and can be confusing or even misunderstood altogether.

Within the "boxed-in" syllabic combinations, the sizes and positions of the letters vary depending on the distribution. With certain vowels, the consonant comes to the left; with others, it is placed above. and when there are two or three consonants (there can never be more), the latter are placed below with the vowels either to the right or in between and all strokes shrunk in size. Within a given framework, the sizes of the letters *m* and *e* for $\boxed{me}$ would be bigger than *m, e* and *n* written as $\boxed{\begin{matrix}me\\n\end{matrix}}$.

One of the major difficulties encountered by Korean linguists was the phonetic transformation of many Korean words. Chicken, to take a most commonly cited example, is 닥 (tak), but when the postposition, 이 (i) follows, an l sound enters: tal-ki. Under the traditional system, the two words were spelled 달기, but this is clearly unsatisfactory. It would be like spelling *mes amis* in French as *me samis* which no Frenchman let alone grammarians would tolerate. The Reformed *Hangul* system settles the problem by standardizing the spelling of chicken as 닭 (talk) with the ㄹ (l) understood to be silent as in the English *salmon*. Unlike *salmon* where it is always silent, the *l* is sounded in the Korean chicken when the postposition 이 follows. Similar standardizations have been effected for all other words that ring phonetic transformations on consonant-endings. The standardizations permit constancy in the postpositions which otherwise would have to be spelled differently each time as in the 닭 example.

Korean words generally consist of from one to four syllables. There are words that run to seven or eight syllables but these are very rare. For the most part, they are made up of two or three. These are said to constitute 70 percent of the whole vocabulary.

Examples:
1-syllabic words: 코 (k'o) nose; 눈 (nun) snow or eye
2-syllabic words: 사람 (saram) man; 바다 (pada) sea; 나무 (namu) tree
3-syllabic words: 아버지 (abŏji) father; 어머니 (ŏmŏni) mother
4-syllabic words: 두루마기 (turumagi) coat

The above are examples of native Korean words. The development of Korean etymology may enable the future scholar to trace Tungusic, Mongolian and other origins for many words which today can only be considered as pure Korean. We have already noted the common ancestry of certain root-morphomes in Japanese and Korean. The extension of a Korean-Japanese Grimm's Law which reflects corresponding changes in the common Chinese ideographic vocabulary may yield further results in the basic vocabularies of the two languages.

On the other hand, etymology is hardly necessary to recognize the presence of Chinese words in the Korean language. They are said to constitute over 50 percent of all Korean words. During the Japanese occupation, many Japanese words were also introduced. The Japanese language being "taboo" today, Korean words have been coined to replace these (food menus, for instance), but the Japanese influence is to be found in the Chinese ideographic vocabulary for modern inventions that take after the Japanese rather than the Chinese examples. Thus, the Chinese characters for train, automobile, plane or bicycle are different in China and the same in Korea and Japan. Modern culture also has meant the introduction of many Western words and terminologies, especially after the Liberation.

Morphology

a) Individual Korean words are like Chinese without any genders, cases or numbers. The gender is expressed by a character-prefix denoting sex and then used only when quite necessary; the case is expressed by particles known as postpositions, and number by the addition of another particle denoting the plural number.

b) The order of words in a typical Korean sentence is: subject first and predicate last with object or complement in between.

Examples:

사람(이)	밥(을)	먹소
saram(i)	pab(ŭl)	mŏkso
man(nom.)	rice(acc.)	eats

The man is eating rice.

선생님(이)	학교(에)	가오
sŏnsaengnim(i)	hakkyo(e)	kao
teacher(nom.)	school(dat.)	go

The teacher is going to school

As obvious, 먹소 and 가오 are the verbs for "to eat" and "to go." They come at the end of the sentences. 밥 (rice) in the first sentence is the object because it is followed by the postposition reflecting the accusative case (을); 학교(school) in the second sentence is governed by the postposition for the dative case (에) and therefore means "to school," (cf. Lat. scolam). Both object and dative adjunct come between the subject and predicative verb.

c) Modifier precedes subject, object or predicative noun.

Examples:

젊은	사람(이)	많이	있소
chŏlmŭn	saram(i)	manhi	isso
young	men(nom.)	many	are

III PEOPLE, LANGUAGE

There are many young men.

어린 학생(이) 영어
ŏrin haksaeng(i) yŏngŏ
young(child) student(nom.) English

공부(를) 열심히 하오
kongbu(rūl) yŏlsimhi hao
lesson(acc.) ardently studies

The young student is studying his English lessons very hard.

The adjectives, 젊은 and 어린, come before the nouns, 사람 and 학생 which they modify; the verbs, 있소 and 하오, are modified by the preceding adverbs, 많이 and 열심히.

The postpositions we have referred to are so called because, unlike the prepositions of Western languages, they come after the nouns they modify. Not "to school," but "school to." Here are some examples:

Nominative 이, 가
Accusative 을, 를
Dative 에, 에게

e) Adjectives or verbs undergo no declensional or conjugational changes. Instead, special particles are added to the stem to indicate the tense or the voice.

Examples:

먹 (stem for "eat")
먹는다 (mŏngnūnda) present
먹었다 (mŏgotta) past
먹겠다 (mŏkketta) future
먹이다 (mŏgida)-(to causative let eat, feed)

높 (stem for "high")
높다 (nop'ta) present
높았다 (nop'atta) past
높겠다 (nop'ketta) future
높이다 (nop'ida)-(to causative heighten)

f) Adjectives are used as predicatives without the help of predicative verbs.

이 산은 높다
i sanūn nop'ta
this mountain (nom.) high.

This mountain is high.

생명은 짧다
saengmyong (ūn) tchapta
life (nom.) short

Life is short.

g) Since the Korean sentence tends to be indicative, relative pronouns are few.

내가 본 그림을 주시오
naega pon kŭrim(ūl) chusio
I(nom.) seen picture(acc.) give

Give me the picture which I saw.

h) One characteristic of Korean, unknown to many other languages, is the usage depending on the age or status of the people to whom one is talking. Different words are used depending on whether one is using the familiar form of speech between equals (differentiated in turn among adults and children), the form used for addressing the young or persons of lower status, and the honorific form for which there are special nouns, pronouns, verbs and, invariably, ending-particles.

common form honorific form
rice 밥 (pap) 진지 (chinji)
sleep 자다 (chada) 주무시다 (chumusida)

The rain is falling.

비가 온다 비가 옵니다
(piga-onda) (piga-omnida)

Sleep well.

잘 자라 안녕히 주무십시오
(chal chara) (annyŏnghi chumusipsio)

Conclusion

Certain general observations may be made about the Korean language as a result of a long process of history.

Firstly, there is the permeating influence of the Chinese language. Its effects upon Korean life and the difficulties posed for the development of a pure alphabetical system of writing cannot be overestimated. The marriage of the Latin and Anglo-Saxon elements in the formation of modern English was a marriage of kindreds, but the marriage of Chinese and Korean was a marriage of languages that were genetically different. Native ideas and modes of thinking as expressed through the medium of the Chinese ideography had to be "forced," so to speak. Education was a matter of learning by rote and memorizations from Chinese texts. The Korean language entered the schoolroom only to help guide the pupil to mastery of Chinese meanings.

Secondly, there can be no doubt about the uniformity of the Korean language. True, Korean like any true language has its dialectical differences, broadly classified into northern, mid-Korean and southern dialects with the northern ones again sub-divided into Pyongan-do and Hamgyong-do and the southern into Chungchong-do, Cholla-do and Kyongsang-do but the differences are not too great compared to the dialects of most other countries. The pronunciations, syntax and accidence of the language were all clearly fixed over a long period of time.

Thirdly, the Korean language may be said to stand between the inflected languages of the Indo-European family and the isolated structure of Chinese. Individual Korean words that provide the basic meanings of the Korean sentence have learned the stern discipline of the Chinese language which concentrates on each unit of meaning or 'concept.' On the other hand, the flexibility of its vocal harmony and the existence of postpositions and ending particles as separate parts of speech give Korean enough scope to express the moods and tenses of the speaker as any European language.

Fourthly, the basic nature of the language may be free and expressive and a long history may have cemented uniformity, but development has been anything but smooth. The stratification of society into rigid classes has pushed the language into "dead-ends." On one hand, it became a highly formalized language of politeness with honorific forms more elaborate than that of the Japanese; on the other, the vocabulary has been much misabused by a people to whom the "wear-and-tear" of a language so thoroughly reorientated to Confucian codes of morals and ethics was an eloquent outlet. Few languages equal Korean in the range and constancy of vulgar usage.

The Korean language, in short, is both flexible and rigid at one and the same time. Foreign words enter easily and the chances are that a Korean, say, of the late nineteenth century, if he could return to hear an ordinary conversation among modern-day Koreans, would hardly recognize it as Korean. Not merely the vocabulary but the very pace and intonation are markedly different. On the other hand, the uniformity of writing, developed by long centuries of learning in a Chinese system which demands uniformity as the precondition to the high hurdle of attainment, makes for strong resistance to any undue changes in print. That same Korean ancestor would probably be able, very quickly, to understand a modern Korean magazine with only slight efforts at readjustment. Foreign words can stream in indiscriminatingly and be banished just as easily. Total reforms are envisaged and just as totally discouraged. It all depends on the social climate.

In conclusion, two points may be added to illustrate vividly the stresses to which the Korean language has been subjected as our present legacy. During the early phase of the Pacific War, the Japanese clapped thirty-three members of the Korean Language Society in jail. Five were eventually found "innocent" and released; sixteen were found "guilty" and the remaining twelve circulated from jail to jail for a year while having their cases "pending" at the procurators' office. The sixteen "guilty" ones languished in jail for the duration of the war. Two died in their cells. History has little parallel to offer this punishment of scholars whose only crime was that they loved their own language.

This was the frontline fate of the language. The result in the rear is the unbalanced situation in an ordinary Korean household of today. To pick a random example: the master can take one foreign language for granted, Japanese; he is more confident in that than in his own language. His son certainly cannot take Japanese for granted; he is busy pursuing English, and his old father, at home only with the Confucian Classics which neither son nor grandson knows or cares about, is confident in nothing, not even in the Korean they talk.

IV POLITICS, LAWS

History of Political Institutions

Consultative Organs

As a democratic country, Korea has had a very short history. Her democratic institutions were introduced and established only after the national sovereignty was restored with the defeat of Japan in the Pacific War.

Carefully surveyed, however, the various political institutions which were adopted by the succession of kingdoms that ruled the peninsula reveal certain unique systems which contained some primitive democratic features.

Until a democratic parliamentary system was finally developed in this country, various forms of consultative organs existed either for the conveniences of the rulers or to check the autocratic tendencies of kings.

Hwabaek (Silla)

There was a sort of aristocratic council which served as a consultative body for the kings of the Silla dynasty, according to one of the oldest history books on Korea, the "*Tangso* (History of the Tang Dynasty)". This was called the *Hwabaek* and consisted of influential members of the peers. The *Hwabaek* council met with the king and debated state affairs. Unlike the national councils of the city-states in ancient Greece, however, decisions could be made only by unanimous agreement among the members of the council, and any single member could kill a proposal before the council by expressing his opposition.

According to the Tangso, there were four "sacred places" around Kyongju, the capital of Silla—each in the four directions of the compass. Important decisions were made on huge rocks at each of these "sacred places." It was an old Korean custom to conclude any important agreement on a huge rock to symbolize that it should remain enduring as the rock.

Supreme Councils (Koryo)

There were six top advisors, the *Taesa, Taejon, Taebo, Taewi, Sado* and *Sagong*, who rendered personal advices to the king during the Koryo dynasty (918-1392). In addition, there was a supreme council consisting of top-ranking government officials of ministerial rank, which served as another consultative organ to the state administration.

The supreme council comprised two different kinds of officials—*chaesin* and *chusin*. *Chaesin* were top officials of the three important ministries of the *Chungsomunha* (general administration and inspection), *Sangsodosong* (personnel) and *Samsa* (treasury). *Chusin* were members of the privy council.

Uijongbu (Yi Dynasty)

Uijongbu was the top state council of the Yi dynasty (1392-1910), comprising cabinet ministers and some other ranking officials. The king himself presided over meetings of the *Uijongbu*. It actually handled almost all the administrative, legislative and judiciary affairs of the dynasty.

In fact, the *Uijongbu* was so powerful that King Taejong, the third Yi monarch, stripped it of some of its powers and made it handle largely foreign relations and review death sentences, transferring most other state business to cabinet ministries. His successor, King Sejong, however, restored the old system and the *Uijongbu* became the center of national administration until the 11th king, Chungjong, established the *Pibyonsa* to take over military and other important state affairs.

Although the Yi dynasty was an autocratic government, these organs provided quite an extent of restraints against arbitrary actions on the part of the king.

Judiciary Organs

Ancient Korea

Details are not available about judiciary systems in ancient Korea, but the section on the Wei kingdom in the Chinese *San Kuo Chih* (Annals of the Three States) says that in such tribal states as Puyo and Koguryo (circa 300 B.C.), trials were carried out at tribal meetings. That is, in these early states, a kind of simple people's trial served as the judiciary organ.

As these primitive tribal states developed into the centralized kingdoms of Silla, Paekche and Koguryo during the fourth century, national organs were established to take care of judiciary matters. Such central organs as the *Ibangbu* in Silla and *Chojongjwapyong* in Paekche were instituted in the capitals, while provincial governors executed judicial powers in their respective areas. Trials in these countries, however, were very authoritative and arbitrary.

Koryo

In its early stage, Koryo continued to apply the same judicial system that had been developed by Silla, but later she adopted that of the Tang dynasty in China. The *Uihyongdae* was established in the capital as a central judicial body. In the provinces, governors handled judicial matters in their respective areas, but inspectors called *Yommunsa* were dispatched from the central government to supervise judicial administration.

Legal proceedings depended mainly on cross-examinations. Torture was officially tolerated but there were also certain measures designed to defend the human rights of the accused.

Yi Dynasty

Although there were independent judiciary organs in the central government, provincial governors continued to handle both administrative and judicial matters in local areas. There was a tendency, therefore, for the governors to abuse their judicial authority. Many kings tried to correct this without much success.

In the capital, there were two offices exclusively for judicial administration. They were the *Hyongjo* and *Uigumbu*. The former dealt with general judicial administration, while the latter was a special court convened by the king. There were two other offices—*Sahonbu* and *Hansongbu*—which handled both administrative and judicial matters.

Towards the end of the Yi dynasty, revolutionary changes took place as the Western court system was introduced to Korea. A Court Organization Act was newly proclaimed, establishing courts on three different levels —the supreme court, courts of appeals, and district courts. Government prosecutors' offices were also attached to all courts.

Twentieth Century

The courts provided for under the Court Organization Act continued to function after

Korea was annexed to Japan in 1910. The Japanese, however, established their own court system at the same time. Higher Courts were created to take the place of the Supreme Court and branch courts set up everywhere.

The U.S. Military Government which functioned from 1945 to 1948 as Occupation Authority continued to use the Japanese system without effecting much changes.

Government Organization

Three Kingdoms

Koguryo, founded about a century before Christ, at first had three top officials—*Sangga*, *Taero* and *Paeja*—to preside over the highest administrative organ of the state and to check the dictatorial tendencies of kings. Later, the number was increased to over 10 officials, and the capital and provinces were each divided into five administrative districts. Each district had a governor called *yoksal* who ruled the castles under his jurisdiction. The lord of a castle was directly responsible for administration of his people, having the authority for taxation, labor conscription and organization of military forces.

Paekche, founded between the second and third centuries, patterned itself after the administrative system of Koguryo, also dividing the capital and provinces into five districts each. Under each local district were 10 counties. The governor of a district, called *Pangyong*, had administrative and military jurisdiction over his district, while each county was ruled by an official called *Toksol*. Governmental posts were classified into 16 grades. There were six ministers—prime minister, finance, protocol, royal guard, justice, and national defense. The central government was then divided into a total 22 bureaus.

In Silla, founded between the second and third centuries, there were ministries of defense, foreign affairs and protocol, warehousing, justice, construction, personnel, etc., under the prime minister. Outside the capital, the kingdom was divided into five provinces. Under the provinces were prefectures and counties.

Koryo

There were three ministries—*Chungsomunha* (general administration and inspection), *Sangsodosong* (personnel) and *Samsa* (treasury). The *Sangsosodong* had six departments—personnel, military affairs, census, justice, education, and engineering. Besides, there was a privy council, whose members, together with the three ministers, formed a supreme council, the king's top advisory council. Under local provinces were prefectures, counties and towns.

Yi Dynasty

Confucianism became the main philosophy for administration, and the government system was reorganized to pattern that of China's.

Government employees were classified into two large divisions, *Tongban* (civil service) and *Soban* (military service). These, in turn, were broken down into central and local employees. There were 18 grades in government service.

Uijongbu, consisting of the three ministers and two deputies, was the highest administrative organ in the civil service. There were also six departments, which took care of general administration—personnel, treasury, education, military affairs, justice and engineering.

The land except the capital was divided into eight provinces. Under the eight provinces were four cities, 68 towns, 82 counties, and 175 sub-counties. The local governments of various levels each had six administrative departments like the central government.

Under Japanese Rule

The Japanese Government-General, appointed by the Japanese Emperor, was the supreme administrator in Korea during the 36 years of Japanese rule in Korea. The chief civil administrator, also appointed by the Emperor, was, so to speak, the prime minister of the Korea Government-General. Directly responsible to the two top administrators were seven bureaus for home affairs, finance, industry, agriculture and forestry, justice, education, and police. The secretariat and foreign affairs sections were also directly controlled by them.

The peninsula was divided into 13 provinces, each headed by a governor. The provincial government was made up of two departments—home affairs and police. The Governor also had a secretariat.

In 1919, the Government-General allowed the establishment of provincial councils to advise the governors. Consisting of members partly named by the government and partly elected, the provincial councils, however, had no authority to resolve upon anything, serving only as a consultative organ of the provincial governor.

Later, partial autonomy was allowed cities and towns, and local councils were formed by elected members. The local councils again were under the strict supervision of mayors who were appointed by the government and had very little power in local administration.

Police System

The modern concept of the police was introduced to Korea only with the introduction of Western civilization. There are no existing records which explain anything about police systems in ancient Korea. According to history books on the Three Kingdoms, there was no independent government organ that handled police functions; these were tied up with military or judicial administration.

In Paekche, the three ministries of the royal guard, justice and national defense each had police jurisdiction over their own administrative fields, while in local provinces, governors had their own police.

In Silla, like Paekche, there was no single office which handled police administrations, but the defense ministry and the *Ibangbu* which was concerned with judicial matters shared jurisdiction over police, while in the provinces, local governors were in exclusive control.

There are no historical records concerning the police system in Koguryo, but it is generally assumed that it had a system that was similar or, at least, not too different, from Silla's and Paekche's.

The situation remained the same in Koryo. In the central government, the departments of military affairs and justice each had authority over their own police administration respectively, while in the provinces, the governors controlled everything, including police.

It should be particularly noted that during the Koryo era, there were a few government agencies, although they existed for a short period, established exclusively for police duties. For instance, there was an office, called *Osadae*," which was charged with police duties against corruption of public morals. There was another strictly for night patrols.

A similar set-up continued during Early Yi, giving way to a permanent, exclusive police office in Middle Yi. Called the *Podochong*, it was the first nationwide and permanent police organization in Korea.

In the capital, the office was divided into two district offices, each having a total of 145 men. The breakdown was one chief, three deputies, 70 officers, three messengers, and 64 patrolmen. Thus, a police force of 290 maintained peace in the capital. In local areas, police offices were organized in similar fashion albeit with less manpower.

The *Podochong*, however, had restricted police duties, and did not have a wide range of business as a modern police force has. That is, its activities were limited to arresting general criminals, such as burglars, murderers, and so on. Therefore, those government agencies which had long handled particular police missions of their own continued to retain police authority in their specialized fields not covered by the *Podochong*.

Towards the end of the Yi dynasty, a revolutionary change was made in the police system in accordance with the government's overall reorganization plan through the introduction of Western institutions. A police affairs bureau was newly established and placed under the supervision of the home affairs ministry.

In Seoul, a metropolitan police office was set up under the direct supervision of the home ministry, charged with such duties as general peace maintenance, fire-fighting, and prison administration. In local provinces, the governors had general authority over police administration in their respective provinces.

During the first ten years of the Annexation, Japan employed a combined force of civil and military police to suppress the Korean people. However, nationwide independence movements against Japanese rule after the end of the First World War persuaded the Japanese Government-General in Korea to separate the military from the civil. A police affairs bureau was established in the central government, while provincial governors were given authority over local police administration.

The cruel, uncivilized police methods of the Japanese nevertheless, persisted right up to the Liberation.

The American Military Government, which administered the southern half of Korea from 1945 to 1948, introduced a modern, democratic police system, thus marking a historic, epoch-making landmark in the history of the Korean police.

The new system abolished various undemocratic laws and regulations enforced by and for the police, deprived the right of summary police disposal of minor offenses, abolished the sabre which had long symbolized police oppression of the people, and hired women as regular police officers for the first time in Korean history. The new reforms also included transfer of administrative jurisdiction over public sanitation, economic, and publications affairs to general administrative offices.

This system served as the foundation for the National Police established by the new Republic of Korea Government in 1948.

Fire-Fighting

In the old days when cities had not developed the large populations of today, there was no need for an organized fire-fighting system. But, as the nationwide population grew and more casualties resulted from fires, the people started to adopt real, preventive measures. For the most part, they were crude and primitive, often even superstitious. During Early Yi, the government built large ponds in the cities to retain water for use in case of fire. In Seoul, there were three such ponds —east pond, west pond and south pond. The first modern fire-fighting system was introduced in 1908, when a fire brigade was established within the court. It consisted of 60 fire-fighters and four hand-operated fire-engines.

During the Japanese rule, fire-fighting was placed under the administrative jurisdiction of the police, and fire-fighting teams were organized and developed largely where there were more Japanese residents than Korean. In towns and villages, only nominal brigades were organized with little equipment to cope with disasters.

The original fire-fighting system was charged with combatting fire, floods and other natural calamities. But during the Pacific War, the duties were enlarged to include anti-air-raids, anti-espionage and other auxiliary police duties. Under the control of the anti-calamity section in the Governor-General's Office, government-financed fire stations were established in such major cities as Seoul, Pusan, Inchon and Pyongyang. In other cities and smaller towns, volunteer fire-fighting brigades were organized and locally managed.

The U.S. Military Government in April 1946 completely separated the fire-fighting administration from the police, and established an independent national fire-fighting office in Seoul, under which were organized local fire brigades.

Decorations

Korea's first decoration system was established in April 1900 by royal command. There were seven different kinds of decorations according to merits, and temporary and lifelong pensions accompanied each decoration.

a) The Great Order of "Kumchok"—Limited to members of the royal family, and to those who had already received the Great Order of "Susong."

b) The Great Order of "Susong"—Given to those members of the royal family and distinguished officials who had already received the Great Order of "Ewha."

c) The Great Order of "Ewha" (Pear Flower)—Given to officials who had distinguished themselves after receiving the first degree of the Order of "Taeguk."

d) The Order of "Taeguk" and Order of "Palkwae"—Awarded to both civil and military officials, each with eight different degrees.

e) The Order of Purple Hawk—Decoration strictly for military services. General officers were given the first three degrees, field officers the second to fifth degrees, company officers the third to the sixth degrees, non-commissioned officers the fifth and sixth, and other enlisted men the seventh or eighth.

f) The Order of "Sobong"—Decoration for women. Awarded by order of the Queen. The first degree was limited to members of the royal family and, in exceptional cases, to those who had received the second degree. The sixth degree was the lowest.

Political Parties in Korea

1945—1948

The Korean people won their first modern freedom to engage in politics only with the surrender of the Japanese Empire to the Allied Forces in World War II on August 15, 1945.

The first political group organized after the Liberation was the Preparatory Committee for National Foundation, formed August 17 by Yo Unhyong and his followers at the request of the Japanese Government-General in Korea. The committee completed organization of 145 branch chapters throughout Korea by the end of August with the strong support of Communist elements. The organization gradually became a political federation of various leftist elements as rightist groups soon withdrew.

On September 6, the committee held a national convention to pass a resolution for provisional organization of a Korean People's Republic. This convention elected Syngman Rhee as President of the so-called People's Republic, though he had not returned home as yet from his exile in the United States. Yo Unhyong was elected Vice-President, and the Communist figure, Ho Hon as Prime Minister. Local chapters were reorganized and renamed People's Committees. The national organization was ready to assume the role of national government even after the American occupation troops landed on Korea.

Meanwhile, the Communist Party, which had engaged in continued underground work during the Japanese era, was publicly reorganized as the Korean Communist Party with Park Honyong as head on September 14. Two days later, the Korean Democratic Party was formed by Song Chinu, who had refused the Japanese Governor-General's proposal to organize an interim constitution. This party supported the Chungking Korean Provisional Government which was established in exile in 1919. On September 25, An Chaehong, a rightist middle-of-the roader, who earlier withdrew from the Preparatory Committee, organized the Nationalist Party, while, on November 12, Yo Unhyong, leftist middle-of-the-roader, founded the Korean People's Party.

In north Korea, nationalist groups organized the Chosun Democratic Party headed by Cho Mansik, while Communists established the North Korean General Bureau of the Korean Communist Party with Kim Il Sung as bureau head.

The Korean Independence Party headed by Kim Koo returned home from Chungking where it had stayed with the Provisional Government. They became one of the two major rightist parties (the other was the Korean Democratic Party) after absorbing the Nationalist Party of An and the New Korea Nationalist Party founded by Kwon Tongjin and O Sechang.

Meanwhile, Dr. Rhee returned home on October 16 from the U.S. where he had been in exile, and received a nationwide welcome. Under his leadership, on November 3, a National Council for the Promotion of Independence was organized embracing all the national parties. However, this organization was soon disintegrated due to the differences of opinions between the Communist and other leftist components and those of the rightists, and, on February 8, 1946, the Taehan Association for the Promotion of Independence was formed comprising rightist parties only.

In July 1946, the North Korea Labor Party was born in the north through a merger of the Communist Party and the New People's Party. This was followed in south Korea by the establishment of the South Korea Labor Party through a merger of the Communist, People's and New People's Parties in November.

Those leftists who opposed the merger with the Communists organized the Socialist Labor Party with Yo Unhyong as chairman and Paek Namun and Kang Jin as vice-chairmen. The party was reorganized as the Working People's Party in May 1947, but it soon lost strength when Yo was assassinated on July 17.

Besides these major parties, some 50 or 60 minor ones mushroomed. These won neither the support nor the confidence of the general public.

Constituent Assembly

The South Korean Interim Legislative Assembly under the Military Government enacted a National Assembly Election Law in October 1946, and in accordance with a United Nations Little Assembly resolution, general elections were held on May 10, 1948 to elect members for the Constituent Assembly. Kim Koo's Independence Party, the People's Independence League headed by Dr. Kiusic Kimm and some other rightist and middle-of-the-road groups boycotted the elections.

On June 26, 1949, Kim Koo was assassinated and his party and followers gradually lost political influence.

In February 1949, the Korean Democratic Party, which had 29 seats in the Assembly, merged with several influential groups of the Provisional Government, including P. H. Shinicky and Chi Chongchon, to form the Democratic Nationalist Party. The new party controlled 70 seats in the Assembly.

Meanwhile, pro-government elements formed the Taehan Nationalist Party in December 1949, becoming the largest party in the Assembly with 71 seats. Yun Chiyong and Yi In led this party.

Second-Term National Assembly

Many political groups which had boycotted the first general elections took part in the second held in May 1950. The results were: pro-government—Taehan Nationalist Party 24, Taehan Youth Corps 10, National Society 12, Federation of Korean Trade Unions 2, others 9, total 57; opposition—Democratic Nationalist Party 23, Socialist Party 2, People's Independence League 1, total 26; independent—127.

With the outbreak of war on June 25, 1950, a total of 35 Assemblymen were either killed or kidnapped by the Communists, and the political line-up in the Assembly in the wartime capital of Pusan was: pro-government —New Political Compatriot Association headed by Pak Sungha 70, Republican Club of Kim Tongsong 40; opposition—DNP 40, People's Friends' Association of Sin Kwanggyun 20; independents 9.

In May 1951, the Republican People's Political Association was born through the merger of the two pro-government political groups, controlling a majority of 108 seats in the Assembly. Meanwhile, non DNP elements in the Assembly started a movement to organize a new political party to oppose the Democratic Nationalist Party. This movement received strong momentum after President Rhee issued a statement supporting a new party on August 15, 1951.

The Rhee statement expedited organization of a new political party among his supporters within the Assembly, and, at the same time, encouraged his followers outside the Assembly to form their own new political group. These two groups eventually failed to compromise and in December the former founded a Liberal Party, while the latter also organized a political party with the same name. Kim Tongsong and Yi Kapsong led the new party in the Assembly, while Yi Pomsok, head of the National Youth Corps, became the number-two man in the latter group, next to Rhee.

In April 1952, political turmoil broke over the question of constitutional amendment bills, but Prime Minister Chang Taeksang, with the support of the Liberals in and outside the Assembly, passed a compromise amendment bill with a command of 103 Assembly seats, thus ending a serious political crisis.

A factional strife developed within the unified Liberal Party between former members of the National Youth Corps and other groups in 1953. The intra-party struggle ended in September with the ouster of the Youth Corps elements from the party.

Third-Term Assembly

The May 20, 1954 general elections saw official candidates of the two major parties, the Liberals and Nationalist Democrats, vie for the first time under nationwide party influence. The results: Liberals 116, DNP 15, Taehan Nationalist Party 3, independent 69, others 3.

In November 1954, another political crisis developed when the ruling Liberal Party declared a constitutional amendment bill passed with 135 votes out of 203. A bitter controversy followed the passage as to whether 135 could be regarded as a minimum two-thirds of 203 required for passage of constitutional amendments. The controversy induced 12 Liberals to desert the party, but the party strength was again increased to 136 in early 1956 by absorbing some independents.

Meanwhile, the opposition, with the Democrats as the backbone, mustered over 60 Assemblymen to form a new political group within the Assembly after the political turmoil—the Compatriots' Association for Defending the Constitution. The group, in December 1954, formed a seven-man committee to organize a new party. The committee soon increased to ten members, and planned to embrace in the proposed new party elements of the Democratic Nationalist Party led by P. H. Shinicky, Chough Pyongok and Kim Chunyon, the Hungsadan and Catholics led by John M. Chang, progressives led by Cho Pongam, independent Assemblymen led by Chang Taeksang and Kwak Sanghun, Taehan Women's Association led by Pak Sunchon, and Chosun Democratic Party led by Han Kunjo.

The new party movement, however, soon encountered difficulties in coordinating political philosophies between the conservative faction and the progressive group and a new party, Democratic Party, was formed in September 1955 by elements of the Democratic Nationalist Party, Hungsadan and some independent groups. Cho Pongam, who could not join the new party, later formed his own Progressive Party in November 1956. In October 1957, Kim Chunyon and Pak Yongjong defected from the Democratic Party, and formed the Unity Party with the former as head.

Cho Pongam's Progressive Party was officially organized in November 1956, but the Party's "peaceful unification" theory was found unlawful and he and over ten party leaders were arrested in January 1958. The Party subsequently was outlawed by the government in February and Cho executed the follwing year.

Present

In the May 2, 1958 general elections, the Liberals won 126 seats, Democrats 79, Unity 1, and independents 27. The main features of the elections were the Liberals' general victory by winning a majority in the Assembly, the Democrats' surprising increase in seats by winning urban districts, decrease of independents and minor party members, nine non-competition districts, and a flood of election suits which followed.

A total of 112 lawsuits were filed after the election, and by September 1959, 98 cases were disposed, with nullification of the election results in five districts, partial nullification in two districts, and reversals in three.

In the ruling Liberal Party, Lee Ki-poong has strengthened his leadership, becoming a power only next to Party President Rhee. Under him, two intra-party groups were formed—one led by so-called extremists Im Cholho and Chang Kyonggun, and the other by moderate Yi Chaehak and Han Hisok.

The opposition Democrats won the vice-presidency in the 1956 presidential elections, and also increased its Assembly strength to 79, enough to hold one-third of the total number of seats in May 1958. The party, however, underwent a serious intra-party struggle in connection with the party's presidential nominations between two factions, one supporting Chough Pyongok, the other John M. Chang. The party is now ruled by a five-man supreme committee headed by Chough. The four others are Chang, Kwak Sanghun, Paek Namhun and Pak Sunchon.

The Unity Party won only one seat in the 1958 general election. It has announced that party chairman Kim Chunyon will run for Vice-President in 1960 but that it will support Rhee for the Presidency.

The Democratic Reformist Party led by Sin Suk and the Labor-Farmer Party of Chon Chinhan, both organized in October 1957, were completely beaten by the two major parties in the 1958 elections. They later issued a joint statement calling for emergence of a third political party, but have found little popular reaction.

There are such minor parties as the Independent Labor Party led by Yu Rim, the Chosun Democratic Party led by Kim Pyongyon and the Taehan Women's Nationalist Party led by Louise Yim but they are not actually functioning as national parties.

Election

Presidential Elections

The first presidential and vice-presidential elections were held on July 20, 1948 in a plenary session of the National Assembly by Assembly members.

Syngman Rhee was elected as the first President by 180 votes out of 197, while Yi Siyong won 133 votes for the Vice-Presidency.

The second presidential elections were held on August 5, 1952 through popular vote in accordance with the constitutional changes made earlier.

Out of a total of 8,259,428 voters, 7,275,883 took part in the election. Dr. Rhee was re-elected by polling nearly 80 percent of the total ballots cast, defeating three other presidential candidates. Besides Rhee, Yi Siyong, Hugh Cynn and Cho Pongam ran.

Ham Taeyong was elected Vice-President

out of nine candidates. The eight other were Yi Pomsok, Cough Pyongok, Yi Yunyong, Yi Kapsong, Chon Chinhan, Louise Yim, Paek Songuk and Chong Kiwon.

In the third presidential elections held on May 15, 1956, the Liberal Party supported Dr. Rhee and Lee Ki-poong as presidential and vice-presidential candidates, while the Democratic Party named P. H. Shinicky and Dr. John M. Chang as its standard-bearers. Shinicky, however, died on May 5 while on a campaign tour. This left Cho Pongam of the Progressive Party, as Rhee's only opponent.

Some 86 percent of the total 9,606,870 eligible voters participated in the election.

Rhee and Chang were elected as President and Vice-President respectively. Rhee polled 5,046,437, some 56 percent of the total votes cast, while Chang won 4,012,654 against Lee's 3,805,502.

Assembly Elections

First Term. The first general elections were held on May 10, 1948 under a United Nation's resolution passed on November 14, 1947. Some 7,800,000 Koreans registered for balloting out of an estimated 8,130,000 eligible, and 7,480,000 took part in the first elections to elect 198 National Assemblymen.

Second Term. A total of 2,230 candidates campaigned for 210 seats throughout the country with an average competitive rate of 11 to 1. This compared with the 5 to 1 rate in the first elections, and the 6 to 1 in the third elections in 1954.

Third Term. Over 90 percent of the total voters participated in the third general elections held on May 20, 1954. The Liberals won 114, the Democratic Nationalist Party 15, Independents 67 and others 7 for a total of 203 seats in the Assembly.

Fourth Term. In the forth general elections held on May 2, 1958, 9,840,655 took part out of 10,164,428 eligible voters. Excluding some 320,000 voters in nine districs where candidates were unopposed, this meant 90.6 percent of the total voters cast their vallots. The Liberals won 126, Democrats 79, Unity Party 1, and independents 27 for a total of 233. Through the elections, a real two-party system is considered to have taken shape for the first time in Korea.

Another feature of the fourth general elections was that the ruling Liberal Party won its seats largely in rural areas, while the opposition Democratic Party overwhelmed the Liberals in urban areas. This was not because the party planks of the two parties had any particular appeals to the voters of the areas where they won, but was rather because of the fact that the urban dwellers were more critical of the administration and sentimentally sympathetic with the opposition.

The Liberals polled some 75 percent of the total votes cast in Kangwon-do and 68 percent in Chungchong Namdo, while the Democrats won 87.5 percent in Seoul.

Before the election, the Liberal Party conducted a series of negotiations with the Democrats with a view to revising the Election Law in order to install several new clauses insuring fair elections. Included were a public management system of election, measures to prevent election frauds and irregularities and a 500,000 hwan(1,000 dollars) deposit by each candidate to bar insincere candidacies.

The new Election Law was overwhelmingly passed on January 1, 1958 with the support, in the final stage, of Dr. Chough Pyongok, who represented the Democrats, and Chang Taeksang, representing the independent group, and was proclaimed on January 25.

The Liberal Party nominated 218 party candidates for the elections while the Democrats had 215 party nominees. Besides the two major parties, the Unity Party and the Labor-Farmer Party also had some candidates.

There were a total of 10,164,428 eligible voters, or 47.2 percent of the total population of 21,526, 344. Excluding 323,773 in the nine electoral districts where candidaters were unopposed, 90.6 percent of the total voters, that is 8.923,905 voters, took part in balloting, and only 916,750 abstained. The number of invalid votes was 347,148, or only 3.9 percent of the total ballots cast.

The Liberal Party had 126 elected, or 54.1 percent of its total candidates, the Democrats 79, or 33.9 percent, the Unity Party 1 with 0.4 percent and independents 27 with 11.7 percent.

By occupation, farmers topped with 31, followed by office workers 26, press and publication 9, lawyers 6, businessmen 3, industrial workers 3, education 2, medicine 2, brewery 2, mining 2, engineering 1, fishery 1, rice refinery 1, others 9, 38 had no permanent jobs.

In breakdown by age, there were 9 Assemblymen in the 30-34 age bracket, 39— (35-39), 46— (40-44), 55— (45-49), 41— (50-54), 24— (55-59), 19— (60-64). None was over 65.

The breakdown by education showed that 134 were college graduates, 79 had high school education, 19 primary school education. 1 was self-taught.

The average number of votes polled by a successful candidate was: Liberal 15,937, Democrat 19,585, Unity 22,219, independent 15,912, and the overall average 19,338.

The average age of the Assemblymen was 46, with the highest 64 and lowest 30.

After the elections were over, prosecutors, offices investigated a total of 1,065 cases of alleged election irregularities, but of these, only 79 were officially indicted.

Summary of Present Election Laws

There are four laws governing elections on various levels. They are the Presidential and Vice-Presidential Election Law, the House of Councillors' Election Law, the House of Representatives' Election Law, and the Local Autonomy Law which governs local council elections. The law for House of Councillors' election, however, has not yet been enforced.

A) Voting right and eligibility

Any one who is over 21 years of age can vote in elections. This is applied to elections at any level, but in local council elections one must reside in a certain area for over six months to acquire the voting right in the particular election.

Anyone over 25, unless he falls under the categories specified by law, has the right to run in the House of Representatives' and local council elections, and anyone over 35 can do so in the House of Councillors' elections. To be eligible for running in presidential elections, one must be over 40 and have residence in the country for more than three years.

B) Election district

In the House of Representatives' election, each county, or city having up to 150,000 men can elect one member, and in case a county or city has more than 150,000 men, it can have another district for each additional 100,000 men. At present, there are 233 election districts in South Korea—16 in Seoul, 25 in Kyonggi-do, 13 in Chungchong Pukto, 22 in Chungchong Namdo, 24 in Cholla Pukto, 32 in Cholla Namdo, 38 in Kyongsang Pukto, 40 in Kyongsang Namdo, 20 in Kangwon-do, and 3 in Cheju-do.

In the presidential election, the entire nation constitutes only one election district, while districts for the House of Councillors' election have not been decided yet.

C) Voting district

One or more voting districts may be established in each "dong," "ri," "op" and "myon." This applies to all national and local elections.

D) Vote-counting district

To insure secrecy in balloting, the vote-counting district does not coincide with the balloting district, but all the ballots cast are taken to the election committee of the election district and tabulation is made there.

In the presidential election, one vote-counting district is set up in each city and county, while cities having more than 300,000 men can have more than one vote-counting places.

E) Election committees

Election committees are independent organizations that administer elections and judge whether election laws are rightfully enforced.

There is a Central Election Committee in Seoul with nine members, and each province, including Seoul City, has a provincial election committee with seven members. Under the provincial committees are local district election committees, one in each election district, also with seven members, and voting district election committees with five members. There also is an election committee in each 'city,' 'op' or 'myon' with seven members.

In each election committee, the number of committee members belonging to one political party cannot exceed one third of the total number. The term of each member is four years.

F) Candidacy

According to the House of Representatives' Election Law, any candidate must apply for registration as a candidate at the district election committee attaching a letter of recommendation signed by over 100 but not more than 200 voters.

One cannot run in both national and local elections at the same time, and any government employee or member of an election committee must resign, if he wishes to run in an election, no later than 180 days before the term of the incumbent expires.

A candidate must deposit 500,000 hwan at the election committee concerned.

G) Election campaign

The House of Representatives' Election Law provides various restrictions or prohibitions in conducting an election campaign. Following are summarized items:

(1) An election campaign may be carried out from the day when a candidate shall have registered his candidacy at the election committee and until the day before election day.

(2) Those who are not candidates or registered election campaign workers shall not engage in election campaigns.

(3) A candidate may have one campaign worker per 1,500 heads in his district. Campaign workers must carry certificates issued by the election committee.

(4) Students and minors are excluded as campaign workers.

(5) A candidate may print one poster per 50 heads in his district, and an additional 50 posters per one campaign speech rally.

(6) A candidate may distribute small-size leaflets bearing his name.

(7) A candidate may distribute leaflets, with his background data, platforms and greetings printed, to each household twice.

(8) A candidate may have signboards, placards and other campaign signs of standard form.

(9) During the campaign period, publications, dramas, movies, and other advertisements supporting or discrediting any particular candidate or party are prohibited.

(10) A candidate may use one loudspeaker and two campaign cars.

(11) A candidate may run only one newspaper advertisement.

(12) Campaign speeches are prohibited from 10 p.m. to 6 a.m.

(13) An election campaign shall not be allowed before the specified campaign period.

(14) No person shall receive contributions from foreigners or foreign organizations in connection with elections.

(15) The Central Election Committee decides the maximum amount of expenses to be allowed for each campaign worker.

H) Election lawsuit

The election law provides two kinds of lawsuit concerning elections. One is to challenge the legality of an election in general, and the other is to challenge the legality of the election committee's pronouncement of the successful candidate.

If any candidate or voter has complaints about the legality of an election, he can file a lawsuit at the Supreme Court against the chairman of the election committee concerned within 30 days of the election day.

If any candidate has objection to the return of a candidate he opposed, he may file a lawsuit against the successful opponent at the Supreme Court within 30 days of the announcement of the election results.

The Supreme Court can then nullify the result of an election when it finds that there were enough violations of the election laws to affect the election result.

Legislature

Development of Modern Parliamentary System in Korea

A modern Western-style parliamentary system was instituted in Korea only after the end of the second world war. Following the first general election in Korea on May 10, 1948, the Constituent Assembly was first convened on May 31, 1948, and three more general elections have been held since.

The Constituent Assembly elected Dr. Syngman Rhee as its first Chairman by an overwhelming vote of 188. In his opening address, Dr. Rhee said that the Asembly would maintain the spirit of the Korean Provisional Government established in Shanghai after the 1919 independence movement, that an election should be held as soon as possible in north Korea to fill the 100 seats left vacant in the Assembly, and that the American forces should remain in south Korea until the organization of new Korean armed forces.

The first tasks facing the Assembly were to institute a Constitution and a National Assembly Law.

To begin with, the Assembly first chose 10 Assemblymen representing each of the provinces. These in turn elected 15 persons to draft a National Assembly Law. The drafting committee submitted a 69-article draft to the plenary session, which passed it without revisions on condition that it be subject to changes so as not to conflict with the Constitution to be promulgated.

When the Assembly wanted to organize standing committees according to Article 16 of the Assembly Law, the lawmakers were confronted with a problem: who was to promulgate the Assembly Law and make it official. The question was resolved under an Assembly resolution that the Assembly Chairman shall promulgate any law by signing it until a Constitution is instituted.

To work on a draft Constitution, the Assembly elected ten Assemblymen, who in turn chose 30 persons as members of the Constitution Drafting Committee.

The drafting committee first planned to adopt a parliamentary cabinet and bicameral systems. The Korean Democratic Party, which at the time had a dominating influence in political circles, chiefly advocated and pushed through these two ideas. But Chairman Rhee was opposed to these ideas and, after a total of 16 meetings, the drafting committee resolved to adopt a presidential cabinet and unicameral systems.

The final draft, however, included some features of the parliamentary cabinet system, too, and it was passed at the 28th plenary session of the Assembly. The Constitution was finally put into force on July 17, 1948.

As Dr. Rhee was elected first President of the nation, the Assembly elected P.H. Shinicky to replace Rhee and also elected Kim Yaksu as Vice-Chairman.

Constitutional Amendments

Shortly before the two-year term of the Constituent Assembly members was to expire, 78 members, directly or indirectly affiliated with the Korean Democratic Party, proposed a constitutional amendment bill to adopt a genuine parliamentary cabinet system, but the bill was consequently defeated in the Assembly.

In November 1951, the Administration, in the wartime capital of Pusan, proposed a constitutional amendment bill to institute a bicameral system, but this one was also eventually defeated in the Assembly.

In April, 1952, a group of lawmakers proposed a constitutional amendment bill, which included a parliamentary cabinet system instead of the presidential cabinet system and a unicameral system with limited non-confidence power against administration. To this, the Administration submitted a counterproposal which included popular election of the President and a bicameral system. Over these two constitutional amendment bills, the Administration and Legislature clashed so severely that a serious political crisis developed.

Through a series of negotiations between the two parties, a compromise bill was drafted and passed by the Assembly. Under the revisions made to the Constitution, a bicameral system and popular election of the President as proposed by the Administration were established, while the Legislature was given the right to submit non-confidence motions against individual cabinet members.

On January 23, 1953, the Administration proposed a constitutional amendment bill allegedly to change the rather state-controlled economic system into a more liberal economic set-up. The proposal provoked another controversy. While the lawmakers were almost equally divided into pros and cons, the Administration withdrew its proposed bill without putting it to a vote.

On September 8, 1954, the ruling Liberal Party, with the support of 136 Assemblymen, introduced a constitutional amendment bill enabling the first President to run for more than two terms and abolishing the Prime Minister's post from the cabinet.

The bill, put to a vote on November 27, 1954, appeared at first to have been defeated with a vote of 135 to 60 with seven abstentions out of the 203 Assembly seats. Two days later, however, the Liberals proclaimed the bill passed, claiming the minimum two-thirds votes out of 203 to be 135, thus reversing the earlier Assembly pronouncement that the bill has been killed.

Summary of Present Parliamentary System

Organization of Assembly

As provided for the National Assembly consists of a House of Councillors and a House of Representatives. Under the present law, the former comprises 76 seats, while the latter has 233 seats. The term of office for Councillors is six years, with one half of the members to be elected every three years, while the term for the lower house is four years.

The Vice-President is to preside over the House of Councillors, and over any joint Assembly session that may be convened.

The Speaker of the lower house and two Vice-Speakers of each house are elected by members for a two-year term.

Each house is to have standing committees as specified by law to study legislative matters in their respective fields, when special legislative matters come up, special committees are to be formed.

Each house is also to have "negotiating groups" to achieve coordination among the different political groups on legislative functions.

The Assembly is to have a secretariat to take care of clerical matters, legislative data, publications, reference library, etc.

Members

Members of the National Assembly are held responsible only by the Assembly for statements or votes made within the Assembly. (Art. 50, Constitution)

During sessions of the Assembly, no member shall be arrested or detained without the consent of the House of which he is a member except in case of flagrante delicto. Even if a member has been arrested before the opening of a session, he shall be released during the session upon the request of the house to which he belongs.

Members of the Assembly shall receive

adequate compensation and travel expenses and may travel on government-owned trains, ships and airplanes free of charge.

No Assembly member can hold any national or local public office except for Cabinet posts, or otherwise provided by law.

Assembly members are forbidden to insult any citizen or refer to the private life of any in the Assembly.

Powers of Assembly

The Assembly has the right to enact laws, revise the Constitution, study the budget, inspect the administration, confirm presidential emergency measures, ratify treaties, approve issuance of national bonds,—review a statement of state accounts, impeach the President, Vice-President, Cabinet members, Justice and other officials provided by law, review qualifications of members and take disciplinary measures against members.

The House of Councillors has the right to consent to the appointment of Justices, Ambassadors, Ministers, the Prosecutor-General, the Chairman of the Board of Audit, and other officials designated by law.

The House of Representatives has the right to vote a non-confidence motion against individual Cabinet members.

Recommendations of Assembly

Resolutions by the Assembly on the national administration should be sent to the executive branch, but the executive branch shall have discretion to adopt or reject Assembly recommendations, and they shall have no conforming power upon the administration.

Standing Committees

The term of members of Assembly standing committees shall be one year.

All bills must be referred to competent committees for study, except when the Assembly decides otherwise by resolution.

The present standing committees of the House of Representatives:

Committee on Legislation and Justice, Committee on Home Affairs, Committee on Foreign Affairs, Committee on National Defense, Committee on Budget and Audit, Committee on Finance and Economy, Committee on Reconstruction, Committee on Agriculture and Forestry, Committee on Commerce and Industry, Committee on Education, Committee on Public Health and Social Welfare, Committee on Communication and Transportation, Committee on Discipline and Qualification, and Committee on Steering (14).

Committees can appoint a special professional staff to assist members. They may participate in committee hearings, and at the request of the Speaker, may also express views at the plenary session.

Assembly Sessions

The Assembly shall have regular and extraordinary sessions. The regular session begins September 1 every year, while special sessions shall be convened upon the request of either the President, one-fourth or more of the Representatives for the lower house, and more than one half of the Councillors for the upper house.

The first special session immediately following a general election shall be convened within ten days after the terms of new members begin.

The term of a regular session shall be 90 days, and that of a special session not more than 30 days, but terms may be extended by Assembly resolution.

A majority shall constitute a quorum for a session and a majority vote of the members attending is necessary for legislative action unless otherwise provided by law.

Introduction of Bill and Legislative Procedures

A bill may be introduced by any member with the support of not less than ten members. A bill must be studied by competent committees, and reviewed by the Committee on Legislation and Justice before it is reported to a plenary session. The Assembly must act on it through three readings. Readings may be shortened or omitted by Assembly resolution,

Relationship of the Houses

The House of Representatives has priority in examining a budget bill. A bill killed in the lower house must not be sent to the upper house. In case a bill is not adopted within 60 days, excluding adjournments, after it has been sent by one house to the other, the house which sent the bill may consider the bill rejected by the other.

A joint Assembly session may be called to iron out the differences between the two houses in case each house has a different version from the other on a same subject.

Relationship with Executive Branch

Bills passed by the Assembly shall be sent to the Executive Branch and the President must promulgate them within 15 days. He also has the right to veto them.

Representatives can pass non-confidence resolutions against individual cabinet members, while cabinet members may attend Assembly sessions to answer questions and state their views.

The Assembly may request cabinet members to attend sessions for interpellations. The Assembly may also request executive offices to make their publications available.

Judicial Organization

General Introduction

Under the Constitution of the Republic of Korea which is based upon the principle of mutual independence of the legislature, the executive and the judicature, the judicial branch enjoys a strictly independent position apart from other state powers.

In addition, the court has the right to ask for convention of the Constitution Committee to determine the constitutionality of any law in case its constitutionality is in question, and the Supreme Court has the privilige to join in the Constitution Committee. Therefore, it may be said that the Republic of Korea's judicial branch is in a rather superior position compared with the other two branches.

Under the Constitution, the court has jurisdiction over civil, criminal and administrative trials, and has the right to request study of the constitutionality of a law as well as to take part in the Constitution Committee.

Organization of Court

The nation's highest court is the Supreme Court; under this are the Appellate and District Courts. Therefore, any legal case may go through three stages—a District Court, Appellate Court, Supreme Court.

Supreme Court

The Supreme Court consists of no more than nine Justices, including the Chief Justice, and no more than eleven judges. It comprises three departments—Civil, Criminal and Special.

A legal case before the Supreme Court is handled by a five-man collegiate court, including one Justice, but important cases are handled by a collegiate court comprising only Justices.

In case a new interpretation of a law other than what has been offered previously is deemed necessary, a special court consisting of all Justices and all judges concerned is convened for joint judgment on the case in question, with two-thirds of the component members required to constitute a quorum in the collegiate judgment.

The Supreme Court being the nation's highest court, it gives out the final verdict on any legal case. That is, it takes care of appeals for retrial of any legal cases disposed of by lower courts, and appeals for retrial of any military tribunal case.

The interpretation of any law given in a verdict by the Supreme Court supersedes that of a lower court concerning the same case.

The Chief Justice supervises general administration of the Supreme Court and court administration of lower courts. The Office of Court Administration is attached to the Supreme Court to take care of general court administration.

Appellate Court

An Appellate Court consists of the President and a specified number of judges.

An Appellate Court comprises three departments—Civil, Criminal and Special.

Any legal case before an Apellate Court is tried at a three-judge collegiate court.

An Appellate Court gives judgment on appealed cases against the decisions of lower courts and complaints lower court orders.

District Court

The lowest level of trial are the District Courts.

A District Court consists of President of a District Court and a specified number of judges.

A District Court may have branch courts within its area of jurisdiction.

A District Court Comprises a civil department and a criminal department.

Any cases before a District Court is tried by a single judge; when a collegiate judgment is necessary, a three-judge collegiate court is convened.

The President of a District Court may empower his judges to travel through his area of jurisdiction, when necessary, to try minor offenses. The accused in any summary court by a circular judge can request formal trial at the District Court within seven days of the verdict.

Justices and Judges

Qualifications

According to a provision of the Constitution, the Court Organization Law has laid out the qualifications for Justices and Judges. The purpose of the provision is to secure qualified persons as judges and also to assure the independence of the judicial branch by eliminating possible interventions by the administrative branch in appointing judges.

The law specifies the qualifications for judicial officials as follows:

A) Justices of the Supreme Court and judges presiding over Appellate Courts must have served for more than ten years as follows:

(1) Judge, prosecutor or lawyer.

(2) The qualifications of a judge, prosecutor, or Law Practice (with due qualifications of judgeship or attorneyship) at the Secretariats of the National Assembly, Ministry of Justice, Ministry of National Defense, Office of Court Administration, or Office of Legislation.

(3) Professor (with due qualifications of judgeship or attorneyship) at publicly authorized law colleges.

B) Judges of the Supreme Court, judges presiding over District Courts and chiefs of department of Appellate Courts must have served for more than five years in any of the positions listed above. Judges of Appellate Courts and chiefs of department of District Courts must have served more than three years in similar positions.

C) Qualifications for District Court judgeship are:

(1) Judicial probationers who have passed a formal examination after practicing the regular subjects for more than one year.

(2) Persons who are qualified to be prosecutors or lawyers.

(3) Persons who, with due qualifications to serve as a judicial probationer or in superior offices, have practiced law more than

two years at the Secretariat of the National Assembly, Ministry of Justice, Ministry of National Defense, Office of Court Administration or Office of Legislation.

(4) Persons who, with due qualifications to serve as a judicial probationer or in superior offices, have taught as professor or assistant professor at publicly authorized law colleges.

Appointment of Judges

The President appoints the Chief Justice of the Supreme Court at the recommendation of the Judicial Council, subject to confirmation of the National Assembly. Appointment of a Justice by the President through the same procedure is subject to confirmation of the House of Councillors. Judges are appointed by the President at the recommendation of the Chief Justice by resolution of the Justices' Council.

Tenure of Judges

The tenure of juges is ten year, but judges can be reappointed. The retirement age for the Chief Justice is 70; for other judges, it is 65.

Right of Court to Review Law

The Supreme Court has the authority to review any order, ordinance or administrative action to determine its contsitutionality, while any court can ask the Constitution Committee to determine the constitutionality of any law.

The Constitution Committee consists of the Vice-President, five Justices, and five members of the National Assembly.

Government Organization

Central Government Organization

The Constitution of the Republic of Korea, promulgated in 1948, adopted a presidential system patterned after that of the United States, with some features of the British-style parliamentary cabinet system added to it. Also influenced by the Nationalist Chinese Constitution, the Inspection Committee and the Civil Service Committee were established as independent government agencies directly responsible to the President.

The President

The President of the Republic of Korea is a constitutional organ heading the executive branch, and as such, represents the Republic in relations with foreign nations.

Article 2 of the Government Organization Law, promulgated on July 17, 1948 as the first law of the Republic, provides that "the President, as the head of the Executive Branch, shall direct and control all organizations of the Executive Branch in accordance with laws and regulations, and may suspend or repeal administrative orders or dispositions of the Cabinet Ministers in case such orders or dispositions are deemed improper or illegal."

The President was first elected by the National Assembly, but since the first constitutional amendment made in 1952, has been elected by universal, equal, direct, and secret vote of the people.

State Council (Cabinet)

The State Council is a collegiate body composed of the President and members of the State Council and is the organ that approves important state policies on matters within the scope of the powers of the President. Decisions of the Council are made by majority vote.

The original Constitution provided for a Prime Minister who served as vice-chairman of the State Council and had the right to recommend appointments and dismissals of members of the State Council to the President, but the premiership was abolished by adoption of the second constitutional amendment in 1954. Instead, the Minister of Foreign Affairs, as the senior member of the State Council as provided in the Government Organization Law, coordinates and exercises general control over all matters referred to the meetings of the State Council.

Ministers of Executive Branch

Heads of the Ministries of the Executive Branch are appointed by the President from among the members of the State Council.

There used to be twelve ministers—Home Affairs, Foreign Affairs, National Defense, Finance, Justice, Education, Agriculture and Forestry, Commerce and Industry, Social Affairs, Health, Transportation, and Communications. The second constitutional amendment merged the Ministries of Social Affairs and Health into a single ministry of Health and Social Affairs, while establishing a new Ministry of Reconstruction, for the same total number of 12 ministries.

Under the Constitution and the Government Organization Law, each Minister can issue "Ministry Orders" concerning matters within the scope of his powers and duties, control and supervise his subordinate officials, and take various administrative actions.

Each Ministry has a Vice-Minister, Bureaus and Sections.

In addition to the twelve Ministries, there are the Office of Public Information, Office of Legislation and the General Affairs Bureau of the State Council under the direct supervision of the President.

The Civil Service Committee, established under the original Constitution, has been reorganized as the civil service section under the General Affairs Bureau, and the Inspection Committee, which was charged with supervision over government officials, has been abolished.

Board of Audit

The Board of Audit is a collegiate administrative organ to inspect and supervise the settlement of the national revenue and expenditure by various organs of the Government.

The Board of Audit is under the direct supervision of the President, and has an independent position in carrying out its duties against members of the State Council.

The collegiate body of Auditors is composed of no more than seven officials including Director and Deputy Director.

Local Government Organization

Local administrative organs exercise administrative authorities over specified local areas under the supervision of central administrative organs. They are largely divided into two categories of ordinary local organs and special local organs. The former means general administrative offices such as provincial and county governments, while the latter includes such specialized agencies as local monopoly bureaus, taxation bureaus and communications bureaus.

Mayor of Special City and Provincial Governor

The Mayor of Seoul Special City and Provincial Governors are the primary administrators of local government appointed by the President, and supervise general state administration in given districts.

The Mayor of Seoul and Provincial Governors can take various administrative actions as specified by law, and can issue Municipal or Provincial Regulations.

The Municipal Government of Seoul has six Bureaus of Home Affairs, Finance, Industry, Construction, Social Affairs, and Police, while Provincial Governments have four Bureaus of Home Affairs, Education and Social Affairs, Industry and Police. The only exception to this is Cheju-do which has only three Bureaus of General Affairs, Industry and Police.

Seoul City has a Deputy Mayor who assumes the duties of the Mayor in case the latter is unable to perform his duties. In Provincial Governments, Directors of the Home Affairs Bureau act for Governors in such cases except in Cheju-Jo where the Director of General Affairs Bureau does so.

County Chiefs and Ward Chiefs

County (gun) Chiefs are appointed by the President at the recommendation of Provincial Governors, and exercise administrative authority over respective 'gun' (county). Ward (ku) offices are established in cities having more than a 500,000 population, and ward chiefs are also appointed by the President.

Chiefs of Police Stations

A Police Station is established in each city, ward, or county with a police superintendent or captain as its chief to take care of security, public hygiene, military conscription and other police affairs. The President can establish police stations in specially designated districts other than aforementioned.

The President can also designate special administrative areas where Fire Stations are to be established to handle fire fighting and other relative matters in designated areas.

Chiefs of Dong and Ri

Chiefs of "dong" or "ri" (lowest administrative district) are not administrative officials but are organs to assist chiefs of local autonomous organs.

Local Autonomous Organs

The local autonomous system in the Republic of Korea originates in Articles 96 and 98 of the Constitution and the Local Autonomy Law.

The local autonomy system was put into operation in 1952 when the first local elections were held under the autonomy law.

Local autonomous organs include the governments of Seoul City and Provinces, those of cities and towns, and offices of education districts.

Various autonomous organs have councils whose members are elected under the Local Autonomy Law. Provincial councils must have a minimum of 20 councilmen for a population of up to 500,000, and the Seoul City Council a minimum of 35 for the first one million men. Other city councils have 15 for the first 100,000 men, "op" councils 13 for the first 30,000, and "myon" councils 11 for the first 10,000 men. Additional members are added as specified in law in proportion with the size of population exceeding the set minimums.

Local councils supervise general administration in respective areas and resolve upon administrative matters other than those which fall under the exclusive jurisdiction of the chiefs of concerned local autonomous organs.

Under the new Local Autonomy Law passed in December 1958, chiefs of local autonomous organs, namely mayors and "myon" chiefs, are appointed by the President or provincial governors. Mayors are appointed by the President at the recommendation of provincial governors, while chiefs of "op" and "myon" are appointed by provincial governors at the recommendation of "gun" (county) chiefs.

Police and Fire-Fighting

The Republic of Korea's police force is the National Police controlled by the central Government, local autonomous police forces are not allowed. Police duties not only cover the maintenance of public order but also include fire-fighting, traffic control, public hygiene, and some other lines.

The Bureau of Security, Ministry of Home Affairs, is charged with general police administration under the supervision of the Minister of Home Affairs.

In Seoul and local provinces, the Mayor

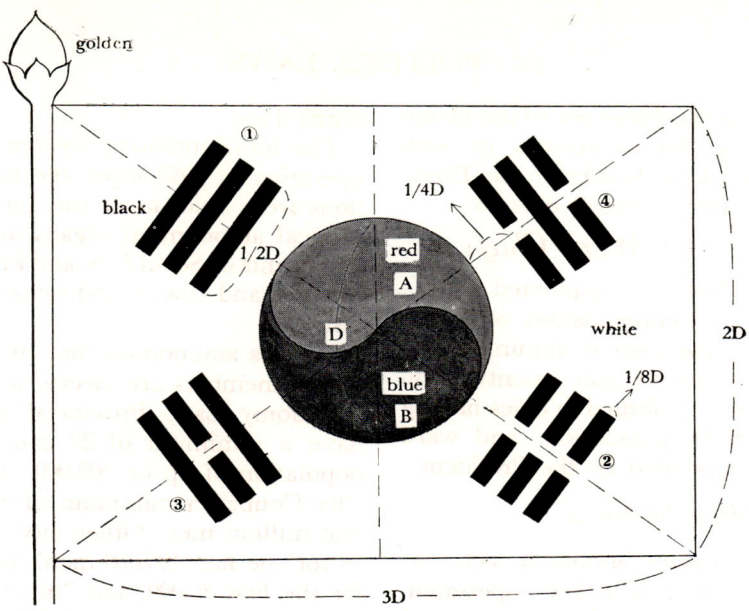

Symbol of Korean National Flag, the Taegukki (D is diameter of the circle)

A (Red): symbol of the sun and dignity.
B (Blue): symbol of male and hope.
① means heaven, spring, east and benevolence.
② means earth, summer, west and righteousness.
③ means sun, autumn, south and moral.
④ means moon, winter, north and wisdom.

The Taegukki
Enacted as the national flag of Korea in August, 1882.

↑ Declaration of Independence of the Republic of Korea
On August 15, 1948, the Republic of Korea was newly born as an independent free democratic nation. People are shown have congratulating themselves upon the epoch-making event.

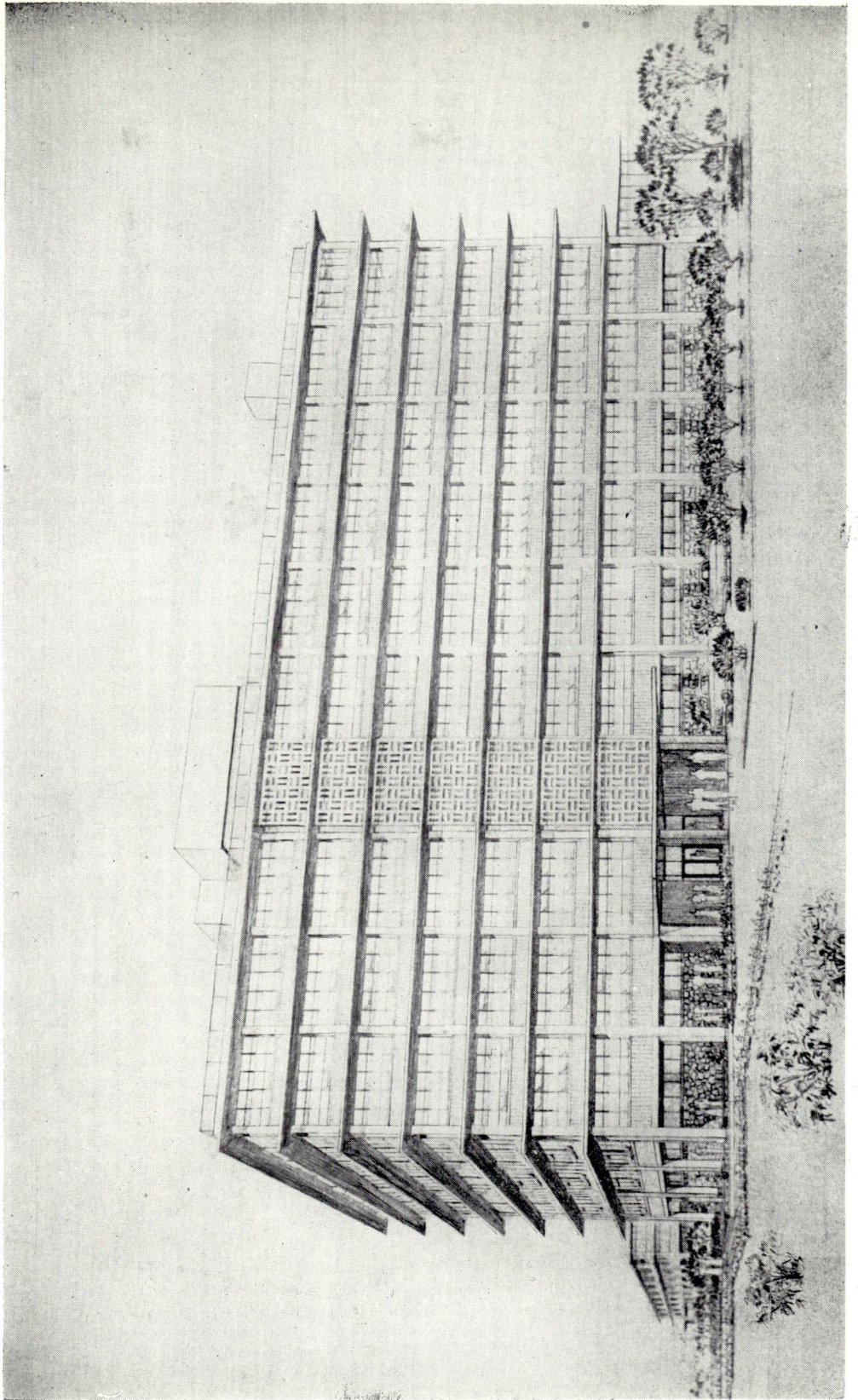

↑ Government Building

A model picture of an eight-storey government building with a two-storey attached building that is to be built in the center of Seoul, the capital city of Korea. According to the plan made by the Pacific and Engineers, an American contractor, Benell and Co., the successful bidder, will soon start the 17-month work at a cost of 2,057,234 dollars and 691,437,181 hwan, in Korean currency.

↑ **National Assembly Building**
 A model picture drawn according to plans for a new National Assembly building work on which was started in May, 1959. One of the highest buildings in the Far East (130m), this 24-storey structure will have 450 rooms. Planned by young Korean students who are studing in Tokyo now.

IV POLITICS, LAWS

and Provincial Governors supervise police administration in their respective areas with the assistance of Police Chiefs who head provincial police bureaus.

Police Stations are established in cities and counties, and under each police station are police sub-stations and police boxes.

Police officers are classified into six ranks —chief, superintendent, captain, lieutenant, sergeant, and private.

A National Institute for Scientific Criminal Investigation is attached to Police Headquarters in Seoul in order to conduct researches, identification of criminal evidence, autopsy, and the like.

National Police also have a police college to train police leaders and to give refresher courses for general police officers.

In case of emergency, military forces may take the place of police in maintaining public order under martial law declared by the president.

Under the general martial law, the martial law commander takes over administration concerning military and judicial affairs, while under the emergency martial law, the commander takes over the entire administration in the affected area and all the administrative or judicial organs come under his direct supervision.

Troops may also be called in to help police in maintaining public order in case of natural calamities or other emergencies.

Fire-fighting is part of the main police duties under the present system, and fire stations are established in cities and counties designated by the president.

At present, there are 24 such fire stations throughout the Republic, with four of them in the capital city.

In addition to these fire stations which are controlled by the National Police, there are volunteer fire-fighting units in all other cities and towns to cooperate with police officers in fighting fire and other natural disasters.

Decorations

There are three kinds of decoration awarded by the Republic of Korea. They are Orders, Medals of Merit, and Service Medals.

Orders

a) Grand Order of "Mugunghwa" (Rose of Sharon)

The highest decoration of the Republic of Korea, worn by the president, may also be awarded to chiefs of state of foreign nations. The Rose of Sharon is the national flower of Korea.

b) Order of Merit for National Foundation

This is awarded in recognition of outstandingly meritorious services rendered in foundation of the state. The order is classified into three categories: First, Second, and Third Grades.

c) Orders of Military Merit

These decorations are awarded to those who distinguish themselves with outstandingly meritorious military services, and are classified into four categories, each of the four being again broken down into three grades—Gold Star, Silver Star and No Star. The four are:

(1) Order of Military Merit "Taeguk"— highest grade military service decoration.

(2) Order of Military Merit "Ulchi"—second grade.

(3) Order of Military Merit "Chungmu" —third grade.

(4) Order of Military Merit "Hwarang" —fourth grade.

Therefore, the Order of Military Merit "Taeguk" with Gold Star is the highest of all military decorations.

d) Orders of Civil Merit

These are awarded to government employees who distinguish themselves with outstandingly meritorious services in their performance of duties and are classified into four categories—Blue Stripes, Yellow Stripes, Red Stripes and Green Stripes.

e) Orders of Cultural Merit

Awarded to Korean and foreign personnel in recognition of their outstandingly meritorious contributions to the fields of diplomatic service, military affairs, social relief, development of national economy, and other services rendered in the interest of the improvement of national welfare and productivity. The orders comprise three categories—Republic of Korea Medal, Presidential Medal and National Medal.

Medals for Merit

a) National Foundation Medal—awarded to those who render meritorious services in the national foundation.

b) Diligence Medal—awarded to government employees who render meritorious services within and beyond the call of duty.

c) Defense Medal—awarded to those who render meritorious services in the defense and security of the nation or to those who save the lives of others at the risk of their own.

d) Cultural Medal—awarded to distinguished men of education, arts or other cultural fields.

e) Public Welfare Medal—awarded to those who donate great sums to educational, welfare or public establishments.

f) Industrial Service Medal—awarded to those who make great contribution to industrial development of the nation.

g) Labor Medal—awarded to private office employees for meritorious service.

Service Medals

a) Special Medal for Wounded Veteran—awarded to disabled war veterans.

b) Medal for Wounded Veteran—awarded to wounded veterans.

c) Anti-Guerrilla Warfare Service Medal—awarded to participants in campaigns against Communist guerrillas before the Korean War.

d) Korean War Service Medal—awarded to those who served during the war.

e) Medal for Families of War-Dead—awarded to bereaved families of servicemen killed in action.

f) Medal for Bereaved Police Families—awarded to bereaved families of national policemen killed in action.

Brief History of Korean Laws

Unwritten

It can be generally assumed that there must have been some form of law to govern community activities in prehistoric Korea since it has been proven that there were primitive communities in those days. However, there are no evidences offering any detailed description of these ancient laws. The only clue may be obtained from the Chinese Classical history book, "Annals of the Three States; Chapter Wei," compiled A.D. 290, which mentions the customs and manners of ancient Korea. The book gives us a rough idea of what the law was like.

According to the classic, the tribes which then inhabited the northern part of the peninsula, namely Koguryo, Puyo, Okcho and Yemaek, had, in general, common customs and manners. Koguryo regarded the tenth month of the lunar calendar as the first month of the year, and, accordingly, proclaimed it a month for national celebration. Tribal leaders gathered for a nationwide convention during this month, and a special prayer to Heaven lasting several days constituted the main national ritual. Major offenses were tried at the convention and the guilty received capital punishment while their families were made slaves. There were no prisons. Regards marriages, a wedding was arranged after the bridegroom had paid a certain amount of goods and money to the bride's family and the newly-wedded man was required to live at his in-laws' house until a child was born.

In Puyo, thieves were ordered to make monetary restitution of the stolen article to 12 times the amount of value. Adultery was punished by death for both parties. A special feature was that a woman's jealousy was regarded as one of the worst crimes, and women found guilty of this offense were executed and their bodies abandoned without burial on mountaintops. If an elder brother died, his widow was married to his younger brother. Otherwise, Puyo's laws and customs were similar to Koguryo's as were Okcho's and Yernaek's.

There are no historical records concerning the three states of Mahan, Pyonhan and Chinhan, so nothing definite about their laws is known.

Chinese legal institutions were introduced to Korea along with all other Chinese forms of culture during the period of Lolang colonization (108 B.C.-A.D. 313).

Written

According to the first Korean history book, the *Samguk Sagi* compiled in 1145, the first written law in the peninsula was promulgated in 373 by King Sosurim, 17th king of the Koguryo dynasty. The text, however, has not been preserved, so we do not know the details of this law. According to a chapter on Korea in the Chinese historical book, old Tangshu, a man convicted for treason, was burnt to death by torches at a public congregation and his entire property confiscated by the state.

Other fragmentary provisions under the first Korean law, according to the Chinese classic, included the following: the death penalty was given to anyone who surrendered to the enemy by opening the gates of a castle or was responsible for the loss of a battle; thieves had to pay 12 times the value of stolen articles; persons allowing a horse or cow to die were made slaves.

In Paekche, the *Samguk Sagi* further tells us, to receive a bribe as a government official or to steal government property constituted a crime punishable by life imprisonment in addition to a fine amounting to three times the original amount or value involved.

In Silla, according to the same book, laws and regulations were promulgated in 520, and government employees classified. In 654, a 60-article criminal code was adopted and, in 758, two experts on law employed by the government. There could be no further doubt about the existence of written laws.

It is in the Koryo era, succeeding Silla in 918, that some systematic state laws and institutions were established for the first time. During the first year of its foundation, the Koryo dynasty was preoccupied with military and security affairs and had little time to pay any attention to proclaiming new laws and regulations. Therefore, the laws and regulations of the Silla dynasty were taken over intact by the new regime. By the following year, its position was more or less stabilized and the kingdom began to devise its own administrative system, among other things, revising the Silla laws. The revisions were modelled partly on the legal institutions of the Tang dynasty which was then reigning in China.

The series of changes undertaken over the ensuing years culminated in a major reform by King Songjong in the year, 982. There were further minor changes after this, but these were the result of powerful Mongol influences and did not offset the basic structure of 982. The reform instituted during Songjong's reign constitutes the backbone of the laws and institutions of the Koryo dynasty.

Koryo had a comprehensive 71-article code, covering various fields, including treason, thievery, marriage and household problems, government organization, and prisons. This was largely patterned after the general code of Tang, but the precise name of the author and the exact year of promulgation are not known. It is generally assumed that the code was enforced by Songjong.

The basic spirit of the criminal laws of Koryo lay in the fact that, on one hand, strict and adequate punishment was meted out for offenses already committed while, on the other, advance warnings were given to prevent crimes.

During the early years of the dynasty, the laws were strictly conformed to as intended, but gradually they were modified under the pressure of public opinion. Towards the end of the dynasty, a new code was compiled by Chong Mongju to replace the old but this was never put in force and the text is lost.

Among the government agencies which handled court and legal affairs were the *"uih yongdae"* and the *"sahondae."* The *"uih yongdae"* was established by the first king, Taejo, for criminal and civil trials. The *"sahondae"* was first established as an inspection agency in the reign of the sixth king, Songjong, but was also vested with some judicial powers. Both agencies underwent a number of changes but their basic functions remained the same.

There were five kinds of punishment under the Koryo laws: *"taehyong,"* *"changhyong,"* *"tohyong,"* *"yuhyong"* and *"sahyong."* The punishments, in that order, comprised one, 50 lashes; two, 50-100 lashes; three, 1-3 years' imprisonment; four, 800 1,200-kilometer distant banishment; and five, death by hanging or decapitation.

Yi Dynastic Laws

The laws and regulations of Koryo were generally adopted by the Yi dynasty in its early formative years. By the latter half of the 15th century, the new kingdom had completed its work of revision, the old laws constituting the basis of the reforms. The Yi was the first dynasty to undertake a systematic compilation of law thus ensuring the organization.

The first comprehensive code compiled was the *"Kyongje Yukchon"*, promulgated in 1394 by the Yi founder who, like the Koryo founder, was Taejo. This was a compilation of all existing laws and regulations, sorted into six major categories of administrative, finance, education and protocol, military, criminal, and engineering.

This original code was followed by another compilation of laws in 1415 by the third king, Taejong. This included the laws instituted after the compilation of the first code. The second one was revised in 1426 by the fourth king, Sejong.

As the number of new laws and regulations increased and the earlier codes proved to contain some shortcomings, King Sejo undertook the compilation of a new comprehensive code to include all the laws promulgated since the foundation of the dynasty. This was later known as the *"Kyongguk Taejon"*; many other codes were compiled subsequently, but this remained the basic code of the dynasty.

The *"Kyongguk Taejon,"* however, was not completed during the reign of King Sejo. Only two of the six major categories, finance and criminal, were completed while he was in power, the rest was completed in 1469 and finally promulgated in 1474 by his successor, King Songjong. Other major codes compiled since the promulgation of the *"Kyongguk Taejon"* include *"Taejon Soknok," "Sugyo Chimnok" "Sok Taejon," "Taejon Tongpyong," "Taejon Hoetong," "Mangi Yoram," "Chonyul Tongbo"* and *"Yukchon Chorye."*

The codes of the Ming dynasty in mainland China were adopted in most cases, and, unless otherwise stipulated by the government, Ming laws applied as they stood.

The criminal code of the Yi dynasty provided specific durations and procedures for preliminary investigation and indictment of a legal case; it also stipulated that the confession of an accused constituted the most important evidence in examining a judicial case. Theoretically, any case could go through court examination on three different levels, with a final review of important cases by the king. In addition, there were provisions to guarantee fair trial. However, it is very doubtful whether the officials concerned adhered to all these provisions in practice.

For over 400 years, the "*Kyongguk Taejon*" was observed as the nation's main code. It was discarded in 1894, when the so-called "*Kabo Reform*" was forced upon the state by Japanese militarists following their victory over China.

Although the reform was forcibly carried out by the Japanese with or without the consent of the Yi dynasty, it should be noted that this was the first importation of modern governmental and judicial systems into the hermit kingdom, which until then had been isolated from the outside world.

The triumphant Japanese drove out pro-Chinese reactionaries from the court and forced several reforms upon the government. One was a 14-article "*Hong Bom*" which was proclaimed in December of the eventful *Kabo* year. The new law stipulated, among other things, a national budget system, reforms in local government organization, legislative procedures, and employment of talented people. The *Kabo* reform was the first step in the modern reorganization of the government and legal system of the country. Administrative and judiciary organizations were patterned after those of the Japanese government, and made independent of one another. The various judicial institutions, such as courts and prosecutors' offices, were also organized and administered for the first time in Korean history under separate, independent laws.

Following the conclusion of the so-called second protocol between Korea and Japan, the nation became a protectorate of the Japanese government and more Japanese systems were imported. In 1910, Japan finally took over Korea as a colony.

Japanese Laws

The Japanese Government-General for Korea was established as the supreme administrative organ of the country and Japanese laws generally enforced over Korea. Save for the political provisions governing elections to the Japanese Diet, the law on administrative lawsuits, and laws concerning family relationships and inheritance rights, Japan's civil, criminal, commercial, civil procedure, criminal procedure, and other general codes were applied to the Korean people.

As these laws were originally patterned largely after the German school of the early 20th century, the Korean people, familiar only with Oriental judiciary systems for centuries, were confronted overnight by strange, new workings of law. However abrupt, there was little trouble in executing these modern laws since the people rapidly adapted themselves to the new legal set-up.

Under the Japanese rule in Korea, the Governor-General was vested with all powers except military administration. Therefore, there was no need of the separation of powers as under the modern system of government. Since the laws in Japan proper were also applied in Korea, there was no legislative organ separately established for this country. In case any special law was felt to be necessary for the Korean people only, the Governor-General instituted one with the approval of the Japanese Emperor. The Governor-General could also issue ordinances for general administration of the peninsula, while provincial governors were able to institute provincial ordinances to be put in force in respective administrative areas.

There were courts on three different levels —the highest court in Seoul, three appellate courts in Seoul, Pyongyang and Taegu respectively, and, under these, a great number of district courts. However, there was no stipulation on administrative lawsuit. All these court systems were put under the supervision of the Governor-General. Under the Japanese military system, a Korea Army was established with its headquarters in Seoul. The army had two infantry divisions, one brigade and two regiments. The Governor-General, however, had no authority over the military administration in Korea.

Current Laws

The Constitution of the Republic of Korea was drafted under the stresses of the acute "cold war" separation at the thirty-eighth parallel. It was drafted as the basis of government for all Korea but, in fact, was applicable only to the south. Eleven years later with a war in between, it remains, *de jure*, the Constitution for all Korea; *de facto*, only of the south.

The original draft of Dr. Yu Chino, President of Korea University, who drew up the Constitution provided for a parliamentary system patterned after the Weimar Constitution of Germany, but a presidential system replaced this during preliminary debate of the draft at the National Assembly in accordance with the then Chairman of the legislature, Dr. Syngman Rhee. With two amendments to the original constitution in 1952 and 1954, the power of the president was further strengthened.

In the 1952 amendment, the election of the president was lifted from the National Assembly as provided for in the original Constitution and extended to nationwide suffrage. The revision was made in the teeth of legislative opposition. The 1954 amendment abolished the constitutional premiership and offset the constitutional two-term limit imposed on the presidency by allowing the first head of state to run as many terms as he wished.

One other major feature of the 1952 amendment has yet to be realized. This was the provision for establishment of a bicameral system to replace the unicameral as provided for under the original Constitution. Elections to an upper senate body have not been held for several reasons.

The judiciary branch of government is made up of the Supreme Court in Seoul, three Appellate Courts in Seoul, Taegu and Kwangju respectively, and, under these, a number of District Courts. The Chief Justice of the Supreme Court is appointed by the president at the recommendation of the Council of Justice and with the confirmation of the National Assembly. Other Justices are also appointed by the president at the recommendation of this Council.

Although the Constitution provides for a final review of any court-martial cases by the Supreme Court, pertinent laws have not been instituted yet to carry out this clause. As a result, military personnel under the present system go through only one trial and the decision of the trial becomes final subject to review by higher officials.

Under the Korean Constitution, anyone is entitled to file an administrative suit against any decision or measure by an administrative organ. Thus, he can first file suit with the supervising office of the original agency concerned, and then, if this is not upheld, he can file another one with a Court of Appeals, and, in the last resort, bring the case before the Supreme Court for final decision. In other words, unlike France and Japan where separate administrative courts handle such cases, civil courts are charged with handling administrative suits in Korea after the Anglo-American systems.

When the Republic of Korea government was established in 1948, it decided to retain the former Japanese laws unless otherwise stipulated by the Constitution or resolved by the National Assembly. Therefore, some of the main Japanese codes are still effective. The government has tried to replace them with new laws and is still trying. So far the civil, criminal and criminal procedure codes have been substituted; the commercial and civil criminal codes have yet to be newly instituted.

It should be particularly noted that Korean laws are still largely patterned after the German, although her political system takes after the American. This is, perhaps, true in Japan and China as well. Under thirty-six years of Japanese rule, the Korean people adapted themselves to the German model and were so thoroughly saturated with the German concept of law that it is well-nigh impossible to change it, at least, for the time-being.

The April Revolution and the May Revolution

The popular uprising of April 1960 put an end to the reign of Dr. Syngman Rhee and the Liberal Party. Dr. Rhee's rule lasted 12 years beginning in July of 1948 when the Government of the Republic of Korea first came into being, until the student-led April uprising forced him to resign from the presidency. His 12 year-reign, including three years of war, was characterized by numerous political abuses and popular discontent. The nation calls the April uprising the "April Revolution."

A transitional government was formed under the leadership of Ho Chong to amend the constitution in favor of a new cabinet system. August 1960 saw the birth of a new cabinet with Dr. John M. Chang as Prime Minister. However, the Chang Cabinet proved to be as corrupt as the Rhee regime and even more incompetent. Political instability grew during Dr. Chang's short and incompetent rule.

In May 1961, the military staged a coup d'etat under the leadership of Maj. Gen. Pak Chonghui. All branches of the armed services announced their support immediately and a military junta was established with Lt. Gen. Chang Toyong as chairman. This is called the "May Revolution."

The military ruling body began to introduce drastic changes into the political, economic, and social spheres of the nation's life. The junta pledged to transfer power to new and conscientious politicians as soon as the revolutionary tasks had been fulfilled.

Historically on not a few occasions, Koreans have staged popular uprisings to have tehir demands met. For all that, the first occasion when their attempt met with success came only on April 19, 1960. There have been also many occasions in Korea's history when the military turned to politics and took over the power. However, no military group has ever staged a coup with the intention of turning over the rule to civilian control immediately upon completion of its self-announced mission of "political house-cleaning." The first military coup free of any political ambitions in Korean history came on May 16, this year. Though in the form of a military coup, the "May Revolution" was intended to fulfill the tasks of the "April Revolution" of the previous year, to establish a genuine democratic republic by solving the political crisis formed by internal corruption and external threats. In short, the May coup was a continuance of the April Revolution, providing the stage upon which to put into practice the April spirit.

The April Revolution

In order to triplicate his four-year term in the presidency, Dr. Syngman Rhee had to resort to various political abuses, including merciless oppression of political opponents and opposition parties. The nation had to go through violent trials whenever one Rhee term ended and a new one began.

The people's discontent and anger reached the limit with the illegal election of March 15, 1960 and exploded. In Taegu, students protested the illegal means employed by the Government in preparation for the March elections in a largescale demonstration on Feb. 28. It was the first non-government organized demonstration of the scale. Students in other cities followed suit in spontaneous demonstrations. On March 15, the day of the elections, the students and citizens of Masan staged violent anti-government street demonstrations to attack police and other government buildings. The fiercer the temper of these demonstrations, the more brutal the police oppression. The second largescale anti-government demonstration in Masan erupted on April 11. The avalanche of the demonstration hit Seoul and Pusan on the 18th of the same month. On the following day, demonstrators clashed head-on with the police in Seoul, Pusan, Kwangju, Taegu, Chongju, Inchon and Mokpo. On the same day, in Seoul, more than 30,000 demonstrators, spearheaded by college students marched on the Kyongmudae, the Presidential mansion, and over 100 were killed by police fire. The Government proclaimed martial law.

On the 25th, a group of 400 college professors marched the streets of Seoul under martial law demanding the resignation of President Syngman Rhee and new elections. Deeply stirred by the daring demonstration of the professors, the citizenry of Seoul rose in anti-government demonstrations of an unprecedented scale on the 26th to force Rhee's resignation. The President submitted his resignation to the legislature on the 27th. The barehanded general public had won against an armed regime.

A transitional government was formed after the downfall of Dr. Rhee. The transitional ruling body functioned under the premiership of Ho Chong. In order to put an end to the dictatorial power exerted by the President in accordance with public demand, the General Assembly changed the system of government, transferring the center of responsibility from President to Prime Minister through a constitutional amendment on May 16 and disbanded itself. A new National Assembly was convened on August 8 as the result of new National Assembly elections held on July 29. Posun Yun and John M. Chang were elected respectively to the presidency and premiership of the newly convened Assembly. A new Government was thus formed.

After the April Revolution

The April Revolution was fundamentally a spontaneous uprising of students and the public and so lacked organization. Consequently, there was no organized revolutionary force which could take over the political power after the old regime. The only discernible change was that the opposition party of the past was the ruling party of the present. The laws governing illegal profiteers and their assets were not enacted until as late as October. The laws, deemed by many as the barometer of the revolutionary conscience, were effected by reluctant hands and, as such, were considered but the minimum of the popular demands.

Constant inner rivalry of the new ruling Democratic Party finally resulted in splitting the party in two. There was no cessation of the struggle for power between the two new party formations even after the split, reducing governmental functions to a state of utter incompetence. The nation lost whatever illusion they first had in the new Democratic Government.

An aftermath of the April Revolution was abuses of freedom. This helped increase social instability already prevalent. Encouraged by the success of the mass demonstrations last April, numerous political groups staged demonstrations on a various scale in the hope that they would help achieve their various aims.

The press, too, suddenly found freedom after so long a period of oppression. Daily newspapers increased threefold in number and news services 30-fold. Many of the papers and wire services existed in name only and played ambiguous roles, harmful to the public. Another abuse of freedom was the appearance of political parties sympathetic to the Communist cause. Korea's greatest national aspiration is the unification of her divided homeland. Taking advantage of this national aspiration, the Communist regime in the north proposed the unification and neutralization of the land and the formation of a joint north-south confederation.

The anti-Cummunist sentiment of the nation was considerably weakened by the propaganda activities of Communist symphathizers who made the most of the nation's aspiration for a unified country and the strong appeal of the term, "peaceful unification." Had the trend persisted, the very existence of the ROK, a republic founded and preserved by the UN, would have been endangered. The Government of Prime Minister John M. Chang totally lacked the means to cope

↑ Nineteenth: "Down with Rhee!"
—Scene of Carnage

↓ Twenty-sixth: "Rhee Is Down! Victory Is Ours!"

↑ "Onward!"

↑ "Long Live Our Soldiers!"

↑ Brute Force

And Casualties ↓

↑ Doggedly They Press on

Proffessors Join in ↓

↓ Time for Order

↓ Children, As Well

↑　The People Triumph

←　Scuffle with Force

↓　The Oppressors Are Tried

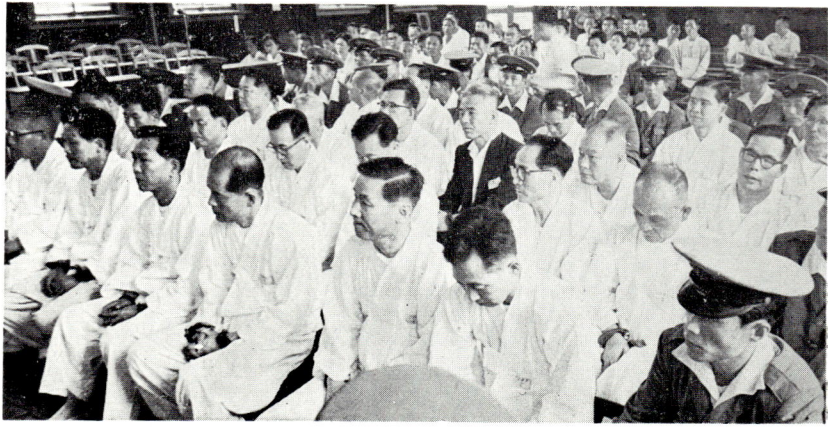

↑ Members of the new cabinet take oath of office

↓ Members of the Supreme Council for National Reconstruction

↑ Marines march on the capitol building on May 16

← Guard duty in a street corner after the coup

↑ War veterans support the coup

↓ Seoul's citizenry hear the news of the coup

↑ The birth of a national movement in support of the revolution

↓ Students march a street after the convention of the national movement

with the oncoming danger.

As lamentable as the utter incompetency of the Chang Cabinet was the fact that there was no opposition party capable of taking over the rule even if Chang were to step out. Over half the seats in the National Assembly were occupied by the ruling party. The strongest opposition was likewise 'conservative, and the progressives occupied a few seats. The conservative opposition would have meant another installment of the deep disappointment the public felt after a few months of the Chang Cabinet, had they the chance of winning power. There were talks of a bypartisan cabinet, but this did not materialize. The public felt no interest in the talks anyway. They knew they could expect nothing from a combined body of the ruling and opposition parties.

The May Revolution

Early on the early morning of May 16, 1961, 13 months after the April Revolution and nine months after the formation of the Chang Cabinet, some military units staged a coup to take over political control. A Military Revolutionary Committee was formed within hours and Lt. Gen. Chang Toyong, Army Chief of Staff, was proclaimed chairman. The commander of the revolutionary forces, Maj. Gen. Pak Choughui, became vice-chairman. A six-clause revolutionary pledge was announced by the Committee on the same day. The Revolutionary Pledge:

1) We shall make anti-Communism the key principle in our overall policy lines and shall rearrange and strengthen our anti-communist readiness which has so far been limited to mere formality and slogans.

2) We shall respect the United Nations Charters, fully comply with our international commitments and strengthen existing ties with the USA and other friendly nations of the free world.

3) We shall root out corruption and accumulated evils from our society and encourage renewed national spirit in order to rectify degenerated national morals and temperament.

4) We shall quickly solve the misery of the masses stricken with desperation and hunger and mobilize all available resources for the reconstruction of a self-sustaining national economy.

5) We shall mobilize all resources to cultivate our strength until we shall be on the same foothold in dealing with the Communists for realization of the national aspiration for unification.

6) We are ready to return to our original duties after turning over the power to new and conscientious politicians as soon as the above-mentioned tasks shall have been accomplished.

This six-point resolution covers the danger Korea faced during the administration of John M. Chang. They were the tasks left over from the past and to be fulfilled by the revolutionary regime. Clause Six reflects the revolutionary regime's determination to build the country into a genuine democratic republic.

After the disbandment of the National Assembly and local legislative assemblies, the revolutionary regime secured its constitutional foothold with the resignation of the Chang Cabinet while retaining Posun Yun as figurehead president. On May 19, the junta reorganized itself into the "Supreme Council for National Reconstruction." The Supreme Council proclaimed the "Emergency Law for National Reconstruction" on June 6, and made it clear that the existing provisions of the constitution would be preserved where there was no conflict with the new Emergency Law. Where there was conflict, the Emergency Law would prevail, it was further expounded.

Article 1; As an emergency measure to protect the Republic of Korea from Communist aggression, to overcome the national crisis caused by corruption, illegality and poverty and to reconstruct a true democratic republic, the Supreme Council for National Reconstruction is hereby established.

Article 2; The Supreme Council for National Reconstruction shall function as the highest ruling body of the Republic of Korea until a General Assembly is formed and Government established through general elections to be held after completion of the tasks of the military revolution of May 16.

The supreme council, consisting of between 20 and 32 active military officers, took over the functions of the disbanded legislative assembly, and assumed control over the Cabinet. It also took upon itself the power to give instructions and to control general activities of the judicial branch of the Government.

Along with organizing the new system and securing its legal basis, the revolutionary regime embarked on social and economic reforms. The fundamental economic policy announced by the supreme council: an economic system proving itself superior to Communism shall be developed with the Government participating competently in general planning. It will guarantee free economic activities, make it possible to overcome the nation's underdeveloped economic and encourage balanced growth of the national economy. The council announced on May 31 that it would stabilize the price of grains and official hwan-dollar exchange rate by encouraging autonomous development of private enterprises as well as through government-sponsored construction of basic industries along with development of the farming and fishing industries.

Within one month after taking over the Government, the supreme council; 1) took over high interest debts of 20% up to a year accrued by the fishing and farming populace, promising to clear these over five-year period; 2) took legislative action to enable the confiscation of illegally acquired wealth from those whose illegal profit made through connivance with the bureaucracy or whose amount of tax-evasion reaches Hwan 200,000,000 ($1 = Hw 1,300), from civil servants who accumulated Hwan 30,000,000 or more through illegal means and from those profiteers who carried out their assets to foreign countries. Imprisonment may accompany the fine.

Along with the disciplinary measures being taken to root out corruption among the civil servants, pay raise is being earnestly considered to guarantee their livelihood. Also being rooted out are the existence of hoodlums nurtured in an atmosphere of political instability and the practice of prostitution. Luxury and disorder in civil life are becoming things of the past.

Article Three of the Emergency Law says, "constitutionally guaranteed fundamental rights of the citizen will be respected unless they conflict with the performance of the revolutionary tasks. Although political parties and social groups have been disbanded, it was promised that the organization of parties and groups would be allowed at the "proper time" when a general election would be held. Non-political groups would soon be allowed to reopen their functions. Newspapers and wire services with proper facilities are allowed to continue their respective operations.

Conclusion

There may be those who would deem the May Revolution, aimed at fulfilling the tasks of the April Revolution, as not the best way out for Korea inasmuch as it stifles some democratic institutions, even temporarily. However, there are factors which must be taken into consideration. Korea is an underdeveloped country and shares a common border with Communism. To save Korea from her inner crisis and outside danger, emergency measures such as the coup were necessary and inevitable. The nation's understanding of these factors, confidence in the revolutionary regime and positive participation in the performance of the tasks will hasten the arrival of the day when a true democracy is firmly planted in Korea's soil.

(Pages 150-1 to 150-4 supplemented on 24th June, 1961)

V INTERNATIONAL RELATIONS AND DIPLOMACY

An Outline of Korean Diplomacy

Diplomacy before Opening of the Country

China and Japan

China and Japan were the only countries with diplomatic relations with Korea until the turn of the current century when the Western Powers began to come to this country to seek trade openings. In dealing with China, Korea always adopted the submissive attitude of the Yi dynasty, paid tribute to Ming. This precedent was followed as Korea regularly sent a mission to China to pay tributes in the form of Korean products. Korea also came to use the name of the Chinese era and to adopt the Chinese calendar.

Dispatch of tribute missions, in effect, served to open trade relations between the two countries as the missions brought home return gifts from China. Adoption of the name of the Chinese era and the Chinese calendar helped introduce the Chinese culture. That about was the sum of Korea's submission to China. The relation of Korea to China was by no means what a protectorate, as defined in international law today, is to the protector country. China, in no way, interfered with the internal and external policies of Korea. It is true that China went to the aid of such small countries as Korea and Annam in the event of aggression from the outside or civil war, but China did so only voluntarily as she regarded it her duty to help these countries.

When Toyotomi Hideyoshi of Japan invaded Korea in the 1590's, the Ming dynasty sent a large force to help Korea but did not demand anything as reward. Nevertheless, Korea did help Ming by sending troops to the aid of that kingdom when the Niuchen tribe, calling themselves Hu-Chin, rose in Manchuria against Ming. Tai-tsung of Hu-Chin, angered and determined to see no more trouble from Korea, invaded Korea with a 30,000-strong force in 1627 and imposed a "brother relationship" to which Korea was compelled to submit. After founding the Ching dynasty in China, Tai-tsung personally commanded a 100,000-man strong expeditionary force to invade Korea again. Ching thereafter took the place of Ming, receiving a yearly tribute from Korea and, like its predecessor, did not interfere with Korea's sovereignty.

As for Japan, for a long time, Korea maintained relations with that country as an equal neighbor. After a long series of piratical raids along the Korean coasts by inhabitants of western Japan toward the end of the Koryo dynasty to the early days of the Yi, the Lord of Tsushima island requested normal trade relations with Korea. The latter accepting this request, the Lord of Tsushima came to handle the diplomatic relations of his country with Korea, and to issue licences for Japanese ships coming to Korea. Three ports, Masan, Pusan and Ulsan, were opened for residence of Japanese trade personnel. In 1510, the Japanese residents at these three ports rose in revolt against Korea and the Korean government closed these ports, thus breaking off trade relations with Japan. These relations were later restored as the Lord of Tsushima punished the Japanese involved with death sentences and proposed reopening of commercial ties. But the trade amount was restricted to half the pre-rebellion level.

In 1592, the Japanese invaded Korea without provocation with a 150,000-strong force and, in 1597, renewed the invasion with a 140,000-army. While Ming helped Korea with a vast force, the Korean navy held command of the sea during the seven years of war. The Japanese withdrew from Korea without gaining anything in 1598 when Hideyoshi died. The seven-year hostilities impoverished Korea, Japan and Ming alike, leaving the worst scars in Korea.

Tokugawa Ieyasu repeatedly sought peace with this country through the Lord of Tsushima till 1606, when normal relations were restored between the two countries. The following two centuries saw the two countries exchange diplomatic missions. In 1609, a Japanese mission was established at Pusan.

Coming of the West

It was not before the early 1900's that Western vessels prowled Korean shores for purposes of trade soundings. In 1839, the government of the Yi dynasty issued a decree to suppress Catholicism, which resulted in the loss of three French missionary lives. In 1886, two French bishops, seven French fathers, seven Korean fathers and a number of Catholics were massacred. Upon receiving a report of this incident from French Admiral Roze at Tientsin, the French charge d'affaires, M. H. de Bellonet, there filed a protest with the Chinese government to which the latter replied that it had no right to interfere with the sovereignty of Korea. The French diplomat then ordered Admiral Roze to raid Kanghwa island off the west coast of Korea. The island was bombarded by three French warships in August 1866 and again by seven warships the next month.

In August 1866, Korean government officials and citizens raided and burnt an American merchantship, the U.S.S. General Sherman, on the Taedong River near Pyongyang, killing the crew. The United States goverment ordered Minister Frederick F. Low in China to go to Korea to negotiate an agreement for rescuing shipwrecked sailors, if any, and, if possible, to conclude a treaty of commerce as well. An American fleet of five warships carrying Minister Low came to Kangwha Strait in May 1871, only to be met by bombardments from Korean coastal artillery. After an exchange of shellings, the American fleet withdrew.

The government of the Yi dynasty tightened its policy of isolating the country against Western Powers all the more after these incidents.

Opening of the Country

Treaty with Japan

In Japan, the Tokugawa Shogunate declined and government reverted to imperial rule with the Meiji Restoration. The Japanese government officially notified foreign envoys in Japan of the restoration of imperial rule in January 1868. The notification to Korea was made in November of the same year through So Yoshitate, the Lord of Tsushima island.

The Korean authorities, however, refused to accept the letter of notification on the ground that a new form and seal were used and that the letter contained such wordings as "Imperial Household" and "Imperial Re-script," which, they believed, only the Emperor of Ching was entitled to use, in documents addressed to Korea. Accordingly, the Japanese Foreign Ministry took over the responsibilities of diplomatic relations with Korea from the Lord of Tsushima and sought direct contacts between its representatives and Korean authorities who rejected these contacts.

Meanwhile, advocates of conquering Korea by force was gaining strength in Japan. General Saigo Takamori, the then chief-of-staff, proposed to be dispatched to Korea for negotiations with the Korean government and that, in case, negotiations got nowhere, force be used. Saigo was officially designated such a negotiator. But his plans did not materialize as Ambassador Iwakura Tomomi and his party, returned from an inspection tour of Europe and the United States, strongly opposed invasion. Supporters of the forceful course quit the Japanese government in protest. For all that, Japan's diplomatic offensive remained unabated.

In September 1875, the Japanese warship, H.I.M. Unyogo, was anchored at the Han River estuary to sound out a route between the west coast of Korea and Niuchang in China. A boat from this warship was sailing in Kangwha Strait in the course of this sounding work when the Korean coastal artillery fired upon it. The day after this firing, the Unyogo came to the scene of the shelling and the Japanese occupied Yongjong island where the artillery was located.

The Japanese government notified the Chinese government of this incident and sought a commitment from the Chinese to the effect that Korea was not tributary to China. The Chinese government's reply was equivocal. The Japanese envoy, Mori Yurei, was told that it was a well known fact that Korea was a tributary of China and, at the same time, an independent state with full sovereignty in both domestic affairs and foreign relations.

In January 1876, a Japanese delegation headed by Lieutenant General Kuroda Kiyotaka as plenipotentiary came to Kanghwa aboard six warships and effected a treaty with this country. The Japanese ambasasador arrived at the site of the negotiations, escorted by 400 armed guards in an apparent attempt to negotiate by threat of force.

The treaty signed on February 26, 1876, officially called the Treaty of Amity between Korea and Japan, stipulated that Korea was an independent state and would have equal rights with Japan. The two countries were to exchange diplomatic missions. Pusan and two other ports were to be opened to the Japanese who were to have extraterritorial rights in Korea and receive treatment as the most preferred nation. It was, in fact, a treaty of inequality designed to give special privileges to Japan and her nationals in Korea. Article 1 of the treaty did provide for independence of Korea but this only served to disavow China's suzerainty.

Treaty with the U.S.

After United States Ambassador to China Low failed to open diplomatic relations between his country and Korea, U.S. Senator A.A. Sargent of California recommended to the president in 1878 that a plenipotentiary be sent to negotiate a treaty of amity and commerce with Korea. The following year, Admiral Robert W. Shufeldt was sent to the Orient with the authorization to work for, among other things, conclusion of a treaty with Korea. In May 1880, the Admiral came to Pusan with a letter of introduction from the Japanese Foreign Minister. He handed a note proposing talks for a Korean-American treaty to the Korean authorities there for relay to the Seoul government. The Korean officials at Pusan refused to accept this letter. Admiral Shufeldt then returned to Japan to seek the cooperation of the Japanese Foreign Minister in delivering the letter directly to the Korean Foreign Minister.

Almost simultaneously came an offer of cooperation from Li Hung-chang of China, who invited the Admiral to Tientsin. The reasons for this move by China, among other things, were:

One—in order to stop the expansionist

ambitions of Japan which had already pried Korea loose from China under the Treaty of Amity, invaded Formosa, and annexed the Ryukyu Islands, Li decided to play the United States against Japan by tying Korea with a treaty to the United States;

Two—it was Li's intention to convince Western Powers by using China's influence over Korea that the latter country remained, indeed, tributary to China, and

Three—anxious as he was for a chance to revise the treaties of inequality China had entered into with Western Powers, Li thought it helpful to this end to see Korea conclude a treaty of more equality with the United States.

Li Hung-chang repeatedly warned the Korean government against the aggressive intentions of Russia and Japan. Diplomatic relations with the United States, Britain, Germany and France, Li counselled, would help Korea curb Japan and stave off the aggressive ambitions of Russia. He advised Korea to conclude a treaty, especially with the United States. The king of Korea delegated him the authority to negotiate on behalf of the Korean government.

The negotiation started between Li Hung-chang and Shufeldt in Tientsin in mid-March 1882. Li proposed that Article 1 of the proposed treaty should stipulate that Korea was a tributary of China with sovereign rights in both domestic matters and diplomatic affairs. Shufeldt firmly rejected this stipulation. If Korea had sovereign rights both internally and externally, he argued, she had the right to deal with the United States as an equal in making a treaty without being bound by what China claimed as suzerainty.

Li threatened to break off the whole negotiation if the United States would not agree to the first article of his draft, which, to him, was the embodiment of his motive for offering good offices. The negotiation ended in a compromise to the effect that provisions concerning the tributary status of Korea would be dropped from the treaty on condition that the king of Korea would send a letter, separate from the treaty, to the president of the United States, explaining his country's relationship with China as defined by Li.

The Treaty of Amity and Commerce between Korea and the United States was signed at Chemulpo on May 22, 1882 and the instruments of ratification were exchanged in May next year. Under Article 2 providing for exchange of diplomatic envoy, the first U.S. Minister to this country, Lucius H. Foote, arrived in Seoul in May 1883. Korea dispatched two special envoy, Min Yongik and Hong Yongsik, to America in August that year, the first Minister to the United States, Pak Chongyang, taking up his post in Washington in 1887. The Treaty contained some unequal features as in provisions governing extraterritorial rights for the United States but, as a whole, it had a lesser degree of inequality for Korea than existing Chinese treaties with Western Powers had for that country.

Follow-up Treaties

On conclusion of the U.S.-Korean Treaty, the British Minister to China, Sir Thomas Wade, approached Li Hung-chang for his good offices on condition that the treaty envisaged by Britain was similar to the Korean-American agreement. A treaty between Korea and Britain was signed on June 6, 1882. The German Minister to China, Von Brant, followed suit and a Korean-German Treaty was signed on June 30.

Britain and Germany, however, refused to ratify these treaties. Britain thought the treaty was less favorable to her compared with those she had effected with other countries of the Far East. The two countries entered into new treaty relations with Korea in 1883, under which they did not maintain ministers in Seoul but consul-generals under the control of their respective Ministers in China.

In June 1884, Russia sent a secretary of the Russian Legation in Peking, C. Waeber, to Seoul as a plenipotentiary to negotiate a treaty. On the treaty coming into force,

V INTERNATIONAL RELATIONS AND DIPLOMACY

Waeber was appointed Minister to Korea and concurrently Consul-General. Russia concluded another Treaty of Overland Trade with Korea in August 1888, under which the City of Kyonghung was opened for trade with Russia.

Diplomacy after Opening of the Country

Sino-Japanese Relations

In July 1882, revolting Korean Army troops raided the Japanese Legation and killed Japanese military instructors. The Japanese Minister, Hanabusa Yoshisada and other members of the Legation, fled to Inchon, where they boarded the English ship, the Flying Fish, to return to Nagasaki. Soon later, Minister Hanabusa and Japanese Legation officials returned to Korea aboard four warships with an escort of 800 officers and men of the Japanese army to discuss post-rebellion measures with Korean officials under instruction from their home government.

In the meantime, the Chinese, in an attempt to forestall the Japanese, had dispatched a 3,000-strong force to Korea. The Chinese abducted Taewongun, Regent-Father of the king and suspected leader of the anti-Japanese rebellion, to put him under "house arrest" in Paoting, China and put the rebellion down for the Japanese. After peace and order returned to Seoul, the Chinese would not withdraw their troops but, instead, attempted to take over the right to train and control the Korean army. This was a clear illustration of China's intention to exercise substantial rights in Korea instead of maintaining an ostensible suzerainty as hitherto. In the face of interventions from the Chinese, the Japanese managed to reach agreement with the Korean government on payment of a 500,000-yen compansation for damage suffered by the Japanese, and the stationing of Japanese guards at their Legation. Thus troops of both countries came to stay in Korea.

Commercial relations between Korea and China had never been specified by a treaty though overland trade activities had continued quite regularly along the border. Now that Japan and Western Powers had entered into official trade agreements, China came to feel the need of one herself. A commercial agreement between China and Korea was effected in September 1882. Unlike other treaties, the tributary status of Korea was expressly stipulated in this Agreement. Li Hung-chang made a further attempt to place Korea's diplomacy under Chinese trusteeship when he sent P. G. von Mollendorf, a German Consul-General in Tientsin, and Ma Chien-chang, to the Royal Government of Korea as diplomatic advisors. Mollendorf, well-versed in the administrative aspects of diplomacy and customs affairs, made a considerable contribution by helping in day-to-day handling of external affairs and introducing order in the customs system. Though mindful of Chinese interests in his early days in Korea, the German advisor kept increasingly in touch with Russian Minister Waeber to connive for a secret Russo-Korean treaty, until dismissed by an angered Li Hung-chang. Two Americans, Denny and Henry F. Merrill, were appointed as new advisors on recommendation by Li.

In order to counter the Chinese political influence that had been growing ever since the anti-Japanese rebellion of July 1882, Japan pledged her support of independence for Korea. She renounced 400,000-yen of the 500,000-yen compensation in 1884 while, on the other hand, trying to boost pro-Japanese influence in Korea by giving loans to pro-Japanese politicians and financing the education of young Korean army officers in Japan.

On December 4, 1884, Kim Okkyun, Pak Yonghyo and other leaders of the *Kaehwadang* (Enlightenment Party) staged a *coup d'etat* while the government was busy opening a Postal Administration Office. The *coup* was effected in close cooperation with Japanese Minister Takezoye Shinichiro and with promised support from the Japanese army. Takezoye immediately occcupied the palace with a Japanese force in support of the *coup*, Six officials, including government Ministers and an army commander were killed. The *Kaehwadang* then set out to form a Cabinet and carry out a reform. On December 6, however, a Chinese force led by Yuan Shih-Kai forced its way into the palace. After a direct conflict between the Japanese force and the numerically superior Chinese troops, the Japanese withdrew from the palace and the shortlived *Kaehwadang* regime collapsed.

Japan sent her Foreign Minister, Inouye Kaoru, to Korea to impose an agreement providing for, firstly, relief of the *coup d'etat* victims; secondly, payment of expenses for building a new Japanese Legation, and thirdly, dispatch of a mission of apology to Japan. In the course of negotiation, the Korean government tried to pin the responsibility on Takezoye, who, the Korean government said, inspired and plotted the violence. Wu Ta-cheng, dispatched by the Chinese government, also tried to intervene in favor of Korea. But the Japanese Foreign Minister turned a deaf ear to all this and pushed through the Agreement.

A provisional settlement was made on this incident of 1884 with signing of this Korean-Japanese Agreement. Its fundamental solution, however, could not be assured unless there were direct negotiations between China and Japan since they were the dominating influences behind the political rivalries of the pro-Chinese and pro-Japanese elements, the relationship that was to develop into military conflict between the two countries. Japanese Plenipotentiary Ito Hirobumi and his Chinese counterpart, Li Hung-chang, started negotiations in Tientsin in March 1885 and a three-point Tientsin Treaty was inked in April that year. This provided for, first, the withdrawal of Japanese and Chinese troops from Korea within four months; second, invitation of instructors from a third country other than China and Japan to train the Korean army, and third, written notification, in case either China or Japan sent troops again to Korea, prior to such dispatch.

While the troop withdrawal from Korea helped avert a headlong clash between the two neighboring countries, Ching continued her efforts to strengthen her suzerainty over Korea by elevating the position of Yuan Shin-Kai, while Japan, on her part, succeeded to make her treaty-guaranteed voice heard in Korean matters and enjoy equal rights as China in Korea.

In the wake of the departure of the Chinese forces, thinking prevailed among some Korean government officials that neither Japan nor China was capable of maintaining the independence and security of Korea, and that it would be more advisable to approach Russia, instead, for protection of the national interests. Mollendorf worked hard behind the stage for a pro-Russian move. The move took shape in 1885 when Kim Yongwon visited Vladivostok with a royal order and let it be known to the Russian authorities there that Korea wished to invite Russian military instructors, and that should the emergency arise she would request the protection of Russia. Mollendorf himself took advantage of a trip to Japan to meet the Russian Minister there and discuss the possibility of Korea seeking Russian protection, inviting military instructors from Russia, and leasing Lazareff (Kyonghung) Bay and its ice-free port to Russia. In June 1885, Secretary Alexis de Speyer of the Russian Legation in Japan visited Seoul to get confirmation from the Korean government on all these suggestions. Seoul refused official acknowledgement of any such suggestion and told the Russian official that the Korean government had already invited military instructors from the United States.

Russia was at the time disputing with Britain over an issue of Afghanistani border demarcation. Rumors of a secret Russo-Korean agreement had reached the English goverment, Britain lost no time to occupy Port Hamilton (Komun) in southern Korea —a move to check Russia. Russia immediately lodged a protest with the Chinese government. Russia threatened that she would be obliged to occupy some Korean port or island if Britain continued her occupation of Port Hamilton. Russia tried, in vain, to negotiate a treaty with China providing for maintenance of the *status quo* in Korea and a non-aggression policy toward Korea, until Britain withdrew her troops from Port Hamilton in late November 1886 on receiving assurances from Russia that she would not occupy Port Lazareff or any other port of Korea if and when the British troops left that port. Balancing of power was long a favorite policy of both Russia and Britain in their relations with Korea and the Far East in general.

Alarmed by the reported Korean approach to Russia, Ching sent the abducted Taewongun back to Seoul, appointed Yuan Shih-Kai in Korea as Minister-Resident for Political and Commercial Affairs and recalled Mollendorf to China. Yuan, with full powers as the envoy of the suzerain state, intensified his interferences in both the domestic and diplomatic policies of this country.

In August 1886, a document in the name of the Prime Minister for Internal Affairs and with the official seal of the king, was sent to Russian Minister Waeber seeking Russian protection. Yuan Shin-kai applied to his home government for dispatch of troops, conspiring, in the meantime, to depose the king and intimidate him and leading officials of the government. The Korean government told Yuan that it had nothing to do with the document. It asked the Russian Minister to return the paper and delivered a document to the foreign missions in Seoul that any paper without the countersignature of the Foreign Minister was invalid. The government further sent an envoy to China to explain its position.

The Korean government, upon the advice of Denny, appointed Pak Chongyang Envoy Extraordinary and Minister Plenipotentiary to the United States in September 1887 to abide by the provisions of Article 2 of the U.S.-Korean Treaty of Amity and Commerce. Yuan Shin-kai, acting under instructions from Li Hung-chang, voiced vigorous objection to this on the ground that Korea, as a tributary of China, should have appointed the envoy with China's approval and that there was no need for expending money to keep a resident envoy in the United Stades since trade relations between Korea and that country were almost non-existent. The Korean government sent another special envoy to China to apply for approval by the Emperor of Ching of Pak's appointment.

The approval was granted on these four conditions: one — that the Korean Minister be designated Minister-Resident so that his status would be lower than that of the Chinese envoy to the United States; two — that on arrival in the United States, the Korean Minister first meet the Chinese Minister and then visit the Department of State through the introduction of the Chinese envoy; three — that the Korean Minister concede seniority to the Chinese Minister in all official appearances; and four—that the Korean Minister consult the Chinese Minister in all diplomatic matters. Minister Pak disregarded the last three conditions when he took up his post in Washington whereupon Li Hung-chang and Yuan Shin-kai demanded that Pak be recalled for punishment.

When the people of Cholla-do province rose in an uprising, the Seoul government rushed troops there. The government forces were defeated so the government turned to China for military help. Li Hung-chang dispatched a force after duly notifying Japan of his action as under Article 3 of the Tientsin Treaty. The Japanese in return notified the Chinese government that they would also send troops to Korea for the purpose of protecting their Legation in Seoul. Shocked and amazed, the Korean government started negotiations with the Japanese *charge d'affaires* for reversal of this decision. Japan insisted that she had the right of troop stationing in this country under the Chemulpo Treaty.

The Japanese Minister, Otori Keisuke, led a Japanese force into the capital while a Japanese brigade under Commander Oshima Yoshimasa landed at Inchon Port. But the capital was as orderly as ever. No one could see any justification for protection of the Japanese Legation and nationals by Japan's own military force. The Japanese Minister counselled his government against further dispatch of troops and started talks with Yuan Shin-kai for simultaneous withdrawal from Korea.

This was rejected by the Japanese military. Japanese reinforcements continued to arrive in Korea. Japan was now looking for an excuse to start war. She suggested to China that the two countries make a joint proposal to Korea for reform of her internal politics. Japan then forced Korea under threat of force to agree upon negotiating such a reform. Korea demanded the withdrawal of Japanese troops and removal of the deadline unilaterally set by Japan for carrying out the reform, before negotiations got underway.

On July 19, Japan regarded this as virtual rejection of the whole Japanese proposal and demanded that the Korean government lay a railway line between Seoul and Pusan and build barracks for Japanese guards in Korea. In a rapid march of events, Japan, on July 20, demanded the withdrawal of Chinese troops from Korea and denunciation of the treaties providing for Korea's stature as tributary to China.

Japanese forces surrounded the Palace and disarmed the Korean National Force on July 23, and Japan declared war on China July 25. While maintaining her troops in the Royal Palace, Japan imposed on Korea at gunpoint a seven-article Provisional Treaty on August 20 and an Offensive and Defensive Alliance on August 26.

Japan won the war, as a result of which both China and Japan recognized the independence of Korea under the Peace Treaty signed at Shimonoseki on April 17, 1895.

Vicissitudes of Japanese, Russian Influences

The Japanese victory in the Sino-Japanese War was followed by the Triple Intervention, which forced Japan to return Liaotung peninsula to China and wash her hands of intervention in Korea on a gradual basis. As the Japanese influence declined, Russia intensified her infiltration into this country. Minister Waeber had taken advantage of his experiences and thorough knowledge of the internal Korean situation acquired over a period of ten years in Korea, to establish close ties with Queen Min and her supporters, known for their strong anti-Japanese sentiments, to wipe the Japanese influence from this peninsula.

The newly arrived Japanese Minister, Miura Goro, decided to use Taewongun in restoring the Japanese influence. His plan called for the father of the King to effect a *coup d'etat* and eliminate Queen Min and her anti-Japanese elements from power. Hard upon dawn on October 8, 1895, a group of Japanese police, soldiers and civilians intruded into the Royal Palace and killed the queen. Taewongun was brought to the Palace to rule and the Cabinet was reorganized.

One *coup d'etat* led to another. A faction counting on Russia and the United States for support planned a violent change of government. On February 9, 1896, some 100 Russian sailors entered into the capital on the pretext of protecting the Russian Legation. On February 11, the king and the prince slipped away from the Palace and took refuge in the Russian Legation.

At the height of the tension created by the threat of a pro-Russian *coup*, Russia and Japan decided that it was necessary to reach a mutual understanding on Korea. In May 1896, Russian Minister Waeber and Japanese Minister Komura initialled an agreement in Seoul. This agreement, signed on June 9 in Moscow by Japanese Plenipotentiary Yamagata Aritomo and Russian Fo-

V. INTERNATIONAL RELATIONS AND DIPLOMACY

reign Minister Rovanoff, said that both countries, agreeing on the principle of maintaining the security and independence for Korea, would share equally in their respective Korea interests. Almost simultaneously, the Russians concluded another agreement with Korean Representative Min Yong-hwan, which provided: one - that Russia would send high-ranking officers to Korea as military instructors; two - that a Russian financial advisor would be sent to the Korean government; three - that if necessary, Russia would grand loans to Korea; and four - that Russia's land cable line would be connected with that of Korea.

This Russo-Korean Agreement was rapidly enforced. Russia sent a group of 20 military instructors with 400 rifles. A Russian named Alexeiff came to Seoul as financial advisor and revenue director. The king stayed in the Russian Legation for one year, handing out many concessions to Russians, Americans, Japanese, Englishmen, Germans and Frenchmen alike.

In 1898, Russian's policy toward Korea underwent a major change. In her overall Far Eastern policy, emphasis had shifted to Manchuria. While obtaining rights to Port Arthur and Dairen on lease grants, she agreed to the preponderance of Japan's position in Korea under the Rosen-Nishi agreement in February 1898.

Russo-Japanese War, the Annexation

Japan concluded an Anglo-Japanese Alliance in February 1902, under which England recognized Japan's political and commercial interests in Korea and also Japan's right to take measures deemed necessary for protecting these interests. Japan then approached Russia, without success, for an agreement which would recognize her preponderant rights in Korea while reserving Manchuria as a zone of dominant Russian interests.

When the Boxer Rebellion broke out in 1900, Russia sent troops to northern China and Manchuria. Russia refused to pull out her troops from Manchuria after the rebellion was put down. In May 1903, which had been set as the second deadline for Russian withdrawal, the Russians not only refused to leave Manchuria but occupied Mukden and Niuchang and stationed troops along the Yalu River.

Japan started direct negotiations with Russia. The Japanese put out a proposal, which said: one - that the independence and territorial rights of Korea and Manchuria would be respected; two - that Japan and Russia would mutually recognize each other's preponderant interests in Manchuria and Korea; three - that a Japanese-Korean treaty would be concluded providing for Japanese advice and assistance in effecting political reform in Korea. Russia submitted a counter-proposal which, while recognizing the special interests of Japan in the Korean peninsula, called for making that part of Korea north of the 39th parallel a neutral zone while excluding Manchuria as a zone of Japanese interest. The Japanese negotiators told the Russians that they would accept a neutral belt 50 kilometers wide on each side of the Yalu River. The negotiations dragged on until February 1904 when the two countries decided to settle their differnces by arms.

At the outset of the Russo-Japanese War, Korea declared neutrality. In total disregard of this declaration, Japan threatened the Korean government into conceding communication rights, fishing rights for Japanese nationals along the coast of the three Provinces of Chungchong-do, Cholla-do and Pyongan-do, and the right to lay railway lines between Seoul and Sinuiju, and Seoul and Wonsan. In August that year, Japan concluded another agreement which obliged Korea to accept a Japanese as financial advisor and a foreigner in Tokyo's employ as diplomatic advisor. The Japanese virtually took over the financial and diplomatc rights of the country through these advisors, Megata Tanetaro and D. W. Stevens. A Japanese police advisor and Japanese educational advisor were also appointed later.

Japan won the war and a Peace Treaty

was signed at Portsmouth on September 5, 1905, Article 2 of the Treaty stipulated that Russia would recognize Japan's predominant interests, political, military and economic, in Korea. The same article also committed Russia against obstruction or interference in any program of direction, protection and supervision that Japan might deem necessary to implement in Korea.

Britain had already recognized Japanese interests as later specified in the Portsmouth Peace Treaty when she renewed her Alliance with Japan on July 29 that year. Again, in secret notes exchanged on July 29, 1905 between the Japanese Prime Minister, Katsura Taro, and the U.S. Secretary of the Army, William Taft, it had been agreed that the United States would recognize Japanese control of Korea, while Japan, in return, would disclaim any aggressive intentions toward the Philippines, then territory of the United States.

Thus, by securing official understanding from these three countries, Japan paved the way to make Korea a protectorate. In November 1905, she sent Ito Hirobumi to Korea as special envoy. Ito concluded a Treaty of Protection. All Korean envoys aboard were recalled and diplomatic missions of the United States, Britain, France, China, Belgium and other countries withdrew from Korea. Korea lost her diplomatic sovereignty completely to Japan.

In 1907, three emissaries of the king carried his credentials in a bid to attend the International Peace Conference at the Hague and call international attention to Korea. Japan found in this the excuse to depose the king and deprive the Korean government of internal reins. In August 1910, a Treaty of Annexation was proclaimed.

Foreign Relations of the Republic of Korea

Relations with the United States

U.S. Military Government

The Japanese surrender on August 15, 1945 left Korea divided, along the 38th parallel, into two occupational zones of American and Russian armed forces. In the south, a United States Millitary Government was set up.

Korea's independence was assured at the Cairo Conference held in December 1943 and reconfirmed at the Yalta and Potsdam conferences. But in reality the 38th parallel partition was retained as the United States and Russia continued to intensify their global conflict. Korea was becoming a focal point of international tension.

The Foreign Ministers of the United States, Soviet Russia, Britain and Nationalist China met in Moscow in December 1945 to decide upon a five-year trusteeship for Korea. Under directives from the Foreign Ministers, a U.S.-Russian Joint Commission met in Seoul in March 1946 to discuss establishment of a Provisional Korean government. In Korea itself, political parties, social organizations and the general public were all denouncing plans for any trusteeship. At the conference table, Soviet Russia insisted that only those organizations and individuals supporting the Moscow Decision be invited for consultation. The United States opposed this on the ground that it would be against freedom of speech to exclude such organizations and individuals simply because they voiced objection to trusteeship. The Commission adjourned in May that year without making any noticeable headway. The talks were resumed in May 1947 but the two sides would not budge from their conflicting positions on this matter of Korean consultations. Whereupon, in September 1947, the United States unilaterally brought the Korean problem before the United Na-

V INTERNATIONAL RELATIONS AND DIPLOMACY

tions.

Meanwhile, the U.S. Military Government set up a Democratic Assembly as an advisory body in February 1946 and established a Legislative Assembly as the law-making branch in December 1946. June of the following year saw the U.S. Military Government reorganized into a South Korean Interim Government.

On November 14, 1947, the U.N. General Assembly passed a resolution on Korea as proposed by the United States over the objection of Soviet Russia and its satellites. The resolution called for a general election to be held throughout Korea under supervision by a nine-member Special United Nations Commission to form an all-Korea government.

As the Soviet command in the north refused access to the Commission which the Soviet Union declared illegal, the Korean question was taken up again by the U.N. on February 26, 1948 through a "Little Assembly" formed to by-pass the Soviet veto in the Security Council and reflect the majority decision of the General Assembly on a workable basis. This "Little Assembly" adopted a resolution calling for election in areas accessible to the U.N. commission body in Korea: i.e., south of the 38th parallel. Under this resolution, elections took place on May 10, 1948 and a Constituent National Assembly was formed,

The National Assembly, convened on May 31, adopted a Constitution for the Republic of Korea on July 17 and elected Dr. Syngman Rhee president on July 20. Sovereignty was proclaimed and the Republic of Korea officially born on August 15, 1948. Lieutenant General John R. Hodge, Commander of the U.S. Occupation Force in Korea, announced the termination of military government.

After Independence

The Republic of Korea Government took over administrative reins from the South Korean Interim Government by stages. The United States immediately extended full support to the infant Republic by appointing John J. Muccio Ambassador to Korea on August 13. On New Year's day in 1948, the U.S. governmet officially recognized the Republic of Korea government. On January 9, the Republic of Korea government appointed Dr. John M. Chang as its first Ambassador to the Uuited States. Consulates-General were successively established in New York, San Francisco, Los Angeles and Honolulu.

U. S. Aid to Korea

Economic aid—American economic aid to this country dates back to the U.S. Military Government days. By 1949, the United States granted Korea 260 million dollars in aid.

In 1949, the United States, seeing the need of continued aid for reconstruction, decided to introduce a large-scale aid program, as implemented in Europe, into Korea. The aid program for Korea came under the direction of the Economic Cooperation Administration in January 1948. The U.S. government asked Congress for 195 million dollars' appropriations to this end.

The 1950 aid program for Korea was carried out under a law governing overall economic aid to the Far East. The U.S. government proposed a bill earmarking 120 million dollars in aid to Korea but Congress rejected this. A compromise bill granting 60 million dollars was later passed by Congress. Congress, however, approved an additional 50 million dollars following the outbreak of the Korean war. Aid for Korea, therefore, totalled 110 million dollars for the period July 1949 - June 1950 fiscal year. About 100 million dollars was scheduled for 1951.

Military aid—The Korean government requested the United States to grant military aid and, in the meantime, maintain American troops in Korea pending buildup of a Korean armed force capable of coping with either civil war or external aggression.

In October 1949, General Douglas A. MacArthur, Supreme Pacific Commander, stated that Korea would receive all defence and security assurances from the United States as requested by the Korean government. But on June 29, 1949, the last contingent of the U.S. forces stationed in Korea departed from Inchon, leaving behind a military advisory group consisting of 500 officers and men.

The United States and Korea signed a Mutual Defence Assistance Agreement on January 26, 1950, transferring all military installations and equipment left by the U.S. Forces to the Korean Armed Forces and legalizing the status of the American military advisory group.

The United States, however, underestimated the strategic value of Korea and judged that it would be militarily impossible to retain the Republic of Korea in the free world. Accordingly, the United States was not enthusiastic in giving economic and military aid to Korea. Nevertheless, Korea continued to press for aid in arms and equipment, putting emphasis on aircraft, tanks and artillery. In March 1949, the government dispatched Dr. Chough Pyong-ok to the United Stares as special presidential envoy to appeal for stepped-up economic and military aid. Up to May 1950, however, no arms or equipment were forthcoming.

Earlier in the year, on January 12, 1950, U.S. Secretary of State Dean Acheson testified before Congress that the U.S. defence perimeter was set along the line connecting the Aleutian Islands, Japan, the Ryukyu Islands and the Philippines. It was made clear that Korea and Formosa were excluded from this perimeter. The United States policy toward Korea continued to fumble until the outbreak of the war, with promises of economic and military aid, on one hand, and belittling of the peninsula's strategic value, on the other.

Since the War

On receiving a report of an unprovoked north Korean attack on the Republic of Korea, the United States lost no time to ask the U.N. Secretary-General to call an emergency meeting of the U.N. Security Council calling on the north Koreans to return north of the 38th parallel. The Council adopted this resolution. The north Korean Communists did not respond to this call, so the Security Council adopted another resolution on June 27, advising U.N. member states to offer military contributions to help repel the aggression. Three hours before this Security Council action, President Harry S. Truman had ordered General MacArthur to throw American Air and Naval forces into action to help the Republic of Korea.

This prompt action signified a drastic change in U.S. policy toward Korea. On June 30, President Truman permitted the U.S. Air Forces to attack military targets in north Korea, ordered the U.S. Navy to blockade the entire coast of Korea, and authorized General MacArthur to use American ground troops in Korea. The United States thereafter played a decisive role as the mainstay of the United Nations Forces in repulsing the aggression.

The three-year hostilities came to an end with signing on July 27, 1953, of the Armistic Agreement, sought by the United States despite objection by the Republc of Korea.

In December 1952, President-elect Eisenhower visited Korea in accordance with an election campaign promise and laid down three fundamental U.S. policies with regard to Korea: one—prevent the war from spreading to the China Mainland, two—uphold the military stand against aggression, and three—strengthen the R.O.K. Armed Forces and continue economic aid to Korea.

While the armistice negotiations were drawing to a conclusion, President Syngman Rhee, on May 30, 1953, proposed to President Eisenhower conclusion of a U.S.-Korean Mutual Defence Pact as an assurance against renewed Communist aggression. President Eisenhower, in his reply, promised that the United States would start negotiation for such a pact immediately after signing of the Armistice Agreement and also that the United States would continue its economic assistance to Korea.

Two top officials of the State Department were sent to Kcrea by President Eisenhower. On July 10, Assistant Secretary of State for Far Eastern Affairs Walter S. Robertson

V INTERNATIONAL RELATIONS AND DIPLOMACY

came to Seoul to lay the groundwork for the proposed pact. Next, Secretary of State John Foster Dulles visited Seoul in August to finalize the negotiations. The Mutual Defence Pact was initialled in Seoul by Secretary Dulles and Foreign Minister Y.T. Pyun on October 1. (The Pact was ratified in November 1954.)

After a series of talks with President Rhee, Secretary Dulles said in a joint statement with the president that the Republic of Korea and the United States would make united efforts to achieve common objectives, including the reunification of Korea. Among the American dignitaries who visited Korea that year was Vice-President Richard M. Nixon, who arrived in Seoul on November 12 and delivered a personal letter from President Eisenhower to President Rhee.

In accordance with Article 60 of the Armistice Agreement, preliminary political talks were opened at Panmunjom in October 1953 between the United Nations and Communist Commands without success. On April 26, 1954 a conference on government levels, as stipulated in the Armistice Agreement, was opened at Geneva to discuss a peaceful settlement of the Korea problem of unification. Foreign Minister Pyun represented the Republic of Korea at the conference which, as expected, ended in deadlock.

After these two fruitless conferences, President Rhee visited the United States at the invitation of President Eisenhower. In the course of a tour that started on July 14, 1954, President Rhee made an address before Congress to advocate a joint attack by two million anti-Communist Asians on the China Mainland. The President availed himself of other occasions during the tour to appeal to the American people on the need of vigorous anti-Communist measures. The president also had a series of top-level talks with American officials, which resulted in signing of a U.S.-Korean Protocol on military and aid problems. Under this Protocol, the Republic of Korea renounced unilateral action to unify Korea by pledging cooperation with the United States and United Nations. It was also agreed in the Protocol that the Mutual Security Act would be applied to Korea.

As a measure to put into practice repeated pledges by the United States of her long-range aid for reconstruction of Korea, the United Nations Command and the Korean government signed an Agreement on economic coordination in May 1952. An Office of the Economic Coordinator, United Nations Command, was established in Seoul under this Agreement.

In July 1953, President Eisenhower proposed 200 million dollars as economic aid to Korea for fiscal 1954 and obtained Congressional approval. This signified the beginning of long-range efforts to help reconstruct the Republic of Korea. The aid amounts since then were 280 million dollars for 1958. In addition to economic aid, approximately the same amounts were granted each year in military assistance except for 1955 when 420 milion dollars were allocated.

The United States withdrew five divisions from south Korea after the end of the bloody war although such withdrawal was not mandatory under the Armistice Agreement. Two other U.S. divisions remained in Korea, however, to stand ever ready to repel any new aggression in cooperation with the R.O.K. Forces.

The United Nations Command moved its headquarters from Tokyo to Seoul on July 1, 1957.

Commercial Relations

The Republic of Korea has been as predominantly dependent on the United States in trade development as in military and economic aid during the past decade. It was, therefore, most urgently necessary to establish normal commercial relations and strengthen friendly ties. After years of negotiation, the Republic of Korea signed a 25-article Treaty of Friendship and Commerce with the United States. The treaty came into force on November 7, 1957 with exchange of ratification instruments.

The problem of the official exchange rate between the Korean hwan currency and U.S. dollar demanded as much attention. Agreement was reached on December 14, 1953 to adopt the rate of 180 hwan to the dollar in determining the value, in Korean currency, of goods imported under the aid program. With economic stabilization yet to be realized, the hwan value continued to decline. This gave rise to a proposal by the United States that a realistic rate of exchange be adopted. The United States and Korea, in a joint statement on August 12, 1955, announced a new rate of conversion— 500 hwan to the dollar.

Relations with Britain

Goodwill Exchanges

Britain was the third country, after the United States and Nationalist China, and the first European country, to recognize the Republic of Korea. Her diplomatic recognition was extended on January 18, 1949.

Together with the United States and Nationalist China, Britain helped Korea regain her independence from the very beginning by signing the Cairo and Potsdam Declarations. When the Korean question was brought to the United Nations, she squarely supported the United States' position. She has been one of the major defenders of the position of the Republic of Korea in the world organization, supporting the Republic of Korea application for a seat in the United Nations every year.

After voting for the third U.N. General Assembly resolution recognizing the Republic of Korea government as the only lawful government in Korea, Britain decided to exchange diplomatic representatives with Korea at the level of minister. Korea appointed Mr. Yun Chichang Minister to that country. Britain's first Minister to Korea was Mr. Vivian Holt. On June 13, 1957, both countries elevated the status of their diplomatic missions to the category of embassy. Mr. Kim Yongu and Hubert J. Evans were appointed the first ambassadors of their respective countries.

Besides establishing normal diplomatic relations, both countries exchanged a number of goodwill missions. The first Korean goodwill envoy to go to Britain was Dr. Chough Pyongok, who stopped there in August 1948 during a world tour he was making as Special Ambassador of the President. National Assembly Speaker P.H. Shinicky and Prime Minister Paek Tujin represented South Korea at the coronation of Queen Elizabeth on June 2, 1953. In 1957, Ambassador to the United States You-chan Yang visited Britain as Special Presidential Envoy to express his nation's gratitude for British military and economic assistance to Korea during the war. In September 1958, Korean Army Chief-of-Staff General Paek Sonyop went to Britain at the invitation of his British counterpart to inspect military installations there.

On the British side, Minister of State for Foreign Affairs Selwyn Lloyd and Army Chief of Staff Sir Harold R. Alexander visited this country in 1953. The Duke of Lancaster, George N. Selkirk, who visited Korea in September 1956, is among the many other British dignitaries who have been here.

Military Forces

When war broke out in 1950, Britain was one of the first countries to respond to the U.N. Secretary-General's appeal for military help to the Republic of Korea. She ordered a nearby fleet of one aircraft carrier, two cruisers, eight battle-cruisers and one patrol boat to go to Korean waters. The Royal Air Force and ground troops immediately followed the Navy to participate in the war alongside the United States and 13 other U.N. allies. The total strength of the British Commonwealth Forces, including contingents from New Zealand, Australia and South Africa was: two brigades, one cavalry regiment, two infantry battalions, one field battalion, air force, navy with seven transports and one hospital ship. The Commonwealth Forces left Korea in September 1956, leaving a group of liaison officers with the

V INTERNATIONAL RELATIONS AND DIPLOMACY

Economic Aid

British economic aid to Korea was also substantial. She made contributions worth 26,840,000 U.S. dollars to the United Nations Korean Reconstruction Agency (UNKRA). She responded to a U. N. Security Council resolution on emergency relief for Korea with 1,333,108 U.S. dollars. The Save the Children Fund, a non-governmental relief organization, has a branch in Korea, spending more than 100,000 pounds sterling a year for children's relief and medical treatment.

In a drastic revision of her foreign trade policy in February 1957, Britain separately announced a partial lifting of the embargo to Communist China. The Korean government lodged a protest with the British government in April to the effect that the British action constituted violation of the U.N. embargo resolution. The protest also pointed out that the lifting would benefit Communist China and, indirectly, north Korea as well. On August 15, Britain announced a total lifting of the general embargo of the whole Communist bloc, including Communist China and north Korea. The Korean government filed another protest. Britain in reply explained that the lifting would affect only non-strategic materials.

Relations with France

France recognized the Republic of Korea on February 5, 1949. She has been one of the strongest supporters of the Republic of Korea government's position in all United Nations debates on the Korean problem.

On April 13, 1949, France appointed M. Georges Perruche, *charge d'affaires* in Seoul, whereas Korea sent Mr. Kong Chinhang to Paris as Minister to France.

Dr. You-chan Yang Ambassador to the United States, visited France as Special Presidential Envoy on a gooodwill tour. Having supported all Security Council resolutions on Korea, France dispatched naval vessels on July 19 and sent a infantry battalion on August 20. The French withdrew after the Armistice Agreement was signed in 1953.

France contributed 142,857 dollars to UNKRA. On June 30, 1957 she sent 74,286 dollars worth of medical supplies to Korea.

France and Korea have subsequently elevated the status of their diplomatic missions to embassy level. Korea's Ambassador to France is General Chong Ilgwon.

Relaions with West Germany

The Republic of Korea approached the Federal German Republic in 1953, soon after the signing of the Armistice Agreement, for establishment of Korean Consulate-General in west Germany. The initial Bonn reaction was that exchange of commercial representatives alone would suffice. Eventually, Germany agreed to the Korean suggestion and on March 5, 1957, two countries decided to exchange Ministers. South Korea appointed Mr. Son Wonil Minister to Germany while the German Consul-General, Dr. Richard O. Hertz, was appointed Minister in Seoul. Both envoys were promoted to ambassadorial rank on August 1, 1958 following elevation of diplomatic representation.

A number of visits have been exchanged between the two divided countries. The first Korean dignitary to visit Germany was National Assmbly Vice-Speaker Cho Kyonggu who was invited by the Speaker of the Bundestag. The Ambassador to the United States, Dr. You-chan Yang visited Bonn in 1957 during his European goodwill tour as President Rhee's special envoy. In early 1957, Mr. Kim Ilhwan, the then Minister of Commerce and Industry, made an inspection tour of Germany at the invitation of the Bonn Government. On the German side, the Vice- Chancellor and Minister of Economics, Dr. Ludwig Erhard, was the only dignitary to visit here. Besides, there are about 90 Korean students studying in west Germany.

When Chancellor Konrad Adenauer talked with United Nations officials during a tour of the United States in 1954, he offered a west German Red Corss Hospital for Ko rea as a contribution to the world organization's efforts to help rehabilitate this country. The hospital opened in Pusan in December 1954. West Germany also responded to a U.N. Security Council appeal for emergency relief in Korea with 47.619 dollars in 1953.

As the overseas market of her prosperous economy expanded, west Germany's exports to Korea increased. In the first half of 1959, she was the top exporter to this country, selling 10,185,000 dollars worth or 25 percent of Korea's total imports.

Relations with Italy

Italy and Korea decided to exchange diplomatic representatives on December 24, 1956. Mr. Kim Yongkee and Mr. Giorgio Spalazzi were appointed Ministers to represent Korea and Italy respectively. The two countries agreed to exchange ambassadors on December 18, 1958. Minister Kim was promoted to the rank Ambassador but Italy's representative was yet to be appointed in 1959.

Italy was another country visited by the Ambassador to the United States, Dr. Youchan Yang, during his goodwill tour to Europe in 1956.

As Italy was not a member of the United Nations until November 1956, she was not in a position to send troops to Korea during the war. She did contribute to the United Nations cause, however, by keeping a field hospital in Korea to give medical treatment to both U.N. troops and Korean civilians. She donated 2,00,933 dollars to the United Nations Korean Reconstruction Agency (UNKRA). This was in addition to 300 cases of food and the 50,000 dollars she sent to Korea in response to the U.N. Security Council's appeal for emergency relief in Korea.

Relations with Vietnam

The Republic of Korea extended recognition to Vietnam immediately after her declaration of independence from French rule in March 1950. On December 8, 1953, a Korean delegation headed by Dr. George L. Paik visited south Vietnam to discuss formation of the Asian People's Anti-Communist League. Korea sent another delegation led by Lieutenant General Choi Dukshin to Saigon in August 1955 in an effort to further strengthen friendly ties with a country Korea held in high esteem as a fellow anti-Communist outpost in Asia.

The Republic of Korea lost no time to recognize the Republic of Vietnem government of President Ngo Dinh Diem in October 1955. Both countries entered into normal diplomatic relations in 1956 by opening Legations in Seoul and Saigon in May and June respectively. In April 1958, Korea promoted her Minister in Saigon, Choi, to the status of Ambassador.

President Ngo Din Diem made a state visit to this country in September 1957 at the invitation of President Rhee and pledged united anti-Communist efforts. President Rhee returned a similar visit in December 1958.

Korea suggested a provisional trade agreement with south Vietnam on February 25, 1957. While she received no definite reaction from Vietnam, the two countries concluded a Tariff Agreement in December 1958. The Agreement which came into force on January 15, 1959, provided for Vietnam to reduce the tariff rate for imports from Korea by half with Korea, in turn, extending the most preferred-nation treatment to Vietnam in import tariffs. A group of Korean marine experts inspected Vietnam in November 1957 and a Korean economic mission has twice visited that country—in December 1957 and May 1958.

Relations with the Philippines

The Philippines, which regained independence on July 4, 1946, voted for the U.N. General Assembly resolution on Republic of Korea Government recognition on December 12, 1948.

The Republic of Korea Government sent Mr. Y.T. Pyun to the Philippines as a goodwill envoy in February 1949. In December that same year, Mr. Pyun visited the Philippines again as a Special Envoy of the President to attend the inauguration of President Elpidio Quirino. The Philippines extended official recognition to the Korean government on March 3, 1949. She has consistently supported for a seat in the United Nations.

One of the most enthusiastic contributors to the U.N. cause to fight the Communist aggression in Korea, the Philippines dispatched one brigade under the United Nations Command and sent 10,000 tons of rice plus medical supplies for Korean relief.

The Korean government appointed Mr. Kim Yongkee first envoy to the Philippines in November 1953: Mr. Kim's legation was opened in Manila January 1954. The Philippine Legation was established in Seoul in November that year. The two countries decided on November 11, 1957 further to strengthen their ties by elevating their diplomatic missions to Embassy level.

Korea participated in the first International Trade Fair held in Manila in 1953. In June 1956, a Philippine Trade Mission came to this country. The Korean government proposed a Provisional Trade Agreement to the Manila government in February 1957. This proposal was followed by a visit to the Philippines of a Korean Trade mission in May 1958. These moves indicate that the two countries are coming to close commercial ties.

Relations with Nationalist China

The relations between the Republic of Korea and China have a long historial background of Sino-Korean relations. When Korea regained her independence from the Japanese, it was remembered with appreciation that throughout the Japanese rule, numerous Korean exiles had fled to China and that the Chinese government rendered all possible assistance to the exiled Provisional Korean Government in China.

One of the first things the Republic of Korea government did was to send Dr. Chough Pyongok to China as a goodwill envoy in April 1948 to express Korean gratitude for this past. On November 7 that year, a Special Mission of the Republic of Korea was established in Nanking. This mission gave way to the Korean Embassy in December 1949. The first Korean Ambassador to China was Mr. Sin Sogu. The Chinese Nationalist government set up a consulate in Seoul in 1947 and, after extending official recognition to the Korean government on January 4, 1949, opened an Embassy in July that year.

Korea's attitude to Nationalist China has been most sympathetic since she lost the mainland to the Communists and moved to Formosa. Placed as they are under the direct menace of Communist aggression, the ties between the two countries have all the more been strengthened. On July 3, 1950, Nationalist China offered three infantry divisions, with 20 transport planes, to take part in the Korean War. The United Nations Command, however, turned down the offer.

President Chiang Kai-shek visited this country on August 6, 1949 for talks with President Syngman Rhee. After a number of conferences at Chinhae, the two leaders issued a communique stressing the friendly ties between their two countries and pledging a united anti-Communist front. President Rhee returned the visit on November 27, 1953. A communique issued then by the two leaders to stress the need to organize a united anti-Communist front eventually led to formation on June 15, 1959 of the Asian Peoples' Anti-Communist League. President Chiang sent Foreign Minister George Yeh to Korea in August 1956 to represent Nationalist China at the inauguration ceremony of President Rhee.

Close relations have also been maintained in the commercial field. The two countries concluded an Aviation Agreement on March 1, 1952. Exchange of visits by economic experts has been frequent. In November 1955, a Chinese Trade Mission came to Korea. This was followed by a visit to Formosa in

March 1956 by a Korean Trade Mission headed by Mr. Kim Ilhwan, then Minister of Commerce and Industry. In January 1958, a 20-man Korean Economic Mission to the Southeast Asia dropped in at Formosa and another 14-man mission visited that country in May.

Relations with Turkey

Turkey voted for the Republic of Korea government in the 1948 U.N. General Assembly and extended recognition on August 13, 1949.

Turkey was one of the first countries to respond to a United Nations call for contribution of military forces to the allied command in Korea in 1950. Though the shooting war ended in 1953, the Turkish contingent of some 6,000 officers and men are remaining in Korea against any possible repetition of a Communist breakthrough.

Turkey has also played a prominent role in the United Nations resolutions on Korea by maintaining representatives with the initial United Nations Commission on Korea and the present United Nations Commission for the Unification and Rehabilitation of Korea (UNCURK). Turkey and Korea announced establishment of normal diplomatic ties in March 1957, appointing Dr. Kamil Idil and General Chong Ilkwon their respective Ambassadors.

The Ambassador to the United States, Dr. You-chan Yang, included Turkey in his 1957 goodwill tour of Europe. On April 25, 1958, Turkish Prime Minister Adnan Menderes arrived here for a three-day tour. The Turkish National Assembly also sent a goodwill mission headed by Speaker Resik Koraltan to Korea in September 1959.

Relations with Japan

Korean-Japanese Conferences

While Japan was under allied occupational control from August 15, 1945 through February 13, 1951, Korea did not have direct diplomatic relations with Japan but, instead, dealt with the Supreme Command Allied Powers (SCAP) which acted on behalf of the Japanese government. It was through negotiations with SCAP that Korea concluded a Provisional Trade Agreement and a Financial Agreement with that country and settle other urgent problems pending between the two countries.

Korea had many interests to protect in Japan when that country surrendered to the Allies. Foremost was the problem of two million Koreans resident in Japan at the time. The Korean Mission was established in Tokyo soon after the Japanese surrender as SCAP, recognizing all these interests, ordered the Japanese government to accept the presence of such a mission.

Korea was not a signatory to the signing of the Japanese Peace Treaty signed on September 8, 1951 but she was entitled, under Article 21 of the Treaty, to privileges laid down in Articles 2, 4, 9 and 12. The Korean government felt it necessary to open negotiations with the Japanese government before the coming into force of the treaty mainly to discuss problems involving Korea as a result of these Articles but also, partly, to restore normal diplomatic relations between the two countries. This prompted the Korean government to propose a Korea-Japan conference.

The First Conference. The first Korea-Japan conference opened in Tokyo on October 20, 1951 with an observer team from SCAP sitting in. The conference adopted five subjects on the agenda and agreed to set up committees for their discussion. The five subjects were:

One - Legal status of Koreans resident in Japan and their treatment. Though many of two million Koreans in Japan had returned home since the Japanese surrender, there were still nearly 700,000 Koreans remaining in Japan. The Korean government was most concerned about the legal status and treatment in Japan of these Koreans since a majority of them were taken to Japan as forced laborers during the Pacific War.

V INTERNATIONAL RELATIONS AND DIPLOMACY

Two - Vessels. SCAP Instruction No. 2168 and U.S. Military Government in Korea Ordinance No. 33 called for returning to Korean waters of all vessels that were in Korean waters on August 9, 1945 and of vessels which had been registered in Korea. But Japan has been trying to settle the whole problem by giving 15 merchant ships totalling 5,610 tons and nine fishing boats totalling 336 tons, plus five lend-lease vessels, to Korea "as a gift for development of the marine industry of Korea." Rejecting this position, the Korean government has been urging Japan to show a sincere attitude pursuant of SCAP instruction and the Military Government ordinance.

Three - Property claims. Korea put forward her basic demands in this matter when she proposed that art objects,, old books, original map prints, gold and silver bars taken from Korea to Japan during the Japanese occupation be returned, that Japanese securities owned by Koreans be honored, and that payment for Korean labor recruits be settled and due compensations paid.

The Japanese countered with claims to properties formerly owned by Japanese residents in Korea during the Japanese occupation. The conference was seriously deadlocked over this issue.

All Japanese properties in Korea, both state-owned and private, were vested in the U.S. Military Government in Korea under Military Government Ordinance No. 33 issued on December 6, 1945. The vested properties were then transferred to the Republic of Korea government under the First Agreement between the United States and the Republic of Korea on Properties and Finance signed on September 20, 1948. The Japanese government recognized the legal validity of this deposition of former Japanese properties under Item B, Article 4 of the Japanese Peace Treaty.

The Japanese government waived the property claims at preliminary talks of the fourth Korea-Japan conference in December 1950.

Four - Peace Line and Fishing. Japan is bound to negotiate a Fishing Treaty with Korea under Article 9 and 21 of the Japanese Peace Treaty. Korea has proposed negotiations to discuss implementation of these articles but Japan has refused to respond to the proposal under a variety of pretexts.

The MacArthur headquarters had earlier proclaimed what was called a MacArthur line as demarcation for Japanese fishing areas. It was anticipated, however, that this demarcation would be lifted with the coming into force of the Japanese Peace Treaty. The Korean government saw the need of a new line to protect marine resources in Korean waters from indiscriminate catching by fishermen of a third country. The government felt that as the country was still in a state of war, such a line was further necessary to prevent the infiltration of espionage agents by sea route. On January 18, 1952, the government proclaimed a Presidential Declaration of Sovereignty over Adjacent Waters that set up a Peace Line - a fishing demarcation between Korea and Japan has persistently refused to recognize this line on the ground that what she called the freedom of high sea fishing would be violated. Ensuing dispute over the line has emerged as one of the most important issues pending between the two countries.

Five - Establishment of basic relations. Differences were as irreconciliable over this subject. Korea proposed that normal diplomatic relations be restored after all pending questions had been settled, whereas Japan took the position that basic diplomatic relations be established first.

Apart from the timing of normalization of relations, both sides showed substantial difference over the contents of a Basic Treaty. To Korea, the Treaty of Protection of 1905 and the Treaty of Annexation of 1910 were invalid documents from the beginning. The Korean government proposed that this position of Korea be clearly stipulated in the Basic Treaty. But the Japanese government insisted that the Basic Treaty should not provide for retrospective invalidity of the two Treaties but instead should declare them invalid for the future.

The whole conference was broken off on April 15, 1952 without registering progress in any of these five subjects.

The Second Conference. General Mark W. Clark, then United Nations Commander with headquarters in Tokyo, proclaimed on September 27, 1952 a Sea Defence Zone around the Korean peninsula, which extended beyond the peace line and barred Japanese fishing boats from this zone for reasons of military operations. Then General Clark invited President Rhee to visit Japan as his guest. The president arrived in Japan on January 5, 1953. As Clark's guest, he talked with the Japanese Prime Minister. This top-level meeting led to reopening of the Korea-Japan Conference on April 15, 1953.

The most controversial discussion at the resumed conference centered around the problem of some convicted Koreans and needy Koreans in Japan whom the Japanese government had ordered deported and the Korean government had refused to accept. The Korean delegation said that the deportation order was a violation of the spirit of a joint Korean-Japanese draft on the status and treatment of Koreans living in Japan, which had been adopted at the first Conference. The Japanese decided to detain these Koreans indefinitely.

Before any substantial progress was reported, the Japanese proposed indefinite recess of the conference on July 23, 1953 apparently to wait and see the outcome of the projected political conference on Korea at Geneva.

The Third Conference. The United Nations Command lifted the Defence Zone on August 27, 1953. The Korean government, dissatisfied with this act, warned on September 7 against any crossing of the Peace Line by Japanese fishing boats. As Korea seized Japanese boats found fishing on the Korean side of the Line in defiance of the warning and punished the fishermen under Korea's Maritime Law, the Japanese government proposed resumption of the conference. The third conference opened in Tokyo on October 6, 1953.

The conference had hardly got down to work to reconcile differences over property claims when the Japanese delegate, Kubota Kanichiro, made certain remarks which provoked the Korean delegation so much that it walked out of the conference. According to the Japanese delegate at a meeting of the committee on property claims: one, under normal practices of international law, Korea has not regained her independence before Japan has concluded a Peace Treaty with Korea; two, disposal by U.S. Military Government of Japanese properties in Korea is against international law; three, the Japanese rule in Korea did some good to the Korean people; and four, the Cairo Declaration on independence for Korea was an expression of "war hysteria."

On October 21, the Korean delegation called off the conference, declaring that it would be useless to continue any talks unless the Japanese changed their basic attitude toward Korea.

The Fourth Conference. Preliminary talks started in late 1957 as the Japanese government withdrew the Kubota statement as demanded by Korea and waived claims to former Japanese properties in Korea. The talks came to a successful conclusion on New Year's Eve with the signing of documents concerning reopening of the conference and mutual release of detainees.

On January 7, 1958 the meeting of the working group started to translate the agreement reached at the preliminary talks into detailed plans. The meeting agreed upon the mutual release of detainees. Under the agreement, Japan would release 474 Korean detainees who had been resident in Japan since before the end of the Pacific War and repatriate to south Korea 1,259 other Koreans who had smuggled into Japan, whereas Korea would repatriate 922 Japanese fishermen held at Pusan after serving their prison terms. A new difficulty arose in this connection as 95 of the 1,259 Korean detainees scheduled to be repatriated to south Korea refused to return to the south and elected, instead, to go to north Korea.

The working group also discussed the return of Korean cultural treasures, but the Japanese submitted a list of only 106 items in the Tokyo National Museum as the objects she was prepared to restore.

The working group meeting meandered through some more complications before reopening of the full conference on April 15, 1958. The conference agreed at the outset that as the Japanese had dropped property claims, the Committee on Property Claims would officially be redesignated as the Committee on Korean Property Claims. It was also agreed that two Subcommittees – on vessels and on property claims – would be set up under this Committee. The other three Committees on the legal status of Koreans resident in Japan, basic relations, and Peace Line and fishing were to remain intact.

While the conference was in progress, the Japanese government released 25 Koreans said to have elected to go to north Korea from the Omura detention camp without seeking consultation with the Korean government. This caused the conference to be deadlocked for three months. In Committee discussions the Japanese were preoccupied with settlement of the fishing dispute and paid little attention to other subjects, including Korean property claims. The conference dragged on for eight months without making any tangible progress until adjourned on December 20, 1958.

The conference originally scheduled to reopen in early 1959 did not meet until August 12, 1959 because of new tension caused by a Japanese decision in February to deport part of Korean residents to north Korea. At the resumed conference the Korean delegation tried to stop the projected deportation to north Korea by taking up this problem in the Committee on the legal status for Koreans living in Japan. The Japanese opposed this and insisted that the problem should be discussed separate from the legal status.

Economic Relations

The economic relations with Japan have occupied a unique and important place in the overall foreign trade activities of this country. The economic relations with Japan may well be divided into three stages.

The first stage covers the period between the establishment of the Korean government in 1948 and the severance of trade relations with Japan in August 1955. Early in this stage, when Japan was still under occupational control, commercial exchanges were reciprocal.

Reciprocity ended, however, with the outbreak of the Korean War. A great portion of aid money from friendly countries, especially from the United States, was spent for procurements from Japan. As the war progressed, a drastically increasing number of orders for war materials were placed from Japan. The open account for private trade between Korea and Japan also registered a huge balance in favor of Japan.

After the war ended, the Korean government tried to improve the balance. But Japan discouraged imports from Korea by restricting the foreign exchange allocation or the import quota for purchases from Korea. The Korean government, on its part, restricted imports from Japan on July 1, 1955 by chalking off 200 Japanese items from the import list. On August 18, the government cut off all trade relations with Japan.

The second stage coincides with the period of the trade rupture. The drastic measure was designed to make Japan remove restrictions against imports from Korea and live up to the Provisional Trade Agreement. This trade cut-off represents the most drastic action the Korean government has ever taken in foreign trade since it was founded in 1948.

The third stage is the period from the trade resumption up-to-date. After the trade ban was lifted, the government subjected all commercial transactions with Japan to prior permission of the Korean Mission in Japan so that imports might be balanced with exports. This regulation was superceded by a new Trade Regulation on May 7, 1958, which has remained in force up to now. Designed to bar those Japanese firms engaged in business transactions with Communist countries from trade with Korea, the new Regulation provides that all Japanese firms desiring to do business with Korea should obtain certificates from the Korean Mission in Japan to the effect that they have no Communist ties.

Pending Questions

One – Korean Residents in Japan. Koreans still living in Japan are estimated to number 600,000 to 800,000. Most of these Koreans were forcibly taken to Japan to meet labor shortages during the Pacific War and, since the Japanese surrender, have been unemployed or underemployed. The problem of these Korean residents has further been complicated by north Korean Communist propaganda directed at them.

An early solution to the whole problem can only be made when the Japanese government agreed to the Korean suggestion that all Korean residents be recognized as nationals of the Republic of Korea and then, that those desirous of returning to south Korea be repatriated while those choosing to remain in Japan be granted permanent residence.

Two – Peace Line. The tension existing between the two countries over the past few years is largely attributable to Japan's refusal to recognize the Peace Line and seizure by Korea of Japanese fishermen within the Peace Line for punishment under Korean law. It is hoped that Japan will come to understand that the Line was designed to maintain continued productivity of fishing grounds around Korea and agree to negotiate a fishing agreement with Korea.

Three – Detainees. With the coming into force of a new Immigration Law, the Japanese government decided to apply it to Korean residents alike. Under this Law, those Koreans found guilty by the Japanese court were not released in Japan upon serving their prison terms. They were, instead, designated for expulsion from Japan and sent to an alien detention camp. The Japanese authorities also detained those Koreans who had failed to register under this Law. Called "violators of the procedural regulations," they were placed in the same category as smugglers and held in the detention camp pending repatriation.

These Koreans did not enter Japan under the same circumstances as aliens from other countries, and they should, accordingly, be distinguished from other foreigners in Japan. The Korean Mission in Japan held that they should have been granted the right of permanent residence in Japan and given equal treatment as the Japanese. The Mission succeded to reach an agreement with the Japanese government on April 2, 1956. This provided for:

Firstly, that Korea would repatriate Japanese fishermen held at Pusan after they have served their prison terms, and,

Secondly, that the Japanese government would release those Korean detainees who entered Japan before the end of the Pacific War, and that the Korean government would accept their repatriation. However, the released detainees themselves would decide whether they should remain in Japan or be repatriated.

Despite this agreement, the Japanese government later demanded that all detainees, upon release, be repatriated to south Korea. After the Korean government rejected the demand under provisions of the agreement, the Japanese government sought ways and means to expel 48 of them who, the Japanese said, wished to go to north Korea. The Japanese repatriated 22 of them to the north aboard a Norwegian ship.

A complete deadlock over the issue of detainees ensued. The deadlock persisted until the end of 1957, when both sides signed another agreement on mutual release of detainees. But this was the beginning of a new problem as both sides continued to detain each other's nationals after the agreement was effected.

Four – Tokto Island. Tokto, or Takeshima as the Japanese called it, is an uninhabited island made up of twin rocks. It is located 85 miles from the nearest Japanese territory of Oki Island and 49 miles from Ullung Island of Korea.

V INTERNATIONAL RELATIONS AND DIPLOMACY

Japan placed this island under the control of the governor of Oki Island, Shimane Prefecture, under the Prefecture's Public Notice No. 40 on February 22, 1905. The Japanese insisted on their claim to the island on the ground that Korea did not protest against the 1905 Japanese action.

In February that year, Japan was at war with Russia. She had imposed a number of Agreements on Korea, thereby holding arbitrary control over the diplomatic rights of Korea. Korea was by no means in a position to protest to Japan in any matter at the time.

Historically, the island is no doubt Korean. For years following the Japanese surrender in 1945, Korea's sovereign rights over the island were never disputed. SCAP Instruction No. 677 issued on January 29, 1946 put Tokto beyond Japanese territorial rights and the MacArthur Line showed that the island was Korean. It is also clear beyond doubt that the intentions of the Cairo Declaration lay in bringing Japan back to her status before the Sino-Japanese War of 1894.

Relations with Thailand, Other Southeast Asian Countries

Thailand, a staunch anti-Communist member of the Southeast Asia Treaty Organization, was another United Nations member country which fought the Communist aggression in Korea.

Thailand recognized the Republic of Korea in October 1949 and agreed to exchange diplomatic representatives on the level of Minister in October 1958.

When another anti-Communist country, the Federation of Malaya, was born in Southeast Asia on August 30, 1957, the Republic of Korea readily extended recognition. In informing the Federation of Korea's official recognition on September 2, the Republic of Korea also expressed readiness to open normal diplomatic relations with that country.

Further efforts to strengthen ties with Southeast Asian countries were made when a non-governmental mission, headed by Dr. George L. Paik, left in November 1953 for a one-month tour of Nationalist China, south Vietnam, Burma, the Philippines and Indonesia. A second mission led by Mr. Yi Pomnyong left in February 1954 on another goodwill tour to Singapore, Malaya, the Philippines and south Vietnam. This mission returned to Korea to see another mission depart in April that year for Southeast Asia.

On the basis of the groundwork laid by these missions, South Korea proposed the organization of an alliance of anti-Communist peoples in Asia. The proposal bore fruit on June 15, 1954, when the inaugural conference of the Anti-Cummunist Asian People's League was held at Chinhae, Korea. The League held the second conference at Manila in March 1956, the third conference at Saigon in March 1957, the fourth conference at Bangkok in April 1958, and the fifth conference at Seoul in April 1959.

Relations with Australia and New Zealand

Australia and New Zealand have played a commendable role in anti-Communist defences of Southeast Asia and the Columbo Plan area by maintaining close diplomatic cooperation with the United States since the close of World War II.

Australia recognized the Republic of Korea on August 15, 1949 and friendly relations have since developed rapidly between the two countries. The Korean government established a Consulate-General in Sydney with Mr. Lincoln Hoon Kim as Consul-General. Australia has voted for all United Nations resolutions on Korea. She has, in fact, been a leader alongside the United States for recognition of the Republic of Korea government as the only lawful government in Korea, democratic unification of Korea, and United Nations membership for this country.

Australia has had representatives with all the three United Nations Commissions on Korea to help achieve the United Nations objectives in Korea.

When the north Korean Communists invaded the Republic of Korea, Australia ordered her ground, naval and air force units in Japan immediately to go to the support of the outnumbered R.O.K. Forces in response to a U.N. Security Council appeal. The Australian forces remained in Korea until August 1957 as a major contingent of the British Commonwealth Division. Australia also helped in U.N. reconstruction and relief efforts for Korea by contributing more than four million dollars to the funds of the United Nations Korean Reconstruction Agency (UNKRA) and the U.N. emergency relief program in Korea.

New Zealand has been as consistent a supporter of the Republic of Korea in all U.N. debates on Korea. She answered the U.N. Security Council call for troop contribution to the Korean war within a month by dispatching army and navy forces. She was another generous contributor to the fund of UNKRA and the U.N. emergency relief program.

The Korean government has long been making preliminary efforts for commercial agreements with these two countries.

Relations with Other Countries

Scandinavia

The Republic of Korea established normal diplomatic relations with Sweden, Denmark and Norway in March 1959. The Korean government appointed her Ambassador to Britain to be concurrently Ministers to the three countries, which on their part named their Ambassadors to Japan to hold the Korea posts additionally. Of the three, Denmark and Norway cast supporting votes for the U.N. 1948 Assembly resolution on Korea.

All the three countries dispatched hospital units to Korea during the war and generously contributed to United Nations funds for Korean relief and reconstruction. Sweden sent a field hospital unit to Korea on July 20, 1950. A Danish hospital ship immediately followed suit, arriving on July 22. A medical unit from Norway came to Korea on March 6, 1951.

After the shooting war ended, the Scandinavian countries made concerted efforts to build a National Medical Center in Seoul through the United Nations and, to that end, made significant contributions to UNKRA: 336,615 dollars plus 230,011 dollars worth of medical supplies and 500 tons of sugar from Denmark, 1,075,300 dollars plus 74,677 dollars for emergency relief from Norway, and 374,962 dollars in addition to 48,326 dollars for emergency relief from Sweden.

Other European States

Other than Britain, France, Germany, Italy and the Scandinavian countries, European states which recognized the Republic of Korea are Belgium (August 15, 1949), Greece (August 7, 1949), Iceland (February 12, 1950), Luxembourg (August 29, 1949), the Netherlands (July 25, 1949), and the City of Vatican (April 13, 1949). Portugal and Spain indirectly recognized the Republic of Korea by supporting the 1948 U.N. Assembly resolution. The Vatican has representatives in Korea. The Korean government is trying to exchange envoys with Switzerland.

The Ambassador to the United States, Dr. You-chan Yang, visited most of these countries – Austria, Belgium, Greece, Luxembourg, the Netherlands, Portugal and Spain – during his 1959 goodwill tour of Europe.

Many of these countries came to the aid of the Republic of Korea, both militarily and economically, during the Korean War. Their military contributions were: an infantry battalion and reinforcements from Belgium in September 1950 and in March 1951 respectively; an army unit, reinforcements from Greece in September 1950, in July 1951, also in July 1951 and in October 1951 respectively; a company of ground troops from Luxembourg in March 1951, and a battalion from the Netherlands in July 1950. The Netherlands also sent a warship to join the naval force of the United Nations Command.

V INTERNATIONAL RELATIONS AND DIPLOMACY

Economic help extended Korea by these countries are listed as follows: 179,477 dollars from Austria, 1,200,000 dollars and 300 tons of sugar from Belgium, 171,282 dollars and a bulk of soap, notebooks, and medical supplies from Greece, 45,400 dollars worth or 125 tons of cod-liver oil from Iceland, 1,052,632 dollars from the Netherlands, 1,144 dollars from Monaco, 313,954 dollars from Switzerland and 10,000 dollars from Vatican.

Commercial relations between these European countries and Korea are not close as yet. The government is trying all it can to move closer to them to use their valuable assets in capital and technology for reconstruction of her economy.

Mideast and Near East

It is true that no country in these areas, except for Turkey, has direct relations with the Republic of Korea. But Mideastern and Near Eastern countries do demand the diplomatic attention of Korea as their voices, expressed through the Afro-Asian group in the United Nations, are increasingly being heard in international affairs.

Egypt, Iran, Lebanon, Syria, Turkey and Iraq have voted for all the U.N. resolutions on Korea. Iraq announced her individual recognition of the Republic of Korea on September 24, 1954.

No country in the Middle and Near East, again with the exception of Turkey, sent troops to join the United Nations Cnmmand during the Korean War but Egypt, Lebanon, Saudi Arabia and Israel made some contribution, such as medical supplies from Israel, to UNKRA. In appreciation of their help, the government sent General Kim Chongyol to Iran, Iraq, Lebanon and Saudi Arabia besides Turkey in 1957.

Latin America and Canada

Although Korea has not exchanged diplomatic missions with Central and South American countries, almost all of them have recognized the Republic of Korea. They are (dates of recognition in parentheses): Chile (May 27, 1947), Brazil (June 14 1949), the Dominican Republic (June 20, 1949), Bolivia (July 14, 1949), Cuba (July 18, 1949), Costa Rica (August 12, 1949), Haiti (August 13, 1949), El Salvador (September 3, 1949), and Venezuela (March 3, 1949).

Other countries - Argentine, Columbia, Guatemala, Honduras, Mexico, Nicaragua and Panama - took part in collective recognition of Korea when they voted for the 1948 U.N. Generel Assembly resolution.

In appreciation of support from these countries, the government dispatched Mr. Kim Tongsong to Central and South America as a goodwill envoy in December 1958. Another goodwill envoy, Ambassador You-chan Yang, visited Latin America again in June 1956. Two of these countries have sent goodwill missions to Korea - Cuba in March 1957 and Guatemala in December 1956. Columbia is the only country in this area which had troops under the United Nations Command during the Korean War. She sent one infantry regiment of 1,300 officers and men in November 1950. This followed the arrival in Korean waters of three naval ships from Columbia in October. The Columbian regiment withdrew on October 27, 1954.

Other countries helped Korea economically during the war. Among these countries were Argentine, Brazil, Chile, Costa Rica, Ecuador, Guatemala, Haiti, Honduras, Mexico, Uruguay and Venezuela. Columbia also contributed economically besides fighting.

The Dominion of Canada recognized the Republic of Korea on April 9, 1949. Canada has supported the Republic of Korea in all United Nations discussions of the Korean problem ever since it was first taken up in 1947. Furthermore, Canada played a positive role in the establishment of the Republic of Korea government by appointing a representative with the United Nations Commission that supervised the general election on May 10, 1948.

The Dominion was one of the 16 U.N. allies in the Korean War. She also willingly helped the United Nation in its efforts for emergency relief and reconstruction in Korea.

Union of South Africa

The Union of South Africa indirectly recognized the Republic of Korea by supporting the third U.N. General Assembly resolution on December 12, 1948, which approved the R.O.K. government as the only lawful government in Korea. The Union maintained a contingent with the United Nations Command during the Korean hostilities.

Korean Missions Abroad

Korean Embassy in China
  Ambassador   : Kim Hongil
  Address   : 44, Jenai road, Section 3, Taipei Taiwan.
  Telephone   : 43371
  Cable Address: GONGKWAN TAIPEI

Korean Embassy in the United States
  Ambassador   : You Chan Yang
  Address   : 2322 Massachusetts Avenue, N.W. Washington D.C., U.S.A.
  Telephone   : Adams 4-4112
  Cable Address: KORIC WASHINGTON D.C.

Korean Embassy in United Kingdom
  Ambassador   : Kim Yutaik
  Address   : 36, Cadogan Square, London, S.W.I., United Kindom
  Telephone   : Kensington 8025
  Cable Address: GONGKWAN LONDON

Korean Embassy in Turkey
  Ambassador   : Shin Eungkyun
  Address   : Kavaklidere Posta Caddesi, Alacan Sokak No. 9, Ankara, Turkey
  Telephone   : 20489
  Cable Address: GONGKWAN ANKARA

Korean Embassy in the Philippines
  Ambassador   : Lincoln Kim
  Address   : 1730 Indian Street, Marate, Manila, Philippiens
  Telephone   : 55396
  Cable Address: GONGKWAN MANILA

Korean Embassy in Vietnam
  Ambassador   : Choi Dukshin
  Address   : 107 Rue Nguyen Du, Saigon, Viet-nam
  Telephone   : Saigon-474
  Cable Address: GONGKWAN SAIGON

Korean Embassy in Germany
  Ambassador   : Sohn Wonyil
  Address   : Koblenzer Strasse 124, Bonn Germany
  Telephone   : Bonn 26391
  Cable Address: GONGKWAN BONN

Korean Embassy in France
  Ambassador   : Chong Ilkwon
  Address   : 33 Avenue Mozart, Paris 16, France
  Telephone   : MIR Abeau 4928
  Cable Address: GONGKWAN PARIS

Korean Embassy in Italy
  Ambassador   : Kim Youngkee
  Address   : Via Lovanio 6 Rome, Italy
  Telephone   : 863,331
  Cable Address: GONGKWAN ROME

Korean Mission in Japan
  Ambassador   : Yiu Taiha
  Address   : 5,1-chome, Takeya-cho, Asabu, Minatoku, Tokyo, Japan
  Telephone   : 45-4004
  Cable Address: DAEPYO TOKYO

Korean Mission to the United Nations
  Ambassador   : Ben C. Limb
  Address   : 350, Fifth Avenue, New York 1, N. Y., U.S.A.
  Telephone   : Oxford 5-4990....4992
  Cable Address: ROKMISUN NEWYORK

*   *   *

Korean Consulate General in Los Angeles
  Consul   : Kang Yongkyoo
  Address   : 5525, Wilshire Boulevard, Los Angeles 36, California
  Telephone   : Webster 1-1331
  Cable Address: GONGKWAN LOSANGELES

Korean Consulate General in New York
  Consul General: D. Y. Namkoong
  Address   : 9, East 80th Street, New York, N.Y., U.S.A.
  Telephone   : Butterfield-8-3904-3905
  Cable Address : GONGKWAN NEWYORK

Korean Consulate General in Honolulu

V INTERNATIONAL RELATIONS AND DIPLOMACY

Consul General: Oh Choongchong
Address : 1113 Hassinger Street, Honolulu, U.S.A.
Telephone : 67906
Cable Address : GONGKWAN HONOLULU

Korean Consulate General in Hong Kong
Consul General: Kang Choonhee
Address : 67-71 Queen's Road, Central, Hong Kong
Telephone : 27116
Cable Address : KORCON HONGKONG

Korean Consulate General in San Francisco
Consul General: Choo Younghan
Address : 3500 Clay Street, San Francisco, California, U.S.A.
Telephone : Walnut 1-2252, 2253
Cable Address : GONGKWAN SANFRANCISCO

Korean Consulate General in Sydney
Consul General: Song Bon Limb
Address : 50, Darling Point Road Darling Point, Sydney, Australia
Telephone : F. B. 1961; 4155
Cable Address : GONGKWAN SYDNEY

Korean Mission in Geneva
Minister : Kim Yongshik
Address : 45, Avenue Wendt, Geneve Switzerland
Telephone : 34.70.58
Cable Address : DAEPYOBU GENEVA

The United Nations and Korea

Elections in the South

The heads of government of the United States, Britain and China, in the Cairo Declaration issued on December 1, 1943 during the Second World War noted the conditon of slavery in which the Korean people were placed and promised to make Korea liberated and independent in due course. This international pledge, reaffirmed by the Potsdam Declaration of July 26, 1945, was accepted by Japan in her instruments of surrender of September 7, 1945.

Russia's entry into the war against Japan complicated the prospects of Korea's independence. The United States and Soviet Russia decided on divided occupation of Korea to enforce the surrender of the Japanese. In December 1945, the Foreign Ministers of the United States, Britain, China and the Soviet Union met in Moscow to end the occupational division of the country and bring about unified independence for Korea. The Foreign Ministers agreed on a maximum of five years of trusteeship by the four powers under directives of the Foreign Ministers. A Joint United States-Soviet Commission met in Seoul to discuss establishment of a provisional Korean government to rule during the period of proposed trusteeship.

As nationwide opposition to the four-power trusteeship mounted, the Joint Commission ended in the United States bringing the Korean problem to the United Nations on September 17, 1958. This was the beginning of the close relation between the world organization and Korea.

The United Nations General Assembly passed a resolution on November 14, 1947 calling for holding general elections, under supervision of a United Nations Temporary Commission on Korea for a free, democratic and independent government of Korea. As the Communists in the north balked the Commissionin's mission, however, the Little Assembly of the United Nations adopted another resolution calling for general elections in areas accessible (south of the 38th parallel) to the U. N. Commission. The year of 1948 saw the election held in south Korea and the resultant establishment of the Republic of Korea government.

Born under the authority and with the cooperation of the United Nations, the Republic of Korea government was endorsed by the

U.N. General Assembly on December 12 that year as the only lawful government in Korea. In making this endorsement, the General Assembly also decided that foreign troops would be withdrawn from Korea and that the U.N. Temporary Commission on Korea would be replaced by a permanent U.N. Commission with the mission of eventually achieving the initial objectives of the United Nations in Korea.

The Republic of Korea government sent a delegation to the fourth U.N. General Assembly in September 1948. It asked the U.N., firstly, that the U.N. Commission on Korea be strengthened and remain in Korea; secondly, that member states of the United Nations officially declare that they be responsible for the security of Korea, and thirdly, that the Republic of Korea be given U.N. membership.

Considering this request, the General Assembly passed a resolution on October 21, calling for the continued presence in Korea of the reinforced U.N. objectives carried out. The General Assembly adopted another resolution on November 22, calling on the Security Council to take up the proposed membership for the Republic of Korea.

War from the North

When the north Korean Communists attacked south Korea on June 25, 1950, the Republic of Korea government promptly reported the fact to the U.N. Commission. Pointing out that the Communist invasion was detrimental to the peace and security of the entire world, the government requested the Commission to order the Communists to stop the aggression and, in the meantime, to call the attention of the Security Council to the situation. The government made an official request to the United States for arms aid. The U.S. government immediately accepted the request and ordered General MacArthur to rush arms to Korea.

The United States called for an emergency meeting of the U.N. Security Council on June 25. The United States told the Security Council that the north Korean Communist action constituted a breach of peace as specified in Article 39, Chapter 7 of the United Nations Charter and demanded that the Council bring about an immediate ceasefire and withdrawal of the north Korean Communist troops north of the 38th parallel. A resolution tabled by the United States also called on U.N. member states to extend no aid to the north Korean Communists. The resolution was adopted with the Soviet Union absent and Yugoslavia abstaining from voting.

The north Korean Communists ignored the resolution. The Security Council met again on June 27 to pass another resolution, also tabled by the United States, which recommended to the U.N. member states to furnish the Republic of Korea all assistance necessary for repulsing the armed aggression and restore peace and security in the Korean area. Still another resolution, also proposed by the United States, came up before the Council on July 7 to organize the first police force in history ever to be formed by an international organization. The resolution called for establishing a unified command under the U.N. flag with an American as commander. The United States took the initiative, under the mandate of the resolution, in organizing the U.N. force. Sixteen countries responded to this resolution to fight in Korea and 53 others rendered assistance to the Republic of Korea.

A few hours before the July 7 resolution was adopted, President Harry S. Truman announced that American Army, Navy and Air Force units in Japan had been ordered to go to the aid of the R.O.K. Forces. On July 8, President Truman appointed General MacArthur United Nations Commander. Congress, on its parts, allocated a huge sum of money as aid to the Republic of Korea. On July 30, Congress decided to refuse aid under the Marshall Plan for those countries which would not cooperate with the United Nations Command.

Soviet Russia imputed the blame for the Korean War to the Republic of Korea and the United States, boycotting all Security

Council, resolutions. On July 4, Andrei Gromyko of Russia demanded withdrawal from south Korea of American troops and charged that blockade of the Korean and Chinese coasts by the U.S. Navy was an act of aggression.

On July 13, Prime Minister Jawaharlal Nehru of India sent a memorandum to the United States and Soviet Russia, offering good offices, in settling the Korean War. As prerequisites to Indian good offices, he proposed that the north Korean Communists withdraw north of the 38th parallel and that Communist China be admitted into the United Nations. Russia agreed to the Nehru proposal but the United States rejected it.

Russia returned to the Security Council on July 27. With her representative as chairman under the rotation basis, Russia intentionally blocked the functioning of the Council to prevent it from taking any action on Korea. In October 1950, the United States sponsored a resolution at the General Assembly which called for the veto-free General Assembly to decide upon U.N. action concerning international peace and security. The resolution, passed by the General Assembly, enabled the United Nations Forces in Korea to act under directives from the General Assembly, instead of from the Security Council.

Both the free world and the Communist bloc submitted resolutions on Korea to the fourth U.N. General Assembly. The Communist resolution sponsored by Russia and four other Communist countries called for: one - ceasefire; two - immediate withdrawal of all foreign troops; three - elections throughout Korea; four - establishment of a joint commission consisting of equal numbers of representives from the legislatures existing in the north and south to discuss preparations for the all-Korea election and establishment of a central Korean government, and five - creation of a U.N. Commission, with neighboring countries of Korea included as members, to supervise the general elections. The resolution was voted down 46 to 5 with eight abstentions at the Politicial Committee on October 4.

The other resolution was submitted by Britain, the Philippines, Australia and five other countries. It called for: one - all adequate measures to safeguard security throughout Korea; two - elections under United Nations supervision to establish a unified, independent and democratic Korean government; three - continued presence U.N.C. troops in Korea until the achievement of the afore-mentioned objectives, and four- establishment of a United Nations Commission for the Unification and Rehabilitation of Korea (UNCURK). The Western resolution was passed by the General Assembly on October 7.

The day after the resolution was adopted, General MacArthur called on the Communists to surrender, adding that should no immediate response be forthcoming, his command would take military action to implement the mandate of the United Nations.

Red China's Entry

On the heels of the R.O.K. troops who crossed the 38th parallel on Octorber 1, the U.N. Force march north on Octoler 8. On October 17, President Rhee made public his views that the Republic of Korea government should hold administrative reins in the north and, accordingly. declared that the government would soon dispatch officials there.

R.O.K. troops reached the Korean-Manchurian border in late October 1950. All north Koren was virtually occupied when masses of Chinese Communist troops were thrown into Korea to open a new phase in the war.

Seriously concerned about the Chinese armed intervention, President Truman hinted at a press conference that an atomic weapon might be used in the Korean War. The firm U.S. attitude toward the Chinese Communists alarmed European countries, which feared a new world war. Britain, among others, played a leading role in bringing pressure on the United States to modify its attitude.

In this growing tension, the Security Council sat in an emergency session with invited representatives from the Republic of Korea and Communist China sitting in. The Council passed a resolution, tabled by the United States and five other countries, demanding immediate withdrawal from Korea of the Chinese Communists. As Soviet Russia vetoed the resolution, however, the Council discussion of the Korea situation came to an end. The General Assembly was to take up the Korean problem.

The United States on December 4 submitted a resolution to the General Assembly impeaching the Chinese Communists. Strong support for the resolution was voiced outside the United Nations. President Rhee demanded that the world organization punish the Chinese Communists. In the United States, Congress passd a resolution in January 1951 demanding that the United Nations immediately condemn Communist China as an aggressor in Korea. In the General Assemby itself, an overwhelming number supported the U.S. presented resolution on February 1, 1951.

Meanwhile, in Korea, the war took a new turn in March 1958 as the Chinese Communists were pushed back north. Earlier on February 5, President Rhee, declaring that the partition at the 38th parallel was no longer existent, advocated a renewed march north by the allied forces.

In March, General MacArthur released a public statement to the effect that if the United Nations Forces were permitted to extend operations to the Chinese mainland, they could defeat the Chinese Communist troops in Korea.

The statement was met with enthusiastic support in Korea but it cost the General his position as United Nations Commander. President Truman relieved the General on April 11 on the ground that he had ignored instructions from the United States government. This was obviously a result of the pressure Britain and other European powers had been applying upon the United States. It was also a clear manifestation of United States policy to limit the war to the Korean peninsula while seeking a settlement through diplomatic negotiation.

Armistice Negotiations, Problem of Unity

P.O.W. Deadlock

The policy to localize the war led the United Nations to seek an armistice with the Communists. United Nations' efforts for an armistice immediately encountered determined opposition from the Republic of Korea.

On May 26, 1951, President Rhee expressed his objection to any armistice that would leave the country divided again along the 38th parallel and declared that the R.O.K. armed forces would march north alone. The National Assembly also registered its objection to the armistice which would not presuppose withdrawal of the Chinese aggressors from Korea and complete and independent unificaton under the sovereignty of the Republic of Korea. On June 29, the Assembly adopted a resolution officially voicing its opposition to an armistice along the 38th parallel.

On June 23, 1951, an armistice overture came from Jacob A. Malik, then Soviet Russia's representative to the United Nations, who proposed that negotiations be opened for an armistice and that the two belligerent sides withdraw from the 38th parallel. After consulting with its U.N. allies, the United States ordered United Naions Commander General Mathew B. Ridgway to open negotiations for an armistice with the belligerent commander.

The first official reaction of the Republic of Korea came on June 30, when Foreign Minister Y.T. Pyun issued a statement saying that the Republic would go along with her allies in the armistice negotiations if withdrawal of Chinese troops, disarmament of the north Korean troops and other conditions were accepted. The Ambassador to the United Stases, Dr. You-Chan Yang also laid down the terms of the Republic of Korea—one, withdrawal from north Korea of the Chinese Communist troops; two—disarmament of the north Ko-

V INTERNATIONAL RELATIONS AND DIPLOMACY

rean forces; three—United Nations' measures to prevent any third power from giving military and economic aid to north Korea, and four—free general elections in north Korea under the supervision of the United Nations. He made it unmistakably clear that the Republic of Korea opposed an appeasement armistice along the 38th parallel.

The United States sidestepped the objection from the Republic of Korea and continued negotiation. On July 26, armistice negotiators agreed on (1) adoption of the agenda, (2) setting up of a demilitarized zone, (3) provisions for policing the armistice, (4) exchange of prisoners of war and (5) recommendations to the governments concerned.

The most ticklish issue discussed throughout the negotiations was exchange of war prisoners. The Communists demanded exchange of all prisoners whereas the United Nations Command proposed that freedom of choice by prisoners themselves be respected in deciding whether they should be repatriated.

The positions of the two sides remained practically unchanged until July 26, 1952, when the armistice conference adjourned indefinitely. On March 28, 1953, the Communist Command in Korea agreed to resumption of negotiations, proposing immediate exchange of seriously wounded and sick prisoners of war. In Peking, Communist China's Premier Chou En-lai proposed on March 30 of the same year that all prisoners wishing to return home be repatriated and that those refusing repatriation be transferred to neutral countries.

R.O.K. Opposition

The Republic of Korea continued to oppose an armistice. President Rhee, in a statement on April 11, said that the Republic of Korea would under no circumstances accept an armistice that would permit the Chinese Communists to remain in Korea. He reiterated the determination of the Republic of Korea to march north to achieve national unification if such an armistice were signed.

As Republic of Korea objections mounted, the United States made all efforts to modify the Korean position while seeking a compromise with the Communists. General Mark Clark, United Nations Commander, often flew to Seoul from his Tokyo headquarters to find a common ground between the Republic of Korea government and the United Nations.

With the talks in Seoul between General Clark and Presideut Rhee were rewarded with little success, Presi dent Rhee brought the matter to the top level. In a letter to President Eisenhower on June 6, he proposed that the United States and the Republic of Korea conclude a Treaty of Mutual Defense as guarantee of security for the Republic. President Eisenhower, in his reply, said, however, that negotiations for such a treaty would be started only after an armistice had been achieved in Korea.

The armistice conference itself was progressing rapidly at Panmunjom. Agreement was reached on June 8 on provisions governing exchange of prisoners. The Republic of Korea's objection to an armistice reached a new height as a wave of demonstrations took place with millions of Koreans participating and the leaders of the three armed branches of the Republic sat in an emergency meeting to reaffirm their determination to march north.

The Armistice Agreement was all but formally signed when President Rhee released 27,366 anti-Communist prisoners of war from detention camps in south Korea on June 18. The action took the United Nations allies by surprise. The United States sent Assistant Secretary Walter Robertson to Seoul as President Eisenhower's special envoy in an attempt to pursuade the Korean government to desist from wrecking the armistice negotiations.

The Armistice Agreement was signed on July 27, 1953 between the United Nations Command and the Communists, finally bringing the long and bloody three-year war to an end.

Geneva Political Conference

Preliminary Talks

The Armistice Agreement provided in Article 60 that a high-level political conference would be held at Geneva within three months after the signing of the Agreement for the purpose of negotiating withdrawal from Korea of foreign troops and a peaceful settlement of the Korean problem. On August 28, 1953, the U.N. General Assembly passed a resolution, which, while approving the signing of the Armistice Agreement in general, supported convening of a political conference in particular. In passing this resolution, the United States proposed that representatives of both sides face each other across the conference table whereas Soviet Russia insisted on a round-table conference.

Under the mandate of the resolution, representatives of the United Nations and the Communist sides met at a preliminary political conference at Panmunjom on October 26, 1953. The Republic of Korea government, not being a signatory to the Agreement, was represented at the conference by Vice-Foreign Mnister Chung W. Cho as observer. The preliminary conference, by nature, was to make only procedural arrangements for the full political conference. But the Communists resorted to propaganda tactics by insisting that Russia and India participate in the Geneva political conference in the capacity of neutrals. The Panmunjom conference soon adjourned indefinitely without achieving any results.

R.O.K. Reservation

The Big-Four Foreign Ministers' Conference, meeting at Berlin in February 1954, decided that the political conference as stipulated in the Armistice Agreement be held on April 26 at Geneva. The Korean government at first announced that it would boycott the Geneva conference but President Rhee later changed his mind and agreed to send a government representative to Geneva on condition that the conference be limited to 90 days and that, after the stated period, the U.N. allies would waste no further time seeking a peaceful solution of the Korean question through negotiations with the Communists.

Dulles Backs R.O.K.

At the outset of the conference, the Republic of Korea representative, Foreign Minister Y. T. Pyun, proposed that free elections be held only in north Korea under the supervision of the United Nations and that the Chinese Communist forces complete withdrawal from the north before the elections. Support of this Republic of Korea position promptly came from Secretary of State John Foster Dulles. Speaking before the Conference, Secretary Dulles reminded the Communists that a feasible plan for reunifying Korea had already been presented in the U.N. General Assembly resolution of October 7, 1950. He urged that cooperation be given to UNCURK in achieving the unattained objective of the United Nations and that the Chinese Communists leave north Korea.

Pyun's 14 Points

The British Commonwealth nations also expressed their appreciation of the Republic of Korea stand. But anxious as they were to seek a peaceful settlement, the Commonwealth representatives called on the Republic to accept general elections throughout Korea instead of in north Korea alone as proposed by the Republic of Korea government. Taking this Commonwealth opinion into consideration and feeling the need for a unified allied stand to counter proposals by the Communists, Foreign Minister Pyun on May 22 submitted a 14-point proposal for reunification of Korea, which follows:

"1. With a view to establishing a united, independent and democratic Korea, free elections shall be carried out under United Nations supervision in accordance with the previous United Nations resolutions thereanent.

"2. The free elections shall be held in

north Korea which has not been accessible to such elections and in south Korea also in accordance with the constitutional processes of the Republic of Korea.

"3. The elections shall be held within six months from the adoption of this proposal.

"4. Before, during and after the elections, the United Nations personnel connected with the supervision of the elections shall have full freedoms of movements, speech, etc. to observe and help create conditions of a free atmosphere throughout the entire area for election. Local authorities shall give them all possible facilities.

"5. Before, during and after the elections, the candidates, their campaigners and their families shall enjoy full freedoms of movement, speech, etc, and other human rights such as are recognized and protected in democratic countries.

"6. The elections shall be conducted on the basis of secret ballot and universal adult suffrage.

"7. Representation in the all-Korea legislature shall be in direct proportion to the population of all Korea.

"8. With a view to apportioning the number of representatives in exact propotion to populations in the election areas, a census shall be taken under United Nations supervision.

"9. The all-Korea legislature shall be convened in Seoul immediately after the elections.

"10. The following questions, among others, shall be left to enactment of the all-Korea legislature:

"a) Whether the President of unified Korea should be newly elected or not;

"b) Concerning amendments of the existing Constitution of the Republic of Korea;

"c) Concerning the disbandment of military units.

"11. The existing Constitution of the Republic of Korea shall remain effective except as it may be amended by the all-Korea legislature.

"12. The Chinese Communist troops shall complete their withdrawal from Korea one month in advance of the election date.

"13. The phased withdrawal of the United Nations forces from Korea may start before the elections, but must not be complete before effective control over all Korea is achieved by the unified Government of Korea and certified by the United Nations.

"14. The integrity and independence of a unified, independent and democratic Korea shall be guaranteed by the United Nations."

Nam Il's Proposal

The Communist proposal, as forwarded by north Korean Foreign Minister Nam Il on April 27, may be summarised as follows:

With a view to achieving the national unification of Korea as soon as possible and founding a democratic, independent and unified country,

1. General elections shall be held on the basis of opinions freely expressed by all the inhabitants of Korea in order to form a unified government of Korea;

2. An all-Korea Commision shall be formed with representatives from north and south Korea as members in order to prepare for, and hold, the general elections, and also to work out measures for close economic and cultural ties between the north and south, and;

3. The general elections shall be supervised by a Neutral Nations' Commission.

The two-month conference ended in deadlock with both sides branding the other aggressor and neither giving way on its position of what constituted free elections. Whereupon, the Korean War allies represented in the Geneva negotiations issued a communique clarifying their position and called off the conference.

The 15 U.N. member states that fought in Korea and took part in the Geneva conference (the Union of South Africa did not send a representative) submitted a report on the conference to the Secretary-General of the United Nations on November 11. Accepting this report, the ninth U.N. General Assembly passed a resolution on December 10, 1954, approving the report and reaffirming the United Nations' objective to achieve a unified, independent and democratic Korea under a representative government by peaceful means, thereby to completely restore peace and security in the Korean area. The resolution thus accepted two basic principles laid down in the communique by the 16 Korean War allies as United Nations principles. The two principles were: firstly, that the United Nations has the right to mediate in bringing about a peaceful settlement of the Korean problems, and secondly, that genuinely free elections should be held under the United Nations supervision to establish a unified, independent and democratic Korea. The principles were reaffirmed in the resolutions on Korea adopted by all subsequent sessions of the General Assembly.

Communist Bids

Disasters wrought by the Korean hostilities and rewardless efforts at the Geneva political conference strengthened the belief of the Republic of Korea government that all negotiations with the Communists would be fruitless. Nevertheless, the Communists continued their peace offensive. The north Korean Communists published a statement on February 5, 1958 saying that reunification of Korea could be attained only through direct negotiations between north and south Korea. On February 7, the Chinese Communists also issued a statement in support of the north Korean stand. The Chinese said that unification would not be brought about unless general elections were held under neutral nations' supervision after all foreign troops had withdrawn from both north and south Korea.

The British government on behalf of the 16 U.N. allies inquired of the Peking government whether the "neutral nations' supervision" as mentioned in the Chinese statement of February 7 would be undertaken under the authority of the United Nations and also whether a Communist-proposed all-Korea legislature to be elected would be formed in proportion to the populations of north and south Korea. Instead of answering these questions, Communist China, in its reply of May 6, repeated their demand for unconditional withdrawal of all foreign troops from Korea and opening of negotiations for Korean unification.

Efforts for U.N. Membership

Soviet Votes

The Republic of Korea government submitted an application for United Nations membership to the Secretary-General on January 19, 1949. The Security Council decided 9-2 to refer the application to the Membership Committee, which in turn supported the application 8-2. On April 8, a Membership Committee report on the Korean application was tabled before the Security Council. The Nationalist Chinese representative presented a resolution admitting the Republic of Korea into the United Nations. It was supported 9-2, the negative votes being cast by Soviet Russia and Ukraine. As Russia had veto power, the resolution was not passed.

The fourth General Assembly took up the proposed membership for the Republic of Korea and passed by 50-6 votes with three abstentions a resolution which, noting that the Korean application had received nine supporting votes and one Soviet veto at the Security Council, asked the Council to reconsider the application. The General Assembly's special resolution, however, failed to persuade Russia to drop her veto against Korea's membership application.

The Soviet veto was keeping other applicants also from admission into the United Nations. In an attempt to end this deadlock, the General Assembly in December 1955 discussed the possibility of granting membership to 18 applicant countries in what was called a package deal. The United States and Nationalist China took advantage of the package deal and proposed at the Security Council that in view of the United Nations role in the birth of the Republic of Korea, it should be added to the countries included in the package deal. The proposal mustered an overwhelming support of 9-1 with one abstention at the Security Council but it failed again to be passed as the opposing vote was cast by Soviet Russia.

Communist Change

The Republic of Korea delegation to each General Assembly has asked the United Nations to take resolute and positive measures for admission of the Republic. In Korea, the National Assembly adopted a resolution on July 16, 1956 calling for forming a National Committee which would sponsor a nation-wide campaign for United Nations' membership. The Committee succeeded to obtain 10 million signatures for a petition and sent it to the Secretary-General.

The 11th, 12th and 13th General Assemblies adopted resolutions calling on the Security Council to discuss Korea's application again. Each time the Soviet Union used her veto power.

It is noteworty that in recent years, the Soviet Union has departed from its original policy of unconditionally opposing admission of the Republic of Korea to propose that the Republic of Korea and the north Korean Communist regime be given seats in the world organization simultaneously. This change in the Soviet attitude may well be interpreted as part of a move designed to make the West admit that there exists two governments in Korea and thereby pave the way for north-south negotiations for unification on an equal footing.

Membership in U.N. Agencies

While the Republic of Korea has been barred from the United Nations because of the Soviet veto, she has been admitted into most United Nations' subordinate organizations or specialized agencies. It is now an active United Nations member in many of these agencies.

The U.N. subordinate or specialized agencies of which the Republic of Korea is member follow:

Economic Commission for Asia and the Far East (ECAFE)

The Republic of Korea was admitted as associate member under a resolution adopted at the fifth general meeting of ECAFE held at Singapore in October 1949. It became a full member under an Economic and Social Council resolution of October 1954.

The Korean government has sent representatives or experts to all types of meetings held under the sponsorship of ECAFE. Through contacts at these meetings with representatives from countries with similar economic conditions, Korean officials have gained valuable knowledge and technical know-how which have been of great help in formulating and implementing economic policies in Korea.

World Health Organization (WHO)

The Republic of Korea was accepted as full member at the second general meeting of WHO held at Rome in June 1949. Under an Agreement signed between WHO and the Korean government on September 21, 1951, the Organization has given technical assistance and sent experts with the capacity of advisors to Korea every year.

Food and Agriculture Organization (FAO)

Ever since the Republic of Korea was admitted as full-fledged member on November 25, 1949, it has sent representatives or experts to all types of meetings organized by FAO to obtain up-to-date technical knowledge. A Basic Agreement governing technical assistance was signed between FAO and the Korean government in December 1953.

United Nations Educational, Scientific and Cultural Organization (UNESCO)

The fifth general meeting of UNESCO held on June 14, 1950 approved Korea's entry as full member. UNESCO has since granted a generous amount of aid including scholarships under its educational program, gift coupons and assistance in construction of a text-book printing plant.

In January 1954 the Korean UNESCO Committee was formed for closer cooperation and cultural exchanges with both UNESCO headquarters and other member countries.

International Monetary Fund (IMF) and International Bank for Reconstruction and Development (IBRD)

The Republic of Korea joined the International Monetary Fund as well as the International Bank for Reconstruction and Development in August 1955. At the time of admission, there was much argument about the advisability of the membership of the two organizations. The argument centered around the regulation restricting the freedom of member countries in deciding or changing foreign exchange rates and preventing member countries from taking restrictive measures in handling foreign exchange.

The government saw more benefit in joining these two monetary organizations of which 54 countries, including the United States and Britain, are members. In fact, Korea has received foreign exchange supplies on a short-term basis from IMF and loans from IBRD for reconstruction of the country's war-ravaged economy.

International Rice Commission

The Republic of Korea joined this organization which is subordinate to the Food and Agriculture Organization on November 21, 1953. Korea as one of the world's major rice-producing countries has set up an Agriculture Center and has maintained contacts with foreign experts at international meetings for the purpose of increased production and betterment of quality.

Indian and Pacific Fishery Council

The Republic of Korea was admitted into this body, also a subordinate agency of the Food and Agriculture Organization, in January 1950.

Universal Postal Union

The organization accepted the Republic of Korea in December 1949. As a signatory to the new Universal Postal Agreement adopted at the 13th Universal Postal Conference in July 1952, Korea has started ordinary and air mail services with all the countries in the world except Communist nations. She has opened ordinary parcel services with 70 countries and air mail parcel services with 19 countries.

International Civil Aviation Organization (ICAO)

The Republic of Korea joined this organization in December 1952, upon expressing its support of the organization's objective to maintain safety and order in international civil aviation and to secure sound and economical operation of international civil aviation on the basis of equal opportunities for all members.

International Telecommunication Union (ITU)

The Republic of Korea joined ITU on October 19, 1950 when it subscribed to its purpose of establishing international cooperation for rational utilization, betterment and extension of international telecommunication services.

The ITU membership has enabled the Republic to exchange telegram services with all non-Communist countries and telephone services with 56 countries. As an ITU member, the Republic of Korea was also allocated some 500 frequencies and signals ranging from HL to HM.

World Meteorological Organization (WMO)

The Republic of Korea joined this organization in February 1956 to adjust the coun-

V INTERNATIONAL RELATIONS AND DIPLOMACY

try's meteorological work to the world standard and also to exchange meteorogical information with other countries.

Other International Organizations

International Atomic Energy Agency (IAEA). The Republic of Korea became a member of IAEA in August 1957 in order to receive aid from the organization in unclear explosion materials and equipment and in peaceful use of atomic energy.

The admission into IAEA followed conclusion of an Agreement with the United States for use of atomic energy for non-military purposes in February 1956. The Agreement provides for the United States assisting Korea in establishment of a research reactor and lending materials necessary for its operation to Korea.

International Wheat Council (IWC). The International Wheat Agreement is designed to guarantee importer countries wheat supplies at stable prices and to secure markets for exporter countries.

The Republic of Korea became a signatory to the Agreement in December 1953, although the country has not benefited by it because of the flow of agricultural surpluses into the country from the United States.

International Cotton Advisory Council (ICAC). The purpose of this organization is to maintain stability of cotton prices, regulate cotton supplies and exchange information about cotton. Seeing the need for obtaining assistance through an international organization in importing cotton, the Republic of Korea joined the Council in March 1954.

International Office of Epizootics (IOE). Korea joined the organization in November 1953.

International Red Cross (IRC). The Republic of Korea's Red Cross Society was unanimously admitted into the International Red Cross Federation at the executive committee meeting of the Federation in September 1955.

Overseas Korean Residents

Majority in Japan

Toward the end of the Pacific War nearly two million Korean were resident in Japan. Some had gone to Japan as they chose to live there. Others had been taken there to meet shortages of military and labor manpower. Still others were there studying or employed by Japanese. The second largest number of overseas Koreans were in Manchuria where about 1,500,000 were living.

A large portion of these Koreans returned home after the Japanese surrendered in 1945. There is no knowing how many Koreans are left in Manchuria, the China Mainland and other Communist areas and how they are living now. The number of Koreans, including students, now resident in free world countries follows (as of the end of 1958):

	Non-Student	Student	Total
Japan	675,962	10,382	686,344
United States	1,687	3.372	5,059
Formosa	382	37	419
Hong Kong	139	1	140
France	35	92	127
West Germany	3	73	76
Belgium	1	39	40
Vietnam	34	—	34
Britain	—	24	24
Other Countries	52	54	106
Total	678,295	14,074	692,369

As shown in this table, an overwhelming majority of overseas Koreans are in Japan. A minority living in Nationalist China and other Southeast Asian countries originally went to those areas as fishermen, forced laborers of the Japanese Army, or employees of Japanese firms. Remaining there after the Pacific War ended, most of these Koreans are salaried workers or businessmen.

Approximately one-third of those resident in Japan are fully employed and well established; another third are underemployed. The remaining one-third, unemployed at the bottom of the social scale, are dependent on relief from the Japanese government, which is said to be spending more than 1,000 million yen a year for this underworld people.

Repatriation Problem

The Korean residents in Japan are divided into three categories, members of the Association of Korean Residents in Japan which supports the Republic of Korea, members of the Federation of Koreans in Japan which is inspired by the north Korean Communists, and middle-of-the-road elements who are loyal to neither the Republic of Korea nor to the Communist regime in the north. The Republic of Korea government has maintained a Mission in Japan in order to improve the economic and social status of Korean residents, assist Korean residents' organizations, and help educate Korean children. The efforts of the Mission have been much frustrated as the conditions of the Korean residents are complicated and the Communists have carried on obstructionist campaigns.

In February 1959, Japan started negotiations with north Korea to deport Koreans in Japan to the Communist north. Despite vigorous opposition by the people and government of the Republic of Korea, the first groups of Koreans were sent to north Korea with assistance from the International Committee of the Red Cross in December 1959. Since most of those Koreans reportedly wishing to go to north Korea are originally from the south and find it extremely difficult to make their living in Japan, it is hoped, among other things, that the Republic of Korea government will settle problems of compensations for them and transport their properties home at the first opportunity so that they will change their mind and choose to return to the south.

Since the establishment of the Republic of Korea government, many Koreans have smuggled to foreign countries, mostly to Japan. Many have been arrested on arriving in Japan and after a period of detention in Japan, they have been returned to south Korea in mass repatriations.

Also calling the attention of the Republic of Korea is the problem of Koreans drafted for forced labor during the Japanese days and detained in Sakhalin by the Russians after the Pacific War. Only a fraction of them are reported to have been repatriated to Japan.

Cultural Exchanges

Introduction – Formation of Korean Culture

In order to pass judgment on whether the concept of Korean culture as generally accepted by Korean themselves or by foreigners is right, one must first understand the complex traits of Korean culture. Understanding of Korean culture in its true perspectives, however, has yet to be acquired.

Two factors, among other things, may be listed as reasons for lack of such understanding. First, there was no systematic attempt by Koreans themselves to study the traits of their culture. No such attempt was witnessed in the pre-modernization years. During the modernization period, any such attempt was hampered by the fact that Korea was a colony of Japan. Second, since the end of Korea's colonial subjugation, efforts have been made to understand the Korean culture in its proper perspectives. But as no groundwork was laid in the past, it has been too heavy a burden for Koreans to acquire such understanding within a short span of time.

It is by all means a significant and necessary thing to use philosophical methods to acquire such understanding but that is not the purpose of this treatise. We will rather attempt to review contacts with the outside world and thereby illustrate the transitory nature of Korean culture and its place in world culture, for the Koreans imported the cultures of neighboring nations and adapted them to their own cultural life over a period of many centuries until they came to have an advanced culture of their own.

Contacts with Chinese Culture

The origin of the Korean people is traced back to a northeast Asian tribe which used the Altai language. They migrated from west to east until they came to the northeastern area, where they started moving southward. They passed through the Liaotung area and then crossed the river into the Korean peninsula. This route of migration represents the pattern of the formation of Korean culture.

While the Koreans lived in Manchuria, in Liaotung and partly in the peninsula, they gradually advanced their primitive culture under the influence of two different cultures. One was the Scytai culture of north-Asian origin and the other was the Chinese culture to the west. Of the original Korean and the two alien elements, the factor with the most widespread and far-reaching influence in the formation of the Korean culture was Chinese. This was indeed the foundation of Korean culture and the dominating factor in advancement of the Korean social structure.

The influence of Chinese culture ranged from techniques in ironware, metal-work, lacquerware and architecture, to introduction of Chinese characters, and study of Confucianism, historical science and literature through Chinese books, and to cognizance of culture and formation of thoughts, especially political. The introduction of all this was crowned with importation of Buddhist culture which brought classical Korean culture into full bloom.

The most advanced classical Korean culture is almost exclusively Buddhist. But the Buddhist culture as seen in classical Korea was a culture developed on the foundation of Chinese culture and is by no means identical with the original Indian culture. Generally, what is called Buddhist culture in China, Korea and Japan is a combination of the Indian and Chinese cultures.

Formation of the classical culture was completed in the days of the unified Silla dynasty and a new age or a period of complete assimilation of the Chinese culture was ushered in with the advent of the Koryo dynasty. This period saw new types of contacts with nomadic and agricultural tribes to the north, the Chinese and the Japanese. The period also witnessed nomadic or Western Islamic elements flow in through Liao, Chin and Yuan. Some Lamaist influence with Tibetan colors was also brought in during this period.

The Yi dynasty period cut a strong contrast with this period which was characterized by the complexity of its culture. The Yi dynasty adopted the Confucianist philosophy of the Sung dynasty of China as its political ideology. The dynasty conformed social thoughts of the educated to Confucianism. This period of conformity saw, toward its end, another element—a Western element—infiltrate into the Korean culture.

Pre-Modernization Contacts with Japan

Contacts with Japan during the period of the classical culture should not be overlooked as the culture of the Three Kingdoms of Silla, Koguryo and Paekche was exported to Japan almost in its entirety. As Japan was a comfortable place to live in and could be reached in one or two days' sailing, many Koreans migrated to Japan during the period of the Three Kingdoms to introduce the Korean culture there. Remnants of what they took to Japan can be found in cultural treasures kept in Syosoin at Nara, many cultural patterns of the Nara Age and some literary works. Such as E.F. Fenellosa who discovered the value of Japanese fine art traced the origin of the ancient art of that country to Korea of the Silla-Koguryo-Paekche days. The influence of Korea in formation of the Japanese culture is mentioned in literature also. Sinten-Seisiroku of Japan is one example which has detailed account of such influence.

The Japanese came all the more to appreciate the cultural advances of Korea as they invaded Korea in 1592 and looted the country of its cultural treasures such as books and chinaware.

The cultural relations between Korea and Japan were reversed as Japan was beforehand with Korea in modernization.

Contacts with Western Culture

Korea's cultural contacts with the west did not start until the turn of the 19th century. Korea of the mid-17th century, viewed by Hendrik Hamel to be in the process of capitalization, must have looked strange to Dutchmen who sailed to the Orient. Korea remained a land of mystery to those Westerners who sailed along the Korean coast until French Catholic fathers landed in Korea in 1836 to take a firsthand look at Korea, understand Korean culture and, in the meantime, import things Western directly to Koreans. The first to come to Korea was Father Pierre Maubant who smuggled into this country in 1836. He was followed by about 20 Catholic fathers who came before the 1836 and 1866 massacre of Catholics. Their primary objective was, of course, to establish the Catholic faith in Korea. To that end, they tried to understand Korea and the people, on the one hand, and taught Latin and French to Koreans, on the other. Their knowledge of Korea and her people served as a guide for the Western world in understanding Korea. What was more important to Koreans was that their presence here gave them their first direct and largescale contact with Western culture.

Contacts with Protestants

Arrival of Protestants further promoted Korean contacts with the outer world and introduction of Western culture into Korea. It is true that education during the colonial days under the Japanese also helped open the country to Western culture. But contacts with Protestants proceeded with enlightenment during the Japanese control and brought Western culture more directly into this country. The official door of Korea was opened for communication with the Western culture when the Korea-American Treaty of Amity and Commerce was concluded in 1882. European and American commodities and missionaries started flowing into premodernized Korea in great numbers.

Protestant missionaries inspired the Koreans with recognition of self and taught them about the advanced capitalist society. New education, medical science, democracy and recognition of self were among the main gifts presented to them. On the other hand, Protestant missionaries tried voluntarily to discover and introduce to the outer world the elegance of Korean culture and the classical beauty of Koreans.

Contacts with Modern Western Culture

Korea started importing Western culture after witnessing China and Japan undertake modernization. Introduction of Western culture on a national scale came after 1894 when Japanese capitalists invaded this country and, alongside with Europeans and Americans, sought rights and interests in Korea, bringing in modern commodities to give Koreans general access to the Western culture they represented. Inspired by this glimpse at Western culture, the Koreans themselves tried actively to import Western capitalist culture in a movement to establish a new culture. "What I Saw and Heard during

V INTERNATIONAL RELATIONS AND DIPLOMACY

My Trip to the West" by Yu Kiljun was a guidebook in this new culture movement.

Active contacts with the Western world were shortlived, however, as the Japanese, invading this country in 1894, eliminated Western interferences and founded their monopolistic control of Korea by 1905. Korea's contacts with the Western world throughout the Japanese occupation were scarce with only a limited number of Koreans going to foreign countries other than Japan as students on a private basis and a restricted number of Western books were imported. There were some efforts by Europeans and Americans to understand the Korean culture. But their books on Korea were nothing more than travel sketches with the exception of a few which reached the academic level.

After World War II

As Japanese interferences and restrictions were ended with the close of World War II, the country was opened for free cultural contacts with foreign countries. But since the Japanese left the country, there has hardly been any genuine cultural exchange although there have been many phenomenal contacts. It would need more time before genuine cultural exchanges have been founded.

The Liberation from the foreign colonial domination has, however, oriented the country's cultural development in a new direction. As many rapid changes have taken place under the newly adopted democratic political structure, an entirely new approach has been adopted also in importation of the foreign culture. It cannot be totally denied that the old approach had a feudalistic tinge. In the past, emphasis was placed on nationalism rather than on democracy in seeking international exchanges. Foreign cultures were accepted as advanced culture without much attention paid to whether they were feudalistic or modern.

The old approach was repudiated in 1945. The Korean culture of the present time is in a period of transition from the Japanese colonial culture to the American and European cultures. This rapid transition has given rise to a new problem of cultural tradition. Importation of foreign cultures in a transitory period is apt to be mere imitation. While busily imitating the American culture that has come with economic aid for the past 15 years, Korea has made some mistakes in propagating and introducing the traditional Korean culture to foreign countries. This is largely attributable to lack of understanding of the Korean culture in its essence. It will not be of much help, either, in promoting genuine understanding of the Korean culture, if foreigners, for their part, continue to rely on Japanese books in studying the Korean culture, view the culture of Korea as identical with that of China or as Arnold Toynbee did, treat the culture of Korea as supplementary to that of Japan.

Mutual understanding of the other's culture is the very prerequisite to genuine cultural exchanges. With the close of World War II, a new phase was ushered in for such genuine understanding between Korea and foreign countries.

Study of Korea by Westerners

Western studies of Korea are of great significance to illustrate Korea's contacts with the Western world from the earliest days. But whether they help significantly in understanding Korea will have to be determined only after they have been carefully compared with Korean studies by Koreans themselves.

Early Studies

Western knowledge of Korea came primarily through letters from Christian missionaries in India, China and Japan, records of voyages to the Orient, and some charts which mentioned Korea.

1) Letters from missionaries—Earliest letters introducing Korea to the Western world were written by missionaries in Japan to their headquarters in Europe. (See "Cartas que os Padres e Irmaos da Companhia de Jesus escreverao des Reinos de Iapao & China aos de mesma Companhia da India e Europa, des annos de 1549, ate o de 1580. 2 parts. Evora 1598.")

Later missionaries in Japan obtained more knowledge about Korea through the Japanese who invaded Korea in 1592 and through the Korean prisoners they brought back. Their descriptions of Korea are found in many literatures. (See "Lettre annuelle du Japon, de Mars 1593 a Mars 1594, ecrite pon le P. Pierre Gomez au P. Claude Acquaviva, general de la Companie de Jesus, Milan, 1597," and "Lettre annuelle du P. Louis Fores au P. G. Acquaviva, Rome, 1598.")

More fragmentary references to Korea were to be found in a comprehensive survey of all literatures and letters by missionaries, especially those who had served in Japan. They are still kept in Portugal. A fair cross-section of these missionaries' references to Korea is at present available from such literatures as H. Cordier's manual of books on China and Japan, and a manual by Johannes Laures, S.J., included in the Kirishitan Bunko—A Manual of Books and Documents on the Early Christian Missions. In Japan, with special reference to the principal libraries in Japan and more particularly to the Collection of Sophia University, Tokyo, Sophia Univercity Press, Tokyo, 1940. A further collection of references to Korea in particular can only be expected of present Western scholars.

Another book that deserves mention in this connection is "Histoire de la Religion Chretienne au Japon, depuis 1598 jusqu'a 1651, comprenant les faits relatifs aux deux cent cinq martyrs beatifies le 7 Juillet 1867, Paris, 1869." The primary purpose of this book, however, is to study Japan, not Korea.

2) Voyage records—One of the oldest mention of Korea in voyage records was made after the ninth century in an account by an Arabian geographer who referred to this country as Sila. Later Portugese merchants who had been to the Indian area referred to Korea as "Gore" and to Koreans as "Gores." Another important literature which mentioned Korea was "Albuquerque. Bris de. Commentarios do Grande Afonso de Albuquerque Capitao, 4 edicao, Lisbon, 1557", which was translated into English with the title, The Commentaries of the Great Afonso Dalbuquerque, 4 vols., Hakluyt. First, No. 53, 55, 62, 69, London, 1875.

The first eye-witness account of Korea was provided Europeans by a shipwrecked Dutch sailor. On August 15, 1653, 36 crew members of a wrecked Dutch ship drifted on the shores of Cheju island. Twenty-two survived until February 1663 when they were moved to Yosu, Sunchon and Namwon in three separate groups of 12, 5, 5. The group at Yosu escaped in September 1666 and returned to Amsterdam in July 1668 via Nagasaki and Batavia. One of them, Hendrik Hamel, published a book, an Account of the Shipwreck of a Dutch Vessel on the Coast of the Isle of Quelpart. Together with a Description of the Kingdom of Corea, to give the Western world the first reliable description of this country. The book provided the most reliable guide up to the middle of the 19th century for Westerners who began sailing to Korean coasts. A detailed bibliography about the Hamel shipwreck account is found in Henrie Cordier's Bibliotheca Sinica, Vol IV, col. 2941-2944 and Bibliotheca Japonica, Col. 402-406. A comprehensive bibliography of almost all Korean materials is contained in the Introduction, the Hamel Shipwreck Account with translation and notes. A representative study of the Hamel shipwreck account with corrections and notes attached may be found in "Verhaal van het vergaan van het jacht de Sperwer en van het wedervaren der schipbr-

V INTERNATIONAL RELATIONS AND DIPLOMACY

eukelingen op het vasteland van Korea, 1653-1666, met eene beschrijving dat rijk, door Handrik Hamelt. Uitgegeren door B. Hoetink. Hague 1920. Worken uitgegeren door de Linschoten vereeniging XVIII."

This study, in corrections of the text and illustratory notes, used Western studies of Korea, China and Japan together with old European books as references, thereby raising the understanding of the history of relations between Korea and the Western world to a new level. This may well be ranked at the top of Western academic studies on Korea.

As supplementaries to these voyage accounts there are some discoveries about Korea by several people who sailed to Korean waters. Among them are:

"Galaup de la Perouse Voyage autour du monde pendant les annees 1785, 1786, 1787 et 1788, Paris, 1797." (A survey of I'le de Dyelet).

"W. R. Broughton, Voyage of Discovery to the North Pacific Ocean, London, 1804" (This is the result of a survey HMS. Providence conducted in the north Pacific area between 1795 and 1797.)

"Basil Hall, Account of a Voyage of Discovery to the West Coast of Corea and the Great Loochoo Island, London, 1818, 1820."

"John Macleod, Voyage of HMS Alceste along the Coast of Corea, to the Island of Lewchew, 1818".

"Edward Belcher, Narrative of Voyage of HMS Samorang during the Years 1834-46, London, 1848, 2 vols."

The fact that all major voyages to the Orient since LaPerouse were made by Englishmen clearly shows that England was very active in her advances into the area since she was interested in exploiting the vast areas of the Orient as markets. France, Russia and Germany, also undertook voyages to the Orient but England excelled them all in carrying out elaborate, scientific surveys. Basil Hacll's account of his voyage was later translated into French, German and Dutch.

Recent Studies

When Europeans came to the Orient on propagation missions or for the purpose of opening trade relations or seeking colonies, they set themselves to study the local, political, economic and cultural conditions as well as languages. This was likewise true of Korea.

1) Achievements of French missionaries – With a Korea parish set up in Rome and placed under the direction of the Foreign Countries Mission Propaganda in Paris in 1831. French missionaries started smuggling into this country, on one hand, to understand Korea, on the other, to propagate the Christian faith. Their activities are described in such books as C. Dallet's Histoire deP' Eglise de Coree, 2vols., Paris, 1874; Dictionnaire Coreen-Francais, Par les Missionnaires de Coree de la Societe des Missions etrangeres de Paris, 1880; and Grammaire Coreenne, par les Missionnaires de Coree de SME de Paris, 1881.

Dallet's history of Korean churches is the most basic literature ever written on Korean Catholicism. Its introduction is a collection of the most direct and realistic records of the political, economic and legal phases of Korea. The Korean-French dictionaries and the Korean grammar books written by the French missionaries contributed to both understanding of Korea by Westerners and study of the Korean language by other Westerners. They were also a great help to Korean linguists.

2) More recent achievements—After Korea's official relations with foreign countries were established toward the end of the 19th century, short essays on Korea came to be printed in academic journals specializing in Oriental affairs. Essays on Korea were contributed by students of Sinology. In dealing with Korea, they relied on personal experiences but more basically they depended on Dallet's book for necessary data. The two most authentic studies of Korea that followed Dallet's were completed by John

Ross and W.E. Griffis. John Ross attempted to make a historical survey and a comparative study of Korea in all fields in his book, History of Corea Ancient and Modern with Description of Manners and Customs, Language and Geography. London, 1891. Griffis' book, "Corea, the Hermit Nations, London, 1882," using all Occidential studies of Korea, China and Japan and some Chinese and Japanese books, showed relatively correct understanding of Korea's history, culture and foreign relations. His book continued to be supplemented until 1907 as Korea's foreign relations developed.

Study of Korea greatly improved in quality as a series of short essays began to appear in Korea Repository (1892-?), Korea Review (1901-1906), Korea Magazine 1917-1919) and Transactions of the Korea Branch of the Royal Asiatic Society, which were published by missionaries in Seoul. Especially, a few articles in the Royal Asiatic Society's Transactions attained the level of Sinology (Sinica) and Japanology (Japonica).

With enough headway made to justify a school of "Koreanology, Coreana," a number of scholars set about collecting and studying the pioneer achievements in Koreanology with a view to bibliographical classifications. On the Catholic side, Bishop Gustav Charles Mutel and Father Leon Pichon collected historical records related to Catholicism and published a bibliography. The Anglican Church collected a large library of Chinese books on Korea. The Landis library, as it was called, was collected by Bishops Napier Trollope and Eli Barr Landis in Inchon and, after the death of Dr. Landis, by Father Trollope alone. Of the Protestant missionaries, H.G. Underwood was one of the first to start a collection. His library was inherited and enlarged by his son, H.H. Underwood. The library of Norman Clark Whittemore, missionary in Pyongan Pukto, was another expensive collection. All these libraries were almost entirely destroyed during the Pacific War, the chaotic post-Liberation period and the Korean War. Only remnants are now available.

H.H. Underwood later compiled a "Partial Bibliography of Occidental Literature on Korea, Seoul, 1931," relying mainly on collections by Englishmen and Americans. In his introduction, Occidental Literature on Korea, Underwood explicitly stated that it was his intention to correct Western misimpressions of Korea. His bibliography which was the first presentation of an Occidental study of Korea in its full scope was supplemented by E. and G. Gompertz in 1935.

As for Korean history in general, "The History of Korea, 2 vols. Seoul, 1905, By H. B. Hulbert," was the only book that helped Westerners understand Korea although it contained some shortcomings. The author also wrote a five-volume chronological survey of the Yi dynasty entitled, "Annals of the Great East." These two books, together with a third, "The Passing of Korea, New York, 1906," which described the decline of the dynasty, formed a landmark in the study of Korean history by foreigners. Hulbert's works served as the orientation for Western studies of Korean history for years.

Occidental studies of Korean history may be divided into three phases, the first being the phase referred to as "early days." In the foregoing chapter of this article, the second from 1882 to the Sino-Japanese War in 189-45 and the third from 1895 to the Russo-Japanese War and the estalishment of the Japanese Residency-General in 1904-5, Hulbert's work was done during the third phase. Occidental books on Korean history published before 1894-5 were generally written for the purpose of understanding Korea, China and Japan and thereby improving the policies and positions of Western countries in the Far East. Many books written especially by Englishmen before the Russo-Japanese War were inspired by such motives. In fact, almost all accounts of journeys to the Orient by Englishmen were written for the purpose of understanding the three Far Eastern countries and thereby contributing to better English interests in the area. Typical of such accounts are Angus Hamilton's "Korea, London, 1904" and Isabella Bird Bishop's "Korea and

Her Neighbors, New York, 1897." Hamilton's book was widely read in Europe where a German translation was published immediately after the original. Mrs. Bishop's book, noted for the elegant and flowing style of the author, greaty helped introduce Korea's international position as well as her natural and cultural conditions of life.

The fact that England attached no little importance to Korea was clearly shown by two notable visits. The first was made by the Hon. George N. Curzon, then Governor-General of India, in the course of a Far Eastern tour out of which came the book, "Problems of the Far East Japan, Korea and China, in 1894." Almost simultaneously, two members of the Royal Geographic Society, Captains A.E. Cavendish and H,E, Gould-Adams, visited Korea and climbed Mount Paektu to publish their travel account, "Korea and Sacred White Mountain," in the same same year as Curzon's work.

Russia showed no less concern by sending legions of military officers, scientists and, especially, geographers to Siberia and Korea. Such works as "Puteshestvie V Ussuriiskom Korae, 1867-1869, Petersburg, 1870," by Nikolai Nikhailovich Prjevaliskii, who was a soldier, explorer, and geographer, and "Flora Man-churia, 1901, 1907 (A Botanical survey of Man-churia)," by V.K. Komarov, a member of the Royal Geographic Society of the Tsar, were strongly indicative of Russia's intentions toward the Far East, whatever the personal motives of the authors. Komarov, it should be added, also carried out an extensive survey of Eastern territory, embracing Russia, Manchuria and the area of the Tumen and Yalu Rivers in 1895-97. The Russians also conducted soundings of Korean waters off the eastern coast. In 1900, the Finance Ministry of the Russian government compiled and edited all these studies of Korea into one volume, entitled, "Opisanie Korea." This work, indeed, presented a most realistic picture of the country. It was a striking contrast to Hamilton's study in that it was designed to help formulate Russian policy toward Korea whereas Hamilton, whose work was based on personal observations, was rather motivated by the desire to introduce an objective picture to the world. In other words, it may well be said that the Russian work was a preparation for the invasion of Korea whereas Hamilton's interest was to forestall Japanese penetration by opening wide the doors of the peninsular kingdom.

With the tightening reins of the Japanese Residence-General into all aspects of Korean life, it became extremely difficult for Westerners to carry on any satisfactory studies in Korea. The inflential and well-organized Royal Asiatic Society was about the only body which could maintain continued and systematic studies. Only a very few works that told the real story of the Korean tragedy went out to the world at all. The notable contributor was F.A. Mckenzie, whose "Tragedy of Korea, (London, 1908)" and "Korea's Fight for Freedom (London, 1920)," described the history of Japanese aggression in Korea and of Korean aggression as climaxed by the Samil movement. Needless to say, such books as Allegne's "The New Korea (New York, 1936)," which defended Japan's position in Korea, were given every encouragement under the Government-General. Only one book may be said to have countered the effect of the Japanese misimpressions piled over the years upon a forgotten story that was Korea. That was the work of Dr. James Earnest Fisher, entitled, "Democracy and Mission Education in Korea (Teachers' College, Columbia University Contributions to Education, No. 306, New York, 1928)." Written with a critical, objective eye, the book may justly be called a monumental achievement in Occidental approaches to Korea. Dr. Fisher's main interest was in analyzing Korean conditions under Japanese control, mainly in the field of education. At the same time, he had some critical comments to make about the activities of the foreign missionaries in the country.

Another significant contribution was "Modern Korea (New York, 1944)," by Andrew J. Grajdanzev. This book dealt objectively with the conditions of Korean life under colonial control to correct the distorted records of the Japanese Government-General. His post-World War II successor may be said to be the late George M. McCune, whose "Korea Today, published by the Harvard University press, was an analytic study of divided Korea

Contemporary Studies

The territorial division of the Korean peninsula as the result of the Japanese surrender meant the presentation of the country to the world from two entirely different angles, the liberal Western approach and the Marxist interpretations of the Soviet bloc. So far as the former was concerned, it was Grajdanzev and McCune who laid the groundwork for contemporary Western studies of Korea.

Western efforts to study present-day Korea against her historical background presented a totally new phase after the Liberation which brought the southern half of the country into direct contact with the West, first through the United States Military Occupation, and through the establishment of a government committed to increased political, economic, military, educational and cultural ties westward. The increased contacts inevitably resulted in a large volume of reports about Korea, a volume multiplied by the outbreak of the war and the presentation of new problems by a country wrecked and bankrupt by a war of international significance. These numerous reports await a thorough analysis not only by Westerners but, more importantly, by Koreans themselves.

At least one such study has already been made by an American. This is Carl Berger's The Korea Knot: A Military-Political History, Philadelphia, University of Pennsylvania Press, 1957. The author made a systematic survey of Korea from World War II through the separation of the 38th parallel in 1945, the U.S. occupation period, the establishments of the rival Korean governments, the outbreak of the war (Berger calls it a civil war) down to the armistice signing. The author used all available reports on Korea since the Pacific War, from U.S. government sources, newspapers and magazine articles, in order to lend emphasis to the final query: who would untie the Korean knot?

One new field, little dreamed by the 19th century missionaries, was the military. A great galaxy of soldiers, civilians and war correspondents have turned out any amount of studies about Korea from the military point of view as a result of the war. Their place in the Western library of Koreanology, however, has yet to be determined.

The most urgently required task, however, is a comprehensive bibliographical undertaking of all Korean literature since 1945, either from Western or Korean hands.

VI NATONAL DEFENCE

Background

Three Kingdoms Period (57 B.C. to A.D. 668)

The concept of military power in Korea arose from the beginning with the formation of tribal communities. By the Three Kingdoms period, there were all sorts of military posts in all three states, the *Chwagunju*, *Ugunju* and *Taejanggun* in Silla; the *Taemodal* and *Malgaek* in Koguryo; the *Wisajwapyong* and *Pyonggwanjwapyong* in Paekche. The most advanced of all the military structures of the ancient days was that of Paekche. The post of *Wisajwapyong*, created early in the 3rd century A.D. was responsible for the *Sugwi* system, by which local garrisons took turns carrying out garrison duty in the capital. On the other hand, the *Pyonggwanjwapyong* commanded troops stationed all over the country except in the capital. In order to assure an effective *Sugwi* system, compulsory service was imposed on all citizens of the kingdom. With further complications of military duties, more command posts were created, and Silla, at least, was creating ranks. By then, the kingdom's military were divided into Infantry and Cavalry. On the other hand, the garrisoned troops of Paekche in the capital were divided into 5 units, each attached to 5 administrative divisions. Each unit was under the military commander of the capital's administrative divisions. The strength of each unit, called the *Pugun* ranged anywhere between 500 and 1,100.

Unified Silla (669—935)

The successful unification of the peninsula by Silla meant the expansion of its territory to include all of former Koguryo and Paekche. The expansion naturally brought changes and the new military structure became largely modeled on that of China. It was divided into 23 organizational branches and had five grades of military garrison.

Koryo (936—1391)

Koryo started out by rejecting all complicated structures of its predecessors with a simple organization but, with its domination of the peninsula, repeated Silla's experience by adopting the Chinese model. Its *Pubyong* system was but another name for Paekche's *Sugwi* in which garrisons of rural areas made up of farmer-soldiers were put on duty in the capital on a rotations basis. Koryo had six commands, each consisting of 38 units called *Yong*. Each *Yong* consisted of 1,000 men. Military service was compulsory in Koryo to all male citizens between 16 and 60. When a citizen was conscripted and reached the age of 20, a certain acreage of land was leased to him from the government. On this he raised crops in his spare time between military duties. The lease was withdrawn when he reached 60. At the end of the 10th century, Koryo's total manpower strength reached 120,000. Military ranks were laid in five orders and special posts created for military administration as a strictly independent channel of the command.

In the 12th century, when political power was concentrated solely in the hands of non-military officials, troops were put under the power of politicians, thus creating confusion in the garrison system of the *Pubyong*. Koryo's military power thus became vested in the hands of a handful of high politicians. A revolt of the military commanders changed masters but not the tendency of a handful of men keeping their own private military set-up. The new wielders of power were military men and typical military factions came in.

This trend remained until around 1270 when, in face of the growing Mongol threat, political power began to be concentrated in the central government. The various militaristic sects began to dissolve into a coordinated royal force. By 1356, the old five-command system was revived.

Yi Dynasty
(1392—1910)

The Yi dynasty modeled its military system on that of latter-day Koryo. The supreme command rested with the *Samgundo Chongjebu* (Supreme Command of the Three Armies) which handled both orders and administrative channels. The *Samgundp Chongjebu* was a five-command system similar to that of Koryo. Each Command comprised five *Yong* and each *Yong* was made up of 1 *Chonggun*, 3 *Chungnangjang*, 6 *Nangjang*, 6 *Pyoljang*, 8 *Sanwon*, 20 *Wi*, and 40 *Chong*. There were one *Sangjanggun* and two *Taejanggun* in each of the Commands. Besides the five Commands, there were Royal Guard Commands bringing to 10 the total number of Commands.

The government's functions were thoroughly reorganized with the establishment of the *Uijongbu*, the supreme governing body of national politics. This body had six administrative branches called the *jo*, handling personnel affairs, finances and taxation, protocol and education, military administration, jurisdics and engineering. Responsibility for operational command rested with the *Samgundo Chongjebu*, keeping command and administrative channels strictly separate.

In 1552 the *Kunjoktogam* was set up. This was an office responsible for putting in order the records of citizens either in service or eligible. The nation's total standing military manpower was estimated at 12,000. Like Silla and Koryo, the Yi dynasty had compulsory service. Men aged between 16 and 60 had to serve the country when called. A youth reaching the age of 20 was given a certain acreage of land to till in between military duty hours. Rural garrisons composed of draftees took their turns and went to the capital to fill in garrison duty there.

In 1593, when the Japanese landed on Korea in the notorious Hideyoshi invasion, volunteers came to the aid of the government forces. Among them were a large number of priest-soldiers. To command this priestly army, an independent command, known as the *Tochongsop*, was organized. A Training Command was also set up for the purpose of training volunteers. After the war, this Training Command and four other newly organized commands were garrisoned in the four military districts into which the national territory was divided.

In 1879, Korea was opened to the outside world with the signing of a trade agreement with Japan. A cultural survey mission sent by the government to Japan returned to introduce various changes into both governmental and social structures. The most remarkable progress in the military field was the organization of a training corps called the *Pyolgigun*, Hired Japanese

VI NATIONAL DEFENCE

instructors gave modern military training to cadets selected from among the sons of high government officials. In 1882, the order of command was simplified when the five-command system became reorganized into a two-command one. Yet other changes were to come.

Following the revolt of military leaders in the year, 1882 and the Tonghak Rebellion, Korea became a stage for a tripartite struggle for power among Russia, China and Japan. To keep pace with the rapidly changing tides of the day, Yi Korea had to undergo sweeping changes in her political and social life. Thus the Kabo Reform of 1894. The military was no exception to the drastic effects and the two-command system yielded to a new six-command one. The Training Command, was replaced by a Royal Guard Command. The Yi military structure remained thus until it was dissolved under growing Japanese pressure in 1907.

Seapower

The origin of the Korean navy was to be found in 1466 when Sin Sukchu built warships modeled on that of foreign prototypes. In 1593, the year following the Hideyoshi invasion, the redoubtable Admiral Yi Sunsin was named Commander-in-Chief of the Yi naval power for the Kyongsang-do, Chungchong-do and Cholla-do provinces. His "Turtle Ships," covered with thick layers of wood from top to bottom and armed with cannons and small arms, were a nightmare of the Japanese navy.

His remarkable genius as commander saw every sea battle end in the defeat of the Japanese in contrast to land battles in which they almost never knew defeat.

In 1681, Pangoyong, the Defence Command, was set up in Kwangnyangjin and commanded naval powers stationed in Kwangnyang and Nogang.

In 1866, the first three large-sized battleships were built. It was only after the Kabo Reform of 1894, that naval power was put under the supreme command of the government's military governing body.

Army

Before the War
Foundation of the Constabulary

The sharp ideological cleavage stemming from the "cold war" separation of Korea at the thirty-eighth parallel saw the outgrowth of various military and para-military groups all over the southern half of the country. The occupation forces of the United States Military Government, which took over from the Japanese colonial authority the responsibility of maintaining order and establishing security after disarming the Japanese military, at first, responsed to this national trend and, on the 13th of November of 1945, established a National Defence Command within the transitional occupation structure.

The National Defence Command had as one of its sub-structures, a Military Administration Bureau, consisting of Army and Naval Departments. Respecting the fact that U. S. assistance was an absolute necessity for the growth of a strong defence structure in the free state to follow and reasoning that the English language would serve as an important advantage for a speedy growth, the Command established a Military English Language School on December 5 of the same year with an enrollment of about 200 students from among applicants with past military experiences in Japan, Manchuria and China. Of these, 110 were educated to become officers. The experiment terminated, the school was closed.

The Three-Power Allied Conference in

Moscow, dealing as it did with Korea's fate, heightened the intensity of the struggle between the Communist and anti-Communist forces. The consequent social disorder was even more aggravated by the existence of private military organizations provoking bloody incidents. Disturbed by this disorderly trend, the Military Government banned all existing military and semi-military groups on January 15, 1946 and established the South Korean National Constabulary on the same day.

This Constabulary embarked on the organization of a defence force on a regimental level as its first job and, between January through April of the same year, completed the formation of eight regiments. The strength of each ran anywhere between one company and one battalion. Also established was the South Korean National Constabulary Officer Training School which began to administer the first U. S.-style military training on May 1 the same year. The month of May further saw the reinforcement of the constabulary forces by more than seven regiments and the enlistment of volunteers into the ranks.

The National Defence Command which had been renamed the National Defence Headquarters, in the meantime, was christened again as the Department of National Defence that same month. At the same time, the South Korean National Constabulary became the Korean National Constabulary. Along with these changes in nomenclatures came a change of organizational structure. Every three regiments were incorporated into one brigade and, from December 1, 1947 through April of the following year, five brigades in all were organized.

Birth of the National Army

The establishment of the Government of the Republic of Korea on August 15, 1948, meant a change in the character of the Constabulary forces from occupational to independent status. Accordingly, it became known as the National Army beginning September 1. Four days later, the Coast Guard likewise started out on a new career as the Navy. These developments gave new momentum to the efforts of the Department of National Defence to better the already substantially improved quality of the defence forces.

On November 30, 1948, the Armed Forces Organizational Act came into effect. Under this Act, the Army Headquarters was established and fourteen branches of service—Infantry, Cavalry, Artillery, Engineer, Signal Corps, Ordnance, Quartermasters, Finance, Adjutant, Inspector-General, Medics, Military Police, Aviation and General were set up. At the same time, the Army moved a step further and promoted each of its seven Brigades to Division.

Meanwhile a new branch was set up within the Army Headquarters under the Emergency Presidential Act of November 20, 1948. The new branch, called the Office of Militia Administration, started to train volunteers at the Militia Training Center established on April 4, 1949, with the object of building up ten militia regiments with a total strength of 20,000.

However, the volunteer system was changed to a compulsory one with the enactment of the Military Service Law on August 6, 1949. On the 31st of the same month, all existing militia projects were cancelled and their staff members given new duties at the Draft Boards in all the Provinces where they were assigned.

In November of the same year, a Youth Guards Project was born to give military training to youth under service age. However, this project did not bear much fruit due to the inexperience of those attending to actual training duty.

Communist Uprisings

Meanwhile, the Communist regime in north Korea was busy laying the groundwork for its southward thrust. The National Army, naturally, was its main target of infiltration. With the help of the South Korean Labor Party (Communist), infiltrators from the north established cells within the Army to

↑ Air Force Academy, Seoul
 The training institution for regular Air Force officers of Korea. Also only high school graduates can apply for the entrance examination; all cadets are appointed Second Lieutenants after finishing a 4-year course,

C 46 Skymasters
Ttransport planes of the ROK Air Force.

Formation Flight of Jet Planes
The skies of Korea can now be defended by Koreans themselves.

T-6 Advanced Training Planes
"Kongukho," the plane that was donated by the people of Korea.

Jet Training under the Leadership of a U.S. Air Force Instructor →

← Discussing an Operation before Action

↓ Headquarters of the ROK Air Force, Seoul

↑ Headquarters of the ROK Navy, Seoul

↑ Navy Band

↓ ROK Navy Honor Guard

↑ Naval Academy
   Chinhae, Kyongsang Namdo. The training school for regular Naval officers. The cadets are selected from among high school graduates through entrance examinations. After completing 4-year courses, all cadets are appointed Ensign and get B. S. degrees.

↓ Landing Ship for Tanks (L.S.T.)

↑ Fall of Pyongyang City
After the restoration of Seoul, U. N. Forces marched up to the north and, in autumn of 1950, finally entered the north Korea capital city of Pyongyang.

↓ A Rifle Unit

↓ A River-Crossing Operation

↑   A 155-mm Howitzer Battery of the ROK Army

← Maneuvers
   Landing operation for the Marines.

Tanks Parade on the Street
↓   Saluting President Rhee on his birthday.

↑ ROK Military Academy

Located in suburban Seoul. Government-operated training school for regular Army officers. Cadets are selected from among high school graduates who have passed the entrance examination, and are appointed Second Lieutenants after completing a 4-year course.

↑ New Recruits' Ceremonial Parade at the Military Academy

← Cadets at the English Class

Headquarters of the ROK Joint Chiefs of Staff

A combined headquarters of the chiefs of staff of the ROK Army, Navy and Air Force set up to concentrate operation, coordinate military administration and assist the President in all military affairs.

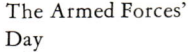

Academy of National Defence

In Koyang, Kyonggi-do, An advanced institute for studying military affairs, politics and economics relating to national defence.

The Armed Forces' Day

October 1st is the big day for all branches of service, Army, Navy, Air Force and Marine Corps. There is always a big combined parade on this day.

United Nations Forces
Sixteen countries joined the Korean War to protect freedom from Communist aggressors.

U.N. Cemetery in Pusan, Kyongsang Namdo
Soldiers and officers of the Allied forces who were killed during the Korean Conflict are buried here.

ROK Armed Forces' Cemetery in Seoul
Every War dead of the ROK Army, Navy, Marine Corps and Air Force lies here.

↑ Refugees Coming Down South
   When U. N. Forces retreated from the north after Communist China's intervention in 1950, many people of north Korea, longing for freedom, decided to take refuge in the south. This picture shows Pyongyang citizens crossing the Taedong River along the wrecked bridge. They feared nothing but Communism.

←
Armistice Conference
U. N. Forces' delegates to the Armistice Conference coming out of the conference building. From left to right: Major General Howard Turner, Admiral R.E. Libby, Admiral Arleinh Burke, Major General Yi Hyonggun of ROKA, Vice-Admiral C. Turner Joy, Chief of the Delegation.

Triumphal Entry into Pyongyang (Oct. 29, 1950)
↓   Pyongyang citizens heartily welcoming President Rhee.

VI NATIONAL DEFENCE

stir up propaganda and unrest. One festering sore was the island of Cheju where a violent uprising on April 3, 1948 continued unabated into the initial phase of the newly-established Government. Two regiments—the 9th and the 11th—were sent to the scene to crush the revolt. Just how effective the Red infiltrations had been was demonstrated soon after by the desertions of a number of men and officers of the 11th Regiment to join the rebels. The Army took thirteen months to completely re-establish order on the troubled island.

The next crisis broke out at the Cholla port of Yosu when one battalion of the 14th Regiment suddenly turned rebel while embarking on a Cheju-bound ship on October 19. They destroyed the munitions stockade and, with the dark, rushed the city proper to occupy it. The armed insurgents numbering around 2,000, then moved to nearby Sunchon and occupied that city as well the following day.

The Army promptly established an emergency field headquarters in Kwangju and sent brigades—the 2nd and the 5th—and two regiments—the 6th and the 15th—into the area to meet the situation. By November 16, the revolt was crushed (with the help of naval units) and the end of smaller uprisings within the Taegu and Pohang garrisons at about the same time marked the beginning of the Army's success in its vigorous house-cleaning efforts.

The Sensitive Parallel

With the thwarting of their subversive tactics against the Republic of Korea, the north Korean Communist authorities stepped up preparations for an open war. On many instances since early May of 1949, they resorted to armed violation of the tenuous border line that separated Korea into two incompatible states. The biggest crisis was that of May 3, 1949 when the Communists pushed a 400-man strength forward to occupy Mount Songak and another strategic hill north of Kaesong. Only after a most furious skirmish were the Communists driven back the next day by the 11th Regiment. Through this and other armed clashes, the Pyongyang regime hoped to probe our defense potentials and increase the feeling of southern insecurity in preparation for their war surprise.

War

The Invasion

At 4:00 a.m. Sunday, June 25, 1950, the Communist Army began a general offensive all along the 38th parallel on the patently absurd pretext that the Republic of Korea had first attacked northern territory. Four hours later, north Korean Premier Kim Il Sung "officially" proclaimed war against the Republic of Korea. The military balance of power on the two sides stood as follows:

a) North Korea
   (Men)
   People's Army   6 Divs.   94,500 men
   Security Force   3 Divs.   24,000 men
   Air Force   1 Div.   1,800 men
   Armored   1 Div.   10,000 men
   Navy   2 Divs.   15,100 men
         Total strength—182,400 men
   (Arms)
   Tanks   242
   Armored vehicles   60
   Aircraft (Yak-9, IL-10, and others) 211
   Vessels   30
   A-A Guns   30
   Self-propelling Guns   170
   Other Artillery   2,445

b) Republic of Korea
   (Men)
   Infantry   8 Divs.   80,000 men
   Auxiliary units   17,000 men
         Total strength—97,000 men
   (Arms)
   Armored vehicles   27
   Rocket Launchers   1,900
   Howitzers (105-mm)   40
   Aircraft (AT-6)   10
   Vessels   30

Retreat and Counter-Offensive

The ROK troops had to fall back before

the absolute numerical superiority of the onrushing enemy. The site of the Army Headquarters was moved to Taejon before the enemy occupation of Seoul within a few days of the outbreak of the conflict. On July 13, the Army had to move its Headquarters again to Taegu. Meanwhile, the enemy, after crossing the Kum River and occupying the Honam, or the Cholla Provinces, concentrated its pressure on the Naktong River sector from the west. By the time the enemy reached within 130 miles north of Taegu, seven-eighth of the total ROK territory was in his hands. His final goal, of course, was Pusan, the southernmost port city of the Korean peninsula. By then, under a resolution of the United Nations "little assembly," the United Nations Command was set up in Tokyo with General Douglas MacArthur as Supreme Commander. Troops of 16 countries— the U.S.A., Great Britain, France, New Zealand, South Africa, Belgium, Australia, Thailand, Turkey, Columbia, Ethiopia, Luxembourg, Greece, the Netherlands, the Philippines and Canada— were dispatched under the unified command to secure the last beachhead of Korea against the Communist aggression. The United Nations troops held their ground, the morale of the enemy began to wear out and, on September 15, the U.N. troops made a historic behind the enemy landing at Inchon under the personal command of General MacArthur to recapture Seoul three months to the day it had fallen. The victorious Allied troops continued to march northward and, on September 20, the late General Walton H. Walker, then in command of the Eighth U.S. Army, gave the order to cross the thirty-eighth parallel. The Communist capital of Pyongyang was captured on October 19, and the combined military might of the U.S. and ROK forces had reached the Yalu by October 10 when the Chinese Communist Forces which had been concentrating along the river began to cross into north Korea. Again the U.N. side had to withdraw before a formidable force of 4 armies totalling 230,000 men. The Chinese crossed the 38th parallel on December 31 and continued its southward thrust along the pattern of the earlier north Korean thrust. Seoul fell into the enemy's hands for the second time on January 4, 1951. The U.N. side built up a new defence line along the route connecting Osan, Changhowon, Chechon, Yongwol and Samchok and held this firmly. A new counter-offensive was launched with the objective of mass destruction of the enemy whose primary strength came from human-sea tactics. Seoul was retaken on March 14, 1951 and the positions of both sides became stabilized more or less along the thirty-eighth until the opening of the armistice talks at the village of Panmunjom, north of Kaesong.

The Armistice Talks

While the armistice talks dragged on at Panmunjom without visible progress, the enemy lost no time in building up his considerably weakened might. The one-year period from July 1, 1951 to June 30 of the following year saw only sporadic fighting now and then all along the line. In this period, it became routine for the U.N. to destroy the enemy's potential military might through largescale air bombing operations deep inside the enemy territory. The enemy built up his strength to around one million men during this period. Then came the fiercest combats of the Korean War. On September 6, 1952, the enemy tried to take the strategic Capital Hill, northeast of Kumhwa. The enemy's attack on the hill was repelled 30 times by the Capital Division of the ROK Army which was defending the hill. Twenty thousand rounds of artillery shells fell daily. On September 29, the enemy gave up his attempt to take the hill and changed his objective to adjoining White Horse Hill. Again bloody combats were fought and again the hill was secured thanks to the bravery of the Ninth ROK Division.

There were a number of other occasions when the enemy finally decided to give up his attempts at territorial conquests after formidable losses. The merciless stalemated

VI NATIONAL DEFENCE

war continued right up to the armistice signing on July 27, 1953.

After the War

After the Armistice was signed, the Army started to streamline its order of command to meet the threat posed by the Communists' military build-up in violation of the Armistice agreements. On December 15, 1953, the 1st Army Group Command was established. Its duty was to coordinate and command frontline combat divisions. The 2nd Army Group born on October 31, 1954 was to control and coordinate overall supply operations to the units under the command of the 1st Army Group. Five Military District Commands were set up under the 2nd Group's command. For military training purposes, 10 Reserve Divisions also were organized. Other developments:

a) Establishment of General Education Command (Aug. 1954)

b) Establishment of Military Staff College (Oct. 28, 1951)

c) Opening of 4-year Military Academy (Oct. 30, 1951)

d) Opening of Nonsan Recruit Training Center (Nov. 1, 1951)

List of Army Chiefs of Staff:
1st Col. Yi Ungjun Dec. 15, '48 – May 9, '49
2nd Maj.-Gen. Chae Pyongdok,
    May 9, '49 – Oct. 1, '49
3rd Maj.-Gen. Sin Taeyong
    Oct. 1, '49 – Apr. 10, '50
4th Maj.-Gen. Chae Pyongdok
    Apr. 10, '50 – June 30, '50
5th Maj.-Gen. Chong Ilgwon
    June 30, '50 – June 23, '51
6th Maj.-Gen. Yi Chongchan
    June 23, '51 – July 23, '52
7th Lt.-Gen. Paek Sonyop
    July 23, '52 – May 5, '53
8th, 9th Gen. Chong Ilgwon
    Feb. 14, '54 – June 27, '56
10th Gen. Yi Hyonggun
    June 27, '56 – May 18, '57
11th Gen. Paek Sonyop
    May 18, '57 – Feb. 23, '59
12th Lt.-Gen. Song Hyochan Feb. 24, '59 –

Navy

The Fledging Navy

With the nation surrounded on three sides by sea, liberated Korea was faced with the formidable task of protecting their territorial waters from any outside threat. Most keenly aware of this need was a group of farsighted and marine-minded men around Sohn Wonyil who later was to become the first Commander-in-Chief of the fledgling Korean Navy. This group called itself the Marine Affairs Group. The Group was incorporated into the Marine Bureau, a branch of the United States Military Government, to form a Coast Guard on November 11, 1945. The newly-organized Coast Guard undertook upon itself the duties of defending Korean coasts from any unlawful violation, of halting smuggled merchandises and of rescuing vessels in distress. The Coast Guard was put under the jurisdiction of the National Defence Command of the Military Government in December of the same year. It was thus organized as the official naval organization with the backing of a Military Government ordinance. It had two 100-ton class and one 40-ton class ships along with a few smaller boats.

With the change of the National Defence Command into the Department of National Defence in June of 1946, the Coast Guard was officially designated the Korean Coast Guard. The unit began to build up its sea power and on April 7, 1940 succeeded in completing the construction of a 300-ton class ship, christened the K. S. S. Chungmugong. Chungmugong No. 2 was to follow in May

1951. The Coast Guard further constructed three hydro-planes around this period, and imported a number of ships from abroad to establish 66 bases in the strategically located ports of Inchon, Kunsan, Mokpo, Pusan, Pohang and Mukho. The total strength then was: 6 LCI's, 1 YO, 11 JMS's, 19 AMS's.

The Coast Guard launched its new career as the Navy with the establishment of the Government on August 15, 1948. Under the Naval Chief-of-Command, chiefs of staff Operations and Vessels, were appointed to be assisted by the sub-structures of Personnel, Finance and Supply, Operational, Vessels, and Service Preservation Bureaus.

In June 1949, the Navy organized the Committee for Ship Purchase Funds in an effort to raise enough cash for four PC-type ships from the United States. The outbreak of war saw the ROK Navy with 70 ships, large and small, and a manpower complement of 7,000.

War

From the first day of war on June 25, 1950, the Navy blockaded the enemy coasts east and west in cooperation with U. N. seapower. It also helped the ground forces by bombardments of enemy-held territories and supply movements. The Navy sank a 1,000-ton class ship carrying an enemy landing unit of 6,000 men, 20 miles east of Pusan.

September 15, 1950 marked the historic Inchon landing which changed the tide of the war. A total of 206 ships, including the main body of the U. S. 7th Fleet participated. At about the same time, on the east coast, another landing operation was carried out at Changsadong. The Navy retook Pohang and, on August 19, was in command of Mukho close to the 38th Parallel. By the time of the Inchon landing, all the southern Korean ports once taken by the Communists were again in the hands of the Republic of Korea Navy. With the rapidly advancing ground forces, the Navy forced the war to the north both on the east and west coasts up to the time of the Chinese Communist intervention. With the general Allied retreat before the new enemy invasion, the ROK Navy, in cooperation with U. N. seapower, succeeded in withdrawing hundreds of thousands of refugees from Wonsan. The total number of men, troops and refugees, that the Navy helped to bring to safety amounted to 331,000 during the early days of the Chinese intervention. With the opening of the armistice talks in June, 1951, the Navy concentrated its efforts on bombardments of the enemy's coastal areas and numerous supply operations.

After the Armistice

After the signing of the armistice, the Navy embarked on a vigorous reorganization program aimed at strengthening its order of command and increasing its effectiveness. In August of 1951, a new post of Waterways Officer was established, to be followed in November by the Weather Officer. In July 1952, Offices of Planning, Operations and Signals were born. In May of the following year, the Office of Chief-of-Staff for Logistics was organized and, in the following month, an independent Bureau of Waterways.

In the educational field, an Educational Department was reorganized into a General Training School in 1952 and the former Coast Guard Cadet School was renamed the Naval Academy in 1949.

In 1951, the then existing three Task Forces were incorporated into the 1st Fleet. The Fleet was renamed in 1953 as the Republic of Korea Fleet. In June, 1955 the Naval Amphibious Operation Corps and Training Unit were born. The same month also saw the birth of the Naval Staff College.

The ROK Navy took over control of the seas surrounding the Korean peninsula from the United Nations Command in March of of 1955.

With the completion of a dry dock in Chinhae in July of 1950, the Korean Navy was able, for the first time in the history of

Korea, to handle repair works on large modern ships.

Marine Corps

The ROK Marine Corps was organized on April 15, 1949 and officially started its career on May 5 of the year with Presidential Act No. 88. The total strength of the Corps then was 300 officers and men. The organization of the Corps was first proposed by Admiral Son Wonil, then Commander-in-Chief of the Navy, and other military leaders who felt that a special branch of the armed forces specialized in amphibious operations was highly desirable after the Communist revolt in the port city of Yosu in November, 1948. The Corps' first Commandant was Maj./Gen. Sin Hyonjun, then Lieutenant-Colonel.

The Corps was stationed in Chinju near Mount Chiri, the main stage of action for the Communist guerrillas who fled into the mountains after the failure of their uprising in Yosu and Sunchon. The Marines fought these guerrillas until they were shipped to Cheju on February 28, 1950.

The island was then seething with unrest as rebel remnants carried on the April revolt of the previous year. Mopping-up operations among snowy hills were to become the daily routine for many months to come. Then came June 25, 1950, and, to intercept the onrushing enemy, the Corps made a hurried landing near Kunsan within a few days of the outbreak. It had, of course, to withdraw before long. During the ensuing days when the United Nations' forces held fast the Pusan beachhead, the Corps made itself famous in the bloody combat for Chindongni near Masan, the southernmost tip of the Communist offensive. For this operation, the first Presidential unit citation with the promotion of whole members was given to the Marines. They joined the 1st U.S. Marine Division in spearheading the historic Inchon landing and pursued the retreating enemy to Seoul. The Corps reached the outskirts of Seoul from the west only after bitter skirmishes with the desperate Red garrison of the capital city. Two days later, on the 27th, PO/1st Class Yang Pyongsu and Seaman Choe Kukpang raised the national flag on the roof of the Capitol building. Along with the steadily advancing Army troops, the Marines moved up to Wonsan, an east coast port city of north Korea, and engaged itself in mopping-up operations there.

The severest trial for the Corps was to come with the Chinese intervention in late October. In sub-zero weather the ROK Marine Corps rearguarded the retreating friendly troops which found the rigors of the northern winter exceptionally unendurable.

In July 1951, the Corps took over the sector around the mountain range of Taebaek. While in this sector, the Marines saw their bloodiest fighting at Tosolsan. It wrested the hill from the enemy after killing 3,381 and capturing 39. Another memorable battle of this period took place on the Kim Il Sung hill, so named by the enemy after his leader.

Overlooking the East-central plains between Inje and Yanggu, it was a strategic prize. The Marines under the command of Colonel Kim Tongha succeeded in wresting it from the enemy after days of furious bayonet-fighting.

Early in 1951, the Corps moved its leathernecks to the islands of Yangdo, Yodo and Taedo along the east coast and to Chongdo, Chodo, Paengnyongdo, Taechongdo, Sochongdo and Yonpyongdo along the western coast line. The troops, stationed in those islands until the signing of the Armistice Agreements in Panmunjom, posed a constant threat to enemy supply lines along the coasts and a morale booster for the disgruntled population under Communist rule.

During and after the war, the Corps incessantly grew in combat potentialities as an amphibious operational force. These potentialities were exhibited to the fullest extent on April 28, 1959 when a joint US-ROK exercise landing operation was carried out in the Yongil Bay area on the southeastern coast.

Air Force

The Early Days

The forerunner of today's ROK Air Force was the Korean Aviation Association organized in August of 1946 by a group of aviation-minded people who gathered around Choi Yongdok. Seven of these people with flying experiences in foreign aviation societies enlisted in the Infantry School as a preparatory step towards founding an air unit of the Korean Constabulary in April of 1948. They were Choe Yongdok, Kim Chongyol, Pak Pomjip, Chang Tokchang, Yi Kunsok and Kim Yonghwan. An Air Base Unit of the Korean Constabulary was organized on May 5 of the same year with Choe Yongdok as its first Commanding Officer. On July 7, the Air Base Unit was renamed the Air Base Headquarters. Its total manpower strength was eight officers and sixty-two enlisted men. There was not a single plane.

Then, on September 13, ten L-4 Trainers were handed over to the Air Base Headquarters from the American military and, with it, an Aviation Unit and an Air Base Unit were founded. The first planes with the Taeguk marking of the national flag were flown by Korean pilots on September 15, 1948 for the first time.

After acquiring 10 trainers, the Headquarters reinforced its ranks with 397 newly-enlisted men. In October, it acquired another 10 trainers of the L-5-type from the U.S. military and, on December 2, took over control of Youido Air Base.

The Air Base Headquarters was reorganized into the Air Branch Headquarters on December 1, 1948 and, on January 14, 1949, the Army Aviation Cadet School was founded in Kimpo with Lt. Col. Kim Chongyol as its first President. On the same day, the Women's Aviation Training Unit was also founded. This Unit, commanded by Captain Yi Chonghi, admitted 15 trainees. At the same time, the overall strength of the Army Air Branch was considerably reinforced with the enlistment of thirty-two airmen. The number of officers was brought up to 150 on April 15, 1949 when a group of servicemen graduated from an aviation course given at the Army Aviation Cadet School. It was on June 10 of the same year when the first cadet group of ninety-seven entered the Cadet School as aviation students.

On October, 1948, Communist infiltrators who had rooted themselves deeply inside the National Army in its Constabulary days succeeded in sparkling a revolt in the southern port of Yosu. The Air Branch, though it had only 20 planes of the trainer-type, gave a valuable helping hand to the ground forces engaged in operations with effective coordination, reconaissance flights and psychological warfare. Its worth was proved again in the uprising that erupted on the rebel stronghold of Cheju on January 24, 1949. Meanwhile, various developments in the Korean military were pointing to the independence of the Air Branch from the Army. On June 28, 1949, an Aviation Bureau was established as a first step toward such independence and, finally, on October 1 of the same year, the Air Branch became the independent ROK Air Force. Appointed as the first Chief-of-Staff was Colonel Kim Chongyol. The new-born Air Force had 22 planes and a manpower strength of 1,100.

VI NATIONAL DEFENCE

In March, 1950, the Air Force, with funds donated by the people bought ten T-6-type planes to be used for training purposes from the United States.

War

The war came eight months after the birth of the Air Force. With only 22 trainer-type planes, the ROK wings had to cover the airborne aspects of a defensive war. It carried on reconaissance and messenger flights single-handedly until planes of friendly nations under the U. N. Command began to show up in the air over Korea. On July 2, 1950, the Korean Air Force had its first fighter planes when ten F-51 Mustangs were handed over by the U.S. Air Force stationed in Japan. Two days later, Korean pilots with a two-day training course flew these craft from Japan to Taegu. The following day, it was engaging the enemy in the air. It was in this period when Brigadier-General Yi Kunsok, the then Air Wing Commander, drove his burning plane upon an enemy tank group over Anyang. After July 10, the ROK Air Force cooperated constantly with the combined air force of the U. N. C. With reversal of the war tides north, the Air Force moved its operational bases from Taegu and Chinhae to the north Korean capital of Pyongyang and then flew strafing missions over Sonchon, Kanggye and Anju sectors until forced back south with the Chinese Communist intervention. During these operations, Major-General Pak Pomjip was killed over Hamhung.

On October 11, 1951, the 10th Fighter Squadron flew its first independant operational mission. It flew a total of nearly 4,000 operational missions during a one-year period. The first man to complete a round one hundred missions was Major Kim Tuman.

Ever since December 4, 1951, when a group of 10 officers were dispatched to the U. S. Air Force Staff College for training purposes, a great number of officers was dispatched to various Air Force Schools in the U. S. The U. S. Air Force Advisory Group was first sent to Korea on August 15, 1952. The ROK Air Force strengthened its structure with the organization of the 10th Fighter Wing. The then existing 1st Fighter Wing was reorganized into the Training Wing. On May 30 of the same year, Captain Yu Chigon became the first man to set a record of 200 operational missions. Throughout the war, the Air Force flew 5,000 missions over enemy supply routes and 2,851 missions to cover ground operations of friendly forces. A total of 39 officers were credited with over 100 missions each. At the end of the war, the Air Force had 118 planes of various types, including eighty F-51 Mustangs and a manpower strength of 12,000.

Post-War Period

August 20, 1954 was a memorable day for the ROK Air Force. On that day, the first educational course on the maintenance of jet planes was started for the ROK airmen at a USAF base in Japan. On September 9 of the same year, flying lessons for jets were started in the United States. Other developments;

Dec. 1, '54 – Lt.-Gen. Kim Chongyol assumes the post of Chief-of-Staff.
Dec. 9, '54 – Commencement of first flying course for jet planes in Osan.
Jan. '55 – Commencement of flying course for C-46 Transporters.
Apr. 29, '55 – 6 C-46's turned over to ROKAF.
June 20, '55 – 5 F-85 Sabrejets turned over to ROKAF.
Aug. 17, '55 – 10 T-33 jet trainers turned over to ROKAF.
Oct. 5, '55 – 10th Fighter Wing reequipped with F-86's. Birth of the 5th Mixed Air Wing.
Nov. 4, '55 – Commencement of supply operation for the 3 service branches.
Dec. 1,' 56 – Replacement of Lt.-Gen. Kim Congyol by Lt.-Gen. Chang Tokchang. as Chief.-of Staff.
July, '57 – USAF radar system on east coast.
August, '57 – USAF K-8 (Kunsan) Base taken over.
Jan. '58 – USAF air route control taken over.
Dec. 1, '59 – Replacement of Lt.-Gen. Chang Tokchang by Lt.-Gen. Kim Changkyu as Chief-of-Staff.
Sept. 15, '59 – Birth of the 11th Fighter Wing.

VII FINANCE, ECONOMY

Outline of Korean Finance

Summary

The most difficult problem to grip Korean finances following the Liberation of 1945 was inflation, as was the case with most of the other nations at the end of World War II. The wartime system of economic controls collapsed with the Japanese defeat. To make matters worse, Japan recklessly issued banknotes soon after the Liberation when production of industrial goods was dropping sharply due to the chaos accompanying the territorial division and the various other bottlenecks that impeded production. Consequently, it was inevitable that a vicious inflationary spiral, the potentiality of which had been accumulating from the Japanese war efforts of World War II, should prevail in post-Liberation Korea.

The United States Military Government that replaced the imperialistic Japanese Government-General was, under the circumstances, not only helpless but they further aggravated the situation. To meet the resultant drop in national income and tax revenues, the Occupation authorities executed unbalanced budgets annually, covering red-ink finances merely through additional banknote issues.

The budget deficit stood at 32% in F.Y. 1946, 20 in F.Y. 1948. Actually, however, almost one-half of the budget expenditures had to be covered with additional banknote issues, as revenues dropped far below the budgeted amount before lagging production, while expenditures increased over the budgeted figures before inflation.

The government of the Republic of Korea, which was established in August 1948, made the arrest of inflation and gradual industrial development the current administrative goals. To that end, it established various economic policies and principles to balance state finances. Despite such efforts, however, the government was unable to avoid a 11 billion hwan (35.5% of budget) deficit in F.Y. 1948 and another 51.6 billion deficit in F.Y. 1949 budget, due to the vast financial requirements incidental to the establishment of government and to the release of funds required to suppress the Yosu rebellion and restore the ensuing damages.

Consequently, inflation worsened and the Korean financial world was on the verge of total collapse. To save the situation, a Korean-U. S. Economic Stabilization Committee was organized. The committee adopted a 15-item principle for economic stabilization in March 1950. This principle was designed to bring about an intermedium in economic stability, rather than economic rehabilitation, by overcoming inflation. In accordance with this principle, a fully balanced budget was worked out for F.Y. 1950 for the first time since the Liberation. As a result of the effective execution of the balanced budget, the Korean economy began gradually to be stabilized.

However, the abrupt outbreak of the war brought all government efforts toward economic stabilization to naught. The war destroyed almost all industrial facilities and paralyzed tax administration. Thus, the government had to fill ever-increasing war expenses with borrowings from the Bank of Korea. In order to prevent further deterioration of inflation, the government executed the budget on a monthly basis, stepped up taxation, issued bonds, collected land tax-in-kind, and took various other measures. However, the government failed to achieve any tangible result. This was due chiefly to the hwan loans extended incessantly to the U. N. armed forces ever since the outbreak of the Communist War.

In April 1952, the Agreement between the Republic of Korea and the Unified Command on Economic Coordination was concluded to facilitate the repayment of hwan loans to the U.N. Forces. Because of lapse in time between loans and reimbursements, inflation continued to be stimulated. To make matters worse, foreign economic aid lagged far behind schedule. In February 1953, the government resorted to monetary reform despite the war which was still going on. Though the government stepped up its stringent financial policy as well as efforts to secure more revenues, it was impossible to stabilize finance or economy, due to ever-increasing expenses and inflation.

The armistice in 1953 and the commencement of full-scale foreign aid projects, following the armistice, made it possible to draft overall rehabilitation projects. Commencing in 1954, the government compiled an economic rehabilitation special account to deal exclusively with all projects required for economic rehabilitation and industrial development. Nonetheless, inflation persisted due to the delay in implementation of aid projects.

The government began implementing a new financial stabilization program in FY 1957, making it a principle to control money supply at the level of the end of 1956. Thanks to powerful implementation of this program, the Korean economy began to show signs of stabilization for the first time since the Liberation. The tempo of the increases in commodity prices dropped from 81.8% in 1955 to 18.5% in 1957, and in 1958 the commodity price index dropped by 6.6% from that of the previous year.

Characteristics of Korean Finance

The Korean finance is marked by the fact that until recently the govenment's budget was always in the red, and supplementary budgets had to be compiled. In fact, the Korean finance for the last decade following the establishment of the government was a history of combatting run-away inflation.

Table 1. Ratio of Deficit to Government Revenues for General Budget

Unit: 1 million hwan

Year	Total Revenue	Borrowing	National Bonds	Ratio of Deficit
1950	2,485.3	1,525.7	–	11.4
1951	6,533.2	–	400.0	6.1
1952	22,118.0	–	1,200.9	5.4
1953	55,505.6	20,200.0	2,000.0	40.0
1954	112,225.2	23,200.0	3,300.0	23.6
1955	209,480.4	–	13,499.1	6.4
1957	218,576.8	9,500.0	15,000.0	11.3
1958	287,129.0	22,666.9	18,000.0	14.0
1959	308,942.0	6,473.6	5,000.0	6.3

The second major characteristic of Korean finance is the fact that it depends largely upon foreign aid. Foreign aid accounted for 44.9% of the total revenue in 1958, and 36.1% in 1959. Inasmuch as it is practically impossible to compile budgets prior to the confirmation of the scale of American aid for Korea, compilations were often delayed and it was not often that the government was able to submit its budget bill within the legally stipulated deadline to the National Assembly.

The fact that Korean finance depends upon foreign aid means that the ratio of revenues in the form of taxes is relatively small. The tax revenues accounted for only 35.4% in 1958 and 49.5% in 1959. This signifies that the finance is much beyond the national economic capability. The tax burden of the Korean people for F.Y. 1957 stood at 19.1% of the national income of that year, and the national tax alone represented 16.1% of the national income. These figures may seem to indicate that the tax burden of the Korean people is less heavier than that borne by advanced nations. But in substance it is far heavier. Moreover, the fact that the rates in such under-developed countries as India, the Philippines, Pakistan, etc., are far less than that in Korea attests to the fact that the Korean people are bearing an excessive rate in the tax burden.

Table 2. Rate of Tax Burden for Korean People

Unit: 1 million hwan

Year	National Income (A)	Tax Burden(B)	Local Tax, Etc.	Total Tax Burden	B/A	C/A
1952	184,067	12,627	2,794	15,421	6.9%	8.4%
1953	227,726	24,822	5,844	30,606	10.9	13.4
1954	343,167	45,998	15,207	61,205	13.4	17.8
1955	542,123	81,173	24,718	115,891	15.0	21.4
1956	784,619	126,710	22,566	149,276	16.1	19.1

Table 3. Rates of Tax Burden (Major Nations)

%

Country	1953	1954	1955	1956
U.S.A.	22.2	20.4	19.4	22.1
England	28.4	28.5	27.0	28.2
West Germany	28.8	27.2	25.9	24.9
France	24.7	25.0	23.6	23.8
Japan	15.8	14.8	14.5	12.5
India	4.0	4.5	4.7	—
Philippines	8.3	8.6	—	—
Pakistan	6.4	5.6	—	—
Burma	9.1	17.9	15.0	—

National Public Finance

Summary

It is possible to identify the traces of public finance in three stages—period of adjustment (August 15, 1945—June 25, 1950), wartime (June 25, 1950—July 24, 1953) and period of rehabilitation (post-armistice). All three stages share two characteristic points: budget deficits and excessive expenses for national defense.

Let us review briefly the sources and fluctuation of the financial scales:

Given 1949 as the constant, expenditures were up four times and revenues eight times by F.Y. 1959. Military expenses accounted for about one-half the total expenditures. In revenue, foreign aid has accounted for about 20% of the total since 1954.

The percentage of foreign aid to the revenues in the general budget, including the economic rehabilitation account, stood at 51% in 1957, 45% in 1958, and 36% in 1959.

About 80% of the foreign aid which averaged 40%-50% of the total revenues for the general budget has been utilized for economic rehabilitation projects. In 1955 and thereafter, foreign aid amounting to over 100 billion hwan or an amount close to this figure has been budgeted annually. Let us review the traces of Korean finance on an annual basis.

VII FINANCE, ECONOMY

Major Financial Indications Based on General Budget

Unit: 1 million hwan
Constant value: 1949-100
(Readjusted to General Budget for F.Y. 1958)

EXPENDITURES

Year		[1]) Military Expenses	[3]) Composition Ratio	Non-Military Expenses	Composition Ratio	Expenses for Military & Police and Military & Police Relief Included in Non-Military Expenses	Composition Ratio	Total	Percentage
1949	(Executed)	239.5	26.3	671.6	73.7	82.6	9.1	911.1	100.0
1950	(Executed)	317.6	54.5	265.1	45.5	96.8	16.6	582.7	100.0
1951	(Executed)	353.5	53.4	308.7	46.6	64.2	9.7	662.2	100.0
1952	(Executed)	451.3	44.0	574.4	56.0	65.9	6.4	1,025.7	100.0
1953	(Executed)	1,415.7	56.5	1,089.4	43.5	247.0	9.9	2,505.1	100.0
1954	(Executed)	1,818.5	49.3	1,902.9	50.7	397.6	10.8	3,721.4	100.0
1955	(1st supplementary budget)	1,127.2	48.3	1,205.1	51.7	245.9	10.5	2,332.3	100.0
1957	(Budget)	1,343.9	49.5	1,557.0	54.1	288.5	7.8	2,900.9	100.0
1958	(Budget)	1,603.8	47.3	1,786.0	52.7	277.7	8.2	3,389.8	100.0
1959	(Budget)	1,783.4	46.1	2,084.1	53.9	349.9	9.0	3,867.5	100.0

REVENUES

Internal Revenues	[2]) Composition Ratio	Taxes	Composition Ratio	Foreign Aid	Composition Ratio	Total	Composition Ratio	Margin	Price Index	[4]) Value Adjusted
458.1	50.3	135.5	14.9	2.2	0.2	460.3	50.5	(−)450.8	260	100
198.6	34.1	102.6	17.6	31.5	5.4	230.1	39.5	(−)352.5	1,084	417
699.4	105.6	420.6	63.5	−	−	699.4	105.6	(+) 37.2	2,427	933
908.4	88.6	460.7	44.9	146.4	14.3	1,054.8	102.8	(+) 29.1	5,451	933
1,677.8	67.0	893.0	35.6	72.3	2.9	1,750.1	69.9	(−)755.0	5,989	2,303
2,433.1	65.9	1,560.9	42.3	661.4	17.9	3,094.5	83.8	(−)626.9	8,567	3,295
1,760.3	75.5	1,157.8	49.6	572.0	24.5	2,332.3	100.0	0.0	16,135	6,206
2,248.7	76.7	1,290.2	44.0	569.4	19.4	2,818.1	96.1	(−)112.8	22,070	8,488
2,503.0	73.8	1,609.1	47.4	684.2	20.2	3,187.2	94.0	(−)202.6	20,128	7,742
3,122.5	80.7	2,420.6	62.6	663.9	17.2	3,786.4	97.9	(−) 81.1	20,757	7,983

Note: [1]) Net military expenses.
[2]) Revenues from national bonds and lotteries included.
[3]) Composition ratio refers to total expenditures.
[4]) Price index refers to average index for each F.Y., except F.Y. 1958 (average of January-September) and F.Y. 1959 (average of September).
(Disparity in total figures are due to the application of the principle of rounding off figures to the nearest number.)

F.Y. 1950

The inflation that persisted since the Liberation reached a serious height by the end of 1949. To make matters worse, the U.S. House of Representatives vetoed E.C.A. aid to Korea. The veto, though withdrawn later, so seriously endangered the Korean economy and finance that it became a most urgent task for the government and people to overcome the crisis. The government organized a Korean-U. S. Economic Stabilization Committee to study ways and means of overcoming the crisis. Agreement was finally reached with the U. S. government on March 4 to adopt a 15-item program for economic stabilization with the object of attaining intermediary stabilization rather than overall rehabilitation in the economy.

According to the budget for F.Y. 1950, which was compiled by the government in accordance with this 15-item program, the revenues and expenditures under the general budget were balanced at 1,505,850,000 won*. The scale of the budget, including special accounts, reached 316.8 billion won. The budget was significant in that it was balanced for the first time since the Liberation.

The government began executing the balanced budget faithfully in order to control inflation. However, the abrupt outbreak of the war in June obliged the government to abandon the balanced budget and, instead, compile and execute a monthly budget for the period of July through October.

Of the 29.8 billion won spent through October, 28.6 billion was covered with government borrowings from the central bank. The economic stabilization plan collapsed completely.

In October, the government compiled the fifth supplementary budget amounting to 164.5 billion won, mainly to meet war expenses. Following the invasion of Red Chinese troops, the government had to compile a sixth supplementary budget to cope with the deteriorating war situation. The entire 58.7 billion won expenditures under the sixth supplementary budget was met with direct borrowings, bringing the total borrowings to 139.5 billion won to help cover total expenditures that reached 302.6 billion. Inasmuch as it was rather difficult to determine financial resources for the compilation of these supplementary budgets at a time when the U. N. Forces were retreating to the Osan-Wonju line, the government had to compile a seventh supplementary budget in March 1951. Under this budget, the government's borrowings increased to 186 billion won and the total budget

*The old currency converted to hwan at 100-1 in February 1953.

deficit, including deficits in special accounts, was 211.2 billion.

F.Y. 1951

The characteristic feature of the budget for F.Y. 1951 was that the total revenues and expenditures were well coordinated, despite the fact that the government was under wartime financial duress. Moreover, tax revenues accounted for 56% of the total revenues for the general budget. Also notable is the enactment of the Fiscal Law (September 7) and the Land Income Tax Law (September 9) in 1951.

The original budget and supplementary budgets adopted in F.Y. 1951 were as follows:

Unit : million won

	General Accounts	Special Accounts
Original	333.1	947.802
1st supplementary	—	11.817
2nd "	62.047	93.522
3rd "	223.103	314.591
Total:	618.25	1,367.732

F.Y. 1952

The government, having succeeded in executing the budget in a balanced manner for the previous fiscal year, generally followed up this policy in compiling the F.Y. 1952 budget. At the same time, the supplementary budget was discarded.

Thus, the new budget which was passed by the National Assembly in April 18 envisaged a scale of 981.9 billion won for the general budget and 2,748.7 billion, including special accounts.

Of the total expenditures in general budget amounting to 976.8 billion won, excluding the amount transferred to the communication's special account, war expenses accounted for 499.9 billion won, or 51% of the total expenditures.

681.7 billion won, or 69.5% of the total revenues, was covered with tax receipts, and the balance with other government receipts. Nonetheless, the execution of the budget hit various snags, outstanding of which was the lagging repayments of won loans advanced to the UN Forces.

F.Y. 1953

The government wanted to rehabilitate the country and win the war at one and the same time. However, as commodity prices had increased tenfold in two years of war, the government had to moderate its policy to meet expenditures with the national burden, relying upon foreign aid to help finance the budget. The total expenditures of the general budget stood at 28.4 billion in the new hwan currency, while net total expenditures stood at 73.351 billion hwan. War expenses accounted for 78.8% of the next expenditures. Another remarkable point is that industrial rehabilitation expenses increased from 1.5% in the previous year to 6.3%.

Of the total expenditures, 30.4 billion hwan, or 41.47%, was covered with domestic revnues, while the remaining 58.53% was covered with foreign aid. With the conclusion of the armistice agreement, the government compiled a supplementary budget to finance rehabilitation projects.

F.Y. 1954

With the confirmation of $200 million in F.O.A. aid fund following the armistice, the Paek-Wood* Agreement was concluded to lay the groundwork for financial stabilization and economic rehabilitation. Anticipating that foreign aid would continue to occupy the major portion of the budget, the Government revised the fiscal law to make the fiscal year identical with that of the United States, so as to ensure effective utilization of U.S. aid funds. The F.Y. 1954 budget was, accordingly, compiled to cover the period April 1954 through June 1955. The general budget totalled 56.9 billion hwan while the net total budget, including special accounts, reached 295.5 billion. Of the total net expenditures amounting to 108.8 billion hwan, war expenses accounted for 79.4 billion, or 73% of the total.

60.2 billion hwan, or 55.34% of the total expenditures, was covered with domestic revenues including 46.1 billion in net revenues in the general budget, and the remaining 44.66% (48.6 billion) from counterpart funds (aid funds). However, due to friction between the Korean and U. S. governments over the utilization of aid funds, the government twice had to compile supplementary budgets.

F.Y. 1955

The government endeavored to realize economic rehabilitation by effectively utilizing I.C.A. aid funds, and the budget drafted toward this goal was passed by the National Assembly on July 31. The new budget was marked by the fact that a) remunerations of public officials were raised, b) subsidies for local autonomies increased, and c) more funds earmarked for investment projects.

Consequently, expenditures increased to 167.9 billion hwan, including 75.1 billion for ordinary administrative expenses and 91.1 billion for national defense. The expenditures were covered with 88.3 billion hwan in internal revenues, 32 billion in military aid fund, 22.5 billion in the counterpart fund, 5 billion from national bond issues, and 20.1 billion in loans from the central bank.

F.Y. 1956

The compilation of the budget for F.Y. 1956 was much delayed due to dissensions over the use of counterpart funds to cover defense expenses, tax reform, and further improvement in the treatment of public officials. The budget bill was finally presented to the National Assembly on November 7 and passed on December 30.

The expenditures reached 218.6 billion hwan, including 114.1 billion for defense ex-

---

*Paek Tujin, then Premier and Finance Minister of the Republic of Korea; C. Tyler Wood, U. N. Command Economic Coordinator.

penses. The expenditures were covered with 145.5 billion hwan in internal revenues, 48.3 billion in counterpart funds and 9.6 billion in loans from the central bank.

F.Y. 1957

The budget for F.Y. 1957 was compiled to stabilize commodity prices, promote balanced development of the national economy, and better the living standards of the people. The total expenditures in the general budget totaled 323 billion hwan, an increase of 7.8 billion (0.3%) from the previous year. But substantial expenditures less 15.7 billion hwan "book-expenditures", including 1.1 billion subscription to the International Bank for Rehabilitation and Development, dropped by 7.9 billion hwan.

The total revenues reached 307.3 billion hwan, an amount comparable with the 305.6 billion expenditures of the previous year's budget.

F.Y. 1958

The total expenditures stood at 396.3 billion hwan (including 19.4 billion for supplies), an increase of 29 billion as compared with 367.3 billion (including 44.3 billion for supplies) over the previous year due chiefly to increased compensation for public officials. If the increase from these compensations is deducted, it means a drop in expenditures by 33.9 billion hwan. When the 9.2 billion hwan in book-expenditures are deducted, the substantial decrease amounts to 24.7 billion.

The 389.8 billion hwan net expenditures were covered with 249,2 billion in internal revenues and 140.6 billion in revenues from foreign aid.

Local Public Finance

Introduction

In principle, the local finance should be promoted toward enabling local autonomies, education districts and city boards of education to make their ends meet. Instead, it has been relying virtually upon national subsidies.

The fluctuations in government subsidies for local finance and their ratio to government expenditures since F.Y. 1945 were as follows. (Unit: 1 million hwan)

Year	Subsidies	Ratio	Year	Subsidies	Ratio
1945	4.3	24.2%	1952	1,370.3	6.4
1946	13.4	11.9	1953	2,815.9	4.6
1947	14.08	10.9	1954	4,153.0	3.7
1948	18.8	6.0	1955	16,451.0	18.0
1949	44.1	4.8	1957	24,575.0	17.0
1950	62.0	2.6	1958	47,400.0	14.0
1951	395.7	6.4	1959	71,900.0	18.0

Note: The principle of rounding off fractions to the nearest number was applied for calculation of percentages.

The conspicuous drop in the composition ratio during 1950-1954 is attributable to the increased requirements for national defense arising from the war. The increases in government subsidies in 1955 and thereafter reflect increased financial requirements, resulting from the expansion of the local autonomous bodies as well as economic and financial stability achieved as a result of the implementation of economic rehabilitation projects.

Further review of the financial resources for F.Y. 1958 shows that the government subsidies for the local autonomies (excluding Seoul Special City, Kyongsang Namdo and Kyongsang Pukto, Cholla Namdo and Cholla Pukto, Pusan City, Taegu City, and Inchon City) reached 20.1 billion hwan while their own revenues totaled 6.6 billion hwan, including 4.1 billion in local taxes and 2.5 billion in non-tax revenues.

In addition, the local administration ex-

VII FINANCE, ECONOMY

penses under the jurisdiction of the Ministry of Education totalled 31.4 billion hwan which was covered, as follows:

Source Amount (Unit 1 billion hwan)	
A. Self Revenue*	6.2
Supplement to household tax	3.3
Special dues	2.9
B. National subsidies	31.2
Repayments of land income tax	5.2
Subsidies for new projects	1.5
Subsidies for financial deficit	4.2
Subsidies for public health and welfare	3.4
Subsidies for salaries of primary and middle school teachers	16.9

*Refers to revenues of education districts and city boards of education.

For F.Y. 1959, 20.4 billion hwan, or 70% of the total financial requirements of the local autonomies (27 billion hwan), was met with national subsidies. The local administration expenses under the jurisdiction of the Ministry of Education totaled 53.4 billion hwan, 51.4 billion was met with national subsidies, the self revenues of the local autonomies accounting for only 2 billion.

Thus, the total local financial expenses, including education expenses, totalled 71.9 billion hwan, almost double the amount for the previous year (47.4 billion), a consequence chiefly attributable to the increased remuneration for local public and education officials in proportion to raises for the civic servants in the central administration.

Tax System

Introduction

Korea has yet to emerge as a full-fledged tax-financed nation, in view of the fact that foreign aid accounts for 36% of the total revenue. Moreover, non-tax revenue represented 14% of the total revenues. Though the rate of tax to the total revenue is lower than that of other nations, there is no denying that there has been remarkable development in less than a decade. When the government was established in 1948, only liquor and business taxes were levied. In fact, there was no full-scale tax administration until after the outbreak of the war. It is a widely acknowledged fact that the tax system develops most during wartime, and Korea was no exception.

The requirement for vast war expenses and wartime national administration prompted the development of tax administration. As a result, the land income tax was initiated, marking the turning point in the tax administration of Korea toward a full-fledged tax-financed state.

Eventually various uncoordinated, non standardized taxes were levied by the government. It will take quite a while before the numerous kinds of taxes are screened, balanced, and a sound tax structure established.

Kind of Taxes

There are twenty-one national taxes: individual income tax, land income tax, juridical persons tax, education tax, inheritance tax, property revaluation tax, business tax, customs duties, foreign exchange tax, liquor tax, commodity tax, electricity and gas tax, transit tax, vehicle tax, horse-race tax, registration tax, tonnage tax, stamp tax, mining tax, restaurant tax and theater admission tax. In addition, there are such local taxes as household tax, education tax, and other indirect taxes. It is surprising to note that there are more variety of taxes in Korea than in any other country.

Another characteristic point is the conspicuous centralization of taxation, as evidenced by the fact that many taxes which should normally be collected as local are levied as national.

Had there been no war, there is no doubt that a major portion of these national taxes would have been turned over to local autonomies following their organization. Unfortunately, the centralization of taxes remained uncorrected due to ever-increasing financial requirements on the part of the central government necessitated by the war.

The current tax structure is as follows:

Tax	Tax Revenue	Percentage	Percentage of GNP
Direct Tax			
National Tax	27.8	28.8	2.6
Local Tax	4.4	4.6	0.4
Sub-total	32.2	33.4	3.0
Indirect Tax			
National Tax	55.4	58.2	5.3
Local Tax	8.0	8.4	0.8
Sub-total	63.4	66.6	6.1
Total			
National Tax	83.2	87.0	7.9
Local Tax	12.4	13.0	1.2
Total	95.6	100.0	9.1

Unit: 1 billion hwan constant price–1955

Thus, the rate of tax burden stood at 9.1% of the Gross National Product (G.N.P.) in 1957. Moreover, the national taxes accounted for 87.1% of the total tax revenues, while local taxes accounted for only 13%.

The direct taxes represented 33.4% of the total tax revenues, as against 66.6% of the indirect taxes. This is because the classification system of G.N.P. was applied. If the traditional budget classification system was applied, the rates of the direct taxes will increase much more than 33.4%.

Comparison with foreign nations also shows that Korea's rates stand high among the underdeveloped nations. This is so because the land income tax occupies a larger portion and the currency economy has yet to find universality.

Anyhow, there is no denying that the rate of direct taxes is much higher than that of other nations, a fact attributable to the various primitive economic factors which have been impeding sound and balanced development of the taxation system.

Tax Structure

The composition rate of each tax to the budget of F.Y. 1957 was as follows:

Tax	Budget	Percentage	Percentage of GNP
National Tax			
Income tax	8.7	9.3	0.8
Land income tax	17.3	18.3	1.7
Juridical person's tax	3.3	3.5	0.3
Inheritance tax	0.1	–	–
Assets revaluation tax			
Sub-total	(29.4)	(31.1)	(2.8)
Business tax	4.6	4.9	0.4
Customs tax	14.9	15.8	1.4
Liquor tax	5.1	5.4	0.5
Commodity tax	12.9	13.7	1.2
Electricity, gas tax	1.4	1.5	0.1
Transit tax	1.1	1.2	0.1
Registration tax	0.8	0.8	0.1
Tonnage tax	–	–	–
Stamp tax	0.9	1.0	0.1
Restaurant tax	0.8	0.8	0.1
Theater admission tax	1.1	1.2	0.1
Monopoly profits	10.1	10.7	1.0
Sub-total	(53.7)	(56.9)	(5.1)
National Tax Total	(83.1)	(88.0)	(7.9)
Local Tax			
Household tax	2.0	2.1	0.2
Education tax	3.0	3.1	0.3
Indirect tax	6.3	6.7	0.6
Local Tax Total	(11.3)	(11.9)	(1.1)
Grand Total	(94.4)	100%	9.0

Unit: 1 billion hwan constant price–1955

From this table, it is clear that the indirect taxes make up the backbone of the tax revenues, as the commodity tax, liquor tax and monopoly profits represented 13.7%, 5.1% and 10.1% of the total tax revenues respectively. Moreover, customs tariffs alone accounted for 15.8% of the total tax revenue.

Another characteristic point is that the land income tax represented 18.3% of the total. Though the business tax acounted for 4.6% of the total tax revenue, it does not differ substantially from the commodity tax inr that it is not a business profit tax. Furthermore, inasmuch as individual income tax belongs to the category of classified income tax, there is no fundamental difference be-

VII FINANCE, ECONOMY

tween business income and business taxes, nor has the juridical persons tax been synthesized with the individual income tax.

Thus, the tax system in Korea has yet to be systematized. The salient points of major taxes are reviewed below:

Individual income tax: Only classified incomes are synthesized, applying discriminatory graduated rates, as follows:

Income less deduction	Tax (base plus graduated amount)
₩ 100,000 or less	9%
Over 100,000 – below 200,000	₩ 9,000+10%
200,000 400,000	19,000+13
400,000 600,000	45,000+17
600,000 800,000	79,000+22
800,000 1,000,000	123,000+28
1,000,000 1,500,000	179,000+35
1,500,000 2,000,000	354,000+43
2,000,000 4,000,000	569,000+52
4,000,000 6,000,000	1,609,000+61
6,000,000 8,000,000	2,829,000+70
8,000,000 10,000,000	4,229,000+79
10,000,000 up	5,809,000+88

The deduction is allowed at the rate of 120,000 hwan for each taxpayer plus 6,000 hwan or less per each dependent, proportionate to the number of dependents.

Land income tax: This tax is a combination of the household tax, income tax and land tax, and is levied also by applying graduated rates, as follows:

Total yield less deduction	Tax (base plus graduated amount)
0– 5 sok	7%
5–10	0.35 sok + 9
10–20	0.8 +14
20–30	2.2 +20
30–40	4.2 +27
40–50	6.9 +35
50 up	10.4 +37

The deduction rate is 4 sok per tax payer.

Juridical persons tax: The proportional tax system is adopted, levying 30% for income less than 30 million hwan and 40% in excess of 30 million hwan.

Local Share of Taxes

Taxes were shared by Seoul Special City, other cities and the rural community as follows:

Tax	F.Y. 1959 Revenue	Seoul	Other cities	Rural Community
(I) Total National Tax	193,237	71,149	48,758	34,093
(A) Pure national tax (total)	138,369	56,399	32,245	10,490
Income tax	21,732	9,104	7,480	5,148
Juridical persons tax	4,807	3,708	1,586	143
Registration tax	2,604	1,432	829	343
Assets revaluation tax	391	138	190	63
Foreign exchange tax	34,741	34,741	–	–
Inheritance tax	314	137	63	114
Mining tax	94	–	–	94
Liquor tax	11,014	3,667	4,862	2,485
Commodity tax	30,397	4,102	17,235	2,100
Customs tax	32,275	–	–	–
(B) Taxes of local tax nature (total)	54,864	14,748	16,513	23,603
No. 1 land income tax	19,094	57	796	18,241
No. 2 land income tax	1,248	591	404	254
Business tax	10,898		9,505	1,587
Transit tax	2,403	769	1,446	188
Education tax	9,900	3,863	3,919	2,118
Vehicle tax	4,215	1,370	2,048	797
Amusement tax	1,599	779	595	225
Theater admission tax	2,302	1,545	698	59
Electricity and gas tax	3,205	968	2,103	134
(II) Repayments and subsidies to local autonomies	72,353	4,261	16,199	5,893
(II)–(B)	17,489			
(I)–(II)	120,884			

The table shows that national tax sources are concentrated in cities, especially in Seoul. Moreover, those taxes, which should naturally belong to the provinces, account for a considerable portion of the national tax revenues. Even these tax sources are also concentrated in cities, except for the land income tax.

Consequently, even if all the national taxes of local or provincial nature are turned over to the local autonomies, the latter will have a combined deficit of 17.4 billion hwan on the basis of the F.Y. 1959 budget scale.

An Outline of Korean Economy under Japanese Rule

Exploitation before the Samil

Following the Sino-Japanese and Russo-Japanese Wars, Japan came to establish a solid footing on Korea. She started her exploitation of this country with readjustment of land ownership and, in 1905, implemented a land ownership investigation project on a nationwide basis. In fact, this project marked the beginning of Japan's so-called protectorate government.

In 1906, Regulations Governing Authentication of Ownership of Land and Houses and Regulations Governing Mortgage of Land and Houses were proclaimed to legally confirm foreign ownership of land and houses in Korea. In early 1910, a Bureau of Land Investigation was established to implement these regulations. This Bureau was renamed the Temporary Land Investigation Bureau in August 1910, shortly after the annexation of Korea to Japan.

The Korean Civil Affairs Decree, the Real Estate Authentication Decree, etc., were promulgated in 1912. In 1918, the land investigation project was terminated. Japan earmarked part of public land and forestry for the royal Yi family, while placing the rest under the management of the Oriental Development (colonization) Company. Eventually, over 50% of the total arable land in Korea came to be dominated by Japanese landowners and Japanese capital released through the Oriental Development Company and the Industrial Bank.

Korea's greatest contribution to Japanese imperialism was made in her role as provider of foodstuff. In 1920, Japan drew up an increased rice production program designed to bring about self-sufficiency in foodstuff. She stepped up efforts to boost rice production in Korea, following the outbreak of the Sino-Japanese War. However, the high farm-rent tended to impede the realization of this adjusted rice production program. Nonetheless, beginning with the Showa era (1925), Korea exported six million to ten million tons of rice annually, averaging eight million tons a year. Such exports were made possible through importation of cereals from Manchuria.

Japan's exports to Korea increased year after year following the Annexation. For example, exports to Korea accounted for 1,229,410,000 yen out of the 3,576,370,000 yen total exports Japan recorded for the year 1939.

As late as 1930, China ranked first in Japan's foreign investment, followed by Korea, Manchuria (including Mongolia), and Formosa. But, thereafter, Japan concentrated her investments in Korea, in conjunction with her switch-over to a wartime structure. As a result, Japan's investment in Korea in 1941, excluding political investments, reached over 7 billion yen.

Whereas the paid-capital of Japanese firms having main offices in Korea totalled 1.75 billion yen, that of Korean firms totalled only 170 million yen.

Exploitation after the Samil

Within a decade since Japan began colonizing Korea, the Korean economy came to be completely dominated by Japan. Land, mines, transportation, communications, and financial institutions were all monopolized by Japanese.

In 1919, the population of Korea stood at 16,783,518, of which 85% were farmers. Of the farming population, tenants accounted for 76.9%, while landowners and independent farmers accounted for only 3.4% and 19.7%, respectively. The arable area totalled 4,522,669 *chongbo*, and arable area per farming household averaged only 1.7 *chongbo*.

Except for textiles, Japan did not develop any industry in Korea. In 1919, Korean plant workers numbered 41,873. They were paid 40% to 60% of the wage scales paid to Japanese workers. Korean plant workers were obliged to work over 12 hours a day. Inasmuch as industrial development was being impeded due to Japan's colonization policy, the labor movement was contained. Nonetheless, the number of strikes increased from eight or nine in 1915 to 84 in 1919.

In the political field, Japan candidly resorted to government-by-force. Patriots who campaigned for independence were either shot or burned at the stake. Such Japanese rule further provoked the resistance of the Korean people. Moreover, the revolutionary movement that swept the world following the First World War added fuel to their movement for national emancipation. Thus, the Samil (March 1st) Independence Movement of 1919. On March 1, 1919, thirty-three representatives of the Korean people proclaimed a "Declaration of Independence". A total 1.5 million Korean people participated in this movement and 20,000 (farmers accounted for 56%) persons were killed at the hands of the Japanese imperialists. As a result of the independence movement, Japan replaced the government-by-force rule with what was supposed to be a "culture administration".

Having laid the groundwork for exploitation of Korea with the termination in 1918 of the "land investigation project", Japan moved ahead with her policy of colonization. In August 1920, Japan's Customs Law replaced its Korean counterpart. Simultaneously, Japan implemented an increased rice production program. The rice was taken away from Korean farmers at cheap prices and, in return, industrial products, including clothing, were sold to the farmers at high prices. Thus Korean farmers, especially independent and tenant-farmers, became bankrupt, and the number of tenants increased. Korean land and mine workers were paid only one-half to two-thirds of the wages paid their Japanese counterparts. Under such social conditions, farmers and laborers fought back and one dispute followed another. Students also began to stage anti-Japanese campaigns. In 1928, a resistance movement was launched in Wonsan, followed by a students' movement in Kwangju in 1929 which touched off a nationwide student uprising. Still earlier, in 1925, the Koryo Youth Society was organized, followed by the organization of the Farmers' Alliance with a membership of 100,000. In December 1925, the famous "Sinuiju Incident" broke out.

On April 20, 1926, King Yijok, the last king of the Yi dynasty, passed away, and the 20 million Korean people were overcome with deep sorrow. A special committee was organized on May 2nd that year to launch an independence movement on June 10th, the day set for the king's funeral service. On the designated date, a major anti-Japanese independence demonstration was staged. The June 10th independent movement is marked by the fact that a slogan calling for the return of land to farmers was adopted together with other slogans. In this sense, the June 10th movement was of historical import.

Korea and the Japanese War Effort

With her penetration of Manchuria in

1931 and of China Proper in 1939, Japan's exploitation of Korea was stepped up. Farmers suffered the most. They were the first target of military and labor drafts. They were also obliged to make deliveries of rice and other grains to fill the quotas allotted to them.

Since 1937, Japan stepped up development of underground resources. She relied upon Korea for her supply of major minerals, gold, iron ore, coal, copper, tungsten, graphite, bismuth, etc.

War industry in the field of metal refinery, light metallic industry, and chemical industry was also developed in Korea to help Japan's war efforts.

The number of Korean workers increased to 733,000, including 550,000 plant workers and 183,000 mining workers. Female workers accounted for 8% of the total. Thirty percent of the laborers employed by plants employing 30 persons up were women.

On an age basis, teen-agers of 15 years or less accounted for 22% of the total workers in plants employing 30 persons or more, while those 19 or less accounted for 26%. Thus, the teen-ager represented 48% of the total labor force.

Laborers drafted for work in Korea totalled over 2.616 million; another 723,000 were sent to Japan and South Sea islands.

In short, the whole course of Japanese imperialism was a long and systematic process to seize Korean land, exploit the Korean people, and, finally, expend millions of Korean lives.

Financial Status

Outline of Financial Status

The total banknote issue increased from 48 million hwan as of August 15th, 1945 to 116.319 billion hwan by the end of 1958, while bank deposits increased from 33 million to 121.241 billion hwan and bank loans from 71 million to 158.983 billion hwan.

The United States Military Government in Korea set its budget for F.Y. 1946 at 8.013 billion hwan for revenues and 11.86 billion hwan for expenditures. Financial difficulties prevailed even after the establishment of the Republic of Korea government. The government was finally able to come up with a balanced budget for F.Y. 1950, setting both expenditures and revenues at 31.684 billion hwan. In the same year, the R.O.K.-U.S. Combined Economic Board was established. A 15-item principle was adopted to arrest inflation and stabilize the economy. But due to the abrupt outbreak of the war in June 1950, all efforts to stabilize the national economy came to naught.

The government's budget deficit in F.Y. 1950 reached 2 billion hwan. Moreover, the loans to the U.N. Forces made during the period August 1950 through March 1951 totalled 1.135 billion hwan, accounting for another major factor in runaway inflation.

The armistice was negotiated in the latter part of 1952, and, as an agreement was also reached for the reimbursement of hwan loans made to the U.N. Forces, the government came to renew its efforts to readjust its financial status and stabilize the national economy. But the continued requirements of vast amounts of money for national defense harassed all efforts at stabilization.

With F.O.A. and other aid funds provided by friendly nations, the government established an overall financial policy so as to ensure balanced execution of the government's budget, stabilize and develop the national economy. Consequently, the government minimized expenditures and appropriated military expenses from the counterpart funds account, while attempting to reduce the national burden to within 20% of the Gross National Product. However, delay in the implementation of foreign aid projects resulted in the collapse of the balanced budget and inflation prevailed unabated.

Foreign aid increased gradually and aid funds came to account for one-third of the total revenues amounting to 167.9 billion hwan under the budget for F.Y. 1955. War expenditures under this budget reached 91.1 billion hwan while other expenditures totalled 75.1 billion hwan.

Revision of Fiscal Year

Inasmuch as foreign aid came to occupy a larger portion of the government's revenues, the government, as of F.Y. 1955, decided to revise the fiscal year starting in April to correspond with that of the United States.

In F.Y. 1957, the government stepped up its stringent financial policy in an attempt to maintain the 500 hwan per $1 foreign exchange rate set in September 1955. Moreover, the fiscal year was once again revised to correspond to the calender year so as to make it possible closely to reflect U.S. aid appropriations for Korea in the government's annual budget.

The government was able to balance its budget in F.Y. 1957, as $277 million in American economic aid for F.Y. '57 was increased by another $50 million, and, in addition, $44 million worth of U.S. surplus agricultural products were made available.

The general budget scale for F.Y. 1957 increased to 27.8% of the Gross National Product, up 2.6% from 25.1% of the general budget for the previous year due to increased remuneration of the public officials, continued issuance of national bonds, hikes in prices of monopoly products, etc. Ordinary expenditures were increased to 99.5 billion hwan and expenditures under the general budget to 218.6 billion hwan up 60.1% from the previous year. This may seem quite impressive an increase. But if the rate of increase in commodity prices is taken into account, it does not represent a conspicuous rise.

The budget scale for F.Y. 1958 reached 323 billion hwan (including 60 billion hwan earmarked for rehabilitation projects), but war expenditures accounted for 124.2 billion hwan. Six years after the armistice, a vast amount was still being consumed for maintenance of the huge defense force.

Despite such a great handicap, the Korean economy has grown up steadily. The commodity price index was contained within the 125% level of the Seoul wholesale price index adopted September 1955, due chiefly to continued American aid as well as to the tight financial and banking policy adopted by the government.

Recent Financial Status in Korea

Ordinary government expenditures for F.Y. 1959 stood at 396.2 billion— 308.9 billion hwan under the general budget (161.1 billion hwan ordinary expenditure, 140.6 billion hwan in national defense, 7.2 billion hwan for national bonds) and 87.3 billion hwan under the counterpart fund special account (56.4 billion hwan for government economic rehabilitation projects, 26.4 billion hwan for private economic rehabilitation projects, 1.6 billion hwan for transfer into the foreign supply special account, and 2.9 billion hwan for other purposes). This represents a decrease of 30.1 billion hwan from that of the previous year (including supplementary budget for F.Y. 1958). It also represents a 22.8% of the Gross National Product estimated for F.Y. 1959.

On a composition ratio basis, military expenditures accounted for 35%, ordinary government expenditures for 44%, and government and private economic rehabilitation projects for 21%.

These expenditures are to be met with 249.46 billion hwan in domestic tax revenue (of which 233.2 billion hwan, or 13.4% of Gross National Product, is internal tax revenue), 140.26 billion hwan in foreign aid (counterpart fund) and 6.47 billion hwan in borrowings from the Bank of Korea. Consequently, the domestic revenue (excluding borrowings) to the aid fund ratio is 64 to 36, whereas that under the previous year's budget was 54 to 46.

The 140.27 billion hwan revenue under the counterpart fund special account was estimated under the assumption that $290 million in aid funds—$249 million under I.C.A. programs and $45 million under the U.S. Public Law 480 programs—will be made available.

Improvement is also noted in the banking field. The money supply has declined since February to 206.709 billion hwan as of the end of June. The margin between bank deposits and outstanding loans dropped, reflecting economic and social stability.

The city banks' rediscounts by the Bank of Korea dropped from 43.6% in 1955 to 50.2% in 1956, 32% in 1957, 22.9% in 1958. In 1959, the city banks began depositing their idle funds with the Bank of Korea. Consequently, commodity prices were stabilized and interest rates for private loans dropped. In view of the favorable turn of the financial situation, the government began contemplating various measures to ease control on bank loans, and abolished the ceiling system in March 1959.

Nonetheless, the suspension of trade between Korea and Japan and the reduction in America's economic aid for Korea for F.Y. 1960, began adversely to influence the commodity price trend, and the Seoul wholesale price index came to exceed the 125% line set for the maintenance of the current official foreign exchange rate, thus obliging the authorities concerned to again implement a stringent financial policy.

Should the release of funds required for the increased investment at this time when the attainment of economic self-sufficiency is in sight be contained, due to the deterioration of relations between Korea and Japan and to a cut in United States' aid appropriations, development of national economy will be impeded. (Principal economic indications are shown below for reference.)

Unit in millions

Year	Money Supply	Bank Deposits	Bank Loans	Economic Aid and Relief Supplies Rec'd.	Price Index
	HW	HW	HW	$	
1945	114	34	40	4.9	12
1946	249	105	120	49.5	55
1947	495	224	275	175.4	100
1948	696	347	365	179.6	163
1949	1,211	599	783	116.5	223
1950	2,831	558	877	58.7	334
1951	7,304	2,403	2,248	106.5	2,194
1952	14,325	5,816	6,492	161.3	4,751
1953	30,316	12,316	18,136	194.2	5,951
1954	58,079	25,418	22,649	153.9	7,629
1955	93,523	45,283	37,988	236.7	13,816
1956	120,925	72,032	72,411	326.7	18,623
1957	145,186	80,776	109,281	382.9	22,070
1958	192,553	115,068	158,856	321.3	20,619
1959*	206,709	138,602	174,316	—	21,950

*as of June 30th.

Securities Exchange

Establishment of Korea Securities Exchange

The Korea Securities Exchange was established on March 3, 1956 with a capital of 300 million hwan. The Exchange thrice increased its capital (in November 1956, May 1957, and May 1958) by 100 million hwan respectively boosting the total to 600 million hwan. In the three years since its establishment, a total of 104.7 billion hwan worth of shares (21.3 billion hwan) and national bonds (83.4 billion hwan) were transacted. The reason for the withering in transactions of the shares as compared with the national bonds is attributed to the fact that shares of major enterprises have not been offered to the public while shares of no more than sixteen enterprises are being offered at the Exchange. Moreover, except for investment shares of the Exchange itself and the Seoul Textile Company, shares available at the Exchange are limited. Especially, investor willingness in the four city banks was reduced as a majority of their shares became monopolized by a handful of persons after an auction of the vested shares. Another factor responsible is the limited number of floating shares of such major enterprises as the Seoul Electric Co., South Korea Electric Co., Korea Shipbuilding Corp., Korea Marine Corp., Korea Forwarding Co., Korea Rice Warehouse Co., etc. Public willingness in investing in securities was all the more lowered as almost no dividends were paid the shareholders, save for shares of the Korea Securities Exchange, Yonhap Securities Co., and the Seoul Textile Co.

The relatively favorable investment in national bonds is attributable to the vast amount of national bonds available, guaranteed reimbursement and payment of interests by the government.

First Year's Achievements (April 1956—March 1957)

Table of First Year's Achievements

Kind	Spot transactions (HW)	Ratio (%)	Future transactions (HW)	Ratio (%)	Total (HW)	Ratio (%)
Shares	450,815,100	13	10,563,162,800	61	11,013,977,900	53
National bonds	2,976,618,540	87	6,692,304,000	39	9,668,922,540	47
Total	3,427,433,640	100	17,255,466,800	100	20,682,900,440	100

As noted in the above table, future transactions exceeded spot transactions five times over, while transactions in shares slightly exceeded those in national bonds. The active implementation of aid projects, attainment of economic stability, distribution of dividends by the Seoul Textile Company, etc., stimulated investment in shares. Thus, the Exchange brought in a total of 131,480,623 hwan, while spending a total of 106,587,821 hwan, earning a net profit of 24,892,802 hwan. It became possible for the Exchange to pay an annual dividend of 6%.

Second Year's Achievements (April 1957—March 1958)

Table of Second Year's Achievements

Kind	Spot transactions (HW)	Ratio (%)	Future transactions (HW)	Ratio (%)	Total (HW)	Ratio (%)
Shares	149,920,000	12	6,383,686,000	15	6,533,606,000	13
National bonds	7,956,353,740	88	34,990,462,000	85	42,946,815,740	87
Total	8,106,273,740	100	41,374,148,000	100	49,480,421,740	100

In the second year of operation, the Exchange came to assume a quite different phase. Transactions in shares dropped from 53% to 13%, while those in national bonds increased from 47% to 87%. The conspicuous decline in transactions in shares was attributed chiefly to the monopolization of vested bank shares by a handful of persons as well as to the limited numbers of shares of major enterprises available in the securities market. Another factor responsible for this is the fact that practically no dividends were paid for the shares offerred at the Exchange. The spectacular increase in transactions in national bonds was attributed to the fact that the government punctually redeemed national bonds plus interests at due dates. The increased requirements for national bonds in the form of securities or mortgages also stimulated investment in national bonds.

The Korea Securities Exchange netted a profit of 32,226,612 hwan in the second year of operation, the total income and expenditures being 250,967,682 hwan and 219,741,070 hwan respectively. Consequently, the Exchange was able to pay the 6% annual dividend.

This table is marked by an increase in the transactions in shares as the securities' market improved. During May, the Exchange transacted a total of 4,600,882,74 hwan, including 1,764,894 hwan in shares and 2,835,088,740 hwan in national bonds. The figures represent an increase of 48.9% in transactions in shares over the previous month due largely to the transactions in investment shares of the Korea Securities Exchange.

In fact, the transactions during the month marked the peak since January last year, when the Exchange recorded transactions reaching 2,838,920,600 hwan, including 1,185,290,000 hwan in shares and 1,653,630,600 hwan in national bonds.

With the increased offerings of the 10th national bonds, the transactions in national bonds increased by 71.5% bringing the overall increases in transactions to 1.762 billion hwan worth, a 62.1% increase from the previous month.

Especially, transactions in the 10th national bonds increased sharply, perhaps influenced by the rumor which prevailed around the end of the month to the effect that the 10th national bonds will be redeemed next year.

Third Year's Achievements
(April 1958—March 1959)

The Korea Securities Exchange suffered a setback at the beginning of the third year, due to a crisis caused by excessive speculation on the part of some of the dealers in securities.

The Korea Securities Exchange endeavored to recover from the crisis and even increased its capital by another 100 million hwan. The Exchange also opened new improved premises. As a result, the Exchange was able to record total transactions at 34,621,021,600 hwan, including 3,831,064,000 hwan in shares (11%) and 30,789,948,600 hwan (89%) in national bonds. Though the total transactions stood below the level of the previous year, it was, nonetheless, 50% more than the record for the initial business year.

Fourth Year's Achievements
(April 1959—)

The fourth business year will not be completed until the end of March 1960. Therefore, the Exchange's achievements on a monthly basis are reviewed as below:

Table of Achievements in April

Kind	Spot transactions	Ratio	Future transactions	Ratio	Total	Ratio
	HW	%	HW	%	HW	%
Shares	107,000,000	21	1,078,290,000	46	1,185,290,000	41
National bonds	399,020,600	79	1,254,610,000	54	1,653,630,600	59
Total	506,020,600	100	2,332,900,000	100	2,838,920,600	100

VII FINANCE, ECONOMY

Table of Achievements in May

Kind	Spot transactions	Ratio	Future transactions	Ratio	Total	Ratio
	HW	%	HW	%	HW	%
Shares	243,769,000	28	1,521,125,000	48	1,764,894,000	38
National bonds	616,474,400	72	2,219,513,000	52	2,835,987,400	62
Total	860,243,400	100	3,740,638,000	100	4,600,881,400	100

Table of Achievements in June

Kind	Spot transactions	Ratio	Future transactions	Ratio	Total	Ratio
	HW	%	HW	%	HW	%
Shares	184,000,000	20	1,041,000,000	69	1,225,000,000	28
National bonds	791,000,000	80	2,287,000,000	31	3,078,000,000	72
Total	975,000,000	100	3,328,000,000	100	4,303,000,000	100

Note: Figures below one million are omitted.

The total transactions in June dropped by 297 million hwan. Transactions in shares were off 539 million hwan from the previous month, while those in national bonds were up 24.2 million hwan. The decline in transactions in shares was attributed to the decreased offerings of investment shares in the Securities Exchange. Spot transactions increased by 13.4%, while future transactions dropped by 11%, accounting for the termination of speculation over the investment shares of the Exchange.

The fluctuations in quotations of shares in April, May, and June were as follows:

Quotations of Securities (Part of Spot Transactions)

Unit: Hwan

	April			May			June		
	Maximum	Minimum	Average	Maximum	Minimum	Average	Maximum	Minimum	Average
Korea Securities Exchange	0.80	0.55	0.68	0.93	0.68	0.80	0.87	0.75	0.84
Hungop Bank	-	-	-	-	-	-	2,450	2,150	2,380
Seoul Textile	5.50	5.50	5.50	-	-	-	-	-	-
South Korea Electric (new shares)	-	-	-	-	-	-	4,200	4,200	4,200
Korea Forwarding Co.	-	-	-	-	-	-	2,500	2,000	2,250
Korea Marine Corp.	150	150	150	-	-	-	150	150	150
7th national bond	78.50	78.50	78.50	-	-	-	-	-	-
8th "	72.70	70.50	71.34	82.50	73.20	77.46	-	-	-
9th "	68.50	65.30	66.32	71.00	61.00	66.68	77.00	72.50	75.96
10th "	44.70	37.50	40.48	62.80	40.10	52.11	64.00	53.00	58.50
11th "	45.80	41.30	43.23	51.60	42.50	46.95	55.70	48.50	51.89
12th "	37.50	33.10	35.94	46.60	37.80	43.45	47.80	42.20	45.72

Commodity Prices

Commodity Price Index in Korea

Systematic findings to calculate the commodity price index and thus determine the trend was first undertaken by the old Bank of Korea in 1910. But this project was later taken over by the Bank of Chosen and then by the present Bank of Korea in 1950.

Except for July 1945 prior to the Liberation, and for a ten-month period immediately following the outbreak of the war, the index has been incessantly determined.

The method of index calculation underwent changes with a change in form of the agency handling this function. In the beginning, the national wholesale price index was calculated on the basis of a simple arithmetical average system with July 1910 as 100. This method was revised in 1939 in favor of a simple geometrical average system (1936-100). In 1949, it was again revised in favor of a weighted average system (1947-100). The last revision was made in 1955 when the weighted arithmetical average system was adopted.

Commodity Price Trends

Under the Japanese rule, the Korean economy was unable to develop in a balanced manner as the Japanese set the pattern to fit into an overall Japanese economic system. As a result, Korea developed a lame-duck industrial structure. It was no wonder, therefore, that commodity prices began to increase sharply following the Liberation, as most ordinary commodities, except agricultural products, had to be imported.

Furthermore, the outbreak of the war and resultant releases of war expenses and loans to U.N. forces brought a vicious inflationary spiral, that, in turn, was further accelerated by sharp decline in production.

Thus the rate of commodity price increase surpassed that of the currency inflation until 1954 when a monetary reform was implemented.

Economic order began to be gradually restored since 1955 with the implementation of balanced budgets, tight monetary policy, and increased importation of aid-funded as well as non-aid funded goods. The rate of increase in commodity prices dropped below that of the increase in money supply.

Seoul Wholesale Price Index
1947-100

Year	General Index
1945 (August)	17.0
1946	55.0
1947	100.0
1948	162.9
1949	222.8
1950 (June)	348.0
1951	2,194.1
1952	4,750.0
1953	5,951.0
1954	7,628.5

Commodity Price Trends since Attainment of Economic Stabilization

The year 1955 and thereafter is referred to as a period of economic stabilization. It was in 1955 when the present official foreign exchange rate of 500 hwan per $1 was adopted and an agreement reached between the Korean and United States Governments to readjust the exchange rate when and if the Seoul wholesale price index (September 1955-100) were to exceed the 125% line for a six-months period. Consequently, the government adopted various financial measures to maintain the 125 line, including a policy of controlling the total money supply at the level of the end of F.Y. 1954 in an attempt to stabilize commodity prices on the basis of the quantitative theory of money.

However, the Seoul wholesale price index exceeded the 125 line in March 1957 and resistered 126.9%, due chiefly to increases in grain prices. These increases were the result of poor yields in agricultural products plus the failure to ensure smooth implementation of the program for importation of surplus agricultural products from the United States,

Seoul Wholesale Price Index
September 1955–100

Year	General Index
1955 (September)	100.0
1956	105.0
1957	124.5
1958	116.3
1959 (January)	119.1
(February)	119.2
(March)	115.2
(April)	114.2
(May)	121.8
(June)	123.8
(July)	123.9
(August)	127.9
(September 18th)	134.0

The fundamental condition for stabilizing commodity prices may be said to be the effective utilization of aid funds and other foreign exchange. It is believed that the government policies adopted in this respect have been largely instrumental in bringing about the price stabilization.

Economic Trends Following June 15th Measures

(Suspension of Trade with Japan)

Following the measures adopted on June 15 last year to suspend trade with Japan, the Seoul wholesale price index has continued to increase beyond the 125 line. It stood at 125.3% as of the end of July, 127.9% as of the end of August, and has reached the 130 level beginning in September.

Such steady increases are attributed chiefly to the suspension of trade with Japan, resulting in increases in the price of export dollars for Japan, which, in return, increased the prices of other foreign exchange.

The suspension of the Japan trade resulted in the storage of goods supplies ordinarily imported from Japan, thereby increasing the prices of stocks. Moreover, importation from areas other than Japan of goods normally imported from Japan means higher costs, which, in turn, means higher market prices.

The severence of commercial ties with Japan has also tended to increase the prices of local products manufactured with imported raw materials.

Foreign Trade

Resume of Foreign Trade in Korea

Foreign trade in Korea is regulated by the Trade Law and other related laws and regulations and government policies. Since the establishment of the government, foreign trade has gradually become systematized. In December 1957, the Trade Law was promulgated, followed by the promulgation of the Decree Implementing the Trade Law in March 1958.

Recent annual exports in Korea averaged $20 million to $30 million, while imports averaged $50 million to $60 million. The over imports are covered with invisible trade earnings.

Exports have been made to Japan, the United States, and Hong Kong. At the same time, efforts are being made to develop markets in Southeast Asia, with exportation of rice to the Ryukyus as a turning point. Major import markets for Korea are Japan, the United States, Italy, West Germany, etc.

Major export items are minerals, raw materials, and foodstuffs, while imports comprise finished products, semi-finished products, raw materials, and capital goods. According to statistics compiled by the Customs Bureau of the Ministry of Finance, of the imports and exports by commodity groups in 1958, foodstuffs accounted for $2.45 million, inedible raw materials for $10.57 million, animal and vegetable oils and fats for $162,000, mineral fuels for $297,000, chemicals and medicines for $10,000, machinery for $5,000, manufactured goods classified by material for miscellaneous manufactured articles for $148,000, and others for $383,000.

For imports, foodstuffs accounted for $16.88 million, inedible raw materials for $6,709 million, mineral fuels for $1.042 million, animal and vegetable oils and fats for $1.1 million, medicals and chemicals for $7.425 million, manufactured goods classified by material for $14.1 million, machinery for $7.265 million, miscellaneous manufactured acticles for $9.49 million, and others for $1.036 million.

Thus inedible raw materials accounted for 63.2% of the total exports, foodstuffs for 15.2%, and manufactured goods classified by material for 15.2%, while foodstuffs accounted for 36% of the total imports, manufactured goods classified by material for 30.1%, and machinery for 13.6%.

The characteristic of Korea's foreign trade is that, whereas its export consists chiefly of minerals and fishery products, there is a variety of import items.

For exports, tungsten once accounted for about 70% of the total exports. In 1958, it still ranked first among the exports, with a record of $2.453 million, or 14.9% of the total, followed by iron ore with $2.225 million (13.5%), dried fish and shellfish with $1.45 million (8.8%). Other major export items are graphite, bismuth, anthracite coal, agar-agar, inedible seaweeds, ginseng, bristle, non-ferrous metallic ores, fluorspar, raw silk, silk waste, oak bars, fresh fish, and shellfish.

Because of the variety of import items, no single item, except alcoholic beverages imported for U.N. forces, account for over 5% of the total imports. Major import items are rayon yarn ($3.235 million-4.9%), molasses, Chinese medicines, paraffin, caustic soda, dyestuffs, antibiotics, ammonium sulphate, newsprint, woollen yarn, iron and steel products, etc.

On a settlement currency basis, exports for U.S. dollars totalled $4.967 million, while those for sterling totalled $2.122 million and those to the Open Account Area (Japan) totalled $10.724 million. Imports through the Open Account (Japan) totalled $10.1 million, while those from the dollar and sterling areas totalled $42,275 million and $63,000 respectively.

Foreign Trade Policy

As stipulated in the Constitution, foreign trade is subject to the government's direct control in accordance with the law and incidental regulations. Exports are allowed, providing they do not infringe upon the Trade Law and the Decree Implementing the Trade Law or other incidental regulations nor undermine domestic industries, while imports are limited to industrial machinery, raw materials, and other items contributing to the development of domestic industries.

Though Article 5 of the Trade Law stipulates that the permits of the Minister of Commerce and Industry are required for exports and/or imports, a system has been adopted to automatically allow for exportation or importation of items classified as ordinary trade items, so as to simplify trade procedures and facilitate foreign trade. The Trade Law regulates such special transactions as barter trade, trade on a D/P basis, etc., and a performance bond is required for these special transactions so as to ensure proper transactions. Trade with Commu-

VII FINANCE, ECONOMY

nist territories has been banned, and even trade with countries dealing with the Communist bloc is rigidly controlled.

In order to encourage exports, government subsidies are available for exports.

In addition, special measures are adopted for traders who explore new overseas markets.

Foreign Aid

Summary of Foreign Aid

Foreign aid discussed here refers to grant-type foreign economic aid provided by the United States and U.N. since the end of World War II. Korea has received a total of $2.47 billion worth of foreign economic aid during the period from the Liberation to the end of F.Y. 1958, 77% ($1.89 billion) of which was granted by the United States, and the remaining 23% ($580 million) worth provided by the United Nations.

$585 million worth of foreign aid was provided Korea, including over $500 million GARIOA funds, and $73 million in E.C.A. funds. Most of these aid funds were spent in the importation of relief and urgently required daily necessities such as foodstuffs, clothing, fuel, fertilizer, and agricultural products.

Foreign economic aid received following termination of the war reached $1.89 billion–$36 million in ECA (Economic Cooperation Administration) and SEC (Supplies Economic Cooperation) funds, $457 million in CRIK (Civil Relief in Korea) funds, $1.154 billion in ICA (International Cooperation Administration) funds, $126 million in US Public Law 480 funds, and $120 million in UNKRA (United Nations Korea Reconstruction Agency) funds.

Utilization of American Economic Aid

The United States appropriated a total of $1.5 billion in economic aid for Korea as of the end of June 1959 to help restore war damages (estimated at over $3 billion by the Office of Public Information), stabilize and develop the Korean economy. $1.28

Status of Foreign Aid

Unit: $1,000

Year	GARIOA	E.C.A.	S.E.C.	I.C.A.	PL480	Sub-total	CRIK	UNKRA	Sub-total	Total
1945	4,934	–	–	–	–	4,934	–	–	–	4,934
1946	49,496	–	–	–	–	49,496	–	–	–	49,496
1947	175,371	–	–	–	–	175,371	–	–	–	175,371
1948	179,593	–	–	–	–	179,593	–	–	–	179,593
1949	92,703	23,806	–	–	–	116,509	–	–	–	116,509
1950	–	49,330	–	–	–	49,330	9,376	–	9,376	58,706
1951	–	10,080	21,892	–	–	31,972	74,448	126	74,574	106,546
1952	–	–	3,824	–	–	3,824	155,534	1,965	157,499	161,323
1953	–	–	232	5,571	–	5,803	158,787	29,580	188,367	194,170
1954	–	–	–	82,437	–	82,437	50,191	21,297	71,488	153,925
1955	–	–	–	205,814	–	205,814	8,711	22,182	30,893	236,707
1956	–	–	–	271,048	32,955	304,003	331	22,334	22,665	326,668
1957	–	–	–	323,266	45,528	368,794	–	14,103	14,103	382,897
1958	–	–	–	265,645	47,890	313,535	–	7,747	7,747	321,282
Total	502,097	83,216	25,948	1,153,781	126,373	1,891,415	457,378	119,334	576,712	2,468,127

billion worth of goods were already imported. In addition, the United States provided $165 million worth of U. S. surplus agricultural products in the form of grant-type aid and $60 million in D.L.F. (Development Loan Fund). Aid being furnished by civilian relief organizations in the United States reaches about $30 million annually.

Of the $1.5 billion economic aid funds, about $500 million was earmarked for investment projects, while about $1 billion was earmarked for the procurement of saleable goods, including raw materials. In addition, over $20 million was allocated for technical aid division.

Counterpart funds are collected from the procurement of goods through private or government channels at the official exchange rate for deposits in the counterpart fund account for use in economic rehabilitation projects or transfer into the national defense account.

As of the end of June 1959, counterpart funds totalled 516.6 billion hwan, including 130.7 billion hwan, collected under the MSA 402 and Public Law 480 programs.

In the investment field, $195 million and 136.2 billion hwan or 40% and 35% of the total dollar and hwan funds earmarked for investment projects respectively were earmarked for transportation division for importation of diesel locomotive engines, rehabilitation and construction of new railways, renovation of highway and bridges, reconstruction of harbor facilities, etc. Investment for mining and industry division accounted for $185 million and 66.7 billion hwan, or 38% and 16% of the total dollar and hwan funds earmarked for investment projects respectively. The funds were used for increased production of coal, expansion of electric power facilities, rehabilitation and construction of communications facilities, construction of the Chungju Fertilizer Plant, and over 200 small and medium enterprises. 5% ($25 million) of the total dollar amount and 23% (89.3 billion hwan) of the total hwan amount for investment projects were earmarked for irrigation projects, antierosion projects, forestry projects, and the fishery industry. The balance was used for health and sanitation, education, housing, social welfare and other administrative purposes.

In the saleable goods procurement program, $200 million, or 20% of the total funds was earmarked for the importation of U. S. surplus agricultural products, $295 million (29%) for fertilizer, $281 million (28%) for raw materials for the manufacturing industry, $129 million (13%) for POL* and coal, $64 million (6%) for machinery, and the balance ($32 million-4%) for miscellaneous items.

The $22 million earmarked for the technical aid program was used for the invitation of foreign engineers and the dispatch of Koreans for training abroad in agriculture, industry, public administration, social welfare, and other fields.

Importation of U. S. surplus agricultural products under U. S. Public Law 480 reached $165 million. This program was first implemented in 1956 when the market prices of agricultural products increased sharply due to unfavorable crop yields. Wheat, rice, barley, corn, millet, raw cotton, and other agricultural products were imported under the program.

The counterpart funds collected under the Public Law 480 program are deposited in the account of the U. S. Embassy and 85% of the deposits are returned to the Korean government in the form of grant-aid for use in the national defense account, while the balance (15%) is held by the U. S. government for promoting the sale of U. S. agricultural products, cultural exchange and various other programs.

With the American foreign economic aid beginning to gradually bear fruit, the United States has implemented a new aid system, namely the Development Loan Fund Program in parallel with the ICA program. Under the loan-type aid system, funds are to be provided at low interest

*petroleum, oils and lubricants

VII FINANCE, ECONOMY

rates on a long-term basis to help underdeveloped nations. Another characteristic of the new aid system is that the loans are to be reimbursed with local currency. Korea applied for D.L.F. loans totalling over $100 million and was granted about $60 million as of the end of June this year.

The D.L.F. applications approved thus far were for construction of the Chungju Hydroelectric Power Plant with $43.5 million, expansion of wireless facilities with $3.5 million, expansion of the Oriental Cement Plant with $2.14 million, construction of a soda-ash plant with $5.6 million, and construction of small and medium enterprises with $5 million.

Utilization of U. N. Economic Aid

The United Nations, armed with a resolution of the General Assembly, dispatched troops of sixteen U. N. nations to help expel the Communist aggressors in Korea, and set up a U. N. Korea Reconstruction Agency (UNKRA) to channel economic aid for the reconstruction of war devasted Korea.

Of the $120 million UNKRA aid funds, $84 million was earmarked for the rehabilitation of industrial facilities-$8 million for agricultural division, $44 million for mining and industrial division (construction of the Mungyong Cement Plant, Inchon Plate Glass Plant, paper mills, textile mills and power plants, etc.), and the balance for communications, transportation, housing, education, and public health and social welfare. The remaining $40 million was used for the importation of fertilizer and grain. UNKRA also provided counterpart funds amounting to 14 billion hwan. The UNKRA projects were terminated as of the end of June 1958.

Results of Foreign Economic Aid

The Joint American-Korean Economic Committee an organization composed of representatives of the governments of Korea and the United States, has been assuming the role of a nerve-center in the implementation of aid projects. In order to augment aid administration, the Foreign Supply Management Law was enacted in 1958. In addition, the Industrial Development Center and the Community Development Committee were established.

Results of the foreign aid began to show in F.Y. 1957 in the form of increased production. In 1958, the vicious inflation was finally overcome and the production level surpassed that of the prewar, thus paving the way for long-term economic development.

Public Enterprises

Introduction

Public enterprise refers to enterprises financed by the government and dedicated to the welfare of the people in accordance with the spirit of the Constitution (Article 15). Public enterprises in Korea include railways, electricity, water, tobacco and salt; there are also partial public enterprises that are supported half by state and half by private capital, such as the Korea Marine Corporation and the Korea Coal Corporation.

Let us review the status and operation of some of the major public enterprises.

Monopoly Enterprises

These are enterprises monopolized by the government to raise government funds. They are, in fact, "relics" of Japanese imperialism for the Japanese initiated these monopolies to raise the funds neccessary to implement their colonial policies in Korea.

The government once sought to denationalize the tobacco enterprise in an attempt to settle its many thorny problems, including deficit operations, arising from the poor quality of tobacco and cigarettes produced. The attempt failed because it proved to be a difficult matter to sort out the intricate pattern of the interests tied in to the enterprise, and even if any theory is at all applicable, the financial scale is so vast as to make private enterprise a virtual impossibility.

The fact that it is government monopoly makes it difficult for the Korean tobacco industry to improve upon the quality of cigarettes. There is no competition and the Office of Monopoly, accordingly, has little incentive to produce novel ideas or encourage technical capabilities.

Recently, the Monopoly office has become preoccupied with scrapping private salterns in an attempt to settle the problems arising from surplus production of salt.

The Office estimates this year's total receipts from its monopoly enterprises at 62.6 billion hwan, of which 37.9 billion hwan is set aside to cover its own expenses and the balance (23.7 billion hwan) is to be transferred into the general budget.

Whereas the Office is raising a net profit of 23.7 billion hwan from tobacco annually, no profit is raised from salt despite the fact that it is spending 12 billion hwan annually on the salt monopoly enterprise.

Korea Coal Corporation

The Korea Coal Corporation is an enterprise backed by government investment and loans. Of the combined national coal output from 3 million to 4 million tons annually, almost one-half is produced by the Korea Coal Corporation.

The six coal mines operated by the Korea Coal Corporation contain vast deposits. Some of these mines go hundreds of meters underground. Besides, the dominant resources of the Corporation, there are hundreds of other coal mines, large and small that are privately operated.

The Korea Coal Corporation produced over 1.5 million tons of coal worth 12.6 billion hwan during 1958. However, the net profit that year reached only 20 million hwan even after returns from all other receipts of the Corporation.

The total assets of the Korea Coal Corporation as of the end of 1958 stood at 17,569,550,000 hwan including fixed assets amounting to 6,478,840,000 hwan and credits totalling 4,090,120,000 hwan, miscellaneous assets and properties. On the other hand, the Corporation's liabilities totalled 14,032,980,000, hwan including borrowings amounting to 5,461,950,000 hwan.

Thus, the total liabilities of the Corporation, including the 600 million hwan capital which has been spent, amount to a sum identical with its total assets including the 21.22 million hwan profit. If the balance sheet of the Corporation is drawn up arithmetically, the Corporation will be left with only 20 million hwan carried-over profit and facilities worth 600 million hwan.

Though the total assets of the Corporation increased by about 18% over the previous year, the fixed assets correspond to only one-third of the floating assets.

A review of the composition ratio of the capital of the Corporation shows that general liabilities account for 62%. Inasmuch as the Corporation has debts corresponding to 102% of its paid capital, it is not only paying a vast amount in interests but is also being obliged to release coal on a credit basis.

Consequently, the operation of the Corporation has become more difficult, impeding efforts to lower production costs and expand production facilities.

Electric Enterprises

All electric enterprises in Korea are semi-

VII FINANCE, ECONOMY

government and semi-private. Presently, there are three newly-constructed thermo-electric power plants in addition to the three old thermo-electric power plants, with a combined capacity of 236,500 KW. In addition, there are six hydroelectric power plants with a combined capacity of 142,310 KW.

However, the actual combined power output of these twelve power plants range from an average of 200,000 KW to a maximum of 270,000 KW.

On the other hand, the contracts concluded by the two suppliers of electricity (the Seoul Electric Company and the South Korea Electric Company) with the end-users exceed 500,000 KW. If electric power clandestinely used is added, the substantial demand for power will far exceed 500,000 KW.

A ten-year electric development program designed to fill total demand by the end of 1961 is being implemented. Nonetheless, it is believed that by the time the program is completed, bringing the total power output to 350,000 KW, the total power requirements will have been increased to 610,000 KW.

Thus, there will still be a 260,000 KW shortage in the supply of electricity, even if it is assumed that the ten-year power development program is successfully implemented. Under the present circumstances, however, there are many factors indicating that it will be difficult to improve the power situation.

It is believed that the failure to rationalize operations, to ensure rational distribution of capital, and the lack of efforts to pursue economic interests are attributable to the lagging development of these major enterprises.

National Income

Estimates of National Income

Following the establishment of the government, the Bureau of Economic Planning of the former Office of Planning estimated national income by expenditures, while the Tax Bureau of the Ministry of Finance and the Research Department of the Bank of Korea estimated national income by occupation and production respectively. The National Income Committee was organized in December, 1952 to coordinate the three estimates on national income. Beginning with F.Y. 1953, authorities concerned arranged for exclusive Bank of Korea estimation of the national income by industrial origin.

But beginning with F.Y. 1959, the Bank of Korea began estimating the national income by expenditures and national income by occupation as well as national income by industrial origin.

Changes in National Income

The Gross National Product on the basis of ordinary prices increased by 43% in six years from 39 billion hwan in F.Y. 1953 to 167.05 billion hwan in F.Y. 1958. This does not represent substantial economic development as it shows that inflation prevailed throughout.

The industrial structure changed conspicuously when viewed in terms of currency income. The gravity of the first industry dropped from 45.5% in F.Y. 1953 to 38.4% in F.Y. 1958. (Reference table 1). This was attributed to the fall in the price of farm products rather than fall in production.

In the case of the second industry, the gravity increased steadily from 12.9% in F.Y. 1953 to 17.2%. This is attributed to increased investment by both government and private entrepreneurs in the second industry.

The composition ratio of the third industry dropped from 45.9% in F.Y. 1953 to 45.5% in F.Y. 1955, to 44.4% in F.Y. 1956, to 43.4% in 1957 and 42.7% in 1958.

Though the ratio has been declining gradually, it is, nonetheless, maintaining higher rates than other industries due to active trade under foreign aid funds.

Meanwhile, a review of the changes in the Gross National Product by constant prices shows that the Gross National Product index increased by 28.4% in F.Y 1958 from F.Y. 1953.

The national economy developed 6% in F.Y. 1954, 4.4% in F.Y. 1955, dropped 0.5% in F.Y. 1956, and developed by 9.7% in F.Y. 1958, thus showing an average annual increase rate of 5.7%.

Agricultural production, which accounted for about 40% of the gross national product, largely influenced the fluctuations in the Gross National Product.

Though the rate of increase in national income is lower than that indicated in the Gross National Product by ordinary prices, it increased, nonetheless, by 43% during the period, reflecting increases in the commodity prices.

Review of the composition of the national income by occupation shows that, whereas the remuneration of employed persons accounted for 29.8% in F.Y. 1953, it accounted for 36.4% in F.Y. 1958 (reference table 5).

This means that the earnings of salarymen and wage-earners had relatively increased in parallel with the expansion of the economic scale.

For all that, the rate is much lower as compared with that of advanced industrial nations.

There were same fluctuations in the income of non-juridical persons' enterprises during the period (reference table 4), but the composition ratio dropped in F.Y. 1958 from F.Y. 1953.

Total expenditures fell short of the Gross National Product but the shortage was covered with foreign economic aid funds.

Although gross domestic capital formation and the government expenditures have been increasing relatively, private consumption expenditures have been declining.

The gross fixed capital formation increased from 7.1% in 1958 to 12.4% in 1958, and the Government expenditures from 9.6% in F.Y. 1953 to 14.4% in F.Y. 1958. But private consumption expenditures dropped from 86.8% in F.Y. 1953 to 81.8% in 1958 (by ordinary prices).

Analysis of National Income

The Gross National Product for F.Y. 1958 estimated by ordinary prices stood at 167.05 billion hwan, up 161.89 billion hwan compared with that (161.89 billion hwan) of F.Y. 1957.

However, the Gross National Product estimated by constant prices stood at 109.96 billion hwan in F.Y. 1955, an increase of 6.4% over the previous year (103.39 billion hwan).

The national income based by ordinary prices reached 148.35 billion hwan in F.Y. 1958, up 2% from 145.42 billion hwan of the previous year. But this falls below the 3.2% increase noted from gross national income estimated by constant prices, a fact attributable to relative increases in indirect taxes and capital depreciation reserves.

The rate of national economic growth in F.Y. 1958 dropped to 6.4% from that of the previous year (9.7%).

Assuming that the average annual rate of national economic growth is 6%, it is not difficult to anticipate that the Gross National Product will reach 210.6 billion hwan in FY 1962.

Korean economy developed steadily during the period F.Y. 1953—F.Y. 1958 when viewed in terms of national income. It is no exaggeration to say that the foundation has been laid for further and steady growth of the economy hereafter.

VII FINANCE, ECONOMY

Table 1.

Gross National Product by Industrial Origin (by ordinary prices)

Unit: billions of hwan

Industry	1953 Value added	Ratio	1954 Value added	Ratio	1955 Value added	Ratio	1956 Value added	Ratio	1957 Value added	Ratio	1958 Value added	Ratio
Agriculture, forestry and fishery	177.0	45.4	212.0	37.3	396.9	41.9	525.8	43.3	663.5	41.0	641.1	38.4
Mining	4.0	1.0	5.1	0.9	7.5	0.8	11.5	0.9	17.0	1.1	19.2	1.2
Manufacturing	34.4	8.8	58.4	10.3	100.4	10.6	131.6	10.8	171.6	10.6	191.8	11.5
Construction	9.5	2.4	21.3	3.7	34.9	3.7	39.4	3.3	60.0	3.7	62.6	3.7
Electricity, water, & sanitation	2.0	0.5	3.0	0.5	5.9	0.6	4.5	0.4	12.4	0.8	16.9	1.0
Transportation, & communications	7.7	2.0	14.0	2.5	27.5	2.9	37.5	3.1	55.8	3.4	58.9	3.5
Wholesale and retail trade	61.3	15.7	93.8	16.4	147.4	15.6	196.3	16.1	247.3	15.3	245.5	14.7
Finance, insurance & real estate	3.5	0.9	3.6	0.6	7.8	0.8	9.7	0.8	17.8	1.1	22.9	1.4
Housing owned	31.4	8.1	56.2	10.0	64.4	6.8	77.3	6.3	108.8	6.7	113.2	6.8
Administration & national defense	27.3	7.0	47.7	8.4	61.4	6.5	69.5	5.7	114.0	7.0	128.6	7.7
Services	26.2	6.7	46.9	8.3	79.6	8.4	100.4	8.2	136.5	8.4	155.8	9.3
Gross domestic product	384.3	98.5	562.0	98.9	933.7	98.6	1,203.5	98.9	1,604.7	99.1	1,656.5	99.2
Rest of the world	5.7	1.5	6.2	1.1	13.6	1.4	13.7	1.1	14.2	0.9	14.0	0.8
Gross national product	390.0	100.0	568.2	100.0	947.3	100.0	1,217.2	100.0	1,618.9	100.0	1,670.5	100.0
Indirect tax	17.0	4.4	33.1	5.8	52.4	5.5	67.0	5.5	103.5	6.4	128.5	7.7
Subsidies	0.7	0.1	0.5	0.1	0.8	0.1	0.9	0.1	6.9	0.4	15.7	0.9
Capital reserves	14.6	3.7	24.7	4.4	39.8	4.2	53.8	4.4	68.1	42.0	74.2	4.4
National income	358.6	92.0	510.9	89.9	855.9	90.4	1,097.3	90.2	1,454.2	89.8	1,483.5	88.4
Gross national production	1,000.0		145.7		242.9		312.1		415.1		428.3	
Rate of increase of gross national product from previous year	–		45.7		66.7		28.5		33.0		3.2	
National income index	100.0		142.5		238.7		306.0		405.5		413.7	
Rate of increase of national income index from previous year	–		42.5		67.5		28.2		32.5		2.6	

Table 2. Trends of Composition Ratio of Gross National Product by Industrial Origin

Industry	1953	1954	1955	1956	1957	1958	Average
First industry	42.0	40.6	41.8	38.9	39.6	40.1	40.5
Second 〃	12.1	14.0	15.2	16.7	17.2	17.2	15.5
Third 〃	45.9	45.4	43.0	44.4	43.2	42.7	44.0
Total	100.0	100.0	100.0	100.0	100.0	100.0	100.0

Source: The National Income of Korea (Bank of Korea)

VII FINANCE, ECONOMY

Table 3. **Gross National Product by Industrial Origin (1955 constant price)**

Unit: billions of hwan

Industry	1953 Value added	1953 Ratio	1954 Value added	1954 Ratio	1955 Value added	1955 Ratio	1956 Value added	1956 Ratio	1957 Value added	1957 Ratio	1958 Value added	1958 Ratio
Agriculture, forestry and fishery	361.6	42.2	388.7	42.8	396.9	41.9	370.5	39.3	412.2	39.8	445.6	40.5
Mining	7.6	0.9	6.3	0.7	7.5	0.8	10.6	1.1	11.9	1.2	19.5	1.2
Manufacturing	69.4	8.1	80.8	8.9	100.4	10.6	119.1	12.6	134.4	13.0	141.8	13.0
Construction	27.8	3.2	38.6	4.3	34.9	3.7	30.3	3.2	38.7	3.8	41.3	0.7
Electricity, water & sanitation	15.4	0.6	6.6	0.7	5.9	0.6	5.8	0.6	6.2	0.6	7.5	3.4
Transportation & communications	18.1	2.1	19.5	2.2	27.5	2.9	30.8	3.3	35.5	3.4	36.9	15.0
Wholesale and retail trade	141.5	16.5	145.2	16.0	147.4	15.6	145.6	15.4	154.9	150.1	164.5	1.3
Finance, insurance & real estate	10.3	1.2	6.5	0.7	7.8	0.8	6.9	0.7	10.8	1.0	14.0	6.3
Housing owned	59.7	7.0	62.0	6.8	64.4	6.8	66.6	7.1	68.6	6.6	69.9	5.1
Administration & defense	72.5	8.5	67.4	7.4	61.4	6.5	59.0	6.3	57.2	5.5	56.1	8.1
Services	65.5	7.7	72.7	8.0	79.6	8.4	84.6	9.0	90.4	8.7	95.3	98.8
Gross domestic product	839.4	98.0	894.3	98.5	933.7	98.6	929.8	98.6	1,020.8	98.7	1,086.4	1.2
Rest of the world	16.9	2.0	13.4	1.5	13.6	1.4	12.9	1.4	13.1	1.3	13.2	1.0
Gross national product	856.3	100.0	907.7	100.0	947.3	100.0	942.7	100.0	1,033.9	100.0	1,099.6	100.0
Gross national product index	100.0		106.0		110.6		110.1		120.7		128.4	
Rate of growth			6.0		4.4		-0.5		9.7		6.4	

Table 4. **Trends of Gross National Product**

Unit: billions of hwan

Year	Gross product by ordinary price	Comparison with previous year	Index	Gross product by constant price (1955)	Rate of growth	Index
1953	390.0			856.3		
1954	568.2	45.7	145.7	907.7	6.0	106.0
1955	947.3	66.7	242.9	947.3	4.4	110.6
1956	1,217.2	28.5	312.1	942.7	-0.5	110.1
1957	1,618.9	38.0	415.1	1,033.9	9.7	120.7
1958	1,670.5	3.2	428.3	1,099.6	6.4	128.4

Source: The National Income of Korea (Bank of Korea)

Table 5. **Composition Ratio of National Income by Occupation**

	1953	1954	1955	1956	1957	1958
Income of employed persons	29.8	33.9	32.8	32.1	33.5	36.4
Income of non-juridical person enterprises	60.3	54.2	57.8	59.0	57.1	53.9
Property income	10.2	12.3	9.8	9.0	9.2	9.5
a. Rentals	7.4	9.2	6.6	6.1	6.5	6.7
b. Interests	2.8	3.1	3.1	2.9	2.7	2.7
Indirect tax on juridical persons	0.2	0.3	0.3	0.4	0.4	0.8
Income of Government assets and ordinary enterprises	0.4	0.3	0.2	0.2	0.7	0.3
Interest on public bonds	0.1	0.1	0.1	0.1	0.3	0.6
Interest on liabilities of consumers	0.8	0.9	0.8	0.6	0.6	
National income	100.0	100.0	100.0	100.0	100.0	100.0

Source: The National Income of Korea (Bank of Korea)

/ VIII INDUSTRIES

VIII INDUSTRIES

Outline of Korean Industry

Quality Replacing Quantity

Korean industry made remarkable progress in the first few years after the war, reaching a peak in 1957. Thereafter, it receded. The pace of expansion has slowed down since 1958 and production, on the whole, has declined. Most industries began to place more emphasis on improving quality as well as on efficient operation of existing facilities. Efforts, therefore, have been concentrated on lower production costs, attractive goods, and markets. In other words, the sellers' market became the buyers' and quality has replaced quantity as industry's guide. On the other hand, agricultural production, which still ranks first in the nation's economy, has increased remarkably since 1957.

The bumper crop of that year was an all-time high since the end of World War II, and the trend has been up since then. Thus, Korea has become self-sufficient in food.

This outstanding progress since the armistice is attributed to improvement on farmlands, liberal application of fertilizers and pesticides, and improved technology under the government's agricultural guidance program. Favorable weather conditions in recent years are also a factor.

Another significant event which has affected the Korean industry has been the signs of economic recessions throughout the world. The effects on Korea were first felt in late 1957.

Increased imports did not bring about correspondingly increased deficits in Korea's international balance of payment. The trend has had the effect of curbing postwar inflation, thus contributing to a stabilized economy. On the other hand, depressed market conditions in the world has brought down Korean exports with the result that export industries hover around the lowest production levels in recent years. Especially hard hit was the tungsten industry, once the largest export industry of Korea.

The slackened pace of Korean industrial progress since 1958 in contrast to the former rapid tempo is an indication that Korean economic growth has now reached a stage of stability. Formerly, Korean industrial ventures were inclined to be speculative, taking advantage of the spiralling inflationary trend of the period immediately following the Korean armistice. With stabilization of the country's political as well as economic conditions and especially as a result of the tight financial situation caused by the government's drastic anti-inflation policy, many industrial ventures have been weeded out, while others were forced to curtail operations with overstuffed inventories and surplus facilities. Thus, the time has come for the

Korean industry to adjust itself to new demands by improving operational efficiency.

Trend in Industries

The mining industry has achieved a remarkable rate of growth in recent years. The rate of progress is eloquently indicated by the production index numbers of the three-year period from 1955 to 1957. Against the 14.6 percent increase of all industries and 23.6 percent increase of manufacturing industries, the rate of increase in mining was 25 percent during the period.

Among the various mining industries, coal and metal showed the largest growth, while metal mining indicated slight increases. In 1958 the most outstanding increase was registered by non-metallic mining industries. This was mostly due to increased production of limestone in response to the country's vast expansion of the cement manufacturing industry.

The production of anthracite, on the other hand, was decreased in 1958, because the all-out efforts of the government to increase coal had been so successful that the nation's coal requirements were entirely satisfied by 1957. Presently, therefore, some of the coal mines have been forced to curtail operations, awaiting the moving of coal stockpiles. Korean coal mines, however, by no means face a dark future, for the government has been encouraging use of anthracite as a substitute for bituminous coal, a large quantity of which has to be imported each year from Japan.

Exports of mineral products accounts for more than half of Korea's total exports. Considerable quantities of metal ores and non-metallic ores have been exported each year but the production of such minerals has been dictated by overseas market conditions, because of the fact that underdeveloped conditions of Korean industry does not offer domestic markets.

Some of the major minerals exported to foreign countries are talc, whose production and exports have been increased in recent years; lead ore and metal bismuth, both of which indicated increased production but decreased exports; and tungsten, which showed decreased production but increased export.

The manufacturing industries have achieved a rapid rate of progress since the armistice. The tempo of advancement, however, had to be slowed down since 1957. Especially significant has been the relative depression of the textile industry, which accounts for 48 percent of Korea's manufacturing industries. By 1957 the textile industry had been expanded sufficiently not only to meet the entire domestic requirements, but also to seek overseas markets. Nevertheless, the textile industry's rate of progress declined from 32.8 per cent in 1957 and again by to 4.4 percent in 1958.

The metal and machine industries have also shown diminishing rates of progress in recent years because the country's requirements for durable consumer goods and maintenance machinery parts were satisfied by 1957, and the expansion has reached a saturation point.

The food processing and chemical industries, on the other hand, enjoyed a boom in 1958. Producing consumer goods mostly, expansion here lagged behind other industries up to the year, 1957, a fact considered to be the reason for the progress made by these industries in 1958.

Metal machinery industries, including iron and steel, shipbuilding and vehicle manufacturing, have been making steady progress, but the development has remained insufficient to elevate the nation's manufacturing industries to self-sufficient levels. Narrow domestic markets, technological backwardness and insufficient capital have also been factors blocking satisfactory development of the country's overall industry.

Under such economic conditions, textile and food processing industries constitute the backbone of Korea's manufacturing industries as in the case of practically all other industrially underdeveloped countries of the world.

VIII INDUSTRIES

Utilization of Land

Farm Land

Utilization of land in Korea is limited relative to her total acreage because of the predominantly mountainous nature of the country. Nevertheless, it is generally conceded that there still remains considerable room for more extensive as well as intensive utilization of the land. The most intensively utilized is farm land, upon which a dense agricultural population is concentrated. There being too large a population on too limited farm land, the maximum possible utilization has to be realized. Increased production of agriculture through increased productivity of farm land has accordingly been attempted by employing concentrated labor force on the farm. At the same time, the ever potential unemployment of surplus labor force in vast numbers within such limited farm lands has been an effective factor to divide the farm lands into fragments fit only for small-scale farming on tiny patches of paddies, which, in turn, has effectively blocked efficient utilization of what small farm lands there are.

The total acreage of cultivated land in Korea relative to its total acreage of territory is by no means small in comparison with some other countries of the world such as the U.S., Brazil, Japan, Austria, etc., for according to a 1948 FOA report, the total acreage of cultivated land in Korea is 23.8 percent (5,156 acres or 2,021,961.6 *chongbo*) of the total acreage of the land. The above figure, however, is somewhat misleading, for Korean agriculture is almost exclusively devoted to grains, whereas in other countries agricultural production is much more inclusive of other products, for which a considerable portion of land is used.

Recently available statistics indicate that the national average of cultivated land per farmer in Korea (1.1 acre) is the smallest in the world with the only exception of Japan. 4,686,000 farmers (1954) share 5,156,000 acres of farm land (1957) in Korea whereas the average is 72.4 in Austria, 58.8 in the U.S., 61.9 in France and Portugal, 4.9 in Brazil and 0.8 in Japan.

As to the utilization of farmland in Korea, statistics compiled in 1957 show that out of the total 9,501,128 *chongbo* or 23,287,275,000 acres of land cultivated, 8.6 percent or 1,106,697 *chongbo* is rice paddies, 17.7 percent or 815,175 *chongbo* is uplands, 21.02 percent is forests and 7.7 percent is used for other miscellaneous purposes.

Pasture

Land utilized exclusively for raising livestocks is practically nonexistent in Korea, for hay and other forage of cattle are collected by human labor in rice paddies, uplands or forests. Therefore, it is, somewhat hopefully, agreed that some of the land which remain unused may be utilized in the future for livestocks.

On the strength of such a bright prospect, the Ministry of Agriculture and Forestry conducted a general survey in 1957 on pastures in order to ascertain the correct figure for the total acreage, nature of soil and extent of their possible utilization. The survey shows that 44 pasture lands covered in the survey are about 8,000 *chongbo* in acreage, of which 2,700 *changbo* or 34 percent proved to be suitable for cultivating forage, 50 percent of the total acreage or 4,000 *chongbo* was found to be suitable as grazing grounds for cattle leaving but a mere 18 percent or 1,300 *chongbo* as land declared unfit for livestocks.

Table 1

Possible Utilization of Pastures in Korea, by Province, 1957

Unit in *chongbo**

Province	No. of Units	Fit for Cultivation	Fit for Forage	Fit for Nothing	Total Acre.	Slope of Plane Max.	Slope of Plane Min.
Kyonggi-do	5	170.7	266.4	144.6	581.7	15	3
Chungchong Pukto	5	490.4	738.8	217.2	1,446.4	30	0
Chungchong Namdo	4	749.0	121.8	61.0	931.8	30	5
Cholla Pukto	4	112.3	491.3	–	603.6	15	0
Cholla Namdo	5	125.8	278.5	11.0	415.3	23	1
Kyongsang Pukto	6	270.0	982.0	566.0	1,818.0	25	3
Kyongsang Namdo	5	63.6	357.0	183.6	604.2	25	11
Kangwon-do	5	471.0	400.0	90.9	961.9	30	0
Cheju-do	5	319.0	365.2	36.5	720.7	10	2 (average)
Total	44	2,771.8	4,001.0	1,310.8	8,083.6	22	2.7

Source: Ministry of Agriculture and Forestry

*one *chongbo* equals 2.451 acres

Forests

Forests and fields, covering 16,274,380 *chongbo* constitute 73.2 percent of the total acreage of Korea (22,258,007 *chongbo*). So high is the figure percentagewise that, so far as the portion of land covered with forests and fields in the total territory is concerned, Korea, with its fields and forests, blanketing about three times as much ground as farm lands, ranks second or third in the world. A mere 52 percent of the forests is preserved, the remaining 48 percent being wasteland awaiting effective preservation and control. To make matters worse, 670,837 *chongbo* of the preserved forests are more wasteland requiring immediate erosion control while an additional 1,076,260 *chongbo* require forestration. What forests there remain have a tree density of only 8.6 m³ per *chongbo* on the average.

The preserved forests have recently been increased by 278,688 *chongbo* since 1956, but this is no more than a de jure increase realized through expansion of territory as a result of the war and adjustment of forest registers in each provincial government. The total acreage of forests and fields as of the end of 1957 is 6,708,568 *chongbo*, which is a decrease of 38,982 *chongbo*, brought about through arrangement of forestry registers after a recent survey on forests and fields within the area "restored" to south Korea as a result of the war.

Total preserved forests as of the end of 1957 is 3,486,938 *chongbo*, which is a decrease of 1,977 *chongbo* from the July 1956 figures of 3,488,915 *chongbo*, while the forests not preserved is 2,028,474 *chongbo*, a decrease of 47,428 *chongbo* from 2,085,902 *chongbo* of the preceding year.

Total acreage of forests requiring immediate erosion control as of the end of 1957 is 670,837 *chongbo*, which is a decrease of 15,383 *chongbo* from the preceding year, while 1,076,360 *chongbo* require forestration—a decrease of 129,897 *chongbo* from the figure of the preceding year. Both of these decreases have been realized through erosion control and forestration works carried out during the year.

As to the ownership of the forests and fields, 20.6 percent of the total forests or 1,382,914 *chongbo* is government property, leaving 79.4 percent of 5,325,654 *chongbo* in the hands of private owners, according to the statistics compiled by the Forestry Bureau, Ministry of Agriculture and Forestry, in 1958.

← Mungyong Cement Plant
　Belonging to Taehan Cement Industrial Co., Ltd. Largest in Korea. Built in 1957. Annual product: 200,000 tons.

↑ Metal Pipe Manufacturing Works
   Kia Industrial Co., Ltd.
   Inspecting products.

A Spinning-Mill in Operation
↓ Kumsong Textile Co., Ltd., Anyang.

Bottling Process in a Brewhouse
↓ Oriental Brewery Co., Ltd., in Yongdungpo, Seoul

The Whole View of the Chungju Fertilizer Plant
The first urea fertilizer plant in south Korea. Construction started in 1955. Annual production capacity: 85,000 tons.

↑　Ammonia Storage Tank at Chungju Urea Fertilizer Plant

↑ Ring Spinning

Nylon Textile Plant
Taechang Textile Co., Ltd.
↓

↑ Whole View of Plate-Glass Works in Inchon

↓ Ceramic Works

Tanginni Thermal Power Plant
The rated capacity is 47,500 Kws, but at present the plant generates 29,000 Kws.

← **Masan Thermal Power Plant**
Equipped with 32,000 KVAs. Maximum capacity is 54,000 Kws.

→ **Yongwol Thermal Power Plant**
Four 31,250 KVAs. Due to outworn machinery and equipment, 50,000 Kws is the maximum.

A Substation of Hwachon Hydro-Electric Power Plant
↓

↑ A Whole View of Hwachon Hydro-Electric Power Plant
    The fifth of the water power plants in Korea, generates 87,000 Kws chiefly to supply to Seoul and Inchon.

   Supung Dam
     This immense dam in the Yalu River was built in 1942. Water power plants of this dam can
↓ generate 600,000 Kws.

← Steel Works
　Taehan Heavy Industrial Company.

Products of the Above Steel Works →

↓ Electric Magnetic Crane

↓ Crane Boat

Sangdong Mine →
Yongwol-gun, Kangwon-do. A tungsten mine. Produced 782 tons in 1956.

←
A Coal Mine

A Miner Working with the Chuck →

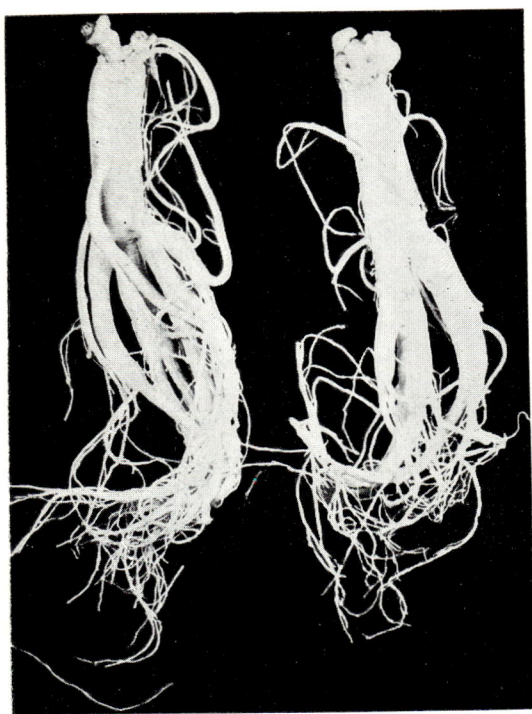

↑ Rice in the Paddy-Field

←
Ginseng
Famous tonic herb that grows only in Korea. Chinese used to consider ginseng as valuable as gold. Mostly exported to Hong Kong.

Raw Silk
↓ Breeding silkworms is the most important subsidiary occupation of farmers.

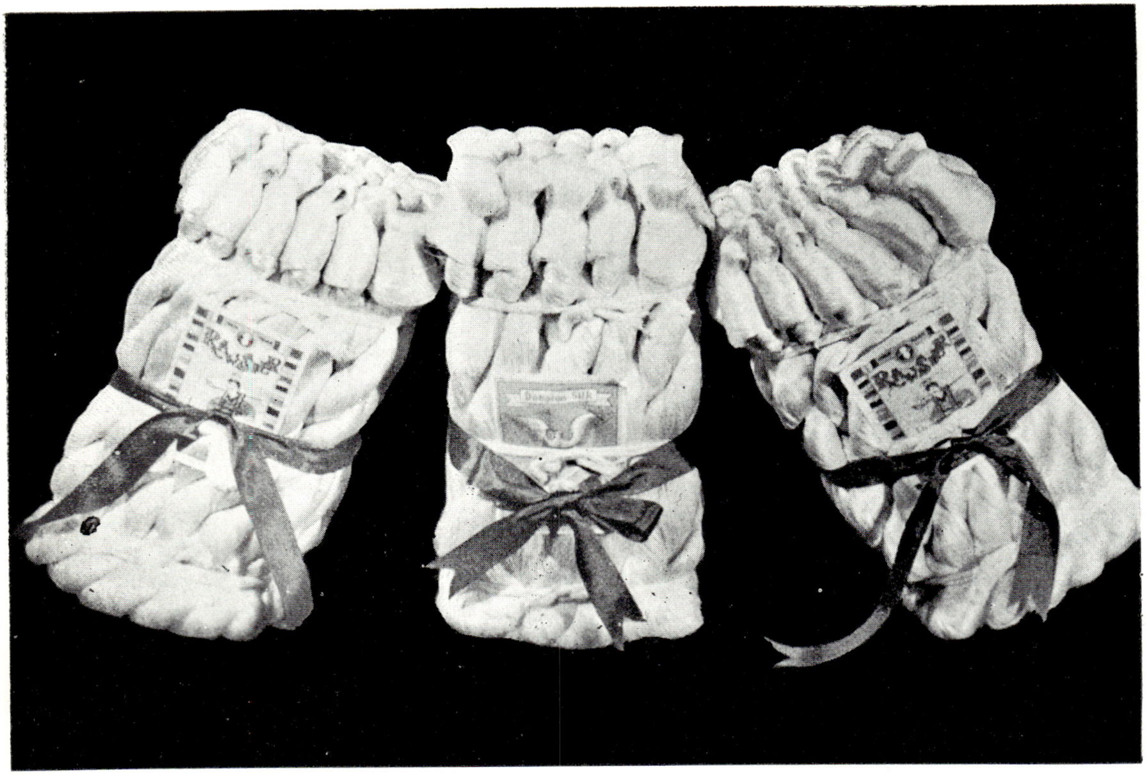

Tobacco Cultivation →
One of the government's monopoly business.

Ginseng Cultivation
↓ Also a government monopoly

↑ Hop Cultivation

A Part of an Experimental Paddy of Hydroponics
↓ First time in Korea.

Tilling →
Primitive methods are still employed in farming.

←
Transplantation
Farmers' busiest season in the year comes when rice is to be transplanted.

↑ Weeding
Even children help.

←
Harvest

↑ Pruning Fruit Trees

←
Cabbage Field
   Cabbage, next to rice, is also a very important farm product.

      Apple Cultivation
↓   The most prosperous field in fruit cultivation.

↑ A Lumbering Spot on the Upper Part of the Yalu River

↓ A Sheter Wood at Suwon

↑ A Primeval Forest of Larches
Northern border.

← **Pasture at Cheju Island**
The largest ranch in Korea was established here by government with the help of General James A. Van Fleet, former Eight U.S. Army commander.

Anyang Ranch, Kyonggi-do →

↓ Cattle-market

A Whole View of Cheju Island Ranch

← Salt Fields at Puan

↑ Lavers Farming
Lavers grow around poles which are put into the sea. The dried lavers of Korea are the best in the Far East.

↓ A Fish Pond at Chinhae

A Scene of Cuttle-Fish Drying →

↓ Agaragar Drying

↓ Pollack Drying

↑ Fishing in the Wintertime

↑ Oyster-culture

↓ Fishing Boats for Pelagic Fishery

↑ Chain Stores in Sinsin Department Store, Seoul

Hwasin Department Store at Chongno Street, Seoul

Midopa Department Store, Seoul

Tonghwa Department Store, Seoul

↑ The Bank of Korea

← The Commercial Bank of Korea

↓ Interior View of a Bank

↑ The Seoul Chamber of Commerce and Industry

↓ Displaying Room in National Commercial and Industrial Exhibitional Center

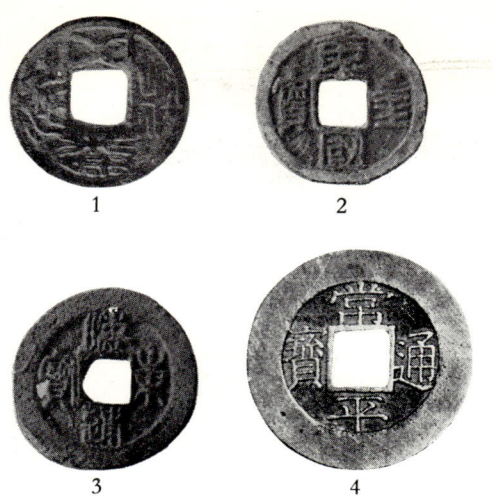

Old Coins and Paper Money

1. "Sangpyong Ojujon," used in Koryo dynasty
2. "Koryojon," used in Koryo dynasty
3. "Haedong Tongbo," cast in 1102, Koryo dynasty
4. "Sangpyong Tongbo," cast in 1693, Yi dynasty
5. "1 Won," cast in 1909
6. "5 Won," cast in 1909
7. "10 Won," cast in 1909
8. "100 Won," cast in 1950
9. "1,000 Won," cast in 1950
10. "500 Won," cast in 1952
11. "1,000 Won," cast in 1952

1

5

6

2

7

3

8

4

Coins and Paper Money Now in Circulation
1. "100 Hwan," "50 Hwan," "10 Hwan."
   (left; reverse, right; obverse,)
2. "1 Hwan"
3. "5 Hwan"
4. "10 Hwan"
5. "50 Hwan"
6. "100 Hwan"
7. "500 Hwan"
8. "1,000 Hwan"

VIII INDUSTRIES

Natural Resources

Exploitation of various natural resources to serve as the basis of Korean economic and industrial development is presently considered as one of the most urgent programs. Utmost efforts are being exerted for exploitation of the natural resources for motive power, such as electricity and coal together with other underground and marine resources.

Coal

Anthracite, lignite and a small amount of peat are produced in south Korea. Bituminous coal, which is essential for industrial uses, is not produced.

Deposits of coal throughout Korea, both north and south, are estimated to be about 1.7 billion tons of anthracite, of which 650 million tons are in south Korea; and 500 million tons of lignite, three million tons in the south.

The demands for coal both for industrial and home consumption have increased to such an extent in recent years that the government has prepared and been executing a ten-year plan for increased production starting with 1957 as the initial years. The plan aims at an increase of 35 percent or 2.5 million tons to be realized in the initial year of 1959: two million tons by the government-owned Korea Coal Corporation and 1.5 million tons by privately owned coal mines. The ultimate goal of the ten-year plan is to produce 1,204 million tons by the closing year of 1966.

Emphasis for increased production has so far been placed upon government-owned coal mines, but during 1959, an ICA fund amounting to $535,000 was allocated to several privately-owned mines in order to promote mechanization of facilities together with promotion of up-to-date technology such as test drilling and gallery extension test methods. Furthermore, a $636,000 ICA fund is being used during 1959 to conduct a survey on coal fields, in addition to $200,000 which is being utilized for surveys in the Hwason area especially for the purpose of meeting coal requirements for the newly constructed Naju Fertilizer Plant.

In the meantime, steady efforts are being made to substitute domestically produced anthracite for bituminous coal by the Ministry of Transportation, whose locomotives have been burning two million dollars' worth of imported bituminous coal into smoke each year.

In an effort to discourage consumption of bituminous coal, the government has also banned the use of bituminous coal as fuel, permitting anthracite only for such a purpose, while gassification of coal is being seriously considered. (some West German firms having been asked to examine the possibility.)

Other Underground Resources

The government, in order to promote exploitation of mineral resources, has been engaged in numerous surveys and researches, including aerial surveys, geological surveys, researches on open air mining, test drilling, gallery expansion test methods, etc. The findings of such surveys and researches are to be incorporated into the geological maps as well as mineral bed distribution maps of the entire country. During 1959, a total of 55,256,500 hwan has been budgeted in order to continue such surveys and researches, which, when concluded, are expected to furnish a basis for establishing a development plan for mineral resources.

One of the difficulties in managing mining industry in Korea has been attributed to obsolete facilities. To remedy such a situation, mechanization of facilities is being carried out, especially for mining and sorting facilities for gold, silver, copper, iron, tungsten and other export minerals. For instance, the government has allocated subsidies amounting to 19 million hwan in 1959 to be used as an improvement fund for mines in an attempt to realize an increase of 30 percent in total output over the 1958 production.

The quality of export minerals is being considerably improved at the Sangdong Tungsten Mines, where a chemical process plan has been completed to start operations since May, 1959. The Changhang Refinery of Samsong Mining Company is also expected to complete its expansion program by the end of 1959 to increase the output of gold, silver and copper.

Production of major minerals during the first quarter of 1959 is as follows:

Gold: 469,397 gr., an increase of 22.8 per cent over the same period of the preceding year.

Silver: 1,562,778 gr., an increase of 3.5 per cent over the same period of the preceding year.

Copper: 736 tons, a decrease of 74.7 per cent from the same period of the preceding year.

Iron: 77,411 tons, an increase of 28.6 per cent (expansion of the Yangyang Mines being a major contributory factor for the increase).

Tungsten: 73,500 kgs., a decrease of 73.6 percent (the major cause being contraction of production forced by sharp decline in the export price of tungsten).

Lead: 270 tons, a sharp decrease as much as 78.5 percent from the same period of the preceding year. Since lead is not produced independently but in combination with gold or silver, its production parallels the rise or fall of gold and silver production.

Graphite: Of the two kinds of graphite, triangular graphite, despite abundant deposits in south Korea, was produced for the first time at the Sihung Mine at Puchon Gun, which started operations belatedly, in February, 1959 with UNKRA aid funds, the output being 85 tons during the first-quarter period of 1959. On the other hand, a total of 362 tons of amorphous graphite was produced, a decrease of 13.9 percent.

Talc: 4,554 tons, an increase of 25 percent, (mines located in Tongyang, Chongwon, Chungju, Sinbo and Namyong).

Kaolin: 12,069 tons, an increase of 147.4 percent. ($64,705,000 earned through exports.)

Caustic Lime: 119,667 tons, a slight increase.

As to other non-metallic minerals, there are slight increases in the production of silica, andolusite, and asbestos, slight decreases in the productions of fluorite and monaziteore, ($123,916 of the former earned through exports).

Electric Power

Present facilities can generate 364,810 Kws, to which will be added 620,000 Kws at the completion of an expansion program slated to increase 330,000 Kws of hydroelectric power, 240,000 KWs of thermal electric power, and 50,000 KWs through atomic energy. Under a ten-year expansion program, therefore, the total electric power output in south Korea is expected to reach one million KWs.

As a part of the ten-year plan, a 150,000 KW Chungju Power Plant is under construction in 1959 with a govenment budget of $4,350,000 together with 1.5 billion hwan in Korean funds. Also scheduled is construction of a 30,000 KW thermal generating plant at Kunsan with a 8.1 million hwan. The government is also contemplating construction of a 60,000 KW thermal generating plant in the southern district in order to minimize excessive loss of power in transmission over long distance — inevitable under the present conditions for lack of generating facilities near the district.

In the meantime, more efficient and effective maintenance of the present facilities is being studied seriously, for existing facilities are mostly obsolete and, therefore, inefficient. For example, the Yongwol Generating Plant is to undergo an intensive overhaul to increase the output by 40,000 KWs with a $2,690,150 ICA fund and 738,350,000 hwan from the government. The Changpyong Hydroelectric Plant dam is also scheduled to undergo reinforcement works during 1959 with a $3,000,000 ICA fund and 54 million hwan government fund.

Rehabilitation and expansion of generating facilities in the war-devastated areas are, in the meantime, being carried out in seventy places, with works already started in 13 places with a 37.7 million hwan government budget fund, while 48,100 hwan is earmarked for the expansion projects in the Yangyang area to meet increasing power requirements for the industrial district.

On the other hand, the loss of power during transmit has been estimated to be as high as 32 percent of the generating output. The government is accordingly planning to improve transmitting facilities with a 1.5 million dollar ICA fund together with 1.9 billion hwan in government budget in order to reduce the loss by 7,000 KWs, thus saving 1,365.5 million hwan annually.

The total power output during the first quarter of 1959 is 191,184 KWs, which is about a 10 percent increase over the same period of the preceding year. The increase is attributed to suitable rainfalls for hydroelectricity.

Agriculture

Agriculture, in recent years, may have been somewhat lagging behind the manufacturing and mining industries in Korea. Nevertheless, considerable improvement has been seen compared with the situation before the war. The bumper crops produced at the highest levels since the Liberation for the consecutive years, 1957 and 1958, may be attributed partly to favorable natural conditions, but the greater portion of the credit is due to human endeavors. Man-made contribution to such increased agricultural production may be attributed to improvement of (1) farm land, (2) breeding, (3) fertilizing and farm management, (4) top soil through deeper plowing, and (5) labor facilities or increased utilization of cattle on the farm.

Such improvements in the field of agriculture were realized through government policy, which initiated a farm land reform program in 1949 for the purpose of raising the social standard of farmers. A five-year plan for increased agricultural production was carried out from 1953 to 1957, to be followed by another five-year plan starting from 1958. The Agriculture Guidance Law was enacted in 1957, as a result of which the Academy of Agriculture was established in June, 1957. At the same time, farm land improvement program has reaped bounteous crops, while increased importation of commercial fertilizers and production of pesticides for agricultural uses further contributed to the cause. In order to facilitate agricultural financing, a special bank exclusively devoted to the purpose was established on May 1, 1958 in compliance with the Agricultural Bank Law enacted in February, 1957. On the other hand, the Federation of Farmers' Cooperatives was founded in October, 1958 to expedite more systematic administration of farmers' cooperatives throughout the country. Another program of the government is the "open market operations" of agricultural products by the government as well as the system of loans to farmers on rice collect security, both intended to maintain stabilized agricultural economy.

Farm Households

The total number of farm households in south Korea is 2,210,914 according to the statistics of 1957, which also indicated an increasing trend in the number of large-scale and "extremely small-scale" farm households, as against a decreasing trend in the number of small-scale farmers. In 1957, "extremely small-scale" farm households, tilling lands of less than three *panbo*, totalled 421,936, and those families which worked on farms from three to five *panbo* were 523,298, increases of 2,276 and 768 households respectively over the previous year. The number of households tilling farms of five *panbo* to one *chongbo* totalled 672,328, a decrease of 3,780. The number of farm households working on less than five *panbo* was 945,234, an increase of 2,044 over the preceding year, while those who cultivated farms of five *panbo* to one *chongbo* showed decrease. As to medium-scale farmers who till one to three *chongbo*, the total number of households was 585,429, an increase of 11,335 over the preceding year.

This tendency in the increase of "extremely small-scale" farm households is attributed to (1) extreme poverty preventing the family members from seeking employment elsewhere, (2) setting up separate families by sons except the eldest who inherits the farms, and (3) sales of farms due to economic hardships. On the other hand, small-scale farm households are on the increase by expansion of farmlands as well as purchases of farms from others. It is undeniable that such increase of medium- and large-scale farmers working on more than one *chongbo* is favorable for efficient management of the land, but, at the same time, proper consideration is due to the "extremely small-scale" farmers to lessen their plight.

A total 2,172,019 households are engaged in either rice paddy or upland farming. This is 98.2 percent of the total number of farm households, indicating that Korean agriculture is almostly exclusively devoted to rice and wheat production.

The size of the agricultural population has been increasing year after year. As of the end of 1957, the agricultural population was 13,591,000, an increase of eight percent or 146,162 persons over the preceding year. The average number of families per farm household is also on the increase: in 1956 it was 6.11 persons, which was increased to 6.15 in 1957 and again by 6.2 persons, by 1958.

Improvement of Farm Land and Land Reform Programs

The number of farm households which has received farmland as a result of the land reform program was 952,731 and 596,801. Farmland belonging to absentee landlords was distributed to the former and the latter received government-owned land. The total acreage of farm lands thus distributed is 352,499 *chongbo* of rice paddies and 117,611 *chongbo* of uplands. Payment by the beneficiary of the land reform for the land distributed, however, has yet to be completed, for so far only 87.7 percent of the total amount has been collected.

Factors causing delay in payment for the distributed land has been attributed to the facts that (1) the annual installment payment in kind amounting to 30 percent of the ordinary year crops proved too heavy a burden on the part of the farmers, who had to suffer lean years in 1951 and 1952; (2) the war inflicted considerable damage and loss on livestocks implements as well as crops, (3) most of the beneficiaries found it hard to pay 30 percent of the crops because of too small-scale farming they were engaged in, and (4) the Temporary Land Income Tax, incoming effective since 1951, levied 5 to 24 percent of tax in kind on crops produced from the farm distributed through the land reform program.

Payment by the government to the former land owners who had to sell their farms to the government, has not been completed by the end of 1958. The 169,803 former land owners who sold 267,877 *chongbo* of farmland to the government were originally scheduled to receive complete payment by the end of May, 1955. But 94.8 percent of 15,541,319,000 hwan has been paid to the former owners as of the end of 1958, the remaining portion still awaiting settlement.

A land distribution program similar to the one carried out following the end of World

War II was undertaken after the Korean War for areas north of the 38th parallel line that were "restored" to south Korea as a result of the cessation of the conflict. Under the program, 3,783 *chongbo* of farmland was distributed to 8,254 farm households in December, 1956, the price of the land being payable in yearly installments of 15 percent of the crops.

As to the improvement on farmland, the government has placed major emphasis upon irrigation projects, as indicated in the above table.

For the farmland improvement program, the government allocated a budget amounting to 22.5 billion hwan in 1958 to be used for improvement and maintenance of the existing irrigation facilities, construction of small-scale reservoirs and cultivation of waste lands. Thus the improvement works for 209 districts covering 128,505 *chongbo*, initiated in 1957, are being carried in 1959, and the works are expected to be completed by the end of 1959 in 64 districts, covering 1,492 *chongbo*. These districts are expected to increase the annual rice production by 139,000 *sok* as a result of improved irrigation system as of 1959. The remaining 145 districts are scheduled to enjoy satisfactory irrigation systems by 1960, when the projects will be completed.

Fertilizers and Farm Implements

Chemical fertilizers have been an absolute necessity for Korean farmlands, for small patches of land has been cultivated year after year by generation after generation of farmers over thousands of years. Large requirements for commercial fertilizers were met up to the end of World War II by the fertilizer plant at Hungnam in north Korea. With the division of the land after the Liberation, however, Korean farmers were forced to rely entirely upon commercial fertilizer imported through foreign aid programs.

During 1958, the total consumption of chemical fertilizers reached 942,856 tons, which were divided into 617,467 tons of nitrogeneous manure, 314,477 tons of phosphote manure, and 10,912 tons of potash fertilizer. Such excessive application of nitrogeneous fertilizer especially since the end of World War II lowered productivity of the land by oxidizing the farms as much as 70 percent and also by attracting pests.

For the purpose of improving such oxidized farmland, therefore, the government has started construction of calcium oxide powder plants in Tanyang and Sosa with a $500,000 ICA fund to produce 50,000 tons of calcium oxide powder annually. Another endeavor by the government to prevent deterioration of the farmlands by excessive application of chemical fertilizers was distribution of a total 36,567 tons of natural lime to farmers.

On the other hand, a large number of agricultural implements has been supplied to farmers due to the government subsidies and Agricultural Funds financed from government budget funds. Total production of farm machinery in 1958 reached 2,352,425 units, an increase of 24 percent over the

Table 2. **Farm Land Improvement Projects of the Government from 1954 to 1955**

Year	Projected Completed	Acreage Benefited	Increased Production	Gov'nt Subsidy	Financing by Loan	Other Fin. Res.	Total
		chongbo	sok	million hwan	million hwan	million hwan	million hwan
1954	86	27,881	79,624	381	599	3	983
1955	1,159	406,015	183,190	4,597	6,850	113	11,560
1957	1,574	164,876	322,065	11,273	6,500	-	17,773
1958	1,505	139,564	346,751	9,885	10,800	-	20,685

Source: Farm Land Section, Ministry of Agr. & Fores.

Agricultural Products

Total production of grains in fiscal 1959 is estimated by the government to be 28,773,000 *sok* against the annual requirements of 30,114,000 *sok*. Therefore, the balance of 1,341,000 *sok* is planned to be imported through foreign aid programs. The requirements for grains are based on the Ministry of Agriculture and Forestry's estimate that 13,046,057 farmers will consume 16,667,000 *sok* and 8,678,077 non-farming population will require 7,919,000 *sok* in addition to the government's requirements for grains which is estimated at 1,707,000 *sok*. This 1959 estimate of grain requirements was an increase over the preceding year's demands by 858,000 sok. The increased requirements are based upon expected increase in population and livestocks as well as the government's stockpiles of grains, which will be 1,300,000 *sok*.

As to the total supply of grains during fiscal 1959, the government estimates 28,773,000 *sok*, an increase of 3,905,000 *sok* over the preceding year, to be realized through record-breaking bumper crops. The total grains supply estimate is divided into 2,299,000 *sok* government stockpile, 6,966,000 *sok* summer crops, 1,291,000 *sok* beans crops 663,000 *sok* fall crops of miscellaneous grains, and 958,000 *sok* production of potatoes.

A significant feature of the 1959 food supply and demand schedule of the government is that the estimated annual shortage of grains is set at 1,341,000 *sok*, a marked decrease from the preceding year's estimate of 4,388,000 *sok*. This is an indication that Korea is moving towards self-sufficient economy as far as food production is concerned. If large quantities of grains are imported through foreign aid programs, however, as in the case of the preceding year when 5,000,000 *sok* were imported to meet the estimated shortage of 4,388,000 *sok*, surplus grains will flood the market, bringing the prices of grains down too far below cost to the detriment of the farmer. To prevent such a situation, adequate measures will have to be taken to export rice.

To clarify the points discussed above, the food supply and demand schedule for fiscal year 1959 prepared by the government is as follows:

Table 3. Food Supply and Demand Schedule for F. 1959 throughout South Korea

Requirements for:				
Farmers	16,667,000 *sok*	3.5 *hop* daily by	13,046,057	persons
Non-farmers	7,919,000 *sok*	2.5 *hop* by	8,678,077	persons
Government	1,707,000 *sok*	3.0 to 6 *hop* by	777,914	persons
Seeds	1,053,000 *sok*			
Soybean sauce and cakes	768,000 *sok*			
Brewery	500,000 *sok*			
Livestocks	200,000 *sok*			
Reserves	1,300,000 *sok*			
Total	30,114,000 *sok*			

Supplies:	
Government grains stockpiles of the preceding year	2,299,000 *sok*
Rice crops of 1958, estimate	16,596,000 *sok*
Summer crops of 1959, estimate	6,966,000 *sok*
Bean crops of 1958, estimate	1,291,00 *sok*
Misc. fall grains crops of 1950, estimate	663,000 *sok*
Potatoes crops of 1958, estimate	958,000 *sok*
Imported grains	—
Total	28,773,000 *sok*
Balance, shortage	1,341,000 *sok*

VIII INDUSTRIES

Korean agriculture, after many years of stagnancy since the end of World War II, was finally brought back on the right track in 1958, when 16,594,865 *sok* of rice was produced. This was due to the five-year plan, initiated in 1958 to improve seeds, eliminate harmfull pests, increase application of domestic manure in the place of commercial fertilizers, and use chemical fertilizer more efficiently. Thus record-breaking bumper crops were fetched in 1958 despite draughts, floods and other natural disasters which plagued the land during the year.

The production of wheat and barley reached an all-time high since the end of World War II in 1954, when 6,530,000 *sok* was produced. In 1958 the production was 6,260,000 *sok*, and the estimated barley and wheat crops of 1959 is 7,230,688 *sok*, which is over the highest record set in 1954.

The production of beans and miscellaneous grains in 1958 was 1,270,000 and 810,000 *sok* respectively.

The production of potatoes and sweet potatoes in 1958 was 1,460,000 *sok*, which cannot be favorably compared with previous records. Nevertheless, the total agricultural production amounting to 26,410,000 *sok* sets an all-time record high since the end of World War II.

Important side-lines of the farmers are cotton, silk and livestocks.

According to Ministry of Agriculture and Forestry statistics, 37,005,221 *kun* of cotton is harvested from 71,332 *chongbo* to furnish 7,451,000 *kun* of raw cotton to spinning mills.

As of 1958 there are 417,783 families producing raw silk on 36,740 *chongbo* of silkworm fields. The number of farmers engaged in raw silk production is gradually decreasing due to shortage of mulberry trees. The farmers are furnishing only 43 percent of the raw silk requirements by 26 spinning mills in Korea whose annual demands for raw silk is about two million *kwan*. Also unfavorable international market prices for raw silk has not been conducive to export of raw silk. However, the government in collaboration with U.S. economic assistance authorities, prepared a five-year plan in 1958 to boost the production of raw silk by three million *kwan* in order to reach the annual production of 4.5 million *kwan*, out of which 20,000 bales are scheduled for export to earn one million dollars in foreign exchange. For this purpose the government allocated a budget of 3,475 million hwan, which will be used to increase the productivity by 300 percent and also to improve quality so as successfully to meet competition in the international markets.

Animal husbandry, devastated by war, is gradually reaching the pre-war standards.

Presently there are 966,734 heads of cattle, which is a two percent increase over the 1957 figure. The number of hogs, (1,350,416 as of June, 1958), was also increased by 9.5 percent in a half-year period. More than 2 million chickens are raised on the farms.

The government, which saw the completion of the first five-year plan for improvement of animal husbandry, established the second five-year plan in 1958 to realize increased production and exports to foreign countries. The goal of the five-year plan is set at 1,000,249 heads of traditional Korean breeds, 2,840 heads of beef-giving cattle, 3,360 of milk-giving, 26,043 of horses, 1,505,700 of hogs, 19,418 of milk-giving sheep, 4,162 of wool-giving, 843,1000 rabbits, 10,024,000 poultries, 270,115 cases, of honeybees, 125,469 to of meat, 673,470,000 eggs, 205,943 hides, 12,429 kg. of wool top.

The vegetable production of 1958 was 296,505,000 *kwan*, an increase of 5 percent over the ordinary year's production. Of the total vegetable production, 36.5 percent were radishes raised on 32,755 *chongbo*, and 30 percent Chinese cabbages raised on 30,559 *chongbo*. The production of these traditional Korean vegetables in 1958 showed about 18 percent decrease below the preceding year due to unfavorable weather conditions.

The 1958 production of cabbages, onions and cucumbers, which is being increased gradually year after year, was 4,301,000 *kwan*, 8,167,000 and 8,448,000 respectively. Also, 7,648,000 *kwan* of water melon and 3,520,000 of Korean melon were produced in the year.

The production of red pepper, used widely in Korea as the favorite spice, was increased by 3.2 percent for a total 7,573,069 *kwan*.

Garlics, increased each year under a five-year plan initiated in 1958, is expected to total 7,641,100 *kwan* per annual production in 1962.

The 1958 production of fruits reached 40,446,000 *kwan*, an increase of 31 percent over the ordinary year's output. The increased production of fruits is attributed to increased acreage of orchards as well as improvements in technology, including effective application of pesticides to meet increasing demands for fruits. Of the total fruit production, 54.4 percent are apples, the others pears, grapes, persimmons, all of which have increased 0.3 to 20.7 percent over the preceding year.

As agricultural products unique in Korea, Korean jute, "fine jute", and sedge grass may be mentioned. The former is being used by farmers as raw material for clothing, its production in 1958 being 1,801,416 *kwan*, while 199,215 *kwan* of "fine jute", used also for weaving linen-like clothing, was produced in the same year. The production of fine sedge grass, which is used to make straw mattresses and cushions, is 423,340 *kwan*, while 1,635,374 *kwan* of "cho" weed was produced to be used as raw materials for traditional Korean paper.

Agricultural Financing and Farmers' Cooperatives

The Agriculture Bank, established in 1958, and based on a special law bearing the name of the bank, is devoted exculsively to agricultural financing.

During 1958 the Bank furnished funds amounting to 78,856 million *hwan* including collateral loans to farmers secured by rice.

The Farmers' Cooperatives Law was enacted and promulgated on February 14, 1957. Presently all farmers' cooperatives in the country are placed under the Federation of Farmers' Cooperatives, established October 10, 1958.

Forestry

Outline

The ratio of forest area to total acreage of the country is so high in Korea that it is sometimes compared to Finland's, but the similarity with Finland stops right there. The adverse effects of forests left unpreserved as well as the low density of trees in the forests of Korea furnishes nothing but one of the worst examples in the world. To be more specific, 73 percent of the total area of south Korea or 6,747,550 *chongbo* is covered with forests, but the density of trees in the forests is on the average no more than 8.7 m^3 per *chongbo*, the accumulation of trees being 58,557,000 m^3 over the entire forest regions. Of the total area of forests and fields, 49 percent is wasteland on which practically no tree grows, and what few trees stand on the remaining 51 percent of the forests are mostly seedlings. As a matter of fact, less than 20 percent of the area grows what may properly be called useful trees. In particular, areas not covered by trees are rapidly turning into wasteland. Of these, about 700,000 *chongbo* require urgent erosion control, without which the land will deteriorate into conditions defying rehabilitation.

The conditions being such, frequently recurring floods have been a serious roadblock against the advances of various industries.

To remedy such an alarming situation, the following measures are usually suggested:

a) The denudation of forests, increasing

each year, had to be checked, and endeavors exerted to increase the accumulation of trees in the forests.

b) Forestation and erosion controls must be enforced on wastelands and denudated forests.

c) Studies on more effective utilization of forestry products.

d) Measures to substitute coal for firewood as fuel.

Supply and Requirements

The annual requirements for timber is 900,000 m³, of which about 400,000 m³ is imported through ICA assistance programs, the remaining erquirements being produced within the country. This is too much of a strain for the country in view of the conditions of forestry mentioned above. One of the largest consumers of trees in Korea is the *ondol,* the traditional Korean floor heating system, which annually requires 16,060,000 tons of firewood. The *ondol* floor burns in enormous quantiy not only all kinds of trees and sometimes even timber which could be put to better use, but also the leaves that are gathered in the forests. So serious is the problem of stopping the widespread use of firewood for the *ondol* alone that unless this age-old custom is changed, reconstruction of forestry is considered practically impossible.

To improve the situation, efforts are being made to increase importation of lumber through ICA economic assistance programs; and preservation of forests is being attempted by cutting trees in the "virgin forests" located in relatively isolated mountains. At the same time, use of anthracite in the place of fiirewood is being encouraged by the Government, particulary for homes in urban districts. To meet firewood requirements in rural areas, special forests for firewood are designed as preserves.

Forestration

The government has designated four kinds of forests as one measure to improve the situation.

1) For firewood and farm forests. Intended to secure fuels, forage, fertilizer, etc., for farmers. Trees grown are mostly acacia and other shrubs of the lowest quantity.

2) Community Improvement Forests. Intended to improve soils of farm lands as well as to furnish farmers with forest products.

3) Lumber forests. Relatively fertile lands are selected to grow various kinds of pine trees, the Japanese *Sugi,* and *Hinoki* among others, for future lumber production.

4) Forestration for "Special Purpose" Trees. Intended to increase monetary income of farmers by growing oak, ginkgoes and other kinds of trees that are used for other than lumber purposes.

The total forestration area is 110,000 *chongbo* as of 1958, for which the Government has allocated a 1,900 million hwan budget.

Erosion Control

Relatively largescale erosion control was started only in recent years with foreign economic assistance funds, for, urgent as the work, limited economic resources of the coun try had not been conducive to the carrying-out of a project over a large area rapidly deteriorating into wasteland.

The most widely used method for erosion control is a system similar to the Upper Watershed Management, used in the U.S., for the purpose of reaping the maximum effects with minimum cost. Primarily intended to curb erosion of top-soils, this method also aims at expansion of farm lands and more effective utilization of forests.

The ten-year erosion control plan, established by the government in 1946, failed to accomplish its original purposes because of the outbreak of the war and insufficient government budget. However, a new, five-year plan was prepared in 1957 to restore 237,670 *chongbo* of waste land with a 1.9 billion hwan fund.

Forest Association

A total of 21,540 Forest Associations are in operation throughout the country. The members of this organization are composed of all household families residing within each association district regardless of the status of the family's ownership of forests.

This organization, voluntary in nature, is encouraged and supported by the government so as to develop community well-being as well as to protect forests. A special feature of this association is that even those who do not own forests are included in the membership.

Presently this organization is engaged in management of forest, forestation in projects and some erosion control work.

The importance of these Forest Associations is widely recognized, since the task of rehabitating forests in the future is considered largely dependent on this organization.

Research and Education

The Central Forestry Laboratory with two branch Laboratories and on seedling experimental stations are engaged in researches and experiments in the field of forestry. Their activities are futher supplemented by the work of each Provincial Forestry Experimental Station.

Forestry education is given by eight forestry colleges, five of which are independent institutes specializing exclusively in forestry.

Unique Forest Products

Oakmushroom, pine mushroom, cork-oak bark callnuts sedge baric and medical herbs, may be cited as, products unique in Korea. Presently only nominal quantities are exported to foreign countries. The future export prospect for cork-oak bark, however, is promising because of its high elasticity as well as its highly effective quality against penetration of moisture and gas.

Manufacturing Industries

Trend of Manufacturing Industries

The production of various manufacturing industries showed an increase of 3.2 percent in 1958 over 1957, according to production relatives compiled by the Bank of Korea, but this increase is a small one compared with the 31 percent increase in 1957 over the preceding year. This seemingly sluggish pace of improvement, however, has to be considered as a sign for the better, for it is a result of readjustment among the manufacturing industries seeking improved quantities of products, balanced supply for the market demands as well as more efficient management, in contrast to the situation prevailing until 1957, when prospects for easy profits because of the ever-present inflation lured reckless investment of capital to manufacturing industrie, that concentrated upon increased production in complete disregard of other factors. Therefore, it has to be realized that the manufacturing industries have now reached a stability point after the turmoil of the post-war period. In the meanwhile, the large-scale factories, constructed with ICA and government funds in 1957 and 58 for producing steel, cement, window pane, explosive powder, newsprints, auto tires, etc., added color and variety to manufacturing products, while promoting advances in other basic industries. On the other hand, the stabilization of manufacturing industries, curbing new investments in their own fields, drove capital to fields that were enjoying unprecedented prosperity, such as construction, commerce and real estate. Metal goods' manufactures also had to step backwards as requirements for durable goods and maintenance parts were mostly fulfilled by 1957, offering limited demands for the products. Other large-scale industries such as steel, shipbuilding, locomotives, boxcars, etc'. have yet to overcome technological and managerial backwardnesses.

Government Policy for Manufacturing Industries

The government, in both 1957 and '58, placed major emphasis on increased production to facilitate the supply and demand of industrial products by attempting to stabilize the inflationary tendency through pegging the exchange rate of the dollar for the hwan at 500 to 1, and, at the same time, by expediting completion of basic industries under construction. Thus, the Mungyong Cement and Inchon Window Glass Plants were completed in 1957, and completion of other plants, including a fertilizer factory, a newprint mill, and an explosive powder plant, is being pushed.

The second rehabilitation project for the Korea Explosive Powder Company was completed, while the Chungju Fertilizer Plant with an annual production capacity of 85,000 tons of urea is under construction with $30,550,000 and 2,750,33.100 hwan.

The Korea Heavy Industry Corporation, which produces steel, has also completed a rehabilitation and expansion program.

Repair works on the blast furnace of the Samhwa Iron Works have been completed while the Chosun Machinery Company is preparing plans to produce diesel engines. Other plans include construction of an oil refinery and establishment of a new hydroelectric power plant at Chungju.

In the field of small and medium-size industries, the government is pursuing policies formulated in 1957. Loan funds were increased, and other measures taken to increase productivity in these areas as well as to improve qualities in search of the export market.

Conditions in Each Manufacturing Industry

The production of manufacturing industries was 11.1 percent of the gross natural product in 1958, as against 10.7 for the preceding year. The increase was realized by the following industries: chemical (14 percent), food processing (12.2 percent), ceramics (5.7 percent), textile mfg. (4.4 percent).

On the other hand, the metal and machine industries declined by 6.4 percent and 15.7 percent respectively.

Textile Industry (Spinning & Weaving Industries)

Requirements for textiles, once extremely urgent, have now reached a saturation point, and the present aim of industry, accordingly, is the improvement of quality to increase domestic consumption and find export markets. Although no expansion work was carried out in 1958, production was increased by 4.4 percent, accounting not only for larger quantities but also improved qualities with added varieties. However, 92.6 percent of the fibers produced was cotton yarn, and only limited quantities of synthetic fibers despite rapidly increasing demands. In the field of weaving, 68.5 percent of total production was cotton, 1.5 percent wool, 1.0 percent silk, 7.3 percen stable fiber, 7.3 percent rayon, and 1.5 percent nylon.

Spinning plants were equipped with 432,492 spindles as of the end of 1958. All in all, the industry's bid for efficient utilization rather than expansion of facilities has proved successful.

The outputs of cotton yarn in 1958—96,450,000 pounds—and of cotton cloth—211,817,000 yards—are sufficient to meet the entire requirements of the country, i. e., the goals of self-sufficiency have been met in this field.

Raw cotton used as raw materials during 1958 totalled 110,770,000 pounds, of which only 80,000 pounds were produced within the country, the rest having been imported through foreign aid programs. Predominant in the Korean textile industry are large-scale mills, but there are also many small and medium size ones that have produced 62,807,000 yards of cotton cloth in 1958.

Woollen textile mills are also turning out sufficient quantities to meet the domestic demands. There are ten major mills, including the Cheil Wool Company and Taemyong Woolen Textile Company that are equipped with a total 37,040 spindles. One of the major difficulties of the woollen textile industry is the shortage of wooltops, necessitating occasional halting of operations whenever the supply is turned out. In 1957, a total of 4,839,000 pounds of wooltops were used to produce 4,011,000 pounds of wool yarn, and in 1958 4,164,000 pounds of raw materials were used to produce 3,643,000 pounds of yarsted wool yarn.

As to woollen cloth, 13 large-scale mills and other small and medium size plants throughout the country produced 4,630,000 yards in 1958.

Silk production has not been developed as might be expected because of the encroachment of synthetic fibers, thereby betraying hopes for export possibilities. Silk, however, is important to fulfill domestic requirements, and efforts are, therefore, being made by the government to encourage its expansion, particularly through increased production of raw silk, insufficient supply of which has been one of the difficulties of the silk industry; for instance in 1958, production of raw silk within the country furnished only 50 percent of the industry's requirement.

The number of silk and rayon machineries, total 15,451 with an annual production capacity of 69,527,000 yards. Requirements for rayon are being increased year after year because of low prices and variety of products. In 1958, therefore, the production of rayon (492,000 yards) was increased by 20 percent over the preceding year, accounting for 20.2 percent of the entire textile goods produced, thus ranging only next to cotton in its production quantity. The bottleneck is unreliable supply of raw materials, which have to be imported at ever fluctuating prices.

The nylon industry, which has been enjoying remarkable prosperity in recent years because of ever-increasing popular demands suffered a slight setback in 1958, producing 4,511,000 yards or a three percent drop from the preceding year.

The stable fiber industry has been steadily declining since 1957 as a result of unsuccessful competition with such synthetic fiber as rayon. In 1958 the production (22,500,000 yards) was reduced by 23 percent below the preceding year. Nevertheless, stable fiber occupies third place in the textile industry.

The underwear knitted goods industry has concentrated on improving quality in recent years, and, in 1958, an increasing portion of its raw materials was assigned to synthetic fibers in the place of cotton to cater to popular demand. Production of knitted underwears in 1958, being 49,912,000 units, was increased by 4 percent over the preceding year, while 51,139,000 pairs of socks and 15,403,000 pairs of gloves were produced in 1958, showing a decrease of 6 and 5 percent respectively.

Food Processing Industry

Sugar Refining. Seven large-scale sugar refineries with a total annual capacity of 205,800 tons, have had to cut operations down to 15 percent of the entire capacity in order to prevent surplus production in 1957. The situation was somewhat modified in 1958, when 25 percent of the total operational capacity was used to produce 51,050 tons of refined sugar.

Flour. There were 14 flour mills with a total annual production capacity of 24,656 B. B. L. as of the end of 1957. The number was increased in 1958 to 22 mills with production capacities of 42,721 B. B. L.

Actual production of flour in 1958 was 257,619 tons, an increase of 13 percent over the preceding year.

The industry is dependent on imported wheat as the major source of supply of its raw materials. It is also suffering from surplus production for only one-third of its capacities were utilized in 1958.

Beverages. Production of beverages has been increased steadily in recent years due to low prices of raw materials coupled with increasing demands. In 1958, total production of alcholic beverages was 2,486,000 *sok*, which was an increase of 14 percent over the preceding year. Of this, 68,728 *sok* were beer produced by the two large breweries, the Tongyang Beer and Chosun Beer Companies.

Production of "*takju*" was 1,645,775 *sok*, "*yakju*" 109,248 *sok*, "*soju*" 492,017 *sok*, and "*chongjun*" 46,628 *sok*. Production of alchol (133,591 *sok*) was also increased by 24 percent due to lower prices for raw materials and increased demands.

Soybean sauce and bean mash, both formerly produced at home, have gradually become factory offers. Production in 1958 was 212,000 *sok* and 9,850,000 *kwan* for the sauce and mash respectively.

Chemicals

Major products of the chemical industry are such consumer goods as rubber goods, soap, matches, leather goods, paper, etc., while the production of basic raw materials is still in infancy due to inadequate facilities and difficult technological problems. The overall production of the chemical industry, however, showed a 27 percent increase over the preceding year, attributable to considerably increased production of salt, rubber and plastic goods. On the other while, production was decreased slightly for paper, dyes, carbite, matches, sulphuric acid, and oxygen. Production of laundry soap, automobile tires and newsprint was slightly increased in the year.

Ceramics

Remarkable progress has been made in the ceramic industry, thanks to the efficient operations of the Oriental Cement Plant, the Mungyong Cement Plant which has commenced operations with an annual production capacity was 200,000 tons, and the Inchon Window Glass Plant with an annual production capacity of 120,000 cases. A total of 25,310,000 units of chinaware were produced in 1958 to meet domestic demands, whereas production of 455,177 tons of bricks supplied the construction industry with sufficient materials.

Metals

The metal industry is still extremely meager despite its importance for modern industrial development. Continued support and encouragement of the government in this field has so far produced little effect.

Machines

The machine industry in Korea still remains in such an infant state that its products are no more than some machine parts and replacement tools, such as motors, automobiles, textile machines, automobile parts and accessories, various electrical appliances and instruments. Important products are replacement parts for machinery, the production of which was decreased by 15.7 percent in 1958 because of reduced demands, indicating the still backward state of things in the Korean manufacturing industry as a whole.

As major products of the machine industry, a total of 5,459 motors and 3,171 pumps were manufactured in 1958, each showing a 20 to 30 percent decrease below the preceeding year.

Production of textile machines is, under present conditions, technically impossible save for some replacement parts, which are produced in negligible quantity. Production of sewing machines, which was started 1955, was increased to 42,102 sets in 1958, but the quality is not high enough to compete successfully with foreign-made goods. Production of bicycles, which has steadily been declining, was 24,678 sets in 1958, — only half of the present production capacity.

Locomotives and boxcars are produced in small quantities at small-scale plants, which are operated primarily for repair and maintenance works on imported foreign vehicles. Automobiles were first produced in 1956 by the International Vehicles Company Ltd., which turned out 237 cars in 1958. Some of the automobile parts produced, such as springs, pistons, and valves, are so excellent in quality that they may be favorably compared with foreign goods.

Electrical goods are being produced increasingly in large quantities due to the improved power situation. Major electric goods produced are sockets, bulbs, transformers, dry and wet batteries.

Mining Industry

Mining industry has made remarkable progress in Korea since the end of the war, in line with the overall economic development of the country. The tempo of rapid advancement, however, was somewhat slackened in 1958, when total production was increased by 8 percent over the preceding year. Taking 1955 as base period, the production increase was 8.2 percent in 1958 and 34.9 percent in 1957. Such a trend is born out by the production for each branch of the mining industry: coal mining was up 33.8 percen in 1957 and 9.7 percent in 1958; metal mining was up 31.7 percent in 1957 and 10.5 percent up in 1958, on the other hand, non-metallic mining which was 40.5 percent up employed the 3.5 percent increase in 1958 is a somewhat sluggish tempo of advancement compared with the annual average increase of 9.7 percent during the two preceding years. The real income of the mine workers, however, was increased substantially over the preceding year due to increased number of skilled labor.

The above conditions are clarified in the table below.

Mining Production

Coal

Anthracite coal mining reached a surplus

Table 4.   Major Indicators of Mining Industry in Korea, 1957 & 1958

	1958	1957	increase or decrease
Production relative (base period 1955)	184	170	+8.2 %
Exports of minerals	$9,041,000	$11,188,900	−19.2
No. of mining districts in operation	2,096	1,952	+7.4
No. of mines in operation	1,396	1,285	+8.6
Mining fund released	6,177	4,717	+31.0
Wholesale price relatives of minerals (base period 1955)	108.4	113.7	−4.7
Export price relatives of minerals (bass period 1957)	66.3	100.0	−33.7
Export price relatives of metallic minerals (base period 1957)	63.5	100	−36.5
Monthly pay for miners	35,700 hwan	31,600 hwan	+13.0
No. of newly organized mining enterprises	36	28	+28.6
Investment by the new ventures	163.3 million hwan	182.7	−10.6

Sources: Bank of Korea Research Dept. Ministry of Commerce and Industry

in 1957, was down 9 percent in 1957.

The total number of mines in operations was increased by 12.9 percent in 1957 but only 8.6 percent in 1958. Such a trend is further reflected in the number of miners: production stage in 1958 as a result of a steady expansion program since the end of the war. Surplus coal carried over from the preceding year, therefore, was disposed of through curtailment of operations in government-owned coal mines and adjustment of supplies, with the result that 14 percent less was produced than originally scheduled. Nevertheless, the 1958 production amounting to 2,671,000 tons was a 9 percent increase over the preceding year. Privately-owned coal mines played increasingly important roles against government-owned mines in recent years, for the ratio of production by the former to the latter changed from 38:62 in 1957 into 45:55 in 1958, even though government coal mine production still exceeds the privately-owned.

Confronted with a situation in which it had to compete with private coal mines, the government enterprise was forced to attempt reduction costs and quality improvement through more efficient management, shifting from the former policy of all-out production increase. One aspect of such an endeavor by the government-owned coal mines is reflected in the fact that productivity per worker was increased from 14.63 tons to 24.35 tons a month. On the other hand privately-owned coal mines was able to make progress by overcoming previous handicaps in high production costs and poor transportation facilities. Whereas the number of workers employed by government-owned mines was decreased to 8,151 as of the end of 1958 from 11,466 of 1957, showing a decrease of 28.9 percent, privately-owned mines employed 35 percent more workers in 1958 for a total 7,016.

Bituminous coal, which is not produced in the country despite large demands, has to be imported in large quantities each year. Importation of bituminous coal amounting to 700,000 tons in 1958, however, represented a 5.6 percent decrease below the preceding year, reflecting the government policy of substituting anthracite for bituminous coal in order to attain a self-sufficient economy.

The table indicates the extent of this self-sufficiency.

Metallic Minerall Mining

The rate of increased production achieved by the metallic mining industry, somewhat sluggish as it has become in recent years, shows a more favorable trend compared with the coal and non-metallic mining industries, as indicated by the following table for major products of the industry.

Increased production of gold was due to favorable market conditions as well as government support and encouragement. Large-scale gold mines increased production while small-scale mining ventures curtailed operations, the former becoming more and more predominant in recent years. For instance, gold mines belonging to the Changhang Refinery and Taemyong Mining Company produced 85.4 percent of the total gold production. Production of 62 kg. of placer gold, which is a 400 percent increase over the preceding year, is attributed to the Taechon Mines, which is equipped with modern facilities imported out of a $591,500 UNKRA aid fund. Only the three large-scale gold mines of Kubong, Muguk and Changhang produced more than 300 kg. of gold in 1958, the remaining small-scale mines each producing not more than 20 kg. during the year.

Production of silver declined in 1958 due

Table 5. Production and mportation of Coal 1955–1958

Unit in m/t

Year	Domestic Production	Importation	Total	Extent of Self-sufficiency
1955	1,308,324	1,065,241	2,373,565	55.1%
1956	1,815,371	972,990	2,788,361	65.1
1957	2,441,217	741,378	3,182,595	76.7
1958	2,670,889	700,142	3,371,031	79.2

VIII INDUSTRIES

Table 6. Production of Major Metallic Minerals in Korea, 1958 Compared with 1957

Minerals	Unit	1958 Production	1957 Production	Increase or decrease
Gold	kg.	2,242	2,071	+10.8
Silver	kg.	7,707	8,626	−10.7
Copper ore	m/t	7,644	9,168	−16.6
Lead ore	m/t	2,435	1,844	+13.2
Zinc ore	m/t	669	564	+18.6
Bismuth ore	m/t	300	363	−17.4
Metallic bismuth	m/t	347	149	+132.9
Iron ore	m/t	261,025	185,412	+40.8
Ferro-manganese ore	m/t	-	3,205	-
Molybdenum	m/t	68	27	+151.9
Tungsten ore	m/t	3,012	3,825	−21.3
Nickel ore	m/t	70	225	−68.9

Source: Mining Bureau, Ministry of Commerce and Industry

to decreased market demands, in contrast to iron ore production, which is being increased through expansion of facilities to meet increasing export requirement. The Samhwa Iron Refinery renewed operations in 1958 after completing its scheduled rehabilitation project, but the market demands for the product lagged so far behind the production capacities that operations were drastically curtailed, only 5,000 tons of iron ore being used during the year, the remaining ore being exported to Japan. Such being the situation, exploitation and development of iron ore mining is intended for exports to earn foreign exchange rather than for meeting domestic requirement.

Table 7. Production of Iron Ore in Korea
1956-1958 Unit in m/t

Mines	1958	1957	1956
Changdong	21,429	11,455	-
Chungju	39,580	48,838	34,368
Yangyang	133,058	74,842	8,914
Kumgok	1,052	4,373	6,732
Taehan	21,500	7,500	-
Others	44,406	38,404	12,853
Total	261,025	185,412	62,867

Source: Ministry of Commerce and Industry

Production of copper ore was 7,644 tons in 1958 showing a decrease of 16.6 percent below the preceding year. This was partly due to unfavorable financial conditions of the Changhang Refinery, which had to delay payment for the ore purchased from copper mines. As a result, large-scale mines had to curtail operation. The small-scale were relatively unaffected by the situation.

Table 8. Copper Production of Major Mines
1956-1958 Unit in m/t

Mines	1958	1957	1956
Talsong	1,566	2,866	3,770
Ilgwang	0	40	841
Chijok	0	318	360
Uisong	0	0	1,170
Haman	0	150	485
Kunui	34	165	0
Sihung	0	0	203
Kunbuk	4,122	4,345	2,320
Others	1,922	1,283	5,189
Total	7,644	9,168	14,708

Source: Ministry of Commerce and Industry

Lead ore production was generally increased in 1958 for a total 2,435 tons—a 32 percent increase over the preceding year.

Production of tungsten ore was decreased considerably because of unfavorable international market prices. The production of 3,011 tons in 1958 wasa decrease of 21.3 percent below the preceding year. All major tungsten mines including Talsong, Okbang, Wolak, Taehwa and Sangdong were forced

VIII INDUSTRIES

Table 9. Lead Ore Production of Major Mines
1956–1958   Unit in m/t

Mines	1958	1957	1956
Sihung	228	270	524
Pongmyong	-	-	10
Ilgwang	-	200	-
Sanmak	270	390	-
Chunyang	20.5	20	-
Tadok	-	20	-
Others	1,916.8	945	2,368
Total	2,435.3	1,845	2,902

Table 10. Production of Non-Ferrous Metals in Korea, 1958 and 1957 Compared.
Unit in m/t

Metals	1958	1957	Increase or Decrease in %
Amorphous Graphite	94,026	147,342	-36.2
Crystalline Graphite	145	260	-44.2
Asbestos	20	87	-77.0
Pyrophyllite	5,843	4,680	+24.9
Talc	10,106	6,600	+53.1
Fluorite	1,621	5,120	-68.3
Diathometh	470	1,335	-64.8
Kaolin	21,565	6,622	+225.7
Limestone	670,715	14,796	+433.1
Silica Sand	3,840	1,111	+245.6
Barite	-	7	-

to curtail operations during the year, while 44 other small-scale mines more or less maintained the preceding year's production.

Bismuth ore is produced in combination with tungsten. Accordingly, its 1958 production had to be decreased to 300 tons in proportion to the tungsten output. However, 347 tons of metal bismuth was produced in the year to offset the situation to some extent.

Production of both molybdenum and zinc ore was somewhat increased in 1958, while nickel ore production declined as much as 68.9 percent, and production of manganese ore, which was 3,205 tons in 1957, was reduced to zero in 1958.

Monazite Ore

A record-breaking output of monazite ore was achieved in 1954, when 1,005 tons were mined in response to increasing demands for atomic energy. Higher production cost and decline in the international market prices, however, reduced productions to 355 tons and 322 tons in 1957 and, 58 respectively, of which 241 tons and 166 tons were exported.

Non-ferrous Metals

Major non-ferrous metal productions for recent years are as follows:

Crystalline graphite is produced by the Sihung Mine, which commenced operation in September, 1958 with modern facilities installed through UNKRA aid programs. Other mines, in the meantime, suspended operations. Amorphous graphite, however, is being produced by more than 40 mines, including Wolmyong-Tuksu, Taehan, Pongmyong and Munhwa Mines, all of which have curtailed operations.

Fluorite production was decreased as much as 68.4 percent below the preceding year. Fluorite mine beds in Korea are usually of small size and so shallow that most of the large mines formerly operated have been abandoned, giving way to numerous small-scale mines.

Production of kaolin reached an all-time high since the end of World War II in 1958. Thirty-four mines produced a total 21,565 tons during the year, but exports were not increased correspondingly. Domestic requirements have also reached a saturation point.

Production of talc was increased 53.1 percent, a lion's share of the increase going to the Oriental Talc Mine, which produced 55 percent of the total output of 10,106 tons. This prosperous state of affairs must be attributed to the Chungju Talc Powder Company, which started operations in February, 1958, as well as to increased export to Japan.

Pyrophyllite production was increased 24.9 percent over the preceding year despite decreased exports due to increased demands within the country for manufacturing fireproof construction materials.

VIII INDUSTRIES

Production of limestone established an all-time record high in 1958 in response to enormously increased demands by the Inchon Window Glass Manufacturing Plant and Mungyong Cement Plant, both of which started operations in recent months with up-to-date facilities.

Production of silica sand spurred by large export requirements as well as the demands of the Inchon Window Glass Plant was also increased by as much as 245.6 percent.

Recent export trend of minerals is indicated:

	1958	1957	1956
Mineral exports, total, in $1,000	9,041	11,189	14,323
Increase or decrease in %	−19.2	−21.9	50.7
Exports of all goods in $1,000	16,667	22,172	23,056
Increase or decrease in %	−24.8	−3.8	25.7
Mineral exports: All goods exports in %	54.2	50.5	62.1

Government Policy toward the Mining Industry

It has been one of the basic policies of the government to sell government-owned mines, which account for more than half of the entire mines in Korea, to private citizens, but much still remains to be done to accomplish the set aims.

Loans to the mining industry, made with government permission or endorsement by banks and similar financial organizations, were considerably increased in 1958 over the preceding year, indicating the government's active support of the industry.

The government has also lowered freight charges and mining tax rates recently in an attempt to reduce production cost of minerals, and improve upon both facilities and technological shortcomings.

Fishery

Outline

Korea is so favorably located for fishery that its products embrace 75 varieties of fish, 20 kinds of shell-fish and 15 species of sea-weeds. Fishery, indeed, accounts for a significant portion of the nation's gross national production. Until the end of World War II, the share (15.4 percent) compared with for agriculture, but in recent years, fishery accounts for 16.8 percent, whereas agriculture has declined to 38.4 percent.

Fishery is also one of the most important foreign exchange earners of Korea, for the industry earned 22 percent or $3,670,000 of the $16,780,000 gross export amount in 1958. The foreign exchange earning from fishery is next only to that of the mining industry.

The total number of people engaged in fishery was 613,724 (189,720 households) in 1958. That the industry is important is further evidenced by the fact that the industry furnishes 85 percent of the nation's animal protein intakes.

Important as it has been, the country's fishery had to wait until 1956 to make any substantial progress for the industry, until that time, had to resort to primitive methods, using available ancient facilities subsequently shattered by the war. The remarkable progress in the post rehabilitation and expansion program for the industry started to show its effect in 1957, when a record production was achieved. In the following year of 1958, the total production of fishery amounting to 395,193 tons proved to be close to the preceding year's all-time high.

Taking 1955 as the base period, progress over recent years may be indicated by the yearly production index: 132 in 1956; 156 in 1957; and 152 in 1958.

The 1958 fishery output was divided into the following proportions: 73.3 percent for fishes, 4 percent—shell-fishes, 7.3 percent—sea-weeds and 15 percent—miscellaneous.

Production of Fishery

Fish

Fish accounts for more than 70 percent of the country's fishery production. Of these, the saury pike, Alaska Pollack, anchovy, yellow croaker, hairtail, shrimp, mackerel and flat fish, among others belong to the group with a total annual catch of more than 10,000 tons. The vast catches in 1958, amounting to 280,000 tons, a 4 percent increase over the preceeding year's all-time record high, was achieved through mechanization of facilities and improvement in technology, including the utilization of fish-school detectors and modern fishing-nets.

Shell-fish and other cultured Sea foods

Shell-fish, forming the backbone of the country's sea-food cultivations, registered a 30.3 percent increase in 1959 over the record output for 1958 when the volume was 16,000 tons. Compared with the 1957 output, however, the production of sea-weeds and other fishery products declined by 17.4 percent and 22.3 percent respectively, the output of sea-weeds being 28,759 tons, and that of other fishery products, 59,359 tons.

Various expansion programs of the government for cultivation of sea-foods, in the meanwhile, started to show favorable effects since 1956, when 5,608 tons of cultured sea foods were produced. In the succeeding year of 1957, a 10-percent increase was realized for a total 6,353 tons, followed by a still further jump of 34 percent in 1958, or 8,219 tons. The cultivation of oyster, (6,215 tons or 76 percent of the year's total cultured sea-foods output) predominates a field, which has made both rapid and steady advances in recent years.

The production of laver for 1958 was the lowest since 1953, thanks to the lean year of 1957, than which '58 was only a slight improvement. The decline in recent years may be attributed to resistance of the Japanese buyer, who is the only potential customer of laver in substantial quantities.

In an attempt to tide over the difficult situation brought about by the unfavorable diplomatic relations between the R. O. K. and Japan, the government has prepared a plan to facilitate conversion of laver cultivation to oyster culture. Initiated in 1957, the five-year conversion plan, primarily intended to relieve the economic plight of small-scale fishermen against declining export possibilities of laver, succeeded in establishing a record production of oyster in 1958 with 215 tons cultivated over 21,618.000 of oyster beds, an increase of 41 percent, over the preceding year.

Another five-year plan to expand cultivation of useful shell-fish and seaweeds, utilizing sand banks and shoals which extend far and wide along the country's coasts, was put into practice in 1958. The plan attempts to increase raising grounds for four kinds of shell-fishes and two spices of sea weeds by 20 million *pyong* during the scheduled five-year period by each annual expansion of four million *pyong*. In the first year of the plan, 51 percent of the original goal was reached with 170 million hwan in government subsidy.

Exploitation of natural resources in major rivers which run through the country was also started in 1958 with the government's five-year plan for fresh water fish breeding. This plan, if it is realized according to schedule, will increase fresh water fish output by 40,000 tons a year by adding 250 fish farms and 50 fish-hatching stations at the completion of the plan.

Durring the initial year of the expansion plan, 15,000,000 hwan in government budget was spent for 35 civilian fish-breeding farms, while two government-operated hatching stations distributed 16.5 million eggs to civilian fish farms.

Fishery Products Processing Industry

The marine products processing industry has enjoyed relatively high prosperity during the past three years since 1956. The industry's production relatives for each recent year, with 1955 as the base index at 100, was 142 in 1956; 166.8 in 1957 and 143.8 in 1958, indicating an increasing trend.

Using 38.1 percent of the year's total marine production or 151,000 tons as raw materials, the processing industry produced 57,000 tons in 1958.

Among various fishery products processing industries, preservation of 57,217 tons of fish by either salting or drying was the only field which suffered a decline in 1958, due to decreasing demands for such forms of preserved fishery products.

The number of fish canning plants in Korea was increased from 35 in 1957 to 39 in 1958. They are equipped with combined annual production capacities of four million cases of canned fish. Especially noteworthy is the virgin export of canned fish to the U. S. and the completion of a "model" fish canning plant during the year out of a $325,000 UNKRA (United Nations Korea Reconstruction Agency) economic assistance fund. Also, a total of 578,000 cases of canned fish were sold to the U. N. forces stationed in Korea during the year.

Production of agar-agar declined to 270 tons in 1958, 266 tons of it being exported. The decline is attributed to the rise of the synthetic equivalent: in addition to 45 natural agar-agar plants already existing, three synthetic agar-agar plants with combined capacities of 360 tons a year had been under construction since 1955 with a $635,000 ICA fund. One of these plants is already operating.

The frozen fish industry, by turning out 165,000 tons of products, showed a slight rise in 1958 over 1957. Ice used by the industry is supplied by 64 ice plants in the country, which have a combined production capacity of 1,557 tons a day and are equipped with a 8,415 tons refrigeration capacity.

Exports of Fishery Products

Korea's export of marine products amounted to 11,000 tons in 1958, earning $3,670, or 22 percent of the country's gross export amount of $16,780,000 for the year. The figures indicate a steady pace of recovery from former conditions, the export amount of $3,914,000 in 1954 having declined by about half in 1955, the result of unfavorable export to Japan. Some recovery, though, was made in 1956 and notably in 1957, when the export figures climbed back to $3,428,000. The largest foreign exchange earner was dried cuttlefish, which was credited with $1,427,000, followed by live and fresh fishes ($713,000), agar-agar ($643,000), and fish liver oil ($147,000).

Half of the exports went to Japan for $1,716,000, while $1,033,000 worth of products were exported to Hong Kong, followed by the U. S., which imported $285,000 worth.

There were two notable features of the marine export picture in 1958. First, the Japanese buyer resistance which meant that only $41,000 of laver could be exported that year. On the bright sight, however, export markets were found, for the first time, for frozen shrimps against the acceptance formerly of only dried.

Facilities of the Fishery Industry

The 37,142 total number of fishing boats, in 1958, was an increase by 629 over a year ago. Barges, on the other hand, dropped by 244 to 990 during the same period. The barges, being mostly obsolete, have been decreasing rapidly both in number and tonnage, whereas increasingly large-size fishing boats with motors are replacing small-size, hand-operated boats, reflecting the tendency towards deep-sea fishing, away from traditional inshore takes.

A total of 216 fishing boats amounting to

VIII INDUSTRIES

3,024 tons was built during 1958 with a $400,000 ICA fund in addition to 86 small-size fishing boats constructed with CARE assissance for an additional 402 vessels to the nation's fishing fleet.

Fishing nets, in the meantime, are produced in sufficient quantity within the country to meet the entire requirements, while domestic production of modern nets also became a feasibility in 1958, thus dispensing with the need for importation.

The production of fishing nets (851 tons in 1958) showed a 48 percent increase over the preceding year's output of 583 tons. Production of fishing ropes also is sufficient to satisfy the entire demands, for although the 1,319 tons produced in 1958 meant a decrease of about 10 percent, the industry as a whole was not adversely affected. The fishing oil situation has become much improved in recent years, contributing to increased catches during fishing seasons. During 1958, a total of 246 drums of oils were supplied to fishermen, an increase of about 30 percent over the preceding year's supply.

Korea's fishery, however, is faced with problems which must yet be overcome if it is to make further substantial progress. The most urgent are improvement of technology and modernization of facilities, especially in the field of fishing boats, about 40 percent of the present boats being obsolete and requiring immediate replacements.

Finance and Foreign Aid

Financial conditions have been somewhat depressed, reflecting the tight overall financial plight for the nation's economy. The total balance of loans made by banks and other financial houses to the fishery industry stood at 3,818,000,000 hwan as of the end of 1957 indicating no more than a 2.7 percent increase over the preceding year. The loan amount accounts for 1.9 percent of the total balance of loans furnished to the country's entire industries indicating a considerable decline from the preceding year's share of 2.9 percent. Of the loans, 419 million hwan was granted for facilities, and 3,399 million hwan as operating fund. Some portion of the loans was granted to small-scale fishermen at low rates of interests through fishermen's associations out of a 200 million hwan fund established by the government.

The economic assistance program of UNKRA and ICA to Korea allocated a total $13,238,500 during a five-year period from 1953 to 1957. Of the amount 64.3 percent or $8,516,700 was allocated for facilities, leaving 35.7 percent or $4,721,800 to be spent for consumer items. Actual importation of the economic aid goods during the five year period, however, was 61.7 percent of the fund allocated or $8,170,800. Whereas 98.1 percent of the fund allocated for importation of consumer items have been spent, only 41.5 percent of the amount earmarked for importation of facilities were paid out. However, construction and installation of facilities is being carried on with capital goods imported through the assistance program. They are presently 40 to 90 percent complete.

Problems of Korea's Fishery

Considerable as the progress of Korea's fishery may appear as in the case of all other industries of the country since the end of World War II, Korean fishery is not without its own evident weakness. The fundamental causes of inherent handicaps of the country's fishery is deep-rooted in the former colonial policy of Japan towards Korea, for under the Japanese rule Korean fishery had not been offered an opportunity to adapt itself to modern mechanization needs of the industry, merely following age-old traditional methods handed down generation after generation. Furthermore, the Japanese ruler did not see fit to develop Korea's industry as an integrated single unit in the service of the nation.

Such being the case, Korea's fishery requires positive support and government protection, probably more than for any other industry.

The first and foremost requirement for Korea's fishery is improved finance through adequate loans. Under the tight financial situation of the country prevailing since 1955 as a result of the anti-inflation policy adopted by the government, the industry received too nominal loans from banking institutions to reap any substantial benefits. Relieving the financial strain by facilitating loans, therefore, is considered essential at the present moment if marine exports are to be developed to increase the nation's foreign exchange earnings, and also to better the economic plight of small-scale fishermen, who have been burdened with private loans at usurious interest rates.

Secondly, modernization of technology as well as conversion from inshore to deep-sea fishing must be promoted. This may be achieved through employment of modern devices such as more extensive utilization of fish-school detectors, aerial detection of fishes, and installation of wireless communication facilities aboard fishing boats, in addition to invitation of foreign experts to Korea for the purpose of instructing Korean fishermen in up-to-date "know-how". Expansion and improvement of fish canning plants are also one of the most effective means to promote deep-sea fishing.

Thirdly, both the government and fishery industry are required to strive for expansion of overseas markets. Whereas the government is required to make serious attempts to create favorable export conditions through improved diplomatic relations—especially with Japan, the largest potential customer— the fishing industry itself is urged to enhance the quality of products and lower costs by sounder management.

Government Monopoly

Production of tobacco, salt and Korean ginseng is monopolized by the government, which derives a sizable portion of its budgetary incomes therefrom. The war inflicted severe damage on the monopoly industry, which, in the first place, remained on a relatively small-scale up to that time.

After the end of the war, the government placed prior emphasis upon rehabilitation of the tobacco industry, which has now become sufficiently developed to supply a large quantity of superior quality products comparable with foreign goods.

Production of salt was not sufficient until recent years, and more than 100,000 tons had to be imported each year until the outbreak of the war, which further reduced what limited facilities and salt fields there had been. So effective, however, has been the government's expansion program of the salt industry that presently its surplus product is seeking overseas markets in Southeast Asia.

The monopoly business contributed 21,200 million hwan to the 1958 government budgetary incomes, showing an increase of 3,200 million hwan over the preceding year.

Tobacco

Tobacco fields cover 21,061 *chongbo*, where 15,934,000 kg. of American breed, 181,000 kg. of Yongwol breed, and 10,323,000 kg. of traditional Korean breed were produced in 1957. The American breed was recently increased considerably in response to the popular smoking demand for superior quality to cut tobacco of traditional quality. Tobacco is grown by farmers who are obliged to sell the entire tobacco crop to the government whoss Monopoly Bureau retains exclusive processing and distribution rights on a wholesale level.

The leaf tobacco is processed into cigarettes and cut tobacco at the four plants of Seoul, Chungju, Chongju and Taegu, all equipped with modern cigarette manufacturing machinery, including filter-tip cigarettes finishing and cellophane wrapping facilities.

VIII INDUSTRIES

Table 11. Production of Tobacco
1949–1956   unit in kg.

	1949	1953	1954	1955	1956
Cigarettes	6,031	10,979	11,900	12,605	12,848
Cut tobacco	7,613	4,488	3,270	6,178	5,576

Table 12. Production of Tobacco (by Brand)
1957–1958   unit in 1,000 pcs.

Brands	1957	1958
Arirang, cigarettes	0	287,531
Sasum, cigarettes	240,031	315,612
Paekyang, cigarettes	1,289,520	1,545,050
Chindallae, cigarettes	2,435,961	1,897,709
Parangsae, cigarettes	6,487,248	7,372,632
Hwarang, cigarettes	2,489,424	2,291,712
Moran, cut tobacco	194,808	186,840
Pungnyoncho, tobacco	5,654,205	7,039,008
Aeyonyon, tobacco	469,050	391,740
Total	19,260,247	21,327,834

The proceeds from the sale of tobacco and cigarettes in 1958 amounted to 45,585,-000,000 hwan, a 5.2 billion hwan increase over the preceding year.

Salt

The government has carried out a five-year plan to increase production of salt to meet the entire salt requirements of the country by extending support to privately-owned salt fields. The fields were, thereby, increased to 1,953.5 *chongbo* (government-owned) and 9,367 *chongbo* (private), producing 367,125 tons for 1958. There are presently three large-scale salt field centers owned and operated by the Government Monopoly Bureau together with more than 900 small-scale salt fields under private ownership and management.

The salt sold to domestic consumers through the government is about 270,000 tons a year. Since sufficient quantities are produced within the country, the salt industry is presently faced with the problem of improving its quality.

Korean Ginseng

Production of Korean ginseng, which has long been favored throughout the east as an extremely effective tonic, received a crushing blow from the war, which brought down the demarcation line with north Korea below the 38th parallel line in the east coast including the town of Kaesong, long the center of ginseng cultivation. After numerous experiments with topsoils and weather conditions throughout south Korea, however, the government succeeded in locating places where cultivating of Korean ginseng was comparable with the former production center of the unique Korean tonic. Thus, various places were designated as ginseng fields, which now cover 1,365,000 *pyong*, from which 1,400 *kun* was produced in 1957. However, the production is no more than 4.8 percent of 1949, when Korean ginseng production was most prosperous. The place occupied by ginseng in the government monopoly business is small in comparison with others, for estimated net profits for 1959 are 50.43 billion hwan from tobacco, 12 billion hwan from salt, whereas only 0.15 hwan is expected from the ginseng monopoly. Because of bright export possibilities, especially for Far Eastern markets, the government is endeavoring to increase ginseng production.

IX TRANSPORTATION AND COMMUNICATIONS

Transportation

General Survey

As was the case in other countries of the world, stage-coaches, carts, and other primitive transportation means were long used in Korea until the arrival of the railroad, the automobile and other modern transports.

The first modern introduction was the street-car which came in 1898, followed by the railroad in 1899, the automobile in 1911, and aircraft in 1929. Ports were opened for trade and sea transportation with the arrival of foreign steamships for the first time in 1876.

Taking into consideration the rather short period of some 60 years since modern traffic first came in, it may safely be said that Korea has seen great strides. In fact, these modern means of transportation played the vanguard role in the introduction of Western civilization into Korea. With them came modern civilization, which has eventually brought a sudden change to all phases of Korean society.

During the 36 years between 1910 and 1945, transportation in Korea was controlled and developed by the Japanese government. From 1946 to 1950, it underwent new development with restoration of the national sovereignty. The war dealt an indescribable blow to the entire field of transportation and the postwar era has necessitated a new phase in rehabilitation and reconstruction.

Korea's railroad transportation is controlled and managed directly by the Ministry of Transportation, which in 1947 absorbed all privately-owned railroad systems.

Highway and air transportation is under administrative supervision of the Transportation Ministry, while sea transportation falls under the administrative jurisdiction of the Office of Marine Affairs, Ministry of Commerce and Industry.

Being state-owned, the nationwide railroad system has a unique characteristic compared with those of many foreign countries where railroad systems are privately managed. In both scale and efficiency, it is consigned to a most important role in the entire field of transportation.

The national railroad was overstrained during World War II, and suffered another trial in 1945 when the networks were cut by the thirty-eighth parallel. Despite the destruction of war, a reconstruction project, underway since 1953, has brought it up to a remarkably efficient level.

This surprising progress could not have been realized without U.S. aid which up to 1959 has totalled $208,698,400 and another 28,791,681,000 hwan in Korean currency. Some 29 percent of the total aid amount has been spent in reconstruction work, while the rest has been used for general maintenance, administration, and modernization.

The U. S. aid contribution has also been helpful in developing highway and air transportation. Various problems were solved under the aid programs, ranging from highway paving to gasoline imports. Technical assistance has been provided for the development of domestic flight services, while the international airport in Seoul has been rebuilt and modernized, bringing Korea into the framework of international air services. Korea is a member of the International Civil Aviation Organization (ICAO).

Railroad Transportation

Brief History

The first railroad in Korea was opened September 18, 1899, between Seoul and Inchon, covering a distance of some 33 kilometers. This was 74 years after the first line in the world was opened in England 1825, and 69 years after the first American rails in 1830. Both Korea's knowledge about the modern railroad and technical assistance in laying the first tracks here came from the United States.

In building the first Seoul-Inchon line, several foreign powers, including Russia, Japan, France and the United States, each bid hard to win the contract. Japan was the strongest competitor but there was a strong anti-Japanese sentiment among high officials of the Korean government at that time, and the contract, accordingly, was awarded to the American, James R. Morse, in March 1896.

Although Mr. Morse won the contract, he encountered financial difficulties soon after he started construction, and the Japanese, after all, took over the project following a series of negotiations with Mr. Morse. The Japanese completed the work in five months, a surprisingly short time. Mr. Morse, no doubt, had a good blueprint and foundation on which the Japanese built, but it is equally certain that the latter had long before planned a Seoul-to-Inchon line. As a matter of fact, their records show that as early as 1885, the Japanese had surveyed the land, climate and economic conditions of Korea, and in 1892, specifically made a preliminary survey for a Seoul-to-Pusan line as part of an eventual plan to link with the Trans-Siberian railroad.

In 1901, Japan obtained the right to build a railroad between Seoul and Pusan, and, with her victory in the Russo-Japanese War of 1904-05, won sole monopoly in building all major railroad lines in the country, including the link between Seoul and the northwestern city of Sinuiju on the Manchurian border. As if to make things certain, Korea was forcibly annexed to Japan in 1910. Thus Japan took over absolute control of railroad transportation in Korea.

It should be noted here that before Japan took over complete control, the Korean government had made a decision of great significance. It adopted the standard 1.435-meter gauge over a considerable amount of objections from the Japanese who were using the narrow gauge. Since the first railroad line was designed by an American, whose country used the standard, Japan had no other choice but to follow suit. It meant that the Japanese could bring little of their own railroad equipment to Korea.

For all that, Japanese railroad work was carried on steadily over the ensuing years. Pusan and Masan were linked in October 1905, Seoul and Sinuiju in April 1906, Seoul and Mokpo in January 1914, Seoul and Wonsan in August 1914. Thus, by 1915, the combined length of Korean railroad lines stretched 1,000 miles.

From 1917 to 1925, railroad management was entrusted to the South Manchurian Railroad Company.

In 1927, the Japanese government launched a 12-year plan for expansion of the network, and, by September 1928, several additional trunklines were opened while the government purchased some privately-owned lines and rebuilt some narrow gauge ones into the standard.

After the Manchurian Incident in 1932,

Japan expanded the Seoul-Pusan and Seoul-Sinuiju lines to double-tracks. With the outbreak of the Sino-Japanese hostilities in 1937, the Japanese put more emphasis in increasing railroad efficiency, establishing three local offices in Seoul, Pusan and Hamhung. They also built many railroad plants to further their war efforts. However, with the Pacific War and the unfavorable turn of the tides, less efforts were spared to improve the railroad system, and the latter part of the war saw things become quite overstrained.

Railroad facilities were almost worn out and there were scant replacements of essential parts and equipments despite the intensive demands of the all-out war effort. By the time of Hirohito's surrender in August 1945, Korea's entire railroad networks were literally in critical shape.

As shown above, the railroad system in Korea grew up with Japan's expansionism and militarism, serving to further her war efforts. The Allied victory freed Korea of Japanese rule but the land was divided and so was the railroad system.

Status of the Korean railroad in August 1945 was as follows.

Total length	6,362 kms
No. of locomotives	1,167
No. of coaches	2,027
No. of boxcars	15,352

Of the above, south Korea shared only:

Total length	2,642 kms
Locomotives	488
Coaches	1,280
Boxcars	8,424

As American occupation forces arrived in Korea to take over the administration in September 1945, the railroad system was placed under the administration of the Department of Transportation of the U.S. Military Government. Due to such sudden change in administration, coupled with Communist sabotage, management went through a short period of chaos. Only after several changes in organization and management, and with the utmost efforts of officials and employees alike, was the railroad restored to normalcy by the latter half of 1947.

With the establishment of the Republic of Korea government in 1948, the railroad entered a new era of increased efficiency and played a significant part in the government's industrialization projects. It was at a new peak of efficient management when the war broke out in June 1950.

Needless to say, rails were important to the warmakers and, for that very reason, suffered tremendous damages. It made significant contributions to Allied military transportation needs during the first months of the war when the U.N. Forces took the offensive in September 1950. With the advance into north Korea, railroad engineers followed the armies to take over railroad operations there. Railroad detachments were established in Pyongyang, Wonsan, Haeju and Sinuiju, all of which bore a substantial share of military transportation work until the withdrawal back south in January 1951.

Railroads at work

Despite the severe damages of war, the railroad system in south Korea returned to normal through a series of temporary repair and rehabilitation projects in June 1951. Since the armistice in July 1953, a fullscale rehabilitation program has been carried out and the railroad now bears only a few of the war scars.

Reviewing the damages and status of rehabilitation in terms of statistic figures, the railroad lost some 40 percent of its total facilities and equipments. Locomotives suffered a loss of 61 percent, coaches 64 percent, boxcars 57 percent, and diesel cars 86 percent.

While a total of 77,421,978 passengers and 6,421,452 tons of various goods were handled by the networks in 1949, the number of passengers in 1951 dropped sharply to only 24,071,469, although the total freight tonnage was increased to 13,022,714, owing to increased military supplies. The respective figures in 1953 were 46,096,645 and 12,238,066, in 1954 58,174,016 and 9,269,393, and in 1958 70,

100,566 and 12,093,758.

A significant change in the course of the postwar development is that conventional steam locomotives are gradually being replaced by diesel engines. There are now 69 such diesels operating in south Korea, with more slated to be imported from the United States.

As of now, some 16 billion hwan (32 million dollars) is annually saved by using these diesel engines which are more powerful and useful than steam.

Another significant point to be noted is that the national railroad has started to use domestic anthracite instead of imported coal for the remaining steam locomotives since early 1959.

Hitherto, some 20 million dollars in foreign exchange have been spent annually for imports of foreign coal for steam locomotives.

At present, some 5.8 million passengers and one million tons of goods are handled monthly on the average, with a daily net income of some 100 million hwan (200,000 dollars).

Following are figures for 1958 and the first six months of 1959:

		net income hwan
1958	70,100,566 (passengers)	23,100,665,423
1958	12,093,785 (tons)	12,545,088,661
1959 (Jan.–June)	34,485,613 (passengers)	12,553,499,195
1959	6,756,150 (tons)	6,930,854,075

Modernization of Facilities

In addition to the replacement of conventional steam engines with diesel as briefly mentioned above, the replacement of old coaches with new is another major project in the overall modernization program of the railroad.

Although both locomotives and freight cars attained a state of 100 percent recovery from war damages, only some 60 percent have been restored in the case of coaches.

In view of the fact that the shortage of coaches now presents the most serious single problem to the development of a modern railroad system in Korea, the Transportation Ministry started an extensive rehabilitation project in 1959. It plans to rebuild 100 coaches and import 300 new ones during 1959. It also plans to manufacture a total of 10 coaches in domestic plants, with two of them already in operation since August. Out of 1,168 coaches now in use, over 300 coaches are makeshift ones used since the war. The shortage of coaches is expected to be solved soon if the Ministry's rehabilitation plans work out.

As for freight cars, there are now 9,889 in operation, an increase of 1,465 over August 1945. Some 600 to 700 cars are being remodeled or repaired every month. Thus there is no problem of shortage so far as the number of freight cars is concerned.

However, as the nation's industry grows and there will soon be more demand for railroad freight, the Ministry is planning to import some 100 modern freight cars, and, at the same time, convert some 300 wooden box-cars to steel.

Augmentation of long-used railroad tracks is also under way in 1959 with 350,000 dollars in American aid and 1,280,000,000 hwan in Korean currency.

In addition, another program to improve and modernize railroad safety facilities, railroad plants and communications facilities was carried out in 1959 with a total budget of 620 million hwan.

Under the program, obsolete safety facilities and communications instruments are being replaced with modern ones, while two diesel engine factories are being built in Pusan and Taejon. A modern teletype network is being expanded to cover the entire railroad system.

Construction Project

Since the Republic of Korea government was established in August 1948, a total 243 kilometers of new lines have been constructed. Most were laid where industrial development was to be expected. In general, they had to be opened despite unfavorable terrain for rails. These included the 86.4 km-long Yongju to Choram line in Kyongsang Pukto, connecting the central part of Korea with the industrial Samchok-Mukho area on the eastern coast across the 680-meter high Taebaek ranges, the 60.7-km long Chechon-Hambaek line which links central Korea with the Hambaek mining area and the Yongwol thermal power plant; and the Chomchon-Unsong line (22.5 kms.) in Kyongsang Pukto, which is essential for the development of the neighborhood Mungyong coal mining area. The construction of these three major industrialization lines was temporarily interrupted by the war, but all have been completed since. The Yongju-Choram line was opened in December 1955, the Chechon-Hambaek in March 1957, and the Chomchon-Unsong in 1957.

Completion of these lines marked a significant achievement for the government in that all three run across the steep Taebaek mountains from central Korea to eastern areas that are rich in mineral resources.

The construction of the Yongju-Choram line cost 6,239,011,912 hwan in Korean currency and $4,184,180 in American aid money, and consumed a total 4,833,291 mandays; the Hambaek Line 2,510,400,233 hwan and $2,188,000 in money, 2,256,140 mandays; the Mungyong 3,020,578 hwan and 34,672 mandays.

In addition to these, the 10.5-km long Sachon-Kaeyang line in Kyongsang Namdo was opened in May 1953 and the 11.8-km. Kunsan-Okku of Cholla Pukto in February 1953. These two lines were constructed during the war in view of their importance in transportation of military supplies.

Another important railroad line was the one between Chungju and Pongyang in Chungchong Pukto for a distance of 35.2 kms, construction on which began in November 1955 and was completed in December 1958. The line was built for the Chungju fertilizer plant, and is another major line linking central Korea with the east.

Besides these, there were four more minor lines built in recent years.

These ten new lines built since 1948 totalled 243.3 kilometers in length, cost 14,389,586,348 hwan and 8,762,080 dollars in foreign exchange, and consumed 9,540,883 mandays.

There are several new construction projects now under consideration, including the line between Nunggok and Uijongbu, northeast of Seoul, for a distance of 28.6 kilometers, construction on which will be initiated before the end of this year.

Present Status of Korean Railroad
Total length of track   4,575.2 kilometers
Total length of passenger lines
                           2,977.6 kilometers
No. of railroad stations   473
No. of locomotives (diesel)   69
                 (steam)   465
No. of coaches   1,168
No. of freight cars   9,889
No. of employees   27,171
Average volume of transportation per month
            (passengers) 5,800,000 men
             (goods)   1,000,000 tons
Average no. of trains running daily   500
Average daily net income   1,000,000 hwan

Highway Transportation

Automobiles were introduced to Korea for the first time in 1911 when two cars were imported—one for royal use and the other for the government. This was followed by the initiation of taxi service in April 1912, bus in 1913, and freight by truck in 1926.

The highway transportation business in Korea since saw rapid growth in a short period, and the number of bus companies reached 539 (as of 1931), of taxi 261 (as of 1933) and of trucking 671 (in 1936). These Korean-owned passenger and freight service companies were largely reduced or taken over by the Japanese during the Pacific War, and very few were operating when the war ended in August 1945.

The Liberation brought back prosperity and many wealthy Korean businessmen engaged in the services. The number of cars prior to the outbreak of the war in June 1950 was: 1,328 buses, 1,573 taxis, and 3,120 trucks,—total, 6,021.

The combined number of these and other privately-owned or non-commercial cars was 16,351 in 1950, but it was roughly estimated that about 75 percent of these cars were either lost or destroyed during the war. More specifically, 67 percent of the buses, 77 percent of taxis and 76 percent of trucks suffered damages. With the shooting war over, the number of cars started increasing again, reaching a total of 28,372 in December 1958. The figure included both commercial and private cars as well as vehicles for government use (excluding the military). Considering the number of cars lost or destroyed by the war, the increase over a short period of five years was too sharp to be caught up by the improvement of national and local highways that had also suffered a tremendous amount of damages during the war. In addition, there was the problem of fuel, Korea being a country which solely depends upon imported petroleum products for automobile fuel. Having taken several government measures to hold down, however slightly, the sharp upward trend in the number of cars running in south Korea, officials now see a rather stabilized situation. According to the latest government figures available, the number of automobiles as of May 1959 was 29,172. The breakdown: private cars 6,162, government vehicles 3,983, vehicles for commercial purposes 19,027, including 3,812 buses, 4909 taxis and 10,306 trucks.

The Ministry of Transportation is now considering a series of measures which the Ministry hopes will improve the overall operation of highway transportation means. One of the measures under consideration is to encourage the use of diesel to replace conventional gasoline engines. It is unofficially estimated that some 500,000 drums of gasoline, all imported, are annually consumed by vehicles running in south Korea. If diesel engines take the place of gasoline engines in any substantial quantity, it will mean the saving of quite a large amount of the foreign exchange south Korea badly needs to rehabilitate her general economy.

The heavy use of major highways in transportation of military supplies during the war, coupled with other damages incidental to a modern war, brought the highway networks throughout the country to a state of near critical condition right after the shooting war ended. To make matters worse, a total of 1,453 highway bridges were lost or damaged.

In the years following the armistice, joint projects by the Korean government and the U.S. aid mission here were steadily launched to improve the highway conditions. Main military supply routes, of course, were given priority. Many new roads were built. Many others are being built or expanded. In addition, road pavement projects have been carried out throughout the country with a primary emphasis on highways linking major cities.

Meanwhile, street-cars are playing another important role in transportation of passengers in the two major cities of Seoul and Pusan as well as in Hampyong. With American aid, south Korea imported 53 street-cars in 1956 and another 15 in 1957 to make up for the loss during the war. At present, a total of 207 street-cars are running in Seoul, 79 in Pusan, and 4 in Hampyong. They are handling some 377,000 passengers a day in average.

Sea Transportation

Korean ports were first opened to international trade and navigation in 1876. Japanese ships immediately became the dominating foreign ships, and, during the 36 years of colonization, Japan virtually monopolized sea transportation enterprises in Korea.

When Japan took over Korea in 1910, Korea possessed only 40 steamships with 7,815 tons, and 33 sailboats with 1,090 tons, for a total of 73 ships with 8,905 tons.

The figures rose as follows in 1938.

Steamships	681	100,293 tons
Sailboats	1,096	143,008 tons
Total	1,777	243,301 tons

When the Pacific War ended in August 1945, Korea possessed a fleet of various vessels with a total of 230,000 tons. During that war, a considerable number of ships owned by Koreans were confiscated by the Tokyo government for the war effort. Many of these were not returned even after the war.

To make up for the shortage of ships in south Korea, the Ministry of Transportation, through a series of negotiations with an American aid mission here, obtained a total of 40 ships in April 1948 as part of the American aid program to Korea. These included 12 LST's and 11 FS-type ships among others.

The number of ships as of June 1949 stood as follows:

Passenger boats	72	3,356 tons
Freight boats	3,767	97,061 ,,
Fishing boats	3,175	42,578 ,,
Barges	359	32,753 ,,
Total	7,373	175,748 ,,

During the first year of the war in June 1950, south Korea lost 1,874 ships of various types with a total 53,010 tonnage. However, there were some 400 north Korean boats fleeing into south Korean waters, as a result of which, the total numbers of bottoms and tonnages showed a slight increase respectively over the figures for 1949. The breakdown showed:

Passengers boats	133	9,493 tons
Freight boats	3,136	101,990 ,,
Fishing boats	5,051	52,953 ,,
Barges	248	19,475 ,,
Total	8,568	183,911 ,,

The number of ships in south Korea continued to increase even during the war years, and, in 1952, there were 9,828 ships with a total 224,475 tons, while the number increased to 10,011 with 236,528 tons in 1953.

As of the end of 1958, the total tonnage of south Korean ships jumped to 325,742, or almost double compared with that of 1949, although the number of ships showed only a slight increase. The breakdown:

Passenger boats	188	10,493 tons
Freight boats	2,028	152,632 ,,
Fishing boats	6,767	89,029 ,,
Barges	573	53,131 ,,
Others	370	20,457 ,,
Total	9,926	325,742 ,,

Of the total number of ships, 8,996, or 91 percent, were less than 100 tons, only 46 ships were 500 tons or more.

Included in the number of ships as of 1958 were 322 ships with 119,575 tons, that had been imported through American aid and other programs. They were broken down to:

Freighters	79	102,412 tons
Fishing boats	199	8,699 ,,
Passenger boats	3	177 ,,
Tug boats	5	174 ,,
Barges	29	2,448 ,,
Tankers	5	5,589 ,,
Others	2	76 ,,

During 1958, Korean passenger boats handled a total of 3,570,000 people while major ports handled 4,318,000 tons of exports and 1,184,000 tons of imports.

Korea's shipbuilding industry was a very limited one under the Japanese rule. The first dock which could accommodate a 10,000-ton ship was built in Pusan in 1938. There were some 70 shipbuilding plants towards the end of the Pacific War, but most of these plants were engaged in repairing of ships rather than building. In 1944 these plants built a total of 18,000 tons of ships, but only 7,800 tons of ships were built in 1945.

Shipbuilding in south Korea continued to be slow during the first few years of the nation's independence, and 1946 saw only 25 ships of over 50-ton capacity built. However, the industry started to return to normalcy as other industries and, in 1947, a total of 40 ships of over 50 tons were newly built, with a total tonnage of 17,000.

The upward trend continued until the war broke out in June 1950, and like other industries, south Korea's shipbuilding industry suffered extensive damage. Thus, the Taehan Shipbuilding Corporation, the largest in south Korea, and other plants built only 526 tons of ships in 1951 and 729 tons in 1954. But the figure jumped to 2,096 in 1955 as the government launched a rehabilitation program with aid from the United States and the U.N. Korean Reconstruction Agency (UNKRA). In 1956, a total of 4,105 tons of new ships were built under the aid programs, 3,809 tons in 1957, and 4,590 tons in 1958.

A five-year program is currently underway, and in 1959, a total of 5,597 tons are to be either newly built or remodeled to replace older passenger boats and freighters.

Air Transportation

Air transportation service was first introduced to Korea in April 1929, when a Japanese airline company started a scheduled flight service between Japan and Manchuria by way of Korea.

In 1936, Sin Yonguk, now president of the Korean National Airlines (KNA), established the New Air Services Company to initiate domestic flight services.

In November 1948, Mr. Sin founded the KNA to start regular flight services between Seoul and Pusan, Kwangju and Kangnung, with three "Stimson" airplanes.

Shortly before the outbreak of the war, the Ministry of Transportation launched an aviation development program, under which airports in eight major south Korean cities would be expanded or newly built with modern air transportation facilities. This was to enable the nation to catch up with the rapidly advancing aviation field of the world. However, the war completely frustrated the program just initiated by the Ministry. In addition, the war brought tremendous damages to existing aviation facilities in south Korea.

With the armistice, KNA soon resumed its regular flight services between major cities, while initiating an international flight service between Seoul and Hong Kong. For domestic services, KNA now has regular flights between Seoul and Pusan, Cheju Island, Kwangju, and Kangnung. Its Hong Kong service has been suspended since August 1959 as south Korea failed to extend the air service agreement with the Hong Kong government.

At present, therefore, KNA planes fly to Taipei, where the planes are connected with CPA (Cathay Pacific Airways) flights to Hong Kong. KNA's service with Taipei was started in September 1959 after its Hong Kong service was suspended indefinitely. In addition to its Taipei service, KNA has another international flight service, but this is not scheduled regularly.

Earlier in 1959, KNA obtained a permit from the United States government for a flight service into the U.S.A. Starting September, it began a twice-a-month non-scheduled flight service between Seoul and Seattle.

Northwest Airlines and Civil Air Transport are two foreign airlines which have regular flight services with Seoul. NWA has now four flights a week between Tokyo and Seoul, while CAT flies thrice on the same route.

Seoul's Kimpo International Airport is now undergoing an extensive expansion program, completion of which means a new comprehensive airport office building and improved facilities for flight safety.

South Korea is a member of the International Civil Aviation Organization (ICAO), and is trying to modernize airport and aviation facilities to catch up with international standards.

Communications

Telecommunication Service
Early Period

Telegraphy. The first telegraph service in Korea was inaugurated in August 1885 between Seoul and Inchon. One month later, in September, the Seoul-Pyongyang service and, in October, the Pyongyang-Uiju services were opened. In June 1888, the southern circuit between Seoul and Pusan was opened, and in June 1891, the northern circuit between Seoul and Wonsan by way of Chunchon was initiated. Thus, the beginnings of telecommunications service were laid and extended into a nationwide network within the space of a few years.

Telescriptors made in the United States were used in this early period, and the Morse code employed in communicating messages through hand-operated transmitters. Government offices were major customers of the service, but private customers gradually increased, particularly after the western circuit between Seoul and Uiju via Pyongyang was opened. International communications service became possible by linking the western and southern circuits with Japan and China.

Telephone. In 1896, a telephone switchboard was installed in the royal court exclusively for use among various government offices. In March 1902, telephone service for government use was opened between Seoul and Inchon, and a telephone exchange for the public between Seoul and Inchon followed suit in June of that year. Similar services were opened between in Pusan and Yongdungpo in March. Gradually, they were spread throughout all major cities. Swedish-made magneto-type telephone sets were used during this period. Customers were mostly government offices and major business firms, with only 65 circuits available for general use.

Telecommunications Service under Japanese Rule

The Japanese government took over the telecommunication system in Korea in 1910 when Japan annexed Korea. The Japanese expanded, improved and modernized the communications service, but their primary objective in all this was to lay the seeds of imperialism in Korea and the Asian mainland. The idea of public service for which the modern system of communication was intended was largely ignored under Japanese management.

Telecommunications Service after Liberation

The Korean government took over the telecommunications facilities after the Liberation. The demands of the Pacific War had so overstrained these facilities that the government could do little more than merely keep them in working order up to the outbreak of the Korean War in June 1950. Before the war, there were, in Seoul and Pusan combined, 12,000 telephone subscribers of automatic telephone systems with 16,000 terminals, and 27,600 suscribers for hand-operated systems with a total of 56,300 circuits. In addition, there were 157 telegraphic and 450 telephone circuits to be used for telegraphic and long-distance telephone services.

Over 80 percent of these communications facilities were damaged during the war, and nationwide services paralyzed with only a limited number of circuits utilized for emergency purposes.

Since 1952, an extensive rehabilitation program has been carried out with funds provided by the government and American aid programs. By the end of 1957, the communications facilities were restored to the prewar level, and, by June of 1959, telephone subscribers numbered 66,000—an increase of 80 percent from the prewar total. At the same time, automatic telephone facilities were doubled, and common battery subscriber service facilities were increased by 2.5 times. The number of telephone-telegraphic circuits was almost doubled to 1,168; about 19 percent is carrier equipment.

Telegraphic service has been greatly improved with the adoption of wire teletype facilities between major cities, and wireless facilities have been improved offering better services between isolated islands, ship-to-shore services and weather forecast networks.

As to international communications services, Korea has direct telephone and telegraphic circuits with the United States, Hong Kong,

Kimpo Air Port
An exterior view of the Terminal Building of Kimpo Air Port (The door to Seoul).

← Youido Air Base, Seoul City

Kangnung Air Base →
In an east coastal town.

← A interior view of the Terminal Building of Kimpo Air Port.

↑ A Freighter Anchoring in the Harbor at Pusan

↑ A ferry steamer between Cheju Island and the mainland.

Dock-Yard
↓ Taehan Shipbuilding Corporation.

← Steam Locomotive and Passenger Cars

→ A Coasting Vessel

↓ A Merchant Ship (The Namhae-ho)

↑ Seoul Railway Station
   The most crowded rail-road terminal in all Korea.

↓ A Special Express with Diesel Locomotive

← **Revolving Bridge over Yalu River**
A 944-meter long bridge across the Yalu between the borders of Korea and Manchuria.

Kupo Bridge
The longest (1,060 m) bridge in Korea over Naktong River.
↓

Taedong Bridge
Across Taedong River in Pyongyang (616m).
↓

Water Pipe Bridge over Taedong River, Pyongyang
↓

Railway Bridges over Han River, Seoul

Although the bridges were damaged vitally during the Korean War, they were repaired as shown in this picture.

Han Bridge

A 840-meter long bridge across Han River. Seriously damaged during the war, it was completely restored in 1958.

↑ Rush Hour in Seoul

The Highway Connecting Seoul and Pusan (The Kunpo Junction) →

↓ Sightseeing Buses

Postage Stamps of Korea
(From Left to Right)

1st Line
1. Regular stamp designed Taeguk
   Issued on Dec. 4, 1884
2. Regular stamp designed Korean flag and plum flowers
   Issued on Mar. 15, 1901
3. Regular stamp designed Taeguk and plum flowers
   Issued on Jul. 22, 1895
4. Emperor Kojong's 40th anniversary of coronation commemorative stamp
   Issued on Oct. 21, 1902

2nd Line
1. Regular stamp designed falcon holding globe and rapier
   Issued on Jun. 1, 1903
2. General election commemorative stamp
   Issued on May 10, 1948
3. 10th anniversary of the formation of United Nations commemorative stamp
   Issued on Oct. 24, 1955
4. 50th anniversary of the foundation of Rotary International commemorative stamp
   Issued on Feb. 23, 1955

3rd Line
1. Liberation of Korea commemorative stamp
   Issued on May 1, 1946
2. Regular stamp designed Mapae (A copper medal used for ancient mailing delivery)
   Issued on Apr. 1, 1951
3. Regular stamp designed ginseng plant
   Issued on Jul. 1, 1949
4. Regular stamp designed Tokto Island
   Issued on Sep. 15, 1954

4th Line
1. Inauguration of second president commemorative stamp
   Issued on Sep. 10, 1952
2. Special stamp for X-mas and New Year designed gala dressed children
   Issued on Dec. 11, 1958
3. Participation of 14th Olympic Games commemorative stamp
   Issued on Jun. 1, 1948

5th Line
1. Regular stamp designed a portrait of King Sejong
   Issued on Jun. 15, 1957
2. 10th anniversary of the formation of Republic of Korea commemorative stamp
   Issued on Aug. 15, 1958
3. Regular stamp designed Chomsongdae (An observatory built in Silla dynasty)
   Issued on Jan. 21, 1957

6th Line
1. Red Cross fund stamp designed field hospital
   Issued on Aug. 1, 1953
2. Postal Day commemorative stamp
   Issued on Dec. 4, 1956
3. 50th anniversary of foundation of Boy Scout commemorative stamp
   Issued on Feb. 27, 1957

↑ A Panoramic View of the Central Post Office, Seoul
Completely destroyed during the Korean War, rebuilt since then.

↑ Parcel section of the Central Post Office.

↓ An interior view of a District Post Office (Kwanghwamun Post Office in Seoul).

↑ Bureau of International Telegraph and Telephone.

↓ An interior view of the Central Post Office.

↓ A tower of aerial wires for telegraph

↑ Telegraphic control room

→ A tele-typewriter in a news service

↓ An interior view of the Bureau of Telegraph, Ministry of Communications.

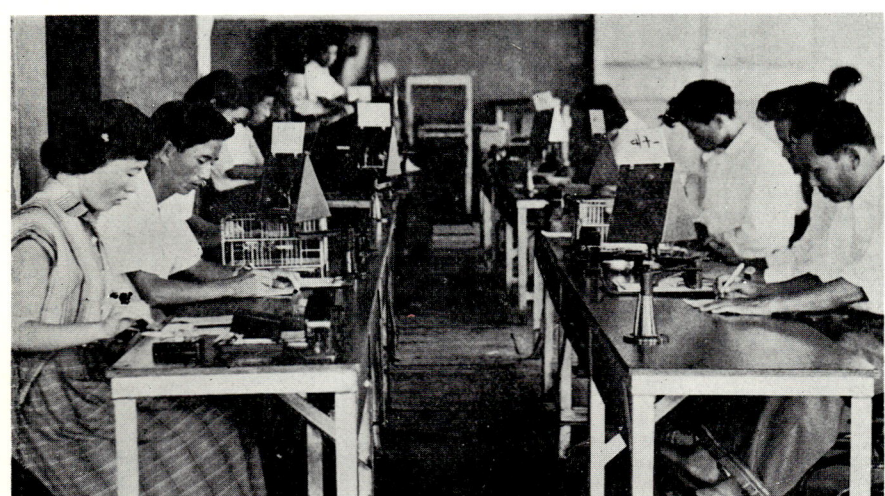

Tokyo, Manila and Taipei, while many other foreign countries can also be connected through relay systems.

Compared with the prewar days, overseas telegraphic service has been increased by four times, and the telephone by 10. In April 1958, Radiophoto circuits were installed between Seoul, Tokyo and San Francisco. An agreement has been signed for a $3,500,000 loan from the Development Loan Fund (DLF) to modernize telephone facilities in south Korea, as a result of which, the number of telephone subscribers is expected to be increased to about 120,000 by the end of 1960 when automatic phone service will have been expanded in major cities.

Present Status

Characteristics of Korea's Telecommunication Service. In some countries of the world, telecommunication service is state-owned, while in others it is managed by private firms.

In Korea, the government has been controlling the service since it was first introduced here. This is so because it is easier and simpler under state management to standardize facilities, keep the rates down, and maintain the confidences that are involved in using the service.

Private communications systems are allowed under license for the exclusive purposes of the military, security, traffic and other specialized organizations and enterprises.

Telegraphy. Some 2,800,000 telegrams are handled annually by 664 telegraph offices scattered throughout the country. Messages are delivered within one hour in most cases.

Teletype writer facilities are used for services between major cities, while small towns and villages still depend upon wire or telephone communication systems. Teletype writer facilities are gradually being expanded, and teletypewriter exchanges are expected to be installed in 1960.

Facsimile and radiophoto services are also in use among major cities, while a mobile telegraph service is occasionally made available for isolated villages on special occasions. Among the various kinds of telegraphic service are the railroad telegrams for train passengers, message service for soldiers, low rate letter telegrams for isolated areas, and special greetings and condolence messages. Yet, a comparatively small number of people utilize these services in Korea. In average, 14 telegrams per 100 Koreans are sent annually.

Telephone. A total of 332 telephone offices serve 66,000 subscribers throughout the country. The number of subscribers is rapidly increasing in the cities.

The magneto, common battery and automatic systems are all in use in Korea, but the latter two systems are becoming more widely used.

As of June 1959, the breakdown of telephone facilities follows:

Magneto system	36,476 circuits	42%
Common battery	17,600 „	21%
Automatic system	32,200 „	37%
Total	86,276 „	

By the end of 1960, there will be 154,100 circuits available to serve 120,000 subscribers, with 85,100 circuits in the automatic system, 24,000 circuits in the common battery, and 45,000 circuits in the magneto.

The number of toll calls have increased by 230% to 443,857 a month in 1959 compared with 1949, and long-distance service is being expedited with the adoption of the intermediate toll dial among major cities.

Telephone facilities in Korea need a great deal of improvement to rank with other countries. Plans are underway to install the automatic system in any district with over 1,500 subscribers. Common battery or community dial system will be used in smaller areas.

Long Distance Circuit Network. There are 228 circuits for long distance telegraph service, and 938 circuits for long distance telephone service. About 35 percent of the total are leased to the military, police, and other enterprises for their exclusive use. There are 70 circuits in an underground cable between Seoul and Pusan. These and other major cities are further linked by open wire carrier circuits with a number of relay stations. When the radio system to be installed between Seoul and Pusan, Mokpo and Cheju, and Pusan and Kwangju is completed, long distance calls will also be made possible by using roundabout circuits even if any direct circuit is out of operation.

There is an increasing tendency for banks and other major enterprises to lease long-distance circuits for exclusive use of private teletype services. In this connection, the Ministry of Communications is currently planning to install the telex system to improve the service.

Wireless Service. The wireless facilities were originally installed for communication between the mainland and off-shore islands. Fisheries were the major customers. However, the facilities were largely expanded during and after the war to be used for communication among mainland points, as cable circuits suffered extensive damages. There are now 30 wireless stations with 36 radio circuits. Major news agencies and weather stations have their own nationwide radio networks for dissemination of news and weather forecasts. In addition, there are six coastal wireless stations for communication with ocean-going vessels. Stations in Pusan and Mokpo, also, have short-wave services.

International Communication. South Korea maintains six direct cable circuits for international communication—one each with Tokyo, San Francisco, Hong Kong, Taipei, Manila and west Germany. Communication is possible with any country of the world except Communist countries. Eight languages— Korean, English, French, Chinese, Japanese, German, Italian and Turkish—are authorized for cable use by the Korean International Telecommunications (KIT) in Seoul, its Pusan branch, and major post offices handling international communications.

As to the international telephone service, there are seven circuits—two with Tokyo, and one each with San Francisco, Hong Kong, Taipei, Manila and Singapore. Calls are also possible with 53 different foreign countries through relay stations. With the installation of Vodas, general telephone subscribers can call foreign points directly from their homes or offices. With the installation of SSB (Single Side Band) system now complete, telephone service between Korea and the United States, Japan and European countries has been greatly improved and expanded, while international calls will be possible from major cities throughout the country.

Meanwhile, radiophoto service has already been opened with 39 major countries of the world through the two circuits with San Francisco and Tokyo.

Mail Service

Brief History

Korea's first mail service started in 487, when the government established postal stations to handle government communication. The stations were established to accommodate government couriers and other officials travelling on official business. The system eventually became the basis for modern postal service.

The Koryo dynasty in its early days classified postal routes into three divisions according to their importance, and established post offices at each postal station along these routes. These offices were again sub-divided into six categories, and were assigned soldiers to operate in the postal service. First class posts were given 75 men, second 63, third 45, fourth 30, fifth 12, and sixth 7.

For military courier service, bells were used to signify the degree of importance, three bells representing messages of a most urgent nature, two bells less urgent, and one for ordinary tidings.

In 983, post office chiefs were appointed to take charge of each station, and in 1274, a courier system, known as the "Mapae" (literally horse medal) was first instituted. "Mapae" is a round, bronze medal indicating the official grade of the bearer with a number designating how many horses were to be supplied for his journey.

In 1458, the government further recognized the importance of postal service and strengthened the organization, increasing the number of postal stations to 583. These were divided into 40 zones with a supervisor for each.

In 1597, a courier service network was established patterned after that of the Ming dynasty in China to handle not only military messages but general government communications.

There were two types of courier service— one on horseback, the other on foot. For the former, postal stations were set up at every 10-kilometer point, with one supervisor, five soldiers and five horses, while for the latter system, stations were established at every 12-kilometer point, with one supervisor, and two soldiers.

After a series of such developments, Korea's first modern postal system was introduced in March 1884 with the establishment of the General Office of Postal Administration by King Kojong. Hong Yongsik, who urged the adoption of a modern postal system after returning from an inspection trip to Japan and the United States, was appointed director. But the new system was abolished only seven months later by the outbreak of the *Kapsin* Revolt and revived in June 1895, some 11 years later. America's postal system was largely patterned at the counsel of Clarence Greyhouse, an American engineer employed by the government. Actual postal business was initiated on November 25 of that year in Seoul, Chungju, Andong, Taegu and Tongnae, and Japanese technicians were employed to assist.

On November 14, 1897, a French expert, M. O. E. Clemencet, was newly hired to replace Japanese technicians as the postal system was further enlarged. On January 1, 1900, Korea was admitted to the Universal Postal Union (UPU) and, on March 23, an Office of Communications was established to handle postal service.

The Japanese, meanwhile, started their own postal service in Korea to serve Japanese residents in Korea. Finally, on April 1, 1905, Japan signed an agreement under which she took over postal and communications services in Korea. Needless to say, she continued to control them throughout her 40-year domination of Korea.

With liberation from Japanese rule in August 1945, Korea again took over the postal service system, and Korean delegates attended both the 13th UPU conference held in Brussel from May 14 to June 30, 1953, and the 14th UPU meeting in Ottawa August 1957.

Present Status

There are 648 post offices and 10 sub-offices scattered throughout the country, with a total of 6,671 employees, including 3,486 mailmen. The number of mail boxes totals 4,557, stamps are sold at 4,306 stands.

During 1958, post offices handled 105,974,794 letters of ordinary mail, 4,912,131 letters registered mail, and 603,259 parcels. The figures included 328,533 sea mail letters, 1,615,010 air mail, 6,392 sea parcels, and 14,685 air parcels to and from foreign countries. In other words, the Korean wrote about five letters a year on the average.

In addition to ordinary mail and postal services, the post offices now handle registered mail, delivery and content certified mail, special delivery mail and special greetings. Free postal service is given to military personnel and candidates for office during election time.

Korea now exchanges ordinary postal services with 88 countries outside the "Iron Curtain," and air mail with 70. For the international post, Pusan, the major port, sends out sea mail three or four times a month, and receives seven to ten monthly incoming deliveries.

Outgoing air mail leaves for the United States, Japan, Hawaii, Canada and Latin American countries via Northwest Airlines on Mondays, Wednesdays and Fridays, while deliveries from these countries arrive on the same days plus Saturdays. For China, Japan, Hawaii, Hong Kong, Europe and other areas, air mail leaves and arrives via CAT on Tuesdays, Thursdays and Saturdays.

In the past, air mail to European countries was sent by way of Hong Kong, but nowadays a new relay system has been introduced, whereby they are sent aboard SAS planes from Tokyo over the northern route to Copenhagen which then relays to each point in Europe. The new system has reduced the time required for the European service by some 17 hours, while lowering postal rates, at the same time.

In domestic postal service, the combined length of postal routes are: railroad, 56 districts—11,405 kilometers; highway, 428 districts—18,973 kilometers; seaway, 46 districts—2,302 kilometers; on foot, 86 districts—1,243 kilometers; and air routes, 6 districts—870 kilometers.

A total of 269 kinds of postal stamps have been issued since August 1945.

Conclusion

Generally speaking, Korean transportation and communications may be said to be well on the road to full modernization. Everything is in better order than we can reasonably expect in an overcrowded country marked by vivid contrasts in its means of transportation and visited by the holocaust of war that took a heavy toll of communications equipment. The modern signs are obvious, in the cities, at least, from the stream of traffic. At the same time, hordes of rack-carriers may still be found at railway-stations as a sharp reminder of an overwhelming state of under-development. However seemingly rapid the pace of reconstruction, it should be remembered that these are complex fields demanding long-range plans to be really serviceable to the people. As Kyung Cho Chung points out in "Korea Tomorrow":

"Educational and promotional work, instituted at all levels, would demonstrate to the people the pivotal importance of improved public services, such as transportation, communication, fast postal service, better roads, farm-to-market and arterial highways, increased potable water supplies, city planning, adequate sewage systems, and the maintenance of flood-control installations."

X SOCIAL PROBLEMS

General View

Study in Contrasts

Social problems in Korea are conspicuously different from those of advanced countries in scope, in nature and in the course of development. The main reasons are: one, lack of sufficient premises for the prerequisites that created the modern social problems of the advanced countries under the capitalistic system, and two: the Communist war that caused such wild fluctuations in the basic livelihood of the people. Korean problems have emerged in the absence of progress of a capitalistic economy; in other words, they are born out of the underdeveloped economic and social structures of the country.

The social problems of the advanced countries are economic in nature for they arise out of the relationship of conflicting economic interests that have collectively developed the civic body of society. More specifically, they are posed by advanced capitalistic systems threatening in whole the livelihood of the gainfully employed and the security of the general public. It can be said that the social problems of advanced states are the inevitable products of the development of capitalistic economic society.

On the contrary, Korea's industrial and social structures are a typical example of economic backwardness. A predominantly agricultural land, 78 percent of the labor population are concentrated on the farms and only 3 or 4 percent in the secondary industry. This means that even if there is the possibility of developing the same kind of social problems, to be found in advanced nations, their importance and influences can not be so great as to affect the whole social life to any serious extent because they would involve only the 2-4 percent of the labor population. The nature of the disputes arising out of modern labor-management relations contrast sharply with those of the West.

Thus, although postwar Korea has moved toward the idea of a civic modern society in a legal sense, various feudal elements still remain in the actual social structure to affect "free" labor relations and constitute obstacles to the economic development projects that have recently been stepped up. Social problems in Korea are badly entangled in complicated vines that are difficult to sort out clearly enough to enable progress. The feudal economic and social structures run against abstract modern ideas as provided for under laws and ordinances; they do not fuse into one. This fact, added to the defective combination of excessive labor power and too poor means of production create the need of urgent solutions to difficult problems.

The unique phenomenon of Korean social problems, one hardly to be found in advanced countries and probably to be described as a characteristic of Korea alone, is this;

inasmuch as these problems do not arise from matters of conflicting relations among the social ranks, they do not assume great gravity. According to a survey made by the Ministry of Public Health and Social Affairs at the end of 1957, there were altogether about 8,400 firms with a usual staff of five employes or a combined total of 248,000. This means that only approximately 1/200 of a labor population of 13,000,000 are working on the second industry. This is half the announced total of 480,000 or 1/15 the number of the potential jobless estimated by the Office of the Economic Coordinator, United Nations Command (OEC UNC), at 3,600,000 and including all unemployed and potential unemployed of farms, middle and small business firms. Thus, the number of industrial workers is very small in proportion to the whole and the problem of unemployment in industry of very minor importance compared to the problems of potential unemployment on the farms and in middle and small business firms. What is more, skilled workers are very few in number and their labor cannot be regarded as constituting a social rank because of their lack of labor consciousness and capacity for unity.

Certainly, the conflicting interests arising from the economic relations of Korean social ranks cannot be construed as societywide problems.

The Urgent Problems

Taking all these factors into consideration, we might well say that the most urgent social problems are unemployment (including potential unemployment), vocational orientation and job openings. The dilemma is the impossibility of maintaining normal employment conditions because management scales are too small. As mentioned above, the total number of firms usually employing more than five is 8,400 for a combined total of 240,000 employes, an average of 35 or 36 per firm.

Furthermore, it is only in a very small number of state-owned industries, public enterprises or semi-public enterprises that big management and trade unions representing thousands of workers have concluded agreements by which wage scales as well as working conditions are set and employment contracts implemented. Thus employment contracts in Korea are made, on one hand, with middle and small enterprises which are in trouble for lack of capital funds and facilities, and, on the other, with labor groups that are unskilled and weak in organizational capacity. Under such circumstances, management, at one and the same time, could not but rely heavily on labor elements for production while not paying enough to maintain minimum standards of living. Consequently, even if there are agreements which provide for working conditions, wage provisions or other pertaining provisions often become invalid. They are mere formalities.

As shown in the results of a survey conducted as of the end of last June, the average monthly wage for a worker is 41,000 hwan compared to 46,600 hwan, the minimum needed estimate per month. For all that, the number of labor-management disputes on wage issues are rather few. In 1957, there were 53 cases of disputes but only half were caused by wage issues. In 1958, too, out of 38 cases, about half only were touched off by wage demands. In most cases, labor demands are to clear arrears.

The conclusion is self-evident: management is not capable of meeting even the low wage scales that are below the mimimum needs. The defaults are not always caused by limited capacity to pay for there have been many cases in which big firms and enterprises were indicted on arrearage charges. Aggravating the tendency is the practice, on the part of middle and small enterprises, to employ relatives, it being convenient to rely on the large family system of mutual dependence.

General labor contracts, it may readily be gathered, reflect the characteristics of a backward economic structure. The labor problem does not even play any conspicuous role when it should properly be at the heart of all social problems. The state may be stepping up economic development projects but because of meager national capital and small-scaled enterprises, the trend inevitably has been to adopt methods of capital savings and labor contractions. The result is that improvement in labor conditions and needs are ignored and management is compelled to accumulate capital at the expense of worker wages.

However weak their position, the living standard of laborers who can maintain a regular income is economically better than that of the unemployed or potential unemployed. Accordingly, the state must regard the labor problem as the immediate urgency. There are over ten times more individuals who are quite bereft of the means of livelihood than the number of factory workers, embracing large numbers of foodless farmers swarming the big cities and the bereaved families of innumerable war dead. Policy, therefore, has been mainly directed at tackling the chronic starvation created by the war. On the other hand, this has prevented policy from ever being applied to the fundamental task of maintaining the whole labor power of the nation in fresh trim. Although Korea is following the example of advanced nations by establishing acts for fixing labor standards, creating a trade union movement, providing for labor-management mediations, and a labor committee, all such noble-sounding laws and ordinances have thus far failed to function properly in meeting the actual requirements of the labor problem. Every fine measure for protecting labor has been virtually introduced from the examples of advanced states, providing for such basic rights as group and unity negotiations, duly approved by the Constitution. The labor legislation on paper is perfect and wonderful.

In reality, however, the standard of the labor legislation is obviously too high to be applied to the present industrial set-up and, sometimes, even obstruct the development of middle and small enterprises. On the other hand, the activities of trade unions which were born after the Liberation seem to be directed rather to political interests than to the promotion of the labor status. The reason is that the unions are organized not from the bottom up but from the top down. The target is set first on the basis of principles approved by the Constitution and then, in line with this target, politicians or educated men occupy the upper berths, leaving the lower positions to later consideration.

Hence, the Administration's help is needed for organizational work and technical difficulties are met unless educated persons participate. This means the influence of political parties and interference by government at the stage when organization work is underway. The strong political influence can disappear only when government launches full-scale development projects and labor steps up productivity and can demand its due share by positively cooperating in the development of small-scale enterprise.

Social problems in Korea, then, are not merely economic, and labor problems do not necessarily arise from such considerations as working conditions and the interests of a labor movement. Therefore, solutions can not be found if we merely introduce systems and structures from advanced nations. It is more important to maintain labor's livelihood by relating the ranks of the unemployed and potential unemployed to the means of social production, mobilize untrained labor power for industries by programs of vocational orientations and training, relate labor power to industrial organizations by job openings. Korea's social problems cannot be solved only by capitalistic ways of economic development. Relief projects which, in other countries, might take the form of social security measures, here assume merely a provisional nature. The tasks of relieving the war victims assume the proportions of a most serious social problem; it is a central task and, obviously, no headway can ever be made unless this problem is removed from that center.

In short, the most urgent problem to be solved is to provide a living for the people. Housing and other problems that are the normal concern of social workers to protect the people from unexpected calamities are only a secondary matter in Korea, critical though they be.

Social Security

For Urbanites

Article 19 of the Constitution of the Republic of Korea provides that: "those who have no capacity for maintaining a living owing to inability to work from old age or illness are provided by the state under provisions of laws."

No concrete legislations, however, have yet been drawn up to render this provision at all effective. Because of the hard living conditions created by war damages, the government has had to concentrate on such problems as the rehabilitation of basic industries and combatting inflation at the expense of other important issues. Throughout the three-year conflict, there were relief projects for the innumerable victims of war under foreign aid and the Ministries of Home Affairs and National Defense were preoccupied with indemnity funds for bereaved members of the war dead. These perennial reliefs in no sense constitute social security as understood in the West.

After 1957, when the Korean economy began to be stabilized, voices were heard from numerous quarters demanding a proper system of social security. As a result, the Ministry of Public Health and Social Affairs prepared a bill soon after to provide unemployment insurance for mental and industrial workers of urban areas. In 1959 came a pension bill to consolidate the effects of the insurance measure. Meanwhile, emergency relief bodies have been set up on a voluntary basis in every factory and mutual assistance programs are being put in practice to guarantee some degree of livelihood for employes after discharge or retirement. Quite a number of the big enterprises have regulations covering compensations for injuries in accordance with the provisions of the Labor Standard Act. The trade union of the Seoul Electric Company and workers of the Ministry of Transportation, in particular, are enjoying the most effective benefits under these regulations.

A comprehensive social security system to the benefit of all may not come for quite some time yet. Only limited ordinances would appear possible in the meantime. More immediately, the range of beneficial effects can and are being further extended by measures to stabilize the living conditions of urban inhabitants.

Population

Abnormal Rates

The most acceptable figures of total Korean population during the Japanese domination were 13.3 million in 1910, 17.3 million in 1920, 20 million in 1930 and 23 million in 1940. They reflect a rapid increase of 1.5% per annum.

However, the following table shows that the population of south Korea during the 11 years since the Liberation increased by 5.8 million as of the end of December 1957, and the total number of Korean nationals was estimated at 21.8 million, excluding north Korean, as of 1954.

As shown by Table 1, the great acceleration in the rate of population growth took place in south Korea during the first five-year period; that is to say, from the Liberation of

X SOCIAL PROBLEMS

Table 1. Population of South Korea since 1944
(in millions)

Year	Population	
1944	15.9	
1946	19.3	
1947	19.9	
1949	20.2	
1952	20.5	(excluding persons in military service) estimated 0.7-8
1955	21.5	(do.)
1957	21.8	(do.)

August 1945 to the war stalemate of spring 1951. The increase during that time was 27% against only a 9% climb since then.

This abnormal jump in the population figures for the southern half of Korea during 1945-51 was the product of the largescale series of mass migrations accompanying both the effects of national liberation and territorial division of the country into a totalitarian north and a free south. The shifts ended only with the stalemate of the war and the armistice talks which froze the armed boundaries of the opposed Communist and allies forces to prevent further passage of northern refugees.

There were two main trends: from the north and from overseas emigrants. The total number of northern refugees was about three to four millions in two main waves of Communist excesses and war disruptions. Owing to the food shortages and the political oppressions, some two to three millions moved from the north to the south by spring of 1946. The official estimates list the total as 65.7 thousand but these figures were based on the number of individuals who had been processed through the refugee camps by January 31, 1949. Certainly, many more times that number bypassed these camps.

The fortunes of war resulted in another great wave of migrations, specifically during the United Nations retreat from the north which sucked up an officially estimated number of 750 thousand refugees and which probably totalled one million. These migrations have decreased the population of north Korea from 12-13 millions in 1944 to 8.3 million as of 1954.

The period immediately following the Liberation also saw great influxes of Korean emigrants who had lived abroad for long years. At the end of World War II, it was estimated that there were a total of 3,290 thousand such Koreans: 1,550,000 in Japan, 1,500,000 in China (mainly Manchuria) and the rest in scattered South Pacific and other areas. According to estimates of the Korean government, 1.4 million emigrants returned from Japan and 430 thousand from other areas as of January 1950.

Four or five millions, therefore, are the most probable figures to account for the extraordinary expansions in south Korean population figures. The only offsetting factors, one might say, were the war casualties, including the numerous south Korean civilians forced north by the retreating north Korean forces after the Inchon landing.

The expansion created abnormal conditions overnight, It not only meant major changes in population sizes and the resultant changes in age distribution and structure of the working class populations, but was largely responsible for the collapse of economic foundations, chaos in political circles, decrease in productivity and the colossal ranks of unemployment. As the refugees mainly moved into the larger towns and cities, the ratio of rural to urban populations was also influenced. According to the official estimates, the urban population increased 72.2 percent during the five-year period as against 26.5 for the rural. This discrepancy, however, has not proved to be permanent for many have gradually been absorbed into the rural areas.

Back to Normalcy

The post-Liberation era has been marked by confusions making for inexact political or economic records. The same inevitably holds true for population figures. The official estimate is that the rate of population increase in south Korea was 9.7 per thousand in the five-year period from 1945 to 1950 but the figure is doubtful. Against this, the birth rate, reported officially, fell from 34 per thousand per annum in 1940-44 to 19 in 1945-50 and the mortality rate was also reduced from the normal level of 18.9 per thousand to as low as 9.3. Improved medical facilities, of course, account for the tendency but even so, the drop is rather too sharp to be explained by this factor alone. As to the birth rate, it may be supposed that the decrease was due to the pressure of unsteady social life, lower standards of living resulting from social disorder and economic collapse, and later marriages. Nevertheless, it is highly doubtful whether the estimated rate at all conforms to the actual decrease. The government itself has pointed out that "birth statistics have not been correctly registered."

However, as can be seen from Table 1, the population increase during the five years from 1953 to 1957 was estimated at 15.2 per thousand per annum. As for the number of men in millitary service, it has generally been estimated at 200,000 but the actual figure has never really been known to any degree of exactitude. As a result, as pointed out in the Nathan Report prepared for the U.N. Korean Reconstruction Agency to serve as the basis for reconstruction policy-making, the state of natural increase of the south Korean population after the war would be more or less 15.2 per thousand, as during the period of Japanese domination.

The age distribution of the Korean population during the Japanese period had a typical "La Tour Effel" pattern like other rural countries of Asia, though the abnormal population movement in the six years since the Liberation has brought about some changes affecting stability. The earlier position was mainly due to the high rate of infant mortality. A private survey covering the period from 1926 through 1936 reported that "only 60 percent of the males and 58 percent of the females lived to attain the age of fifteen; half of the males were dead by the age of 27 and half of the females by the age of 31. There is no available figure on child death rates, but the infant rate in some certain census years can be shown in Table 2 below.

As the result of the high birth rate despite the high infant mortality, the ratio of the age group under 14 to that over 15 has shown a slight tendency to increase during the Japanese domination, as can be seen in Table 3. On the other hand, the age group over 60 constitutes only six percent more or less of the whole population. The age group over 60, of course, are handicapped for physical work. The burden of child dependency falls heavily on the working are groups, inevitably increasing the general poverty of the Korean family.

Table 3. Percentage of the Four Major Age Groups

Year	under 14	15–39	40–50	over 60
1925	39.7	37.3	16.0	6.6
1935	40.4	37.4	16.1	6.1
1944	43.3	35.0	15.4	6.3
1949	41.6	37.9	15.0	5.4
1953	37.1	40.6	16.6	5.7
1956	38.7	39.2	16.5	5.6

1) Figures from 1949 on apply to south Korea only.
2) Source: Economic Year Book 1957. Bank of Korea

However, since the Liberation, the ratio of the under-14 age group has decreased, registering 4 percent in 1953. On the contrary, the 15-36 and 40-59 groups increased by one or two percent in each case. This trend can be explained by the fact that the influxes from the north during the first few years after the Liberation mainly served to swell the populations in the working age groups. The war dead, of course, included all ages and sexes but these were cancelled out by the war refugees from the north who were also largely in the working age groups, the figures in each case approximating one mil-

Table 2. Infant Deaths per 1,000 Births and in Ratio to Total Deaths

years	per 1,000 births	Percentage of infant to total mortality
1936	80.7	11.6
1939	403.9	20.4
1943	108.1	21.4
1944	115.6	17.4
1948	70.9	14.2

1) The 1948 figures are for south Korea only.
2) Source: Economic Year Book, Bank of Korea, 1958

X SOCIAL PROBLEMS

lion. In other words, the accretions to the working population from population shifts were much greater than the losses from the working ranks as war casualties.

Both birth and death rates have dropped very sharply, especially infant mortality for the latter. This was an abnormal post-Liberation tendency as greatly affected by the political and social changes. Among other things, it has greatly altered the age structure of the population. As an abnormality, it must be regarded only as a temporary phenomenon.

That it is so is indicated by the return to natural distributions shown by recent figures. Recent government statistics as well as the Nathan Report has shown increases in the birth rate and decreases in the death. As the figures for 1956 in Table 3 show, it may be said that the age distributions, at least in south Korea, are returning to pre-Liberation normalcy.

Labor Problem

Characteristics

The conditions under which labor operates have been outlined in Chapter 1 of this series on social problems, entitled: "General View."Labor but enjoys a fragmentary status in an industry offset by lack of capital formation in a country almost 80 percent rural.

To amplify at the risk of some repetitions, an average enterprise employs 36 to 37 workers. Production facilities are poor; in fact, it would be no exaggeration to say that only a few factories, semi-official plants installed after the Liberation, business firms established with foreign aid or government assistance, and government-controlled industries, are equipped with modern facilities. The labor problem arises mainly from the fact that a surplus labor potential is unable to be geared to factory methods of operation that are based on relatively small productivity. The difficulties are compounded against the background of the feudal heritage. Feudalism with its emphasis on the family and encouragement of paternalistic dependence in society may long have yielded its economic foundations but the psychological strains are there and while the modern Korean may be able to turn a deaf ear to the individual employer's demand for loyalty, he is unable to defy him. This gives the individual employer all the advantage for he is able to demand loyalty and apply pressure upon collective bargaining laborers so heavily as to extract their service, if not quite their loyalty, without a contract. The laborer has the choice either of working and deferring, or idling and starving.

Then there is the waste of woman power. The traditional concept of the woman's position at home is still so strong that married women avoid occupations even if they are there in the offing. The social prejudice

Table 1: Labor Population and Industrial Statistics of Employment and Unemployment

Figure in 1,000, as of November 7, 1956

Labor Population	11,716	Active Labor Force	8,565
Agriculture	5,602	Fishery	200
Fishery (as related to permanent employment of five or more person)	35	Manufacturing (as related to employment of five or more workers)	225
Domestic Manual Work	500	Commerce	400
Government Agencies	298	Indigenous Employees for UN Command	45
Specialists	30	Transportation	35
Unemployed	1,135	Others	60

Data: Survey conducted by R.O.K.-U.S. Combined Economic Board.

discourages women from acquiring skills and even if they do so, society prefers to hire male hands even for jobs that are elsewhere a woman's prerogative, like nursing.

Table 1 is an outline of the backward economic structure that handicaps labor. The Table shows that workers in second industries and domestic work together constitute less than one-seventh to one-eighth those in the first industries, and the second industry laborers alone are only one-fourth to one-fifth the total number of unemployed. Accuracy of these figures is, however, very doubtful, for the survey conducted separately by the Ministry of Home Affairs as of the end of December 1957 says that the labor population totalled 10,300,000 while the jobless and unemployed numbered over 467,000. An annual report presented to the National Assembly by the Reconstruction Bank in the preceding year estimated the labor population at or around 8,500,000 as of the first day of September 1956 and the unemployed at 1,300,000. Furthermore, the R.O.K.-U.S. Combined Economic Board, which prepared Table 1, asserted that in addition to approximately 1,100,000 fully employed, there were also unemployed potentials submerged in farm lands and medium or small industries, bringing the aggregate total of unemployed in this country to 3,600,000. It goes without saying that these statistics have been prepared on the basis of different data and different methods. The great discrepancies in the figures were apparently caused by the fact that with the labor market in Korea still unexplored, no accurate picture was humanly possible. The labor market remains stalemated to this day and there are no signs of orderly exploration in sight.

To make matters worse, labor contracts are mostly concluded through nepotic relations due, of course, to that family system we have described. This restricts job opportunities for "outsiders" and encourages the more unscrupulous foremen to play broker. The unemployed, for their part, find the broker, however expensive, more dependable in landing them jobs than private or official employment agencies. The Ministry of Public Health and Social Affairs announced in 1957 that the 140 government agencies established in all major cities had not been able to function properly. The announcement was an understatement, to say the least. Not a single worker has yet applied for a job through any such regular channel.

Wages, Etc.

Labor wages, affected as they are by the disordered state of the labor market and the limited capabilities of the enterprises to meet them, have never reached the minimum costs of living as estimated by the Health Social Ministry. Nominal payments, however, increase every year (see Table 2). It is, indeed, a virtual impossibility to expect nominal wages to reach any parallel with the actual costs of living under the extreme fluctuations reckless postwar inflation has brought to commodity prices and which were checked only at the end of 1957. The frequent interventions of the Health Social Ministry in labor disputes, arising from matters of overdue wages of several months' standing, were necessitated, if not by the feebleness of the particular trade union concerned, then by the dragged-out internal quarrels among the ranks of the Korean Federation of Trade Union itself, quarrels which not uncommonly have lasted a year.

Table 2:

Year	Workers	Wages (in Hw. 1.000)
1955	Mine workers	25.9 (average)
1956	Mine workers	31.6 (average)
Jan. 1957	Mine workers	35.4
May 1957	Mine workers	35.4
Sept. 1957	Mine workers	36.3
1955	Manufacturing laborers	19.1
1956	Manufacturing laborers	22.3
Jan. 1957	Manufacturing laborers	23.4
May 1957	Manufacturing laborers	23.1
Sept. 1957	Manufacturing laborers	24.8

Data: Survey on labor situation prepared by The Ministry of Public Health and Social Affairs in 1957.

These figures would undoubtedly be increased if wages could be made in kind as well as in cash.

Table 3 on the substantial wages index reveals slight differences from Table 2. The accuracy of this index is also doubtful for regardless of the nature of the collective agreements thus far concluded, there have been no clearcut provisions therein to govern either the wage computation or the method of payment; instead, terms of payment have been effected only under obscure, abstract sounding principles. "Wages sufficient to maintain a minimum level of livelihood shall be guaranteed," and so forth. Where wages have been met by payment-in-kind as well as cash, they have been intended only to soothe the unionists, invariably with ideal language as a "sop" to a union movement, negligent, in the first place, on the substantial economic front. No wonder accurate indices for substantial wages are foiled.

Table 3: Index of Substantial Wages(1943)

Year	Mining worker	Manufacturing worker
1955 (average)	210.9	164.9
1956 (average)	208.8	147.4
Jan. 1957	253.6	167.6
May 1957	237.1	168.1
Sept. 1957	240.9	164.6

Date: Survey on labor situation prepared by the Ministry of Public Health and Social Affairs for 1957.

The problem of wage deferment, of course, is but another unprecedented cause of labor disputes. A firm labor stand at this extremity has produced a tendency to include in collective agreements a provision governing payment pure and simple.

Labor conditions are very difficult to outline. Although working hours have been stipulated as being 8 hours a day and 48 hours a week, on the average their observances are mostly neglected except in big industries. Especially in the cases of medium and small industries, some workers are reportedly engaging in ten to twelve hours of work voluntarily, and the provision in the Labor Standard Act on vacations with full wage is considered to be an empty check-in-effect. There is, in most cases, too wide a gap between actual labor conditions and provisions of the said Labor Standard Act. Provisions on Protection of Women Workers and on Child Labor may be listed as examples. One reason for the inefficiency of the labor regulation is that its legislative aim has been set too high to be met by medium and small industries which constitute 70-80 percent of the country's manufacturing industries.

Trade Unions

In spite of these unfavorable conditions, trade unions have been organized. The history of Korean trade unions began in 1920 when the Chosun Kongjehoe (Korean Cooperatives) was activated as the first movement of organized labor and became strengthened in 1924 with the formation of the General Union of Laborers and Farmers with a membership of 40,000. The following year saw the workers of the Seoul Electric Company stage Korea's first organized strike and in 1929 came the famous general strike in the port city of Wonsan. The labor organizations, it should be pointed out, were not of the nature familiar to the advanced countries of the West for the strikes they called were part of a political movement against Japanese domination. Not wages but national independence was the aim.

The situation was changed overnight with the Liberation of 1945. Two organizations were formed and immediately turned against each other as inevitable reflections of the political tensions of the times among the ranks of labor. The leftists were the first to organize themselves with the formation in December that year of the Chosun Nodong Chohap Chonguk Pyonguihoe (National Council of Trade Unions), better known by its abbreviated form, Chonpyong. The rightists retaliated with the formation of the Taehan Nodong Chohap Chongyunhaphoe (Taehan Federation of Trade Unions). The Nochong, as the rightist body was called, was formed on March 1, 1946, anniversary day of the famous Samil Independence Day of 1916. As a revolutionary movement, the Chonpyong naturally stood sharply opposed from the very beginning to the Nochong which proclaimed the rights of free workers based on trade unionism. Bitter fighting took place between the two organizations with the rightists generally on the defensive against a strong leftist bid to wreck its power. In September 1946, however, the Nochong seized the leadership of south Korea's labor movement after the collapse of a major leftist bid with a railway strike instigated by the Chonpyong.

In March 1947, the U.S. Millitary Government declared the Communist Party illegal so the Chonpyong went underground to carry on its disruptive work. By the time the Republic of Korea government was formed in 1948, however, the desperate leftists were generally put down and the rightists were able to reorganize the labor movement unimpeded. The Nochong thus had 680 trade unions with a total membership of 127,600 and, in December 1946, sent Korea's first representatives to an international gathering, the first plenary meeting of the International Conference of Free Trade Unions in London where they obtained full ICFTU membership. The outbreak of the war next year, however, hit this rightist labor movement so critically that its various organizations were either totally incapacitated or near-dissolution.

The war meant exile for the head office in the provisional capital of Pusan. It also meant that all outstanding problems had to be piled up under wartime conditions. The labor movement again assumed political direction and produced dissension as a result. In November 1951, the squabbles among the high-ranking officials of the Nochong came to a head with the labor dispute in the Chosun Spinning Company. The internal strife posed obstacles to rank-and-file activities among the trade unions and there was a question of the Nochong falling apart. By the Seoul restoration of 1953, however, the Nochong was able nearly to complete its reorganized power and return somewhat to its prewar levels with 194 unions under its wings for a combined membership of 112,700. Considering the fact that the membership figures claimed by the organization before the war had been somewhat exaggerated, it is fair to make the claim of the prewar status.

The post-armistice history of south Korea's labor movement, unfortunately, has not been promising despite improved economic conditions. Since 1955, the economy has been constantly progressing, in some fields, economic power has nearly doubled the prewar level, e.g. the textile and machinery industries. Notwithstanding all this and, in contrast to the constant increase in memberships, the struggle for hegemony at central headquarters has been so persistent as to become annual affairs. No year passes without several months of dedication to slanders and deceptive practices under the public's nose. It should be added that the platform had been revised as far back as November 1952 to prevent just such dissensions. The main feature of the reorganization had been to replace the chairman with a system of collective leadership. For all that, bickerings have gone on.

Today, the Nochong embraces 560 unions with a total 240,000 memberships. Among the affiliated industries are textile, railway, seamen, miners, electric workers, communications workers; it also controls five vocations, unions for cooks, barbers, Korean laborers for the U.N. Command, horse-and ox-cart pullers, and makers of synthetic resin. In most cases, collective agreements have been reached but the provisions are no more than nominal. Fine ideals about the rights of free labor are mentioned but the key provision which makes free labor work, wages, is couched in ambiguous language. The main provisions are about recreational facilities, holidays, rests and such other "sops" to forestall complaints and maintain "dignity."

For all that, the labor movement, far from being lost, may be held to be progressing on solid ground with every passing year. Labor disputes are decreasing in number. That in itself does not prove anything. What does spell hope lies in the fact that what disputes occur are concentrated increasingly on problems of deferred wages and wage increases. The core of the problem is being met.

Here are the figures. In 1958, 15 out of the 32 labor disputes that year, or almost 50 percent (a good percentage considering the circumstances) arose from issues of overdue payments. The other disputes were about working hours (1), sanitary conditions (1), discharges (6), right of collective bargaining (6) and three other minor reasons. This tendency may be more clearly understood by comparing with the previous year. In 1957, there were 77 disputes but only a few were about wages.

Nobody is taking Nochong excesses lying down. There has been one instance when the head office was resisted very seriously by a rank-and-file member organization. Nochong must 'clean house' or, go under and there are signs that the organization is undergoing another reorganization, this time starting out from the ranks.

Labor Acts

Legislative actions have been taken to cope with labor problems, but so far, only one fundamental labor law has been enacted, and just about enough to adjust impeding problems at that. During the period between October 1945-October 1947, the U.S. Military Government and South Korean Interim Administration had pressed for a series of legislative actions to protect the rights of labor. Their aim was "to prevent production from possible decline that might result from the hostile relation between labor and management." It was the first legislative action of the kind. Other major legislations were as follows:

USAMGIK Decree No. 14—Laborers' Wage Protection Act (Enacted Oct. 10, 1945)
USAMGIK Decree No. 19—Law on Protection of Laborers (Enacted Oct. 30, 1945)
USAMGIK Decree No. 97—Laws on Pronouncement of Public Policies Concerning Labor Problems and on Establishment of Labor Department (Enacted July 23, 1946)
USAMGIK Decree No. 121—Law on Juvenile and Child Labor (Enacted September 18, 1946)
Legislation No. 4 of the Interim Governnemt—Law on Protection of Minor Laborers (Enacted May 16, 1947)

Besides these Occupation decrees, major legislative acts under the Constitution of the Republic of Korea, were completed during the wartime years of Pusan. They included:

Trade Union Act: (4 chapters 52 articles) Enacted March 8, 1953
Executive Decree thereof enacted April 20, 1953
Labor Standard Act: (12 chapter 115 articles) Enacted May 10, 1953
Executive Decree thereof enacted May 20, 1953
Labor Dispute Mediation Act (5 chapters 30 articles) enacted April 20, 1953
Law on Labor Committee (4 chapters 20 articles) enacted Feb. 8, 1953. Executive Decree thereof enacted April 20, 1954.

Korea is an underdeveloped country and its labor problems reflect the acute insecurity of labor's position. Their character inevitably will change with development of the substantial economic programs currently underway. Such important matters as job opportunities, vocational guidances, minimum wage laws and social security must yet be attended to. They are lacking even within possible limits. A large portion of labor prerequisites, however, have been fully satisfied.

Accidents

No adequate legislative action has yet been taken to cope with the high rate of labor accidents apart from the Labor Standard Act of the U.S. Miltary Government. The only brake provided against the numerous disasters occuring in factories is the provisions of the Labor Law enacted in 1953. They fall far short of providing enough relief.

For example, the number of accidents as compiled by the Bureau of Labor of the

Ministry of Public Health and Social Affairs for 1958 was 396. Against the damages, the compensations made to the victims involved totalled only 122,432,000 hwan. Of this total, 115,004,360 went to the surviving families of those laborers who had been killed; only 7,427,640 went to the injured who undoubtedly numbered far more.

Expenses for Labor Accidents (1958)

Figures in 1,000

Industry	Killed Total	Funeral	Compensation	Diseases and Injuries Treatment	Rest	Compensation For Disabled
Gross Total	122,432 (396)	14,623 (112)	100,813 (119)	3,533 (95)	1,389 (43)	2,074 (27)
Mining	95,150 (313)	11,297 (86)	78,116 (94)	2,881 (70)	1,174 (41)	1,682 (22)
Manufacturing	17,339 (18)	2,515 (10)	14,472 (4)	–	–	352 (4)
Construction	6,256 (37)	325 (6)	5,607 (12)	324 (19)	–	–
Electric, Gas, Water-Pipeline, Sanitation	458 (4)	130 (2)	328 (2)	–	–	–
Commerce, Finance, Real Estate	–	–	–	–	–	–
Transportation, Storage, Communication	3,229 (24)	356 (8)	2,290 (7)	328 (6)	215 (2)	40 (1)
Motor Repair	–	–	–	–	–	–

* Figures in brackets show number of accidents.
* Data furnished by Bureau of Labor, Ministry of Public Health and Social Affairs.
* Statistics exclude accidents to farming, forestry, hunting and fishing since no compensations have been made in these fields.

The yearly increases in compensation as shown in the following table reflect the increase in accidents in direct proportion to industrial development. Accidents have a way of assuming calamitous proportions in Korea. A fire, for instance, can raze a whole district of cramped up, wooden shacks. Deaths and injuries amount to the thousands among the labor ranks almost every day in the cause of their work. According to statistics prepared

Industries	Total	Killed Male	Female	Total	Male	Female	Injured Total	Male	Female
Gross Total	266	265	1	126	126	–	140	139	1
Mining	74	74	–	30	30	–	44	44	–
Manufacturing	55	55	–	25	25	–	30	30	–
Construction	71	71	–	30	30	–	41	41	–
Electric, Gas, Water Pipeline, & Sanitation	38	38	1	25	25	–	13	13	–
Transportation, Storage & Communication	28	27	1	16	16	–	12	11	1

* Data furnished by Bureau of Labor, Ministry of Public Health and Social Affairs.
* Statistics exclude accidents from farming, forestry, hunting, fishing, and fields of commerce, finance real estate and motor repairs.

by the Health-Social Ministry's Bureau of Labor, 126 workers were killed and 140 permanently incapacitated for work in 1958 alone. Above is the breakdown for the year.

Rates and Curves

The frequency rate for accidents may be computed by the following fraction:

$$\frac{\text{Number of Accidents} \times 1{,}000{,}000}{\text{Aggregate no. of laborers per year} \times 2{,}400}$$

(Yearly working hours per capita)

As the denominator is equivalent to the gross total of working hours, the frequency rate at the working site is calculated per 1,000,000 hours. The rates thus worked out are probably lower than the actual figures, but at any rate, tendencies can be determined. Such computations show that the highest death rates occur in the following fields: mining, cargo-handling and technical industries, in that order. Among the industries the highest death rate is to be found in the metal refineries, followed by spinning. Mining work claims the highest total of work suspensions as a result of injuries, followed by cargo-handling, construction work and the metal industry at relatively low rates. The light industries and transportation are even lower. It is also a well understood fact that newly-built factories under reconstruction programs are rather vulnerable to accidents. This is due mainly to two causes: one, the workers are not fully familiar with the new facilities; two, they are, for the most part, made up of apprentice hands.

The findings reveal these further trends. Mishaps occur mostly in the first two or three hours of work with gradual decreases by the noon-time break to pick up again in the first two hours upon resumption of work. The trend is similar in the experiences of advanced countries. The volume of work runs parallel to the accident rates. Night work is accompanied by fewer accidents. As to weekly trends, the frequency rates between holidays run almost parallel to the curvature of the weekly production. The annual chart shows higher frequencies in spring and summer and the reverse tendency in autumn. The seasonal changes are attributed to failing physique, increased fatigue and slow response to work with warmer weather. Generally speaking, the young are more prone to accidents than the old and the unskilled or new hands are more frequently the victims. The rates jump with overtime work or speed-up labor. Female hands are less accident-prone as the 1958 chart shows. Even in regular work, men are more apt to get themselves in trouble than women. Accidents befalling the latter cause minor wounds for the most part. They rarely suffer great misfortunes.

The 1958 statistics further show that 45 percent of the accidents resulted in deaths. The death frequency rates are highest in mining and construction work, the former also claiming the dubious privilege for the highest rates of injuries, critical or minor. Without exception, injuries are to the hands or feet. Accidents to limbs depend upon the nature of the work, but totally, hands claim 30 to 50 percent of the injuries as against 20 to 35 percent for the feet, and then again, it is fingers that are mostly involved.

Finally, the cause of accident is mostly the fault of the workers themselves. Compilations show that 60 to 70 percent of the total number of accidents may be attributed to laborers, mainly from excessive strain. Drinking, lack of sleep, the attitude to work, low intelligence quota, frustrations in ever attaining a minimum level of living and insensibility on the job to make up for the frustrations all help to pile up the accident rates.

Unemployment Problem

Characteristics

The most conspicuous characteristic of the unemployment problem in Korea is its potentiality. This may be attributed to the fact that the labor market in Korea is based on a unique structural background of the Korean economy.

The productive structure in Korea, like other economically underdeveloped countries, is marked by the duality of modernized production running parallel with the manual productive methods carried over from previous stages. This duality was bound to bring forth corresponding duality in forms of employment which in turn led to enormous numbers of the potential unemployed. Accordingly, unemployment in Korea assumes the typical form of potential unemployment prevailing in underdeveloped countries along with a few, if not many, aspects of the substantial unemployment found in advanced countries.

To be more concrete, it would be proper to state that unemployment in Korea has resulted from over-feebleness of the second industry both in scope and extent compared to the first and third industries. In other words, overpopulation from the first industry, without having been absorbed into the conditions of modern employment created by the second industry, remain submerged under the surface; only a very small proportion sustains a vagrant status while other small proportions have disappeared from the surface to engage in manual work, hand-processing labor, domestic labor, petty (shack) store-keeping or peddling.

The main cause of unemployment may very well be attributed to the incomplete combination of labor and production methods arising from relatively fewer industrial facilities.

Statistical Review

To elaborate upon the unemployment picture in detail, the problem may be clarified to a larger degree by reference to the break-downs of population according to age and occupational structure as described in Table 1. This table was prepared on the basis of the census conducted by the Ministry of Home Affairs in December 1956. The census shows that the total populaion of this country had reached 20,724,000 excluding those in active military service, foreigners, prisoners, police detainees and seamen. Of this total, the actual labor force was estimated at 10,307,000, excluding juveniles under seventeen years of age, the old over sixty, high school students, housewives and the physically disabled. The break-down of population on the basis of each major occupation is shown in the following

Table 1: (Figures in thousands)

Farming	5,694.5	Fishery	72.7
Mining	20.9	Industry	204.5
Commerce	405.0	Transportation	66.9
Public Service & Free Enterprises	380.0	Miscellaneous	446.4
Unemployed	357.7	Jobless	110.0

(Annual Economical Review, 1957, Research Dept, Bank of Korea)

Table 1 includes the actual labor population plus family supports. Therefore, it is very difficult to determine the actual labor force though it may be possible to grasp the outline of the unemployment structure in Korea. The present state of employment indicates that over seventy-eight percent is engaged in the first industry lines of farming and fishery, and about ten percent in the second industry; the rest comprises the unemployed and jobless. And among those engaged in the first industry, particularly in farming, three million are women who, therefore, constitute the majority of the industry's physical labor force. The remaining labor population may be classified into the following two categories: Unemployed, seventeen percent or over 357,000, and jobless, ten percent or 110,000. According to the 1956 annual report submitted to the National Assembly by the Reconstruction Bank, however, the labor population as of the first day of September 1955 was estimated at around 8,500,000 and the unemployed at around 1,300,000 of a population figure of 21,526.000. On the other hand, the R.O.K.-U.S. Combined Economic Board claims that there are 3,600,000, unemployed in Korea, including potential unemployment in the fields of small and medium enterprises.

As may be noted in the above estimates

made public so far, none, at least, can be credited with accuracy in the number of unemployed because there is too wide a difference in the estates of each statistics prepared separately by the different agencies, on the basis of different data and preparation methods. It should be pointed out that the numerical differences are too wide to be admitted no matter how rudimentary the methods of computation and how dependent they were on mere guesswork. Accordingly, it may be asserted that the structure of the labor populations is so disorderly in itself that clear definitions or classifications cannot be made on the basis of fixed standards. In other words, the overwhelming majority of the labor population in Korea is concentrated on farm lands as is the case in other underdeveloped countries, industrial labor is estimated at less than one-twentieth of the farm labor. Further, the industrial labor population is mostly engaged in such work as mining and construction work which require relatively less skilled labor capabilities. This factor may also be noted in the extent and scope of the second industry. According to a survey prepared by the Ministry of Social Affairs as of the end of March 1957, the number of business firms employing more than five laborers totalled 640,084, with the combined number of employees totalling over 244,000. This survey shows not only the fragmentary nature of Korean business enterprises but also the productivity of the Korean labor population. As a result, there is no doubt, as the R.O.K.-U.S. Combined Economic Board has pointed out, that, in addition to the visible and substantial unemployments noted in the unemployment statistics, there is *de facto* unemployment submerged in the first and third industries, while the smaller factories are made up of large potentials swelling the ranks of the unemployed at any moment.

An Incomplete Problem

The failure in land reformation after the Liberation brought about poorer conditions in agricultural production, which in turn took the form of family labor designed only to meet the needs of self-consumption. Rural overpopulation, which in advanced countries had been absorbed into the third industry, remained stalemated in Korean farming villages to become parasitic on the rural life, for only a very small portion of the overpopulation was presumably engaged in petty store-keeping (shacks), hand-manufacturing, retailing, peddling, etc., or in private family labor. Therefore, it may be said the most conspicuous characteristic of unemployment in Korea is its incomplete condition in the domain of the first industry, such as farming and fishery. This serves as incentive to the invisible, incomplete state of unemployment in medium and small commercial enterprises as well as in transportation.

According to the afore-mentioned announcement by the Ministry of Public Health and Social Affairs, the monthly net income does not exceed 23,000 hwan while the minimum cost of living for an average family of 5.2 requires 35,000 hwan, bringing the monthly deficit of a laborer's family to 12,000 hwan. There are many occasions when the monthly net income of a public servant falls far short of the living cost as estimated by the Ministry for a 5.2 family. If the populations, whose employment statuses are improper or whose monthly net incomes are far below the minimum cost of living under labor conditions, are to be included in the category of the potential unemployed (without restricting the range of the potential unemployment to those who are partially or otherwise incompletely employed, defined according to working hours or working days) most of the labor population, under the present, inadequate industrial structure of this country with its low wage system and excessive overpopulation, may, in a sense, be well considered as potentially unemployed.

It goes without saying that some forms of unemployment are like those in advanced countries. Korea also has seasonal unemployments and unemployment affecting certain lines of work and workers in a prosperous turn of business. Apart from the seasonal cause, however, such instances of unemployment have risen largely from external incentives and not from the inherent self-contradictions in the industrial structure itself. For this reason, detailed discussions of problems relating to such causes should be dispensed with in Korea. They can but get in the way of close examinations into the applicable aspects of the problem and thus hinder the economic development of the country. Also dispensable is the question of unemployment arising out of technical inabilites which are inevitable at the pace of industrial development we expect.

Last but not least, there is the very serious possibility of reductions in the personnel of future possible changes in the foreign military aid programs. Discharged veterans will undoubtedly be a source of increased potential unemployment in the rural areas. This problem, however, cannot satisfactorily be dealt with here.

Measures

To sum up, unemployment in Korea has the following three characteristics:

1) While incomplete unemployment in rural areas is relatively highly rated, incomplete unemployment or the number of neglible wage-earners in the urban areas is by no means small, the extent of visible income-earners is very strictly limited.

2) The source of labor is too short of technical capabilities to be absorbed immediately into the modern industry; at the same time, its abundant availability renders the accumulated position of labor very weak in dealing with production.

3) Lack of clear objectives makes it inevitable for labor populations to roam certain areas with little fluidity; accordingly, there is little possibility of the potential unemployed emerging to the surface. In other words, the resources of the Korean labor market are being left untapped.

Korean unemployment is not of a nature that may be resolved by the establishment of such institutions as employment agencies or unemployment insurance benefits as in advanced countries. As detailed discussions of the necessary measures to cope with the problem should be studied in relation to any economic development program, a brief outline of measures being taken by other underdeveloped countries are hereunder listed for reference:

1) Legislative action on minimum wages, registration of technical specialists, employment stabilization, measures against unemployment and unemployment insurance.

2) Establishment of employment agencies that can cope with the triple functions of grasping the actual conditions of labor, effecting standardization of emblyment and helping toward measures against unemployment.

3) Special attention in the course of compulsory education to the promotion of unemployed technical labor.

4) Implementation of capital savings and collective labor methods of production to expand opportunities for new employments.

The Woman's Question

Law and Tradition

Along with political, social and economic democratization, the woman's problem has begun to draw public attention. There is no basic measure to meet the problem of women in labor because it is still impossible to execute sound social policies. As a result of the unprecedented war havoc after 1950, the number of war widows increased sharply and a great many women are now in a state of potential unemployment camouflaged.

In the leading part of Article 8 of the

Constitution, clause 1 provides that "all people are equal under the law....." and the latter part of the same clause as well as clauses 3 and 4 contain supplementary provisions to the same effect. The latter part of the clause 1 provides that "the people will never be discriminated by sex, religion or social status in all fields of political, economic and social life." It should be noticed that there are no restrictive provisions which substantially stipulate the principles of equality; they are illustrative provisions. Races, languages, political views, social and national origins, property or lineage are no causes for discrimination. As to equality of the sexes, discrimination is prohibited by public laws and private laws. Both sexes have equal suffrage.*

Equal rights in marriage are also provided in Article 2. Article 17 of the Constitution guarantees the right and duty of labor. It provides that "every one has the right and duty to work and the labor of women and minorities is specially protected." It goes without saying that this provision, too, like Article 18, is intended to protect the workers. The "labor conditions" provided in clause 2 of Article 17 mean the conditions for wage scales, working and rest hours, payment, employment terms, and dismissal. Of course, it is for safeguarding the interests of labor that the state upholds these conditions and does not leave them to one's discretion. To meet these requirements, there is the Labor Standard Act (No. 286).

The phrase, "special protection", in clause 3 of Article 17, means to prohibit unjust treatment and discrimination toward women and minorities on the pretext of lower efficiency than that of male adults, and to establish laws to give them special protection on the basis of human rights and national health, taking different physical conditions into consideration.

In this connection, it should be remembered that women's rights under the family system of Korea is based on the paternal

*There are exceptional cases like military service where women do not share in the rights and duties duly provided.

lineage. The system came through the Koryo and 500 years of the Yi dynasty and has become a hard-crusted convention. The tradition gave birth to the concept that the place of the female is under the male and, so long as this tradition continues to exist, equal rights for both sexes and the free activity of women in society may not be expected no matter how vigorously the laws proclaim equailty.

According to statistics made in 1957 by the Ministry of Home Affairs, female employees amounted to 3,745,700; of this, the largest number—3,069,473—was in the fields of agriculture and fishery and second largest in commerce, followed by the manufacturing industry.

Number of Female Workers
As of December 31, 1957

Total	Agriculture & Fishery	Mining	Manufacturing	Construction	Public Works
3,745.770	3,069,473	2,651	36,992	2,155	4,682

Commerce	Transportation & Communication	Civil Servants	Service	Others
165,788	2,511	12,691	71,047	377,780

Data provided by Ministry of Home Affairs

Labor Conditions

Female labor consists of three main features.

A) Unlike male labor, it is generally in manual work. Women are physically more weakly constituted than men and can hardly stand the burden of heavy work. Where the amount of work per hour is the same as that undertaken by males, say, in middle-grade factory work, there may not be any conspicuous difference in the extent of fatigue in the first three to four hours but thereafter, the female begins to show increasing signs of fatigue over the male.

B) Women's labor is generally of a temporary nature and is, therefore, untrained for the most part except for household functions and particular lines like medical treatment and educational work. This is so not because female talents are different from the male's but because they have not received the same vocational education and because their maternal activities have been somewhat limited by various social conventions. For this reason, the absolute majority of female wage-earners are to be found within the age brackets of 15 to 25. Their terms of working are also, on the average, very short compared to those for men.

C) There are periodical waves of inefficiency caused by menstruation and other physiological crises peculiar to the female. The waves affect not only outright mental or physical functions but also increased loss of time and other handicaps resulting from the strain of heavy pressure on the job.

These handicaps have often been used as a pretext for limiting employment and discriminating in payment in favor of the male despite the existence of laws guaranteeing the same opportunities and wages for the same amount of work. The handicaps are properly to be overcome by reforming the educational, social, deep-rooted family, and conventional systems. Intensive attention should be given to strengthen measures for protecting the labor of women. In other words, such labor should be accorded special protective measures in view of the inherent physical nature involved. Importance should be accorded such measures for the sake of maternity rather than any theoretical concept of female labor. Limitation in working hours, prohibition against late night work, prohibition against work in mining pits, rest periods before and after parturition are among the more obvious of the measures to be included.

Comprehensive studies have been undertaken to ascertain the differences in the physical comportments of the male and female. The results in general show that female workers are behind the male of the same age brackets in weight and height. The earlier the female engages in labor, the worse her physical condition, a deterioration common to factory workers, domestic workers or workers in other related fields. In view of the fact that most of the female hands in the factories are from rural provinces, it cannot be denied that the cause is attributable to social, economic and hereditary factors. It is well ascertained by various surveys that such diseases as tuberculosis is carried in the rural provinces to a serious extent.

Further, according to statistics, female workers in food factories have been found to sustain comparatively higher rates of contractions; mental workers also evidence very high rates. Factory workers or, for that matter, women living in the general vicinity of factories, show poor percentages of child deliveries compared to their rural sisters though there are no proofs to tell definitely whether the cause lies in factory work. What has been proved by various studies is that most cases of infant deaths were caused by excessive labor during pregnancy.

Subsidiary work on farms and in the textile, chemical and food manufacturing industries as well as in offices, demand the largest amount of female labor. On the farms, the labor is provided mostly by members of the farm households; employed labor, including factory hands, are mainly represented by unskilled or juvenile workers.

When taking the physical handicaps into due consideration, female labor is found to be subject to the following necessary conditions: (A) limited on the basis of an energy regeneration rate of 2.0; (B) excluded from work that is too intensive in nature or that requires long hours of walking or handling of heavy things, and (C) confined to non-dangerous work.

To conclude: the Liberation has brought emancipation for the Korean woman but the traditional hold persists against the emancipatory process. The tradition retains its strong influence because the Korean woman can find no confidence in "emancipation." In the words of Simone de Beauvoir, she is "Liberated for nothing." The woman's question, like the farmer's, lies at the core of complex social problems.

Juvenile Problem

One of the gravest tasks confronting Korea today is the problem of juvenile rehabilitation. Apart from legislative principles and some measure of welfare needs, the problem has as yet to be actively tackled. The main reason for this lag may be attributed to the fact that the government has been hectically preoccupied with the immediate relief of the orphan and other destitute ranks created by the recent war. Far from devoting the fullest attention necessary to propel sufficient remedies, the standing juvenile problem has more recently been pushed back as of secondary importance before other impending measures of immediate relief.

The main emphases have been placed upon compulsory education, technical education, protection of child labor and institutional guidance for the juvenile delinquents. Here, we shall only attempt to discuss the problems of child labor, war orphans and juvenile delinquents, leaving aside a host of other important, long-range problems such as vocational education and illiteracy.

Child Labor

The rate of child labor in Korea is three to four percent higher than those of other advanced countries like England. According to a survey conducted by the Bureau of Labor, Ministry of Public Health and Social Welfare in 1957, of the total 244,000 workers employed in the second industries (only the workers in such business enterprises employing more than five persons), juvenile workers ranging from 14-18 years of age (juveniles finish primary education at the average age of 14) totalled over 25,000, including 10,000 boys and 15,000 girls. They constitute 10.4% of the total second industry employment.

As these figures merely show the number of juvenile workers in the second industries, they may increase both in number and rate to a greater degree when the juvenile workers engaging in family labor in the field of agriculture, one of the first industries, and others especially in medium-small commercial enterprises, in the third industries are to be included. It is believed that with young people ranging from 20-23 years of age serving in active military service, the need for juvenile labor is being further accelerated. It is stipulated in paragraph B, article 17 of the Constitution that "juvenile labor shall receive special protection." And article 50 of the fifth chapter of The Labor Standard Act also provides that "juveniles under 13 years of age shall not be employed." Prohibition of night work in article 56, working hours set forth in article 55 (7 hours a day, 42 hours a week), prohibition of underground work in article 56 and payment of travel fare to the home town in article 62 are chiefly provided to deal with the problem of child labor. Article 63 provides that "an enterprise employing at all time more than 30 juvenile workers under 18 years of age shall provide education facilities" and that "details concerning the education facilities referred to in the foregoing paragraph shall be stipulated by presidential decree." Of all these provisions, prohibition of night and underground labor, limited working hours and labor age are being observed only in big industries; it is very difficult to go along with the rest of the provisions. It may be that the scale of second industries is too small to implement the provisions, but the main cause stems from the fact that net incomes of the persons responsible for supporting families are far less than minimum costs of living in most cases, wherefore earnings from juvenile labor are added to the livelihood and, in some cases, juvenile workers voluntarily engage in excessive labor in violation of the labor regulations. It appears that provisions concerning education facilities for workers and payment of travel fare to the home town have become no more than empty prescriptions. Other impending activities, such as vocational training (with the exception of the Central Boys' Vocational Training Center and the Program of an-art-for-a-student in school education) and educational assistance are yet to be materialized.

In the absence of accurate statistics, the comparison of juvenile workers' wages with the adults' cannot be clarified but it is generally estimated that the former are paid around one half on the average adult's wage. This may be partly because the basic wage weighs very little in the wage structure of Korean laborers in general. Some even argue that this low wage system has brought forth these adverse to the original legislative intention of provisions concerning the protection of child labor. With few exceptions, virtually no industry is providing welfare and safety facilities for juvenile workers.

Protection of War Orphans and Vagrant Juveniles

There are other juvenile welfare facilities such as mass accommodation facilities for war orphans and detention centers for juvenile vagrants called Sonyonwon. Reference to the Sonyonwon shall be omitted in this article. With the increase of adequate facilities, protection activities of war orhpans and juvenile vagrants are being gradually expanded. As the above table indicates, necessary facilities have been established in all provinces and the number of juveniles accommodated are increasing every year.

Most of these facilities were set up after the Korean War. It was reported that before the war, there had been only 120 such set-ups throughout the country and the juveniles accomodated numbered around 20-30 per cent of the present-day figure. They were built mostly with government funds and foreign materials, and there were some private set-ups established by religious organizations after the war but they are all under public agencies today. There are various foreign aid agencies, such as UNCACK, UNKRA, U.N. Command and OEC and these agencies have established ten hotels and 35 welfare and relief set-ups for children.

Prospects for active juvenile vocational guidance activities seem to be very bright with the completion of the National Social Workers' Training Center and the Central Juvenile Vocational Training Center, and in line with these establishments, the project of the Juvenile Vocational Training Center is underway with the 1957 ICA funds. Another project for juvenile training center is being undertaken jointly by the Korean Government and OEC. Nevertheless, being still at the stage of organization all these establishments are unable to bring about definite results. The juvenile welfare set-ups presently in operation total 490 and their prime objectives are to accommodate crippled youths, orphans and juvenile delinquents, and other facilities are National Sangsimwon aimed at treating the mental infirm and the Central Kamhwawon to give proper guidance to juvenile delinquents.

Number of Facilities and Juveniles Accommodated in 1957

Province	Facilities	Number of Juveniles Accommodated
National	4	786
Seoul	67	8,208
Kyonggi-do	75	7,406
Chungchong Pukdo	15	1,005
Chungchong Namdo	53	5,171
Cholla Pukdo	30	3,701
Cholla Namdo	46	7,762
Kyongsang Pukto	65	6,844
Kyongsang Namdo	104	10,887
Kangwon-do	23	1,904
Cheju-do	8	1,155
Total	490	54,829

Problem of Mixed Blood Children

A report indicates that the number of mixed blood children taken care of in 1957 alone reached 24,000, and this has become one of the impending social problems, but detailed discussion on the matter shall be omitted herefrom. As may be noted in the above explanation, juvenile protection activities in Korea have so far been very sporadic. It is imperative to systemize these activities, and there are increasing demands in some circles for legislation like the one adopted in England under the name of "Child Welfare Law." In other words, there are strong demands for united legislative actions with a view to tackling problems of mental deterioration and degradation of the young generations that might accompany the increase of war orphans and vagrant juveniles, supervising and controlling protection facilities and activities to prevent the maltreatment of children so as to improve the physical health of infants of high death rate and carrying out special vocational training activities of young people to enable them easily obtain jobs.

Housing Problem

Acute Shortages

The housing problem in Korea is a critical issue, one which calls for immediate attention. The major cause for this may be found in the natural increase in population and the accompanying changes in the social system. The problem became even worse after the war. More than 595,000 houses were either burned down or destroyed in the course of the war and some four million refugees fled Communist-dominated north Korea to the south in the period between August 1945 and January 1951 when the war was deadlocked. Furthermore, more than two million Koreans abroad returned to the southern part of the peninsula since the Liberation. The housing problem of Korea is hardly to be equalled anywhere else in the world. (It has been reported that even on such an advanced continent as Europe, three percent of the total population is living in caves or under other circumstances unsuited to human habitation and that the U.S. itself suffers from a shortage of around 3,340,000 houses). In addition, the mass movements of the rural population to city areas has aggravated the situation in the city while its accompanying factor, mass poverty, has compelled the concentrated population to shelter themselves in rented rooms.

In an effort to solve this problem, the government has been building numerous houses with foreign assistance while private enterprises have striven for construction of apartments and other accommodations out of their own funds. These joint efforts may well be said to have borne fruitful results when, at the end of 1957, a total of some 593,000 houses were reported to have been rebuilt, or equal to the amount destroyed during the war. For all that, the shortage resulting from natural calamities and natural increases in population is still approximately 420,000. This quantitative shortage has also made it inevitable for the populace to lodge in crowded houses and has brought about deterioration in the quality of dwelling facilities. Korean houses are characteristic of the backward living standards from virtually every point of view, density, materials, sanitation, cultural facilities. An average structural width per house is only 10.4 *pyong* while density per house exceeds five persons, and the main construction materials consist of nothing more than such primitive things as lumber, straw and mud. They constitute the major structural parts of wooden, straw-roofed houses. The electricity utilization rate is only 18.9 percent. These are grim facts which have made it imperative to improve the housing standards at any cost. In order to meet these qualitative shortcomings, the government has been encouraging the construction of modern-type houses by advertising for prize contests of new housing designs, propagating model houses and supporting and assisting in the production of home-made housing materials while striving to cope with quantitative problems by extending all possible aid to every housing project. The above figures show the extent of reconstruction completed after the war.

tance agencies, the government has exerted its effort on such temporary set-ups as refugee camps, houses for resettling farmers and for the rural people in recovered areas and others to meet the emergency. The housing structure itself remains to be improved.

The most notable accomplishments were the housing projects planned by the United Nations Korean Reconstruction Agency in 1953-1954 and the one conducted under the ICA Aid Program. UNKRA has built in major cities what are known as Reconstruction Houses with foreign aid materials, with the government financing part of the expenses for the construction. These projects provided the occupants with the opportunity to possess houses for themselves on the basis of 6-8

Housing Situation before and after the War

Provinces	Shortage Before the War	Destroyed	Reconstructed 1st	2nd	3rd
Seoul	192,260	60,082	9,919	32,333	42,252
Kyonggi-do	322,861	64,045	40,950	56,179	97,159
Chungchong Pukto	203,770	34,803	6,747	24,098	30,845
Chungchong Namdo	336,812	20,743	11,471	26,437	37,908
Cholla Pukto	375,758	74,747	29,980	23,219	53,197
Cholla Namdo	522,608	91,328	28,667	30,995	59,662
Kyongsang Pukto	530,044	80,945	12,949	54,062	67,011
Kyongsang Namdo	580,217	80,945	43,204	64,916	108,806
Kangwon-do	181,068	106,092	27,561	54,525	82,086
Cheju-do	30,031	723	6,015	7,800	13,815
Total	3,275,429	614,453	217,463	374,564	592,741

Housing Construction with Foreign Aids

In the face of the extreme housing difficulties, initial efforts have been concentrated by the government on mass housing construction as measures to accommodate the needy. With the cooperation of foreign assis-

Houses Built under the Government's Housing Program

Classification	1951	'52	'53	'54	'55	'56	'57	Total
Camps	10,225	-	-	-	-	-	-	10,225
Temporary winter house	-	14,700	-	-	-	-	-	14,700
Relief	10,100	7,000	13,100	-	-	-	-	30,200
Recovered farm house	-	-	13,700	-	-	-	-	13,700
Temporary house in recoverd area	-	-	-	1,000	-	-	-	1,000
Resettler's house	-	-	13,883	43,188	43,189	20,333	10,459	131,052
Blind veterans'	-	-	-	-	40	-	-	40
AKF house	-	-	-	-	100	-	-	100
Reconstruction house	-	-	-	-	1,940	3,090	3,834	8,864
Rehabilitation house	-	-	-	-	-	935	821	1,756
Wounded veterans'	-	-	-	-	-	186	-	186
House built with loans from former Japanese property	-	-	-	-	-	-	5,690	5,690
Total	20,325	21,700	40,683	44,188	45,169	24,644	20,804	217,513

year instalments. Rehabilitation Houses under similar projects were solely financed in the form of loans by the government's Housing Fund, construction of which were performed by government registered contractors, the Korea Housing Administration, Army Engineering Corp and private business interprises. These houses were distributed to applicants who would be charged with the responsibility to complete the repayment by yearly installments with fixed interests. The main features of this type of houses are their permanent inhabitability, quite apart from those built temporarily for the victims.

The ICA Assistance Program provides, under yearly housing projects underway since 1957, foreign exchanges to procure housing materials from abroad an internal counterpart fund to make loans to the Housing Union consisting of private construction enterprises and end-users with a view to financing part of the construction. The occupants are liable to repay the loan within ten years. The housing projects to be carried out under the Government Housing Program are as shown in the lower table of the preceding page.

The direct and indirect housing policies of the government have resulted in the reconstruction of 540,000 out of the total war damages of 610,000 units. Yet the shortage remains critical, involving insuperable problems of sanitation, density, vulnerable shacks and lodging tenements. The enormous increases in the ranks of the homeless or vagrant families are undeniably hotbeds for crimes and epidemics. Structurally also, Korean houses are far behind modern accepted standards.

For reasons of the barest requirements of sanitation not to speak of better surroundings, especially in the rural areas, the government still has a long way to go to raise housing standards and improve housing settlements for the general populace.

Korean Family

Chongbop Family System

The traditional family, under which the father assumes the headship on the basis of the male lineage, is still the prevailing unit in Korean society. This family system, called the *chongbop*, is based on the practical application of Confucian ethics and, as such, is not a unique Korean tradition. Created by the Chou dynasty of China where it bound society for several thousand years, sometimes presenting itself as a moral criterion and at other times being interwoven with existing judicial institutes, the *chongbop* was first introduced to Korea at the close of the Koryo dynasty. Initially it was known as the *yegyo*, or Rituals.

Since every political and social organization came under strong Confucian influence during the long reign of the succeeding Yi dynasty, the *chongbop* inevitably became entrenched in the Korean family and persisted for almost six hundred years as an inviolable tradition. The close of the nineteenth century saw the system challenged seriously for the first time by the import of modern ideas from the West. Leading Korean thinkers saw the desirability of liberating the tight Korean family maintained at the expense of society and, no doubt, the system would have collapsed of its own weight under the inevitable changes of the times. The system, however, was saved in the twentieth century by a Japanese colonial policy which wanted to prevent the modernizaion of Korea by Koreans themselves and saw in the maintenance of this outdated family, the core of its instrument.

The result was that, although a relatively early start had been made toward the formation of a civic society under the Japanese domination, Korean society could never end the process by modernizing the family system. However heterogeneous its features, Japanese colonial administration helped preserve the individual status of the huge family system under the pretext of respecting Korean customs and traditions. It related a system of farm tenant slavery to the feudal ruling class, thus strengthening the privileged position of landlords while blocking the flow of national capital into modern industries and thereby preventing numerous members of the huge families from being absorbed in modern business. The mutual inter-dependence of family members became intensified, the families made up uncalculating, unselective, unreasonable communities, poverty prevailed and potential unemployed increased to a large degree. Years of the *chongbop* system created almost incurable social problems.

The Liberation has been accompanied by the adoption of democratic systems both in political and social life, but it has brought no changes to the *chongbop* despite general expectations. The system has been too deeply rooted in Korean life to be eliminated in any short period of time, thus posing itself as a great obstacle to the application of democratic theories in actual practice. The main principle of the *chongbop* is the continuance of the father line. The common consciousness of lineage among the family members is strong and several such families, bound by this strong consciousness of blood into a common clan, constitute a community. Regardless of how distant the kinship, the male lineage is treated as representative of the family, and a family is supposed to live under a common roof as far as possible, no matter how large it may be. The *chongbop* ideal is for nine generations to live together in one household. Such ideal households are bound by exclusivism toward society and rivalry against one another. The stronger their inner resistance, the more restricted the actions or good intentions of the individual members toward the outside. In short, we have unrealistic, outdated groupings of large families looking up to the continuance of the family through the male line and sharp limitations in the freedoms of individual members in social behavior as a result of an anachronistic way of life. In some cases, even their freedom to vote or choose an occupation are restricted, aggravating the evil effects of an anti-social attitude that is hardly conducive to the encouragement of democratic principles.

As the *chongbop* requires continuance of the family line as its prerequisite, the tendency is for high respect to be accorded the dignity of one's ancestors and individuals of a higher lineage position demand unconditional respect from those in lower positions. These attitudes have their unfavorable effects upon the complexes of the descendents who find themselves in statuses that comprise an important factor in the structure of the social order. As the family line is maintained through the male, the discrimination between the male and female descendents is very conspicuous and the predominant position of man over woman is a social tradition. Men are given priorities in education as well as in domestic life and development of their social outlook is, accordingly, delayed. The strict adherence to the order of the eldest male descendent as the lawful inheritor makes for great restrictions in the exchange of opinions between men and women. The old adage that "males and females shall not sit together at one place after seven year of age" blocks the woman's role of lineage maintenance to a large degree. Married women do not retain the occupations they had before their nuptials with the result that there is an absolute scarcity of skilled female workers in Korea. Illegitimate children and the descendents of concubines are extremely maltreated and can suffer disgrace from the slightest misdemeanor whereas legitimate sons can and often do indulge in outrageous misbehavior.

As may be supposed, the head of the huge household possesses a very powerful authority over the rest of the family and can exercise control over their every action. His rights are recognized by pertinent laws and regulations: Right of Approval (in marriage, divorce, adoption, repudiation of an adopted child, separation of household, registration of an illegitimate member of the family), Right of Exclusion from the Family Registrar (of the indiscreet widow, for example), Right of Property Custody, Right of Guardianship (of persons of minor age), Right of Inheritance and Appointment of Residence. The wife and children of the household head are under his control at all time, enabling him to intervene in almost all aspects of their lives and assume a self-righteous posture before the uncritical dumb. The rise of many class distinctions among the family members and the centralized authority of the household head cement class consciousness, despotic habits and disgraceful obedience into a tradition to pose a no mean obstacle to any democratic progress in Korea. Moreover, the extreme state of mutual inter-dependence makes labor a family rather than a social affair. Even in public industries, instances are to be found where kinfolks constituting the ranks of senior officials number more than half the workers. In this latter connection, it should be pointed out that signatories to labor contracts are the head and members of the family who sign such documents to the neglect of the provisions provided for under the Labor Standard Act of the government. The organization of trade unions is hindered and collective bargainings or agreements become mere formalities. The habit of mutual help in the economic life of the family also means obstacles to the development of a social security system.

For all these reasons, the large family units under the *chongbop* system bring forth very harmful effects on political institutions as well as on all fields of social and economic activities. It may very well be said that the elimination of the *chongbop* is a necessary prerequisite to any development of democracy. Nevertheless, the system cannot be abolished until and unless unfavorable social and economic factors of a pertinent nature are removed. It is necessary beforehand to create such conditions as to enable the heads of small family units and their direct lineal descendents to lead reasonably secure collective lives. This calls for an economic system permitting people to live on individual incomes without relying on the farmland of the family possession for their livelihood because a deeply rooted social bondage can not be cut off without individual attainment of economic independence. Such problems as a minimum wage system and social security for the unemployed, the old and the disabled must be tackled. Needless to say, such reforms, prerequisites to the end of the *chongbop* system, have to be accompanied by modernization of the personal status law to help end the *chongdop* by developing the small family unit.

Aftermath of War

Against this gloomy picture, it may truthfully be said that since many upper class landlords have lost their properties as a result of war, many real estates, such as farm-lands and forests, are no longer under the *chongbop* system and that the tenants have become landowners, the large family unit showing a tendency of revising its nature, especially in urban areas. Nevertheless, as a persistent tradition of several hundred years, it has not shown the possibility of undergoing any drastic change. Rather, it is logical to assume that as matters now stand, with the farmers constituting almost 80 percent of the total population and small or medium enterprises making up the overwhelming part of business enterprises, the system will continue to exist for some time. Both the provisions in the draft personal status law to continue the system of family headship and the reluctance of prevailing opinion to place any restrictions upon the authority of the head reinforce this assumption.

In this sense, it may be said that social and economic developments may not be expected until resolute measures, taken to transform the old system of family registrations to the current one of present residence, are reflected in social institutions to such a degree as to bring about the complete transformation and modernization of society.

Public Welfare

It is no exaggeration to state that public welfare work has thus far been limited mainly to relief activities for victims of natural calamities and dislocations of the Communist War. Relying largely upon materials from the United Nations, its specialized agencies, friendly nations and religious and social organizations, relief activities have been conducted on merely temporary and first-aid bases. The objectives have been to help refugees and other needy people to attain self-supporting livelihood. In a society where a complete social security system has been put into effect, relief work should be woven into the system and financed from the national budget, that is, from the taxpayers' money, but the possibility of such implementation is very dim because of the feudalistic huge family system under which each family feels responsible for supporting each other, both morally and materially, thus leaving those unable to obtain family support—the poverty-stricken, old, or otherwise unfortunate —objects of welfare work. This may also be one of the reasons way the farming population, occupying more than 80% of the total labor force, is in a state of potential unemployment in extreme poverty and that most of them may be considered in a way as mere objects of relief. At the same time, most industries, except for a few largescale basic industries established after the war, are so small in scale that the total number of employees is less than half the substantial unemployed and their wages far less than the minimum living costs. It is for this reason that appropriations out of the national budget to social work can hardly be expected at this moment.

Thus, in many cases, welfare activities have been limited to the visible, poverty-stricken people residing in cities and the work has tended to be restricted to temporary forms of relief, such as saving the victims from impending cold and hunger. This disorderliness, unsystematization and impermanence in relief activities are mainly due to the fact that with the available materials and budget being sharply limited, it is hardly possible to extend full assistance to such numerous needy people. Also because the Republic is a recently born state visited by the heavy tolls of modern warfare, the government has had to give first priority to postwar reconstruction and to the firm establishment of a self-sustaining economy as the fundamental national objectives, thus leaving little room for attention to orderly social relief work. The following chart shows the province-by-province breakdown of suf-

Year-by-Year Breakdown

Province	1951	1954	1956	1957
City of Seoul	427,832	125,856	286,050	104,589
Kyonggi-do	2,279,111	228,247	212,650	757,891
Chungchong Pukto	375,985	93,928	251,200	178,518
Chungchong Namdo	458,575	124,996	127,074	236,490
Cholla Puko	723,176	236,406	657,599	661,553
Cholla Namdo	929,796	439,742	559,471	479,618
Kyongsang Pukto	731,936	561,351	1,024,874	606,390
Kyongsang Namdo	869,832	758,603	967,625	717,869
Kangwon-do	852,082	120,186	151,532	265,729
Cheju-do	132,089	33,645	92,210	126,777
Total	7,780,414	2722,960	4,330,285	4,135,424

ferers in each fiscal year. This excludes the relief targets of religious and other social organizations, it being undetermined yet exactly how many needy people have benefited from the relief activities conducted by these organizations.

Foodstuff and clothing occupied the overwhelming part of relief materials, apart from a few medical good for first aid use. Construction materials for resettlements were negligible. An average three *hop* of grains have been distributed per capita as in the following table.

Grain Distribution to Needy People

Year	Total Quantity (Figure in 1,000 tons)	Recipients (figure in 1,000)
1951	320	1,981
1954	201	1,287
1956	31	201
1957	34	219

All the foodstuff, fuel and clothing brought in under the United Nations' Relief Program and/or from friendly nations, besides those introduced by religious and social organizations, reached as high as approximately 1,789,000 tons from 1950 up 1957, including more than 449,000 tons of foodstuff. In addition to these public welfare agencies, there were 77 foreign private relief organizations as of 1957. Both religious and social in nature, many of these organizations are still actively engaged in relief work. The materials they have brought in are shown in the following table:

Year	Food	Clothing	Medical Goods	Misc.	Total
1953-1955	20,216	8,205	420	4,671	33,512
1956	36,538	1,991	135	1,312	39,976
Total	170,713	14,309	1,157	8,439	194,618

Apart from these temporary relief activities on first-aid basis, a long-term resettlement project, for war victims has been underway since 1952, sponsored jointly by the Korean and U. S. governments. Under the project, a total of 126,100 families have been resettled throughout south Korea as of the end of 1957, a total of 693,000 individuals.

These houses were built with lumbers, nails and cements brought in under the ICA assistance program. The resettlers are engaged in farming, reclamation of wasteland, stockbreeding and labor in salt-fields, and the government is giving them full support by providing them with farming tools, fertilizers and other materials to enable them to attain self-sustaining status.

Besides temporary relief, other welfare activities are also being conducted, but they are all on a small scale except for the old, women, and bereaved families of the war dead, military and police. Welfare work for the old was to provide aged people without dependable family support with food and other commodities for minimum daily living in accordance with the "Korean Relief Act" promulgated during the Japanese period. Some aged were taken into asylums. As of the end of 1957, there were 37 such facilities, providing for some 2,600 old men and women.

Social work for protection of women has been limited mainly to relief and guidance work for war-widows. It is estimated that widows requiring assistance (including 60,000 war-widows) total 200,000 of whom 20,000 have been reported to have sunk into the depths of misery. In addition to the guidance work, about 70 national houses-for-mothers-and-children have been set up along with some vocational centers.

As relief work for the survivors of dead soldiers and policemen have already been discussed elsewhere, detailed discussion might as well be omitted here. The work is being performed in accordance with the "Servicemen Protection Act" and "Policemen Protection Act" promulgated in April 1950. The objectives are:

1) To give proper support for their living according to status. (Aid in medical treatment, midwifery, child education and funeral, vocational assistance and help in marriages.)

2) To obtain jobs for wounded veterans. (National Vocation Guidance Center, National Revival Center and other specialized

3) To carry out special pension institutions for wounded soldiers and policemen. The recipients number over 123,400.

Such is the outline of the social work thus far performed or being carried out in Korea. Neither government-sponsored services nor social relief activities by private organizations have gone behind temporary, first-aid measures to cure the wounds inflicted by the war. Such continuous national welfare works as resettlement projects, relief activities for the old and protection of widows, for families of servicemen and policemen alone, have taken on business like features of modern welfare work.

Natural Calamities

Natural Disasters and Accidents

Natural disasters in Korea are marked by the severity of the effects compared to causes. The main cause is unadjusted natural environments. In rainy seasons, lower parts of areas along rivers are subject to the threat of overflow and houses and cultivated land are often flooded or even washed away by steams of water rushing out through crushed embankments. Preventive measures are sought and discussed every year but this problem cannot be settled in a brief space of time.

For the way of life in rural regions does not easily allow such settlement. In rural regions, construction of houses and supply of fuel rely entirely on trees and plants on nearby hills. People cut them down at random without reasonable replanting to make up for what is gone. As a result, the forests become denuded. Denuded forests give way to violent landslides making river-beds higher and then comes the river-overflow. In short, the cause of river-overflow lies in deforestation and deforestation prevails due to the living condition of the Korean farmers. The same reason applies to fire disasters.

Most Korean houses are made of wood and the ground on which a house is built is limited. Especially in heavily populated big cities and towns, spaces between houses are so short that the possibility of catching fire is immense and once a fire is out, the amount of losses is great contrary to one's expectation due to the spreading fire.

Traffic accidents and some other disasters occur owing mainly to unadjusted natural environment. No matter whether in urban or rural regions, causes of traffic accidents lie in narrow roads and sharply increased traffic volume since the Liberation and lack of safety facilities and supervision over vehicle maintenance.

According to statistics made by police authorities covering the period from 1957 to 1958, the amount of damages caused by tempests is estimated at more than 26,000,000,000 hwan.

The break-down:
Casualties: 345
Buildings destroyed: 32,300
Ships damaged: 96
Livestock lost: 1,460
Highways damaged: 7,770 places

Traffic accident:
Casualties: about 6,000
Commercial cars: about 2,000 cases
Personal cars: about 1,500 cases
Trucks: acout 550 cases
Military cars: about 1,000 cases

These accidents occurred mostly in cities and towns. Another important cause is that vehicle operators in cities and towns are forced to work for 15 to 16 hours a day in violation of labor provisions. As for fire, statistics covering one year from October 1957 to early October, 1958 show that 1,480 cases, occurred bringing total figures of damages and casualties to 1,670,000,000 hwan and 250 persons. Compared with the previous year, the number of cases was increased by 190 while the amount of losses decreased by 70,000,000 hwan and casualties decreased by 110.

Ninety percent of the disasters are accidental and can be said to be caused by denseness of houses and the native systems of floor-heating and chimneys. Explosion accidents occurred over 320 times in ten months starting January, 1958 and 650 persons were killed or wounded. There accidents occurred mostly by careless handling of explosives which had been thrown away during the war except for 43 cases which occurred while fishing with explosives. This is evident since most of the victims were children. However, this kind of accident is no longer regarded as an outstanding problem since explosives are very sensitive to moisture and the length of time they can be stored is limited.

As mentioned above, flood, drought, fires and traffic accidents constitute main disasters in Korea. For this reason, preventive measures cannot but be passive and basic counter-measures are very difficult. For causes of flood and drought to be eliminated by making forests green with abundant wood and to make forests green, something must be done to the way of life of Korean farmers. Traffic accidents and fire disasters cannot be expected to be dealt with adequately unless present structures of cities and towns are basically reformed and styles of houses are entirely changed.

Thus prevention of disasters in Korea can not be realized in a short period of time but rather require long-term synthetic development projects. As a matter of cause, temporary preventive measures can be taken before trying to find basic count-measures and government is concentrating on these temporary measures. For example, government is stepping up projects to prevent flood and is leading planting campaigns. Nationwide campaigns like the "fire preventing week" intended to arouse the people's attention can be another example.

Furthermore, to prevent fire disasters and traffic accidents, the government has established strict punishment regulations. Of course, these cannot be basic counter-measures. Overflow rivers cannot be prevented merely by construction of embankments and droughts cannot be prevented only by launching irrigation works. Traffic accidents and fire disasters cannot be prevented by public campaigns or punitive regulations. These problems should be settled synthetically and from many different angles.

Along with synthetic development projects for the country, there must be long-term preventive measures.

XI HEALTH PROBLEMS

General Preview

Before Western Science
Primitive Period

Primitive Koreans most certainly knew something about medicine. By instinct or experience, they must have learned many ways to cure an illness or heal a wound. Evidences, however, are very scanty.

Mythology attributes the birth of the Korean race to one, Tangun, born supernaturally of a son of God who descended upon earth with three thousand spirits. Among them were the spirits of Wind, Rain and Cloud. They served as ministers to Tangun and were entrusted with the tasks of controlling problems of food, illnesses and justice among his subjects.

All this, of course, is unreliable. Old literature, however, has something to tell us about problems of health in connection with this legend. Thus, we are told, garlic and moxa were used as medicine in addition to spells and prayers to cure the sick. Undoubtedly, beasts of prey and natural disasters were the chief enemies of man on this peninsula and, of the two, the latter was probably more dreaded. Some measure of defense could be taken against animals by huddling together in community life but against a vicious epidemic, they were totally helpless.

The Korean people are believed to have originated somewhere on the steppes of Central Asia. From this cold region, they migrated east toward warmer land, finally settling down upon the Korean peninsula. Here, they worshipped the sun as the one and only God and, in time, developed a "chosen people" mentality like the Jews. They were very fond of religious services for which they cleansed their minds and bodies and wore snow-white clothing. They had no way to prevent any epidemic but this emphasis on cleanliness probably did much, in the long run, to serve as prevention against diseases.

In food, too, the ancient Koreans reflected their religious bent for clean, light and pure objects, a taste encouraged by the introduction of Buddhism during the Three-Kingdom period. Thus, they ate only chickens among the fowls, while fat greasy meat was avoided. The favorite food was fish. It was only in the Yi dynasty (1362-1910) and the replacement of Buddhism by Confucianism as the state religion that the diet became heavier. Beef and pork became essential items not only for Confucian festivals but for the daily meal, a habit encouraged with the introduction of Western culture and the importance of meat-eating in Western dietetics. In the countryside, however, many farmers still do not like meat. Undoubtedly, the main reason is the meager livestock available, but, at the same time, we may easily recognize in their resistance an undeniable yen for stoic simplicity that was the stamp of our ancient forefathers.

Astrology was also employed by primitive Koreans as a means to prevent epidemics. Thus, old records tell us that "the dead had to be buried within the day," or that "ice was used for the dead in summer."

Medieval Age

There are no records that make any mention about hygiene during the primitive period. Pending evidences to the contrary, we shall then assume that primitive Koreans had no knowledge about hygiene and kept their health and vigor primarily by the habit of cleanliness.

Hygiene first came in with the introduction of Chinese civilization following the founding of the Chinese colony of Lolang in the northern part of Korea. This opened the road not only to Chinese but Indian medicine which came with Buddhism shortly after. These were mixed to produce the science of herb medicine which flourished from the middle of the Three-Kingdom period. The Three Kingdoms, especially Silla, not only created public hygiene systems but also provided for a complete medical education with medical institutions of learning, thus encouraging a science that was to become the father of Japanese medicine.

During the subsequent Koryo dynasty, the advantages of medical knowledge spread among the general public. In the court, there were two posts, the *Taeuigam* (Grand Medical Supervisor) who attended to the high officials, and the *Heminguk* (Public Charity Bureau) which dispensed medicine for commoners. Besides the *Heminguk* in the court, there were several charity institutes in the country to care for poor patients and helpless old folks without charge. The royal household, of course, had their own exclusive centers, the *Sangyakkuk* (Medical Bureau) and the *Sangsikkuk* (Food Bureau), the latter guaranteeing the quality of the king's table.

As yet, there are no records of any concrete measures taken against epidemics. The most we can point to, therefore, is herb medicine. Its overall efficacy is highly problematical. In the first place, it was effective only for the elite classes which alone could afford the expenses and even the nobles depended on Taoistic moderations rather than on the herbs for their health. Certainly no positive measures for the health of the general public was contemplated.

Yi Dynasty

From the earliest prehistoric days to modern times, epidemics was the cause of great disasters to peninsular life as they have been for mankind in general. The oldest record of such an outbreak has been placed at 15 B.C. in the *"Samguk Sagi"*, oldest historical reference book on Korea. Knowledge of seasonal influences on epidemic waves, such as humidity and temperature, were known but little more. Typhus, small-pox, influenza and cholera were all regarded as the same kind of sickness and termed *aek*. That being so, it is difficult to get any detailed information about the epidemic history of Korea. Regarded as a chronic plague, the *aek* sickness is one that was left unchecked, its nature unknown, for over two thousand years. Only in 1894, after the introduction of Western science, did it become possible to discriminate among the various kinds of diseases. In that year, for the first time, scarlet fever, measles and cholera were separately identified.

The biggest recorded outbreak occurred in the year 1750. According to a report from the provincial governments for the month of May of that year, *aek* accounted for a total of 124,000 lives that month. Including unregistered victims, the actual toll was estimated at over 300,000. In September, another 67,870 died. Modern researches on cholera list 32 outbreaks between 1489 and 1946 with the greatest case in 1796 when nearly 400,000 lost their lives. Typhoid fever, dysentery, smallpox and other diseases prevailed just as often.

The outbreaks of the eighteenth century occurred when herb medicine was at its height of development. Many authoritative scholars issued popularized booklets on herbs for distribution to every home in order to combat such "mass killers." Herbs, however, could do little, if anything, against them because, traditionally, they had been prepared for individual use rather than as public hygiene. Korea may be an underdeveloped nation but in epidemics, the difference is sharp between the old days and the modern era when almost all causes of epidemics have been eliminated to such an extent that the most ordinary practitioner is hardly able to find a victim.

A study of the medical system of the Yi dynasty shows that it was almost the same thing as that of the previous Koryo although in all fields of culture, differences were great. The top medical authority, *Chonigam*, was only another name for the *Taeuigam* with the same function of supervising the court physicians and examining the qualification of would-be practitioners. Only in 1885 was this post abolished in favor of a modern system. As in Koryo again, the Yi dynasty also had medical institutes to care for the general public, the *Heminwon* and the *Hwalinso*.

Within the essentially similar systems, however, the Yi dynasty saw some improvements in differentiating branches of medicine. They were conditioned, of course, by the fundamental weakness of herb medical practice with its tendency to indulge in futile subjective metaphysics and neglect objective approaches to anatomical or physiological problems. Despite the handicap, the Yi doctors were able to divide their practice into departments of surgery, obstretrics and gynecology. Above all, they also provided for women's participation in medical work for early in the dynastic era, an unprecedented institute was set up for girl medical students. Called the *Cheseangwon*, this institute trained a combination of nurse and doctor-assistant called the *uinyo* whose main task was to ease child-bearing and practise acupuncture. Because women were seldom allowed to step outside of the home in feudalistic society, these *uinyo* were in very popular demand.

King Sejong was greatly concerned about the state of public health as he was in many other things intended to improve the general lot. Thus, he visited more than thirty hot-springs all over the country and commanded his scholars to study the waters in order to establish them as public health centers.

Western Medicine

Korea's first contact with Western medicine came during the Three-Kingdom period and Koryo. The carrier was Buddhism which brought elements of Indian, Persian, Arabian and Roman medical knowledge but, it would appear, without any appreciable influence on Korean doctors who were quite completely under the spell of Chinese herb medical practices.

The Hideyoshi invasion from Japan at the close of the sixteenth century brought further elements of Western medicine, the Dutch and Southern schools, but again with little influence. Only in the late half of the nineteenth century did it really take hold in Korea. The first concrete practice came during the 13th year of King Kojong's reign in the form of a quarantine imposed on the port of Inchon and the initiative was undertaken not by Westerners but Japanese.

The Inchon quarantine of 1875 may be considered as the herald of the treaty port openings in Korea. The turning-point in the history of Korean medicine came immediately with the promulgation of certain regulations for preventive and sterilization measures. Eight years later, a stream of Japanese and American doctors followed suit to offer Western medical services and education and the first government medical school and hospital was established in 1899. This institute and the *Chejungwon*, a Royal Hospital, opened in 1885 by the American missionary-doctor, Horace Newton Allen, were the first two organizations to offer both educational and hospital facilities at the same time.

In short, we may summarize the introduction of Western medicine as follows: in the historical period, knowledge came through the medium of books translated into Chinese; this exerted little influence on Koreans. In the modern period, the Americans and Japanese, the latter learning their science from the German school, introduced Western medicine in both practical and educational fields; this proved decisive.

The first practical steps in public health administration were; the Japanese enforcement of port quarantine and creation of a public health bureau to prevent epidemics; promulgation of a small-pox act.

The Japanese Era

The long period of Japanese domination saw the problem of epidemics resuming its historical force of uncontrollable proportions, identifiable now but inexorable just the same. The administration was driven to drastic measures to combat the various diseases throughout the country. The police, entrusted with the job of controlling the germs, created public health divisions in all its provincial bureaus. Japanese doctors with a working knowledge of bacteriological or hygiene problems were put in charge of these divisions; public physicians were assigned as technical assistants at county and other local levels of the police. Two centers, one for bacteriological and serum research work, the other for hygiene experimentations, were established in Seoul to provide for pharmaceutical and hygienic tests; branches of these centers were installed in the provincial governments.

All these measures, however, did not turn the tide for the primary concern of the Japanese authorities was to check a frontierless threat rather than ensure the health of the Korean people. They wanted to contain the dam rather than seek the cure, and if only Koreans could provide the basis for their own health, they were not given the chance for modern medical knowledge is necessary to combat diseases and important posts were never offered to Koreans, not even to qualified doctors.

The authorities, therefore, concentrated their efforts merely on negative measures. Posters, booklets, movies and lectures galore may have warned against diseases as often as possible but there was at no time any positive approach to the problem. Only an enlightened policy can guide the people to combat germs but enlightenment was never forthcoming. The net effect of the Japanese campaigns was to arouse public fears and increase faith in superstitious remedies. Only in the last days of their administration did the Japanese belatedly built sanatoriums and adequate nursing schools in order to ease the threat of a particularly widespread outbreak of tuberculosis. These positive measures were taken because the T.B. crisis hit the Japanese community and the patients were mostly Japanese

In short, the Japanese policy on public health was dictated by the same merciless course of imperialistic aggrandizement that sacrificed Korean interests in all walks of life.

The immediate facts are readily available when we examine the record in the clinical field, the necessary instrument of public health promotion. To begin with, there were acute shortages in medical institutions, drugs and other clinical necessities. Moreover, the general practitioners served only those who could meet the bill; the poor majority, who could only afford part of their hospital fees or not at all, did not receive adequate treatment at any time because there was no such thing as social welfare. Few Koreans mastered enough knowledge about modern public hygiene to prevent illnesses, any the less prolong life or elevate living standards. Textbooks on hygiene dealt only with simple outlines and medical studies received less attention than other fields.

The Liberation Era

One of the first steps of the subsequent United States Military Administration was to embark on a strong program of public hygiene, the extent of Japanese apathy and negligence in the field coming as a revelation to the health-minded Americans. The first order issued by the Occupation authorities on September 24, 1945, barely a few days after the landing of the first G.I.'s on Korean soil, was to separate public health concerns from the province of the police and direct them into positive channels through a Department of Public Health. For the first time, principles of contemporary hygiene were applied in their own right. The Americans were also quick to realize that only Koreans could really care for their own health. Few Koreans being trained for hygiene work, the Occupation authorities sent many Korean students abroad for a well-rounded education. It was these medical students, among the earliest of all kinds of students going abroad, who provided Korea's true basis for public health work upon their return home. Men like Hwang Yongun, Choe Changsun, Choe Chechang, Choe Myongyong, Han Pomsok, Chu Inho, Paek Haengin, Yun Yuson, Kim Tongchol and Song Hyongnae deserve special mention not because they were the first Korean students of modern hygiene but because of the active work they have been carrying on in this field.

Following the establishment of the Republic of Korea government, relations between this country and the United States grew firmer with increased opportunities for expansion of the Korean medical field. Indeed, it is no exaggeration to aver that every progress in Korean hygienes owes a debt to ever-improving American knowledge. From the beginning, the Korean government considered the training of hygiene specialists and the reinforcement of hygiene organizations as the two top priority problems to be tackled. Extensive studies were also undertaken over the years to ascertain the basic conditions of Korean health in order to devise appropriate measures. On the other hand, we must admit that there have been responsible men who have slowed the process, due undoubtedly to the general apathy of the country engendered over the long years of the bankrupt Japanese age.

The most promising step has been the recent establishment of a School of Public Health in the Medical College of the Seoul National University under government supervision. Such a school was in the planning stage as early as the U.S. Occupation period only to be delayed repeatedly down the years which saw the vacancy filled by occasional lecture sessions and private institutes of the American-Korean Foundation.

Today, Korea has more than fifty doctors with Master Degrees in public health from overseas study. One of the government's two top priorities may be said to have been satisfactorily tackled, at least more than we can reasonably expect. What about the other? Have our hygiene establishments been strengthened?

Reorganizations have been attempted in accordance with the provisions of the government Organization Law of 1949 but things have never gone smoothly. The problem is poor administration. At the top, the Ministry of Public Health and Social Affairs of the central government has undergone such frequent changes in structure that it has hardly provided effective guidance. At the levels of the provincial governments and the Special City of Seoul, public health and hygiene belong to separate, independent departments, thereby preventing the necessary basis for close harmony in problems that are essentially interrelated. Below the provincial governmental level, there are virtually no effective agencies in existence. All told, there are only some 20 public health centers and 500 public dispensaries. These operate sporadically, distributed nationwide on occasions of annual health campaigns.

Present and Future

Necessary Measures

Before suggesting some measures necessary to sound hygiene, let us review the background of Korean health problems.

The Korean peninsula is located at nor-

XI HEALTH PROBLEMS

thern latitudes of the temperate zone. This has led to a cultural development of which we are both proud and happy. The changes of the four seasons are distinctive and water is everywhere abundant. This makes the land one of the best places to live in. These exceptional advantages of nature have helped the Korean people to live along and continuous history. It has also contributed to the habit of white clothes and clean homes.

Basically, then, Koreans are a health-minded people, naturally inclined to hygiene. Their diet has consisted mainly of rice and vegetables and they have, generally, led plain lives, loving nature and not asking much of society. The way of life was tolerable under the feudalistic structure of society when Korea was a "hermit nation." But in this turbulent age of rapid social, technological and scientific transformations, it has become outmoded and unsatisfactory.

What is more, the problems multiplied by the conditions of modern life have been aggravated by the low per capita incomes caused by an explosive population growth that has known no checks. Statistics show that as of December 1958, the total population of south Korea was 22,633,468; the life expectancy was 45 in the male and 49 in the female; the birth rate was 35.6 and the death rate 20.6 (the last two figures according to 1955 census). The mean rate in the increase in Gross National Production (G.N.P.) was 7.06 percent and the annual per capita income 70-75 dollars. This low standard living is the basic obstacle to hygienic improvement.

Following are some of the more urgent problems which await solution:

Environmental Sanitation

The Korean land is beautiful and the average Korean keeps himself clean but the society in which he lives combines all the unsanitary excesses of underdevelopment. The minimum indispensable measures are to provide adequate water service, control drainage, excrement or trash, and secure better food diets. All efforts to tackle these problems are still far short of satisfactory.

Waterworks service is available only in the larger towns and cities and only 60 percent of the urban population rely on a system of 68 water plants which, for the most part, are of the slow sand filtration type. According to statistics of the Ministry of Health and Social Affairs, the percentage of the total population supplied with waterworks (approx. 300,000 metric tons a day for a daily consumption of 60 liters) is only 14 percent.

This means that only a mere two and a half million people, little more than one-tenth the total population, are at all adequately served. The overwhelming majority must depend on rivers, ponds or wells, especially the last, of which there are 129,275 public wells and 232,684 private. The government treats the public water supply with liquid chlorine of 1-2 p.p.m. (parts per million) concentration and public wells with calcium hypochlorite.

For all that, the gross inadequacy of a proper supply and distribution system means that the threat of water-borne diseases is ever-present.

Only a small part of drainage works is covered, leaving enough room everywhere for flies, rats and other pests to breed. Human excrement is disposed of by the traditional method of the pit privy and sewers to be used as manure on the farms without adequate processes of treatment. The result is the constant threat of endemic diseases, typhoid fever, dysentery, clonorchiasis (liver fluke) and paragonimiasis (lung fluke). A survey on the last two parasitic diseases has been conducted by the use of purified skin test antigen on about 10,000 persons, in all localities. On the basis of the positive reactor findings, it is estimated that 4,5000,000 are infected with clonorchis sinensis and up to 1,5000,000 with paragonimus watermani.

Inasmuch as the agricultural economy is founded on a traditional application of all waste nitrogenous matters, however inadequately treated, nothing short of an overall agricultural economic reform can lead to improvement. In the meantime, the parasites are a constant threat.

Malnutrition caused by lack of animal protein, fats, the vitamin B group, and ashes, is a national malaise. Combined with the high contraction rates of parasites, it amounts to a truly serious problem.

Despite the ever-present dangers, epidemiologic inspections, supposedly a routine precaution, are conducted only when there is an actual outbreak of an epidemic or infectional disease. The problem of environmental sanitation is being badly neglected when it should be the first priority in any movement to improve the state of public health.

Year	Victims		Deaths		Fatality Rate
	No.	Mortality Rate	No.	Death Rate	
1950	16,757	—	2,728	—	—
51	172,486	845.5	3,602	164.7	19.5
52	10,227	49.6	1,367	6.6	13.4
53	7,052	32.8	849	3.9	12.0
54	2,982	13.9	373	1.7	12.5
55	3,209	14.6	909	4.1	28.3
56	1,458	6.6	214	1.0	14.7
57	1,963	8.7	197	0.9	10.0

Community Infection

Improper sanitary works and neglige nce of routine epidemiologic check-ups brings us to the second problem, namely, the control of community infections. Mass vaccinations and inoculations to parallel the sanitary conditions of the community's surroundings may help to ensure mass immunizations although they are no more than passive measures. Thanks, however, to the development of many antibiotics and insecticides, acute cases of communicable diseases are diminishing as shown by the above table.

Chronic communicable diseases, on the other hand, have yet to be controlled. The most common is tuberculosis which has increased latest figures to 800,000 needed hospital cases and a 7.5% rate of contraction. Leprosy accounts for 45,000 patients. These, together with annual recurrences of Japanese B-encephalitis and poliomyelitis, are the most serious problems yet to be solved.

Medical Profession

The registered numbers of physicians, dentists, herb practitioners, midwives and nurses per ten thousand population in 1957 are shown by the following chart:

Classification	Total	Per 10,000
Physicians	6,782 (male 6,069, female 713)	3.2
Dentists	1,125 (male 1,054, female 71)	0.5
Herb-doctors	2,373 (male 2,359, female 14)	1.1
Midwives	2,878	1.4
Nurses	2,962	1.4

The chart indicates that the number of medical professionals is far from enough to ensure the general public health. The shortage is further aggravated by the extreme tendency to concentrate in the large cities. Thus, Seoul has one doctor to every 800 persons.

One of the most important problems for government authorities, therefore, is to train more and better active medical professionals. This requires ample improvement in institutes of medical education. Medical and medical educational installations as of 1957 are shown here.

Educational Institutes

Medical Institution	No. of School	No. of Enrollment, Each Year
Medical College	8	950
Dental College	2	250
Nursing and Midwifery School	25	2,000
School of Public Health	1	40

↑ Red Cross Hospital in Seoul

↓ National Medical Center, Seoul (Scandinavian-sponsored)

← Seoul National University Attached Hospital

Severance Hospital Attached to Yonsei University →

← Capital Army Hospital, Seoul

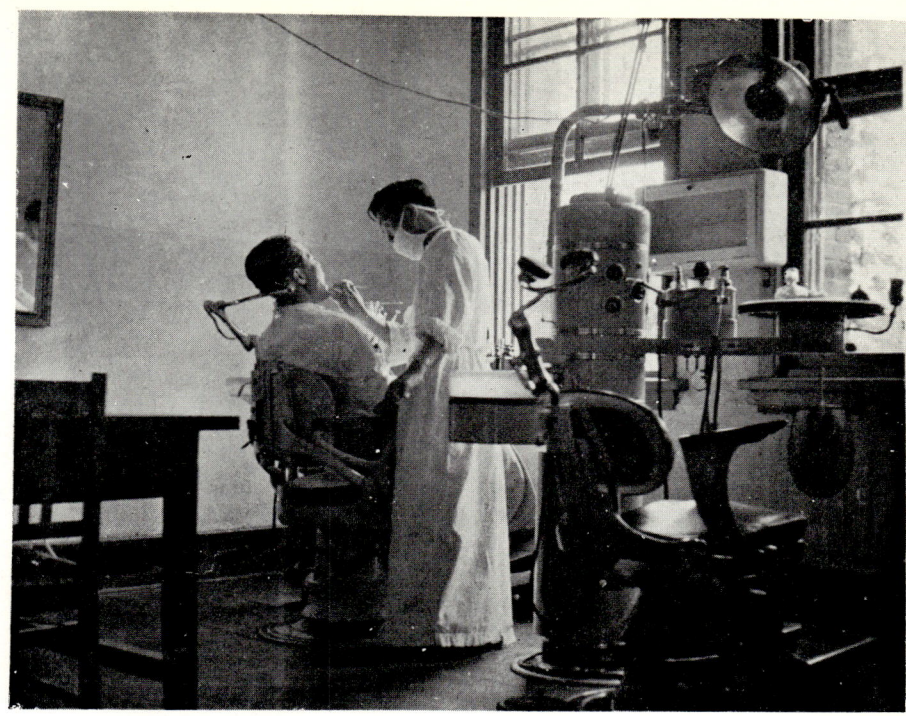

↑   The Interior Facilities of Dental Clinic

↓   A Pharmacist Laboratory in Hospital

↑ Suction Pump Tower for Waterworks

↑ Switch-board Room for Watershed

↓ Water Tanks for Filtration in Kuui-ri Watershed, Seoul

Medical Installations

Total	Hospital and Clinic				Dental Hosp and Clinic	
	Gen Hosp	Hosp	Clinic	Limited Clinic	Hosp and Clinic	Limited Clinic
6,824	50	96	2,626	281	551	90

Herb Clinic		Dispensary	Sanatorium (TB Leprosy)
Clinic	Limited Clinic	Industry, School, Offices, etc.	
793	482	72	46

Midwifery Office	Health Center	Relief Dispensary
1,202	22	513

Herb-Doctors

As a previous chart shows, there is one herb-practitioner in every ten thousand citizens, a figure that reflects the lingering confidence of the people in the traditional method of cure.

Herb-medicine suffered a fatal blow when the traditional order of society crumbled before the onrush of the modern political revolution. The Japanese, very proud of their newly acquired knowledge of the Western sciences, looked down with disdain upon the prevalence of herb-medicine in Korea, denying its worth as an honorable profession. They may have given Korean herb doctors licences to carry on their practice but discriminated against their legal and social status. On the other hand, some Japanese scholars, centered on the faculty of the Keijo (Seoul) Imperial University, recognized the scientific values of the ancient Oriental medicine and conducted a series of remarkable research work which, however, have yet to be publicized.

The Liberation of '45 was a liberation for all and herb-practitioners were no exception. They greeted the event as opportunity for free development of their medicine. But the new public health authorities proved to be as scornful of their profession as the Japanese had been. This incurred resentments among their ranks. Indeed, many young scholars of herb-medicine, infuriated by the unexpected denial, turned to Communism to express their protest against the U.S. Occupation and what they considered to be an insult to their status and calling.

Despite this loss, indefatigable efforts have been made by other doctors, resulting in the birth of a private educational institute in 1948 that, in subsequent years, has grown to the dimensions of the present-day Tongyang (Oriental) Medical School.

At the time of the Liberation, the total number of herb-practitioners was 1,657. Since then, the figure has been considerably boosted by graduates of the herb medical college and doctors qualifying themselves through state examinations conducted under the revised Medical Acts of 1952. In 1959, the total was 2,643.

The increase, however, is greatly dwarfed by the total 7,000 practitioners in Western medicine who are being reinforced yearly from the many colleges providing education in the advanced sciences. Then, again, we must remember that too many of them are oldsters, a fact that would suggest a decisive malady in herb medical practice.

Acupuncture is an inseparable part of herb medicine and so is practised by most of the herb-doctors. It can, however, be considered as an independent profession in its own right. A total 2,230 acupuncturists were officially qualified during the Japanese administration. Of these, 200 are blind men who learned massage and other techniques under a rehabilitative program for the crippled.

Up to the Liberation, the clients have been mostly restricted to the rural population. Today, however, there are three hundred and odd herb-doctors in Seoul alone, serving urban generations of both sexes, young and old.

The Administration authorities reportedly are considering not to issue further licences to prevent deterioration in standards. Indeed, herb-medicine is confronted by many obstacles natural to the conditions under which it carries on an old tradition. Its practitioners, however, see no reason why it should not develop into a full-fledged profession able to hold its head in the modern world.

They may have a point but first the obstacles must be overcome. Intellectual confidence must be acquired and simpler and better dispensary methods developed if they are ever to make the point.

Future in Hygiene

Because of the prolonged state of political instability, casting its shadows over all social, cultural and economic efforts at improvement, no normal rate of progress can be expected in public hygiene. The continued division of the land and the destructions of war have exacted a heavy toll from the nation's will to advance. In two fields of public health programs, therapeutics and preventive services, damage has been especially considerable.

The pace, however, is forward. Foreign aid, especially from the United States, has without doubt done much to spread general enlightenment about the problems involved. Of course, it was instrumental in combatting the immediate threats. The sudden diminution in the number of acute epidemic victims, donations of many "miracle" drugs and new medical equipments, and the training of many young students overseas, are examples of the great contributions they have made.

Above all, the expansion of present installations and construction of new ones, together with the training of yet more medical students abroad as part of annual programs will certainly serve as the driving power for future progress.

The turning-point will be the day when the government will allot enough budget in keeping with the importance of public health (only one percent is presently allocated as compared to the reported minimum of eight in most other countries). With the money must come positive efforts to ensure that organizational work and functions of public health administration and services are consistent. On that day, we need not be prophets to predict that it will only be a matter of years before the state of Korean health administration catches up with the levels of the advanced countries. The health of the Korean people will then be assured in a welfare state and hygienics will assume its proper role as a valuable branch of science.

Herb Contribution

The reappraisal of Oriental culture is a new worldwide trend among scholarly circles and the study of herb-medicine is included as a typical natural science of practical value.

Admittedly, the Oriental world has been somewhat biased in their excessive reliance on herbs. Subjective speculations and phenomenological idealisms have gone hand-in-hand once too often in the name of experience to explain symptoms of the human mind and body. Research work on the true causes of the ailment was unduly neglected.

On the other hand, Western medical science is also not without its weaknesses, and we contend that the two great medical schools of the East and West can heal their respective Achilles' heels by mutual exchange, thereby integrating both into one new school of medicine for the future.

Indeed, we may notice some signs of such integration movements. One evidence is the increasing use of *sanghwatang*, a good but cheap herb preparation against fatigues and anaemia. Heavy dosages of aspirin- phencetine-caffein (A.P.C.) tablets or antibiotics often fail to relieve the individual of cold or exhaustion, but a *sanghwatang* concoction, either in powder or tunic, is completely effective after a few days' intake. At any rate, it is now one of the "best-sellers" in drugstores that otherwise deal in Western pills.

The Western acceptance provides herb-doctors with two lessons. First, they need feel no sense of inferiority before modern science when this science itself is disposed to accept certain fundamentals of their medicine. Secondly, accepting, they must uphold their profession in the spirit of modern science. This requires an objective approach to the patient rather than subjective preoccupation with herbs for their own professional sake. However effective the drugs, the people will not accept them if they are not developed to meet their tastes or serve their demands.

Some practitioners of Western medicine, especially among the younger generations, are utterly scornful about the efficacy of herb drugs. They point to outmoded theories and unscientific ambiguity in the language of the herb-doctors and conclude that it is only for old folks and ignorant people unable to free themselves of habitual customs or emotional attachments. In my opinion, however, people are not so foolish as all that. Certainly, they are too economy-minded to pay for negative or fraudulent results. At any rate, there are enough intelligent people in my corner, members of the National Assembly who drafted the Herb Medicine Act and most of the leaders in journalism who registered sharp opposition to a proposal for doing away with herb medical practices altogether.

Disenchantment was pronounced among progressive circles in the latter days of the Yi dynasty. This was understandable since they were the first recipients of the advanced state of Western sciences. At the same time, however, they and subsequent generations have been so fascinated by the power and grandeur of the new civilization and culture that the tendency has been to accept them all without digesting them properly or subjecting them to adequate criticisms.

Meanwhile, the abrupt postwar enthusiasm of Westerners in Oriental culture has led to reappraisals of Eastern heritages and spurred vigorous East-West exchanges. Regards herb medicinal practices, the principles on which they are based were set more than two thousand years ago and little, if any, developments have evolved since then. As a time-honored form of treatment, they are not to be supinely antiquated under the rapid changes of modern science. No satisfactory readjustment, therefore, is likely in the near future.

The truly great task of coordinating Eastern and Western medical sciences is best done by close cooperation between modern researchers, armed with sound scientific knowledge, and herb-scholars with abundant experiences. An administration of insight and imagination could well encourage such cooperation to speed the process. Such rejuvenation will surely elevate herb medicine to an unprecedented height of efficacy in both Occidental and Oriental efforts to improve the health of man.

XII THOUGHTS AND RELIGIONS

General Remarks on Korean Thought

Introduction

The primitive thinking of any and every people is rooted in religious ideas. Korea is no exception. Her thinking, which has never been able to divorce the religious and social aspects to any clear degree to make one independent of the other, is undoubtedly to be traced back to a primitive form of religion. Some thinkers would do this rather deliberately to give the bias to religion while others want to minimize the religious influence in human life by stressing social trends. Inasmuch as this author is not in a position to take a definitive side on the issue of religion vs. society, he shall confine himself objectively to the strict historical facts known to us.

Primitive Thought and Religion

Some features of primitive Korean thinking may be ascertained from the national ethos. The primitive ethos of the Korean people belonged to the prevailing one in Northeast Asia. The root was Shamanism, the animistic form of worship common to all tribes of the region. Although other powerful religious forces and modes of thinking entered Korean life in the process of the historical development of the country, Shamanism to this day retains a powerful hold on the credulous folks. Not all the intermingling with superior religions has robbed it of its essential role of appeasing the adverse spirits. The result is that Shamanism as practised today preserves much of its original features.

In bygone days, people were worshipping mountains everywhere from Shantung through the Manchurian plains and down the Korean peninsula. Their forms of worship have come through the mists of antiquity and a long civilization, and may be found, virtually intact in all the remote rural areas of Korea. As a historical evidence, the primitive belief is well expressed in certain pictures appearing on the walls of Koguryo tombs on the Manchurian side of the Yalu border as well as in those preserved in and around Pyongyang.

The Three Kingdoms and Unified Silla

With the development of the primitive Korean communities to a degree sufficiently vigorous to establish statehoods, came contacts with the advanced culture of China. The Three Kingdoms began to learn Chinese political, social, ethical ideas. The outstanding feature of Chinese civilization, of course, was Confucianism. Confucian concepts of social harmony and moral precepts permeated Korean intellectual thinking from the outset to play a most important part in moulding the Korean national character. The second great foreign body of thought during the Three Kingdoms was Buddhism. Since Buddhism arrived through China which adopted the Mahayana or "Greater Vehicle" school of Buddhism, it follows that this was the version of the Gautama's teachings that dominated Korea. The Hinayana or "Lesser Vehicle" school, however, was not without its influence in Korea for the southern kingdom of Paekche was able directly to communicate with India and some Korean scholars, disposed to refer to the original source, studied there.

Silla

Buddhism was introduced into the Silla kingdom at the height of its prosperity to be merged with the traditional and Confucianistic beliefs into a complete body of Silla thought. A concrete example is the five commandments of the *Hwarangdo*, which incorporated the Confucian virtues of filial piety and loyalty to the monarch, the Buddhist restraint on taking animal life, and the native *Hwarang* concept of chivalry and patriotism. The impression has prevailed that the *Hwarangdo* or "Way of the Flower of Manhood" was a school devoted to martial valor. The undue emphasis on the warlike *Hwarang* should properly be regarded as prejudiced. What should be stressed was the spirit that would harmonize all the teachings then known to the kingdom. It was this rather than the military exploits of this or that *Hwarang* warrior that provided the keynote for the successful unification of the Korean peninsula under Silla. The famed Pulguksa and Sokkuram temples in Kyongju were the symbols of that harmonizing spirit.

Among the many brilliant priests of the Silla days of glory, the name of Wonhyo stands out as the representative thinker of the age. Wonhyo did not care to go to the Tang kingdom of China although that was the fashion for all the other scholars. Instead, he studied intensively at home. His subject, naturally, was Buddhism and the fact that he could concentrate on his studies in Korea goes to show that Buddhism was developed sufficiently to enable a devoted scholar to understand it without the necessity of an expensive foreign travel. The many books on Buddhism which he wrote reveal that the scope of his studies had been very comprehensive. His works, held in high esteem by the T'ang kingdom, show that Wonhyo was not merely a Buddhist scholar but a universal-minded individual interested in harmonizing all teachings known to him into a single integrated whole. In Buddhism itself with its various splits and deviations, he tried very hard to reconcile the traditional Mahayana school of religion from its active reaction as represented by the *zen* sect. In short, his ceaseless search for a harmony to all man's teachings corresponded with the national aspiration to unite the three kingdoms into one.

Thus, the tone of Silla culture was one of harmony and unity culminating in the establishment of the *Hwarangdo* institutes. At the core was the appreciation of natural beauties and the teachings of the Buddha as expressed in Mahayana literature. A harmonized spirit was inculcated in the *Hwarang* youths and this, in turn, expressed itself in flexible approaches to society and such inspirations in the field of literature as the *Hyangga* poetry which, for the first time, employed Chinese characters adapted to Korean pronunciation.

Not all was harmony, however. Wonhyo's Buddhist rivals were scholars who insisted on laying the foundation of Silla culture upon Buddhist epistemology. Side by side with the unifying but flexible concept of the *Hwarangdo* of which Buddhism was but a part, was the logical insistence on strict Buddhist doctrines based on spiritual motives, of which the outstanding scholar was Wonchuk. The *Hwarang* school was able to catch the siprit of the moment to unite the land under Silla but it was the doctrinaire school which was to assert itself in the united kingdom to grow into the state religion of Buddhist Koryo. Buddhism became orthodox; *Hwarangdo* wilted.

Koryo

Indeed, *Hwarangdo* may be said to have served its purpose with the success of Silla. Success achieved, the school, based on intuition, had little chance to compete with the incorporated systems of traditional thoughts as represented by Confucianism, Buddhism and Taoism. So long as the kingdom lasted, the school survived; the kingdom falling, it declined sharply.

The spiritual promise of Silla was about an everlasting life in the other world by a glorious fulfilment in this one, but with the dynastic change came the anxiety to secure the present life on earth. In other words, the people wanted religious consolations that were both realistic and practical. They found this outlet by worshipping the spirits of their departed ancestors. This ancestor-worship, the core of Confucian teachings, was based on principles of geomancy and, as such, was no doubt an extreme form of escapism for it entailed the worshipping of the elements, wind, water, mountains, and so on. It was, however, realistic in that the people sought worldly blessings as compared to the spirit of the *Hwarandgo* in which worldly things did not count. Against the aristocratic tenor of the Silla spirit, ancestor-worship lent itself to popular appeal.

The history of Koryo, it must be remembered, was a history of recurrent pressures and invasions from warlike peoples in the nomadic plains between the civilized states of China and Korea. This made for a feeling of great insecurity which only served to heighten the popular urge for escapism. The mentality was suited to Buddhism which soon became the dominant religion in the kingdom, embracing all classes of believers.

The hold of Buddhism remained tight in the popular mind but the aristocracy, widening the gap between the classes, was making the religion more and more a purely academic affair. Famous priestly scholars were collecting and printing Buddhist sculptures and literature and involving themselves in a maze of complicated doctrines the farther they sought. The extreme was reached by the monk, Taegak, who wanted to create a completely new world as based upon the Buddhist Scriptures known in Korean as the *Taejang*. These were scriptures prevailing in the Sung kingdom of China and, as such, was naturally Continent-centered; i.e. centered on the Central Kingdom. Taegak went beyond this mere concept to consider other countries outside China for the foundation of Buddhism. The *Taejang*, or Tripitaka Koreana as it is known in English, is, indeed, the most monumental work on Buddhism in the world.

Meanwhile, the ruling feudal class was gradually parting company with Buddhism. This was due primarily to the transition from Silla to Koryo which resulted in the changes of personal fortunes among the leading classes. In any such transition, a power vacuum is created between one set of nobility and another into which the new religion, championed by the newcomers, streams in.

Thus, the Buddhist priests surged in with the new Koryo kingdom and the Confucian scholars with the Yi. Feudalism has received a temporary setback but it renews consolidation and reasserts itself to find the religious class holding undue powers in the state. The feudalistic opposition to Buddhism was all the more reinforced by the fact that the temple was losing its religious and ethical significances to become a secular and merely ceremonial institute. Against Buddhism, the feudal lords turned to Confucianism which challenged the former with ethical ideas that were more realistic and practical. On theoretical grounds, there was no real issue, a fact which can be clearly recognized from the works of such priests as Wonhyo who were perfectly able to reconcile both teachings.

The outstanding scholar who criticized Buddhism, Choe Sungno, did not take exception to the prevailing religion on any theoretical grounds whatever but questioned its practical or ethical ones by pointing to its corruption. What was more important, King Songjong, reigning in Choe's days, found it necessary to oppose and, if possible, destroy those feudal lords of the ruling class whose interests were deeply bound in Buddhism. The royal opposition to the state religion was clearly political and what he sought was political criticisms of his courtiers. His need was answered by the Confucian scholar, Choe. Indeed, upon reading Choe carefully, we might assert that the scholar was also influenced by the king, that the two complemented each other from different approaches. In other words, Choe's criticisms not merely made no issue on ideological grounds but it was a political maneuver to guide the king in his opposition to the vested interests of the Buddhists. On theoretical grounds alone, these interests could afford to counter-challenge the newly rising forces. The recorded history of the Koryo dynasty shows us that after Korean acceptance of the Sung philosophy, the struggle between the Buddhist and Confucianist forces were political and economic rather than ideological.

When the new school of Confucian philosophy of the Sung dynasty was first introduced to Korea, Korean scholars did not understand its philosophical imports. They had to steep themselves in studying the new words, phrases and terminologies before they could even begin to understand it. This took a long span of time. For a while, Confucianism and Buddhism co-existed with the practical ethics of the former and the latter's concept of future life taken for granted together. The clearest testimony to this co-existence was the works of Chong Tojon, a great Confucian scholar toward the end of the Koryo dynasty. His criticisms of Buddhism on ethical grounds were excellent but, like his predecessors, he had no cause to quarrel with its theories. The same went for the next great Confucian scholar, Kwon Kun. A period of silence was needed before such scholars as So Kyongdok, Yi Toege, Yi Yulgok and Ki Taesung appeared to grasp the significance of the Sung philosophy. The new theory of human nature, the *li-chi* doctrine of the Chu Hsi school, captured the imagination of the kingdom and led to the replacement of Confucianism with Buddhism as the state religion of the new Yi dynasty. It had taken a very long time for the new Confucian school to be really understood. In the opinion of this author, it required two centuries of study from the end of Koryo and the early years of Yi before it could take deep root in Korea.

Yi Dynasty

The dynastic change of the fourteenth century was not only political but social and economic, and since the aristocratic class of Koryo constituted a combination of both political power and Buddhism, the new Yi regime had to find a new center of faith to consolidate its own political foundation. That faith was provided by the philosophy of Chu Hsi.

The scholar who laid down the theoretical cornerstone for the new dynasty was Chong Tojon. His works were inspired by the ancient Chou system of government as expounded by Confucius and his followers culminating in the interpretations of Chu Hsi.

The kingdom acted vigorously upon this cornerstone. In order to make good kings out of the Yi successors with no political experience and encourage candidates for sound civil servants, schools were established in towns and villages. Altogether, it took almost one century before the new dynasty could consolidate itself by eliminating all conflicts in the court and suppressing the traditional political powers and vested interests.

To sum up: the Chu Hsi philosophy was adopted as the guiding principle of the new regime in the fields of education and politics but it was only in the sixteenth century, or 200 years after the founding of the kingdom, that it was really understood and formulated. Thereafter and until the end of the dynastic life, it was to become an immovable doctrine.

Chu Hsi did not develop in a straight line according to its inherent ideas. Instead, it became an instrument of political strife, giving rise to many rival doctrines. Schools of epistemology, human nature and rituals were born and fought one another. There were, in fact, so many schools that some scholars claim Confucianism was more highly developed in Korea than in China, its homeland. A monopoly of the state, everything in Korean life, including the individual's way of thinking and social behavior, had to conform to Chu Hsi philosophy; all other ideas were barred, and suppressed as heresy. Among others, the new progressive theory of the Chinese, Wang Yang-ming, had to be banned. Despite severe suppressions, however, some scholars managed to embrace this theory about the unity of knowledge and conduct, or theory and practice.

From the end of the sixteenth century, there arose the Silhak school of real or practical learning whose followers attempted to put into practice the original Chu Hsi teachings undermined by strict orthodoxy. The school was for the most part championed by members of the *Namin* or "Southerners" faction. This was one of the two factions born around the year, 1575, and the nucleus of many more similar political groupings that were to indulge in increasing struggle for power in the subsequent Yi years. From now on, scholars were to belong to one or the other of these various factions and their ideas were to be affected by the rise or fall of the factional color they wore. The *Namin* faction, once powerful, fell out of favor in due course of time and it was as the 'out's' that brilliant scholars arose within its ranks to advocate political reforms and industrial development in changing trends of the modern age. Originally, they espoused Chu Hsi but later they became increasingly influenced by new teachings in the Ming kingdom, among these, Wang Yang-ming's theory which we have mentioned. They were also the first Koreans to be affected by Western thoughts, especially scientific knowledge, which were coming through China from a Europe on the high tides of the recent Renaissance. Yi Sugwang, Yu Hyongwon, Yi Ik, Hong Taeyong, Pak Chiwon, Yi Toksu, Pak Chega,

Chong Yakyong, Hong Manson, So Yugu, Yi Kyugyong and Kim Chongho are but only a few of the representative *Namin* scholars who wanted to ameliorate the state of affairs they found in Yi society. To the contrary, the government was monopolized by die-hard conservatives who, in the face of the reform movements, went all the way down the path of official corruption and national poverty till it was ripe for plucking by foreign invaders advancing on the "Hermit Kingdom" in the nineteenth century age of imperialisms.

One branch of the Sohak, or Western learning, was represented by Catholicism by way of China in Chinese translation. Whether it was accepted as a philosophy or for practical ethical purposes is hard to tell. Many scholars, however, rejected its philosophical contents. Catholicism, which would equalize all classes and demand a loyalty higher than the earthly monarch in Seoul, appealed to the masses with the result that it found itself engaged in a continuing state of conflict with authority for one hundred years up to the middle of the nineteenth century. There were many massacres but persecutions only forced Catholicism to take deep roots, contrary to conservative expectations.

In the middle of the nineteenth century, there lived a great thinker in Kyongju, named Choe Cheu, better known, perhaps, by his literary penname, Choe Suun. The deep concern he felt for the poverty of the peasantry drove him to study every idea, old or new. The result was a fresh native religious inspiration called the Tonghak school. This religion combined the three Oriental basics of Confucianism, Buddhism and Taoism with an infusion of Catholic spirit towards the first and foremost goal of saving the soul of the peasantry. We are, however, outrunning this general account for first it is necessary to mention the increasing cleavage between government and society.

The wave of Catholic massacres in 1801 was but the first of many waves in the next four decades. They reflected the extreme degrees to which government would carry

XII THOUGHTS AND RELIGIONS

on its unquestioned authority, blind to the consequences of the deep social cleavages. Corruption and disorders ran wild in the capital, while minor officials and the landed gentry shamelessly cheated, oppressed, and exploited the farmers in the countryside, learning all sorts of ingenuous schemes by which to impose extravagant interest rates, compulsory labor, etc.

A series of peasants' rebellions now followed of which the Tonghak was the last and greatest. The first such revolt took place in the year 1811 in the northern province of Pyongan Pukto under the leadership of a northerner, Hong Kyongnae. The government was able to suppress this insurrection but not the causes that had led to it, the unrest and distress of the farmers which were only deepened and spread all the more widely over the country. The next great outbreak came in 1862 when the peasants of Chinju in the southern province of Kyongsang Namdo besieged the government troops on that armed fortress. Chinju sparked off unrests on Cheju island, in other Kyongsang areas, and in the Pyongan provinces of the north. In fact, the spirit of rebellion continued up to the outbreak of the Tonghak movement in 1894.

The founder of the Tonghak sect, as we have noted, was the Kyongju *yangban*, Choe Cheu, or Choe Suun. Inasmuch as he stressed the importance of a truly Korean answer as against the answer from the West, namely, Catholicism, to the social problems of the times, he has been regarded as anti-West in his thinking. Actually, he was not anti-Western but pro-Korean and far from rejecting Western learning, he studied that, too, and absorbed some of its ingredients into his Eastern learning.

The need, he felt, was a religious direction in the country rather than from Heaven or Rome to save the farmers from their impossible plight. For championing the farmers, he was arrested and executed but remained the spiritual leader of a growing movement which was to break out in a politico-religious revolt that the government could suppress only with outside military help.

The increasing foreign influences confronted Korean thinkers with the basic issue of opening up the kingdom to the world or keeping it closed. Most progressive scholars favored the former because they saw the necessity of modernizing Korea and preferred to meet the challenge of the times rather than ignore it. But the progressives were too uncertain and succumbed easily to temptations and chameleon-like changes that made them easy victims of foreign influences. The most steadfast thinkers were men of the caliber of Yi Hangno. As a traditional Korean, he was a Confucian scholar and an admirer of Chinese civilization. This made him both anti-Japanese and anti-Western, but unlike the die-hard conservative scholars, he clearly felt the changes of the times.

Yi neither ignored the modern trends of the times like the conservatives nor embraced them without understanding like the progressives; the necessary changes had to be made upon Korean initiatives. Many Koreans who were Confucian-orientated followed Yi, including Paek Nakkwan who reached the conclusion that the best course was an "Open Door" policy once Korea was strong enough to stand on her own two feet.

While all this soul-searching was going on in the "Hermit Kingdom," the conflict of Power interests descended upon it. In Korea, it was focussed among Japan, Russia and China, with the other by no means disinterested Western Powers in the second row. Korean politicians and scholars found themselves divided into this or that foreign camp.

To thinkers like Yi Hangno and Paek Nakkwan, however, the clearest danger came from a Japan which was disclosing her hidden intentions of conquest from 1894 on. In a world of vacillating attitudes toward the foreign powers, Yi and Paek remained consistently anti-Japanese; that is to say, pro-Korean. Yi turned to partisan warfare after the Japanese Annexation to lead a host of volunteer anti-Japanese fighters. Paek was arrested by pro-Japanese officals of the Korean government and put to death.

Western ideas of democracy were first propagated in Korea by an organization known as the Independence Association. The first and foremost aspiration of its members was to rid Korea of foreign control. They wanted a democratic Korea but first it had to be an independent Korea. That was why they called their organization Independence Association.

The newspaper they published had as its main objective the inculcation of independent ideas among the masses. Scholars like Chu Sigyong and Chang Chiyon embarked upon a systematic study of the Korean language to the same end. Yet other scholars, like Yu Kiljun and Paek Ilgyu, tried to introduce capitalistic ideas for the general public could not have independent political ideas without independent economic means. In short, the Independence Association stood for Western modernization of Korean society by means of letters.

Modern Era

The Independence Association was championing ideas which were already streaming into the peninsula through foreign missionaries, especially American, who began opening Protestant missions from 1884 on. The missionaries were not only Gospel-carriers but also on-the-field social reformers. They built schools, hospitals, charity institutions. Capitalistic interests followed to obtain grants for building railroads, telegraphic lines and other modern means of transportation and communication. In the meantime, the Independence Association, of course, was encouraging Western ideas of liberty and equality. All such efforts to modernize Korea were terminated with the Japanese Annexation of 1910.

What Japan wanted was a colony based on a feudalistic structure of society and bound by Confucianism. The Japanese rulers, therefore, preserved and even encouraged these features of Korean life but vigorously suppressed all new trends of thought from the West and everything nationalistic. The young Korean generations, however, could not be stopped from thinking and accepting such ideas as anarchism, socialism, and communism to liberate Korea. In their ardent wish for independence, they made no fine distinctions between them and when the Liberation did, indeed, come, they were too impatient to adapt foreign systems of ideology to unworkable Korean conditions and lacked sufficient time to process them through the grains of careful academic scrutiny. To this day, Koreans have not determined what is really applicable.

In other words, the overall desire of a long-lost state of national independence drove many Koreans into unrealistic ideologies and even superstitious faiths. Various forms of superstition dominated the Korean masses who were poor both materially and intellectually. The Japanese government did not try to eliminate them but rather protected them. They corrupted the Korean mind and intellect. Confucianism, Buddhism and Christianity, all of which had promoted nationalism, had to fight against corrupted thinking in their ranks when the Liberation came in 1945.

The ideological conflicts of this kind which are often to be met in colonized countries were experienced in Korea not only in the religious field but also in the fields of science, culture, politics and economy. They offer basic problems that must be solved not only in Korea but all over the world. Korea is, however, one of the countries which must find an urgent solution to the ideological struggle because it confronts the Korean mentality with the most complex situation known in Korean history. This complexity is at the root of all the unrest, mental suffering, escapist trends and mental deadlocks of the Korean people today.

Confucianism in Korea

Introduction

It is needless to expound Confucianism itself for this is well understood by the interested Western scholar or layman. However, in order to make this article intelligible to foreign readers who are not familiar with Korea and to make them understand how Confucianism came to exert such a great influence upon Korean life and thought, it would be helpful to point out some salient points of Confucianism.

According to recent researches made by Oriental and Western scholars, the *ju* class was made up of dispossessed descendents of the Chou aristocracy to form a middle class between the helpless and ignorant peasantry and the aristocracy by the time Confucius was born. The fortunes and dignity of the *ju* declining, all they could depend on for a living was their talents and knowledge in the six arts of ceremonials, music, archery, charioteering, writing and numbers. Such critical periods as the "Spring and Autumn" or the Warring ages only swelled the ranks of new experts and when official education was broken down, private teachings flourished, giving birth to "the hundred schools."

Confucius was one of these newly-born private teachers. Determined to devote himself to learning at the age of fifteen, he studied all the available classics to present himself, at the age of 33, to the public as a great teacher of ethics, politics and the classics. He also visited many of his contemporary thinkers and scholars and travelled widely all over China, preaching his doctrines or practising them in official positions. It was his resolution to save the world from chaos and he finally concluded that the best way was education. Young folks in every walk of life flocked to his door to hear him speak.

The main thesis of Confucius was that human nature is endowed by a universal set of principles, among which the fundamental was the principle of *ju* or reciprocity. This principle is extended to basic human relationships where they are manifested, such as between king and subject, father and son, man and wife, old and young, friend and friend. The principle was basic to every school of thought: philosophy, psychology, ethics, politics. On this basic, the second most important principle was practical ethics in the form of loyalty, by which Confucius meant the primary instinct of being true to oneself and finding forgiveness thereby. This *li* principle, as it was called, was to be observed by everybody. As such, it becomes supreme, governing practical life in manners, rituals, ceremonies and etiquette. Further, the key to the *li* was to be found in filial piety as the most natural, intimate and fundamental factor in the society of human relationships. Filial piety was, indeed, considered to be so important that Confucius saw in it the fountain-spring of all virtues. From which, it would appear, the Master may have thought of consolidating and pacifying the restless world with the authority of father and monarch.

Confucius was modest enough to say that he had nothing new to teach but was only trying to restore the practices observed in the "good old days" of the Chou dynasty. From which, we can conclude, among other things, that the *ju* philosophy did not begin with Confucius. Nevertheless, he was so much its protagonist that the Western world came to call this philosophy Confucianism. Apart from the historical fact of precedence, it remains true that Confucius' words are the kernel of the subsequent *ju* philosophy.

As mentioned above. there were hundreds of rival philosophies in the days when Confucius was alive. But Confucianism was so generous and broad-minded that it absorbed all the good points of all other doctrines. China after Confucius underwent a long historical process of social, cultural and political changes, each phase with its corresponding impact upon Confucianism. At each turn, the philosophy adapted itself to the circumstances to absorb whatever the foreign elements. So much so that a certain Chinese scholar has remarked that present-day Confucianism may hardly be recognizable to its founder.

Whatever the degree of transformation, the fact remains that Confucianism did most in moulding the national character of the Chinese people, affecting as it did every phase of Chinese life. The same may be said of its influence upon Korean life at a slightly moderated plane. The influence is not entirely accidental for there were many traditional outlooks in ancient Korean life that were susceptible to the teachings. First, Koreans were humane or, at least, wanted to be so considered. To *Tangun*, the mythical founder of the nation, has been attributed the phrase: *"hongik ingan"* (love humanity) as the national precept. Such also was the general spirit of Confucianism.

Secondly, Koreans were a peaceful and moral people. Various Chinese records have noted these traits. There are passages that tell us that although Koreans were fond of excessive merry-making, they were at no times immoral. Such also was the spirit of Confucianism.

Thirdly, historical records also show that Koreans respected age and, accordingly, held filial piety in the highest esteem.

Last but not least, Koreans were religious-minded and worshipped over-ruling powers. That, too, was in line with what Confucius taught.

All these factors enabled Confucianism to be accepted in Korea without much opposition. To the contrary, the whole positive system of philosophy that was Confucianism was so overwhelming that it exerted a great influence on the conscious planes of Korean life. Inevitably, the philosophy underwent transformation in Korea as it did in China. To observe its actual trend and developments, it will be necessary to provide it against the Korean historical background.

The Moulding Element

Confucianism was introduced to the peninsula so early that its date cannot be ascertained from the historical records. The earliest reference is contained in the "Annals of the Three Kingdoms" of the Koryo dynasty which says that universities based upon the Tang system were established in the Three Kingdoms. Apparently, Confucianism was taught and studied, along with other courses, in these universities.

On the basis of the dated records, Koguryo had the earliest university (372). Records for Paekche universities are missing but it is certain that the kingdom must have had an earlier institute than Koguryo. This we infer from the recorded fact that a Paekche scholar, Wang In, went to Japan in the year, 285, carrying a copy of Confucius' Analects with him as well as a primer on "One Thousand Characters." Wang In was but the first of other scholars sent by Paekche to Japan in order to introduce the Confucian classics to the island kingdom.

The establishment of higher educational institutes came late in Silla as compared to the other two kingdoms for this state was busy training *Hwarang* warriors to attain a position of supremacy on the peninsula. Once Silla rose to such a position and united all Korea under its sway, attention was turned to culture and education. They established a university in 682 and scholars went to the Tang kingdom to bring back 50 volumes on ceremonies and literature. The higher educational institutes of Silla taught Confucian classics and mathematics, the Analects and the Book of Filial Piety as compulsory courses.

The chief aim of higher learning in those days was to train administrators who had to be well-versed in history and compositions to enable them to devise good policies and draft sound laws. As the commentary

XII THOUGHTS AND RELIGIONS

school was dominant in the Han and Tang dynasties of China, so was it naturally in Silla. Scholars were concerned not so much with the spirit as with the letters of Confucian doctrines. Spirit or letter, all phases of Chinese culture penetrated a recipient Korea and Confucianism began to exert deep influences on all phases of Korean life, political, social and moral. Thus, it came to play an important part in moulding the Korean national character.

In 717, King Songdok sent a high-ranking official, named Kim Sujong, to the Tang kingdom and the scholar returned to Silla with images of Confucius and ten of his disciples. These were enshrined in the university and sacrifices offered up to them. King Hyegong (765-779) went so far as to attend the classes where Confucianism was studied. Confucius was not only respected but idolized and venerated.

The Master was also being intensively studied by outstanding Korean scholars, notably Sol Chong and Choe Chiwon. Sol Chong, son of the famous Buddhist priest, Wonhyo, was a teacher of the Confucian classics at the university. Choe Chiwon, at the age of 12, went to the Tang kingdom where he passed the state examinations, became secretary to a famous military commander, and secured his fame with an article denouncing a notorious traitor. He returned to Silla at the age of 28 but, instead of seeking official positions, spent the rest of his life visiting beautiful places and cultivating himself. The books left behind by Sol Chong and Choe Chiwon are our best representations of Silla Confucianism. To them, the reader must be referred for further information. Suffice to note here that Confucianism came to flower during the three hundred years of Unified Silla when a united kingdom at peace could think of self-cultivation rather than preoccupy itself against threats of external aggression.

Path of Career

The founder of the next dynasty of Korea, Koryo, attributed his success to Buddha's favor. The Koryo monarchs, therefore, encouraged Buddhism. which became a state religion. But this did not mean the decline of Confucianism. The founder himself had a Confucian university established in Pyongyang and the fourth king, Kwangjong (950-975) introduced a state examination system for the first time upon the recommendation of a Chinese scholar.

These examinations consisted of two courses, poetry and written essays on current affairs. One had to be well-grounded in Confucian classics and literature, prose and poetry. It encouraged a trend that made Confucianism a subject for study not as a system of belief but for pure learning. Buddhism was the moral core that bound the people in unity; Confucianism was the individual's road to a career.

On that basis, Confucianism made great strides. King Songjong had a professor in Confucianism stationed at each province of the Koryo realm in order to instruct students everywhere. In Kaesong, the capital, he established a universsity where Confucianism was studied although it would appear that the students there were more interested in Chinese literature than in the Confucian classics. Perhaps, the thirst for office via the state examinations was more intently felt in the provinces.

The reign of King Munjong (1047-1082) saw the rise of a great scholar. This was Choe Chung, known as the Confucius of Korea. The main reason for this high merit was his recommendation that university teaching be divided into nine classes. Thanks to Choe Chung, Confucian learnings flourised but not for long. Wars and the military revolt that destroyed the power of the throne discouraged Confucian studies and all kinds of learning in general. This state of educational bankruptcy was to remain for more than 200 years. Not until the reign of King Chungyol (1275-1308) was another great scholar to rise and restore Confucianism from neglect. This was An Hyang upon whose recommendation, governors were commanded by the throne to contribute funds for setting up scholarships, the king himself generously contributing to the purpose. An also sent a scholar, named Kim Munjong, to China in order to import pictures of Confucius and his 72 disciples and renew the practice of sacrificing to their memory. In his latterly days, he learned to respect the modern Chinese commentator on Confucianism, Chu Hsi, from whom he took his penname. The disciples who gathered around An numbered by the hundreds. Paek Ijong, Wu Tak and Kwon Pu were but only a few of the eminent scholars he produced.

The end of the Koryo dynasty which saw the Buddhist priests steeped in corruption produced more and more outstanding scholars of Confucianism. The most popular one was Chong Mongju, a very gifted individual who was devoted to studies throughout life from childhood. Together with Yi Songgye, the founder of the next Yi dynasty, he protested against the corruption of the Koryo kingdom and participated in the revolt that overthrew a degenerated system. Unlike Yi, he refused to replace one ruler for another and suffered martyrdom for his loyalty to an impotent Koryo monarch. The stuff of Confucian wisdom, loyalty and courage, Chong Mongju is the founder of the Korean school of studies in human nature.

Way of Life

A State Religion

From the outset, the founder of the new Yi dynasty made it the cornerstone of national policy to reject Buddhism and adopt Confucianism as the national teaching. A center of faith was necessary to command allegiance and necessity dictated this transfer for the Buddhist temple, once flourishing in the brilliant days of Koryo, became so tyrannical an institute in its declining years that the new dynasty could hardly expect to control or educate the people by continued espousal of Buddhist teachings.

Shortly after transferring the seat of his capital from Kaesong to Seoul, Yi Songgye established a Confucian institute, the Songgyungwan, in the east sector of the new capital. Next, he established four further schools north, south, east and west of the city.

Finally, he had schools built throughout the provincial districts to inculcate respect for Confucius and Mencius among the popular masses. Confucianism was really coming into its own, exerting influences not only in political life but also on such important occasions of popular ceremonies as coming of age, marriage, funeral services, and ancestor-worship rites as well as the system of moral self-autonomy.

Besides the able and resourceful monarch, the new kingdom started out with many outstanding scholars imbued with a renewed sense of purpose and direction. There was Kil Chae (1353-1419). Like his teacher, Chong Mongju, Kil distinguished between "house-cleaning" and "house-wrecking." Chong was assassinated after the fall of Koryo. Kil retired from political life in order to devote himself to the education of the young in the spirit of Confucian loyalty. His example was carried on by his disciple, Kim Sukcha, and by the latter's son, Kim Chongjik. Kim Chongjik, who had studied under his eminent father, proved even more exceptional a man of learning and integrity and turned out many more dependable inheritors of the Confucian tradition.

With Cho Kwangjo (1482-1519), the Confucian scholars could no longer take everything for granted. Cho was a very precocious youth who sought out a disciple of Kim Chongjik, Kim Yongpil, in exile to study Confucianism at his feet. He spent many years in the mountains near Kaesong to emerge a matured master of the Confucian classics and quickly establish his fame in society as a leading scholar of the day. The attention of the reigning monarch, Chungjong, was drawn to this talented young man and Cho enjoyed a succession of top government posts in charge of learning and morality. The royal favor gave him ample opportunities to put his Confucian teachings into practical politics and he insisted upon ideal government by spreading Confucian teachings among the masses, by proper selection of officials from men of learning and character, and by revising the rules of community self-governing. Altogether, Cho proved too drastic and impatient and so fell out of royal favor. Conservatives and scheming officials conspired to drive him out of official life and he was executed at the age of 38.

Height of Development

The fate of this well-meaning but unfortunate young scholar spelled a break in Confucian enthusiasms. Many scholars then and later became chary of pursuing their Master's harmonious society in practice and refused to accept governmental positions that were offered. Instead, they turned to withdrawn life and devoted themselves to thorough academic studies and controversies in quiet, remote and scenic places in the mountains and along the river-banks. This atmosphere produced a host of metaphysical scholars, such as Cho Sik (1543-1620), Kim Inhu (1510-1560) and So Kyongdok (1489-1546), to mention only a few. So, in particular, had a doctrine that was intrinsically his own. His world was the physical one and his doctrine, accordingly, a monolism known as the *ki*, i.e. matter. So's metaphysics for the theory of the universe holds that before the beginning of the world, there was an extreme state of voidness (太虛, literally: the Great and Original Void), from which everything in the world stems. As for *ki*, there was no beginning or end of the matter. So was a true student in that he stood above blame or reputation, poverty or worldly concerns. He produced many outstanding scholars.

The first Korean scholar who really understood the Confucian innovator of the Sung dynasty, Chu Hsi, was Yi Toegye (1501-1570). The Chu Hsi school of thought was introduced in the latter years of Koryo but, as we have noted in "General Remarks," it took some two hundred years before the Korean Confucianists could digest the new philosophical vocabulary in which it was couched. Yi Toegye, penname of Yi Hwang, was born in Kyongsang-do province. He passed the state examinations at the age of 34 and, although enjoying several high positions in government, preferred to devote himself to academic studies. His doctrine, based, of course, on Chu Hsi's *li-chi* principle, holds that the universe is composed of two vital elements, *yi* and *ki* (*li* and *chi* in Chinese; meaning respectively, mind and matter). Accordingly, human nature is also composed of *yi* and *ki*. In opposition to disciple Ki Taesung's doctrine of dualism, Yi Toegye taught a monolism based on Chu Hsi which makes *yi* the root of *ki*. To support the thesis, he advanced the theory that the "four ends" come from *yi* which is metaphysical while the seven emotions arise from *ki*, the physical force. The "four ends" in Chu Hsi's metaphysics follows: the root of sympathy is benevolence, that of righteousness, shame; that of courtesy, concession, and that of wisdom, reason. The seven emotions are pleasure, anger, sadness, fear, love, hate and desire. Against his master, Yi Toegye's disciple, Ki Taesung, held that sympathy, shame, concession and reason, drawn from the seven emotions, are the "four ends" of the mind, or *yi*. Like Yi Toegye, the *yi* preceded the *ki* but more elements of the *ki* made up the *yi* than was suspected in Toegye's philosophy. Master and disciple argued the matter for a long time, the latter finally yielding.

Another great scholar of this period was Yi Yi, better known by his literally penname, Yi Yulgok (1536-1584). A native of Kangwon-do province, he learned to write characters almost as soon as beginning to speak and it is said that he composed an essay denouncing one, Chin Pokchang, a national traitor, at the age of seven. When he was 16, his mother died. This made him so sad that he sought comfort in Buddhism by retreating into the Diamond Mountains in order to study the Buddhist Scriptures. At the end of a year, he decided that Buddhism was not the true way so he returned to society and Confucianism. He studied many schools of thought and became a great scholar and statesman by his ability to reconcile them all. Of course, he enjoyed many ministerial positions, including the post of national defense, but minor officials prevented him from putting his ideas into practice. Instead, he found himself putting his talents for reconciling various schools of thought to the tasks of reconciling the various party splits which were rising to the foreground in his days. To the loss of the nation, his efforts proved vain. For his patriotism, loyalty and unstinted efforts to put up a harmonious front, he met with untimely death. Evidently, Yi Yulgok was wrapped up in administrative affairs but he did not neglect his young disciples.

Yi Yulgok's doctrine contained many points similar to that of Yi Toegye. Unlike the latter, he had to meet many more metaphysical arguments that had gone into the basic conception of a universe composed of *yi* and *ki*, without the pioneer's reputation in the whole sphere of Chu Hsi philosophy. Thus, he maintained that although *yi* and *ki* can be separated in space and that the two cannot exist anterior or posterior to one another in time, the fact remained that they are not of the same entities, the reason being that while *yi* is the principle of the universe, *ki* is the material by which the *yi* operates. He held that this principle applies equally to man inasmuch as man is a little universe.

Yi Yulgok's personality and learning earned him many intimate friends among the outstanding scholars of the day and produced many remarkable disciples. A large Yi Yulgok following formed a school which developed a main trend of discussions to the effect that the *yi* and *ki* were simultaneous products and, for that reason, the *ki* had to be regarded as equally as the *yi*. Thus, matter, at last, reached the state of mind and they became known as the *ki* school. The scholars who championed this view were mostly inhabitants of the Kyonggi-do and Chungchong-do provinces.

On the other hand, the followers of Yi Toegye became known as the *yi* school. Kyongsang-do was the home of "mind forever over matter."

The Realistic School

All this absorption in abstract pursuits of the *yi* and the *ki* had their inevitable reaction. In Korea, no less than in Europe: no matter, never mind. Fed up scholars, concerned nonetheless by the fate of Confucianism, expressed fears that such metaphysical subtleties were driving the Master's teachings into a shell and that the well-nigh idle arguments provoked by the metaphysicians were only creating narrow partisan spirits and wide party splits.

Out of this spirit of dissatisfaction arose a new school called the Silhak. Its followers pointed out that the state was losing sight of the essential qualities and real purposes of Confucianism and only by a return to the original teachings of Confucius and Mencius could confusion be cleared away and welfare brought to state and people. Hence: Silhak which means Real Learning. The representative scholars of this school, Yu Hyongwon (622-1673), Yi Ik (1681-1763), An Chongbok and others, concentrated upon studying practical problems such as economics, educational systems, legal systems, and the like.

Two scholars suffice to reflect the spirit of this Real Learning. One was Pak Chiwon (1737-1805), a great writer as well as scholar. Among other progressive programs, he advocated land reform to divide farms equally among the poor peasants. Pak Chiwon also visited China on several occasions. There he came in contact with the new sciences of the West which he introduced to Korea along with Chinese scholarship.

The more significant scholar was Chong Yakyong (1762-1836), better known by his penname, Chong Tasan. A native of Kyoggi-do, Chong won early recognition for his scholarly distinctions from the king and served in many important government posts.

His brilliance, however, made him many enemies who constantly sought an excuse to pull him down from royal favor. Their chief instrument lay in the new forbidden religion from the West, Catholicism. Chong's brother, likewise an eminent scholar of a discredited faction (*Namin*), was a Catholic and Chong himself was interested in the religion. The king, Chongjong (1777-1800), however, was behind him and, although he was downgraded now and again for reasons of "guilt by association" with heresy, he returned to high position each time. Once his royal protector died, however, Chong had no chance so he retired to his native town to bury himself in learning. With the enthronement of Sunjong, he was exiled to Kangjin in the southern province of Cholla Namdo. There he remained for 19 long years, studying and writing. He was allowed at last to return to his native place where he spent the rest of his life in retreat. He died at 75, leaving behind a prodigious amount of work, totalling some 500 volumes and dealing with almost all branches of learning, from commentaries of the Confucian Classics to practical subjects of the day, like medicine and agriculture.

A Sage Dethroned

Although the Silhak school lived its day, it was not a full day. Some of its adherents made minor positions in government but as a whole, they were out of power and so failed to weave the programs of their vigorous school into the seams of national policies. The policy-makers of the state were, for the main part, conservative, busy upholding the status quo, refusing to introduce any foreign ideas of culture, rigidly adhering to a policy of seclusion that was to earn Korea the name of the "Hermit Kingdom" in the outside world. Whatever the bias of the powerful state, the onrush of the foreign influences and the tides of new ideas could not be blocked. The only effect of the seclusion policy was to suppress the ideas and encourage foreign intervention in a weak kingdom in search of markets. Korea became a plum, ripe for plucking and Big Powers centered their conflict upon her head. Korea contributed to the cause of war between China and Japan and between Japan and Russia. Japan, emerging the victor, the Big Powers granted her a "colonial sphere" and the ripe plum that was Korea dropped on her laps.

Under Japanese domination, all phases of Korean life were strangled. Korean Confucianists were persecuted by the Japanese but the Japanese authorities encouraged Confucian concepts of loyalty to the center of authority, the center being the Japanese Emperor. The Songgyungwan had to go, not because it taught Confucian teachings *per se* but because it represented the highest organised center of such teachings and, as such, was a reminder of Korea's proud past. Accordingly only the name was changed. As the Kyonghakwon, the institute was allowed to function for such purposes as offering sacrifices to Confucius' memory.

The Songgyungwan resumed its original name and duties right after the Liberation. It has been elevated to the level of a modern university, the only one with ancient buildings. Thus, Confucianism is still beng studied. However discredited it may have been in the face of modern industrial demands, it has its devotees, young and old, in the country. The young can only study the subject shorn of all disillusions for these they have experienced in life. They can but seek the essential qualities of Confucian wisdom.

Korean Buddhism

Introduction

Buddhism is a body of teachings of Sakyamuni who had studied all schools of philosophy and the creeds of all religions known to ancient India and combined them into one coherent doctrine that rejected every extreme view in the others. His teachings were exported to China where the highly developed culture and learning of the ancient Chinese modified them to suit the needs of Chinese society. We may, therefore, rightly call these teachings Chinese Buddhism. Korea imported this Chinese Buddhism and, in turn, adapted it to Korean culture. The teachings here may be called Korean Buddhism. In other words, Korean Buddhism is a cultural product of Korea whose seed was Chinese Buddhism. While many elements are common to original Buddhism, Chinese Buddhism and Korean Buddhism, the three national systems are, on the other hand, different from one another in many respects. From the beginning, Buddhism in Korea absorbed the mythological elements while containing its philosophical and scientific dissertations. Hence, it was not merely a religion nor a system of philosophy. It has, rather, been a culminating form of Korean culture, embracing all fields of mythology, religion, literature and the arts. For this reason, we are justified in calling the Gautama's teachings here Korean Buddhism.

What are some of the characteristics of Korean Buddhism? First of all, compared with Buddhism in India which was propagandistic and Chinese Buddhism which was highly sectarian, Korean Buddhism has been a unifying medium.

Secondly, compared with other countries, Korea has preserved many volumes of Buddhist scriptures rarely found in other lands. Priest Uichon deliberately collected Buddhist literature, compiled a bibliography of these scriptures and the Tripitaka Koreana and a complementary thereof which he published is a great source book on Buddhism. His bibliographical work has survived intact till this day to serve as one of the greatest reference material on Buddhist bibliography. The Tripitaka Koreana was printed during the Koryo period. This monumental work, with contents well arranged and wooden types which have been preserved till today, was an epoch-making event in the whole history of printing.

Thirdly, Korean Buddhism has exercised influence upon every phase of Korean life. It moulded not only many artistic products, but also Korean customs and manners.

International Exchange

During the periods of the Three Kingdoms and Unified Silla, many Korean priests studied the doctrines of Buddhism and contributed much to their understanding and deeper knowledge both at home and abroad. Koryo, in fact, supplied China with Buddhistic literature at a time when the Central Kingdom was running short of Buddhistic inspirations. Thanks to Koryo, the religion revived there. Even more important, Korea exported Buddhism to Japan, thus becoming instrumental in the conversion of the islands into a Buddhist nation.

Cultural Significances

In the days of the Three Kingdoms, Koreans believed in the Heavenly Emperor. The ultimate object of human life was held to be to understand and realize the intentions of this Heavenly Emperor. Accordingly, it was only man's duty to worship Him: all great men were regarded as His descendents. Since, also, all important affairs of man were supposed to be judged by this Heavenly Emperor, they thought it necessary to communicate with Him by offering up sacifices. In short, the whole of human life was controlled by a supernatural being who was the final judge and arbiter of all human affairs.

It was to this kind of society that Confucianism was introduced with its ethical basis on the relationship of man and man. As such, it was really quite a revolutionary concept for ancient Koreans. Shortly after Confucianism, came Buddhism. Eager as they were for foreign cultures, Koreans welcomed Buddhism which soon permeated all segments of society. In this manner, Korean culture became enriched in scope and degree.

Buddhism is a religion as well as a philosophy. As it spread among Koreans as such, it began to influence Korean arts, music and

XII THOUGHTS AND RELIGIONS

all branches of scientific learning. The secret of Buddhism's success was that it gave Koreans what they lacked, sense of security and a feeling of hope. This, in my opinion, was its great and important contribution to Korean life.

As Buddhism became associated with secular matters, construction of temples and pagodas and publication of scriptures came to be regarded as a symbol of protection for the state against enemy powers. In other words, Buddhism provided defense and security.

Let us trace the development of Korean Buddhism, so closely connected as it has been with the ups and downs of the national fortunes, step by step by referrring to its actual historical process.

Koguryo

At about the same time when the Korean peninsula consisted of the three kingdoms of Koguryo, Paekche and Silla, China was divided into 16. One of these kingdoms was Chien Chin whose monarch, Fu Chien, was said to have made it mighty by virtue of espousing Buddhism. This Chien Chin kingdom rendered help to Koguryo in its war against Yen. Consequently, Koguryo sent an envoy to Chien Chin in order to invite back a priest, Shun Tao, and import Buddhist scriptures and images. This event marked the first recorded introduction of Buddhism to Korea (372: 2nd year of King Sosurim). Shun Tao was followed soon by the coming of another Chinese priest, A Tao. In 375, the Koguryo government built two temples, the Songmunsa and Ibulnansa, for Shun Tao and A Tao respectively. These were the first temples in Korea.

Korea had a fairly well-advanced culture before the introduction of Buddhism. For instance, in the Koguryo capital, there was a college where the king himself delivered lectures on morality. The cultural precedents made it easier for the new religion to be accepted and spread among the people. In 20 years there were nine temples in the capital alone.

The first known Korean monk to go abroad was Priest Nang who went to China to study the Buddhistic theory of the void. It was he who systematized hitherto desultory theories on Buddhism into a coherent whole. Other priests, Hyeja, etc., also contributed much, some going abroad as missionaries.

In the meantime, a third great foreign religion, Taoism, was imported from the Tang dynasty so there were three sets of teachings, Confucianism, Buddhism and Taoism, competing with each other for supremacy. For a spell, Taoism was the victor over its two rivals. Because of the religious conflicts, some Buddhists took refuge abroad and Korean Buddhism entered a phase of confusion. The Koguryo kingdom also declined and, finally, fell in the midst of these religious conflicts.

Paekche

Thirteen years after Koguryo introduced Buddhism, an Indian priest named Maranata came to Paekche from Chin. The Paekche king, Chimnyu, went as far as the suburbs of the capital in order to welcome him. A temple followed within the year and ten priests studied and preached there. Paekche developed Buddhism into a state religion and later sent Buddhism to Japan, stimulating all phases of Japanese culture for in addition to the religion went Korean knowledge about arts and architecture. In due course, Buddhism in Paekche relapsed into a formalistic, ritualistic affair with its attendant waste of the national treasury upon buildings and overseas propaganda. The kingdom decayed. Monuments of better days, however, remained standing: artistic temples, statues, images and pagodas. Some of them have survived till this day, attesting to the spirit of Paekche. They are now registered as national treasures.

Silla

Because of it geographical position and

worship of national gods, Silla was isolated from international cultural contacts and rather reluctant to absorb foreign influences. Unlike Koguryo and Paekche where the initiative was taken from the top, Buddhism first came to Silla as a popular movement. It needed to be brought to the attention of the top as a sound basis on which to rest the national strength and prosperity. The Chinese priest, A Tao, is said to have visited Silla from Koguryo. Moreover, there was a legend going on to the effect that the Buddha himself was in Silla to preach the doctrines. The martyrdom of Ichadon, Buddhist convert and popular national hero, decided the king, Pobhung, who finally introduced Buddhism and later proclaimed it formally as the national religion. Thereafter it made great strides. In the reign of Chinhung, the Koguryo monk, Hyeryang, was naturalized as a citizen of Silla. Hyeryang founded a Buddhist association, called Palgwan, with the king as head.

With prosperity of the dynasty came the conviction among the ruling class that Buddhism was the means to educate the people and make the kingdom endurable. The religion was not only considered as soul-saving; it was also regarded as a necessary force for spiritual unity in the realm to pave the way for the political unity of the peninsula under Silla's hegemony.

In the reign of King Chinpyong, the monk, Wongwang, formulated five commandments for the people as inspiration for this spiritual unity. In the reign of Queen Sondok, the monk, Chajang, compiled a theory that held that Silla was the Buddhist land *par excellence;* it was a theory intended to disarm the neighboring kingdoms of Koguryo and Paekche. Chajang also had a nine-storeyed pagoda built in the temple grounds of the Hwangyongsa as a symbol of Silla's national spirit and defense. He also had plans to consolidate the national foundation to provide a Buddhistic basis for general mass enlightenment. Finally, he built the Tongdosa temple to which he drew the monks of the kingdom as a concrete example of monkish austerity, thereby hoping to enhance the general morality.

Unified Silla

When Silla united the Korean peninsula, it became necessary to consolidate the foundations of a single political state with one language and one school of thought. The task fell upon Wonhyo, the outstanding Silla priest. Wonhyo gave up the idea of going to the Tang kingdom halfway and, instead, visited all the famous priests and scholars throughout the three erstwhile kingdoms. All the scriptures, commandments and treatises written by previous Korean scholars were brought to his attention for rearrangement into a single coherent system. This system was meant to serve not only as a national religion for Silla but as a universal one for all mankind in general. Wonhyo was not only a member of the vested class, enjoying literature, but an active participant in the military affairs of the state. In the latter days of his life, he returned to secular life to enjoy secular pastimes and amusements, such as singing, dancing and drinking. As a broad-minded priest, he managed greatly to popularize Buddhism in all walks of life. As the profound scholar, he left a bulky number of works behind him when he died at the age of 70. Of the 99 books he wrote, containing a total 240 volumes, 20 have been preserved to this date. Wonhyo was but one of many other outstanding priests and scholars who helped build up Buddhism for a united Korea.

Denominations

The pursuit of Buddhist studies from many angles during Unified Silla resulted in the creation of different schools, of which there were five main ones. The guiding principle in the teachings of each was based upon some particular point in the Scriptures: the Nirvana which led to the Yulban school, the Disciplines which had its headquarters in Tongdo temple, and so forth. Besides schools, there were nine "headquarters' temples" known as the "nine mountains" in scattered parts of the peninsula. These belonged to the sect known as *zen* Buddhism.

As the religion penetrated increasingly into Korean spiritual life, it also began to express itself in outward forms, temples, pagodas, etc. Some of the famous temples built at this time are extant today: the Tongdosa in Yangsan, the Wolchongsa in Pyongchang, the Haeinsa in Hapchon, the Pomosa in Tongnae, the Yujomsa in Kosong, the Hwaomsa in Kurye, the Songgwangsa in Sunchon, Tonghwasa in Taegu and numerous others all over Korea.

Korean Buddhism of this period was also exported abroad for there were many Silla emigrants. Thus, it is said there was a Silla settlement in the Shantung province of China where temples were built after the model in the motherland.

Arts

Unified Silla's development of Buddhistic forms in fine arts was even more remarkable. A wooden engraved image of the Buddha, produced in the reign of King Kyongdok, is said to have been sent to Tang where that broadminded Chinese monarch, Tai-tsung, expressed great admiration. The reign of Queen Sondok saw the building of an observatory based on Buddhist cosmology. Of all artistic achievements, the most brilliant and still extant ones are the temples, Pulguksa and Sokkuram, familiar to every Korea tourist.

Buddhist forms of artistic expressions were not idle work for, as we have already noted, the religion was seriously intended to defend the state. They were originally rendered with national defense and protection against the enemy in mind. With a united Silla at peace and enjoying prosperity, art became confident and expressed itself in delicate lines of proportion and harmony.

Koryo

Buddhism was the foundation upon which the Koryo kingdom established itself. It reached its height during the middle of this 400-year old dynasty, and left many believers over to the subsequent Yi dynasty. The priest of Unified Silla, Toson, helped Wanggon establish his new Koryo kingdom. The new dynastic king, in turn, helped Toson in his efforts to consolidate the kingdom on the basis of Buddhism. He had ten temples built in or around Kaesong and Pyongyang, and erected a nine-storeyed pagoda as a symbol of protection. He also edited ten articles of instructions for his successors. Needless to say, they were based on Buddhism, the first article claiming that his kingdom had been founded by virtue of the protecting hand of all the patron saints of Buddhism, the sixth article making observances of Buddhistic ceremonies compulsory on all loyal subjects. These ceremonies made Buddhism a social affair of the people as well as a professional one for the priests.

In Official Life

With Buddhism becoming an increasing affair of state and society, it became necessary for the government to acquire the services of trained Buddhists in national administration. A state examination system for Buddhist priests was, therefore, started to serve side by side with the regular Confucian system for selection of civil office candidates. The Buddhist courses were two, *zen* and doctrines, and the candidates thus selected were appointed to proper positions in order of rank. There were two offices in the government to handle all the administrative affairs of the priests and their temples.

Popularization

At the outset of the Koryo kingdom, the monk, Chegwan, insisted that the unity of the Three Kingdoms had corresponded with the unity of the three phases of Buddhism; namely, doctrines, disciples and priests, into a single whole. This was called the Chontae school of Buddhism. The mantle of the peninsula unity falling upon Koryo, this school prevailed in the kingdom. Further, it spread to China.

The Chontae school, in turn, encouraged the rise of the Buddhist school of Hwaom Scriptures. The most significant contribution of this school to Korean Buddhism was to translate some of the Buddhist literature into the vernacular Korean language. This consisted of a set of ten prayer songs of the Pohyon Bodhisattva which even the unlearned commoners could learn to read and chant. In this way, Buddhism became popularized and Buddhistic ceremonies observed by the common people.

Zen Buddhism

To elaborate upon the formation of the Chontae school, according to a proposal submitted by a group of famous Buddhists: in Tang, the three branches of Buddhism had been unified into one *zen* school; now that the kingdom of Koryo had also unified the Three Kingdoms into one, it was only fitting that the king should adopt this school so that he and his descendents might reign forever. With the establishment of the Chontae school upon this basis, Korean Buddhism underwent a denominational change. Instead of the "five teachings and nine mountains," it came to be called the "five teachings and two sects." The Chontae school derived its name from a mountain. The name of another mountain went to the second school, Choge. Although known by different names, Chontae and Choge were both based on the same philosophy of the *zen*. They were, so to speak, two heads of the same thing.

Not only denominations, but the meaning of the "five teachings" also underwent a change. Before Chontae, the "five teachings" meant to emphasize each of the five Buddhist creeds. Now, it came to mean some of the creeds or some of the names of places where huge temples existed.

Thus, the monk, Taegak, the source of *zen* inspirations, ushered in the elaborate form of Buddhism so typical of Koryo.

Tripitaka Koreana

The one significant feature of Koryo Buddhism from the very beginning was the publication of Buddhist literature. Taegak was, especially, a zealous pursuer in this field. Son of a king, Munjong, he studied and became the priest of Tongdogsa temple. He also had occasion to visit the Sung kingdom where he collected many volumes on Buddhistic literature and, upon returning home, searched for more everywhere in the kingdom.

There was a political meaning to this program. In the reign of King Hyonjong, there was a barbaric invasion from a certain state, called Kulan, in Manchuria. The Koryo kingdom, fresh and ambitious, stood as one against the invader. Even the monks fought back bravely. The kingdom also remembered that Buddha was the protector of the state so the king, believing that the enemy could be repelled by the Gautama's influence, had his royal Buddhist subjects summoned together to print the Scriptures. It was an arduous effort but worth undertaking as an impressive demonstration of their serious faith. After some forty years, a total of 5,048 books were published. In the meantime, the enemy had withdrawn, presumably overwhelmed by Buddha. The books were retained at the Puinsa temple as a symbol of national protection.

The reign of King Kojong saw the kingdom succumb to the invasion of Genghis Khan's Mongols. The enemy burned down the Puinsa temple and the books so recently preserved there. They also destroyed that other monument of national protection, the nine-storeyed pagoda of Temple Hwangyongsa in Kyongju. Far from being disheartened, the king fled to Kanghwa island while his soldiers were fighting the world conquerers on the battlefield. Firmly believing that Buddha's influence would preserve the kingdom, however much the Mongols overran the mainland, Kojong appointed a monk to the post of editor to cast new wooden types capable of printing 160,000 pages. It took hundreds of scholars and technicians seventeen years to complete the consummating task. In the meantime, the Mongols, too, had withdrawn, carrying with them the submission of the kingdom. These mammoth projects, twice duplicated under the pressure of foreign invasions, are known as the Tripitaka Koreana. They are the most complete collection of Buddhist literature in the world. The first types, as we have seen, were destroyed. The second have been preserved at the Haeinsa temple to this day.

Decline

By the middle of the Koryo dynasty, then, Buddhism reached its height in Korea. It became so popularized and secular that ceremonies became occasions for social gatherings rather than solemn religious rites. Toward the end of the dynastic era, Korean Buddhism suffered the common fate of all religions exposed to undue temptations and surfeited by material possessions. The new Confucian school of Chu Hsi rose to accuse the Buddhist monks of corruption. For all that, Buddhism continued to turn out a great many monks of wisdom and personality. Toward the end of the dynasty, some priest-scholars went to China to study. Upon returning home, they tried their best to revify Buddhistic interest and subject the religion to fresh reform. But the day of Koryo was over and, with it, the supremacy of Buddhism as the state religion.

Yi Chosun

The Yi dynasty adopted Confucianism as the national teaching and applied pressure on Buddhism. Sometimes, it was drastic, at other times, relaxed but the intention was clear and constant. In every possible way, it meant to throttle a religion it despised. The Buddhist influence shrank and the priests escaped from the public into the mountains.

At the outset, the attitude was tolerant. The founder of the new dynasty was a Buddhist himself and his very first step in assuming power was to appeal to the people in Buddha's name to prevent disorders. In this, he had the help of an outstanding monk, Muhak.

The first drastic step was taken by the third king, Taejong. This ruler ordered the amalgamation of the many denominations into a few, reduced the number of temples, confiscated temple properties, conscripted temple servants, abolished the priestly official posts, prohibited the erection of temples in royal cemeteries and cast military weapons out of wrecked Buddhist images or temple utensils. The policy of suppression increased in severity throughout Taejong's reign. It was practical necessity that governed the harsh measures. Temple properties and estates, for one thing, were confiscated in order largely to help the newly-founded kingdom out of its financial difficulties. The doctrines of Buddhism themselves were not molested. To the contrary, the monk, Hanho, was able to write and publish a famous book denouncing the severe persecution of Buddhism. So long as the authority of the state was unchallenged, one could champion or denounce any religious theory.

Translations

The next king, Sejong, was quite a different monarch from his predecessor. He believed that it was wrong to suppress Buddhism and so decided to make himself the Buddha's Protector. Sejong, of course, was the inventor of the Korean alphabet, the *Hangul*. He thought it a pity that while all the neighboring countries had the Buddhist Scriptures translated into their respective national languages, Koreans should remain dependent upon the Chinese translation. The king himself, therefore, set out to render some of the Scriptures into Korean with added commentaries. It is impossible to estimate the contribution Sejong made to popularize Buddhism among the masses.

The real effort at translations, however, began with Sejo, the seventh king. A devout Buddhist believer, he created an office in charge of Buddhist affairs as soon as he ascended to the throne and, like Koryo, had many Scriptures translated into Korean. Many monks likewise undertook translations of this or that Buddhistic literature in their various temples.

The next two kings, Songjong and Yonsan, revived the policy of suppression. Under Myongjong, a great scholar-priest, Pou, exerted all his influence to offset this policy but whatever chances of recovery were stifled by the Confucian scholars around him.

Soldier-priests

The invasion of Korea by the Japanese warlord, Hideyoshi, saw the emergence of a monk, Sosan, as a great military leader. Thanks to Sosan, whose services were well appreciated by the government, Buddhism was tolerated and regained some of its old vitality.

Sosan was by no means the only priest to respond to the royal appeal for nationwide resistance to the Japanse invaders who were overruning the country and ravaging everywhere. Sosan rallied 1,500 monks around him to offer resistance. So did Priests Samyong, Noemuk and Kiho who had 700, 1,00 and 700 monkish soldiers respectively under their banners. All told, there were no less than five thousand foot-soldiers on the battlefields who were drawn from the Buddhist ranks. This patriotism gave Buddhism a respite and the policy of suppression was relaxed in the next few years after the end of the Japanese wars. The reign of King Injo, however, saw an even more drastic policy of suppression in which monks were barred from entering the cities.

Not only in war but in peacetime, too, the Buddhists proved their mettle by mobilizing labor from the monkish ranks in public work programs. The most notable instance was the Namhan mountain fortress which they built under the direction of one, Priest Pyogam. The invasion of the Manchus once again provided priestly leaders the opportunity to repeat the patriotic example of their predecessors in the Hideyoshi wars.

But the course of the Confucianist kingdom was not to be deflected by any amount of Buddhist loyalties. From Hyojong onwards, sons of good families were disbarred from priestly careers and those who were already in the temples were urged to return to secular life. Many priests submitted protests to the government against this policy but in vain.

Unbroken Heritage

As stated above, Buddhism suffered heavy pressures not because the Yi government thought there was anything wrong in Buddhism *per se* or saw in the religion the source of harmful influences on state or society but because the policy was a positive one of adopting Confucianism as the state religion. Outlawed from public life, the priests withdrew into secluded lives to steep themselves in indrawn studies of the Scriptures, writing and meditating. They preserved whatever property they could salvage from the overall policy of suppression and slowly increased their holdings.

To sum up: the Buddhists stood up to persecutions of a dynasty lasting over 500 years. In times of emergency, they did more than their share. Thus, they have maintained their heritage to this day.

Present Situation

When Korea was annexed to Japan, the authorities decreed regulations for Buddhist temples. These provided for a general headquarters under which were 31 temples under which again were more than 1,200 small temples. Each temple was headed by a chief monk under whose supervision all temple affairs were carried out by three departments of General Headquarters.

When Korea was liberated from Japan, the Buddhists held a general conference at which time they passed a resolution to the following effect: that the Buddhist organization is a self-governing body, that all regulations of the Japanese period shall be abolished, that the headquarters shall be established in the capital, that each province shall have one Buddhist council, that all temples in every province shall be administered by its respective council, that headquarters shall supervise all provincial coun-

↑ Reading Mass at Catholic Church

↑ Chonghyon Catholic Church
The biggest Catholic Church in Korea is also the Korean Catholic Parish Center.

↑ Yongnak Presbyterian Church
4,000 believers attend every holiday occasion.

↓ Interior of Chonghyon Catholic Church

↓ Catholic Sisters of Charity

↑ Charity pots of the Salvation Army

↑ Head Office of the Chondogyo
(see "Tonghak" in Chapter XII)

↓ The Salvation Army Academy, Seoul

↑ Buddhist Monks at Temple Mass

↑ Bhiksuni; Priestesses

↓ Buddhist Believers Holding Mass

cils and, at the same time, that headquarters has the power to make resolutions and inspections.

In 1946, this headquarters held its general conference at which time a new constitution was drawn. Presently, all affairs pertaining to Buddhism are carried on under this constitution.

Originally, all temples were landowners with hundreds of thousands of farm or forest landholdings. With the land reform, they were turned over to the government and, although compensated by issuance of bonds, the temples, for the most part, became economically strained. About 60,000 *pyong* of land, however, were subsequently restored for purposes of recovery and many temples have opened new forestlands.

At present, Korean Buddhism counts a total 6,723 monks, 90,000 lay members and 1,531 temples. Many of the monks are actively engaged in education, journalism, politics, industry and other fields. Nowhere are they more active than in education. The Buddhists operate one university body with four colleges and a graduate school, three other colleges, seven high schools, 13 middle schools, other higher civic schools, kindergartens, lecture-halls and *zen* halls. Altogether there are 33 Buddhist institutes engaged in educational work and the promotion of general culture.

Furthermore, the Buddhists also run 12 social welfare institutes, such as orphanages, asylums for the old, and free inns for the poor. They are financed by more than ten factories which were established out of the land reform bonds they drew as compensation for the government's land confiscation under the Land Reform Program.

Christianity in Korea

Catholicism

Catholicism was first introduced to Korea in the seventeenth century as a result of documents carried back by Korean diplomatic missions travelling to and from China. The introduction of this religion to Korea was, therefore, a departure from the usual experience of the Church for normally Rome had to send forth missionaries to the land of conversion. In other words, the first Korean Catholics became converts not by direct contact brought from Rome but by indirect carried forward by Korea. The first Korean convert was not baptized by a foreign missionary on Korean soil but by the foreign missionary of a foreign soil. It was Koreans who brought the teaching back to Korea, thus anticipating the inevitable arrival of foreign missionaries at some latter date.

The Catholic doctrine was received from the outset as a new source of truth and knowledge by a number of outstanding scholars tormented by the nature of the incessant factional strife among the general run of scholars who were making a mockery of Confucius' teachings by making the sage an instrument for private gain and squabbles. These reform-minded scholars were genuine Confucianists casting about for a solution to the strait-jacket in which the ancient teachings seemed to be inextricably bound with the resultant cleavage between corrupted officialdom and deepening poverty of the peasantry. They were, therefore, responsive to fresh ideas. They embraced the Silhak or True Learning school of thought emanating from China. Now, from China again, a religion came, armed with fascinating principles of science and universal laws from the farther west. They called the new thing *Sohak*, or Western Learning. Among them was that brilliant scholar we have mentioned in our chapter on Confucianism, Yi Ik. He and his disciples, An Chongbok, Yi Kahwan and Chong Yakyong, undertook earnest studies in this Western Learning.

Yi Ik and his disciples remained good Confucianists. Others in their ranks were more deeply attracted by the promises of the Gospel, among them, Chong Yakchon, Kwon Ilsin and Yi Tokcho. From the first year of King Chongjo's reign (1777), these men gathered at a little temple by the River Han to study the dogmas of Christianity and launch a religious movement. In 1783, one of them, Yi Sunghun, went to Peking as a member of a usual diplomatic mission. There he was baptized and returned to Korea to baptize his fellow believers in turn. Yi Sunghun's return marked the beginning of a full-fledged Catholic movement in Korea.

From its inception, the Catholic movement was persecuted mercilessly by a government pursuing an extreme policy of isolation. Catholic doctrines were considered to be both dangerous and presumptious, in short, a heresy. To a Confucian-orientated society, it was alarming that ordinary folks could share allegiance between Rome and Seoul, not to speak of God in whose name Rome demanded its share of the allegiance. The government's reaction was, therefore, out of all proportions to the strength of the movement and persecutions were thorough and acute.

In 1789, a Korean Catholic, Yun Yuil, addressed a petition to Mgr. Alexander de Gouvea, the Portuguese Bishop stationed in Peking, requesting the dispatch of a priest to Korea. Mgr. de Gouvea forwarded this request to Pope Pius XXVI, together with a report on the "Hermit Kingdom." The Pope approving, the Chinese priest, Chou Wen-mou, was sent to Korea in 1795. All these communications, of course, had to be undertaken in the greatest of secrecy and when Chou came, it was to slip across the Yalu border in disguise.

In the meantime, the Catholic adherents had swelled from 4,000 to 10,000 by the year, 1800. So long as the *Namin* faction had some degree of influence in governmental circles, the Catholics were relatively safe for the *Namin* were the enlightened party, its scholars comprising the Silhak and Sohak enthusiasts we have mentioned. But the outbreak of an intensive factional fight at the turn of the century led to the downfall of the *Namin*. The only force standing between the Catholics and government was, thereby, removed and there was a severe massacre of the believers. Among the numerous outstanding Catholics killed in that year were the *Namin* members who espoused the religion. Even some members of the royal family who had become converts were given the capital punishment. The Pope's bishop, Chou Wen-mou, was also killed. All told, over 300 Catholics were formally executed. There is no telling how many were killed otherwise in what is known as the *Sinyu* massacre after the name of the year according to the lunar calendar.

Persecutions, however, had the opposite effect upon Korean Catholics. Instead of disavowing the religion, they sent further appeals to the Bishop of Peking for other priests—in 1811, 1815 and 1824. The Korean plight reached the ears of Pope Leo XII and, on September 1, 1828, the pontiff instructed the *Missions Etrangeres de Paris* to undertake the mission of spreading the faith in Korea. Moreover, on September 9, 1831, Pope Gregory XVI established the first Roman Catholic Church for Korea. French missionaries thereafter came in disguise to preach the Gospel underground. Realizing the need of training Korean believers for the priesthood, the missionaries also dispatched three Korean boys to Macao where they enrolled in a seminary.

In the fifth year of King Honjong in 1839, persecution flared anew in the *Kihae* massacre. Among the victims was Kim Taegon or Father Andre Kim, one of the three Korean boys who had studied in Macao and returned home as Korea's first ordained priest. Besides Father Andre, the *Kihae* massacre claimed the lives of three of the twelve French priests in the country, three chambermaids in the court, and over 200 other believers. Never had persecution of a religion been harsher in Korea. The kingdom was determined to stamp it out. To the con-

XII THOUGHTS AND RELIGIONS

trary, the religion persisted underground and won yet more converts.

Catholicism with its denial of privileged class statuses and the equality of all men under a Father in Heaven was a potent appeal in the country. On the other hand, because it was new and dangerous, it was difficult to spread popularity. The main purpose in the early days was to entrench it in Korean soil despite government and outlawry.

In the last year of Choljong in 1853, the number of believers had grown to more than 20,000. Three years later, a seminary was established in the Chechon town of Chungchong-do. Catholicism even entered the palace to make converts there. Even Princess Min, wife of the Regent Taewon, was sympathetic to the faith. The all-powerful Regent himself was not hostile to Catholicism as such. What he was dead set against was foreign meddling in the political affairs of the isolated kingdom. So long as Catholicism remained a religion and nothing more, he was willing to overlook things. But now came a grave *faux pas* committed by the Catholics themselves.

The colonial powers at this time were trying to ply Korean ports open for trade. The Regent drove them off with gunboats. The pressure, however, was constant and the Regent had his hands full trying to maintain the "Closed Door" policy. In the year 1865, the Russians breathed down the Regent's neck from the north to demand "diplomatic" negotiations. At this juncture, a Catholic delegation approached him with a suggestion that he invite Anglo-French intervention to check Russia. Anglo-French influence would favor Catholic growth in the country unlike the influence of Orthodox Russia. Their proposal, however, infuriated the Regent to whom the "Closed Door" policy was the fixed principle and all foreign powers equally undesirable. That Catholicism existed in Korea was an open secret but it was supposed to be forbidden and it was bad enough that a Catholic delegation should approach the Regent, any the less offer a proposal that went against his grain. Their folly invited the third and worst waves of massacre, known as the *Pyongin* massacre. The persecution lasted three years, claiming the lives of nine French missionaries and over two thousand Korean Catholics. These were legal deaths, the victims being beheaded, hung, beaten to death, or dying in prison cells. If the number of Catholic lives unlawfully taken in the rural areas by the wilful government retaliation is included, the *Pyongin* massacres took a toll of over 8,000 martyrs, almost half the total believers in the country.

However, international political trends were changing Korea's destiny to the advantage of Catholicism. The Yi kingdom was becoming increasingly aware that isolationism was impossible. Taewon's iron rule was finally snapped in 1872 when political power went to Queen Min and the "Closed Door" policy gradually yielded to an "Open Door." With the foreign treaties, freedom of religion was tolerated, tacitly if not officially. The long era of Catholic persecutions was over. Catholicism came increasingly to public attention and such contacts, as the direct assistance rendered by Bishop Butel to Emperor Kojong, changed the climate to a friendly one. In 1908, a special group of missionaries was invited by Korean Catholics to emphasize the educational role of the Church. Catholicism was entering the general stream of social enlightenment as Confucianism and Buddhism had done.

At the time of the Japanese Annexation in 1910, the Catholic statistics were as follows: one bishop, 46 missionaries, 15 Korean priests, 59 Korean nuns, 73,517 believers and 69 churches. Subsequent years saw the number of believers and churches steadily increase. More foreign influences also came, the Maryknoll Church from the United States and the Columban Fathers from Ireland. For all that, Japanese hostility was not conducive to Catholic growth. At first, the Japanese did not dare touch the Church but with increasing years of occupation came increasing boldness. They occupied churches for use as military barracks, drafted seminary students and priests into the Japanese Army, expelled foreign missionaries from the country. Seventy-nine Korean Catholics died martyrs to the Church rather than submit to Japanese pressures to renounce their belief. Their souls were blessed by the Pope in a special ceremony conducted in Rome on July 5, 1925. Despite Japanese excesses, the Church grew. On V-J Day, there were seven bishops, two parish priests, 102 missionaries, 103 Fathers and 4oo Brothers and Sisters.

The Liberation brought the first real freedom of worship to Korea. The Vatican formally recognized the government of the Republic of Korea on April 17, 1949 and dispatched Mgr. Patrick F. Byrne of the United States as Apostolic Delegate to Korea. One year later, came the Communist War which took the lives of five bishops, 82 priests, and 150 Brothers, Sisters and seminary students as well as untold numbers of ordinary Catholics. The territorial division of the country, moreover, has left thousands of believers in north Korea.

Against these disadvantages, the church has made remarkable strides in the south. Presently, there are eight parishes, four bishops, 230 Korean priests, 199 foreign priests and over 417,000 believers. The church also operates two colleges, five vocational schools, 20 high schools and 22 middle schools.

Protestantism

Protestantism was first introduced to Korea by a Hollander, named Weltevree, during the reign of King Injo in 1627. Shipwrecked on Korean shores with three other Dutch sailors, Weltevree happened to be a very ardent Christian and decided that it was his mission to preach in the strange country where he found himself. He assumed a Korean name, Pak Yon, and preached the Gospel wherever he went and whomsoever he contacted. Some years later, another Dutch vessel was wrecked off the coast of Korea and the "Hermit Kingdom" had another 36 Dutchmen as guests. From these, too, Koreans heard about the Christian religion.

These were, of course, isolated contacts that introduced Protestantism but incidentally. Not for almost two hundred years was Korea to hear about Protestantism again. It was Catholicism which introduced Christianity in the intervening years, in no uncertain terms as we have seen in the previous section. The first intentional Gospel work was carried out in 1832 during the reign of Sunjo and it was again a Hollander. In June of that year, a Minister Charles Gutzlaff landed at the inlet of the Kum river in Chungchong Pukto and preached the Gospel for forty days. He also undertook translations of the prayerbook.

Minister Gutzlaff was followed by a more persistent Protestant, Minister Robert Thomas of the Church of England. Thomas came in September 1865 and preached for two months on various islands along the Ongjin coast in Hwanghae-do before he had to flee to China before the fury of the Regent, Taewon. In August of the following year, he was back aboard an American merchant marine. The boat sailed up the River Taedong and Thomas distributed Bibles to the folks gathered along the riverbanks. Of course, he preached, too. This vessel was fired upon by Korean troops near Pyongyang and all its crew members killed. Thomas was taken before the magistrate of Pyongyang for questioning. He was found guilty of treason and beheaded. The story is that just before the axe fell, this English "Man of Christ" gave his Bible to a wrestler who was watching the execution and prayed for the man's soul. Whereby, the wrestler became a devout Christian.

In 1882, the "Hermit Kingdom" signed its first foreign treaty of friendship and commerce with the United States. This opened Korean doors for the propagation of Christian faiths in the country. In succession, the Methodists and Presbyterians came. The two American missionary pioneers, Henry G, Apppenzeller (Methodist) and Horace G. Underwood (Presbyterian), arrived simultaneously at Inchon on Easter Sunday of

1885. Inasmuch as the Methodists were divided into Northern and Southern churches, Korea likewise came to have two different Methodist sects. Appenzeller belonged to the Northern Church; the Southern was inaugurated in Korea by E. R. Endrix in 1895.

The two Methodist sects promoted missionary, educational and medical work harmoniously enough down the years. Eventually, on December 2, 1930, they were merged into an independent Korean Methodist Church with Dr. Yang Chusam elected first Superintendent. Presently, there are about 1,000 Methodist churches in the country with a total membership of 300,000.

The Church has been responsible for the establishment and management of the nation's most outstanding schools. Both the Paejae middle and high, Ehwa girls' middle and high, Paehwa girls' middle and high, and the Ehwa Women's University, are Methodist institutes. Many of Korea's outstanding leaders, including President Syngman Rhee, received their education at these schools, some of which already cherishing a history of seventy years or so. The president was a student of the forerunner of the Paejae middle school, the Paejae Haktang, and as such, was one of the first few Koreans to receive a modern education under Methodist supervision.

The Presbyterian Church was developed by missions from the United States, Canada, and Australia. Dr. Underwood's Northern Presbyterian Mission was centered in the Pyongan-do Provinces of the north, the Presbyterian Church of Australia was introduced by J. H. Davies in the Kyongsang-do of the south in 1889, while the Southern Presbyterian Mission of the U.S. was operated by L.B. Tate in the southwestern provinces of the Cholla-do in 1892. W. Mackenzie brought the Canadian Mission to Changyon and Songchon, eventually spreading it to Hamgyong Pukto and over the border to Manchuria.

These various Presbyterian sects organized themselves into the first unified Presbyterian church in September 1912 and christened it the Taehan (Korean) Presbyterian Church of Christ (Yesu). Thereafter, it developed conspicuously, even dispatching missionaries to China. Like the Methodists, they contributed greatly to the progress of Korean education, the advancement of medical science, and the improvement of social welfare. Among the Presbyterian schools, the Sungsil middle school and Sungsil College have proved to be the most prominent.

The Presbyterians were again divided into three sects after the Liberation. The Presbyterian Church of Christ (Yesu), which professes to be the conservative religion, has 2,082 churches with a total 550,852 membership. The semi-conservative Presbyterian Church of Christ (Kitok) has 620 churches with 173,409 members. The Presbyterian Church of Korea (extreme conservative) has 497 churches with 140,000. This makes the total of Presbyterian churches 3,199 with a combined 864,261 membership.

The Puritan Church was introduced by the missionaries, F. Cowman and A. Kilbourne, in 1907. This church professes complete purity and concentrates upon direct preaching rather than indirect efforts through educational, medical or other institutions as in the case of the Methodists and Presbyterians. The Japanese closed down the church but it was reinstated after the Liberation. Today it has 104 churches with a total 27,036 membership.

The Seventh Day Adventists or Church of the Latter Day Saints was introduced to Korea in June of 1904 by the Korean, Im Kiban, and the Japanese, Kunidani. The Seventh Adventists also preach the Gospel directly but they also carry on medical and educational work at the same time. There are 251 churches and 45,500 members.

Other Protestant denominations follow: Episcopalian Church (originating from the Church of England): 18 churches, 2,000 members; Baptist Church, 155 churches, 17,116 members; Episcopalian Church of God: 44 churches, 8,761 members; Jehovah's Witnesses: 20 churches, 1,167 members.

Thus, the total number of Protestant churches is 5,301 with a combined membership of 1,324,258. There are about 350 foreign missionaries and, all told, some eight million dollars are expended annually to finance missionary operations in Korea. The Protestants, in fact, have contributed more in Korea than in any other country.

First, of the 33 patriots who signed the Declaration of Independence in March 1919, 16 were Protestant Christians. Indeed, the Samil Movement was centered around the schools and churches of the Protestant denominations.

Secondly, their Bibles have always been printed in *hangul*, thus contributing not only to the revival of the alphabet in the twentieth century but to general mass enlightenment.

Thirdly, the Protestant churches operate seven universities, 14 theological schools, 35 middle or high schools for boys, and 18 middle and high schools for girls.

Fourthly, the churches operate a total 525 social welfare institutes, including nursery schools and old people's homes.

Fifthly, the churches have helped improve social conditions by launching anti-vice campaigns.

Sixthly, the evangelizing missions undertaken by Protestants has improved conditions in prisons, military barracks and schools.

Seventhly, the churches have helped train the Korean youth physically through the Y.M.C.A. and its programs. The "Y" building on Chongno, Seoul was destroyed during the war but is now being rebuilt. A modern Y.W.C.A. building, on the other hand, has already been built in Myongdong, Seoul.

Eighthly, annual funds of about 8,000,000 dollars or one billion hwan for operations of the 350 foreign missionaries in the country contributes to improvement in foreign dollar exchanges.

Last but not least, the Protestant churches are strongholds of democracy.

Protestant or Catholic, the Christian religion provides a spiritual backbone for the current struggle of the Korean people against Communism.

The Tonghak Movement

The Founding

The significant changes that were coming to Korea both within and in her relations with an expanding world in the latter half of the nineteenth century accumulated in the rise of a native religious movement drawing its inspiration from both historical Korean experiences and the currents of modern reforms. This was the movement known as the Tonghak. Before we describe the religion and its history, it is necessary to outline the career of its founder, Choe Cheu (penname Choi Suun).

Choe was born in 1824 in Kyongju, onetime capital of Korea under the dynasty of Unified Silla. His father was a noted Confucian scholar and the family was a famous one that traced its ancestry back to the glory that was Silla. His mother died when he was an infant and the death of his father when he was sixteen quickly reduced the family to straitened circumstances. The boy's youth was, therefore, a lonely and economical one. He was naturally gifted with rare talents and he studied hard. He felt very strongly about the injustices of society and the corruption in official life and the anger he harbored against the existing order drove him to seek a way out of established institutions. His intensive studies led him to the conclusion that the traditional teachings of Confucius, Mencius and Buddha would not save

Korea and his mind turned increasingly to the proposition of a new religious teaching that would unlock the keys to a better future.

When Choe was eighteen, he embarked on a pilgrimage in order to find the answer to this troubling proposition. His search was to lead him to all odd corners of the country over the next fourteen years, observing and studying the way people in all walks of life were living everywhere, always seeking the clue to the new truth that tugged. Finally, at the age of thirty-two, he came across a book, entitled, Chonso (literally, Heavenly Writing). This was the clue he had been seeking for. He stopped roaming and, over the ensuing years, concentrated his studies on the Chonso alone. At last, at the age of thirty-eight, he found his answer and went forth to preach aloud.

What he had to offer was a Way to God for the Korean people under a doctrine that man and heaven were one. There was a new religion afoot in the land at this time, Catholicism, which also challenged the existing order by teaching that God was above state and all men were alike in His eyes regardless of their status in society. Inasmuch as many people were apt to confuse his religion with Catholicism, he had to clarify his teachings. His religion was called *Tonghak* which means Eastern Learning as distinguished from Catholicism which was known as *Sohak*, or Western Learning, and he accentuated the differences at every opportunity between that which was of the East from that which came from the West. He pointed out that since he had been born and raised in the East, his concept of God inevitably had to be different from that of the West. On that score, he explained that man could not be saved simply by passive acceptance of God. Only through his own efforts could Man cultivate His good graces and finally become identified with Him. He then put all this against the perspective of Korea's past experiences. Confucianism and Buddhism were true religions but they were only part of the great truth as incorporated in the Chondo, the Heavenly Way. The Way, he concluded, was at hand, the natural fruit of time-honored Korean ways of thought and tradition.

Let us recapitulate Korea's experiences. The first Koreans, we are told, were sun-worshippers for they were a people who had migrated east toward sun and warmth from their cold origins in Central Asia. The Korean state was born when the Son of God longed for human reincarnation and fulfilled his longing through the union of a bear and a tiger. From this mystic beginning, Koreans down the ages worshipped the innumerable spirits of nature abounding.

The coming of Chinese civilization during the Three Kingdoms period saw one great religion after another streaming into the country, Confucianism, Buddhism and Taoism. Each established itself and cast its spell over all three kingdoms while these variously struggled for supremacy. First Paekche, then Koguryo and finally Silla swayed. When Silla came into its own, it was to unify the peninsula. Her instrument was the Hwarangdo, or Way of the Flower of Manhood, which carried the sword to Silla's neighbors with religious faith in state and king and brought a prosperous era during which Buddhism flourished. Buddhism continued to do so during the subsequent Koryo dynasty but latter-day Koryo saw the religion degenerate to succumb together with the kingdom to the new Yi dynasty which replaced Confucianism as the official religion. Confucianism, ever resilent, now reached its peak of prosperity and power and, with these, in turn, degenerated. By the time, Western Learning was introduced, the government was saddled with a feudalistic structure ridden with corruption. The new religion from afar appealed greatly to the masses suffering unprecedented economic hardships. This spiritual consolation from the West, however, was only one side of the coin. On the other was the manifest intentions of the Western Powers to exploit the Korean market. The Western Powers competed with one another while the Yi kingdom stood at bay, challenged from both within and without. It was high time to raise Korean spirits and fortify Korea's soul. Here was the religious inspiration that gave rise to Choe Suun's Tonghak movement.

There was basically nothing new in Choe's religion. What he did was to absorb all the religious traditions known to him irrespective of whether they were of Korean or foreign origin. It was intensely nationalistic but devoid of any narrow nationalism. All religions, from primitive Shamanism to Western Catholicism, had embodiments of truth in them. All peoples had to find their separate roads to God's common embrace and Korea's way was the Tonghak way. Far from being ancient in garb as the suggestion might be, it spoke a new language, comparable to the language of modern ideas.

Development

The new Tonghak religion, its founder boldly proclaimed, marked the beginning of a new age, a fresh civilization, the coming of the Kingdom of God on earth. Unlike Christ, he rejected the idea of a kingdom in heaven. Paradise belonged to the here and now and he was confident that man could create it on the very soil on which his audience was standing.

But before Koreans could even begin to establish this Kingdom of God on earth which was their kingdom, they had to be liberated as a people. As the guiding principle to win such liberation, he proclaimed that man was God (人乃天). By this, he apparently meant that man was possessed of a God-like nature, which gave him the power to throw off a tyranny that was man-made and not in accordance with God's ways. Because they had God-like attributes, all men had dignity; because they had dignity, all men were free and equal; because they were free and equal, they had to be liberated from all kinds of inequality and oppressions. With particular reference to Korea, because his audience was Korean and he was familiar only with the Korean case, the masses needed to liberate themselves from the yoke of feudalism and corrupt officialdom within, repel the threats of alien invasions from without.

Choe Suun believed in color and festival-like gatherings for there had to be brightness to the people's lives if such lofty ideals were to be achieved. He edited sacred scriptures and occult prayer-books to guide the people in the new direction and helped the process by creating miracles that healed the people of many diseases to demonstrate the real power of the new faith. The masses, either in physical or mental distress, rallied to him and became ready converts. He left the ruling classes cold for these were strongly dominated by the Confucian philosophy of Chu Hsi. The ruling classes, however, could not but remark the increasing strength of this strange new native religion. They became alarmed and, four years after he began his preaching, Choe Suun was arrested by the authorities and executed on March 10, 1864 at the age of forty-one. The execution took place in Taegu for the Kyongsang-do provinces were the center of the new movement. Choe's martyrdom only increased the strength of the Tonghak believers beyond Kyongsang-do. Under the leadership of Choe Sigyong, his successor, the movement went underground and spread among people in all walks of life with the rallying slogan: "All men are equal." For more than thirty years, Choe Sigyong actively promoted the movement clandestinely while compiling numerous religious articles. By 1871, the movement had generated enough power to take on outward shape and spark off popular insurrections at Yonghae and Mungyong in which more than ten thousand followers participated.

In 1892-93, the Tonghak staged "non-violence" demonstrations in Changye, Poun and Seoul itself. Their aims were threefold: (1) that Founder Choe Suun, executed as a heretic, be declared innocent of this charge; (2) that the kingdom drive off foreign influences and eliminate corrupt officials; and (3) that freedom to worship be guaranteed.

In Seoul, the government wanted to disperse the demonstrators by mobilizing its troops. Instead, the government decided that it was wiser to persuade them to disband and return to their homes and jobs. The Tonghak complied and the government at once resorted to sterner repressions and severer exploitation of the peasantry.

The following year, 1894, the Tonghak staged an even bigger revolt, the famous Kabo Tonghak Movement, crying "Down with Tyranny" and "Down with Westerners and Japanese." Armed rebels, reinforced by peasants, swept all over the southern areas and marched toward the capital. The government rushed troops southward only to be defeated. The government, therefore, appealed to China for help which was promptly forthcoming as were the Japanese under the policy of "me too." Confronted by the overwhelming strength of two foreign armies, the Tonghak rebels did not stand a chance. The revolt was speedily crushed and 400,000 followers lost their lives, including Choe Sigyong and Chon Pongjun, the two prominent leaders. The movement had not been in vain, however, for the feudalistic tyranny of the Yi kingdom, at least, came to an end.

The calamity, however, did not end the Tonghak movement. The sect was reorganized by the next leader, Son Pyonghui. Soon after this, Son decided to set out on a world trip to inspect conditions in various countries. However, he got only as far as Japan where, with other progressive Korean politicians, he interested himself in political movements back home. While in Japan, the Tonghak leader was instrumental in bringing over many selected young Koreans of promise for further studies.

In 1904, when the Russo-Japanese War loomed imminent, Son instructed his comrades at home to form a political party. The platform of the Progressive Society, as the Tonghak's political organization was called, demanded change in the mode of living of the common people, elimination of corrupt officials and change of government by popular force, if neccessary, in order that Korea might consolidate the foundation for political independence. The reaction of the people was spontaneously enthusiastic as everywhere mass meetings took place and demonstrators shouted slogans for "New Life!" and "Expel Corrupt Officials!" But the movement was betrayed within the party ranks itself when Yi Yonggu, the leader Son had left behind to deputize for him, sold the Progressive Party out to the notorious pro-Japanese group known as the Iljinhoe. This put a virtual end to the Tonghak's political bid.

Son was naturally indignant when he heard this news. In a countermove to heal this serious damage, he decided to divorce politics from religion and changed the name of Tonghak to Chondogyo. He issued a statement to that effect at home and abroad and established worship centers in each county with headquarters in Seoul. Yi Yonggu and his followers, finding themselves expelled from the Tonghak movement by this move, retaliated by establishing the Sichongyo. Son returned home to become the first Taedoju, head of the Tonghak "church." Before long, he delegated the post to Kim Yunguk who, however, defaulted and went over to the Sichongyo. The deputy Taedoju, Pak Yonho, accordingly, was elevated to the top post.

When Korea became annexed to Japan, the Chondogyo established more than 30 schools and more than 100 preaching stations throughout the peninsula. It became more than obvious what was afoot. The leaders were preparing for the day of restoring national independence through means of new education and mass training.

In 1919, when the Samil Independence Movement broke out, Son Pyonghui became its first and foremost champion while the Chondogyo proved to be the most important of all organized bodies behind the nationwide struggle. Son was arrested by the Japanese gendarmes and died in prison. Japanese repressions were harsher and harsher on the Chondogyo sect than on any other organized body. The more than 30 schools, so recently established, were forced to close down and were taken over by other agencies.

The Chondogyo, however, did not relax

their efforts. They published numerous periodicals for intellectuals, educators, women, laborers, farmers and children, dealing with all problems that might enhance the national spirit and provide new knowledge ever in the cause of Korean independence. In affiliation with Christian and other organizations, they established youth organizations, peasants' societies, workers' associations, women's associations, children's associations. Many of the believers went underground following Japan's invasion of China and, toward the close of the Pacific War, they had an active clandestine party, called the Osimdang, which functioned until the Liberation of 1945.

Present Situation

The Chondogyo, which had its membership shrunk under Japanese oppression, stood a good chance of expansion when Korea was liberated. But the chance proved to be a limited one under the blow of the territorial division for there were many more followers in the north. They staged a Samil Movement there in 1948 in conjunction with their fellow-adherents of the south to be subjected to bitter Communist suppression. In 1949-50, the Chondogyo northerners formed a secret organization called the Yonguhoe and developed a political movement all over the northern zone. Again the northern regime cracked down hard and the prisons of Pyongyang bulged with "reactionaries." The outbreak of war provided the Chondogyo members with opportunity to fight their oppressors as guerrillas in the rear and the occupation of the northern zone by United Nations forces enabled thousands of young believers to come south when the Chinese Communists attacked.

Meanwhile, in the south, the adherents, smaller in numbers and not so severely tested as their northern comrades, began to reorganize preaching stations, reviving "church" districts in each county and providing halls in each *myon*. The central headquarters in Seoul was reshuffled with instruction, executive, decisions and disciplinary departments. Such organs as the Tonghak Association, Tonghak Women's Association and Tonghak Students' Association, were formed under the headquarters. The Tonghak Association, founded in 1957 in order to spread the ideals and aims of the movement and apply them in practice, has branches in each county, overseas branches in Japan, Hawaii and even Cuba. Present membership is shown below:

The Sichongyo also has its headquarters in Seoul although its influence is diminishing. There are other minor sects, derived from the same Tonghak movement, such as the Sangjegyo and the Suungyo, with negligible followings.

As of 1955

Areas	No. of Churches	No. of Priests and Preachers	No. of Adherents
Seoul	9	656	81,320
Kyonggi-do	22	1,143	193,535
Chungchong Pukto	29	946	142,860
Chungchong Namdo	27	1,203	197,465
Cholla Pukto	38	1,193	187,891
Cholla Namdo	32	951	179,191
Kyongsang Pukto	27	1,150	186,855
Kyongsang Namdo	32	1,321	213,086
Kangwon-do	12	609	109,642
Cheju-do	7	75	3,896
Total	235	9,247	1,495,741

Chondogyo Doctrines

(A) Man is Heaven.

The basic idea of the Chondogyo is that man is heaven. By this is meant that each and every man cherishes God. This is no primitive pantheism but the God that every individual has within him. The relation between God and man is that between the Maker and the made, which puts God in the keeping of each individual's conscience. According to the founder, Choe Cheu, by pursuing your goal from eternity to eternity, you will reach a state of enlightenment and through enlightenment realize yourself. This is the foundation on which the new man and the world can be created.

Inasmuch as man has God within himself, Choe said, you must serve man as you would serve God. This doctrine leads to the principles of freedom, equality and peace; this next doctrine leads to the principles that matter and spirit are one and the same, that body and mind are one and the same, that politics and religion are one and the same; this further doctrine leads to realism which, among other things, demands that the Kingdom of Heaven be realized on earth. The Kingdom of Heaven on earth will come into being but only when the nation has been preserved, morality prevails throughout the world, and every man is saved. Moreover, all these principles can be realized only when the individual has attained Spiritual Enlightenment, National Enlightenment and Social Enlightenment.

(B) Doctrine of the Supreme Force (*Chigiron*)

The Chondogyo holds the ontological doctrine that the Supreme Force governs the whole universe. This, Choe Cheu, called *Chigi* (至氣). The entity has two attributes; one of repulsion, the other of harmonious attraction. The entity is another name for God. The Supreme Force governs universe, nature and society; it is omnipresent but it cannot be recognized by organs of the senses; it is neither matter nor mind; it is the original entity of reality and appearance, matter and mind. That is why the Chondogyo holds that we must develop a perfect state of mind and body, that politics and religion are the same thing.

(C) Doctrine of Non-Thusness and Thusness, and Doctrine of Doing by Non-Doing (Epistemology and Philosophy in History of the Chondogyo)

The Chondogyo regards Non-Thusness and Thusness as methods of epistemology and Doing by Non-Doing as the process of everything in the universe. Thusness is appearance, phenomenon; None-Thusness is reality, real entity. In order to reach real metaphysical reality, we must go beyond the phenomenal world through the process of scrutinizing the present condition, its cause and future and effect. This is the intellectual process through which we reach the world of Thusness as well.

The Doctrine of Doing by Non-Doing means that every development is the outcome of self-movement. The idea is similar to Lao Tze, the only difference being that the Chondogyo view is more positive, emphasizing changes and progress.

(D) Serve Man as You Would Serve God with Sincerity, Respect and Truthfulness.

The ethics of the Chondogyo may be summarized in the four words of the Chinese phrase: shin jen yu tien (Serve Man Like Heaven); that is to say: "Serve man as you would serve God."

From this principle, the following three practical moral precepts are derived: Sincerity, Respect and Truthfulness. By Sincerity is meant the true, the positive, the mentally tenuous attitude; by Respect is implied to respect Heaven, respect man and respect things; by Truthfulness is meant faith and honesty in dealing with one's fellowman.

(E) Sacred View

In view of the extreme individualisms and totalitarianisms prevailing here and there, now and then, throughout the world, the Chondogyo holds that cooperation is the key to all social problems, the way to eliminate deadly competitions in all forms of opposition.

(F) The Kingdom of Heaven on Earth

Traditional religions have regarded this earth as a temporal one, thereby seeking eternal life of bliss in the other world. The Chondogyo rejects this idea, believing that man can create the ideal world on earth.

Doubtless, such ambition on man's part may require everlasting efforts. However, in view of the undoubted development of science, progress of human culture and slow but sure promotion of justice and equality, we may hope that some day mankind will reach this ideal world. On the basis of this reasoning, the Chondogyo holds the "Kingdom of Heaven on Earth" as one of its creeds. As expounded previously, in order that humanity reaches that ideal world, national sovereignty must be preserved, morality must prevail everywhere in the world, and every man must be saved and delivered from all kinds of man-made sufferings. Only then can eternal peace come to mankind.

(G) Enlightenment Movement, Practical Program

As stated previously, to achieve this lofty ideal, enlightenment must proceed. Enlightenment comprises spiritual, national and social awareness. By Spiritual Enlightenment is meant the individual's liberation, elimination of mental defects, changes in the idea of men from the old to the new; by National Enlightenment is meant that every nation and every legitimate group of people must be liberated from alien domination; by Social Enlightenment is meant the elimination of all obstacles that hinder progress in society to the end that rampant individualisms and terrible totalitarianisms may be replaced by social cooperation. The three Enlightenments are the cornerstone for eternal peace in the world.

Chondogyo Rituals

The Chondogyo believer must observe two thing, the *simgo* and the "five *kwan*." in order that he might lead a life of Sincerity, Respect and Truthfulness.

A) *Simgo* means literally "inform mentally." In other words, before and after an act of any kind, going out or coming into the home, before or after sleep, before or after eating, to mention only a few activities in life, we must inform God of what we are about to do or what we have just done—in silence.

B) The "five *kwan*" are the following five religious rituals: chanting of the Chondogyo prayer, clean water, congregation, a gift of rice, and prayer.

The believer must chant the officially prescribed prayer text every day as often as possible. The purpose is to purify the heart.

Clean water means that unlike other religions which require many kinds of food, fish, meat, fruit, vegetables, etc, in offering sacrifices, for the Chondogyo believer, a bowl of water is good enough.

Chondogyo believers must save a spoonful of rice at each meal; at the end of the month, he should dedicate the rice thus saved to the "church."

The believer must keep three kinds of prayer. First, he should hold prayer-meetings with his family at nine o'clock every evening by placing a bowl of clean water in the center of a circle; secondly, the family must hold a prayer-meeting every Sunday night; thirdly, a special prayer-meeting must be held on days decided by the "church."

Anyone who fails to observe the "five *kwan*" is not qualified to be a believer.

Taejonggyo

Preamble

Thousands upon thousands of years ago, the universe was created and one of its components was the earth upon which minerals, vegetables, animals and other things were created. However, since there was no intelligence in the animals, man included, the world remained a dark place for countless numbers of years. It was merely a physical world. Hwanin (Creator—Hwan: bright entity; In: first cause), looking down at this dark world, thought that its development depended upon human intelligence. Accordingly, he decided to grant three divine instruments, a mirror, a sword and seeds to Hwanung (God of matter and principle of the world—Hwan: bright entity; Ung: great) and send him and three thousand spirits down to earth. Among the three thousand spirits were those who knew the secrets of clouds, rain, lightning and wind. They descended under the shade of a tree called Paektan (sandalwood) atop Mount Paektu. This was the beginning of civilization in the world.

In compliance with Hwanung's wishes, the God General, Chiu, commanded the three thousand heavenly heroes to burn down the forest, build roads and teach unintelligent mankind how to speak. They drove the people out of caves and taught them how to build up villages. Since the people did not understand language, the divine heroes taught them what they ought to know and do through music which is the expression of harmony in the universe.

Legend says that the farmers' music which still prevails in Korean villages was originated before speech during this mythological age. The Divine General, Chiu, was a brave and wise hero. The Korean verb, *chuda* (putting things in order) is said to have derived from him.

As community life progressed, the divinity, Kosil, taught the people how to cultivate the land, raise domestic animals and eat cooked food. Another divinity, Chuin, taught them the marriage system. Even today, farmers resting from work in the fields for a drink or a meal, first raise the cup or the bowl up in the air and call, "Kosere," which means to offer food or drink to Kosil.

With the progress of civilization, the divinities taught the people medicine, irrigation and flood control. Since it was impossible to preserve civilization merely by word of mouth, the divinity, Sinji, invented characters whereby the divinities hoped to preserve and develop civilization.

This was the first stage of progress. By then, the people had learned to wear clothes instead of animal skins, to dwell in houses instead of caves, and to lead community life.

Way of Life

So the people began to lead community life. Here, the Diving King, with the help of the other divine heroes, gathered the people together and, promulgating the Way and Truth of Heaven, ordered them to worship God with sincerity, fulfill their human destinies by preserving and developing their conscience, and lead lives of goodness and beauty. Further, he expounded the philosophy of the universe, the principle that man and the universe is one and the same, the principle that life has three cycles of the past, the present and the future, and the principle that the universe began with the grand extreme and that this grand extreme, in turn, became chaos out of which the five elements were produced. And he taught them about the principles of motion and rest. The original spirit enters into the matter. This is the principle which gives birth to the human baby. This is the principle which governs everything on earth.

God creates everything in the physical world and gives birth to human beings in society. Accordingly, the Heavenly God is also the Human God. God is mind. Therefore, the heavenly mind and the human mind is one and the same and to deny God is to deny the mind. Furthermore, since matter and spirit are the same, the body and the mind are inseparable and, for the same reason, man and the universe are the same, man being a little universe. Again for the same reason, nothing exists without spirit or life. Since life is light, the whole universe may be regarded as a body of light. Since death is darkness, the Taejong-gyo regards life as immortal. Life is active and intelligent; it is the seat of intelligence and the body is its instrument of action. Things looked at outwardly have no mind and no life. Such a view of the universe is to regard the universe as dark. And this is a false view because it denies the existence of God who is the original source of life, mind, nature and every other thing that exists.

From these principles, we may derive practical lessons, the canons of the Taejonggyo; namely, to cultivate and practise morality, to encourage spirit and foster character and personality. If we practise these canons, we shall get rid of diseases and enjoy immortality, and the world shall become peaceful.

The Canons

In accordance with the fundamental principles of the universe, the Taejonggyo regards Heaven as a pure and active being and the earth as unclear and inactive; it regards the male as active and the female as passive. For this reason, we ought to keep our minds pure and active so that we may preserve our lives forever. In Heaven, there are three hundred and sixty pockets of air and in the human body there are three hundred and sixty holes. Through these holes, the body inhales the cosmic spiritual air. By inhaling these cosmic elements, we can suppress the five elements of the body and increase the state of purity which makes our body and mind pure, cool, at rest. Then we may be at peace with the world and with ourselves and that is the guiding principle of health and longevity.

Customs and Culture

Hence, Koreans worship Heaven which is the source of light and life. For the same reason, they worship the sun. This has given rise to the custom of getting up early in the morning and of bowing towards the sun in the belief that the sun is the symbol of Heaven. Koreans believe that man is the symbol of Heaven. Koreans believe that man is the son of the sun. The son of the sun came down to this land of Korea which is situated in the east. According to the philosophy of the five elements, the east is wood and wood is benevolence. Now the man of benevolence enjoys longevity. Furthermore, it is believed that in the Mountain of the Three Gods, that is to say, the Paektusan, there are sacred plants to eat which is to live long without diseases. All these beliefs make up the core of the Taejonggyo, or the Teachings of the Heavenly Gods who descended on Korea.

The Taejonggyo teachings were incorporated into Korean customs, morality and culture. The scriptures handed down consists of many writings dealing with the metaphysics, philosophy, practical ethics, rituals and other properties of the Taejonggyo. They are the essentials of the Taejonggyo which was formulated at a later period.

The basis of communication between man and Heaven and between man and man is sincerity. Sincerity between father and son is filial piety; that between king and subject is loyalty; that between man and his environment is selflessness. Owing to these teachings and their application in practical life among the people, Korea used to be called the "Eastern Land of Courtesy," "The Land of the Gods," and the like.

The ritual of this religious faith is to offer sacrifices to the Heavenly Gods and spirits. The offering of sacrifices has been the custom of all Koreans, low and high.

Brief History

And so, the teachings of the Heavenly Gods who descended upon this land of Korea marked the beginnings of the morality, customs and culture of primitve Koreans. Following upon the footsteps of this Heavenly Host, Tangun, founder of the Korean nation, spread Heaven's Way among the people and consolidated the political founda-

XII THOUGHTS AND RELIGIONS

tion of a state. In short, Tangun established the Heavenly Teachings as a national religion.

Later on, during the Koguryo dynasty, King Tongmyong called this Teachings of Heaven-Worship; in Silla, the Hwarangdo owed its success to these Teachings; in Paekche, they called this religion the Chonsingyo; in the Koryo dynasty, they called it the Wanggomgyo after the name of the divinity, Wanggom, and in the Palhae (Pohai) dynasty, it was the Chinjonggyo. The Yi dynasty, which adopted Confucianism as the national teaching, suppressed this religion. As a result, it was forced to withdraw from community life into the mountains and remote places. Yet, the believers did not cease to believe in its truth and did their best to promote the welfare of humanity.

In 1910, one, Na Chol, revived this religion and called it the Taejonggyo, *tae* meaning great, *jong* standing for Tangun, and *gyo* meaning teaching. Its creeds are to worship the trinity of the godhead, the principle of communication, knowledge and preservation, and the principle that holds human nature, life and spirit as one and the same. Basically, the Taejonggyo is a revival of an age-old religion of the Heavenly Gods. Our account here is the Taejonggyo version.

Present Status

The Taejonggyo has its headquarters in Seoul. Headquarters consists of a senior committee, three departments on morality, economy and politics, and attached institutes for research and culture. Besides, there is a provincial headquarters in each province under which are district stations in counties or towns. Its following has never been determined.

Shamanism and Aberrations

No story on Korean religion can ignore that primitive faith in the elements, generally known as Shamanistic worship. Shamanism, or more properly speaking, the myriad forms of animistic worship derived from a common ancestry in time immemorial, is still very much a potent force in Korean village life. Elsewhere, in "Manners and Customs," examples are given of Shamanistic practices that are occasions for the outburst of supercharged emotions into defiant superstitious channels and that make the Korean countryside perpetual nights of gongs and clamors. Here, we can only trace the barest outline of its history.

As we have seen, the Yi dynasty rejected Buddhism which flourished in the Koryo dynasty and adopted Confucianism as the national teaching. This left a gap in the spiritual needs of the humble Korean. Confucianism was essentially a sane philosophy appealing to the learned. It could not replace the hold Buddhism had on the humble Korean when the temples fled into the mountains. Instead, Shamanism, ever potent in the countryside, surged in to fill the gap left by the absence of Buddha's potent powers in the supernatural. Thus, the decline of Buddhism not only meant the increase of Confucianism in the upper ranks of society but the increase of Shamanism as well in the lower strata. Confucianism permeated society from the top; Shamanism reared up from the depths of the primitive rural community. Buddhism's expulsion was Shamanism's opportunity and the farther the former retreated, the nearer the latter advanced. The familiar robes of the Buddhist monks disappeared and the witches became conspicuous not only in villages but in the towns as well. The nature of Shamanism has ever been to surge and triumph at every given opportunity.

This led to great increases in the number

of professional Shamans or anybody who had anything to do with the magic rites. As Shamanists were regarded as belonging to the lowliest of occupations, the officials and scholars of the Yi dynasty did not deign to record any statistics. Any estimate, therefore, must largely be guesswork. Based on the poll-tax for this class in official documents from 1801 to 1834, we offer the following province-by-province estimate as the number of Shamanists averaged during the Yi kingdom:

Kyongsang-do	522
Cholla-do	415
Seoul	181
Chungchong-do	175
Hamgyong Namdo	129
Kyonggi-do	32
Kangwon-do	62

These revenue documents do not list the number of Shamanists in Hwanghae-do, Hamgyong Pukto and Pyongan-do provinces. Applying estimates to the north in proportion to the given figures, we may consider the total number of professional Shamans to have been about 2,000 in the nineteenth century. If to that, we add the men-Shamans who were not included in the poll-taxes on the basis of latter-day proportions between the two sexes, we may add another 650 to the 2,000. Not only that but the women-Shamans listed represent only those who were registered in order to be taxed. There were certainly numerous others who were not so registered. Taking this fact into consideration as well and, bearing in mind that each Shaman undoubtedly had several assistant-Shamans, we may conclude that the number of people earning their livelihood by practising Shamanist rites must have totalled no less than 5,000.

The more reliable reports drawn up during the 30's of this century estimated the total at about 12,380. The province-by-province distribution is as follows:

Cholla Namdo	1,945
Kyonggi-do	1,865
Pyongan Pukto	1,236
Chungchong Namdo	1,226
Hwanghae-do	1,009
Kangwon-do	887
Kyongsang Namdo	883
Pyongan Namdo	833
Kyongsang Pukto	721
Cholla Pukto	713
Hamgyong Namto	598
Chungchong Pukto	292
Hamgyong Pukto	172

These figures show only the number of professional Shamans. If we include the non-professionals, the total must be very much greater.

Besides Shamanism, Korea has had countless numbers of other semi-religious faiths, some derived from the outstanding Tonghak movement of latter-day Yi. The origins of the Tonghak and the derivations thereof have already been dealt with. Suffice to say that whenever a system of values disintegrates for reasons of sudden social changes, economic strains or political upheavals, people fall into a state of great anxiety. If they cannot adjust themselves to the circumstances rationally, they resort to a religion. The numerous semi-religions of Korea are, then, the outcome of the numerous social, political and economic insecurities in the lives of the Korean people.

Traditionally Korean society was divided into two stern classes, the *yangban* aristocracy and the *sangnom* or *sangsaram* lower classes, including slaves. The latter was supposed to give absolute obedience to the former for the *yangban* represented the ruling class. Education was a *yangban* monopoly and the illiterate masses had to look up to the aristocrats for guidance and protection. When the ruling class became corrupt, the masses lost all sense of security and, gripped by anxiety, became an easy prey to any semi-religious sect making extravagant promises.

As mentioned above, Confucianism became the fabric of life for the aristocrats. In time, the system degraded as nobility evoked the Sage's name to wrangle official appointments, quite forgetting its original purrpose of ethical practices. In short, the aristocrats lost the basis of their authority to rule the masses. At the same time, while the worldly were making a mockery of Confucius' name, the scholars indulged in hair-splitting arguments about Confucian metaphysics that led to the formation of factions and inculcation of factional spirits. Consequently, economic conditions worsened and corruption reigned unchecked. Those in power did not try to retrieve the situation by creating industries to provide jobs for the hungry; they exploited the hungry even more.

The people were ready for any religious appeal. Christianity coming in at this time worked so well among the masses that no amount of official suppressions could stamp it out and neither Confucianism nor Buddhism could prevent the increase of this new religious force. If Christianity was to be stopped from reaching the poverty-stricken masses, it was necessary to offer another religion with a comparable social program strong enough to challenge it. This gave rise to a number of semi-religious movements, of which, the most outstanding, of course, was the Tonghak. The idea was to offset the appeals of Christianity by stressing Eastern features so they all tended to create miracles by a merging of Oriental teachings, Confucianism, Buddhism and Taoism. Recent Korean history has given occasion for such semi-religions to rise time and again. Every national crisis produced a host: the downfall of the Yi dynasty, the Samil Movement, the Liberation, the Communist War. As quickly as they sprout in the wake of a national crisis, they decline when national security is felt, and when security proves somewhat lasting, they are extinct.

Following is a list of current semi-religions:

Songdokkyo (Way of Sacred Virtues)
　Creed: purity and right-mindedness cures us of disease.
Kumgangdo (Way of the Diamond)
　Creed: to promote morality by encouraging Confucian principles and virtues.
Sangjegyo (Way of God)
　Creed: Heaven redeems all people.
Taegukdo (Way of the Extreme)
　Creed: worship Heaven, cultivate oneself: such is the way to comfort mind and body.
Samhwangdo (Way of the Three Gods)
　Creed: right-mindedness and charity.
Chonji Taeangyo (Way of Serenity)
　Creed: observe the teachings of Haewolson; then shall you have comfort of mind and body.
Taehan Chonnigyo (Korean Heavenly Teachings) Creed: worship the Creator.
Ilsimgyo (Way of Single-mindness)
　Creed: faith in the Confucian ethics.
Sonbulgyo (Way of the Hermit and Buddha)
　Creed: partly Buddhistic, partly Taoistic.
Pochongyo (Way of Heaven)
　Creed: worship Heaven, clarify virtues, uphold virtues, love others.
Mirukkyo (Way of Miruk)
　Creed: worship the Taoist spirit, Buddhistic metaphysics and Confucian ethics.
Pohwagyo (Way of Pohwa)
　Creed: benevolence, righteousness and right mind and spirit.
Pyongsan Taedohoe (Pyongsan Association)
　Creed: to establish a national religion and morality.
Taehan Pyongsan Sonbul (Taehan Pyongsan Association)
　Creed: merge the three Oriental teachings, Buddhism, Taoism and Confucianism, by eliminating the irrational elements in them.
Suungyo (Teachings of Suun)
　Creed: Confucian virtues and Buddhist compassion.
Tangungyo (Way of Tangun)
　Creed: to unify the nation by worshipping the National Founder and to protect Confucian virtues.
Taeulgyo (Teachings of Taeul)
　Creed: spiritual cultivation and saving

the nation.

Ilgwangyo (Single Way Teachings)
Creed: undetermined.

Chongdogyo (Right Way Teachings)
Creed: to establish the Kingdom of God on Earth.

Kwansonggyo (Way of Kwansong)
Creed: to rectify the world by worshipping Kwansong.

Chilsonggyo (Teachings of the Seven Stars)
Creed: to produce patriots by worshipping the Seven Stars (the Plow)

Chonhwangjigyo (Teachings of Chonhwang)
Creed: to save the nation by cultivating the mind.

Samnyonggyo (Way of the Three Spirits)
Creed: to merge the three Oriental teachings, Confucianism, Buddhism and Taoism.

Tonghak Sangjegyo (Way of the Eastern Supreme Spirit)
Creed: right mind, spirit and world.

Modern Korean Thought

Introduction

It is a hazardous task to attempt dealing with a subject like modern thought in Korea because no clear demarcations have yet been discerned to separate the thinking of the present-day Korean from his predecessors. This is all the more the case when we consider that a difficult subject like this is properly dealt as a science in the thinking processes of any people. Yet some explanation is in order inasmuch as it is certain that the present-day Korean's opinions of everything around him is as different from his ancestors' as daylight is from night. However different, his way of thinking in the modern world is colored by a national frame of mind centered for centuries on unquestioned faiths in such religio-philosophical faiths as Buddhism, Taoism, and, especially, Confucianism. A typical young modern Korean may express flat disinterest in Confucianism but he remains, all the same, bound by the Confucianist approach of disciplinary habits to work and study, life and play. Such discipline is the core of the Confucian faith.

At any rate, the need to recognize and understand today in order that we may foresee the Korea of tomorrow is tempting enough to assay an outline on modern Korean thought, whatever the meager results.

The first question we must ask ourselves is: just when did this "modern thought" begin in Korea and how deeply or broadly has it penetrated the Korean mind? A question like this requires answers to other prior questions. What constitutes "Korean modern thought?" What do foreigners understand by the term? How modern is it in relation to international trends of thought? Others must attempt to answer these questions. Suffice to explain that by "modern thought," we mean, simply, that the Korean has found himself on another plane of life from that of his ancestors and whatever he thinks about to readjust himself accordingly is modern thought.

To return to our premise: in order to demarcate a line which may have marked the advent of the world of new ideas, we must recall the traditional thinking of the Korean people. This has been dealt with in the former chapters of this book. The present author, therefore, will dispense with belaboring the reader about traditions and assume the arbitrary line of 1894 as the necessary demarcation. That was the year of the Kabo Reforms that brought such reverberating shocks to the tottering feudalistic structure of the Yi dynasty. True, Korea had contacts with the West before this. Hideyoshi brought Western firearms to Korea in order to conquer her, shipwrecked Dutchmen brought Western instruments, Catholic priests opened our eyes to Western achievements, and more substantially, foreign treaties from 1882 on brought in many foreigners scattering any amount of new ideas. But it was the Kabo Reforms which shock the Chosun kingdom both politically and socially and gave rise to streams of Korean movements for modernization of society.

From 1894 on, Western and Japanese capitals began to invade Korea in order to compete with one another for exploitation of Korea's markets and natural resources. Hard upon these foreign investments came new ideas which inevitably replaced feudalistic ideas of politics and society. Confucianism was split into two schools under the impact. The positive school, as ever admiring Chinese culture, stuck loyally by a declining dynasty to oppose all foreign influences, particularly, Japanese militarism; the negative school retreated from everything, old or new. The political world became sour with the domination of men who either followed Japanese policies or collaborated with representatives of the Japanese government. On the other hand, this levelling process provided a basis for the introduction of new ideas and the opportunities, in turn, resulted in conflicting schools of thought about how to bring about modernization.

The Search for a Capitalistic Outlet

The movement to reform Korean society after 1894, then, was a movement at modernization. However, this proved impossible at the close of the nineteenth century for the political and economic conditions of the kingdom were neither ripe nor favorable. The politicians, steeped in degenerated times, were simply not up to the task of meeting a bold, selfless and demanding challenge, and even if we assume that there were enough great men among them who understood the nature of the aggressive Japanese capitalism that was applying pressure on Korea in order to rob her of independence, and opposed it fully, the internal feudal economy of the kingdom was too weak and the economy of a modern Japan, allied with England, too strong. Not only economically but even spiritually, the power of the old ideas was tottering while there was no other ideological system prepared to brake the tides of corruption. Politically, Korea was bankrupt and Japan, certain in its aim of imperialistic expansion in an age of imperialisms, meant to fill that vacuum.

But this is hindsight and we are concerned with Korean thinking in very critical years, however imminent the evidences of impossibility. From 1882 on, that is to say, when the "Hermit Kingdom" was at last opened by the signing of the United States treaty, Koreans came in increasing contact with Westerners, especially the American missionaries who not only brought the Bible but knowledge of Western medicine and education as well. Through such contacts and from the lessons of China and Japan, Korean leaders became convinced that Korea had to be modernized. The obvious answer was to replace feudalism which was on the brink of self-destruction with capitalism and many wanted to effect this transformation at one bound as Japan had done.

This, of course, proved to be an impracticable task in the face of the circumstances within and without. Impractical or impossible, we are here concerned with what Koreans were thinking about the needs of modern reforms. Many intellectuals urged a capitalistic solution during this critical period and even long after the Japanese domination. Two examples will suffice here.

Yu Kiljun (1856-1916) lived at a time when capitalism was swiftly developing imperialistic wings throughout the world. Realizing the danger of Korea falling into the status of a colony directly from feudalistic society, he sought a program that might save the land this fate by modernizing upon the feudal structure. Feudal Korea would have none of this and he was continually hounded by conservative elements who were anti-Japanese and pro-Chinese. At first, he strove for economic and political reforms. After Korea became a colony, he turned his efforts to educational ends.

Yu's outstanding work was a book, entitled: "Soyu Kyonmun" (What I Saw and Heard in the West). Printed in Yokohama, Japan, it wasv a revolutionary work for the era, for its size (20 Chapters, 555 pages), for its new style of mixing the *hangul* letters and Chinese characters, and, above all, for its contents. The purpose of the book was to modernize Korea by imforming the reader of what the Western world was doing and accomplishing. He emphasized the rights of the people, nationalism, international spirit. He emphasized the contrasts he saw between the West and his native country and explained that what he found at home was poverty and weakness of an underdeveloped agricultural land while what he found in the West were high standards of living under a highly developing system of commercialism. Yu thus reminds us of the commercial state theory which once prevailed in Europe. As the first book to persuade Koreans to accept a capitalistic system of society, his was the first work of a modern tenor to reach the Korean reading public.

Like Yu, Paek Ilgyu also tried to introduce the capitalistic spirit into Korea. His main work, "The Economic History of Korea," was published in San Francisco in 1920. At that late date, it was rather an overdue work but, as a development of Korean modern thinking, it was monumental. In the preface, he made this effective point: "if we study the economic history of Korea more deeply, we may be able to foster an education in economics which may prove to be the key to the economic independence of Korea. Economic independence will accelerate political independence." An overseas student with an M.A. from the University of Southern California, Paek was absorbed in the cause of national independence throughout his foreign travels. By showing the inter-relation between economic and political independence, he reemphasized the meaning of the sweeping Samil movement for independence that broke out in 1919. No Korean has yet followed his footsteps by clarifying the problems of contemporary Korean society as succinctly as he.

National Consciousness

Korean movements for national independence, resistance against Japanese domination, and anti-Japanese movements are not easy to understand. Too much emotions were involved over too long a period of time to present a clear picture other than a single spontaneous stream like the sweeping Samil or the joyous Liberation. At one extreme, we might say that the Korean people achieved nothing. The Samil was a failure, after all, and the Liberation was incidental to the U.S.'s prosecution of a war. At the other, we might conclude that every Korean who retained his national identity successfully earned his independence and liberated himself for the open aim of the enemy was to erase that identity. Clearly, such extreme conclusions will not do for Koreans are not all heroes or all cowards but a people like every other people, loving peace and hating tyranny. The clear picture lies somewhere in between.

Such a picture, however, is far from emerging for the history of the Korean people's fight for independence has yet to be studied thoroughly. There is simply no literature sufficient enough that enables us to grasp the ideological thought behind it for a thought there must be besides emotions. To obtain any clear picture, we must pass a phase of research work into the data, records and other written or factual materials, collecting and systematizing them as objectively as we can. In all fairness to ourselves, we must concentrate, particularly, on the records of those who laid down their lives for the cause of independence, the known patriots, the massacred ranks, and the unsung individuals in nameless cells.

XII THOUGHTS AND RELIGIONS

So much for the independence movement or the anti-Japanese resistance. Despite the Japanese, the process of modernization begun in 1894 continued throughout the colonized period. Great numbers of Koreans pioneered in modern thinking to pave the path to national democracy. To be a modern thinker was to stimulate the spirit of nationalism in the people and that was the lifelong tasks of men like Chang Chiyon and Sin Chaeho. Chang (1861-1821) was a prolific writer who reflected the spirit of modern times in numerous newspaper articles and a great volume of books. Sin (1880-1936) started out as a student of ancient Korea, devoted his life to the cause of Korean independence, and died in a Japanese prison cell. His fate was by no means exceptional.

Another name that cannot be omitted is Chu Sigyong. As the pioneer in a scientific approach to the Korean language and the systematizer of Korean grammar, Chu played a very important role in reawakening the national consciousness of the people. This was so because the Korean language was enemy to Japanese imperialism and the linguists who followed in his footsteps were incarcerated in prison for years. How to relate this resistance of language to direct political action remains to be described. Consciously or otherwise, the linguists must have seen in this a means to foster the national spirit that would speed the day of national independence. One of them, Choe Hyonbae, has suggested as much. The viewpoint of the linguists themselves may be biased but certainly to uphold language was to resist an enemy which tried to erase it. At the very least, by championing language, Chu and his successors reminded the people of their national birthright.

Finally, the American Protestant missionaries who began arriving after 1884 were also instrumental in reawakening the national consciousness. It was in Protestant churches that Koreans first heard about democracy and national birthrights, out of the Protestant climate that the Independence Association was formed and from Korean Protestant ranks that the spearhead came for the Samil Movement. The most outstanding work reflecting the Korean spirit of nationalism through Protestant inspiration is "The Spirit of Independence" by the man who later became president of the Republic of Korea, Dr. Syngman Rhee. The importance of this book cannot be underestimated. It must be carefully read against a proper Korea background in order to be rightly appreciated. What is more, only such a correct appreciation can lead to an understanding of the political trends of Korea after 1945. This most important book breathes the spirit of Korean independence in that Protestant climate of the late nineteenth century.

A New Logic

Under the mounting pressure of the long period of Japanese imperialism, the nationalistic and democratic yearnings of the Korean people found a new logic to the intolerable situation. That logic was directly related to social thinking in modern Japan.

Many Koreans may have accepted new trends of thinking directly from the West but the main trends came via Japan. It was mostly under the influence of Japanese thinkers that anarchists or socialists were born. The only counter-balance was the trend of Communism that flowed from the Soviet Union rather than Japan. The route was from Siberia through the Kando Province of Manchuria with its large Korean community and over the northeastern border into the Hamgyong-do provinces, traditionally the stronghold of opposition to government in Seoul. All these social theories were accepted unconditionally by Koreans as means of national liberation before being fully digested as such. For that reason, they have never really been well studied or understood.

Voluntary movements against Japanese domination began toward the end of the nineteenth century. At first, as we have seen, they emanated largely from Confucianism. After the downfall of the Yi kingdom, many Koreans, living either in exile or studying at home or in Japan adopted many other social or political theories that seemed to offer the most likely prospects of defeating the designs of Japanese imperialism. The search continued in the clutch of Japanese colonialism. This was the era of Korean nationalism.

Meanwhile, the national economy was crumbling. Save for the landlord class which collaborated with the Japanese colonizers, the farmers were reduced to a state of virtual banktuptcy. Many quit the country altogether, some going to Japan and others to Manchuria. Those who remained were at the mercy of wilful Japanese exploitation. Increasingly, then, Korean intellectuals who saw the plight of the farmers first-hand became preoccupied with the land problem. Most of them found the answer in Socialism or Communism Thus, Koreans split themselves into two camps: socialist and nationalist.

Under Japanese rule, the two camps shared a common goal of anti-Japanese resistance and national liberation. With the Liberation, the split became acute and the conflict fierce and naked. Ideological confusion reigned over an atmosphere of a joyous liberated state. Almost immediately, too, the Russo-American "cold war" sharpened the conflict and drove the oppositions apart, each on one dominating side of an "iron curtain." Confusion was ended. In its place stood two hostile, uncompromising ideologies, separated by a line neither acknowledged. The north has gone Communist. The south has adopted the model of American democracy. Here we are concerned only with the south for the fate of the north is tied solidly with the Communist bloc which is another story.

The Republic of Korea, which is the official English name for the southern state, has adopted liberalism as its guiding principle. The society is, however, unyielding in its stagnancy with remnants of feudalism and remnants of Japanese imperialism all piled together in a world of contradictions, not to speak of the fears and insecurities created by the recent thrust from the north. These are seriously hindering elements that must be corrected in order to clear away enough of the contradictions before a liberal climate can prevail to any satisfactory degree. The problems are basically political and the present mood, even in college lecture-classes, is escapism from politics and, indeed, from all reality save for the perusal of Western authors. Yet they are Korean problems and, as such, must be weighed and studied by Koreans themselves in or out of school. The fountain-heads of clarifications must come not only from classes on the social and humanistic sciences but, more importantly, from students of philosophy. The last subject of interest in the current escapist mood is philosophy. Yet all problems must, first of all, be explained philosophically.

Not all problems are the result of internal divisions. Many have stemmed from the division of the country into two zones by outside Powers. This compounds the task of the Korean student of philosophy for he must find one from all the currents of the world in order to unlock the key that can unify the conflicting ideas at home. Other Powers may decide to unify Korea by a show of hands but it is the Korean people themselves who must be prepared to unify themselves. Otherwise, although opportunities may come, we may fail to make use of them through sheer lack of self-determinant consciousness such as had proved the case from the middle of the nineteenth century up to the Japanese Annexation in the beginning of the twentieth.

Literary Heritage

One tradition which Korea inherited in the Japanese years and which must be held in high esteem is the spirit of literature that was born. Many patriots expressed themselves in the form of literary creations. We have yet to analyze the trends of this literature sufficiently to link its spirit with the spirit of social and political movements.

What we see clearly in the creative literature of the era is the spirit of transition from feudalism to modern society. The proletariat literature which reflected the sufferings of the Korean people under the yoke of Japanese imperialism and colonialism did not develop into a full-fledged one but went into channels of political resistance. The overall literary trend was, therefore, a harmony of realism and romanticism. In other words, it did not merely reflect social conditions but expressed national aspirations.

A third school wanted to get away from it all. The men of letters here felt suffocated by the reality of the harsh conditions they were living in and sought escapism, even to the point of suicide. The late poet, Yi Sang, for instance, spent his entire life in a suffocating atmosphere. One of his poems, entitled: "Fatigue," may be considered as a striking description of the anxiety and unrest in his days. It was a prayer for salvation of the Creator and, as such not merely the prayer of a young man of 28 in the year 1937. It is the prayer of many a young man today.

The Korean youth yearn to be delivered of all the difficulties caused by political and economic factors in their society. This is at it should be but only if they remember never to be isolated but engaged in world-wide movements of such liberations for all youths have political or economic problems and the Korean youth cannot be isolated from the problems of their generation everywhere. Korean problems being particularly acute, the Korean youths are heavily handicapped. For instance, "Paddy-Fields," a story written by the late writer, Choe Mansik, describes the discontent caused by the economic unrest and political conflicts in his Japanese days. This discontent has hardly been alleviated to this day.

To find the new philosophy that may clear the thorny path to a bright future requires a backward gaze at the past; in other words, Korean history. To study that is surely the point of departure for us today.

Differing Generations

To understand Korea, we must, above all, realize that there are many angles of opinion. As a certain American missionary has observed, democratic ideas and new education are the key to understanding Korea today. There is a great difference between Koreans educated under the Japanese system and those educated under the post-Liberation system. And there will be more differences among the elementary school children, secondary school pupils and college students when these in turn reach maturity.

In general, the Japanese-educated above the age of forty are less progressive than the younger generations who received their education after the Liberation, and the gap has been increased even more by the separation of the country and the recent war. The older generation does not understand the rising ones. Steeped in feudalistic ethics of thought, they are prone to put the younger Koreans under an authoritarian system at home or in the school and this the latter do not accept. Herein is one basic source of conflict between the old and the young.

Above all, the older Koreans assume a pessimistic attitude about the younger generations, thus betraying lack of historical understanding about their country.

XIII EDUCATION

Introduction

Aims

The Korean people have historically displayed a great deal more devotion to the whole of the nation or community than to the pursuit of selfish individual interests. Outstanding examples of this self-denying spirit of the people can be found in the ideals of the *Hwarang* during the Silla era and, more recently, in the Samil Independence Movement of 1919.

This prevailing sense of devotion to the interest and welfare of the whole explains how the concept of the *Hongik Ingan* (serving the general good of all men) developed and was established as the guiding philosophy of the state through the many centuries of the nation's history. It was with this national ideal in mind that the Ministry of Education of the present government formulated the following basic objectives in education.

  a) to realize the ideal of the *Hongik Ingan*
  b) to perfect the personality
  c) to cultivate abilities to manage an independent life and develop the essential qualities of a good citizen
  d) to contribute to the growth of democracy in the nation
  e) to work for the co-prosperity of mankind

In order that these objectives may be achieved, it was further decided to adopt the following seven points as the more concrete aims of education (Article 2 of the Education Act):
  a) health and spirit of perseverance
  b) spirit of national independence and contribution to world peace
  c) upholding cultural and educational heritages of the nation and contributing to world civilization
  d) creative initiative and rational way of life
  e) freedom and responsibility; faith and cooperation
  f) effective use of leisure and development of esthetic sense
  g) sound management of the individual economy

Stages

With the end of the Second World War, education in Korea turned a new leaf. The colonial education under the totalitarian Japanese rule was quickly replaced by what was a beginning of a new democratic way of education. In the initial period of the Military Government of the United States and the provisional civic government, one which was inevitably marked by a certain amount of chaos and confusion in transition, two major tasks were tackled first; to reform the educational system and to expand the educational facilities. It was also a period of a nationwide campaign to study and learn the Korean language which had been suppressed by Japan. Hundreds of institutes teaching the reading and writing of the language sprang up all over the country.

Awakened to democratic ideals of education, educators everywhere sought new educational methods to replace the old totalitarian methods.

Meanwhile, an Education Advisory Committee organized under the U.S. Military Government set up a policy emphasizing the responsibility of education to help create an enlightened citizenry devoted to democracy and national independence. Five major aims of education defined by the Committee were:

a) To establish firmly a sense of self-respect as citizens of an independent nation and to foster a spirit of international cooperation and friendship

b) To encourage a spirit of living up to one's principles and appreciation of the value of labor, to cultivate a sense of responsibility, mutual faith and technology and contribution to the civilization of mankind

d) To elevate the national standards of health and foster stamina and power of perseverance

e) To promote appreciation of the arts and encourage creative activities, and to develop a virtuous, well-rounded personality

When the national government was inaugurated in 1948, Dr. An Hosang was instituted as the first Education Minister. He based his policies on the *Ilminjui* (One People's Principle), a nationalistic and anti-Communist doctrine he personally advocated. Dr. An organized all high school and college students into a Student Defense Corps in order to check Communist activities in the campus by strengthening nationalistic regimentation of the students.

Dr. Paek Nakjun (L. George Paik), the second Education Minister, stressed vocational training and technical education at a time when the need for economic reconstruction was urgent. He has encouraged all students to learn a trade or skill while in school. Dr. Paek also placed emphasis on educating a free and responsible citizen to enable the students better to adjust themselves to the new political and social institutions of democracy. It was during his tenure that military training for high school and college male students began as part of the national policy to successfully fight the Communist War.

The nation was still at war when Kim Pomnin became the third Education Minister. He initiated a book translation program in order to alleviate a serious shortage of textbook and reference materials. He also helped organize the National Academy of Arts and the National Academy of Sciences.

The fourth Education Minister, Dr. Yi Songun, carried out a program of retraining teachers to cope with the adverse effects of the war on the standards of the teaching staff. Mr. Yi strongly advocated a policy to inform the students of the atrocities committed by the Communists and the evils of Communism based on the experiences of the war years.

Dr. Choe Kyunam, the fifth Education Minister, emphasized teacher training and technical education. He also maintained that the responsibility of education lay primarily in the cultivation of moral virtues.

Among the major policies adopted by the present Education Minister, Choe Chaeyu, are expansion of the compulsory education system, improvement of education in science and technology, and development of the national culture.

The most significant development in the field of education since the end of the Second World War was the enforcement of compulsory education based on the principle of equal opportunity. Compulsory education is now applied to a six-year period between the ages of six and twelve, and plans are underway to extend this period to nine years.

Meanwhile, John Dewey's progressive educational philosophy was a substantial influence. His "Democracy and Education" was translated and published in Korea, his ideas discussed at teachers' college and his principles propagated by a number of U. S. education missions that visited Korea.

However, some of the new methods of education have met with criticism from those educators retaining the traditionally Conservative outlook. Some claimed that excessive freedom granted to students caused a general decline in morality. Some critics maintained that part of the new curriculum was not suited to the realities of a developing nation. Co-education also was a point of debate in some quarters.

It should be noted that there are private schools as well as public schools and that religious foundations of various faiths—Buddhism, Confucianism and Christianity—are allowed to operate private schools.

History of Education

This history of Korean education will be reviewed in four parts: from Old Chosun to Silla, Koryo, the Yi dynasty up to the *Kabo* Reform of 1894, and from 1894 to the present.

Part 1 (From Puyo to Unified Silla)

Beginnings

The oldest available historical references to formal education in Korea concern what is known in history as the "Three Kingdoms Era." In the earlier period of Puyo and the primitive Three Han states, there were no educational institutes. Education in the ancient days consisted of family heads teaching filial duties and loyalty to the clan. Farming, manual work and warring skills were taught within the family and the tribe.

The Hwarang

It was during the Silla dynasty that a unique system of training young men, known as the *Hwarang-do* (literally, Way of the Flower of Manhood) was developed. Originally women headed this organization but later, during the reign of King Chinhung, handsome and intelligent young men were selected to head the group. The *Hwarang*, as they were called, received an education that consisted of academic training and military skills. In fact nearly equal emphasis was placed on both the study of history and philosophy and the teaching of various forms of warlike techniques. Men of virtue and intellect were often selected from this group to serve the state as statesmen and military leaders. The guiding principles of *Hwarang* education can be found in the five morals established by Priest Wongwang. They were: loyalty, filial duty, trustworthiness, valor and justice. Members of the *Hwarang* also made a practice of visiting places of scenic beauty to develop a sense of beauty and broad-mindedness.

A noble spirit of chivalry resulted from such education, which also included recitation of poems and rendition of music. In time of war, the *Hwarang* youth fought valiantly on the battlefields. Kim Yusin, who played a key role in Silla's unification of Korea, was one of several great men of Silla who were *Hwarang* in their youths.

Koguryo Schools

There were two types of educational institutions in the kingdom of Koguryo, a private establishment called the *hyangdang*, and a state-operated institution known as the *taehak*. Historical records show that there was a considerable number of *hyangdang* where youths studied the Chinese classics, literature and histories, and learned the art of archery. The *hyangdang* is considered to be the predecessor of the *sodang* which flourished in the Koryo dynasty.

XIII EDUCATION

The *taehak* was first established in the second year of King Sosurim (A. D. 372). It was a school for youths of the upper classes whereas the *hyangdang* was for students from ordinary families. Chinese classics, histories and literature were again the mainstay of the *taehak* curricula although it is assumed that certain military skills were also taught. Both the *taehak* and *hyangdang* were systems copied from the Chinese and, as such, served significant purposes in the importation of Chinese culture.

Unified Silla

The major educational institute of the post-unification period of Silla was the *Kukhak* (literally State School), which was formally established in the second year of King Sinmun (A. D. 682). Some historians, however, believe that it was established in the fifth year of Queen Chindok (A.D. 651), when a number of *paksa* (professors), *chogyo* (assistant professors) and *taesa* (12th grade officials of the state) were nominated as officials for the new school.

At any rate, the *Kukhak*, an institute for public service, was a nine-year course primarily teaching Confucian classics. Students' ages ranged between 15 and 30. The school had three departments, all teaching the Analects of Confucius and Hsiao-ching (a dialogue on filial duty) but each offering different sets of additional classics. One taught the Notes on the Rites (*Lichi*) and the Changes, another offered the Tsochuan Annals and Poems, and the third the Writings of Old and a selection of Chinese literature. Each department was staffed by one professor and a number of assistant professors. The fact that all courses offered the Analects and Hsiao-ching as essential classics shows the emphasis on Confucian morality.

There was also an optional course in mathematics, which was taught by a professor or an assistant professor, according to historical records. The records do not show the number of students attending these courses. Only those whose official ranks did not exceed the *taesa* (12th grade) were admitted.

The school expelled those with poor academic records but allowed promising youths to stay longer than nine years. All students were graduated after attaining the ranks of *taenama* or *nama*, one or two grades higher than the *taesa*.

The *taehak*, headed by *kyong* (president), changed its name to *taehakkam* during the reign of King Kyongdok and regained its original nomenclature since the reign of King Konghye.

In the fourth year of King Wonsong (A. D. 788) a system of public service examination was established to select officials on the basis of scholarship. This was the Three Standards System. The high standard required mastery of the Tsochuan Annals, Notes on the Rites, the Analects and Hsiao-ching. The middle standard required mastery of the Analects, Hsiao-ching and the etiquette chapter of the Notes on the Rites. The low standard called for mastery of Hsiao-ching and the etiquette chapter of the Notes.

Any scholar who mastered the Five Classics (the Changes, the Poems, the Writings of Old, Notes on the Rites and the Annals) the Three Histories (Saki, Hanshu and Second Hanshu) and the writings of the One Hundred Scholars (of the period of the Warring States of Chun-chiu) was considered to have reached a superior standard and given a high post. The new method of selecting public servants on the merit of the applicants' scholarship gradually replaced the old custom of selecting high officials only from the aristocracy.

Part 2 (Koryo Education)

Confucianist Emphasis

The educational trends during the Koryo dynasty were strongly influenced by Confucianism which was the dominant philosophy of the period. During the dynasty, the public educational institutes developed further, the public service examination system was firmly established, and private schools also flourished.

Buddhism, which at the beginning of the dynasty, was as strong an educational influence as Confucianism, lost much of its strength during the middle period of the dynasty. The prevailing attitude was to regard Confucian teachings as sources for political wisdom and to view Buddhist teachings as moral lessons for individual behavior. The excessive emphasis on the study of Confucian classics resulted in general disregard of military needs and training. Consequently, the nation found itself tragical'y unprepared before the series of invasions launched by rising nations on the Central Asian steppes. The invasions caused heavy damages on educational institutes of all kinds.

Early Institutes

In the early days of the Koryo dynasty, there were three state-operated schools for training government officials. The major state institute of the dynasty, *kukchagam*, was founded by King Songjong in the eleventh year of his rule (992). Later, the 16th king of the dynasty, Yejong, organized a foundation called the *yanghyongo* to manage the school and built a largescale building for the institute.

It was during the reign of the 17th king, Injong, that elaborate systems for the state school were formally set up. The school had three major department, *kukchahak*, *taehak* and *samunhak*, each accomodating 300 students. Students were enrolled at different departments depending on the rank of their parents. For instance, the *kukchahak*, the first ranking department, admitted only those whose families enjoyed the third "*pum*" (grade) or higber rank in government service. The greater part of the curriculum of the nine-year school was Confucian classics. Students who finished more than three years of study at the school were eligible for public service examination. Attached to the *kukchahak* were three other departments, *yulhak* (law), *sohak* (geography and astronomy) and *sanhak* (mathematics), which admitted children of lower-ranking officials and private citizens. The three auxiliary departments were all six-year courses.

The school consisted of seven major faculties called "*che*." The seven taught the Changes, the Writings of Old, the Poems, *Chou-li*, Notes on the Rites, the Annals and Military Science respectively. The *kangyeje*, the faculty for military training, was later abolished.

In the Provinces

The *hyanggyo*, sometimes called the *hyanghak*, (both meaning, literally, 'Province School') was also a state-operated institute. While the *kukchagam* was established in the capital, an unknown number of *hyanggyo* were erected in various provinces during the reign of King Injong. These provincial schools taught Confucian classics in much the same way as the state school but on a smaller scale. Students were from families of lower-ranking officials or private citizens. Good *hyanggyo* students were selected and given the opportunity to study at the *kukchagam*.

Another kind of state school was established by King Wonjong, the 24th king of the dynasty (1272). It was called the *tongso haktang* (literally, East-West Schools) since it was a twin set of schools for Confucian studies located in the eastern and western parts of the capital. This system was later changed into what is known as *obu haktang*, a set of five schools erected in and around the capital. These schools were similar to the *hyanggyo* in nature.

Private Schools

Inheriting the tradition of private schools of the Silla dynasty and witnessing a temporary decline in state education, a number of prominent Confucian scholars founded private schools, called *sahak*, in the capital during the reign of Munjong, the 11th king. A large number of graduates from these private schools passed the state examination to become scholar-administrators. Choe Chung, a former Prime Minister, was the most prominent of 12 founders of such schools. His *kuje haktang* (Nine-Faculty School), established around 1053, flourished greatly and soon came to be regarded as an authoritative center of Confucian scholarship.

The educational standard of the 12 schools known as the Twelve *To* was similar to that of the *kukchagam*. Meanwhile, another kind of private school, called *sodang*, was developed during the dynasty as institutes for educating youths from common classes in basic Confucian classics.

The Kwago

Kwago, the public service examination, was formally inaugurated by Kwangjong, the fourth king (958). The system spurred the study of Confucian classics and development of private institutes for teaching the classics. Examinations during the dynasty generally tended to stress Chinese prosody and literature.

Part 3 (Growth of Yi Schools)

Outline

The Confucian tradition which had exerted a great influence upon the thoughts and education of the Koryo dynasty influenced the following Yi dynasty with even greater force. The interpretation and analysis of Confucian classics by the Sung scholars of China was readily accepted as the orthodox philosophy in Korea. The ideals of Confucian teachings were adopted as the ideals for good government by the Yi kings. Consequently, Confucian scholars received royal favors and were given important official positions. During the first half of the dynasty, the scholars emphasized ideology and metaphysical studies; consequently their academic achievements were largely unrelated to the realities of the nation. There was a period when rivalries among various groups of scholar-statesmen brought about a series of bloody *coups d'etat*.

The latter half of the dynasty, however, saw the emergence of a group of scholars with greater interest in practical sciences than in ideologies. They were influenced by the method of historical researches developed by Ching scholars. Such leading scholars of this school as Yu Pangye, Yi Ik, An Chongbok and Chong Yakyong undertook serious studies in economy, history, laws and geography of the nation.

The Sodang

The pattern of the educational institutes in the Koryo dynasty mostly remained intact throughout the Yi dynasty. The only new development was establishment of the *sowon*. The highest state institute, which was called the *kukchagam* in Koryo, was now called the *songgyungwan*. Formally opened in the seventh year of King Taejo (1398), the *songgyungwan* consisted of two main establishments, *munmyo* and *myongyundang*. The former was a shrine honoring Confucius as well as leading Korean scholars of the Confucian tradition. The latter was the school building. The school accomodated about 200 students of 15 or more years of age.

King Taejong, the third king, established five additional schools in Seoul (1411) but the number was reduced to four by Sejong, the fourth king (1445). Each of the four schools, known as *sahak*, admitted 100 students. The curricula of the *songgyungwan* and *sahak* were almost identical.

The number of *hyanggyo* increased greatly during the Yi dynasty, but its educational function was reduced considerably after the advent of the *sowon*. The *hyanggyo* also had its *munmyo* and became a center for various ceremonies held by the citizens of the province or town where it is located. The ceremonies included regular Confucian worship ceremonies honoring exemplary filial men, patriots and other men of virtue, and meetings to honor the aged. The *sodang* was freely established by various groups of private citizens for the education of the young, sometimes in preparation for higher learning at the *sahak* or *hyanggyo*. The numerous *sodang* fell under four different categories depending on whether the school was managed by, one—the schoolmaster; two—a private volunteer; three—a group of volunteers, and four—the cooperative village. The curriculum consisted of Confucian classics, Chinese and Korean classical literature, and calligraphy. Recitation of classics was the principal method of teaching.

Sowon, a new type of educational institute, came into being in the 38th year of Chungjong, the 11th king (1543), when a provincial district chief, Chu Sebung, founded the *paegundong sowon*. Fundamentally a private institute, the *sowon* taught Confucian classics for fees and held Confucian rites twice a year. With private contributions and royal grants, the *sowon* built itself into a financially powerful foundation owning farmlands as well as books. The number of *sowon* grew quickly and reached over one hundred by the reign of Sonjo, the 14th king. Since prominent scholars were invited to teach at these institutes, the *sowon* also assumed the role of a center for academic gatherings and debates. *Sowon* received royal blessing when Myongjong, the 13th king, granted each a tablet on which the name of the institute was written with a royal brushstroke.

Part 4 (Modern Education)
A Royal Decree

As the fruits of Western civilization reached Korea with increasing impact through China and other contacts in the last few decades of the Yi dynasty, the need to renovate the centuries-old educational institutions mounted. But the basically isolationist policy of the monarchy and the feudalistic sentiments of the people hampered and delayed introduction of modern Western ways of education.

In the 19th year of King Kojong's reign (1882), a royal decree opened the gates of the state-operated schools to common citizens. Until then, the schools admitted only those who belonged to the upper class, known as *yangban*. The *Hansong Sunbo*, an official gazette, was first published in that year also.

The Missionaries

In 1885, American Protestant missionary groups began founding modern high schools in Seoul, including a girls' school, the first such institute in Korea's history. In 1894, the *kwago*, the public service examination with undue emphasis on Confucian classics, was abolished and reorganization of the education system began. In 1985, new educational principles were proclaimed. In 1905, the Japanese government began intervening in the educational affairs of Korea, directly or indirectly, as a result of the First Korean-Japanese treaty. While public schools were gradually placed under Japanese control, private schools made determined efforts to cultivate a spirit of resistance and to spearhead a movement to enlighten the people at large.

Perhaps the greatest influence on education of the period derived from missionary schools established and managed with Christian spirit and Western methods. Sciences and humanities of the Western tradition taught at the missionary schools awakened Korean educators to the need to modernize education in Korea. By stressing the spirit of national independence and dignity of the human being, these schools laid the foundation for growth of democratic spirit in the country. It may well be said that these new schools founded by foreign Christian missionaries opened the road to new education.

A missionary group of the Northern Methodist Church of the United States opened the first missionary high school, Paejae, in 1885. The group was represented by Henry G. Appenzeller. The school, with its modern curriculum, well-organized system, and new educational philosophy, was truly the pioneer of modern education in Korea. Another boys' high school, Kyongsin, was established by a Presbyterian group in 1887. Opened in 1886, the Ehwa Haktang, a Methodist foundation, became the first girls' school in Korea. Five other missionary high schools were founded in major cities during the period, all exerting impressive influence on Korean education.

As for higher education, Sungsil College was erected in Pyongyang in 1906 and Yonhui College (Chosun Christian College) in Seoul in 1915, both as missionary foundations.

Language Schools

The emphasis in public educational facilities of the period was first placed on foreign language schools. An English language school for training interpreters was established in 1883. The *yukyong kongwon*, a public school established in 1886, employed American teachers who taught English texts through interpreters. In 1894, the school was closed down and the Kyodong Elementary School, the first of its kind, was established in its place. In 1897, the first senior primary school was opened. The number of elementary schools in Seoul soon increased to eight, and the number in provincial cities soon totalled 57, most of them located in Kyonggi-do, the province surrounding the capital. In 1899, the Hansong Middle School was established with a curriculum emphasizing practical sciences and public welfare.

The first teachers' training high school was erected in 1895. Language schools for Japanese, English and Chinese were also opened that year and a Russian language school followed the next year. In 1900, a German language school was established. The number of school years set by these language schools varied, and there were not many graduates. Meanwhile, the *songgyungwan* continued to receive much official attention as an establishment for teaching Confucian classics and for ceremonies honoring scholarly sages of old. Other public educational institutes established during the period between 1895 and 1900 included a medical school, a commerce and industry school, a law institute, a mining school, a junior military school, a military academy, a postal institute and a communications school.

Hangul Learning

Another significant development in the last few decades of the Yi dynasty was the study of the Korean language undertaken with official encouragement. In 1907, a reasearch center for the study of the Korean alphabet, *hangul*, and ways of standardizing the written language were established within the Education Ministry. "Grammar," written by Yu Kiljun (1909), and "Sounds of Speech (1910)," written by Chu Sigyong, were significant results of the new efforts in the widest and fastest possible propagation of the simple Korean alphabet among the people. These were pioneer works in the study of the national language which continued despite harsh methods employed by the Japanese to suppress and obstruct them throughout the colonial period.

The last years of the dynasty saw the advent of various quasi-social academic associations which undertook educational and cultural activities in order to accelerate enlightenment of the people. The *Tedong Hakhoe, Sobuk Hakhoe, Honam Hakhoe, Kwandong Hakhoe,* and *Kyonam Hakhoe* were all such academic associations which contributed much to the awakening of the populace to the need of education and knowledge. Meanwhile, a considerable number of private high schools was established with contributions from private individuals and groups. These schools helped develop a spirit of independence in the nation and resisted pressures of Japanese colonial policies.

Another group of institutions which played a leading role in the resistance were four modern newspapers, *Tongnip Sinmun* (The Independence News), *Hansong Sinmun, Cheguk Sinmun,* and *Taehan Maeil Sinbo*. The *Tongnip Sinmun*, first private-own newspaper, was published in 1896.

Student Resistances

Japan's colonial education in Korea began in 1910 with Governor-General Terauchi Masatake's policy of training Korean students as workers rather than educated men. Practical skills and knowledge were stressed at the expense of liberal arts education. The ulterior motive seemed to be to pave the way for submission to the foreign rule by stabilizing individual economic conditions. As a result, new schools opened were mostly primary schools and technical schools, and no serious attempt was made to expand secondary and college education facilities.

Statistics show that only seven public middle schools, including two for girls, and four 3-year colleges, existed in 1919. Only four percent of Korean children were receiving schooling at that time, while in Japan 90 percent of the children were attending schools.

In 1919, students all over Korea took part in the Samil Independence Movement and denounced Japan's colonial and authoritarian ways of education in Korea. Saito Minoru, the new Governor-General, consequently, announced what he called a new policy of cultural education and soon organized an education research committee commissioned allegedly to eliminate discriminatory treatment against Koreans. Upon recommendation of the committee, made up of 25 Japanese and only three Koreans, the school system in Korea was changed to conform with that in Japan.

However, this was merely part of Japanese efforts to assimilate Koreans with Japanese and weaken the spirit of independence. The schools in those days devoted more time to teaching the Japanese language than to teaching the mother tongue of the students. Emphasis was placed on Japanese history courses at the expense of Korean. The only university, the Seoul Imperial University, was established in 1928 but admittance of Korean students was restricted.

The number of elementary schools increased gradually in the 20's and 30's, but discriminations against Koreans were obvious in higher education, appointment of teachers, and enrollment practices. In 1929, open violence erupted between Korean students and Japanese students in the city of Kwangju, located in the southwestern part of the peninsula. The incident quickly touched off a nationwide student movement against Japanese rule.

Governor-General Ugaki Kazushige who assumed the post in 1931 advocated improvement of education in farm communities. Ugaki encouraged education of practical skills and attempted to steer students into technical schools instead of high schools and colleges that they might become leaders of local communities rather than leaders of national stature.

Totalitarian Methods

Totalitarian methods dominated public school education in Korea during the rule of Governor-General Minami Jiro which began in 1938. Korean language lessons were replaced by Japanese language lessons, except in the first three grades of the elementary school.

Efforts to Japanize Koreans swept the schools as the Japanese authorities attempted to utilize education as the means to induce loyalty to the Japanese Emperor among the people. The aims and contents of education in those days were in line with the imperialist intents of the Japanese government. Korean teachers and students were ordered to make visits to the Shinto shrines, and a number of American missionary schools was shut down for refusing to comply.

After Japan declared war on the United States and Britain in 1941, the education system was adjusted to meet the war needs. The middle school course was shortened to four years from five; preparatory college and college courses were also shortened from three to two years. Names of schools readily identified as the result of foreign missionary christening or reflecting the traditional Korean heritage were changed to new names that were invariably Japanese. English language lessons were terminated and Korean teachers and students told to speak only in Japanese at school and even at home. The Japanese authorities also pressured Koreans into Japanizing their names. To meet the manpower shortage at the height of the war, Japanese authorities began conscripting Korean students into Japanese military services as volunteers. Schools were virtually closed in the last months of the war as students were mobilized to serve the war effort as large labor forces.

XIII EDUCATION

Table 1. Showing the number of schools for Koreans and the number of students thereof.

	1912	1919	1925	1935	1941
Industries for primary education	18,212	24,774	20,516	10,352	9,353
Primary schools	350	517	1,254	2,358	3,118
Students	44,638	89,288	407,292	716,730	1,576,352
Short course schools	–	–	–	579	1,618
Students				35,695	57,428
Miscellaneous Private schools	1,317	690	671	367	236
Students	55,313	34,970	72,267	60,710	57,428
Sodang	16,540	23,556	18,510	6,807	4,105
Institutes for secondary education	44	107	96	199	309
Middle Schools	6	18	32	45	78
Students	918	3.841	12,128	20,412	35,792
Technical schools	19	22	44	60	95
Students	1,456	2,034	5,311	12,016	26,794
Technical continuation schools	19	67	20	94	136
Students	636	1,252	892	3,829	8,614
Normal schools	–	–	–	4	11
Students				920	3,414
Continuation normal schools	–	–	14	4	11
Students			1,696	563	1,989
Colleges	1	6	9	15	19
Students	93	588	1,053	2,722	3,639
Preparatory colleges	–	–	1	1	1
Students			91	112	219
Universities	–	–	1	1	1
Students			47	210	304

Table 2. Showing the number of Korean teachers

	1912	1919	1925	1935	1941
Institutes for primary education	3,829	3,250	8,039	9,846	11,673
Kindergarten	–	28	203	481	674
Primary school Public	1,037	1,664	5,180	7,251	8,222
Private	67	102	338	483	432
Short course school	–	–	–	514	1,443
Miscellaneous schools	2,725	1,456	2,318	1,117	902
Sodang	(16,771)	(23,795)	(19,101)	(7,271)	(4,755)

(Continued on next page)

(Continued from page 369)

		1912	1919	1925	1935	1941
Institutes for secondary education		63	150	287	867	1,347
Middle school	Public	16	21	38	72	135
	Private	14	73	161	304	404
Technical school	Public	25	23	59	68	155
	Private	5	2	10	76	137
Technical continuation school	Public	3	31	19	73	126
	Private	-	-	-	6	82
Miscellaneous school		-	-	-	268	308
Institutes for advanced education		1	21	64	142	290
Normal school		-	-	13	17	32
College	Public	1	7	6	15	87
	Private	-	14	45	110	170
University	Preparatory school	-	-	-	-	-
	Colleges	-	-	-	-	1
	Total	3,893	3,421	8,390	10,855	13,310

Education System

Administrative Systems

The educational administration in Korea holds that its ultimate objective is to evolve itself organizationally into a system which ensures neutrality and independence from politics on the basis of local self-autonomous function.

The highest authorities in educational administration are the President, the Minister of Education, and, if necessary, the Minister of Home Affairs. The authorities subordinate to these three men include the Provincial Governor, the City Education Board, and the Superintendent of the Education District. The Central Education Board and the Provincial Education Boards have functions that are primarily advisory.

The chart on page 371 illustrates the channels of authority in educational administration.

The Central Education Board and Provincial Education Boards

The function of the Central Education Board is to study educational policies and measures of national import and make recommendations to the President and the Education Minister. The Provincial Education Board has a similar function at the provincial level. These boards are not administrative organs, but they have a limited control over the administration. For the Education Minister and the Provincial Governor are obliged to refer to the Boards for approval of any revisions or changes that they wish to make in Board recommendations.

The Central Education Board consists of 30 members of prominent scholars and educationists recommended by Seoul Special City Education Board and every Provincial Education board one member each, and by the Education Minister for the rest. They are appointed by the President.

The Provincial Education Board consists of the members elected by every Education District and city Education board one member each, and the 3 members selected by the Provincial Governor concerned.

Educational Self-Autonomy

The Education Districts and the City Education Boards were first established on

XIII EDUCATION

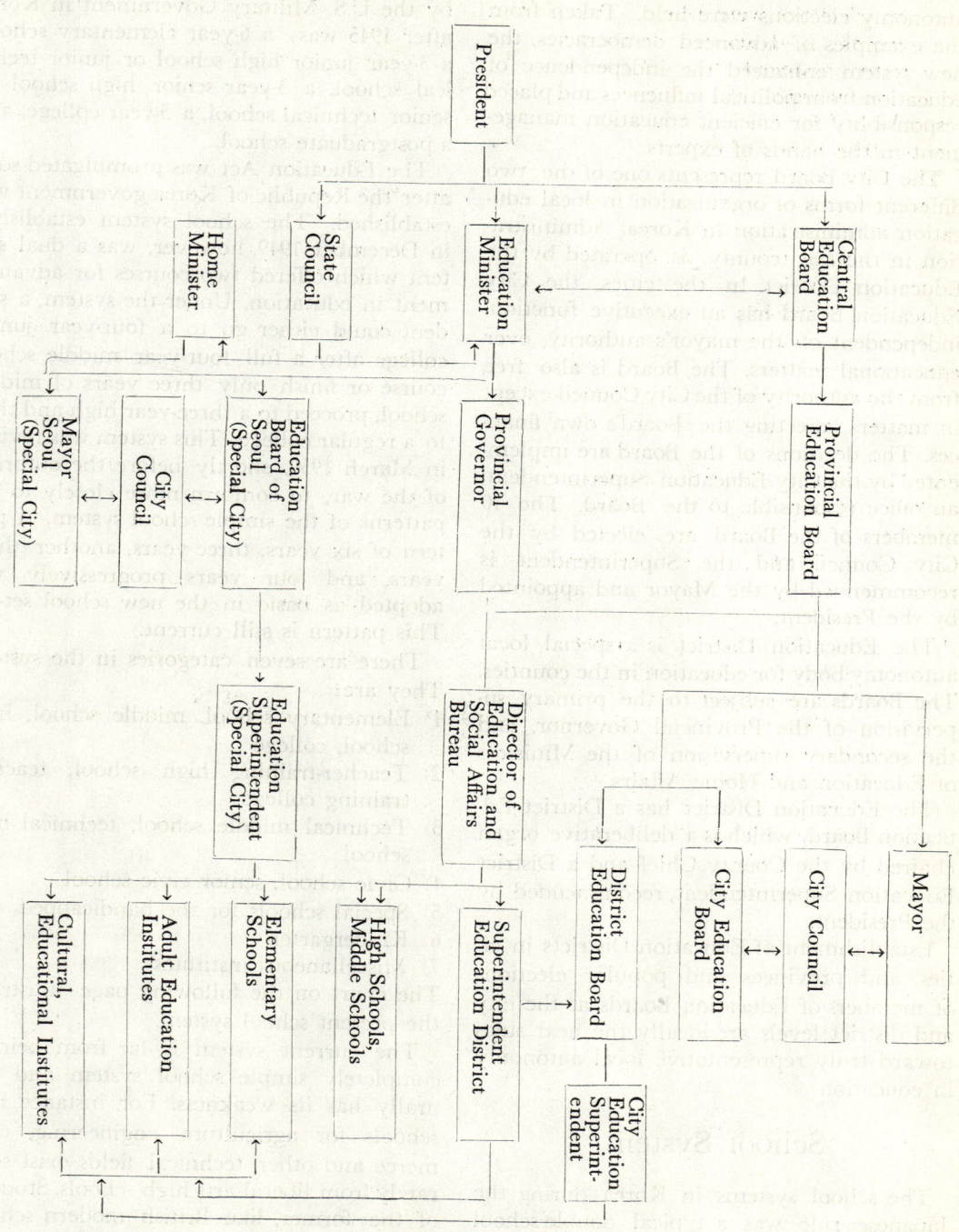

June 4, 1952, two months after the first local autonomy elections were held. Taken from the examples of advanced democracies, the new system enhanced the independence of education from political influences and placed responsiblity for efficient education management in the hands of experts.

The City Board represents one of the two different forms of organization in local education administration in Korea. Administration in the *kun* (county) is operated by the Education District. In the cities, the City Education Board has an executive function, independent of the mayor's authority, over educational matters. The Board is also free from the authority of the City Council except in matters affecting the Board's own finances. The decisions of the Board are implemented by the City Education Superintendent, an office responsible to the Board. The 10 members of the Board are elected by the City Council and the Superintendent is recommended by the Mayor and appointed by the President.

The Education District is a special local autonomy body for education in the counties. The Boards are subject to the primary supervision of the Provincial Governor, and the secondary supervision of the Ministers of Education and Home Affairs.

The Education District has a District Education Board, which is a deliberative organ chaired by the County Chief and a District Education Superintendent, recommended by the President.

Establishment of Education Districts in cities and provinces and popular elections of members of Education Boards at the city and district levels are ideally the next steps toward truly representative local autonomy in education.

School System

The school systems in Korea during the Japanese rule was a typical double-school system, but efforts were made to establish a democratic (or simple) school system after the liberation of the nation from Japanese domination. The new school system adopted by the U.S. Military Government in Korea after 1945 was: a 6-year elementary school, a 3-year junior high school or junior technical school, a 3-year senior high school or senior technical school, a 3-year college, and a postgraduate school.

The Education Act was promulgated soon after the Republic of Korea government was established. The school system established in December 1949, however, was a dual system which offered two courses for advancement in education. Under the system, a student could either go to a four-year junior college after a full four-year middle school course or finish only three years of middle school, proceed to a three-year high and then to a regular college. This system was revised in March 1950, shortly before the outbreak of the war, to conform more closely to the patterns of the simple school system. A pattern of six years, three years, another three years, and four years progressively was adopted as basic in the new school set-up. This pattern is still current.

There are seven categories in the system. They are:

1) Elementary school, middle school, high school, college
2) Teacher-training high school, teacher-training college
3) Technical middle school, technical high school
4) Civic school, senior civic school
5) Special schools for the handicapped
6) Kindergarten
7) Miscellaneous institutes

The chart on the following page illustrates the present school system.

The current system is far from being a completely simple school system and naturally has its weakness. For instance, high schools for agriculture, engineering, commerce and other technical fields exist separately from liberal arts high schools. Students of the former, like British modern schools and the German Realschule, are placed at a certain disadvantage in competing with regular high school graduates at college en-

XIII EDUCATION

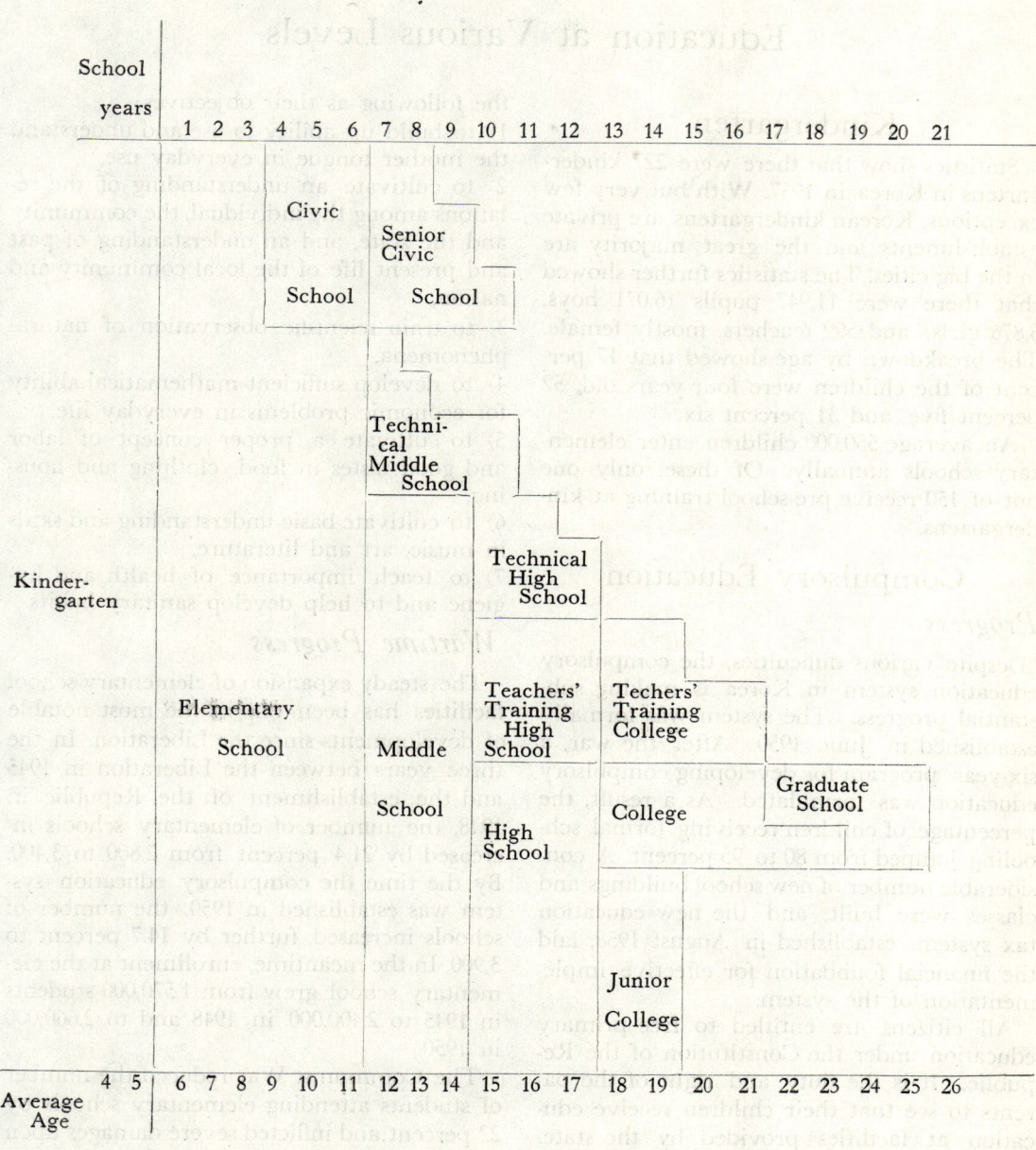

trance examinations. However, these defects born of necessary adjustments of the school system to the realities of the nation. The ideal remains the principle laid down by the Education Act that all citizens are entitled to equal opportunity for education, regardless of their creed, sex, social and economic status, and in accordance with their abilities.

XIII EDUCATION

Education at Various Levels

Kindergarten

Statistics show that there were 227 kindergartens in Korea in 1957. With but very few exceptions, Korean kindergartens are private establishments and the great majority are in the big cities. The statistics further showed that there were 11,947 pupils (6,071 boys, 5,876 girls) and 599 teachers, mostly female. The breakdown by age showed that 17 percent of the children were four years old, 52 percent five, and 31 percent six.

An average 550,000 children enter elementary schools annually. Of these, only one out of 150 receive pre-school training at kindergartens.

Compulsory Education

Progress

Despite various difficulties, the compulsory education system in Korea is making substantial progress. The system was formally established in June 1950. After the war, a six-year program for developing compulsory education was formulated. As a result, the percentage of children receiving formal schooling jumped from 80 to 95 percent. A considerable number of new school buildings and classes were built, and the new education tax system, established in August 1958, laid the financial foundation for effective implementation of the system.

All citizens are entitled to free primary education under the Constitution of the Republic. It is the duty and right of the parents to see that their children receive education at facilities provided by the state. The city education districts are obliged by laws to make available and manage educational facilities to accommodate all children of school age within their jurisdiction.

Aims

The elementary schools in Korea regard the following as their objectives:
1) to build up ability to use and understand the mother tongue in everyday use,
2) to cultivate an understanding of the relations among the individual, the community and the state, and an understanding of past and present life of the local community and nation,
3) to train scientific observation of natural phenomena,
4) to develop sufficient mathematical ability for economic problems in everyday life,
5) to cultivate a proper concept of labor and good tastes in food, clothing and housing,
6) to cultivate basic understanding and skills in music, art and literature,
7) to teach importance of health and hygiene and to help develop sanitary habits.

Wartime Progress

The steady expansion of elementary school facilities has been one of the most notable of developments since the Liberation. In the three years between the Liberation in 1945 and the establishment of the Republic in 1948, the number of elementary schools increased by 21.4 percent from 2,800 to 3,400. By the time the compulsory education system was established in 1950, the number of schools increased further by 14.7 percent to 3,900. In the meantime, enrollment at the elementary school grew from 1,570,000 students in 1945 to 2,400,000 in 1948 and to 2,660,000 in 1950.

The Communist War reduced the number of students attending elementary schools by 22 percent and inflicted severe damages upon school facilities. Following the armistice signing in July 1953, efforts to expand compulsory education were renewed. The six-year program initiated in 1954 sought to bring to 96 percent of school age children the benefits of compulsory education. As life gradually returned to peacetime normalcy and the national economy recovered progressively, from war damages, new schools were built and damaged ones rebuilt.

War Damages

The size of the enrollment grew rapidly under the program, reaching 3,216,217 in 1956 (90.5 percent of school age children) and 3,790,352 in 1958 (94.2 percent). Only 74.8% of the school age population were attending schools in 1948, and 81.8 percent in 1950.

The number of elementary schools in the nation, meanwhile, increased from 3,400 in 1948 to 3,092 in 1950 and to 4,474 in 1958. The six-year expansion program accounted for an 11.24 percent increase since 1954.

Classroom shortage became very acute as the enrollment grew steadily although rebuilding of school facilities was in progress. It still remains a major educational problem in Korea. A total of 7,544 classrooms were burned down during the three-year war, and 15,473 others were partially damaged. In other words, 72.2 percent of the classrooms that had existed before the war were affected by the conflict. Much recovery was accomplished with material assistance of friendly foreign nations and contribution from private citizens who eargerly sought rapid expansion of educational facilities. In the six-year period from 1953 to 1958, a total of 16,559 classrooms were built. The annual breakdown: 2,397 classes in 1953, 457 in 1954, 7,365 in 1955, 843 in 1956, 2,891 in 1957, and 2,606 in 1958.

The war period was also marked by a serious shortage of teachers. The number of teachers in 1954 was only 1.5 percent more than in 1948. However, the number grew rapidly under the six-year program. There were 59,593 teachers in 1958, a 42 percent increase over the 1948 figure. This meant that an average of one teacher was available for all classes. The annual breakdown of teachers: 41,355 in 1948, 47,246 in 1950, 31,976 in 1951, 37,320 in 1953, 41,975 in 1954, 47,020 in 1955, 52,635 in 1956, 56,707 in 1957, and 59,593 in 1958.

Tasks Ahead

It is true that substantial progress was made in developing compulsory education in the past eight years, but there are a number of important improvements yet to be made before a reasonable standard of education is attained. To cite only a few: the classroom shortage must be overcome, dilapidated facilities must be repaired or rebuilt, more school funds must be raised, teaching aids and other equipment must be supplied in more abundance, size of the average class should be reduced, and free distribution of textbooks must be made possible.

These are no easy tasks and all will undoubtedly require many years of tireless efforts. The legislation of a Compulsory Education Financial Grant Law, which will provide better financial support to schools in rural communities, has been proposed and is being pushed. A new long-range program with improving school facilities is also under consideration. All these efforts form part of the nation's drive toward badly needed improvement in the quality of the compulsory education to match the quantitative increase.

Secondary Education

Secondary education in Korea consists of three-year middle schools followed by three-year high schools. A majority of the secondary education schools are liberal arts institutes, but there are some vocational or technical schools at the high school level.

The demand for secondary education increased tremendously and suddenly immediately following the end of the Second World War, and the trend has continued. The demand was so great that providing sufficient facilities and maintaining a reasonably high standard in the rapidly expanding field was a constant challenge and a major problem. Today the problem still remains to a large extent.

The number of middle schools has nearly tripled in the past 13 years. There were

248 middle schools with 94,027 students in 1945, 380 schools with 278,512 students in 1948, 524 schools with 225,518 students in 1951 803 schools with 419,787 students in 1954, and 1,031 schools with 428,264 students in 1958. The high school figures were: 65 schools with 39,986 students in 1951, 272 schools with 112,631 students in 1954, and 345 schools with 159,090 students in 1958.

In 1946, there were 183 six-year technical schools with a total of 1,738 classes for 99,642 students. Now there are 277 technical high schools with 2,851 classes for a total of 102,559 students. The percentage increase since 1952 was 57 percent in the number of schools, 80 percent in both the number of classes and students.

Partly because of war damages but also from lack of funds, many of these technical schools lack proper lab and research facilities. To remedy the situation, the Education Ministry has set up a five-year plan to spend 3.107,799,000 *hwan* for improvement of facilities. According to the plan, 130 of 250 classes of public technical high schools will be equipped and furnished with necessary improvements for lab and field work. Twenty-two private high school classes will be similarly equipped by 1962 under the plan.

A further increase in the number of high schools and middle schools is considered essential. In 1957, about 44 percent of 336,289 primary school graduates entered middle schools. It is estimated that 700 new middle schools will be needed within five years to accommodate the increasing number of applicants.

The present division of secondary education into liberal arts schools and technical schools is considered by many as unsatisfactory and undemocratic. There is a strong demand for a system of comprehensive high schools.

Teachers' Training

The teacher shortage was one of the major problems that confronted the U.S. Military Government after the Liberation of the couuntry in 1945. The number of primary schools was increasing rapidly, and it was difficult to train a large number of qualified teachers in a period of social and political disorder.

The Military Government expanded the facilities of nine existing teacher-training schools, established six new ones in 1946, and added another one in 1947. The Republic of Korea government placed all teacher-training high schools under central governmental control in 1950 in order to facilitate adequate programming of teachers' training on a national scale. The massive damages of the Communist War inflicted upon these schools were repaired satisfactorily by 1958 under various foreign aid programs and contributions of private Korean citizens.

One-year continuation courses to train graduates of liberal arts high schools as teachers were established at teacher-training schools after the Liberation. In 1956 the shortterm training course was deemed no longer necessary and was consequently abolished.

At present, there are 18 teacher-training high schools with a total of 11,826 students. These schools have 198 classes and a combined total of 395 teachers.

There was no teacher-training colleges in 1945. The first such to be established was the teachers' training college of the Seoul National University. In 1947 another college was erected in Taegu, in 1954 the two-year school at Kongju was promoted to a full teacher-training college, and in 1955 two two-year teacher-training colleges for the arts were established in Pusan and Kwangju. Besides these government establishments, the private Ehwa Women's University has a similar four-year college, and a two-year college for women and a co-educational institute were founded in Seoul 1954 and 1956 respectively.

The three government-operated four-year colleges now have 28 classes and 3,530 students in all. The number of students of all teachers' training colleges, government and private, now stands at 7,057.

In the period between 1947 and 1958, eight two-year teacher-training institutes were operated by nine colleges to train high school teachers in the arts and various technical fields. These institutes were closed down as soon as adequate numbers of qualified teachers became available out of graduates of formal teachers' college.

Colleges

The higher education institutes in Korea can be divided into three major categories: colleges, universities and junior colleges. Some of the universities and colleges have graduate schools. Colleges and universities have four-year courses, except for medical colleges which have six-year courses. Graduate students are required to attend the graduate school more than one year before applying for masters degrees and a minimum of an additional three years before applying for the doctorate. The junior colleges have two-year courses.

A university consists of at least three colleges, including one in the science technology field. The degrees conferred on graduates of colleges and graduate schools include bachelors degrees and masters degrees in literature, theology, fine arts, music, law, political science, economics, commerce, science, engineering, medicine, dentistry, pharmacy, agriculture, veterinary science, and maritime science. The doctorates include doctor's degrees in literature, philosophy, theology, economics, law, medicine, science, pharmacy, engineering, agriculture and veterinary science.

Policy decisions of national universities are made by university councils which consist of the respective presidents, college deans, professors and a number of prominent educators.

Colleges Increased

The number of colleges has increased more than five times in the past 14 years from 25 to 131. The number of professors and students also rose by 200 present and 800 percent respectively.

The National Seoul University was opened in 1946 during the military government period. About the same time, a number of private higher education institutes—such as Posong, Yonhui, Ehwa, Hehwa and Myongyun—became formal colleges. In 1947 a series of new colleges came into being in Seoul and other provinces. By 1949 there were four universities consisting of 22 colleges, 26 independent colleges, four junior colleges and eight college-level institutes. The total enrollment of these schools was 28,000 students.

During the war, many universities and colleges in Seoul and northern provinces took refuge in Pusan. In 1951 the government established the Wartime Combined University, absorbing students of various colleges which could not afford independent management.

In order to avoid concentration of colleges in the capital city of Seoul, the government in 1953 founded three new national universities in the provincial capitals of Taegu, Chonju and Kwangju. It was in 1953 that most of the colleges returned to Seoul from the wartime capital of Pusan. The records show that in 1952 there were eight universities, 27 colleges, and 10 college-level institutes with a total enrollment of 31,342 students. In 1954 there were 13 universities, 31 colleges, seven junior collges and 15 college-level institutes with a total enrollment of 62,663 students. The increase in the number of students between 1952 and 1954 reflects the beginning of a tremendous renewal of interest in college education which was interrupted by the war.

However, the hasty expansion of colleges in the post-war period brought about a deterioration in the standard of advanced education. As a result efforts had to be made after 1954 to provide adequate facilities for colleges and elevate scholastic standards. Some 1,000 graduate students were sent abroad for further study to become professors upon their return. Since 1956, a total of 140 foreign professors have been invited to lecture at Korean colleges. The number of graduate schools in Korea stood at 22 in 1958.

Aid Contribution

Generous assistance of the United Nations

Korean Reconstruction Agency (UNKRA) and United States aid programs have played major roles in the tasks of repairing and rebuilding a total 776 college classrooms and 2,346 college labs destroyed during the war. New buildings and facilities which various colleges added to their campuses between 1955 and 1957 to meet the standard required by the presidential decree on college establishment standards surpass greatly the scope and value of college assets that existed before the war.

Statistics on advanced education institutes in Korea at present are fairly impressive: 79 colleges and universities (aggregate total of colleges including these within universities comes to 154), some 80,000 students and 3,000 professors. The student figure equals 0.36 percent of the total national population (21,321,000) and 4.2 percent of school age population (estimated at 1,643,000). These percentages still compare unfavorably with 5.2 percent and 32.1 percent respectively of the United States and 0.67 percent and 8.83 percent respectively of Japan.

Despite continued efforts, improving general scholastic standards of colleges and closing gaps between the better colleges and lesser ones, in particular, remains as major problems to be solved. It is regretted that financial backing for these efforts is largely limited because of general weaknesses of the national economy.

Of 15 universities and 32 colleges in Korea, nine universities and 24 colleges are private foundations. Nearly 50,000 of the 80,000 Korean college students are attending these private schools, with the remainder attending state-operated schools.

Technical Institutes at College Level

Besides regular high schools training professionals in the fields of technology and sciences, there are more than 100 institutes giving professional instructions to graduates of middle schools. One of the two types of these institutes is the technical school, and the other the advanced technical school. The courses at these schools last one to three years. Advanced technical schools sometimes have a continuation course for specialized fields.

At present there are 61 technical schools (one public, 60 private) and 66 advanced technical schools (five state-operated, 13 operated by provincial governments, 48 private). The technical schools have altogether 302 classes and 6,752 students and the advanced technical schools have 270 classes and 6,665 students. The totals are 572 classes and 13,417 students.

The subjects of instruction at these schools are: agriculture, mechanical engineering, dressmaking, beauty culture, accounting, electric engineering, nursing, shorthand, driving, merchandizing, chemical engineering, home economics, horticulture, forestry, veterinary, radio, communications, textile engineering, architecture, engineering drawing, shipbuilding, navigation and knitting.

Civic schools

The purpose of the civic schools is to give elementary schooling to those youths who have passed the school age without attending primary schools. The civic schools are three-year schools teaching primary school lessons. They have adult classes to teach reading and writing of the Korean language to illiterate adults. All illiterate adults born before 1910 are required to attend language classes in civic schools for more than 200 hours a year.

The following figures show the trend in civic schools in recent years. In 1946, there were 8,287 schools, 777,868 students and 12,228 teachers; in 1950 13,072 schools, 37,043 classes, 1,039,631 students, 20,409 teachers; in 1953 3,215 schools, 4,378 classes, 188,801 students, 6,708 teachers; in 1955 2,533 schools, 4,929 classes, 224,213 students, 6,124 teachers; in 1957 2,439 schools, 4,895 classes, 184,721 students, 5,713 teachers.

Some 400 advanced civic schools are being operated in Korea to give middle school lessons to grown-ups and youths who finished elementary schools or civic schools. These schools offer one to three years of training to students. Statistics prepared in 1958 show that there were ten advanced civic schools operated by the state and 412 others run by private citizens or foundations. The former had 43 classes, 72 teachers and 1,525 students altogether, and the latter 1,147 classes, 1,987 teachers and 43, 468 students in all.

The advanced civic schools were created after the pattern of similar establishments in Denmark, and efforts are being made to emphasize training of civic virtues and community outlook. For this purpose, enrollment of adults at these schools is being encouraged.

Special Education

There are four state-operated schools and 12 private institutes for the education of handicapped youth. Although the government policy requires the Special City of Seoul and the provinces to establish at least one school for the handicapped, progress along this line has been hampered by preoccupation with recovery of other educational facilities from war damages. Two of the four state-operated are in Seoul. They are the national schools for the deaf-and-mute. The other two are a school for the deaf-and-blind in Pusan and another such department attached to the Cheju North Primary School on Cheju Island. The private institutes are all on the primary school level, except one in Taegu which provides for middle school level education.

The state schools are training 340 blind pupils, 531 deaf pupils and 36 special instructors. The private schools are training 418 blind pupils and 348 deaf for a total of 766 pupils.

Curriculum and Textbooks

Curriculum

The new curricula prepared after the nation's liberation in 1945 stressed Korean history, written Korean and civic morals in line with a policy to emphasize democracy and nationalism in education. The curricula and time allotment tables for various schools during the military government period reflected efforts to wipe Japanese ways and manners from the students' life and education. A drive to abolish use of Chinese characters and use only the Korean alphabet in writing was an example of nationalistic policies of this period.

The establishment of the republican government was followed by the promulgation of the Education Act in December 1949. On June 2, 1950, the Education Ministry adopted regulations for the Curricula Study Council. The first meeting of the Council was held in Pusan in March 1953.

The Council was chaired by the Vice-Minister of Education. The Deputy Chairman was the chief of the curricula and textbook bureau of the Ministry. Thirty-two non-school representatives of the Council included educators, lawyers, businessmen, politicians, journalists, writers, military personnel and scholars. The other 38 members of the Council represented various levels of scholars.

The Council created 13 sub-commitees staffed by a total of 683 scholars and teachers. The Council decided time allotment tables for primary schools, middle schools, high schools and teachers' training schools. Except for the primary school curriculum, the curicula included optional subjects. Extra-curricular activities of students were stressed, and time was alloted for them also. A minimum of one hour weekly was to be devoted to anti-Communist teachings and moral training at lower schools. Morals were included in the curricula of high schools and teachers'

Time allotment table for primary school curriculum

Subject	1st grade %	2nd	3rd	4th	5th	6th
Korean	25—30	25—20	27—20	20—23	20—18	20—17
Arithmetic	19—15	10—15	12—15	15—10	15—10	15—10
Social Life	10—15	10—15	15—12	15—12	15—12	15—12
Science	10— 8	10— 8	15—10	15—19	10—15	10—15
Health	18—12	15—12	15—10	10—12	10—12	10—12
Music	12—10	15—10	8—10	8— 5	8— 5	8— 5
Art	10— 8	10— 8	8—10	7—10	10— 8	10— 8
Field Work	—	—	—	7— 8	7—10	7—10
Extracurricular Work	5— 2	5— 2	5— 8	5— 8	5—10	50— 1
Total (100%) (Above breakdown figures show percentages)						
Total no. of hours a year	840	875	945	980	1,050	1,080
Weekly average hours	24	25	27	28	30	31

Time allotment table for middle school curriculum

Subject	1st grade (hours)	2nd grade	3rd grade
Compulsory*			
Korean	140	140	140
Mathematics	140	105	105
Social Life	175	175	140
Science	140	140	140
Health (Physical training)	70	70	70
Music	70	35	35
Art	70	35	35
Technical Training (Home management for girls)	175	175	175
Extracurricular activities	70— 105	70— 105	70— 105
Optional*			
Technical Training (Home management for girls)	35— 245	35— 245	35— 245
Foreign Language	105— 175	105— 175	105— 175
Others	0— 105	0— 210	0— 280
Totals	1,190—1,330	1,190—1,330	1,190—1,330
Weekly average	34— 38	34— 38	34— 38

*Optional does not mean that the students have a choice; the schools have the option to choose from them. Compulsory similarly means that all schools must teach the subjects.

Time allotment table for high school curriculum

Subject	1st grade (hours)	2nd grade	3rd grade
Compulsory:			
Korean	140	140	105
Social Sciences	105	105	35
Morals	35	25	35
Korean History	—	105	—
Mathematics	140	—	—
Sciences	140	—	—
Physical Training	35	35	35
Music & Art	—	140	—
Technical Training (Home management for girls)	105	105	105

XIII EDUCATION

Subject	1st grade (hours)	2nd grade	3rd grade
Optional:			
Korean	105	105	105
World History	—	—	105
Geography	—	105	—
Analytical Geometry	—	—	105—210
Geometry	—	—	70—140
Physics	—	140	—
Chemistry	—	140	—
Biology	—	140	—
Geology	—	140	—
Military Training	140	140	140
Philosophy or Pedagogy	—	—	210
Physical Training, Music & Art	—	0—210	—
Foreign Languages (English, German, French and/or Chinese)	0—175	0—175	0—175
Professional Training	0—420	0—700	0—700
Extracurricular Activities	70	70	70
Total	1,190—1,365	1,190—1,365	1,190—1,365
Weekly Total	34— 39	34— 39	34— 39

training schools as a regular subject. Because of emphasis on technical skills in education, middle schools were to spend at least 15 percent of the entire school hours for technical training, and high schools at least 10 percent.

College Curricula

College students are required to study certain subjects as basic liberal arts training. The required subjects are Korean, foreign languages, philosophy, cultural history, introduction to natural science, physical training and one optional subject. Students are allowed to take up study of subjects other than their own major fields but they are required to limit the study to one-third or less of the efforts for their major.

A credit system is used in colleges, except junior colleges. Credits are granted on the basis of one credit for study of one hour weekly during one semester. Forty credits for one semester are considered as a standard, and a maximum of 24 credits can be obtained in one semester.

Graduate students become eligible for submitting a master degree thesis when they have studied more than one year in school and obtained 24 credits. They can apply for doctorates after three years of study and obtaining 60 credits.

Text-Books

The first text-books distributed nationally with state approval after the Liberation were "Basic Korean," compiled by Hangul Hakhoe, and "National History Text-book," compiled by Chindan Hakhoe. The Education Advisory Council established by the Military Government later established curriculum regulations and initiated a text-book publication program. Text-books prepared and published during the Military Government period for use at various grades of primary schools and high schools throughout the nation covered these subjects: Korean, arithmetic, social studies, science, music, handicraft, farming for primary schools; and Korean, business and trades for high schools.

Following the establishment of the national government, a number of laws and regulations were put into effect to govern compilation and editing of text-books. Among them were presidential decrees on compilation of national text-books and Education Ministry-approved text-books (both dated

April 29, 1949) and an Education Ministry rule on the text-book compilation council (dated June 2, 1950).

At present there are 34 kinds of national text-books and 20 kinds of Ministry-approved text-books in circulation. Fourteen more kinds of text-books are being prepared currently. Meanwhile, 36 kinds of teachers manuals were also prepared for primary and middle school staffs, and additional 28 kinds of manuals were to be published shortly.

The principal of the school has the right to choose text-books, but he must give priority in his selection to national text-books published by the Ministry of Education. If national text-books are not available for a certain subject, he can select from Ministry-approved text-books. If neither is available, the principal may choose from auxiliary text-books sanctioned by the Ministry.

As a rule, the primary schools use only national text-books, while middle and high schools use Ministry-approved or other text-books. Since the Liberation, a deluge of text-books for secondary education schools appeared in the market, and the government, feeling the need to weed out the unsatisfactory, demanded revision of many text-books in 1949.

Following the outbreak of the war, the government banned text-books written by Communists. As the war hit the publishing activities of the nation severely, the supply of text-books was disrupted greatly. The Education Ministry recommended a loan for a joint stock company of text-book publishers so that the text-book crisis might be overcome quickly.

The private text-books authorized for use in schools now total 527 kinds in 1,066 volumes. Of these, 23 kinds are for primary schools, 237 for middle schools and 267 for high schools.

The most notable development in text-book publication in Korea was the completion of a modern text-book printing plant near Seoul in Sept. 1954. UNKRA and UNESCO made available $235,000 for importing modern printing equipment for the plant. It was a joint project of the U.N. agency and the Korean government. As a result of the new plant, 1955 and 1956 saw record publications of text-books for primary and secondary schools.

In 1957, the first largescale free distribution of text-books was made to 6,826 children of poverty-stricken islands off the mainland. The same group of children have received continued free distribution from the government every semester.

During the war, the Free Asian Foundation and UNKRA donated large quantities of printing paper for text-book publication but this gratis supply stopped soon after the armistice. Since then, American aid dollars have been purchased by text-book publishers to import foreign paper.

The following table shows annual publication of national text-books in recent years.

	Primary School (volumes)	Secondary School	Total
1951	13,191,727	363,465	13,555,192
1952	11,045,691	836,079	11,881,770
1953	15,353,595	898 590	16,252,185
1954	19,235,085	1,251,169	20,486,254
1955	23,204,310	1,038,000	24,242,310
1956	23,601,200	1,646,080	25,247,280
1957	19,599,500	1,671,515	21,271,015
1958	9,925,942	1,292,000	11,217,942
Total:	135,157,050	8,996,898	144,153,948

Financial Management and Facilities

Government Finance in Education

Primary School

In accordance with the constitutional provision that all children are entitled to free education at primary schools, the financial needs of primary schools are met by the national treasury. The national treasury is the source for salaries paid to teachers and for subsidies granted to educational districts whose revenues are insufficient to meet expenditures. The Compulsory Education Financial Grant Law provides for equitable distribution of revenues between urban and rural districts.

During the U.S. Military Government days, elementary education was financed from household surtax and special surtax as well as subsidies from the national treasury. Financing of compulsory education, begun in June 1950, became extremely difficult after the outbreak of the war. However, tax-collections from rural populaces for financing education became simpler in 1951 when the farmers were allowed to pay levies in kind.

An ambitious six-year program for development of compulsory education was initiated after the armistice, but financial difficulties in educational administration continued because of heavy fiscal needs for rebuilding and repairing school facilities. Consequently, the method of raising educational funds was changed in 1958. A new tax called education tax was introduced to replace the household and special surtaxes, which had been the revenue sources for education funds. The new education tax, which was divided into national and local education taxes, was collected by the education district or the city board of education instead of the provincial administrations. An estimated annual revenue of 10.4 billion hwan was expected from the new source, a 70 percent increase over the past. About the same time, the salaries of all government employees were doubled. The two developments prompted general efforts to reduce the extraordinary levies from the parents by the Parent-Teacher Associations (P. T. A.'s).

The following are financial figures for compulsory education in 1958 on a nationwide scale:

	(Hwan)
Ordinary Expenditure:	33,149,578,300
Subsidies from Treasury:	
Salaries for Teachers	18,718,337,100
General account	8,235,054,400
Local district revenue:	6,196,186,800
Classroom Building Expenditure:	5,818,760,100
Subsidies from Treasury:	1,500,000,000
Local district revenue:	4,318,760,100
Grand Total:	38,968,338,400

Secondary Schools

Financial needs of secondary schools (middle schools and high schools) are met largely by tuition fees and other levies from students. Only part of the needs is met by subsidies from the national treasury and revenues or contributions of provincial or city administrations and foundations. This situation means that a heavy financial burden is placed on the parents of the students and that the opportunity for education is not available to every competent student.

In the case of public middle and high schools, one half of the salaries for the teaching staff is borne by the national treasury and the other half by the Special City of Seoul or the provinces, which are the founders of the schools. However, all other expenses are met by levies from the students. Levies on students of private middle and high schools are being restrained by rules governing the school foundations, which are non-profit public welfare corporations.

The following are figures showing the nationwide financial contributions to secondary institutes in 1958:

	(Hwan)	(%)
Revenue:	5,179,088,944	100
Subsidy from treasury	534,595,348	10
Local district revenue	627,113,116	12
Tuition fees	1,763,152,500	34
Initiation fees	65,555,000	2
Foundations	181,640,480	4
PTA fees	1,214,782,500	23
Donations	792,250,000	15
Expenditure:	5,179,088,944	100
Salaries	1,620,014,224	31
Welfare expenses for teachers	882,540,500	17
School expenses	1,552,042,220	30
Activities expenses	332,242,000	6
Repair and maintenance	792,250,000	16

Colleges

The financing of national and other public universities and colleges are primarily the burden of the government treasury. Tuition and entrance fees are collected from students but they meet only five percent of overall expenditures. Private colleges depend more heavily on levies from students since average revenues of the foundations are very limited. The Education Act provides that the national treasury subsidize private colleges, but current state subsidies to private institutions are nominal.

Under these circumstances, colleges and universities in Korea have been depending on supporters' associations which impose heavy levies on students' parents. The revenues through these supporters' associations are used to augment salaries of professors and to expand and improve facilities. They form more than 50 percent of the school expenditures. The Education Ministry has recognized this fact and proclaimed regulations to govern management of the associations in 1953. Under the rules, the Ministry sets ceilings every year for levies imposed by the associations on students.

The membership of these associations is made up mainly of students' parents. Management of the associations is controlled by a general assembly, a board of governors, and an executive committee. The groups have played a major part in rebuilding and expanding school facilities in the difficult post-war period and have enabled the colleges to provide the faculties with a minimum livelihood.

The following are figures showing revenue breakdowns for various types of colleges and universities in 1957.

	Treasury or private foundations (Hwan)	Tuition & other fees	Supporters' Associations
National univ. & colleges	1,364,166,112	312,832,132	2,236,090,370
Public univ. & colleges	156,822,950	116,192,079	222,831,308
Private univ. & colleges	1,489,660,776	1,995,695,563	4,622,690,519
Total:	3,010,649,838	2,424,719,774	7,081,612,197

School Facilities

Cut-Downs

In accordance with the Education Act, the Education Ministry has established standards for colleges and universities for sites, buildings, equipments, athletic fields, etc. In view of the fact that many Koreans were blocked from the benefit of advanced education by the Japanese authorities during the colonial period, the government has been encouraging establishment of new colleges in addition to one university and 25 colleges that existed before the Liberation. As a result, the number of colleges (including those within universities) has risen to 131. In the course of this rapid expansion in ten years, inclusive of the war years, a number of colleges came into being without proper facilities or faculties. After the armistice, both the schools and government officials have set their minds on improvements in all fields. The Education Ministry is calling on colleges to meet the official standards within five to six years.

An official investigation committee of the Ministry ordered suspension of enrollment at two colleges in 1956. It also ordered a total reduction of 6,710 students in enrollments at 32 other colleges. In 1957, the committee called for another reduction of 1,600 students in enrollment at ten colleges. Expansion of other facilities in a recent one-year period follows:

Increases of 85,436 *pyong* in building space, 247,123 *pyong* in sites, 81,551 *pyong* in athletic fields, 451,353 volumes in libraries, and 1,082 new professors.

Foreign Aid Boosts

In order to help recover from war damages sustained by 50 percent of the nation's

↑ The Head Office of Seoul National University, Seoul

↓ College of Liberal Arts and Sciences, Seoul National University, Seoul

← Hongik College, Seoul

→ Sukmyong Womens' University, Seoul

← Hanyang University, Seoul

↑ Chungang University, Seoul

↑ Ewha Womens' University, Seoul

↓ Yonsei University, Seoul

↑ Susong Primary School, Seoul

→ Kyonggi High School, Seoul

↓ Kyonghui University, Seoul

→ Songgyungwan University, Seoul

← Tongguk University, Seoul

↓ Korea University, Seoul

← Kyongbuk National University, Taegu, Kyongsang Pukto

↑ Chonnam National University, Kwangju, Cholla Namdo

↑ Chonbuk National University, Chonju, Cholla Pukto

A Creche
 Forgetting the absence of mama, babies are happy enough with nurses.

Sketching
 The baby-painters are busy representing the beautiful scenery on their canvasses.

Going to School
 Girls of every school wear their own uniforms.

School Children's Excursion
  Parents, sisters and even grandmas often join in.

Family Outing
  School boys or girls enjoy their week-ends with parents on outdoor excursions away from home.

Excursion into a Mountain
  Teachers and students enjoy themselves playing games or singing songs.

At Class →
Every class consists of more than fifty students in average.

← **Sewing**
High school curriculum contains such practical exercises as sewing and homekeeping for girls, technical works for boys.

An Intermission
A ten-minute intermission between every fifty-minute class in primary, middle and high schools.

Boy Scouts
This international movement is quite widespread in Korea.

← National Library, Seoul

→ Library of National Assembly, Seoul

← A Library Crowded with Students

↑ Aerial Wires of K. B. S. In suburban Seoul

↑ The Korean Broadcasting System, Seoul (HLKA)
   The First Studio in Namsan, Seoul is a newly-built building. The old one in Chongdong is used as the Second Studio of the KBS.

↓ A Radio Drama is on the Air

↑ "Who is It?"
   One of the popular programs for school boys and girls.

↑ The Building of Chosun Ilbo Daily, Seoul
  Founded in 1920. One of the four leading newspapers in Korea.

  The Building of Tonga Ilbo Daily, Seoul
↓ Founded in 1920. One of the four leading newspapers in Korea.

←

The Building of Kyonghyang Sinmun Daily, Seoul

Founded in 1946. One of the four leading newspapers in Korea.

The Building of Hanguk Ilbo Daily, Seoul

Founded in 1954. One of the four leading newspapers in Korea

↓

↑ Tongnip Sinmun (Independence News)

↑ Hwangsong Sinmun (Imperial Capital News)

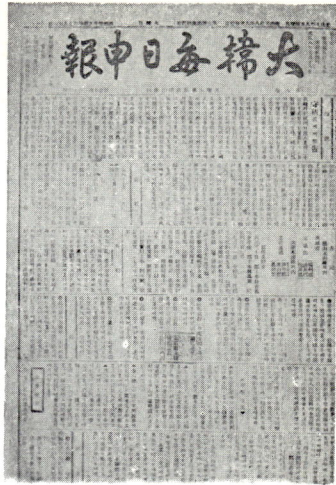
↑ Taehan Maeil Sinbo (Korean Daily News)

↑ Tonga Ilbo (East Asia Daily News)

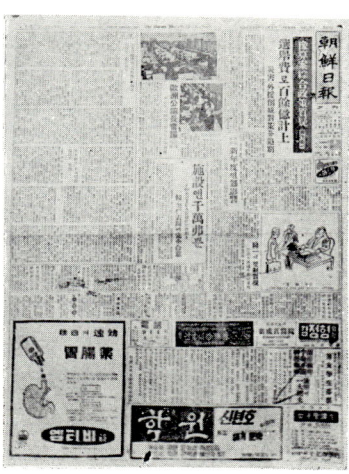
↑ Chosun Ilbo (Chosun Daily News)

↑ Kyonghyang Sinmun (Kyonghyang Daily News)

↑ Hanguk Ilbo (Korean Daily News)

↑ The Korea Times (English)

↑ The Korean Republic (English)

↑ Magazines Issued in Korea

↓ Editorial Room of a News-Paper Office

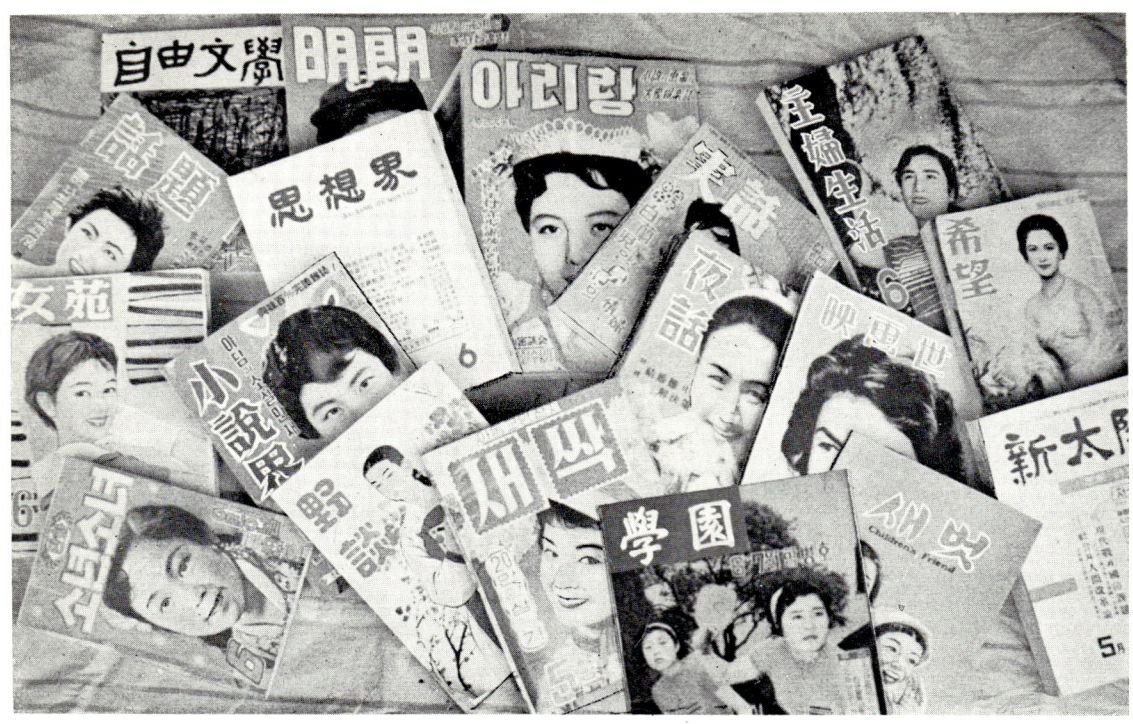

classrooms and 80 percent of technical facilities, vast sums in foreign aid have been appropriated for school facilities.

In the five-year period beginning 1952, $16,673,742 in aid grants and 6,334,855,000 hwan in counterpart funds generated from sales of aid goods were allocated in American economic aid projects in educational fields, and $10,821,744 and 423,104,000 hwan in counterpart funds were allocated for UNKRA projects. Meanwhile, AFAK funds amounting to $4,125,000 were also spent for educational facilities. AFAK, which stands for Armed Forces Assistance in Korea, is a special aid agency of the U. S. military forces stationed in Korea.

At the time of the founding of the Republic in 1948, there were 47,451 classrooms in the country, which together were capable of accommodating only 81 percent of 2,673,478 students.

During the war, 10,891 classrooms, or 23 percent of the total, were completely destroyed and 12,063 classrooms, or 25 percent, were partially destroyed. As a result, nearly half of the students were left without classrooms. Many had to study in outdoor classes.

During the latter part of the war, 1,000 new classrooms were built with materials provided by the Civil Assistance Command, an American organization, and 1,000 other classrooms were rebuilt with aid from another American relief aid program. Other expansion and recovery programs effected in the years since the armistice included: 3,769 classes newly built with UNKRA funds 1953-1956; 1,730 classes newly built or rebuilt with American aid 1956-1957; 2,326 classes built with AFAK funds and materials in 1954-1957; 230 classes built and 244 rebuilt with various other aid funds; 4,723 repaired by funds raised by schools themselves.

As a result, some 61 percent of classrooms completely destroyed during the war was restored and 53 percent of classrooms partially destroyed were rebuilt. Meanwhile, 9,883 classes for primary schools, 109 classes for teachers' training schools, and 126 university classrooms were newly built under government projects between 1955 and 1958. Various provincial and city governments accounted for recovery or construction of 7,686 other classes. At present, there is a combined total of 51,600 classrooms in the nation, an increase of 4,149 since 1948. Of this, 34,933 are for primary schools, 12,256 for middle and high schools, and 4,411 for universities. The officials estimate that 38,725 more classrooms are needed — 28,151 primary, 3,582 middle and high, and 6,992 university.

Foreign assistance also accounted for great strides in recovery of vocational or technical educational facilities. With $1,262,462 and 171,218,000 hwan in counterpart funds, six engineering high schools and one fishery high school were re-equipped and expanded under UNKRA projects. Since 1956, $2,169,801 of ICA funds have been allocated for importing equipment for 51 technical schools, and 501,638,000 hwan in counterpart fund have been spent to expand building facilities. These projects have greatly improved facilities for training vitally needed skilled and professional labor at strategic industrial locations. Latest efforts under foreign aid programs have been directed at reorientation programs for professors, vocational assistance, and observation tours of foreign institutions by school administrators. Thirteen professors have returned from foreign tours under UNKRA projects, and 23 under ICA projects.

A great emphasis was placed on the recovery of teacher-training high schools after the war. As a result, 80 percent of 443 classrooms destroyed or damaged during the war were rebuilt by 1957. Extensive programs for reorientation of professors for such schools were also conducted. A sum of $144,000 out of UNKRA and ICA funds has been spent to purchase educational equipment for 18 teachers' training high schools. An additional $1,397,483 has been allocated for exchange of professors with the United States and $850,000 for building material.

Emphasis in foreign assistance was placed on improvement and reconstruction of facilities of medical and other technological colleges. With $10,729,245 and 2,995,269,000 hwan in counterpart funds, the Korean Maritime College was newly built and equipped, the Medical School of the Kyungbuk University was rehabilitated, and the National Seoul University received technical assistance and underwent expansion of facilities for its colleges of medicine, engineering and agriculture. Books and laboratory equipment valued at $442,195 were also purchased under foreign aid programs and distributed to nine colleges.

UNKRA has also spent $88,173 for audio-visual education projects, $15,469 for literacy campaigns, $300,000 for training leaders of farm communities; ICA has contributed $149,000 for audio-visual education projects, $208,476 for recovery of the central meteorological observatory, $96,000 for training nurses, and $72,000 for training atomic scientists.

Private Foundations

Steady Growth

The 20 private primary schools operated by various foundations have been receiving government subsidy in the form of salaries for teachers since 1958. The government has been giving partial subsidies to these schools since 1955 in order to alleviate the financial burdens of parents. The schools are technically commissioned by the education authorities to provide for primary education.

There are 195 private foundations each operating one or more middle schools and 154 foundations managing both middle schools and high schools. The schools run by the private foundations total 1,631, or nearly one-third of the national total. Since the government approved establishment of foundations for erecting and managing secondary education facilities in 1948, the number of such foundations has steadily grown. The number of foundations established each year was: 83 in 1948, 17 in 1949, 21 in 1950, 26 in 1951, 51 in 1952, 43 in 1953, 48 in 1954, 38 in 1955, 15 in 1956, 6 in 1957 and one in 1958.

The Ministry approves the creation of such foundations on the basis of studying the local needs. Projected school facilities and equipment, possibility of solvent operation, and availability of competent teachers are all considered.

College Foundations

There are 38 foundations established for the purpose of managing college-level schools in Korea. The number of such foundations grew steadily since the Liberation until 1955 when the government set the minimum requirements of colleges and began to withhold approval of foundations failing to satisfy the requirements. Although it is difficult to assess the exact sums of endowments from such college foundations because of price fluctuations and frequent changes in assessments, the 1958 assessments showed that the largest endowment amounted to 3,732,496,000 hwan and the smallest one to 10,000,000 hwan. The aggregate of endowments of 37 college foundations (excluding one foundation which depends entirely on donations from religious organizations) was 31,407,697,913 hwan. One of the minimum requirements set by the government was that the college foundation should have profit-yielding assets valued at ten times its annual ordinary expenditure for school management. On this basis, the aggregate should reach 74,787,775,510 hwan to meet the requirement.

The gains profits for the 37 foundations totalled 651,409,539 hwan in 1955. The largest individual gain was 82,630,000 hwan; on the other hand, 11 foundations earned nothing. Figures for 1956 and 1957 respectively:

	'56	'57
Combined gains:	764,446,105	848,718,867
Largest individual gain:	110,325,000	109,837,460
No. of foundations drawing nil:	10	11

XIII EDUCATION

Teachers' Training and Group Activities of Teachers

Teachers' Training
Work-Shop Method

The status of teacher-training high schools and colleges has been generally outlined in previous chapters. The students receive government rents in limited amounts. In addition to subjects taught at ordinary high schools, the curricula of the teachers' training schools include principles of pedagogy, history of education, educational psychology, educational methods and apprentice teaching. It is planned to elevate the high schools to junior college level to further raise the standard of primary school teachers.

Teachers for middle schools and high schools are trained at two-year teachers' training colleges.

The Education Act of the Republic of Korea emphasizes the general theory that teachers need to continue studying their specialized fields of knowledge and wisdom to keep abreast with constant progresses in human civilization. The principal object in reorientation of teachers in the period immediately following the Liberation was to instill democratic ways of education in the place of totalitarian ways preached by the Japanese authorities. Numerous lecture meetings were held in Seoul and provincial cities to that end.

The main objective of teacher reorientation after the establishment of the independent government was to raise both the general caliber of teachers and the standard of curricula. The curricula were adjusted after the outbreak of the war, notably by the introduction of the work-shop method of reorientation by the first U.S. education mission to Korea. This type of education was familiarized especially after the government moved back to Seoul from Pusan in 1954 through a series of annual lectures. Large audiences were denied these lectures and participants carefully selected to ensure effective discussions and studies of the work-shop method. Since 1956, it has become a rule to select 50 teachers from schools all over the country to take part in intensive seminar work in conjunction with the central educational research center.

So far, the reorientation programs have been based on numbers of hours but a plan is being drawn up to introduce the credit system in view of the proposed establishment of education colleges. Plans call for establishment of educational research centers in provincial cities to adopt reorientation programs around the year. So far, programs were conducted during the summer and winter holidays.

The number of primary school teachers receiving reorientation totalled 10,993 in 1953, 12,749 in 1954, 15,475 in 1955, 12,357 in 1956, 5,303 in 1957, 4,544 in 1958 for a total 71,421 teachers in seven years. Number of middle school teachers: 4,797 in 1953, 3,302 in 1954, 6,357 in 1955, 7,612 in 1956, 935 in 1957, 942 in 1958; total-18,145. High school teachers: 2,484 in 1953, 2,793 in 1954, 3,684 in 1955, 1,429 in 1956, 832 in 1957, 1,182 in 1958; total - 12,404. The aggregate total of teachers who underwent reorientation between 1953 and 1958 was, therefore, 102,770.

U.S. Educators

Four groups of prominent U.S. educators have visited Korea in recent years to help develop democratic practices in Korean education. The first three groups were sent by the organization known as the Unitarian Service Committee, bringing Korean teachers in all fields and grades education into contact with up-to-date teaching methods and specialized knowledge in education. The first group, consisting of seven educators, arrived in August 1952 to help in reorientation programs for 700 teachers on such subjects as school administration and curricula. The second group, consisting of six educators, came in August 1953 to hold discussion meetings with a wider field of Korean teachers on a farther range of subjects, such as educational philosophy, teacher-training, curricular improvements, guidances for students' lives, etc. The third and largest group was financed by UNKRA. Composed of 13 educators headed by Dr. Harold Benjamin, this group came in 1954 and its members were stationed at teachers' training colleges in Seoul. Taegu and Kwangju to render first-hand assistance in management and lectures.

The fourth group was from the George Peabody College in Nashville 5, Tennessee, U.S.A. Headed by Dr. Willard E. Goslin, and working under an ICA aid project, the professors of this group came in 1956 and, in the course of an extended stay, dealt with various problems encountered by Korean educators from reorientation programs to text-books. They also conducted many seminars for Korean teachers.

Reorientations

Annual programs in teacher reorientation have been given since 1953 at all technical and vocational schools in Korea. These programs consist of summer and winter lecture series with particular emphasis on problems of acquiring technical skills in teaching. The number of teachers who have attended these lectures total 3,000, representing schools of agriculture, engineering, commerce, fishery, home economics and various other courses.

In 1958, a five-year program got underway in recognition of the importance of raising the quality of vocational school teachers. The plan calls for retraining 710 teachers every year except the fifth and last year when the total was 723. This meticulous breakdown was arranged in order to bring the entire staffs of all vocational schools under the program, the combined total of teachers being 3,563.

Yet another reorientation program embraces teachers in the various crafts to help secondary school students develop skills in learning a trade during their normal course of education. This program consists of summer lectures every year. More than 1,500 teachers have attended them since they got underway in 1956. Subjects dealt with have included metal works, carpentry, radio, beauty culture, photography, horticulture and husbandry.

Teacher Licenses

The Education Civil Servants Act, promulgated in April 1953, laid down the principles regarding qualifications of teachers with detailed regulations following in October 1953 and November 1954. Under this Act, licenses for principals, assistant principals and education supervisors are granted by the Minister of Education after due deliberation on their qualifications. Licenses for teachers are normally granted after examinations to test their qualifications, but there have been instances when they were granted only after deliberations. The examinations are conducted by a central committee formed for the express purpose.

In the seven-year period between 1951 and 1957, 2,573 out of 21,719 applicants passed examinations for primary school teacher licenses, 449 out of 6,590 applicants for middle school, and 765 out of 6,670 applicants for high school. Between 1951 and 1958, the Education Ministry issued licenses to 6,455 principals, 8,984 assistant principals, 3,593 first class regular teachers, 58,421 second class regular teachers, 37,758 associate teachers, 1,719 special teachers, 185 superintendents, 29 supervisors (for a total of 118,033 license issuances). Much of the authority to issue licenses was transferred from the Ministry to local educational authorities in 1955. Between 1956 and 1957, the local authorities issued licenses to 1,650 assistant principals of primary schools, 2,781 first class regular teachers, 13,113 second class regular teachers, and 7,145 associate teachers (for a total of 24,689 licenses).

Group Activities of Teachers

Federation

Group activities of Korean teachers are built around the Korean Federation of Education Associations. This body is made up of the ten education associations in the Republic of Korea, one for each of the nine provinces and the Special City of Seoul, to enable the educators of the region concerned to gather for good fellowship and undertake joint efforts to improve the regional education. The Federation embraces 60,000 members and sets forth as its aims the improvement of the economic and social statuses of Korean teachers as well as to contribute to progress in Korean education and culture.

The scope of the Federation's mission is all-embracing. It undertakes to engage in research work and studies pursuant to all problems in Korean education, carry out cooperative movements to better the economic lot of its member-teachers, uphold the independence of education from political or economic pressures, publish books and conduct exchange programs with foreign nations.

The policy decisions of the Federation are made at conventions attended by delegates from the 10 associations. The Board of Governors is the executive organ of the Federation and affiliated with the organization are such bodies as the welfare cooperative, the central educational research center, the committee for protection of educators, the committee for educators' code of morals, the committee for educational autonomy and the audio-visual education committee.

Inaugurated on November 23, 1947, the Federation has contributed much to the educationdom of Korea throughout the years. It began by publishing a monthly magazine, New Education, in July 1948. In June 1949, it recommended to the government a revision of the proposed Education Act so as to ensure higher salaries for teachers. December 1949 saw the first publication of another magazine, New Classroom, dealing with problems in teaching materials. In January 1950, the Federation sponsored a lecture series on educational administration. In July of the following year, the Federation dispatched teams of speakers to explain to provincial audiences the significance of local autonomy in education administration. The Federation celebrated the first Education Week (Oct. 6-12) in 1953. It inaugurated the welfare cooperative in February 1956. It adopted the Educators' Code of morals in September 1958.

Research Center

The central educational research center was established by the Federation on March 1, 1953, to provide Korean educators with opportunities to study the theory and practice of good education. It is made up of a 30-member executive committee and two departments, Research and Study, Guidance and Propagation.

The center has completed or is undertaking 37 research and survey projects. It has conducted 25 reorientation programs under commission from the Education Ministry and has published 43 reference books. The research and survey projects are as follows:

1) Computative skills in primary schools.
2) I. Q. tests in primary schools.
3) New directions in Korean education.
4) Functions of various schools under the present system.
5) Development of primary school-children's social consciousness.
6) Guidance in students' work.
7) Career preparedness of teacher-training students.
8) Competence tests in science for primary schools.
9) Preparation for national entrance examinations of primary school graduates (conducted in March 1958).
10) Critical analysis of middle school entrance examinations (conducted in March 1957).
11) Validity of entrance examinations conducted by middle schools in Seoul.
12) Status of education in villages near

Seoul.
13) Status of middle school teachers.
14) Methods in teaching mathematics.
15) I. Q. growth.
16) Social consciousness of children in general.
17) School surroundings.
18) Juvenile delinquency.
19) Criminal offenses in school premises.
20) Competence in science.
21) Development of child vocabularies.
22) Standards of high school texts in English and mathematics.
23) General criteria of the Korean people.
24) Group studies of primary school classes.
25) Quality tests for middle schools.
26) Reading.
27) Qualifications for professional careers.
28) High school problems.
29) Quality tests for teachers.
30) Education in Kyonggi-do Province.
31) Vocabularies of primary schoolchildren.
32) Middle school entrance examinations.
33) Analysis of entrance examinations (high schools and colleges).
34) Student guidances in careers and advanced studies.
35) Homework of primary schoolchildren.
36) Status of teachers.
37) School functions.

Welfare Cooperative

The welfare cooperative of teachers serves as a social security system based on mutual help among its voluntary members. It implements policies to ensure against unemployment and otherwise to promote the welfare of teachers, for instance, providing life and old age insurances not only for the teachers but also their dependents. With the support of members and the efforts of the Federation, the cooperative has managed to maintain its independence despite competitive pressures from commercial insurance companies.

Some 30,000 teachers have joined the cooperative in the three years since its founding. This is only 40 to 50 percent the total of number of teachers. The reasons for the limited participation are believed to be the imbalance between steep rises in prices and pay raises and the general instability of society. However, since the powerful Federation is managing the cooperative, it is expected to grow in scope steadily in the future.

The Board of Governors of the Federation has the duty to decide general policies of investment activities by the cooperative. The Board chairman appoints a committee to make decisions on actual investments, to set the ceiling on investments, to control profits and returns. The committee also serves as the body to deliberate requests for disbursements and determine amount of disbursement. The payments made by the cooperative do not necessarily exceed those of insurance companies but the cooperative is unique in seeking to be fair and considerate in making the payments. The cooperative grants twelve kinds of payments. Welfare accounts such as payments for on-duty injuries, sickness and delivery of children occupy about 50 percent of the current payments. Payments to bereaved families occupy 25 percent, age-limit retirement payments 14 percent, and ordinary retirement 10 percent. Pensions for the retired and the bereaved families, and increases in rates of payments are being planned. Other activities planned for the future include hospital expenses for ordinary injuries and sickness of members and their dependents, partial compensation for property losses, contribution to expenses for wedding and funeral ceremonies of dependents, establishment of hospitals for members, low-interest housing loans for members living in rented homes, low-interest loans to educational institutes, consumers' cooperative activities, and establishment of low-cost hotels for traveling members. The cooperative paid various grants to 1,549 persons in the total amount of 15,098,380 hwan in nearly two years since its founding.

Teachers' Code of Morals

The Teachers' Code of Morals was drafted by a five-man drafting committee appointed by a 50-man committee on the code which met in Seoul on June 20, 1958. The drafting committee studied similar codes of the United States, Britain, Soviet Russia, Japan and other nations before drafting the code for Korean teachers. The resulting draft was later approved by the full committee.

The preamble of the Code, adopted by the 12th convention of the Federation on September 19, 1958, stresses the vital influence of teachers' behaviors and characters upon students, the importance of education as a major contributor to growth of democracy, and the ideals of human dignity and equal opportunity. The Code called on all teachers to unite in their efforts to fulfil the mission of leadership with patriotic devotion.

The first of five chapters of the Code is entitled Students. It sets forth as the basic duty of teachers the development of a noble character and a spirit of independence in the student. It further calls on the teachers to respect the human dignity of students, to treat them with fairness irrespective of their ability and family backgrounds, to pay due attention to needs and desires, to refrain from divulging their personal defects and secrets, to help them select and prepare for careers, and to help them develop high ideals and cooperative spirit.

The second chapter entitled Home asks the teachers to try to establish close cooperative relations with students' parents, to keep the parents informed of educational policies of the school and of students' progress, to reflect the parents' opinions in school guidance, to refrain from taking advantage of the parents' economic and social positions, and to cooperate fully in the management of the PTA.

The third chapter entitled Society states the role of teachers as the nucleus in friendly and cooperative relations between the school and the community. It calls on the teachers to carry out faithfully their duty and responsibility as citizens, to contribute to development of civic virtues in the community, to inform themselves of social conditions of the community and help solve its problems, to reflect the needs of the community in planning school activities, and to refrain from politically partisan activities.

The fourth chapter entitled Profession urges the teachers to uphold the dignity of the profession by abiding by the laws and respecting peace and order, cultivating a wholesome atmosphere through friendly cooperation with their colleagues, participating actively in planning and carrying out plans decided and agreed upon, employing no dishonest means to seek promotion or transfer, seeking no material gains through abuse of professional position, and supporting group activities designed to promote advancement of teachers' welfare and social status.

The fifth chapter entitled Culture calls upon the teachers to try and command the respect of students and society by maintaining propriety in speech and behavior, to seek self-betterment through constant study and active participation in group studies, to use leisure hours wisely for wholesome recreation and developing good tastes, and to find happy and harmonious family life.

Extra-Curricular Activities

Student Movements before the Liberation

Student activities before the end of Japanese colonial domination in 1945 consisted mainly of anti-Japanese independence movements and activities. All extra-curricular activities of students were designed to promote the cause of independence. Students all over the country participated in the 1919 Samil Independence Movement, many defying death and persecution by Japanese authorities. An even more striking evidence of students' patriotism was the Kwangju Student Incident of 1929, in which Korean students revolted against discriminatory treatment by Japanese officials. Following the 1919 movement, the Japanese authorities had switched their colonial policy from oppression to assimilation efforts, but their appeasement policies failed to blunt the spirit of resistance among Korean students. On November 3, 1929, a group of Korean students in Kwangju clashed bodily with a group of Japanese students, and the incident touched off nationwide anti-Japanese movements, in which 54,000 students took part. The students represented 194 schools, including 54 primary schools.

Extra-Curricular Activities after the Liberation

Student Volunteers

Student activities during the military government period were marked by efforts to bring about ideological unity in the campuses and endeavors to develop moral and physical capabilities to contribute to betterment of the community and the nation. The Student Defense Corps, which now constitutes the backbone of all student activities, was organized with these objectives in mind. Since its foundation in 1949, the organization has successfully wiped out Communist elements from the schools.

More than 27,000 students entered the military services to take part in the fighting against Communist forces during the war. A special force, called Students' Volunteers, suffered 1,394 casualties during the conflict.

The official time allotment table for various schools, which went into effect in April 1954, has set aside a certain number of school hours for extra-curricular activities as if they were part of the curriculum. As a result, the primary schools and middle schools have included student activities in their curricula. These activities include meetings and groups organized through popular representation to discuss individual skills and abilities, professional careers and the development of artistic tastes.

Defense Corps

Pupils of primary schools are organized into Children's Societies with the class and school as units to carry out extra-curricular activities under the guidance of teachers. The objectives of these Societies are to develop community spirit and teach the pupils to appreciate the importance of labor and healthy life. The Children's Society of each school has one president and one vice-president, who are assisted by a secretary and a clerk. The society comprises children's societies at class levels and may also comprise various clubs organized for specific fields of activities.

In secondary schools and colleges, nearly all extra-curricular activities are directed by the Student Defense Corps. There may also be various clubs, religious organizations and chapters of the United Nations Student Association. At the college level, a number of academic research groups are also operating actively. The corps seeks to train students' ability in self-government within the limits of school regulations, to help develop creative abilities and individual tastes, to encourage labor and confer, if possible, a skill or a trade to all students, to encourage various sports and military training, and to promote anti-Communist thinking, national consciousness, and understanding of the concept of collective securiy.

The student head of the corps of a school is the chairman of the student committee, who is elected by delegates from the classes. The students are also grouped, in the manner of military forces, into platoons, companies and battalions. Commanders of these units serve under the chairman of the student committee. The chairman also coordinates the activities of the various department; for general affairs, discipline, arts and literature, welfare, handicraft and engineering, sports, etc. The dean or principal of the school heads the school corps, and the professors serve on the guidance committee of the corps. Student defense corps are organized in all public and private schools in Korea, and all teachers and students except those of primary schools are bound to become members. The school corps are consolidated into city and provincial corps, which in turn are consolidated into the national Student Defense Corps. The president of the country serves as the president of the naional corps, and the Education Minister is chairman. All high-echelon corps are advised by the guidance committees which include in its membership key government officials of the area. Independent from the corps are religious student bodies such as the Y.M.C.A., Y.W.C.A. and Catholic students organizations, which maintain national coordination and relations with similar or parent organizations abroad. These organizations as well as the Korean chapter of the U. N. Student Association, which was organized in 1954 independently from the corps, are governed by the students themselves.

Activities

A list of any program of extra-curricular activities drawn up by the Students' Defense Corps leaves nothing to be desired. They promote all the undeniably good things of life. At the same time, there is always an item or two lumped with the universal desirables to indicate that the students are up to the mark in the contemporary world. Thus, the programs list such categories as literature and arts, athletics, practical skills, recreation, religion, civic duties and virtues, enlightenment of the masses—and U. N. The emphases are on sports, military training, mental and bodily discipline and anti-Communism. The students are obliged to pay the dues that go into the maintenance of the Corps' activities.

The Central Corps has been vigorous in carrying out its various programs on a nationwide scale. It publishes a students' weekly and holds oratorical, athletic or literary contests. Inevitably, they have erected a monument to commemorate anti-Japanese student movements of the past and have sponsored a students' conference of Asian anti-Communist nations. A notable aspect is the enlightenment movement in which student teams travel to rural areas to stage literacy campaigns and offer lectures during the summer vacations. These movements are usually backed by newspaper firms, the Korean Association of UNESCO, and the Ministry of Education.

The records chalked up so far: total number of students, 21,123; total number of farmers "taught" the Korean alphabet, 74,884; total number of *hangul* lectures, 27,193; total numbers of speeches, 15,798; total number of roundtable discussions, 94.

Education of General Public

Literacy campaigns have shown much progress, but much remains to be done to help cultural advances in rural communities through effective use of mass communication media for general enlightenment. Another educational task is to spread knowledge and information concerning scientific methods of farming through vigorous audio-visual education measures.

Adult Education

Because the Japanese colonial rulers tried to capitalize on the ignorance of the ruled, some 78 percent of the adult population were unable to read the Korean alphabet at the time of the Liberation. A concerted drive of the government, civic leaders and schools to wipe out illiteracy was initiated promptly. The drive took the form of numerous *hangul* institutes for adults, which in 1947 alone numbered 30,538 with a total attendance of 1,625,340 persons. The function of these irregular institutes was turned over to adult classes of the civic schools shortly before the Communist War. After a period of inactive status during the conflict, the adult classes swung into action from 1954, holding 70 to 90 days of *hangul* lectures every year during leisure periods in farming communities. Following figures show the progressive improvement of literacy rates among grown-ups above twelve years of age: in 1945 7,980,902 out of 10,253,138 were illiterate (78%), in 1948 5,311,080 illiterate out of 13,087,405 (41%), in 1953 3,145,259 illiterate out of 12,269,739 (26%), in 1954 1,709,020 illiterate of 12,269,739 (41%), in 1955 1,524,041 illiterate out of 12,269,739 (12%), in 1956 1,419,205 illiterate out of 13,911,678 (10%), in 1957 1,145,283 illiterate out of 13,713,873 (8.3%), in 1958 562,982 illiterate out of 13,713,873 (4.1%).

There is a tendency among the aged to fail to use the knowledge of *hangul* and forget it eventually. To combat this, supplemental lectures are being conducted in addition to regular adult classes in some areas. More than 300 book centers of limited scope have been established to encourage reading among the newly initiated. The trends in adult classes of civic schools are shown by the following figures: in 1946 777,868 attended 8,287 schools, in 1950 1,039,631 attended 37,043 classes, in 1953 188,801 attended 4,378 classes, in 1955 244,231 attended 4,929 classes, in 1957 184,721 attended 4,859 classes.

During the period from the Liberation and until shortly after the establishment of the Republic, a large number of lectures on the Korean language and history and democratic principles were held for audiences who were educated during the Japanese rule. During the war many groups of lecturers visited camps housing refugees who fled from the Communist-ruled north to preach democratic ideals.

In 1954, adult schools were established in major cities and were opened to the general public who sought to improve their knowledge, skills or taste. A total of 12,100 adults (7,698 male and 4,402 female) received the benefit of these establishments which offered short term courses on nearly forty different subjects. 10,501 persons attended 237 different courses at 22 adult schools in 1956. 6,996 attended 201 different courses at 20 schools in 1957.

UNKRA established the Fundamental Education Center in Suwon in November 1955 to train farm leaders. The school was turned over to UNESCO in September 1957. The first 60-man class graduated from the two-year school in March 1958 and went to their home districts where they in turn train farm youths in courses lasting four to five months. This unique center aims to train its students to understand the problems of the Korean people, to have an interest in solving these problems, and to enable the students to make personal contacts with villagers in a manner that will stimulate the villagers themselves to realize and analyze their own problems and to find and carry out their own solutions to such problems.

Preservation and Utilization of Cultural Heritages

The nation abounds in valuable historical records and excellent works of art created over the centuries. The government selected 368 pieces of architecture, calligraphy, paintings, sculpture, historical documents, handicraft, and archeological materials and designated them as national treasures. It also designated 106 points of historical interest as historical sites. Nothing that the Japanese had taken away many works of historical and artistic significance and that the three-year shooting war had inflicted severe damages to many of these cultural heritages, the government in recent years spent a sum of more than 250,000,000 hwan for preservation and repair of national treasures and historical sites.

The government exhibited many of the national treasures at special displays held in Washington, New York and six other key American cities in late 1957 and early 1958. The exhibits drew a large number of visitors and were believed to have succeeded in creating or promoting proper understanding of Korea's cultural background.

Sciences and Arts

The National Academy of Sciences was established in July 1954 in accordance with the Culture Protection Law, which guarantees freedom of academic research and seeks to promote the status of scientists. The academy, comprising 80 members, is the representative organ for scholars and scientists and provides counsels at government request. It also promotes cultural exchanges with foreign nations.

Although government assistance to scholars and scientists has been limited, some fifty outstanding scholastic organizations have sprung up in recent years and are very active. The government proposed to grant 50,000,000 hwan to help these groups conduct academic researches.

The National Academy of Arts was also established in July 1954, comprising four departments for literature, fine arts, music, drama and allied arts. The government annually sponsors a national art exhibition, where 2,082 select works of creative art were shown between 1953 and 1958. In order to help the developing film industry, the government exempted domestic movies from taxation in March 1954. A total of 184 feature films were produced in Korea between 1952 and the summer of 1958. Fourteen of them have been exported to Hong Kong, Formosa, the United States, and Japan. Meanwhile, more than 800 American and European movies have been imported with government permission during the same period. There are 160 theaters and movie-houses, 48 dramatic and other entertainer groups, 44 movie production companies, 38 distributors of foreign movies, and 144 registered movie actors and actresses.

Libraries

The libraries in Korea underwent little improvement during the military government period because of the prevailing chaotic situation. Only notable happenings before the war were establishment of the school for librarians in the national library in Seoul in April 1946 and organization of the Korean Library Association in April 1947. The war came when the national library and college libraries were rearranging the set-up to meet Korean needs, training badly needed library staff, and increasing the number of books little by little. Recovery of the national library and other public libraries from severe war damages has made little progress so far because of lack of funds. The following figures on libraries show that only in the field of college libraries are there signs of improvement and expansion.

In 1950, there were 16 public libraries with 607,956 volumes of books, 17 college libraries with 1,072,058 volumes, and 14 libraries of special nature with 483,272 volumes. In 1955, 12 public libraries, 1,784 capacity, 476,844 volumes; 43 college libraries, 4,194 capacity, 1,297,034 volumes; 15 special libraries, 526 capacity, 187,374 volumes. In 1957, 17 public libraries, 3,126 capacity, 539,944 volumes; 65 college libraries, 11,384 capacity, 2,079,141 volumes, 42 special libraries, 1,730 capacity, 442,153 volumes.

Eighty students graduated from the national school for librarians before the war, but the school remains closed since the war. In April 1957, a library department was established in the Yonsei University, and later a one-year library school for college graduates was established in the library of the university. The former now has 50 students, the latter 17 students.

The Korean Library Association became a member of the International Federation of Library Associations in 1955 and a member of the Asian Federation of Library Associations in 1958. The Association has sent representatives to a number of librarian conferences held in Europe and the United States.

Museums

The first public museum in Korea was established in 1916 when collections of historical Korean relics by Japanese scholars were displayed in the Kyongbok Palace. Later museums were built in Kyongju (1924), Pyongyang (1933), Kaesong (1931), Puyo (1939) and the Seoul Imperial University (1940). After the Liberation, new museums came into being in Inchon, Taegu, Namsan, the Korea University, the Kyongbuk University, the Chonnam University, and the Ehwa University. The growing efforts to preserve and study historical relics were interrupted by the outbreak of the war in 1950. Thanks to efforts of interested persons and officials concerned, the collections in the museums largely escaped war damages. The government sent a number of staffers of the Nationl Museum to the United States in 1949 to study museum management.

The number of items of the major museum collections are as follows: 52,861 at the National Museum in Seoul, 5,000 at Kyongju, 1,228 at Puyo, 556 at Kongju, 5,494 at the Namsan Museum (which was recently annexed to the National Museum), 895 at Taegu, 534 at Inchon, 10,871 at the art museum of the Former Royal Household, and 2,500 at the Seoul National University Museum.

UNESCO Korean Committee

Korea's official relations with UNESCO began in 1949 when a Korean delegation attended the international UNESCO conference. On June 14, 1950, shortly before the outbreak of the war, Korea was granted membership in UNESCO by a vote of 27 to 1. But the ratification of the membership by the National Assembly was delayed until October 1952 because of the emergency condition created by the war. The presidential decree on organization of the Korean committee was made in July 1953 and the committee was finally organized on January 20, 1954, with a membership of 60.

Although long-range programs could not be carried out by the committee because of difficult post-war circumstances, the committee did its best to give publicity to UNESCO and its significance throughout the nation. The committee also sponsored a number of public lectures, held exhibitions of reproductions of Leonardo da Vinci's works and children's paintings, both presented by UNESCO headquarters, and organized student volunteers into rural enlightenment teams who travelled through provincial areas to instruct farming methods and lecture on hygiene and home economics.

The committee compiled and edited the UNESCO Korean Survey to introduce Korean culture to the world in line with the ten-year East-West cultural exchange program of UNESCO. The 740-page document penned by 170 experts was published in Korean in May 1957 and work began on its English version in 1958.

Other activities of the committee includes coordination and distribution of UNESCO aid projects which benefited Korea in the way of printing paper for text-books, gift coupons for school equipment, and books for colleges.

Problems in Using the National Language

The Education Ministry organized in 1953 a committee for study of Korean usages and commissioned it to solve problems in usage of the mother tongue. The committee, composed of 50 prominent educators, scholars, politicians and journalists, set up five sub-committees to study the problems concerning the Korean alphabet, Chinese characters, technical terms, transcription of foreign words, and elimination of Japanese words from Korean usage.

In response to criticisms against the spelling system which was devised by scholars before the Liberation and is now in current use, further studies were made to determine the possibility of simplifying the spelling system. But no new formula to supersede the current system emerged from the studies made by the committee.

The committee selected 1,300 Chinese characters on the basis of frequency in usage, and the government is encouraging use of Chinese characters within that limit. This is part of a progressive drive to abolish Chinese characters from Korean writing. However, a greater number of Chinese characters are appearing in newspapers and other popular publications as well as academic works.

Efforts to Koreanize technical terms after the Japanese are bringing about gradual results. The government is providing various academic and scientific research groups with special funds to devise new technical terms to replace those copied from the Japanese vocabulary.

After careful study of ways to transcribe foreign sounds in the Korean alphabet, the committee announced a formula of Koreanization in September 1958. The formula was a result of two years of extensive study and discussions among committeemen. The committee is also studying a standard formula for transcribing Korean proper names in the Roman alphabet.

Students Abroad

Number of Students

Procedures for obtaining official permission to study abroad were simplified as a result of new regulations put into effect on January 1957. A special government committee sets and studies basic policies governing students' study abroad. The government also set up a committee for placement of returning students in the cabinet secretariat.

In the deliberation of application for studying abroad, priority is given to students in natural science fields, particularly engineering and technical fields, whether the students are paying their own expenses or are being sponsored by government or foreign aid organizations, such as UNKRA, ICA and the American-Korean Foundation. Students and government officials travelling to the United States on observation or inspection tours are given special three-month English courses at the Foreign Language Institute to augment their linguistic ability prior to their departure.

Students who received government permission to study abroad between 1951 and September 1958 numbered 4,628 in total. 2,359 were students studying sciences and technology. The breakdown by years: 128 in 1951, 403 in 1952, 631 in 1953, 1,129 in 1954, 1,079 in 1955, 520 in 1956, 435 in 1957, 301 in 1958.

A great majority of the students went to the United States, while the others went to 18 other countries, mostly European. The breakdown by country of destination: 4,136 (United States), 135 (France), 105 (West Germany), 61 (Formosa), 48 (Canada), 27 (Italy), 21 (the Philippines), 23 (Belgium), 19 (Britain), etc.

132 of the students went abroad under government scholarships or official scholarships offered by foreign governments. In the case of students receiving Korean government scholarships, their school expenses, living allowances and travel expenses are covered entirely by the government.

Male students must complete at least one year of military service before proceeding to study abroad. Students desiring to further their study abroad can apply for permission if they have obtained B average or better scholastic records in college and received recommendations from the college. Applicants must pass special examinations conducted by the government four times a year. Qualifications tested in the examination include the students' determination to continue academic pursuit, patriotic and national pride, linguistic ability, financial resources, and physical fitness.

The students' stay abroad is limited to two years as a basic rule, but can be extended another two years upon recommendation of the Korean diplomatic missions abroad and approval by the special committee on students abroad. However, any further extension of their stay can be granted only when the students are engaged in research in atomic science, are deemed capable of obtaining doctorates, or are engaged in studies vitally important to the nation.

In view of the large number of Korean students studying in foreign countries, the government is planning to station education supervisors at strategic locations to assist the students and encourage them to return home as soon as their projected study is completed. The Education Ministry figures as of September 1958 show only 641 students (507 male, 134 female) returned home between 1952 and 1958. The breakdown by years: 5 in 1952, 41 in 1953, 70 in 1954, 92 in 1955, 137 in 1956, 197 in 1957, 99 in 1958 (by September).

The government annually sets aside $300,000 of foreign exchange for travel expenses of students and $2,520,000 for school expenses and living expenses so that the parents may transmit a maximum of $140 a month to the student at the official exchange rate.

Government Assists

The government is helping education of Korean residents in Japan and Formosa. Assistance for the education of Koreans in Japan has been hindered greatly by the strained diplomatic relations with that country, where there are an estimated 600,000 Korean residents. The Education Ministry conducted a survey of education of Korean residents in Japan in February 1956. The government spent 1,500,000 hwan in 1957 and 4,000,000 hwan in 1958 to improve facilities of residents' schools and subsidize teachers' salaries, to distribute Korean text-books, to invite teachers of the schools for reorientation, and to offer scholarships to students. Realizing the need to assist the resident schools in Japan more actively and on a larger scale, the Ministry is planning these other measures: to establish a model school for Korean residents in Japan, to stimulate general improvement of educational standards, to dispatch specially selected teachers of the Korean language, Korean history, music and athletic training, and to station education supervisors in Japan to provide more effective guidance.

Meanwhile, the government has been supplying text-books and sending financial subsidies to a primary school for Korean residents in Formosa. The subsidies have been used to help pay teachers' salaries and improve school facilities of the school, which is operated by the Korean embassy in Taipei. The Education Ministry is also helping select teachers to be sent to the school in Formosa.

XIV MASS COMMUNICATIONS, PUBLICATION AND PRINTING

Newspapers and the Press

Brief History

The newspaper, as we understand the term today, was first printed in Korea in the year, 1578. It was a paper published by civilians after the pattern of a periodical published by the royal court. Intended for circulation among intellectuals of the time, the paper was published by what may be called a group of professional newspapermen for the newspaper meant bread and butter. Upon finding out what had been going on behind his back, the king, Sunjo, had everybody concerned with the paper arrested and condemned to exile. The officials of the court who were responsible were also forced to resign. This is the first record of press persecution in Korea.

The incident, however, does not mean that all kings of the Yi dynasty suppressed civil opinion for a channel was kept open for royal subjects to submit opinions to the king in a "Memorial to the Throne".

In October 1883, another paper, *Hansong Sunbo*, was published by a group of revolutionaries who were advocating "Enlightenment" by speedy acceptance of Western civilization. Such men as Kim Okkyun, Pak Yongho, So Kwangbom and Hong Yongsik, known as pioneers in Westernization, got together to print the paper. They had the support of a court faction that favored the "Enlightenment" movement.

In December 1894, however, the paper, which had been published once every ten days, was attacked by a mob instigated by the Conservative faction of the court.

Undaunted, So Chaepil,* one of the leaders of the "Enlightenment", came out with the "Independence News".

A four-page tabloid issued three times weekly, "Independence News" was different from its predecessors in that it was written entirely in the Korean alphabet, whereas the others had employed both Chinese characters and Korean *hangul*. The paper stood wholeheartedly behind the "Enlightenment", and editorial columns of the paper urged the need for Korea to adopt a constitutional form of government based on democracy. So influential was the paper that it encouraged not only the modernization of Korea but also the publication of many other newspapers.

Korea had hardly obtained a foothold on a modern world of enlightenment, however, before the light was extinguished in a modern world of imperialism. As a result of her victories in war, first over China and then

* Who subsequently fled to the U.S., there to settle down and take out American citizenship under the Anglicized name of Philip Jaisohn.

over Russia, Japan arrogated to herself the right to control Korea's destiny and one of the first things she did was to suppress public opinion, freedom of assembly and freedom of the press. The Japanese military commander-in-chief, stationed in the capital city of Seoul, subjected Korean newspapers to military censorship.

All papers, reflecting anti-Japanese views, were banned. Among the papers thus proscribed was the *Hwangsong Sinmun*, which had become one of the most influential voices in the country.

In order to deal with this situation, a group of patriotic-minded newspapermen invited an Englishman to help bring a paper out. The Englishman, Ernest T. Bethell, was named publisher of the paper as a brake against whatever Japanese persecutions were inevitably in store. It must be remembered that Japan was an ally of Britain at the time and not willing to cross a valuable partner. Thus it was that the *Taehan Maeil Sinbo* (Korea Daily News) was born on August 10, 1905 under a foreign masthead.

The editorial staff of this newspaper, owned jointly by Anglo-Korean stock, included the names of many patriots who later had to seek political refuge abroad. Relatively free of the Japanese military censor, the *Taehan* stood at the forefront of all anti-Japanese movements, thus setting the pace for other newspapers. So keen, vigorous and influential was the daily in voicing Korean protest against Japanese domination that the Japanese Governor-General, Ito Hirobumi, was once heard to remark that "one word of the *Tachan Maeil Sinbo* has more influence than all the words of this Ito."

With the Annexation of 1910, what relative freedom the press could get by was all put to an end. All seven newspapers published by Koreans, including the *Taehan Maeil Sinbo*, were permanently suspended.

It was not until the memorable uprising of March 1, 1919, the Samil Independence Movement, that the Korean press again found its voice. Spurred by a whole people's protest against Japanese domination, many underground newspapers were printed.

The bid, however, was shortlived. The Samil Movement was crushed under the heels of Japan's military might and all Koreans who had had anything to do with the underground presses were arrested and executed by the gendarmes. About the only thing the Samil Movement succeeded in doing was to voice to a deaf world the aspirations of the Korean people for independence.

The Korean will, however, shook Tokyo somewhat and the semi-military governmental structure in Korea was replaced by a "civil administration" that permitted press publication. Thus, in 1920, the *Tonga Ilbo*, *Chosun Ilbo* and *Sidae Ilbo*, three dailies which were to play a most important role in fostering education, culture, sports, arts and other social movements. Under the watchful eyes of the police censor, the originally meager papers were later developed into 12-page dailies with both morning and evening editions.

The relentless militarism of Japan, however, brought forceful measures to bear upon Korean culture and education, designed no less than to erase language and letters. As a result, the three papers were closed on August 10, 1940, leaving Korea without a newspaper to express Korean opinion. Even before this, the press could not function smoothly under the censor's nose. Both the *Tonga Ilbo* and *Chosun Ilbo* were ordered to suspend publication four times, and *Sidae Ilbo* twice. Editors were executed and the printing presses confiscated. Instances of bans and seizures of an objectionable issue or two were innumerable.

Throughout the subsequent Japanese era, Korean papers had to operate in the teeth of gendarme restrictions in order to keep alive reminders of a nation's birthrights.

The Liberation of Korea from Japan on August 15, 1945, shattered the shackles imposed upon the Korean press and nation at one stroke. Numerous papers of various political shades and colors sprouted with the sudden liberty. By this time, the northern half of the country had fallen into the orbit of Soviet Communism and south Korea was flooded with Communist propaganda and literature, spearheaded by the newspaper, *Chosun Inminbo* (Korean People's Press) which first came out in September 1945.

The *Tonga Ilbo*, resurrected after a long state of suspension as the foremost Nationalistic paper in November of the same year, forthwith assailed the leftist daily. The *Chosun Ilbo*, at the same time with the *Tonga*, also resumed publication in December of the year, wavering for some time between left and right and finally veering definitively toward the latter. Numerous dailies, all two-to-four-page tabloids followed, swelling the ranks of the two ideological camps. The bitter press rivalry reached its climax with the announcement of the proposed Big Power trusteeship for Korea supported by the left, violently opposed by the right. The issue compelled each newspaper to take a clear stand, willing or not. The result was confusion with copyrights changing hands and editorial staffs fired by one side to be rehired by the other. This was by no means all. Mobs, hired by the rival political powers, descended upon newspaper buildings to threaten editorial offices and wreck printing presses.

To put an end to all this confusion and also to shield itself from the attacks of the Communist press, the United States Occupation authorities issued an ordinance in May 1946, requesting all periodicals to register with the Military Government. Altogether 242 dailies, weeklies, monthlies and news agencies complied. For all that, the confusion remained.

It was ended only with the establishment in August 1948 of the government of the Republic of Korea which forbid the left. Politics settled down on a basis of normal functions and the press followed suit. The leading dailies, such as the *Tonga Ilbo, Chosun Ilbo, Seoul Sinmun* and *Kyonghyang Sinmun*, gradually began to increase their circulations throughout the country. Local papers also started to make progress.

The sudden outbreak of war sent all the dailies down south with the government. Over the ensuing months, newspapers had to struggle against overwhelming odds to issue wartime editions from one corner of the land. Only with the armistice was the press able to return to Seoul and resume normal operations.

Today, there are a total 581 dailies and other periodicals with a combined circulation (for the dailies) of 1.2 million copies; i. e. one copy for every ten persons.

The dailies total 41, of which two are in English and one in Chinese, the last intended primarily for the considerable Chinese community.

Newspapers in Seoul

Newspapers published in Seoul are known as "centrals" and find a nationwide clientele as against the "locals" that are published in provincial cities for limited provincial readership. The "centrals" have made remarkable progress since the end of the war.

The major newspapers of Korea were able to benefit from U. S. economic assistance to Korea only after the armistice and the return of the capital to Seoul in 1953. With resumption of normal operations, the wartime tabloid edition was rapidly replaced with the usual two-page format which was later increased to four pages. Six-page papers, with morning and evening editions next followed, and this again was expanded to eight pages. This rapid pace of progress must be attributed to the U. S. cultural policy which, from he first, expressed positive interest in the Korean press as a natural ground to breed familiarity with democratic concepts. U. S. government help came in two ways: one, many individual pressmen were invited to the U. S. for retraining; and, two, newsprint aid came under the economic assistance program of the International Cooperation Administration (ICA).

The progress has not been without its dark side. Some publishers, for instance, have been too prone to use cheap low quality newsprint when they were certainly in a position to pay more concern to their substantial numbers of readers, while others were able to derive "fat" incomes from advertisement spaces without paying employes sufficient salaries to maintain a living. Such "economy" was motivated by a competitive zeal for money alone, each rival paper intent on nothing but increasing the number of pages "at any cost." Contents, under the circumstances, were completely ignored.

The competition for more pages, pure and simple, began in 1957 when both the *Chosun Ilbo* and *Kyonghyang Sinmun* came out with two-page morning editions and four-page evening editions. Before that, all the major dailies were carrying two-paged morning and evening editions. The *Seoul Sinmun* overshot the new mark with four pages for both morning and evening early in 1958. Left far behind, the two other "majors," *Tonga Ilbo* and *Hanguk Ilbo*, caught up in late 1958 with four pages in the morning and two in the evening.

The bug refused to bite further and, by the end of the year, the leading papers, *Tonga*, *Chosun*, *Kyonghyang* and *Hanguk*, settled down to four-paged morning and two-paged evening editions. Only with the current year has attention been turned to contents.

Of all the Seoul dailies, the up-and-coming *Hanguk Ilbo* has been remarkably successful in competing with other papers of long standing. Assuming a 100-percent commercial stand in contrast to most of the other papers that are to a greater or lesser degree politically influenced, the *Hanguk* has built up a circulation of 140,000 in a surprisingly short period of time. The paper's chief weapon against the durable "traditionals" has been to challenge the prestige of "authoritative editors" on rival staffs by recruiting many young talents.

The two dailies of long established tradition are the *Tonga Ilbo* and *Chosun Ilbo*. The *Tonga* is the organ of the opposition Democratic Party while the *Chosun* is considered politically neutral. Actively supporting the government are the *Seoul Sinmun* (also a "traditional") and the *Yonhap Sinmun*. The *Kyonghyang Sinmun,* which has a Catholic foundation, is also a leading opposition. It has recently been ordered suspended. Other dailies with smaller circulations are *Segye Ilbo*, *Pyonghwa Sinmun*, *Kukto Sinmun* and *Chayu Sinmun*, all of which suffer financial straits.

Make-ups are more or less identical. The political news, foreign and domestic, go on the front page with the editorials while the economic news are to be found on page two with news commentaries. The third page is devoted to "human interest" stories and the fourth is the "culture" page.

Advertisement spaces are provided for in the lower parts of all pages. They fall in three categories: "regulars," "interims" and "specials." The "regulars" are run for over a long continuous period, usually lasting about a month, covering space for movies, medical drugs, books, foods, cosmetics, etc.

The "interims" take care of public announcements and the "specials" are for political campaigns or platforms.

The advertising rates are charged on the basis of production cost per issue, the balance between the production cost and estimated proceeds from subscription fees furnishing the basis on which is added a profit margin. The rates thus derived differ depending on the size of circulation. The circulation, however, is kept confidential so that potential advertisers are often baffled. Furthermore, the underdeveloped conditions of Korea's overall industry do not encourage advertising agencies, what active few there are being the result of mergers.

Most papers actively sponsor "cultural" programs (the press has always played a significant part in raising the nation's cultural standards).

Hardly a month passes by without some fare, concert, opera, dance or a sporting event that is not sponsored by some newspaper firm.

The papers also sponsor such non-profit contests as short stories, essays and the marathon. Highlight of this last, by far the most popular of track events, was the international marathon race, sponsored by the *Hanguk Ilbo* on September 28, 1959 in commemoration of the Seoul restoration nine years ago.

The distribution network of the papers are spread throughout the country with numerous "promotion centers" in Seoul and branch offices in the provincial cities and towns. As these branches are mostly under managements independent of the "head office" in Seoul, contracts are made with the main office concerning minimum paid subscriptions to be sold, sales commission rates, and local news topics from the province to the capital. In some instances, the "main office" in Seoul exercises direct control over such local branches through its own capital investment. The branch office sometimes sets up sub-branches.

The papers are delivered by newsboys and in the large cities, also hawked in the streets.

Provincial Newspapers

There are 26 newspapers and 29 weeklies published in the provinces. Since late 1958, they have been operating under heavy financial disadvantages as a result of the pressure from Seoul.

The successful encroachment of the leading Seoul dailies upon the provinces with comparatively bulky editions, attractive make-ups, and authoritative articles have left local papers with decreasing numbers of subscribers and sharp declines in advertising clients. Practically all provincial papers are operating in the red. Nevertheless, some papers are trying to overcome the unequal situation by playing up news of local interest.

The major "locals" are the *Kukche Sinbo* and *Pusan Ilbo*, both published in Pusan. Other publications in Kyongsang Namdo are *Minju Sinbo*, *Chayu Minbo*, *Kyongnam Ilbo*, and *Masan Ilbo* The provincial capital of Kyongsang Pukto, Taegu, has two competitive dailies, the "Taegu Daily News" which enjoys Catholic backing, and the *Taegu Ilbo* which is controlled by a businessman group. These two overshadow the remaining two Taegu publications: *Yongnam Ilbo* and *Sisa Ilbo*.

Besides dailies, the provincial cities and towns are also served by two or three weeklies.

Student Papers

Publication of student papers in Korea had to wait until February 1952 when the Seoul National University came out with edition No. 1 of a weekly, University Press, at the wartime capital of Pusan. Before the Liberation of '45, the college, (then Keijo Imperial University) had a weekly called the *Jodai Gakubo*, but this was Japanese-controlled and intended for the Japanese student. Publications were discouraged even with the Liberation because of the political turmoil which swept through the nation, dividing college students into two hostile camps. Under such circumstances, the school authorities withheld permission for publication of student papers for fear of possible exploitation of the young by unscrupulous politicians.

The University Press has not missed a single issue since the first issue. Its survival and improvement has encouraged other colleges to publish weeklies of their own.

The Korea and Yonsei Universities got started in 1953 following the road back to Seoul. Others followed suit. At present, there are student papers registered with the Office of Public Information, 10 weeklies, 21 monthlies, 3 papers issued every ten days, and 1 bi-monthly. All these papers are members of the National University Pressmen's Association. Unlike their professional counterparts, the college papers have not been very active in sponsoring cultural programs as might have been expected.

Press Service

Until the Liberation, wireless press services in Korea were furnished solely by the Japanese wartime monopoly, the Domei News Service. With the Liberation, Korean staff members promptly took over the facilities. There were the usual leftist attempts to dominate only to be frustrated by the U. S.

Military Government which, instead, asserted its Occupational rights to take over. USAMGIK used the facilities to form an organization called the *Kukche Tongsin*. The aim was to familiarize the Korean people with USAMGIK activities and a prominent Korean journalist, Kim Tongsong, was named editor.

Meanwhile, leading Korean entrepreneurs were busy forming the first Korean news-agencies and making bids for worldwide services. The *Chosun Tongsin* signed a contract with United Press and became the first Korean organization to transmit the services of a major world news agency to the Korean public.

The original client of the Associated Press was the *Yonhap Tongsin* but *Yonhap* was unable to benefit from the contract because it lacked sufficient facilities. On the other hand, *Kukche* had excellent facilities but it could not find any American agency willing to sign a contract with a USAMGIK organ. Either for this reason or otherwise, Military Government withdrew from the management and turned over the facilities to Mr. Kim Tongsong. *Yonhap* and *Kukche* then merged into the *Haptong Tongsin* which contracted for A.P. service.

Several minor agencies were formed, offering specialized services, mostly of trade and business interest, but none functioned effectively. For the reading public, there were only two agencies worth mentioning, the *Haptong* and the *Chosun*, the latter soon renamed the *Hanguk Tongsin*. Major or minor, all news agencies were crippled by the war which took its usual heavy toll of men and tools in the press as in all other fields.

A conviction was born during the darkest days of the war that all news agencies should be merged into one powerful body. An attempt was actually made in Pusan during the first phase of the war (the north Korean offensive) with the formation of the *Taehan Tongsin* but without success.

The *Taehan* returned to restored Seoul to meet with objections from the other news agencies which had remained in the occupied capital and which saw little reason to be subjected to its control. Whatever the merits or demerits of the argument, all agencies were hurriedly uprooted once more by the second phase of the war (the Chinese Communist intervention).

This time, men, tools and the news agencies all reached Pusan for a long three-year exile. Far from mergers, five new firms were formed. On the other hand, of the "Big two," only the A. P. client, *Haptong*, remained stabilized. The U. P. client, which had changed hands many times, finally to melt into the *Taehan*, was beset by grave financial difficulties. Two of its most important executives had been war casualties. It had to merge itself into a new management one final time before it could qualify as a major firm. The name of the new service was the *Tongyang Tongsin* and it promptly signed a new contract with the U. P. organization.

Back in post-armistice Seoul, *Haptong* and *Tongyang* competed vigorously with new expansion schemes under new capital investments. The competition took the form of new equipments, installation of teletypes, telephoto receiving sets, etc. At the same time, the number of news agencies multiplied and capital was available for the formation of yet other major firms signing contracts with established worldwide networks. Presently, there are no less than 14 agencies, of which four in the majors, the *Haptong*, *Tongyang*, *Tonghwa Tongsin* and *Segye Tongsin*. All four have contracts with American, British, French and other foreign news agencies.

The Korean news agency is effective only when it has a contract with a reputed foreign service. It is a one-way traffic for the Korean news agency buys the foreign service and transmits this to the Korean public but does not, in turn, sell. Only on rare and limited occasions does the Korean agency send a correspondent abroad. At home, it not only transmits the foreign news to the newspapers which, in turn, offer them to the public but also maintains its own staff of reporters for domestic news gathering which also goes to the papers which, naturally, have their own staffs doing the same thing. The combined circulation of readers on which the news agency indirectly depends totals no more than one million.

The intensity of the competition among the news agencies may be pinpointed by the *reductio ad absurdum* of the rivalry a few years ago between *Haptong* and *Tonghwa*. *Haptong* found itself confronted with a newcomer aspiring to the majors by approaching A.P. for a contract. Considering itself the sole A.P. client, *Haptong* protested when A.P. signed a separate contract with *Tonghwa* but to no avail. From the A.P. point of view, there was no reason why it should not sign two contracts in Korea as anywhere else. From the *Haptong* point of view, a rival agency was deliberately trying to undermine its foundation. The upshot was that A.P. drew two sources of income in Korea for the same service while the limited and indirect Korean reading public derived the same foreign news from two different channels.

Broadcasting Service

Introduction

The precise date when radio came to Korea is known. It was on February 16, 1927 when the Seoul Broadcasting Station went on the air on call signal JODK and wave lengths of 550 and 1500KC's with a power output of just 1 KW. Management was composed of a board of directors who were all Japanese under the strict control of the Government-General and the audience was very much limited. Nevertheless, the "magic box" was a startling novelty in the country and enthusiasm was great.

The early programs were rudimentary. Consisting mostly of news, market price quotations and weather forecasts, given in both Japanese and Korean, it was virtually a one-man operation and the announcer was by no means professional. This meager fare was increased in 1929 when Japanese programs were relayed to Korea to take up most of the broadcasting time. Facilities were also expanded in 1933 with the addition of AM and shortwave transmitter sets, each with a 10-KW power output. A separate channel in the Korean language was granted, at the same time, but subject to strict censorship, an effective jamming system providing against any program considered hostile to Japanese policy. Nonetheless, it was a rare opportunity for the Korean to listen to a broadcast in his own native tongue and the broadcaster exploited the channel to the maximum possible extent to foster interest in native culture, language and the arts.

The following year, 1934, saw Radio Seoul beaming to both Japan and Manchuria and going on the air with a symphony orchestra of its own. It also saw yet tighter restrictions from the censor with the formation of a Broadcast Deliberations Committee, made up of members who were mostly gendarmes responsible for "thought control," army officers and Government-General officials.

In September of the same year, Pusan also went on the air on call signal JBAK and 1030 KC's with a power output of 0.25 KW. The network now began to expand in earnest: Pyongyang in 1936, Chongjin in 1937, Iri and Hamhung in 1938, and Taegu and Kangnung in 1941. Mokpo, Masan, Taejon, Wonsan, Kwangju, Chunchon, Haeju and Sinuiju were added during the Pacific War years. The addition of Chongju in June of 1945 completed the Korean Broadcasting Networks with its center at Seoul which by now was operating with a 50-KW transmitter. The radio was important to the Japanese war efforts and the networks had to be rushed in line with the all-out nature of the hostilities upon which the Japanese Empire had embarked.

The circumstances under which the Korean radio staffs had to work leaves little to the imagination. Nevertheless, they did manage to get nationalist ideas and sentiments across. That they did so in the teeth of the remorseless Japanese overlord is very much to their credit. Not until the very day of Liberation on August 15, 1945 was there the slightest let-up to their paradoxical trials.

With that eventful day, the broadcasting networks throughout the country were at once taken over by the Korean staffs and placed under the control of the U. S. armed forces of Occupation. The censor's hand vanished and overall changes effected.

One example suffices to give an inkling of what the change meant. The Korean had hitherto been familiar only with the Japanese pronunciations of the political, economic, technological and other vocabularies of a modern scientific world. In no time, the radio made them familiar with the Korean renditions.

The establishment of the Republic of Korea government in August of 1948 saw the networks reorganized as a governmental organ under the Office of Public Information. Even before independence, in September 1947, Korea became a member of the *International Telecommunication Union* which allotted the initials, HL, as the international code for the country. With the war, Radio Seoul fled south like the rest of the country and had to double up with Radio Pusan. Programs were placed on a wartime footing and mobile broadcasting units were organized to furnish news and entertainment to the members of the Korean armed forces as well as the numerous refugees in their dislocated camps. The war, of course, had inflicted severe damages on radio facilities. It also opened up new fields; for example, Cheju, which was the unwitting recipient of a station in view of its strategic wartime importance.

With the armistice, the Korean radio networks, called the Central Broadcasting Station but known in English as the Korean Broadcasting System (KBS), embarked on a steady program of rehabilitation over the ensuing years. The first foreign language program was offered in English in September 1953, followed soon by Chinese (with the primary object of conducting psychological warfare against the armed Chinese presence in the north), Japanese in 1955 for Japan and, particularly, for the large Korean community there, and French in 1958 for Southeast Asia. In 1956, television was first introduced and the following year saw the first round-the-clock broadcasting. The 10-KW shortwave and AM transmitter sets installed in 1953 were but a prelude to the installation of two 100-KW sets in subsequent years, enabling the "Voice of Free Korea" to reach Hawaii and the North American continent. Awards were instituted to encourage both program quality and technological advances, a Radio-TV Center was inaugurated and, in December of 1957, KBS boasted a brand-new building atop Namsan Hill overlooking the capital.

Private stations were also formed in the post-armistice period.

There are three such at present, the Christian Broadcasting System in Seoul (1954), the Inchon station of the Evengelical Alliance Mission (1956) and the Pusan Cultural Broadcasting System (1956). A fourth will be on the air within the year.

Round-Up

The Korean air is dominated by the government station—KBS. Under the direct control of the Office of Public Information, the network is on the air 24 hours a day with its key station in Seoul and 12 provincial stations as well as three mobile units. The private stations are on the air for only limited hours. Television, also limited, has been cut to half-hour programs by courtesy of the radio-TV networks of the United States Armed Forces as a result of a fire which destroyed KBS's sole TV station early last year.

The total number of radio receiving sets in the country is estimated at about 350,000 for the most part in the large towns and cities. In other words, there is one radio to every 58 persons. To ensure the widest possible audience, the government has been setting up "amplifier villages," where programs may be heard by an entire community through a radio set mounted on a powerful amplifying system.

KBS (Korean Broadcasting System)HLKA. Broadcasts over two channels. Channel 1 - 170 KC's, 100 KW's - is directed at the popular audience at home with news, musical, sports and other entertainment features. Channel 2 - 970 KC's, 100 KW's - concentrates on programs of higher intellectual levels. It is also the channel for overseas broadcasting, notably the "Voice of Free Korea". The foreign language programs, consuming 54 hours a week totally, are directed towards North America, Hawaii, Southeast Asia, Japan and the Chinese Communist forces in the north, the last presented by the Chinese (Nationalist) Embassy in Seoul. On the other hand, KBS is also the medium for the Korean language broadcasts of the "Voice of America" and the "Voice of the United Nations Command."

The 12 stations in the provinces serve the key Seoul station by transmitting most of the programs over Channel 1 and some of Channel 2. From three to six hours a day, however, these stations offer programs prepared locally for local interest. The 12 stations are as follows: HLKB, Pusan; HLKG, Taegu; HLKD, Masan, HLKF, Chonju; HLKH, Kwangju; HLKN, Mokpo; HLKI, Taejon, HLKQ, Chongju, HLKM, Chunchon, HLKR, Kangnung, HLKL, Namwon, and HLKS, Chongju. The three mobile stations are located at Tongnae, Yosu and Pohang.

Channel 1 is broadcast from a modern building with up-to-date equipment and studios through a giant 100-KW transmitter station in the suburbs of Seoul. Channel 2 is in downtown Seoul but its 100-KW transmitter is in the City of Suwon, south of Seoul, whence the overseas broadcasts emanate.

As a governmental network, KBS depends upon the government's budgetary allocations.

CBS (Christian Broadcasting System) - HLKY, Seoul. Dial, 840 KC's, power, 10 KW's; on air 62 hours a week; served by Station HLKT in Taegu with power output of 250 KW's; programs, mostly musical, religious.

DBC (television) - HLKZ - TV, Seoul. Commercial, 100 KW's; completely destroyed by fire in February 1959—pending rehabilitation, offers hour-long programs over AFKN-TV (U.S. Armed Forces Korea Network). Note: there are only about 10,000 TV sets and the general public depends upon public screens.

TEAM, the Evangelical Alliance Mission- HLKX, Inchon. Power output, 20 KW's; on the air 100 hours a week in four languages, Korean, Chinese, English, Russian; programs, mostly musical, religious.

MBC, the Munhwa (Cultural) Broadcasting Company- HLKU, Pusan. Power output 1 KW; 50 hours a week; strictly commercial, backed by 30 sponsors.

Seoul Cultural Broadcasting Station - HLKC, Seoul. Approved by government and expected to function sometime in 1960. 905 KC's, 5KW's; commercial.

Allied Stations. The United States Armed Forces provide G.I.'s serving in Korea with their own radio-TV service through the medium of the U.S. Armed Forces Korea Network. AFKN provides news, "Stateside" programs and disc jockey shows on a round-the-clock basis through 11 stations. TV hours are limited.

The Voice of the United Nations Command (VUNC) is transmitted to the suburbs of Seoul from its station in Okinawa. Mostly propaganda, programs are offered in Korean, Chinese and English daily from 5:30 p.m.—11:30 a.m.

Printing and Publication in Ancient Korea

Before Koryo

There is no historical evidence to determine just when Korea began to write. Certainly when she did so, it was in Chinese.

The assumption is that the Chinese character was first used by the Korean during the Lolang period of Chinese colonization (108 B.C.). Inscriptions appearing on tombstones and other remains from this age may be said to bear this out. With equal force of logic, it may be concluded that it was the Chinese colonists who wrote these inscriptions and that the Korean had no hand in the matter.

Whatever the case, the Chinese ideographical form of writing was prevalent among the Korean elite during the period of the Three Kingdoms. Since its foundation as a state, Koguryo was compiling her own history, and, by the reign of the 26th king, Yongyang, (A.D. 590 - 618) had accumulated 100 volumes of the *Yugi* (Reminiscences). The scholar, Yi Munjin, is noted for editing the *Yugi* in a five-volume *Sinjip* (New Edition of the Reminiscences).

The *Paekche Sogi* (Written Records of Paekche) was compiled by the scholar, Kohung, in A.D. 375 as the first historical product of the kingdom which transmitted Chinese culture, including the Chinese form of writing, to Japan. Other recorded histories of the kingdom, such as the *Paekchegi, Paekche Pongi,* and *Paekche Sinchan,* were also transmitted to Japan in latter years after the fall of the kingdom.

Silla, situated in the southern part of the peninsula, was the last of the three kingdoms to learn the Chinese character. She received it from Koguryo in A.D. 392 and her first history was compiled by the scholar, Kochilbu, in A. D. 545 during the reign of the 24th king, Chinhung.

Besides history, it is presumed that the three kingdoms were also busy compiling other kinds of books. These were mostly hand-copied editions with the use of brush, but some undoubtedly were printed in woodblock for Korea was by now turning out excellent quality wood, paper and ink, all proven ideal for bookprinting. The epitaph of the 19th king of Koguryo, Kwanggedo, erected in 414, and the inscription on the "hunting memorial" of Silla's King Chinhung in 565 furnish us with a reasonable ground to assume that woodcut block printing had developed considerably in the early stages of the "Three Kingdoms."

The number of Confucian scholars and Buddhist priests increased after the Silla Unity. Many of them were invited to Tang China to compile books, notably the famous scholar-poet, Choe Chiwon (857-?) whose collection of works called the *Kewonpilg yongjip* is still preserved in China, and whose poems have long been appreciated in Japan. Outstanding Buddhist priests were Wonhyo, who annotated the *Hwaumgyong* (Ava Tansaka Sutra) in 43 parts, 70 volumes, Wonchuk, who edited and translated Buddhist scriptures into Chinese in 23 parts, 103 volume, and Hecho, who compiled a travelogue on India, the *Wangochonchukkukchon,* (circa 727) as a significant contribution to the interchange of culture between East and West. Many of these works, several preserved to this day, are presumed to have been printed with woodcut blocks.

Woodcut was certainly used by Silla since the reign of 31st King Sinmun (681-692) for Buddhist and Confucianist scriptures. By then, Buddhism was established as the state religion and scholastic pursuits given every encouragement. The most noteworthy work was rendered by the scholar, Sol Chong (692 -?), who devised a comprehensive reading system for the difficult Confucian scriptures and published a woodcut print edition of the "Nine Classics" by this unique method.

The Koryo Dynasty

Buddhism was to exert yet more influence upon publications during the Koryo era and Confucian studies continued to be encouraged. Especially significant was the invention of metal type printing and the mammoth publication of the Tripitaka Koreana.

The publication of the Tripitaka Koreana was started in 1011 by royal command of the eighth king, Hyonjong, from more than 5,000 volumes of Buddhist scriptures imported from China. It took more than 60 years to engrave all the woodcut blocks necessary for completing a project comprising more than 6,000 volumes. Subsequently, the prince-priest, Uichon, undertook publication of the Supplementary Tripitaka with Buddhist scriptures collected from the Sung, Liao and Japanese kingdoms. It took him seven years to complete the work which consisted of 1,010 parts and 4,740 volumes. Some portions of the original editions of these truly gigantic efforts have been preserved.

The Mongol invasion reduced the enormous piles of woodcut blocks to ashes and the entire Tripitaka project had to be undertaken once more. This was done immediately in 1236 and, after sixteen years of continuous efforts, the work was completed in 1,539 parts and 6,805 volumes.

Most of the woodcut blocks have been preserved until today and are presently stored at Haein-sa Temple in southern Korea, providing us with one of the most important sources for study of Buddhist history.

In the field of Confucian and other non-Buddhist learning, numerous books on the Confucian classics, history, geography, jurisprudence, and literature were published with the active encouragement and support of successive Koryo monarchs. There was a court organ then devoted exclusively to book publication with branch offices in many parts of the country. Metal printing types were invented and used in 1232 for the first time in the world — more than 200 years before Gutenberg.

The earliest book which is presently known to have been printed with metal types is the *Sangjongyemun* (Letters on Authentic Etiquette in Detail). Published sometime between 1232 and 1241, 28 copies of the 50-volume book were reprinted with "metal types". The metal cannot be ascertained precisely, but copper or an alloy of iron and copper is presumed to have been used in view of the high state of metallurgical development in Korea as evidenced by the various examples of exquisite metal workmanship throughout the ancient ages.

The Yi Dynasty

The type, originated by Koryo, was developed fully and used extensively during the early period of the Yi dynasty. Accepting Neo-Confucianism as the guiding principle of the state, the Yi dynasty suppressed Buddhism and destroyed many Buddhist temples and images, which hitherto had served as excellent material for metal-type casting.

The court printing house, "Office of Literatures", published a Direct Interpretation of the *Taemyongyol* (Criminal Code of the Ming Dynasty) in 1395 from woodcut blocks, and printing facilities were expanded in 1403 with the establishment of a "paper manufacturing office" and metal type foundry. Copper prints numbering tens of millions were cast by the court organ as the first project of its kind.

The Sung Classics, printed from woodcut blocks were used as base for the metal types. Printing in *kemi*, as the type came to be known, turned out to be a clumsy affair, for sizes were not uniform and wax had to be poured between the types before they could be properly set. The fourth king, Sejong, therefore, ordered Minister of Industry Yi Chang to cast more uniform types based on the letters of the *Chaji Tonggam Kangmok*, woodcut printing of the Yuan dynasty. Grooves were engraved on the type-case to keep the types in place while printing. The improvement enabled printings of 20 to 40 pages a day. King Sejong also had more than 200,000 copper types cast to supplement the preceeding types. Called the *kapin* type, they were to be used extensively over a long period of time. Sejong is further credited with having two other types cast in subsequent years: lead in 1436 and copper in 1450.

Printing types were increased still further in 1452 when the fifth king, Munjong, ordered casting of the *imsin* copper type and, in 1455, his successor, Tanjong, directed casting of the *ulhae* type, which came in three different sizes.

The seventh king, Sejo, who was a devout Buddhist, cast the *ulyu* type with copper in 1465 for the purpose of publishing the Wongak Sutra, but the types turned out to be irregular. The ninth king, Songjong, redressed matters twenty years later by casting more than 300,000 *kapjin* types. All of the metal types cast up to that time were made of copper with one exception. The 11th king, Chungjong, used bronze for his *pyongja* type.

These various type castings met the continuing and increasing demands for the publication of various Confucian literary works and history books. Especially since King Sejong, biographical records of each king were written down and three copies of each printed edition stored in three "history libraries". So many books had become available and still more in demand by the reign of 14th King Chungjong that he went so far as to attempt establishing a book publishing house in Seoul in 1519. Politics interfered and the attempt failed. Nevertheless, he managed to cast *kimyo* bronze types. The 14th king, Sonjo, cast the *kapin*, an iron-and-copper type in 1573. Book publication had become so popular by that time that many "intelligentsias" became professional writers by publishing the *Chobo*, a periodical sold on subscription basis to court officials and the *yangban* nobility. A royal ban, however, put an end to this "newspaper" enterprise in less than a year.

Thus, the printing technique of Korea reached its zenith in the 1500's but not for long. The foreign aggressions, of the Japanese in 1592 and the Ming Empire in 1627, toppled the nation from its supremacy in this field. Prominent printers were, in fact, taken to China and Japan to promote printing standards.

With much of her types lost or destroyed by the invaders, Korea had to revert to "primitive" woodcut blocks to reprint the various books which had survived the wars. The first efforts at recovery was made by the 18th king, Hyonjong, who cast more than 52,000 iron and copper types in 1668 to print the biographical record of his predecessor, Hyojong. Since that time, his types were used for biographical records of every king, thus becoming known as the Record Type.

The "renaissance" period during the reigns of the 21st and 22nd monarchs, Yongjo and Chongjo, produced a great number of printing types, resulting in a "boom" revival. The number of copper types cast over the ensuing years follows: 150,000 in 1772, 150,000 in 1777, 80,000 in 1782, 320,000 (of various sizes) in 1792, and 300,000 in 1795. The total 870,000 thus recast after the devastations of two wars were, however, mostly destroyed again in a large fire in 1857, leaving only 170,000 types available. To replenish the stock, 170,000 more were cast in 1858. These have been preserved and are presently stored at the National Museum in Seoul.

In addition to the active court undertakings, many private citizens produced metal prints and ceramic types to publish "lineage records" and literary works. The best known was the publication of the *Changgokpildam* (a collection of works by the Prime Minister) printed with small types cast by Kim Sokchu. The privately cast types were so excellent that the court purchased them in 1695 for official publications.

This prosperous "industry" began to decline during the late Yi period because of political instability and troubles from within and without the country. The modern printing techniques of the West was introduced by way of Japan, which was then exercising a definite influence on Korea. With influx of Western civilization from 1876 on, publications underwent a drastic change along Western lines. Thus, in 1883, the government started publication of an official bulletin, *Hansong Sunbo*, first issued once every ten days, but later becoming a weekly. Published by the government office, the *Pakmunguk*, the Hansong Weekly was continued until 1888. It was a Roman Catholic mission to Korea which made a great contribution to the spreading of Western printing techniques during the early days of Westernization. The Roman Catholic mission, suffering several religious persecutions, had previously published several books with woodcut blocks in 1862 and 1864, but the missionary work had to be suspended after the great persecution of 1886. A Father Ridel fled to Manchuria where, in cooperation with a Korean Catholic, he compiled a Latin-Korean Dictionary, Korean-French Dictionary and a Korean Grammar.

These early Catholic efforts proved to be the stepping-stone for Korea's subsequent adoption of Western printing techniques on a large scale.

Book Publication

Suppressions and "Boom"

It was about eighty years ago that modern, lead-point types were first utilized extensively in Korea. The country was just beginning to be Westernized and numerous periodicals as well as books were published in the next twenty old years until the Annexation.

Japan lost no time after that grave event to suppress Korean publications which were nationalistic in sentiment and, therefore, strongly anti-Japanese. The result was that formerly active publications were stifled by the Japanese censor who banned practically all books written by Koreans, except scientific publications and fictions of apparently non-political nature.

The strict censorship was somewhat relaxed after 1919 when the Japanese policy of semi-military suppression was replaced with what was then called "civil administration." As a result, not only many periodicals but also many books started to come off the printing houses. Political suppression, however, remained in full force so that most of the books published were literary works. Even fictions had to suffer innumerable expurgations and frequent sales bans.

The "China Incident" brought the mailed fist back and all publications were placed under the control of a wartime organ that monopolized the distribution of books and rationing of printing paper.

With the Liberation, the Korean people's desire for learning through the medium of their own written language exploded with such fury that innumerable publication houses sprang up. Many new firms rapidly became prominent and new life infused upon the Pakmun Publishing Company, Hangsong Book Company and others of long standing.

The "golden year" of book publication in Korea was reached in 1946 when more than 160 publishing houses of various sizes and political backgrounds flooded the market with hastily printed books and pamphlets. Whatever was printed sold so well that the total number of books reached nearly 1,000 and about five million books were estimated to have been sold in that year alone.

The "boom" was carried over 1947, when the number of publishing houses increased to 581. The number of books totalled 950 with the following breakdown — politics 102; religion 23; economics 24; literature 124; social affairs 25; philosophy 22; history 48; linguistics 9; biographies 25; reference books 151; textbooks 150; and miscellaneous, 197.

The number of publishing houses kept increasing in 1948, but sales now declined sharply. The "boom" was over. Instead, attractive binding, formats and better-grade paper replaced the haphazard products of yesteryear when coarse paper was used for the most part and bound in any way that suited the whims as well as pockets of the publishers.

Number of companies in 1948, 792; number of books printed, 1,200; breakdown of books -- politics, 48; religion, 29; economics, 19; literature including fiction, 170; social affairs, 28; philosophy, 30; history, 32; biographies, 23; reference books, 187; textbooks

131; and miscellaneous, 103.

In 1949, the publishing firms totalled 847, and in 1950 the war reduced them to practically zero. In all, the publishers of south Korea had offered 5,000 titles to the reading public in the five-year period between Liberation and war. Many firms sprang up only to wither and drop but several built themselves on a solid foundation and developed into the future.

The war created a "wasteland" in the entire field of book publications. Only tiny trickles of reference works and textbooks were forthcoming in the early stage of the hostilities. With the favorable turn of the wartides, however, the publication field started to come to life once more and, by the end of 1951, a total 359 companies were registered with the government. A total 786 books were published that year of which 454 were textbooks, reference works, and comics, 111, fictions and song-books.

As the war situation became somewhat stabilized in 1952, the number of publishing houses increased to 387, and a total 1,333 titles were printed, an increase of 550 over the preceeding year. Publishing houses became very busy trying to replenish the stocks lost during the war.

Unlike newspapers, magazines and other periodicals, book publications were unable to make a comeback with the armistice and the end of the Pusan exile. The armistice year of 1953 actually saw 89 doors closed, leaving 461 which together issued 1,108 books during the year. Breakdown of the books; reference books, 258; fictions, 250; law books 56; linguistics 56; dictionaries, 48; books for children, 80; and miscellaneous, 360.

Post-armistice Squeeze

Nineteen fifty-four was the beginning of the gloomy years. Squeezed between high production costs and sharp decline in sales, 155 companies closed shops, leaving 584, about half the number of publishing houses active in the post-Liberation "boom" years. The trend continued in 1955. Bookstores and publishers, putting much faith in the usual "peak" season that fall, dumped their books in the market when their expectations failed to pay off. They were encountering an unprecedented buyer's resistance. Altogether 133 publishing houses folded up, leaving 500 to carry on. The emergence of many popular magazines during the year was interpreted by book publishers as a warning signal that the people's reading habit had changed from books to magazines.

The lowest ebb was reached in 1956. Business transactions among publishers, wholesalers and retail dealers were almost at a standstill. Bookstores sold books at discount rates, wholesalers closed shop one after another, and publishing companies dumped their wares 50 to 80 percent below cost price. Only 40 to 50 publishing firms managed to put out books, and most of these were not new editions but reprints of old ones. Most were on the verge of bankruptcy.

The "depression" showed no signs of a let-up in 1957. The number of books published dropped down 1,000 and sales figures showed a corresponding decrease. Indeed the "leanest year" since 1945 was the lot of the Korean publishing company.

The first postwar break came only in 1958. Several companies with large capital investments ventured into the publication of de luxe dictionaries and tomic works. Their new efforts were distinguished from former examples by attractive bindings and liberal use of good-grade paper. The enormous capital outlays for such books as the Encyclopedia, Standard Korean Dictionary, New Korean Dictionary, World Literature Series, Korean Literature Series were received with great enthusiasm.

In other words, the risk undertaken by a few publishers broke the spell of "depression." It was, however, a success story of only six or seven out of six to seven hundred struggling firms. The overall picture was still far from bright, and it remains so today. Reference books for students, formerly considered one of the best money-makers, has ceased to be profitable because of the severe competition among publishers and the decreasing purchasing power of students. Nonfiction sales have declined so steadily that the first printing of 1,000 copies is hardly ever cleared.

Among the many causes which have kept the publishing business depressed for several years, the gravest is considered to be the fact that too many publishing houses compete with one other with more or less identical books without adequate planning and with decreased perchasing power on the part of the buyer in the midst of an overall economic recession.

While most of the publishers have adopted a cautious attitude, a few are venturing out into the field of serial publications with the tides of the times. Thus, "Series of New Culture," "Series on Ideology and Culture," "Cultural Series of Women's Life," "World Literature Series," "Korean Literature Series," etc., are now in print. The tendency is likely to continue for some time.

One noteworthy event in the last two years has been the increased popularity of foreign books translated into Korean, e. g. "Dr. Zhivago." Although, Korea is not a member of the International Copyright Convention, the problem of foreign copyrights has started to be discussed.

There are presently about 600 publishing houses registered with the government, together accounting for 843 titles during the first half of 1959. The breakdown: 193 reference books, 143 works on sociology and economics, 137 literary works, including fiction, 64 books for children, 46 histories, 43 books on language, 32 books on academic researches, 32 books on engineering, 31 books on law and politics, 25 religious works, 12 philosophical works, 9 books on industry, and 76 miscellaneous.

Magazines

Popular, If Not Profitable

The monthly magazine, *Sonyon* (Boy), published in 1908, was the first magazine ever presented to the Korean people with a format and contents of what might properly be called a magazine in our contemporary sense of the word. True that prior to the Boy, the *Korea Chagang Wolbo* (Self-Reinforcement Monthly) was published in 1906, and the *Taedongbo* and *Kihohunghak Wolbo*, first published in 1907 and 1908 respectively, were periodicals, but their formats and contents did not entitle them to the term, magazine, as we understand it today.

With Choe Namsun, a poet and one of the most prominent historians, as editor-in-chief and publisher, *Sonyon* was a vital magazine, seeking after "modern Westernized life" with sharp criticisms against the contemporary feudal society. As a publication serving the "enlightenment" movement of the time, the magazine covered wide fields of literature, philosophy, religion, geography, astronomy, and even anthropology. The "Boy" indeed represented the awakened spirit of the times after a long period of hibernation under the feudal system.

Sonyon, however, was so vigorous in attacking Japanese encroachment of Korean sovereignty that the Japanese authorities had it banned after the Annexation. Undaunted, Editor Choe put out the *Chongchun* (Youth), for grown-up readers of the "Boy", following a similar line as the Boy but on a higher intellectual plane.

These two magazines, "Boy" and "Youth" made significant contributions to the Westernization of Korea, and their contribution to the subsequent modern literary movement was considered definite because of the style of writing adopted.

During the 20's, a large number of magazines were published as a result of the active social movements then in progress after the Independence Movement of 1919. They were so popular, if not profitable, that during the six-year period from 1923 to 1929, no less than 20 magazines appeared.

Practically all of these publications were short-lived affairs, a few not lasting one issue and most petering out before the tenth. The magazine which went beyond the 30th issue was considered exceptional. These amounted to only a handful.

Among the magazines, the most numerous were organ magazines of literary associations. There were also quite a number of women's and children's magazines.

Medium for Nationalism

Magazines were then published not as a business venture but to promote the independent spirit of the Korean people against Japanese domination. They were, therefore, heavily tinctured with political ideals, usually Nationalism or Socialism. Representative of the nationalistic sentiment was the *Chosunjikwang* (Light of Korea); on the other hand, the *Kaebyok* (Creation of the Universe) preached the virtues of Socialism with more zeal than any red magazine of the times.

In the '30's, more and more magazines were published as profit-making ventures. Accordingly, they were offered in more attractive formats. Among some 60 magazines issued by daily newspaper firms enjoyed the largest circulations while the *Samcholli*, (3,000 Ri) published by the poet, Kim Tonghwan, as a private venture exerted as much influence as any of its newspaper-backed rivals. Relatively important literary magazines of the time were the Poetical Literature and Korean Literature. Most of the others were organ magazines of literary associations and did not live long.

The 40's saw magazine publications wither away as a result of increasing Japanese suppressions that accompanied the worsening war crisis. Influential magazines of the 30's, including the *Samcholli*, disappeared. The suppression of the Korean language compelled a few magazines to fill up space with articles written in Japanese. It was a "dark age" for the Korean magazine.

After the Liberation, publication was resumed with a new lease on life. So many magazines have been published that altogether more than 3,000 different magazines were available at one time or another. Most of them, however, did not survive the turbulent years that followed the Liberation. Magazines presently enjoying relatively long lives are: *Arirang, Yadam* (Historical Fiction), True Story, World of Fictions, (popular); Contemporary Literature, *Sasangge* (Ideological World —intellectual), *Hakwon* (Garden of Learning) for students, New Friends for children, Feminine Garden and Women's Living for women. There are several other monthlies currently published, but their influence is limited.

Publication of magazines in Korea has always been a risky venture except in the case of popular magazines. No more than four or five have lasted five years.

Printing Industry of Korea

Introduction of Western Printing Methods

Western printing was first introduced to Korea in 1885 by the American Christian missionary, Dr. Henry Gerhard Appenzeller, who printed the Korean Language Bible at his mission school, the *Paejae Haktang* (Institute of Learning) in Seoul.

This epoch-making event in Korea's long history of printing took place with installation of a U. S.-made automatic paper cutter operated by a motor fed with petroleum. The printing shop also cast English and Korean types for publication of the Bible and other religious tracts.

Subsequently, when the Government Bulletin and *Hansong Sinbo* (News) were published in 1895, lead types were brought in from Japan. However, operation of a largescale modern printing shop had to wait until 1903 when the Korean government established the Mint in Seoul to print bank notes and government bonds. Later the Mint was renamed the Korean Government Printing Bureau, and, following the Annexation, continued to function officially under the Governor-General.

The Mint was presumably equipped with considerably large facilities, for it is believed that more than 200 Korean printers were employed at the printing department of the Mint in 1909.

In the meantime, some private printing shops began to emerge. In 1905, an O Taehwan established the Paengmun Printing Shop in Seoul as the first modern printer. Another printing company was soon founded with facilities that included lithographic equipments. Two more followed in 1907.

The printing shops enjoyed so much prosperity during the early days of Westernization that in 1908 not less than five new companies ventured into the field.

A steadily growing printing industry, however, had to suffer a temporary setback in 1919 when the Independence Movement flared up. Kim Honggyu, superintendent of the Posongsa, and Kim Nyonje, chief typesetter of the Sinmun-kwan, were imprisoned for printing the "Declaration of Independence" at their shops. The Posongsa, moreover was set afire by the Japanese police. The Japanese correctly recognized the importance of such printing facilities.

Development of Printing Industry

The Samil marked the closing chapter of the initial stage of Korea's printing industry. After 1919, Western civilization poured into the "Land of Morning Calm", as a result of which publication of books increased by leaps and bounds. Largescale printing shops were established in succession.

Private printing shops, which had formerly been located exclusively in Seoul, were established in provincial cities also, so that by 1943, one-fifth of the country's printing shops were scattered throughout the country outside Seoul and its suburban areas, even though about one-third of the workers were living within the city limits.

During this period of growth from 1919 to the end of World War II, the printing industry established itself as one of the important industries of the country. It was, however, manipulated by powerful Japanese capital.

One of the "giants" of the printing industry was the Chosun Book Printing Company, Ltd., successor of the former Printing Bureau of the Japanese Government-General.

Incorporating itself in 1923 as a private company, it printed Bank of Korea notes, government securities, Government Bulletins, textbooks and all other print materials for the Governor-General. Housed in huge buildings the Chosun Book Printing Company was equipped with the best facilities in the country, including two-color offset printing machines, employing 650 workers.

The second largest firm, the Chosun Printing Company, Ltd., which was the first to installa monotype machine in Korea, had the capacity of printing about 300 reams a day. There were other large printing shops in operation, such as Chikajawa Printing Company, Tanioka Printing Company, Otsuka Printing Shop, and Daikaido.

The "China Incident" resulted in a wartime "boom" which bestowed upon the printing shops of Korea some share in the printing jobs accumulating for the Japanese military authorities. The industry was so expanded that by 1945 there were 735 printing shops in Korea employing 11,150 workers, who attended 1,475 printing presses, 30 offset presses, and 30 lithograph presses among other machines.

Practically all of the printing shops, however, were controlled by the Japanese and the influence of Korean businessmen was exceptional. Nevertheless, when the Federation of Korea Printing Industry was organized in 1943 two Koreans—Pak Inhwan of the Central Printing Company and No Songsok of Taedong Printing Shop, held executive positions in the wartime control agency.

After the Liberation

When the "Liberty Bell" tolled on Chongno street, announcing Korea's liberation from Japan in August, 1945, Korean workers formerly serving Japanese masters promptly took over their printing shops. Ownership of large printing shops, such as the Chosun Books Printing Company, Ltd. Chikajawa Printing Company, Tanioka Printing Shop, Otsuka Printing Company, and Daikaido Printing Company, were formerly transferred to the U.S. Military Government in Korea, which later transferred the "enemy properties" to the Republic of Korea government to be sold, in turn, to private businessmen.

The Liberation created increasing demands for printing as the people sought reading materials printed in the Korean language, long supressed under Japanese rule. Despite sufficient facilities, the Korean printing industry had to struggle against lack of competant printing technicians, for all Japanese printers who had formerly dominated the scene had been driven out of the country. As a trade organ, the Korea Printing Culture Construction Association was organized one month after the Liberation in 1945, and incorporated in 1948 as the Korea Printing Association to embrace all printing shops in the country.

The war destroyed 85 percent of all printing facilities in Seoul. Provincial printing shops which escaped the holocaust, however, enjoyed thriving wartime business without competition of the largescale printing shops in Seoul which were in ruins.

After the armistice and the government's return to Seoul from Pusan, rehabilitation was started in earnest. Up-to-date printing facilities were brought in from foreign countries, and the competition among printers was resumed with renewed intensity.

At first it was a competition for sheer size: any printing shop with larger facilities was the winner, but with rehabilitation and expansion schemes well underway, superior printing techniques attracted more business.

The principal printing shops now in operation in Seoul are the Haptong Book Publishing Company, which spent 20,000 dollars for its facilities; Mungyo (Educational) Books Publishing Company, and the printing shops of the Korean Republic Corporation, Government Monopoly Bureau, International Publicity League, and Tonga Publishing House.

Altogether 93 printing shops are equipped with modern facilities brought in from foreign countries with a total capital investment amounting to more than $ 3,310,000 through foreign economic assistance programs.

The progress of printing technique, which was once considered one of the gravest difficulties, has kept so well in pace with expansion of facilities in recent years that all printing needs both for domestic and overseas distributions are printed within the country. Especially noteworthy has been the improvement in printing types as many printing shops devised and cast new improved types.

Co'or printing, however, still presents difficulties because of the lack of technique on the part of Korean printers. To break the bottleneck, the trade organ, Korea Printing Association, is training apprentices at its Korea Printing Technique School. Also, the Seoul Technical high school has been offering training courses since 1955 as the first and only accredited school ever to furnish such training to Korean students.

The printing industry, as a whole, has been moving towards gradual conversion from former small-scale ventures to largescale enterprises with enormous capital investments.

XV SOCIAL SCIENCES

Outline

The Classical Heritage

Social science in the broad sense of the word germinated in Korea during the Three Kingdoms Period (57 B.C. - A.D. 936), especially in Silla. But social science as we understand the term today was introduced to Korea at the beginning of the 1900's from the West through Christian missionaries. After the Japanese Annexation of Korea in 1910, however, it was Japan which brought this science of the West in large measure, spreading its knowledge through formal education. Under the Japanese domination, the Korean people were deprived of the freedom to pursue independent studies; therefore, Korea was without any systematic pursuit of social science when the Liberation came in 1945. The ten-odd years since that break, then, have been a period of readjustment, of consolidating the ground for future development.

The earliest studies in social science, during the Three Kingdoms period, were devoted mostly to compilation of history and development of Buddhist philosophy. Representative works of history were the Songso by Yi Munjin (Koguryo), the "Written Records of Paekche" by Kohung, and "National History" by Kochilbu (Silla).

The most notable works in the field of Buddhist philosophy, on the other hand, were developed in the "Supplementary to the Tripitaka Koreana," written by the eminent priest-scholar of Silla, Uichon. The precise, academic treatment of the subject placed the Supplementary at the top of similar publications issued during the period.

Studies of history were further developed during the Koryo period. Kim Pusik compiled the "Annals of the Three Kingdoms," betraying a powerful influence of Chinese views on history, while the priest-scholar, Ilyon, compiled "Reminiscences of the Three Kingdoms" in five volumes, a work based on the Buddhist theory of history.

Side by side with Buddhist philosophy, Confucianism was implanted to establish itself as a branch of studies related closely to the politics of the time. During the introductory period, Confucianism furnished aristocratic "intellectuals" with no more than basic knowledge, but later, acceptance of the Sung school of learning provided for free, philosophical interpretations of the Chinese classics.

As neo-Confucianism gained ground, Buddhist philosophy as well as its ethical codes were subject to critical scrutiny, eventually leading to an assertive movement for "land reform" in order to readjust the distribution of wealth.

Neo-Confucianism became a dominant force with the Yi dynasty, which supressed Buddhism as a basic national policy. It was gradually modified and finally developed into a distinct theory, producing two opposing schools—one led by Yi Toegye and the other by Yi Yulgok.

Meantime, "Western Learning" came in the middle of the 16th century through Ming China, to spread among certain "intellectual" circles. Western sciences of Renaissance vintage and Roman Catholic philosophy exerted considerable influence and produced several scholars.

On the other hand, a utilitarian trend of studies, which began to assert itself since 1592, culminated in "Real Learning", which developed itself into a powerful force by critical attacks against the existing social, economic and political institutions. Later, the growth of "Northern Learning" added a further variety. None of these schools, however, succeeded in establishing an independent theory that could organize the related fields of studies into an integrated whole.

The Modern Reorientation

It was only after Korea was annexed to Japan in 1910 that social science as such was substantially introduced.

The German school of law and legal science, especially, gained a strong hold in Korea. So powerful was the influence of the Japanese lawyers (who borrowed their codes as well as theories from the Germans) that it still lingers, even though there have been attempts to ride on the currents of Anglo-American legal systems and theories in recent years.

In the field of political science, the country has been kept busy introducing various Western ideas through translations and interpretation of Western writings.

Economics, during the Japanese domination period, was concentrated on historical study of the Korean economy. The trend has continued through the Liberation of 1945, and findings in this field today are published in the "Economic Study," bulletin of the Korean Economics Association.

Other fields of social science, such as philosophy, logic, ethics, psychology, sociology, history, archeology, geography, Korean and foreign linguistics have made considerable progress since that time through direct contacts with Western countries, contacts denied under the former Japanese domination.

Fruits of the studies pursued in each subject of social science have appeared in academic magazines as well as bulletins put out by academic associations; moreover, numerous collected essays are published on special occasions.

Also notable has been the continued publication of photostat editions of rare Korean classics.

Books published by scholars, on the other hand, have been mostly text-books for university students.

Philosophy

Birth of a Light

The first transcendental concept entertained by ancient Korea was light. Our prehistoric ancestors were worshippers of light and named many rivers, mountains, kings and even national events after it.

The first predominating philosophy in the historical period of the "Three Kingdoms" was Buddhism. So flourishing was the teaching that the priest, Tonang, developed the theoretical basis of the "Three-Ideas Sect" in Koguryo, while Wonchuk of the Silla kingdom stood at the forefront of interpreting his theories on "Intellectualism." Both theories were later incorporated into a single theory by the outstanding Silla priest, Wonhyo. During the Koryo period, Chinul analyzed the two *Zen* sects to coordinate them into the "Choge," thus inaugurating Korea's unique tradition of Buddhistic ideology.

In the field of Confucian philosophy, which replaced Buddhism as the decisive influence of the Yi dynasty, the most significant event was the development of "Sung Learnings" by Yi Toegye and Yi Yulgok The basic themes they laid down provided the issue for the theoretical controversy that still remains without a definite conclusion among Confucian scholars. Whatever the differences on psychological or epistemological grounds, Confucianism not only inspired Korean scholars to hold the idea of "respect" in the highest esteem but tried to apply it in daily life.

Western scientific ideas were introduced to Korea after the middle of the Yi dynasty through the Roman Catholics. Independent of Western thoughts, however, the scholar, Pak Yonam, entertained such novel ideas that he advocated a revolution of the earth. The new forces of Western science combined with native talents were developed into what was called "Real Learning," which involves such practical studies as astronomy, geography, agriculture and other modern sciences. The ideal of "Real Learning," however, was soon stifled by a policy of state confinement and persecution of Catholic adherents during the late Yi dynasty.

Against the alien Western sciences, a new religious movement based on traditionally Oriental studies emerged as "Eastern Learning." This was a humanistic school of thought, based on native experiences with the object of awakening the masses. "Eastern Learning" preached that "man is god; therefore, honor man as you would honor god."

"Real" or "Eastern," the ferment of new ideas were attempts to meet urgent needs for a change. The effective change was one of a long Japanese domination which deprived the Korean people of the freedom to engage in philosophical speculation. Despite police intimidations, however, Korean philosophers managed to organize a Philosophical Society to hold monthly meetings and occasional public lectures in addition to publishing a bulletin. They also rendered valuable service by promoting nationalistic ideas among the people against Japanese despotism.

Philosophical studies were invigorated after the Liberation and the ensuing confusion of thoughts ended with the establishment of the Republic of Korea government. Philosophical interest could now be pursued along a stable course within the framework of democracy.

Relatively many books on philosophy have been published, notably a dozen outlines of an introductory nature and several books on contemporary philosophy and thoughts. Elementary courses on philosophy are taught at all universities as required courses, while specialized courses in the field are offered at the department of philosophy, which most of the liberal arts colleges have established.

Practically all Korean philosophers are members of the Korean Philosophical Association, which publishes an organ magazine, "Philosophy," in addition to sponsoring public lectures and annual conventions.

Current trend of philosophical studies in Korea may be summarized by the fact that the British and American schools have recently been attracting wider attention in contrast to the past popularity of the German and French. Also, an increasing number of young students are interested in pursuing philosophical studies on a scientific basis. Therefore, they are more interested in analytical philosophy or logical empiricism together with pragmatism. On the other hand, some segment of the young generation seems fascinated by existentialism for Kierkegaard and Nietzsche are also popular.

Students are covering all fields of Western philosophy from Plato and Aristotle to the present, but the general public is still so much preoccupied with existentialism that more than ten introductory books originally written in the Western languages were translated into Korean for publication. Translation of books on scientific philosophy, on the other hand, still remains insignificant.

In the field of Oriental philosophy, comparative studies with Western philosophy are actively pursued. It is an attempt, on the part of Korean scholars, to find the key which will open the door to Korea's future prosperity.

Only by constant studies in this field will the Korean scholar be able to make whatever contribution is theirs to the world philosophy of tomorrow.

Ethics

The Korean people have long believed that they have been a homogeneous race for 4,000 years, but it was only about 1,300 years ago that the people had a national ethics—one built upon foundations more solid than the mere concept of homogeneity.

The ethical idea of ancient Korea was based on the *Hwarang* spirit, to which is attributed the Silla success in uniting the Korean peninsula for the first time more than one thousand years ago.

Until about 50 years ago, the Korean people, confined within the Oriental cultural sphere, lived under the influence of the Oriental ethics of Buddhism and Confucianism. Encroachment of Western ethical ideas on the traditional Oriental ethics was considerable during the course of Korea's gradual adoption of Western civilization, but it was only since the end of World War II that they came into close contact with Western ethics. For the first time, then, the Korean people were confronted with a worldwide humanistic ethics.

As an independent nation, the Korean people are presently absorbed in Western ethical trends and ideas while maintaining, at the same time, the national ethics of an independent nation.

Ethics as a theoretical, academic study rather than a broad basis for moral education is maintained by professors of philosophy departments of every Korean university. The academic and theoretical studies of ethics are occasionally announced at public meetings of the Korean Philosophical Association, but more often they are published in books and college magazines.

Study of ethics may fall into five distinctive groups. One group tends to follow the ethical ideas of existentialism, reflecting not only the worldwide post-war fashion but the current unstable conditions in which the Korean people find themselves. The second group is attracted by social ethics under the influence of Russell and Dewey. The third is more interested in the "ethics of pure reason" as a new attempt to study the practical philosophy of such German philosophers as Kant, Fichte, or Hegel, devoing themselves also to inquire into ethics connected with the historical philosophy. The fourth inclines towards study of "religious ethics," which may be further subdivided into Christian ethics and Buddhist ethics. (The contributor does not feel justified to include Confucian ethics in the religious category.)

To the last group belong those who are trying to develop a "unique Korean ethics." This group is composed not only of students of Oriental studies but also of scholars majoring in studies of the West. Many books on ethics originally written in Chinese by the Korean philosophers of the past have been translated into the Korean language. A representative study in this field by a non-Korean is "Chong Tasan—A Study in Korea's Intellectual History" by Gregory Henderson, which is included in the "Collection of Buddhist Essays" published by Tongguk University in Seoul. "A Study of Korean Thoughts" by Pak Chonghong, may also serve as a representative work on the subject from a Korean pen. Besides these, there are many books on ethics written by Korean authors as well as translations of the foreign authoritative works. In conclusion, it should be emphasized that Korean ethics was, in the words of Chung Kyungcho in "Korea Tomorrow," so general in its diffusion over the centuries as to constitute the mores of the people.

Logic

The Korean language was originally developed more for expressing sensual or intuitive feelings than for abstract reasoning; accordingly, the merits of the language may well be found in artistic expressions, particularly in the form of poems. In contrast, the Korean vocabulary on abstract reasoning has not been subdivided and the language, as a result, has so far failed to develop itself along logical lines. Most of the scientific terminology, therefore, rely on Chinese words and verbatim transliteration of Western. Inevitably, a formal development of reasoning methods as inherent in the Korean language itself has yet to be realized.

The Hindu logic of ancient India was studied during the Silla period by such eminent priest-scholars as Wonchuk, Taehyon, Songyang and, of course, Wonhyo, who even wrote a book on the subject. Their efforts, however, failed to yield any fruit as *Zen* Buddhism prevailed over Hindu logic in later years. For that matter, Confucian logic become a subject for independent study only until quite recently when Kim Kyongtak published his treatise on the theme.

Logic as an independent branch of study was recognized only after the introduction of Western philosophy, and its development was noteworthy only with the Liberation that gave the Korean people unrestricted freedom to publish and study.

Study of logic started its normal course of growth right after the Liberation with textbooks on the subject published by An Hosang, Yi Chaehun and Kim Yonggi, all of whom presented formal logic in their books. Subsequently, Pak Chonghong wrote "General Logic," in which he brought up a "logic of creation," suggesting that creation or construction should be subject to logical reasoning instead of attributing it to some mystic inspiration.

Numerous text-books on logic followed, all similar in contents. In the meanwhile, Kim Chunsop, who had been teaching symbolic logic and mathematical logic at a university, wrote a book, in which the subject of his lecture was introduced to general readers by an explanation on the differences between traditional formal logic and symbolic logic. Since then the importance of symbolic logic has been accepted by an increasing number of Korean students and there is not a text-book on the subject today that does not include a chapter or two about it. However, most references are of introductionary nature, and it will be some time before an extensive study is made.

Epistemology, on the other hand, was studied by An Hosang and Pak Chonghong, who published a book on the subject. Korean translations of Hegel's "Encyclopedia" have also been published in two versions as representations of the science of dialectics to the Korean people.

In recent years, the logics in Oriental "Divination" has attracted the attention of several scholars, including Pak Chongdal, who is credited with several essays on the subject. Such studies are an attempt to clarify the reasoning method of the East by emphasizing the importance of the "Golden Mean" instead of rejecting it as in the case of the formal logic of the West. Applying symbolic logic to the ancient Oriental logic, Yi Chongdal is trying to arrive at a scientific treatment of the "Divination" logic while Kim Kyongtak is attempting to clarify and interpret it on the basis of the logic of growth. Meanwhile, Pak Chonghong is trying to develop a "logic of creation" systematically in order to reach a conclusion on general logic.

Far more efforts, however, must be made before the entire field of logics can make any substantial headway.

Sociology

Sociology in Korea is studied in an unfavorable climate that refuses to recognize its due importance. The handicap existed at the outset of the Liberation for the Japanese domination had left but a negligible number of persons majoring in the subject.

When the Seoul National University established courses in sociology soon after the Liberation, the chairs were filled with persons who had studied the subject in Japan. During the early days, therefore, sociology was studied on the basis of Japanese studies, and books available on the subject were mostly Japanese works.

Since Japanese sociology followed after the German school, at least, until the end of World War II, Korean studies were not much more than a carbon copy of German sociology, as reflected in a few "Outlines of Sociology" published as text-books during this time. Under the strong influence of the German school, therefore, sociology tended to be considered as a branch of philosophy.

Nevertheless steady efforts were continued to develop the study. Especially influential were several articles written by young students of sociology appearing in the academic magazine, Hakpung (Academic Trend).

The war infused fresh blood into sociological studies, for many American books on the subject as well as various economic assistance programs to develop such studies exerted great influence.

After the introduction of post-World War II sociological studies of the West, to which the Korean students had no access until that time, American theories began to be asserted at college lectures. With gradual stabilization from the wartime confusion, yet further ground was gained. Thus, a Department of Sociology was established at both the Kyongbuk and Ewha Women's Universities.

On the other hand, Yi Mangap and Yi Haeyong, two prominent professors of Seoul National University, were sent to the U.S. under a Rockfeller Foundation aid program to study sociology, thus paving the way for increasing Korean contacts with American sociologists. Such personal contacts were instrumental in shifting Korean studies away from Japan and toward the U.S. Accordingly, sociology has become an optimistic science on the pattern of inductive, empirical, American methods. Many theories were rearranged and interest in social surveys deepened. In 1957, the Korean Sociology Association was formed to hold at least one annual convention a year to announce findings of recent researches and surveys, as well as to exchange information among the members.

In the meantime, survey works have become active. For instance, a survey on "the composition of Korean agricultural villages" was undertaken under Professor Yi Mangap with an Asia Foundation aid grant as a preliminary work for sociological analysis of agricultural society. The survey also marked the first application of American methods to a Korean sociological survey. Professor Choe Munhwan, on the other hand, is trying to ascertain whether surplus labor force on the farm is forcing Korean farmers to leave the farms for urban areas. Professors Ko Hwanggyong, Yi Mangap and Yi Haeyong are also conducting a survey on the family system of the Korean farmer.

Other colleges are carrying surveys on the urban family, the monogenic village and other pertinent structures in Korean society.

In this way, sociology has ceased to be a mere theoretical study but is moving towards establishing itself as a science of positivism in order to furnish a sociological interpretation of Korean society on a scientific basis. Findings from such researches and surveys are expected to lay a firm ground on which to rest future pursuits in sociological studies.

One problem which has yet to be faced is to find a method to combine the different sociological theories in Europe and America into one unified system which is applicable to Korean society.

Korean sociologists have so far been too preoccupied with basic research and survey works to deal with the problem. But the issue will, without any doubt, present itself in the near future.

Psychology

The Recent Spurt

Psychological studies have made remarkable progress in Korea in recent years, both in the theoretical and applied fields, under strong American influence. True, psychology was introduced to Korea during the Japanese domination, but the then-relatively new science was not brought closely to society and so few were interested that not more than ten Koreans majored in the subject. After the Liberation, the practical as well as experimental aspects of psychology have been stressed and social recognition of psychology as a science has gained firm ground.

The following colleges with departments of psychology offer courses in psychology for M.A. and B.A. degrees, the Seoul National University, the Ewha Women's University, the Chungang (Central) University and the Songgyungwan University.

Besides Master courses, undergraduate courses are offered at all other colleges. The universities have so far produced about 200 Masters of Arts in psychology, who are presently working side by side with the considerable number of persons who received their M.A. or Ph.D. degrees in the U.S. and Japan.

The universities are confronted with various difficulties in laying a firm groundwork. Some are attempting to operate research and survey laboratories for specialized fields, such as empiric psychology and psychometrics.

Survey and research activities are carried out mostly by universities which publish the findings. Noteworthy in the theoretical field is the pursuit of experimental aesthetics, psychometrics, physiological psychology and anthropology, while the applied field so far published covers education, industry, military affairs, and personnel counselling.

Such researches and surveys have so far remained somewhat trifling, but more extensive activities are expected with improvement of facilities and increased research funds.

Services rendered society by psychological studies are presently limited to the contributions made through psychometrics, counselling and personnel management.

Psychometrics, especially, has made a significant contribution with numerous standard tests made available after 1945, about which nothing was known before the Liberation. To be specific, in addition to various classification tests made available for the military forces, standardization has been completed for achievement test, general intelligence test, differential aptitude tests, personality and temperament tests and interest tests. These standard tests have been utilized mostly by elementary and high schools and their adoption by society in general is also becoming popular. The Krepelin test for industrial personnel administration has recently been completed on a successful, experimental basis.

In preparing such pychological tests, priority has been given in the order considered most urgently required by present-day society.

In the field of counselling, which started attracting the interest of society two or three years ago, services have been made available for students of many schools, while some business and government organizations including state penitentiaries, furnish personnel counselling by professional psychologists.

Counsellor training is being given school teachers and university students, although more intensive researches and developments are yet required.

The contribution of psychology to the country's industry has been insignificant except for one or two industrial pioneers. Wider application must await overall industrial growth.

Psychological studies have yet to reach the level where professional journals and books can be published. Presently, publications are mostly text-books for university students, books on physiology and childcare designed for popular readers, and translations of Western works.

The Korean Psychological Association, organized in 1945, embraces a membership of about 50 professional psychologists, who participate in the Association's annual convention and monthly meetings. The Association functions under a president, a vice-president and four executive committee members, General, Research, Survey and Education. It is, however, still without an organ journal of its own.

It has to be admitted that psychology is not presently enjoying proper recognition presumably because of its relatively short history. With the emphasis on formal education, psychology is also placing priority in the field of education. At least one students' counsellor should be hired by every high school. A considerable number of industrial psychologists should also be trained to meet possible future demands of the Korean industry. Side by side with such applied psychology, basic theoretical researches will have to be carried out.

Psychology is still an infant science in Korea. Growth depends upon overall development of the nation.

History

Korea has always attached importance to history and the history of the country has, accordingly, been recorded without interruption since the ancient days. Since this history was recorded by the men in power, the focus was upon the sovereign of the state. Important recorded histories of ancient Korea which have been preserved until today are the "Annals of the Three Kingdoms" and the "Reminiscences of the Three Kingdoms" (57 B.C.—A.D. 918) as well as the "Dynastic History of Koryo" (A.D. 918—1392). Whereas the "Reminiscences of the Three Kingdoms" was written by one author, the other two are official works recorded by royal command. Most of the old recorded histories adopted a chronological and biographical style of writing as was the case in China.

The most authentic history of the Yi dynasty (1392—1910) was recorded in the "Annals of the Yi Dynasty" which covered in detail everyday occurences. This book is one of the most voluminous works of the kind now available, and are comparable with the "Annals of the Ming Dynasty" as well as the "Annals of the Ching Dynasty" of China in both magnitude and authenticity.

Numerous other recorded histories of Korea disappeared after the invasions of Korea by the Mongols early in the 13th century, Japan at the end of the 16th century, and the Manchus at the beginning of the 17th.

Study of history along modern Western lines was started at the beginning of the present century. It was subject, however, to innumerable restrictions under Japanese despotism and, for the most part, therefore, was pursued by Japanese historians. Among the few Koreans establishing themselves as authoritative historians during the early period of Japanese advantages, the most noted was Choe Namson. Choe is credited with many books on a Korean history based on the interests of the Korean people in contrast to Japanese historians whose objectives were to serve the Japanese government, mainly by furnishing historical data for a colonial policy. Creditable as his works certainly were, Choe did not go beyond popular education.

It was in the 1940's that history was approached scientifically on any extensive scale. In addition to the orthodox treatment, some scholars attempted to inquire into Korean history from a materialistic point of view.

After the Liberation, the first goal set was to revise Korean history by correcting the many distortions practised by the Japanese historians. Chindan Societies originally organized during the Japanese domination under the leadership of Dr. Yi Pyongdo have redoubled their efforts to publish the results of researches undertaken by members, while the Korean Historical Association and the Historical Society of Korea have also been publishing bulletins in addition to sponsoring occasional public lecture meetings. Also active is the Korean Western Historical Association as well as the Asiatic Research Center of the Korea University, the Institute of Far Eastern Studies of the Yonsei University, and Taidong Cultural Research Center of the Songgyungwan University.

Furthermore, all of these organizations publish photostat editions of precious classics. As a result, "Modern" editions of the Annals of the Yi Dynasty have become readily available to all students of Korean history.

Korean history occupies the central position in any study of history today; Oriental and Western histories are handicapped by the limited number of foreign books available. Nevertheless, interest is growing with increased cultural and political contacts between Korea and the outside world.

Such steadfast efforts on the part of Korean historians have succeeded in elevating the standard of historical researches in Korea to such a high level that as far as Korean history is concerned, the standard of researches has already surpassed that of former Japanese historians. One of the most significant events in recent years, which serves witness to the progress is the projected publication of the five-volume History of Korea currently being written as a joint project by Dr. Yi Pyongdo, Professor Kim Sanggi, Dr. Yi Sangbaek, Dr. Yi Songun and Dr. Kim Chaewon. With a Rockefeller grant, two of the five volumes have already been published. Being a crystallization of more than ten years of efforts by the nation's more eminent historians, the monumental works, when completed, is expected to provide a foundation for future development in the study of Korean history.

Systematic treatment of the nation's political history has been completed, leaving as future assignments the completion of social, economic and ideological histories. In order to attain the final goal, extensive collections and rearrangements of historical data scattered throughout the country are being carried out. Yet more extensive cooperative projects among the historians utilizing such historical data, and closer contacts with foreign historical circles are expected to assure an amazing progress.

Archaeology

Development

In Korea, as well as in China, archaeological activities have begun with epigraphic studies.

In the seventeenth century, Yi U and his brother, Yi Kan, the grandsons of the 14th king of the Yi state, Sonjo (1568—1609), were very much interested in the study of "memorial stones" and afterwards compiled the "Collection of Inscriptions of Memorial Stones in Korea" in five volumes with two supplementary volumes introducing more than 300 ancient inscriptions.

Kim Chaero (1682—1759) also collected inscriptions of the Koryo and Yi dynasties, and succeeded in publishing 226 volumes of the "Kumsongnok" (Collection of Epigraphic Inscriptions) and 20 supplementary volumes. All but 39 of his 246 volumes works have been lost.

Kim Chonghui (1786—1860), who was the greatest painter and calligrapher in Korea under the pennames, Wandang and Chusa, also was one of the greatest epigraphists. He made an advanced study of Korean epigraphy and kept in touch with the epigraphists of Ching (China) personally or through writing. His works on epigraphy comprise five volumes of the "Wandang Chip" (Works of Wandang) and a 1-volume "Kumsok Kwannok" which is a monograph on the inscription of the memorial stone of Silla King Chinhung.

With the start of modern Japan's penetration in 1870, Japanese historians found manifold opportunities to study Korea's ancient history. In 1900, field surveys on ancient remains were begun, while during the long Japanese period in the first half of the century, many archaeological works were carried on by private scholars, as well as by government agencies, such as the "Committee for Investigation of Ancient Remains" and "Society for Research into Korean Antiquities."

In 1916, a museum was established in Seoul for the purpose of keeping and showing the antiquities which had been collected as a result of these efforts. Other museums were established later in Pyongyang, Puyo and Kyongju.

These archaeological works can be divided into three periods; Prehistoric, Proto-Historic and the Three Kingdoms. Regionally, they are divided into several areas, such as, the Tungkou Area in the Yalu Valley (Koguryo Tombs), the Pyongyang Area in north Korea (Lolang and Koguryo Tombs), the Kyongju Area (Silla Tombs), and the Puyo Area (Paekche Tombs). Besides tombs, temple sites, pagodas, Buddhistic images and the like in every region are also important archaeological objects.

However, the most important thing is the excavations of ancient Koguryo tombs in the Pyongyang area. When the rich materials and frescoes were discovered in the tombs, they were introduced to the whole world through many luxurious publications, contributing much not only to the study of ancient Korean culture but also to that of China's Han dynasty.

On the other hand, in south Korea, Silla's ancient tombs (of the 5th and 6th centuries) were excavated here and there in the Kyongju area. Of these, the Kumgwanchong (Gold Crown Tomb) and the Sopongchong (Lucky Pheonix Tomb) have made a great stir in the world for their golden crowns, as well as for other priceless contents. Among the international figures who have admired them was the archaeologist-monarch King Gustav of Sweden who happened to be in Japan on a visit then as Crown Prince and who came over to Korea to see the Sopongchong dug out. The tomb was, accordingly, named after his country, *so* being the abridged form of Sweden as well as the character for luck; *pong* meaning phoenix after the design of the fabulous bird that appears on the golden crown.

Since 1945, when the Japanese left Korea, archaeological activities have become the absolute prerogative of Korean archaeologists. They have carried on vigorous work on the remains of every period throughout the country. In the south, the works have been done chiefly by the National Museum in Seoul. Among the works, the new excavations of Silla tombs and archaeological survey over the nearby islands are the more important. Especially remarkable was the excavation of the Hou Tomb in 1946, though this was already introduced to the world through the National Museum Research Publication.

The war and resultant confusion has put an end to all these endeavors. Since then, all that the National Museum has done has been to check up on various remains damaged during the war and to conduct emergency surveys over new artifacts discovered by chance. These unexpected discoveries, made in the course of the construction and repair work which was suddenly increased after the war, would have been more satisfactory, if they had been excavated undamaged. Due to unscientific methods, however, not a little of the valuable monuments and sites were damaged when dug out. The National Museum which has been chiefly instrumental in carrying on archaeological activities is a government agency. It has branches in Kongju, Puyo and Kyongju.

Scope

No definite remains of the Old Stone Age have yet been uncovered in Korea although there is undoubtedly the possibility of such discoveries in the future. The New Stone Age or Neolithic Age has been the upper limit of research activities for Korean archaeologists so far; in fact many remains of the New Stone Age have been discovered throughout the country. Of these, the most remarkable are the Shellmound and Dolmen. In particular, the Dolmens, which are scattered in groups here and there, are densely concentrated in Korea as compared to other Far Eastern countries; study on the origin of these isolated Korean Dolmens is an inevitability.

Then there is the Comb Pattern Pottery, one of the major pottery types of our New Stone ancestors. The interesting point about this ancient pottery is its striking similarity to that of the Baltic region and eastern Russia, lending considerable weight to any theory about a connection between Korea and Northern Europe across Siberia.

Coming into the Archaeolithic Period, Shellmounds, like Dolmens, gradually increased in numbers extending even to North Kyushu across the sea in Japan. Shellmounds of this period have been discovered mostly on the south coast of Korea. The main purpose of studying this ideal archaeological subject is to gauge the influence of the Chinese Metal Culture during the period, thus to establish an Absolute Chronology.

The end of the Archaeolithic Period was followed by the historic Three Kingdoms (from the beginning of the Christian Era to the 7th century). Some remains and sites now appear that are considered to be a transition between the two periods. To establish this as a fact is another major task of the Korean archaeologist.

As a historical period, we should go to the historian rather than the archaeologist for established facts about the Three Kingdoms, but so few written records are available that we must still depend on the latter.

One of these three kingdoms, Koguryo (37 B.C.—A.D. 668), embracing southern Manchuria and northern Korea, has left numerous tombs in the Tungkou area in Manchuria (Tungkou was the early Koguryo capital). The well known frescoes, which decorate the walls of the ancient tombs and are one of the greatest works of art in East Asia, are very important to any student of Oriental painting. They were contemporaneous with the art of the Six Dynasties of China.

The tombs of Paekche (18 B.C.—A.D. 660), in southwestern Korea, were discovered in the vicinities of Seoul, Kongju and Puyo. Like the Koguryo tombs, these also contain stone chambers— some built with bricks— beneath the mounds. The chambers have entrances through which the burial contents have long since been looted, principally by Tang invaders of the 7th century. Luckily, however, some are so small and simple in structure, that they were saved and remain intact to this day.

Silla (57 B.C.—A.D. 935), the third kingdom, started out in southeastern Korea and succeeded in uniting all Korea under her rule in the 7th century. Many mountainous tombs of the Old Silla Period are scattered in and around the capital, Kyongju. These have wooden chamber tombs instead of stone like the Paekche and Koguryo. The wood decayed and the soil of the mounds overhead fell into the chambers completely filling them up. This has made it difficult to rob the tombs of their burial contents, with the result that almost every tomb has remained untouched and brilliant treasures uncovered. The main problem is to determine the dates when these tombs were built.

Folklore

Religious Rites of Ancient Times

Some of the ancient Korean folklores were recorded in a few Chinese literary works, such as "The Hanshu-Tung-I-Ch'uan," "the Hou-Hanshu-Tung-I-Ch'uan" and "The Wei-Chih-Tung-I-Ch'uan." According to these records, the Korean race observed regular religious rites to worship heaven during and prior to the Three Kingdoms period. The ceremonial rites, in which all members of the clans participated took place after the spring seed-planting season and fall harvests. After the rites, which included much drinking and dancing, important problems of the clans were discussed as an inevitable part of the occasion. Not only heaven but various lesser gods of the universe, were worshipped.

This polytheistic tradition has been transmitted down to posterity over a period of many centuries, It influenced the folk customs of the Korean people and gave birth to Shamanistic rites in a latter period.

Shamanism

Shamanism has come to exert the most profound influence on the customs of the Korean people, so much that some scholars advance Shamanist interpretations in the Tangun legend of Korea's foundation. As a matter of fact, the earliest literature of Korea is tinged with Shamanistic beliefs.

Shamanism was deeply rooted among the folk customs of the people through the Koryo and Yi dynasties. Shamanist services, therefore, became so much a patronized affair that the mediums could neither avert impending tragedy nor render supernatural power through incantation and exorcism. Since the introduction of Western science at the turn of this century, this primitive superstition has lost much of its former magical attractions but its lingering influence is still considerable. Presently, the most powerful stronghold of Shamanism is Cheju Island off the southern coast of the Korean peninsula.

Geomancy and Fortune-Telling

Next to Shamanism, geomancy and fortune-telling have exerted further influence. Imported during the Three Kingdoms period from China, the magic art of fortune-telling was used extensively throughout the periods of the Three Kingdoms, Koryo and the Yi dynasty. Whenever an important problem of the state arose, the fortune-teller was consulted and his prediction respected. Individuals also patronized him in an attempt to know their future personal fortunes.

Geomancy, on the other hand, played a decisive role from the Three-Kingdoms period until the end of the Yi dynasty in the selection of sites for capital cities, buildings of all kinds and, especially, the burial grounds of ancestors. The black art of locating the most ideal sites have lost its potency since the 1900's as a result of the diffusion of Western science. But it still retains its power among the less educated segment of the population, who are obsessed by the belief that selection of sites under the principles of geomancy is a matter of serious importance, entailing grave consequences.

Folklore of the Korean people share many things in common with the Chinese. In addition to geomancy, fortune-telling, and some features of Shamanism, the same lunar calendar has been used by the two countries since the Three Kingdoms. Even at the present day, all traditional national events are observed on the dates of the lunar calendar.

Folklore Literature

Korean folklore, however, is not without some of its unique aspects. The earliest records on the subject are the Annals of the Three Kingdoms and the Reminiscences of the Three Kingdoms. Being primarily a book of history, the Annals of the Three Kingdoms contains many historical legends, through which we can get a considerable knowledge of folklore of the early days. The Reminiscenses of the Three Kingdoms, on the other hand, is so rich in accounts of folklore that the book may well be regarded as a collection of data on the subject. The two books are the only literature available for the study of folk customs and manners of the Korean people prior to as well as during the Three Kingdoms.

The Yi dynasty produced many books which contain fragmentary descriptions on folklore. The most widely known are the Songho Sasol by Yi Songho, the Yongje Chohwa by Song Hyon, the Sannim Kyongje (Forestry Economy) and the Newly Supplemented References to Literature, both by Chong Tasan. Hong Songmo wrote the *Tonguk Sesigi* (the Korean Almanac), and the fourth king, Sejong, is credited with three geography books in which folklore is described.

Establishment of the folklore as a science in Korea, however, had to wait until the 20th century. Introduced through Japan in the twentieth century, Western methods were first adopted by Cho Sokhang, who was later identified as a pioneer in the field. Son Chintae and Kim Chaechol soon followed suit, the former leaving many essays and data, in addition to "The Study of Ethnic Culture" and "The Study of the Ethnic Legends;" while Kim Chaechol wrote "The History of the Korean Drama." The poet, Kim Soun, in the meantime, rendered an outstanding contribution by publishing "Anthology of Korean Folksongs."

Scientific studies of folklore under the Japanese domination, however, were subject to severe restrictions for the Japanese Governor-General looked upon such efforts with the utmost suspicion. One of the important reasons why folklore has failed to grow must be attributed to the weak foundation laid during the Japanese domination period under such unfavorable circumstances.

Present Conditions

After the Liberation from Japan in 1945, forklore began to attract ever-increasing interest of the people. The newly aroused interests in the Korean language, literature and history sought materials from folklore to further their respective studies. But the post-World War II turmoil produced no work of significance on the subject, except "The Study of Korean Folksongs" by Ko Chongok.

Since the Korean armistice in 1952, however, folklore has been accorded renewed attention of the academic circles. Thus, in 1953 chairs of folklore were established at the Kukhak University in Seoul and Chungnam University in Chungchong Namdo. In the following year the Sukmyong Women's University in Seoul followed suit.

Continued interest in the subject gave birth to the Korean Folklore Society, which publishes bulletins and the establishment of a Committee on Folklore; the Korean Language and Literature Society. The Korean Anthropological Society was also organized to touch upon folklore as an inevitable part of its own studies, while the Society for the Preservation of the Korean Masque was born to be engaged in works in its specific field.

Currently active scholars are Yim Tonggwon in folklore and folk-songs; Yi Hongu, Chang Sahun and Song Kyongin in Korean classic music and dance; Kim Taegyu and and Cho Chihyon in Shamanism; In Sokchae, Choe Sangsu, Yi Tuhyong, and Chang Hangi in classical drama; Kim Tonguk in the masque; Chi Hyongyong geographical names; Chang Chugun and Chang Toksun in legends.

Geography

A Rich Heritage

Study of geography as a science dates back to ancient days, but authentic data to endorse the long centuries of development have not been preserved. Since the Yi dynasty, however, numerous books on geography have survived, attesting to the high level of Yi geographical studies.

The first geography book during this period was published by that enlightened monarch, Sejong. Included among the Sejong Sillok (Sejong Records), it was a collection of geographical data compiled from each province of the country. Edited about 500 years ago, an inkling of "modern Korean geography" is to be found in this book, prior to the age of modern geography inaugurated in the West by Varenius.

In addition to this publication, Sejong also made a significant contribution to the country's meteorology through his own invention of a hytometer in 1442—nearly 200 years before the invention of a similar instrument by the Italian, Benedetto Castelli in 1639. The invention of the hytometer was apparently inspired by the king's interest in the country's rainfall because of the importance his kingdom attached to rice-paddy farming predominant in the nation's economy. The continuing development of meteorology is further indicated by the evidence of a tide mark installed as a depth sounding apparatus during the late Yi dynasty period at the Chongge River which runs through the capital city in order to measure the amount of rainfall in the upstream regions.

The "Sejong Sillok Book of Geography" was followed by the Tongguk Yoji Sungnam (Findings throughout the Provinces) during the reign of King Songjong, with a later revision, under Chongjong, as a Newly Supplemented Edition. Being a voluminous publication composed of 25 books in 55 volumes, the revised edition, describing the country's geography extensively, is presumed to be the work of many hands, indicating the rise of a large number of geographers.

Such great interest in geography led to the development of a historical approach to the subject, resulting in the "Tongguk (Korea) Book of Geography," a work which marked the first step towards the study of historical geography in the country. Subsequently, during the reign of King Chongjo, Chong Tasan published the Taehan Kangyokko (Study of Korean Land Boundaries) as well as the Chosun Sugyong (Korean Hydrography), in which the author described the influences of rivers on the country's economy.

During the late Yi period, Yi Chonghwan published the Taengniji, in which he described the country's geography from the viewpoint of both natural and descriptive geographies, indicating a possible influence of modern European studies as introduced to Korea through China. This book is indicative of the apex reached in geographical studies in Korea prior to the formal introduction of Western geography.

In addition to such monumental works, there were numerous publications of lesser magnitude during the Yi dynasty. Development of geographical studies was accompanied by publication of a similarly large number of maps. Among the most famous was the Taedongyo Map of Korea by Kim Chongho. World geography was first introduced through the "Samin Pilji"(Essential Knowledge for Governors and Subjects), which was a Korean translation of a work by an unidentified Englishman published during latter Yi.

Native interest in geography suffered a setback with the Annexation in 1910. During the Japanese domination that followed, major studies were carried on by the Japanese, through whom the methodological treatments of Friedrich Ratzel, Paul Vidal de la Blache, Alfred Hettner and other European geographers were introduced to few Korean students. The interest aroused by the Western approach among the limited number of scholars, however, did not lead to any publication approaching the magnitude of the Tongguk Yoji Sungnam. The most significant contribution of the Japanese era was a 1/50,000-scale topographical map in more than 700 sheets covering the entire territory.

With the Liberation, fresh blood was infused into Korean geographical interest with the introduction of Western geographical studies direct from America and Europe.

However, the German school, already familiar, still predominates. The Ratzel theory of environment, which once held Korean students of geography in a firm grip, has been replaced by the influence of Dietrich and Alfred Hettner. Thus the theory of "reciprocal action between man and nature" influences most students of geography, with a few standing firm on the ground held by the Ellsworth Huntington school. The la Blache school of methodology, meanwhile, continues to weave its spell in certain quarters.

The renewed growth of geographical interest is expected to challenge the Yi examples in originality, but not at any early date so soon after the termination of hostilities.

One "virgin field" which has remained uncultivated is applied geography, for Korean geographers have been denied participation in preparations of any overall land exploitation plan. To bridge the gap between academic pursuits and the practical daily lives of the people through applied geography is surely one of the most important assignments for future students of geography.

Economics

Under the Japanese

Korean scholars have always held economic history in the highest esteem in any study of the national economy. It was the basic principle maintained even under the despotic Japanese rule.

Study of economics in the modern sense of the term began in Korea after the Japanese Annexation of 1910. On the heels of this tragic event came a number of Japanese economic experts who undertook the task of surveying Korea's economic conditions. On the other hand, few Korean economists, notably, Chang Kichang and Yi Kakchong, published independent research findings on the agricultural and private mutual trust fund systems prevailing between the years 1917 and 1920. At that infant stage, efforts consisted solely of attempts to clear up partial segments of the nation's economy.

Subsequently, many essays on Korean economic history and agriculture were published by professors of economics at Posong (present Korea University) and Yonhui (present Yonsei University) colleges during the early 30's.

The first significant work was Professor Paek Namun's "The Economic History of Korean Society" published in 1933, which was soon followed in 1937 by the eminent scholar's "The Economic History of Korean Feudal Society." Several other works on Korean agriculture were also published during the decade, notably by Pak Kukchae, Kang Chongtaek, Pak Mungyu and Yi Hungyu.

As the Japanese Empire plunged deeper into the war crisis of the 40's, Korean students of economy began to feel the effects of the Japanese wartime policy. But the basic attitude of studying the national economy along nationalistic lines, was maintained, despite Japanese discouragements. Thus in 1940, Yu Chahu published his "A Study on Korean Currency," to be followed by the publication of "Markets in Korea" by Mun Chongchan in 1941, and Choe Hojin's "The Economic History of Modern Korea" (Yi Dynasty Korea) and "The History of Korean Agricultural Communities," both published in 1942. As indicated by the titles of these works, the Korean economists under wartime conditions are placing the major emphasis on a circular sector of the nation's economy, reflecting its growth through alien capital investments upon the particular sector dealt with.

Korean economic studies finally rode on the tide of modern economics in 1943 with publication of Professor Yun Haengjung's "Problems of Modern Economics" and Professor Ko Sungje's translations of Michel Kalecki's "Essays in the Theory of Economic Fluctuation," 1920 and J. M. Keynes's "General Theory on Employment, Investment and Money."

The study of economics in Korea until the Liberation in 1945 may, therefore, be summarized as follows:

Firstly, no complete systematic study of feudal economic history was evolved, especially in the field of agriculture, in which a due appraisal of rural productivity was conspicuously absent.

Secondly, appraisal of overall industry, including manufacturing, lagged far behind inquiries into the agricultural field, which had been accorded prior emphasis.

Thirdly, independent channels in the field of theoretical economics were open predominantly to Japanese economists, closed to Korean.

Liberation Fever

Following the Liberation in 1945, Korean economists revived interest in their chosen field to a feverish pitch. An economic research organization was formed so as to enable the few scholars available, reinforced by several economists returning home from foreign soils, to pursue studies on Korean economic history. The political turmoil, however, soon put an end to this ambitious scheme.

Incidentally, two publications in 1946—"Social Science Essays" by the Korean Social Science Research Center and "Academy" by the Chosun Academy of Science—contained articles on economics which were predominantly socialistic, and, as such, indicative of the trends of the post-Liberation era.

In retrospect, it is understandable that students of economics should lend a willing ear to the gospel of socialism at one time or another, for most Korean students under Japanese despotism wanted to arm themselves with knowledge of economics as an effective ideological tool against the Japanese. Their eager minds poured forth both the ideas of Adam Smith's *laisser faire* economics and Marx's socialism simultaneously.

The nationalistic sentiments of the economic students, on the other hand, found expression in the study of Korean economic history which became a most active field during the post-Liberation period. Thus numerous works on the subject have been published since 1945. Recent publications include Professor Ko Sungje's "A Study on the Industrial History of Modern (Yi dynasty) Korea" in 1959, Professor Choe Hojin's "Korean Economy and Economics" in 1958, "A Short History of Korean Agricultural Technology" in 1950, Chon Soktam's "Economic History of Korea" in 1949 and Yi

Pungman's "A Study on the Economic History of Korean Society" in 1948, Kwon Taesop's "The Basic Structure of Korean Economy" in 1947.

The study of Korean economic history was so popular until the outbreak of the war in 1950 that the subject was a required course at the economics departments of all the universities. In the meantime, other fields of economics than history also made steady progress.

One tide of economic theory after another has swept through the country since the introduction of modern economics to Korea. No further new ideas are likely to present themselves, at least for the time being. On the wake of the Liberation in 1945, socialistic economics seemed to have such a sweeping influence on economic studies that university lectures on the classic theory of the Adam Smith school tended to fall on deaf ears. Cool thinking, however, gradually replaced the once agitated state of mind in academic circles as politics followed a definite course. Economic students began to adopt a more sincere attitude after the war.

The prevailing attitude of the students is that the underdeveloped conditions of Korean economy do not lend themselves readily to adoption of the economic theories and policies that are practiced in advanced foreign countries.

Therefore, both classic and Keynsian economics are being studied, the scholars seeking an opportunity to adapt their respective schools to the nation's economic policies. At the same time, there is widespread interest in economic development and policies for underdeveloped countries in general.

Education

Education in Korea has not been systematized as a science as in the U.S. and Britain where it falls within sound scientific frameworks. This is so because ideologies have dominated the functions and purposes of education throughout the long history of the country. The path was provided, first, by the Buddhist teachings of the Three Kingdoms period (57 B.C.—A.D. 936), then by Confucianism in the Koryo period, Neo-Confucianism in the Yi, Christianity during the Japanese era, and, finally, by the present idea of progressive education.

In the prehistoric eras of Tangun and Kija, though there were no systematic concepts of education, the people were taught such virtues as worship of God, respect for others, and loyalty to the state. With the historical period of the Three Kingdoms, however, "institutes of learning" were founded in Koguryo, while Silla, which finally united the land, was guided by a state policy providing for education in the Chinese Classics as based on Buddhist teachings to the end of training political leaders. Koryo education, strongly influenced by China, had as its main objective the training of court officials.

The "civil service examination" system, introduced from China, played a decisive role in this respect. By the latter period of Koryo, "practical" education had quite replaced the abstract philosophy of Buddhism and importance was attached to such studies as astronomy, the almanac, mathematics, medicine, geography and other natural sciences.

Buddhism, so predominant in education down the centuries, was rejected by the Yi dynasty in favor of Neo-Confucianism. Education, based on Chu Hsi's school of the Master Sage, rapidly gained firm ground to exert a powerful influence among the people. The principle of "greater justice and moral obligation," on one hand, and flunkeyism," on the other, became deep-rooted, and any concept of a democratic education, to say nothing of education for women, was beyond the wildest imagination.

The idea of modern Western education was introduced to Korea in 1886 through American Christian missionaries and the first such system of education established in 1895 in the Japanese. The royal Korean government subsequently established Western-type schools for popular education and also trained official interpreters at a foreign language institute. The several mission schools, founded, by the meantime, by the American Christian missionaries, were teaching not only Western culture but also Western concepts of democracy.

The forced annexation of Korea to Japan in 1910, however, nipped the idea of democracy in the bud, and Japan utilized education as a means to attain its ends of colonial policy. Educational idealism after the German school of Herbert was introduced by the Japanese in order to exert a powerful influence on middle and higher schools of learning, thus giving rise to the popular concept of studying for study's own sake among certain intellectual circles. This school of thought still lingers. Elementary education, on the other hand, was influenced by Pestaroch, especially by his theories on practical education.

When Korea become liberated from Japan in 1945, the ideas of Japanese education based on totalitarianism and the American idea of a democratic education intermingled to usher in a new stage at once when the country was placed under the administration of the U.S. Military Government. The concepts of pragmatic education, especially Dewey's, exercised powerful influence. Thus progressive, democratic education has become a dominant factor and the Education Law of the state proclaims that the goal of democratic education is to provide "extensive benefits to all humanity." The Education Law was enforced in 1948 as the legal basis for education. Under this law, six-year elementary schooling is compulsory for children between the ages of seven to twelve at state expense.

Legal Science

A Short History

Legal science has had but a short history in Korea without as yet developing any marked features suited to the country. For two thousand years, it had a tradition of law based on Oriental ethical concepts.

The break came in 1899 when a decaying Yi kingdom was forced to adopt a modern system of law under Japanese pressure. Outstanding as the legal theory and jurisprudence of the past certainly were, Korea willy-nilly had to accept the German school after the Japanese example.

When Korea was liberated in 1945, practically all lawyers in the land cherished the notion that the Korean legal system, based on the Japanese and, therefore, the German, was one of the best in the world. Such being the case, when U.S. Military Government officials presented American law books to Korean lawyers, the latter were unimpressed. Lawyer and law professor found it all very interesting but in their full awareness of the differences between the German-Japanese-Korean and the Anglo-American schools of thought, they could find but little to attract them in a legal science that was based on case-methods. They were and still are more attracted to German-Japanese law books except in the field of international law.

Constitutional Law

The Constitution of the Republic of Korea is modelled after the Weimares Verfussungsrecht of Germany, but the American presidential system has been incorporated through two amendments. Nevertheless, the constitutional law of Korea is still definitely influenced by the German school, as are her scholars, such as Dr. Yu Chino of Korea University who drafted the Constitution, Professor Pak Ilgyong and Professor Han Taeyon, both of Seoul National University, all three of whom have developed their theories in commentaries based on the works of such Germans as George Jellinek, Carl Schmitt and Theodor Maunz. The only notable exception is Dean Mun Hongju of Pusan National University, whose commentary superimposed many American theories on the German groundwork.

Criminal Law

Legal science on criminology has long followed the controversy between the classic and modern schools in Germany. As soon as the works of Germany's Edmund Mezger and Japan's Shigemitsu Tando evolving a new theory on this controversy became known in Korea, many young law students immediately accepted their conclusions. Dr. Hans Welzei's "Die Finale Handlungslehre" became a big issue, Professor Hwang Sandok of the Seoul National University introduced the book to Korea promptly, and published a translation of H. Welzel's "Das neue Bild des Strafrechtssystems, 3rd edition" in 1957. Professor Yu Kichon of Seoul National University, on the other hand, uses American case-methods in his intepretation of the Korean Criminal Code.

Civil Law

A new civil code was enacted in 1958. The commentary by Professor Kim Chunghan of Seoul National University thereon betrays the marked influence of Professor Sakae Wagajuma of the Tokyo University. The Japanese, in turn, were influenced by Karl Renner's "Die Rechtsinstitute des Privatrechts und ihre Soziale Funktion 1929."

International Law

Professor Yi Hangi of the Seoul National University betrays the influence of Professor Jessup of Columbia University in his recent work, "Science of International Law" published in 1958, while Professor Pak Chaesop of the Korea University, a one-time student of Harvard, seems to be guided by the theories of Professor Verdross Wien.

Legal Philosophy

Legal philosophy follows what may be called the Kelsen-Otaka line after Hans Kelsen of Vienna and Japan's Dr. Otaka. Tomoo. Kelsen taught Otaka in the 30's and the latter, in turn, influenced the two prominent professors of law in Korea, Yi Hangyong (Korea University) and Hwang Sandok (Seoul National University), both of whom have published books on legal philosophy. In 1957, however, Professor Hwang started moving toward establishment of a Buddhistic legal philosophy, thus breaking away from Kelsen's, as indicated in his dissertation, "Recent Natural Science and Legal Philosophy," 1957. Professor Yi Hangyong, on the other hand, has attempted to combine the sociology of modern law with the legal theories of Confucius in his "Outline of Legal Philosophy," 1955. Meantime, works by the U.S.'s Roscoe Pound and Germany's Gustav Radbruch have been translated into Korean, but their effects have been insignificant. Nor are present-day works on legal philosophy by Japanese scholars attracting any attention in Korea.

One note of regret is the conspicuous absence of even a single scholar studying the history of Korean law, a fact all the more deplorable because two professor (Prof. Hyon Sunjong and Prof. Kim Chunghan), at least, are specializing in European legal history. The cause of this is attributed to the war which destroyed most of the ancient literature on the subject. However, since much of this loss has now been recovered, we may expect brilliant works on the history of Korean law in the near future.

The relative inactivity among Korean legal circles is blamed primarily on the destruction of practically all works and efforts of the post-Liberation period by the war, and the vacuum still lingers. Another reason is believed to lie in the lack of opportunities to study law in Germany, since Germany is considered more rewarding in this field than the U.S. where most overseas students inevitably go.

The failure to bring the theoretical and practical aspects of legal science closer together in Korea has also been considered one of the decisive factors for "practice" offers little incentive to the pursuit of science.

Political Science

Political science as a branch of modern social sciences began to make progress in Korea only since the country's liberation from Japan. True that prior to 1945, fragmentary studies were carried on by individual Korean scholars, but fragmentary they remained with no systematization.

With the Liberation as a turning-point, a definite stage was reached and many universities established departments of political science as well as of politics and economics. Most of the professors who filled the chairs of the newly created departments had been educated in Japan, and their lectures, accordingly, did not go beyond the German concepts of the Staats Lehre or Staats-Rechts Lehre that were taught by their Japanese professors.

It required considerable efforts to remedy such a situation and, for some time, the professors had to devote themselves to the translation and interpretation of other Western political ideas. It was during this time that many books by R.G. Gettell and H.J. Laski were translated and published in Korean. The war swept everything under the rug and it was only three years later, after the armistice signing, that studies were resumed and numerous text-books published on political science.

As before the war, political science entails preoccupation with the translation and interpretation of foreign political ideas. In other words, Korea is as yet making no systematic study of the science to fit her own needs; she is still seeking the means to her own end and destiny.

Political science, like all other social sciences, cannot find an absolute principle which applies universally. Each nation has to have its own political theory applicable in a particular time and space. Therefore, the political ideas born out of the modern civic societies of the West do not lend themselves to ready adaptation to present-day Korea. Nevertheless, students of political science, Korean or otherwise, must seek a common principle that can be valid for all lands and races. So far as Korea is concerned, conditions compel her scholars to leave such a mission to the students of tomorrow.

In retrospect, the progress in political science over the past 14 years has, by no means, been trivial in view of the political handicaps that have plagued the nation, handicaps climaxed, of course, by a hot "cold war." However small the measure of progress, it presents a hopeful outlook for a definitive trend in future progress.

Linguistics

The science of linguistics goes back to 1490 with the invention of the Hangul alphabet by that truly enlightened monarch,

Sejong. His Hunmin Chongum (Formation of the Korean Alphabet) was followed in short order by translations of two Chinese classics, the Ku-chin-yun-hui (Yuan) and Hung-wu-cheng-yun (Ming) in which he utilized his novel system of phonetics. This was again followed up by two Chinese pronounciation or "rhyming" dictionaries, the Sasong-tonggo and Tongguk-chongun. The most original of Sejong's works, "Formation of the Korean Alphabet," contains references to the origins and ramifications of languages as well as phonological contrasts, altogether indicating a surprisingly high standard of research.

During the 16th century, the Chinese, Mongolian, Manchurian and Japanese languages were studied, leaving important data for modern research workers.

It was in the 17th century, however, that linguistic studies were really revitalized, producing such outstanding scholars as Hwang Yunsok, Sin Kyongjun and Yu Hui in the 18th. Most of their efforts consisted in collecting data and comparative studies of sounds and dialects. Decline set in late in the 19th century when Western research methods were introduced by missionaries who were unable to do anything significant in the field.

Korean linguistics underwent a drastic change by adoption of Western methods in 1884. That was the year of the Kabo Reform. Several linguists arose, the most outstanding being Chu Sigyong, whose works have guided all linguists and grammarians up to this date.

The Japanese Annexation, however, forced suspension of Korean linguistic researches until the nationwide independence movement of 1919. That shaking event permitted a revival and the Koreans plunged into renewed study of their neglected language with an enthusiasm born of long deprivation. Scholars undertook such urgent and practical works as Korean spellification, the adoption of a normative language, and preparation of standard grammar. It was during this time that the Korean Linguistic Society was organized.

Subsequently the linguists concentrated on philological studies which, in due course, gave way to historical researches. It was during this period that Choe Hyonbae, the leading authority on the Korean language today, achieved his first striking success in the field of Korean grammar. Yang Chudong, another living authority, won distinction for his study of folk songs and ballads of the Silla and Koryo eras. Many essays on Korean phonetics, phonology, morphology and dialects were also published by such scholars as Kim Yungyong, Yi Huisung, Pang Chonghyon, Kim Songi, Chong Insop, and Yi Sungnyong. Study of Western linguistics, on the other hand, lagged far behind for the scholars were too preoccupied with the problem of Korean word formations.

The Pacific War crisis brought increasing pressure to bear against the native language and its champions. Publications written in Korean were officially banned and linguists thrown in jail. All studies were stopped for the duration of the war.

The Liberation, not surprisingly, brought instant revival of unprecedented interest. All academic associations which had been disbanded by the Japanese sprang to life again and many scholars who had gone underground emerged from obscurity to present innumerable publications at once. It was at the high-tide of language enthusiasm that the Communists warred on the south. The linguistic circles represented a heavy casualty at the hands of the invaders. Young scholars, however, have rapidly filled the sorely-felt vacancies since the armistice and outstanding progress has been made in recent years in the entire field of Korean linguistics.

One of the most remarkable achievements has been the development of historical researches. Outstanding successes have also been made in the fields of phonetics, morphology and word formation. Important work has also been done in the field of comparative studies, undertaken after long years of neglect, much interest, for instance, going into descriptive linguistics as introduced mainly from the U.S. Normative grammar is being studied again along with renewed interest in historical grammar, while the science of dialothology has interested a few particular groups that are busy collecting dialects throughout the country.

The progress made in each specialized field of linguistic studies has led to the publication of innumerable essays in numerous academic bulletins, such as "The Korean Language and Literature," "Tongbang Academy Bulletin," "Asia Research Bulletin," "Chindan Academy Bulletin," "Hangul," and "Linguistics."

Korean Linguistics and Literature

Japanese Excesses

Scholars of the Korean language and literature kept their interest alive through the critical Japanese period of 40 years. The obstacles they were up against cannot be exaggerated. Japan frankly wanted to wipe the language off the land, and forbade its official use. With an intimidating police on constant guard against anything likely to remind the people of their true national rights, the scholars, perforce, had to confine their studies to the Korean classics. They confined themselves to the systematization and interpretation of these works during the dark age. The considerable fruits of certain Japanese scholars served as motivation for the Korean linguists. The first of these, Yongga Koo-jon (selection of Yongga) by Maema Kyosaku, was published in 1924. Okura Shinpei attracted continued attention with such works as "Study of Idu and Hyangga" (Community Folk Songs), 1929; "The History of Korean Linguistics," 1943; and the "Study of Korean Dialects," 1944.

Against these Japanese contributions, Korean linguists came out with such outstanding publications as Choe Hyonbae's "Korean Grammar" in 1937, and the "Korean Phonetics" in 1942; "Outline of the History of Korean Poetry" by Cho Yunje in 1937; "The History of Korean Literature and Linguistics" by Kim Yungyong in 1938; "The Korean Linguistics" by Pak Sungae in 1935; and "A Study of Old Korean Songs" by Yang Chudong in 1942. Other works of considerable significance published at this time were "The History of Korean Drama," 1939 by Kim Chaechol; and Chong Nosik's "The History of Korean Changguk" (Classical Music Drama), 1940; "The History of Fiction in Korea," 1933, and "The History of Chinese Linguistics in Korea," 1931.

Other works deserving mention were "History of the Korean Language," 1923, by Kwon Tokkyu; "The History of Korean Literature," 1922 by An Hwak; "The History of Literature in Korea," 1926 by Kwon Sangno; "Sijo Yuchwe," 1928 (Korean Classic Poetry) by Choe Namson; "Korean Folk Songs," written in 1933 by Kim Soun; "Selected Sijo of the Generations," 1940 by Yi Pyonggi; and the "Dictionary of Korean Proverbs," 1940, by Pang Chonghyon and Kim Sayop. Research efforts also appeared in such magazines as the Chindan Academy Bulletin, first published in 1934, and the literary magazine, Munjang, first issued in 1939.

In addition to these original works, Chinese classics were reprinted under Choe Namson's supervision by the Kwangmunhoe, a cultural association devoted to ancient literature. The established publishers, the Pangmun Bookstore, meanwhile, were putting out a series of "literary editions" and the Chungang (Central) Bookprinting House had a concurrent series on Korean literature.

Works published during the Japanese domination period, however, were mostly of an introductory nature with a few exceptions, because the unstable social conditions of the time were not conducive to extensive training of younger generations. Few Korean scholars struggling against tremendous odds had to preoccupy themselves with the difficult task of collecting basic data. Therefore, studies of Korean linguistics until the Liberation were predominantly devoted to collections, arrangements and annotations of such basic data. The Korean linguists of the time, however, left a lasting mark on the history of Korean linguistics with a Draft of the Standard Spelling Method for the Korean Alphabet which was completed in 1933. Japanese persecution in the '40's of members of the Korean Language Association involved in compilation of the "Korean Dictionary"* was the culmination of their intention to murder the Korean language.

The Liberation of '45 set afire the people's enthusiasm in their own language. Public lectures attracted capacity crowds that were only too anxious to readjust themselves to a neglected 'basic.' Development was rapid but the war came all too soon to scatter the numerous data collected in the zeal of the post-Liberation years.

Since the armistice stabilization, however, Korean linguistics have made renewed progress. Important works may be listed as follows: "Yoyochonju," 1947 by Yang Chudong; "A Study of Korean Poems and Songs," 1948, and "The History of Korean Linguistics," 1949, by Cho Yunje; "A Study of Korean

*Completed only in 1957 under a Rockfeller aid grant.

Phonetics," 1949, and "The Study of Phonetics," 1956, by Yi Hisung; "The Outline of Korean Linguistics," 1949, edited by the Korean Linguistic Association; "A Study of Songs of the Yi Dynasty Period," 1955, by Kim Sayop; "History of the Korean Language," 1955, and "The Annotation of Archaic Words," 1955 by Kim Hyonggyu, and the "Dictionary of Archaic Word Data," 1946, by Pang Chonghyon.

While old, established scholars were busy with interpretation of Korean classics, a crop of younger students were inclined to take up comparative study of linguistics and literature, which in turn, prompted revaluation of the classics on a scientific basis.

Publication of classics has also been spurred in recent years by extensive collections and systematizations. Many photostat editions of rare classics are being published by universities such as Yonsei and Tongguk as well as by leading publishing firms.

Voluminous Chinese linguistic works are also being duly systematized, interpreted and otherwise researched by the younger Korean students of linguistics. Korean grammar, too, is likely to be fitted into a unified framework in the not too distant future. Literary horizons are altogether bright and promising in every respect.

Foreign Literature

It has been over fifty years since foreign literature was first introduced to Korea. Throughout that time, academic studies in foreign literature were subject to innumerable difficulties. For one thing, the Japanese colonial policy towards Korea was anything but encouraging to the study of such literature and, inevitably, there were but few Koreans who were able to major in the field.

The first sign of any worthwhile pursuit in the field of Western literature appeared in the magazine, "Overseas Literature," in 1926, which carried the translation work of a few Korean students who were then studying in Japan. The magazine was the product of a close-knit, expanding literary association, and the contributors were members of this body, many of whom have become leading educational figures today, such as Yi Songun, President, Songgyungwan University; Son Usong, Dean, College of Liberal Arts and Science, Songgyungwan University; Chong Insop, Dean, Graduate School, Chungang University; Kim Chinsop, former head of the Literature Department, Songgyungwan, etc. At that time, Korea had no institution of higher learning offering specialized courses in literature; therefore, most students who wanted to study the subject preferred to go to Japan where such courses were readily available.

These students, however, returned home to find obstacles all the same. On one hand, they had difficulties in earning a livelihood; on the other, they were denied ready access to new foreign publications. Nevertheless, they succeeded in translating a considerable number of foreign literary products and to get their works printed in newspapers and magazines. In particular, the "Liberal Arts Commentary" and "Munjang" (Sentence) of the '30's rendered significant contribution to the study of foreign literature. The ambitions of thirsty young Koreans, however, were soon frustrated as Japan warred on the West in the '40's and prevented any cultural movement of this nature. The teaching of English at school was positively discouraged and all channels to the importation of foreign books remained closed up to the date of Liberation. The students had nothing more to go on but whatever classical literature was available.

The Liberation enabled Koreans, for the first time, to pursue foreign literature unmolested, and many colleges and universities, either expanded or newly founded, established literature departments where those who had majored in foreign literature during the Japanese period hastened to train the young generations. At the same time, many students went abroad to study literature, returning in after years to specialize in their chosen field.

The war inflicted untold damages but interest was resumed with renewed intensity after the armistice. English, French and German cultural bodies cropped up one after another, and the stepped-up tempo of all these literary stirrings brought earnest endeavors to the increase of cultural exchanges between the East and the West. The numerous essays appearing in college academic bulletins are indicative of the trend.

Such exchange has become greatly facilitated with the foundation in 1959 of the Comparative Literature Society of Korea which has subsequently become a member of the International Comparative Literature Association.

Translation of foreign literary works has also become so active a proposition that many publishers are busy putting out one "series" after another, a "series" comprising as many as fifty volumes.

The steadfast efforts of the professors and the talents of numerous students in the field of foreign literature are Korea's assurances of a fine future in spreading knowledge of the West, in particular, increasing East-West cultural understanding, in general. Their efforts are expected to pave the way to the outflow of Korea's literary efforts.

XVI NATURAL SCIENCES

Preface

This entry will survey the overall historical characteristics of natural science in Korea, leaving the detailed analyses to the specific entries.

The beginning of the activities that may be considered relevant to natural science was as early as the diffusion of Chinese culture into Korea. Although it is difficult to make an exact chronology of the early contacts between Korea and China in fields with some relevancy to natural science, it is known that from the Three Kingdoms period (57 B.C.-A.D. 936), Korea received from China written works in astronomy, chronology, mathematics and medicine.

Feudal Korea saw a wide circulation of these works in original Chinese throughout the country. Not being pedagogic, these volumes served as valuable, practical guides for the agricultural society.

For example, Chuchan-Shanshu (Nine Chapters in Arithmetic) was a useful reference book in farming, and the Chinese books in medicine were essential for Koreans in advancing their own medical learning to the point of publishing later *Silla-Pobsabang* and *Paekche-Sinjippang* and the development of superior medical herbs which were highly valued in China.

In chronology and mathematics, also, Korea remained a passive recipient of advanced Chinese culture of the Three Kingdoms period, as pointed out in the *Samguk-Sagi* (Annals of the Three Kingdoms). However, the Korean orthodoxy in Chinese learning resulted in the retention of many aspects of Chinese learning of the period even after they were all but forgotten in China proper.

During the Koryo period, internal disturbances in China caused loss of many cultural treasures, and China began to reseek its own cultural heritage from Korea. While it was at this time from Sung (China) that Korea received the basic stock of learning, Sung was in continuous internal disruption and finally was conquered by the nomadic Mongols who established the Yuan Empire. During the Yuan period, a new calendar system was adopted. Although there were indirect influences from the Islamic culture on Korea, it was received second-hand after earlier assimilation by the Chinese.

In cartography, from the Three Kingdoms period, the influence of the West is discernible in a variety of suddenly-appearing new techniques.

During the Yi dynasty, there were strong trends toward adopting and systematizing foreign academic doctrines. This was due largely to fourth King Sejong's political and cultural accomplishments. In many fields of learning, astronomy, chronology, mathematics, meteorology, and others, there were many progressive scholarly activities. It was during this period of re-orientation that the famous rain gauge was invented, the calendar revised, with due reference to the Arabic solar calendar, and mathematics were vigorously taught to the public.

Especially noteworthy was the interest shown in meteorological works, and many expeditionary units were dispatched to Kumgangsan, Kanghwa and Cheju mountains to obtain meteorological data. In cartography, by actual survey and by means of panorama sketches, it was possible to project a map of Korea which has considerable resemblance to the more exact map of Korea used today.

In medicine, after a long period of merely copying and borrowing from Chinese sources, the time came when the Korean began to revise and improve upon the original to a very substantial degree; and in agronomy also, especially in silk worm breeding, the Korean showed ingenuity in supplementing the Chinese original with comments and revisions as they were deemed necessary through their own research and experience. These activities were interrupted by internal and external disturbances which culminated in the Japanese invasion of Korea in the sixteenth century. Renewed Korean attempts at recovery of cultual heritages at the close of the nineteenth century were in vain. These attempts were not confined to the world of learning, but encompassed the practical reform of economy and society as a whole. The stimulus for them was primarily domestic, but not to be overlooked is the role Western ideas transmitted to Korea through China played in giving energy to the movement. Because of this latter role, the movement is often called 'Western Learning.' Yet the substance of the movement was primarily traditional.

The representative fields of 'Western learning' were astronomy, algebra, hydrology, chronology, and others, and serious efforts were made to restore the high standard of learning attained by King Sejong in agronomy, medicine, astronomy, and meteorology, etc. There were innumerable publications in agronomy as well as in medicine such as *Tongui-Pogam* (literally, Eastern Medicine Rare Survey) and in many other fields of learning. The highlight of this movement was the completion of Kim Chongho's map of Korea entitled *Taedongyojido* based on an actual survey of the land.

While it would seem that Korea was greatly Westernized in methodological outlook, by copying what was Western through China and Japan, there was little imprint of experimental techniques of the West on Korea at the end of the nineteenth century. Western influence was more in the form of inspiration toward improvement and modernization than in direct technological borrowing.

After the close of the nineteenth century, however, through the Japanese colonial administration and the work of Western missionaries, Koreans began to obtain training in scientific pursuits, but the scope of the popularization of science in Korea was rather limited up until the 1945 Liberation, and since that Independence date, Koreans have been striving for progress in scientific pursuits. The initiative is now in the hands of Koreans, and in a short span of time, their own accomplishments in learning, research and publication in the field of science have been very considerable. In many fields, Korea is lagging far behind, but the prospect is brighter than at any time before in the modern history of the country. This is not to say, however, that the conditions allow for optimism. There are difficulties. The dependence of Korea on foreign countries, expecially America, for technical and economic support, gives rise to caution that scientific undertakings are not on a pure Korean foundation.

The government is confronted with the important task of bringing about conditions conducive to progress in scientific pursuits for the younger generation by making available the necessary facilities and grants-in-aid. Individual accomplishments of scholars obtaining their training abroad are important, but there seems to be the necessity of a far-reaching program for scientific development, especially a largescale allocation of

XVI NATURAL SCIENCES

resources for such a program. The efforts that have been made by the scientists in Korea under very unfavorable conditions are commendable indeed. But the development of new facilities for research and development must increase in direct proportion to the number of new graduates in respective fields if Korea is to gain optimum use of its trained human resources.

Mathematics

The ancient history of mathematics in Korea closely parallels that of China. In fact, the various cultures of old Korea were often originated in China and subsequently introduced to Korea over few centuries. Around 750 B.C., Chou established the so-called Six Arts which included the Art of Numbers. The art of numbers was divided into nine forms. This is said to be the foundation of what is later known as Nine Chapter Arithmetic. Some mathematical books of the Chou era are still available today. Among them are *Chou-pi-suan-ching* and *Chin-chang-guan-ching*. The former is mainly concerned with astronomy and, interestingly, contains the heliocentric theory. The latter was a basis of Nine Chapter Arithmetic. In what follows, we will look into it rather closely. It is divided into nine chapters which together constitute every-day arithmetic. Each chapter contains appropriate problems and each problem in turn is divided into three parts: question, answer and method. The method here, unlike solutions in today's mathematics, does not contain reasoning but merely shows how to compute the answer. In this sense, mathematics then was a skill rather than a science. It is, nevertheless, interesting to note that it uses fractions as well as positive and negative numbers. Thus the concept of negative numbers was used in China well before a similar notion was invented in Western nations, although it arose in case of China, as an intuitive object from such considerations as 'increasing and decreasing' and 'gaining and losing," rather than as a theoretic extension. Following is an examination of Nine Chapter Arithmetic by selecting one problem from each chapter.

Chapter I Rice-fields. This mainly deals with measurements.

Q*: Find the area of a field which is 3 1/3 *po* ** wide and 5 2/5 *po* long.

A: 18 square *po*.

Chapter II Grains. This shows how to exchange different kinds of grains.

Q: How much beans can one get with 3 1/30 *tu* *** of millet?

A. 2 73/100 *tu*. (A list of the exchange rates among various items is given in the text.)

Chapter III Proportional Distribution.

Q: Three persons have 560, 350 and 180 coins respectively. They together must pay 100 coins to pass the custom office. They want to pay in proportion. How much must each pay?

A: 51 41/109, 32 12/109, 16 56/109.

Chapter IV Square and Square Roots.

Q: The area of a square is 55,225 square *po*. Find the length of a side.

A: 235 *po*. (In the text, methods of squaring and extracting square roots are shown and they are similar to the standard methods of today.)

Chapter V Volumes.

Q: Given a 51,824 feet **** long cylinder of which the base is a trapezoid with an upper side of 18 feet, lower side 3 6/10 feet and height 18 feet. Find the volume.

A: 10,074,585.6 cubic feet.

Chapter VI Balance.

Q: A person leaves the capital and reaches

* Q and A denote question and answer respectively.
** *Po* is a unit of length.
*** *Tu* is a unit of volume.
**** The foot used here is a Chinese foot.

Ch'i in five days. A second person leaves Ch'i and reaches the capital in seven days. If the second person left Ch'i two days ago and the first leaves the capital now, in how many days will they meet on the way?

A : In 2 1/12 days.

Chapter VII More and Less.

Q : A certain number of persons want to buy jointly an item at a certain price. If each pays 8 coins, they overpay 3 coins. If each pays 7 coins, they pay 4 coins short. Find the number of the persons and the price of the item.

A : 7 persons and 53 coins.

Chapter VIII Equations. This chapter shows how to solve systems of simultaneous equations by using "counting sticks." Counting sticks are of two colors, red and black. Red sticks are for positive numbers and black ones for negative numbers.

Q : If one sells 2 cows and 5 sheep and buys 13 pigs, then he earns 1000 coins. Also, he can give 3 cows and 3 pigs in exchange for 9 sheep. Finally, if he sells 6 sheep and 8 pigs, then he must pay extra 600 coins in order to buy 5 cows. Find the itemized prices.

A : 1,200 coins per cow, 500 per sheep and 300 per pig.

Chap. IX Right Triangles.

Q : Given a right triangle of height 3 feet and base 4 feet. Find the length of the hypotenuse.

A : 5 feet.

The relations among the lengths of the sides of a right triangle have been known in China since quite early times. In the era of the Three Kingdoms, Liu Hui of Wei, who wrote the appendix to Nine Chapter Arithmetic, sharpened the value of the ratio of the circumference of a circle to its diameter which was until then known as 3. He started by inscribing a regular hexagon in a circle. Then he doubled the number of sides each time until a regular 96-angled polygon was inscribed, from which he derived an approximate value of $\pi - 3$ 3.141024. Later at the end of Liu Sing dynasty, Tsu Ch'ung-chih of South Hsu-chon obtained a more precise result: 3.141526 $<\pi<$ 3.1415927. In terms of fractions, it was claimed that the exact value of π was 355/113 and an approximate value 22/7. This result was included in his book "Chui-shu."

Throughout Chinese history, the center of philosophy was occupied by politics and ethics. Mathematics then was merely a part of the cultural background. It was in the Sui and Tang dynasties when mathematics were officially established as part of the national examination for governmental services. Naturally, this was soon imitated by Korea. As computing tools, Chinese used "binding ropes" at first, then later bamboo-made rods. "Suntsu-Suanching" published in Sui and Tang would be a suitable text-book. It explains how to use counting sticks. They are placed vertically for the first, 100-th, 10000-th places, etc., and horizontally for 10-th, 1000-th places, etc. They are placed left to right.

```
              1 2 3 4 5 6 7 8 9
vertical      | || ||| |||| ||||| ⊤ ⊤ ⊤ ⊤
horizontal    — = ≡ ≣ ≣ ⊥ ⊥ ⊥ ⊥
```

For instance, | ⊥ ⊤ = ⊤ stands for 16728. Red and black sticks were used to denote positive and negative numbers respectively, while triangular (positive numbers) and square (negative numbers) cylinders were used sometimes. Zero was denoted by O. For polynominal equations, square-shaped arithmetic boards, made of paper or wood, were used. The following picture shows the equation $x^2 - 7x + 12 = 0$ placed on an arithmetic

10^4	10^3	10^2	10	1	10^{-1}	10^{-2}	10^{-3}	⋯		
萬	千	百	十	一	分	厘	毛	⋯		
									商	answer
			—	‖					實	constant
									法	X
									廉	X^2
									隅	X^3
										X^4

board. Extra columns for explanations were included for the convenience of the reader. As is seen here, an extra stick was always placed for the linear term.

This method of solving equation is similar to Horner's method. Polynominal equations are also treated in the famous book "Suan-hsueh-ch'i-meng" (1299) by Chin Shin-chien of the Yuan dynasty. This book was soon introduced to Korea but was no longer available in China after the seemingly endless revolutions. It was, curiously, Korea which later made this book available in China again. Through the Japanese invasion of Korea in 1592, this book became available in Japan and became the "Bible" of Japanese mathematicians. The method therein allows one to solve polynomial equations of any degree and obtain answers in infinite decimals. Thus they had irrational numbers. It was typical of Oriental people that they accepted the existence of irrational numbers only intuitively but did not look at them as Western people did in the theory of equations. Another important result in "Suan-hsueh-ch'i-meng" is one on progressions. For instance, the following results were obtained:

$1+2+\ldots+n = (n^2+n)/2$,
$1^2+2^2+\ldots+n^2 = (2n^3+3n^2+n)/6$,
$1^3+2^3+\ldots+n^3 = (n^4+2n^3n^2)/4$ and so on up to the 11-th powers.
$1+(1+2)+(1+2+3)+\ldots+(1+2+\ldots+n) = (n^3+3n^2+2n)/6$,
$1+4+10+20+\ldots$ (each term here is a partial sum of the above) $= (n^4+6n^3+11n^2+6n)/24$,
$1+5+15+35+\ldots$ (each term here is a partial sum of the above) $= (n^5+10n^4+35n^3+50n^2+24n)/120$, etc.

Also some results on difference equations and linear equations are contained.

Another work which deserves mention is Suan-fa-tungtsuan (1592) by Cheng Ta-wei of the Ming dynasty consisting of 16 volumes. It is simply written and quite interesting. It can be mastered without an instructor. This was also introduced to Japan during the Japanese invasion of Korea in 1592. This book was translated into Japanese and appeared as Jingoki in the Wasan (Japanese mathematics) circle. Problems it contains include:

Q : Across the fence, one hears some people trying to distribute silver coins equally among themselves. He knows neither the number of people nor of coins. If each takes 7 coins then 4 will be left over. If each takes 9 then 8 will be short.

A : 6 people, 46 coins.

Q : I can see a seven-storeyed tower in the distance. Red lights are seen on each floor, doubling in numbers going down. Together 381 lights are seen. Now can you tell me how many lights are on the top ?

A : 3.

Q : One hundred cakes and one hundred monks. Each senior monk takes three cakes. Each junior monk takes one third. How many senior and junior monks ?

A : 25 seniors and 75 juniors.

Q : Three good daughters of Chang's family are married.

They want frequently to be back home to help their parents.

The first daughter wedded in the eastern village, comes home every three days.

The second daughter living in the western village comes every five days.

The smallest daughter lives far south. Yet she comes home every seven days.

When will they meet at home to drink tea together ?

Wise men will kindly answer.

A : In 105 days.

Shu-chiu-chiang by Chin Thiu-chao treats more advanced mathematics. "Shu-li-hsing-yun" published in Ching dynasty reveals the introduction of Western mathematics. This book was soon introduced to Korea.

Among mathematical books written by Koreans, *Mukssachip* by Kyong Sonching and *Kusuryak* by Choe Sokchong should be mentioned in addition to the *Sanhak-chungeui* by Nam Pyonggil which treats more advanced mathematics. *Sansul-Kwankyon* by Yi Sanghyok which was published in the 6th year of King Cholchong (1855) contains the power series of trigonometric functions. Due to the traditional national policy of seclusion, new mathematics were not introduced until the late part of the Yi dynasty during which books such as *Sanhak-Tongnon* and *Sanhak-Sinpyon* were published and widely read. Nevertheless, such a long tradition in Korea in mathematics helps the new generation in producing good mathematicians in every field, particularly after World War II. By way of conclusion, it should be noted that Professor Chang Kiwon of Yonsei University perhaps is the leading figure in the field of history of Korean mathematics.

Physics

In ancient times, in every country of the world, natural sciences were represented by astronomy and meteorology. In Korea, from the Koryo period, the scientific learning of astronomy carried from China was circulated, and the stone-built astronomical observatory in the year A.D. 647 during the Silla period is still in existence.

In A.D. 505 the use and methods of storing ice for summer were known and there was an extensive program for the construction of ice storage. As has been well-known, movable type was made of wood in 1395, of copper in 1403, and of lead in 1436. Two hundred years before Castelli (Italy), Koreans made a copper rain gauge in the year 1442. These are some of the Korean contributions to natural sciences.

During the pre-Japanese period, efforts were made to advance studies and research in natural sciences, but they failed to attain an original experimental character. However, later in the Japanese period, Chosun Christian College (the forerunner of the present Yonsei University) set up the Department of Physics and Mathematics, and Keijo Imperial University instituted the Department of Physics in the College of Technology, so that advanced studies in physics were formally initiated. This was the cradle period of Korea's studies in physics.

Since Keijo Imperial University admitted only a nominal number of Koreans, many Korean aspirants for advanced studies in physics were compelled to go to Japan or America. As of August 15, 1949 there were but eleven who had properly completed a college education in the field of physics, among whom only two were graduates of Keijo Imperial University, eight of them from colleges in Japan and one from an American institution.

After the Liberation many of the former colleges acquired the status of university, and there have since been many new universities. At present there are twenty-three institutions of higher learning which maintain separate departments of physics, and the total number of students these departments admit annually is approximately 560.

In 1948, the physicists who returned from their tour of study abroad organized the physical Society of Korea and sponsored lectures and seminars but the organization was hampered in its activities by systematic Communist sabotage. The reorganization of the Society took place at Pusan during the Korean War. Dr. Choe Kyunam was elected the president, Professors Pak Choljae and Kwon Yongdae the vice-presidents.

Since 1953 there have been numerous lectures and seminars sponsored by the Society and in 1954 the Society became affiliated with UNESCO.

In 1954 faculty members and students in the field of physics organized the Physical Society of Seoul National University, and since then continued to publish a "Journal of Physics" annually contributing to the world of Korean physicists. Yonsei University has a similar organization and has been publishing a similar journal.

In the meantime, the number of graduates in the field of physics increased to a considerable degree, and the students in this field continue their studies in such countries

XVI NATURAL SCIENCES

as the United States, England, West Germany, Austria, France, Canada, etc. There are at present ten physicists who hold Ph.D. degrees.

In connection with the Atomic Energy Council projects, an atomic reactor is being installed, and scholarships administered by the government for nuclear scientists enabled many of them to continue or properly conclude their studies abroad.

The laboratory facilities available at the time of the Liberation were considerable, but all of these important facilities were destroyed during the Korean War. With the assistance of the United Nation Korean Reconstruction Agency, seven of the universities in Korea set up their laboratories anew and many other private institutions of higher learning followed.

The major scientific equipment currently installed in Korea:

1. Cyclotron, 30 cm, 1 MeV p-beam
   (Seoul National University)
2. Nuclear Research Microscope, ORTHOLUX (Seoul National University)
3. X-ray apparatus
   (Seoul National University, Korea University, and Yonsei University)
4. Geiger-Muller counter
   (Ministry of Defense, Seoul National University, Tongguk University, Kyongbuk University and Seoul Normal College)
5. Mass Spectrometer
   (Ministry of Defense)
6. Electron Microscope
   (Ministry of Defense, and Kyongbuk University)
7. Spectrograph
   (Ministry of Defense, and Songgyungwan University)
8. Supersonic Wave Generator
   (Ministry of Defense)
9. Shock Tube
   (Tonga University)

Chemistry

Historical Summary of Chemical Studies

As in many other fields of intellectual pursuit, Korea has a laudable record in chemical studies. Achievements in the application of chemical knowledge to everyday life, medicine, weapons and other artifacts were considerable.

There have been many changes in the attitudes of chemists during the course of the long history of this science in Korea. There was a time when, as in many other regions, the chemical pursuit was almost exclusively alchemical.

Modern chemistry was introduced to Korea as a part of general modern science from Europe. Korea encountered it along with Christianity during the Ming and the Ching periods of China. Although there was a strong indigenous movement of scholars for a positivistic epistemological system, this was suppressed by the feudal isolationist policy.

During the Japanese period, there was a serious program for teaching chemistry to Koreans, but the program was much too devoted to producing half-educated Korean chemists for the purpose of colonial administration. Due to the peculiar geo-political position of Korea, Japan constructed in Korea many chemical factories for metal refining, leather processing, sugar refining, and such plants as ceramic factories, paper mills, cement, synthetic fibre, mitrates, carbide, sodium plants, etc., but all of these were destroyed during the Korean War in 1950 and immediately following.

Present state of Chemical Studies

It can be said that the chemical studies by Koreans in the contemporary period did not start until the Liberation. While only a limited number of Koreans obtained their advanced education in chemistry during the Japanese period since the Liberation, the number of students doing advanced studies in chemistry increased markedly and many of them have had opportunities to learn abroad in the United States and other countries. There are at present many Korean chemists teaching advanced courses in American universities and continuing their research at various foreign institutes. There has been continuous qualitative as well as quantitative improvement in the laboratory facilities available in Korea for studies in chemistry.

There is still room for considerable improvement however. Advancement since the standstill of the Korean War was bound to be marked and development statistics can lead to deceptive optimism.

Training in Chemistry

There are twenty-four institutions offering courses in theoretical chemistry; the leading institutions among these are Seoul National University and Yonsei University. These institutions have an annual admission quota for 3,000 B.S. candidates and 120 graduate students for higher degrees. There are about 250 Korean students studying chemistry abroad, mainly in the United States. There are, in addition, a considerable number of chemists who returned to Korea from abroad after obtaining advanced degrees in chemistry. However, the supply of chemistry professors is not adequate.

Research facilities are utterly lacking, and even the basic equipment for teaching of college chemistry courses are not nearly adequate, not to mention the dearth of essential books. That many of the Korean students of chemistry abroad attain distinction is, however, proof that the training of theoretical chemistry in Korea is superior. Besides teaching theoretical chemistry, many professional schools offer courses in applied chemistry, e.g. agricultural college, medical school, pharmaceutical college, engineering school, etc. Many of these professional schools offer such courses as biochemistry, organic chemistry, inorganic chemistry, Analytic Chemistry, etc.

Major Activities of Chemists

While the number of chemists in Korea is limited, there are many accomplished chemists in various fields of chemistry, and the majority of these chemists are engaged in professorial work. They have had, in most instances, obtained their training in America, France, England, Germany, Japan, etc. In addition, there are quite a few Korean chemists teaching at foreign institutions of higher learning, for example, Professor Yi Taegyu (physical chemistry), University of Utah; Professor Choe Sangop (physical organic chemistry), Boston University; Professor Ham Poksun (organic synthetic chemistry and biochemistry), University of Paris. Since there are many Koreans now working toward professional degrees abroad, it it expected that the shortage of chemists felt at present will soon be dissipated. A unique characteristic of Korean students of chemistry is that, due to the lack of laboratory equipment, on the one hand, and to the sound training they receive in mathematics and theoretical physics, on the other, they usually go into the fields of physical chemistry, quantum chemistry, theoretical organic chemistry, dynamic biochemistry, and biochemistry.

Research facilities are at present practically non-existent, except for the workshops of professors, as far as theoretical chemistry is concerned. For research in applied chemistry there are a few laboratories connected with government administrative functions:

Central Chemical Laboratory
   (Health, food, drug, etc.)
Central Technological Laboratory
   (Chemical industry)

Ministry of Defense Laboratory
   (Weapon, military supply, etc.)
Geological Survey of Korea
   (Geological and ore analysis)
Seoul National University Medical Herb Laboratory (Herb analysis)
Quarantine Laboratory
   (Vaccine, serum, etc.)
Atomic Energy Laboratory
   (Radioactive matters)

These laboratories are adequately equipped through government funds and foreign (especially American) aid supplies. The Atomic Energy Laboratory, for example, which was scheduled to be completed by the end of 1959, is a project initiated by the Korean-US Agreement on the Peaceful Uses of Atomic Energy signed in February 1956 and to be placed under the direct jurisdiction of the Office of the President. It is intended to do all laboratory work pertaining to the isotopes of fissionable matters. Korea has been repeatedly represented at the atomic energy conferences sponsored by UNESCO in recent years. The government has granted 84 scholarships for students of nuclear science to study abroad during the period from 1955 through 1958 and 21 were granted in 1959. In addition there are 14 students in the field who are supported by foreign scholarships.

The atomic reactor currently being installed, Triga Mark II type, is primarily for instruction purposes, but it will facilitate production of isotopes and research works. It is expected to contribute much to the study and development of nuclear science in the Republic of Korea.

The first meeting of nuclear scientists in Korea was held in June 1959. The most important items dealt with were 13 theses concerning I^{131}, Ca^{45}, P^{32}, C^{14}, Fe and other radioactive isotopes and 6 theses dealing with various radioactive minerals in Korea. This was a significant milestone in the development of science in Korea, and it is noteworthy that the Seoul National University maintains an Atomic Research Committee.

There are various organizations of academic character, i.e., the Chemical Society of Korea and the Pharmaceutical Society of Korea, both of which publish bulletins periodically.

Prospects

Although chemical learning has a very ancient background here, it is still in a formative period as a modern science. The modest but real achievements of Korean chemists during the short span of years since it acquired modern outlook indicates that it is under-equipped and this contributes to underdevelopment. As soon as adequate facilities are made available, it is expected that Korea will make decisive contributions in chemistry especially in the fields of physical chemistry and biochemistry.

Medical Science

Western Medicine

Western medicine was introduced to Korea through two routes – one, directly from the United States; two, indirectly from China and Japan.

Credit for opening the first route should go to the American doctor, Horace Newton Allen. It was Dr. Allen who first impressed upon the Korean public the efficiency of Western medicine by curing numerous wounded soldiers during the outbreak of the *Kabo* revolt of 1884. He was subsequently appointed physician to the *Chejungwon*, hospital for the royal household, and soon began teaching American medicine to selected Koreans.

Other American doctors followed his trail to the *Chejungwon*, culminating in the arrival of Dr. O. R. Evison, a former professor of Canada's Toronto Mediccal College, who was sent by the North American Presbyterian Board in January 1893. This mission group soon after reorganized the *Chejungwon* as a charity hospital when changing political conditions made it impossible for the royal household to maintain the establishment. Dr. Evison, however, continued to render what has proved to be significant contributions. In 1899, he established an attached medical school and taught pathology, pharmacology, bacteriology and hygiene from text-books he had translated himself while serving as head of the *Chejungwon*. In 1900, he built a hospital with a 15,000-dollar donation from an Ohio pastor, Mr. D. H. Severance, after whom the hospital was named. From the outset, Dr. Evison not only practised but also taught medicine. From an enrollment of four students, his classes grew to provide Korea with one of the most outstanding establishment, the Severance College and Hospital. The College has amalgamated with the Yonhui University (Chosun Christian University) in recent years to provide the Medical College to the combined Yonsei University body of colleges. The Hospital, however, remains independent.

The names of Allen and Evison stand, indeed, as monuments in the introduction of Western medicine to Korea.

The first application of Japanese medicine came in 1880 with the return from Japan of Chi Sogyong, pioneer student in Western medicine. Chi specialized in small-pox vaccination, and the little establishment he set up to train specialists in small-pox was the first of its kind undertaken by a Korean.

In 1895 (32nd year of Kojong), a Bureau of Public Health was installed and preventive measures against epidemics put into effect. Thus, ports were quarantined and small-pox vaccinations extended. A major mission was undertaken jointly by the state medical school and Dr. Evison's private medical school when they were charged with the responsibility of curbing an epidemic outbreak in Manchuria in 1900.

From the opening of the twentieth century, the Japanese began to play an increasingly important role in expanding the Korean medical field. In 1907, they founded a Korea Hospital in Seoul by annexing the state medical school and its attached hopital and, in 1909, they were instrumental in strengthening public medical institutions. For all that, American medicine continued to prevail everywhere through the Severance institutions even after the Annexation.

There is little evidence to determine what contributions exactly the Chinese had rendered in introducing Western medicine to Korea. All we can say is that they contributed in some way.

There were quite a number of medical colleges by now and they were turning out many Korean doctors. A number of students went abroad.

The present system of medical education, largely patterned along American lines as all educational systems after the Liberation, follows:

Graduates of regular high schools are entitled to receive two years of premedical course which in turn makes them eligible for four more years of medical course. At the end of these six years, they are given diplomas but can obtain practitioners' licences only after qualifying themselves by passing an examination given by the Ministry of Health and Social Affairs.

There are nine medical colleges in Korea today: namely, the Medical College of Seoul National University; Medical College of Yonsei University; the Sudo Medical College; Medical Department of Catholic College; Medical College of Pusan National University; Medical College of Chonnam University; Medical College of Kyongbuk University. These institutions together turn out more than five hundred doctors every year.

There are approximately 6,500 physicians in Korea. Although they are relatively well distributed over the country, the tendency is to prefer big cities to rural communities. This leaves many rural areas without even a single doctor.

Chinese Herb Medicine

Ancient Koreans presumably used some

varieties of herb as medicine. Certainly, during the Lolang period of Chinese cultural importations, they must have exchanged medical knowledge with the Central Kingdom. There is reference in old Chinese medical records to the effect that the people of Korea used some kind of operational knife or needle made out of stone at the time. The oldest Chinese book on pharmacology extant (452-536 B.C.), proves that herb medicine was known in Korea, if nothing else.

Officially, however, the use of Chinese medical drugs began in the year A.D. 561, long after they had been developed and improved in China and other countries of Asia. It was introduced to the Koguryo court by a citizen of Han, Chih Tsung, who carried many books of medicine and acupuncture with him. From Koguryo, it spread to Paekche and Silla. The foreign medicine, known for six hundred years, now became promptly adjusted to the Korean way of life and to the Korean constitution.

Records show that the Three Kingdoms (57 B.C.-A.D. 936) laid the premium on the health of the state and the pursuit of medical practice. The Silla rulers, Sinmun and Kyongmun, are noted for creating medical doctorates to encourage the profession, the former toward the close of the 7th century, the latter toward the end of the 9th. The doctorates indicate the extent to which the profession had gained social recognition.

In this connection, it should be mentioned that Japanese knowledge of Chinese medicine came through Korea, especially from Paekche and Silla. The worldwide reputation that the city of Osaka today enjoys as the world capital for drugs may be traced back to the Koguryo citizen, Tongnae, who was invited by a Japanese Emperor in A.D. 459 to teach medicine in Japan. He and his descendents practised medicine for generations in that country under the exceptional patronage of successive Emperors.

By the middle of the Three Kingdoms era, Korea had learned all there was to know from China and began putting out original works instead of referring to Chinese books.

Thus there was the *Silla Pobsabang* (literally, Monks' Prescriptions of Silla) and the *Paekche Sinjippang* (New Prescriptions of Paekche). Outstanding works of the succeeding Koryo dynasty were the *Chejung Ippyobang* (Effective Public Prescriptions) and *Ouichjal Yobcng* (a Gist of the Court Physician's Prescriptions), published in 1160 and 1226 respectively.

Yi Medicine

It was during the Yi dynasty that herb medicine truly flowered. No less than one hundred and fifty books were turned out on the subject during some five hundred years of supremacy ended only with the introduction of Western medicine from the West.

The first most important work was the "*Hyangyak Chipsongbang*," a collection of prescriptions for cures in the provinces. The conviction that the acquired knowledge on Chinese medicine should be based on native-grown herbs was not new to the Yi kingdom. Koryo herb doctors were also interested in their profession to meet Korean natural resources and, in the latter half of the Koryo dynasty, one, Kwon Chunghwa, produced a work called the "*Hyangyak Kanibang*." This book offered simplified prescriptions for use in indigenous herbs. During the enlightened "Sejong age" of the Yi dynasty, three outstanding medical scholars, Yu Hyodong, No Chungye and Pak Yungdok, re-edited Kwon's "*Hyangyak Kanibang*" and added abundantly to its sparse contents. The result was "*Hyangyak Chipsongbang*." Published in 1433, in 85 chapters and 30 books, the work is regarded as a monumental effort in independent Korean medicine.

Supplementing this concentration on local herbs was a comprehensive work on a whole range of the Chinese medical heritage. At least sixteen scholars, including No Chungye who had participated in the "*Hyangyak Chipsongbang*" project, delved into one hundred and fifty Chinese works of the Tang, Sung, Yuan and the early Ming periods in order to classify the name of each disease in their proper order and category. The result was the "*Uibang Nuchwi*" (Comprehensive Prescriptions), published in 1445 in 266 chapters. A valuable source of reference to the total accumulation of Chinese medical literature, the *"Uibang Nuchwi"* was looted by the Japanese warlord, Kato Kiyomasa, during the Hideyoshi invasion and is now kept as national treasure in Japan.

The *"Tongui Pogam"* (literary, Eastern Medicine Rare Survey), published 1597-1611 in 25 chapters, is interesting in the light of a modern school of thought. A practical attempt as contrasted with former theoretical approaches, the central idea of its author, Ho Chun, lay in his conviction that diseases arose from the disharmony of three elements, *chong, ki* and *sin. Chong*, among other things, referred to hormones; *ki* was related to involuntary nervous systems or what in modern medical parlance may be called bioelectric responses; *sin* referred to damages caused by mental attributes upon the nerve center. On the whole, the theory was identical to the more aloof school of stresses and impulses so widely discussed in the contemporary world of medicine. His research methods knew nothing of modern chemicophysical experimentation but, rather, entailed the closest observations and examinations of a deductive theory that, in detail, is at once more specific and through the five organs of our senses. It was more systematic than the modern stress theory.

Ho Chun's emphasis that mental and physical sanitation in medical treatments was secondary is not far from the contemporary psychosomatic approach. That he could probe the cause of human ailments in such a detailed manner and yield findings unsurpassed by modern medicine is one sound reason why herb medicine is still a practical need today. With the *"Tongui Pogam,"* the superiority of Korean medicine was acknowledged throughout the Orient. The book is printed not only on Formosa but also in China proper as an essential handbook for herb medical cures.

Other Important Works

Uimun Pogam(Doctor's Handbook) and *Chejung Sinpyong* (New Public Edition) by Chu Myongsin, published 1724 and 1799 respectively as concised editions of the *Tongui Pogam*;

Tongabang Yukkiron (Oriental Theory of the Six Elements) by Cho Chongjun, published 1749 - one of the best works on pediatrics;

Magwa Hoetong by Chong Yakyong in 1788, a complete book on scarlet fever;

Taesan Yorok by No Chungye, published 1434, deals with the essence of obstetrics, antenatal training puericulture, baby care, etc.

Taesan Chipyo, a concise book on child-births by Ho Chun (1608);

Mulmyongo (a study of names) by Yu Hui is a reappraisal of traditional pharmacology, supplemented by a song-book called Yaksongga, which is supposed to help the begginner remember the effect of herbs by chanting;

Saam Chimgugyol and *ChimguKyonghombang*, 16th and 17th century works on acupuncture;

Chong Pibang which offers surgical remedy for tumor;

Poju Muwonnok (1744) and Revised *Muwonnok* in *hangul* (1790), the crystallization of long experience in medical jurisprudence as competent as any modern works.

Finally, there was the *sasang* theory of herb medicine, first made public in 1901 by Yi Chema (1837-1899). A revolutionary theory, it divides individuals into four types according to their constitution and temperament as follows;

a) *Taeyangin* (big lung, small liver)
b) *Taeumin* (big liver, small lung)
c) *Soyangin* (big pancrea, small kidney)
d) *Soumin* (big kidney, small pancrea)

Sasang treatment is guided by these types rather than by the nature of the disease. Thus the treatment may differ even in the case of the same disease if types are different.

Modern Apathy

Decline in herb medical practice set in during the last years of the Yi dynasty and continued throughout the long Japanese rule. The heady promises of the Liberation had their effects on herb practitioners as on everybody else, but lack of scholars and public apathy blocked their expectations. The most concrete achievement was the establishment of a private educational institute in March 1948 by the herb druggists. The institute made regular college status in 1953 and opened a new pharmacology course in 1955, rechristening itself as the Tongyang Uiyak Taehak (College of Oriental Medicine). Three hundred and fifty graduates of this college gained official status as herb practitioners after the Medical Act of September 25, 1952, and many others obtained qualification through government examinations. Today, there are a total 2,643 men qualified to give herb medical cures as by the last count in September 1959.

It must be remembered that herb medicine has to be encouraged under the most discouraging circumstances. There have been bitter, collective attempts by practitioners of Western medicine to suppress its revival. Even without such opposition, only little about herb medical researches can trickle out to the general public in the face of popular knowledge about Western pharmaceutics. About the only noteworthy works in recent years were Cho Honyong's *Hanuihak Wonnon* (Fundamentals in Herb Medicine), issued in 1935, and No Chunghwi's essays of 1951.

Herb medicine must tread a very slow and intermittent path. It is, however, considered to be a most important field, requiring not neglect but more research work. This undoubtedly will be forthcoming when social conditions are improved.

Pharmacology

Primitive mankind has universally attributed illnesses either to gods or evil spirits. They relied upon prayers or spells for cures. They noticed other things, too: here was a herb which caused vomits, there a bark which resulted in loose bowels, and over there, a plant which killed the animal. Out of such observations arose the use of herb medicine. With increased knowledge, they started to dry up and store herbs for off-season use.

Old Korean literature tells us that our ancestors used moxa and garlic as medicine. Throughout the two thousand years from Tangun through Puyo to the historical Three Kingdoms Period, the people believed that deities produced diseases. However, they made some progress in pharmaceutical cures, learning, among other things, how to make plaster for external wounds and boil tunic for internal ailments. Boiling in itself meant that they knew something about chemistry.

During the Three Kingdoms Period (57 B.C.-A.D. 936), exchange of medical knowledge with China was strongly promoted. Koguryo as the nearest state to China was especially vigorous, importing not only Chinese pharmacology but also Indian medicine which came with Buddhism.

In the era of Koguryo's King Pyongwon, many medical books were imported, the "Hungti Taching," "Huiwaitien," "Waiching," "Shennung Pentsaoching," "Wuchin Pentsao," "Tungchun Yolu," "Pentsaoching" and "Mingi Pelu." Silla imported most of her medical library from Koguryo or Paekche, in addition to outstanding works like the "Tang Pentsao," "Pentsao Shihi" and "Haiyo Pentsao" which indicated that the kingdom was influenced more by the Sui and Tang dynasties than by any previous period. In the time of the Wei and Chin dynasties, Korean pharmacology was hardly recognizable from the simple practices of their primitive ancestors, so completely had its character been changed under long Chinese influences.

The "Shennung Pentsaoching" describes every characteristic of Oriental medicine and, as such, is one of the most valuable of medical works. It lists 365 herbs to correspond with the number of days in the year. Those herbs are divided into three categories – good, better, best. The best, listing 120, are subscribed for liberal use as body building tunic.

The better, listing 120 herbs, are for cures of ailments and physical weakness. The good, classifying 125, were rather poisonous and prescribed for diseases only. The manner of classifications eloquently suggests their Taoist origin.

The book instructs, among many other things, (1) how to make a suitable mixture, (2) how to collect and dry the herb, (3) whether or not to boil, (4) whether or not to make the medicine in tablet or powder form, boiled in water or liquor, (5) when to take the dosage. In short, it deals with the whole range of pharmacology.

The "Pentsao Kangmu" was a book on alchemy and shared greatly in developing early Korean medicine. Alchemy came from the West and was intensely practiced in China, where they not surprisingly tried to transform cheap metals like copper, iron and mercury into silver or gold in quest of the elixir of life.

The references in Chinese literature to the superb art of Koguryo alchemy underlines the advanced chemical knowledge of that kingdom, a fact reinforced by the murals appearing on its tombs.

In Paekche, medicine was already an independent vocation. The doctor and the pharmaceutist belonged to separate professions. The high tide of development was reached after the Silla Unity when medical research work, centering on the "Shennung," was extensively pursued along lines of original researches and based on experience and observation.

During the Koryo era, which introduced Sung medicine, medical institutions became yet more firmly consolidated and medicine became a truly original and independent practice. A *taeigam* (literally, grand medical supervisor) was newly installed in office to supervise medical affairs and a bureau of the court physician, the *Sangyakkuk* or *pongiso*. Public hospitals were also built and much knowledge about Western medicine resulted from close contacts with the Yuan kingdom. Above all, medical education was enhanced. Two medical schools were established, one in Pyongyang and the other in Songdo, the Koryo capital. Doctors were also dispatched to the provinces to spread enlightenment and state examination system for medicine founded.

The early Yi period saw these great strides:

(1) One medical instructor was stationed in every province.

(2) Emissaries were sent abroad to study the differences between foreign and domestic herbs. They published the results of their findings in the *Hyangyak Chesaengjip Songbang* (a Collection of Prescriptions for Domestic Herbs), and *Uibang Yujip* (a Collection of Prescriptions). The first medical books written by Koreans, these books were sent to Japan after diplomatic relations were opened between the two countries.

(3) Charity hospitals, called the *Heminso*, were built for poor patients, *Hwalinso* establishments for the general public. In the court, there were two kinds of physicians, the teamaker (*Sangta*) and the medicine-maker (*Sangyak*) whose functions were to prepare the royal herb bowl. Both court and public physicians were graded in eight and eleven orders respectively.

(4) Ho Chun edited his "*Tonguibogam*" (see Chinese Herb Medicine) by order of King Sonjo.

Industrial progress and trade prosperity increased drug exchanges. The encouragement of *ginseng* production needs special mention, for *ginseng* was the most famous of all herbs.

Ginseng was freely traded until the advent of Koryo when supplies began to grow shorter every year. By the Yi era, it was good for export in the form of tribute only. Cultivation now began to be encouraged in Kyongsang-do province. The successful example there was later emulated in Cholla-do. By King Chongjo's reign, the herb was processed into red *ginseng* and exported to China. This accelerated production and the site of *ginseng* cultivation moved to Kaesong where the soil and climate is best suited, leading to the development of the famed Kaesong *ginseng* of today.

In the latter Yi years, a medical school called Uihakkyo, was founded (Kojong 36).

To this was attached a hospital four years later. This institution, later reorganized as the Taehan Uiwon (Korean Medical Institute), had separate schools for medicine and pharmacology.

With the introduction of Western medicine (see Western Medicine), the number of pharmacies dealing in Western drugs increased. Western medicine stirred demand for Western pharmacology and they were met by the establishment in 1915 of the Chosun Yakhakkyo (Korea Pharmaceutical School), forerunner of the present College of Pharmacology of the Seoul National University.

The Chosun Yakhakkyo, reorganized as the Kyongsong Yakhak Chonmunhakkyo (Seoul Pharmaceutical College) in 1950, was the sole educational institute of its kind before the Liberation. Today, there are thirteen such colleges turning out seven hundred to eight hundred graduates every year.

The colleges offer a four-year course and the graduate acquires licence only after passing the national examination.

Other active establishments are: the Chemical Research Center of the Ministry of Health and Social Affairs, a prominent pharmaceutical research institute whose history goes decades back; Drug Research Center, Seoul National University, another important researcher; Korean Pharmaceutical Society, founded in 1920, issues four journals every year; and Drugs Research Center, Ministry of Health and Social Affairs, which conducts overall research.

The above short history tells us that research work on modern pharmacology, begun only after the Liberation, is still in the cradle. On the other hand, it indicates that Korean herb medicine, developed over thousands of years, has something of value even though it is philosophical rather scientific in approach. Adjustment and modernization of herb medicine is surely one of the missions of Korean pharmacologists today.

Dietetics

Outline of Background

It is generally accepted that dietetics was first introduced to Korea in 1924 by J. D. Vanbushirk, then professor of biochemistry at the Severance Medical College. His is the first known report about the composition of Korean food and its nutritional values.

The first Korean research worker on dietetics was Professor Yi Soksin, likewise a biochemistry teacher at the Severance with a doctor's degree from Berlin University.

In time, nursery schools and women's colleges were giving regular courses in dietetics, while medical and pharmaceutical colleges kept up a modicum of research studies and advanced teaching.

In the last years of the Japanese administration, the importance of dietetics was suddenly recognized. Specialists were assigned to the Health Experimental Center (forerunner of the present Chemical Research Center of the Ministry of Health and Social Affairs) to analyze the contents of Korean food and edible plants. Han Kudong, Dean of the Pharmaceutical College of the Seoul National University, the late Dr. Kim Hojik, and Chae Yesok, Deputy Director of the Chemical Research Center of the Health-Social Ministry, were members of this Center.

During the American Military Administration, the importance of ethics was yet further emphasized and a dietetics division of the Chemical Research Center conducted a vigorous study under the direction of Chae Yesok who made a report on the chemical compositions of common Korean foodstuffs.

Institutions and Agencies

The Ministry of Health and Social Affairs

is the government agency directly responsible for nutritional problems. The Ministry of Education, however, is in charge of the educational aspects while the Ministry of Agriculture carries out campaigns through such instruments as the 4-H Clubs and the Ministry of National Defense maintains its own research institution in the interests of the armed forces personnel.

A list of the active research agencies follows:

1) Dietetics Division, Chemical Research Center, Ministry of Health and Social Affairs
2) Guidance Bureau, Agriculture Center, Ministry of Agriculture
3) Food Nutrition Section, Ministry of National Defense Laboratory.
4) Food Processing Division, Industrial Research Center, Ministry of Commerce and Industry
5) Fishery Center, Office of Marine Affairs
6) Korea Dietetics Society
7) Nutrition Specialist Committee, FAO Korea Association
8) Korea Home Economy Society

In addition to these organizations, formation of a central committee of nutrition is underway as recommended by FAO with key members of the agencies concerned.

Present Aspects in Research:

1) The Chemical Research Center:
Studies biochemical and dietetic contents of Korean ferments;
studies vitamin and amino-acid values of Korean food;
conducts research work to establish method of food analysis and studies high protein foods.

2) The Science Research Center:
Concentrates on improvement of food processing;
thus, changes in nutrimental values from drying, storing and cooking processes, the process of adding vitamin B to polished rice, etc., are studied.

3) Food Process Division, Industrial Research Center;
reports on the nature of bacteria in Korean fermented foods.

4) College bodies:
Medical College, Seoul National University maintains a research team that submits reports on protein, vitamin, cholesterol, inorganic salt quantities in Korean's blood as well as on Vitamin B^{12} quantities in foods. Sudo Medical College maintains a team that carries out research work on seaweed proteins. Catholic College has prepared a report on the basic metabolic contents of the average Korean. A Yonsei University team studies the nutritional values of rural food consumption.

5) Fishery Center, Pusan:
experimenting in edible fish powder.

6) The late Dr. Kim Hojik, outstanding professor and authority on dietetics: has contributed to high-protein baby food by a process of fermenting bean powder, a discovery supported by FAO in experiments along further nutritional and production lines. (Production of this bean milk with FAO recommendation is currently under government consideration.)

Produces and Imports

The population of south Korea was 21,321,136 as of December 1957 and the cultivated area 1,209,661 *chongbo* of rice-paddies plus 819,451 *chongbo* of other arable fields. The soil is comparatively fertile and can supply almost all the food needed.

The chart shows that our prime products are cereals. Milk and other food of animal sources are scarce. This means that Korean food is short on proteins, fats, calcium, Vitamin A & B_2.

We may also note from the chart that sufficient consumption of calories is due to import of American surplus food through aid and trade. Measures are, indeed imperative to foster domestic production of food with enough calory content.

Koreans have not experienced any serious food crisis since 1945.

Yet they are found to be lacking in nourishment.

Effective counter-measures follow;
1) Control of food production and compulsory education in nutritional problems.
2) Enactment of a Nutrition Act, creating a properly recognized status for dietists to take care of mass feeding problems, especially for those hospitalized. Establishment of a nutrition school.
3) Public supervision of food dealers.

Astronomy

The Ancient Days of Astronomy and Astrology

The origin of astronomy in the East dates back to about 7,000 years ago in China and India. Korean mythology of pre-historic days of three to five thousand years ago connotes that astronomical observations took place during ancient times. Some authentic historical documents refer to the earliest astronomical observations as having been practiced during the Three Kingdoms period. Chinese methods were used, but even before that time, astronomical observations must have been practiced in Korea, because Korean mythology is studded with many astronomical references, which may reasonably be interpreted as having been based on facts rather than myth or hearsay.

It can therefore be readily assumed that early Koreans having been engaged primarily in agriculture, must have been sufficiently interested in the changes of the four seasons to undertake studies in the movements of constellations as the only reliable means to predict accurately seasonal changes, which meant changes in their own daily lives.

It would not be without foundation to presume that the beginning of astronomy in Korea goes back to the prehistoric period prior to the Three Kingdoms era.

The earliest astronomical studies in China and India produced the lunar calendar, which together with other studies of astronomy were imported to Korea. Therefore, the astronomy of ancient Korea is similar and related in method to the Chinese.

The ancient astronomers of the East, after successful formulation of the lunar calendar by observing the movements of the sun and moon, turned their interests to other mysterious stars in the sky, identifying the Stars of Gold (Venus), Wood (Jupiter), Water (Mercury), Fire (Mars), Soil (Saturn) as well as the fixed stars and planets. Continued observation of the stars in an attempt to predict movement of the five planets failed to produce the desired knowledge. Impressed ever more profoundly by the seemingly patternless movements of the five planets, the Chinese astronomers in about 400 B.C. attributed them to divine will. The assumption was soon developed into an accepted conclusion that being based on divine will, the movements of the five planets were indicative of fortunes not only of each individual person but also of the stars and the universe, eventually giving rise to Eastern astrology. This was the beginning of the astrology that is popular commercially even in the West today.

According to the theory, all vestitudes in the universe are caused by changes of five elements-Gold, Wood, Water, Fire and Soil; after which the five planets were named.

Since the five planets were believed to have been created with "masses" of each respective element of the five, the movements of the five planets, are indicative of events which happen in the universe, just as clothes are prognosticators of the season.

Ancient astrology gained popularity and spread to neighboring countries. The astrology of Korea was similar to that of China during the time astrology was also making rapid development and gaining popularity in the West.

The Three Kingdoms Period

Reasonably accurate astronomical observations were practiced in the kingdom of Koguryo as indicated by some references to the subject appearing in ancient records. For example, "The Annals of the Three Kingdoms" in its section on the Koguryo kingdom noted the time of an eclipse in the ninth month in the 72nd year of the reign of King Taejo (A.D. 124). Comparing these records with the entries by Houhan-shu of China and the list of eclipses by Oppolzer of the West on the same natural phenomena reveals that the records by the Koguryo kingdom is the only correct entry among these works.

We can get further glimpses into the astronomy of the Koguryo kingdom by the reference to an astronomical map as existing in the capital city of Pyongyang and also by the astronomical symbols and pictures inscribed on the murals and walls of the period. Such historical data reveal many elements and proof that much reliance was placed on astrology.

The Paekche scientists were likewise engaged in astronomical observations to a considerable extent as indicated in "The Annals of the Three Kingdoms," which lists 26 cases of eclipses observed and recorded.

The Paekche kingdom had a court office specifically designated to pursue astronomical studies. Important functions of the office were preparation of calendars, practice of astrology based on the theory of "five elements" and the "male and female", as well as astronomical observations based on its own methods. The kingdom was also the first to introduce its knowledge on the astronomy and calendar to Japan in A.D. 553 and 602. The calendar used in the Paekche kingdom and which was later introduced to Japan through scholars of the kingdom was the Yuanchia Calendar originated in Sung, China by Ha Sungchon in A.D. 445.

The kingdom of Silla, which had imported astronomy and the calendar from the other two kingdoms, made direct contacts with China after unifying the Korean peninsula during the second half of the 7th century, eventually to develop astronomy to an unprecedentedly high standard. The calendar then in use was the Linte Calender formulated originally in 665 by Li Shun-feng of Tang China, while an astronomical map was imported from China at about the same time through the Buddhist priest-scholar, Tosung. A hydroscope was first manufactured in the Silla kingdom in 717.

"The Annals of the Three Kingdoms" makes frequent references to astronomical observations made by astronomers of the Silla kingdom, indicating considerable development of the science. It appears that the frequent contacts with China and Japan across the seas must have inspired the scientists in their work. But a more important function of astronomy was revison of the calendar brought in from China through observations of constellations, because the Chinese calendar was soon found to require adaptation to the time equation.

The astronomical observatory of the Silla kingdom now standing in the ancient capital city of Kyongju, being the oldest structure of its kind remaining in the world, is a mute testimony to the highly developed state of astronomy during the period. Built in 647, the cone-shaped structure of solid granite, about ten meters high, has an opening in about the middle to allow passage of a man, and the top can be reached through a ladder placed inside the structure. Half of the top is covered with a flat roof, leaving the other half open for observation. It is presumed that various astronomical instruments must have been placed upon the flat roof.

The Koryo Kingdom Period

The Koryo kingdom which inherited traditions of the Silla kingdom inclined towards astrology, for the predominantly agricultural country placed emphasis on its attempts to put nature's whims under control by imploring the gods with methods formulated with astronomical knowledge. The stone observatory which remained until quite recently in suburban Kaesong was symbolic of the development of astronomy during the period.

The significant feature of the astronomical studies in the Koryo kingdom were records on observations of sun-spots. According to the "Book of Astronomy" contained in the "History of Koryo," 34 incidences of sun-spots were noted and entered in the record during the period from 1024 to 1383. Sizes of the sun-spots were recorded as being about the size of an egg, a plum or a chicken. Unscientific as they certainly were by present-day standards, such early interest in the changes of sun-spots is noteworthy.

Throughout its nearly 500 years of tenure, the Koryo kingdom, like its predecessors, relied on China for the calendar. Thus, at the beginning, the kingdom adopted the Hsuanming Calendar originated by Sou Ang of China in 822, later replacing it with the Shoushih Calendar which was compiled by Kuo Shou-ching and others of Yuan China in 1280, thereby conforming with the Gregorian Calendar in its estimate of one year as being 365.2425 days.

The astronomical observations were mostly directed at eclipses of the sun and the moon, movements of constellations and comets, while natural phenomena of the sky considered abnormal were carefully noted and recorded in detail. Among the astronomers, O Yunbu made the most substantial contribution through his issuance of an astronomical map and other works. In the Koryo kingdom period an official court member was charged with measurement of time.

The Yi Dynasty

Various astronomical instruments were produced during the Yi dynasty period, and many of them have survived until the present. On the other hand, not even a fragment of the astronomical instruments of Silla and Koryo remains today.

In the wake of the dynasty's foundation, the astronomical map of the previous age was revised in 1395, and a new system was adopted for measurement of time. Also an astronomical office was established within the court to equip itself with various instruments in 1432. Subsequently a new armillary sphere was manufactured in 1432, and a clepsydra in the following year.

Furthermore sundials were installed at two places in the capital city of Seoul to tell time by measuring the shadows of the sun, and a special instrument was manufactured to observe constellations. The astronomical observatory was also equipped with large and portable armillary spheres.

The most ingenuous instruments devised during the early period of the Yi dynasty under the reign of the Fourth King Sejong (1419-1450) was the automatic hydrosphere. Installed in the instrument was a wooden doll which was contrived to strike a bell to indicate a certain time. A similar time-piece manufactured at the time had the images of a warrior, a woman and the "twelve gods" to strike the bell at certain times.

During the reign of the fourth king, Sejong, officials of the astronomical observatory were dispatched to the Samgak (Triangle) Mountain near Seoul and the Kumgang (Diamond) Mountains to observe eclipses of the sun and the moon, while the Mari Mountains on Kanghwa island were also used from time to time as posts for astronomical observations. Thus during the times of the fourth king, Sejong, more systematic, mechanical observations replaced the former practice of relying mostly on the naked eye. This was hailed the advent of a "golden age" of astronomy in Korea.

After the middle of the Yi dynasty, Western sciences began to make inroads upon the traditional studies by way of China, and in league with the newly rising forces of the utilitarian school of thoughts, exerted considerable influence on astronomy, directing it along more scientific, independent lines. Thus astronomical phenomena were noted and recorded following, systematic criteria which was used in identifying the normal and abnormal phenomena of the sky. For example, the astronomical records of the time contain a specific entry on a comet first discovered on the tenth night of the tenth month in 1664. The observations of the comet were maintained for about 80 nights except on eight cloudy nights to prepare a map, tracing in detail the movements of the comet until its disappearance. This study left rare data for the world's history of astronomical studies.

During the late Yi dynasty, two scholars, Nam Pyongchol and Nam Pyonggil, made outstanding contributions to the development of astronomy through numerous publications on mathematics, astronomy and the almanac. The calendars then in use were both the Tatung version of Ming and the Shihhsion Calendar of Ching. Cf the two, the latter is of two kinds, the prior version being compiled jointly by the German T. Adam Shall von Bell, S.J.; the Indian I. Rho, S.J.; and the Chinese Shu Kuang-chi. This was done by revising the Chung Chen Calendar, while the latter-day version was a joint work of the German I. Kogler, S.J.; the Portugese A. Pereyra. S.J.; and the Chinese Ming An-kuo in 1737. The solar calendar was first adopted during the late Yi dynasty period in 1893, but traditions barred extensive use of the new calendar, allowing only a supplementary to the solar calendar.

Western Astronomy of Modern Times

Modern astronomy of the West was first introduced to Korea in the 1900's. By 1929 an observatory was erected in Inchon near the capital city, installing an equatorial refracting telescope among other equipment. The works of the first Western style observatory included stellar photography and accurate measurement of time by revising the time-difference of chronometers through observations of fixed stars passing over the colure with a merian transit.

Also, a 6-inch refracting telescope was installed atop a building of the present Yonsei University in suburban Seoul, but the wooden tube of the telescope rendered the instrument obsolete by the 1930's.

The outbreak of the Korean War in 1950 destroyed the only astronomical observatory in Inchon, leaving not a trace of the telescopes. Ever since the astronomical field has been left neglected until recently. A chair of astronomy and meteorology, however, was established in 1958 at the Seoul National University, while installations of telescopes are being projected by several universities including the Normal College, the Yonsei University and the Songgyungwan University—all in Seoul. The Central Meteorological Observatory of the government is also planning to install a 15-inch refracting telescope, as funds become available.

Meteorology

The Ancient Periods

Because early Koreans engaged in agriculture as the primary industry of this land, it is not surprising that they concerned themselves rather seriously with the phenomena of weather.

There is some reference to the observation of earthquakes before Christ in the *Samguk Sagi* (Annals of the Three Kingdoms), and there are detailed observational accounts of wind, rain, storm, sleet, snow and frost in the *Koryosa Ohaengji* (Supplement to the Five Elements Theory of Koryo History). The definite shortcoming of these observations was that they failed to be systematic, and the observers were hopelessly caught in the conceptual strait-jacket borrowed from the Chinese theory of Yinyang-Wuhsing, and, consequently, believed that wind, rain, climatic changes, insect pests, fog, snow, and all similar phenomena were conditioned by Water, Fire, Wood, Metal and Soil (Wuhsing, or Five Elements, of Yin and Yang), as shown in "Astronomy".

Thus the meteorological understanding of the time was closely related to astrology. As a result the government maintained *Sowungwan* within the *Sachondae*. The function was to administer all matters pertaining to astronomy, chronology, meteorology, and related sciences. Although there had been repeated reorganization of this agency, it remained very much the same until the end of the Yi dynasty, and, hence, promoted the mistaken conception that meteorology is a part of astronomy, a contention which still remains in Korea. The *Koryosa Ohaengji* has been mentioned here, however, to show that it is the earliest record pertaining to meteorological observations.

Meteorology during the Yi Dynasty

The archaic meteorological activities which had been carried on down to the Yi dynasty experienced a significant reformation during the reign of Sejong (1914–1450) whose era could be said to be the most properous one. Many aspects of this reformation are mentioned in the *Munhon Pigo* (literally, Sundry Records), and some of the instruments invented during the reign are still extant.

King Sejong was himself exceptionally versatile, and he saw during his lifetime many scholars emerging to invent and manufacture a variety of meteorological instruments. In the fifth year of the reign of Sejong (the fifth month), 1423, measurements were made to discover the depth on the ground of rain soakage as about 3 cms, according to the *Chosun Wangjo Sillok* (Chronicle of the Yi Dynasty), and this underlines the degree the meteorological observation at the time concerned itself with agricultural pursuits.

In the fourth month of the seventh year of the reign of Sejong, 1425, a law was enacted to make it compulsory that the local governments (province and county) make reports on the depth to which rain soaks into the ground, and in 1441, the government installed scales on Machon Bridge and the Han River to measure the watertable. It was in the same year that the famous rain gauges which were as modern as those used today were invented. They were made of copper, installed on granite tables, and distributed to the local governments (province, county, town and village). These governments were required to make periodical reports on precipitation. This was the first network of precipitation measurement stations in history. It is regrettable, however, that the records of precipitation are scattered in the *Chosun Wangjo Sillok* (Chronicle of the Yi Dynasty), and the 'raining record' has been lost during the disturbances. The records extant today are considerable, however. There is a series of precipitation records beginning 1770 for the Seoul area and it covers a span of 190 years, compared with 180 years for Rome and Paris which are renowned for the length of such series.

While these activities indicate the progress that was made uniquely and on empirical grounds, they did not attain systematic perfection, as pointed out already, due to their restrictive adherence to the 'Wuhsing' theory.

Contemporary Meteorology

The earliest modern attempt at improved meteorological administration was the Japanese project in June, 1884, of installing various meteorological instruments at the Pusan Bureau of Communication to record and forecast weather conditions of the Strait of Korea. In 1885, quite a few customs offices (Inchon, Pusan and Wonsan) began to conduct meteorological observations, and, in the following year, the Russian Legation in Korea installed its own meteorological instruments. Thereafter the number of meteorological stations rapidly increased and, in 1907, the Inchon Station was made the Central

Station and all others placed under its jurisdiction as branch stations.

After the Japanese annexation of Korea in August 1910, the title of the Central Station was changed into the Weather Observatory of the Government-General of Korea, and again in 1939 into the Weather Station of the Government-General of Korea. After the end of World War II, it came under the control of Koreans and the title was changed to National Central Weather Observatory. At present its jurisdiction extends over 14 weather stations in south Korea, including one at Kimpo International Airport.

The National Central Weather Observatory has up-to-date instruments and makes both daily and long-range forecasts. It publishes the Year Book, Monthly Meteorological Bulletin, and Meteorological Statistics.

Since January 1959, it has maintained a training institute in which meteorological workers are trained for a period of one year before their placement.

Korea joined the World Meteorological Organization in 1956 and has been making contributions to meteorological surveys and projects of free world nations since that time.

In addition, there are meteorological units in the army, navy and air force, with the primary function of supplying weather information necessary for military operations.

Yonsei University is at present making plans to institute a department of meteorology, Seoul National University is already offering courses in meteorology. Besides, there have been lecture courses in the subject at Normal College, Aviation College, and College of Agriculture.

The Meteorological Society of Korea has about 100 members and maintains its office at the National Central Weather Observatory. It carries out a variety of activities related to meteorological work. One of the recent projects of the Society was a prize contest for photographs of clouds which culminated with a photograph exhibition of the entries.

Geology

Summary History of Geological Studies

There are evidences that geological observations and descriptions were made in Europe as early as the seventh and fourth centuries B.C. The earliest recorded reference to geology in Korea were Kim Am's *Pungsu-sol* (Theory of Geomancy), A.D. 800 and *Tosin-Pigyol* (literally, Key to Principle) by an anonymous writer in A.D. 900, both of which deal primarily with divination. Around 1800, So Yugu published *Imwon Kyongjeji* (Forest and Garden Economics) which resembles the famous "De Re Metallica" by G. Argicolla, published in Europe around A.D. 1500. Yi Chunghwan published the *Palyokchi* (Records on Eight Areas, i.e. provinces) which includes a chapter entitled 'Theory of Mountains' around 1600. These indicate that there were many able geological observers, although they failed to contribute to systematic development.

Geological studies remained, however, unscientific in Korea, until 1822 when the government invited a German geologist, Gottsche, in order to undertake a geological survey. Shortly afterwards, a Japanese geologist, Kohuji Humijiro, completed a geological survey of Korea and published its results during the period from 1904 through 1909.

Following the Annexation in 1910, Japan commenced the investigation of mineral deposits which they were later to exploit, and instituted the Geological Survey of Korea in 1918. These investigations were geological in character and, incidentally, contributed to Korea's own geological studies. Especially noteworthy publications in this connection were Kawazaki Shigetaro's Yonchon System, Nakamura Shintaro's Sangwon System, Kobayashi Teiichi's Chosun System, Shiraki Takuji's Pyongan System, Shimamura Shinbei's Taedong System, Tateiwa Iwao's Kyongsang System on tertiaries. These marked the beginning of systematic geological study in Korea. Later geologists pointed out many shortcomings in these works of Japanese geologists.

After the Liberation of 1945, the Geological Survey came under the jurisdiction of Koreans. At the time it was headed by Pak Tonggil who reorganized the Geological Survey with the old staff members and new recruits.

Soon after Koreans launched geological research, the Korean War broke out in 1950 and all the efforts of the first president, Pak, failed to bear fruit. During this initial period, Seoul National University instituted a Department of Geology in the College of Arts and Sciences, and this Department was staffed by Dr. Kim Okchun, Son Chimu and Sin Pyongwu under the chairmanship of the late Professor Kim Chongwon.

When the Japanese monopoly on geological studies was over, many young Koreans were initiated into the field and these early initiates are at present active in the Geological Survey of Korea, various government agencies, irrigation cooperations, coal companies and many other related and pertinent organizations.

In April 1947, the Geological Society of Korea was organized with the staff of the Geological Survey of Korea and the faculty members of Seoul National University who were connected with geological studies. Originally there were only ten members, but the membership has increased to eighty at present. The first president was Pak Tonggil and the current president is Kim Hantae.

The Geological Survey of Korea has been taking part in preparation of Gallagher's Report and has completed a survey of mineral deposits throughout the country. It produced a geological map of Korea scaled at 1:1,000,000 and published the Bulletin of the Geological Survey of Korea, Technical Paper of Geological Survey of Korea, and Report on Coal Field Geology. These were important contributions to Korea's geological studies.

In the meantime, Seoul National University continued its geological research, especially in re-examination of the geological stratigraphy that was considered definitive during the Japanese period. One of the new findings in this Okchon System which was regarded as pre-Cambrian is very likely Mesozoic, so that the Koguryo granite may very well be pre-Cambrian. Many of the concepts of the Japanese geologists concerning the formation of granite in Korea has been found to be misleading and revision has been undertaken accordingly.

Contributors to Geological Studies in Korea

One of the greatest contributors to geological studies in Korea is the late Professor Kim Chongwon whose work entitled "The Stratigraphy of the Chosun System" was an essential reference. His unpublished manuscripts dealt with economic geology, but they were unfortunately lost before publication.

While the late Professor Kim Chongwon concerned himself with stratigraphy and economic geology, Pak Tonggil engaged himself in the field of mineorology and chemical analysis. Pak's discovery of such minerals as diamonds in Korea and his own method of cobalt ore analysis are among his most important contributions.

Present State of Geological Studies in Korea

Geological studies in Korea today are centered around the Department of Geology of Seoul National University and the Geological Survey of Korea of the Ministry of Commerce and Industry. Seoul National University has been conferring about twenty degrees annually in the field, and the thesis produced for them under the direction of Professors Chong Changhi, Chong Pongil,

Kim Ponggyun and others have made valuable and unique information available. As pointed out earlier, there was a significant modification of the Koguryo granite, and other information as a result of the revision of the stratigraphy of the Okchon System. At present the major geological survey undertaking is the investigation of the coal bed structure of Samchok coal field, and of the relationship between Taedong System and Naktong Series and Silla Series.

Since the appointment of Kim Okchun as the president, the Geological Survey of Korea has been carrying on an extensive program of surveying the coal deposits, and metal ore deposits. The results of this program have been highly profitable. Explorations for fissionable materials are being continued, and efforts are being made to introduce up-to-date methods of exploration and expansion of research facilities. The possibility of obtaining uranium concentrated from the uranium ores minable in Korea is being investigated, and the methods of dressing and combining various minerals are being scrutinized. All these activities constitute part of the force behind the development of geological studies in Korea.

Agronomy

Since Korea is one of the world's oldest agricultural societies, there is an extensive and varied history of agronomical learnings. The history of agronomy in Korea may best be treated in two parts, namely, the period before the contact with the West (about 1907), and the period thereafter. As early as the Silla period (57 B.C.-A.D. 935), the government was conducting agricultural programs covering irrigation, seed selection and distribution, insect pest prevention, etc. They carried out what might be called research and experiments, the results of which were recorded and disseminated in Japan.

During the reign of Songdok, A.D. 722, a system of public farming was instituted as an embryonic form of agricultural administration, and King Hungdok (A.D. 826-836), ordered Kim Taeryom to go to Tang to procure ginseng seeds to be cultivated experimentally in the mountains of Chiri at the southwestern part of the peninsula. At that time, the principal crops were paddy rice, various species of barley, beans and millet, and the farming products included silk cocoons, fibres, tea and pastural products.

During the Koryo period (918-1392), a system of three-crops-in-two-years was applied and it was the beginning of articulate farm management in Korea. Also about the same time a variety of farm instruments were invented (shovel, plough, spade, etc.) during the reign of Kongmin who advocated importation of water wheels from southern China. In 1365, cotton plants were imported from what is now Vietnam and many species of vegetables were imported or cultivated in Korea.

During the Yi dynasty, agronomy attained a systematic outlook, and, during the reign of the fourth King Sejong (1397-1450), Chong Cho was ordered by the king to publish *Nongsajiksol* (Agronomical Principle) which is the oldest Korean agronomic book believed to be extant. The countrywide observations which began in 1442 was a part of the rational farming program of the dynasty. The rain gauge used at the time was invented 200 years before Benedetto Castelli (1639), of Italy. Chong Inji, on the other hand, revised the existing calendar to suit farming. By the order of King Myongjong (1546-1567), Kim Yuk edited a botanical work entitled *Kuhwangchwalyo,* which is an abstract of Sejong's *Kuhwangbyokkokpang.* Kim also advocated introduction of water wheels and revision of the existing calendar. The master of agronomy at the time, Yu Hyongwon, (1662-1762) published *Pangyesurok* based on subjective experiences in farming, and brought agronomy into an academic frame of reference.

Pak Chiwon (1737-1805) maintained close contacts with leading Chinese agronomists and published significant agronomical works entitled *Kwanongsocho* and *Nongjongsinso* (Agricultural Management). The former included descriptions of existing farming methods and recommendations for improvement of these methods. A similar work was published by Pak Sedang (1636-1711) and Hong Manson (1643--1715) who dealt with forestry in *Sannımgyongje* (Forest Economics) in four volumes, which covered botany in general as well as insect pest prevention, medical herbs and silk worm breeding. The latter was the reference source for the later publication of Yu Chungnim's *Chungbosannimkyongje* and So Yugu's (1764-1845) *Imwonkyongjeji* (Forest and Garden Economics). So was responsible for importation of sweet potatoes from Tsushima (Japan) and its experimental cultivation at Tongnae and Cheju Island, and, thereafter, publishing a book entitled *Chongjobo* (On Potatoes) for the dissemination of the method of sweet potato cultivation. It stimulated many similar studies completed by Kang Pilli, Yi Changsun, etc.

Thus, during the Yi dynasty, there were activities on a largescale for reclamation, construction of dams and irrigation systems, afforestation, silk cocoon breeding, insect control, in which the progress made was very considerable.

Since 1907, Korea began her contacts with the West and acquired Western techniques in farming. Korea's contemporary of agronomy commenced from this time forward. In 1910, the Japanese government set up a number of model farms, and the leadership of farming was transferred to the Japanese government after the Annexation. Thereafter the agricultural administration became predominantly colonial and Koreans played merely passive roles. Although the Agricultural, Commercial and Technological School was established in Seoul immediately after the Annexation, its academic standard was limited.

The first college of agriculture in Korea was established at Suwon about 1920, and it turned out to be almost exclusively for the Japanese, and only about 25% of its students were Korean. Many agricultural institutions such as Forest Station, Silk Worm Station, Veterinary Station, Agricultural Experiment Station, etc., were established, and Suwon became the center of agricultural research and guidance for all of Korea.

While the college and its branch institutions intended to introduce Japanese practices to Korea, the peculiar conditions in Korea compelled them to initiate programs for farming, livestock and cocoon production uniquely Korean. They, therefore, began works in soil analysis, fertilizer analysis, seedling evaluation, etc. However, Japanese research was primarily on paddy rice. Since the College at Suwon was almost exclusively for the Japanese, many Korean students went to Japan for their training. The Korean graduates of colleges found it difficult to continue their research because most of the institutions did not employ Koreans. The few who found positions with the agricultural experiment stations were used merely as laborers under Japanese superiors.

After the Liberation in 1945, the agricultural organization was wholly revised under the leadership of Koreans. The Agricultural Institute of the government has under its jurisdiction separate experiment stations for agriculture, forestry, livestocks, and others, and, with the help of America and other countries, the research facilities are being greatly improved and many students are being sent abroad for advanced training.

There have been theoretical studies in farming methods, crossing of species, use of agricultural statistics, fertilizer, chemicals for crops and livestocks There are at present 14 colleges of agriculture, and research facilities have been improving both qualitatively and quantitatively.

Those who have returned from their tours of study abroad are expected to make definite contributions to the Korean study of agronomy. The increasing volume of publications on agronomy in recent years and the annual conference of agronomists sponsored by the Agricultural Society of Korea are encouraging signs of the progress that has been made. The plans for application of nuclear science to agriculture have stimulated the agronomists greatly in recent years, and it is hoped that after the present nurturing period of Korean agronomy, it will not be long before Korea can make substantial independent and original contributions in the field.

Fishery

The seas surrounding the Korean peninsula are rich with good fishing resources. Fishing, therefore, has developed naturally and will continue to develop under the demands of modern industry. About 600,000 individuals make their living from the sea, accounting for an annual catch of 400,000 tons.

Before the Liberation, the Fisheries College of Pusan was the sole institute offering higher educational courses in fishery science. It was primarily for Japanese students; only some 5 percent of the student body were Korean, a rate maintained annually. On the other hand, Korean students could choose from four fishery institutes of middle school level under the public school system. They were located at the ideal coastal towns of Yosu, Tongyong, Chongjin and Kiumpo.

After the Liberation, a National Fisheries College was established in Pusan (Pusan Fisheries College) and a similar private institute in the port city of Pohang on the eastern coast. Besides these two levels of higher education, high schools offering courses in fisheries science were established in Yosu, Tongyong, Pusan, Pohang, Kuryongpo, Ullung, Chumunjin, Namhae, Wando, Cheju, Mokpo, Inchon and Taejon. The Pusan Fisheries College has five departments: propagation, fishing, manufacturing, shipbuilding and fisheries economy.

As for administrative agencies, there is the Office of Marine Affairs under the Ministry of Commerce and Industry. The Office has a Bureau of Fisheries which is responsible for fisheries administration. In addition, there is the Central Fisheries Experimental Station in Pusan and the Central Fisheries Inspection Station in Seoul. The Fisheries Experimental Station has branch offices in Inchon, Pohang, Yosu, Chumunjin, Mokpo, and Kunsan. The Central Fisheries Inspection Station's branch offices are located in Inchon, Mokpo, Cheju, Wando, Yosu, Pusan, Pohang, and Chumunjin; in addittion, there are eight sub-branches under the eight branches of the Inspection Station.

The experimental and research work undertaken by the Experimental Station covers four fields; namely, oceanography, fish-farming, fishing, and manufacturing of fish products. In the area of fish-farming, the life histories and farming methods of the carp (*cyprinos carpio*), gibel (*arassius carassius*), snake head (*ophicephalus argus*), sweet fish (*plecoglossus altivelis*), surf smelt (*hypomesus olidus*), cod (*gadus macrocphalus*), Manchurian trout (*brachyniystax lenok*) and herring (*clupea pallasii*) are surveyed and findings described in the progress reports put out regularly by the Experimental Station. The carp, gibel, snake head, surf smelt, etc., are also hatched at the Chinhae Fish Culture Station, Chongpyong Fish Culture Station and other similar establishments for distribution to private fish-farms. The government, on its part, releases fertilized eggs of the carp, Manchurian trout, and surf smelt into rivers, bays, and other Korean waters; hatched cod and herring are released into inlets. In addition, smelt fishes have been hatched for rivers as an annual project, while hatched salmons, trouts and cods are released into bays and inlet waters. The life histories fo the oyster, clam, and other shellfish have likewise been studied in parallel with oyster-culture projects, as have the life histories of yet other species of fish. A documentary book, "Korean Fishes" covering the life histories of over 70 kinds of fresh water fish, was published in 1939 by the Japanese, Uchida Sentaro. In 1955, telapia fish were imported from Thailand for the Chinhae Fish Culture Station; telapias hatched by this station are presently being distributed to private fish-farms.

In the fishing field, the Fisheries Experimental Station's role is to conduct reasearch work to improve fishing gears, diving equipments, trawl equipments, fishing boats, and fishing nets for catching the Alaska pollack, herring, chub-mackerel, anchovy, sardines, yellow corvenia, etc., as well as to survey further fishing resources and describe findings in its progress reports.

In the field of oceanography, efforts have been made to survey currents, temperatures, and resources, chiefly planktons of the adjacent seas. Such findings have also been described in progress reports on oceanography.

In the manufacturing fields, the natural conditions of fish life and quantities of different Korean species are analyzed; manufacturing processes for fish products, the manufacture of fish liver oil, and gelantin processes of fish scales, etc., are surveyed.

In addition, algae cultivation formulae are being surveyed. Findings in this field are also reported in the usual manner.

"Fisheries in Korea" was the sole magazine on fisheries science published prior to the Liberation. Many Japanese scholars utilized this academic journal to present their theories and findings on the science.

The names of Korean fishes, the morphological studies and culture methods of the laver, Alaska pollack, etc. were introduced by the Korean authority, Chong Mungi. In addition, the Korean Natural History Journal carried an article authored by the Japanese experts, Mori Tame and Siba Noboru, on lists of Korean fishes and shell-fishes in Korea respectively. Presently, the Korean Fisheries Society and the Korean Oceanography Society are holding regular academic meetings. The Pusan Fisheries College is publishing its own research journal. Various theories and findings on fishery science have been reported in the journals of the Korean Zoology Society and the Korean Botany Society.

The names of 23 kinds of fishes listed by one, Ha Yon, in the Geography of Kyongsang-do in 1469 represents the oldest existing record on the study of fishery science in Korea. The oldest document on the life history of Korean fishes and classifications thereof is the "Chasan genealogical table of fishes," published in 1805 by Chong Yakchon. The document lists 116 species.

The "Ichthyoloishe Bermeskungon Ausdem 8001" offered by the German, S. N. Herzenstein, in 1872 and "Uber einige neue U. Stlene Fisch harten aus und Ichthyol" of another German, F. Steindachner, in the same year, represent the oldest studies on Korean fish by foreigners. Thereafter, 28 Korean and 19 foreign scholars have come to identify, classify, and study the life histories of 850 species of fish in Korea, in addition to engaging in reseach work on fishing, fish-farming and manufacturing of fishery products. Their works have been summarized in the "Korean Fisheries," published in 1954 by Chong Mungi.

Shell-fishes or mollusks are much favored as providers of protein and fat, but they are more prized as export items, over 10 varieties, including oysters, clams, abalones, and crabs being exported. So far, 311 kinds of mollusks have been identified in Korean waters, by a total number of 18 scholars engaged in this field. Shiba Noboru has 315 listed in an article captioned "Korean Mollusks" (Korean Natura History Journal, No. 18).

The Pusan Fisheries Experimental Station has surveyed and prepared a report on Korean waters; on the other hand, the Central Fisheries Experimental Station is still continuing survey and research work in the same field.

XVII LITERATURE

An Outline of Korean Literature, Its Heritage

Geological, Seasonal and Social Background

The essential contours of the Korean peninsula consist of a major mountain ridge cutting along a north-south line with numerous smaller ridges jutting east and west from the backbone. Except for narrow plains to the northwest and southwest, the land is covered with undulating hills and mountains. Consequently, Koreans of prehistoric times formed small community groups in whatever space was allowed by Nature. The communities were separate entities, until the advent of civilization with government and communications broke down the barriers to free interflow.

The topographical conditions and the seas surrounding the peninsula assured extremely uniform seasonal changes.

The Oriental world has long known Koreans to be a people of quick sensitivities with interest in and concern for the seasonal conditions. The idioms used by the Korean when he wishes to express exultation, fear, or sorrow, are notable for their dependance on the seasons. They prove how deeply the awareness of seasonal changes is rooted in the daily life of the Korean people. These changes, reflected yearly in nature's mass landscapes and the blooming and withering periods, are one key to an understanding of the nation's semantic outlook. The Korean owes his poetic disposition to the unusually bright blue sky which flares over the scenic beauty of a rugged land with a short rainy season. This caused him to hold nature close to his heart.

The lack of a progressive spirit, satisfaction with the relative security of the small valleys, and yearning love of peace of our ancestors are all a natural product of this seasonal environment.

The land mass of China, which borders on the peninsula in the north, played a major role in the development of Korean culture. Buddhism, Confucianism, and Taoism, imported from or through China, brought all-pervading changes to the nation's culture, and shaped its way of thinking. Korea was never reluctant to recognize and accept the merits of the new culture. But the hardy culture of the mountain land was never replaced, only modified. China, of course, was not wholly a benefactor. On numerous occasions, large-scale armed aggressions originating in China overran the land.

The disastrous temporary effects of these aggressions on the spiritual, economic and political life of the nation directed the courses of both the Korean's temperament, breeding a capacity for flexible resistance and his international viewpoint, a watchful isolation guaranteed by alliance with a str-

XVII LITERATURE

ong foreign power. Korea's is a history of positive and negative resistance against the pressures of foreign Powers. This tragic international position coupled with the poetic disposition accorded by nature have made insecurity, an inner sense of uneasiness and poetic optimism inseparable determinants in the formation of the national character. Although Buddhism helped nurture a colorful civilization during the Three Kingdoms period and through Koryo, the undercurrent of uneasiness did not cease. The Confucianist culture of the Yi dynasty preached the virtues of self-control and forbearance, but it did not succeed in erasing from the national feeling a fundamental insecurity. The continuous struggle for power among the officials of the Yi dynasty provided another basis for this negative attitude.

Literature born under these circumstances naturally betrayed a melancholy sentiment, ephemeral and hoarded self-satisfaction, and a reclusive negativeness among its spiritual foundations.

Another important factor in Korean literature was the effect of incessant local political changes. These did not allow a proper climate for establishment of powerful traditions. Literature developed in imitation of Chinese imports. The frequency of the political changes also meant frequent wars which had sharp effects on cultural developments. Numerous cultural properties of the Three Kingdoms disappeared in the smoke and fire of such wars, leaving great blanks in what otherwise might have become an independent cultural progression.

Korean literature was so much an imitation of Chinese literature that it was written in the Chinese ideographic script. Even at its best, it did not have its own tradition. When a new literature was born in a certain ideal period of a progressive Korean realm, it was fated to die with the realm. None of it was ever handed to succeeding periods and kingdoms. All joined the ashes of the dying kingdom. With each new era and new dynasty, the process was repeated all over again.

The Characteristics of Korean Literature

This heritage gave rise to a peculiar temperament in Korean literature. This temperament demanded freedom from all existing moral laws, social concepts and other binding conditions. It is a temperament born of the writer's ego and, in conditioned circumstances, defies the logic which justifies the conditions. This temperament gave flexibility to the resistance of Yi dynasty writers against the all-embracing Confucian order with its moral and ethical concepts. If any tradition is to be found in Korean literature, it is this temperament—a negation of tradition.

Until Korean letters were invented by King Sejong of the Yi dynasty in 1446, the letters used in Korean literature were Chinese characters, the writing from which played the role of a medium in the introduction of Buddhism, Confucianism, and Taoism. The usage of Chinese characters, and the employment of the connotations and ideas inherent in these imported letters, had become so widespread and deeply rooted a practice that the invention of the nation's own letters did not simultaneously give impetus to the development of an independent literature. For over 500 years, the Korean letters, *Hunmin Chongum,* belonged to the lower echelons of the nation, placing those literate unfortunates outside the realm of official life. Few works were written in the nation's own letters which might be placed in the category of classics during the period. It was not until the latter part of the nineteenth century, when recognition of the *Hunmin Chongum* as Korea's very own written language blossomed, that Korean writers realized the importance of the national alphabet and literature began to change its face. This period can be compared with the European Renaissance; through it the ego of a nation became the foundation stone for an increasingly independent culture. Through this renaissance which came so belatedly, Korea began her career as a newcomer in a modern world; her budding independent literature began to feel the impact of Western civilization. The time allowed for the development of modern literature in Korea was extremely limited, however, and forced a hasty tempo, a growth of weeds as well as flowers. The illogicality and backwardness which spots the history of modern Korean literature are a natural consequence of this forced tempo.

This tempo of literary changes and output was furthur hastened with the beginning of the twentieth century, when liberal ideals and the concept of democracy began to reach the land. Koreans were awakening to their place in the world as a nation and began to esteem their own language and letters. In 1896, an all-Korean-language newspaper, "*Tongnip Sinmun*" (The Independence News), was first published. This event may well have been the most important development in the history of Korean literature. Korean letters, preserved thus far only by the loving care of the lower social classes, began to occupy their rightful place in the daily life of all Koreans.

The Birth of Modern Literature

Korea's national plight in and around 1910, when Japan forcibly annexed this peninsula, was characterized by a state of extreme confusions. A backward-looking feudalistic outlook and radical ideals of independence prevailed in quick succession over the field of literature. The nation had little opportunity to establish a firm foothold in the swiftly changing literary tides. Nevertheless, modern literature in Korean came into being, the fruit of a longing hunger for liberty and national integrity over adverse circumstances. Poetry, novels, and short stories, with the goal of enlightenment of the masses controlling their themes, succeeded in prompting the young generation of the day to grasp the meaning of modern concepts. The dreams and ideals thus planted in young hearts led directly to the national independence movement of 1919, a peaceful mass demonstration bloodied on Japanese bayonets. Though the movement failed to bring political independence, it poured a new, progressive spirit into a nation which had so long been passively conservative. Through this movement, which swelled in the waves of the liberalism of the post-World War I period, Korea started to fight its way free from its traditional backwardness, impelled to become one with a world striking out for new horizons.

Korean literature, despite the harsh oppression of alien authorities, kept pace with this tendency.

Classic Literature: Poetry

Poetry

The Prehistoric Days

The poetry and songs of prehistoric Korea have long been a matter of mystery, for no authentic literature on the subject is known to exist. We can, therefore, merely offer a rough outline of ancient poetry through reference to fragmentary descriptions appearing in a few Chinese classics.

It is presumed that poetry of a sort was born and developed through religious rituals and songs accompanying labor. Naturally, such chanting was accompanied by music and dancing, forming an integral whole. References appearing in some ancient records on ancient Korean rites to honor heaven contain descriptions to that effect.

As to when poetry evolved of itself from such modest beginnings, becoming an independent art and setting its own fixed forms, is again a matter of conjecture. The existing few records, however, lead to the assumption that it was during the reign of King Yuri of the Silla dynasty (A.D. 24-57) when such a state was reached. The Song of Tosol was most likely a product of the time. It is the first known Korean poem written in fixed form.

The Poetry of the Three Kingdoms Period

As the country entered the Three Kingdoms period, short lyric poetry expressing individual emotion was presumably developed to supplement the long, narrative forms of the past. Since not a single poem of those times has survived, we cannot appreciate this ancient poetry. "*Samguk Sagi*" (Annals of the Three Kingdoms) and "*Samguk Yusa*" (The Reminiscences of the Three Kingdoms) contain several references to the titles of such poems with some interpretations. We can, therefore, reasonably presume that the *Hern Song* and the *Hoesogok, Bandungsan* (Half-Mountaineering) Song, and the *Mudungsan* (Non-Mountaineering) Song were probably short lyric pieces.

Subsequently, the introduction of music from China as well as further social development during the period seem to have promoted the growth of poetry.

The Hyangga

Sometime after the unification of the Korean peninsula by the Silla kingdom, a new form of poetry known as the *Hyangga* was born. It was new in the respect that these poems—which had previously been word-of-mouth affairs—were written with Chinese characters adapted to Korean pronounciation. The Chinese characters were then the only means of writing.

Altogether, 25 such *Hyangga* have been preserved—14 in "*Samguk Yusa*" (Reminiscences of the Three Kingdoms) and 11 in "*The Kyunyojon.*" They were mostly recorded by Buddhist priests, men of the highest cultural class, who chanted the *Hyangga* at Buddhist festivities.

During the reign of Queen Sondok (632-647), an anthology of *Hyangga*, the *samdaemok*, was published by royal command, indicating the popularity of this poetry during that time. The volume. however, has not survived.

The Kyonggi-Style Song

As Koryo succeeded Silla, Chinese culture exerted tremendously expanded influence. The *Hyangga* began to wane rapidly to be replaced by the *Kyonggi Chaega*. The name of the form was derived from the repetitions of the word "*Kyonggi*", which was inserted between each verse. Its form is unique, with the elements arranged as follows;

The first verse . . . 3. 3. 4. 3. 3. 4. 4. 4. 4. *we* 2. (or 4) *kyonggi hayo*

The second verse . . . 4. 4. we 2 (or 4) *kyonggi hayo*

The above form was repeated to form a chapter or more. The letters used to record the poem were Chinese characters with the pronunciation adapted to Korean sounds.

The emergence and subsequent popularity of the Kyonggi-style Song during the Koryo period were apparently inspired by the "new" literature and music implanted from Sung (China); the composition of the song into chapters followed the pattern set by Sung literature. Furthermore, the peace and prosperity which reigned over the Koryo kingdom must have lent themselves readily to such a long form, more popular in such times than the short form of the *Hyangga*.

Authors of these songs were mostly scholars, such as An Chuk. who was credited with composing the *Kwanddong Pyolgon*, and the *Chukke Pyolgok*. Another, the *Hyangnim Pyolgok*, is also known to have been written during the Koryo period by an unidentified scholar. The work of aristocrats, the songs depicted scenes of luxurious composure tinged with the somwhat decadent air which prevailed in the aristocratic social life of the time.

This mood continued into the Yi dynasty, which produced 13 classical songs of the Kyonggi style, including the *Sangdae Pyolgok* by Kwon Kun.

Song yo (The Popular Song)

While the aristocrats were venting their poetic emotions in Kyonggi-style songs, the common people of Koryo society chanted the *Song yo*. Composed by courtesans and other members of the lower social class, most of the *Songyo* have been consigned to oblivion along with their authors and dates of composition. A few, however. have been saved by the people who kept alive the words and melodies. After the birth of *Hangul* in the early Yi dynasty, however, the songs were recorded, several of them being subsequently recognized as literary masterpieces.

A number of these songs were incorporated into books on Korean classic music and dance. "*The Akchang kasa*" and "*The Akhak Kibom*" (The Criteria of Musical Studies), both written during the Yi dynasty. Among these are: "*Ssanghwajom*" (literally, Double Flower Shop). "*Sogyong Pyolgok*" (Farewell Song at the Western Capital). "*Chongsan Pyolgok*" (Farewell Song of the Blue Mountain). and "*Chongsokka*". Of these, "the Double Flower Shop" is considered best for its candid expression of deep human emotions. The "popular" songs, written entirely in the Korean language, therefore, are appreciated more highly than the scholarly Kyunggi-style songs.

Sijo

The *Sijo*, a stanza of three verses, has been the subject of much controversy among scholars who cannot agree on its origin. But it was presumably born of the turbulent social conditions in the late Koryo period. Such conditions must have demanded a brief, concise form of emotional expression for the long, elaborate forms of the Kyonggi and the "popular" songs did not lend themselves readily to the disposition of the times, the mouldering of a great political revolution.

Both the form and content of the *Sijo* are closer to the "popular song" than to the Kyonggi-style songs, giving us grounds for assuming that they branched from the "popular".

About 10 *Sijo* of the Koryo period are known today. All are considered excellent, depicting well the contemporary emotions of the time. One of the most famous of early *Sijo* was written by Chong Mongju, a Minister of Koryo, who chanted:

Though this frame should die and die,
    though I die a hundred times,
My bleached bones all turned to dust,
    my very soul exist or not-
What can change the undivided heart
    that glows with faith toward my Lord.

During the next Yi dynasty, the *Sijo* commanded increasing popularity, reaching its golden age during the middle of the Yi era.

Many scholars of Chinese classics, who had formerly looked down upon the *Sijo* with contempt, began to work at the short poem. Eventually the *Sijo* established itself as one of the most sophisticated and dignified of poetry forms. Thus, the prominent Confucian scholar, Yi Hwang, wrote "The Tweve Songs of Tosan", and Yi Yi composed "The Nine Songs of Kosan", a part of which follows:

Only I and seagulls know
    Chongnyangsan's thirty-six peaks.
The seagulls are chatterers
    but falling flowers tell the most tales.
Peach petals, do not float down!
    The fishers will know where we are.

The height of *Sijo* development was reached during the seventeenth century. Yun Sundo, the greatest of all *Sijo* masters, belonged to this period. His "Fisherman's Four Seasons" and "The Prayer Songs in the Mountain" are considered the best of all works of the kind, The spring song of "the Fishermen's Four Seasons" runs:

Is that sound the cuckoo's call?
    And is that green the willow's fronds?
The fishermen's hamlet
    is hidden in evening smoke.
Come my boy, the new fish are rising,
    Let's bring out the old nets.
When the clouds have cleared away,
    the sunshine bright and warm
Heaven and earth are unrolled,
    and the sea looks ageless.

The boundless, boundless expanse of waves
    is stretched like shimmering silk.

As the Yi dynasty entered its late period, a prose style of *Sijo* composition came into being, producing, at the same time, lengthy forms of poetry. Also many common people began to write *Sijo*, which had formerly been a semi-monopoly of the scholar and ministers of the court. One of the typical pieces of the late Yi dynasty by an anonymous poet reads:

Stay, O wind and do not blow.
    The leaves of the weeping tree by the arbor are all fallen.
Months and years, stay in your course.
    The fair brow and fresh face grow old in vain.
Think of man: he cannot stay boy forever,
    There's a thing that makes me sad.

After the decline and fall of the Yi dynasty, the *Sijo* drew the same fate. During the Japanese-dominated period, however, it was revived by such men of letters as Choe Namson, Yi Kwangsu, and Yi Unsang. Even today, the traditional, short poems are endeared by many people, and new works are published occasionally, even though the *Sijo* can hardly dream of regaining its former glory. An example of the modern *Sijo* by Yi Kwangsu goes:

Pirobong is glorious,
    but do not ask ask me how grand.
Man's eye cannot encompass it,
    so can his lips describe it?
Should you wish to know Pirobong,
    then go, I say, and see it.

(Pirobong is the highest peak of the Diamond Mountain, whose scenic beauties are one of the prides of the Korean people.)

Akchang (The Music Phrase)

Born and developed as lyrics for the court music of the Yi dynasty, *Akchang* is written

Note: All the English versions of the *Sijo* appearing in this chapter are the work of Richard Rutt, a priest of the Anglican Mission in Korea, and are included in "An Introduction to the Sijo Vol. XXXIV." Transactions of the Korea Branch of the Royal Asiatic Society: Seoul, Korea. 1958.

in Chinese characters, following the patterns of the Kyonggi-style song or Chinese classic poetry. A master of court music, Pak Yon, collected and edited folk songs to make the most significant contribution to the development of the *Akchang*. About ten works, are presently known, including the most famous, *Yongbi Ochonga*.

Narrative Poetry

A new longer form of poetry emerged during the early Yi dynasty. The 4. 4. form of narrative poetry involves a long series of verses. The contents are all inclusive giving an account of one's travel, daily life, or even involving a literary essay or criticism. Therefore, narrative poetry, born during the reign of King Yonsan (1495-1506) of the Yi dynasty, inclines toward prose style of writing in content, though the form is the verse.

The emergence of such a new style is significant in the evolution of the writing, because it may be interpreted as the inevitable process of shifting from the formerly exclusive methods of verses to prose.

An important productive factor in this long, verse series seems to be the political unrest of the time during the reign of the 10th king of the Yi dynasty, Yonsan, whose court, ridden by fierce strife among various factions, drove many scholars and high-ranking officials deep into the country and mountains.

Closeness to nature and her beauties must have created an inner urge in such men of culture to seek expression to their feelings. Finding the traditional forms of the Kyonggi-style song and the short *Sijo* inadequate to express their emotions, they presumably formulated the new, free form of narrative poetry.

Thus the earliest works of narrative poetry depicted the beauties of nature, as in the case of "*Yangchungok*" (A Song in Praise of the Spring) by Chong Kugin (1401-1481).

The greatest of them all was Chon Chol (1536-1593), whose "*Songgang Kasa*" is regarded by some critics as one of the best of all works of Korean classic literature. "Songgang Kasa" (Songs of the Pine River) is composed of four long, independent poems: The Farewell Song of Kwangdong, The Song of Meditation on a Fair Maid, The Song of the Famed Fair Maid, and the Farewell Song of the Star Mountain, of which the first is the most renowned.

During the last period of the Yi dynasty, narrative poetry expanded into an even longer form, sometimes reaching several thousand verses. Most of such lengthy works depicted personal accounts of journeys, as in the case of "*Yonsangi*" by Hong Sunghak, "*Puksonga*" by Kim Hyongjin, and "*Hanyangga*" by Hansan Kosa.

Narrative poetry was composed not only by scholars, but also by the womenfolk, who found an apt means to express the feminine world in such poetry. Thus, for example, the bride's sorrow at leaving her home was chanted in "*Sinhangga*", the joy of an excursion into the flower field in "*Hwachongga*", the woes of an old spinster in "The Song of the Old Maid."

Narrative poetry, which gained so much popularity during the middle of the Yi dynasty, however, shared the fate of the Yi dynasty, decadence and oblivion.

Classic Literature: The Novel

The Age of Mythology

The age of mythology runs from the prehistoric days to the early part of the Three Kingdoms period. Prior to the emergence of novels, narratives and epic literature based on myths, legends and folk-tales were born, to be spread by word-of-mouth among the primitive people of old.

"The Reminiscences of the Three Kingdoms" are studded with such early myths and legends, which are concerned with the founder-gods of the early kingdoms on the Korean peninsula. Thus, the foundation of the earliest Korean state was attributed to Tangun, who was depicted as a son of heaven who had descended to the earth and married a bear (probably symbolic of a man bearing that animal's name.)

The Silla kingdom has its mythological founders in stories about Pak Hyokkose, Sok Talhae and Kim Alchi, while the myths about the establishment of the Koguryo kingdom centered around Chu Mong. The kingdom of Puyo had Hae Mosu and Kum Wa to explain the birth of its founder-kings and the subsequent development of the kingdom. Oviperous origins were attributed to all of the earliest founder-kings of the ancient kingdoms

Numerous legends were built on such myths during the middle of the Three Kingdoms period. The Silla kingdom, for example, had stories of "the Bell of Pongdok Temple," which emitted the sound of a wailing baby which had been cast into the bell, and "the Shadowless Tower;" the early history of the Paekche kingdom was made more colorful with the story of "The Rock of the Falling Flowers," from which 3,000 *kisaeng* courtesans were said to have plunged into the river as so many flowers falling, choosing death before an advancing army of the all-conquering Silla forces. The Koguryo kingdom had a legend about "The Cave of Kirin," the mystic animal whose appearance was said to herald the birth of a saint.

After the unification of the Korean peninsula by the Silla kingdom, an increasingly large number of droll stories emerged. This was in large measure due to the influence of Chinese legends, introduced by Korean scholars who had been to China.

Some of the legends of the time were recorded in "the Annals of the Three Kingdoms" and "Reminiscences of the Three Kingdoms." These include "The Yongwon Woman" and "Kasil", (Silla); "Tomi" (Paekche); "Prince Hodong," "Ondal," and "The

Tortoise and the Rabbit," (Koguryo). "The Story of Pangta," originated in Silla and was transmitted even to China, where it was recorded in "The Yu Yang Miscellanea," edited by Tuan Cheng-shik of Tang. Some of the legends of the period, notably "The Panta legend," were revived later during the Yi dynasty as themes for classic novels.

As one of the typical legends of the time, the story of Ondal, about the fool and the princess, may be cited as appearing in "Annals of the Three Kingdoms:"

In the mid-sixth century, there lived in the kingdom of Koguryo a beggar by the name of Ondal. He was kind and pure in heart but looked so ugly that the people called him Ondal the Fool. Ondal supported a blind mother. At the palace, the king often used to tease the young princess by threatening to marry her off to Ondal the Fool. Now, when this princess became of age, she insisted on this marriage.

Disowned by the king for this attitude, the princess sought Ondal the Fool and persuaded the beggar and his mother to agree to the marriage. With the encouragement and support of the princess, Ondal the Fool became an excellent warrior and, finally, demonstrated his prowess at a contest during a national festival, winning praise from the king himself. Subsequently, when the Chinese forces invaded the country, Ondal the Fool, now the most renowned knight of the kingdom, repulsed the enemy, to be accorded the most honorable recognition of merit from the king. Later, the ex-beggar general marched into the kingdom of Silla to restore the territory of his country, but was killed on the battlefield. At the funeral of Ondal the Fool, the coffin containing his corpse refused to be lifted from the earth, whereupon his bereaved wife, the princess, said soothing words to the soul of the general. This broke the spell and the coffin was lifted.

Popularity of this narrative literature of fantasy continued after the Koryo kingdom replaced Silla in 918, so much so that several books of such stories were published, including "The Suijon" (Unique Strange Tales). Edited by the literary master, Pak Inyang, and published somewhere between the reigns of the 11th and 15th kings of Koryo, the book has long been lost. But about ten of its stories have survived, finding their way into two other books, "*Taedong Unbugunok*" and "*Taebyong Tongjae*," giving us a glimpse of the masterwork.

Among the stories of "Unique Strange Tales," one is about a man by the name of Choe Hang and his concubine. The hero dies from a broken heart because of his parents' stern refusal to allow the hero to keep a beautiful concubine in their home. The soul of the hero, then, appears in the guise of a living man to his beloved concubine, to tell her that he has finally secured his parents' consent to their union. Arriving at the house with the concubine, however, the hero disappears into the house, over a wall, leaving the concubine outside. Next morning, the concubine is informed of her lover's death to her extreme sorrow. The hero, however, is reincarnated a week later, to live happily ever after with the concubine.

Another story of "Unique Strange Tales" is about a tragic love affair of one, Chigi, whose affection for Princess Sondok remains unfulfilled. The "Story of a Tiger's Wish", on the other hand, ends happily: Kim Hyon meets a fair virgin while in the act of a prayer-walking around a Buddhist tower. They fall in love, but the virgin transforms herself back to a tigress—her real identity-and rewards her lover for the night's love, so that Kim Hyon may eventually become a man of high position in the court.

During the middle of the Koryo kingdom, a new form of literature began to emerge, growing side by side with the literature of fantasy. The new verse form of narrative literature, under the influence of Chinese literature, depicted anecdotes, jokes, satires, pornography, and commentaries to entertain aristocrats and scholars. Presently remaining works include "The Novel of the White Cloud" by Yi Kumbo, "Collections for Leisure Breaking" by Yi Inno, "Collections for

Leisure-Supplement" by Choe Cha, and "The Folk Stories of Yokyong" by Yi Chaehyon. From a strict point of view, the verse form of narrative literature was a derivative form of narrative literature

By the late Koryo period, narrative literature became more creative, finally to produce numerous fictional "biographies." Animism was used extensively for most of the works, to provide ominous warnings to human life. The biographical stories preserved today include "*Kugsonjon*" by Im Chue, "*Kugsong-Sangjon*" by Yi Kyubo, "*Chukpuinjon*" by Yi Kog, "*Kosangjon*" by Yi Chom, and "*Chongsichajon*" by Sokik Yongam. Such works of creative literature paved the way for the classic novels of the Yi dynasty.

The Early Classic Novels

After the country entered the Yi dynasty period, narrative literature saw such new works as "*Chondam Haei*" by Kang Himaeng and "*Taepyong Hwahwa Hwalgejon*" (The Biography of Peaceful Leisure Stories of Humor) by So Kojong. In the meantime, Chinese literature maintained its steady flow into Korean society, and practically all classic fictions of China, such as "Annals of the Three States" and the "Four Great Books of (Chinese) Romances" were read widely, contributing to the birth of classic novels.

The first work of such imaginative literature was the "*Kumo Sinhwo*" (The New Story of Kumo) by Kim Sisop. This book, written after the model of "The Chondung Sinhwa" of Ming, is a collection of fantasies, of which five stories have survived to the present. The stories differ from the fiction of the Koryo period in two significant respects: first, the scenes were set in Korea, the older stories invariably choosing China and Chinese characters; secondly, the endings are tragic in contrast to the happy endings which marked all works of fiction produced during the Koryo period.

Growth of the Classic Novel

After "The New Stories of Kumo," numerous novels were published, among which "*Hong Kildongjon*" stood out as the most popular masterpiece. Written sometime during the reign of the 15th king, Kwanghaegun, by Ho Kyun, the hero of the story, Hong Kildong, follows a similar fate to that of the author, who apparently vents his disgust with the social system of the time in the novel. The stage of his story is set in his own contemporary society, and the hero mocks the *yangban* (the uppermost social class of the Yi dynasty) with ingenious tricks, finally to crown himself as the ruler of the far-off island of Yugu (Ryukyus). The creator of this hero, author Ho, was, revealingly, executed as a traitor for attempts to overthrow the existing social system.

Another significant work of fiction was "*Kuun mong*" (The Cloud Dream of the Nine) by Kim Manchung. Here the classic novel was endowed with perfect form. The publication of "The Cloud Dream of the Nine" coincided with the social upheaval of the time, accompanying the transition from the old system, based on Confucianism, to the new institution of utilitarian studies, which was then replacing the traditional guiding principles of neo-Confucianism. It was also the time when aristocratic society began to crumble from its medieval foundation, giving way to the rise of the common people. The verse form of literature was then beginning to ascend from the crown, to give way finally to the prose style of literature. All of the social trends of the time were reflected in its literature.

Being a product of such a period of great social transition, the author of "The Cloud Dream of the Nine," Kim Manchung, tried to find a solution to life in his story by presenting the three basic Eastern philosophies—Buddhism, Confucianism, and Taoism. Despite his background as a Confucian scholar, he closed the work with a strong presentation of the Buddhist philosophy of life—that riches, honors, and fame are like a brief dream during a doze in the spring.

"The Cloud Dream of the Nine" is being widely read even today. Dr. Gale of the

American Protestant Mission has translated it into English. It was published by O'Connor of London.

Besides "The Cloud Dream of the Nine," Kim Manchung wrote, among others, "*Sassi Namchonggi*" (The Conquest of the South by the Sa Family), which was a satirical remonstrance against the institution of concubinage, allegedly directed particularly against King Sukchong, who figured in major court scandals involving queen and rival.

The Golden Age of the Classic Novel

Prose came to yield the scepter over verse forms after the reign of the 19th king, Sukchong (1661-1720), and the literary world became flooded with new works. The most popular, even up to the present, of all works of the golden age of the classic novel was "*Chunhyangjon*" (The Tale of Chunhyang).

Written by an anonymous author, presumably between the reigns of the 21st king, Yongjo (1725-1776) and the 22nd king, Chongjo (1777-1801). the novel was expanded, with so many new parts added during the course of many reprintings that the original version has been lost. Therefore, the presently available versions are known to be the work of many hands. The novel is the story of a romance between the son of an upper class family and the daughter of a socially despised *kisaeng* (professional entertainer) daughter. A male servant of the hero was cast in the important role of spokesman for the common people of the time.

The story itself is simple and naive: Yi Toryong, the son of a *yangban*, falls in love with Chunhyang, the *kisaeng* daughter. After turning down repeated overtures of the hero through his comical servant, Pangja, Spring Fragrance (the heroine's name) finally succumbs. The hero, however, is soon ordered by his parents away to the capital city to further his studies, much against his will. At the tearful scene of farewell, the couple pledges eternal love, the girl promising that she will wait forever for his return. After the hero's departure for Seoul, the provincial governor, enraptured by the beauty of the girl, commands her mother to deliver the heroine up as his concubine. The proposal being firmly turned down, the governor imprisons the girl, and, to satisfy his own lust, inflicts sadistic torture, which Chunhyang endures with amazing fortitude. In the meantime, the hero returns to the town in the guise of a beggar in the role of secret royal inspector of the provincial adminstration. Discovering the tragic fate of his lover, he reveals his real identity, handing out stern punishment to the governor, and rescuing the girl. They live happily ever after.

That the story was received with enthusiastic acclaim was indication that it gibed well at aristocracy, against which the common people harbored deep-rooted resentment.

Besides "*Chunhyangjon*" numerous other novels were published during the time, to be endeared to all lovers of literature. Some of the popular works of the time include such stories of military heroes as "*Im Kyongupjon*," "*Choaungjon*," "*So Taesengjon*," "*Yu Chungyoljon*;" "*Yi Chinsajon*;" family-life stories such as "*Changhwa Hongnyonjon*;" fantasies, including "*Ongnumong*," "*Ongnyonmong*," "*Kumwonjon*," "*Chon Uchijon*," "*Wolbong Sangi*."

Probably one of the most notable works of the period is "*Imhwa Chongyon*," by an anonymous writer. To begin with, its length is overwhelming, for it is as voluminous as Tolstoi's longest. It presents altogether several hundred characters, of whom 70 are cast in important roles. The leading roles belong to four women, Im, Hwa, Chong and Yon, all of whom develop a human panorama of immense scope around the hero, Imsaeng.

The Fall of the Classic Novel

The classic novel, which dominated the literary world during the middle of the Yi dynasty, waned rapidly during the late period of the dynasty. By that time, Western civilization and culture began to pour into the land, sweeping away all traditional systems and ideas. The age of "enlightenment" drove away all old forms of literature, giving birth to what was then called the "new" novels, written after the Western style. From then on, all works of fiction began to be written after the Western style.

Short Outlines of the Classic Novels

Following are very brief synopses of some of the most famous classic novels. It should be noted that literary merit cannot survive condensations of this type, and that characters and societies are not herein developed.

Kuunmong
(The Cloud Dream of the Nine)

Written by Kim Manchung in 1689, "The Cloud Dream of the Nine" is a romantic tale of Oriental resignation—that all fames and glories of the world are nothing but a brief dream.

The events start in a celestial kingdom, where a famous saint sends one of his disciples, Songjin, to the Dragon King on an errand, and a saint-matron dispatches her angels to offer fruits and flowers to the Dragon King. On the way to the Dragon King, they meet and indulge in carnal pleasure. As punishment, they are sent to Yama, the Ruler of Hell, and condemned to earth as humans.

The disciple of the saint, Songjin, is born Yang Soyu, while the eight angels are born beautiful girls and grow up to be either famous *kisaeng* (professional entertainers or courtesans) or daughters of respectable families.

The hero establishes himself as a man of fame securing a high position in the royal court after passing the civil examination at an early age. Various romances develop one after another as the hero meets all of the eight women who had been condemned with him. Finally, all nine members gather to talk about the ephemeral nature of human life, and then go back to the celestial kingdom.

Ongnumong
(The Dream of the Jade Chamber)

The hero, Mun Changsong, in the celestial world is condemned to the earth for playing with five angels in the Jade Chamber. Born Mun Sangsong, the hero meets a famous *Kisaeng*, Kang Namhong, who is one of the five angels also condemned to earth. They fall in passionate love and vow matrimony, but fate decrees otherwise.

Passing the civil examination, the hero becomes the most eagerly sought-after bachelor in the capital city, but he marries the virgin, Yu, another of the five condemned angels, upon the recommdation of his mistress *kisaeng*. The hero, however, is soon forced to marry the virgin, Hwan, by royal command, another fallen angel, and then is exiled to a remote place on a false charge brought against him in a factional intrigue there to meet another one of the condemned angels.

When a remote province of the country is invaded by alien forces, the hero leads his troops to repulse the enemy, which is led by no other than the hero's mistress-*kisaeng*. The invasion force is defeated, and during the course of the combat, one of the enemy general's daughters—in fact another one of the fallen angels—falls in love with the hero. The hero takes her to the capital city on his triumphant return to the court. After leading a prosperous life in harmony with his two legally married wives and three concubines, the hero is finally reinstated to heaven with the five fallen angels.

Inhyon Wanghujon
(The Tale of Queen Inhyon)

Written by an anonymous court lady, "The Tale of Queen Inhyon" is a story of court intrigue involving two queens.

After the death of the first queen, King Sukchong marries Queen Inhyon. Being unable to beget a crown prince, the queen asks the king to take Madam Chang as a concubine, which the king does, much against his will.

After begetting a crown prince, Madam Chang intrigues to advance herself to the position of queen, and finally succeeds, expelling Queen Inhyon.

The king, however, feels remorse as time goes on, and when Madam Chang's faction murders most of the deposed queen's supporters, the king reinstates Inhyon as the queen.

Changhwa Hongnyunjon
(The Tale of Rose Flower and Pink Lotus)

Written by an anonymous author, "The Tale of Rose Flower and Pink Lotus" is a typical story of a cruel stepmother who makes life miserable for the two virgins of the flowery names.

The stepmother of the two maids, Rose Flower and Pink Lotus, in an attempt to slander her stepdaughters, hides a large, skinned rat in their bed at night. Next morning the stepmother accuses one of having a miscarriage, and has the girl, Rose Flower, taken away and drowned.

The other maid, Pink Lotus, is informed of her sister's death in a dream, and following a blue bird, goes to the scene of the murder where, in great grief, she plunges into the waters. The spirits of the two virgins then become ghosts of malice, and frighten the provincial governor to death.

The malicious spirits harrass the people so much that finally a renowned warrior is sent from the capital to the place where the ghosts of the virgins appeal to the warrior to punish their stepmother and clear their names. Stepmother then is executed for her crime and the bodies of the two virgins are reclaimed from the river and given a decent burial. Satisfied, the malicious ghosts disappear.

Im Kyongupchon
(The Tale of Im Kyongup)

Written by an anonymous author, "the Tale of Im Kyongup" is historical fiction depicting the mood of the 1600's.

General Im Kyongup, the hero, is dispatched to the Manchu kingdom by royal command in response to an appeal for military aid. As a commanding general of the Manchu forces, the hero annihilates an alien army of invaders and returns to Korea.

The Manchus then invade Korea as a preliminary to an attack on Ming. The hero's successful stand against the invading Manchus at the frontier compels the enemy to make a detour into the country, and the king surrenders to the Manchus, who take three princesses as hostages. Still menaced by the presence of the hero, the outstanding military general who may someday take revenge, the Manchus attempt several assassinations on the hero's life. Finally, they capture him.

As a prisoner in the kingdom of the Manchus, the hero shows so much devotion to the three captive princesses of Korea that the Manchus are sufficiently impressed to release all of their prisoners with appropriate honors.

When the hero returns to the capital with the three princesses, a rival of the hero slanders him, picturing him as a traitor to the king. The latter, however, imprisons the malicious slanderer. Thus threatened, the rival general murders the hero with an iron bar.

Yu Chungyoljon
(The Tale of Yu Chungyol)

Written by an anonymous author, "the Tale of Yu Chungyol" is a story of vengence in fulfillment of a filial duty.

The hero's father is exiled to a remote place as a result of slander by a treacherous subject of the king. Fleeing from the capital for safety, the hero is separated from his mother when they are attacked by a band of robbers.

Arriving at a house of one of his father's friends in the province, the hero marries this man's daughter, but is soon forced to seek safety deep in the mountains away from the malicious designs of his father's slanderer.

In the mountains, the hero meets a hermit sage and learns the arts of warfare. When he hears that his arch-enemy in the court is rebelling against the king in league with other traitors, the hero goes into the capital, where, by virtue of the military arts he has learned in the mountains, he annihilates the enemy. The king appoints him to the highest position in the court in recognition of his meritorious deeds.

The History of Modern Korean Literature

The Era of Enlightenment

A large-scale social revolution along Western lines began in Korea in 1884 following a political incident which ushered in what was then referred to as the era of enlightenment. The rapid Westernization movement reached its peak in 1894, when another political revolution gave impetus to the trend of the times. The new movement swept through every phase of Korean society, and literature was far from being an exception. A new literary movement began germinating from the very start of the Korean era of enlightenment; it was finally to overrun completely the traditional approach to literature.

In 1996, Yi Injik, who had stood at the forefront of the Westernization movement, presented Korean society with a novel under the title, "The Tears of Blood"—a work which shook his contemporaries and was destined to became the first milestone in the country's compulsive march into literary Westernization.

The Era of "New" Novels

"The Tears of Blood" was followed by several other fictional works in a similar vein, thereby giving rise to the eruption of the "new" novels in the 1910's. What were then called the "new" novels contained many elements of the old, traditional Korean writings, but there was a significant difference from the old stories—their fervent spirit, a compulsion to enlighten the people. Every author of a "new" novel, including pioneers Yi Injik, Yi Haejo, An Kwangmi, and Yi Sanghyop, attempted to infuse modern, Western ideas through his works. Therefore, their fictions preached such concepts as the political sovereignty of the people, economic independence, promotion of Western—style education and science, end to superstition, etc.

From a strictly literary view—point, however, the "new" novels were without exception little more than naive attempts to produce artistic products. Nevertheless, they made a lasting contribution to Korean literature, paving the way for future development and consolidation of the literary revolution.

Rise of Songs

Side by side with the "new" novels, a new form of poetry gained popularity during the 1910's—the song poem. The words of the songs, which retained many elements of traditional Korean verse style, approached Western-style poems in cadenza and treatment of vocabulary. Like the "new" novels, songs of the time promoted the enlightenment of the people as indicated in the titles,"Independence," "Railroad," "Scholarship," "Around the World." Such songs with appropriate music were chanted enthusiastically by the young people for a long time, even when the era of enlightenment was over. In the meantime, writers of the song—poems gradually leaned away from songs, finally to develop the "new" poetry movement.

The Changing Literary Scene

As the country moved into the 1910's, a new literary movement emerged, marking the second stage of modern literature in

Korea. In defiance of the "new" novels and the songs, which were distorted in the shackles of the old traditions, two literary giants of Korea established a radically modern force: Choe Namson in poetry, and Yi Kwangsu in novels.

Choe Namson started his literary career in 1908, publishing the first magazine for children, entitled: "The Boy." He then established himself as a pioneer of the "new" poems by publishing in his magazine such works as "From the Sea," "To the Boys," and "The Boys of New Korea," which were marked by a free style of expression in contrast to the rigid adherence to the formalism of traditional poetry. He made another definite contribution to literature by initiating a colloquial style of writing through such fictions as "The Pink Skirt," "Boys," and "The Star at Dawn".

Yi Kwangsu exerted a much stronger influence through his pioneering works in the field of Western-style fiction. In 1914, he published a short story under the title, "To Our Young Friends", in the form of a personal letter, which proved to be the first really modern fictional piece ever written by a Korean pen. Subsequently, from 1918, he wrote a succession of long novels, including "The Heartless, "The Revival," and "The Pioneer". In 1931, he published "The Soil", which, together with "The Heartless", are considered two of the greatest masterpieces of the time. He is, indeed, considered the undisputed master of fiction throughout the 50-year history of modern literature in Korea.

So great was the influence of Yi Kwangsu that an astoundingly large number of youths aspired to become novelists during the late 1910's.

Young Writers of the "Creation" Circle

A group of young students of literature, then studying in Japan, organized themselves in 1919 into a literary association in order to publish the first Korean language literary association magazine, "Creation," in Tokyo. Leading members of the group, which later became known as the Creation Circle, were Kim Tongin, Chon Yongtaek, Chu Yohan and Kim Ok. Although inspired originally by the works of Yi Kwangsu, the young writers of the Creation Circle in one aspect were in opposition to the early master: they advocated pure art in literature in defiance of Yi Kwangsu's belief that the art forms shuld be used for political enlightenment of the people, a strain which runs quite obviously through all of his works. The basic attitude of the young writers naturally led them to naturalism, marking the introduction of this Western concept of art to Korea.

Among the members of the Creation Circle, Kim Tongin and Chon Yongtaek wrote notable novels, creating pure works of literature untainted by the heavy nationalistic soliloquies of Yi Kwangsu. Chu Yohan concentrated solely on poetry, though virtually all leading members of the Creation Circle published both novels and poems. Especially noteworthy was Chu Yohan's "Fire Play," which stood out as one of the best contribution in the development of Western-style poetry in Korea.

Another significant contribution rendered by the group was the overall improvement of modern Korean writing by forceful attempts to differentiate the tenses—past, present, and future. They used dialects in their works. All three of the leading members of the group—Chu Yohan, Chon Yong taek, and Kim Tongin—later became undisputed masters of modern Korean literature.

The Growth of "The Ruins"

In 1920, a group of young men of letters published their own literary association magazine, "The Ruins". Their literary movement was a continuation of the work begun on the groundwork laid by the "Creation" group. Prominent members of the group were such poets as Kim Ok, O Sangsun, Hwang Sogu, and Namgung Pyok, all of whom introduced symbolism into their works. The popularity of symbolism was in most part due to the French influence of the late eighteenth century. Previously, Kim Ok published his own translated versions of various French poems in 1918 in a weekly magazine, but it was not until publication of "The Ruins" that symbolism became a formidable force among the poets. The decadent school of Symbolism, after the French style, then literally swept through the Korean literary circles of the 1920's, reflecting the utterly desperate feeling which prevailed at that time. Such a state of affairs became inevitable when it finally seemed clear to the Korean people that, in all likelihood, Korea would not be able to free herself from the humiliation of being a subjugated nation forever under Japanese domination. The nation-wide independence movement in 1919 failed to achieve the ends its martyrs so ardently set forth.

The poetry of the period, therefore, brimmed with desperation. A pathetic nihilism was the spirit of the times. The same was true with the novels of that era. Yom Sangsop, a leading novelist of "The Ruins" magazine, together with other writers, such as Kim Tongin and Hyon Chingon, cast frustrated, decadent characters in the role of heroes.

Yom Sangsop, however, had inclined more towards naturalism from the very beginning of his career in 1920, when he published a short story, "The Green Frog in the Specimen Gallery," in "Creation" magazine. Subsequently he published numerous stories, including "The Dark Night", "The Last Night", "A Small Incident", all of which showed his leaning towards naturalism.

Hyon Chingon, who emerged into literary circles at about the same time as Yom Sangsop, also wrote many works in which naturalism played its due role, such as "The Degraded", "One Lucky Day", "Fire", etc. Both Yom Sangsop and Hyon Chingon, together with the three pioneers of the modern Korean novel, Yi Kwangsu, Kim Tongin and Chon Yongtaek, were later to became the "five early masters," who were to be credited as a group with the initial development of modern fiction in Korea.

Romanticism of the "White Tide"

In 1922, the literary association organ magazine, "White Tide," was published by a group of young poets and novelists who were intoxicated with romanticism. The members included such poets as Hong Nojak, Yi Sanghwa, Pak Yonghi, and Pak Chonghwa, and the novelists Hyon Chingon and Na Tohyang. Writing in a romantic vein, they poured out the universally accepted state of decadent desperation in their works, as was the case with certain writers of the "Ruins." Recalling the period, however, one of the members of the "White Tide," Pak Yonghi, was later to write: "The 1920's were a golden period of poems...Every man of letters assumed himself a poet regardless of his ability in poetry."

The "White Tide" group members were later to become prominent figures in literary circles. Among them, the poet Hong Nojak left "I Am The King, Sir" and Yi Sanghwa, "The Madonna," each making a considerable contribution to the growth of Korean poetry. Pak Yonghi later switched to literary criticism, while Pak Chonghwa, after first shifting from poetry to fiction, finally became one of the best historical writers. Na Tohyang, who demonstrated his talent at the age of 19 with "The Play of Illusion", left many works of sentimental romanticism and naturalism before his premature death.

In addition to the "White Tide" group, several other notable poets appeared on the scene about this time. The most prominent of them was Kim Sowol, who wrote many sentimental poems of a romantic strain in the Korean folk song style. Despite his premature death, which put a far too early end to his promising career, Kim Sowol left many quaintly exquisite pieces, such as "The Azalea" and "Flowers in the Mountain" which won immortal fame among his lyric poems, and are still especially treasured by many young lovers of literature in this reconstruction age.

Another poet of the "golden era" was Pyon Yongno, who published works of symbolism, such as "Sulsang Chikchong." Kim Hyongwon, on the other hand, introduced the poetry of America's Walt Whitman through Korean translations, while Kim Tonghwan popularized poetry among the general public through the publication of his long poem, "The Nights on The Frontier", in 1923. Both Kim Tonghwan and Kim Hongwon are considered to have planted the seeds of a so-called proletarian literature soon to blossom through their literary works for the edification of the man in the street.

The Buddhist poet, Han Yongun, who was yet to build his literary fame, started his literary career at about this time also, but it was much later that he published the important anthology, "The Lover's Silence." A Buddhist priest, his works impressed his readers with the profoundness of his philosophical meditation.

Two masters of the *Sijo* (the traditional Korean short poetry form), Yi Pyonggi and Yi Unsang, were also products of the "golden era". Two women, Kim Myongsun and Kim Wonju, were also active poets of the time.

The "New Trend" Group

A new literary movement began to assert itself late in 1923. It was somewhat later referred to as the "New Trend" group literature, which was a predecessor of "the Proletarian" literature which gained wide popularity a few years later.

This new movement was reflection of the socialist action which began to spread in 1920. From a literary point of view, the new movement was in defiance of the romanticism which predominated in the "White Tide" group. However, several members of the "White Tide" group, notably Kim Kijin, stood at the forefront of the new movement, spreading in earnest the gospel of socialist literature. This influence was soon to be seen in the works of Pak Chonghwa, Pak Yonghi, and Yi Sanghwa, who published their works in "The Kaebyok" (The Dawn of History) magazine. The "New Trend" literary works lashed out at the established writers in a fury of criticism charging that the old writers "disregarded the masses". Literature for the "proletarian class" then became a heated topic, a fountain of controversy.

The "New Trend" group literature was characterized by its theme choice of the lowest social class, its portrayal of the abject poverty of the low income mass. This was a vast change from former habits, wherein writers cast mostly middle-class characters in their novels. The "New Trend" merely followed popular requirements of the time and a few bad elements of conscious defiance of the upper social class.

Virtually all works of the "New Trend" group shared common endings: the poetry was concluded with abstract shouting, and all fiction came to a tragic, terrifying end usually with a murder or arson. Such endings were accepted with enthusiastic acclaim at that time, and, naturally, every writer felt impelled to make a lunatic criminal of his hero at the close of his novel.

The best example of this style of fiction-writing was furnished by Choe Sohae with "Starvation and Murder," published in 1925. Other writers of the time who did not belong to the radical group were not immune to its powerful influence. Kim Tongin in his "Potato," Hyon Chingon in "The Fire," and Chu Yosop in his "Rikshawman" and "Murder" showed styles similar to that of the "New Trend" group.

The "Proletarian" Literature

The literature of the "New Trend" group lasted for only about two years, making way for "proletarian" literature in 1925, following organization of the Proletarian Arts League.

The era of "proletarian" literature was thus ushered in. The movement differed from the "New Trend" group in two significant respects: in contrast to individual activities for socialism which marked the "New Trend" group, the proletarian literary movement featured organized activities under a unified command. Furthermore, it was a conscious political movement for socialism in the guise of literary activity, whereas the "New Trend" group placed literature above politics, true as it was that they, in effect, served the same ends.

Such basic differences between the two groups were manifested much too clearly in the essay, "Turning of the Literary Movement," by Park Yonghi, published in 1926. Explaining the reasons for the shift from the "New Trend" to the proletarian literary movement, the author emphasized in the article the importance of a conscious effort to utilize literature as a means to the political ends of socialism. As socialist action swept through the country, the proletarian literature gathered force for several years, finally to dominate literary circles for some time. Serving political gods, however, was not conducive to creating even a passable work of art, and, naturally, none of the proletarian group left any work of importance from a strictly literary point of view.

So powerful and lasting has the socialistic literary movement been that many writers became "sympathizers" of the "proletarian" cause through their works. While Pak Yonghi and Kim Kijin continued their activities as the confirmed representatives of proletarian literature, such novelists as Yi Kiyong, Han Solya, Kim Namchon and several poets, including Yim Hwan, created work which placed them among the "sympathizer group."

The era of proletarian literature was also a period of lively contests for supremacy among several literary groups. As the "proletarian" men of letters rode on the crest of the tide, other writers who had started their careers earlier challenged the upstart socialists. Representatives of the naturalism group were Kim Tongin, Chon Yongtaek, Yom Sangsop, and Hyon Chingon, while the nationalistic literary group was under the command of Yi Kwangsu and Chu Yohan. The "White Tide" group also hastened to the scene of the battle.

The novelists and poets of the nationalist group lashed out at the socialistic writers who denied the very existence of "literature" produced as art. They also resorted to the time-proven formula of recalling the glorious past of Korean literature. Thus, in 1926, the nationalists proclaimed *Hangul* (Korean Alphabet) Day in memory of the formulation of the unique Korean phonetic symbols by the fourth king of the Yi dynasty. They also promoted a revival of the Korean classical poem, the *sijo*. This movement against proletarian literature headed by Yi Kwangsu, Choe Namson, and Yi Pyonggi, gained support from the devotees of naturalism, such as Yom Sangsop and Hyon Chingon.

The hostility between the nationalists and socialists produced what was soon identified as the "compromise" group, under the leadership of the poet, Yang Chudong, and the up-and-coming literary critic, Chong Nopung. They suggested that both the proletarian men of letters and the nationalistic writers in effect were serving a common cause against Japanese imperialism with the pen. The compromise proposal was a reflection of the movement for a unified struggle against Japanese domination through the political assembly, The New Stem Association, organized in 1926.

The "Compromise" group held on to a considerably significant area of the literary stage around 1929, but they clashed head on with the proletarian group. The center of their controversy was the conflicting views on the importance of form for literary success. Whereas the proletarian group advocated the uppermost importance of content, the compromise faction emphasized superiority of form over contents. Prolonged wrangling ensued over the issue, each group publishing essays one after another in their asssociation magazines.

The anarchists also found themselves in violent conflict with the proletarian writers.

The most active combatants for the anarchist camp were the poet, Kwon Kuhyon, and the literary critic, Kosan. In the meantime, another distinct group began to win popular recognition and acceptance, to be identified as "fellow-travelling" writers. They were fellow-travellers of the socialists in that their works were unmistakably sympathetic to or almost identical with the proletarian literature, but the writers themselves did not belong to the socialist literary organization (The Proletarian Arts League). Among the writers who were known as "fellow-travellers", prominent figures were such novelists as Yu Chino, Yi Hyosok, Cha Mansik, Han Intaek, and the poet, Kim Haegang.

Yu Chino's "Shopgirls" and Yi Hyosok's "The Coast of the Russian Territory" won fame for the authors as excellent novelists along the "fellow-travelling" line.

Such widespread inclination towards socialism was inevitable, for it was the rage of the time, and every person who considered himself an intellect regarded it a privilege to join the parade sponsored by international socialism.

The proletarian literature which had established itself as such a dominant force withered rapidly in 1931 under the Japanese suppression of socialism. A new era of literature succeeded the evidently colorful ten-year period of socialist-dominated literary activities.

A New Turn in Literature

Literature was forced to make a new turn in 1931. The year was marked by the outbreak of what the Japanese termed "the Manchurian Incident," which was actually a prelude to the Japanese invasion of China. The sudden rush of events towards overt acts of imperialism and militarism by Japan exerted a profound influence on Korean cultural as well as literary circles. The Japanese police issued one order after another to dissolve all nationalistic and socialistic organizations in Korea. The New Stem Association, which had attempted to place the Korean independence movement under a unified command, was the first to receive the blow. The Korean Artists' Proletarian Federation, which commanded the socialist writers was next. A sudden police raid on the latter ended with many key staff members of the organization in Japanese prisons, and another large-scale police roundup of its members in 1934 left the socialist organ utterly powerless. Finally, in 1935, the body was forced to dissolve itself, thus putting an end to "proletarian" literature.

As the socialist era began to wane from 1931, a new literary trend emerged. It was a movement for *belles-lettres*, a revulsion against proletarian literature. This new movement was already in the making in 1930, when a monthly poetry magazine, "The Poetics," was published by a group of poets who were later to join the ranks of the most important poets in Korea, for the young group was headed by Yi Hayun, Pak Yongchol, Chong Chiyong, and Kim Yongnang. Their movement swelled in 1931, when "The Monthly Literature and Arts" was published as a successor to "Poetics." In this literary magazine appeared the works of several novelists and playwrights, such as Hong Haesong, Yu Chijin, and Hong Il, as well as poems written by the Poetics' group.

A noteworthy feature of the "Monthly Literature and Art" was the extensive introduction of foreign literary works. The year 1931 having been the centennial of the death of Goethe, the magazine alloted liberal space to articles on the German writer. Many foreign works, especially poems, were translated and appeared in the magazine.

By this time a large number of students of literature returned to Korea after studying foreign literature in Japan and other foreign countries. They started the introduction of foreign literature in earnest, gaining widespread recognition. Calling themselves the Foreign Literature Group, such persons as Chong Insop, Kim Chinsop, Yi Hongu, and Kim Kwangsop, together with the initial members of the Monthly Literature and Arts group, published numerous articles on, and translations of, foreign literary masterpieces in both magazines and daily newspapers.

The Foreign Literature Group also started a modern drama movement in 1931, organizing the Drama Arts Study Association. For about five years after the birth of the organization, they staged translated versions of many modern dramas of the West. The woman poet, Mo Yunsuk, and novelist Yi Muyong soon joined the foreign literature group. Previously, during the initial period of the foreign literature group and their Drama Arts Study Association, the members had engaged in bitter controversies with the proletarian group, then enjoying great influence.

In 1933, a group of writers and poets organized themselves into the Nine Men Association and began to assert the importance of art in literature. Among the nine members, Yi Hyosok had cleansed himself of his former inclinations towards "proletarian" literature. It was indeed eloquent testimony that the once-powerful proletarian literature tenants had disappeared from the scene. Of the nine men, the poet Kim Kirim and the novelist Yi Taejun, Yi Hyosok, and Pak Taewon were destined to become masters of Korean literature.

The fall of proletarian literature was evinced by the introduction of "modernism" from Western literary circles. The poetry and theory of Ezra Pound was first introduced by Kim Kirim in 1933, to be accepted as "modernism", cultivating a new field in the poetry movement. Subsequently, T. S. Eliot became popular. Thus, in and around 1933, Korean poetry was in close contact with its Western sister. In 1934, the intellectualism of English and American literature, notably that of Aldous Huxley, was implanted by Choe Cheso, who had majored in English literature. Furthermore, Yi Sang and others began to write psychological novels, contributing to further modernization of literary technique. Under such influence, considerable numbers of modern young writers appeared, including Chang Manyong and Kim Kwanggyun—all attempting to probe into the melancholy world of the introverted psychology of the intelletuals. Thus the few years following 1931 saw the rise of several important forces on the literary horizon.

While the proletarian literature retained only a lingering influence after its decade of glory, the socialistic literature went through a transition period, prolonging its life in the form of literature evoking the "agony" of the times. The "agony" was a product of the era of anxiety, for the men of letters and other intellectuals were now starkly faced with the ominous threat of Naziism and Fascism in Europe, ominous since 1933, along with the intensified Japanese imperialism manifested in the invasion of Manchuria in 1931. Such uneasiness, fear, and anxiety, and the widespread unemployment among intellectuals, were taken up immediately as the theme of literary works by ex-devotees of the proletarian literature group. The writers who formerly belonged to the "fellow-travelling" group also joined the new tide, to produce many a work of gloomy depression. Most writers who started their literary careers about this time also wrote in a similar vein, including the women novelists Pak Hwasong, Kang Kyongae, and Choe Chonghi.

While the era of anxiety was in progress, the winds of humanism from the West began to engulf the world in defiance of the totalitarianism of Hitler and Mussolini. The new thought was introduced to Korea in 1935-36, and literary circles showed an animated interest in humanism for some time. However, the increasing suppression by the Japanese police of Korean intellectuals soon wiped out all signs of the acceptance of humanism in literary circles.

The "Dark" Age

Literature was thrust into a "dark" age in 1937, when Japan started its full-fledged invasion of the Chinese mainland. Every activity of Korean society was placed under the iron grip of Japanese wartime policy. As the war on the China mainland was prolonged with no apparent end in sight, the Japanese tightened their grip still harder, finally to ban the 4,000-year old Korean language at schools and at official functions throughout the Korean peninsula.

The anxiety caused by the Japanese plan to destroy Korean culture was by this time firmly rooted among the people, and, consequently, men of letters expressed their ardent wish to escape from reality. Thus the poets composed songs of "anxieties", "blues" and the spirit of "darkness". Novelists resorted to various devices to express this desire for escape. For instance, Yi Taejun longed after bygone days in his novel, "Real Estate Broker." Han Solya depicted a character of debauchery under the weight of reality in his "Wrestling", Yi Hyosok wrote "The Rose Is Sick" to present a case of morbid reality.

On the other hand, some writers of fiction attempted to escape through satire and cynicism. Don Quixote was the prototype of the hero of Choe Mansik's "Had I Only Believed in Christ" (1937), and Yi Kiyong's "Human Training" (1938). Such literary satire became so popular that the literary critic, Im Chaeso, was compelled to write 'The Satirical Novel" in 1937, expressing his conviction that under the circumstances, satire was the best available means to literary quality.

Besides satire, other devices were chosen to allow full escape from grim reality. Thus, historical fiction became popular, so much so that Yun Paengnam and Kim Tongin published an exclusive magazine of historical fiction in 1938 under the title, "Yadam" (Historical Stories). Such escape into the past gained so much popularity that the theaters staged many historical dramas and were rewarded with resounding financial success.

Finding it difficult to set the scene in contemporary society, an increasingly large number of writers went back to Korean history to choose themes for their stories. Some of the masterpieces of Korean historical fiction were indeed products of this period. Noteworthy works of the time were "The Biography of Im Kokchong" by Hong Myonghi (1936), "Blood on the Silk Dress" (1935) by Pak Chonghwa, "They, the Youth" (1938) by Kim Tongin, and "The Tower without Shadow" (1937) by Hyon Chingon.

The popularity of historical fiction inevitably led literary circles to revive their interest in the past, which became a topic of lively discussion. Many essays appeared in magazines and newspapers under such titles as "The Characteristic of the Time As Depicted in Old Novels", "The Traditions of Korean Literature and the Classics", "The Beggar's God and Oriental Sentiment".

Another popular type of fiction-writing was what was then called "social life" novels. Such novels depicted contemporary society, but a critical description of reality was only conspicuous for its absolute absense throughout these tracts. The author merely wrote about contemporary scenes with, so to speak, the camera's eye, refraining from any comment whatsoever. A representative work of such style was "The Scene on the River Coast" (1936) by Pak Taewon. Many writers who had formerly published fiction of a political bent began to follow the trend. For instance, Yu Chino wrote "Dear Friends" and "The Fall", both in 1939, and Cho Yongman wrote "A Record From Beginning to End", utilizing an extreme form of photographic realism.

Another noteworthy feature of the period was the rise of the "farm novels." True, several authors had already set the scenes of their stories on the farm, as in the case of "The Soil" (1937) by Yi Kwangsu and "The Evergreen" (1934) by Sim Hun, but it was in 1938 that Yi Muyong set the pace for "farm novels" by publishing a series about the rural districts in a deliberate attempt to back-handedly denounce Japanese-dominated urban life as he found it. His works along that line include "Chapter 1, Lesson 1," "The Slaves of the Soil," and "The Farmer." It was, indeed, the gloomy atmosphere of the urban areas that had sent writers to the farm in search of peace of mind.

On the other hand, popular fiction catering to the less sophisticated segment of the population gained force. Virtually all of such fiction for popular entertainment was serialized in the daily newspapers, presenting the readers with stories of melodramatic romance, always with an idealized hero and heroine. "The Jungle" (1936) by Kim Malbong, "The Wild Rose" (1937) by the same authoress, and "The Song of Sacrificial Love" (1940) by Pak Keju, all written in such veins, were received by the popular readers with wild acclaim. Even Kim Namchon published such romantic nonsense as "The Aquarium of Love" (1939), ignoring his own past as the fierce champion of "proletarian" literature.

New Writers of the "Dark" Age

While the old writers were resigned to their fate under the shadow of gloomy reality, a crop of new writers appeared on the literary stage. Whereas the old, established men of letters were brooding over the present and dwelling on the memory of a freer past, the young literary aspirants showed a radically different view of literature and life. These new writers were not burdened with the pleasant memories of the good old days. They simply accepted reality as it was, and tried to build up their literary careers under the prevailing social atmosphere without much ado. So wide was the gap separating the old school and the new, that the young group was identified as the writers of the "new era." They were mostly novelists who won recognition from 1935 to 1940 after making debuts in the two dailies, *Tonga Ilbo* and *Chosun Ilbo*, which sponsored literary prize contests each year and serialized prize winning works.

The writers of the "new era," such as Pak Yongjun, Kim Tongni, Chong Pisok, Kwak Hasin, Hyon Tok, Kim Yongsu, and Choe Inuk, endeavored to write for literature's own sake, in contrast to the old "masters" who felt obliged to tinge their works with political thought. The scope of the young writers' fiction was extensive and colorful. For example, Kim Tongni depicted certain mysterious phases of humanity, incorporating this in the traditional manners and customs, while Chong Pisok showed interest in the local color in his "The Songhwang Shaman Temple". Hyon Tok excelled in writing about the lowest class of society in its minutest details, but apparently with no deliberate sympathy for socialism, unlike such works in the past.

The new breed of young writers steadily encroached upon the literary domains of the established writers of the older generation, finally to occupy an important segment of the local literary world. Their vigorous drive eventually surpassed the old timers' for fame and fortune; within the social framework, they accepted inertia in literary activities, their constant struggle to avoid outright combat with a reality they could not accept.

Despite the unfavorable social conditions, a larger number of literary works were produced than in any previous period. During the five-year period from 1935 to 1941, altogether more than 50 anthologies of poetry were published, an unprecedented occurrence. Also, the number of novels published during this time broke all records, notably due to two literary magazines, published in 1939, "The Sentence" and "The Humanities Review". The two literary magazines made significant contribution to the growth of literature, even though they lived no more than three years. On these magazines, many young novelists and poets found their first audiences, including the poets, Pak Tujong, Pak Namsu, Cho Chihun, and Pak Mokwol, and the novelists, Choe Taeung and Im Ogin. They were indeed the last crop to sprout in the literary field during the Japanese domination period—all literary activities for all practical considerations came to an end at the close of 1941, when Japan plunged into the Pacific War.

After the declaration of war against the allies, Japan stepped up its suppression of the Korean language, placing a ban on the publication of the two literary magazines (The Sentence and The Humanities Review). Thus did Korean literary activities cease until the close of World War II with the defeat of Japan in 1945.

The Post-Liberation Turmoil

The Liberation of Korea from Japan in August, 1945, as a result of the Allied victory, shattered in one stroke all the shackles which had kept Korean literary circles in bond. The men of letters, however, were soon to suffer the fearful pains of the post-Liberation political turmoil. The division of the land into northern and southern areas of occupation by the U.S. and Soviet forces threw the country into utter confusion, and literature had to prepare the ground for resumed activities amidst a growing storm of social unrest.

As soon as the Liberation was assured, several leading men of letters organized the Literary Construction Headquarters in Seoul to embrace all writers. The new organization was soon reorganized under the name of the League of Men of Letters, manifesting itself as an all-inclusive Communist front organ. To counter this movement, several leading nationalist writers grouped themselves together in the All-Korea Association of the Men of Letters in 1946, while another group of writers organized the Association of the Korean Young Men of Letters.

The Communist camp under the League of the Men of Letters and the nationalist factions lashed out at each other until 1948, when order was restored with the establishment of the Republic of Korea government. Then virtually all men of letters came under the Association of the Korean Men of Letters as a section of the Federation of Cultural Groups in Korea.

During the post-war period, not a single literary work of any significance was produced, for men of letters busied themselves with politics, and the hostilities between the nationalist and Communist writers took forms other than the pen. Nevertheless, considerable quantities of literary works were published during the period in such magazines as "The New World", "The Voice of the People", "The White Race", "The New Literature", and "The Literature". The numerous, short-lived magazines and daily newspapers furnished excellent training grounds for aspirants, producing several new writers. For instance, Han Musuk won recognition after publishing her prize-winning novel "History Flows" in "The Sun News," and Son Sohi made her debut in "The New Generation" magazine; and Kim Songhan, O Yongsu, and Hong Kubom in either the "Seoul Daily News" or the magazine "The New World." "The Literary Arts" magazine, which was first published in 1949, also produced many young writers, including Son Changsop, Chang Yonghak, and Kang Sinjae. A small group of young poets, including Pak Inhwan, Kim Kyongnin, and Cho Kyong, asserted themselves with what they called modernism, publishing an anthology under the title "The Chorus Between the City and Citizens".

Novels produced by established writers during the post-Liberation period include "The New Affection" by Pak Yongjun, "The Gallant Horse" by Kim Tongni, "The Wind Blows As Ever" by Kye Yongmuk, "The Wild Lily" by Choe Inuk, "Native Town" by Choe Taeung, "The Hen" by Choe Chonghi, "Chance Encounter" by Om Sangsop, "The Darkening Color" by Chong Pisok, "The Brother" by Im Ogin, and "Sentimental Journey" by An Sugil. Many poets of the old school resumed their activities, including Kim Kwangsop, Yi Hayun, Mo Yunsuk, Cho Chihun, Pak Tuchin, Yu Chihwa, Pak Mokwol, and Chang Manyong.

When Korean literature was thus about to resume its growth after establishment of the Republic of Korea government and a period of experimentation, the Korean War broke out in 1950. During the war, most men of letters took refuge in the free south. The wartime temporary capital city of Pusan at the southern tip of the Korean peninsula harbored many writers. "The New World" and "The Literary Arts" resumed publication in refugee-crowded Pusan, and new magazines came off the presses of that city, including "The Free World," "Thoughts," and

"Hope", which ere filled with fiction and poetry, the writers living refugee lives. Literary works during the Korean conflict, however, were mostly eye-witness accounts of battle scenes. Exceptional were war novels with some artistic merit, "The Partisans" by Pak Yongjun and "The Posterity of Cain" (1954) by Hwang Sunwon being such exceptions.

The Post-Korean War Period

After the armistice in 1952, virtually all men of letters returned to Seoul to resume their careers. But hostility between the two leading groups of writers erupted into a bitter contest for supremacy, dividing all men of letters into two rival camps. One of the groups tried to consolidate its ground by reorganization of the Association of Korean Men of Letters, while its opponents organized themselves into the Association of the Liberal Men of Letters at the end of 1954. The writers of the former group carried their works in the magazine, "Modern Literature," while the rival group had the "Liberal Literature" publish theirs. Although the struggle between the two groups is yet to be resolved, the real writers slowly began to feel the uppermost importance of writing meritorious works of art instead of indulging in such struggles for power. The bitter part of the rivalry thus ceased of itself.

In the meantime, a series of significant events took place in literary circles. In 1954, the Korean Acadamy of Arts was established and began to wield an authoritative influence, and in 1955, the Korean Chapter of the P.E.N. was organized to promote cultural exchanges with Western countries, including in its goals the projected translations of several Korean literary works into English. A group of poets, dissatisfied with the existing associations, organized the Korean Poets' Association to assert themselves, and a crop of young literary critics established the Literary Critics' Asssociation.

Several literary awards were instituted: in 1955, the Asia Foundation, largely supported by U.S. citizens on the American West Coast, set up the Freedom Literature Awards, giving prizes annually to several novelists or poets; in 1957, the Korean Academy of Arts stated its Literary Merit Awards; jointly the Korean Association of the Men of Letters and the Korean Association of the Liberal Men of Letters instituted the annual New Writers' Awards; the Kim Tongin Literary Award was established in memory of the late old master of novels.

Increasing opportunity was offered to writers, both young and old, by a strong flock of magazines newly published since 1958, such as "Modern Literature," "Liberal Public Opinion," "The Thought World," and "The New Sun."

Thus, by 1958, everything pointed to signs that literature had recovered completely from the post-World War II turmoil and the chaos of the Korean War. In 1959, publication of literary works became most active, with voluminous series going to the presses, including the Korean Poets' Series.

Meanwhile, the vastly expanded institutions of higher learning are producing each year hundreds of literary graduates, many of whom aspire to earn their living with the pen. Ever alert to all opportunities to board the literary bandwagon, some of them have succeeded in having their works printed by winning the annual literary contests sponsored by virtually all leading daily newspapers.

In a permanent revolution dating to the birth of mankind, young, intensely ambitious aspirants, identifying themselves as such, are now struggling to break into the hallowed preserves of their established seniors.

But with Korea in the throes of an all-pervading economic, social, cultural revolution, this struggle of the young to "break through" has taken on increased significance. It is far more a form of combat, with the heirs to the ferment of postwar, reconstructed Korea almost desperately determined to shelve their elders.

This is a grim struggle with the defenders mostly older men who have had their principles tempered in the grim fires of a militant anti-colonialism and in the worldwide clash of politics vs. art.

The young writers, buffeted by violent changes in society, knowing a fiery dedication to freedom and to shining images of democracy and advanced technology, have no such principles, indeed seem most to be inconsistent with the realities of the Korean phoenix.

They stand nowhere, yet seek painfully, to tear open the wrappings placed in the past and present by the often too-dedicated pens of their elders.

The new pens are destructive, searching for the beast in man that has led him to the excesses of authoritarianism and cruelty in the past and present. Once presented, this beast is ugly and demoralizing—an anathema to the older writers, but, to the new, a tonic, bitter but necessary to purge society of indigestible images partaken too casually in the mass excitement of feasts beset with causes and false glory.

Korean literary circles see this confrontation flaming wildly within the next few years, for the adversaries can win a prize unknown to their forebears—a Korean nation almost completely literate, where the poor as well as the rich read and write, and the successful writer can truly claim to be a leader and one chosen among his people.

Pitted here are experienced men used to group activity and determined that the principles they hold close shall be disseminated more widely than ever before possible. And pitted here are untried men, wholly individualistic in approach, feverishly portraying Faulkneresque scenes, too driven to apply the Sartre and Camus they pore over in the evenings, many so painfully groping as to spew forth only abstractions but all determined to "awaken" and lead forth to new creativity the newly born Korean, the great mass of the nation that learned to read since the 1945 Liberation.

Modern Literature: The Novel

Emergence of the "New Novels"

The new force towards modernization gave birth to a new style of story-presentation in the 1910's, known as the "new" novel. The word, new, which capped the word, novel, manifested itself as something to be distinguished from the traditional novel. Nevertheless the "new" novel fell short of what may be properly called modern fiction in our present-day conception of the term. For one thing, the "new" novel contained too many elements of the traditional style of story-telling to come under the classification of modern-style fiction. The "new" novel was rather a mixture of the old and new, an inevitable outcome of the early literary movement for modernization. Hence, students of the history of Korean literature refer to the "new" novel as the "transition" novel. The "new" novel, therefore, was destined to bridge the transition period between the centuries-old traditional style of story-telling and the forthcoming Western style of fiction.

The "new" novel swept through Korean literary circles from 1906 to 1915, producing about ten major popular writers. Among the crop of new writers, Yi Injik, treated previously in this section, distinguished himself as the pioneer as well as the most outstanding craftsman. His work, "The Voice of a Devil," in particular, has been on the lips of many a man of letters as the representative work of the "new" novels. Besides this work, Yi Injik is credited with several other major works, including "The Tears of Blood," known as the pioneer work in the movement, "The Silvery World", and "Pheasant Hill". Yi Haejo was noted for his prolific writings.—"The Liberty Bell",

"The Peony Fence," "The Jailed Flowers," and "The Blood of the Flowers," among many others. Other writers of new novels include Choe Chansik ("The Color of the Full Moon," "A Dream in the Spring," etc.,) Muk Chongsu, Yi Sanghyop, Pak Yongjin, Kim Ikchu, Namgung Chon, and Son Uil.

Certainly "new" as they were, the works of such writers could not quite make the break from the bonds of the traditional. They all retained in common many characteristics of the old style. To begin with, their writings failed to adopt completely the prose style of modern fiction, for they were still under the lingering influence of the Chinese verse style, which had dominated story-telling before their time. The themes of their fiction were also inspired by the traditional ideas of age-old Oriental moral preaching—presenting a dramatic case of reproving vice and rewarding virtue. Therefore, the feudal way of thinking was the dominant motive for all the "new" novels. Nevertheless, the "new" novels did embrace a few significant elements of modern literary ideas. First of all, they adopted the prose style of writing to a considerable extent in spite of the powerful influence of the traditional Chinese verse style which appeared in their writings. The "new" novels also used the descriptive style in contrast to the traditional narrative style of the past. Imposd upon their feudal way of thinking were such modern ideas as the equality of men and women, suppression of superstitious practices, etc. They were "new" novels in that they set the scene of the story in the realistic world in contrast to the myths and legends which had supplied materials to the "old" novels. The "new" novels were, furthermore, analytical, and not necessarily chronological, as against the faithful observance of the time sequence followed by the "old" novels.

Such mixtures of the "old" and "new" continued for about ten years, in the early 1910's, paving the way for the emergence of full-fledged "modern" fiction.

Early Stages of the Modern Novel

The publication of "Mujong" (The Heartless) by Yi Kwangsu in 1917 marked the beginning of a new era in the country's literature. This was the first work of its kind to show no trace of the traditional style of fiction-writing. True, compared to present-day standards, the author of "The Heartless" put too much of his own heart into the attempt to enlighten his readers. Thus he tried to explain characters rather than describe them. Immature as The "Heartless" was as a literary work, it stands out as the most significant Korean novel ever written due to its influence as the first work of its kind—in almost complete modern dressing. It was "The Heartless" which laid the foundation for the growth of modern fiction in Korea.

As one of the most popular and prolific authors, Yi Kwangsu kept up his literary activities up to the outbreak of the Korean War in 1950, when he was captured and taken behind the "Iron Curtain" with several other prominent writers. In addition to more then twenty long novels, he left an innumerable number of short stories, poems, essays and literary critiques, all of which exerted a more powerful influence on literary development than the work of any other single man of letters in Korea.

Originally a Christian, Yi later became a devout Buddhist and Buddhist philosophy dominated all his later writings. His religious devotion led to a philosophy of humanitarianism, a concern and regard for all living beings in the world.

All of his novels were built upon the author's basic philosophy of life, which approved of life instead of presenting it as a hopeless affair. This basic attitude of Yi Kwangsu's writings was later subjected to much criticism by other writers. They charged him with a lack of originalistic daydreaming, and a rigged pattern for exposition, which the early modern fiction writer adhered to throughout his career.

Be that as it may, Yi Kwangsu monopolized the literary world for four or five years after the publication of "The Heartless" in 1917, because other literary aspirants found themselves helpless to break the trance of the people, who were enraptured totally under the spell of Yi Kwangsu.

The Era of Literary Group Magazines

The national independence movement in March, 1919, was the beginning of a new era in Korean literature. Until that time the country was without literary circles as such, for Yi Kwangsu was enjoying a virtual monopoly in the field of the novel, while Choe Namson was developing juvenile literature. The independence movement failed to achieve the objective it so ardently aspired to, but the alarmed Japanese government adopted an appeasement policy for Korea under a new "cultural" administration, as opposed to the former period of cultural suppression. Thus several daily newspapers and magazines were allowed to be published. Under such a relatively "favorable" setting, large numbers of young aspirants for literary prominence were able to organize into various literary groups and to publish their works in group magazines.

The period from 1920 to 1930 is characterized by the emergence of numerous literary group magazines, thereby giving rise to the name of the era. Indeed, all men of letters who are presently considered as the established authorities of the old school made their debut during this period in magazine circles. Among the then-and-coming young writers, the most brilliant as well as active was Kim Tongin, who established himself as the most popular writer, next only to Yi Kwangsu, by 1925 with his work, "The Potato."

Advocating art as the prime requisite for literary work, as against Yi Kwangsu's inclination towards enlightenment of the people through literature, Kim Tongin published nearly 100 fictional works before his death in 1951. Two characteristics mark all of his novels. First, they aspire after aesthetical goals, and secondly, they are inclined toward naturalism. His representative works, "Lunatic Flame Sonata" and "The Mad Painter," for instance, remind the reader of Oscar Wilde's Salome for their indulgence in aesthetics while "The Biography of Kim Yonsil" may find their peers in Flaubert's "Madame Bovary" and de Maupassant's "A Woman's Life" for naturalism. Kim Tongin managed to incorporate both of these two contrasting ideas throughout his career, until his death in 1951, but during the latter period of his life, naturalism seemed to have attracted more of his interest. In memory of the author, the Kim Tongin Literary Award has been established for young writers.

Some Other Novelists of the '20's

Other writers of Kim Tongin's generation are presently active, including Yom Sangsop, Pak Chonghwa and Chon Yongtaek, among many others.

Yom Sangsop is noted for his unwavering adherence to realism. He made his debut in 1921 with "The Green Frog in the Spicemen's Gallery," which earned distinction as the first work of naturalism in Korea. He followed up his initial triumph with numerous short stories, numbering more than 100 by this time, in addition to slightly over ten long fictional works which include "Two Minds," "The Three Generations," and "When the Peony Blossoms." His early works, such as "The Dark Night," "Love and Sin," and "The Last Night of the Year," showed much subjective emotion and immature style and structure, but by the 1930's, the early shortcomings had completely disappeared. He shifted from the subjective to the objective as manifested in his mature works, such as "The Death-Bed" of the 1940's and "The Shower," written in the 1950's. Being a faithful realist, his novels are not likely to leave a deep impression upon the minds of young readers, but he is considered one of the most outstanding of writers in Korea. His literary activities claimed for him many prizes, such as the Seoul City Library Award, the Freedom Literary Award, and the Academy of Arts Literary Merit Award.

Pak Chonghwa, who started his literary career as poet, distinguished himself as the most representative writer of historical fiction. Romanticism and nationalism run through all of his works, including "Blood on the Silk Dress," "The Benovolent Mind of Buddha," "The Dawn," and "The Nation." Another characteristic of his novels is his adherence to the authentic history of Korea, which is fully incorporated in his works.

A man of influential activities in the field of social affairs as well as literature, Pak Chonghwa presently holds several important positions. He is the head of the Association of Korean Men of Letters, President of the Academy of Arts, and a professor at Songgyungwan University. His contributions won such widespread recognition that in 1955 the first Literary Merit Award was accorded him from the Academy of Arts.

Chon Yongtaek, on the other hand, has published so few works that the only anthology of his works, "The Woman Who Looks Up at the Sky," contains practically all of his important efforts. A devout Christian, Chon utilizes Christian humanism and idealism as the underlying theme of his fiction.

Late Masters of the '20s'

Other important novelists of the 1920's—now dead, but with lasting influence—are Hyon Chingon and Na Tohyang. Hyon Chingon (1900-1943) left quite a few short stories and nearly ten long novels, such as "The Equator" and "The Tower Without Shadow." His work came under the heading of realism, and are overflowing with the sentiments of the middle class, depicted through his unique, refined technique. These characteristics are amply represented in the short stories, "The Poor Wife", and "The Dormitory Inspector, Old Miss B.," and "Love Letter."

Na Tohyang (1902-1926) attracted the attention of literary circles as a genius. He made his debut at an early age. The romanticism of his early short stories soon gave way to realism as found in "The Windmill" and "The Dumb Boy, Samyong."

Other promising writers of the 1920's who died premature deaths are Choe Haksong and Yi Iksang. Both of them are noted for works which serve as representatives of early "proletarian" literature, which began to sweep through literary circles in the early 1930's.

Among the early novelists of the 1920's, Pang Ingun and Chu Yosop made noteworthy contributions to the growth of literature through their publication of a literary circle magazine, "The Korean Literary Stage," in 1924. They attempted to cater to less sophisticated popular acceptance much too early, it may be said, and in their late years, their activities on the literary stage have dwindled to insignificance.

The Golden Era of the '30's

The 1930's were marked by great changes in literary circles. Literary activity became a full-fledged profession for many writers, rather than an avocation, and unlike the '20's, participation in a literary group and subsequent publication of one or two short stories in a group magazine ceased to automatically qualify a person as a man of letters. Advancement in the overall standard of literary works was also remarkable during the 1930's, so much so that most modern masterpieces were written during the ten-year period.

Among writers who won popular recognition during the first half of the '30's were Yu Chino, Yi Hyosok, Choe Mansik, Kye Yongmuk, Yi Muyong, Kang Kyongae, Kim Malbong, and Pak Hwasong.

Yu Chino, who ceased his literary activities in 1945 in order to become president of Korea University, was better known during his youth as a writer despite his formal training as a lawyer. His early works, such as "The Shopgirls," and "The Butterfly," were considered to be representative of his inclination towards proletarian literature. His later works, however, showed a change of heart, a movement away from socialism in search after some ethical standard.

Yi Hyosok, who died while still very young in 1940, frustrating the expectations of literary circles for this brilliant development, started his literary career with works sympathetic to socialism, as shown in his short story, "The Coast of Russian Territory." Subsequently, however, he became a lyric fiction writer, as evidenced in "When the Buckwheat Flowers." The poetic style of his prose marked his novels, which imparted a sensuous, mysterious feeling to the reader as a unique characteristic of his late novels, such as "The Pollen," "The Hog," and "The Rose is Sick."

Chae Mansik, who died in 1950, was another unique writer, known, however, for his typical Korean satire. Among his many novels, "The Muddy Tide" is considered the best representative.

Yi Muyong distinguished himself as an observer of the rural scene through "The Farmer" and "The Mind Longing After the Soil." Since 1945, his novels have been set in urban areas, finding declining acceptance among his readers, who consider his "farm novels" period as the peak of his creative career.

Kang Kyongae, a woman novelist who died in 1943, attracted attention for her physical charm as well as realistic work. Her best-known works are "Father and Son," "The Human Problem," "Salt," and "The Underground Village."

Kye Yongmuk, whose activities won fame during the second half of the 1930's, maintained his independent position without joining any literary group. "The Idiot Adada" is considered the best of his efforts.

Kim Malbong, a still active woman novelist, established herself as one of the most popular, if not sophisticated, of writers. Her knack of catering to popular acceptance made her one of the authorities among newspaper fiction serial writers. Representative works of her early period are "The Jungle" and "The Wild Rose." Her novels of the 1950's include "The White Night," "Love," and "Going Over the Hill."

Another popular woman novelist who started her career in the 1930's is Pak Hwasong, whose fiction has been well received by the popular reader.

Writers during the Second Half of the '30's

Literature made remarkable progress during the second half of the 1930's—the most fruitful period throughout the history of modern literature in Korea. It was, indeed, in this five-year period that modern literature became complete in Korea, and many works considered classical masterpieces produced.

Nearly 20 writers made their literary debut during the second half of the 1930's. Of them, Pak Yongjin, first chose the farm as the setting of his stories, but later shifted to the city. His works include "When the Cotton Seeds Are Planted," "Body Odor," "The Blue Sky," and "The Shadowy Flower Garden." His recent efforts show an attempt to find a solution to contemporary urban ethical problems.

Kim Yujong, who died in 1937, demonstrated his talent in "Spring, Oh Spring," "The Deep Mountain Valley," and "The Bean Field of Gold." His works are noted for imparting typical Korean atmosphere and satire, depicted with a technique considered more refined than that of his predecessor of the same vein, Chae Mansik. All characters of his fiction are ignorant, poverty-stricken, simple peasants, whose naive joys and sorrows found a humorous but covertly tragic expression as a result of his brilliant pen.

Poet-novelist Yi Sang, who died in 1939, was perhaps more noted for his poetic works, which defied lay comprehension. He infused modern psychology into his works, such as "The Wings," "The Record of Life," and "The Lost Paradise." His influence, therefore, was considerable on effecting further modernization of fiction treatment in Korea.

Paek Sinae, a woman novelist, showed considerable talent in such works as "Abject Poverty," "The Memoirs of a Mad Man," and "A Small Vampire," but her death in 1939 put an end to her promising career.

Kim Tongni made his debut, attracting wide attention, with a work which presented vividly typical Korean traits. His early works, such as "The Picture of the Shaman," "The Rocks," and "The Posterity of Hwarang," depicted traditional Korean characters, realities, emotions, and mode of life with an extremely refined style and structure, so much so that he surpassed Choe Mansik and Kim Yujong. Nihilism and mystic thoughts run through his early fiction. But in his later years, he expanded his literary horizon over humanity, so that his novels could be readily understandable anywhere in the world, as in the case of "The Cross of Saban" and "The Withdrawal From Hungnam." His basic thought also turned towards humanism, as depicted in "The Cross of Saban," which won him the Literary Merit Award of the Korean Academy of Arts in 1958.

Choe Chonghi first wrote mostly in the first person about women, their lives and destinies, as in the case of "The Human Range," "The Sky Range," and "The House of Evil Luck." But later she broadened her themes to include general social affairs. "In The Wind" is a representative product of her later years.

Hwang Sunwon has built up her literary fame by maintaining artistic standards in complete defiance of compromise toward wider popular acceptance of her works. Considered one of today's most artistic writers, her stories overflow with quaint lyricism, as shown in such works as "The Star," "The Crane," "The Lost People," "The Posterity of Cain," "The Lost People," "The Human Grafting." In her long novels, she shows her intense interest in social problems.

Another novelist who began a literary career in the late 1930's is An Sugil. His "The Third Human Pattern" won a Freedom Literary Award from the Asia Foundation. Other presently active writers who made debuts at that time include Kim Kwangju ("The Liberator"), Chong Pisok, whose "Madam Liberty" confirmed his position as one of the most popular authors of less sophisticated fiction, Kim Songhan ("Chusangdan and the Neighbors"), Kim Yongsu ("Criteria"), Yi Ponggu, who is noted for sentimental writing, Kim Isok ("Cuckoo"), and Choe Inuk ("The Image of a Child").

The Post-World War II Period

The 1940's were marked by a literary vacuum forced by the Japanese wartime policy, which suppressed all writing in the Korean language. Literary activities were dormant until the Liberation in 1945.

The political confusion and the subsequent outbreak of the Korean War, however, was not conducive to producing noteworthy works or men of letters. It has been only in the recent few years, that many young literary aspirants have begun to assert themselves. The literary stage is presently crowded with more than 50 new novelists, who managed to join a seemingly ever-increasing army of writers. Most of the young writers, however, have so far failed to cultivate new fields before the literary horizon. True that, whatever the excuse, literary circles have failed to produce a single outstanding man of letters or a noteworthy work since the suppression of the 1940's.

Only time will tell whether the sincere efforts by a few young students of literature will blossom out into a new path for literature, which has become devoid of fresh activity since the 1940's.

XVII LITERATURE

Modern Literature: Poetry

The Pioneers of the "New" Poetry

The "new" poetry of Korea as distinguished from the "old" traditional forms has no more than a sixty-year history. During the brief span of time since around 1910, one *ism* after another clamored for attention among poets, who promptly responded to the "new" ideas *a la mode*. Having been started in imitation of Western poetry, the "new" poem has since been kept busy trying to catch up with Western trends. Such being the case, it would be only fair to say that modern Korean poetry has yet to cultivate its own character, although it is true that the "new" poetry has won wider popular acceptance than the traditional poems.

The first poem after the Western style ever to appear in print was "From the Sea to the Boys" by the famed pioneer in Korean letters, Choe Namson. It was published in the first edition of his magazine, "The Boys," in October, 1909. As publisher-editor of several magazines, and also as a writer of novels and poetry, Choe Namson shattered the rigid formalism which had governed poetry with his poems for young readers.

His pioneering work in the "new" poetry was soon reinforced when Yi Kwangsu added to the movement a considerable number of "new" poems, all published in the magazines of the early 1910's. Thus the two pioneers of Western-style literature, Choe Namson and Yi Kwangsu, are credited also with the introduction and subsequent popularization of the "new" poetry.

Decadent Nihilism of the "Golden" '20's

As Western-style poetry gained increasingly popular acceptance, a significant new event took place in 1919. A new weekly magazine, "The Western Literary Arts News," was published. Among several poets who wrote for the magazine, Kim Ok stood out as the most notable for his introduction of Western poetry through translation. Especially his translated versions of the French poems of the late nineteenth century inspired many a young man of the time to write poetry after the "new" style. In 1919, the literary magazine "Creation" emerged. Herein Chu Yohan published works of symbolism, as in the case of his "Fire Play", and Namgung Pyok published poems of naturalism and romanticism.

In the following year, 1920, Kim Ok, Namgung Pyok, Sangsun, and Hwang Sogu, together with a few novelists, published a literary association magazine, "The Ruins." Virtually all the poets of this magazine showed strong tinges of a growing decadence in reflection of the frustration then prevailing throughout Korean society after the tragic failure of the independence movement of 1919. As a confirmed poet of the decadent spirit, Kim Ok published in 1921 a collection of Western poems translated into the Korean language under the title, "The Dance of Anguish," which notably included the works of Charles Baudelaire and Paul Marie Verlaine. In the meantime, a few literary magazines, two daily newspapers, and one magazine exclusively devoted to poetry ("The Village of Roses") were published in 1920, offering ample space to poets. The predominant tendency of the poetic works appearing through these media was nihilism. For example, "The Sinking of the Sun," by Hwang Sogu, may be quoted to give us some idea of the poetic tendency of that time.

The sun has sunk and
    curled up in a cave with no end.

As the evening clouds appear like mad Lepers' foam,
    The Sun has sunk,
    Amid the darkening eve.
    Into the sorrowful heart of a maid
    Lost in a wide field.
The Sun is sinking.
    As into the hollow eyes of a corpse,
    Lying before an alien Alter.

A group of young poets, including Hong Sayong, Yi Sanghwa, Pak Chonghwa, and Pak Yonghi published the association magazine "The White Tide" in 1922 to present their works of romanticism. This romanticism, however, was distorted by decadent nihilism expressing itself with grim overtones of pessimism, and demonstrating a morbid desire to escape from reality. This prevailing mood of the poets was well represented by "The Sickroom Filled with Moonlight," by Pak Yonghi.

As my heart was about to cease,
    In sighs, tears, regret, and wrath,
    Three pretty virgins entered my sickroom, saying
    "The moon has sent us to lay
    Our hands upon your sick heart."
I, then, knew my snow-white blood of love
    Hidden deep in my heart, asking in gratitude
The Names of the virgins,
    "The sorrow is I."
    "The fear is my name."
    "The indolence they call me."
    Their hands reached silently over my sick heart.
    The madness that seized my heart from that moment on,
Has become an everlasting disease without a cure.

Such sentimental decadence was indeed the most striking feature of Korean literature during the 1920's, a time when cultural obliteration under the "Rising Sun" of Japan seemed certain.

At the same time, socialism, which was sweeping the country, gave rise to an escapist movement of self-abnegation, referred to as the proletarian literature, and treated previously in this volume. It became established firmly by 1925 after the organization of the Proletarian Arts League. Prominently active poets who chanted the socialist line were Im Hwa, Kwon Hwan, Pak Seyong, and Kwon Kyuhyon. They clashed head on with the poets of nationalism, creating heated controversies over the place of politics in literature.

Be that as it may, the poetry field was so crowded by a new crop of young poets, numbering nearly 30 that the period was later recalled as the "golden '20's." Noteworthy books of poetry published during the "golden age" were "The Song of the Jelly-Fish" (1923) by Kim Ok, and "The Beautiful Dawn" (1924) by Chu Yohan. The two publications are milestones in the growth of Korean poetry. They were the first books of the kind ever printed, and have had significant influence as prime representative anthologies of the poetry written during the cradle period of the "new" poetry.

Poetry of Anxiety in the '30's

Anxiety marked the poetry of the 1930's as Japanese militarism became more and more manifest. Literary activities were placed under strict control. As the police state grew, a widespread sense of anxiety and fear colored all literary works of the '30's.

During the early '30's, a group of young writers and poets, including Yi Hayun and Kim Kwangsop, who had studied foreign literature abroad, organized themselves into the "Foreign Literature Group." They published translated versions of many Western poems in the magazines, "The Poetic Literature" and "The Monthly Literary Art." Chong Chiyong and Kim Kirim, on the other hand, attracted attention with their lyric poems, suffused with sentimentalism.

By the middle of the '30's, "modernism" began to assert itself, advocating the thesis that poetry should be composed with a definite consciousness, rather than as an automatic outburst of one's sentiment, which was allegedly a major characteristic of the lyric poetry of the time. The advocates of such "modernism" included Chang Manyong, Chang Soyong and Kim Kwanggyun. Chang Soyong wrote the following "An Antique Flower Vase," to endorse his concept of "modernism."

> The antique pot with its stooped shoulders,
> In the shape of tears,
> Has not the two arms
> Frozen blue.
> As an old nurse
> Is the lonely pot.
> Holding with its dumb lips
> Out-of-season grass in mouthfuls,
> It holds within
> About a little over five *hop* of water,
> Which is longing after the mountain valley.

Although this "modernism" found its major exponent in Chang Manyong, the start was made by Chong Chiyong, who first introduced illustrative poetry appealing to vision in contrast to the musical poetry of lyricism, which laid emphasis on auditory perception. About this time, the woman poet, Mo Yunsuk, won fame for the passionate utterings of the heart, while No Chongmyong chanted her fortitude.

As Japan launched its invasion of the Chinese mainland in 1937, increasingly heavy pressure was brought to bear on Korean literature, with a positive program to officially discourage the use of the Korean language. The Japanese police were so wary of latent nationalism that their censorship of literary works tightened considerably. As a result, Korean poetry became devoid of criticism and thought, replacing these with emphasis on form and rhetorical flourish.

Despite such unfavorable circumstances, two literary magazines, "The Sentence" and "The Humanities Review," kept Korean poetry alive, producing several new poets, including Pak Tujin, Pak Mokwol, Cho Chihun, pak Namsu, and Yi Hanjik. Then total darkness engulfed Korean literature with the outbreak of the Pacific War, which the Japanese authorities seized on to deal a mortal blow to virtually all Korean-language publications as being traitorous to Japan's imperial policies,

Liberated Poetry

The Liberation from Japan in 1945 was greeted with overwhelming rejoicing, as expressed by the pen of Kim Kwangsop;
"The Liberation"

> Oh, the Joy:
> Let the sky rise higher, be bluer.
> Intoxicated are all of us with the
> Brilliant glory: to plunge into thy heart,
> To work, to learn, and to construct.
> We stand erect upon the earth,
> Supporting the glories of heaven.
> This stirring emotion of liberation!
> This universal joy to share!
> On this date of a new history for liberty,
> One solid mass of heat and force have we become,
> Our path, who would dare to block?

But a trap awaited those filled with stirring emotion. For full rejoicing was premature. New tragedy awaited the liberated nation. The post-Liberation political turmoil, a result of the division of the land by the U.S. and Soviet forces, reduced the singing, shouting poets to utter confusion. Separating themselves into the hostile camps of democracy and Communism poets everywhere were lured into the politics of division. The price was their literary merit. During the five-year period from the Liberation to the Red invasion which began the Korean War in 1950, the amount of poetry published was negligible.

The struggle against Communism and a newly intense nationalism were the basic themes of the poetry of the Korean War (which drove most men of letters down to the south as refugees). So many poets managed to survive the war that "The Anthology of War-Time Korean Literary Works, The

Volume on Poetry" (1955) contained the works of more than 60.

Renewed Growth after the Korean War

After the Korean armistice, poetry renewed its growth. Thus the "1953 Annual Edition of Collected Poems" included contributions from nearly 100 poets. The 1954 edition of the anthology carried works by 70, while the number of poetry books published during the year reached more than 30. In addition to such publications, many poems appeared in magazines, notably "Modern Literature and Liberal Literature."

In the meantime, several literary awards were established to promote the further growth of poetry. Annual poetry awards are accorded by the Korean Academy of Arts, the Free Asia Society, the Korean Association of the Men of Letters, the Association of the Liberal Men of Letters, and the Korean Poets' Association.

The poetry of the last few years has indicated a strong tendency towards intellectualism, drifting away from what may be termed emotionalism, which had formerly been predominant. Such inclinations are, no doubt, a reflection of the poets' recognition of the political realities Korea has been forced to face squarely since 1945. It must also have been inspired by the influence of T.S. Eliot, whose works seem to have impressed Korean readers, leading to complete freedom from romanticism, and contributing, at the same time, to the popularity of existentialism among many poets.

> The origin of recollection,
> The city of humiliation,
> An exile in the darkening eve.
> Burying one's neck in a black overcoat,
> One hears the worn-out requiem, which
> Also, no one likes to hear forever.
> Amid the ruins of today,
> May we meet again,
> The mission of 1950.

(by Pak Yunhwan, from his anthology, "The Last Conversation).

The Essay
Essay Undeveloped

The essay as a part of modern Western-style literature has remained mostly literary hack work in Korea. About 20 years ago, Min Pyongmin wrote in an indignant article on the subject that many of the short articles appearing in periodicals must have been written "mechanically in response to requests of magazine editors in line with their business policies.... the essay, which is a form of art, is being trampled by Korean literary circles."

It must be admitted that what made Min Pyongmin indignant more than 20 years ago still holds true. The daily newspapers and magazines are filled with short articles written by men of letters, most of whom put down pointless words about trifling events and their impressions of their own daily lives.

True, some collections of essays are published in book form, but they are very few and far between. Such being the case, it is practically impossible to name a single man of letters who is noted more for his essays than for other forms of literature.

The Two Pioneers

Choe Namson, the pioneer of Western-style art during the 1920's, was the first to write essays. His essays were more significant for the style of writing than for contents. They mostly concerned his personal accounts of journeys around the country. Thus, he published in 1926 "The Pilgrimage after the Spring," a description of his trip to the southern part of Korea, and in 1927, "The Visit to White Head Mountain." The author used traditional Korean expressions and letters much more extensively than was the case in similar writings of the preceeding period, presenting, essentially, a new form of description.

Almost all of the essays written by Choe Namson were semi-academic presentations on Korean history, geography, manners and customs, legends and myths—all of which were inscribed in praise of the land, its people, and its culture.

Another literary master of the early period of Western style literature in Korea, Yi Kwangsu, also produced a large number of essays. His collections of essays, "The Stone Pillow," published posthumously in 1954, is a collection of records of the author's personal experiences while he was living an isolated life, deep in nature. Being a devout Buddhist, Yi Kwangsu wrote much about religious inspiration and meditation, which governed his retreat life.

Recent Years

In more recent years, Kim Chinsop may be cited as the most famous essayist in the strict sense of the term.

He liked to use the word, philosophy, so much so that his numerous essays are studded with the term followed by such phrases as cold, travel, life, naming, money, etc. The collection of his essays, therefore, was aptly entitled "The Philosophy of A Living Man." His style of writing, however, was dominated by everyday-words, cliches, despite his attempts to philosophize on everything under the sun. Meditative passages marked his essays, reflecting the author's philosophy of life, which was always to seek a philosophy in everything. His writings, however, were never depressing, for he liked to use the word "praise" frequently, even if he did not do so as often as he used the word philosophy. Thus, after meditating or philosophizing, he usually came up with a conclusion in "praise" of whatever he was brooding about, as is aptly shown in the titles of many of his essays— "The Praise of Farmers," and of "Housewives," "Rain," "Mother," "Wine," "Life," "Tears," "Flowers," etc.

It has been no more than 40 years since the first essay — of a sort — was written in Korea. Still in its infancy, the modern essay style of Korea is without any noticeable character of its own, probably with one exception — the tendency towards philosophizing on any and every subject under discussion.

Most of the short articles appearing in the daily newspapers and magazines under the headings of essay by men of letters treat trifle subjects in a light vein. Essays which discuss the serious problems of life, inducing readers into sincere meditation, are rare.

Stage Play

Pioneer Days

The founder of the Korean play is Yi Injik. He began the "the new school," a group which channelled its efforts into plays aimed at popular entertainment. Yi Injik studied literature and drama in Japan and, after coming home, started to write stories, using the language of daily Korean life. It was a rebellion against the then existing storytelling technique in which the style of writing employed was the form directly translated from the Chinese. He adapted such stories as "The Silver World" and "The Plum Tree in The Snow", which he himself had written, for stage productions at the Wongaksa, the first theater in Korea. The themes of these two plays were the introduction of the modern educational ethics and criticism of feudalistic customs. Through these themes, the playwrights intended to enlighten the people, drawing them toward a national consciousness for independence.

The "new school" established by Yi Injik played a major role in Korean theatrical history for over 20 years. Its influence can still be noted in the present-day theater of Korea. During the 20 years up to 1931, when the Research Circle for Dramatic Arts was established, a large number of plays was produced by a number of colorless theatrical groups in urban as well as rural areas. Among the plays were "God's Punishment for Scapegraces", "Lae of Laes" "Snow in the Battlefield", "Murdering Brother-in-Law", "The Tear", and "The Robber with a Six-Shooter".

Typical of these infantile plays was "The Robber with a Six-Shooter". The plot goes roughly as follows: The police are harrassed by the uncanny appearance and disappearance of a hold-up man who never leaves any clue behind at the scene of his crime. The criminal works only at night, and is armed with a pistol. In the daytime, he disguised himself as a blind man, or a dandy-looking gentleman. One night, he breaks into a pawn shop and makes away with valuable goods. The police start an extraordinary manhunt for the criminal, but to no avail. Presently, a meeting is held at police headquarters to discuss methods of determining the whereabouts of the criminal. Nothing new is produced by anyone present. Then a young man stands up to say that he will arrest the criminal no matter what obstacles there are. This is the newest man on the police force. Veteran officers laugh at the insolence of this newcomer. The ambitious young policeman keeps vigil every night at a street corner he has decided is likely until one night he sees a blind man passing before him. His 'hunch' tells him that this is the criminal. He pursues the blind man. The blind man suddenly turns into a big, far-seeing fellow who turns on the pursuing officer. Finally a bullet he fires hits the hero in the leg, but the policeman finally ties his rope around the criminal's wrists. Then a second shot from the tied robber hits him again, this time in the chest. By then, this story has reached a nearby police station thanks to a passer-by who saw the bloody fight. A band of policemen finds the heroic young policeman already dead. The veterans who previously made a laughing stock of the dead hero shed tear of repentance...... and so does the audience.

As this primitive plot shows, the plays produced in that period were stories of simple adventure (physical, in most cases), vengeance, and performance of one's duties. This kind of story appealed greatly to the theatre-goers of the day. Authors of most of these plays are unknown. Two of the few playwrights of the day are Yun Paengnam and Cho Myonghi. Yun Paengnam wrote "Fate" and "The Eternal Wife". His writing style is not outside the "new school." However, his sense of humanity gave works characteristics which were not to be found in others' works. Later, he turned to motion picture production and popular novel writing. Cho Myonghi, who wrote "The Death of Kim Yongil," used his own experiences during his schooldays in Tokyo as material for his plays. He later became a poet. The first group formed for modern drama, *Towolhoe*, was organized in the 1920's by a number of students then studying in Japanese schools. It is lamentable that this group's theatrical activities did not surpass the level already established by the "new school." Other than producing original plays of low standard, this group staged translated foreign plays. There were actors and audiences to keep stage production going, but the only notable plays— a few—were written solely by two playwrights, Yun Paengnam and Cho Myonghi.

Modern Drama

Aside from the afore-mentioned *Towolhoe*, the first real movement for modern drama in Korea was marked in 1931 with the organization of the Research Circle for Dramatic Arts. In 1931, the Korean theatrical society began to import ideas from the theater of Europe. The Research Circle for Dramatic Arts concentrated its efforts on theatrical conceptions and on the production of original stage plays. This circle gave birth to such playwrights as Yu Chijin, Yi Kwangnae, Kim Chinsu, Yi Muyong and Yi Sohynang. Yi Muyong was an established novelist when he joined this movement, and Yi Sohyong was already a renowned director.

Yu Chijin was one of the organizers of the circle and besides playwrighting, he also directed on the stage. His early works are: "The Clay House," "The Scene of A Village Where the Willow Tree Stands," "The Bull," "The Waiting Wife," and "The Price Mawl," the last two being adaptations from historical novels. The first two works had the exposure of the social injustice of the day as their themes. "The Bull" is a farmland comedy. The bull plays a life-or-death role in the life of the farmers, whose criteria of values center around this four-legged farm animal. Yi Kwangnae also made an attempt at analysis and criticism of the social injustice then prevailing on the farm under the oppression of the Japanese through two plays—"The Country Teacher" and "The House of the Pomegranate." Compared with these two playwrights, who gathered their materials from farmland life, Kim Chinsu wrote his play with themes centered around the Hamlet-type sorrow of the young intellectuals of the colonial land.

Yi Muyong satirized society's foolishness in his plays "The Daydreamers" and "Recuperation without Payment," and Yi Sohyang also tackled social problems in his "The River Bank" and "Mother." Nam Sedok has to his credit the costume play, "The Rock of Nakhwa." Two newsspapers, *Tonga Ilbo* and *Chosun Ilbo*, responded to the earnest efforts of the Research Circle for Dramatic Arts by offering prize contests for stage plays. The afore-mentioned "The Country Teacher" was part of the harvest of these contests. There are others, including "The Clay Wall," and "The Floating People," which reached the stage through these contests. These two plays, the former by Han Taedong and the latter by Kim Sungu, sketched with a realistic touch the life of the people, victimized by the economic policy of Japanese imperialism. Song Yong, Chae Mansik, and Kim Yongsu were established novelists who tried their hand at playwriting. Song Yong wrote "The Mountain People" and "The New Chairman of the Board," and Chae Mansik gave birth to "I Wish I Were A Christian" and "The Feast Day." Another play, "The Fault," was written by Kim Yongsu in the same period. While modern drama was blooming on the soil of Korea, plays belonging to the "new school" still persisted. Their best representative is "Sorrow Over Love and Trouble Over Money," by Im Songyu.

Japanese Oppression

During the latter days of World War II, the Japanese authorities became hysterical in their censorship of plays. Gone was all freedom of thinking. Use of the Korean language on any public occasion was severely limited, and, eventually, Korean playwrights were ordered to write plays only in Japanese. The playwrights also had to give up the last vestiges of freedom of choice of themes, and work along lines set up by the Japanese, "The Heilung River," "The Northern Legion," and "The Jujube Tree" were plays written those days by Yu Chijin.

After the Liberation

When the nation was liberated from the Japanese rule with the end of World War II, its severely oppressed theatrical society quickly recovered. New theatrical groups were formed, one after the other, and playwrights, actors, actresses, and directors came forward from what in many cases was outright hiding. The theater, depressed for so long, became lively again.

This excitement in the theater was too soon followed by ideological confusion and social insecurity stirred by the struggle between Communism and democracy. Amidst this confusion and struggle were born "The Fatherland," "The Self-Beating Drum," "Wonsul-Lang," (Yu Chijin), "Brain Surgery"

(Chin Uchon), "His Excellency Yi Chungsaeng," "The Wedding Day" (O Yongjin), "The Cosmos," and "The Playground" (Kim Chinsu), and "The Artery" and "The Boss is A Lady" (Kim Yongsu).

These plays reflected the hope for a better world which suffused a nation just liberated from a very harsh colonial rule. The war started by the Communists in 1950 was a severe blow to the theater, which was just rising from an infantile stage. During the war days those anti-Communist plays were written: "I Will be A Human, Too" (Yu Chijin), "Seoul Under the Reds" (Kim Yongsu), "Out of the Waste" (Kim Chinsu), and "War and Flowers" (Han Nodan).

The other playwrights, belonging to a new generation, and who wrote their plays during and after the war:

Choe Pomsok, "The Dream City;" Im Hijae, "The Engine Which Lives on Flower Petals;" O Sangwon, "The Ignored Ones;" Ha Yusang, "Free Marriage;" and Yi Yongchan, "The Family."

Screen Play

The first motion picture in Korea was produced in 1922. The production techniques of the time were to pass before the screen play could acquire its place among the channels of literature.

The most noteworthy picture produced in this backward stage of motion-picture making was "Arirang," written, produced and directed by Na Ungyu, the pioneer of Korean motion pictures. Its theme was the resistance against the Japanese rulers, and the nation's nostalgia for the "good old days." Also produced around the same period were "The Dawn," written by Sim Mun; "The Crossroads of Youth," An Chonghwa; and "A Boat Without an Owner," Yi Kyuhwan. All the screen plays of this period were strongly influenced by the realism then prevailing in the society of literature.

With the introduction in 1935 of the sound track, screen playwrighting became a movement. Those who played major roles in this movement are An Sohong, Kim Yuyong, So Kwangje, Pak Kichae, Yi Kyuhwa, and An Chonghwa. However, creative activities of these people did not bear noteworthy fruit due to the Japanese colonial policy, which directed that everything and all things must contribute toward winning their desperate war.

Then came the Liberation of August 15, 1945. The first motion picture produced in the following period was "Hurrah for Freedom!" written and directed by Chon Changgun. This picture sang the nation's exultation over the Liberation. "The Seagull," "The Home of the Heart," and "The Convict without Crime," which followed "Hurrah for Freedom," handled social problems arising in the post-Liberation days from a realistic approach.

The Communist invasion of south Korea in 1950 brought yet another big blow to the Korean motion picture world. The blow was such that not a single screen play was written nor a roll of feature film produced for the three years of the war. The plight of the industry was only solved through the government's exemption from taxes of the entire motion picture industry. Producers, writers, and directors set the stage for what was to be a new and golden era for the Korean motion picture. However, it was not long before the writers were submerged in disappointment over the tendencies of motion picture production. Every effort of the producers was poured into considerations of box-office returns. Typical productions showing this tendency were "Madam Liberty" and "The Star of the Lost Paradise." Both were based on novels of the same titles by Kim Naesong.

The box-office success of these two pictures established a tendency to avoid the hazards of originality in the creation of a screen play. These were dark days, and in these dark days, there appeared these writers of screen plays: O Yongjin, Yu Chijin, Yi Chongki, Yu Tuyon, Yi Chongson Yi Chinsop, and Yi Pongnae.

The motion picture in Korea does not yet deserve much space in any discussion of art or literature.

The government gives positive financial benefit to those companies which produce films which are exported or which receive awards at international film festivals. This has led to serious concern for quality and, it is hoped, the next few years will provide a substantial basis for discussion of the Korean screen play as literature.

Literature for Children

Literature written for children is the best understood and the most intimately held form of literature regardless of time and place. In Korea today over 200 fables written by Aesop have been translated. "The Wind," a song written by Christina Rossetti, the nineteenth century English poetess, has been sung by Korean children for 20 years now. There is a song written for children in modern Korea by Yun Sokchun that goes:

O Stream,
You who down and down do flow,
Is it to the sea you want to go?

O Tree,
You who up and up do grow,
Is it the sky you want to know?

This is well understandable—where there flows a stream and where there grows a tree. Stories and songs for children, whether written in the Occident or Orient, have a similar, kindly responsive spirit to the dreams of young souls. This is more so when the fables and songs of ancient days are looked into. "Cinderella" (Northern Europe), "Cendrillon" (France), "The Girl Covered With Ash" (German), "Red Dish and Broken Dish" (Japan), "Rat for Soy-Bean and Rat for Red-Bean" (Korea) and "The Story of Changhwa and Hongnyon" (Korea) are all very similar. Madam Kockus, the British researcher of Cinderella, said in her book that she had collected 345 stories from all over the world which were exactly like Cinderella.

Patriotic Motive

The year in which Korean writers and poets started to work on literature for children as an independant channel of literature was 1908, when Chae Namson published the magazine, "The Boys". The publication of this magazine marked the first appearances of stories and songs written solely for children. The magazine, however, did not last long. With the Japanese annexation of Korea in 1910, the magazine was placed under constant censorship by the Japanere authorities until it was finally banned. Other magazines appeared after the abolition of "The Boys," but no literature for children in the true meaning of the word was to be found in them.

Time passed without bearing fruit in this channel of literature until March 1, 1923. On that day, a magazine entitled "The Children" was published by Pang Chonghwan. The magazine led to resumption of full-scale literary activities for children. By then, the arrest, jailing and torture of Koreans were routine tools of Japanese political oppression, an aftermath of the blood independance movement of 1919. The sorrow of a lost nation was even reflected in its literature for children. Sorrow, fear and a sense of helplesness governed works which should have been full of pleasant dreams for a better tomorrow. Only sad stories were translated from the works of the Grimm brothers, Hans Christian Anderson, and "The Arabian Nights," and were liked by the children. "The Half Moon," published in 1924, was the most popular song among Korean children for a long time to come. Written and composed by Yun Kugyong, the song compared the half moon of the night sky to a small beat on the Milky Way, and a lone star with a light-house looking over a vast sea. It helped console the vaguely sorrowful hearts of the young ones.

Korean literature for children was first systematized by Choe Namson and Yi Kwangsu, who were also the pioneers of the modern literary movement of Korea, in cooperation with Pang Chonghwa. The three writers organized a research circle for arts for children in 1923 and named it "The Saektong Circle." Among those who joined in the circle's movement were story writers Ko Hansung, Chin Changsop, and Ma Haesong, and composers Yun Kugyong and Chong Sunchol. Others are Chong Insop and Yi Hongu, who translated foreign works, and Son Chintae, who did research work on the ancient fables. Yun Sokchung incessantly published original works. Other notable writers who published their works through the children's magazines, "The New Boys" and "The Country of Stars" are Yi Chongho, Yon Sanghum, Han Chongdong, So Takchul, Yi Wonsu, Pak Mokwol, Kim Sokjin, Yi Hosong, Sin Myonggyun, Choe Chonggok, Yi Chuhong and Yang Chaeung.

In and around 1924, the proletarian literary movement infiltrated the Korean scene and made the magazine, "The Country of Stars," its organ. The movement made it an objective to waken the children to class-consciousness. The colonial status of Korea made this class-consciousness a part of resistance-consciousness against the oppressing Japanese authority and the big landlords and rich enterprisers who increased their wealth under the protection of the Japanese. Fon a time, this movement was popular to a considerable degree.

With the commencement of the Sino-Japanese War in July, 1937, the Japanese started to conscript Koreans for military and labor services, and banned the usage of Korean letters in all publications. Korean literature, including that for children, faced the imminent danger of total disappearance. With the outbreak of the Pacific War in December, 1941, Japanese oppression reached a high degree of hysteria, and literature written in Korean for Korean children was all but gone when the end of the Pacific War liberated Korea in August, 1945.

The song first sung by Korean children after the Liberation was "The Day of Liberation."

"The Day of Liberation"
Seoul was covered with
Waves and waves of *Taegukki*, (the national flag)
Vehicles full of people were driving
Out of the opened jail-gates,
The bell of Chongno could not cry
Out of its too deep emotion.
Children were out in the streets
Clad in their Sunday best,
And grownups exchanged wordless greetings.
Seoul, covered with *Taegukki*, our flag,
Blind people came out to see the flags,
And hugged each other in tears.

This exultation did not last long. It turned out that Korea was divided into northern and southern parts at the 38th parallel. A people with a history of 5,000 years with the same language, same temperament, and same culture were broken into two to the despair of the nation. Ideological confusion followed, and the nation had to find space for its breathing amidst the relentless struggle between Western democracy and Communistic totalitarianism. Literature was not to be placed outside this struggle. Nor was the literature for children. Only in the efforts to wipe out the poisonous effects of the Japanese imperialism did the two opposing ideological factions find a common objective. In this period, the publications gave back the nation's lost language and letters to children. They were "The Children's Newspaper," "The Weekly School Children" and "The Children's Country." Writers and poets who published their stories or songs in this period were Ma Haesong, Yun Sokchung, Kwon Taeung, Yi Wonsu, Kim Yongil, Pang Kihwan, Kim Yosop, Pak Mokwol, and Pi Chondok.

The three-year period of the Korean War, beginning in June of 1950, brought a disastrous effect on the tendency of Korea's arts for children. During the war, numerous children lost their families and homes, and formed an unhealthy factor in a torn society put into utter confusion by the plights of the war. These waifs made resistance their principle of living without grasping what they were resisting. Taking advantage of this phenomenon, some short-sighted enterprisers flooded the literary markets with mean and malicious cartoons, cheap detective and adventure stories, to the further detriment of the juvenile souls. The only noteworthy aspect of the war in relation to literature for children was the fact that a number of able writers for children, including Kang Sochon, Han Chongdong, Chang Suchol, Pak Honggun, and Pak Kyongjong, were able to flee the Communist north and join the ranks of the writers in the south.

Contests

One commendable phenomenon in the intellectual life of Korean children of recent origin is that major daily newspapers of Seoul and other cities are filling substantial spaces with short stories, poetry, and various articles for children. Also the two broadcasting systems, the HLKA and HLKY complexes, are entertaining children with good and sound dramas, stories and songs in their "children's hours". Writers working through these media now are Yun Sokchung, Pak Mokwol, Han Chongdong, Pak Kyongjong (for songs), Ma Haesong, Kang Sochon, Kim Yusop, Yi Yonghi, Pang Kihwan (for stories), and Yi Wonsu, Kim Yongsu and Chu Pyong (for children's drama).

Korean children under the age of 15 now have not had the bitter experience of the days of Japanese occupation, and do not harbor the instinctive bitterness of the elder generations. However, their yearning for the unification of the divided land and their love of country are as strong as their elders, if not stronger.

The self-pity or the "reclusiveness" which once prevailed in children's literature are nowhere to be found now. The prime objective of Korea's literature for children is the guidance of the younger generation in a progressive and constructive spirit so they may dream and work for a better future.

Introduction of good stories and poetry for children from foreign countries is an important prerequisite for the full development of the children's culture in any country. O Chonsok, Pak Yongchol, Chu Yosop, Chong Insop, Yi Hongu, An Ungyol, and Pi Chondok are writers who are making constant contributions in this area.

A movement to introduce Korean children's literature abroad is also underway.

Another important movement is being started by the school children themselves. In October of each year, the month of culture in Korea, a number of high schools sponsor writing contests for children delegates of primary schools all over the country.

Literary Criticism

A New Theory of Literature

What may be called literary criticism in our modern sense of the term first appeared in 1918 in the magazine, "The Youth." In a strict sense of the term, it was not literary criticism, nor was it intended as such by the author, Yi Kwangsu, the pioneer of the modern Western-style novel in Korea. The article was written as a review of novels submitted for a literary contest sponsored by a magazine; part of it turned out to be literary criticism.

In the article, the novelist presented his views on literature thus, in part: "The recent tendency of fiction towards art, parting from the old, traditional direction toward moral education, is indeed the nucleus of newly-rising literature. Since the old days, literature has made it a rule merely to produce works punishing evil and rewarding good, so that literature could serve religion or ethics. Therefore, literary critics tend to seek a moral in literature, and its absence branded the work as worthless trash. That is a misconception into which a person without new understanding of literature is very likely to fall.....Literature is not by any means a book of moral education nor a supplement to a religious education, but has its own clear-cut ideals and mission. Jealousy may be used as the theme of a literary work, but the work does not necessarily have to aim at exterminating jealousy; using loyalty and filial love in a literary work does not necessarily have to be intended to promote the idea. All that literature needs is to present to the people realistic descriptions of how jealousy or loyalty or filial love may find expression in human emotion...."

Commonplace as it certainly is, the article was the first theoretic presentation of the modern literary view, because, prior to the publication of the article, nobody had ever advanced such a "radical" theory.

Novelists vs. Critics

Literary criticism, then, was developed in the form of controversy between the novelists, on the one hand, and the critics, on the other. This conflict was started by novelist Kim Tongin in 1920, when he presented the critics in a dubious light, casting doubt on the value of literary criticism, and wrote in part: "The critic has neither right nor duty to the writer, and therefore is not in a position to condemn the writer as if he were a trial court judge. All he can properly do is to interpret the works to readers with reverence, as the movie "talker" for a silent motion picture does before an audience."

The article, written as an emotional outburst of the novelist against a bitter denunciation of his novels, did not fail to invite retaliatory blows from indignant critics. Yom Sangsop, who was one of the most influential novelists of the time, promptly met the challenge by writing that, "Such a comparison of sacred literary criticism to the movie talker is an intolerable deed of ignorance as well as an abuse of language."

The controversy over the merits and demerits of literary criticism was soon joined by numerous writers, and two or three years elapsed before it was resolved with a victory for Yom Sangsop.

Nationalism vs. Socialism

As controversy over literary criticism died down in about 1923, another issue presented itself as a result of the emergence of what was then called proletarian literature. The socialist writers gained popularity by 1925 with works based on the materialistic view and intended to serve the political cause of socialism. The writers of nationalism then came to criticize the basic attitude of the socialists, for the proletarian literature distinuished itself from others for its emphasis on content at the cost of technique, focusing attention on social institutions rather than human beings, making literature serve as an agitator of the class struggle at the sacrifice of artistic value of the search for truth.

The nationalist writers, who placed art above all other considerations in literature, engaged in heated controversies over the issue from 1925 to about 1928. Leading critics on behalf of nationalism were Yi Kwangsu, Yom Sangsop, Kim Tongin, Pak Chonghwa,

Kim Yongjin, and Kim Tonghwan, while the prominent spokesmen for the socialists were Pak Yonghi and Kim Palbong.

When such heated debates reached a zenith, another group of writers came out with a "compromise theory." Advanced notably by Yang Chudong, the "compromise theory" was based on the idea that "the class cannot be without the race, neither can the race be without the class." It also suggested a compromise over the issue of content vs. form with the view that "the content cannot be without the form, the form being co-existent with the content." The theory on the content and form gave much food for thoughts to other writers who had been considering the two elements separately. Yang Chudong, the exponent of the "compromise theory", wrote on the issue, "It is a basic activity of the human to recognize content, while according the form (to the contents so recognized) is the activity of the writer. The content is the substance of a being (existence), whereas the form is an expression of the being and value. Therefore, art cannot be with content alone, because the mere existence of a being cannot by and in itself produce value. The form is the prime element to constitute art, because art belongs to the world of value. From the strict sense of art, humanism, socialism, and others are not an ism. An ism in art is restricted to meaning in the form (expression)."

Thus the "compromise theory" showed a leaning towards form, which promptly invited criticism from the socialist group as the "art-is-everything-ism".

The Rise of Professional Critics

The controversies among the socialists and nationalists at the extremes with the "compromisers" in the middle were resolved in the early 1930's after the Japanese supression of socialism. A movement for *belles-lettres* followed, according the uppermost value to asethetic expression for literature. It negated any compromise for popular acceptance and also advocated freeing literature from all political or ideological bonds.

It was inevitable for literature to adopt such a basic view, because, for one thing, the Japanese censorship was tightened after the invasion of Manchuria, suppressing all freedom of political activity. Therefore, writers had to steer their works clear of politics, and concentrate on pure art. Another factor which contributed to the pure literature movement was reflection on the part of the writers themselves. They admitted that they had been too preoccupied with politics to pursue art wholeheartedly.

Starting around 1930, the belles-lettres movement commanded a *bellees-lettres* place for about 15 years, until the termination of the Japanese domination of Korea in 1945. A significant event which took place around 1930 was the emergence of professional critics. Prior to that time, the literary stage was without a literary critic as such, for the writers who published literary reviews were either novelists or poets by profession, and critics only by avocation.

The professional critics gradually manifested themselves, belonging to either of two distinct groups. Such critics as Kim Hwantae, Kim Munjip, and Yi Wonjo attempted to cultivate the theoretical aspects of the pure literature, while others such as So Yunsik, Choe Cheso, Hong Yomin, Paek Chol, and Im Hwa, tried to lure literature along the direction of social utilitarianism.

Among the former group, Kim Hwantae proved his outstanding talent as the best theoretician of pure literature, but his early death left a promise unfulfilled. Kim Munjip, on the other band, established himself as a unique critic for his extraordinary analytical passion. But he dissappeared from the literary scene, and is presumed to have died.

So Inji was more famous for his essays on philosophy and socialism rather than his literary criticism. Hong Yomin, who started his career as a critic, later became a writer of historical fiction,

Paek Chol, who has been continuing his activities to the present, shifted as the trend of each time pointed the way for him to follow: the literature for the "social class" was the attraction he felt during the initial period of his career in the early 1930's, but he advanced opposition to his early theory in the late 1930's, and the Liberation of Korea in 1945 found him advocating a middle-of-the-road literary concept between Communism and democracy.

Communism vs. Democracy

Literary criticism blossomed out into full-scale activity in 1945 following the Liberation of Korea from Japan. The initial activities of the post-World War II period were, in all their outward appearances, a carbon copy of the controversies between the socialist and nationalist men of letters in the '20s.

Literary circles were divided into two hostile groups: the Communists vs. their opponents. The Communist camp, led by Im Hwa, Yi Wonjo, and Kim Chongsok (all of whom choose to go to north Korea during the Korean war, only to receive death sentences from their Communist masters) repeated the claim that literature had to serve the class struggle of Communism. The theoretical arguments for pure literature were advanced by Kwak Chongwon, Cho Yonhyon, Im Kungjae, and the novelist Kim Tongni, all of whom advocated literature for humanity as against the literature for the party, politics, and propaganda of the Communist writers. The opponents of the Communist theory of literature invariably chose democracy. Thus the literary controversies were entangled in a web of politics.

Repeating the pattern set in the 20's, a compromise theory asserted itself. Paek Chol was its lonely exponent. His efforts, however, failed to produce any noteworthy effect. It was again the political situation which finally forced an end to the controversies. The establishment of the Republic of Korea government and the outbreak of the Korean War dissipated all pro-Communist elements.

Presently Active Critics

The post-Korean War period produced a large number of professional critics, including Yun Pyongon, Chon Sangbyong, Hong Sejung, Chon Idu, Won Hyonggap, Kim Ujong, Kim Sangil, Yi Oyong, Kim Chonghu, and Chong Changbom. The established critics, who had started their careers earlier, also continued their activities: thus Paek Chol has to his credit two books, "The History of New Literary Thought", and "The Reconstruction of Literature;" Cho Yonhyon's works include "The History of Modern Literature in Korea," "Designs for Holidays," and "Literature and Its Surroundings." These books, published in recent years together with novelist Kim Tongni's "Literature and Man," and "Discussion on the Modern Novel" by the late novelist, Kim Tongin, are important works for a full understanding of literary criticism in Korea.

Throughout its 50-year history, literary criticism in Korea has always been handicapped by unfavorable social settings, which hampered the normal growth of literary theories. The Japanese domination and the political chaos of the post-World War II period are to be blamed for the literary criticism. So far, literary criticism has been represented mostly by a few monthly reviews of literary works published in magazines and newspapers. Substantial books on the subject, presenting a systematic literary view, have been minimal.

All social handicaps which shackled literary criticism having now become past history, a brilliant future is approaching over the literary horizon. Literary criticism is in a favorable position to make a fresh, new start without any need to free itself from the bondages of oppression, tradition, or convention. A tradition has yet to be established.

XVIII FINE ARTS

General Introduction to Korean Art

History of Korean Art

It was in the eastern part of the Korean peninsula that the first civilization of Korea was born. This area is isolated from the rest by mountains running from the northernmost Paektusan, to the south. Because of this feature, the cultural pattern there is much different than in other areas. Many discoveries, "chipped stone implements" and so-called "comb pattern potteries," distinguish the prehistoric culture of this geographic region from that of the rest. With the beginning of the historic period, however, artistic activities began to decline because the area was too mountainous and too far from the center of the peninsula for any relations to compete with the more rapidly developing portions of the peninsula. Later, the people of this area were often called "non-civilized" by the southern Koreans of the Yi dynasty.

Northwestern Korea, however, advanced its culture to the highest point in the peninsula, maintaining cultural ties with China and areas farther west from the Stone Age forward to the seventh century A.D. Dolmens, the most outstanding remains of the Stone Age in Korea, were discovered mostly in this area. One particular type seems to have originated there. The bronze culture which is supposed to have come from Siberia and northern China also spread through the peninsula with this area as the gateway.

During the period, from the first century B.C. to the beginning of the fourth, the Han Chinese colonies in northwestern Korea, the Lolang Province and the Taifang Province, had much influence upon contemporary Korean art. In A.D. 313 Spartan Koguryo in Manchuria overran the Chinese colonies. Moving its capital to Pyongyang, it got along with the northern Chinese dynasties, particularly with the northern Wei (386-534 A.D.). So close was the relationship that Koguryo developed a unique art combining native elements with the cultural stimulus of Wei.

When Silla conquered Koguryo, it continued to maintain Kyongju, in the southeastern part of Korea, as its capital throughout the dynasty. The center of artistic activities moved south and never returned north so that in the Yi period (1392-1910), the people of the northeast and northwest – especially of the northern borders – had almost no chance to contribute to Korean art.

During the Three Kingdoms period, Paekche (18 B.C.-A.D. 660), in the southwestern part of the peninsula, kept close relations with the southern dynasties of China over both the sea and land, establishing a cosmopolitan culture. Although it was far less militarized than Koguryo and seemed very passive, its culture was outgoing. Ancient Japanese culture and arts were almost exclusively influenced by Paekche and its artists and artisans.

The southeastern area of Korea had a unique culture since the Stone Age. Particulary, Silla (57 B. C.-A. D. 935), having strong military and administrative systems as often seen in other conservative countries, succeeded not only in unifying the three kingdoms under its single dominance in the seventh century, but also in establishing a single unified culture on the Korean peninsula and advancing this to its peak from the eighth century through the ninth.

Trends in Korean Art

Oriental art so-called may be divided into two large schools: the Chinese and the Indian. The Chinese school puts emphasis on inwardness, while the Indian tries to approach both reality and inwardness. It is natural that both Korean and Japanese arts should be closer to the Chinese school since the influence of a near neighbor was constant. It doesn't mean, however, that Korean art is Chinese art. Although the basic iconography, or the fundamental rules of representation, originated in China, differences in impression, subjectivity, drawing and handling of the details produced different effects upon a common object.

The reason that the ancient arts of Korea and Japan were much influenced by that of China was not only their geographical proximity but also their common religion, Buddhism, which was the patron and promoter of their arts. Almost every artistic work was related to Buddhism.

It was indeed only after the introduction of Buddhism from China in the fourth century that art began in the true sense of the word for a people settled since the Stone Age. The sudden demands for Buddhist images, paintings, pagodas and temples meant a hastily trained corps of architects, sculptors and painters, who were apparently educated and influenced by the Chinese artists and art objects already in the country from China. The piousness and devotion of the ancient Buddhists, was a stimulant that made excellent artists of the Korean people in a short period of time. Once they mastered the basic techniques completely, they went ahead to produce characteristically Korean works of art according to their own thoughts and inspirations.

Sino-Korean forms of Buddhist art were, in turn, introduced to Japan to contribute to the progressive Japanese arts culminating in the Asuka and Nara periods. Japanese art, however, was less influenced by that of China partly because of the relative geographical isolation and partly because the islands had their own religion in Shintoism. Korea was a different case. The peninsula also had folk religions, such as Shamanism, but its proximity to China made the upper classes and government officials overwhelmingly affected by Chinese ideas and cultures. Korea's own styles were too much disturbed to be developed with complete independence.

As mentioned above, although Korean artists followed the Chinese line basically, they produced different works from the Chinese with different approaches, different handling and different evaluations. Some, for instance the celadon wares of Koryo, were so excellent and unique that they far surpassed the Chinese. Nevertheless, they were unable to influence the Chinese in the reverse, though having vital effects on the Japanese.

The history of Korean art is divided into six periods as follows:

1) Pre-Three Kingdoms Period. (Before 3rd century)
2) Three Kingdoms Period. (4th through mid-7th century)
3) Unified Silla Period. (mid-7th through mid-10th century)
4) Koryo Period. (mid-10th through 14th century)
5) Yi Period. First half. (15th and 16th century)
        Second half. (17th through 19th century)

← Hunting on Horseback
A fresco in Muyongchong (Dancing Tomb), Psi an, Manchuria
Koguryo dynasty (300~500)

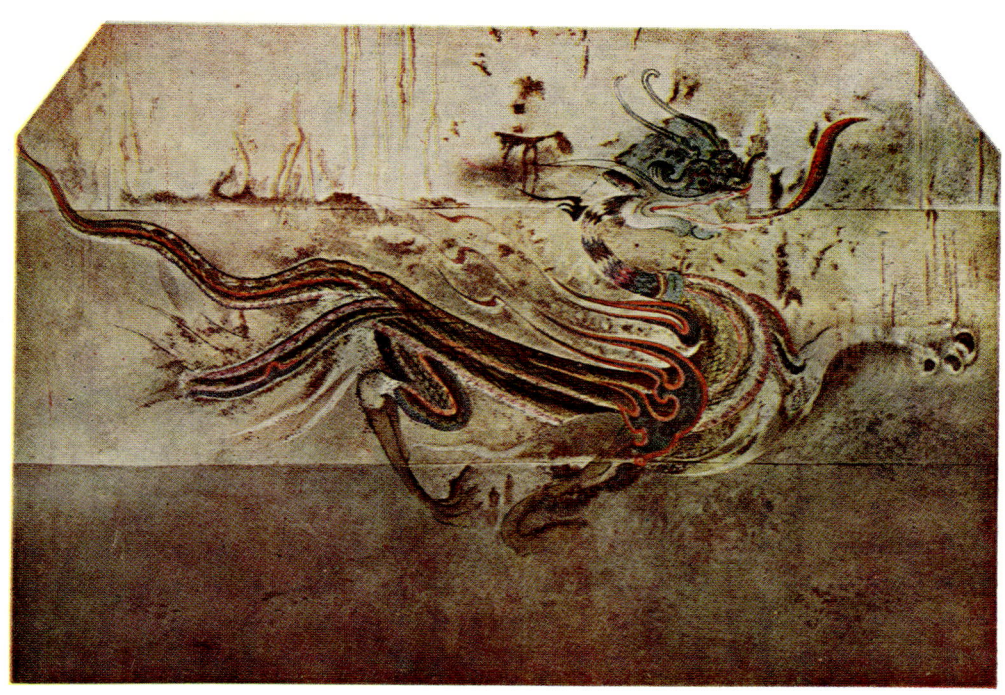

↑ Blue Dragon (One of Four Deities)
A fresco in Taemyo (Great Tomb), Uhyon, Kangso, Pyongan Namdo.
Koguryo dynasty (500〜650)

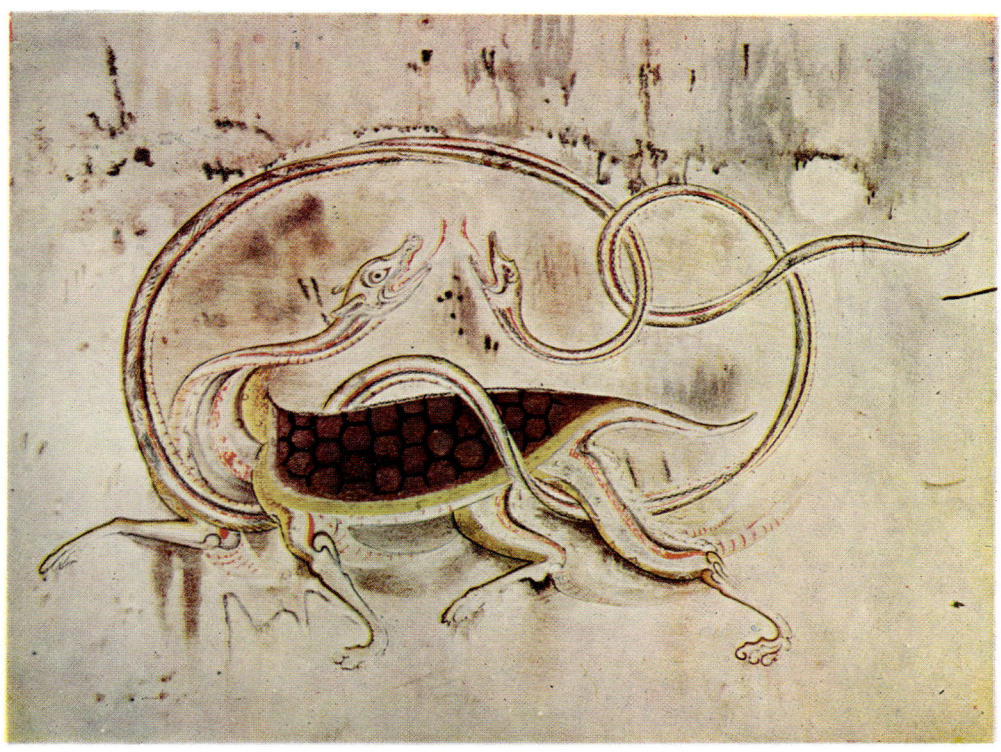

↑ Tortoise-Serpent (One of Four Deities)
A fresco in Taemyo (Great Tomb), Uhyon, Kangso, Pyongan Namdo.
Koguryo dynasty (500〜650)

White Tiger (One of Four Deities)
A fresco in Chungmyo (Middle Tomb), Uhyon, Kangso, Pyongan Namdo.
Koguryo dynasty (500~650)

Flying Angel
A fresco in Taemyo (Great Tomb), Uhyon, Kangso, Pyongan Namdo.
Koguryo dynasty (500~650)

← T'abyok God Statue
   A fresco in Tomb No. 17, Tsian, Manchuria.
   Koguryo dynasty (500)

← Ox Cart
   A fresco in Ssangyongchong (Two Pillars Tomb), Yonggang,
   Pyongan Namdo.
   Koguryo dynasty (500)

↑ Sacred Procession for the Dead
  A fresco in Ssangyongchong (Two Pillars Tomb), Yonggang, Pyongan Namdo.
  Koguryo dynasty (500)

Red Bird (Original: One of Four Deities)
  A fresco in Taemyo (Great Tomb), Uhyon, Kangso, Pyongan Namdo.
↓ Koguryo dynasty (500~650)

↑ Women (Original: A Part of Ox Cart)
  A fresco in Ssangyongchong (Two Pillars Tomb), Yonggang, Pyongan Namdo.
  Koguryo dynasty (500)

↑ Hunting Game in Mountains
Ink and color on silk
By King Kongmin (1330–1374)
Height 9.84″; Width 8.66″, Koryo dynasty

↑ Four Goats
Ink and color
By an unknown painter
Height 13.15″; Width 9.44″, Late Koryo dynasty

↑ Sokka Yorae (Sakyamuni)
By No Yong (14th century)
Height 8.27″; Width 5.11″
Koryo dynasty

 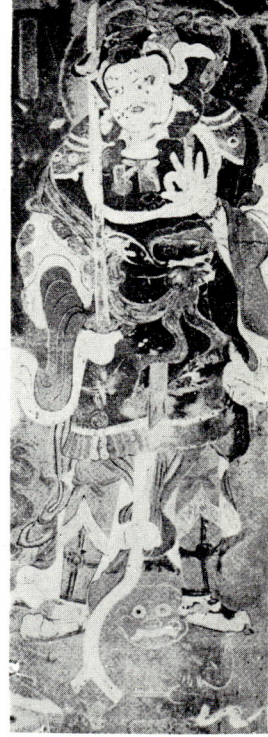

↑ Chonwang (Virupaksa) and Bosal (Bodhisattva)
Two frescos in Pusok-sa Temple, Yongju, Kyongsang Pukto
Late Koryo dynasty (1377)

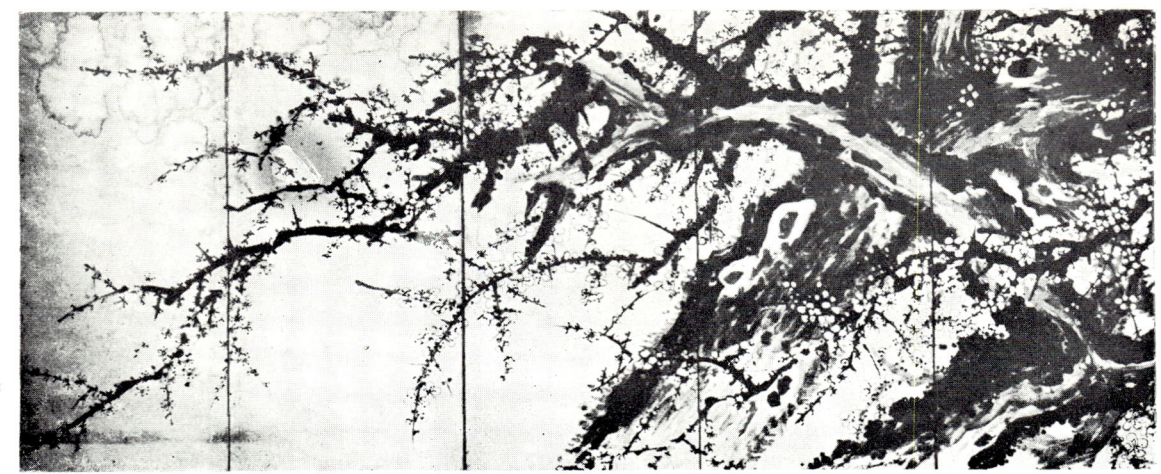

↑ A White and Red Plum-blossom Screen of Ten Pieces
Ink and light color on paper
By Chang Sungop (1843-1897)
Height 35.79″ ; Width 169.41″, Yi dynasty

↑ Two Birds on a Branch
Ink and light color on paper
By Cho Sok (1595-1668)
Height 37.58″ ; Width 12.19″
Yi dynasty

↑ Plum-blossoms
Ink on paper
By Cho Sok (1595-1668)
Height 35.73″ ; Width 22.19″
Yi dynasty

↑ A Man Lying on a Rock
Ink on paper
By Kang Huian (1419-1464)
Height 9.31″; Width 6.20″, Yi dynasty

↑ Utopia in Dream
  Horizontal scroll, ink and light color on silk
  By An Kyon (mid-15th century)
  Height 15.23″ ; Width 41.76″
  Yi dynasty

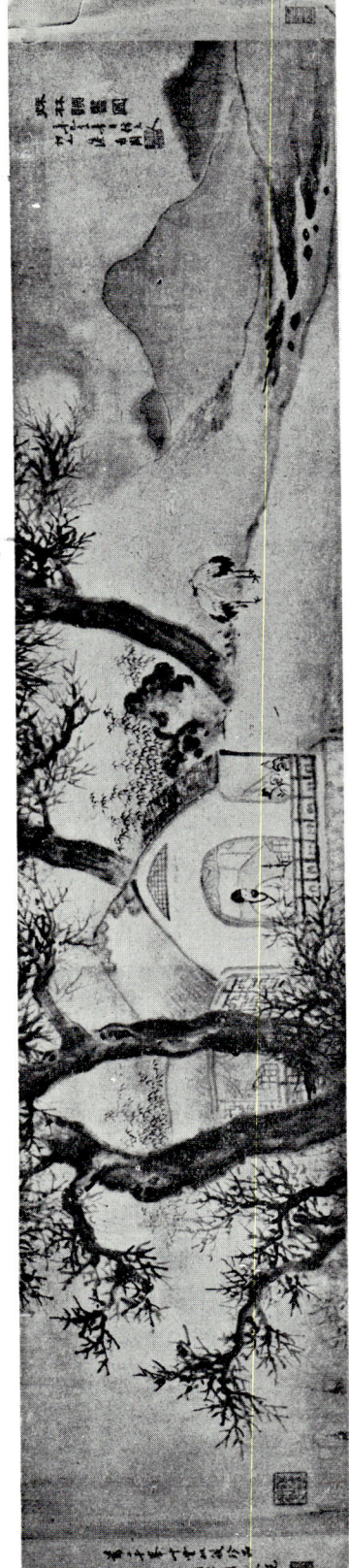

↑ Reading in a cottage
  Ink and light color on paper
  By Yi Hanchol (1808–?)
  Height 10.68″ ; Width 49.03″
  Yi dynasty

↑ A Woman on Horse-back
Ink and light color on paper
By Yun Tokhui (1685–?)
Height 33.40″ ; Width 27.80″
Yi dynasty

↑ Grapes
Ink and color on paper
By Yi Inmun (1745–1821)
Height 14.60″ ; Width 11.93″
Yi dynasty

↑ Wild Ducks by the Lakeside in Autumn
  Ink and color on paper
  By Kim Husin
  Height 13.00″ ; Width 18.48″
  Late Yi dynasty

Enjoying by the Riverside on Tano Day
Ink and color on paper
By Sin Yunbok (1758-?)
Height 11.33″; Width 13.96″
↓ Yi dynasty

Butterflies →
Ink and color on paper
By Yi Kyoik (1807-?)
Height 9.42″ ; Width 10.98″
Yi dynasty

A Summer Landscape
Ink and light color on silk
By Ho Yu (1809-1892)
Height 28.87″ ; Width 22.67″
↓ Yi dynasty

Grapes in Moonlight
Ink on paper
By Yi Kyeu (1573-1645)
↓ Height 42.95″ ; Width 23.26″, Yi dynasty

↑ Hearing Flute Melodies at the Riverside
Light color on paper. Height 14.79″; Width 8.23″
By Kim Unghwan (1742-1789), Yi dynasty

A Tiger
Ink on paper. Height 37.82″; Width 22.55″
↓ By Sim Sajong (1707-1768), Yi dynasty

Two Magpies and Many Cats
Ink and color on paper. Height 56.31″; Width 37.82″
↓ By unknown painter, Yi dynasty

↑ **Genre Scene**
Ink and light color on paper
By Sin Yunbok (1758-?)
Height 11.33″; Width 13.96″
Yi dynasty

Genre Scene
Ink and light color on paper
By Sin Yunbok (1758-?)
Height 11.33″; Width 13.96″
↓ Yi dynasty

Wrestling Match
Ink and light color on paper
By Kim Hongdo (1760-?)
↓ Yi dynasty

↑ Dance enjoying
Ink and light color on paper
By Kim Hongdo (1760-?)
Yi dynasty

Blacksmith
Ink and light color on paper
By Kim Hongdo (1760-?)
↓ Yi dynasty

↑ A Private School
Ink and light color on paper
By Kim Hongdo (1760-?)
Yi dynasty

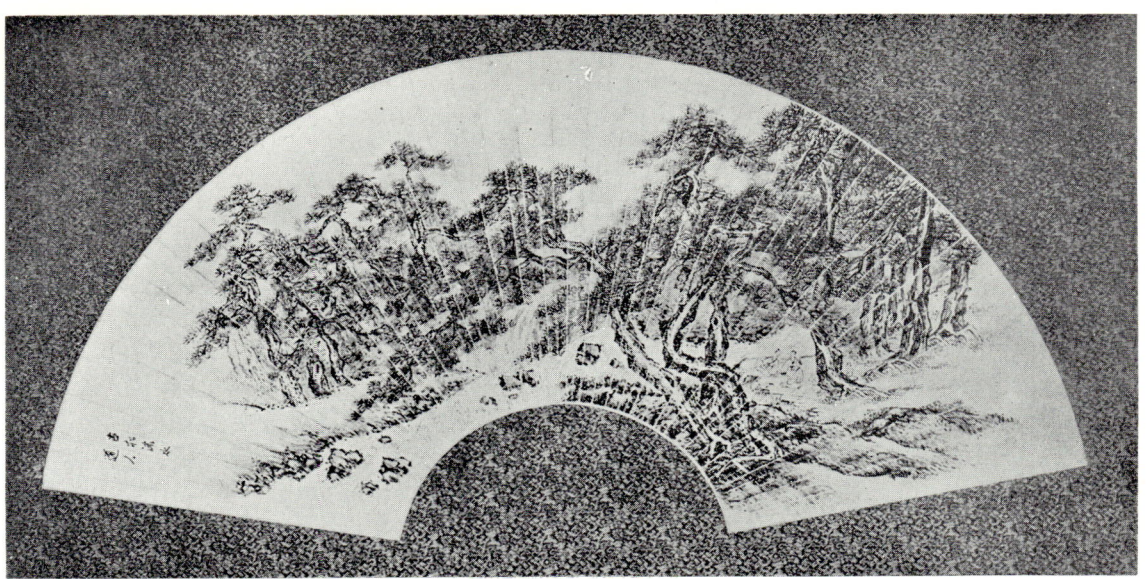

↑ Clear Rivulet under Old Pine Trees
Fan mounted as a scroll, ink and light color on paper
By Yi Inmun (1745–1821)
Height 10.50″; Width 30.17″
Yi dynasty

Dancing Hermits
Ink and light color on silk
By Choe Myongnyong (?–?)
Height 56.67″; Width 34.60″
↓ Yi dynasty

↑ A Hermit on Horseback
Ink and color on silk
By Yun Tuso (1668–?)
Height 38.77″; Width 23.50″
Yi dynasty

↑ Fairy Screen of Eight Pieces
Ink and light color on paper
By Kim Hongdo (1760-?)
Yi dynasty

← Summer Landscape
Ink and light color on paper
By Kang Sehwang (1713–1791)
Height 29.59″; Width 14.32″
Yi dynasty

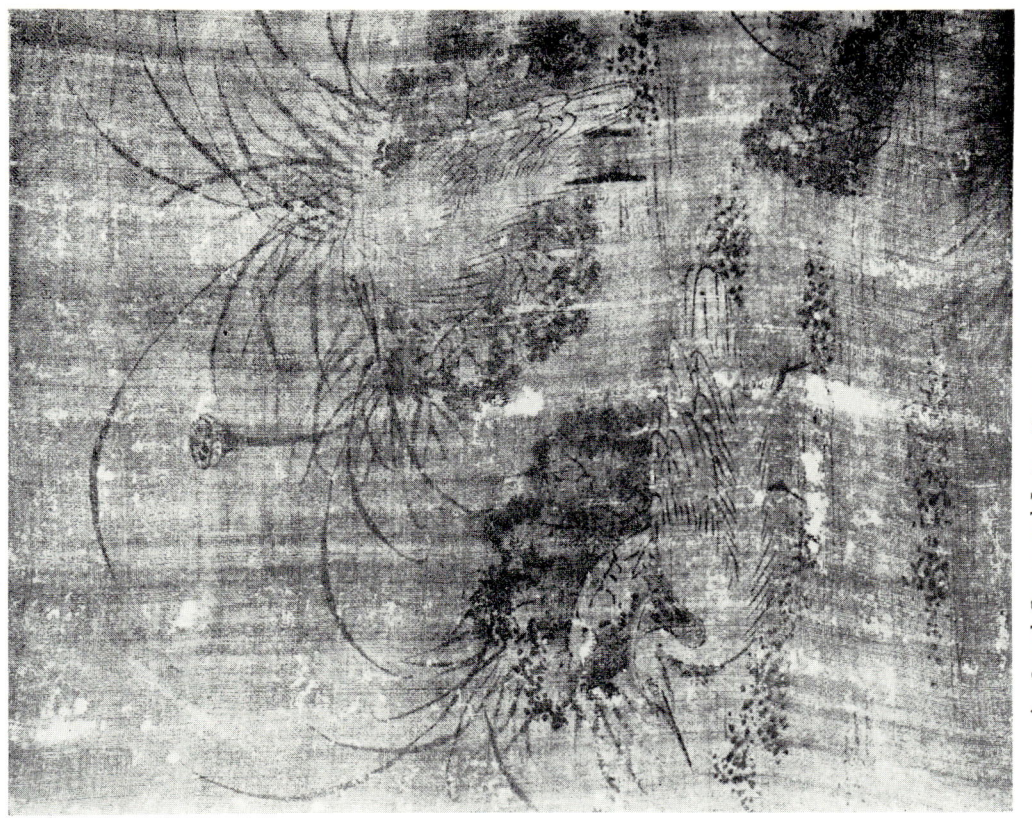

↑ Sacred Cranes and Lotus Flowers
Ink and light color on ramie cloth
By Madam Sin (Saimdang;1512–1559)
Height 9.78″; Width 8.23″
Yi dynasty

↑ Grapes
Ink on ramie cloth
By Hwang Chipchung(1533–?)
Height 10.62″; Width 8.71″
Yi dynasty

↑ A Birds on the Tree ↑
Ink and light color on paper
By Chang Sungop (1843–1897). Height 50.23″; Width 12.29″, Yi dynasty

↑ Kwanum Bosal (Avalokitesvara) Serving by Amita Yorae (Amitabha)
A fresco painted by Tamjing (579~631), a monk of Koguryo, in Kondo (main hall) of the Horyuji Temple, Nara, Japan.
Koguryo dynasty (600)

← Camelopard
A fresco in Taemyo (Great Tomb). Uhyon, Kangso, Pyongan Namdo.
Koguryo dynasty (500~650)

← Monk
A fresco in Taemyo (Great Tomb), Uhyon, Kangso, Pyongan Namdo
Koguryo dynasty (500~650)

↑ Dancing
A fresco in Muyongchong (Dancing Tomb), Psi an, Manchuria.
Koguryo dynasty (500~650)

↑ Persons
A fresco in Ssangyongchong (Two Pillars Tomb), Yonggang, Pyongan Namdo.
Koguryo dynasty (500)

↑ Washing Feet under a Tree
   Ink and light color on paper
   By Yi Kyongyun (1545-?)
   Height 10.98″; Width 7.63″
   Yi dynasty

↑ Snow Covered Mountains
   Ink and light color on silk
   By Yi Chongkun (late 15th-early 16th century)
   Height 7.74″; Width 6.31″
   Yi dynasty

↑ Landscape with Palaces
   Ink and light color on paper
   By Mun Chong (?-?). Height 12.40″; Width 16.82″, Yi dynasty

↑ Two Men under a Pine-tree
Ink and light color on paper
By Yi Chehwan (1783?–1837?)
Height 55.38″; Width 26.25″
Yi dynasty

A Tiger
Ink and light color on paper
By Ko Un (1495–?)
Height 43.43″; Width 21.71″
↓ Yi dynasty

↑ Flowers and Butterflies
Ink and color on silk
By Sin Myongyon (1809-?)
Height 11.57″ ; Width 8.71″
Yi dynasty

↑ Dharma
Ink on paper
By Kim Myongguk (mid-17th century)
Height 32.45″ ; Width 22.91″
Yi dynasty

↑ Cattle Farming
Ink and color on paper
By Kim Turyang (1696-1763). Height 15.51″ ; Width 20.04″, Yi dynasty

Two Cats →
Ink and light color on silk
By Pyon Sangł yoǩ (18th century)
Height 37.28″; Width 17.00″
Yi dynasty

← Crowded Carps
Ink and light color on silk
By Cho Sokchin (1853–1920)
Height 55.47″; Width 25.89″
Yi dynasty

↑ Enjoying Kwak Punyang
Ink and color on silk
By Kim Toksin (1754–1822)
Height 57.26″ ; Width 48.91′
Yi dynasty

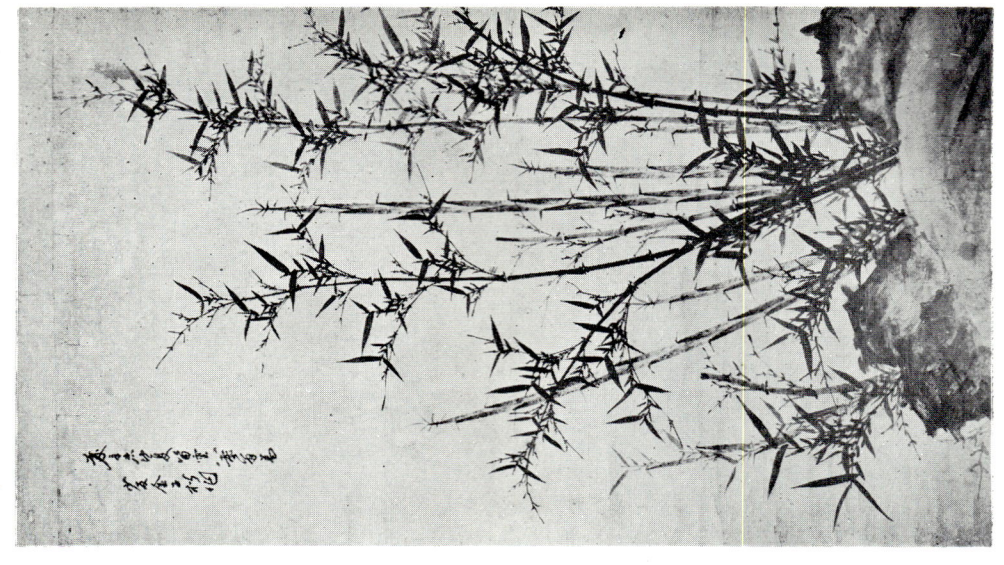

Bamboos
Ink on paper
By Yu Tokchang (1694-1773)
Height 55.89″; Width 36.67″
Yi dynasty

Bamboo in a Storm
Ink on ramie cloth
By Yi Chong (era of King Chungjong)
Height 42.22″; Width 27 44″
Yi dynasty

A Thatched Hut on Mt. Nosan
Color on silk
By Chong Son (1676-1759)
Height 50.17″; Width 27.23″
Yi dynasty

Portrait of Sin Im
Ink and color on paper
By Kim Chinyo (?-?)
Height 17.18"; Width 12.67"
Yi dynasty

Portrait of Yi Sannae
Ink and light color on silk
By unknown painter
Height 39.00"; Width 22.19"
Yi dynasty

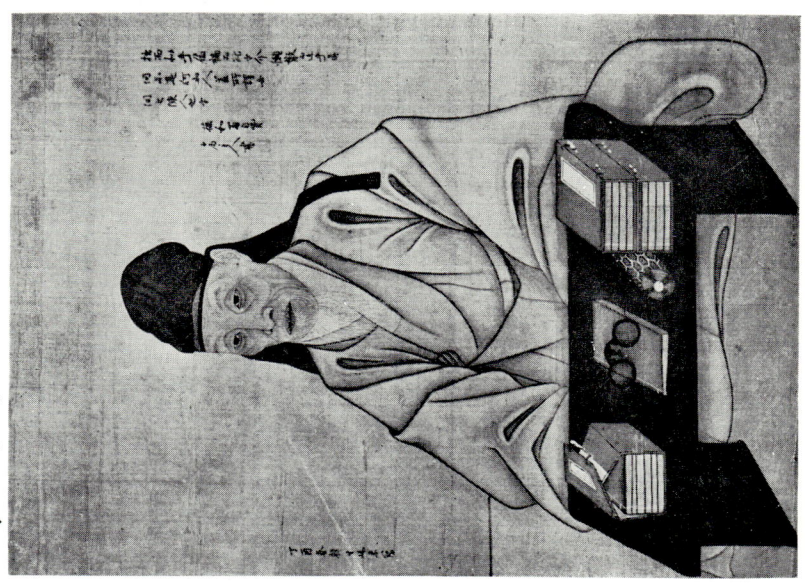

Portrait of Pohwa
Ink and color on silk
By Han Chongnae (?-?)
Height 25.65"; Width 18.36"
Yi dynasty

A Bull
By Yi Chungsop (1916-1956)
Date: Uucertain

Landscape of Songgyungwan
By To Sangbong (1902-   )
Date: 1959

Retrospection
By Pak Yongson (1911-   )
Date: 1959

Still Life
By Yi Chongu (1899-   )
Date: 1927

↑   A Sitting Woman on Chair
   By Kim Insung (1911-   )
Date: 1959

On the Lawn Grass
By Chang Ukchin (1917-   )
↓   Date: 1959

↑ A Late Autumn in Ancient Castle
By Yi Sangbom (1897 -   )
Date: 1959

↑ A Book-Lover on Midnight
By Kim Unho (1893 -   )
Date: 1959

↑ Choksoknu Pavilion
By Pyon Kwansik (1899 -   )
Date: 1960

Summer →
By Ko Huidong (1886-   )
Date: 1960

Early Spring
By Pae Yom (1908-   )
↓ Date: 1959

At the Lakeside →
By Chang Usong (1909-   ), Date: 1959

↑ Autumn
By No Suhyon (1899-)
Date: 1959

An Organism
By Chon Kyongja (1924-) →
Date: 1957

People
By Kim Kichang (1913-)
↓ Date: 1959

← An Inscription of King Hotae's Tombstone
Situated in Tsian, Manchuria.
Koguryo dynasty (414)

An Inscription of a Monument →
Paekche dynasty (about 600 A.D.)

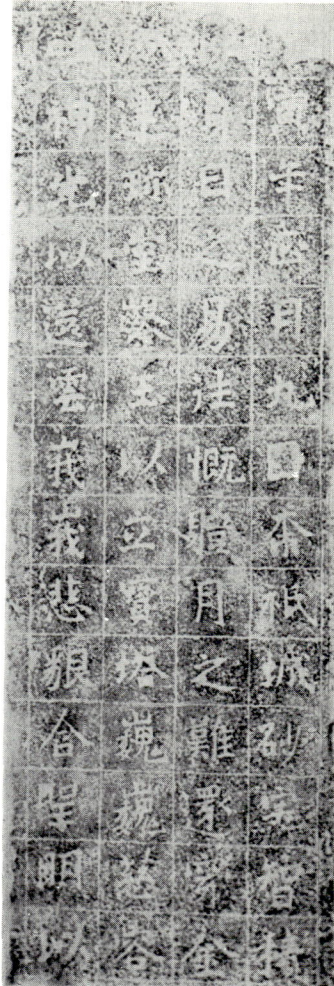

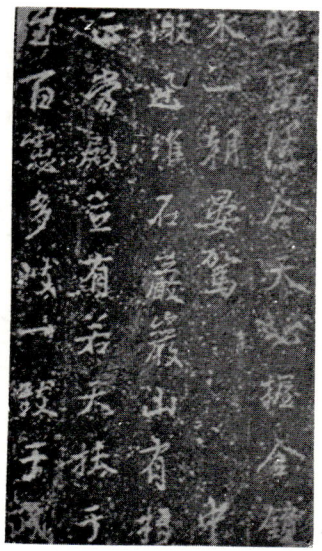

↑ A Monument of Priest Nanghye in Songju-sa Temple
By Choe Ingon (868-944)
Silla dynasty (890)

↑ A Monument of Ojang-sa Temple
By Kim Yukchin
Silla dynasty (801)

An Inscription of Moduru's Tombstone
↓ Koryo dynasty (410)

← A Hunting Monument of King Chinhung
Situated in Hamhung, Hamgyong Pukto.
Silla dynasty (560)

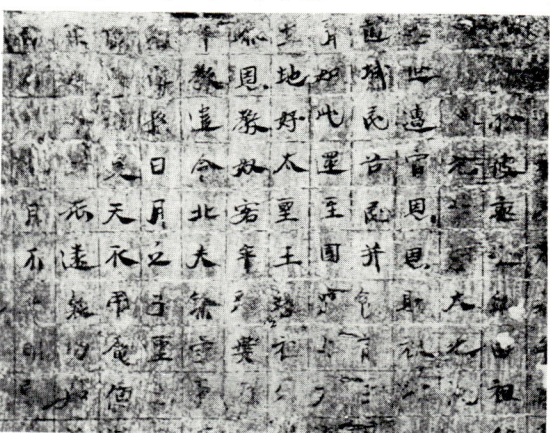

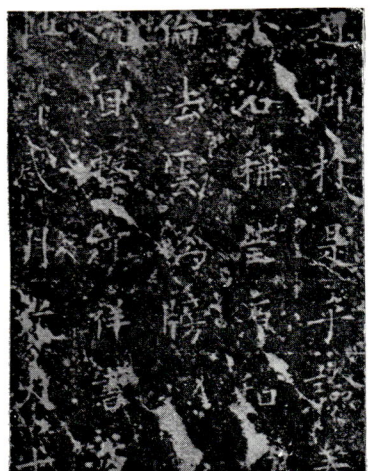

↑ A Monument of Powol Pagoda of Monk Suchol
Situated in Silsang-sa Temple
Silla dynasty (876)

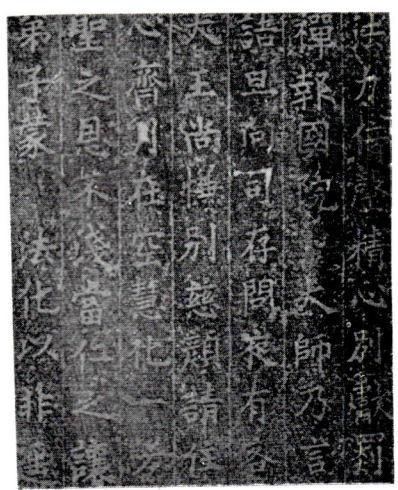

↑ A Monument of Priest Pobin
By Han Yun
Koryo dynasty (978)

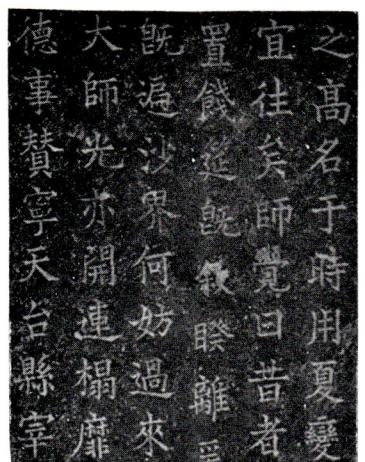

A Monument of Priest Taegak
By O Onhu
Koryo dynasty (about 1100)
↓

↑ A Monument of Priest Sungmyo
By Kim Koung
Koryo dynasty (about 1025)

↑ A Monument of Monk Chinjong, in Bongom-sa Temple
By Chang Sosol
Koryo dynasty (965)

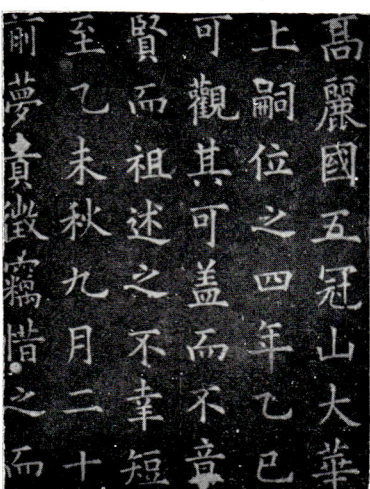

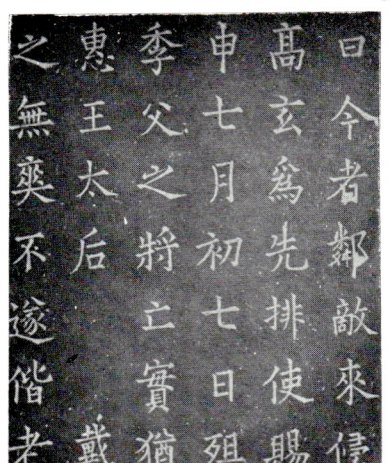

← A Monument of Hyonhwa-sa Temple
By Chae Chungsun (?-1036)
Koryo dynasty (1021)

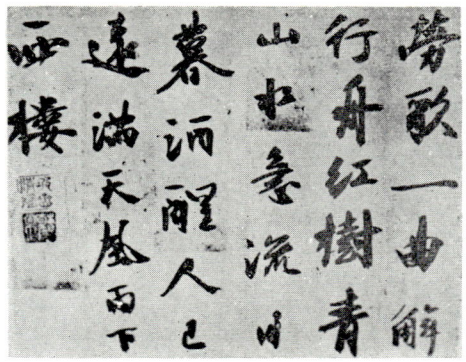

↑ By Song Suchim (1493–1564)
  Yi dynasty

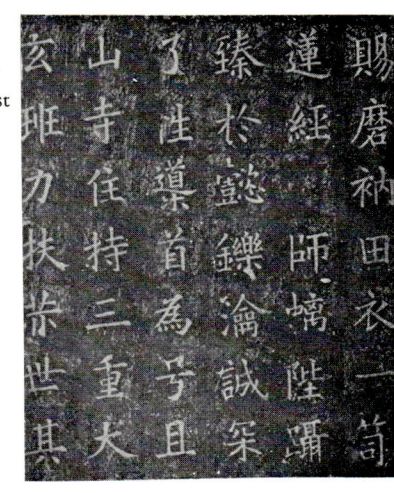

→ A Monument of Priest Chingwang
By An Minhu
Koryo dynasty (1085)

A Monument of Paekwolsaun
By Kim Saeng (711–791)
↓ Silla dynasty

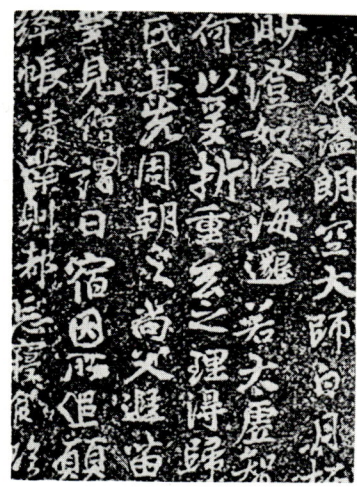

A Monument of Priest Hyongyong
By Yi Wonbu
↓ Koryo dynasty (1119)

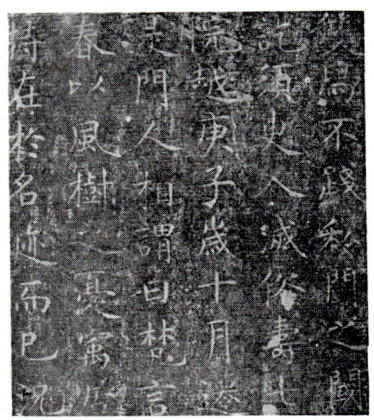

A Monument of Hyegwang Pagoda
of Monk Pobgyong
By Sok Songyong
↓ Koryo dynasty (946)

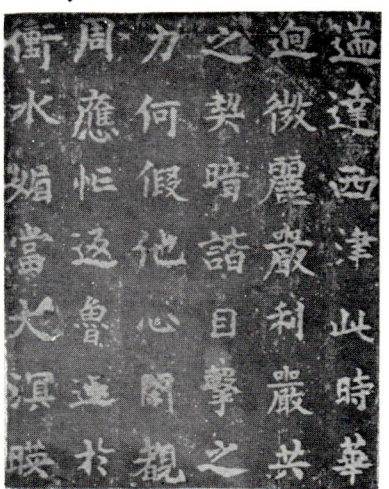

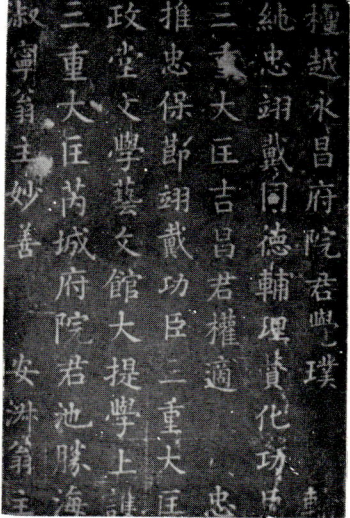

→ An Inscription of Monument
By Han Su (1333–1384)
Koryo dynasty (1378)

← **A Monument of Priest Chingam**
By Choe Chiwon (857-915)
Silla dynasty

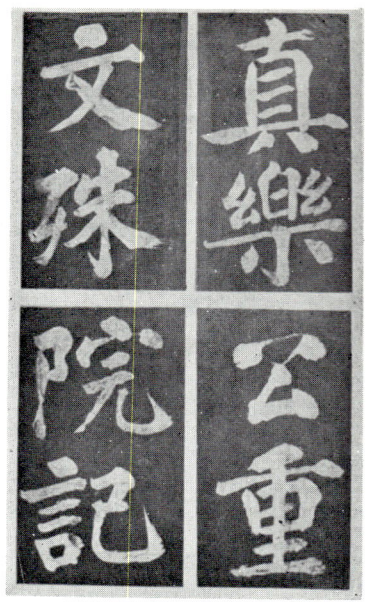

↑ **A Memorial Inscription for Munjuwon Monastery Reconstructed**
By Sok Tanyon (1069-1158)
Koryo dynasty

A Monument of Priest Songak →
By Kwon Chunghwa (1322-1408)
Koryo dynasty (1377)

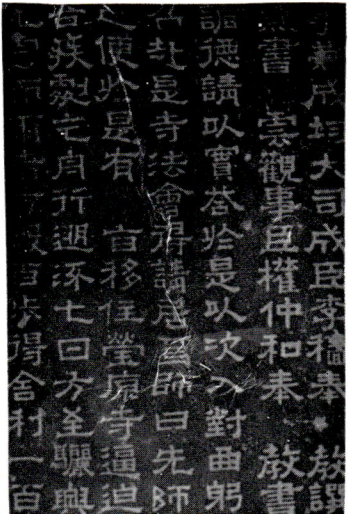

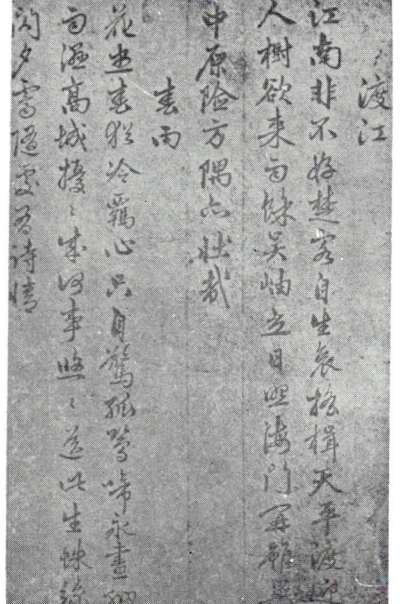

← By Yi Am (1297-1364)
Koryo dynasty

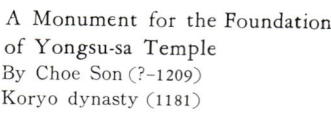

A Monument for the Foundation of Yongsu-sa Temple →
By Choe Son (?-1209)
Koryo dynasty (1181)

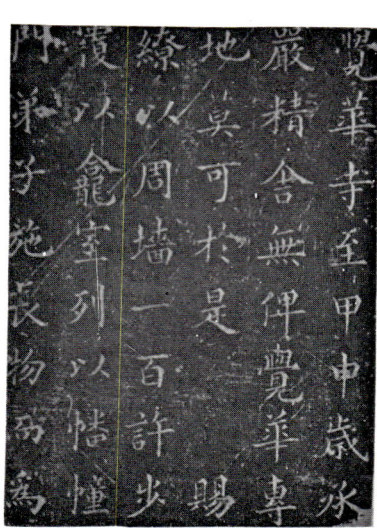

↑ Preface of the Book
"Mokmin Simso"
By Chong Yagyong (1762–1836)
Yi dynasty

→ By Yun Sun (1680–1741)
Yi dynasty

↓ By Kwon Kyu (1478–1548)
Yi dynasty

↓ By Han Ho (1543–1605)
Yi dynasty

↓ By Kim Chonghui (1786–1857)
Yi dynasty

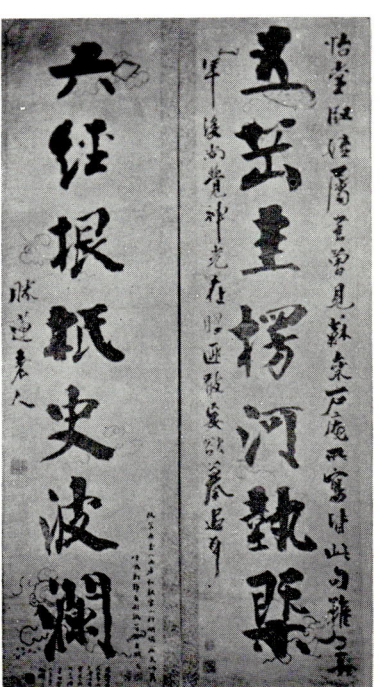

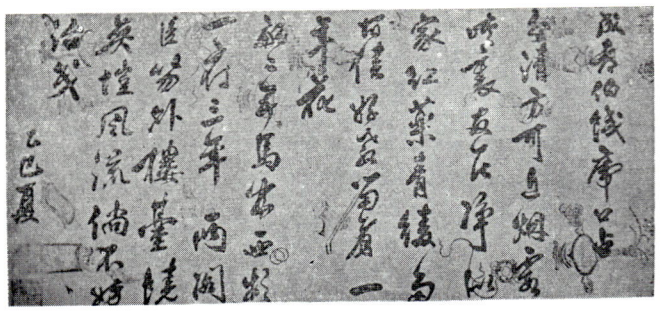

↑ By King Chongjo (1752–1800)
   Yi dynasy

By Yang Saon (1517–1584)
↓ Yi dynasty

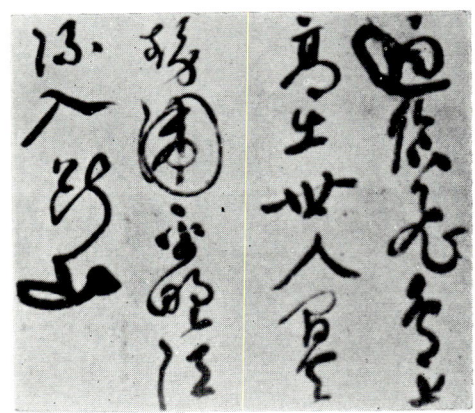

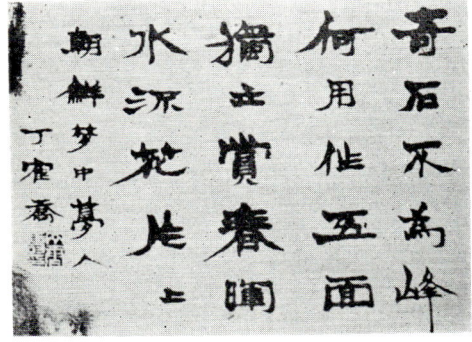

↑ By Chong Hakkyo (1832–1914)
   Yi dynasty

By Min Yongik (1860–1914)
↓ Yi dynasty

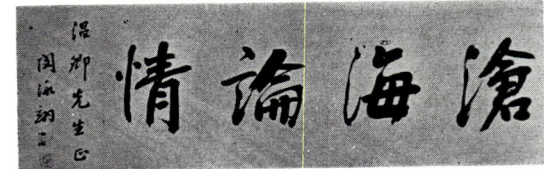

By Yi Kwangsa (1705–1777)
↓ Yi dynasty

↑ By Prince Anpyong, Yi Yong, (1418-1453)
　　Yi dynasty

By Yi Insang (1710-1760)
↓ Yi dynasty

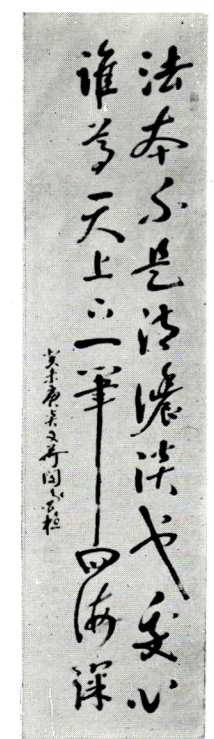

↑ The Cursive Style
　By Min Hyongsik
　(1875-1947)

↑ By Kim Songgun
　(1835-1918)
　Yi dynasty

The Seal Style
By O Sechang
↓ (1864-1953)

By Sin Wi (1769-1845)
↓ Yi dynasty

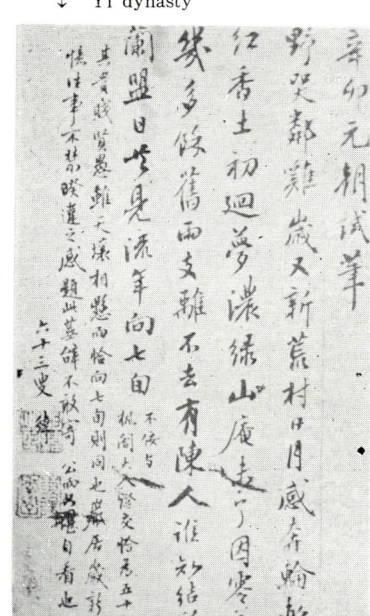

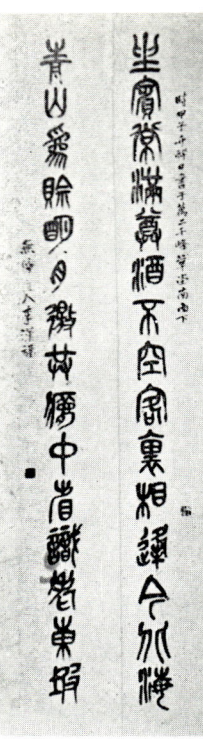

↑ The Seal Style
By Yi Hanbok (1897–1940)

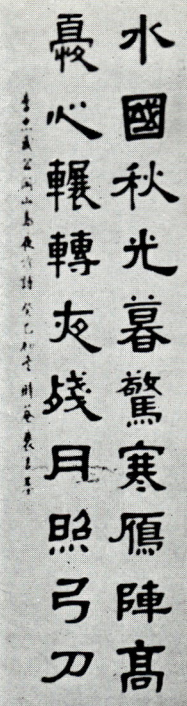

↑ The Seal Style
By Pae Kilgi (1917–)

↑ The Seal Style
By Kim Taesok (1875–1953)

↑ The Cursive Style
By So Pyongo (1862–1935)

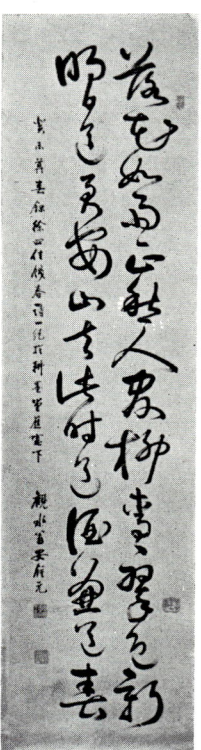

↑ The Cursive Style
By An Chongwon (1874–1951)

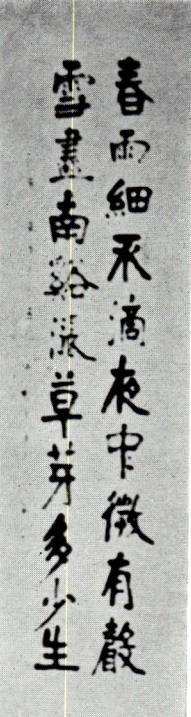

↑ The Square Style
By Son Chaehyong (1903–)

↑ Sitting Miruk Bosal (Maitreya) in Deep Speculation
 A Buddhist image made of bronze found at nearby Andong, Kyongsang Pukto.
 Height 31.69″
 Silla dynasty (500~600)

↑ Sakyamuni in Seated Posture
Granite; Height 2.73m
Silla dynasty
  The principal image in the Cave Temple on Mount Toham near Kyongju. One of the greatest masterpieces of stone Buddhas in the world, it is remarked especially for its elegance and loftiness.

↑ Bodhisattva on Right Wall of the Cave Temple

↑ Bodhisattva on Left Wall of the Cave Temple

← **Avalokitesvara**
Granite; relief on the back wall of the Cave Temple.

Buddhist Triad of Kyongju City, Silla
↓ Granite

↑ Sakyamuni of Koguryo (Late 6th century)
Gilt bronzei; Height 5.25″

↑ Maitreya of Silla (Early 7th century)
Gilt bronze; Height 35.75″

Apsatas of Silla (8th-9th century)
↓ Gilt bronze; Height 4.75″

↑ Bodhisattva of Paekche (6th century)
Gilt bronze; Height 4.25″

↑ Maitreya of Three Kingdoms (6th century)
  Bronze; Height 11.25″

Maitreya of Silla (6th-7th century,
Gilt bronze Height 6.56″
↓

Buddha of Silla (8th century)
↓ Bronze; Height 10.31″

↑ Avalokitesvara and Tamun-
  chon (One of Four Deva
  Kings) of Koryo
  Gold; Life size

↑ Maitreya of Paekche (6th
  century)
  Bronze; Height 4.53″

↑ Maitreya of Three Kingdoms (Late 6th-early 7th century) Gilt bronze; Height 3.62″

↑ Avalokitesvara of Silla (8th century) Gilt bronze; Height 6.25″

↑ Maitreya of Silla (6th-7th century) Gilt bronze; Height 8.25″

↑ Avalokitesvara of Paekche (6th century) Gilt bronze; Height 8.44″

↑ Bodhisattva of Three Kingdoms (Early 7th century) Gilt bronze; Height 4.94″

↑ Bodhisattva of Paekche (Early 7th century) Gilt bronze; Height 5″

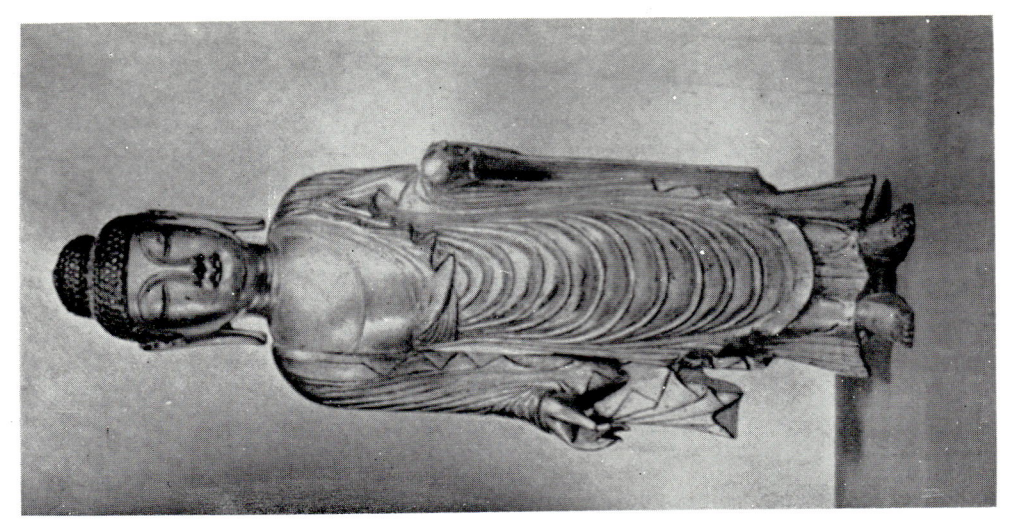
↑ Bhaisajyaguru of Silla (8th-9th century)
Gilt bronze; Height 16"

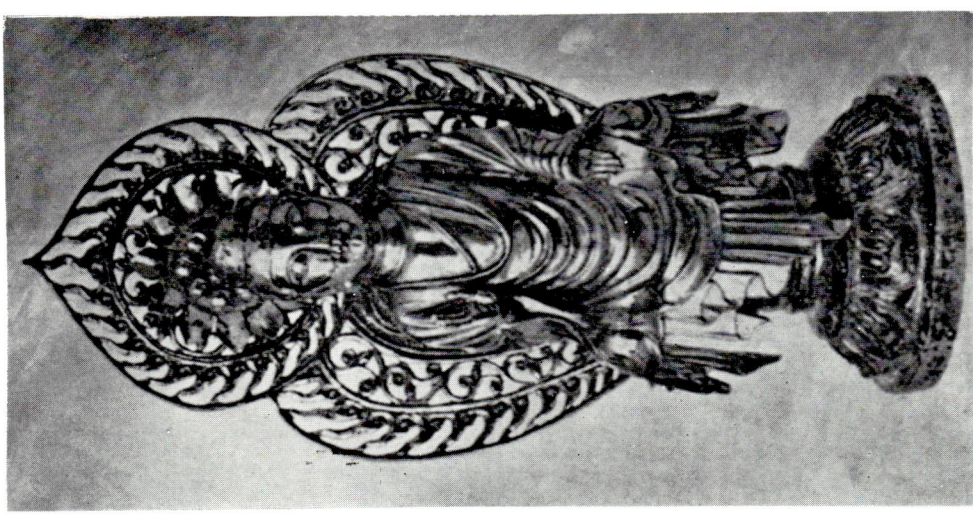
↑ Buddha of Silla (7th-8th century)
Gold alloy; Height 4.75"

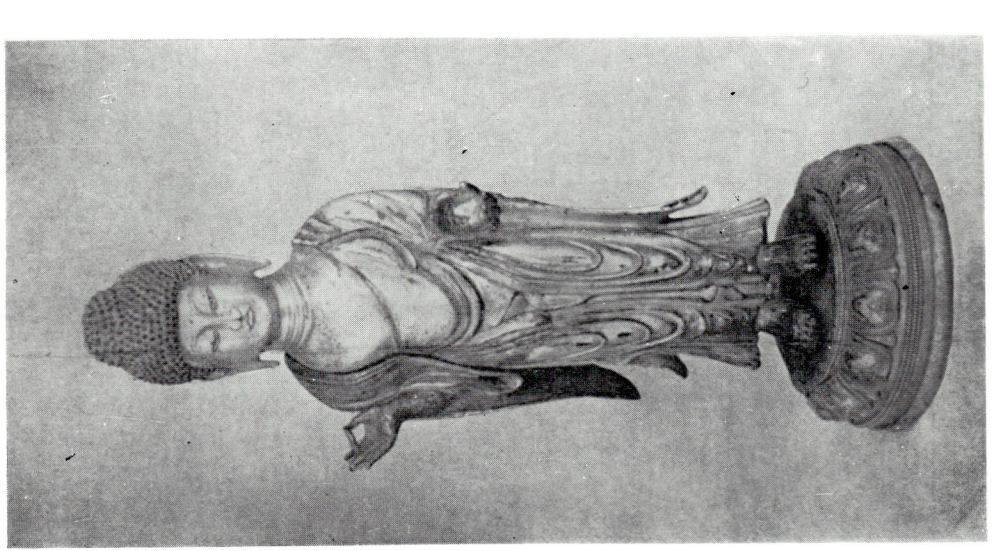
↑ Bhaisajyaguru of Silla (8th-9th century)
Gilt bronze; Height 11.44"

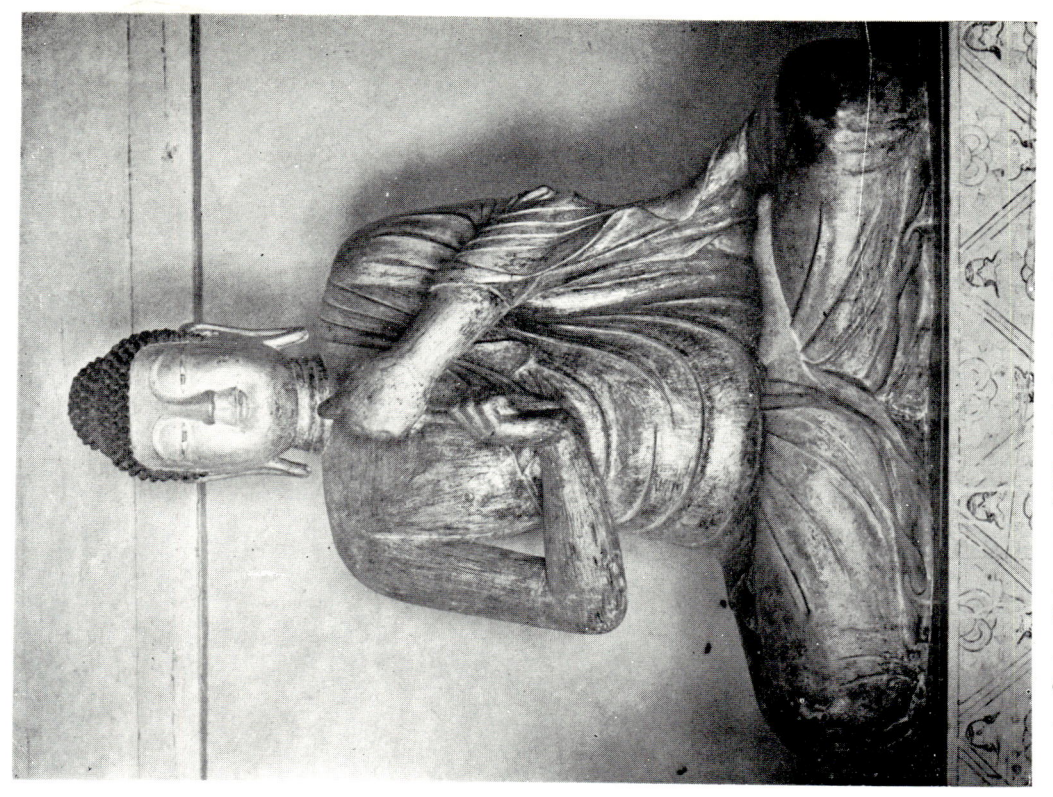

↑ Sitting Vairocana of Silla, Pulguk-sa Temple
   Gilt bronze; life size

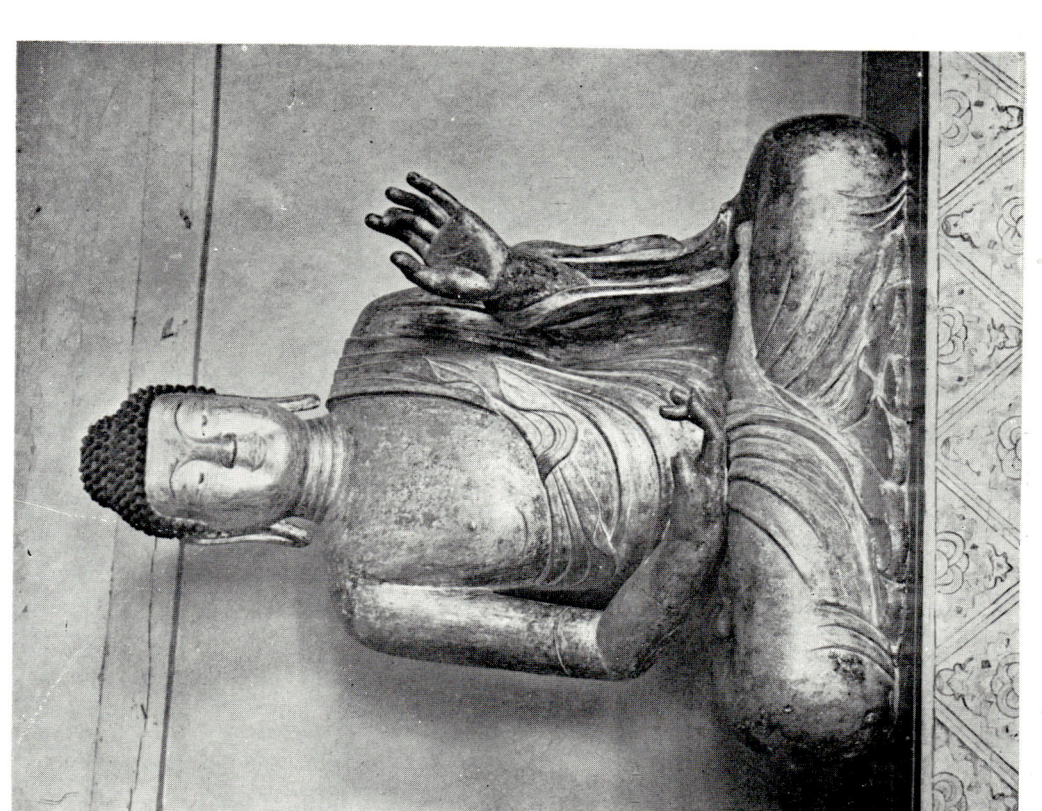

↑ Sitting Amitabha of Silla, Pulguk-sa Temple
   Gilt bronze; life size

↑ Buddhist Shrine
Gilt bronze; Height 11.13″; Width 9.88″; Length 5.19″
Koryo dynasty (13th-14th century)

↑ Seated Buddha of Silla (9th century)
Gilt bronze; Height 8.37″

↑ Avalokitesvara of Silla (7th-8th century)
Gilt bronze; Height 7.13″

↑ Sitting Vairocana of Pian-sa Temple, Silla
Iron

↑ Sitting Vairocana of Tonghwa-sa Temple, Silla
Stone

↑ Standing Buddhas of Suburban Kyongju, Silla
Stone

↑ Sitting Buddha of Suburban Kyongju, Silla
Stone

↑ Sitting Buddha of Puyo, Paekche
Stone

↑ Sitting Bodhisattva of Woljong-sa Temple, Koryo
Stone

↑ Sitting Buddha of Kangnung, Koryo
Granite

↑ Sitting Sakyamuni of Koryo
Clay; Height 2.69m
Principal image of Pusok-sa Temple

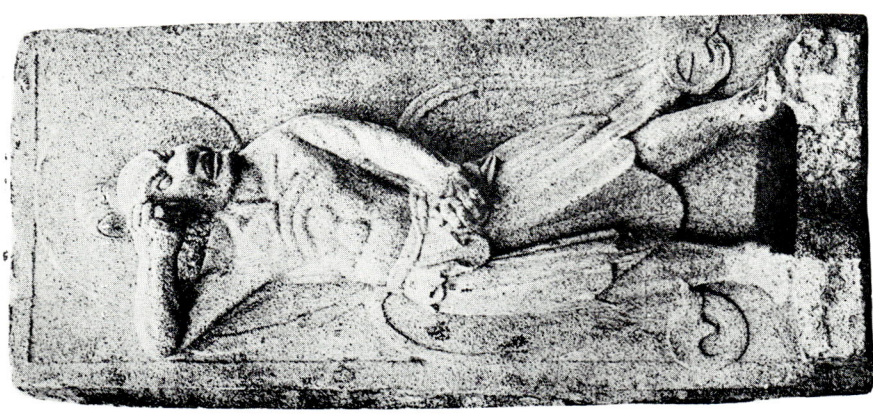

↑ Kumgang-yoksa, or the Oriental Herculeses of Silla Granite: relief one on each side of the entrance to the Cave Temple on Mount Toham near Kyongju.

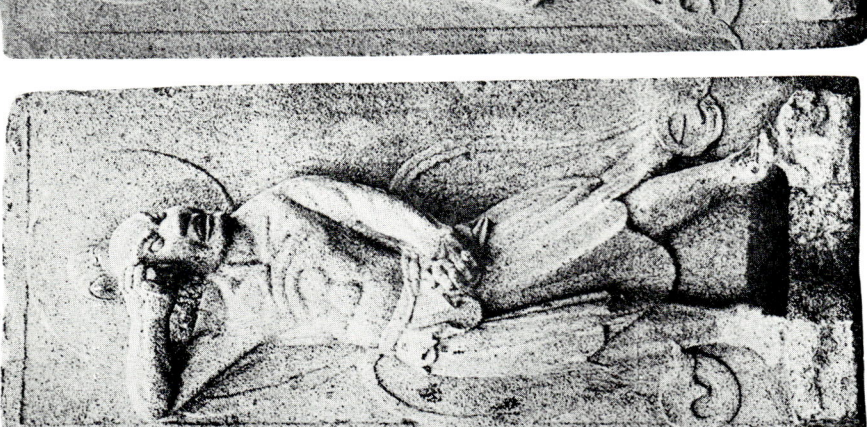

↑ Two Images of Four Deva Kings of Silla Granite: relief on the wall of the entrance to Cave Temple near Kyongju.

↑ Clay Buddha Images of Haein-sa Temple, Yi dynasty

↑ Standing Maitreya of Taejo-sa Temple, Koryo
Granite; Height 11m

↑ Standing Tathagata of Paekche
Stone

↑ Stone Buddha of Silla
Located at the lakeside of Muyongji (Shadeless Lake) in Kyongju.

↑ Tomb Gates of Silla, Kyongju
Stone

← South Side of Four-face Buddha of Silla
Located in Kyongju, Kyongsang Pukto.

Stone Buddha of Koryo
↓ Granite; carved on a rock, Andong, Kyongsang Pukto.

↑ Detail of 13-storeyed Pagoda of Wongak-sa Temple
  A marble tower. On the whole body surface Buddhist images and modelled roofs are exquisitely carved in relief.

↑ Pudo Tower of Pulguk-sa Temple
  Height 2m; late Silla dynasty
  Monument to a Buddhist priest.

↑ Carved Decoration on Stone Steps
  Center of the steps in front of Myongjongjon building within Changgyong-won park (former palace). Carved in relief. Yi dynasty.

↑ Stone Lion
 A part of stone pagoda of Punhwang-sa Temple, Kyongju. Silla dynasty.

↑ Stone Sculpture of the Tomb
 One of stone sculptures standing around the tomb of Kim Yusin, Silla dynasty.

Stone Men within Tonggu-nung Mausoleum
 A mausoleum is often guarded by stone men and stone animals. There are two
↓ kinds of stone men; statues of civil servants (right) and those of military officers (left).

↑ Tombstone of King Muyol
In the mausoleum of King Muyol of Silla Kingdom, Kyongju. The main body of the tombstone is missing, only the head(Isu) and tortoise-shaped pedestal remain now.

↑ Tombstone of the Six Dead Vassals (Sayuksin), Seoul
  The bodies of six loyalists, killed by a tyrant of the Yi dynasty, lie buried here.

↑ Monument of Wongak-sa Temple, Seoul
  The main body of the monument is marble. Built in Yi dynasty (1471), this monument is one of the remains of the temple.

↑ Monument for Yu Inwon of Tang China
  Puyo Museum, Chungchong Namdo.

↑ Tombstone of Admiral Yi Sunsin
  Near Onyang, Chungchong Namdo.

← Bronze Statue of Min Yonghwan, Seoul
   A patriot of latter-day, Yi dynasty.

↑ Bronze Statue of An Chunggun, Seoul
   A patriot who assassinated Ito Hirobumi, first Japanese Resident General of Korea.

Tombstone of Kim Yang, Silla
   The main body of the tombstone is missing and only the tortoise-shaped pedestal remain now in Kyongju, Kyongsang Pukto.
↓

↑ Bronze Statue of Dr. Syngman Rhee
　　Namsan Hill, Seoul

↑ Bronze Statue of Admiral Yi Sunsin
　　Chinhae, Kyongsang Namdo. The naval hero during the Hideyoshi Invasion.

↑ Bronze Statue of General Ulji Mundok
Kwangju, Cholla Namdo.
  An army general of Koguryo kingdom, who defeated the mighty host of Sui (China) in 612 A.D.

↑ Bronze Statue of General MacArthur
Park of Freedom, Inchon City.

Landing Operation at Inchon
↓ Bronze; relief at one side of General MacArthur's statue.

↑ Bronze Bell of Tongdo-sa Temple
Silla dynasty
   Note the Taeguk—symbol of the Korean National Flag—cast around the bottom of the bell.

↑ Bronze Bell in Kanghwa Island
Height 2m; Diameter, at bottom, 1.4m
Yi dynasty (later than 1711)

↑ Dragon-Head-Shaped Hock and Upper Belt of King Songdok's Bell

↑ Flying Figure Carved in Relief on One Side of King Songdok's Bell

↑ Bronze Bell of King Songdok
  Height 11m; Diameter, at bottom, 2.27m; Thickness 0.24m
  Unified Silla dynasty (771)
    Also known as bell of Pongdok-sa Temple or Emille-Jong. A masterpiece reflecting Silla's metal work of art. (See Chap. XVIII-Sculpture)

↑ "Dream"
  By Kim Kyongsung (1915-   )
  Date: 1956

↑ "Flute"
  By Yun Hyojung (1917-   )
  Date: 1955

↑ Jewelry Box with Twin Duks
  By Yi Sunsok (1905-   )
  Date: 1957

← "Bathing"
  By Kim Chongyong (1915-   )
  Date: 1959

↑ Namdae-Mun, or the Great South Gate
One of the oldest structures extant in Seoul, a typical representation of the Yi architecture. Built in 1395 when King Taejo began to build his Seoul City Castle.

↑ Tongdae-Mun, or the Great East Gate
   East gate of city castle of Seoul. Built in 1396.

← A Detail of the First Storey of Tongdae-Mun
   Pojak, or a characteristically structural part between roof and supporting posts. (See the architecture of Chapter XVIII.)

↑ Tongnip-Mun, or the Independence Gate
　In the northern part of Seoul. Built at the end of Yi dynasty by Independence Association to symbolize Korean independence. A stone structure copying a Roman Triumphal Arch.

↑ **Chongum-Mum**
   On the riverside of the Taedong, Pyongyang

   Taedong-Mun
   On the east side of the Taedong, Pyongyang. A castle gate built in early Yi dynasty. One
↓ of the masterpieces of Yi architecture. Note curved lines of roof

Hwahŏng-Mun
A part of Suwon Castle, Noted for beautiful scenery.

↑ Pukhansan Fortress
Built in 1714. North of Seoul. 8 kilometers in length.

↑
Namhansan Fortress
Located in Kwangju-gun, south of Seoul. Built in 1621.

→
Suwon Castle, Suwon, Kyonggi-do
One of strongly Chinese-influenced structures.

City Castle of Seoul
Part of the city wall of Seoul, the
↓ capital of Yi kingdom

West Gate of Samnang Castle, Kanghwa-gun Kyonggi-Do
One of the oldest castles in Korea. Beautiful
↓ Chondung-sa Temple within.

Ruins of Ondalsong Fortress
One of the "Eight Best Sceneries of Tanyang" in Chung Chong Pukto.

Ruins of Cheju Fortress, Cheju Island

Part of the Rampart Wall of Pulguk-sa Temple, Kyongju, Kyongsang Pukto.

Oguk Fortress
Outskirt of Hoeryong, Hamgyong Pukto. One of six fortresses of the Ninchens when they occupied this northern area of Korea.

↑ Toksu Palace, Chong-Dong, Seoul
   Embraces Sokchojon (right, white columned) and Museum of Fine Arts (left columned building behind a large roof) besides many large and small buildings of the palace itself. Built in 1902, but rebuilt four years later after it had been burnt down.

←
Sokchojon
Merely means stone building. Construction begun in 1900 and completed 11 years after. A modern Renaissance style building designed by an Englishman. Here, the U. S.-U. S. S. R. Joint Commission labored in vain to unite Korea. After the War, it has been used as the National Museum.

Chunghwajon →
The main audience building of the Toksu. All the aristocrats, high ranking civil officials and military officers had interview with the king here. The stones standing in the front yard indicate ranks of officials, who were arranged here according to their grades, civil officials in right, military in left.

←
The Museum of Fine Arts
Built in 1938 as a museum to include all the articles of the museum in Changgyong Palace that had been established by King Sunjong in 1907. One of two modern buildings in the Toksu Palace.

↑ Injongjon, Seoul
   The main audience building of the Changdok Palace of Yi Kingdom.

The King's Throne in In-
↓ jongjon

↓ Richly Decorated Ceiling of Injongjon

← **Puyongjong**
　A bower in the Secret Garden of Changdok Palace.

Taejojon, Changdok Palace
↓　The inner palace of the queen.

← **Chongchu-Mun**
　A gate in the Secret Garden.

↓　**Naksonjae, Changdok Palace**

↑ Piwon (The Secret Garden)
  A garden belonging to Changdok Palace. The largest in Korea. Many remains of Yi dynasty architecture preserved here.

↑ Pyobon-Gak
Botanical and zoological specimen gallery in Changgyongwon Park, once a palace of Yi kings.

Sujong
A pond in the Changgyongwon Park. Under the floating lotuses are various goldfish.

Zoo
Also in the Changgyongwon Park. The largest zoo in Korea.

Aeryonjong →
An arbor in the Secret Garden of Changdok Palace.

← **Injong-Mun**
The main entrance of Injongjon of Changdok Palace.

Nongsujong
↓ An arbor in the Secret Garden of Changdok Palace. Samo roof.

Sangnyangjong
↓ A bower in Changdok Palace.

↑ Kunjongjon, Kyongbok Palace, Seoul
Used for king's coronation and other major rituals. Built in 1867.

↓ Decorations on the Ceiling of Kunjongjon

↑ The King's Throne in Kunjongjon

← The Front Stone Steps of Kunjongjon

7 Hyangwonjong at the Center of a Pond in Kyongbok Palace

Kyonghoeru
A great pavilion in Kyongbok Palace of Yi dynasty. Feasts were chiefly held here. Built in 1867. One of masterpiece architectures of late Yi dynasty. Roof is the Palchak style.

Kyongbok Palace Museum

Kyongbok Palace Art Gallery

Sebyonggwan →
A mid-Yi period building. Located in Chungmu city, Kyongsang Namdo.

Taejaegak
← On a cliff facing the Paengma River, near Puyo, Chungchong Namdo.

Nongae Sadang in Chinju, Kyongsang Namdo →
A shrine for Nongae, the kisaeng heroine who lured a Hideyoshi commander of to a riverside and pulled him into the water with her.

← **Chunhyang Sadang**
Shrine of Chunhyang, the heroine in the most popular love story of Korea. Located in Namwon, Cholla Namdo.

↑ **Yongwangjong Pavilion**
　　Located at the riverside of the Taedong, Pyongyang City. During the Hideyoshi Invasion, the peace negotiation was held here between China and Japan.

　Ulmildae
↓　An old pavilion built on a beautiful peak of Moranbong Mountains in Pyongyang City.

Subukchong →
In the old Paekche Kingdom capital of Puyo, Chungchong Namdo.

Paekhwajong
Also located in the old capital city of Paekche, one of the Three Kingdoms in early Korean history. ↓

↑ **Sajaru**
A two-storeyed pavilion in the old Paekche capital, Puyo.

←
Panghwa-Suryujong and the Ruins of Fortress
Located in Suwon, Kyonggi-do.

↑ **Tonggunjong**
　　Located in Uiju, the northernmost town of Korea. When an enemy attacked, this was the first place to strike a signal fire. Rebuilt in 1823.

↑ **Kwandokchong**
　　Located in Cheju City, Cheju Island.

Chuksoru →
Located in Samchok, Kangwon-do.

Chongganjong
↓ Kansong, Kangwon-do.

Kyongpodae
Located in a east coastal city, Kangnung, Kangwon-do
↓

Hwajodae, Yangyang-gun, Kangwon-do
↓ On a rocky cliff on the east coast.

Hyonchungsa, Chungchong Namdo
A shrine for Admiral Yi Sunsin, hero of the Hideyoshi Wars, for his patriotic devotion.

↑ **Yonjudae**
A Buddhist shrine on a high rocky mountain in Kwanak Mountains.

Yudalgak →
Located in a southwestern port, Mokpo, Cholla Namdo.

Yongnamnu
In the beautiful southern town of Milyang, Kyongsang Namdo.

↑ Uisangdae
  Located in Yangyang-gun, Kangwon-do. Together with the nearby Naksan-sa Temple, one of the "Eight Best Sceneries of Kwandong (Kangwon-do)."

An Old Pavilion in Suburban Chinju, Kyongsang Namdo

↑ Kyonggijon
An old building in Chonju City, Cholla Pukto.

Kangsonnu of Sonam-sa Temple
↓ Sunchon, Cholla Namdo

←
Hanbyoknu
Located in Chonju, Cholla Pukto.

Sojangdae →
A pavilion in the Namhansan Fortress.

← **Choksoknu**
Located in Chinju, Kyongsang Namdo. This is where the kisaeng, Nongae, carried a Japanese commander to mutual death in the water.

Tongmyo →
Sungin-dong, Seoul. Built in 1602, the lot is 9,444 square meters and the building area 1,000 square meters. A shrine to worship Kwanu, a Chinese general of the ancient Chokhan Kingdom of China. This worship of a foreigner, strange as it may be, was relatively widespread in Korea.

↑ **Pubyoknu**
　At the riverside of the Taedong, Pyongyang City. Built in the early Koryo period.

↑ **Yonghojong**
　Located in Chosan, Pyongan Pukto, north Korea.

East Gate of Namhansan Fortress
↓　Kwangju-gun, Kyonggi-do.

↑ Chomsongdae
  One of the earliest astronomical observatories in the world. Located in Kyongju, the capital city of Silla Kingdom. Built in 647 A. D., 6.8 meters in height. (See Chapter XVI-Astronomy)

← Tabo Tower
Of Pulguk-sa Temple in Kyongju. Built in 535 A.D., and repaired in 751. One of the greatest masterpieces of stone art works in the Far East. 10.4 meters in height.

↑ Sokka Tower
Also within the Pulguk-sa Temple. Together with the Tabo Tower, best represents the Silla art. Used for preserving Buddha's remains, such as teeth, hairs and bones.

Interior View of Sokpinggo, Kyonju
One of the oldest ice storages in the world. Made of granite.
↓

↑ Sokpinggo, or Stone Ice Storage, Kyongju, Kyongsang Pukto
Made in early Silla dynasty and rebuilt in A. D. 174. Granite ice storage. There are ventilators on the vaulted ceiling and draining arrangement in the center of floor. Height of the entrance is 1.6 m, and its width 1.4 m; Height of the interior 5.21 m, the width 5.76 m,

↑ Stone Lantern of Silsang-sa Temple
Namwon, Cholla Namdo.

Pudo Pagoda of Kap-sa Temple
↓ Kongju-gun, Chungchong Namdo.

↑ Stone Lantern of Pulguk-sa Temple
Kyongju, Kyongsang Pukto.

Stone Lantern of Pulguk-sa Temple
↓ Poun-gun, Chungchong Pukto.

Wanggung Tower
↓ Iksan-gun, Cholla Pukto.

↑ Three-Storeyed Tower Supported by Four Stone Lions
Hwaom-sa Temple, Kurye-gun, Cholla Pukto.

Four-Storeyed Stone Tower of Sudok-sa Temple
↓ Yesan-gun, Chungchong Namdo.

↑ Pomo-sa Four-Storeyed Stone Tower
Tongnae-gun, Kyongsang Namdo.

↑ A Five-Storeyed Stone Tower in the Site of Chongrim-sa Temple, Puyo, Chungchong Namdo.

The Stone Tower of Punhwang-sa Temple
↓ One of the oldest tower in Korea. Originally, it was nine-storeyed tower. Built in 634 A.D., by laying stones cut to brick-shape. Located in Kyongju, the Silla capital.

↑ Nine-Storeyed Octagonanl Stone Tower of Wolchong-sa Temple
 Located in Pyongchang-gun, Kangwon-do. An outstanding example of Koryo stone tower. Height 15m.

↑ Sari Tower of Sinnok-sa Temple
Yoju-gun, Kyonggi-do. Structure of Silla dynasty.

←
Kumsan-sa Temple's Five-Storeyed Stone Tower
Kimje-gun, Cholla Pukto.

A 13 Storeyed Stone Tower Remaining in
↓ the Site of Chonghye-sa Temple

Silsang-sa Temple's Three-Storeyed Stone Tower
↓ Namwon, Cholla Namdo.

↑ Night View of Many-Storeyed Stone Pagoda. Pagoda Park, Seoul
  Built during Yi dynasty (1468). A marble tower composed of 3-storey base and 10-storey tower body. Height 40 feet. Many symmetrical and exquisite Buddha images in relief engraved on whole body surface.

Yujomsa Temple
In the Outer Kumgang (Diamond Mountains). Also a Buddhist temple of Unified Silla period. Fifty-three Buddha images are placed on the branches of an elm tree which the temple was named after. Yu means elm. Of the 53 images, 43 are Silla, showing the refined techniques of the dynasty. Buildings, again, were rebuilt in Yi dynasty.

Sokwang-sa Temple, Anbyon-gun, Hamgyong Namdo
Established in 1392. Especially noted for the beautiful scenery around the temple.

Tongdo-sa Temple
Located in Mount Yongchui, Yangsangun, Kyongsang Namdo. Established in 642. Except for a few Silla stone works, however, all the buildings are of late Yi dynasty. Besides the main buildings, it contains 13 hermitages around the mountain.

↑ Taeungjon of Tongdo-sa Temple, Yangsan-gun, Kyongsang Namdo
   Built in 642, but rebuilt after the Hideyoshi Invasion in Yi period. Stone works remain as they were first laid during Silla dynasty.

↑ Mirukchon of Kumsan-sa Temple, Kimje-gun, Cholla Pukto
   Also a Silla building but rebuilt in Yi period. Seemingly a three-storeyed building on the outside, the interior has only one storey.

← **Taeungjon of Popchu-sa Temple**
Located in Mount Sok-ni, Chungchong Pukto. First built in 553, rebuilt in Yi dynasty. A good example of Yi architecture. Taeungjon means the main building in which the principal Buddha is placed.

Koran-sa Temple
Located on a cliff facing the Paengma River near Puyo, the Paekche capital. A small Buddhist temple that was built in Paekche dynasty (450). Especially noted for a spring, named Koran Spring, and a flower, named Koran-cho, near the temple. Both spring water and flower are said to have been favored by Paekche kings.

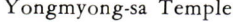

Yongmyong-sa Temple
Located in the Moranbong Mountains of Pyongyang. It is said the temple was first built in the reign of King Kwanggae-to of Koguryo (393 A. D.). ↓

Taeungjon of Sonam-sa Temple
Located in Sunchon-gun, Cholla Namdo. First established in Silla period. But the taeungjon ↓ is of late Yi dynasty.

↑ Pulguk-sa Temple, Kyongju
   Built in 540 by one, Kim Taesong of Silla dynasty, and extended in 756. Rebuilt in 1659 after it was destroyed by fire during the Hideyoshi Invasion. With the stone works it contains, such as Blue Cloud and White Cloud Bridges and Towers of Tabo and Sokka, it is, needless to say, one of the most ancient and beautiful Buddhist temples, representing not only the glorious art of Silla but also one of the greatest masterpieces of art work in the Far East.

↑ Taejokkwangjon of Haein-sa Temple, Hapchon-Gun, Kyongsang Namdo
First built in 802 A.D., suffered seven destructions by fire. Building now extant was built in late Yi period.

↑ Chonchuk-sa Temple
The rocky mountain is Manjangbong Peak.

↑ Samsongjon
Cells of the Haein-sa Temple.

Taeungjon of Sokwan-sa Temple, Anbyon-gun, Hamgyong Namdo

Good example of Yi period metamorphosed style of one of the two major trends in architectural forms of Koryo dynasty. Rebuilt in 1731. Pojak, the decorative structural part beneath the roof, betrays over-gorgeous tendencies. (See Chapter XVIII-Architecture)

Muryangsujon of Pusok-sa Temple

One of the two major styles of Koryo architecture (A-Style, see Chapter XVIII-Architecture). Doubled-eaves, the oldest wooden building in Korea (mid-Koryo dynasty). Length; 19.12 m: width; 11.94 m.

The Whole View of Pusok-sa Temple

Yongju-gun, Kyongsang Pukto. The temple was established in 676 A. D.

↑ Taeungjon of Pomo-sa Temple
   First built in 680, and rebuilt after damages of Hideyoshi wars.

↑ Taeungjon of Yongmun-sa Temple
   Located in Yangpyong-gun, Kyonggi-do. Established in Yi dynasty by King Sejo.

← Hwaom-sa Temple, Kurye-gun, Cholla Namdo
   First built in 544; rebuilt in 1636.

Magok-sa Temple, Kongju-gun Chungchong Namdo
↓   First established in Silla period, and rebuilt in 1782 after being destroyed by fire.

↑ Palsangjon of Popchu-sa Temple, Poun-Gun, Chungchong Pukto
   Originally a building of Silla period (553), but rebuilt in Yi dynasty (1624). Pagoda-like five-storeyed wooden building. 23.2 meters in height. Very unique in structural style, it is one of the rare buildings that show the Silla wooden architecture.

↑ Naksan-sa Temple
   Located in Yangyang-gun, Kangwon-do. First built in the reign of King Munmu of Silla Kingdom, rebuilt in Yi dynasty, and once more rebuilt after the Korean War.
   Sudok-sa Temple
   Located in Mount Toksung, Yesan-gun, Chungchong Namdo. Especially noted for the mural
↓ paintings on the walls of Taeungjon. The murals are said to be the works of Tamjing.

6) Modern. (After 1910)

The general chronological trends in Korean art of each period warrant closer examination.

The Pre-Three Kingdoms period embraces the Aeneolithic and the Lolang periods. Although the Lolang culture had much influence on Korean art, it belonged originally to China rather than to Korea. Therefore, strictly speaking, the Pre-Three Kingdoms period cannot be discussed here in relation to Korean art. In general history, the Three Kingdoms period began in the first century before Christ but there was almost no distinguishable artistic movement until the fourth century. We shall, therefore, include the first four centuries of the Three Kingdoms in the Pre-Three Kingdoms period. It was in the fourth century when genuine art began to develop. And, because there apparently were transient phases in between the periods, Korean art is considered to have changed approximately every three centuries.

The Buddhist images (bronze or clay) of Koguryo and Paekche in the Three Kingdoms period show, in detailed iconography such as drapery treatments or the arrangement of drapery folds, that the artists faithfully followed the Chinese sculpture of the Six dynasties, say, the sculptures of northern Wei, Sui or early Tang. But the faces of those image were no longer so slim and sharp as in northern Wei but round and tender in Koguryo while in Paekche, a unique facial type appeared as a combination of the faces on the original Chinese images with the features of real Paekche people. Conservative and somewhat peculiar Silla also displayed this strong characteristic in its art. In its clay figurines which originated from the Chinese Ming-Chi period, the awkward and naive modelling of the Silla potters brought out different effects from the Chinese original. The images of Maitreyas which had been frequently made in China during the middle of the sixth century became, from the original heavy and clumsy bodies, slimmer with added touches of gloomy and solemn faces emphasizing introversion and introspection.

Such emphasis on introversion continued throughout the next Unified Silla period when Korean art reached its peak during the seventh and eighth centuries. Out of the softly modelling body of a Silla Buddhist image radiates a hidden mystical power which enchants the spectator.

Compared to the Chinese Buddhist images, the Korean Buddhas of the period from the fifth century to the seventh generally became soft and calm. Such softness and calmness obviously came from the soft modelling and the tender expression of the facial expression, showing the modifying skill of Korean artists.

Although Koryo art was generally behind that of Silla, its artists succeeded in producing some excellent art pieces, notably the celadon. Compared to the contemporary Sung celadon, Koryo celadon was more softened, as in the Buddhist image of Silla; its form-and shape consists of curved lines in contrast with the linear Sung while the design and color of the glaze are more elegant and evoke a feeling of greater warmth. That is the expression of the peace-loving, tender nature of a people living in a warm climate under a clear sky amidst surroundings of soft and wavy contours provided by the mountains. However, those who controlled the direction of Koryo art and who introduced and demanded certain forms or patterns of beauty were not the individual artists but the upper classes of society which fancied sophisticated beauty. The born Romanticism and carefree Bohemian nature of the Korean people retreated before the upper trend, then reappeared as refined sophisticated beauty in art.

Such aristocracy, however, did not appear in the art of the Yi period. Yi art was neither artificial nor elegant like Koryo art but bold and dynamic. It was a new style that appealed to reason rather than to emotions. Such revolt against Koryo art could be carried out because the Yi dynasty officials, the patrons and promoters of Yi art, converted to the Neo-Confucian practice of putting pressure upon Buddhism, had no taste for mystical beauty like the ancient aristocrats. The Yi artists, accordingly, were free to work without the need of courting the favors of their customers; that is, they had neither restrictions nor criticisms. This impeded the artists from developing their skills and techniques, but left them free enough to reflect the Bohemian nature of the people in their work. Yi art reflected a taste for "perfectness in imperfectness" and "harmony within disharmony," concepts well-expressed in ceramic wares. Examples are works usually called "peasant's art," which are so original in style and so unique in form that one can easily ascertain something truly "Korean." The same characteristic also appeared in Yi paintings which preferred composition, outline, and minute brushstrokes.

One of the characteristic tendencies shown by Korean artists throughout their long history was that they didn't care about detailed skillfulness. They were struggling for a perfect expression of inwardness and introspection. At no time did they ever want to express themselves through their art. Korean art is so modest and so democratic that it has never made claims for itself whereas Chinese art seems to be proud of the artist's skill and Japanese art to express strongly the artist's individuality in forms or colors. In Korean art it seems that the artist was trying to represent exactly and naively just what he felt by means of the standard techniques or trends of his time. It shows that the artist did this neither in expectation of praise from others nor to get large sums of money. Korean artists produced their art works naturally. They did this as if it were their predestined duty.

The art of China or Japan is likened to a court lady or an actress who has a grand and attractive appearance mostly because of her brilliant make-up and costume, but that of Korea is more like an ordinary housewife, who, although wearing plain clothes and betraying ruggedness and weariness on the face, has a real beauty that radiates from within her soul with a deep philosophy around her person.

Korean Painting

The earliest and most important pictures in Korean art history are the frescoes in the ancient tombs of Koguryo of the Three Kingdoms period, which began about the fourth century. The frescoes vividly reflect the Korean people's everyday life and the characteristics of the period combined with the imported foreign culture of the Chinese continent. Inferring from the sophistication Koguryo already displayed in those earlier days, its art was probably begun far earlier than the fourth century, for long-accumulated abilities of representation appear in those frescoes.

The paintings of Koguryo, and also those of Silla and Paekche, are very valuable not only in Korean art history but in the painting history of ancient China as well. For reflecting movements, trends and styles of Chinese painting, they are all that fills the blank between the Six dynasties and the Tang periods in Chinese art history.

Paintings of Three Kingdoms Period

Frescoes of Koguryo

Since early times, Koguryo, with her proximity to China, had relations with the culture of the Han dynasty. It was also in contact with the ancient Northern culture through tribes to the north and west, especially through the Huns, who had been pressing against the borders for a long time. These contacts stimulated rapid cultural progress, culminating in the "Culture of the Ancient Tombs" of about the fourth century about which our main information comes from the fabulous frescoes left behind. The tombs have been found in two main areas; around Tungkou in south Manchuria, the capital of Koguryo until A. D. 427 and around Pyongyang in north Korea, the capital city after 427. The frescoes, which date roughly from the fourth to the seventh century, were painted to pray for the bliss of the dead and to leave records of their lives. The paintings express the deceased's hope for the continuation of his life from this world to the next, picturing religious symbols for happiness and immortality. Every tomb chamber was a figurative universe, decorated with pictures of the sun, the moon, the stars, the clouds and other celestial objects, as well as of the almighty God. It was also decorated with portraits of the deceased's wife and concubines, and pictures of all the pleasures and actions of life, such as departure for the front, battles, hunts, music and dancing, so that the spirit of the dead might enjoy himself. It is considered that the Koguryo frescoes derive from those of the cave temples in the Middle East, or from the engraved stone friezes and frescoes in the Han dynasty tombs, particularly in Yangchentzu and the northern suburbs of Liayang in Liaotung peninsula because of their proximities to Koguryo. The Han fresco found to bear the closest similarity to Koguryo works is the *Yollakto-hwako* (a picture of feasting), found in the Astana tomb of A.D. 364 in Sinkiang Province. The clothing depicted is especially very similar to that of the Koguryo frescoes.

Koguryo artists ignored distinctions between big and small, far and near. They also lacked perspectives and horizontal representation, and turned the front view to the side to make for diagramic composition. Yet they succeeded in representing the complicated inner world of the Koguryo people, their peculiar thoughts and religious beliefs, such as the faith of the Four Supernatural Beings and the belief in Immortals. The frescoes clearly reflect Koguryo's steady digestion of Buddhism, and new imported culture and techniques, as in the gradual abandonment of the diagramatic illustration for more advanced techniques. This particular artistic evolution probably received a stimulus from the hunting pictures and animal designs drawn and brought by the northern nomadic tribes at that time. A good example is the hunting scene of the *Muyong-chong* (the Tomb of the Dance) in the Tungkou area. The animals, drawn chiefly in lines, are seen running between hills, which are also drawn in thick, wavy parallel lines. This is the basic method of Chinese painting which consists chiefly of lines and *ts'un*, or contours. In spite of the less skilled techniques, those Koguryo frescoes well express the local color and the Spartan spirit of Koguryo people in a very Koguryo-like characteristic atmosphere.

The frescoes of the 6th and 7th centuries, however, show that Koguryo advanced her culture to a higher point. Influenced by the paintings of the Southern and Northern dynasties of China which had made sudden progress in art, Koguryo began to leave real art works in its tombs, such as the "Picture of Four Supernatural Beings" and "Picture of Trees," whose highly skilled techniques and neatly composed formations prove they are not only masterpieces representing Koguryo culture of the sixth and seventh centuries, but also reflect the essence in the paintings of the Six dynasties.

Koguryo frescoes influenced the art of southern Korea. Some very Koguryo-influenced frescoes were found in the tombs of Paekche, and, a few centuries after, in the royal tombs of Koryo. It had influence even on the fresco-tombs of North Kyushu in Japan across the sea.

Among the many recent Koguryo tomb discoveries, the most significant has been the *Tongsumyo* tomb in Hwanghae-do excavated in June 1949. The tomb has a large fifty-foot long fresco of a parade of two hundred and fifty men, painted on its corridor wall, and is dated the 13th year of Chinese Emperor

Tungchin Muiti (A.D. 375). The oldest tomb ever discovered and dated, it has served to revise the dates of Koguryo tombs and, in general, has yielded more knowledge of the early frescoes than hitherto accessible.

Paintings of Paekche and Old Silla

Unlike Koguryo, which bequeathed many pictures to posterity, very few paintings have come down to us from Paekche, and little is known about that kingdom's painting.

A few Koguryo-influenced frescoes, such as the pictures of the Four Supernatural Beings and of the universe, were found in two Paekche tombs near Kongju and Puyo. Reflecting the Paekche characteristics, they are more softened and less powerful than Koguryo frescoes. Because of its geographical handicap, Paekche was behind Koguryo in importing continental culture. But, inferring from the skillful techniques shown in the "Landscape-Decorated Tile" which was discovered at an old temple site near Puyo, Paekche must have made progress in paintings, too, having imported the art of the Southern dynasty by sea and of Koguryo by land. Then, too, the reputation of Paekche artists, acclaimed in Japanese writings of the time, and the refined skill in the portrait of Prince Shotoku of Japan, said to be the work of Prince Ajwa of Paekche, are evidence that Paekche made enough progress to influence ancient Japanese paintings.

The stone chambered tombs of Koguryo and Paekche, preserve the frescoes they contained. But the wooden chambers of the Silla tombs left nothing of their art to posterity. In the *"Samguk Sagi"* (Annals of the Three Kingdoms) is an anecdote of Solgo, talented Silla painter of the mid-sixth or seventh century, who is said to have painted portraits, landscapes and Buddhist pictures. His picture of a pinetree was so realistic that birds mistook it for a real tree. From this story, we can guess that Silla, too, was very advanced in painting.

Paintings of Unified Silla

Silla's unification of the three kingdoms in the middle of the seventh century inaugurated an epoch not only in politics but in the arts as well. Uniting the three different cultures and with the cultural stimulus of its close relations with Tang China, Silla undoubtedly made good progress in painting. But again, as with Old Silla, not a single picture has been found. What little we know is from a few writings about the art and artists of the period.

According to the *"Samguk Sagi,"* there was an Office of Arts in Silla. And, in the *"Hsin-Tang-Shu"* (New Tang Writings) of China as well as in the "Great Artists' Stories" written by Chang Yen-yun, it is written that a Silla general, named Kim Chungui, went to Tang at the end of the eighth century, to become a noted painter. An old Korean account also mentions two priest-painters of Silla, Chonghwa and Honggye.

Paintings of Koryo

Koryo art was influenced by the Sung dynasty of China. Like Sung, Koryo set up an Office of Arts in the court where scholars, priests, aristocrats, and even kings enjoyed painting for pleasure. According to some old writings about Koryo, many of these avocational painters were noted for their remarkable Buddhist paintings and the *Sagunja* painting of the four flowers; plum blossom, orchid, bamboo and chrysanthemum. There was also a group of professional painters, the most famous of whom was Yi Yong in the reign of King Injong (1125-1146). His masterpieces were the "Picture of Yesong River" and "Picture of Chonsuwon," both of which were probably in the Northern Sung style, for according to the History of Koryo, they were praised by the Emperor Kui-Tsung of Sung. It is regrettable that none of these are left. Kings like Kongmin, Honjong and Injong were among the gifted painters of the kingdom, and, naturally, inspired the contemporary painters. The collection of King Kongmin, especially, stimulated the development not only of contemporary Koryo painting but of the subsequent

Yi dynasty as well.

There are not many extant Koryo paintings. A few Koguryo-influenced frescoes were found in the tomb of Kongmin, in other tombs around Kaesong, the capital of Koryo, and in the two temples of Pusok-sa and Sudok-sa. A Buddhist picture drawn by No Yong on a folded screen, now in the National Museum of Korea in Seoul, the picture of Avalokitesvara drawn by Hye Ho (13th century), now in the Asakusa Temple of Tokyo, and the great Buddhist picture in the Metropolitan Museum of Art in New York, are some of the rare pictures of Koryo. Pieces of a hunting scene, said to be the work of King Kongmin, are severally preserved in the Seoul National University, the National Museum of Korea and the Toksu Palace Museum of Fine Arts in Seoul, but little is known about them yet. An ink-painting drawn by Hae Ae, now in a temple in Tokyo, Japan, and a summer landscape by Ko Yonghui, now in Konjiin in Kyoto, Japan, show another aspect of the Koryo style.

Paintings of the Yi Dynasty

After the fall of the Buddhist society of Koryo at the close of the fourteenth century, a new culture began to develop in Korea. Neo-Confucianism suppressed Buddhism and set in motion a cultural movement which brought about remarkable progress in the sciences and arts of the Yi dynasty.

Professional painters were mostly members of the Office of Arts which had been reorganized by the Yi government. In addition, avocational scholar-painters—aristocrats, statesmen, scholars and all other members of the learned classes—were very active in the early Yi period. Among them, a professional painter, An Kyon, and the scholar-painters, Kang Hian in the reign of King Sejong (1419-1449) and Yi Sangjwa in the reign of King Chungjong (1506-1544) particularly display in their ink-painting landscapes skills accumulated since the Koryo period. An Kyon was a master in the landscape of the Kwo Hsi school of Northern Sung, Kang Hian's simple and tight landscapes reflect the court painting school of the Southern Sung, Yi Sangjwa's landscapes the Ma Yuan school, also of the Southern Sung.

With the spread of Confucianism throughout the Yi society, the need for portraits of kings, aristocrats, national heroes and ancestors for purposes of veneration led to rapid progress in this field of painting.

Among the scholar-painters, on the other hand, appeared some who well-expressed the social characteristics of the Yi dynasty in their pictures of birds and flowers and in the *Sagunja* paintings. Yi Am (1499-?)'s pictures of birds and flowers and of animals in rough but rich characteristic brushstrokes are full of charm. The *Sagunja* paintings in black ink without color were favored by scholars and other intellectuals, such as Sin Serim (1521-?), Yi Yon (1542-?) and Cho Tong (1595-?). Remarkable was the appearance of the woman painter, Sin Saemdang, a housewife of the upper class, who painted peculiarly feminine sketches of grass and insects and of seaweed and fish, most of which are still preserved. The appearance of such a woman painter is indication that Yi paintings were making healthy progress.

The Hideyoshi wars crippled Korean arts and it was many years before artistic activities could be resumed in the early seventeenth century when the landscapes and figures of Kim Myongguk, the master painter from the Office of Arts, revived painting. Meng Yung-kuang, a Ching dynasty painter who visited Korea from 1645 to 1648, introduced the delicate and realistic techniques of early Ching representation of nature, as well as its academic style of painting.

In the early eighteenth century, though most painters followed the Northern Sung school, the Southern school of Sung painting began to take root in Korea. Chong Son (1676-1799), of the Office of Arts, was the first to adopt the Southern school, sketching landscapes directly from nature with his free and generous touches and an original *ts'un* (chun in Korean) modelling or shading. His followers were Sim Sajong (1707-1769) who was known even in China and Choe Puk whose magnanimous personality was well reflected in his paintings. Yi painting was reaching a unique peak, with men like Kim Hongdo (1760-?) and Sin Yunbok, painting scenes of the everyday lives of common men and women, to introduce genre paintings for the first time to Korea. In the meantime, Western-influenced painting methods brought from China led to new techniques of portrayal and cubic expressions in the Oriental paintings. A good example is the "Picture of a Dog," one of the masterpieces of that time, which is now in the Toksu Palace Museum of Fine Arts in Seoul. The most successful Southern school painter of this period was Yi Inmun (1745-1822) who painted landscapes of pinetree forests and rivulets with simple but strong and acute brushstrokes. Kim Suchol, who succeeded Yi, was distinguished for his landscapes and pictures of grass and flowers, drawn in a new treatment of cutting strokes. The last of these Yi master artists was Chang Sungop (1843-1897), a playboy, whose unworldly behavior has left many anecdotes but whose techniques were the result of hard self-study.

Kim Chonghui (1786-1856) was perhaps the greatest all-around painter-calligrapher-scholar. His *Sagunja* paintings in ink and his sketches have a matchless refinement which is accredited to his harmonization of poetry, calligraphy and painting, and to his pure and profound personality as a scholar. When he was young, he went to Peiping to study and made the acquaintance of master artists and scholars of Ching. It was probably there that he acquired the extensive knowledge which helped him so much afterwards. He was also noted as an art critic. Among his followers, the most outstanding were Cho Hiryong, Chon Ki and Ho Yu.

To sum up, the Northern school of Sung overwhelmingly dominated Korean painting in the first half of the Yi dynasty, while, in the second half, the Southern Sung school was the recognized painting style. Yi painting was basically simply a branch of Chinese painting. Most paintings were on Chinese subjects; the nearer a picture was to a Chinese master-painter's, the better it was received. Of course, there were some very independent painters such as Sin Serim, Yi Am, Cho Sok and Sin Saemdang, but they formed no schools to succeed them. The original creations of Chong Son and the genre paintings of Kim Hongdo and Sin Yunbok, remarkable though they were, were only the dilettante work of a few gentlemen-scholars, not art for the public.

True, dedicated painters struggled against poverty and slight, and were often deemed eccentrics. Consequently, there was neither painting history nor, except for a few essays by Kim Chonghui and others, was there any criticism of painting until the end of the nineteenth century when Western painting came to Korea.

Modern Paintings

In modern art, Korean people have two different kinds of painting styles. One is the traditional "Oriental painting" which was originally brought from China, and the other that which is called "Western painting" that came from Europe not more than fifty years ago. The distinction is not one of ideas or creative consciousness, but of materials used. But in the early days of Western art in the Orient, there was a great gap between these two kinds of paintings, because of the dissimilarities of their spiritual backgrounds, logic and methods of expression. Naturally, then, the Oriental and Western paintings must be discussed separately.

Modern Oriental Paintings

About 1910, when modern art should have begun, the painters of Oriental painting were still extending the late Yi style, seemingly forever. Among them, however, were some who had enough courage to break the traditional barrier to enter into modern times. These included Kang Chinhui, Chong Taeyu, Cho Sokchin, Kim Ungwon, An Chungsik, and Yi Toyong, all of whom were born and became master-painters toward the close of the dynasty. Most painters, however, insisted on the harmony of painting with calligraphy and poetry, in keeping with the strict ideas of Yi tradition.

The paintings of that time can be divided into two movements: one was the school represented by the Office of Arts which was regarded as craft rather than art because it attached importance to techniques; the other was the academic school which laid stress on inwardness rather than on technique. Generally, though, both lacked the creative spirit and, under the pretext of upholding tradition, repeated old forms, styles and patterns of art without infusing or renewing them with even a trace of creative originality. All that they did was to reproduce and imitate old classical paintings or pictures from the *Kaejawon Hwabo*, a sort of guidebook to paintings which they virtually regarded as a Bible.

Actually, most painters of that time practiced their technical skills by merely reproducing pictures from the *Hwabo*, instead of emerging from their ateliers to create from nature first-hand. Little did they dream that nature in the raw could be transferred directly onto canvas or reproduced through one's individual understanding. Therefore, they were not artists but craftsmen; real art could hardly be expected from them.

The leaders of the two major schools of painting were An Chungsik and Cho Sokchin. Both of these distinguished painters had many pupils. Cho Sokchin, the last official painter of the kingdom, was born in 1853 and was a member of the *Tohwaso* (Office of Arts). An Chungsik, whose paintings are often seen even today, was born in 1861 and had recognized talent in landscape, bird, flower, and figure work. Both were sent by the government to Tientsin, China, to study Chinese paintings. Kang Chinhui, born 1851, was noted for his beautiful painting of plum-blossoms as was Chong Taeyu, born 1852. Kim Ungwon (1855), painted orchids skillfully. Yi Toyong, born in 1885, was a disciple of An Chungsik but was influenced by Chang Sungop afterwards to specialize in landscape and still life. His paintings were good but afflicted with over-modesty to be great. Ko Huidong learned his Oriental painting from both An Chungsik and Cho Sokchin. Interested at one time in Western painting, he returned to the Oriental, bringing what he had learned from the Western school thereto. His style of shadings is closer to the *ts'un* of the Northern school of Chinese paintings, mixed with Western-influenced technique, than to the delicate and modest style of the Southern school which was in fashion then.

To conclude, modern Oriental paintings which succeeded those of the Yi period were separated into two schools by An Chungsik and Cho Sokchin during the 1900's but they were reunited afterwards by Yi Toyong. Ko Huidong should have brought about this union because he was a disciple of both An and Cho but had gone over to Western painting. And there was no one but Yi who could understand both divergent arts perfectly and fuse them into one.

In 1911, the authorities of the Former Royal Household of Yi sponsored the establishment of the *Sohwa Misulwon* (Academy of Arts). Yi Wanyong was the president and the membership consisted of Kim Ungwon, An Chungsik, Cho Sokchin, Chong Taeyu, Kang Chinhui and Yi Toyong. The chief purpose of the Academy was to teach traditional Oriental art to young painters. Only eight years after, however, it had to be closed though it had produced many remarkable painters, such as O Ilyong, Kim Unho, Yi Sangbom, No Suhyon and Choe Usok. In 1918, the first association, the *Sohwa Hyophoe* (Association of Arts), was organized. This group helped greatly to develop the native art throughout the period of Japanese rule as against the *Senten* (Chosun Art Exhibition), the Japanese Government-General's official salon in Korea.

The early exhibitions of the *Sohwa Hyophoe* consisted mostly of Oriental paintings and calligraphies. For instance, at the first exhibition, there were only four Western paintings.

At that time, paintings meant Oriental paintings. In addition to the exhibition of *Sohwa Hyophoe*, there were a few Oriental art exhibitions; such as the memorial exhibit of the works of Cho Sokchin held in Susong primary school in May, 1921, and the exhibition of the Academy of Painting and Calligraphy, which was led by Kim Kyujin, showing 310 works at the First Bank Building on June 16 of the same year. On June 19, the *Sohwa Hyophoe* celebrated its Third Anniversary with a sketch-show in a restaurant in Seoul. In Inchon, Kim Yutaek held a one-man show of his painting and calligraphy in a school building in December.

Distinguished artists of this period were Ko Huidong who had returned by this time from Westerns to Orientals chiefly to paint landscapes of the Southern school, and Kim Yongjin who was a disciple of the Ching dynasty artist, Fang Ming, and a master painter of *Sagunja* and flower pictures in the academic-painting style of Ching. In addition, there were Yi Sangbom, No Suhyon, Ho Paengnyon, Pyon Kwansik, Yi Yongu, Yu Chinchan, Kim Chinu and So Pyongo, all of whom had had pictures on display both in the *Senten* and the *Sohwa Hyophoe* exhibitions. Most of their pictures were landscapes of the Southern school. The *Senten* was an important showcase for such outstanding painters as Yi Hanbok and Kim Unho, both of whom had studied Oriental painting at the Tokyo College of Art, as well as for Yi Yutae, Chang Usong and Kim Kichang, disciples of Kim Unho who chiefly painted figures. There were few more painters who could not be considered of less importance. Pae Yom, a student of both No Suhyon and Yi Sangbom, who was a traditional painter of the Southern school, Yi Ungno who tried to unite the Western and Oriental schools, and Kim Yongsu who was one of the most excellent painters of the period.

On August 6, 1920, a fresco of Oriental painting was completed in Changdok Palace by three leading painters, O Ilyong, Kim Unho and Yi Sangbom. In September, 1922, Ho Paengnyon held a one-man show in Posong School, Seoul. For the purpose of studying the old and new painting styles, the *Tongyonsa* Society was organized in March, 1923, by No Suhyon, Yi Sangbom, Pyon Kwansik and Yi Yongu. The first exhibition of women artists' works in Korea was opened on March 17, 1923, sponsored by the Changsin Institute of Arts which was established just three days before. On March 24, 1923, an art exhibition was opened in Artists' Club, Namsandong, Seoul, by the brothers Hwang of Kaesong, Chongha, Songha, Yongha and Kyongha. The *Sohwa Hyophoe* held its third exhibition beginning on March 31, 1923 in Posong School. Sponsored by the Chosun Art-Lovers' Society, the First Exhibition of Oriental Paintings was held in September, 1923. In August, 1923, the *Sohwa Hyophoe* founded an art school and opened it on November 10 to teach Western painting, Oriental painting and calligraphy. With more than a hundred works, No Suhyon and Yi Sangbom held in Posong School in November, 1923. In an art exhibition which was held in Taegu in November of the same year, more than forty works were hung in the Oriental painting section by So Pyongo, So Kyongje, So Taedang, Pak Hoesan and Ho Kisok. In January, 1924, an art school called the Korean Institute of Art was established in Seoul. The *Sohwa Hyophoe* held the fourth exhibition in 1924 and the fifth in 1925, both in Posong School. Besides, there were some college students' exhibitions, of which the most famous and significant ones were the exhibition sponsored by the Tonga Ilbo, one of the leading newspapers, and the Seoul Dental College.

The *Senten* (Chosun Art Exhibition) which had been opened in 1922, was annually held until the end of World War II. In the first exhibition, Korean painters who had their pictures hung in the Oriental painting section numbered 34 including two reference works of Yi Toyong and Kim Kyujin. Among them, several are still living: No Suhyon, Yi Sangbom, Ko Huidong, Ho Paengnyon, Kim Unho and Kim Yongiin. Pyon Kwansik, Yi Yongu and Yi Pyongjik joined them in the second exhibition, in which 23 works of Korean painters were displayed in the Oriental section. The works of Korean painters in the Original section, however, steadly increased in number year after year.

During this time, there were three major currents in Original painting; the traditional painting school which was tryng to protect and further the traditional, the academic school which pursued the harmony of poetry and art, and the revolutionaries who attempted to inject Western painting methods into the Oriental.

After World War II, Oriental painters worked hard to get rid of the Japanese influence which had pervaded Oriental art in Korea and corrupted it during thirty-six years of Japanese rule over Korea. A persistent search was begun to discover the true characteristics of Korea's own art.

For this purpose, Kim Yonggi and Yi Ungno founded an art institute in Seoul. Unfortunately, the idea was better than the execution and the institute was soon closed. Since Oriental art had within itself too many difficulties to adapt itself easily to modern form, it took a relatively longer time to become a modern art in the true sense than did others.

Painters who have been conspicuous in modern Oriental painting are Ko Huidong for his achievements and position in the history of modern Korean art rather than for his paintings, and Yi Sangbom for his art. Yi, whose works had been awarded "Special Selection" mention ten times running in the *Senton*, is one of the real master artists in Korea. His very democratic personality as a typical Korean appears on his canvases in combination with his noble painting style.

The other painters are those who ventured to put together Oriental and Western art on canvas. Chief among them are Kim Kichang, his wife Pak Naehyon, and Yi Ungno.

Since 1945, when Korea cast off the chains of Japanese rule, many artists have been struggling to establish a genuinely characteristic Korean art. Koreans have finally been able to have their own salon, the National Art Exhibition. There have also been 27 one-man shows and several various art exhibitions. All painters of Oriental art are today working hard to achieve their goals: old masters to keep the tradition, active middle-aged painters to seek the characteristic of Korea, and younger painters to create something radically new.

Western Paintings

It is believed that the first couriers of Western art to Korea were two foreigners, Bosch Hieronymus, a Dutchman, and Remion, a Frenchman. The Dutch painter did a portrait of King Kojong in 1898 and it was reported in a paper of that time that he was paid a goodly commission for the portrait. It was, probably, the first Western picture painted in Korea. Remion, a French surveyor who had been invited to the Railway Bureau also in the reign of King Kojong, was not a painter but had a deep knowledge of art. He painted so many portraits of nobility and royalty that his influence set off discussions about establishment of an art school for Western paintings.

Inspired by this, Ko Huidong and others showed the first Western pictures painted by Korean artists in an exhibition for foreigners held in the French Legation in Seoul in 1905. In 1908, when European art was approaching a glorious peak in Fauvism and Cubism, Korea had her first art student, Ko Huidong, an Oriental painter up to that time. Disappointed with the mannerisms of traditional art, he went to Japan and studied Western paintings at the Tokyo College of Arts. He was followed by Kim Kwanho in 1909, Yi Chinu in 1914 and Yi Pyonggyu in 1916, all students of Japanese artists who, in turn, were followers of the French impressionists; among them Wada Eisaku, Fujishima Takeji, Okada Saburosuke and Kobayashi Mango. Returning home, however, they faced too many difficulties to work at what they had learned in Japan and to enlighten the people who were still bogged down in Middle Age thinking.

The old idea that Oriental art was the

only superior method of painting was hard to overcome.

When a painter went out to a field carrying his paint-box, people teased him saying, "What are you carrying to sell in the box, candy or tobacco?" or "Is that all he learned abroad while spending money?"

Nevertheless, Ko Huidong painted three pictures for a magazine in 1914—a cover picture and two sketches of landscapes–which probably were among the oldest Western paintings in Korea. In 1916, Kim Kwanho returned from Japan, settled down in Pyongyang, his native land, and established an art institute to teach the new methods of Western paintings. His paintings were in the Chavanne style which was then in vogue there and had been quite well received especially among the Japanese painters of the Shirakaba Circle.

These pioneers of Western painting apparently did their best to plant the seeds of the new Western school in the artistic wasteland of Korea. Their failure may be attributed to the fact that Westerns were premature.

Since 1919, the tree of Western painting which had been planted in Korea by pioneers, was getting accustomed to the Korean climate and soon began to grow bigger and bigger finally to blossom fully. On July 20, 1920, Kim Yubang's "The System and Mission of Western Painting," the first art treatise in Korea, appeared in a leading newspaper, Tonga Ilbo. His thesis was that Western art had been accepted in Korea not only because of its technical skill but for its theoretical ideals as well. On March 19, 1921, Na Hyesok, the first woman Western painter in Korea, displayed more than seventy works in the Kyongsong Ilbo building. It was also the first one-man show of Western painting in Korea, and received the first art criticism, "After Seeing the Exhibition of Na Hyesok" by an anonymous reviewer in the Tonga Ilbo on July 22, 1921.

In December, 1921 Yanagi Muneyoshi, a Japanese who loved Korean ancient art so much that he attempted to establish a museum in Korea, held an exhibition of reproductions of Western classic arts, enabling most Koreans to view Western arts for the first time. On October 1, 1922, Mrs. Holmes, a secretary of the British Art Association, came to Korea to talk with Korean artists. In August 1923, two art schools, the *Towolhoe* Art Institute and Art School of the *Sohwa Hyophoe* were established. From 1922 to 1924, there were four major exhibitions of Western art, and many art students went to Japan to study Western painting. On the other hand, Yi Chongu went to Paris in 1925 and studied oil painting for three years there. In 1927, while he was in France, his two works, "Portrait of a Woman" and "Still Life with Figures," were shown in the famous Salon d'Automne. He was the first Korean to have work displayed in a major exhibition of a foreign country. The two pictures show that he painted honestly following the realistic style of pure French Sub-Impressionism after ridding himself of Japanese oil painting style. This is very important because of the fact that up to that time, Western art had been imported into Korea through Japan, but after Yi's trip to Paris, it began to be imported directly from Europe and America. In fact, Chang Pal, who had been in the Tokyo College of Arts, left there and went to America to study Western painting. Others went to Germany and France; Paek Namsun, Na Hyesok, Im Yongnyon, and Pae Unsong. Chan Pal, returning from America, made a mural painting of the Twelve Disciples for the Catholic Church in Myongdong, Seoul. This, however, was religious rather than artistic.

Awakened to their own nationality under Japanese militarism which had become severe since 1930, Korean students in Japan organized an art society chiefly led by the students of *Teikoku* Art School and called it the *Paekuhoe* (White Cow Society), later, the Association of Artists in Tokyo. The Association held an exhibition in the Kyongbok Palace gallery in 1942.

At home, in 1930, Yi Chongu and others organized an art society called the *Mogilhoe*, but six years later this also was forced to close by Japanese government authorities. In 1935, however, another art society called the New Artists' Association was organized and held three or four exhibitions up to the end of the war. Sin Honghyu held a one-man show in June, 1935.

Among the art currents imported from Europe in the decade since 1930, the Fauvist trend of Ku Ponung, Yi Chungsop and Pak Kosok, the Abstractionist trend of Kim Hwangi, and Expressionism were the best known among Korean artists. Few actually painted in such styles. In 1932, Cho Usik wrote about Surrealism in a magazine, but no Surrealistic works have appeared to date. As for Cubism, it fared even worse, because in Korea there was an absence of rationalism and modern industry on which Cubism must stand.

In spite of the fact that they were seriously trying to adopt Western art styles, Korea wasn't ready to accept them yet. Or perhaps, the people were too tired and bothered by Japanese militarism to think of anything else. The new art movement could not move the public except for a few specialists and painters. What is sigificant is that local subjects, such as a cow, a grass-roof or a wheel, were often seen in the pictures of that time. It meant the artists hoped to revert to their natural state, to be Koreans resisting Japan.

In 1939, the *Sohwa Hyophoe,* which had held nineteen exhibitions up to that year, was forced to close down by the Japanese police as was the *Mogilhoe* in 1941. Even art was not permitted to be called that. It had to be "the art of sacred war" or "the art of decisive battle." There was nothing but terror. Freedom was gone, to say nothing of the atmosphere of artistic creativity. From 1940 to the end of the war, all art movements were almost totally halted. And in 1941, the Japanese Governor-General forced Korean artists to organize a semi-official society of artists, the Wonsonhoe, in order to observe their movements and to mobilize them quickly at any time.

The *Senten* (Chosun Art Exhibition), which opened its first exhibition in 1922, held its last 23th exhibition in 1944. Although the trend in the *Senten* was toward colonial and Japanese art, it couldn't be denied that the exhibitions had given opportunities to many young painters of Korea. Of them, the most outstanding were Kim Insung and Yi Insong, both of whom were Naturalistic Realists. Yi showed his sharp intellect most outstandingly through his water colors.

In the first *Senten,* three painters had only four pictures hung. But Korean painters who displayed their pictures in the Western section gradually increased, and in the nineteenth exhibition, eighty Korean painters showed works.

After World War II, when all the Japanese in Korea had withdrawn, Korean painters, as well as Koreans in every other field, were too excited to create anything. Once they realized that they had the privilege of freedom, they found themselves too ignorant of art and too lacking in skill to deserve the privilege. Only those who had real talent and worked hard could make noticeable progress.

In 1946, although many art exhibitions were held in Seoul, most of them belonged to left-wing artists' groups except for a few, including the exhibition of the New-Realism club led by Kim Hwangi. After the government of Korea was established in 1948, leftist movements in art were almost blocked completely and Red artists driven away from every art group. At that time, the New Artists' Association, which had been established before 1945, was reorganized and held its first exhibition. On the other hand the moderates and neutral or independent artists organized the Art Culture Association and called in the undecided painters in the red camps. But some members, who had come down from the north left in protest against the neutrality of the Association. In the meantime, to advance and develop the national arts, the government founded the National Art Exhibition, or the *Kukchon,* and held its first exhibition in 1949. Such an official salon gave incentive to the painters who had slumped into a state of depression because of the political and social conditions resulting from the country being divided at the 38th parallel. In 1950, for the purpose of calling together all painters who did not belong to any artistic group and developing a new art movement, a body called the "Art Association of '50" was set up and was about to open its first exhibition when the war broke on June 25.

After the Seoul restoration on September 28, 1951, there was a nationwide convention of artists held at the National Theater (now the National Assembly building), and every artist became a member of the Korean Art Association, except for a few painters such as Kim Hwangi and Nam Kwan, members of the Art Association of '50 that disbanded of its own accord because most of the members had gone over to the Korean Art Association.

In 1951, when the government moved to Pusan once more, members of the Korean Art Association and other artists did their best to cooperate with the government for victory over the Communists. One of their remarkable projects was the War Painters' Group, which was organized in Pusan and which included thirty painters who had fled from the north after the war. Yi Madong was the head. They belonged to the National Defence Ministry's Bureau of Troops Information and Education as war illustrators, and more than ten of them went to the Eastern and Western fronts. After returning from the front, they held an Exhibition of War Painters' Records in June and November of 1951. Eight painters, attached to the Navy, also held an Art Exhibition of the Sea August and September in Pusan.

As a result of war, the Communist artists went north; on the other hand, northern artists, longing for freedom, came south, among them such gifted men as Pak Kosok, Chong Kyu, Hwang Yomsu, Kim Pyonggi, Yi Chungsop, Han Muk, Yun Chungsik, Pak Sugun, Kim Hungsu and Chang Nisok. In 1952, they held an 'Exhibition of Artists from the North' in Pusan. In addition, between 1952 and 1953, there were seventeen major and minor exhibitions in Pusan and three in Seoul. On November 25, 1953, after the government came back to Seoul, the second National Art Exhibition was opened in Kyongbok Palace art gallery. In January, 1954, the National Museum of Korea sponsored a Special Exhibition of Korean Modern Paintings in Seoul. It was a review-show of the old recognized works of modern painters, but still very significant as it gave the public a chance to see modern Korean masterpieces once more. Throughout the year 1954, there were eighteen art exhibitions including the third National Art Exhibition. Important were the one-man show of Kim Hwangi, the *Mihyopchon* (the Exhibition of Korean Art Association) which was on such a large scale that it could be compared with the National Art Exhibition, and the exhibition of the works of three deceased painters, Kim Chunghyon, Ku Ponung and Yi Insong, which was held in the newly-opened Chonil Art Gallery. From 1955 through 1957, almost fifty exhibitions including the *Kukchon*, the *Mihyopchon*, one-man shows and group exhibitions were held. It was significant that the leading newspaper, Chosun Ilbo, sponsored an art exhibition and that in this period there appeared many group exhibitions which had rarely been seen before. Although the increase of artistic groups and circles should have been welcomed, it must be remembered that this meant many artists cast doubt upon the art movements of such major artistic groups as Taehan (Korean) Art Association and Hanguk Art Association, which were the main parties in a protracted quarrel.

In 1958, seventy-three various art exhibitions were held. Although the increase of exhibitions doesn't mean progress in art, it at least proves that artistic works have been given more frequent opportunities for expression. The same year, Korean artists began to come in contact with other countries, particularly with the United States. On March 22, the Exhibition of Korean Modern Art was opened at the World House Gallery, New York, and in February, Korean print artists showed their works in the International Modern Prints Exhibition held in the Cincinatti Art Museum. Foreigners brought their works to show in Korea, such as the Exhibition of the Minnesota Art College, the Twentieth Century American Painting Exhibition and West Germany's Prints' Exhibition.

Today in Korea, however, no one owns an original painting by a Western master artist and there is no musem of modern art. Korea's Western art has taken only a few steps.

Sculpture

There is no evidence to substantiate claims that Korea ever had its own characteristic sculpture. The *Changsung* (a mile-post statue, resembling an army-general or woman-general and serving a function just like the Indian Totem Pole) and earthen idols are found in the ancient tombs of the 4th and 5th centuries. There is a question whether these objects should be dealt within the category of artistic sculpture.

The history of Korean sculpture was systemized when Buddhism entered into Korea and sculptors began to carve Buddhist images. These have been the main subject of Korean sculpture throughout history. The earliest Buddhist statues are those of the 5th and 6th centuries. Buddhism entered Koguryo in 373 A.D. and to Paekche in 384 A.D. from China by land and sea routes respectively. It was in 527 A.D. that Buddhism came to Silla. We will trace the development of Korean sculptures chronologically beginning with Koguryo.

Buddhist Images of Three Kingdoms Period

Koguryo

Due to its proximity to China, the Buddhist images of early Koguryo were strongly influenced by the Northern schools of the Wei and Chin dynasties. With the scant remains that are available today, it is impossible to determine all the aspects of the sculpture of that time. The Buddhist figurines of tile which were excavated at Pyongan Namdo, north Korea, are a typical example of the Buddhist images of the early stage of that period. These small tile figurines which consist of two kinds of standing Bodhisattvas and seated Tathagatas are sitting or standing on almost artless lotus pedestals wearing old-fashioned and simple but well-proportioned clothes and have gracefully long but stern faces with semilunar lips and swollen usnisas or *Yukke* in Korean (the fleshy protuberances on the crowns of the Buddha heads). These show they are in the style of the Northern Wei dynasty of China. Soon after this discovery, a gilt bronze Buddhist triad with a nimbus was found in Hwanghae-do, north Korea. The triad images, which bore the date of *Sinmyo* year (572 A.D.), have swollen *Yukkes* and lips in little inverted arches in the style of the Northern Wei. Their right hands are upraised showing the palms and the left hands are lowered with the palms facing downward. The flame-shaped nimbus has in its center a lotus carved in relief which is surrounded by arabesques, and the border is composed of flames. In front of the center of the nimbus, Buddha is standing flanked by two Bodhisa'tvas.

A limestone sculpture of two seated Buddhas which was discovered at Pannapsong in south Manchuria is one of those which indicate Koguryo sculpture extended even to the borders, and also one of very important remains for the advanced study of Koguryo Buddhist images.

Paekche

There are more remains of Paekche sculpture than of Koguryo. Among them the most notable ones which bear the typical form of early Paekche sculpture are the standing Bodhisattva of gilt bronze and the seated Tathagata of alabaster, both of which were found on the site of a pagoda at an ancient temple in Puyo. The former is standing on an inverted lotus pedestal, with its hair trailing on its shoulders and the garments crossing in the front to form an 'X'. The latter has a very solemn face though it is carved with ancient less skilled techniques. Both of them are examples of the standing and seated statues with draped clothing in the style of the Northern Wei, which must have been brought to Paekche through Koguryo.

Another gilt bronze Buddhist triad with a nimbus was discovered at the ancient fortress of Puso around Puyo. The triad, which bears the signature of the sculptor, Chon Chiwon, as well as the gilt bronze Sakyamuni with a halo, is a Koguryo-influenced sculpture. However, there are two statues that show the influence of the Southern dynasty in China. Both of them are gilt bronze Avalokitesvaras, one from around Puyo and which is now in the National Museum of Korea in Seoul, and the other the official National Treasure No. 320. They are of late Paekche period and being in harmony with the Chinese Southern influence show very soft and free expressions.

An alabaster thinking Buddha in *Panga*-posture (sitting with one leg pendant, the other crossing it and resting upon its knee), which was excavated at Puyo, is another important remain which indicates how the statues of that posture spread in Korea during the Three Kingdoms period.

Paekche sculpture had great influence on the progress of Japanese sculpture in the Asuka period and inspired them in the production of such masterpieces as the Kudara Konnon, or the Paekche Avalokitesvara, of the Horyuji Temple in Japan and the wooden Maitreya sitting in the *Panga*-posture of Koryuji Temple in Kyoto, Japan. It is unfortunate that none of these remain in Korea today.

Silla

Although conservative Silla was slower than the other two kingdoms to receive Buddhism chiefly due to its geographical handicap, it was quicker to develop it and left more sculptural remains. This reflected well Silla's own characteristics of having digested foreign culture. Especially, Silla made considerable progress in the sculpture of the tomb stelae. Silla's Buddhist images again reflect influences mostly from the Northern Wei of China through Koguryo, but very little from the Southern dynasties of China. Among the hundreds of Silla's remains, the most noticeable ones are thinking Buddhas in *Panga*-posture, as well as stones of Tathagatas and Buddhist triads. The *Panga*-posture Buddha, which depicts a Buddha sitting on a pedestal with one leg crossing over the other and supporting the head on its right hand and contemplating, was believed to be located only in the old territory of Silla. But recently some of the images in that posture have been discovered in other regions too, such as in the old territory of Paekche. Of course the *Panga*-posture, which came into Paekche and Silla from the 6th century through the 7th, had already been in northern China since the 5th century and became fairly refined prior to the 6th century.

The most typical of the masterpieces of the *Panga*-posture images is the stone Maitreya which was discovered in Kyongju, the capital of Silla. A gilt bronze Maitreya found at Onung in Kyongju and now in the Toksu Palace Museum of Fine Arts and another Maitreya in the National Museum of Korea are also masterpieces of the thinking images in *Panga*-posture that are rarely to be seen. A stone Tathagata and two attendant Bodhisattvas, excavated at Kyongju, are also fine works which, on the one hand, show the ancient style of the Northern Wei and, on the other, can transmit the peaceful and tender character of Silla with their mysterious smile.

An image of a seated Tathagata found in

Kyongju and a Dvarapala, guardian deity, engraved on the pagoda of Punhwang Temple in Kyongju are distinguished monuments among the graceful and refined remains of Silla.

The remarkable formative abilities which the people of old Silla displayed in those works were a prelude to the more brilliant development of the sculptures of Unified Silla which followed.

Sculpture of Unified Silla

Since Silla's unifying of the three kingdoms under its single dominance in 667, Korean sculpture made rapid progress. Tombs, which formerly were erected on plains, began to be constructed on hills with the Tang style stone-men, stone-animals and statues of the twelve Oriental zodiacal signs placed before them. Hundreds of remains of sculptural masterpieces have been left to posterity such as the sculpture in the cave temple known as Sokkuram above Kyongju and statues of stone, bronze and iron in various locations.

Above all, the stone works of the cave temple, constructed in the reign of King Kyongdok in the 8th century by a Kim Taesong, were stimulated by frequent construction of cave temples in Tunghuang, Yunkang, Lungmen and Mt. Tienlung from the middle of the 4th century to the Tang period in China. These works show the Silla people's unique and refined skills which had accumulated since the old Silla of the Three Kingdoms period. The almost-ten-foot-tall principal image is Sakyamuni sitting crossed-legged and draping his Kasaya or robe on his left shoulder. The wheel sign, his preaching symbol, was placed in the center of the cave so as to be admired by the many various images which are carved on the wall around it, such as two Bodhisattvas, the ten disciples, an avalokitesvara with eleven faces, and others. Those granite sculptures, in which the Silla people's skillful cubic treatments and their refined techniques of life-giving are displayed, well-reflected Silla's national traits and local characteristics clearly. Also well depicted are the neatly arranged formative techniques in the Tang style. These are the real masterpieces that deserve worldwide reputation.

The two five-feet-tall bronze images of seated Vairocana and Amitabha in Pulguksa Temple, both of which were made in the same period as the cave temple, are masterpieces of bronze images of that time. Among small images, the most typical one is the golden Tathagata, which had an inscription of the date, the fifth year of King Songdok (706 A.D.) on it when it was discovered at the pagoda of Hwangboksa Temple in Kyongju.

Beside those, there are many remains of Buddhist images which are so refined in carving arts and casting skills that they recall vividly the once glorious Silla culture.

Koryo Sculpture

With the passing of the Silla period, when Korean sculpture had reached its peak, the new Koryo era couldn't keep the level that Silla had established.

Koryo sculpture declined because of decreasing demands for Buddhist images, which was—as often said—due partly to the insistence on copying sutras and partly to the spread of the *Song* Sect better known by the Japanese name, Zen, which disregards ritual. And furthermore the slackness of the formative spirit was consequential in the decline of Buddhism.

Therefore, contrary to Silla's Buddhist images which had not only realistic human bodies carved with very refined technique but also somewhat lofty divinities as a result of the religious faith of the sculptors, Koryo Buddhas were merely human-like and had no divinity. Koryo inherited from Silla not the art but only its technique, which gradually declined and became so clumsy that it was compared with craft which one could see only in dolls.

The best among the Koryo remains intact today are a seated Amitabha of Pusoksa

Temple in south Korea and an iron Tathagata which was in Chokchosa Temple in Kyonggi-do but now is in the Kaesong Museum. Both of them are the works of early Koryo, hence bear Silla's thick, formative style. Except those few works of early Koryo, there is almost no remain worth mentioning because Koryo sculpture began to decline very rapidly after the middle of that period.

In the 13th century, influenced by the Yuan dynasty of China whose official state religion was Lamaism, Koryo sculptors made some images of Lamaism for a while. But that also soon declined. Next came the Yi period of Confucianist domination which ended sculptural works in Buddhist images.

Yi Dynasty Sculpture

The movement to exclude Buddhism in the early Yi dynasty dealt a fatal blow to Korean sculpture. Even the Buddhist images that had been preserved in many temples could not be kept any longer, because temples had many difficulties in maintaining themselves and some had to be closed. Under such social conditions, Buddhism could not help declining more and more until at last it survived in only modest form in the country. Although Buddhism was alive, the Buddhists decreased in number and dropped in quality. As a result, sculptors of Buddhist images had no heirs and skills declined day by day. Some Buddhist images of the Yi dynasty period were handed down in some remote temples, but they are only vulgar realistic statues of beautiful girls and handsome boys. This retrogression of Buddhist sculpture, however, was not only noticeable in Korea but in the Japan of that period as well.

Modern Korean Sculpture

From ancient times, sculpture was the mainstream of Korean art. To express real artistic creation, the Korean people always chose sculpture rather than painting or architecture. The elegant and highly advanced Buddhist images of the Three Kingdoms period and the noble stone sculptures of the Silla dynasty are not only the pride of the Korean people but constitute the orthodox formative values of Korean cultures. It can't be denied that Greek sculpture had influence on Korea's through ancient northern societies, and the sculpture of the Middle East nomadic people was also introduced to Korea. But, with refined techniques, Korean sculptors of the Three Kingdoms period and of Unified Silla could create Korea's own beauty on Korea's own stone, granite. Anyway, the Korean people once established a very highly advanced art of sculpture.

The once glorious Korean sculpture, however, began to decline during the Koryo and Yi dynasties, and finally, in the late Yi period, passed away completely, giving way to painting and ceramic art. In that time there were only professional engravers and carvers of stones and metals-that is, skilled stonecutters and alchemists—but no sculptors in the artistic sense.

In 1914, Kim Pokchin entered Tokyo College of Arts in Japan and studied Western-influenced sculpture for the first time. Korean modern sculpture got its start when he came back home and began to teach his many pupils. Although his works were those of the so-called official-school and the realistic style, sculpture came to be realized as an art. Carving on stone, wood, plaster and clay went into the formative creation. Thanks to his pioneering attempts, Korean sculpture became a modern art form.

Teaching sculpture at both the Towol and Koryo Art Institutes, Kim Pokchin created works and techniques encouraging students and developing modern sculpture in Korea. However, even in the exhibition of the *Sohwa-hyophoe* (Association of Arts) which had been established in order to develop Korean arts, no section was provided for sculpture. But the movement was advancing and many distinguished sculptors appeared and gave hope for the future. Among the notable artists were Mun Chongo, Yun Sunguk, Kim Chongyong, Kim Kyongsung and Yun Hyojung.

The stages for displaying their works were the *Teiten* (Japanese Imperial Art Exhibition) and the *Bunten* (Art Exhibition of Japanese Ministry of Education) in Tokyo, and *Senten* (Chosun Art Exhibition) in Korea. In the *Teiten*, Kim Pokchin once displayed a wooden statue of a woman and Yun Sunguk a nude statue, both winning prizes. In the *Senten*, no works of Korean sculptors were displayed until the 4th Exhibition when one of Chon Pongnae's and two of Kim Pokchin's works were displayed. One of Kim's pieces, "Two Years Ago," was awarded third prize. Since then, the sculptural works of Korean artists have been shown every year.

In Korea, after the end of World War II in 1945, the only sculptors were those young artists who had studied in Tokyo, such as Yun Sunguk, Kim Kyongsung, Kim Chinyong, Yun Hyojung and An Changdong. They had to travel a lonely way because in that period sculpture wasn't considered real art. Therefore, in 1946, in order to develop an art movement for sculpture, they organized the Chosun Sculptors' Association. It was, however, divided into left and right factions, and the Association stumbled.

In April, 1946, when the Art College was established in Seoul National University, Yun Sunguk and Kim Chongyong joined as professors of sculpture and some dozen students were under their leadership. That was the second start of Korean modern sculpture. Among the students were Paek Mungi, Kim Sejong, Chang Kiun and Yu Hanwon. They displayed modern sculpture in the first National Art Exhibition. Also exhibiting there were Pak Ilhun and Kim Mansul who had studied sculpture privately and had nothing to do with the Art College. The judge was Kim Kyongsung, while Kim Chongyong and Yun Hyojung were the nominators. Although all the displayed works of seventeen sculptors were still in realistic style, those of the sculptors from the Art College had definite creative ideas.

The Korean War which broke out in 1950 claimed the lives of some Korean sculptors, imposing a shortage of men and ideas to the world of sculpture of Korea.

In 1951, when the government was in Pusan, Yun Hyojung travelled to Europe to attend a meeting of UNESCO. And in 1952 Kim Chongyong and others showed their works in the International Exhibition of Sculpture held in London, in which Kim's sculpture won a prize.

The most distinguished works of that time were Kim Kyongsung's "Nude" which was displayed in the Invitation Exhibition of Modern Artists sponsored by the National Museum of Korea in March, 1952, and Yun Hyojung's "Lone Soul," an Italian-influenced work which showed the sculptor had received a stimulus from Italy while he was in Europe. At that time, each of them made the statues of Admiral Yi Sunsin, one in Chinhae and the other in Tongyong, which were the forerunners of the statue-boom that followed in Korea.

In 1953, after Seoul was recovered and the government came back, Hongik and Ewha Women's Universities set up sculpture courses in their art colleges. Such an increase in sculpture education must be considered an advance because Korean modern sculpture could develop itself mostly through art education. In fact, most of the sculptors who had displayed their works in the National Art Exhibition were the students of art colleges.

The first one-man show of sculpture in Korea was held by Kim Yonghak in August, 1958. The first metal sculpture in the abstract style, made by Song Yongsu, was displayed in the 7th National Art Exhibition.

Having discarded the realistic style of Kim Kyongsung, Korean sculpture has arrived at the abstract style of Kim Chongyong and Yun Hyojung. It is fortunate that Korean sculpture is being modernized, but only in manner, not in theory. Modern Korean sculpture has only a few years of history since the end of World War II. There are still many processes Korean sculptors must experience in the future.

Architecture

General Survey

The basic Korean structural style is the framework or lintel style, which consists of horizontal wooden beams supported on wooden posts. Due to Korea's cold climate, the spaces between the posts were usually thickly plastered with clay or lime over a wicker framework; sometimes they were filled in with a wall of stones or tiles. From early times, the main material of Korean houses, even the palaces and temples, was wood. A number of fine non-residential buildings, such as castles, tombs, pagodas, and gates, were made of stone, particularly of granite, which was available all over the country.

The Korean house is basically square or rectangular, L-shaped, T-shaped or square U-shaped. Public buildings such as palaces, schools and temples which were influenced by Chinese architecture, are not so complicated in shape as the common houses. A public building consists simply of many square houses—connected by corridors.

A peaked roof frame is erected on the beams which span the supporting posts. There are four regular shapes; *Mappae* (a simple two-gable roof), *Paljak* (additional roofs just below both gables), *Wujingak* (four roofs, two square, two triangular; no gables), and *Samo* (four triangular roofs). A *Wujingak* is generally for a large building, while a *Mappae* is for a small house. The most commonly used in ordinary Korean houses is the *Paljak*. The most outstanding characteristic of Korean roofs, and a feature not seen in Western architecture, is that they curve up at the corners. Both ends of the roof-ridge also are curved up. Such curved lines reflect Chinese influence in Korean architecture.

Under the eaves, between roof and supporting posts, is a richly decorated structural part supporting the large and heavy roof. Called *Pojak* in Korean, this is also Chinese influenced. In Far Eastern architecture, a house is often classified by the style of the *Pojak*.

The interior of a house is also very characteristic. Because of the Korean people's custom of sitting on the floor, the floor is higher than in Chinese houses where the people use chairs. Although some of the floors in a Korean house are of wood, most are *Ondol* in which oil papers are pasted on clay-plastered stones under which run several tunnels, enabling the heat from the furnace at the ends of the tunnels to warm the floor. *Ondol* flooring is unique to Korea, originating far back in the Stone Age. The floors of large rooms in such buildings as palaces and temples, however, were once made of tiles or stones, another influence of Chinese architecture. But from the beginning of the Yi dynasty, wooden floors began to be made in some temples, and after about the mid-Yi period, every temple had wooden floors.

Another noticeable feature in Korean architecture is the partition. In the ancient buildings of the Chinese, a building was used for one need instead of being partitioned into rooms. In Korea, too, a building might remain unpartitioned and be used for only one need. But most Korean houses are partitioned into several rooms or combine buildings for different purposes into one house. The partition is considered to have resulted from the neccessity of separating *Ondol* rooms from the wooden floored ones.

To add to those characteristics, Korean palaces, temples, and public buildings are carved and painted with various colors and designs both outside and inside. Although the decoration was at first patterned after that of Chinese buildings, designs and colors were developed differently because of the differences in nature and national traits. The resulting brilliant decoration became one of the most distinctive characteristics of Korean architecture, even though it became, in later years, rather ostentatious.

Historical Survey

From early times, Korean culture was influenced by the more advanced culture of the Chinese continent. Architecture was no exception. The Lolang colonies, which flourished about two thousand years ago, perhaps first brought Chinese influence to bear upon Korean architecture. There are no remains to give details of the architecture of the period, but writing about the social lives of the people of the times lead us to presume that the buildings of that period were by no means primitive. Thereafter, Korean architecture received four or five more series of influences from China up to the Three-Kingdom period, by which time, the influence was complete.

Three Kingdoms Period

It was in the period of the Northern and Southern dynasties that Buddhism spread so widely in China that the culture of the period could be termed Buddhistic. Consequently, when Buddhism was introduced in Korea of the late Three-Kingdom period, the Chinese Buddhist culture naturally accompanied it to raise the culture of the Three Kingdoms to higher levels. With the building of numerous Buddhist temples came rapid progress in architecture. Only a very few stone towers and no wooden buildings have been left to posterity. Fortunately, however, pictures of buildings in the frescoes of the ancient Koguryo tombs give us some idea of the architecture of the fifth and sixth centuries.

In the stone chambers found in almost every Koguryo tomb, big timber columns were pictured on the four corners of the wall; then *Pojak*, beams and other structural materials were also painted between the ceiling and pictures of columns, in imitation of a wooden house in the stone chamber. In a certain chamber, parts of real building materials were used instead of pictures. And the pictures of castles, dwellings and various other buildings of that time were painted in the frescoes on the walls of the chambers. All these show that Korguryo buildings were big in scale and excellent in technique.

The famous Horyuji temple of Japan gives details of the structural form of ancient architecture, as based on the structural techniques of Paekche, one of the Three Kingdoms.

Buildings shown in the carved pictures on the walls of cave temples in Yunkang and Lungmen of north China show much similarity to Korean structures. Nevertheless, the architecture of the Three Kingdoms period did not merely copy the structural methods of the North and Southern dynasties of China.

Unified Silla Period

Under the influence of Tang Chinese culture, Silla advanced her culture to the most glorious point in Korea's history. Pulguksa Temple, the Cave Shrine (Sokkuram) of Kyongju, and many stone works all over the country, show that Silla made progress not only in architecture but in every field of art.

Two stone structures, typical of the advancement of Silla art in the ninth century, are the *Tabodap* (Tower of Many Treasures) of Pulguksa, and Hwaomsa Temple's three-story tower of stone with a decoration of lions. Such excellent and original works are not to be found in contemporary Japan, or even in China. Also the great stone *Chongwun* (blue cloud) Bridge and *Paekwun* (white cloud) Bridge, in the Pulguksa Temple, are world-widely known for their grand and excellent structural forms which reflect the essence of Silla art. Among many of the fine stone works of Silla, fifty or more have been designated National Treasures.

Compared to such brilliant remains in stone, nothing is left of wooden constructions of that period. There is no way to picture the wooden house of Silla but to make what few deductions are possible from the wooden structural techniques employed in stone towers, and the corner-stones and roof-tiles found in the sites of wooden buildings.

A wooden house of Silla was built on a stone platform. Pillars stood on beautifully rounded or squared bases. The roof was tiled and, at the ends of double rafters, neatly decorated tiles, called *Maksae-Kiwa*, were arranged. The two ends of a roof-ridge were decorated with bird-tail-like tiles, called *Chimi*. Not much of the form of the *Pojak* is known except for what can be deduced from the presumably similar or related structural methods in contemporary Japanese wooden buildings, which correspond in some other structural respects with the stone towers of Silla. The architecture of Japan and Korea of that time were similar in many respects, both having their sources in the architecture of Tang. Therefore, although each developed their own unique nature and characteristics, in both countries, palaces, temples and other buildings were built in such numbers as never before, thus reflecting the magnificent style of Tang architecture everywhere. The two and a half centuries of Unified Silla was a golden age for Korean architecture and culture.

Koryo Dynasty

Koryo was named after Koguryo, because it wished to recover the old territories of Koguryo. This dream was never realized, chiefly due to the constant invasions of its northern borders by northern barbarians such as the Kitais, the Niuchens and the Tartars. However, Koryo's high spirit of nationalism had much influence on architecture, which began to gradually adapt itself to Korea's own circumstances. But new architectural styles in China began once again to have strong influences on Koryo before her own architectural style could be firmly fixed.

Koryo architecture can be divided into two styles. One is that which was influenced by the Sung-style structural methods which developed chiefly in the valley of Yangtze River where Sung settled down after being driven south by Chien and Liao. The method is thought to have been introduced to Koryo by Sung merchants. Another style, influenced by the architecture developed in northern China under Chien and Liao, was introduced to Koryo after it came under the influence of the Yuan dynasty.

For convenience's sake, we will call the former, A-style, and the latter, B-style. Both styles, took on an admixture of the traditional constructive methods carried over from the Silla period, and were carried on by Yi architecture; thus, though Korean characteristics were added during their progression, every ancient wooden building now standing belongs to either one of these two styles or to Yi architecture originating from both.

A-style and B-style are distinguished by the arrangement of the *Pojak* between pillars and roof-eaves. In the A-style, the *Pojak* is arranged just above pillars, while in the B-style, it is arranged not only above pillars. The *Pojak*, originating in Han China as the structural part of the house supporting the heavy roof, became in time not only a structural but an ornamental feature. One of the distinctive and effective characteristics of Far Eastern architecture is often classified by differences in the forms of the *Pojak*. However, the basic principle of the structure is common to all styles. First, short horizontal beams are placed on top of the pillars, projecting forward and sideward, on which are placed closely spaced small rectangular blocks of wood. On these are placed another layer of short beams, with small blocks so that the *Pojak* supports the weight of the projecting roof-eaves. Since the *Pojak* consists of just two elements, the short beam, or *Chomcha*, and the small block, or *Soro*; the distinction between A-style and B-style lies in the form and structural method of the *Chomcha* and *Soro*.

An A-style *Chomcha* has a curved line just like a doubled-S on its lower edge while that of B-style is merely an arc. In early A-style buildings, a *Soro* which had a curved bottom was used, but later the same rectangular *Soro* were used in both A- and B-style, the wooden blocks being located one above another, while, in A-style, they were arranged rather freely,

In B-style, the *Pojak* extends forward and to both sides; in A-style, only the extreme points of the *Pojak* extend to the sides. The *Pojak* is generally built up from the higher parts of pillars, but, in A-style, it is built up from just above the heads of pillars where the bottom row of the *Chomcha* are stuck in and other rows are worked up.

While the most distinguishing charateristics of A- and B-styles appear in their *Pojak*, another difference is in the treatment of the ceiling.

B-style structures have a true ceiling; A-style exposes the structural materials of the roof. In B-style buildings, where the roof-beams are not visible to the eye, they are generally made carelessly with poor material. In A-style buildings, which have no ceiling and expose the roof-beams, very careful and complicated methods are employed to give a neat and finished appearance to the exposed beams.

The A-style architecture, introduced from Southern Sung China about the twelfth or thirteenth century, flourished in Korea between the late Koryo dynasty and the early Yi dynasty (14th and 15th centuries). There are many fine buildings of that time remaining in Korea now, most of them designated as National Treasures. The finest are Pusok-sa Temple (12th-13th century) in Kyongju, Sudok-sa Temple (1308) in Yesan, Chungchong Namdo, and Songbul-sa Temple (early 14th century) in Hwangju, Hwanghae-do.

The A-style declined after the mid-Yi period. One reason was its structural defects. The *Pojak*, placed above the heads of posts and projecting forwards but not sidewards, left the side space between the posts unsupported. And too, the simplicity of A-style architecture, while suitable for small houses, gradually lost favor for large buildings which, it was felt, should be more ornate and magnificent.

Thus, in the middle Yi dynasty, when formality held sway under the overwhelming influence of Confucianism, A-style architecture withered away in its techniques and forms degenerated. This tendency to elaboration and ornateness appeared, first of all, in the *Pojak*, particularly, in the *Chomcha*, the short wooden beam. The short beam originally had a curved line like a doubled-S on its lower edge. Even when later, a sharp horn-like piece began to be attached to its end, its contour was still dignified and restrained. Toward the mid-Yi period, however, very complicated curved lines began to be used for the *Pojak*, both sides of each short beam being decorated with carved designs of flowers and grasses, so that the contour became much too ostentatious, leading into meaningless decoration. What distinguishes such a metamorphosed A-style, which is called "*Ikkong*," from the original is the decorative part, or *Hwaban*, which fills the blank space between upper parts of pillars of the old A-style. The *Hwaban*, which was usually of the flower and grass design, was made, as well as for decoration and to eliminate the unsafe blank space between the *Pojak*. It is not known exactly when B-style architecture came to Korea. Apparently, it came later than A-style architecture, because most of the remaining Koryo wooden buildings are of A-style. Only two belong to B-style, a building named *Songkwang jon*, of Simwonsa Temple (1378) in Hwanghae-do, north Korea, and a building named *Ung jinjon*, of Sokwangsa Temple (1386) in Hamgyong Namdo. Both buildings are of the late Koryo dynasty. However, the carving on the stone tower of Kyongchon-sa Temple, built in 1348 to pray for the longevity of the Yuan Emperor and the peaceful reign of Koryo, faithfully follows the B-style form of that time. It is said that some Yuan craftsmen joined in the construction. Whether this is true or not, since the architectural details carved on the tower are very similar in many respects to those of Yuan architecture, the B-style archtecture of that time apparently received influence from Yuan. Korea's B-style architecture began as soon as Yuan started to have influence on Koryo.

Yi Dynasty

A-style, one or two centuries older than B-style, at first predominated in the early Yi dynasty. However, as stated above, A-style soon began to decline due to its structural defects and the unsuitability of its form to the tastes of the period. B-style waxed as A-style waned, and by the sixteenth century, took the place of A-style.

Another reason for the sweep of B-style in the Yi period was that Ming China, succeeding Yuan, developed an architectural style which belonged to the same current as B-style architecture. However, although the architecture of Ming and the B-style of Korea had the same source which had developed in China since Sung and Yuan, Korea's B-style architecture developed its distinctive and unique characteristics, definitely different from those of Ming or of Ching, reflecting the different land and character of the people.

The most distinguishing feature in the B-style of the latter Yi dynasty is, above all, the continuously elaborate decorative elements, particularly in the *Pojak* which was the most conspicuous part of a building. In the early B-style buildings, the *Pojak* had had no decorative element but was simply a solid structural part. However, the horn-like projection evolved from the original short and rigid form growing longer, slimmer, and gracefully curved.

The decorative elements increased more and more. Both sides of the beam began to be carved with designs, carved lotus, or phoenix head. The decorating was done not only on the outside of the *Pojak* but on the inside as well. At first, the decoration was made only on the upper part of the *Pojak*, above the pillars. Later the original duty of the *Pojak* as a structural part was ignored and both outside and inside began to be richly decorated to become a mere decorative panel.

Although such a decoration displays very Korea-like local color, it disregarded the real structural motives vital in architecture. When *Tanchong*, or coloring, began to be applied to the decoration, it became too gorgeous, too rich, and too intricate, driving Yi architecture into a dead end.

Modern Korean Architecture

As a result of Japan's colonialism in Korea, Western architecture which first accompanied the mission work of Catholicism, appeared in quantity. Palaces or government buildings such as the *Sokchojon* of Toksu Palace, the Catholic Church in Myongdong, Seoul, public buildings of foreigners, and stores or dwellings of wealthy merchants were built in Korea under the influence of Western architecture.

The Catholic Church in Myongdong, Seoul, is of Gothic style on a Latin cross shape plain figure designed and supervised by Father Eugene Joan George Coste, a Frenchman. The construction was completed in the same year.

In 1896, a Catholic theological school was built in Yongsan, and in 1891, a Catholic church in Chungnimdong, Seoul. Other Western buildings built in Korea before and after 1900 are the Anglican Church in Seoul, the British Consulate (1898) in Inchon, the housing quarters of a German concern (1884, now the Municipal Museum of Inchon), an English concern, Holme Reger & Co., (1896, now a building belonging to the ROK Navy), Taebul Hotel (1888, now a Chinese restaurant in Seoul), the Catholic Church in Inchon (1893), and a villa of an Englishman, James Johnston (1905, now also a Chinese restaurant in Inchon). All of these buildings were built for the needs of foreigners according to their plans chiefly by Chinese workers.

Those which were built according to foreigners' plans at the request of Koreans are the *Sokchojon* (Stone Building) of Toksu Palace and the Independence Gate in Sodaemun, Seoul.

The *Sokchojon* of Toksu Palace, which was begun in 1908 and completed in 1910, is a Modern Renaissance style building designed by an Englishman, Davidson. The Independence Gate, built in 1898 according to the plan of a Russian, at the request of the Independence Association (*Tongnip Hyophoe*), was simply a copy of a Roman Triumphal Arch.

The culture of Korea was too far behind the times to recognize architecture as an art. Even after World War II 1945, let alone before, Koreans thought of buildings as no more than a place to live in. However, after 1945, Korea began to have cultural relations with advanced countries of the world. As a result, new ideas came and Korean architecture became an art.

Of course, ancient Korean works of architecture were recognized as fine art, some investigations were made by Japanese scholars, and the excellence of Korean ancient structures recognized all over the world. But the investigations were limited to the field of archaeology, leaving aesthetic studies in second place. Furthermore, since the Korean people's modes of living became modernized, so called, modern Korean architects thought only in terms of Western architecture. The trend was fostered by the influence of Japanized Western architecture, which was unsuited to the Korean people's living manner.

Many dwellings, offices, stores and public buildings were erected in Korea, but they were nothing but "structures," having no connection with art. Architecture was ignored even by the official National Art Exhibition, which did not set up a section for architecture until the fifth exhibition in 1957.

Of course, even during the Japanese rule, there were not a few students who studied architecture, and after the Liberation of 1945. it was they who worked in the field of architecture in Korea. But they couldn't claim architecture as an art according to the public understanding of the time. They had to be satisfied as technicians.

When the architect, Kim Chungop, went to Paris in 1951 to attend a meeting of UNESCO, he stayed there and studied architecture under the direction of Le Corbusier. This was important not only to himself but also to modern Korean architecture, for through him, Korean architecture joined international currents for the first time.

The turning point in Korean architecture, came in 1953, when Hongik College established an architectural course in its Art Department and Seoul and Hanyang Universities had architectural courses in their technical colleges.

Korean architecture could now be considered an art. In the meantime, architects Kang Myongsu and Yi Chonsung, went abroad to view modern architecture. World currents awakened Korean architects and advanced Korean architecture. The National Art Exhibition established a section for architecture, and some other exhibitions for architecture were held. Furthermore, new buildings began to be built around Seoul by these new architects.

In the architecture division of the fifth National Art Exhibition in 1957, of the nine works displayed, seven were by judges (Kim Chungop, Kang Myonggu and Yi Chonsung) and an invited artist, Om Tongmun. Only two were by ordinary artists, Yi Yunhyong and Yun Taehyon. In the sixth Exhibition, there were 19 works, mostly by college students, and in the seventh, 12 works were displayed.

In 1957, there were three major architectural exhibitions, the exhibition of the works of Kim Chungop, Hanyang University's architectural exhibition, and Seoul Technical College's exhibition, which displayed such freshness and modernity in both character and structure as to confirm Korea's turn to architecture as a modern art. Due to material and technical problems, however, modern architecture has yet to be fully manifested in Korea.

Handicrafts

In the history of the handicraft arts of Korea, the development of ceramic art places it as the most advanced country of the world next to China. The distinctive features of the age were the golden works which were discovered in the tombs of the Silla dynasty.

Knowledge about the ancient handicraft culture was acquired mostly from handiworks excavated in the ancient tombs of the Three Kingdoms period.

Three-Kingdom Period

The excavated remains from the tombs of the Three Kingdoms' period, especially the rich materials from the Silla tombs as well as the characteristic constructive style of the tombs themselves, form a unique feature in Asia. It was ascertained by archaeological investigations that the unique Silla styles—the golden crowns, gilt bronze ornaments, comma-shaped jewels, bronzeware and earthenware—were introduced not only to Paekche but also to the Kyushu and Honshu areas of Japan. The golden crown, which is composed of a golden circlet with tree-shaped and antler-shaped golden uprights, is a very unique design which is thought to have originated in the Scytho-Siberian culture or in the southwest-Asian culture. Various burial objects in addition to the golden crowns were excavated in the old Silla tombs; included were golden objects including filigree earrings like those of Greece, glassware, glass ornaments, and comma-shaped jewels of hard stone which were ornaments unique to Silla. Most remarkable is the gilt bronze object in open work inlaid with shells of a sort of beetle, Kiljongchung or Tamamushi in Japanese (Chrysochroa elegans), which was also used afterwards in the famous Japanese chest, Tamamushi-zushi of Horyuji Temple. Grey hard earthenware with long legs, found in Silla tombs, are in a characteristic style, the origin also of Japanese Iwaibe earthenware.

Owing to the uniquely constructed chambers, Silla tombs could preserve many art works of handicraft buried within them, whereas the tombs of Koguryo and Paekche have long since been looted of their burial objects because of the stone chambers which were made to be easily broken into. Therefore, few handiworks of Koguryo and Paekche remain today.

Of the few Koguryo remains, the most notable is the gilt bronze ornament in openwork with the decoration of inlaid shells of Kiljongchung like that of Silla. Few earthenware objects which were excavated in Koguryo tombs are, on the contrary, not Silla's own unique style, but after the Chinese. The fact that Koguryo earthenware objects are fewer in number and less skilled in technique bears out the theory that Koguryo people used woodenware for their tables.

The gilt bronze crown ornament, one of the Paekche remains, shows the progressive development of Paekche handicrafts in its decorations of Greek scroll-work and Chinese design of mountains and clouds. Also the refined skills of Paekche handicraft artists appeared in the six kinds of tiles with decorations of landscape, lotus, clouds, phoenix, demon and coiled dragon. Earthenware well reflects Paekche's soft and peaceful character, and it has been concluded that glazed soft pottery was produced in Paekche since early days.

Unified Silla Period

Objects which may represent the handicraft of the Unified Silla period are bells in Buddhist temples. The masterpieces of the bronze bells of Silla which are left in Korea now are the Bell of King Songdok (made in 771 A.D.) now in the Kyongju Museum and the Bell of Sangwon Temple in Mt. Odae (made in 725 A.D.). In 1948, at an old temple site in Yangyang, Kangwon-do, a bell, dated 20th year of Chongwon (804 A.D.), was excavated, only to be scrapped during the Korean War in 1951. A few more outstanding works are now left in Japan.

Typical is the Bell of King Songdok, about eleven feet high and seven and a half feet in diameter, with writing cast on the surface. The writing says that King Kyongdok of Silla started to cast the bell with about seventy-two tons of bronze to pray for the bliss of late King Songdok, his father, but died leaving the work to the next king, Hyegong who completed it in the year of *Sinmyo* (771 A. D.). The mouth of the bell is an obtuse-angle octagon. Lotus and other gorgeous decorations are cast in relief on the surface of the upper part, and a flying devata, or god, is also in relief, drawing beautiful lines around the surface of the middle of the bell's body. The lower part of the surface is decorated with double petalled lotus flowers. The bell is a real masterpiece of metal work which displays the refined technique of Silla artists in those vivid, brilliant decorations as well as in its elegant and wonderful tones. Compared to the contemporary Chinese (Tang) and Japanese (Nara and Heian) bells which usually have some loops around the cylinder of each bell, Korean bells of this and later times, having quickly gotten rid of the original Tang style, devloped into those of a uniquely Korean which was inherited by the bells of following periods. As the "Chosun Bells," they are well known to the world.

Besides such advancement in metal craft, Silla also made progress in pottery and left many fine works of ceramicware and roof-tiles to posterity. Although hard earthenware had progressed in the Three Kingdoms' period, it was in the united Silla period when real pottery, especially the green glazed pottery which probably was introduced from China, was produced and practically used. A small Buddhist coffin for bones with floral decorations and a green glazed tile with the picture of the Four Deva Kings in relief found in a temple site in Kyongju shows that Silla advanced the ceramic art to a higher point. Another example of tile masterpieces are the roof-tiles and tiles with pictures excavated in Kyongju, which are decorated with a Demon's face, fabulous birds and animals, arabesque, and others, so skillfully, so delicately and so elegantly that they far surpass those of Tang.

Koryo Dynasty

While sculpture declined, handicraft progressed rapidly and brightly in the Koryo period, especially ceramic art. The celadon, represented by Koryo ceramics, is extraordinarily outstanding not only in Korean art history but in the ceramic history of the world as well. It is one of those fine art pieces in which chemistry and the formative spirit of human beings were highly and completely harmonized.

The first written records on Koryo celadon, appears in the "Koryo Tokyong," written by Hsu Ching, a member of a Sung mission to Korea in May, 1123 A. D. According to the book, which was about what the author had seen in Koryo, the kingdom had already accomplished the elegantly and delicately glazed celadon of a rare "secret color." The shape of the ware was similar to that of the Tiang-choa ware of northern Sung, while the glaize was similar to that of the Yuechou-yuyao ware of Hangchow in Chekiang Province from the end of Tang period to the beginning of Sung, or to that of the Celadon ware in Lolang of northern Sung.

On the other hand, the most significant Koryo celadon ever discovered in Korea was the celadon pot excavated in Kyonggi-do, at the bottom of which is an inscription engraved as follows:

"The 4th Year of Sunhwa (993 A.D.)
　　Dedicated to the First Room
　　　of the Royal Tablet Shrine.
　　Made by Choe Kilhoe, potter."

The potter, Choe, made the celadon for the Royal Tablet Shrine in 993 A.D. The pot was covered with a sort of unfinished glaze which may be thought of as the forerunner of the Koryo celadon.

These two writings, the writing on the bottom of the celadon pot and that in the Koryo Tokyong, tell that Koryo celadon, receiving technical influence from the Sung wares, was gradually developed during the 130 years from 993 to 1123 when the author of the Koryo Tokyong was in Korea. Most Koryo kilns, which had apparently been operating since the early Koryo period judging from the remains at the kiln-sites, were found at Kangjin and Puan on the south and southwestern coasts of the Korean peninsula far from the capital city. Although some kiln sites were discovered in other places, the mainstream of Koryo celadon was always in the southwestern coast, the nearest area to Yehchou, the production center of Sung celadon. However, the route over the sea between the location was used frequently since the Paekche period. Furthermore, the fragments discovered in those kiln-sites on the southwestern coast are very similar to those of Chinese kiln-sites in Yuehchou both in shape and glaze. Drawing inferences from these facts, it may be concluded that Koryo celadon originated from the southern Sung wares, the technique of which came to Koryo on the south and southwestern coast across the sea.

Although Koryo celadon had its source in China, it made such unique and rapid development in Korea, that the author of Koryo Tokyong praised it highly in his book. The glazes of Sung and Koryo celadons were called *Pisaek*, or secret color, but written in different letters, because Koryo celadon glaze was uniquely refined and much different from Sung's. The elegant shape of the Koryo celadon with slender and beautifully curved lines as well as its wonderfully glazed color, became a characteristic of Koryo beauty.

In the mid-twelfth century, another unique type of design, *Sanggam*, an inlaid-work on celadon, was created. Until the beginning of the thirteenth centry, *Sanggam*-ware was the most favored celadon in Koryo. Devotion to the delicacy of celadon glaze began to lessen, at the start for the thirteenth century; however, fine *Sanggam* celadon were still produced, especially golden decorated porcelains, such as the celadon noted for the monkey and peach decoration inlaid with golden paste which was excavated at Manwoldae, Kaesong. From the fourteenth century, the last century of the Koryo dynasty, celadon began to decline along with the fortunes of the kingdom. The end of the period, saw the beginning of a new pottery development, the *Punchong* ware of light greenish blue.

Besides celadon, of course, there were various ceramics and porcelains in the Koryo period. But the mainstream of ceramic art was always in celadon. Such mass production of refined celadon and advanced inlaid-work gave stimulus to the rest of the handicraft field, as well as to Koryo culture itself. The result was fine works of bronze and lacquerware. The typical bronze works are the incense-burner of Tongdo-sa temple in Yangsan and the bronze water-pourer, or sprinkler, decorated with willow-trees and mandarin ducks inlaid in stering silver, which is now in the National Museum in Seoul. The most remarkable of Koryo handicrafts was lacquerware inlaid with mother-of-pearl. It was so excellent that Hsu Ching, the author of Koryo Tokyong, said in his book, "..... the lacquerware with mother-of-pearl inlaid is so delicate and so dear....." According to the History of Koryo, a supervising office for the production of lacquerware was established in 1272, and the Office of Arts employed mother-of-pearl specialists in addition to painters specializing in lacquer. Also, it is written in the History of Koryo that lacquerware with mother-of-pearl decorations was presented to the Liao dynasty of China in the reign of King

Munjong (1947-1082) of Silla. From those facts, it is thought that Koryo also made progress in the field of lacquerware, a progress traceable to periods far earlier than the Koryo dynasty. It is very unfortunate, however, that none of these works is left in Korea now, except the lacquer-box with mother-of-pearl decoration of scroll and Indian letters which is now in a temple in Nara, Japan.

Yi Dynasty Period

Confucianism, which dominated the Yi period, brought no minor changes in the field of handicraft art. The practical idea of Confucianism had such influence on handicrafts that every handiwork had simple, practical, and non-aristocratic beauty. Throughout the dynastic era of five hundred years, ceramic, which was not only the representative craft of the dynasty but also one of the important industries of the time, was divided into two major currents of style. One was the *Punchong* (light greenish blue) pottery, successor to the declining Koryo celadon; the other was white porcelain which was refined after having received influence from the white porcelain of the Ming dynasty. This also originated from the white porcelain of Koryo.

Development of white porcelain continued throughout the Yi dynasty, while both the technique and style of the *Punchong* pottery became extinct after the Hideyoshi Invasion. Compared to the aristocratic Koryo celadon, the Yi white porcelain is generally simpler, spontaneously reflecting what is truly Korean better than works of any previous period. White is precisely the color the Korean people have traditionally favored. The good faith, spontaneity and grief which appear in the honest forming of the white porcelain evoke an intimate feeling of the heart. This color and form, being in harmony with bold designs, compose the basic beauty of the Yi dynasty.

The *Punchong*-ware which developed rapidly since the end of Koryo was perfected in the Yi dynasty to reflect the fresh and naive character of the period. The white porcelain was slowly improved in quality, and, in the reign of King Sejong, was used in the court as king's ware. In the reign of King Sejo, some more advanced types of pottery appeared, such as the *Chonghwa* white porcelain which had long been popular, the white porcelain decorated with *Sokkanju* (a kind of red clay), and the red-dotted white porcelain, all which were fusions of the tradition passed down from the picture-celadon of Koryo with the influence received from the *Chonghwa*-ware of the Ming dynasty.

According to a report of the time, there were 136 works of pottery kilns and 185 works of porcelain in the Yi dynasty. The white ware was called porcelain, while the *Punchng* and other wares were called pottery in that time. After the Japanese invasion, however, these works of both pottery and porcelain were mostly destroyed and ruined —particularly the production of *Punchong*-ware was rendered completely extinct, so that even the court itself could hardly acquire the wares. Furthermore, the Japanese were almost fanatically devoted to pillaging the ceramic techniques of Korea and in deporting even potters to Japan. Hence, for the first time in Japan, kilns for white porcelain were founded in Arita and other northern Kyushu areas by the kidnapped potters of the Yi dynasty.

The factor which made white porcelain survive was the establishment of *Kwangju-Punwon*, or the Kwangju-branch, which was supposed to be a porcelain kiln that belonged to *Saongwon*, a government office in charge of food and banquets at the court and established in 1468; therefore it meant the branch office of the *Saongwon*. The government-operated kiln supplied several kinds of porcelain to the court until the end of the dynasty. At that time, however, *Hoechong*, the color material for the *Chongwha* porcelain, which had been imported from China, became so hard to get that government prohibited civilian use of *Chongwa*-porcelain except for the court. Consequently, other porcelains, such as *Sokkanju* and the red-dotted variety, were widely spread among the civilians.

Due to the fall of the Ming dynasty and the Manchu invasion in 1636, however, Yi ceramics became depressed again until consolidation of the Ching dynasty in China, when Yi pottery rose briskly once more. But, even during those ages of difficulties, Yi porcelain achieved a very refined blue-white glaze, and the potters, in order to save the *Hoechong*, devised new decoration methods. Among them the *Kaechang* (literally translated, Opening Window), a method to fill a decoration only in a certain previously outlined section, and another method in which a decoration was to be put only on the upper part of a line which divided the surface of a pot by the ratio of one to two.

In 1752, the *Kwangju-Punwon*, which had been in Kumsa-ri, was moved to the place now called Punwon-ri. From the end of the eighteenth century, *Hoechong* began to be used again so frequently that some *Chonghwa* porcelains were overly decorated with *Hoechong*. From the reign of King Sunjo to the dictatorship of Taewongun, ceramics were produced and favored by the people. Many masterpieces were among them.

Since the decline of the Yi dynasty in the second half of the nineteenth century, *Kwangju-Punwon* could not be maintained as before. Corrupt officials appeared who, in their way, contributed to the deterioration day by day. Local kilns were worse off. They turned out such crude products that the porcelain were called "*Sang-sagi*," or vulgar ware. In 1883, at last, the *Kwangju-Punwon* was run by private concerns, which, for the purpose of mass production, employed Japanese potters and tried to modernize the production facilities. But such a reverse-import of Japanese technique resulted in indiscreet confusion in the long, traditional Yi technique, hastening the decline of Yi ceramics.

As already stated, the ceramic tradition established a characteristic feeling in the stream of Korean art, the name of which, however, was also heightened by the Yi dynasty bamboo and wood working with very refined design of unique, simple but sound beauty. Being neatly designed but not too luxurious, the furniture of wood and bamboo were appropriate for the traditionally-built Korean houses, showing their practical and simplified beauty. They are of various kinds, such as desk, script-box, square table, box for ink palette, dressing-case, lantern, chest, tray and others. However, all of them have a unique and uniform beauty, which indicates that wood-working also had a deep-rooted tradition from an early period. The woodworkers made good use of every kind of wood that could be obtained in Korea, such as pagoda-tree, ginko, Paulownia, pear and persimmon.

All the wood and bamboo work, lacquerware with mother-of-pearl and *Hwagak* (woodwork decorated with colors and pieces of the horn of an ox) were of various kinds and available for the luxuries of aristocrats or for everyday use by common people. But especially, the products for the common people were excellent, having unique characteristics, originality and native beauty within them.

Modern Handicrafts

Korean people were not aware of their own talents for handicrafts until very recent days, chiefly due to the fact that they thought handicraft was not an art but a workman's craft. Therefore, when modern foreign handiworks were brought into Korea at the end of the Yi dynasty, they failed to attract the attention of Korean citizens though all of the articles were valued and appreciated in the court.

After the Japanese domination over Korea, the Former Royal Household of Yi, stirred by some Japanese Yi pottery-lovers, established a factory for art works in Korea. However, it produced so many crude imitations of Yi pottery that they are still a cause of confusion in studies of Yi dynasty art.

The activities of modern handicraft, nevertheless, began by recognizing and succeeding the ancient handicraft art. The one who first informed and propagated to the Korean people the intrinsic values of Yi pottery and handiworks of other periods was not a Korean but a Japanese, named Yanagi Muneyoshi. In May, 1920, he came to Korea and declared the superiority of Korean handicrafts through lectures to Korean gatherings. In 1921, he came again to Korea and held a musical concert to raise funds for the establishment of a People's Museum of Korea, which afterwards developed into a center of handicraft movement in Korea. He also exhibited more than four hundred pieces of Yi pottery in Seoul in October of 1922.

But what really made the Koreans awake to their superiority in handicrafts was the wonderful remains of the ancient handiworks that were excavated by Japanese art specialists. The distinguished and excellent remains gave the artists self-confidence and stimulus to make their own works. Thus began the era of modern Korean handicrafts. In 1925, Kim Songgyu displayed some of his lacquerware decorated with mother-of-pearl in the World's Fair held in Paris and, in 1928, Yi Sunsok had a one-man show of designings in Seoul. In 1922, a women's art institute was established and embroidery was the main subject taught there by Chang Sunhui and others. However, the remarkable works were mainly seen in the *Senten*, which set up a handicraft division composed of three section from the eleventh exhibition. Of the many artists who were active in the *Senten*, Chang Kimyong, Kim Chaesok, Kang Changwon and Kim Chinap are still outstanding.

Particularly the lacquerware-artists—Kang Changwon, Kim Chingap, and Chang Kimyong, as well as Paek Taewon and Pak Yongju — were the forerunners of modern handicrafts of Korea who had worked with both the traditional and the new techniques. In February, 1946, after World War II, they organized the Chosun Handicraft-Artists' Association sponsored by the U. S. Military Government in Korea.

Modern handicraft of Korea, however, wasn't fully started in 1953 when handicraft courses were established in every art college and handicraft based upon contemporary theories began being taught. Those who have shown up well in the National Art Exhibition and others are almost always the students of handicraft.

In 1955, the Korean Handicraft-Artists' Association was organized, and in the same year, with the aid of the Rockfeller Foundation of America, the Formative Cultural Institute of Korea was established. Through this organization, Chong Kyu went to Rochester and Yu Kangyol to New York to study modern handicrafts. Kim Chongsuk also went to America for the purpose of establishing a handicraft course in Hongik University upon returning.

The major handicraft exhibitions that were held in Korea were the embroidery exhibit of Pak Yuk in Pusan 1952, the Formative Cultural Institute's first exhibition of newly-made potteries held in 1957, and Paek Taewon's solo exhibition of his handiworks in November, 1957. The National Art Exhibition has been the main stage for handicrafts. At the first exhibition, 36 works were displayed and the judges were Chang Sonhui, Kim Chunghyon and Kim Chaesok. In the second, 35 were shown and judges were Kim Chingap, Yi Sunsok and Chang Sonhui. In the third 29 were displayed, in the fourth 36, in the fifth 45, in the sixth 48, and in the seventh 30. The chief works which were displayed in the National Art Exhibition were of lacquerware, embroidery, designing and dyeing. The dyeing of Yu Kangyol opened a new field in handicraft arts of Korea.

In conclusion, Korea's modern handicraft, having a history of achievement and being close to the everyday lives of people, could hardly depart from tradition. Since 1950, however, influenced by the new art currents of the world, especially by modern designing, Korean artists of handicrafts are facing an artistic challenge and adventure to create a new handicraft art. They are now at the crossroads of the national tradition and world currents in modern handicrafts.

Calligraphy

Three Kingdom Period

Korean calligraphy began when Chinese characters were first introduced to Korea. The oldest known writing of Korean people is of the Three Kingdoms period, an inscription on the tombstone of King Hotae in Tungkou, Koguryo's capital city, in south Manchuria. Inscriptions are carved on all the four sides of this 22 feet high pillar, which, compared to the Chinese tombstones of Han dynasty, is relatively unadorned and of nearly raw stone. The tombstone itself and even more the writing manner of the inscriptions, which is more simple but grand and magnificent old *Ye*-style without brush stretching, seems to show the grand mind of Koguryo artists. The difference from the Chinese writing method is very important to the history of Oriental calligraphy. The inscription on the tombstone, which was erected in 414 A. D. by King Changsu, the son of King Hotae, is a record about the great achievements of King Hotae, the greatest hero of the Three Kingdoms.

Another old writing of Koguryo is the chronicle of Moduru, a vassal of King Hotae, a rare find, comparable to the Chinese wooden tablets of Han dynasty, in one of the ancient Koguryo tombs around Tungkou. Instead of frescoes as in most of Koguryo tombs, the walls of Moduru's tomb contain his chronicle in handwriting. Although the writing is not so outstandingly nice, one must consider the handicap that it was written directly on lime-plastered wall. There is a clumsy yet naive strength to it, and it is a very important landmark in the study of Koguryo calligraphy. Paekche, another one of the three kingdoms, left to posterity only one inscription, carved on the Monument of Sataekchijok, and discovered after World War II. It too is one of the most significant inscriptions in the history of Oriental calligraphy, the emotional and excellent writing-style shows a very important aspect of the brilliant culture of Paekche. Written in the style of the Chinese Six dynasties, its solemnity, correctness, and elegance is as good as any inscription of contemporary China.

Silla's only remaining inscriptions are to be found on the four so-called hunting monuments of King Chinhung (540-575). Written in *Hae*-characters of the Six dynasties, they are notable for their clear and simple antique style.

Of these Three Kingdoms inscriptions, the Paekche writing is the finest. This and the antique and simple style of the inscription of King Hotae's tombstone, best represent Three-Kingdom calligraphy.

Unified Silla Period

It is to be regretted that in the tombstone of King Taejong Muyol, who unified the three kingdoms, the main body has been lost and there remain only a tortoise-shaped pedestal and *isu*, or capstone. On the *isu*, there is a writing, "The Grave of Taejong Muyol the Great," in the characters of the *Chon*-style, which is said to be the writing of Kim Inmun, the son of the king. Although it is not exceptionally outstanding, it is a good example of *Chon*-style. The *Chon* (seal character)-style, which had been very fine up to the Chin period, degenerated until the Ching period, when it was refined again by Teng Wan-pe.

Korean calligraphy was affected by the

contemporaneous Chinese writing methods. In the Unified Silla period, therefore, the *Haeng*-style was that after Wang Hsi-chih of Tongchin, and the *Hae*-style was of the three masters of Tang, Ou Yang-hsun, Yu Shin-nan and Chu Sui-liang. Ou Yang-hsun's style especially had much influence not only on the calligraphy of Silla but on that of the Koryo dynasty as well, and most writings of both dynasties were of this style. The Hwaom Sutra, engraved on stone at the beginning of the Unified Silla period, is a very correct and outstanding example of the Ou-style. Inscription on a monument of Sachonwangsa Temple is also in the Ou-style; it is regrettable that only few characters are left on its fragments. If it were complete, it would be one of the finest inscriptions of Silla.

The inscription on a monument of Mujang-sa Temple in the *Haeng*-style of Wang Hsi-chih, is one of the most refined writings in the history of Original calligraphy, being on a level with Wang's own writing in the introduction to the famous Chinese book, "Nanjonggo," and the preface to the "Chipcha-songyo." There are two theories about this epigraph. According to the "Haedong Kumsok Chongmok (Index of Korean Epigraphs)," the "Tongkuk Kumsokpyong (Review of Korean Epigraphs)," the "Taedong Kumsokso (Writings on Korean Epigraphy)" and the Writings of Hong Ryangho, the Mujangsa Temple epigraph was written by Kim Yukjin, though the inscription says only that he dedicated it. Since the characters are so similar to the writings of Wang Hsi-chih himself, some think the inscription is a collection of characters copied from the writings of Wang. A part of the inscription was discovered about a hundred years ago by Kim Chonghui, the great calligraphic master, bearing three characters very similar to ones in the introduction of the "Nanjonggo." This inscription was introduced by Kim Chonghui to his Chinese teacher, Ong Pangkang, and became widely known and admired in China. Even as a collection of the characters from Wang, it still is remarkable for its faithfulness to the original.

Another ancient inscription, the calligrapher of which is known, is also in the *Haeng*-style of Wang Hsi-chih, written on the monument of a Buddhist priest, Sinhaeng Sonsa (813), powerfully but elegantly by Sok Yongop. Also outstanding is the epigraph on the mounment of Pojosonsa, the *Hae*-characters of which were written by Kim Won and the *Haeng*-characters by Kim Onkyong. Kim Won's *Hae* characters are written with strong dignified brush-strokes. The *Haeng*-characters are as dignified as the *Hae*, though also in the Wang-style. Notwithstanding, the inscription is one of the most excellent epigraphs of the Silla period.

Choe Chiwon, the famous literary man who went to China to study, passed the national examination, even got an official post in the Tang government but afterwards came back to Korea, was also notable for his calligraphy, though his calligraphy was far behind his literary fame. The inscription of the monument of Chingam Sonsa is especially noted for its high dignity and strong brush-strokes in the Ou-style *Hae*. Choe Indon, whose writing was gentle and neat, was also on a level with his cousin, Choe Chiwon. These were typical artists of the Silla age. There was also a calligrapher, Kim Saeng, who was as celebrated in Silla as Wang Hsi-chi was in China. It is regrettable that nothing remains of his writing except a collection of the characters taken by Sok Somok from his inscription of the monument of Paekwol-saun, a quotation from Choe Indon of the Koryo period. Though it was written in the Wang-style *Haeng*, neither in dignity nor in quality does it live up to his fame. This may be because of adequate copying or clumsy carving, and of course, he cannot be definitively judged by this one inscription. It is to be regretted that there are no other verified remains of his writing.

Another outstanding inscription of Silla is that of the monument of Wollang Sonsa, strictly and correctly written by Sok Sumong in the style of Tang. The unknown calligrapher of the inscription on the Powol Tower of Sucholhwasang expressed high dignity in the correct and solemn *Hae*-characters in the Ou-style. Had it not been defaced it would be the finest work of Silla and of Korean epigraphy, comparable to works of the three great masters of Tang.

Koryo Dynasty

Although the use of Chinese characters became even more widespread in this period than in Silla, little of its calligraphy has been left to posterity. Koryo, as we have said, inherited from Silla, the Ou-style *Hae*-writing and the Wang-style *Haeng*.

Yi Hanchu's inscription of Taehyong Taesa, written in the Ou-style, has some epigraphic characteristics though the writing is a little vulgar. The *Tongguk Kumsokpyong* (Korean Epigraphic Review) comments that the inscription of Popkyongdaesa written by Ku Choktal is "powerful and keen." The *Sochong* remarks that there is an inheritance from the Chinese Northern dynasty and that the brushstroke is odd but fine. Although somewhat unskillfully following the Ou Yang-tung of China, there is something in it of the Northern dynasty. Yu Hunyul's inscription of Muwi-sa Temple, said by the *Tongguk Kumsokpyong* to be in the Yen Chenching style, is not in the Yen-style but the Ou-style and in fact is close to Ou Yang-tung's own writing. Also, according to the same book, Chang Soyol's inscription of Chinjongdaesa is so poor in the Yen-style and the Yu Kongkwon-style. However, the fact is that it is not in the Yen-style but in a style close to Wang Hsi-chih's and Yu Shihnan's writings, and is a very elegant masterpiece of Koryo Inscriptions.

Other outstanding calligraphers of the Koryo dynasty were Han Yun, Chae Chungsun, An Minha, O Onhu, Kim Koung, Paek Hyonne and Min Sangje. All of them were masters of the Ou-style. Yi Wonpu wrote in the combind style of Yu Shihnan and Ou Yanghsun. The most famous and outstanding calligrapher of the time was Sok Tanyon, who wrote *Hae*-characters in the Yen-style and the *Haeng*-characters in the Wang-style. The oldest Korean remains in the Yen-style are the works of this calligrapher, who studying for himself, succeeded in mastering the Yen-style in the midst of the overwhelming influence of the Ou-style.

King Chungson, the 26th monarch of Koryo, having abdicated the throne to King Chungsuk went to Peiping, where he erected the *Monkwondang* (House of Ten-Thousand Books) and was in close contact with Chao Tzu-ang, the master calligrapher of Yuen to whom he introduced the Korean calligrapher, Yi Cheyen. Through Yi, the writing style of Chao Tzu-ang (also called Songsol) was introduced and swept Korean calligraphy, holding sway until the beginning of the Yi dynasty. Yi Am and Yi Cheyon, making the Songsol-style their own, became the first great masters of Koryo calligraphy. Other remarkable calligraphers in the Songsol-style were Han Yu, Kwon Chu and the Chinese brothers, Sol Changsu and Sol Mongsu, who became naturalized Koreans. Noticeable calligraphers, not of the Songsol school, were Chae Yudan, who wrote *Hae*-characters in the Ou-style, Choe Son, master of *Hae*-writing, and Kwon Chunghwa, who was distinguished in *Ye*-writing. Hong Kwan was also famous in that period, but no remains of his works are left.

Yi Dynasty

The Songsol-style continued to dominate the early Yi period. Such books as the *Chonjamun* (A Thousand Characters—primary reader on Chinese characters), the *Chokpyokpu* (famous Chinese poetry), and others, were written in the Songsol-style, reproduced by the order of the government, and were widely spread among the people. Even then in the reign of King Sejong the Wang-style was decreed the standard for government copywriters, the mainstream of calligraphy was always the Songsol-style. Prince Anpyong, the third son of King Sejong, having mastered the Songsol style, was a

↑ Gold Crown and Two Pendants
Excavated from Kumgwanchong (Gold Crown Tomb), Kyongju, Kyongsang Pukto
Height 17.50″ ; Diameter 7.25″
Old Silla dynasty (350~450)

↑ Various Gold Pendants
Excavated from Kumgwanchong (Gold Crown Tomb), Kyongju, Kyongsang Pukto.
Old Silla dynasty (350〜450)

↑ Two Pairs of Gold Ear Pendants
Excavated from Tomb No. 52, Hwangu, Kyongju, Kyongsang Pukto.
Length 3.19″ (left) ; 2.75′ (right)
Old Silla dynasty (5th~6th century)

↑ Ornaments (Glass Beads)
Excavated from Kumgwanchong (Gold Crown Tomb), Kyongju, Kyongsang Pukto.
Old Silla dynasty (5th~6th century)

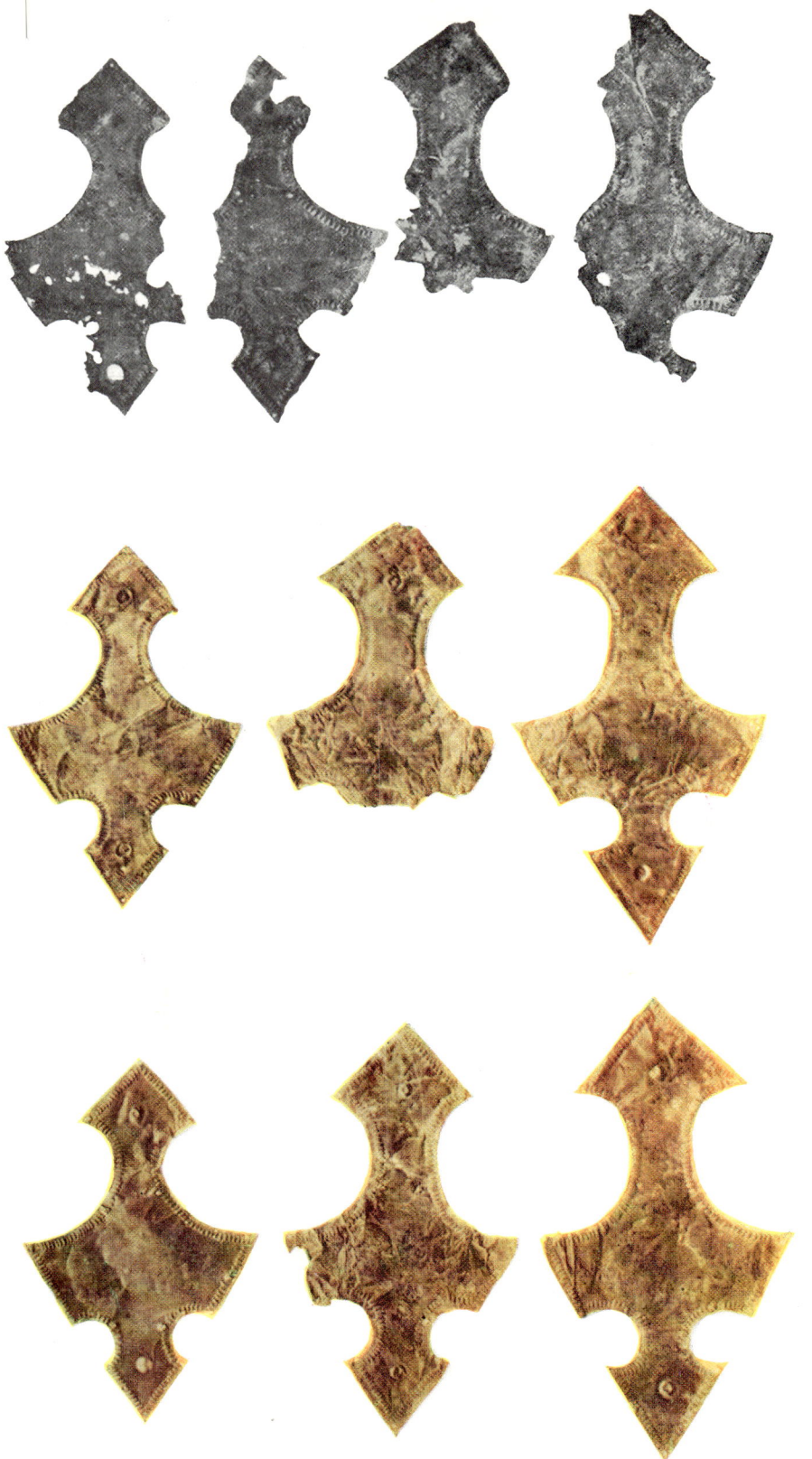

↑ Gold and Silver Cross-Shaped Ornaments
Excavated from Kumgwanchong (Gold Crown Tomb), Kyongju, Kyongsang Pukto.
Height 4.31″~7.00″; Width 2.94″~3.61″
Old Silla dynasty (350~450)

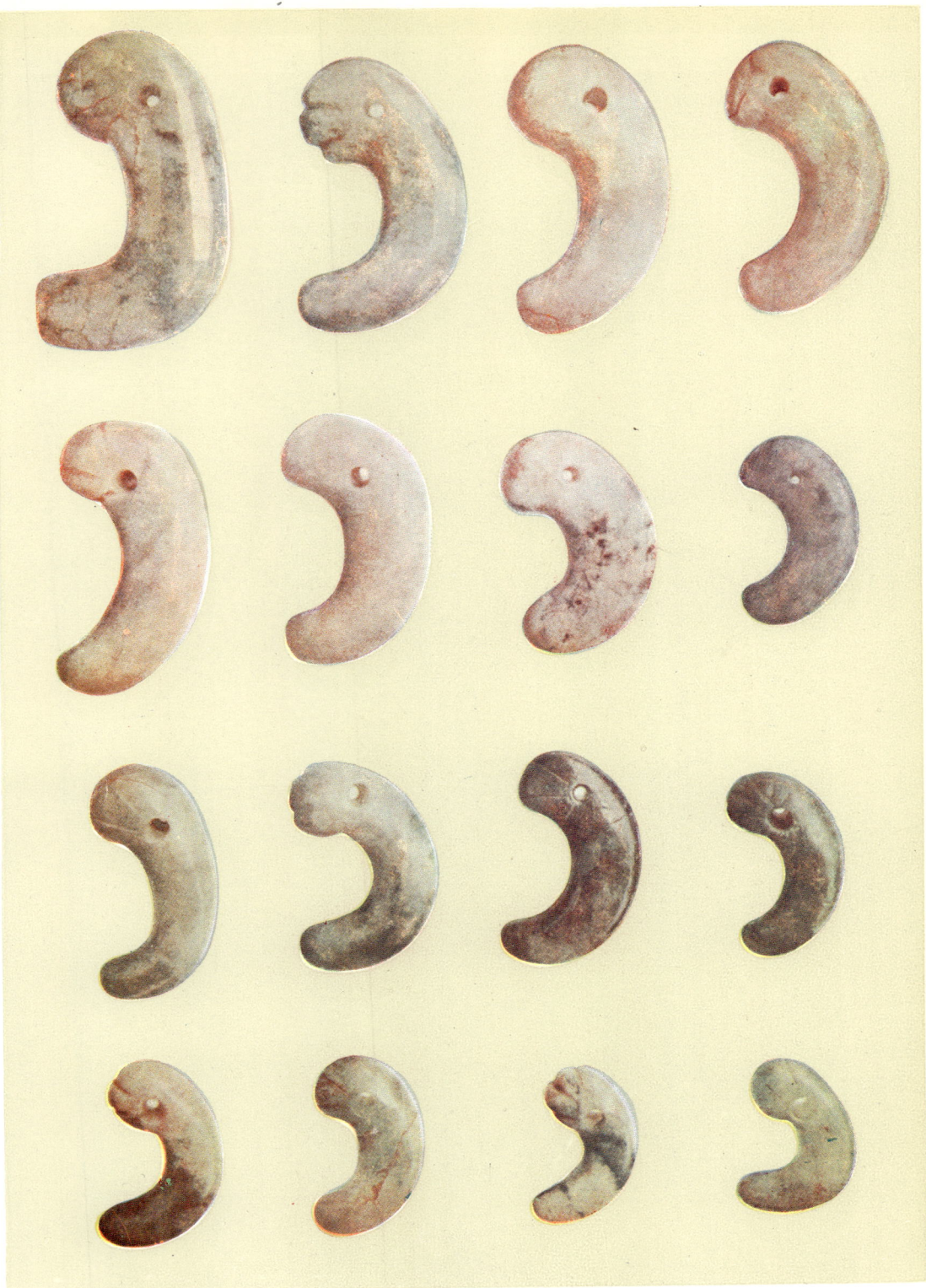

↑ Comma-Shaped Jewels
Excavated in Kumgwanchong (Gold Crown Tomb), Kyongju, Kyongsang Pukto.
Old Silla dynasty (350〜450)

↑ Toksu Palace Museum of Fine Arts, Seoul

↓ Kyongbok Palace Museum, Seoul

Corridor of Toksu Palace Museum of Fine Arts ↓

← **Kyongju Museum**
  Kyongju, Kyongsang Pukto

Puyo Museum
  Puyo, Chungchong Namdo →

← **Kongju Museum**
  Kongju, Chungchong Namdo

Showroom of Toksu Palace Museum of Fine Arts →

↓ Printing block of the complete collection of the Buddhist Scriptures preserved in Haein-sa Temple. Made in Koryo dynasty.

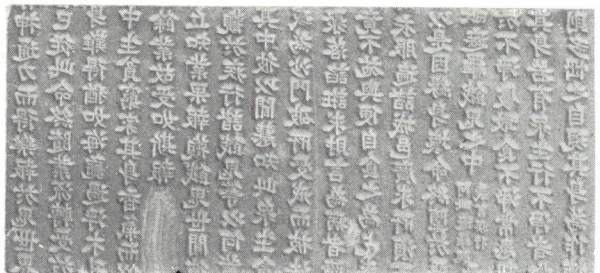

↓ Preserving room of the printing blocks of the complete collection of the Buddhist Scriptures, Haein-sa Temple

↓ A Page Printed by the Above

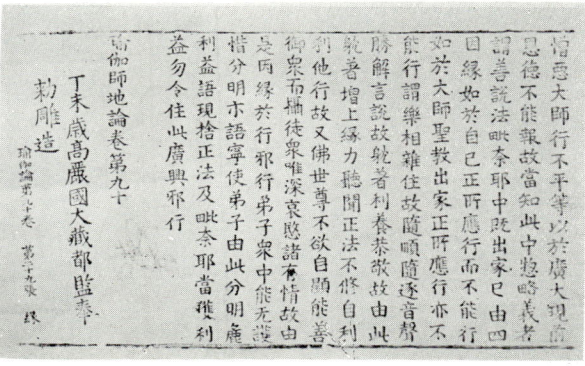

← Parts of the 80,000 printing blocks preserved in Chondung-sa Temple, Kanghwado Island

↑ A printing block of the complete collection of the Buddhist Scriptures preserved in Chondung-sa Temple.

Another Ancient Printing Block
↓ Preserved in Keryong Kap-sa Temple, Chungchong Namdo.

Sundial
→ Made of copper, in the reign of King Sejong.

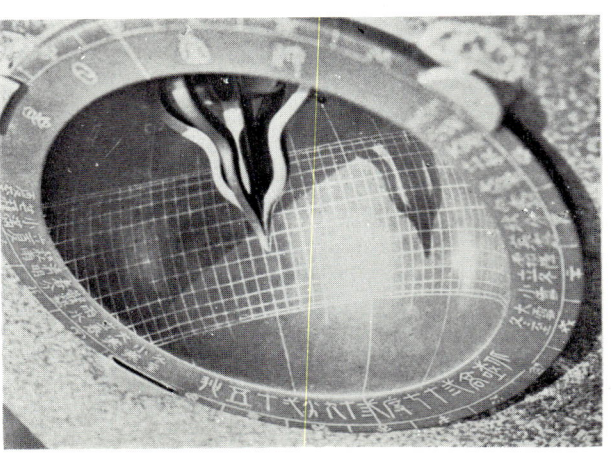

Rainfall measure
  Sejong, the fourth king of Yi dynasty, ordered to make a rainfall measure for each province, for the first time in Korea and in the world—in fact, 200 years prior to the Western countries.

↑ Hour-Glass
  Also made in the reign of King Sejong. It has various chimes to tell hours.

An 18th Century Map of Kyong-sang-Do
  From an atlas, "New Revised Edition of Tongguk Yojisungnam."

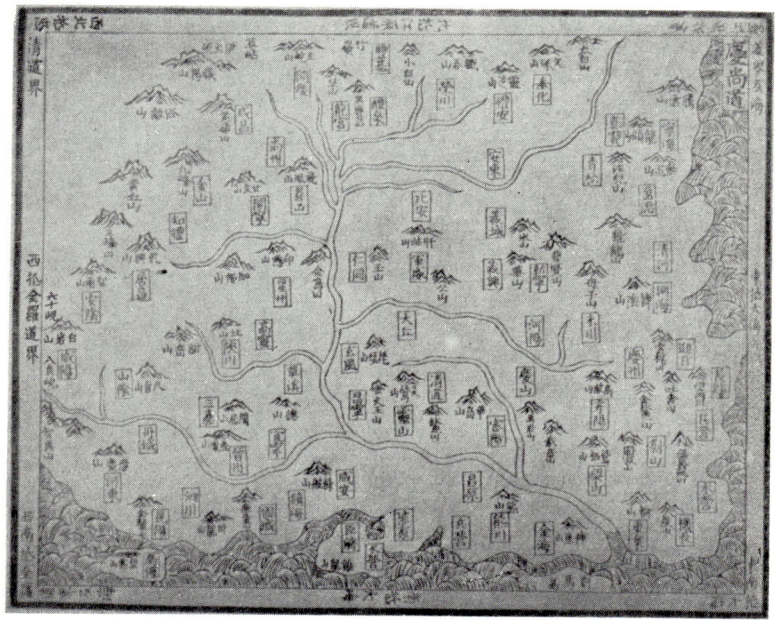

"Taedong-Yoji-Chondo (Map of Korea)"
Made by Kim Chongho in Yi dynasty (1861).

Bronze Mirror with Figures and Tree in Relief
Diameter 7.69″
Koryo dynasty

Bronze Mirror with Decoration of Figures and Carriages
Diameter 9.54″
Lolang period (1st–2nd century)

↑
Bronze Mirror with Dragon in Relief
Diameter 6.80″, Koryo dynasty

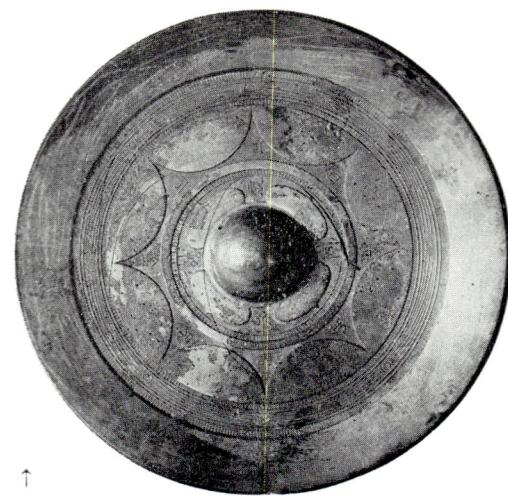

↑
Bronze Mirror Discovered in Sogamdong
Diameter 9.19″, Koryo dynasty

↑
Polygonal Bronze Mirror
Diameter 9.75″, Koryo dynasty

↑
Hexagonal Bronze Mirror with Twin Dragons
Diameter 11.32″, Koryo dynasty

↑
Bronze Mirror with Twin Phoenixes in Relief
Diameter 9.69″, Koryo dynasty

↑
Bronze Mirror with Twin Carps in Relief
Diameter 7.52″, Koryo dynasty

↑
Bronze Mirror with Utopian Landscape in Relief
Diameter 8.59″, Koryo dynasty

↑
Bronze Mirror with Floral Decoration in Relief
Diameter 3.52″, Koryo dynasty

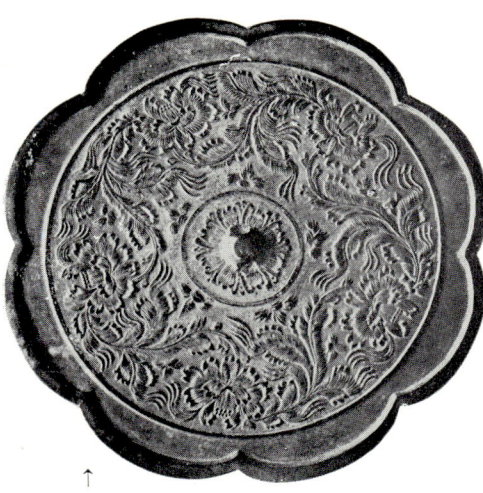

↑
Octagonal Flower-Shaped Mirror
Diameter 8.59″, Koryo dynasty

↑
Bronze Mirror with Figures and Landscape in Relief
Diameter 10.68″, Koryo dynasty

↑
Bronze Mirror with Flying Mandarin Ducks in Relief
Diameter 6.94″, Koryo dynasty

↑
Bronze Mirror with Lucky Animals in Relief
Diameter 5.15″, Koryo dynasty

Bronze Wall Mirror in the Shape of Bell
Length 6.68″; Width 4.41″
Koryo dynasty

Bronze Hand Mirror
Diameter 4.95″; Length, including handle, 8.83″
Koryo dynasty

Square Bronze Mirror
Length 5.19″; Width 5.37″
Koryo dynasty

Cross-Shaped Bronze Mirror
Diameter 4.53″
Koryo dynasty

↑ Iron-Made Mirror Stand with Gilt Bronze Ornaments
Height 9.29″, Koryo dynasty

↑ Iron-Made Mirror Stand with Incised Decoration Filled with Stering Silver
Height 10.11″, Koryo dynasty

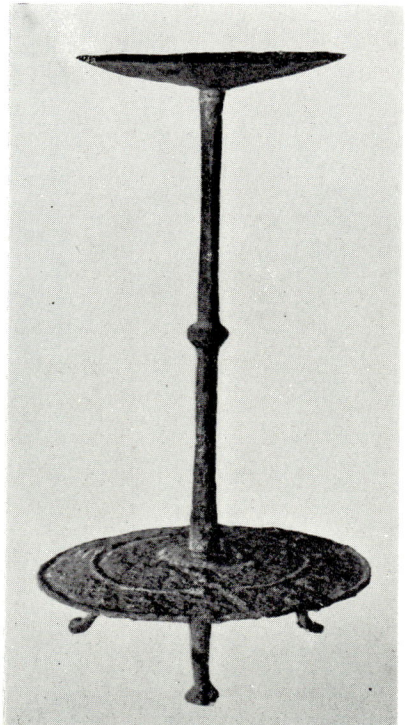 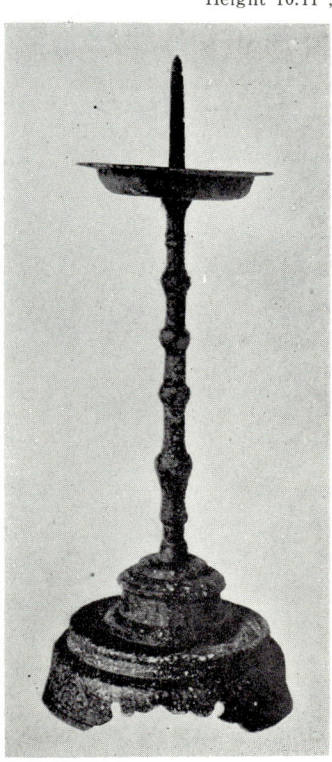 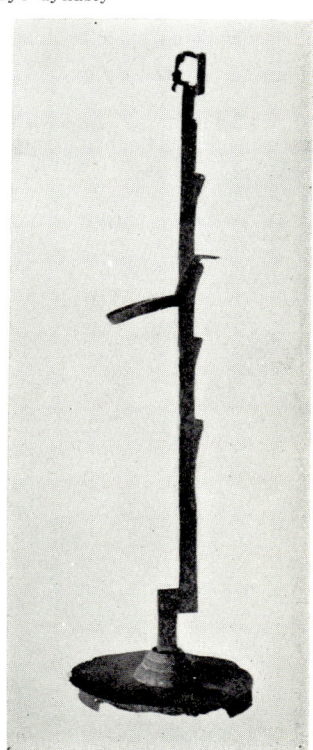

↑ Iron-Made Candle Stick
Height 18.97″, Koryo dynasty

↑ Bronze-Made Candle Stick
Height 13.95″, Koryo dynasty

↑ Bronze-Made Candle Stick
Height 32.27″, Koryo dynasty

↑ Bronze Drinking Bowl
Diameter 6.62″; Height 2.27″
Koryo dynasty

↑ Gilt Bronze Lock Set
Length 8.59″; Width 8.59″
Koryo dynasty

↑ Bronze Water-Pourer with Incised
Decoration Filled with Gold
Diameter 5.13″; Height 14.36″
Koryo dynasty

Bronze Wine Pot with Cover
Diameter 6.32″; Height, including cover, 10.02″
↓ Koryo dynasty

↑ Bronze Bowl and Cover
Diameter 6.44″; Height, including cover, 5.19″
Koryo dynasty

↑ Ornamental Bronze Plate for a Coffin
Figure of a woman is painted.
Koryo dynasty

↑ Bronze Razor
Length 8.89"
Koryo dynasty

Ancient Tools (From left to right)
Candle scissors, ordinary scissors, pincers, tweezers, all are made of bronze.
↓ Koryo dynasty

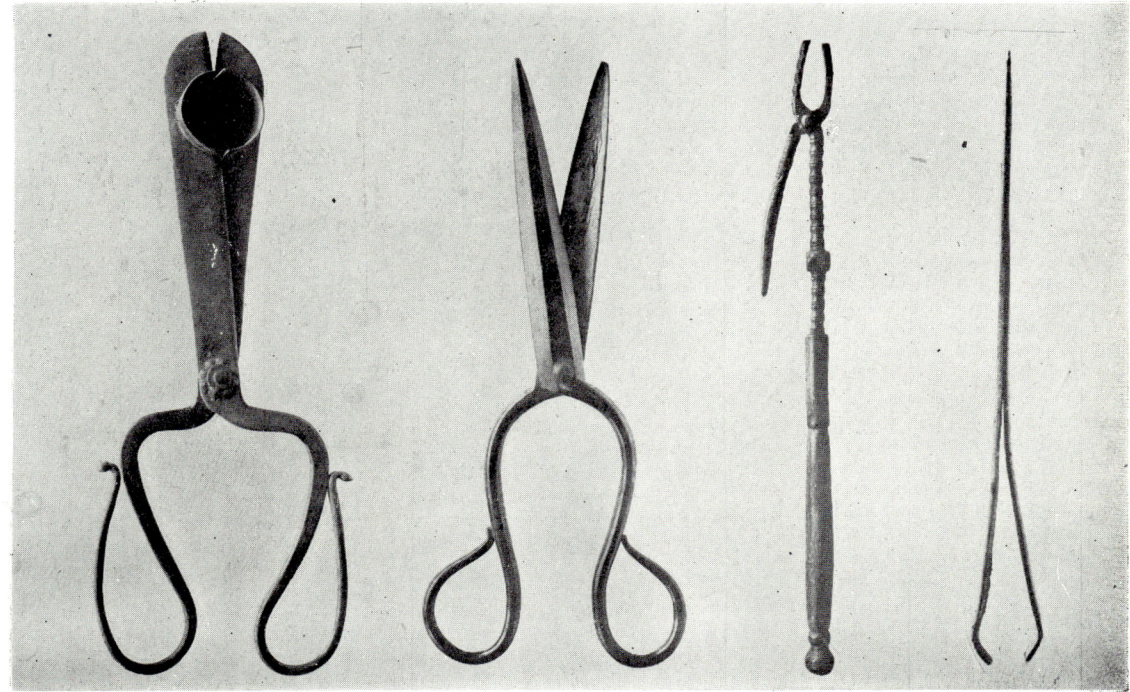

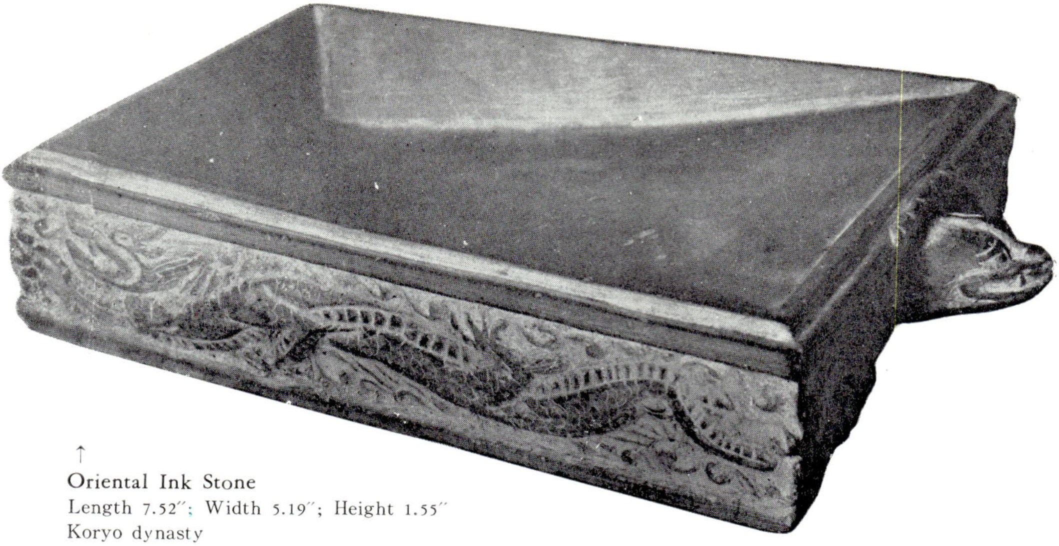

↑
Oriental Ink Stone
Length 7.52″; Width 5.19″; Height 1.55″
Koryo dynasty

↑
Oriental Ink Stone
Length 7.16″; Width 4.12″; Height 0.84″
Koryo dynasty

Stone Drinking Bowl
Diameter 6.80″; Height 2.63″
Koryo dynasty
↓

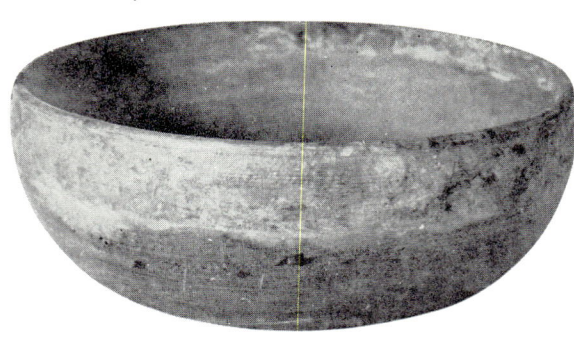

← **Wine Pot Made of Stone**
Height, including cover, 8.95″
Koryo dynasty

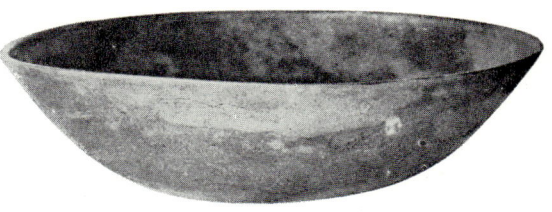

↑
Stering Silver Bowl with Incised Decoration
Diameter 4.35″; Height 13.1″
Koryo dynasty

↑
Stering Silver Bowl with Incised Decoration of Eight Flower Petals
Diameter 4.12″; Height 11.99″
Koryo dynasty

↑
Stering Silver Wine Cup Stand
(See right-hand.)

↑
Side View of the Left Stand and a Wine Cup on It
Diameter of the stand 6.50″; Height, including cup, 5.05″, Koryo dynasty

↑
Oil Pot
Lacquerware with inlaid decoration of mother-of-pearl.
Koryo dynasty

↑
Rosary Case and Cover
Lacquerware decorated with inlaid mother-of-pearl.
Koryo dynasty

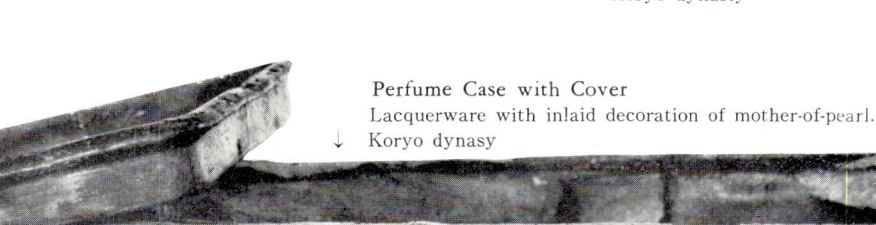

Perfume Case with Cover
Lacquerware with inlaid decoration of mother-of-pearl.
↓ Koryo dynasy

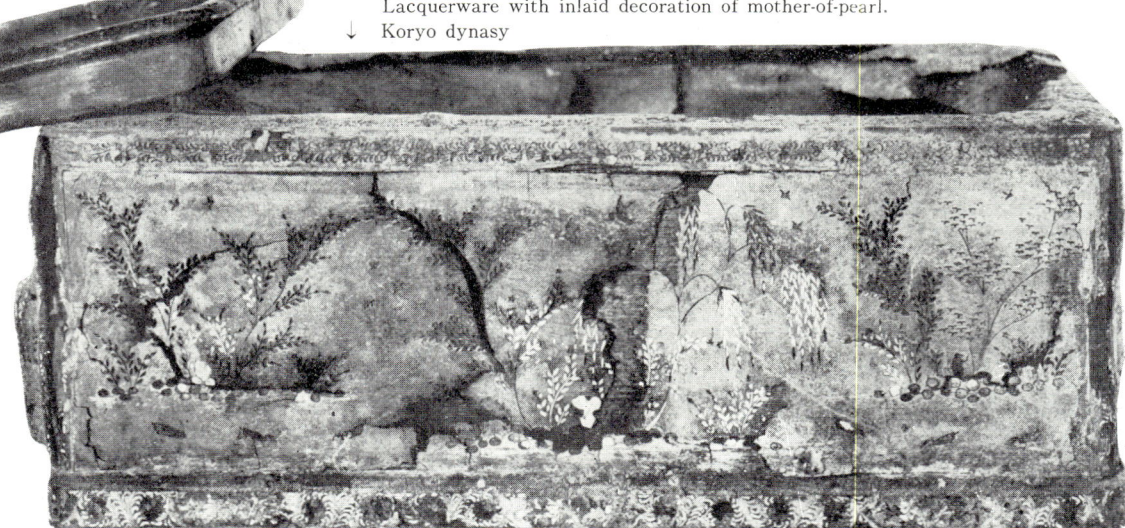

↑ Lacquered Basket with Color Design
Excavated from Chehyopchong (Painted Basket Tomb), Taedong, Pyongan Namdo.
Length 15.27″; Width 7.70″
Lolang dynasty (350~440)

↑ Cloudy Patterns of the Lacquered Table
Excavated from Chehyopchong (Painted Basket Tomb), Taedong, Pyongan Namdo.
Lolang dynasty (0〜100)

Urn
Imprinted floral pattern and yellowish green glaze.
Excavated in Kyongju, Kyongsang Pukto.
Height 6.30″
→ Silla dynasty (7th~8th century)

↑ Vehicle-Shaped Vessel
Whitish gray Kaya pottery
Excavated from an ancient tomb in Kyongsang Namdo.
Height 7.32″ ; Length 10.12″
Three Kingdoms period (6th century)

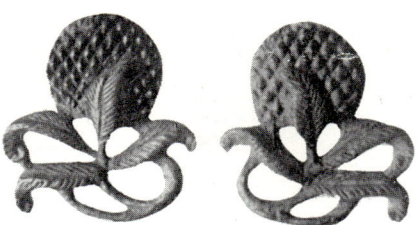

↑ Gilt Bronze Ornaments

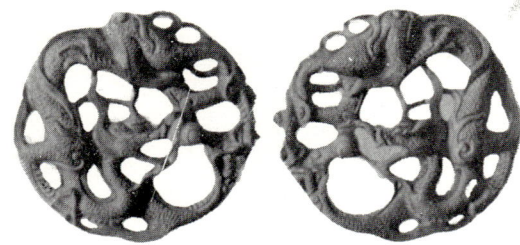

↑ Gold Ornaments

↑ Gold Ornaments

↑ Gold Ornaments

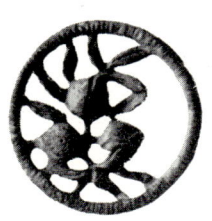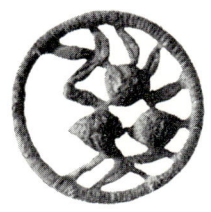

↑ Gilt Bronze Ornaments

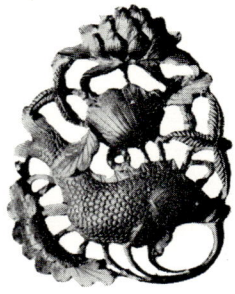

↑ Gold Ornaments

↑ Gilt Bronze Ornaments

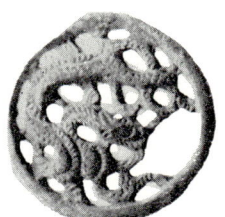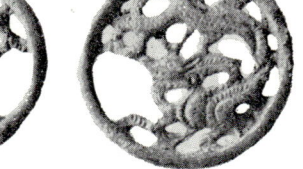

↑ Gilt Bronze Ornaments

All the above ornaments are about actual sizes. Koryo dynasty.

↑ Silver Beads
Discovered at a Silla's tomb in Chinju, Kyongsang Namdo.

↑ Comma-Shaped Jade and Golden Ear Pendant
Discovered at a tomb of Imna period located in Chinju.

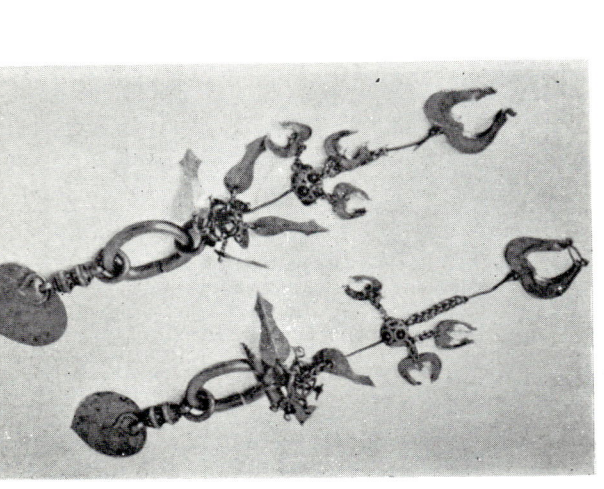

↑ Golden Ornaments of a Crown
Excavated from the Chung-sang Tomb of a Paekche King. Paekche period

Golden Ear Pendants in the Shape of Bamboo Leaves
Excavated from the Gold Crown Tomb, Kyongju.
Old Silla dynasty
↓

← Ear Pendants
Gold with glass bead ornaments
Excavated from the Gold Crown Tomb, Kyonju.
Length 3.63″
Old Silla dynasty (5th-6th century)

↑ Gilt Silver Pocket Knife
Length 9.06″
Koryo dynasty

Gold-Decorated Ornamental Tube
Length 2.80″
↓ Koryo dynasty

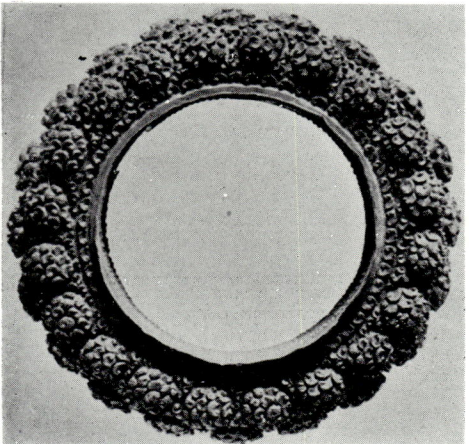

↑ Gilt Silver Bracelet
Diameter 3.58″
Koryo dynasty

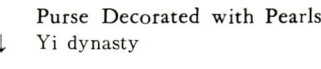

↑ Dragon Head Ornament, Bronze
Length 3.58″
Koryo dynasty

Fan Decorated with Pearls
↓ Yi dynasty

Purse Decorated with Pearls
↓ Yi dynasty

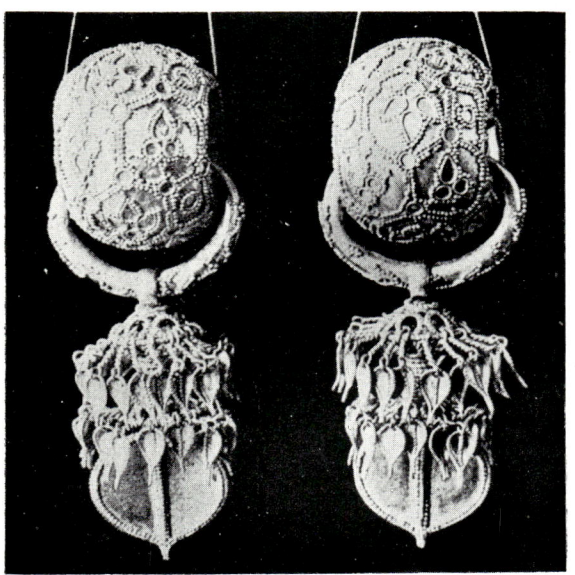

↑ Gold Ear Pendants
Excavated from Pubu (husband and wife) Tomb of Silla dynasty, Kyongju.

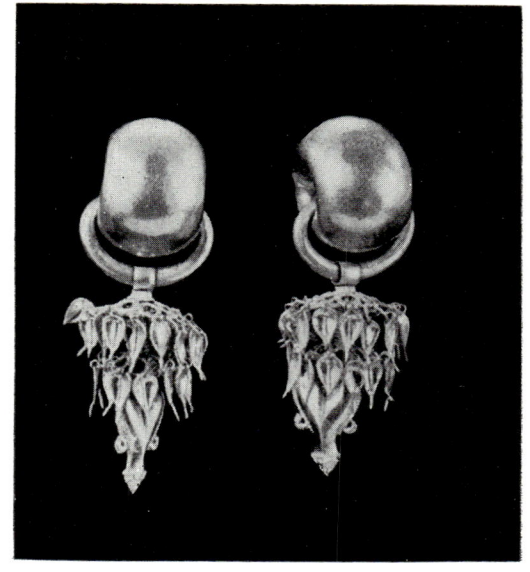

↑ Gold Ear Pendants
Excavated from a tomb of old Silla dynasty (5th-6th century).

← Rings, Gold
Excavated from Gold Crown Tomb, Kyongju. Height 0.25″; Diameter 0.69-0.75″
Old Silla dynasty (5th-6th century)

Bracelets, Gold
Excavated from the Gold Crown Tomb, Kyongju.
Height 0.19″; Diameter 3.13″
↓ Old Silla dynasty (5th-6th century)

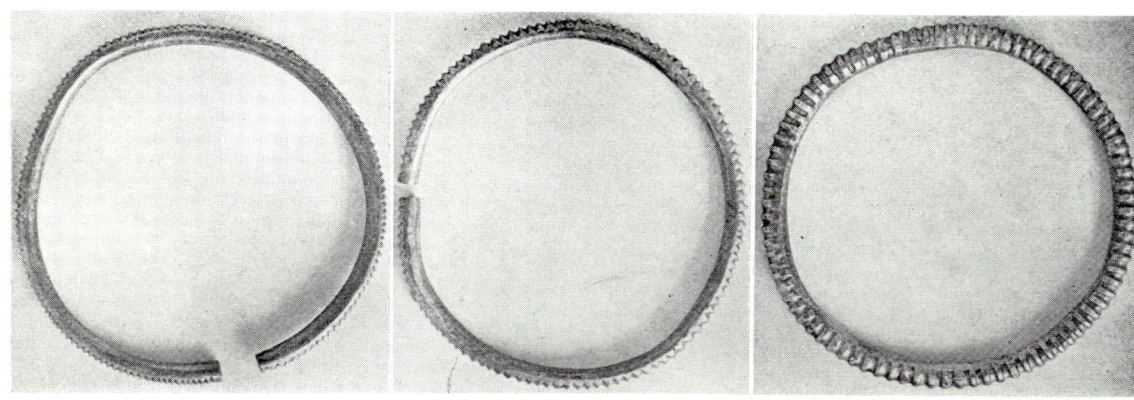

↑ Buckles, Silver
The left with incised decoration.   The right with decoration in relief.
Length, each, 4.89″
Koryo dynasty

↑ Gilt Bronze Buckles
With decoration in relief.
Length 4.17″
Koryo dynasty

Gilt Bronze Ornaments of a Coffin
Openwork. Length 8.35″; Width 10.73″
↓ Koryo period

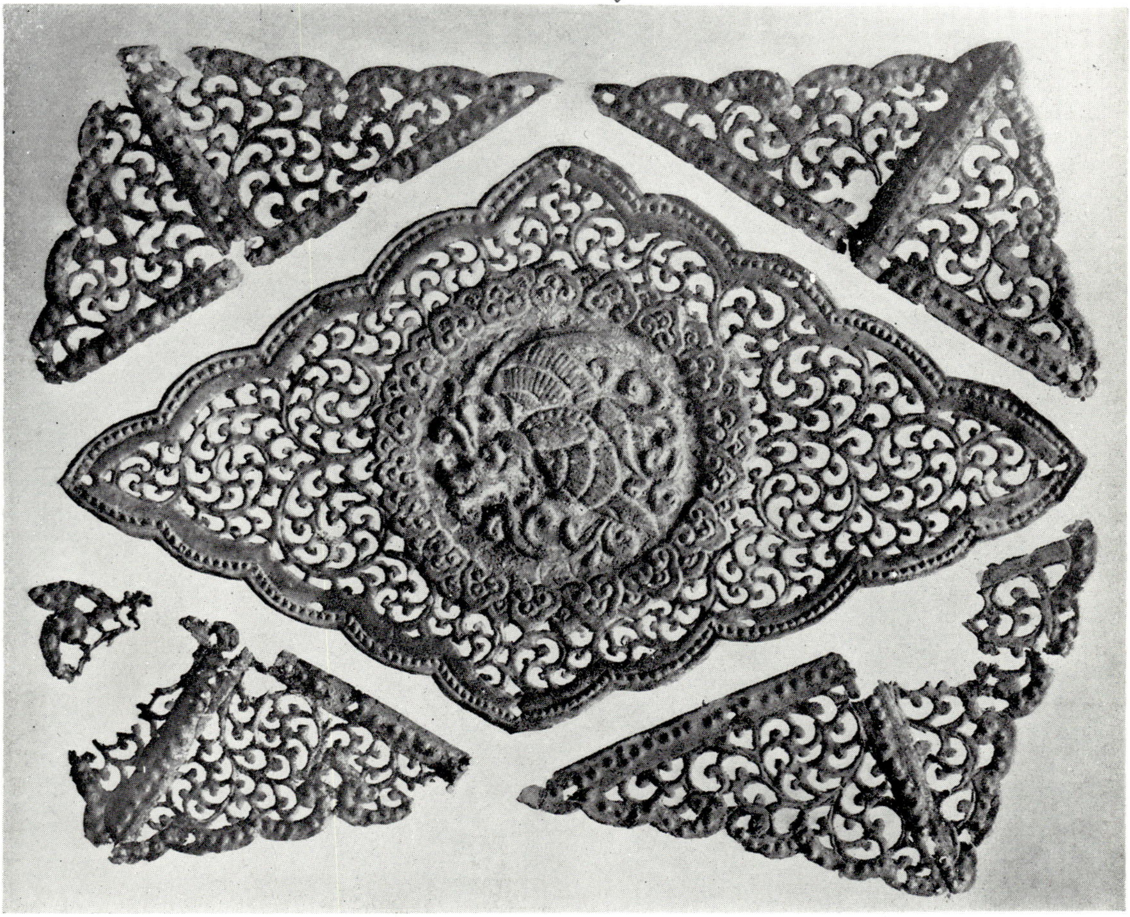

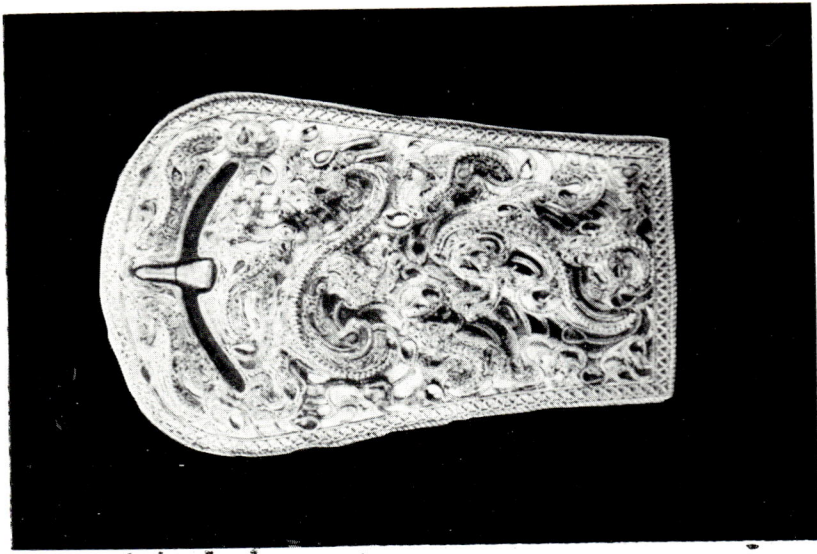

← Buckle
Gold with turquoise ornaments.
Excavated from Tomb No. 9.
Pyongyang.
Height 2.56″; Width 3.75″
Lolang period (1st-2nd century)

Gilt Bronze Ornament with Openwork →
Excavated from a Koguryo tomb.

Ornamental Part of Crown
Excavated from Chungsang Tomb of Paekche kingdom. Nungsanni, Puyo.
Left: The obverse
Right: The reverse
↓

← Tiles
Excavated at the riverside of the Taedong, Pyongyang, Pyongan Namdo.
Lolang period

← Tiles
Used in the Tomb of Chang Mui, the Governor of Taifang Province,
Four Chinese Colonial period

↑ Tile (Left; Upper-View, Right; Side-View)
Excavated From the Chonchu Tomb of Koguryo
Koguryo period

↑ Tile (Left; Upper-View, Right; Side-View)
Excavated from Mount Chonpung
Four Chinese Colonial period

↑
Tile
 Discovered at the site of Sepodong Fortress, Anbyon-gun, Hamgyong Namdo. Okcho Period

↑
Tile
 Excavated at Taedong-gun, Pyongan Namdo, the old territory of Lolang. Lolang period

↑ Tiles (Left; the Obverse, Right; the Reverse)
 Discovered at Pungsan-gun, Hwanghae-do, the old territory of Taifang Province. Four Chinese Colonial Provinces period.

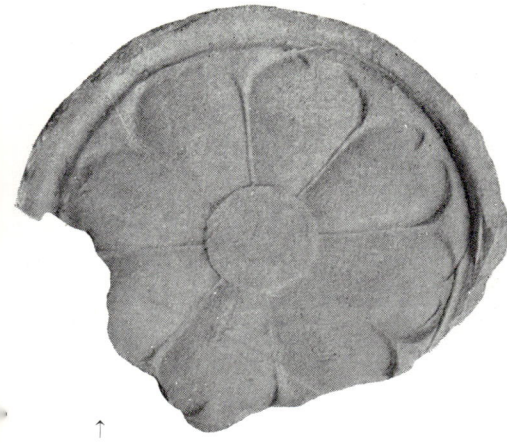

↑
Tile
 Discovered at Puyo, Chungchong Namdo. Paekche dynasty

↑
Tile
 Discovered at the ruins of Kaya State's palace in Kyongsang Pukto. Kaya period.

↑ Landscape Tile
  Excavated at the site of a temple in Puyo.
  Paekche dynasty (7th century)

↑ Phoenix Tile
  Excavated at the site of a temple in Puyo
  Paekche dynasty (7th century)

↑ Tile (face and side)
  Excavated at the lakeside of Anap, Kyongju.
  Silla dynasty

Tile
  Excavated at Kyongju.
↓ Silla dynasty

← Tile Used in the Five-Storey Pagoda of Sinnuk-sa Temple

↑
Tile
From an ancient tomb in Kyongju.
Silla dynasty

↑
Tile of the Ruined Sinbok-sa Temple
Silla dynasty

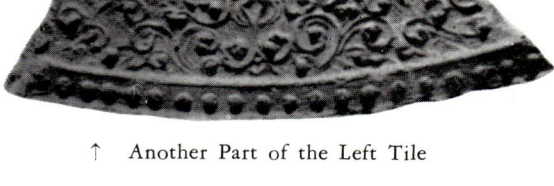

↑ Another Part of the Left Tile

↓ Another Part of the Left Tile

↑ Tile with Arabesque
Excavated from the lakeside of Anap around Kyongju.
Silla dynasty

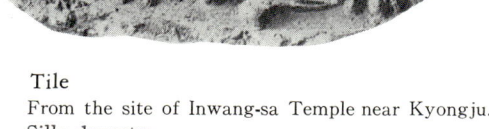

Tile
From the ruins of Sachonwang-sa Temple near Kyongju.
Silla dynasty
↓

Tile
From the site of Inwang-sa Temple near Kyongju.
Silla dynasty
↓

↑ Tiles
Excavated from Tosongni at the riverside of the Taedong, Pyongyang.
Koguryo period

↑ Tile
Discovered in Pyongyang.
Koguryo period

↑ Tile
Discovered at the site of Sansongni Fortress, south Manchuria. Koguryo period.

↑ Tile
From the Chonchu Tomb of Koguryo.
Koguryo period

← Tile
From Oesong, Pyongyang.
Koguryo period

Tile
From Tungkou, south Manchuria.
Koguryo period →

↑ Water Pot, Cover and Bowl
Celadon graze; reticulated, modelled and incised decoration.
Pot, Height 7″; Diameter, at base, 4.13″
Bowl, Height 3.5″; Diameter, at mouth, 7.19″. Koryo dynasty (12th century)

Wine Pot and Cover
Celadon glaze; modelled and incised decoration.
Height 12.12″; Diameter, at base, 3.37″
↓ Koryo dynasty (12th century)

Vase
Celadon glaze; incised decoration filled with white and black slips, and painted decoration in copper oxide.
Height 13.63″; Diameter, at base, 5.19″
↓ Koryo dynasty (13th century)

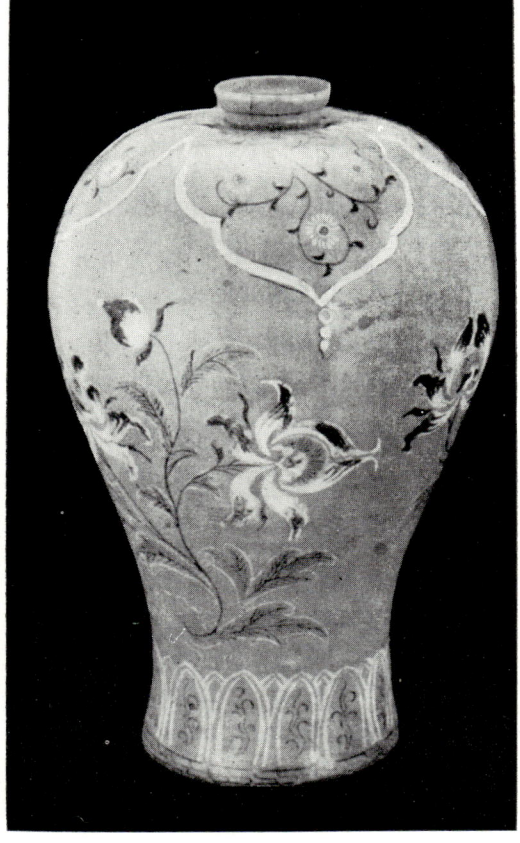

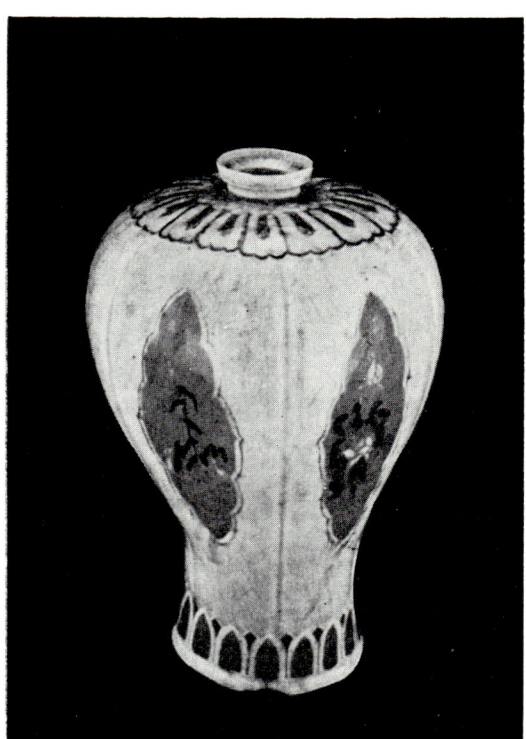

Vase
Koryo white ware; incised panels filled with celadon which have incised decorations filled with white and black slips.
Height 11.31″; Diameter, at base, 4.13″
Koryo dynasty (12th-13th century)

Wine Bottle and Cover
Koryo white ware; undecorated.
Height 12.5″; Diameter, at base, 3.31″
Koryo dynasty (13th-14th century)

Wine Cup and Stand
Koryo white porcelain; reticulated and incised decoration.
Height 4.94″; Diameter 5.19″
Koryo dynasty (11th-12th century)

Ovoid Incense Burner on Three Legs
Koryo white porcelain; modelled and perforated.
Height 3.5″; Diameter 3″
Koryo dynasty (11th century)

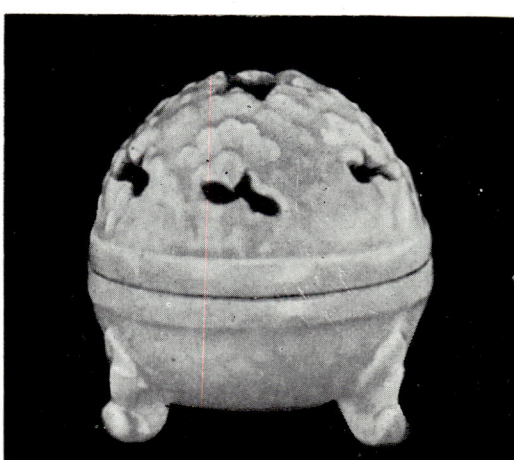

Tall Necked Wine Bottle
Celadon glaze; incised decoration filled with white and black slips.
Height 11.75″; Diameter, at base, 4.31″
Koryo dynasty (13th-14th century)
↓   The stopper is missing.

↑   **Jar with Flattened Sides**
Celadon glaze; stamped and incised decoration filled with white and black slips.
Height 11.63″; Diameter, at base, 4″
Koryo dynasty (13th-14th century)

Jar with Flattened Sides
Celadon glaze; stamped and incised decoration filled with white and black slips.
Height 10″; Diameter, at base, 4.5″
↓   Koryo dynasty (13th cenutry)

Jar with Slightly Flattened Sides
Celadon glaze; stamped and incised decorations filled with white and black slips.
Height 10.31″; Diameter, at base, 5.13″
↓   Koryo dynasty (mid-13th–early 14th century)

↑ Jar with Four Handles, and Cover
Celadon glaze; incised decoration filled with black and white slips.
Height 9.54″; Diameter 1.49″
Koryo dynasty.

↑ Vase
Celadon glaze; modelled and incised decoration filled with white and black slips.
Height 10.9″; Diameter, at base, 3.69″
Koryo dynasty (12th-13th century)

↑ Incense Burner
Celadon glaze; modelled and incised decoration
Height 6″; Diameter, at base, 4.81″
Koryo dynasty (11th-12th century).

↑ Vase
Cream colored porcelain; painted decoration in black.
Height 8.23″; Diameter, at shoulder, 5.73″
Koryo dynasty

↑ Vase
Celadon glaze; painted peony design in underglaze iron
Height 10.62″; Diameter, at shoulder, 6.56″
Koryo dynasty (mid-13th century)

↑ Vase
Vase with graffito tree peony design painted in black slip
Height 8.35″ ; Diameter, at trunk, 5.38″
Koryo dynasty (10th~13th century)

↑ Bottle
Temmoku glaze; design of spot
Height 7.75″ ; Diameter, at trunk, 6.44″
Koryo dynasty (10th~13th century)

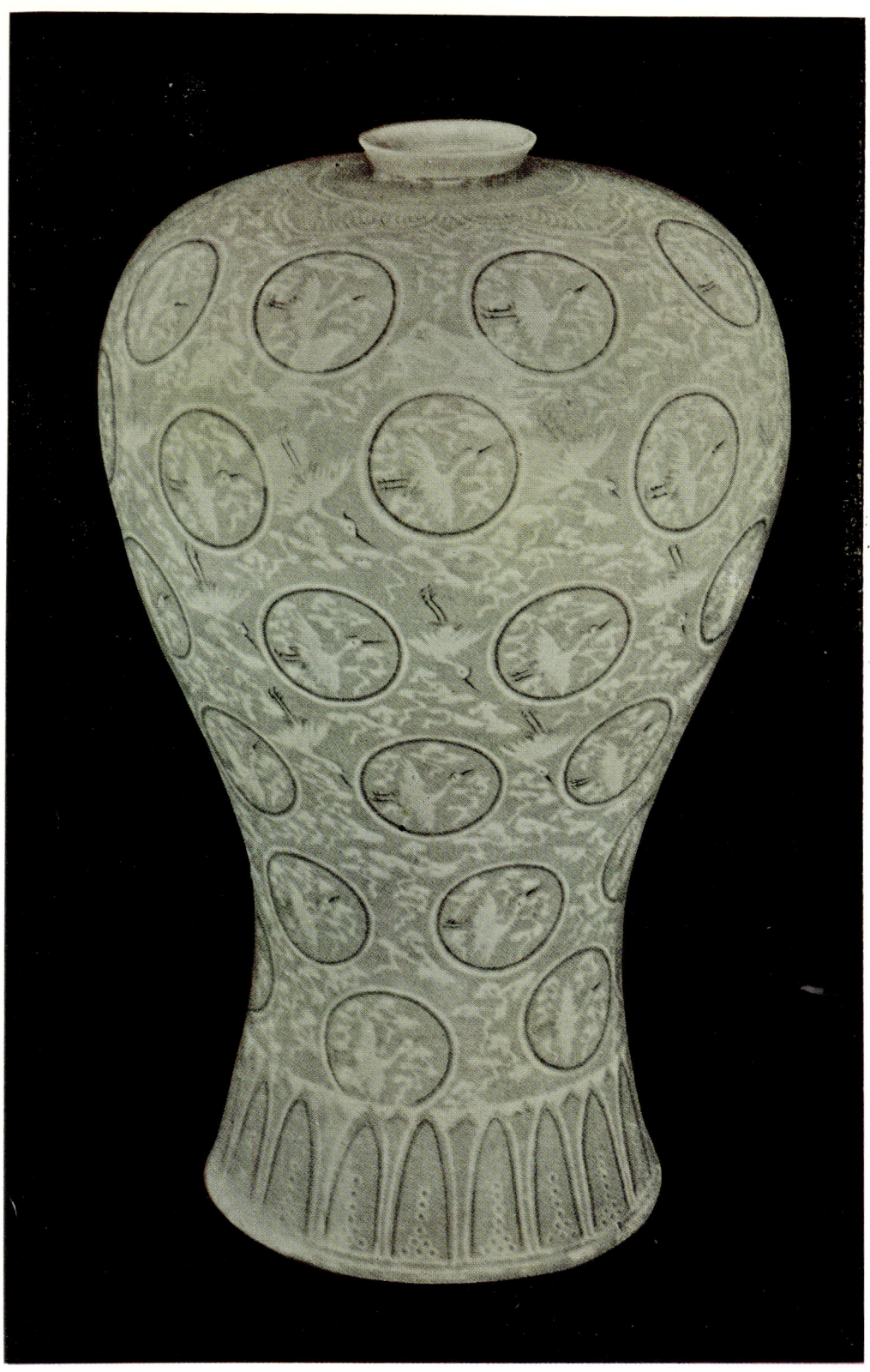

↑ Vase
Celadon glaze; incised decoration filled with white and black slips
Height 16.25″ ; Diameter 9.87″
Koryo dynasty (late 12th century)

↑ Vase
   Celadon glaze; inlaid twin phoenix design in underglaze iron
   Height 6.92″ ; Diameter 4.77″
   Koryo dynasty (13th century)

Vase
Celadon glaze; incised decoration.
Height 9″; Diameter, at base, 3″
↓ Koryo dynasty (12th century)

↑ **Jar**
Celadon glaze; incised decoration filled with black and white slips.
Height 5.91″
Koryo dynasty (11th-12th century)

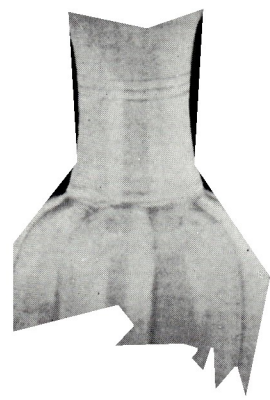

↑ **Circular Box without Cover**
Marbled celadon glaze.
Diameter 4.21″
Koryo dynasty

Water Jar
Celadon glaze; modelled, and incised decoration filled with white and black slips.
Height 7.88″; Diameter, at base, 6″
↓ Koryo dynasty (12th-13th century)

↑ **Bowl**
Celadon glaze; incised decoration filled with white slips.
Height 3.86″; Diameter 6.18″, at base, 3.74″
Koryo dynasty (13th century)

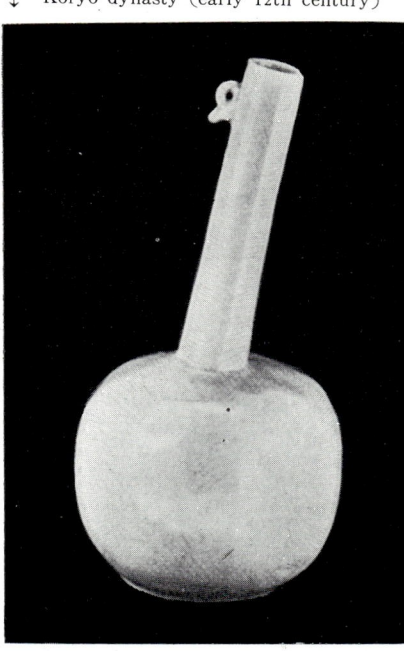

Wine Bottle
Celadon glaze; incised decoration.
Height 12.8″; Diameter, at base, 4″
↓ Koryo dynasty (early 12th century)

↑ **Round Box and Cover**
Celadon glaze; modelled and incised decoration.
Height 2.52″; Diameter 4.81″
Koryo dynasty (12th century)

Wine Bottle
Celadon glaze; undecorated.
Height 7.56″; Diameter, at base, 2.88″
↓ Koryo dynasty (early 12th century)

Wine Bottle
Celadon glaze; undecorated.
Height 9.88″; Diameter, at base, 2.3″
Koryo dynasty (early 12th century)
↓ A double gourd shape.

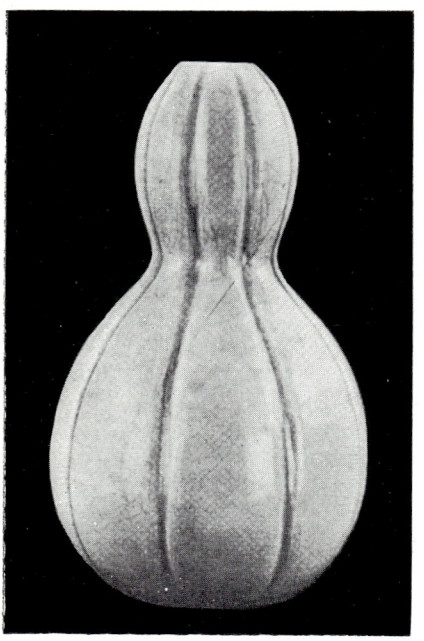

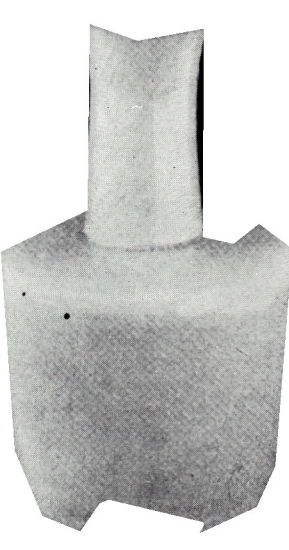

↑ Wine Cup and Stand
Celadon glaze; incised decoration.
Height 3.88″; Diameter 5.88″
Koryo dynasty (11th-12th century)

↑ Wine Cup and Stand
Celadon glaze; incised decoration.
Height 4.63″; Diameter 7.38″
Koryo dynasty (early 12th century)

Five Dishes →
Celadon glaze; undecorated.
Height 0.63″; Diameter 4″
Koryo dynasty (11th-12th century)
  They were probably intended to hold sauces.

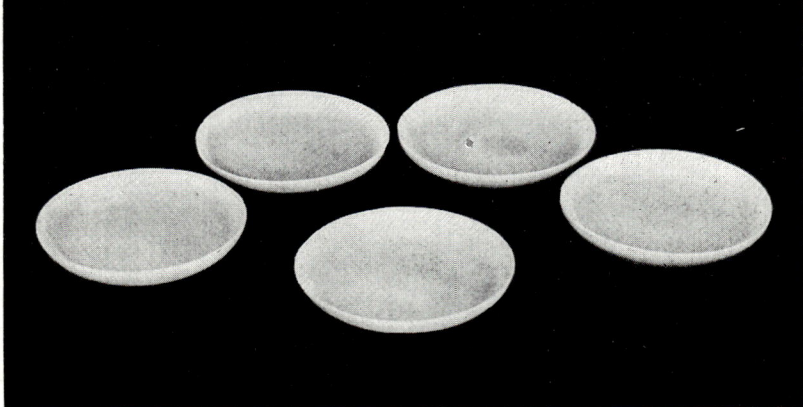

← Brush Stand
Celadon glaze; reticulated, modelled, incised and underglaze iron decorations.
Height 3.5″; Width 7″
Koryo dynasty (early 12th century)
  Dragon-heads are at both ends.

↑ **Incense Burner with a Reticulated Ball Cover**
Celadon glaze; reticulated, modelled, incised and underglaze iron and white slip decoration.
Height 6″; Width 4.9″
Koryo dynasty (12th–13th century)

Incense Burner
Celadon glaze; modelled, incised and underglaze iron decoration.
Height 7.19″; Diameter 6.25″
Koryo dynasty (12th century)
↓   A mythological beast is seated on the cover.

Writer's Water-Dropper
Celadon glaze; incised and white slip decoration.
Height 4″; Diameter, at base, 1.88″
Koryo dynasty (12th century)
↓   A lotus bud shape.

Incense Burner
Celadon glaze; modelled, incised and underglaze iron decoration.
Height 8.38″; Width 6.38″
↓   Koryo dynasty (11th-12th century)

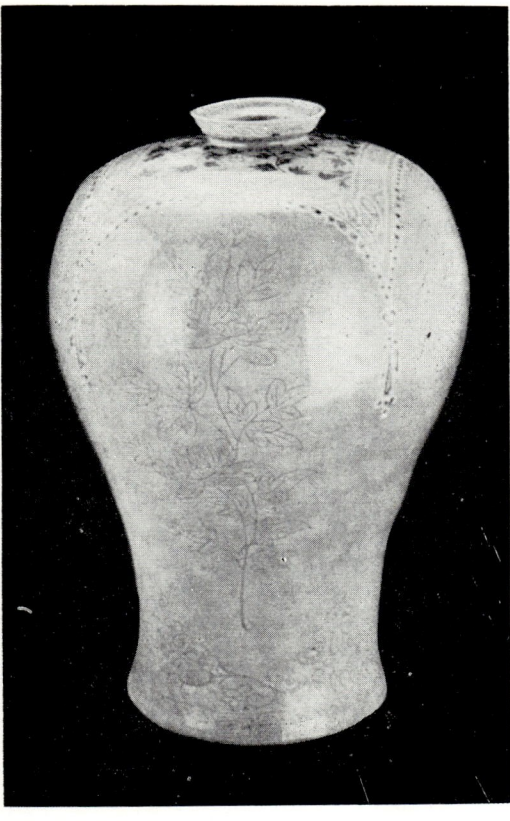

↑ Wine Pot and Stopper
Celadon glaze; incised decoration filled with white and black slips.
Height 13.69″; Diameter, at base, 3.88″
Koryo dynasty (late 12th century)

Wine Pot with Lid
Celadon glaze; incised decoration filled with white and black slips.
Height 8.38″; Diameter, at base, 3″
↓ Koryo dynasty (late 12th century)

↑ Maebyong Vase
Celadon glaze; incised and with incised decoration filled with white and black slips.
Height 13.75″; Diameter, at base, 6″
Koryo dynasty (12th-13th century)

←
Drinking Bowl
Celadon glaze; incised decoration filled with white and black slips.
Height 3.5″; Diameter 7.88″
Koryo dynasty (early 12th century)

Black is used only for the legs, beaks, eyes and tail feathers of four white cranes which are placed around the exterior.

Drinking Bowl
Celadon glaze; incised decoration filled with white and black slips.
Height 3.63″; Diameter 7.88″
Koryo dynasty (12th century)
→

Wine Cup and Stand
Celadon glaze; incised and with incised decoration filled with white and black slips.
Height 3.75″; Diameter 6.25″
↓ Koryo dynasty (12th-13th century)

Drinking Bowl
Celadon glaze; incised decoration filled with white and black slips.
Height 3.63″; Diameter 8″
↓ Koryo dynasty (13th-14th century)

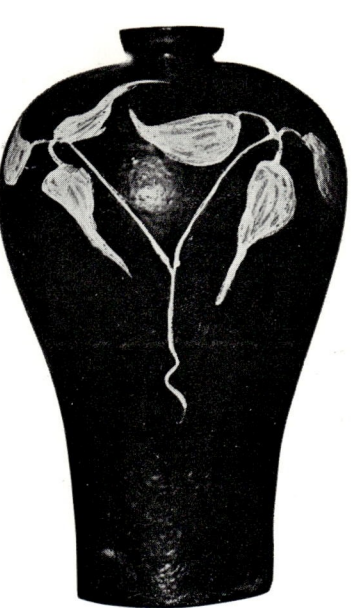

Vase →
Black ware; celadon glaze, decorated with underglaze iron oxide combined with ash, underglaze iron and incised lines filled with white slips.
Height 11.13″; Diameter, at base, 3.75″
Koryo dynasty (13th century)

← **Maebyong Vase**
Celadon glaze; painted in underglaze iron.
Height 11.25″; Diameter, at base, 3.75″
Koryo dynasty (late 13th-14th century)

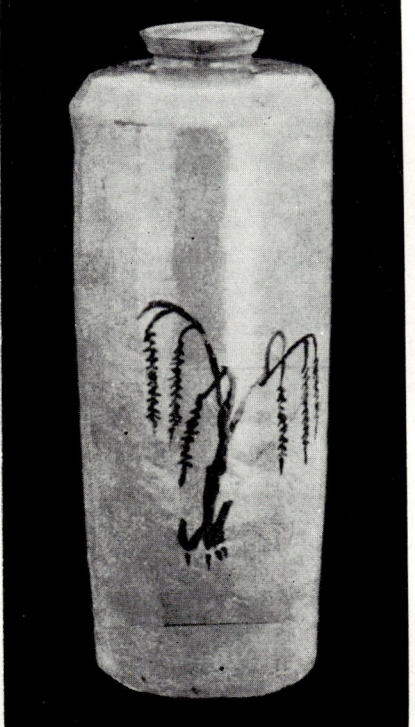

Drinking Bowl
Celadon glaze; incised decoration filled with white and black slips.
Height 2.62″; Diameter 7.75″
Koryo dynasty (12th century)
↓ The pomegranates also decorate the interior.

Drinking Bowl
Celadon glaze; incised and with incised decoration with white and black slips.
Height 2.5″; Diameter 6.87″
Koryo dynasty (12th century)
↓ The interior also has white chrysanthemums.

↑ **Cylindrical Wine Bottle**
Celadon glaze; painted in underglaze iron.
Height 12.44″; Diameter, at base, 4.31″
Koryo dynasty (13th-14th century)

Jar and Cover
Celadon glaze; incised decoration filled with white and black slips.
Koryo dynasty

Jar with Four Handles, and Cover
Celadon glaze; incised decoration filled with white and black slips.
Height 5.8″; Diameter 4.11″
Koryo dynasty

Tile Plate
Celadon glaze; incised decoration filled with white and black slips.
Length 9.42″; Width 11.94″; Height 0.12″
Koryo dynasty

Vase with Four Handles
Celadon glaze; modelled and incised decoration.
Height 9.38″; Diameter, at base, 3″
Koryo dynasty (12th century)

↑ **Vase with Lotus Decoration**
Celadon glaze; incised decoration.
Height 12.05″
Koryo dynasty

Writer's Water-Dropper
Celadon glaze; modelled and underglaze iron decoration.
Height 4″
Koryo dynasty (early 12th century)

Wine Pot and Lid
Celadon glaze; incised decoration filled with white and black slips.
Koryo dynasty (late 12th century)

↑ Wine Pot Shaped as a Tortoise-Dragon
Celadon glaze; modelled and incised decoration.
Height 0.63"; Diameter, at base, 4.25"
Koryo dynasty (11th-12th century)

↑ Wine Pot Shaped as a Carp-Dragon
Celadon glaze; modelled and incised decoration.
Height 9.5"; Diameter, at base, 4"
Koryo dynasty (end of 11th-early 12th century)

↑ Wine Pot and Cover
Celadon glaze; modelled and incised decoration.
Height 11.38"; Diameter, at base, 3.75"
Koryo dynasty (11th century)

↑ Wine Pot and Stopper
Celadon glaze; modelled and incised decoration.
Height 6.50"; Diameter, at base, 3.94"
Koryo dynasty (12th century)

Oil Bottle
Celadon glaze; incised decoration filled with white and black slips.
Height 1.88″; Diameter 3″
↓ Koryo dynasty (12th century)

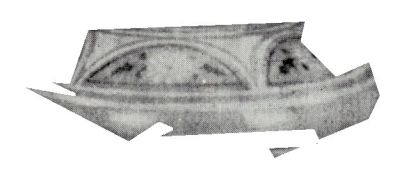

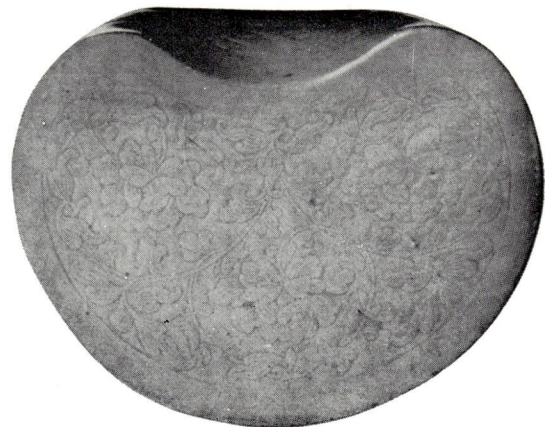

↑ **Pillow**
Celadon glaze; reticulated, modelled and incised decoration.
Height 4.5″; Width 10.5″
Koryo dynasty (11th-12th century)

Maebyong Vase
Celadon glaze; painted in underglaze iron.
Height 10.88″; Diameter, at base, 3.63″
Koryo dynasty (13th century)
↓

Maebyong Vase
Celadon glaze in underglaze iron.
Height 10.13″; Diameter, at base, 3.63″
Koryo dynasty (13th century)
↓

Maebyong Vase
Celadon glaze; painted in underglaze iron.
Height 14.50″; Diameter, at base, 4.56″
Koryo dynasty (13th century)
↓

↑ Round Tea Box and Cover
Celadon glaze; incised decoration filled with white and black slips.
Height 2.38″; Diameter 3.06″
Koryo dynasty (12th-13th century)

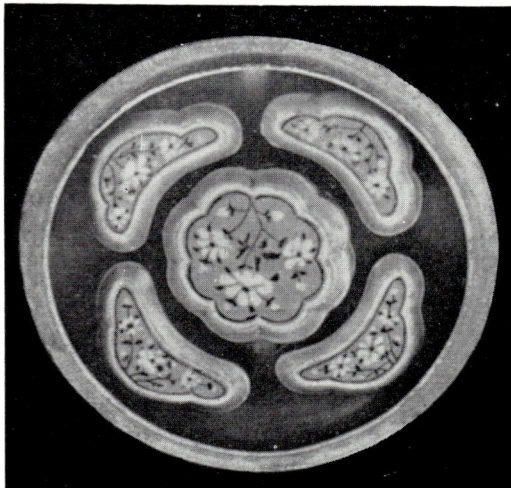

↑ Round Cosmetic Box and Cover with Five Boxes Inside
Celadon glaze; incised decoration filled with white and black slips.
Height 3″; Diameter 7.5″
Koryo dynasty (late 12th-early 13th century)

↑ Ewer
Celadon glaze; incised decoration filled with black slips on whitish surface.
Height 7.56″
Koryo dynasty

↑ Jar
Celadon glaze; painted in underglaze iron.
Height 5.08″
Koryo dynasty

↑ Wine Pot
Celadon glaze; modelled, incised and white slip decoration.
Height 7.25″; Diameter, at base, 4.5″
Koryo dynasty (11th-12th century)

↑ Incense Burner
Celadon glaze; modelled stamped and incised decoration.
Height 5.12″; Diameter 4.87″
Koryo dynasty (11th-12th century)
 Follows the form of the Chinese three legged bronze thing.

Ewer, Cover and Bowl
Celadon glaze; incised decoration.
Height 9.56″
↓ Koryo dynasty

↑ Wine Pot and Cover
Celadon glaze; modelled, undecorated.
Height 7.38″; Diameter, at base, 3.38″
Koryo dynasty (11th-12th century)

↑ Water Pourer or Sprinkler
Celadon glaze; incised decoration.
Height 13.5″; Diameter, at base, 3.69″
Koryo dynasty (12th century)

↑ Water Pourer or Sprinkler
Celadon glaze; incised decoration filled
with black and white slips. Height 14.19″;
Diameter, at base, 3.56″
Koryo dynasty (late 12th century)

Dish
Celadon glaze; incised decoration.
Height 0.63″; Width 3.88″
↓ Koryo dynasty (11th-12th century)

Bowl
Celadon glaze; undecorated.
↓ Koryo dynasty

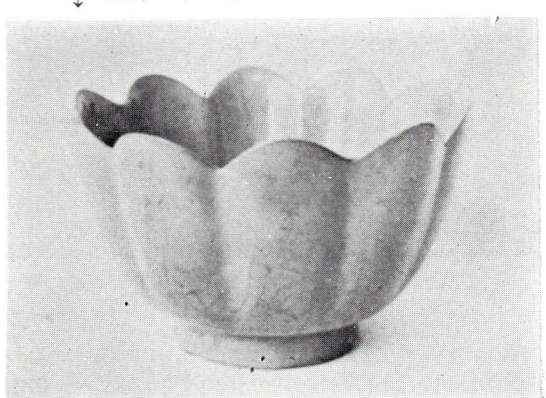

↑ **Bottle**
Cream-colored porcelain; painted in underglaze iron and underglaze blue.
Height 6.69″; Diameter, at base, 3.75″
Yi dynasty (mid-17th–mid-18th century)

↑ **Jar**
Chonghwa white porcelain.
Height 11.61″; Diameter 6.36″
Yi dynasty

Tea Bowl
Ko Ido ware
Diameter 5.55″
↓ Yi dynasty

←
Jar
White porcelain with openwork.
Height 10.49"; Diameter 10.06"
Yi dynasty

↑ Faceted Wine Bottle
White porcelain.
Height 8.93"; Diameter, at base, 3.31"
Yi dynasty

←
Jar and Cover
Iron painting over brushed-slip; Kyeryongsan ware.
Height 11.14"; Diameter 8.78"
Yi dynasty

↑ Bottle
Bottle with birds and tree design in underglaze blue and cinnabar
Height 10.38″; Diameter, at trunk, 5.38″
Yi dynasty (17th~18th century)

↑ Vase
　　Blue and white vase with framed landscape design
　　Height 18.49″; Diameter, at trunk, 13.72″
　　Yi dynasty (18th~19th century)

↑ Food Jar
 Cream-colored procelain; painted in underglaze iron
 Height 12.05″ Diameter, at trunk, 10.92″
 Yi dynasty (17th~18th century)

↑ Bottle
Multi-plane bottle with pine and kite design in underglaze cinnabar
Height 10.71″ ; Diameter, at base, 3.58″
Yi dynasty (18th~19th century)

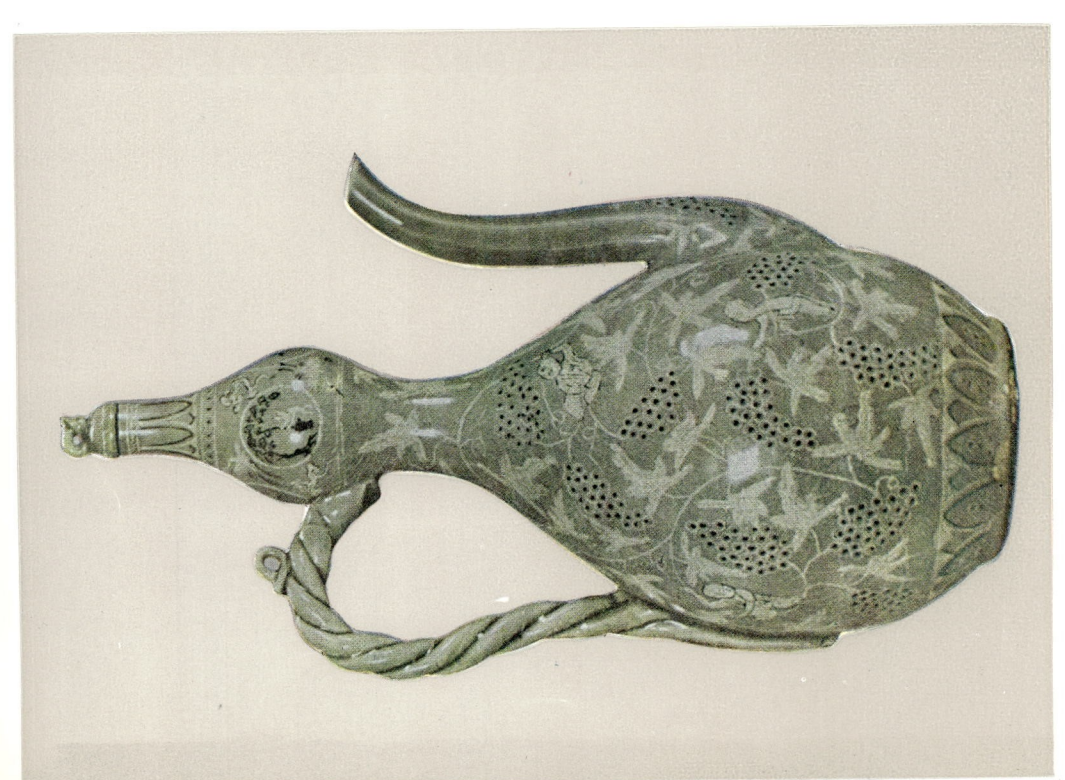

↑ Jug
Celadon glaze; gourd-shaped jug with inlaid vine and children's design
Height 14.96″ ; Diameter, at trunk, 6.54″
Koryo dynasty (13th century)

↑ Bottle
Bottle with floral design in underglaze blue and cinnabar
Height 6.68″ ; Diameter 9.77″
Yi dynasty (17th~18th century)

↑ Bottle
Multi-plane bottle with over-all undergaze cinnabar slip
Height 8.11″
Yi dynasty (18th~19th century)

Flower-Pot
Chonghwa white porcelain.
Height 3.87″; Diameter 6.32″
Yi dynasty

Faceted Wine Bottle
Chonghwa white porcelain; painted in underglaze blue.
Height 13.82″
Yi dynasty

Faceted Bottle-Vase
Painted in underglaze copper red.
Height 14.21″; Diameter, at base, 4.53″
Yi dynasty

←
Octagonal Jar
Chonghwa white porcelain.
Height 9.77″; Diameter 10.01″
Yi dynasty

Tall Necked Vase →
Chonghwa white porcelain; painted in underglaze iron and underglaze red with relievo.
Yi dynasty

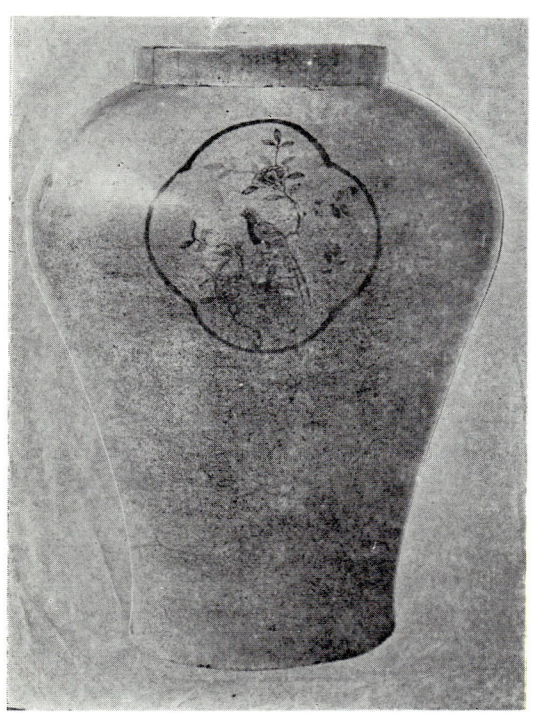

←
Jar
Chonghwa white porcelain; painted in underglaze iron.
Yi dynasty

Bottle
Chonghwa white porcelain.
Height 7.24″; Width×Length, at base, 3.03″×1.26″
↓ Yi dynasty

Jar
White porcelain; painted in underglaze iron.
↓ Yi dynasty

↑ Jar
Painted in undergalze red.
Height 10.75″; Diameter 9.47″
Yi dynasty

Wine Bottle
White porcelain; painted in underglaze blue.
Height 7.25″; Width 7″
↓ Yi dynasty (17th-18th century)

↑ **Food Jar**
Punchong ware; decorated white slip applied with a broad brush and painted in underglaze iron.
Height 6.19″, Diameter, as base, 2.63″
Yi dynasty (late 14th-early 15th century)
From a kiln located at Kyeryongsan, Chungchong Namdo.

Writer's Water-Dropper
Chonghwa white porcelain; modelled and painted in underglaze red.
↓ Yi dynasty

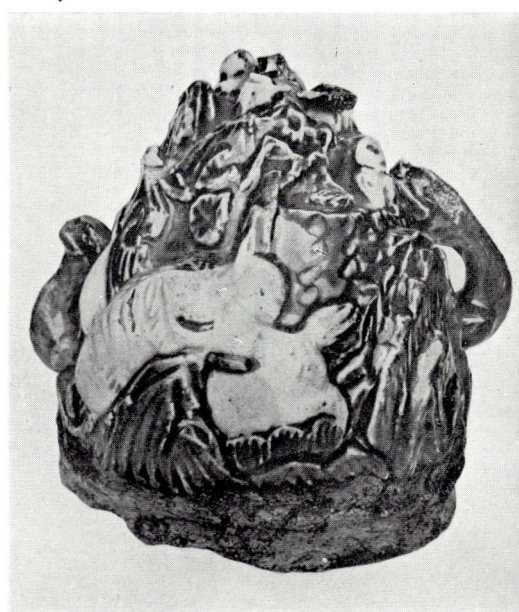

↑ **Brazier**
Chonghwa white porcelain; relievo.
Height 6.74″; Diameter 6.62″
Yi dynasty

Jar
Black ware; decoration relievo.
Height 10.76″
↓ Yi dynasty

↑ Pilgrim Bottle
Punchong ware; brushed slip and engraved.
Height 8.38″; Diameter 7.09″
Yi dynasty

↑ Food Jar
Cream-colored porcelain painted in underglaze iron.
Height 13.75″; Diameter 11.5″
Yi dynasty (17th–18th century)

Pilgrim Bottle
Punchong ware; engraved.
Height 9.42″
Yi dynasty
↓

Food Jar
Whitish porcelain; painted in underglaze iron and underglaze blue.
Height 12.69″; Diameter, at base. 5.19″
Yi dynasty (17th–18th century)
↓ It has a whitish paste.

↑ **Jar**
Punchong ware; engraved.
Height 14.31″; Diameter 11.68″
Yi dynasty

↑ **Jar**
Punchong ware; stamped decoration filled with white slip. Height 16.05″
Yi dynasty

Wine Bottle
Celadon glaze; incised and stamped decoration filled with white and black slips.
Height 11.5″; Diameter, at base, 3.25″
↓ Yi dynasty (early 15th century)

Wine Bottle
Punchong ware; decorated with white slip applied with a broad brush and painted in underglaze iron.
Height 11.69″; Diameter, at base, 3″
Yi dynasty (15th-16th century)
↓ From a kiln located at Kyeryongsan mountain.

Brush Stand →
Chonghwa white porcelain; painted in underglaze iron.
Height 6.11″; Diameter 5.69″
Yi dynasty

←
Jar and Cover
Punchong ware; incised decoration.
Yi dynasty

Brush Stand
Chonghwa white porcelain; modelled and painted in underglaze red.
Height 3.52″; Length 5.73″
↓ Yi dynasty

↑ **Wine Bottle**
Punchong ware; celadon glaze, stamped decoration filled with white slip.
Height 10.56″; Diameter, at base, 3″
Yi dynasty (15th-16th century)

Jar
White porcelain; painted in underglaze iron.
↓ Yi dynasty

Food Jar
Grayish porcelain; painted in underglaze iron.
Height 14.25″; Diamater 14.75″
↓ Yi dynasty (17th-18th century)

↑ **Bowl**
Punchong ware; decorated with white slip applied with broad brush.
Diameter 7.09″
Yi dynasty

Bowl
Punchong ware; incised decoration.
Height 3.16″; Diameter 7.64″
↓ Yi dynasty

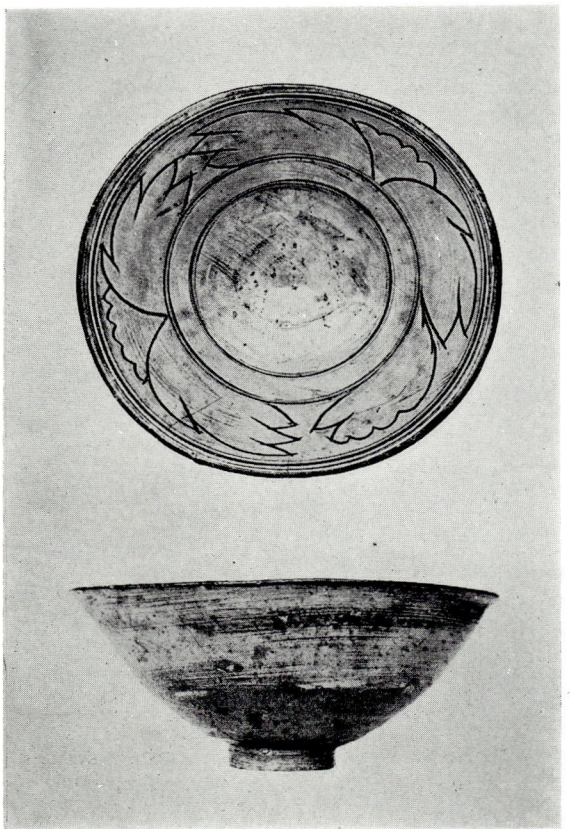

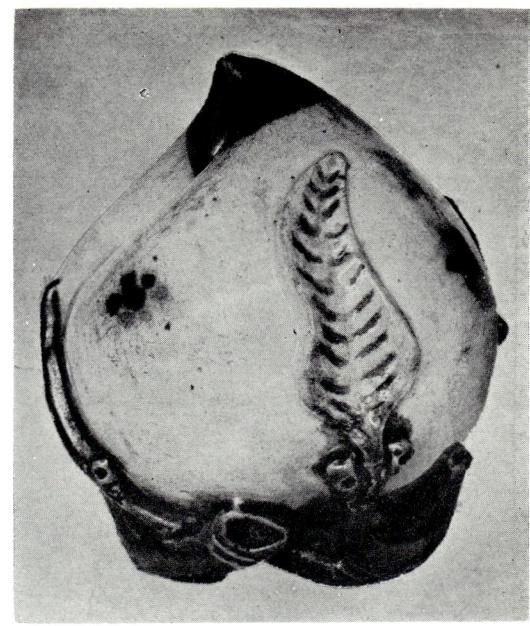

↑ Writer's Water-Dropper
Chonghwa white porcelain; modelled and painted in underglaze red.
Yi dynasty

→

Wine Pot
Chonghwa porcelain; modelled and painted in underglaze iron.
Height 5.73″; Length 7.04″
Yi dinasty

↑ **Brush Stand**
Chonghwa white porcelain; painted in underglaze red with openwork.
Height 5.61″; Diameter 5.57″
Yi dynasty.

Dish
Chonghwa white porcelain.
↓ Yi dynasty

Tea Cup
Incised decoration filled with black slip.
Diameter 4.92″
↓ Yi dynasty

Bowl
Decorated with white slip applied with broad brush.
Height 2.33″; Diameter 7.22″
↓ Yi dynasty

↑ **Jar**
Painted in underglaze iron brown.
Height 11.42″
Yi dynasty
   A northern Korean pottery, different from those of the south.

Tea Kettle
White porcelain; relievo.
↓ Yi dynasty

↑ **Brush Stand**
Chongnwa white porcelain; openwork.
Yi dynasty

← Brush Stand
White porcelain; incised with openwork.
Height 5.87″
Yi dynasty

Jar with Four Loops →
Punchong ware; brushed-slip.
Height 17.29″; Diameter 11.20″
Yi dynasty

← Brush Washer
Chonghwa white porcelain;
painted in underglaze iron.
Yi dynasty

Jar →
Early Chonghwa white porcelain.
Height 11.02″
Yi dynasty

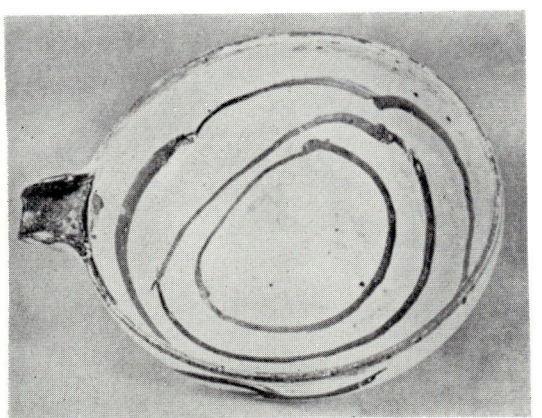

↑ Bowl with a Spout
Kyeryongsan ware; decorated with white slip applied with a broad brush, and with black lines in underglaze iron.
Height 3.5″
Yi dynasty

Flask
Black glaze; undecorated.
Height 10.27″
↓ Yi dynasty

Jar
Painted in underglaze iron brown.
Height 8.62″
↓ Yi dynasty

↑ **Wine Bottle**
Dark-blue glaze.
Height 6.65″; Diameter, at mouth, 0.86″, at body, 3.27″, Yi dynasty

↑ **Bowl**
Punchong ware; incised decoration filled with white slips.
Height 1.73″; Diameter 6.14″, Yi dynasty

Square Bottle
Chonghwa white porcelain.
↓ Yi dynasty

Octagon Bottle
Chonghwa white porcelain; written Chinese character in underglaze red.
↓ Height 7.87″, early Yi dynasty

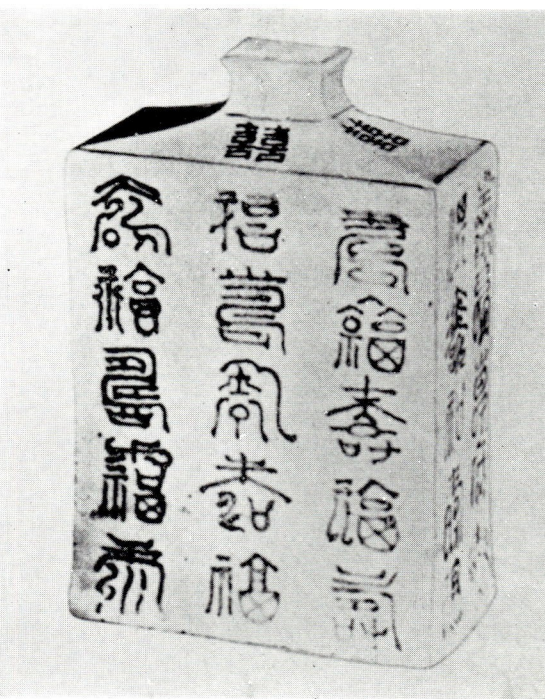

Dish
Chonghwa white porcelain.
Yi dynasty
↓

↑
Dish
Chonghwa white porcelain.
Diameter 6.57″
Yi dynasty

Writer's Water-Pot
White porcelain; light bluish glaze.
Height 1.63″; Diameter, at base, 2.25″
Yi dynasty (late 18th–19th century)
 A product of Kwangju Punwon, the Yi government-operated kiln.
↓

↑ **Ritual Vessel**
Decorated with incised lines.
Width 8.27″; Length 6.73″
Yi dynasty

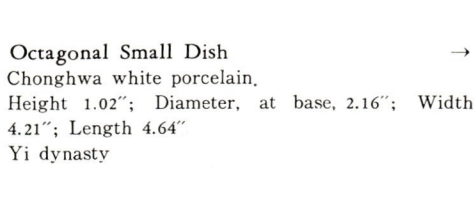

Octagonal Small Dish   →
Chonghwa white porcelain.
Height 1.02″; Diameter, at base, 2.16″; Width 4.21″; Length 4.64″
Yi dynasty

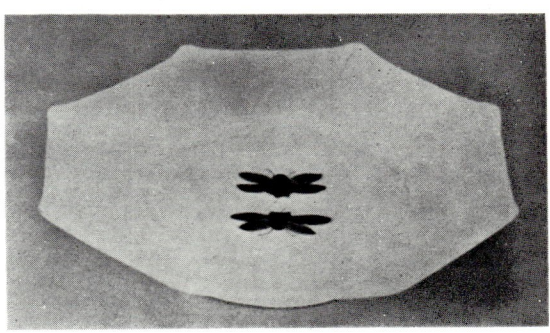

←
Foot Bowl
White porcelain; painted in underglaze blue.
Height 5.31″; Diameter 9.75″
Yi dynasty (18th–early 19th century)
  From the Puwon kiln located in Kwangju-gun, Kyonggi-do.

Jar
White porcelain; painted in underglaze iron.
↓ Yi dynasty

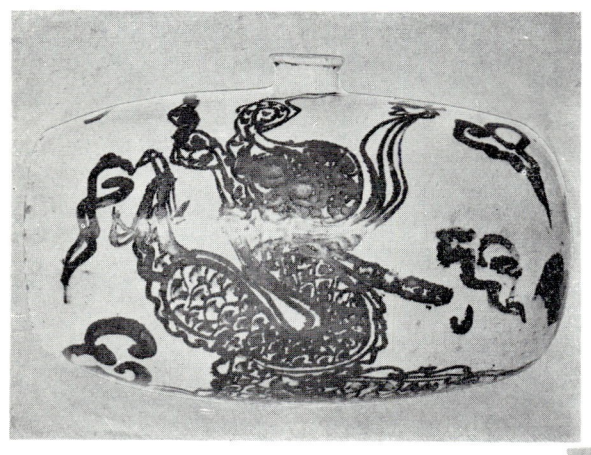

↑ **Dish**
Early blue and white Chonghwa porcelain.
Diameter 8.62″
Yi dynasty

→
Minature Buddhist Shrine
Punchong ware.
Height 5.98″
Yi dynasty

Yomnang Purse →
A fancy embroidary work somewhat like a Western evening bag for a lady. Improved from a traditional Korean treasury purse.

Sewing Basket
↓ A rush work.

← Rice Container
Made of a block of log.

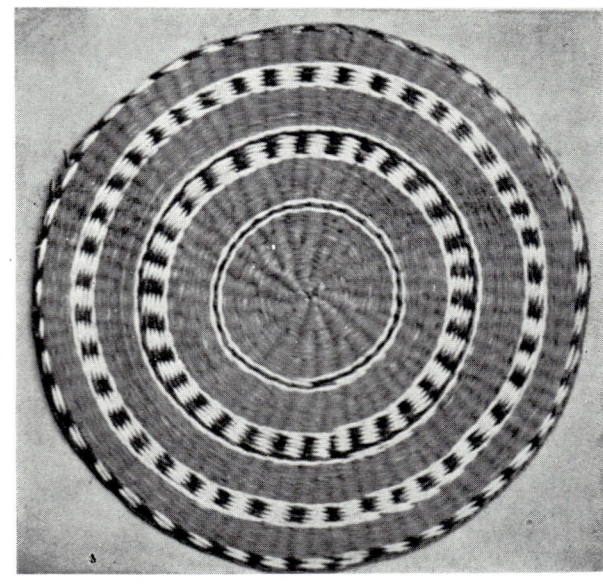

A Round Mat →
A rush mat used on the wooden floor.

← Wrapper for Rice Container
A paper-made wrapper to keep rice warm.

← Bamboo Basket with Cover
　　It is very useful for putting candies, cakes or paper-made articles in it.

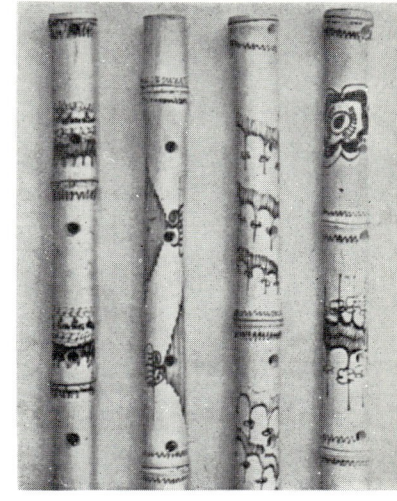

↑ Bamboo Flutes

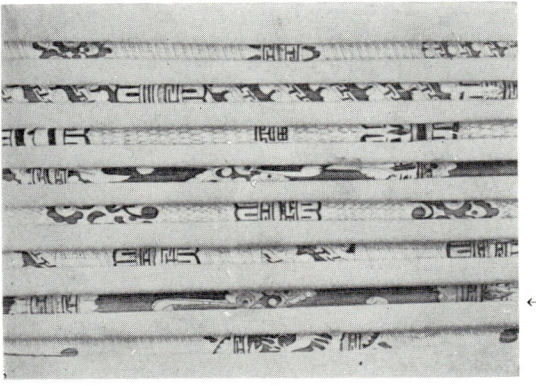

← Tobacco-pipes of Bamboo

A Shutter of Wardrobe
　Lacquerware with mother-of-pearl →

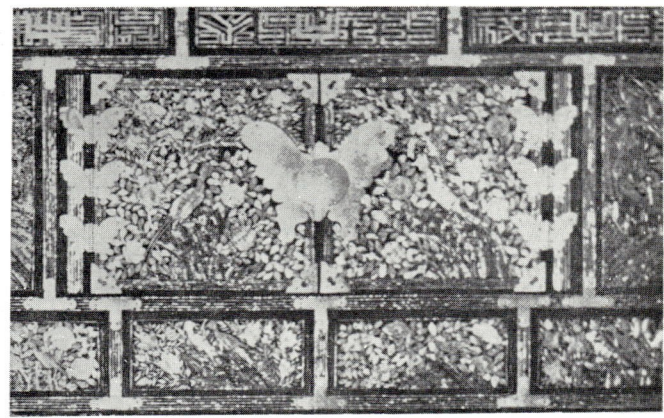

← Brazier
  Made of brass used as a heater.

Soban →
  A small dining table.

← Cuspidor
  Made of brass and used for an ashtray in addition.

Wooden Container
Used for washing tablewares and storing vegetables or grains. →

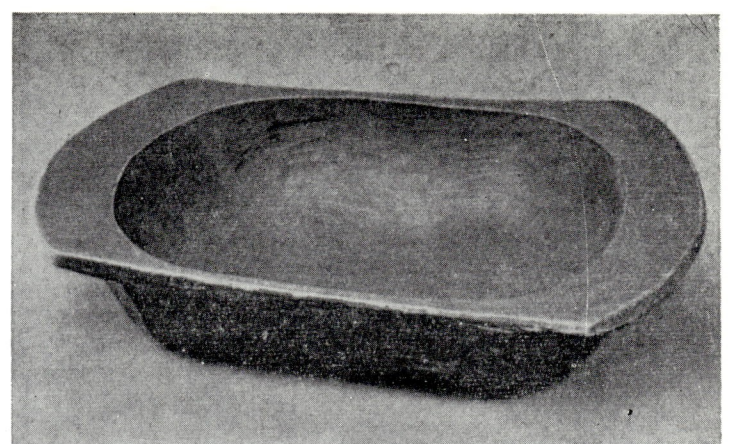

← Dipper
A gourd with a handle.

South-Korean Gourd
An indispensable utensil in Korea for washing rice. →

← Stone-jar
Used for boiling herb.

Stone-pot →
A pot made of stone. Cooked with this, food tastes far better than with a metal pot.

Rice Bowl
A brassware for winter season as it keeps warmth better than a chinaware.
↓

A Brass Jug
↓ Used for water or liquor container.

Combs
A wooden comb of traditional type (lower), and horn combs of Western type (upper).

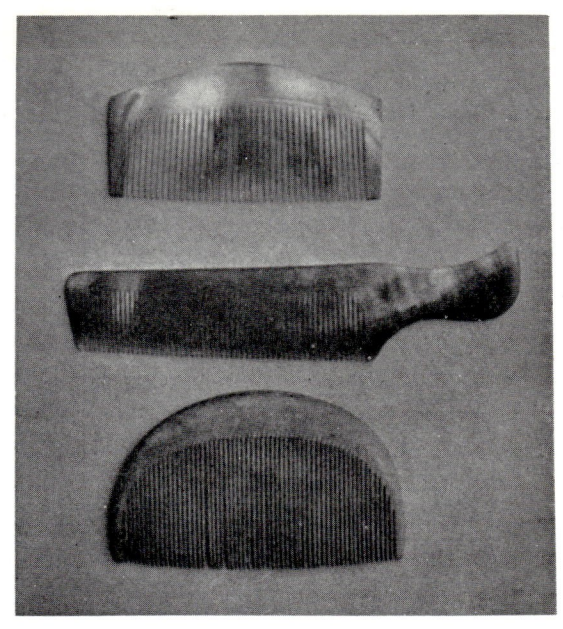

Wicker Baggage
A common baggage for travellers. The larger one is a cover. Made of dried willow branches.

Bamboo Basket
A large-size round basket made of bamboo sheath. It is uniquely Korean; not to be found in Japan or China.

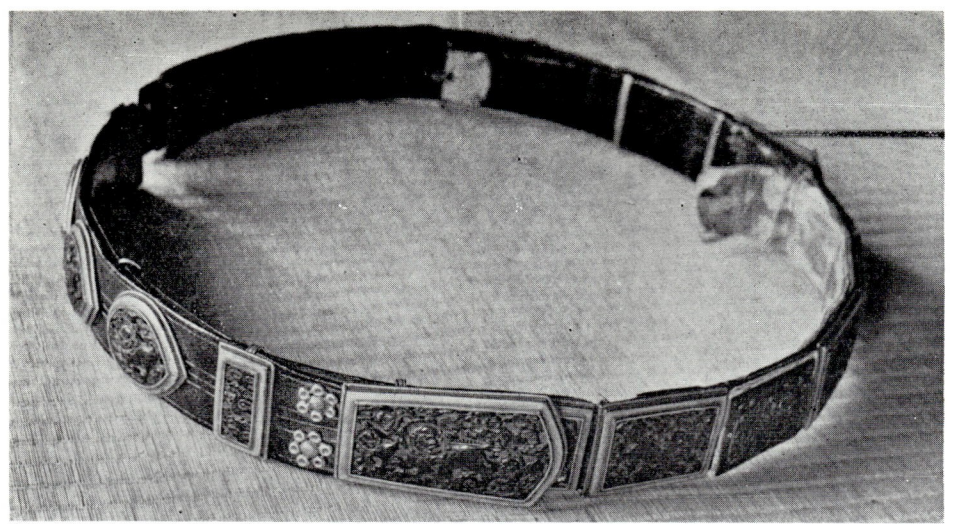

↑ Kwandae(Belt)
 A belt worn by a government official of Yi dynasty over his court dress. The jade decorated on the center of the belt shows the grade of the wearer.

Marunsin or Shoes for Dry Day →
 Shoes for ladies of upper class. Made of leather or Oriental paper covered with various kinds of silks.

Lantern
 Such special lanterns are often hung in front of Buddhist temples. ↓

Fan with Taeguk Decoration ↓

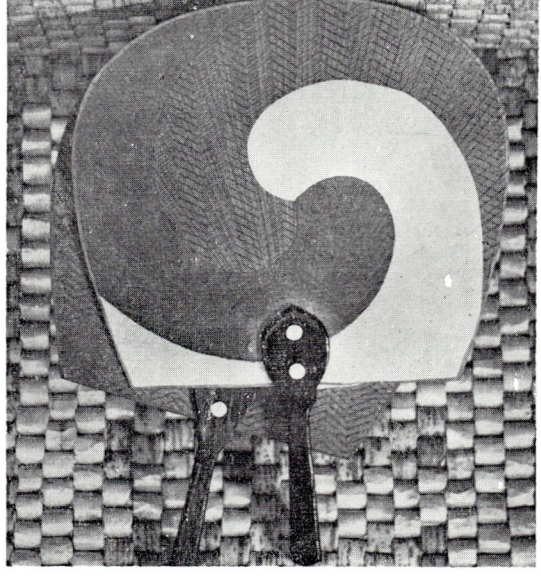

Straw-shoes
Used to be worn by low-class people or travellers, but no longer used nowadays except by farmers.

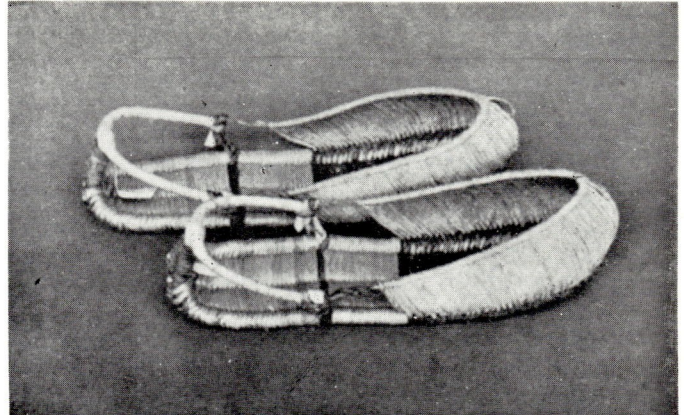

Wooden-shoes
A sort of rain-shoes.

Rubber-Shoes
The most common shoes in Korea. The shoes shown in this picture are for a woman.

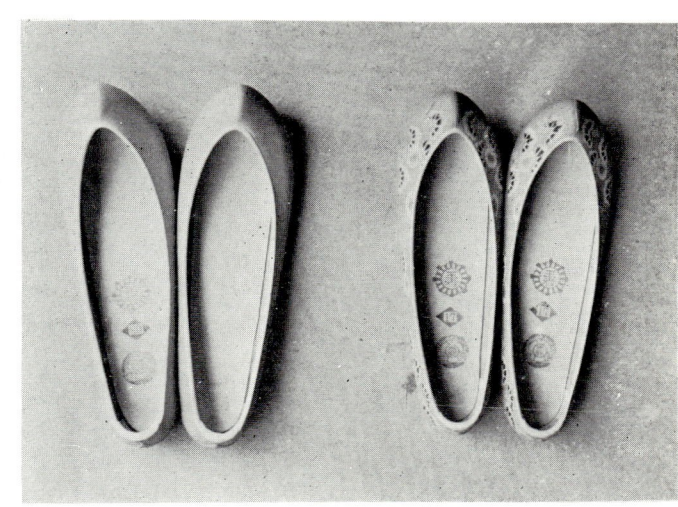

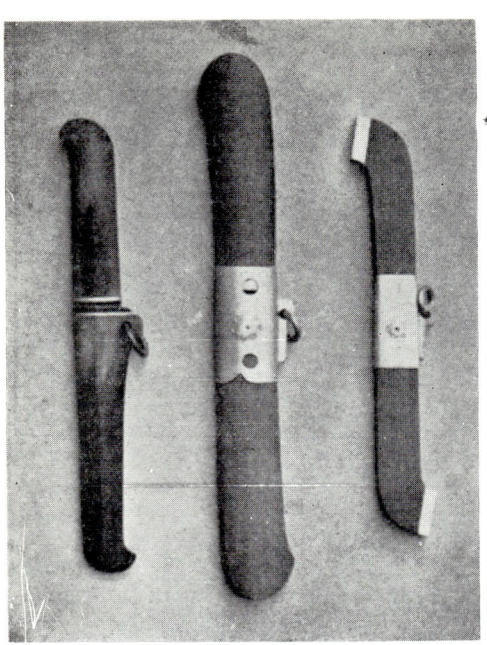

Changdo
Right: The haft and the sheath are made of wood and decorated with nickel ornaments.
Left: A pocket-knife for self-defence and ornament with such curved ends as can be seen on tips of socks, shoes, or fans, which are traditional.

Washing-club
A club for beating laundries to get rid of dirt and soap. The smaller one is for the younger. (About 45 cm)

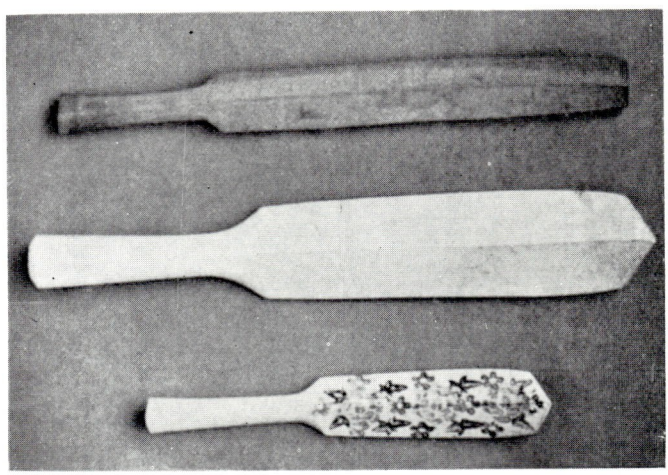

Ironing Stone
Used for fulling cloth by beating with clubs. (Width: 55 cm, Length: 20 cm, Height; 10 cm)

Cupboard and Box
 A useful furniture designed with combination of old and new styles or figures.

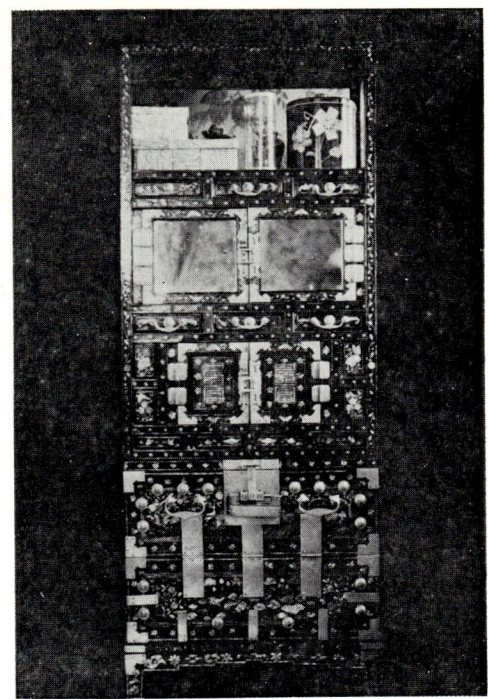

↑ **Chest of Drawer**
 A typical chest of drawer, Yi dynasty. Note the figure with mother-of-pearl on lacquerware.

Furniture Store
 All lines of modern furniture are available in stores like this.

↑ **Mirror-stand**
 A classical type.

↑ Wooden Furniture
   Many new decorative styles have been introduced to Korea for making of desks, seats, book-cases, tables, etc.

Lacquerware with Mother-of-Pearl
   Often used for figures as shown here. Most Korean homes are furnished
↓ with lacquerware.

genius who lightened the early Yi dynasty, though he lived only 36 years. He became the leading figure of the artists' circle of his time. His contribution to the famous epilogue to the *Towondo* (a picture story of Utopia), written when he was 30, nevertheless, shows such an indomitable spirit and noble dignity that it was called "the first under heaven."

The epilogue contains also the writings of many other brilliant calligraphers of that time, such as Sok Chonbong, Kim Chongso, Pak Paengnyon, Yi Hyongno, Song Sammun, Sin Sukchu, Chong Inji and Kang Choktok. Most of their writings are in the Songsol or analogous-styles.

In the first half of the Yi dynasty, Wen Chenming-style and Mi Fu-style were also imported, and with Wang-style, dominated only Yi calligraphy. Among the many remarkable Wen Chenming-style calligraphers of the first half of the Yi period, Song Suchin was typical. In the reign of King Songjo, Han Ho (Han Sokpong), one of the most famous calligraphers in the history of Yi dynasty, succeeded in developing a unique style which he devolved from the Wang-style. Yi Kwangsa commented, "It is so gross, yet the brushstroke is remarkable ...... both goodness and badness are mixed up in this gifted calligrapher." Wandang said of his work, "Sokpong's Calligraphic Album has extreme highness as well as extreme lowness." Nevertheless, the vulgar Sokpong-style swept the country and had such a great influence on the calligraphy of the time, that most schools made it their standard writing style. This so-called school-style was called "the vulgarity of Korea," yet Sokpong deserves the name of genius for his success in creating a uniquely Korean writing style.

In the latter half of the Yi period, however, "the vulgarity of Korea" was swept away by the appearance of the noble but sound Paekha-style, created by Yun Sun, one of the most important figures in Yi calligraphy.

Notable calligraphers of that period were Ho Mok, in *Chon* (seal)-characters, Yi Kwangsa, refined in *Haeng*-characters though far behind Yun Sun, Kang Sehwang, both calligrapher and painter, Chong Yakyong who was a great scholar as well as good calligrapher, and Sin Wi, versatile in calligraphy, painting and poetry, and there also were Yu Hanji who wrote beautiful *Ye*-writing, Yi Samman who had a powerful though vulgar brushstroke, Yi Insang, and Cho Kwangjin. King Chongjo wrote in the Mi Fu-style with dignity, liberty and powerful brushstrokes, first among the calligrapher-kings of Korea.

Above all was Chusa (Kim Chonghui), the greatest master artist and scholar. Chusa went to Peiping as a child to study. Under the intimate influence of the Chinese master, Ong Pangkang, and the epigraphic fashions of China at that time, he created a very original writing style which has had influence on Korean calligraphy till this day. The first epigraphist of Korea, Chusa, best represents Korean calligraphy throughout its history.

Other calligraphers of that time were Chong Hakkyo of *Ye* and *Haeng* writings, Kim Songkun of the Mi Fu-style, Kwon Tongsu, Chi Changhan and Chi Unyong. Min Yongik, who exiled himself to China after the Japanese dominance over Korea, was distinguished in both calligraphy and painting. Especially, his collection had much influence on Korean calligraphers. O Sechang was a master calligrapher in seal-characters and was also outstanding in seal impression. His valuable work, the "*Kunyok Sohwajing* (Collection of Korean Calligraphy and Paintings)," consists of calligraphy and paintings extracted from two hundred and seventy works of literature. Kim Tonhui was refined in *Hae*-writing, combining the Yen-and Hwan Tingchien-styles, and advanced his technique of *Ye*-writing to a high point. He established the *Sangsohoe* to educate younger artists, that his writing style for a while had considerable vogue and a sort of technicalism that resulted from his writing style has still some influence on

Korean calligraphy of today.

Besides these calligraphers, there should be noted of the late Yi dynasty So Pyongo, whose writings were bold and free-hearted, An Chongwon who was skilled in every style and wrote modestly and elegantly, Kim Taesok of the seal impression, Hyon Chae of *Cho*-writing, and Min Hyonsik of the characteristic method he created. Yi Hanbok was distinguished for a particularly broad knowledge of calligraphic styles. An Chungsik and Yi Toyong, the famous painters, were also talented in calligraphy.

Of calligraphy in the Korean alphabet created in 1446 in the reign of King Sejong, there is almost nothing to be mentioned. Scholars and officials of the Yi dynasty, devoted to Confucianism and the emulation of China, thought Chinese characters were the only medium of writing and treated the original Korean alphabet with contempt, calling it *"Onmun* (Colloquial Letters)."

At one time, in 1504, the alphabet was even banned. Therefore, most remains of Hangul calligraphy are to be found in private letters, and in stories and songs written by women, who were then almost all uneducated. Consequently, it is very difficult to systemize the development of the *Hangul* calligraphy. Since it was written almost exclusively by women, the writing style was effeminate and slender, and was called the Court-style because it was written generally by palace maids. Some of the writing methods of Chinese characters were used, but there was a unique writing method of *Hangul*.

Modern Korean Calligraphy

While numerous styles are to be found in modern Korean calligraphy because every calligrapher follows his own individual tastes, there are four or five main groups.

The first style group is that of the old calligraphers 70 to 80 years old, such as Kim Yongjin who is more noted as an Oriental painter, Song Chihon, Yi Konsik and Yi Pyonghui.

The second is a group of calligraphers in their 50's. Typical is Son Chaehyong who was a disciple of Kim Tonghui, the creator of the technicalism which is a very characteristic writing style as well as a weakness in Korean calligraphy. His followers are Chong Hyonbok, Kim Kisung, Chong Hansop and Cho Suho.

The third is a group of calligraphers seeking a sound base for the development of Korean calligraphy in the study of classics and calligraphic theory, and overcoming the tendency to place great emphasis on techniques. Such calligraphers are Pae Kilgi, Yu Higang, Choe Chunggil, Yi Kiu, Choe Hyonju, Hyon Chongni, Pak Pyonggyu, and others.

The Brothers Kim Chunghyon and Kim Yonghyon may make the fourth category, being a little different from the calligraphers of the third group.

Some other calligraphers have each their own characteristics, so that they cannot be categorized as belonging to any of these groups. They are Cho Tongho, Kim Yunchung, Yu Chiung, Chong Haechang and So Tonghyun, most of whom are between 50 to 60 years old.

To conclude, Korean calligraphy suffered a period of decline after World War II, but it was revivified with establishment of the Korean government, and has been moving forward since then.

Photography

It is commonly believed that photography was introduced to Korea by American missionaries when they first came into Korea about a hundred years ago. However, it is perhaps more likely that a Japanese photographer, named Tei Jiro, who is recorded to have died in Korea in 1885, brought photography to Korea around that time.

The first Korean who dealt with photography professionally was Kim Kyujin (also known as Haegang), an Oriental painter, who studied photography in Japan in 1895 or thereabouts, and became the first court photographer in Korea. Mun Chijang became the first news photographer in Korea, joining the Tonga Ilbo newspaper in 1923. "Still Life—Glass" by Im Ungsik (Eung-sik Limb), then an amateur photographer, was the first Korean art photograph to be published, in the Japanese magazine, "Photo Salon," in 1934. Other early photographers were Choe Subok, Chang Pyongjin, O Pyongdo, Yi Songyun, Pak Pilho, Pak Samsik, Chong Unsang, and Yi Hyongnok. In 1939, the pictures of Cho Myongwon and Chong Mongjae appeared in a Japanese annual photo-publication, and at the same time, the picture of So Sungsam was accepted for the All-Japan Figure Photo Exhibition. In 1941, Yi Haeson's work appeared in an exhibition celebrating the Japanese year of 2600.

From about 1933, photographic societies began to be organized. The largest was the All-Korea Photographic League, which had more than ten minor organizations under its influence though only one of them was strictly Korean. Another major organization was the Amateur Photo Club (A.P.C.), which had branches in Seoul, Pusan, Taegu, and many other places, established by the Japanese monthly magazine, the Photo Report. Most Korean photographers of that time were members of these organizations.

After World War II, when all Japanese in Korea had withdrawn, many photographic societies such as the Korean Photographic Institute and others were organized, but they were loosely coordinated and, consequently, contributed little toward progress of photography. In fact, until the outbreak of the Korean War, the photographers were held in low respect and often ridiculed and slighted by artists of other callings.

After the Korean War, all photographers were linked under the strong Korean Association of Photographic Art (KAPA), which was organized in Pusan. It was the first strong, conscientious organization among photographers since photography had been brought into Korea. The KAPA worked brilliantly. Abroad, it displayed some works of member artists in the International Photo Salon and others. Domestically it held several photo exhibitions and campaigned to have a photography section set up in the National Art Exhibition.

Although the Korean War was a period of tragic suffering for all Koreans, it brought some good fortune in the field of photography. First, it changed the Korean people's opinion about foreigners for the better, hence, Koreans were able to be in closer relations with foreign countries, which, in turn, began to pay regard to Korea. Second, many cameras and photo accessories came into Korea after the war. And lastly, Korean youths came to see, hear and think of things very realistically after having experienced unforgettable tragedies during the war. They were finally rid of the old restraint of ideas that believed photography could exist only within the framework of painting, then tried to represent the everyday life of man freshly and realistically, and the social phenomena objectively. There had been severe debates between the school of realism and the advocates of the idea of subordination to painting from then till 1956 or '57, when the former overwhelmingly won out in the field of Korean photography.

At the tenth exhibition of KAPA in 1958, some Modernistic works were shown chiefly by college students. Although the future of Modernism cannot yet be foreseen, it is evident that younger artists are looking for something new and different. Notably, they are trying to convey personal and psychological impressions, in their works to extend the limits of photography. Naturally, Modernism will be the opposite of Realism in the near future.

Although Korean photographic printing techniques have progressed somewhat compared to previous days, real photographic journalism is not in Korea yet, chiefly because of its high cost. Therefore, the works of photographic artists are only shown directly through exhibitions which are held annually by every photo organization. The government-sponsored National Art Exhibition contains every section of arts, but that of photography is not yet included because of objections by members of the Academy of Arts which is the advisory body to the Exhibition organizers. This despite what KAPA has done to persuade them to establish a section in the Exhibition for photographic art.

There are few photo magazines in Korea now. They are, however, mostly news-picture magazines, such as the Donghwa News Graphic (monthly), the Free Korea's Graph (monthly), the Kukche Podo (International Report, quarterly) and the Pictorial Korea (annual). There once was a genuine photo magazine, Photographic Culture, but its last issue was published in November, 1958.

Those institutions which have photography courses in the art colleges are Seoul National University, Pusan National University and Ewha Women's University. In 1959, Yi Hyesuk won the master degree in photography for the first time in this country. In the same year, Yi Chongsang went to West Germany to study color photographic techniques.

It was not until 1952 that works of Korean photographers began to be shown in foreign countries. In 1952, a picture of Im Ungsik was the first Korean entry to win a prize in an international photo salon held in Japan sponsored by ARS Co., a Japanese photographic publisher. Since then, twenty-six pictures of nineteen photographers have appeared in exhibitions and publications of foreign countries. Several Korean photographers showed their works and won prizes in an annual international photo salon sponsored by Asahi, the leading Japanese newspaper. Those who won prizes in the Asahi salon of 1954 were Yi Pyongsam, Kim Hanyong and Chong Insong. Chong had two color pictures which were awarded prizes. Also in the same salon of 1955, the works of Na Chilsong, Yi Yunsung and Im Ungsik were accepted; in 1957, Kim Kwangsok, Yi Kyongjong and To Pongjun; in 1958, Pak Yongdal and Yi Haemun; and in 1959, An Chongchil and Chong Pomtae.

In 1955, a picture of Im Ungsik appeared in the Photographic Annual of 1955 in the United States, and in 1959, works of Kim Haengo, Yi Hyongnok and Chong Pomtae were accepted in an international photo contest sponsored by the publication U.S. Camera. In the same year the pictures of Han Yongsu and Kim Chongtae were inserted in the World Photographic Annual published by Heibonsha of Japan. A photograph by Kim Kwangsok was displayed in Photo Maxima of the U.S., while one by Kang Yongho appeared in the international photo salon held in Australia.

The reason that only twenty-six were selected out of many works which had been sent to those foreign exhibitions and publications was that Korean photographers lack the basic theories and creative ideas with which a real art work could be produced. Basic technical skills were also lacking. But the twenty-six who have displayed internationally were not inferior in quality. In fact, compared to the other arts, photography is one of the advanced arts in Korea. It has been proved in the international galleries though its reception at home has been cool.

The most memorable event in the photographic history here was the "Family of Man" show in Korea in 1957. About 300,000 men and women saw the display which caused a great sensation.

Widely-noted photographers who have been to Korea are David Douglas Duncan, Carl Mydams, Hank Walles, John Dominis, Margaret Bourke-White, W. Bishop, Horace Bristol, Donald S. Welles and Jyun Miki.

XIX DANCE, MUSIC

Dance

Essential Nature of the Korean Dance

Dance has played a major role in the rituals of the Korean people as in the case of other peoples. The essential nature of the Korean dance is that it has always been a part of their daily lives. As an excellent example to illustrate the point, we can cite our farm dance which has, indeed, been an inherent part in the daily life of the Korean farmer.

Techniques and rules of the farm dance offer us clues to the original posture and movements of the Korean people, because agriculture was the foundation of all things in the country until quite recently. The farm dance offered young men of Korea an opportunity to express their feelings without any restrictions imposed by convention or ethics. The *mot* and *hung*, the two most important elements of the farm dance, emerge from the naive atmosphere of the dance.

The two words, *mot* and *hung*, are extremely important in the Korean dance, and proper appreciation of the terms is very helpful to understand the real nature of the Korean dance as a whole. The word, *mot*, connotes some kind of beauty. For instance, it refers to symmetrical beauty, exotic attractiveness, inner beauty. Therefore, when one find a spiritual inner beauty aside from outwardly aesthetic features, we express our feeling with the word, *mot*. The word, *hung*, has a similar meaning, and, in the dance, connotes a state of everlasting exhilaration. The ideal of the Korean dance, then, is enjoyment of the *mot* and *hung* rather than demonstration of techniques or dancing for dance's sake.

As a matter of fact, one can never judge an execution of the Korean dance by technical aspects alone, nor do the dancers, for their part, attempt to excel in technique for its own sake. The real beauty of the Korean dance is to be found in a perfect combination of the *mot* and *hung*. This is, indeed, the essence.

Another feature of the Korean dance is its emphasis upon shoulder movement. The concept of time is dispensed. The dancer may either move or just stand still, for the "spiritual" executed in quiescence is, indeed, the ultimate of the Korean dance.

Such has been the fundamental philosophy of the original Korean dance, but the ethical philosophies of Buddhism and Confucianism exerted tremendous influences. Thus, the court dance was created. On the other hand, dances of foreign lands such as China, Tibet, and the South Sea areas, were modified to serve as Korea's folk dance, combining elan, grandeur and elegance.

Therefore, the folk dance involves far more advanced techniques than the court dance.

Another important characteristic of the Korean dance is precedence of rhythm over movement, for rhythm plays an active rather than a passive role. It means that one does not dance to rhythmic accompaniment but creates one's own rhythm while dancing. The fact that all of the past masters of the Korean dance were also excellent drummers lends eloquent testimony. Every performer whoever won fame for unequalled mastery of the Korean dance started out his or her career as a drummer. The old drummers of Korea, as they beat drums, could not suppress their feeling but had to stand up and dance in spite of themselves. Such a dance, then, was rhythm incarnate moving.

The profound taste and character of the Korean dance, therefore, lies in covert techniques, for the dancers appear to move and, at the same time, stand still while in a state of uncontrollable exhilaration. To some audiences, the dancer may appear as if he or she were everlooking movement. For all that, movement is a basic element of the Korean dance.

History of the Korean Dance

There are no authentic records describing the Korean dance in any detail, but several literary works of the courts handed down to later generations tell us of the features of ancient Korean dance. The *Akhak Kuebom* (Criteria of Musicology) and the *Siyong Mubo* (Current Dance Music of the Yi Dynasty) is available to understand the dances of that period. In fact, these are described so intensively that we can recreate them today. The two books also contain references to some of the representative dances of each dynasty since Silla. Also important is the recent uncovering of the Dance Tomb of Koguryo* for the mural within the tomb discloses some features of Koguryo dances.

The court dances of Korea are presently preserved at the National Academy of Korean Classic Music.

Korean dances fall under four distinctive groups according to the features of the dances: ritual, court, folk and modern.

The ritual dance includes the *il-dance* performed at Confucian shrines at the time of festivity, and the dances executed at Buddhist temples on the occasion of festive worships, such as the *pob-drum*, *para* and butterfly dances. Most of them have been preserved until today.

The *il-dance* was first introduced to Korea during the Chunjong period of Koguryo 3,000 years ago from China, the original Chinese ritual being modified and developed.

The *il-dance* is divided into two kinds: the military and civil dances, the number of dancers varying according to the symbolic ranks represented by the dance. The "emperor" is performed by a group of eight *il* or 64 persons, the "barons" by a group of six *il* or 36 persons, and "the honorable men" by four *il* or 16 persons. This dance is composed of a series of simple movements executed with certain symbolic goods held in hand. For the "civil dance," each performer holds a kind of flute in the left hand and a pheasant feather in the "military dance," a shield with a dragon painted on it is held in the left hand, and a hatchet in the right. At the Confucian shrine, the "civil dance" always precedes the "military dance," for the former is called "the dance of maintaining peace and prosperity," while the latter is "the dance of achieving the glorious assignment."

Among the Buddhist ritual dances, the "drum dance" is performed by a juvenile priest wearing a hood and beating a drum in front of Buddha's image. The *"para dance"*

---

*The Dance Tomb, located in Tungkou in the Manchurian province of Chian, once part of Koguryo territory, was discovered in 1940 and identified as having been built during the Koguryo era. The interior walls of the tomb are covered with murals depicting the customs of the Koguryo people, including a dance scene performed by a gronp of 14 men and women.

is executed in the Buddist temple by a set of five or six priests, each holding a cymbal-like percussion instrument, which is crushed together as they move about. The "butterfly dance" is made up of quiet movements performed by dancers wearing butterfly-like costumes.

Court Dance

The court dance, also referred to as the "*chong-jae*" or "*pob* dance," is rendered on festive occasions at the court. What is popularly called the classic dance of Korea refers to the court dance — a practice in order to distinguish this from the folk dance. The court dance is a combination of dance and music, including vocals, executed either by courtesans in case of the royal household festivities or by juvenile dancers at feasts where outsiders are invited.

In both cases an "usher," called the *chukkanja*, leads the dancers onto the stage and narrates the theme of the dance about to be performed. The "usher" also presents the audience with an epilogue at the end of the dance.

The court dance is of two kinds: *hyangak* and *tangak*, the former being traditional and the latter adaptation of various Chinese dances of ancient origin.

There are more than 50 different court dances presently known, among which the representative ones are the *Chosun* Dance of the Koguryo period, the Sword and the *Choyong* Dances of the Silla period, the *Kiak* Dance of the Paekche period, the Ball and Crane Dances of the Koryo period, and the *Hangjang* and the Nightingale-Singing-in-the-Spring Dances of the Yi dynasty. Contents of the court dances are explained with vocal singing which always accompanies the dance, and the luxurious costumes are based on the philosophy of the period. All of the dances resort to slow movements suggesting grandeur.

The preservation of the court dance is significant to the Korean people in that it has retained the elegant dance of ancient Korean women without degrading itself in the course of transmission to posterity.

Folk Dance

The Korean folk dance includes the Farm Dance originating during the Three Han period, the Sword, Priest's, *Hannyang*, *Changgu*, Male, and Mask Dances, the Five Clown Dance, Lion Dance, *Sandae* Play Dance, *Pongsan* Mask Dance, etc.

The folk dance differs from the court dance in that whereas the court dance is formal, restrictive, and feminine with emphasis on elegance, the folk dance is masculine, animated, fast in tempo and there is no restraint on the dancers, costume and movements.

Farm Dance

The farm dance is the most primitive and exciting of all Korean dances. On the occasion of harvest, seed planting, and other festivities, male farmers of a village gather together in a square under a flag on which is inscribed the words "Agriculture is the foundation of the universe." Accompanied by rousing sounds of various drums and brass instruments, the farmers clad in brightly striped costumes whirl about madly beating a small drum grasped in each dancer's hands. As they spin like tops, their restless necks send long tapes attached at the top of their hats in long arches floating in the air. Origin of the farm dance hat has been buried in oblivion during the course of its long history, but it still plays such an important part in the farm dance that strenous practice of neck movements is essential if one wishes to be an expert. This emphasis on the neck movement, unique in the Korean farm dance, is similar in nature to the neck dance of India.

Sword Dance

The sword dance, also called the *Hwangchangnang* Dance, is performed by females in group or solo, each dancer holding a sword in each hand. Originally a court dance since Silla, it was later adopted by the people, and has remained a folk dance ever since.

The sword dance is based on a legend of ancient Korea. During the Silla period, a young boy, named Hwang Changnang, was so famous for dancing with a sword in each hand that he became a professional itinerant dancer. The fame of the dancer, in the meantime, spread so far and wide that it reached the ears of the king of Paekche, an enemy kingdom of Silla. Upon invitation of the enemy-king, the boy-dancer presented his sword dance in front of the monarch. In the middle of his dance which enraptured everybody in the audience, including the king, he thrust the sword with which he was dancing into the king, killing him instantly. He was subsequently executed by Paekche, but the people of his country, Silla, were so impressed by the young dancer's patriotic daring that the people began to imitate his sword dance, wearing a mask which resembled the persecuted patriot's face in memory of the hero. The seemingly innocent swords in the hands of dancers proved so deadly, however, that later the swords were replaced with the "dance-sword." Short wires connect the blade of the "dance-sword" with the handle. In this way, the swords send out a rattling noise as the dancer brandishes them in dancing. The metallic sounds are one of the most important factors adding grace and color to the dance.

Originally masculine and animated, the sword dance gradually transfigured itself into a graceful feminine dance. Nevertheless, we can find some basic features of Korean dancing: of all sword dances of the East, ours is the only one which does not call for "swordmanship" on the part of the dancer, for the swords in the Korean dance serve a supplementary rather than a major role.

Priest Dance

The priest dance embraces within itself the most characteristic beauty of Korea among all Korean dances, for the entire repertoire of Korean dances are condensed into this.

The original version of this dance is presumed to have been started in Korea with the introduction of Buddhism into the country, but the latter-day version of the priest dance is not a religious one performed by Buddhist priests but a folk dance adapted from the original Buddhist ritual dance.

The priest dance is divided into two kinds. One was developed during the early stages of the Yi dynasty by the people as a protest in caricature against the hierarchy of the times. The dance, therefore, insinuates apostasy of the Buddhist priests who had been the privileged leaders of the Koryo kingdom. Later the ridicule through this dance was directed towards the leading class of the Yi dynasty, the *yangban*.

The other kind of priest dance is based on a humanity-theme in contrast to the cynical antagony of the first. Wearing the Buddhist priest's hood and costume and holding a drum stick, the dance expresses agony, ascetic feeling and spiritual exhaultation of human flesh and blood. The dance, therefore, calls for trained techniques. Feature of this dance is that when the dancer has swirled himself to a climax, he or she stops dancing to beat a drum on the floor. This beating of the drum is generally interpreted as "attainment of salvation" (the Nirvana) in Buddhist philosophy. It insinuates that having become blind and mute in front of the Buddha, human flesh and blood can only resort to drum-beating in prayer for salvation. We may get an inkling of the philosophy and meditation of the East in this dance.

Drum Dance

This dance is performed with the long, slim *changgu* drum of Korea slung across the shoulder. Other Korean dances rarely call for techniques more elaborate and acrobatic than this dance. Therefore, it may best be described as a series of acrobatic movements, demonstrating skill in drum beating at a tempo. The *changgu* drum used for this dance was first introduced to Korea from China during Koryo; accordingly, the acrobatic beauty and techniques exhibited in this dance are Chinese in nature. It is believed that the introduction of the *changgu* drum added color and variety to Korean dancing, for the monotonous rhythms of previous dances became delicate developments in the latter-day dances through incorporation of the *changgu* drum into the original tunes. The left side of this drum is covered with calf skin, while the right side is made of horse skin so that the former may sound low notes and the latter high. The low notes insinuate the gentle and slow but steady nature of the calf while the high notes suggest the nimble movements of the horse. In recent years, the role of the *changgu* drum in this dance has been relegated to a secondary place, the dance itself becoming the dominating factor of the dance.

Another significant contribution of the *changgu* drum has been that the percussion instrument encouraged impromptu execution in all Korean dances, for drum beating drove everybody to unique "shoulder movements" despite themselves.

Difference of Korean Dance from Ballet

The Korean dance differs fundamentally from the ballet of the West in that whereas ballet seeks overt beauty of forms through rigidly controlled elaboration of techniques, the Korean dance attempts covert aesthecism of the inner spirit through discretion. Another basic difference between the two is that the Korean dance places emphasis on the upper half of the body, while ballet's importance is in the lower portion of the dancer. In the Korean dance, the image introduced by the shoulders is responded by the arms, while the head moves in affirmation.

This does not, however, mean that the Korean dance does not call for techniques of stretching and bending of the knees or movement of legs, but the legs in the Korean dance move in support of the upper half of the body and not for demonstrating the technique of leg movements for their own sake. Throughout our history of the dance, therefore, legs have always remained hidden behind a long shirt.

The ballet is performed on the toes, but the Korean dance is executed on the heels, for the Korean dancer steps forward with his or her toes up. Such steps undoubtedly run counter to the natural movement of the body, but it is an important attribute to the introverted spiritualism of the Korean dance in that it holds body movements in check. Free movement of the Korean dancer is further restricted with his or her loose-fitting costume in contrast to the tight fitting costume for the ballet which facilitates unimpaired movements. At the sleeves of the Korean dancer's costumes are attached long cloths called *hansam*, covering the hands completely and yet further hindering movement of arms. But the technique of handling this apparently cumbersome *hansam* is one of the most important parts of the Korean dance.

Modern Dance

The Western dance was first introduced to Korea in 1926 when the Japanese dancer, Ishii Baku, modern pioneer of his country, presented a public performance in Seoul, billing his art as "modern dance." The term, "modern dance," therefore, has been used in Korea as indicating both Western dance and new dances of all kinds as against the old, traditional dancing.

The introduction of Western dances to Korea by Ishii Baku coincided with the rage in Europe of the "new dance" movement. Ishii was one of the few Japanese who studied ballet in the early days under the Italian master, G. V. Rossi, and he was profoundly influenced by the new dances of Duncan, Dalcroze, Diaghilev while he was in Europe in 1915. He exerted definite influence on the modern dance of Korea, for practically all Korean dancers of modern times who later won fame once studied under him.

What they called "modernization of Korean folk dances," however, was nothing more than superficial adaptation of the traditional. Nevertheless, their version of the modernized Korean dance was warmly received in Japan where it was originated and developed. The Korean dance students were, therefore, later put in the embarrassing position of having to import the modern Korean dance from Japan, because the distorted fabrication of Korean dancing along what they believed to be modern lines was enthusiastically received by Korean audiences. Awed by such overwhelming response, younger dance students of Korea concentrated on imitating their idols instead of attempting to originate and develop their own modern versions.

Lasting as his influence was, Ishii Baku was not the first to introduce Western dancing to Korea. Several public performances preceded the arrival of the Japanese pioneer of the "modern dance." They were staged at the Wongaksa Theatre, the first Western-style hall of public entertainment built in Korea, or the Y.M.C.A. building in Seoul. For instance, there was a public performance in 1923 of a troupe composed of Korean residents in Siberia. The *Hopark* dance of Russia was first introduced by a member of the troupe who fascinated the Korean people to such an extent that it soon became a rage.

Another memorable event of the early period of Western-style dancing involves a white Russian girl, remembered only as Helen. Helen presented Seoul audiences with her native dances as a side show in a public performance staged as a relief program for white Russian exiles.

In the meantime, professional female dancers of the Yi dynasty who had formerly served the Korean court, were driven out of the palace after the fall of the kingdom, and drifted into high-class Korean restaurants. Thus, the traditional court dance of Korea found its refuge in drinking houses, and former courtesans degenerated into *kisaeng* girls, the Korean equivalent of the Japanese *geisha*. That a later Korean generation condemned dancing so sternly is readily understandable when we remember the historical fate of the Korean dance.

The first presentation of Western dancing by Westerners took place in 1927 when a Russian troupe, called the "Slavinskaya Choir," arrived in Korea to present a program of Russian dances. There were also public performances by Fujida Shigeru, Sakai Chieko and Torifuji Yoshitaro, Japanese dancers who had studied the authentic Russian folk dance in Moscow. The third presentation of Ishii Baku's dance in 1928 impressed the Korean audience with employment of the electric phonograph. The year also saw a memorable ballet performance by a German ballerina.

The first Korean to present a public performance of Western dancing was Miss Pae Kuja, a former revue girl of the Japanese circus, Amakatsu. Her program which included "Arirang" and "The Queen of Gold and Silver" was an adaptation of traditional Korean folk dances along "modern" lines. She opened her own dance studio in Korea in 1929. In the same year, Miss Choe Sunghi, who had been studying under Ishii in Japan, returned to Korea also to open her own dance studio. Her first public performance took place in 1930 with a program which included "They Seek after the Sun," "The People Look for Liberation," "Song of the World," "Sorrow of India," etc. The audience, however, did not respond favorably, and the gap between her and the popular audience of Korea widened still further at her next public performance some time later.

The year 1931 was marked by the arrival of the world-famous Sakharov dance team whose performance left a deep impression on Korean dancers.

The first presentation of Mr. Cho Taekwon's modern dance following his return from Japan was not a success, but it was significant in that he was the first Korean male dancer of the modern school. Subsequently both Miss Choe Sunghi and Mr. Cho Taekwon concentrated on modernization of Korean folk dance, but the public response went against their efforts. Miss Choe later took her dances to Japan, where they were enthusiastically received, paving the ground for her future as queen of the modern Korean dance.

In 1938, the *"Neue Tanz"* of the Mary Wigman school was introduced to Korea by the Japanese, Eguchi Takaya, and in 1939, the great Pavlova herself presented classic ballet to Korea.

As the country's enthusiasm for dance mounted steadily, increasingly large numbers of Koreans went to Japan to study the art. The modern dances of the Ishii Baku school, however, retained the reign of Korea's modern dance until the end of World War II.

Present Conditions

Apart from what is popularly called the "modern dance" of Korea, the traditional folk dance has been preserved until today, due particularly to the efforts of Mr. Han Songjun, whose contribution to systematization of folk dances was rewarded with an Art Award from the Japanese government. Then there was Kim Chono, whose authentic folk dancing was also widely appreciated.

After the Liberation of Korea in August 1945, all dancers organized themselves into a Korea Dance Artists' Association. Many went to north Korea during the war, while those remaining in the south organized a Korea Dance Group to keep dancing alive in Pusan refuge. The activities of such leading young dancers as Im Songnam, who studied the ballet in Japan, is considered one of the most promising with his ideal physique and the high standard of his creative works. His modern ballet, "The Man in Gray," is generally singled out as a demonstration of wonderful technique.

Song Pom, who has not studied abroad, trained himself in the ballet as well as in dances of both the Korean and Indian schools to create a highly personal style of his own. He attempts to excel in "modern ballet", but his version seems somewhat different from the usual interpretation of the dance. His "Departure for the Front" is considered a masterpiece.

Miss Kim Paekpong, who came to south Korea from the north during the war, has been attempting to create a new style based on traditional forms in contrast to practically all other contemporary dancers whose attempts at modernization of classical Korean dance met with failure because of their superficial imitation of the old combined with the new. Miss Kim, however, has yet to find basic principles on which to build her new style.

Korean dance students today are being trained at small private studios, for there are no schools exclusively devoted to dance instructions. Public performances usually incur financial losses, and no subsidy is extended by the government. Moreover, the Ministry of Education has not authorized establishment of any department of dance at accredited schools. In short, the handicaps are many for the young men and women of Korea who aspire to be great dancers.

As a professional organization, the Dance Association embraces many members, unlike the Dance Instructors' Association which naturally is made up only of instructors.

On the other hand, several universities sponsor annual dance contests for high school students, while a newspaper in Seoul has recently made it an annual affair to hold a "Premiere of New Dancers."

In the meantime, practically all Korean dancers are cherishing the hope that their dancing, if based on traditional Korean rhythm, will some day find a welcome reception in the world's leading theaters.

Korean Traditional Music

There are three kinds of music in Korea today; native music, Chinese music that was imported many years ago, and the classical and jazz music of the West introduced during this century. One hears little of traditional music compared to Western, and most Western music is light. Thousands of radios throughout the land make music easily available. The strains one hears are usually Western music and popular Korean songs that imitate Western beats from blues to mambo. On the other hand, the taste for and appreciation of Western classical music is remarkable. Modern music students demand nothing less than Bach and Beethoven in their formative years, and audiences have learned to expect this.

Christianity is responsible for the importation of Western music and much in its instruction. The influence of church music extends far beyond the church boundaries to arrest the minds of people everywhere, in villages as much as in the cities.

Ancient Instruments

According to mythical legend, Korea is said to have been founded in the year 2333 B.C. However that may be, archaelogical evidences, turning up such findings as ships, swords and porcelains, would suggest that state ceremonials were established in the prehistoric era. This, in turn, would indicate that music had a place in prehistoric Korean life for music has always been closely bound with Oriental state and religious ceremonies.

Over in China, music was a most important part of all rituals and formal educations during the Chou dynasty (1125-250 B.C.). Indeed, a minister was appointed whose sole responsibility lay in the supervision of rituals and music. With the state offering positive encouragement, intensive studies were pursued by scholars in these fields. In particular, the Duke of Chou, premier and regent of King Cheng, was largely responsible for the importance of this dynastic era in the history of Chinese music. He laid down plans which led to the establishment of a Board of Music and a number of master musicians were retained to collect and write lyrics while eulogies in praise of the righteousness and virtue of the royal ancestors were composed and music played on instruments of bronze and jade. The musical instruments of this period are said to have been the original Chinese. Many of these were introduced to Korea in the prehistoric era and they have been used ever since to this day.

Coming down to the historical Three-Kingdom period, first there was Koguryo. The people of this kingdom lived very much in the open air, and were fierce, impetuous, strong and hardy. They were fond of music and pleasures at night. It was during the Koguryo era that the black harp (*komungo*) was invented by a minister, Wang Sanak. It is said that a Chinese *kum* (harp) of seven strings was sent to the kingdom of Koguryo, but no one knew the art of playing it. An announcement was accordingly made to the effect that a reward would be given to any one who could be found to play the instrument but no one could be found. So Wang Sanak remade the instrument, instead, and composed some one hundred melodies on the new model. One day, while he was playing upon it, a black crane came and danced to the tune. The instrument was, therefore called a Black Crane Harp, and later, simply, the Black Harp or *komungo* in Korean.

Ancient books on Korea make passing references to music in Paekche so we know that there was music in the second of the three kingdoms, but nothing more beyond that mere fact.

The third Silla kingdom is responsible for the development of the *kayagum*, the king of Korean harps. A purely native invention, it has remained the most important of all Korean instruments up to the present day. Strictly speaking, it belonged to the principality of Kaya, after which the name derives. The inventor, one, U Ruk, composed twelve compositions on the harp at the command of a Kaya monarch, as a result of which his fame as a musician spread to Silla. When Kaya fell to Silla, U Ruk went to the latter kingdom where he was made court master of music. Three men were appointed to study singing, dancing and instrument-playing from him. It is said that they learned eleven tunes, but chose only five because they thought the tempo of the others was too fast. At first U Ruk was greatly displeased, but finally sent them to play before the king. For his part, the monarch was greatly pleased, but the ministers of the state objected because they said the tunes belonged to a ruined kingdom and, as such, should not be accepted by Silla. To which the king made reply that Kaya had been destroyed because its ruler was in the wrong, and that the faults of a king had nothing to do with music that was good.

In the *Samguk Yusa*, the Reminiscences of the Three Kingdoms, a legend is told of a certain flute, called the *manbasik*. Translated it means, "the million waves became peaceful." The instrument was so called because when the flute was played by the king, the waves became calm. During the reign of King Sinmun, so the legend goes, there was a mountain in the Eastern Sea (Japan Sea) shaped like the head of a tortoise. On the mountain was a bamboo tree which parted into two in daytime and joined together at night. The king ordered this tree cut down and from it he made a flute. Now this Sinmun is credited in history with invention of the *taegum* (large flute). So we have one and the same monarch figuring legendarily in the invention of the *manbasik* and historically in that of the *taegum*, but what the relation was between the two instruments is not known. The *taegum*, *kayagum* and *komungo* make the Three-Kingdom period a a very important one in the history of Korean music. All three instruments have undergone very little changes in over a thousand years.

Unified Silla, which brought Paekche and Koguryo under the single dominion of the third kingdom, enjoyed a period of peace and prosperity. It imbibed much from China which, under the concurrent Tang dynasty, was at the height of its artistic splendor. The great Tang king, Hienchung, was not only a patron of music but an able composer himself, building a concert within his palace and participating in musical performances himself. After the Tang dynasty, Chinese music became even more spontaneous and less scholarly. Save for Confucian temple music, little, however, seems to have been handed down. Korea, on the other hand, was a diligent pupil of China throughout these brilliant ages and, in turn, became the teacher of Japan as may be gathered from old Japanese documents to the effect that Paekche citizens went there to teach music.

Music also seems to have been nurtured during the Koryo dynasty (918-1,392) but the history of Korean music does not list any important musical instruments or compositions for this period. In the ninth year of King Yejong, the Sung Emperor, Huitsuan, sent a whole range of varied Chinese instruments plus 11 volumes of music notes to the kingdom. These instruments were used for monthly sacrificial rituals and seem to have been the beginning of sacrificial music in Korea.

Yi Music

The period of the Yi dynasty, ushered in 1392, marked great advances in original compositions, new arrangements of old ones, the remaking of old instruments and the compiling of a guide to music. Yi Taejo, founder of the last Korean dynasty, was apparently a great music-lover. In the midst of annoyances from officials who would upset all affairs of the new state he was building up and through all the attendant disorders of shifting the capital from Songdo to Seoul, he nurtured music till it rose to its greatest height in his lifetime. There are said to have been more than 800 musicians attached to the court.

The enlightened age of King Sejong, Taejo's grandson, saw musicians make lasting contributions in an age of flourishing culture. Sejong is only too well-known as the inventor of the *hangul* alphabet. What is not well-known is that he used the music scale as his foundation. Thus, in the old Korean encyclopedia, an account of the *hangul* alphabet appears under the sub-heading: "music." From Sejong onwards, the *hangul* was used to record witty sayings, folk lores, folk songs, and love songs. Little wonder that much music should be composed in praise of this illustrious king. Tradition says that the famous melody, "The Melody of Eternal Life, One Thousand Years," was composed in 1450 by the scholar Chong Inji of the old Confucian College of Seoul in praise of Sejong and his father, Taejong. Chong Inji is also famous for the song in 124 stanzas, "Dragon Flying to Heaven," which he completed in collaboration with two other scholars to eulogize the Yi dynasty. The "Dragon" was sung, in particular, at major gatherings of Confucian scholars, sacrificial rites and festive occasions in the palace.

The single most outstanding individual contribution to the entire realm of Korean music was made by the Sejong musicmaster, Pak Yon. Recognized as the greatest musician Korea has ever produced before or since, Pak Yon was composer, conductor and instrument-maker in one. His collection of musical instruments, old and new, totalled 75. He was also the organizer of the Imperial Music Department in his days and the modern National Traditional Music Institute claims him as founder of the Prince Yi Conservatory which was the predecessor of the institute. A large portrait of him hangs there today. Pak Yon was also responsible for providing the ritual music for Korean Buddhism. His tastes were discriminating so that of the three prevailing kinds of music, he considered the last named to be of low class and, accordingly, had its volume greatly reduced. He also disliked the idea of women musicians and used his influence to have the court bar them from performing. In this, he encountered much opposition from other officials but he succeeded, nevertheless, in cutting down on the number of female performers along with the country music. It is the prejudices of a great musician, therefore, that is to blame for the scarcity of folk songs today.

Sejong's successor, Sejo, was also a music-lover. His contribution to musical history was in remaking instruments and paring down the number to sixty. Unfortunately, he turned to Buddhism in his latter years, thus neglecting more opportunities to enhance the musical standards of an essentially Confucian state.

In the reign of Sejo's grandson, Songjong, who ascended the throne in 1470 and left behind a considerable legacy of artistic works, the most significant of all treatises on Korean music was written. This was the *Akhak Kwebom* (literally, "A Normal Study of Music") by a musicologist, Song Hyon. The date of this remarkable history, consisting of nine volumes bound in three books, is 1493. The contents may be outlined as follows:

Volume I Tone, Pitch, Scale and Theory.
II Position of Instruments of the Orchestra.
III Description of Chinese dances as related in "History of the Koryo Dynasty."
Description of Korean dances as related in "History of the Koryo Dynasty."
IV Chinese Dances actually performed.

V Korean Dances actually performed.
VI Description of Musical Instruments used in Chinese Sacred Music.
VII Description of Musical Instruments used in Chinese Secular Music.
Description of Musical Instruments used in Korean Music.
VIII Description of Accessories used in the Chinese Dances; fans, tables, etc.
IX Description of Costumes used by Musicians and Dancers.

The high tide of traditional music was reached during Pak Yon's time. After Pak Yon, it has steadily declined. The one center of preservation was the Prince Yi Conservatory which claimed Pak as their founder. Outstanding individuals of the Conservatory also have carried on the tradition, notably Myon Tchadok, a Yi citizen of Chinese descent. Myon studied Chinese writing, classics, harp, chimes, zither and violin and graduated from the Prince Yi Conservatory in 1862. In succession, he was supervisor of orchestras (1864), Master of Music (1889) and Third Director (1895) of the Conservatory. In 1904, he was promoted to fifth grade official of the state, in 1911 he was Master Administrator, and in 1916, succeeded to the Director's chair of the Conservatory. In this post, he worked at the Conservatory to a ripe old age, distinguished by many high decorations. We are especially indebted to him for his great contribution to Korean music.

As mentioned in the early part of this chapter, the Prince Yi Conservatory has recently made a new start as the National Traditional Music Institute. Under the jurisdiction of the Ministry of Education, the institute preserves over sixty kinds of traditional instruments and provides much data on old music, including music whose origins date back to the Sung dynasty in China and the Koryo kingdom in Korea.

Trends in Music

Korean traditional music is slow and simple in tempo and rhythm, in comparison with Western music. In an age favoring quickness and complexity in all fields, therefore, it naturally has been less popular than Western music. Thus for a long time since the introduction of Western music, the traditional music tended to be neglected, seldom appearing on radios, records, theaters, and concerts.

Recently, however, a tendency has been growing among music lovers to give traditional music its rightful place in the life of the people. Particular mention should be made of the work being done at the National Traditional Music Institute, formerly the Prince Yi Conservatory, which used to provide music for the royal family of the Yi dynasty. This institute has been busy training Korean musicians in the tasks of notating, collecting and preserving a library and museum of Korea's traditional musical heritage. The institute now has over sixty different kinds of traditional instruments, including such rare ones as the *pyonjong, pyongyong, achaeng, komungo* and *kayago*.

Following the fall of the Yi dynasty, most of the ancient traditional rituals and ceremonies were abolished. At the same time, traditional music started to decline because it no longer had any practical use. It started to be treated as a sort of useless classics to be preserved purely for the sake of being handed down to future generations. Since the war, many students of traditional music have had to give up their studies. To repair this handicap, the National Traditional Music Institute and authorities concerned have launched an intensive campaign for propagating traditional music and training new young students. Their efforts have been highly successful in the past several years. The radios and theaters have begun to include more traditional classics in their musical programs; the Wongaksa especially has dedicated itself as the theater for old Korean music. Moreover, in 1955, a training center was established with the object of annually training an average of about 30 boys who have just graduated schools in traditional music for six years, thus to lay a firm foundation for handing down a unique heritage to future generations.

There is another organization called the Chongak Center which is dedicated to the propagation and rejuvenation of traditional music. But this is more or less an organization of leisurely people who are interested in learning traditional music purely for the sake of amusement in their leisurely hours. Therefore, its activities have been less active as compared with other professional organizations.

In recent years, the National Traditional Musical Institute has been busy in organizing concerts and operas to interest as many people as possible in the value inherent in the Korean traditional music. The first of these series of attempts was a drama made out of the "Story of Hungbu" in 1958. In 1959, Mrs. Kim Sohui composed a Western-style solo out of a Changgukcho and gave a recital of this at the Wongaksa.

Efforts have been launched by such authorities in Korean traditional music as Messrs. Yi Hyegu, Chang Sahun and Song Kyongnin to systematize traditional music theoretically. In 1594, these scholars organized an Institute of Traditional Music, which, ever since, has been holding a lecture meeting once a month for the purpose of orientating the general public on traditional music. In 1959, Mr. Yi Hyegu, chief of the organization, got a Doctor of Literature for his treatise entitled, "Study on Ujo and Kebaekcho in modern Traditional Music of Korea." Mr. Yi's treatise was instrumental in giving traditional music theoretical systematization.

Since 1957, people began to acknowledge the need of giving a proper reappraisal to the value of traditional music, and in 1958, the Ministry of Education undertook a project for systematizing traditional music as a subject of academic learning. As the first step, the Ministry made records out of the *Pansori-Chunhyangga,* sung by the late Chong Chongyol, the late Yi Hwachungsong, and Mrs. Kim Sohui, the *kayagosanjo* sung by Mr. Sim Sanggon, and a folk song of Cheju Island sung by the team from Cheju Island at a concert of traditional music sponsored by the Federation of Writers in 1958. Subsequently, Messrs. Kim Tongjin, Na Unyong, and Kim Songtae made a collection of the *Chunhyangga,* Mr. Kim Kisu a collection of the *Kayagosanjo,* and Mr. Yi Pyongu a collection of the folk songs of Cheju Island. Out of these intensive works came the first edition of the projected series on Korean traditional music.

"The Seven Proposals for Improving Korean Traditional Music," written by composer Na Unyong, and the "Comparison of Korean Instruments for Solo and Western Orchestra" compiled by Messrs. Kim Tongjin, Kim Huijo and Chong Hoegap can be cited as evidence showing how enthusiastic they are in their zeal for creating musical works out of the heritage handed down from the older generations. Thus, contrary to the past when it was regarded a mean thing to teach traditional music in schools, students have now come to take pride in learning traditional music in schools. The Toksong Womens' College in 1954 sponsored a concert making boys and girls compete in singing traditional music. This, indeed, was a significant event in the history of the Korean traditional music. Recently, schoolgirls are enthusiastic about learning to play the *Kayago.* Mrs. Kim Yundok has established an institute dedicated to teaching *Kayago* to girls from middle and high schools, and the institute now has five university girls and 15 girls from middle and high schools. In 1957, the Ministry of Education issued an instruction to middle and high schools throughout the country to include the *piri* flute in their musical training. Radios, in the meantime, have started to pick up traditional music almost daily in their programs. In 1959, a Department of Traditional Music was established in the Musical College of the Uni-

↑ Fan Dance; Miss Kim Paekpong
A scene from "Witches in a Picture"

↑ Schoolgirls Mass Classic Dancing

↑ Mask Dance
 A folk dance that is masculine, animated, fast in tempo and without restraint on the dancers, costumes and movements.

Fan Dance, or Puchae-Chum
↓ A folk dance.

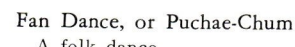

↑ Priest Dance, or Sungmu; Miss Kim Paekcho
  Has nothing to do with Buddhism. Merely a folk dance adapted from a Buddhist ritual dance, the Sungmu reflects the most characteristic beauty of Korea among all other dances.

↑   A Scene from "Flow of Lines"

↓   A Scene from "Witches in a Picture"

↑ Sward Dance; Miss Kim Paekpong
A scene from "Sparks of Life"

↑ Drum Dance, or Changgo-Chum; Miss Kim Paekcho
An acrobatic dancing demonstrating skill in drum-beating at a tempo.

↑ Drum Dance, or Changgo-Chum; Miss Cho Yongja
Taking a pose with Changgo drum slung across the shoulder.

↑ A Scene from "Ancient Style"

↓ A Scene from "A Tale of Our Village"

↑ Fairy Dance; Miss Kang Sonyong
  While the fairy was bathing in a lake, she had her clothes stolen by woodcutter, so she was forced to marry him on earth.

↑ "White Waltz"

↓ "Swan on a Lake"

A Ballerina Taking a Pose →

← A Classic Ballet

↓ "Romantic Suite"

↑ "Swan on a Lake"

↑ "Beautiful Korea"

↓ "Groan of Life"

↑ A Woman Playing Kayagum
One of the most famous Korean instruments. A purely native Korean harp invented by U Ruk, the gifted musician of the Kaya State and afterwards the court musician of Silla Kingdom.

A Woman Beating Changgo
↓ The most popular drum in Korea. Favorable in popular music and festival.

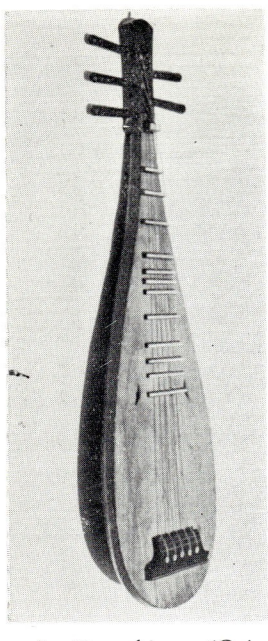

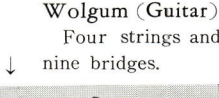

Wolgum (Guitar)
↓ Four strings and nine bridges.

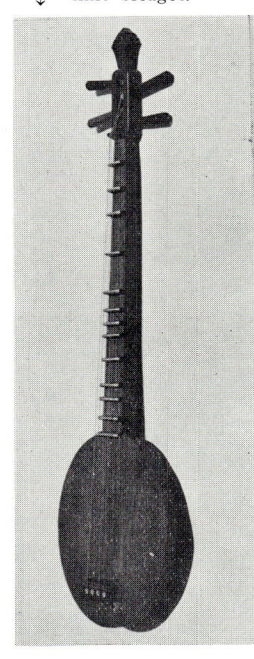

↑ Hyangbipa (Guitar)
Five strings. Plucked by a small stick.

↑ Haegum (Violin)
The bow is attached to the violin and played vertically rather than horizontally.

↑ O (Stopper)
On the back of wooden tiger are 27 teeth in three series. Used to stop orchestral pieces by running a brush of the stick along the back.

Unna
Ten chimes struck by a wooden beater. The tone
↓ varies.

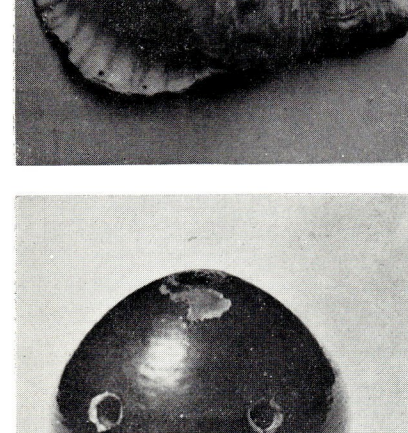

← Nagak (Horn)

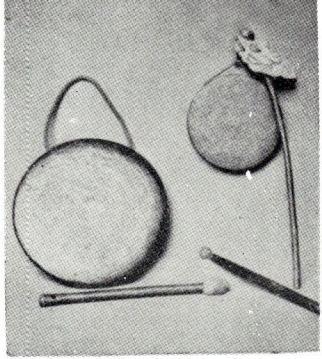

↑ Taegum and Sogum
Gongs. Used in ritual music.

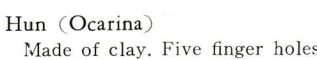

← Hun (Ocarina)
Made of clay. Five finger holes.

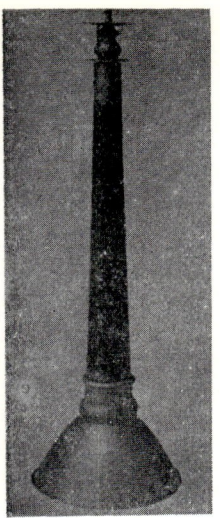
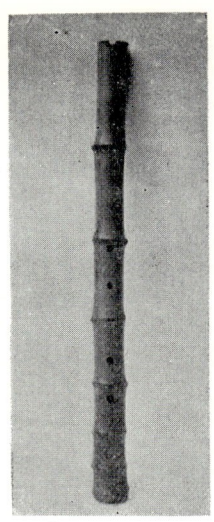
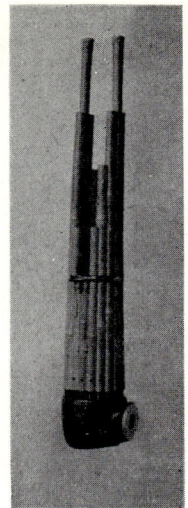
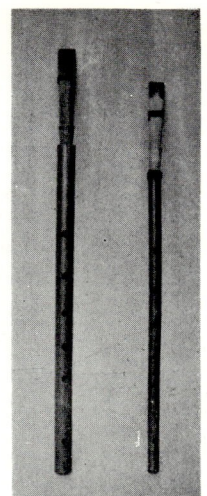
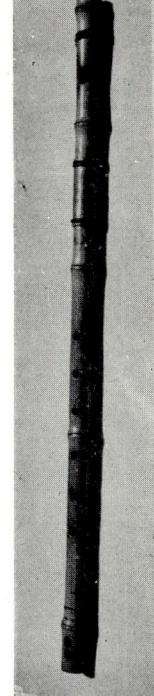

↑ Taepyongso (Clarinet)
　Wooden body with brass funnel.

↑ Tanso (Pipe)
　It has a fivecovered holes. Played vertically.

↑ Saenghwang (Organ)
　17-tube miniature pipe organ.

↑ Piri (Oboe)
　Made of bamboo. Left is Hyangpiri, right, Sepiri.

Taegum (Flute) →

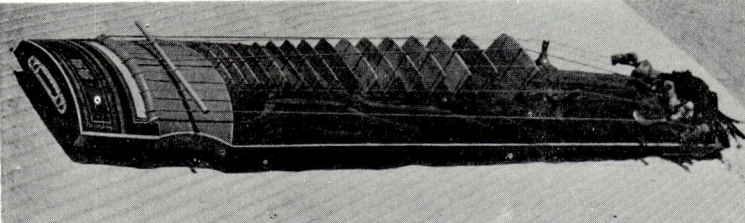

Kayagum
　12 strings stretched over 12 bridges. Plucked by fingers.
　↓

↑ Komungo
　This harp is one of the oldest instruments made in Koguryo.

The National Traditional Music Academy
　To train traditional musicians.
　↓

Kumbo →
　An old traditional music book.

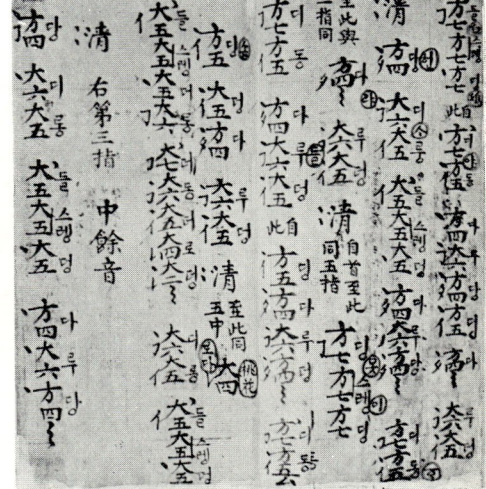

Pyongyong and Masque Dancers
Sixteen slabs of jade, hung in two rows of eight each, in a carved frame. The slabs are seemingly identical but the thickness varies.

Taegum
Korea's own instrument. It is not found in Japan or even in China. At one-third of the distance from the end of this flute is a hole, called Chong, which is covered with a thin membrane taken from a reed. This fibre vibrates and produces a blaring sound.

Saenghwang
It is said that a Dane used the principles of this instrument to invent an organ which developed later into the harmonium, accordion, and finally, pipe organ.

Accompaniment of Korean Traditional Instruments
Dance or Drama performed to the accompaniment of such an orchestra; frm right to left, Changgo, Piri, also Piri, Taegum and Haegum.

↑ **So (Flute)**
A mouth-organ. 16 pipes. The tones are chromatic.

↑ **Pyongyong (Jade Chimes)**
The tone is produced by striking the slabs with a mallet tipped with horn.

↑ **Changgo (Hour-Glass Drum)**
The left side is beaten with the palm of the left hand, the right with a stick held in the right hand.

↑ **Chwago**
An ancient drum used since the Three Kingdoms.

Pyonjong (Bronze Chimes) →
The outside appearances of the 16 bells alike, but the inside dimentions are different. The upper right bell, the thickest, produces high tone, and the lower right bell, the thinnest, low tone.

↑ An Orchestra of Korean Traditional Instruments

All college-students. The instruments in the back row are all Kayagum (harp); the front row, from left to right, Changgo (drum), Komungo (harp) and Ajaeng(cello); the instrument, the girl in the center is holding, is Haegum (violin).

↑ Seoul City Symphony Orchestra
   Western music has made rapid progress in Korea.

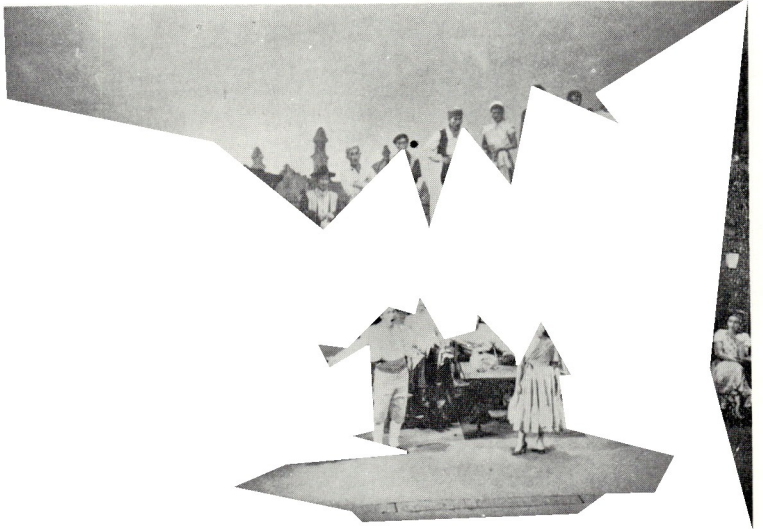

← A Scene from the Opera "Carman"
   Koreans average three operas a year.

The Seoul City Symphony Orchestra
   Gave a concert in Hong Kong on April 20, 1947

← ROK Navy Band

→ ROK Army Band

U.S. Symphony Orchestra of the Air
   At Seoul on concert tour.
↓

versity of Seoul. This was considered one of the major developments in efforts aimed at regaining and developing our unique heritage further.

Classification of Korean Music

(1) *Aak*, Confucian Temple Music: This is oue of the most ancient kind of music now played in Korea. Originated in China, it underwent a lot of Koreanization during King Sejong's reign. The Chinese text consists of eight lines of four syllables each. One note is set to each syllable. The heptatonic melody begins and ends on the same note. The orchestras, one sitting on the terrace and the other on the ground, play alternately.

(2) *Tangak* and *Hyangak*, Court Music: Korean court music consists of two kinds, *Tangak*, Chinese court music invented during the Tang dynasty, and *Hyangak*, indigenous court music. The latter is believed to have been in existence since the 5th century. *Tangak* was introduced into the country in the 8th century. *Tangak* has been played in ceremonies and rites, and *Hyangak* usually with dancing and other entertainment. The orchestra for *Hyangak* consists chiefly of conical oboes which constitute the principal melodies, horizontal flutes, two-stringed fiddles and drums. In *Tangak* bell chimes, stone chimes, and the mouth-organ are also used. *Hyangak* has a pentatonic tone-system while *Tangak* is heptatonic. It has a more complicated rhythm than *Tangak*.

(3) *Chuita*, Military Music: Military music such as the *Muryongjegok*, sometimes called *Taechuita*, was played in military processions and on such occasions as when gates to military headquarters were opened or closed. There were two kinds of military bands. One is louder and marches in front of an important person, such as a king. The other, the softer one, was usually played following a procession escorting an important person. Conical oboes, brass trumpets, cymbals, gongs and drums were used in the front band; the rear one consisted of oboes, horizontal flutes, hour-glass-shaped drums and round drums. These bands were commonly called *Toraji*.

(4) *Changak*, Chamber Music: Chamber music has been a decent form of amusement for gentlemen. *Yongsanhoesang*, originally a Buddhist song, used to be accompanied by dancing, later dropped the text and became purely instrumental music. Without dancing, it used to be played with nine additional pieces of musical instruments. The instruments used in the music are the six-stringed zither, dulcimer, two-stringed fiddle, horizontal flute, conical oboe, and hour-glass drum.

(5) *Sanhyon*, Dance Music: Korean dance music is of three kinds. *Yombul* is grave and slow, *Taryong* is gay and rhythmical, and *Kutkori* is a rippling and comparatively fast music. The instruments used are almost the same as those used in the softer *Chuita* band.

(6) *Sanjo*, Solo Music for twelve-stringed zither or horizontal flute: *Sanjo* was played by a professional musician, accompanied by an hour-glass drum. It has three main sections; slow, moderate and fast.

(7) *Kagok*, Lyric Song: This usually is sung by professional singers, men or women, to the accompaniment of a six-stringed zither, a dulcimer, a small conical oboe, horizontal flute and an hour-glass drum. A complete performance consists of twenty-six pieces of musical instruments and lasts for many hours.

(8) *Kasa*, Narrative Song; Narrative songs such as the *Chunmyongok*, "Sleepy Spring," usually sung by a trained singer, was accompanied by a horizontal flute and an hour-glass drum. The rhythm usually consists of six beats and the tempo is generally slow.

(9) *Sijo*, Short Lyric Song: *Sijo* is almost similar to the *kagok* in tone and text. But it is not as richly ornamented and is accompanied only by an hour-glass drum.

(10) *Changguk*, Dramatic Song: A professional musician sings the dramatic song with a fan in his hands. Declamation, song,

gesture and the accompaniment of a drum all comprise a performance. The long story that takes more than two hours to relate is supposed to make the audience weep and laugh.

(11) *Minyo*, Folk Song: In contrast to the folk songs of China and Japan, those in Korea are characterized by their triple meter and dotted rhythms. Phrases are clearly arranged according to a rule, usually four measures to a phrase. The texts of the Korean folk songs vary according to the localities in which they are sung. According to different musical dialects, Korea is divided into three parts: central, northern and southern.

(12) *Nongak*, Rural Band Music: This is the type of band music which is played by farmers to express their delight at completing transplantations or harvest of rice. As in other Korean folk songs, they are also characterized by triple rhythms in feeling. The band is usually played hopping along village roads and in open grounds. It consists primarily of percussion instruments, but sometimes conical oboes are added.

Korean Musical Instruments

Korean musical instruments are classified according to the eight kinds of material of which they are made,—metal, stone, earth, silk, gourd, bamboo, wood and leather.

A brief explanation of Korean traditional musical instruments follows:

Classification: Metal

Pyonjong (Bronze chimes)

First invented by the Chinese musician, Yuen. Sixteen bronze bells, two rows of eight each, hang in a carved wood standard. Carvings represent dragons, lions, phoenix bird and lotus flowers. The figure of the lion was used to represent "metal." Pheasant feathers and tassels ornament the sides. Bells are almost same diameters at the bottom, but larger in the middle. Outside appearances are the same, but the inside dimensions are different. The metallic mass of the first bell lower right is less than that of the next, the last bell on upper right is the greatest. The thick bells produce high tones, the thin bells low tones. They progress upward with a hammer.

Tukchong (Bronze chime)

A single bronze bell similar to *pyonjong*, but larger. It is used only to start the orchestra.

Panghyang (Iron chimes)

Sixteen iron slabs in two series horizontally arranged on a carved standard tied with cords of twisted silk. The chromatic series correspond to those of the bell chimes, but an octave higher, the thin ones giving low tones; the thick, high. They are struck with a hammer tipped with cow horn. Used in non-ritualistic music.

Yangum (Zither)

Said to have come originally from India. The word *yang* means foreign. The fourteen strings are tapped by a thin rod held in the right hand. Each string is in quadruple, totalling fifty-six strings in all.

Chabara (Cymbals)

These small cymbals are said to have come originally from Egypt through India.

Ching (Gong)

Hung by a cord held in the hand, it is struck with a wooden beater tipped with leather.

Para) Cymbals)

Large and heavy. Usually used in Buddhist temples.

Taegum (Gong)

Large but smaller than *Ching*. Used in Korean ritual music.

Sogum (Gong)

Small, resembling the *Taekum*

Napal (Bugle)

Long, sometimes three feet in length.

Classification: Stone

Pyongyong (Jade chimes)

Sixteen slabs of "jade," hung in two rows of eight each, in a carved frame. The figure of the swan was used in the carvings to represent stone. Length and breadth are almost identical but the thickness varies. Invented by Kyeng, a Chinese, it was used mainly for religious purposes. The tone is produced by striking the slabs with a mallet tipped with horn.

Tukkyong (Jade chimes)

A single slab of "Jade" hung in a frame similar to the *Pyongyong*. It is seldom used, and then to end a piece of music.

Classification: Silk

Kum (Harp)

Seven strings without a bridge, plucked by the fingers. Invented by the famous Chinese, Yumje Sillong.

Tangbipa (Guitar)

Four strings, plucked by the finger. In ancient times a small wooden plectrum was used. Sometimes three thimbles were worn— one on the 2nd, one on the 3rd, and one on the 4th finger. The neck of the instrument turns backwards. Its origin is said to be Persian.

Hyangbipa (Guitar)

Five strings, plucked by a small stick. The neck is straight.

Sil (Guitar)

Twenty-five strings with twenty 25 bridges, plucked by fingers.

Kayagum (Harp)

Modeled after the Chinese *Chaeng*, with 12 strings stretched over twelve bridges, plucked by the fingers. The inventor is the famous U Ruk of Kaya.

Achaeng (Cello)

Seven bridges passing over separate bridges over which is drawn a "bow" made of Fosythia wood The rod of wood itself is resined; there are no hairs on the bow.

Taejaeng (Harp)

The name indicates "big harp," The inventor was Mong Myom. It has fifteen strings, plucked with the finger.

Haegum (Violin)

Differs slightly from the Chinese violin. The Korean violin is played vertically rather than horizontally, and is held on the left knee. The bow, with hairs, is attached loosely to the violin by running the strings between the hairs of the bow and the bowstick. While played, the finger board faces the right, or bow arm.

Classification: Bamboo

Taegum (Flute)

This instrument is purely Korean, and is not found in China. One third of the distance from the end of the flute is a hole covered with a thin membrane taken from a reed. When the breath passes through the instruments, the fibre vibrates and produces a blaring sound.

Tangjo (Flute)

The inventor is Choong of China. The flute is held horizontally and has six finger holes besides the mouth piece.

Chung Kum (Flute)

Medium size. Invented by King Sinmun of Silla.

Chi (Flute)

Six holed, horizontal flute. A wax mouth piece is inserted in the side near the end.

So (Flute)

Resembles the "Pan Flute." It is really a mouth-organ without reeds. It has 16 pipes, arranged so that 1 and 16 are the longest, 8 and 9 the shortest. The tones are chromatic. Played at sacrifices and festivals.

Tangpiri (Oboe)

Made of bamboo with eight holes. Its mouth piece somewhat resembles the Western oboe. Used in both palace and popular music. The posterior holes of the oboe are lower than the anterior. Only in this does it differ from the other *Piri*. The *Piri* of the Korean orchestra corresponds to the violin of the Western orchestra, and is the real foundation. The string instruments are used to supplement the wind instruments so that the tone will continue while the players are taking breath.

Hyangpiri (Oboe)

Made of yellow bamboo, with 8 holes. The posterior holes are higher than the anterior.

Se Piri (Oboe)

The smallest of the *Hyangpiri*. Made of bamboo and soft sounding. It is used in court and popular music, and consists purely of reed instruments.

Tongso (Pipe)

Tone blaring like *Taegum*, because of hole covered with membrane which vibrates when blown. Played vertically, has 6 finger holes. Covers more than two octaves. It is said to have come originally from Tibet.

Tanso (Pipe)

Greatly resembles the *tongso* except that it has no fibre covered hole. Played vertically and has five finger holes.

Yak (Pipe)

Three holes. Played vertically. When used in civil dances it is carried, and not blown. It is blown in classical music pieces.

Chok (Pipe)

Small, vertically held.

Classification: Gourd

Saenghwang (Organ)

The miniature pipe organ is played by blowing out and sucking in the breath. The inhaling helps keep the pipes dry. The bowl was originally made of gourd into which were inserted 17 tubes. Invented by Yuwa, a Chinese woman, it was introduced later into Russia and tried by a Danish professor named Kratzeeuauer. Using the principles of the instrument he invented an organ which he submitted to the academy at Petrograd. The result was the modern harmonium, the accordion and finally pipe organ.

Classification: Earth

Pu (Drum)

Jar of baked clay struck with split bamboo mallet. Used in orchestra giving 10 different tones.

Hun (Ocarina)

Made of baked clay. Five finger holes, 3 anterior, 2 posterior. The mouth piece is at the point.

Nagak (Horn)

First introduced into Korea by King Kongyang.

Classification: Wood

Pak (Castanet)

Clappers shaped like a folded fan. Six leaves 1.152 ft. long, 0.256 ft. wide are held loosely together by a silk cord at the lower end and clapped together. The loose ends are thicker than the bound ends. Two hands are used for playing. It is used to begin and close music.

Tchuk (Starter)

A square wooden box placed on a base, with a wooden hammer or clapper running through the cover. The Korean *Tchuk* has a lid. Used in classical, sacred and festival music.

O (Stopper)

Wooden tiger, crouching on a square wooden base. On its back are 27 teeth in three series. Used to stop orchestral pieces by running a brush of long split bamboo along the back.

Taepyongso (Clarinet)

Wooden body with brass funnel. It is purely a reed instrument, and was used in military processions and festivals.

Classifications: Leather

Kongo (Drum)

Large drum introduced by King Sejong. Used in the lower orchestra. In olden times, it was used for court music.

Chingo (Drum)

Much like the *Kongo*, but not so much ornamented. Used in the lower orchestra for sacrificial music.

Unggo (Drum)

Introduced by King Sejong. It is used together with the *Sakko* and the *Kongo*, placed to the east. It is struck with a single stick at the end of the music. Used in the lower orchestra in court music.

Sakko (Drum)

Same as *Unggo* used in lower orchestra to start music.

Chunggo (Drum)

Kettledrum, used in sacrifices to the god of war.

Cholgo (Drum)

Introduced by King Sejong. used in higher orchestra. It is placed on a box-like table. Came from the Chou dynasty.

Kyobanggo (Drum)

The standard is 2.7 feet in width. It is used in secular music.

Chwago (Drum)

An ancient drum used since the Three Han era. It hangs from a frame standard.

Yonggo (Drum)

Like trap drum, two sticks are used. It is

used in military music.

Changgo (Drum)

Hour-glass shape. Used in secular music, is favorable for popular music and festival. It is beaten with the palm of the left hand at one end and with a stick held in the right hand at the other.

Kalgo (Drum)

Shaped like *Changgo,* but the palm is not used. A stick is used in each hand.

Noego (Drum)

Used in sacrifices to the gods.

Yonggo (Drum)

Used in sacrifices to the human spirits.

Nogo (Drum)

Used in sacrifices to the human spirits.

Noedo (Drum)

Small drums used in sacrifices to gods, to begin music. They are fastened to three-foot handles or sticks, and cords are fastened to the drums. When the handles are shaken, the cords beat against the drums.

Yongdo (Drum)

Small drums used in sacrifices to earth spirits, similar to *Noedo.*

Nodo (Drum)

Small drums used in sacrifices to human spirits, similar to *Noedo.*

Western Music

Introduction

Though it has been only about 50 years or so since it was first introduced into Korea, Western music has been rapidly and greatly popularized in this country. Particularly since the Liberation from Japanese rule, Western music has been actively pursued throughout the country. In this regard, it is to be noted that two major symphony orchestras have been newly organized to give regular concerts and that, despite the high expenses, operas are staged several times a year by enthusiastic singers. These unprecedented developments signify remarkable progress. The fact that several music colleges have been founded since the Liberation and that more students are going abroad to pursue advanced studies are added indications of the high enthusiasm for Western music.

Music students of each age level are encouraged by annual contests; there are also contests for other than music students, for primary school children and high school pupils. Meanwhile, foreign musicians are paying increasingly frequent visits to Korea. All of this cannot but help raise the level of Western musical standards.

Generally speaking, then, a great deal of progress has been marked in the field of musical performances. On the other hand, it is to be regretted that this progress in mere playing has not been matched by creative endeavors.

Church Music

Roman Catholicism reached Korea before Protestantism, but the number of Catholic churches (1139 by the last computations in 1957) is far less than that of the Protestant denominations and the volume of music is even more disproportionate. There is only one Catholic church that is equipped with a pipe organ and a choir. This is a Church in Seoul run by a professor of the Catholic College, the Reverend Yi Mungun, who majored in a musical course at Rome.

Church music, therefore, largely means Protestant music. There are 5,031 such churches in the country and each and everyone of these that are located in the major cities, at least, have their own choirs.

Apart from these choirs, there are several choruses which specialize in church music and give public performances. The conductors of these choruses are mostly men who majored in music in the United States.

Major choruses of this nature are:
  Oratorio Association Chorus:
    conducted by Pak Taejun
  Song Chong (Holy Bell) Chorus:
    conducted by Kwak Sangsu
  Zion Chorus: conducted by Yi Tongil
  Korean Chorus Association:
    conducted by So Sujun

On Easter days, and particularly during Christmas, Handel's "Messiah" chorus is invariably to be heard in many quarters of all major towns and cities. Church music, in short, enjoys great popularity everywhere.

Musical Education

During their six years in primary school, the children sing to the accompaniment of a piano or an organ and learn how to read musical notes. After finishing primary education, they enter junior high schools, and later senior high where they continue their musical education. There are 4,474 primary schools, 1,073 junior high schools and 600 senior highs in Korea.

The number of hours dedicated weekly to musical education in high school courses are:

junior high
year	hours per week
1st	2
2nd	1
3rd	1

senior high
year	hours per week
1st	1
2nd	1
3rd	

In extracurricular hours, high school students train themselves in vocal and instrumental solos and take part in school choruses and brass bands. So far, the Seoul Art High School is the only school specializing solely in a musical education.

Most music schools of college level were established after the Liberation. They are:
  Music College, Seoul University (Seoul)
  Music Department, College of Art, Ewha Women's University (Seoul)
  Music College, Sukmyong Women's University (Seoul)
  Departmant of Religious Music, Theological College, Yonsei University (Seoul)
  Music Department, College of Physical Training, Kyonghui University (Seoul)
  Music Department, Hyosong Women's College (Taegu)
  Music Department, Chosun University (Kwangju)
  Music Department, Sorabol Art College (Seoul)
  Music Department, Sudo Women's Teacher's College (Seoul)
  Music Department, Pusan Normal College (Pusan)

Annual contests to promote music education are given by; one, Ewha Girls' High School for children of primary school; two, College of Music, Seoul National University for high school students of music; three, Ewha Women's University for girls' high schools, and four, Chosun Ilbo (a daily newspaper) for college graduates.

Broadcasting System, Phonograph Records, Etc.

The goverment-operated Korean Broadcasting System has its key station in Seoul. It also has local stations in Pusan, Taegu, Taejon, Iri, Kwangju, Mokpo, Chunchon, Masan, and Namwon. Apart from these stations, there are the following three private broadcasting stations:
  Christian Broadcasting Station, in Seoul
  Korea Evangelical Broadcasting Station, in Inchon
  Pusan Cultural Broadcasting Station, in Pusan

Radio programs of these stations chiefly consist of Western music, mostly played from phonograph records of foreign origin. Broadcasting of actual concerts is less frequent.

A number of trade-marks have cropped up after the war, representing the major producers of phonograph records: Oasis Co., King Star Co., Universal Co., Sinsin Department Store, Midopa Department Store, and Domido Co. Their products are mostly either popular songs or dance music.

The production of classic-music records is so limited that there are only a small number of discs, offering the foremost works of Korea's outstanding composers, such as Hong Nanpa's "Balsam," Hyon Chemyong's (Rody Hyun) "Thinking of Home" and "Breezes," Yi Hungyol's "Rocky Hill," Kim Songtae's "Plant of One Heart," "A White Lily," "Sanyuhwa," "Farewell Song," and "Thinking of Parents," Kim Tongjin's "Hankering for Home" and "My Heart, Daffodil," Kim Sunae's "Four-Leafed Clover" and "Azalea," and Na Unyong's "Moonlit Night."

Taste for Western classical music is indicated in the survey taken September 27, 1959 by the Chosun Ilbo daily among customers of the three main tea-serving music halls in Seoul; Renaissance, Dolce and Seven Star. Results of the survey follow:

Preferential Order	Item
1st	Piano Concerto No.5 by Beethoven (Emperor)
2nd	Symphony No.9 by Beethoven (Chorus)
3rd	Violin Concerto E Minor by Mendelssohn
4th	Opera "Cavalleria Rusticana" by Mascagni
5th	Fantaisie Impromptu by Chopin
6th	Symphony No. 5 by Beethoven
7th	Opera "La Traviata" by Verdi
8th	Symphony No.6 by Tchaikovsky (Pathetic)
9th	Italian Folk Songs
10th	Violin Concerto D Major by Tchaikovsky

(It should be noted that music-hall customers largely consist of young students bred in urban society. Whatever the reasons that bring them to the music-halls in droves, one thing is certain: they lack any sound or confident knowledge of the music they imbibe).

Solos and Chamber Music

When a recital is held at a big theater, such as the Municipal Theater, the organizers are bound to suffer financial loss due to the heavy expenses involved. Unless it features a noted foreign musician or a popular Korean soloist, a recital at such a big theater can hardly expect to derive enough income. As a result, a soloist, who is unable to meet those disbursements, chooses an auditorium of some music college or other educational institution for his recital. Sometimes he may choose a smaller theater like the Wongaksa. In most cases, his performance is limited to the capital. A follow-up tour of the provinces is rare for even the more talented performers.

Numerous recitals have been held since the Liberation and through the war years. The war may have left its heavy mark on Korea's main run of musical talents but by no means dampened enthusiasms. If anything, recitals have been even more numerous in the postwar years. The performers may be divided into three categories.

First, there are the musicians whose names were already established in the prewar years. Such men as the violinist, Hong Chiyu; the cellist, Chon Pongcho, and tenors Yi Inbom and Yi Sangchun, have made their postwar comebacks since 1954.

The second category comprises musicians who either went abroad for advanced studies or plan to go. They are far more numerous than their colleagues in category one and, for the most part, began appearing on the stage from 1957 onwards. The better-known soloists are: Han Tongil, Mrs. Yi Kiwon and Misses Kwak Unsu and Yun Pohi (piano); Im Yujik (violin); Miss Chang Chongja (cello), and Pyon Songyop, Mrs. Yi Kyongsuk and Misses Ma Kumhi and Yi Kyusun (vocals).

The third category are the new young faces who have been making more and more debuts in recent years in hopes of gaining due public recognition. Enthusiasm is greatest here and while it is too early to tell the degree of talents to be found in their ranks, the fact that they are generally keen on developing their skills and techniques inevitably means a state of constant progress from which the best talents should emerge.

Whatever the category, all Korean soloists have one thing in common: they pay little regard to the financial returns from their performances.

In the field of chamber music, the two orchestras that have maintained themselves the most steadily are the String Quartet Band of the Seoul Chamber Music Association and the Academy String Trio Group. The forerunner of the Association was the Experimental Music Society, organized in 1952 in the wartime capital of Pusan by Im Wonsik, leading prewar conductor, and Chon Pongcho, the cellist. The aim of the Society was to give public performances of Western works as yet unintroduced to Korea and new Korean compositions. In 1957, the membership of this Society was enlarged to include several of the better-known musicians, such as the composer, Yi Songje; the conductor; Yi Namsu, pianists Mrs. Sin Chedok and Miss Chong Sunpin and the flutist, Miss Ko Sunja. There was also a new American member, the violinist, Lawrence F. Thompson, who was in Korea to present recitals under the sponsorship of the Asia Foundation. The Society, therewith, developed into the Seoul Chamber Music Association with the accretion of yet many more members, the violinists, Yi Chehyon, An Yonggi and Kim Yongsam and the cellist, Yang Chepyo. Altogether, the Society and the Association have presented 26 performances.

The Academic String Trio Group has been as busily engaged since 1957. Its leader is Dr. Kye Chongsik, a violinist who majored in music in Germany and was one of the foremost performers during the Japanese era. Dr. Kye has not only given many recitals after the Liberation but has also been constantly active conducting string quartets. Dr. Kye on the violin, Kim Tongsong on the piano, and Kim Chongmyong on the cello are the mainstays of the Academy.

Apart from these two major groups, there are other string bands, such as the Paek Heje Trio Group and the Women's Quartet Band. All in all, chamber music is becoming quite a vogue in the field of music.

Orchestra

The delirious joy with which the Korean people greeted the end of Japanese domination on August 15, 1945 revealed, among other things, their unconditional love of music. Joyful musicians banded together right after the Liberation without any secure financial backing whatsoever to form the Korea Symphony Orchestra. In October, only two months after the eventful day, they performed Beethoven's Symphony No. 5 at the Sudo (Capital) Theater to be acclaimed by a whole nation. The orchestra went ahead to offer a diet of good, regular performances in the next few years. It was with this orchestra that a young musician from Manchuria, Im Wonsik, emerged into the limelight as a conductor. The veteran violinist, An Pyongsu, who had studied and played in Berlin, also conducted.

At the height of its success, the Korea Symphony Orchestra began to be undermined by the formation of a new Seoul Symphony Orchestra with better financial resources. The latter orchestra under the direction and supervision of an American conductor, Dr. Rolf Jacoby, an advisor to the Seoul Broadcasting Station, achieved a new landmark by offering the Korean audience the first rendition in this country of Beethoven's Symphony No. 9 at its ninth regular concert with the chorus provided by the Art College Choir of the Music Department of the Seoul National University. The Korea Symphony Orchestra thereafter declined, its ranks were attracted to the Seoul Symphony Orchestra, and it soon disbanded. Its star, in short, was replaced by the Seoul Symphony Orchestra which presented regular concerts with a new conductor, John S.

Kim, up to the outbreak of the war.

The effect of the war was to drive musicians to the armed services which were in the best position to maintain orchestras. Thus, when the Seoul Symphony Orchestra reappeared after the confusions of the war upon a regular stage in wartime Pusan, it was as the Navy Symphony Orchestra. Besides this transformation of an existing organization, there was a new line-up of musicians gathered together under the army's wing to form the Army Symphony Orchestra. An Air Force Orchestra followed in due course. In this manner, symphonic strides were carried over the excesses of the war and the positions of the much-harassed musicians maintained with hopes for the future.

With the restoration of Seoul in 1953, the navy and army orchestras settled down under the regular batons of Im Wonsik and John S. Kim. Both had, in the meantime, undergone specialized courses in the art of conducting in the United States. In effect, they became more matured and confident conductors, with ample opportunities to display their best from the benefits of advanced technical training.

In 1955, a number of noted foreign musicians visited this country at the invitation of John S. Kim, horn-player Peter Altoberi, oboist Michel Nazi, cellist Richard Kay, violinist Kenneth Gordon, and pianist Thomas Bernstein. All of them not only gave solo recitals but also played with Korean orchestras during their stay in Korea. They were instrumental in giving their Korean colleagues many new pointers, particularly in the arts of performing on the horn and oboe which have received but little attention compared to the popularity of the violin or the piano. Besides such individual visitors, we were also privileged to listen to such famous orchestras as the Symphony of the Air (in 1955) and the Los Angeles Symphony Orchestra (in 1956).

The armed services, having seen the nation's symphonic orchestras through the stresses of war, relinquished them to public organizations with the restoration, more or less, of post-armistice stability. In 1956, the Army Symphony Orchestra was taken over by the Korean Broadcasting system to be called the K.B.S. Symphony Orchestra, and, a year later, the Seoul City government assumed management of the Navy Symphony Orchestra which has thus played under three different signboards in a history of less than ten years. Both orchestras were given the opportunity to tour Southeast Asian nations on goodwill cultural missions, the K.B.S. Symphony Orchestra in 1957 and the Seoul Symphony Orchestra in 1958. Also in 1958, two distinguished American conductors, William Strickland and Edward Straus, visited Korea and conducted both these two main Korean orchestras. Subsequently, either one or the other symphonic group has accompanied the foreign musicians who have been visiting Korea in ever increasing numbers in the past two years, culminating in the arrival of an Italian troupe whose main performers, soprano Gabriella Tucci, tenor Gianni Zaza, the bass, Fulinio Gulavasi, and others sang under the direction of Nino Berki conducting the combined Broadcasting and City Orchestras.

Last but by no means least, mention should be made of Eaktay Ahn, Korea's most successful export. Composer of our national anthem, Ahn left Korea during the Japanese occupation to major in music and establish himself as conductor, cellist and composer in Europe and settle down finally in Spain. In 1955, Ahn paid a long-absent visit to his fatherland to conduct the Navy Symphony Orchestra in a concert which featured his own symphonic fantasia, entitled, "Korea."

Opera

The start of opera in Korea was a one-man effort on the part of Yi Inson. Yi Inson was both a doctor and gifted tenor, having studied both fields in Italy. His plans met with serious obstacles from the beginning as he failed to secure an organizer able to meet the heavy expenses involved in the task of presenting an opera. Yi himself, therefore, had to incur his own financial losses. Nevertheless, he went ahead. The opera was "La Traviata." He translated the Italian into Korea, produced the opera himself, played the tenor lead part. Alternate roles for the prima donna were taken by the two main sopranos of the day, Ma Kumhi, Japan-educated, and Kim Chagyong, graduate of Ehwa Women's University. The Korea Symphony Orchestra and the Art College Choir of the Seoul National University's Department of Music provided the best orchestra and chorus supports. The opera was finally performed in the summer of 1948 at the City Municipal Theater to packed houses.

Encouraged by this success, Dr. Yi went ahead with presentation of "Carmen." This time he had a wider range of talents to draw from. The drama expert, So Hangsok, was available for the stage production, one of Yi's more promising students, Song Chinhyok, alternated with him for the main tenor role, the mezzo-soprano, Kim Heran, of the Art College, Seoul National University, had her chance to play "Carmen," and a promising new soprano graduate of Ewha, Kim Pokhi, was Micaela. Instead of the Korea Symphony Orchestra, it was the Seoul Symphony Orchestra, but the conductor was the same person, the popular Im Wonsik. The chorus group was again drawn from the Art College and the children's chorus was made up of candidates from schools, radio stations and so forth. Again, "Carmen" proved a great success. With two straight hits to his credit, Yi Inson went to America and the International Opera group he founded went out of existence almost immediately. He has never returned.

In January 1949, another tenor, Han Kyudong, staged Gounod's "Faust" under the sponsorship of a Franco-Korean Association. Only part one of what was supposed to be an ambitious attempt, however, was presented.

The eve of the war's outbreak saw a unique departure with the successful presentation of Rody Hyun's "Tale of Chunhyang." In staging this operatic version of Korea's most popular love story in modern form, Dr. Hyun enjoyed a distinct advantage. The entire cast and staff, including the orchestra and chorus, belonged to the college of which he himself was dean, the Music College of the Seoul National University. *"Chunhyang"* was a big hit which opened in the latter part of May and was carried over to June. In the latter part of June, the war broke and the next performances of the opera were under wartime conditions in 1952 in the southern cities of Pusan and Taegu. In 1958, it was staged in Seoul again for the third time.

In 1952, a young composer, Kim Taehyon, presented the peratic form of another well-known local story, the Korean version of the Cinderella story, *"Kongji Patchi,"* in wartime Pusan, and, in 1954, Rody Hyun, encouraged by his first *"Chunhyang"* hit, composed the historical "Prince Hodong" in restored Seoul.

In general, an average of one opera was staged every year up to the outbreak of the war. As a result of the dislocations created by a war which destroyed not only the material but the spiritual sides of Korean life, operatic movements, at best, could be carried on only intermittently; often it was threatened with total extinction. Not until 1957 did opera begin to show signs of rejuvenation. With the formation that year of the Seoul Opera Group, operatic interests were rekindled. The first public performance of this group was again "La Traviata." With the exception of soprano Om Kyongwon, the other leading members of the cast, soprano Chang Hegyong, tenor Hong Chinpyo and tenor Yi Wugun were new faces, fresh and promising from the Music College of the Seoul National University. Miss Om's debut was made earlier in the post-armistice period in Rody Hyun's "Prince Hodong."

In 1958, there were three operas, the first presentation of "Rigoletto" by the Seoul

Opera Group with the visiting American Daniel Harris as producer, Rody Hyun's *"Chunhyang"* and "Tosca" staged by a new group, the Korea Opera Association. Many names were becoming identified with opera; soprano Om Kyongwon, tenor Hong Chinpyo, baritones O Kyongmyong and Kim Hakgun, and others. The Prima Opera Group, which hitherto had confined itself strictly to recitals featuring operatic arias, also joined the general bandwagon by giving the full "Cavalleria Rusticana" in April 1959. The same Mascagni opera was again staged the very next month by the Korea Opera Association in its first double-feature, the other being "Pagliacci." The final opera of the year was the Seoul Opera Group's "La Boheme."

Thus, if the recent two years are any indication of a trend, Korea is averaging about three operas a year. All three of Verdi's main operas, Puccini and Mascagni have greatly widened a prewar canvas that, as we have seen, was limited to "La Traviata," "Carmen" and half of "Faust." What is more important, a crop of new young singers have made their debuts on a demanding stage and are likely to stay there until talents are cemented and progress assured on all fronts of future operatic endeavors. Financial arrangements are secure enough to allow for the planning of new repertoires.

Creative Music

In contrast with the outgrowths of student contests, symphonic concerts and full-scale operas, original compositions are scarce and the works of Korean composers, accordingly, are seldom played. What domestic songs reach the public ear are songs either long familiar or the products of men whose reputations in the musical field are safely established. A roster of such prominent names would include Rody Hyun, Kim Sehyong, Yi Hungyol, Kim Songtae, Kim Tongjin, Yun Isang, Kim Taehyon, Kum Suhyon, Im Wonsik, Kim Sunae, Na Unyong and the late Hong Nanpa. "A Capricio for Symphony Orchestra" by Kim Songtae and "Death of a Magpie" by Chong Yunju are the most frequently heard pieces of modern Korean music as are, of course, the operatic works of Rody Hyun and Kim Taehyong.

Efforts have been made to encourage composers though not frequently. As mentioned previously, one of the main purposes in the forming of the Experimental Music Society in Pusan was to feature new works by Korean composers. The Society was responsible for bringing out the works of the new, more promising composers, such as Chong Yunju and Yi Sanggun. In 1956, the Korean Musicians' Association created a "Composers Prize" which carried an award of one million hwan. The final selection was made in the United States, as a result of which nomination for first prize was withheld and the second place award went to the new composer, Chong Yunju, for his "Death of a Magpie." In 1957, the Seoul Symphony Orchestra also provided many composers, old and new, the opportunity to present new works in a program, entitled, "An Evening for Korean Composers."

The composers, for their part, are also making serious efforts to find modern ways of expressing themselves. The tendency is to inject new life into unique Korean music while, at the same time, trying to keep abreast of the latest in modern music. The members of a body called the Creative Music Society and the students personally taught and trained by the composer, Na Unyong, have been particularly active in this respect. The composer, Kim Tongjin, also, deserves to be noticed for the efforts he is making to create a new form for national music. Thus far, however, his efforts have not led to any established place in the repertoires of the concert-hall.

One added and by no means insignificant incentive has been the recent spurt in the output of motion picture films. The movie "boom" means a big demand for musical compositions which, in turn, mean greater rewards for the hard-pressed composer. A "Best Film Music Award" has already been established, the winner of the first prize this year being Kim Taehyon for his work in a picture called "Belfry."

Popular Music

Popular music may be divided into two classes: songs and light instrumental music. The songs can be divided into five distinct categories.

First, there are songs composed in a mixed Korean-Western style. By Western is meant the rhythm and the beat for the mood undoubtedly would appear quite exotic to the Occidental ear. They are largely sentimental love ditties that have made a stock-in-trade of the things in nature or landscape that appealed to the tragic or reminiscent moods of the old poet, the butterfly, the temple and the like. Often, too, the composers are able to yearn about the loved one or missing boats in distant places like Shanghai or San Francisco. Let the titles explain: "Moonlight Over Silla (an old renowned kingdom)," "American Chinatown," "Girl at a Mountain Villa," "The Honam (railway) Line in the Rain," "Miari Slope that Rends the Heart," "Only My Love," "Cowboy of Arizona," and so forth.

Secondly, there are the theme songs for movies. These are usually the works of composers who have majored in Western music. They are far less prolific than the composers of the first category both because the movies as yet rely mostly on Western music and because the demands are somewhat more exacting. The only theme song which may be said to have "stuck" was the one provided by Son Sokpong for the movie, "Gone is the Dream."

The third category are the American disc songs that have flooded Korea no less than anywhere else. Its most avid listeners are the young students of urban communities and it is familiar to everybody else for it floods tea-rooms, bars and other such establishments. From the number of requests made to the Korean Broadcasting System, HLKA, in the past five years, the favorites in order of preference follows; "Que Sera Sera," "The Midnight Blues," "Sail Along, Silvery Moon," "I'll Be Home," "Crazy Love," "Autumn Leaves," "Changing Partners," "Banana Boat Song," "Love Is a Many-Splendored Thing" and "Three Coins in the Fountain."

The fourth category are songs that are state-recommended. Naturally, they have to do with patriotic inspirations, such as march reminders of "Liberation" dedications or "anti-Communist" resolutions. However noble the purpose, these songs seem to make little headway in the face of the competitions from categories one and three.

The fifth category are rearrangements of the old folk songs, which, among other things, has put the "*Arirang*" to march beat with a brass band and provided a mambo rhythm for the farmers' "*Toraji.*" They, too, have not made much headway, first because there are not many folk songs to go around, and secondly, because everybody prefers them the way they are.

Light music in Korea means dance music and this again means everything: waltz, foxtrot, tango, blues, swing, samba, mambo, calypso. Some bands featuring tango or other such popular kind of dance music have enjoyed comparatively good financial income by playing at dance-halls or American parties. The returns, of course, led to the formation of many more such bands. Today, they also play at theaters and are taking part in musical shows.

XX DRAMA, MOTION PICTURE

Definition of the Korean Drama

Music and Dancing Prevalent Themes

Drama in Korea has its origin in the religious rites of prehistoric days as in the case of all other nations. The apparently simple dance movements with musical accompaniment were developed into a Silla drama called the "*choyong*." The *choyong* was not dramatic in the strict sense of the term as we understand it today even though it has certain such elements in that it follows a definite story of a hero. It is a series of dramatic dances rather than drama *per se*. Besides the *choyong*, there were several other "shows" performed for royal and popular entertainment, but again their primary emphasis on dance movements with music accompaniment disqualifies them as drama.

Dancing with music accompaniment has always been important in Korean classic "shows" of all kinds regardless of their official designation as dance or drama. The "*sandae drama*" of the Koryo period contains more definite elements of a drama than the *choyong*. It was performed on stage by masked actors following a script which presents a story with occasional spoken lines, predominant as dances and songs were throughout the play. The *sandae* was further developed during the Yi dynasty when it became one of the official functions of the court. Eventually, it lost royal support to become an entertainment medium for the common people. This most representative of Korean classic dramas found wide popular acceptance and has survived until today, apparently because the subjugated masses of feudal Korean society found solace in a bitter-humorous masque that ridiculed the privileged classes—Buddhist priests and the *yangban* nobility.

Another "show" for popular entertainment during the Yi dynasty was marionettes. The most representative one was the *kkoktugaksi* show presented by itinerant groups. Realistic rather than symbolic, the marionette adhered faithfully to the script. Its scenes and characters as well as the story were different from those of the *sandae* masque, but the exaggerated humor that ridiculed the leading Yi classes was the same. Dance and music is again important throughout the show. The *kkoktugaksi* is performed to this day.

Besides the two representative shows above described, there were other "dramatic" forms of popular entertainment, such as the acrobatic clowning, the *ogwangdae*, *pyolsingud* which was in the nature of a Shamanistic ritual and the *Pongsan* mask dance. All such classic entertainment shows have undergone decline since the introduction of Western culture in the 1900's.

Western Tides

Encroachment of Western-style shows on the classic scene became a definite trend in 1909 when the *Wongaksa* theater was opened in Seoul under state auspices. Until that time, entertainers had been without a theater and had to present their works either on a makeshift stage or on the ground of any village square large enough to accommodate a crowd.

The introduction of Western-style shows produced increasing interest in the "new drama" which, in contrast to the traditional "old drama" with their stress on music and dancing, relied almost exclusively on spoken dialogues. Less serious in its artistic standards but more popular to less sophisticated audiences were the "new school plays" with their romantic stories of handsome heroes and beautiful heroines.

Dramas became so popular among the people in the 1930's that many amateur groups competed with professional men of the theater. Especially noteworthy was the contribution of college groups.

The Pacific War crisis was a temporary setback and the Communist War even more so. Furthermore, the postwar "boom" in motion pictures has proved to be extremely discouraging to any effort on the part of theater performers to stage a comeback. Drama circles today stress "small theaters" for limited audiences rather than maximum financial returns from capacity audiences.

Marionette

Three Survivals

No description of the Korean drama is complete without an important work about the "puppet shows." From the several references on the subject in Chinese classical books, it is presumed that they were performed from the very outset of the Three-Kingdom era. Apparently quite a number of marionettes consisted of considerably wide repertoires, but only three have survived the test of time. We have no inkling of what all the rest was like.

Of the three survivals, moreover, two are not entitled to be called marionettes because they consist of nothing more than simple manipulation of puppet dolls with musical accompaniment and are without script or story. They have completely disappeared from the village scene of Korea. We shall, therefore, describe only the third, the *kkoktugaksi*.

Here is a marionette in every sense of the word. It has a "scenario" which can be followed clearly and a definite cast of characters. It has inevitably declined with the great changes in modern taste but is still played occasionally in village market places. It is a typical example of the ridicule to which the leading classes of feudal Korea were subjected by Korean "showmen" and, as such, shall be treated in some detail.

The Kkoktugaksi

The *Kkoktugaksi* was presented by an itinerant groupe of six or seven members, three of whom usually musicians. The dramatis personnae consisted of *Pakchomji*, the hero; his wife, *Kkoktugaksi*; his concubine, his young brother, two young Shaman women, a nephew, four high priests, the Governor of Pyongan-do, a butler to the Governor, a gunman and a serf. The musicians were also included in the cast as villagers. It had eight acts, each independent of the others.

As the curtain opens to the maddening beat of a brass drum, our hero, *Pakchomji*, is shown starting out on a countrywide tour of all scenic beauties. At dusk, he goes into a village inn for the night. At suppertime, he goes out to ascertain the source of the thudding that has been sounded repeatedly while he was eating. It is the noise of several men beating upon the floor in their excitement over a heated game of gambling. It is music to our hero's ears and he begins to dance in sheer delight, singing a song about the natural beauties of the eight provinces.

The second act opens with one Buddhist high priest dancing with two young female Shamanists. Our hero joins in but after a while of the merry-making, he is chagrined to recognize in the two Shamanists no other than his own nieces and that the priest intends to seduce them both. The hero pleads with the priest to stop the dancing but his pleas fall on deaf ears. Whereupon, he summons his nephew, the village "strongman," who breaks it all up.

Act Three has a ferocious and hunrgy monster devouring all birds that land on a field. The hero no sooner appears to enjoy the peaceful sight of the birds when the monster pounces upon him, biting him with sharp teeth. Along comes the strongman nephew to the rescue. He grapples with the monster in a long and furious fight that is accompanied by a great deal of clamor. In the end, the monster is slain.

In Act Four, our hero searches in vain for his wife, *Kkoktugaksi*. At last, he gives up the search and brings the concubine forth upon the stage when who should appear but the spouse. A quarrel flares between the two women to be settled only when the hero agrees to divide his fortunes equally between them. In the "equal" distribution, the concubine gets all the valuable property of his house, leaving the wife nothing but "trash." There is a good deal of "theatrical gestures" on the part of the tearful *Kkoktugaksi* to express her sorrow and rancor but in the end she leaves the stage. Her destination: a Buddhist temple deep in the Diamond Mountains to become a nun.

In Act Five, the hero is spurned by the concubine and, upon the unanimous advice of the villagers, sets forth on a journey in search of his wife.

Act Six introduces the Governor of Pyongan-do who arrives at the provincial capital and immediately goes pheasant-hunting.

Act Seven opens to the march of a funeral procession for the Governor's wife. The Governor shows no signs of mourning but seems only too glad to be rid of her, much to the scandal of the villagers. The coffin carrier, of a sudden, has pain in the legs and drops the coffin, thus bringing the procession to a halt. Again, the hero's nephew saves the day. He appears nakedly, his huge muscles exposed, and lifts the coffin easily.

In the final act, a Buddhist temple is built on a "holy" mountain to console the spirit of the Governor's deceased wife with a 49-day prayer.

The Props

The stage of the show was set in any village square likely to hold quite a crowd. Four poles were erected to cover about two square meters of ground. Curtains were draped around the poles to hide the puppet manipulators from the public view.

The puppets were carved of wood and clad in appropriate costumes, some with long beards as the characters demanded. Sizes of the dolls varied from 49 to 90 centimeters in length. The show was presented in the evening and the stage illuminated by petroleum burning at the ends of cotton-tipped sticks.

As in the case of the masque, introduced in the next chapter, the marionette conveys a caricature of Buddhist priests who have broken the Buddha's commandments, a triangular love affair involving the concubine of a *yangban* house master, taunts and mockeries of the *yangban* class as a whole — all favorite objects of ridicule among the subjugated classes of the feudal Yi Dynasty.

Masque

Four Categories

The earliest authentic reference to the masque play appears in the "*Samguk Sagi*," which mentions three varieties of the masque as having been performed during the ninth century of the Three-Kingdom period. That the masque continued to be played during the Koryo dynasty is indicated by the "*Koryosa*" which refers to the masque as being among the kind of plays offered in the 23rd year of the reign of King Kojong (1236). During the Yi dynasty, an official post was created with the express purpose of handling masque shows which accordingly prospered as an official function of the court. In 1634, however, this post was abolished and the masque thereafter had to cater to the common people on its own private footing.

The masque shows fell into four distinctive categories, three named after the localities where they were played.

The Sandae

The fourth, called the *sandae* after the royal nomenclature for the office responsible for handling masque shows, is the best known. It is a "spectacular" in 10 acts and 13 scenes with an official title after the main role in each act and scene. Thus, Act One is "The High Priest," Act Two, "The Pock-Marked Priest;" Act Three, "The Dark-Faced Priest;" Act Four, "The Priest of the Blinking Eyes," and so forth. Like the *Kkoktugaksi* puppet show (see Marionette), the *sandae* brought out the triangular affair of the typical *yangban*, his wife and his concubine in its mockery of the Yi nobility, and more than the puppeteers, heaped taunts upon the priestly class.

The *sandae* had an all-male cast, playing and dancing to the accompaniment of traditional Korean drums, strings and brass blaring out tunes based on folk songs, Buddhist invocations, Shamanist invocations and the like. It also had one puppet doll and a set of 24 masks, one for each of the cast. It was performed on a makeshift stage in open air in the village square on holiday occasions, such as the *Tano* festival on the fifth day of the fifth moon, or Shaman prayer-days for rain. Starting after sunset, the show continued deep into the night to the delight of the audience.

This unique Korean drama has lost much popular support. Only one troupe, in fact, is keeping it up in the Kyonggi village of Yangju. A group was organized in Seoul about ninety years ago as the only authentic performers of the *sandae* in latter-day Korea but was forced to disband after fifty years.

The Haeso

The *Haeso* masque, performed in the Haeju area of Hwanghaedo in the north, was also performed on *Tano* occasions. Its origin cannot be traced back but it is presumed to have been born at about the same time as the *sandae*. A seven-act play, the roles varied slightly according to the locality in which it was played, but the overall cast of characters was the same as in the *Kkoktugaksi* or the *sandae*. Its six-piece band also played folk songs and Buddhist incantations from evening until break of dawn. The *Haeso* was also performed in the village square but, unlike the *sandae*, there was no stage. It was financed by donations from the merchants and well-to-do farmers of the village who, in turn, were privileged to occupy the best seats for themselves and their friends.

The *Haeso* was concluded when the masks and costumes were thrown into a bonfire in the belief that they were possessed of evil spirits. The audience gathered around the fire to chant Shamanist invocations.

↑ Yangban (Man of Letters)
A mask used in Korean Hahoe masque

↑ Kaksi (Virgin)
A mask used in Korean Hahoe masque

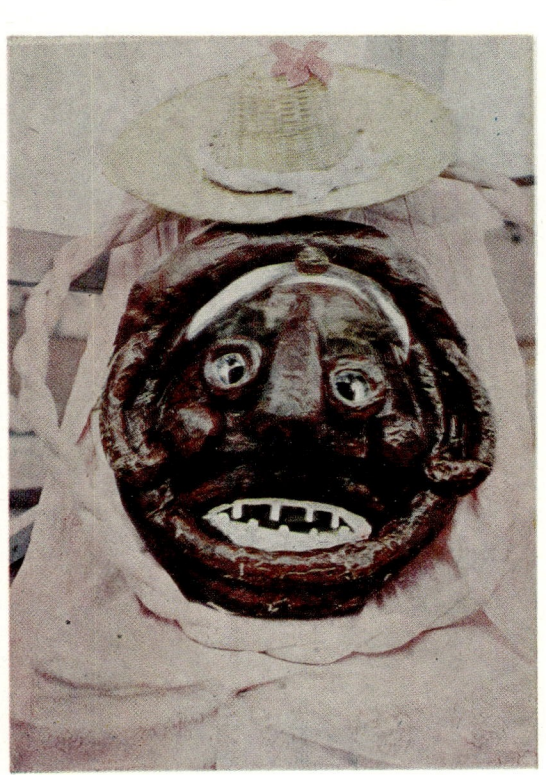

↑ Malttugi (Noble-man's Servant)
A mask used in Korean Okwangdae masque

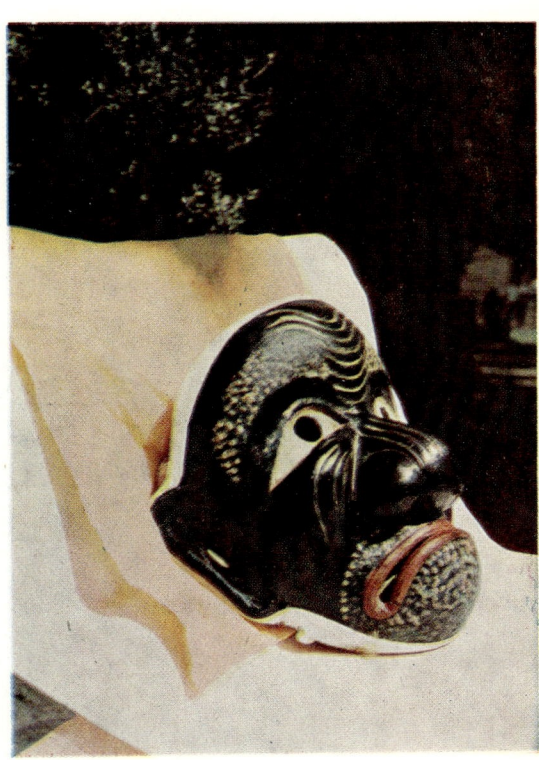

↑ Nojang (Old Priest)
A mask used in Korean Sandae masque

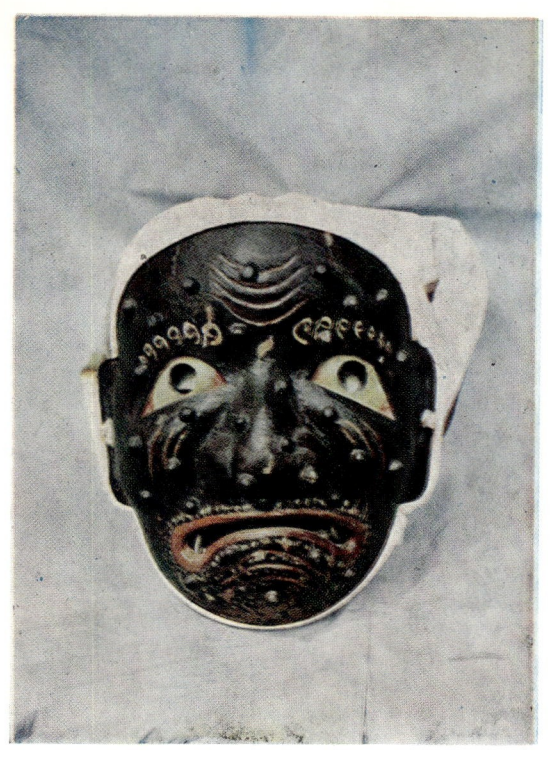

↑ Ohmjung (Boil Priest)
A mask used in Korean Sandae masque

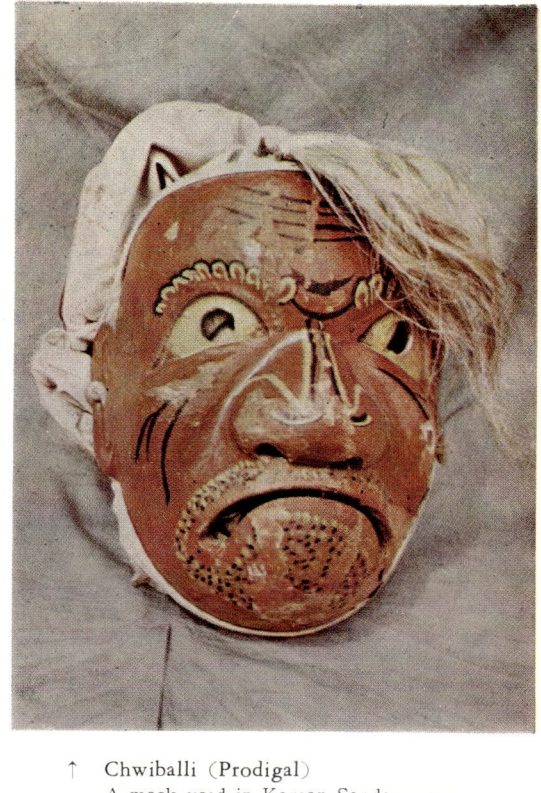

↑ Chwiballi (Prodigal)
A mask used in Korean Sandae masque

↑ Somu (Young Shaman Whitch)
A mask used in Korean Sandae masque

↑ Mokjung (Black Priest)
A mask used in Korean Sandae masque

→ Mr. Park Chomji's concubine
　A scene of Korean Kkoktugaksi puppet show.

← Mr. Park Chomji (Hero)
　A scene of Korean Kkoktugaksi puppet show.

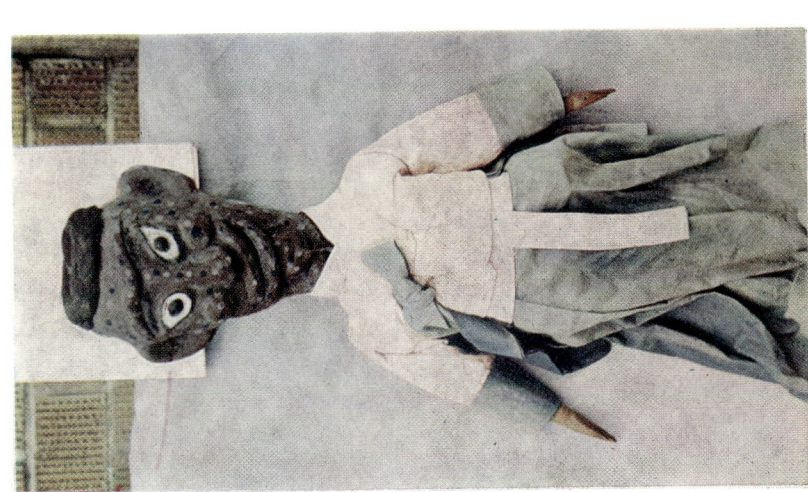

→ Kkoktugaksi (Heroine)
　A scene of Korean Kkoktugaksi puppet show.

↑　Taehan Theater, Seoul
　　Releases foreign films.

↓　Inside of the Taehan, seating capacity: 1,500.

↑ Kukche (International) Theater, Seoul
Releases new Korean films.

↓ Inside with modern conveniences of International Theater

Inside of the Wongak-sa Theater, downstairs. →

↓ Inside of the Wongak-sa Theater, upstairs.

Wongak-sa Theater, Seoul
 Stages classical Korean musical performances, folk-dances, and stage-plays for tourists
↓ and other foreign visitors. The handsome hall was designed in typical Korean style.

↑ **Sigonggwan (Citizen Theater), Seoul**
  Also called Central National Theater. The hall is often used for gatherings of political parties or non-partisan groups.

  Cheil Theater
↓ The biggest theater in Taegu City, Kyongsang Pukto.

Scene from a Korean classical opera.

Scene from the Western operatic version of "Chunhyangjon (Tale of Chunhyang)".

Scene from another Korean classical opera.

↑   A scene from "Song of Love," fork-song drama.

↓   A scene from "Father of King Kojong and his Daughter-in-Law, Queen Min," historical drama.

A Scene from the Motion Picture "Arırang"
  Produced in 1928. Silent. The first attempt to offer resistance against Japanse militarism.

A Scene from "A Fig Tree"
  Produced in 1933. Silent. A comedy.

A Scene from "A Bull without Horns"
  Produced in 1932. Silent.

↑ A Scene from "A Large Tomb"
   Produced in 1930. Silent. Another resistance movie.

↑ A Scene from "Gold Fish"
   Produced in 1929. Silent. A teen-age love story.

A Scene from "Wedding Day"
↓   Produced in 1957. Talkie. Winner of the best comedy prize at the 1957 Asian Movie Festival held at Tokyo.

↑ A Scene from "Nameless Stars"
Produced in 1959. Talkie. Black-and-white. A semi-documentary movie based on the Kwangju Students, Incident of 1929.

A Scene from "No Tragedy"
Produced in 1959. Talkie. Black-and-white. A filmized popular story of the young generation during the Korean conflict.
↓

↑ A Scene from "Wild Rat"
Produced in 1930. Silent. Beauty of the good old days

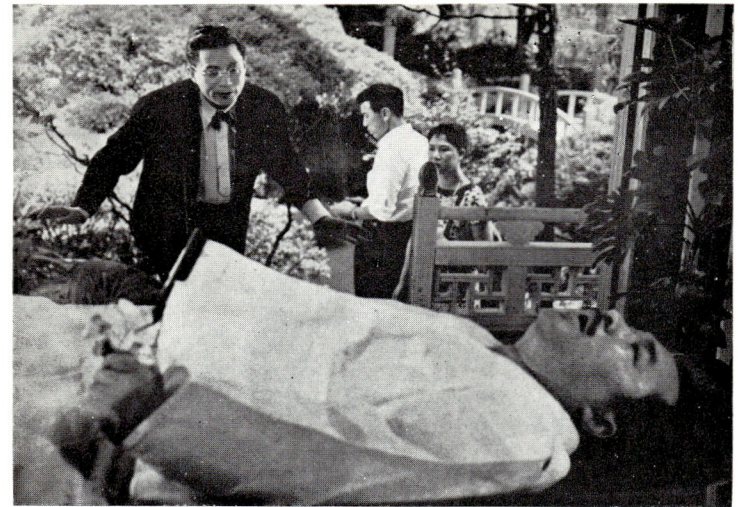

A Scene from "Distraint of Life"
 Produced in 1958. Talkie. Black-and-white.

A Scene from "Three Thousand Maids of Honour and Nakhwaam (Rock of Falling Flowers)"
 Produced in 1960. Talkie. Black-and-white. A historical movie about the end of the Paekche Kingdom.

A scene from "Free Marriage"
 Produced in 1959. Talkie. Black-and-white.

A Shooting Scene of the Movie "Sungbang Pigok (Elegy in a Buddhist Cell)"
The director (center) holds a discussion with actor and actresses.

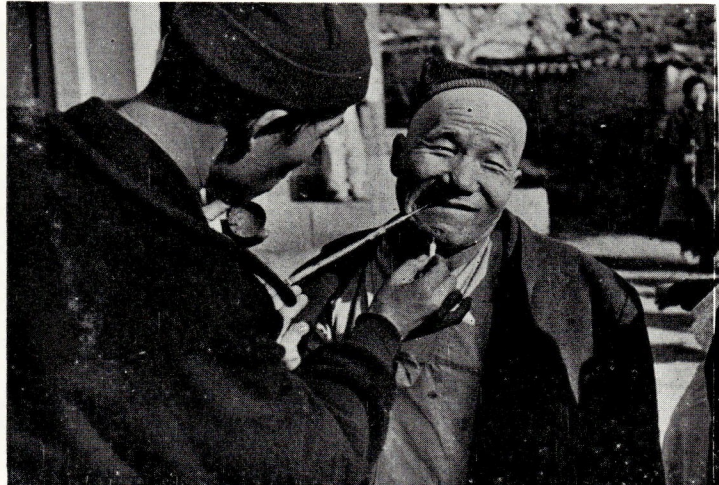

Make-up
More wrinkles for a good old man.

Camera
The actor is seated at right below, half hidden.

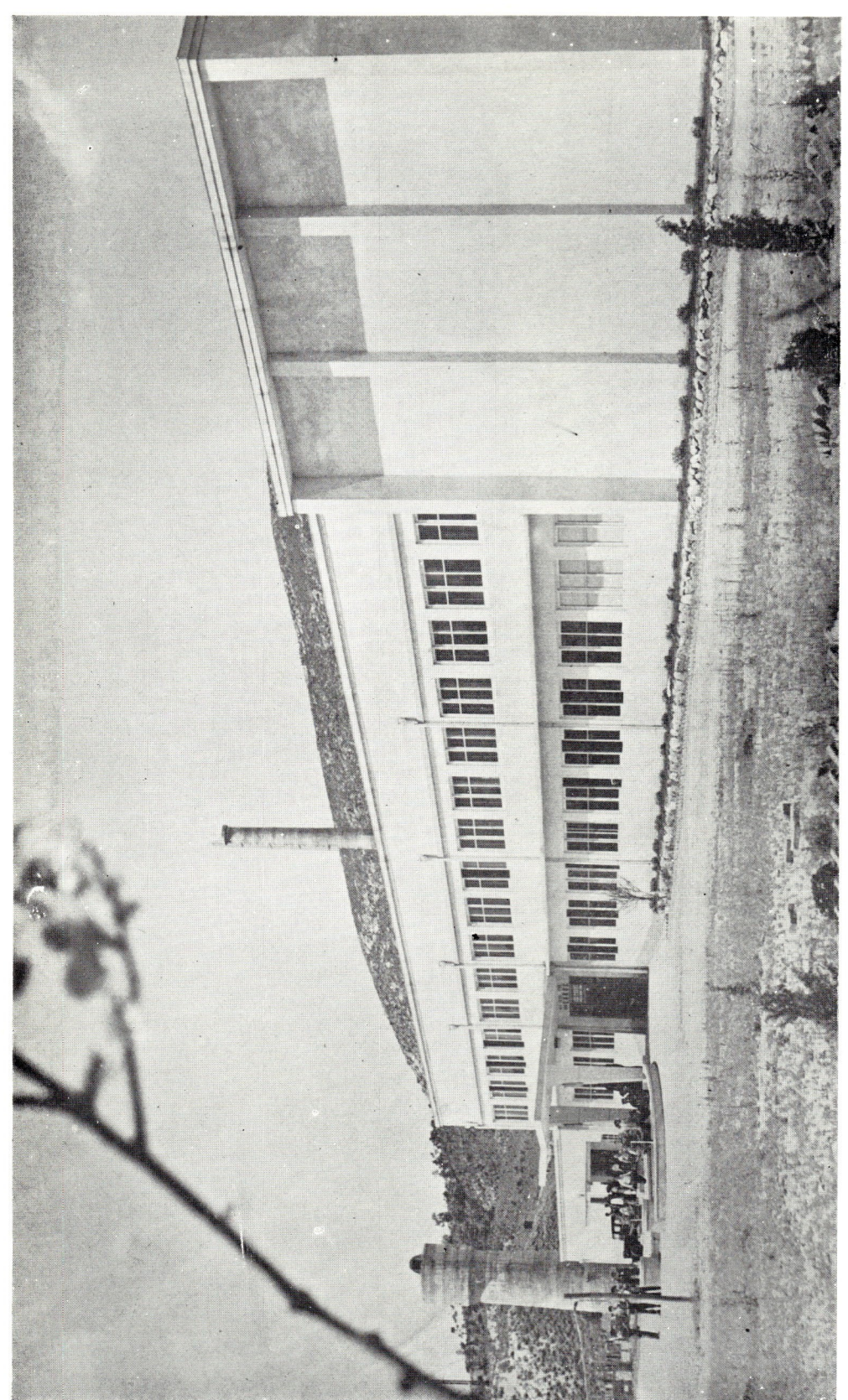

↑ An Exterior View of Anyang Studios
Largest site for motion picture making in Korea. Located in Sihung-gun, Kyonggi-do.

The Hahoe

The *Hahoe* masque in the Hahoe district of Kyongsang Pukto was performed on occasions of Shamanist prayer festivals on the second day of the first moon. According to the old men of the village, its origin goes back five hundred years ago.

Unlike the two previous masks which were staged for public entertainment, the purpose of the *Hahoe* was to appease the spirits of two departed women with potent spiritual powers over the village. They had a shrine and the masque was part of a ritual observed to cleanse the village of evil spirits. That being the case, the villagers were only too glad to contribute to the funds that made the masque ceremonial play possible.

The "Five Clowns"

The fourth type, appearing in Kyongsang Namdo, was an acrobatic affair known as the "Play of the Five Clowns," the clowns apparently being the "Generals of the Five Directions," i. e. generals who took positions to the north, south, east, west and center in accordance with a Confucianistic set of rituals for music and dancing. It was performed by village amateurs under the direction of the old village man versed in the play on the fifteenth day of the first moon.

A Typical Example

As a typical example, the third of these plays, *Hahoe*, is introduced and interpreted here. Actually all four were similar in content and spirit so the *Hahoe*, which the author has studied considerably, may serve for the general canvas.

Outline of the Hahoe

Act I: Enter a young woman, dancing around the stage with rhythmic movements of the shoulders. Enter a priest also dancing with a rosary dangling down his neck and a wooden bell in hand. Priest approaches the woman, winks. She responds and they dance together until the priest finally carries her off on his back. No dialogues in this act.

Act II: Enter a nobleman, pulled onto the stage by his servant. They are joined by a scholar and his concubine. Servant circles his master, throwing gibes at him while scholar trails his mistress, cooing her name. Nobleman and scholar greet one another and engage in conversation which is sheer nonsense. At last, nobleman notices the pretty lady and goes over to give her a peck. Enter a court courier with a document which has nobleman quivering with fear to the delight of the servant who throws more gibes. The document is a demand for payment of a debt. "It's for her," the nobleman spouts, running off the stage.

Act III: Enter an old woman with a cane in hand and a gourd at her waist to beg money of the unresponsive audience. Surprise encounter with a long-missing husband. Old woman busies herself with sundry chores to reestablish home. Quarrel breaks when husband buys a carp. Hubby, angry at all the nagging, destroys furniture and deserts old woman once more.

Act IV: Two actors with lion masks fight each other. Along comes the servant of the nobleman in Act II who scolds them. Lions are frightened and run away. This act is a mime with much clumsy dancing and jumping around.

Act V: A "bull" at the center of the stage. Enter butcher with an axe in one hand, a knife in the other. Butcher spits on the handles of his instruments preparatory to carving up the bull. "How filthy," exclaims one of the audience who is supposed to represent aristocracy. "Here, you do it," butcher retorts. Then he carves out the embarrassing organs of the slaughtered creature. "To whose home shall I send these?" he asks to a burst of laughter.

Meaning of the Play

Act I: The priest who is supposed to live according to Buddhist precepts and certainly abstain from vulgar displays, appears in a commoners' world and carries off a village girl. This was doubtlessly a flagrant violation of Buddhist principles and the mockery of the act was the expression of the commoner's hatred for the depraved priests of the day.

Act II: The commoners also openly insulted the aristocracy whose power was tremendous and whose oppression heavy. The sentiment of hate was shared by actor and spectator alike since both were of the oppressed commonalty. It was the only occasion when they could openly mock and ridicule a *yangban*, and his servant throws gibes which in another time and place would have meant serious trouble.

Act III: Here was a satire directed not only against the ruling classes as such but a reflection of the hardships borne by the common people and the incompatibility of domestic life. It is a vivid contrast with the previous two acts for in one, the hypocritical and timid rich pursue mistresses and create trouble for themselves while, in the other, the commoner's home life collapses through sheer poverty.

Act IV: Another example of incompatibility in Yi society in which tweedledee and tweedledum fight like lions. The lion mime, which also appears in the *Haeso* and other plays, was common to many places as a rite of exorcism to chase the evil spirits away and fetch good luck for the lunar new year.

Act V: Like Act II, it flings insults at the *yangban* and his superficial dignity.

Modern Drama

Trends

Western drama was first staged in Korea in 1909 at the newly opened *Wongaksa* theater in Seoul. The "new drama," as it was known against the traditional dramas of the masque and marionette, was inevitable at a time when the powerful influence of Western culture and civilization began to be felt.

The pioneer of the "new drama" movement was a returned exile from Japan, Yi Injik. It was Yi who made the *Wongaksa* a going concern. He not only wrote the plays for Korea's first real theater but managed, supervised and directed them. He was followed in 1911 by Im Songgu whose works were greeted with standing ovations from the outset. Im, however, stooped to less serious drama later, catering to popular romantic sentiments in what became known as "new school plays." In 1913, another "modernist," Yi Kise, appeared with two more troupes and the theater became a crowded world. By then, a considerable number of professional actors, actresses, stage directors and playwrights were available to put the "new drama" on a solid footing.

Meanwhile, a more serious group, calling itself the Drama Arts Society, was organized in 1921 mostly by returned students from Japan. A significant contribution to this Western-inspired movement was the formation of the *Towolhoe* (Saturday-Monday Society) in 1922 by a group of students then studying in Japan. Such figures as Pak Sunghi and Kim Palbong, later to become eminent writer, came home during school vacations to play major roles in "realistic" plays.

Amateurs though its members were, the Saturday-Monday Society surpassed any other professional group with its high artistic standards and the introduction of "realistic" themes. The Society's repertoire consisted mostly of original works written by its own members but it also included translations and adaptations of world masterpieces. Popular approval was so lasting that in the ten years of its existence, it presented a total of eighty-seven performances—a record-breaking feat for the time. Its influence has been felt ever since in Korean dramatic circles.

Besides the *Towolhoe,* a professional group, called *Chuisongjwa,* also deserves mention for turning out a substantial number of good actors and actresses throughout the 'twenties.

The most significant landmark in the next decade of development was the formation of a Society for the Study of Dramatic Arts in 1931. Organized by men who today constitute the elite of Korea's theatrical and literary circles, this Society presented numerous world masterpieces besides original works by its members. The Japanese Governor-General soon forced it to disband because of its nationalistic tendencies, but its individual members carried on by organizing another body, Drama Study Troupe. Under this signboard, they lasted until the end of the decade when the Japanese again forced dissolution.

The' thirties was a period of socialistic convictions and these were reflected in the theatrical world with the Modern Theater, New Construction and several other groups, all sympathetic to the cause.

The early 'forties was the period of concentrated Pacific War efforts and the theater came to a standstill in intensified Japanese pressure upon Korean language and culture.

The tragic post-Liberation division of the land and the ensuing political cleavage between the two irreconcilable ideologies brewed chaos in Korean dramatic circles. Numerous groups, each with its political color, sprouted one after another and folded up as quickly. Only with the establishment of government and laying down of a definite political line was confusion ended and a National Theater born (1950) that enabled the Korean dramatists to follow a clear course.

The Communist War sent the National Theater south in refuge and the post-armistice initiative was taken by an organ of this Theater, the New Drama Society, which revived interest chiefly in Shakespeare and Yu Chijin, one of the foremost Korean dramatists. The unprecedented "boom" of motion pictures, however, deprived the stage of both talents and audience, and decline set in all too soon.

Nevertheless, several groups went right ahead, creating what is known as a "small theater" movement. This emphasized artistic presentations as opposed to the professional that sought large theaters and better financial returns for the producer. The more serious-minded went further ahead when they organized the Korean National Center of International Theater Institutes in 1958, and engaged in international cultural exchanges.

Importance of the Student Drama

Aside from such professional groups, amateurs—mostly college students—have always attracted the attention of theatrical circles with their powerful influence on "academic" development of the drama. "Students' Drama" began in 1925 and, in five years, drama movements became a fashion in all colleges. The Pacific War years buried these movements under the demands imposed on youth but the Liberation brought them back with renewed intensity, culminating in the first nationwide university students' drama contest in 1949. Drama circles, both professional and amateur alike, welcomed the event as the greatest "festival" ever held in Korea. The significance of the occasion may be readily understood by the fact that many of the playwrights, producers, actors and actresses of today made their debuts at such student annuals. Today, more than ten colleges stage at least one drama a year for the public, and the students concerned have won the respect of professionals for their high artistic standards.

The "new school" has been mentioned. Ushered early into the history of the modern drama by Im Songgu, it has since been a part of theatrical endeavors for the less sophisticated audiences. Romanticism was the dubious theme, the dramatists almost exclusively relying on tear-jerking tragedies. The "new school," however, has almost completely disappeared, at least in the large cities. Only a few actors and actresses remain, banding themselves on countryside tours.

On the comic side of show business, the acrobatic-clown, popularly called *"kwangdae"*, inherited his feat from the traditional masques of Korea, but his field has been confined within itinerant circus tents. The traditions of Korea's "old drama" were better preserved, in part, in the *"changguk,"* the Korean folk opera or musical drama. Origin of Korean music drama dates back to the Three-Kingdom period and was developed to perfection during the Yi dynasty as one of the essential functions of the court.

After the introduction of Western drama, the "music drama" adapted itself to the requirements of the times to seek urban popularity. "Modern" versions of these old dramas were first presented to Seoul audiences at the *Wongaksa* theater in 1912 by a group called *kwangmudae*. The *kwangmudae* was succeeded by a group called "Moonlight Troupe." This group enjoyed considerable prosperity during the' thirties.

The Music Drama

The *changguk* or Korean music drama stood at its zenith for about two years from 1955 to 1956, when nearly 90 percent of all theatrical performances were taken up by the newest revival of the oldest Korean drama, attracting capacity audiences whenever the all-female casts presented their premiere performances as well as "old favorites."

The music drama, superimposing Western dramatic effects upon traditional Korean music, singing and dancing has show signs of decline in the recent few years. Only through more serious aesthetic efforts can the once-prosperous state of the Korean music drama of Korea be restored.

Another form of popular entertainment in the theater has been the *"akkuk"*, which may properly be called musical comedy.

The Korean version of Western "musicals" was started in 1929 when a "musical comedy troupe," calling itself the Golden-Star Opera, presented a program of band music, sing-song girls and jokes at the *Umigwan* Theater in Seoul.

The itinerant band musicians and stage "artists" managed to win popularity from certain less sophisticated quarters to survive the excesses of Pacific War demands. In recent years, such troupes are still touring around the countryside but have virtually disappeared from the metropolitan areas.

Training Courses

The path of the drama today is neither wide nor smooth. On one hand, it has never received government subsidies; on the other, the public is more attracted to movies. For all that, interest persists and students are to be found absorbed either in dramatic arts' schools or in on-the-job training with professional groups.

It was only five years ago that a formal institute for training theatrical professions was first established in Korea by the founding of the Sorabol Arts College in Seoul, offering two-year courses on the subject.

In 1959, Chungang University established a four-year-course in theatrical arts at its Department of Drama and Motion Pictures. There are also six schools in Seoul which train professional workers for the stage in half to one year courses. Altogether about 1,500 persons are presently being trained at such schools and with professional drama troupes, in addition to many college students who are receiving professional guidance as members of university students' drama groups. As already mentioned, such groups have in the past proved most fruitful in producing active stage talents.

Theater

The idea of a theater is new to Korea. As mentioned previously, dramas were performed in open air if not in court. The theater in Korea, therefore, was the outcome of Westernization in the early 1900's. The *Wongaksa* (1909) and *Kwangmudae* (1912) were the first real theaters in the land. Both were forced to close doors during the twenties under the pressure of the Japanese Governor-General.

There are now more than 200 theaters in south Korea, but less than ten percent of them are used for presentation of dramas, and then only occasionally; the rest screen movies.

The one bright spot was the restoration of the *Wongaksa* by the government in 1958. Serious works of drama and other forms of theatrical art are presented there to small, select audiences.

Thorny Paths of Modern Motion Picture Industry

Dominating Medium in Popular Appeal

In Korea, as elsewhere in the world, motion pictures are considered both as the most popular form of mass entertainment and one of the most effective media of expression. They constitute a vital part of the cultural, moral and social life of the Korean people.

Koreans today produce more than a hundred feature-length films a year in their own language. The motion picture production, indeed, is regarded as one of the major industries of the country and present indications point to even greater successes in the years to come. Like the history of the nation itself, however, the Korean motion picture industry had to tread a very thorny path to develop itself, its growth stunted by Japanese occupation, economically stalemated during the Military Government period, victimized by war.

Before the Liberation

The first motion picture was shown in Korea in the year, 1903. This consisted of a few one-reel films brought by the American staff of an electric streetcar company for purposes of advertisement. From this modest start, movie-going was to become a most rapid and widespread pastime, adding cinema houses to the rise of modern buildings and creating a profitable business in film distribution.

In the early stage of the industry, Western films, especially American, dominated the movie theaters. There were smash hits, "The Last Days of Pompeii" and "The King of Kings." These early silent pictures not only met the needs of entertainment; they played an important role in familiarizing the Korean people with Western culture and technological accomplishments.

Especially conspicuous in this connection were U.S. feature films which were representative of the American way of life and devotion to freedom. "Broken Blossoms" (1919) and "Way Down East" (1920) are typical of American offerings that received warm Korean applauses.

The period from 1925 to 1931 is generally considered the golden era of Western films in the Korean motion picture history. Among the smash hits during this period were "Storm over Asia" by the famed Russian director, Vsevold Pudovkin, Germany's "Siegfried," France's "La Rue", and "Robin Hood" which presented Douglas Fairbanks, Sr. for the first time to Korean audiences.

The silver screen enabled the Korean movie-goer to appreciate the differences in the tastes of the various Western countries—the American fares with their emphasis on fun and recreation, the French creations of subtle moods that sent the viewers away reliving the problems of life, the German demonstrations of a proud national heritage, and the British *savoir faire* attempts at a genuine form of art.

It was, of course, a long period of national humiliations and there was a marked divergence in the movie-going habits of the

Korean people and the Japanese population of colonizers, the latter frequenting the Kirakukan and the Taishokan in the center of metropolitan Seoul, the former preferring Chosun Theatre and Umigwan in the northern sector of the city.

Koreans who used to see imported Western silent movies in the early 20's still remember the eloquence of the *"pyonsa"* who were an integral part of screens that carried neither Japanese nor Korean subtitles. The *pyonsa*, or *benshi* in Japanese, were a group of men in the unique profession of providing translations of the dialogues. Though there was no way of knowing whether the *pyonsa* were carrying on any faithful translations, audiences were easily moved by the mesmeric power of their eloquence and enthusiasm. Old movie fans remember the names of such *pyonsa* as Song Tonghwan, So Sangpil and Kim Tonghwan as much they do the great classical films they handled.

With the coming of talkies, the *pyonsa* began to disappear from the stage. The first talkie came in 1928, a sports short featuring a simple music and primitive sound effect screened at the Chosun Theatre. The invention of sound gave impetus to the growth of a powerful Japanese motion picture industry and the year, 1930, marks the sudden influx of Japanese films on the colonial Korean market. Japanese movie houses began to invade native Korean communities and the Government-General itself encouraged Koreans to see *samurai* movies, the Japanese apparently believing that *samurai* swordplay would rid Koreans of nationalist sentiments.

With the undoubted values of Western culture and technology brought home so immediately, Koreans began to concern themselves about producing films on their own resources. The first such attempt was made in 1921 when "Chunhyangjon" (Tale of Chunhyang, a classic love story) was produced. Facilities then available at a Japanese studio in Seoul were used to produce "Chunhyangjon" The success of Korea's most popular love story was less than expected but it was, at least, a hopeful beginning. In 1923, a second Korean feature was produced, "Ssangongnu" (Beady Tears), followed soon by "Changhwa Hongnyonjon" (Table of Changhwa and Hongnyon).

It was perhaps in the year, 1924, that Korean motion picture production began to show prospects of continuity as a normal business enterprise. The first modern motion picture company was founded in Pusan in that year with Japanese funds and investment. Under the supervision of a Japanese director, "Unyongjon" (Tale of Unyong) was produced with An Chonghwa, one of present-day Korea's senior directors, in the leading role. Though heavily Japanese-dominated, both in terms of funds and personnel, this Pusan company provided training for some of the best Korean motion picture talents, notably Yun Paengnam who stood out prominently as a director in this early stage of the industry's development. Yun won his first critical acclaim in 1924 with "Elegy to the Sea," and followed this up with "Image of God" and "Oath under the Moon," both equally successful.

"Oath under the Moon" is recalled especially since it was in this movie that the immortal motion picture idol of Korea, Na Ungyu, was first introduced to the screen. He was a bit-player in that movie but his superb performance attracted the attention of Director Yun who cast him in the starring role in his subsequent pictures, "The Pioneer" and "Simchongjon" (Tale of Simchong), 1925-26. Na's performance in these two films established him firmly as a genius of an actor and the industry's most unforgettable figure. His soaring fame implanted the habit of movie-going in a larger segment of the Korean population and paved the way for an expanded market for domestic films. It encouraged the formation of new motion picture companies, among which, the Chosun Cinema Production (1927) deserves special mention for utilizing his talents in almost every film it turned out.

Na Ungyu won immortal fame not merely because he was a great actor but also because he was a devoted patriot. Every facet of his acting was symbolic of the spirit of deep Korean nationalism and resistance to Japanese militarism. "Arirang" was undoubtedly the best example of his acting abilities and patriotic devotion. The theme of Korea's most popular and undying folk song, the movie version was a lyrical expression of resistance, hope, and heart-rending protest of the oppressed. It is by far the best classic in the history of Korean movie-making. Only through ingenious editing techniques of Na Ungyu was the film able to pass the extremely suspicious nature of Japanese censorship.

Among the many films which featured Na Ungyu as both actor and director during the period of 1928-1935 were: "Ambitious Youth," "Goldfish," "Wild Rat," "Adieu," "Ongnyo," "Samnyong the Dumb," "Minor Incident on Seventh Avenue," "Chongno," "A Strange Account of the Kaehwa Party," and "In Quest of Love." The last, especially, is known for its boldness in exposing the ruthlessness of Japanese colonial administration. A story of Korean peasants chased out of home and farm by the Japanese, it was beautiful cinematographic work, climaxed by the powerful scene of an endless line of dejected emigrants crossing the River Tumen to Manchuria. The movie was originally entitled "Over the River" but the title had to be changed because of censorship objections. From 1934 to 1937 when he died of tuberculosis, Na directed and acted in four more films: "The Wanderers," "The Ring of Fire," "Daffodil," and "Love's Sad Song."

Other directors considered prominent during this period include:

An Chonghwa ("Florist," "Crossroad of Youth," "Ex-Convict.")

Yi Kyuhwan ("Ferry Boat Without a Master," "Yi Toryong.")

Yun Pongchun ("The Tomb," "Terminal," "Tosaengnok," etc.)

Chon Changgun ("Ten Thousand Miles of Blessed Land")

Kim Sangjin ("The Sound of Bell," "Suil and Sunae.")

Pang Hanjun ("Han River.")

The first Korean venture into sound was made by the Seoul Studio in 1935. As in the case of the silent, the first talkie was "Chunhyang" This was followed by "The Frontier (1940) and "Angel Without a Home" (1941), both directed by Choe Ingyu. The introduction of sound and the rapid change in the emulsion speed of the film entailed the necessity of intensive training for motion picture artists and technicians. Among the directors who studied the art of cinematography abroad were Hong Kyemyong ("Youth Brigade"-1938, "The Story of Changhwa and Hongnyon"-1940), Pak Kiche ("The Winds of Spring"-1938), Yi Pyongil ("Spring over the Peninsula"), Kim Yonghwa ("Ethics of a Housewife") and Pang Hanjun ("Songhwangdang" and "The Story of the Giant Whale").

The frantic "war efforts" of the Japanese began to be felt by the motion picture industry from 1938 onwards. Imported Western films, already subjected to heavy customs duties and censorship restrictions, were now banned and, for many years, there was a total black-out on all Western products save for the militant or propagandistic films of the Axis countries. At home, the Japanese tightened their control over all negatives and demanded that all qualified motion picture artists and technicians register themselves with government offices. In 1941, the Government-General, in the injunction which prohibited foreign imports, announced that the motion picture was a means of reorientating national thinking and encouraging popular will to Empire expansion. As a corollary, an organization was formed whereby creative efforts of Korean moviemakers were ruthlessly stifled.

The Korean Motion Picture Company, formed in September 1942, was a quasi-business organization intended to prevent the movie industry from flourishing in Korean hands. It came into being only after all existing production companies were forcibly disbanded and a master-slave relationship between Japanese company executives and their Korean employees established. Korean directors utilized by this company turned out such films as "Volunteers in the Army" and "You and I," films which constituted part of the overall Japanese campaign to induce Korean acceptance of the Japanese Army draft. As a monopoly, the Korean Motion Picture Company exercised control over all phases of motion picture production, supplies, distribution and production schedules.

Liberation and War

In the flush of the sudden liberation in 1945, a state of vacuum and lethargy lasted several months in the field of motion pictures as in all areas of cultural endeavors. An appalling shortage of trained artists and technicians paralyzed the entire movie industry.

Out of this initial state of chaos and confusion, however, the nucleus of a national motion picture industry eventually began to take shape. In early spring of 1946, three movie production offices were opened and a box-office hit scored by the director, Choe Ingyu, with an anti-Japanese military movie, *"Chayu Manse!"* (Hurrah for Freedom!). On the other hand, the director, Kim Sodong, experimented successfully with a domestically assembled sound recording system in a film called, "Story of a Peony Lantern." A steady stream of films followed and new acting talents discovered. The producers and directors in the years after the Liberation preferred nationalist themes, mainly to make the point of unceasing nationalistic movements under the Japanese. The bulk of the turn-out was shot with outmoded 16-mm cameras processed at makeshift laboratories.

The motion picture industry was, perhaps, the hardest hit among all media of mass communications by the war of 1950. The Communists, placing much store in the motion picture as one of the most effective instruments of propaganda, virtually removed one hundred percent of all film-making equipments in their retreat before the Allied counter-offensive and either liquidated or took (voluntarily or otherwise) fifty percent of the best film personnel. ROK troops in their northward push recovered some of the looted equipment but it was by no means a fair return.

Only with the armistice was the Korean motion picture industry able to make some semblance of a comeback with 35-and 16-mm full-length feature films but most betrayed poor technical quality and were handicapped by intense competition from Western imports. Of some 20 produced in the next few years, only two or three allowed the producers to recover their investments. It was another period of chaos, accentuated by the hapless feeling of moviemakers before the onslaught of Cinemascope, Cinerama, Vistavision, and the like, all following one another with disconcerting speed and landing upon the Korean market at an even more greatly accelerated rate.

Postwar Boom of Motion Picture Industry

Tax Exemption Makes Movies a Major Industry

Not until the year, 1956, was the indigenous industry able to show some signs of normalcy and embark on a long stride toward prosperity. Three developments account for this great leap forward.

First, in the interest of the domestic growth of movie-making potentialities, the National Assembly on March 18, 1955 passed a bill that waived admission taxes for all films produced at home. Normally, an admission tax was the rule for all films, imported or otherwise, at the rate of 90/190. At a time when the government of a war-torn country needed every source of revenue, the legislative action was, indeed, a most drastic and radical step. It is the unanimous consensus that this exceptional treatment was the main factor for the "boom" that is enjoyed by the motion picture industry today.

Second, though still primitive and small by any standard, all vital equipment needs were available by now at laboratories of the Ministry of National Defense and the Office of Public Information. In order to be of equal benefit to all, however, such facilities had to be available to private enterprises. The Asia Foundation, a private American aid agency with main offices in San Francisco, was especially instrumental in this connection. It donated $50,000 worth of equipment including a Mitchell camera, lighting stands and bulbs, an automatic Houston developing machine and a modern printer. A non-profit association consisting of leading producers and technicians was formed to handle and manage the donated equipment in the best interest of all private producers. In addition to the equipment made available by the Asia Foundation, Hong Chan, owner of the Sudo Theater in Seoul, opened a mammoth movie studio at Anyang on the outskirts of Seoul. The studio is equipped not only with a stage adequate for all set shootings but also with a most modern sound-recording system.

Third, two Korean films produced during 1955 broke box-office records for all pictures ever shown in Korea, foreign or domestic. These were "Chunhyangjon" and "Chayu Puin" (Lady of Liberty). An estimated 90 thousand people saw this third and most successful version of the "Chunhyang" tale in a 21-day run at the Kukto Theater in Seoul and equally enthusiastic receptions were forthcoming in all rural areas where it was screened. The picture reportedly drew 100,000,000 hwan in box-office receipts against an original investment of 18,000,000 hwan. An even greater success was scored by "Chayu Puin" which reportedly netted 160,000,000 hwan against an original invertment of 50,000,000 hwan in the course of a 26-day run at Seoul's Sudo Theater. Based on a popular novel by the contemporary novelist, Chong Pisok, as serialized in the newspaper, Seoul Sinmun, it is the story of a middle-aged wife of a university professor who deserts her husband to elope with a crafty lover. The value of "Chunhyangjon" and "Chayu Puin" as stimulants to the industry cannot be overestimated. They have succeeded in creating interest in Korean motion pictures at every level of society and in convincing producers that there was now a definite market for domestic movies.

Production

There are no major producers in Korea and no self-contained units owning their own equipment. All Korean producers are, in fact, shoe-string operators. Since, again, production facilities are never immediately available, the making of motion pictures is more or less a sporadic affair. It is a "one picture at a time" industry, as evidenced by the fact that during the period from January to August this year, the 78 feature films released in Seoul involved more than 60 different individual production companies.

Here, as everywhere, production is dictated by the economics of the industry. Often the producer is not an artist but a businessman who rarely hesitates to weigh the economic necessities against artistic values. Budgets over the past two years have varied from 20,000,000 hwan to 80,000,000 hwan (about $80,000). It is generally estimated that it takes 30,000,000 hwan to make an average 35-mm A-class Korean picture. Budget figures include cost of advertising and release prints which are borne totally by the producer.

As Korean film-making is essentially a handicraft operation, no production line economies are possible. However, in recent months, a trend has become conspicuous in which small fund producers are consolidating their financial ability to spearhead largescale production. A sharp rise in the costs of talent and crews resulting from intense competition among the numerous individual producers has engendered the trend. Several major production companies now seek to enforce a system whereby popular stars and directors work on an exclusive contract basis.

Generally speaking, most Korean films are made from published stories serialized in the major daily newspapers and magazines as well as over the radio broadcast. Classic tales and short stories by famous authors that seem to lend themselves to commercial exploitation also receive considerable attention.

The lack of shooting stages sometimes makes the producer the plaything of the weather. However, the Korean climate, other than in the rainy season (June-July), permits reasonably steady exterior shooting. Cover sets, or alternates to exterior locations, have been made available for a large number of productions. Set costs are a comparatively low budget item due to the great amount of location shooting. There are no soundproof shooting stages owned or operated by private producers.

Materials (film stocks, chemicals, etc.) and services (talent, crew) constitute the major production costs. It is estimated that the average picture is budgeted at 30% for raw stock and 40% for talent and crew. Importation of raw film stock is undertaken through trading firms such as the Three Star Trading Company which specializes in the handling of Kodak products. The price of raw film is comparatively high since a 100% tariff is placed upon all raw films imported through regular trading channels. The price of negative raw film was approximately 80.00 hwan per foot as of the end of September 1959.

It is common practice for the lights to be tied in to the main power line but due to the undependability of this utility, cameras are usually battery-operated for all daytime shootings. The ratio of footage shot to the length of the finished film varies with the director but the proportion of two to one is about normal. Period of production, from photography to completion, averages from 60 to 75 days, weather permitting.

Practically all pictures are sound-recorded not directly but at post-synchronized dubbing stages at the Office of Public Information and the Anyang studios. Editing is usually done by the director who is assisted by a cutter. Release prints are reproduced optically, then developed in the processing laboratories at Anyang and Chongnung near Seoul. Original music is often written for Korean films but usually the background score comes from records.

Personnel engaged in production belong to four major organized groups: the Korean Motion Picture Producers Association (Chairman, Chong Hwase: approximately 50 members), the Korean Motion Picture Directors Association (Kim Sodong, Chairman, approximately 30 members), the Korean Motion Picture Technicians' Association (Kim Songchun, Chairman, approximately 80 members), and the Actors' and Actresses' Association (Pok Hyesuk, Chairman, approximately 100 registered members). These professional associations have considerable influence among their members. They are often engaged in activities designed to protect the interests of their individual members. The Motion Picture Producers' Association has recently been incorporated as a non-profit organization and operates on individual membership dues of 1,000,000 hwan per year. It recommends and selects entries in and national delegates to foreign film festivals and negotiates with the government on such problems as tax elimination.

Free enterprise governs, but indirectly the government plays an important role in the Korean motion picture industry. Each production must pass government censors in order to obtain the right of tax-free exhibition. Nevertheless, the present government line is one of official encouragement, as evidenced in the removal of taxes, to the private enterpriser in the field. In view of the present national budgetary needs and the alleged progress of the industry, however, it is speculated that the government may impose a 20-25% tax on box-office receipts for all domestically-produced drama films as of 1960.

Meantime, the problem of financing motion picture production is a continuing one. The funds are largely drawn from loans made by friends or wealthy individuals who succumb to the glamor of the screen. To-date capital for motion pictures has rarely been advanced by banks, nor are bank loans likely to be given until the industry or an individual company becomes completely stable. Rates of interest paid on loans are extremely high and production and distribution slow-downs usually mean that all hope for profits will be consumed through payment of interest on money borrowed. Due to the high cost of production money, distribution and exhibition must begin immediately where production leaves off.

Theaters

Perhaps the most serious single problem facing the home industry at the present time is exhibition. There are at present 160 theaters in the Republic, of which 47 are located in Seoul. There are eight first-run theaters in Seoul and one half of these are devoted exclusively to the showing of domestic films. The seats average 1,000 in Seoul and 700 in the local areas. A great majority of the moviehouses in the rural areas show domestic films, with Western films shown at the rate of one per month or two every three months. The Korean people, as people everywhere, prefer domestic pictures, to those which represent a culture different from their own.

The distributor is the agent of the producer and not a separate company. Even when separate distribution companies are used, there is no minimum guarantee to the producer from the distributor. Prospects for financing pictures with advanced payments from the renter have not been bright, but in recent months many of the theater owners, especially those in Seoul, have undertaken to help finance productions, indicating the start of exhibitions through a theater circuit. These theaters include the Kukche, Myongbo and Kukto, all of which are located in Seoul.

Booking arrangement percentages vary from 65-70% and 35-30% for the producer and exhibitor respectively.

As there are no box-office taxes placed on Korean films, a high proportion of the profits find their way back to the producer. For all that, lack of a regular distribution network results in a decrease, by more than 30%, in the total box-office revenue. The lack of a normal distribution vehicle has led to a system under which distributors wanting to show a film in a specific province buy it on a flat lump sum payment basis instead of percentage. An average of 1,500,000 hwan-2,000,000 hwan is spent on advertisements, usually a 50-50 arrangement between the producer and exhibitor. Six to nine months are required for a picture to be played off.

The admission fare is between 400-500 hwan for first-run houses and 150-200 hwan for third-run. Most theaters run single full-length features continuously. Seats in first-run theaters are reserved. Performances usually begin about 10:00-10:30 a.m., and end in time for the midnight curfew. On the average, first-run houses play one movie a week.

A film may be considered a box-office success if it is shown for two weeks at a first-run theater to an accrued audience of 30,000. Any film which has succeeded in attracting an audience beyond this figure is considered a smash-hit. Because of intense competition, less than 40% of the producers have been able to collect revenues to meet their original investments. The commercially successful domestic films released in 1959 during the period of January-August include:

Title	No. of Days Shown	Audience
"Emperor Kojong and the Patriot, An Chunggun"	30	150,000
"Over the Hill and Over the Sea"	21	110,000
"There's No Telling the Fate of Man"	21	110,000
"The Giant-Midget Team Goes to Nonsan"	21	90,000
"Yu Kwansun, the Heroine"	21	100,000

"No Tragedy"	21	120,000
"No Fault of Hers"	21	90,000

Foreign Films

Foreign films have suffered a sharp decline in box-office income as the result of a shrinking market. As part of the government measure to encourage production of domestic motion pictures, a 115% admission tax has been imposed on all imported Western films, and it is practically impossible for foreign film distributors to expect any sizable revenue from provincial areas. Theaters available for foreign films total less than 10, most of them in Seoul. Tickets are printed at the government mint to prevent fraud in tax payment, thus making things even more difficult. Furthermore, the government is imposing a quota on foreign films at 165 per year, but the annual quota usually consists of about 180 films, thanks to a "bonus quota" awarded 20 additional films. This "bonus quota" is awarded to producers who have made pictures considered to be of high-quality and, as such, are an encouragement to domestic production.

Black-and-white foreign films can usually be imported at approximately one-fifth or less the cost of producing a Korean feature, and an A-class color film with top internationally known stars costs only one-half or less the average domestic production costs. Although better Korean movies have brought about decreased interest in foreign films, block booking tactics is still used by foreign film distributors. The royalty system is not used by foreign film producer-distributor organizations. They lease their films on a flat price per-print basis. This arrangement usually calls for a one or two year life for a print lease. In the case of U.S. films, at the end of the lease period, the print is returned to the American Embassy where the local importer receives a certificate stating that he has lived up to the terms of the contract.

Although rental and leasing fees for foreign films vary enormously, an average black-and-white feature would cost approximately four to five million hwan; color films which as a rule cost at least twice as much to produce, are usually correspondingly high in lease price. The theaters collect 40% box-office tax on all foreign films. This tax, which is collected by the government once a month, is often put out by the exhibitor at high interest short term loans, repayable prior to the tax collection date. Imported films are not dubbed in the Korean language, but sub-titling of prints is undertaken locally. Imported films popular during the first half of 1959 include: "The Best Years of Our Lives" (an estimated 80,000 audience saw this film), "Somebody up There Likes Me" (which drew 60,000), and "Young Lions" (which also drew 60,000).

The following table indicates the number of imported and domestic films since 1951:

	Foreign Feature Films				Domestic
	U.S.	European	Others	Total	Production
1951	5	10		15	
1952	45	19		64	11
1953	48	31	2	81	10
1954	109	43		152	18
1955	99	21	3	123	16
1956	135	15	1	151	36
1957	114	15	1	130	47
1958	174	25	25	224	92
1959 (as of the end of Oct.)				119	90

Because of the bitter past experience and the diplomatic snarl since 1945, no Japanese films have been shown in Korea since the Liberation. A few Soviet films were shown during the period from 1945 to 1947, but entry of films produced in Communist or pro-Commust nations is now prohibited by law.

Scenario Writers and Critics

One of the main problems of the domestic motion picture industry is the shortage of good scenario writers. Only five or six persons are competent to prepare a detailed shooting script. An original scenario is unusual and more than 80% of the films produced are based on adaptations from stories already available in book form. Because of growing indifference on the part of the audience to cheap "soap opera" type movies, writers are becoming increasingly aware of the necessity of providing better quality melodramas. O Yongjin, Choe Kumdong and Kim Kangyun are among the scenario writers considered first-class. Other promising young writers include Yi Pongnae, Yi Hangi, Yi Chinsop, Im Hijae and Yu Tuyon.

Motion picture critics play an important role in stimulating the industry in the production of better quality pictures. On the other hand, a Motion Picture Critics' Association was formed in 1958 to promote friendship among its members and to encourage equitable review of films in the press. The Association is publishing an organ magazine called "Film Critics' Review."

Two monthly fan magazines are being published in Korea, entitled "Kukche Film" and "Movie World." These provide information on all phases of the domestic motion picture industry.

Actors and Actresses

A great majority of Korean screen actors and actresses come from a stage background. Due primarily to the paucity of theaters for modern drama and the resultant difficulty of making a living out of stage acting, practically all of the members of the two major dramatic troupes, Sinhyop and Minguk, have succumbed to the lure of the recent motion picture boom. Actors and actresses draw their pay from the first day of rehearsal to dismissal regardless of whether or not the shooting schedule has been interrupted. Actresses are more popular with the fans than actors and usually draw the highest salaries. Korea now has several outstanding stars with an estimatable box-office value. The so-called "guaranty" paid to these stars range from 1,000,000 to 2,000,000 hwan per picture. Some top stars: actors – Kim Chingyu, Choe Muryong, Pak Am, Yi Min, Hwang Hae and Kim Songho; actresses – Choe Unhi, Kim Chimi, Mun Chongsuk, Chu Chungnyo, Cho Miryong and Om Aengnan.

Directors

The sharp increase in the number of productions has entailed the coming into existence of a large number of new directors some of whom are considered highly promising. As producers are still hesitant to enter into a contract over any long period, the directors are usually hired on a contract per picture basis. The amount of payment such a short-term contract provides varies depending on the skill of the director. It ranges from 1,000,000 to 2,000,000 hwan. Considered first-rate in directing are Yi Pyongil, Yu Hyonmuk, Kim Sodong and Yi Kangchon. The most promising and talented of the new faces are Kim Muk, No Pil, Paek Homin, Pak Songbok and Choe Hun. Men like Yu Tuyon, Yi Pongnae and Kim Kangyun have shifted their profession from scenario writing to directing.

Technicians

For technical personnel, there are neither standard salaries nor well-defined duties except perhaps for the cameramen and lighting technicians. The older established craftsmen are considered to be comparatively well paid while the lower grades draw very low wages. Technicians have no central employment pool and are employed usually upon recommendation of the director or cameraman. On the other hand, there is a Motion Picture Technicians' Association. This is a prestigious body and those affiliated with it do not require proofs of their proficiency. Cameramen work on a picture for a flat payment of 500,000 hwan on an average, while lighting technicians are usually hired on a contract basis and have to furnish their own lighting equipment. The per picture revenue for a first-class lighting technician is usually 1,000,000 hwan.

Set Shooting Stages and Laboratories

Stage facilities and laboratories in Korea are classified as governmental and private. Though available primarily for governmental use, the shooting stages and laboratory equipment of the Ministry of National Defence and Office of Public Information are sometimes rented out to private producers. The Information Office has all basic processing equipments and the Defense Ministry all but an automatic developing machine. Information's film unit is equipped with excellent pieces of equipment made available by the United States Operations' Mission.

The two main studios, Chongnung and Anyang, run their own private facilities. The Korean Motion Picture Culture Associations, Inc., a non-profit organization consisting of representative producers and technicians, controls the Chongnung Studios and makes its facilities available to private producers at low rental fees. The Anyang studio and laboratory, run by a private businessman, undertakes processing for most of the domestic films.

For reasons of high costs, color photography is still at a fledgling stage. Yi Mansu, head of the Korean Color Processing Laboratory, experimented with color photography in the production of yet another "Chunhyangjon" version in 1958 with a raw stock of ANSCO film. The film was not much of a success, commercially or technically, because of inferior quality color processing.

Director Yi Kangchon produced the first black-and-white Cinemascope film in early 1959 at the Anyang Studios. This was followed by two more Cinemascope pictures and a Vistavision, but on the whole, the wide screen is still uncommon.

International Relations

Participation of Korean producers in international film festivals took place for the first time in 1955 when four Korean observers attended the Second Asian Film Festival held in Singapore in May. Korea was admitted to the Federation of Motion Picture Producers in Asia in 1956, when the Federation held its third annual film festival in Hong Kong. At the fourth film festival held in Tokyo, "Wedding Day" (directed by Yi Pyongil) won the best comedy award. The film was shown at the Berlin film festival the same year. In 1959, Korea received two subsidiary awards for best child acting and best choreography in Kuala Lumpur.

In 1957, Korean producers also began to make joint pictures with other countries. Im Hwasu, president of the Korean Entertainment Company, spearheaded co-production efforts, primarily with Hong Kong producers. In two years, he distributed five such feature-length films in Korea. Two other producers cooperated with Taiwan and Philippines' producers to take location shots in tropical settings. These films, however, did not prove financially successful with the result that no producer has sought foreign partnership in 1959.

Korea's admission to the Federation of Motion Picture Producers in Asia has made her industry known to the world, and each year invitations arrive from the organizers of the Cannes, Venice and San Francisco film festivals. Korean producers feel that quality pictures are yet to be made and to date no entries have been sent, except for two movies to the 1957 Berlin festival.

A few well-known foreign motion picture personnages have visited Korea, notably John Ford who stayed in Seoul for about a week in early 1959 to shoot and direct a documentary film on Korea for the U. S. troops stationed in Korea. An Italian delegation, including the actress, Rossana Podesta, was also here in April of the same year. Other visitors have included Jane Russell, Bob Hope and Marilyn Monroe.

Awards

There are five different awards given annually to improve the artistic and technical standards of domestic films. They are:

The Outstanding Domestic Film Award, given by the Ministry of Education

The Pusan Ilbo Film Award, given by the Pusan Ilbo newspaper in Pusan

The Pyonghyop Award, given by the Motion Picture Critics' Association of Korea

The Kukche Film Award, given by the Kukche Motion Picture News Company

The Chonnam Ilbo Award, given by the Chonnam Ilbo newspaper in Kwangju

These awards are given mostly in the fields of directing and acting. The most valued is the one chosen by the Ministry of Education. Winners of Education Ministry awards for 1959 are as follows:

Outstanding Films: "Bell House," "For Love's Sake," "Free Marriage," and "Life's Seizure."

Best Actor: Kim Chingyu
Best Actress: Choe Unhi
Best Supporting Actress: Hwang Chongsun
Best Director: Cho Kungha

Education and Training Institutions

The creation of a domestic motion picture "boom" has entailed the problem of how to meet the growing demand for talent in acting as well as in laboratory processing. Among institutions established to fill the needs in this facet of the industry are:

Sorabol College of Arts, the most popular and well-staffed of this kind, is headed by Kim Sejon and provides a four-year college education in the fields of drama, motion picture, music and literature. Those enrolled in the motion picture department comprise the bulk of its students. The college admits 300 high school graduates each year. The number of applicants for entrance is so large that competition is intense, the rate often being 3 to 1. Because demand among producers for new talent is strong, the college boasts a 100% employment record for its motion picture department graduates.

Chungang University, has recently established a department of arts aimed at providing courses for those seeking a career in motion picture and drama. Facilities for adequate training are in the process of being expanded, and it is expected that the university will turn out able and ambitious youngsters, especially in the field of acting. Stage and laboratory facilities are available to students for on-the-spot training; producers cooperate by undertaking to hire the students as bit-players.

The Central Institute of Art, is devoted to providing short-term courses on the motion picture for some 250 to 300 students. The Institute has a night school for those who have to work during the day. Lectures are delivered mostly by motion picture people with established fame, covering fields of directing, acting, camerawork and script writing. The Institute is remarked for its night students who are from all kinds of professions, even college professors and high-ranking government officials.

The Tongyang Institute of Art, has been only recently established and is patterned after the Central Institute of Art. This Institute is unique in that it makes available courses on music and dance. The Institute has an enrollment of about 400 students.

XXI HISTORICAL REMAINS

Of Tombs and Temples

Introduction

A total of 150 historical remains have been officially registered throughout this peninsular country. These include such immovable relics as the sites of former Buddhist temples, kilns, ancient tombs, and other monuments of greater historical than artistic worth.

The remains may be classified roughly into the following four typical categories: 1) Ancient tombs 2) Sites of Buddhist temples 3) Castles and Mountain fortresses 4) Kiln sites.

Ancient Tombs

Major groups of these ancient tombs, registered as historical relics to be preserved, are located in the western provinces of Hwanghae-do, Pyongan Namdo, Chungchong Namdo, Cholla Pukto, Kyongsang Pukto and Kyongsang Namdo. They are largely monuments of Koguryo, Paekche, Silla and the Kaya states, concentrated notably in such places as Songsanni, Kongju; Nungsangni, Puyo; and Pannammyon, Naju of the Chungchong and Cholla provinces from the various stages of Paekche culture, the wide area of Koryong, Changnyong, Sungan and Kimhae of Kyongsang Namdo where the Kaya states spread, and the Silla cities of Kyongju and Yangsan in Cholla Pukto.

The registry also includes the sepulchral-shaped dolmens of the Pyongan Namdo and Hwanghae-do provinces in the north that prevailed during the period between the late Neolithic and Aeneolithic Ages. There are two different types of dolmen. The northern type of dolmen is made up of a huge, flat stone ceiling supported horizontally by several other stone slabs on the surface of the ground, with the space inbetween the structural stones constituting a grave chamber. One dolmen in Unyul, for example, is made of stone ceilings, eight meters in length, supported by three pillar-shaped stones, thus resembling a present-day table. In contrast, the southern types in the southern part of the peninsula are, in many cases, either of shorter stone supports or without any props at all, the stone ceilings lying on the ground and the grave chamber built underground.

Such dolmen types appear occasionally both in southern Manchuria (northern types) and northern Kyushu, Japan (southern types) but the major concentration is found in the Korean peninsula. It has yet to be determined whether there is any relationship between the dolmens of Korea and Europe. Likewise, the dates have not been established as a certainty.

Koguryo tombs, believed to have been founded in the 5th, 6th and first half of the

7th centuries, around the capital city of Pyongyang, are made of stone chambers built under the earth mounds with mural paintings of departed souls or the "Four Deities" drawn on white plaster-covered walls. Another distinguished characteristic of this type is what is called a lantern ceiling, one believed to have originated in the Near East, with triangular stones piled up on the four upper edges of the main wall.

The following Koguryo tombs, equipped with mural paintings, have been officially registered as historical remains: tomb of the Twin Pillars, the Great Tomb at Uhyonni and the tomb of the Heaven and Earth Deities in Sunchon. The Twin Pillars is made of a square main chamber comprising many square anterooms, with two octagonal stone pillars astride either side of the main entrance. They are reminiscent of the ones that may be found in the stone cave temples of China and India. In the main chamber, one may notice portraits of departed souls drawn on the northern wall, and, both walls adjoining the entrance, processions of Buddhist monks and servants in old-fashioned frescoes. In the case of the Great Tomb, such paintings are of little importance compared with the rectangular anterooms with tri-partitioned ceilings that are lined up along with the main chamber resembling those found in the ancient Chinese tombs.

The tomb of the Heaven and Earth Deities in Sunchon has no usual lantern ceiling. Instead, it has a peculiar-looking one made of stones supported by numerous inverted V-shaped arms, representing a very interesting method of dome-building.

The Great Tomb at Uhyonni is noted for swift, fluent brush strokes and effective use of colors displayed in the mural paintings on the polished, granite walls of the grave chamber. It surpasses by far the contemporary art of China. Ancient Paekche tombs erected around Kongju are believed to have been founded during the first half of the 6th century, the most representative of them all being the one that seems to have been a royal grave, judging from the huge arched ceiling and the way it was built with bricks.

A rectangular grave chamber of huge granite covered with earth can be seen in most of the ancient tombs located around Puyo, capital city of Paekche some 1,500 years ago. On the walls of the chambers, the Four Deities were drawn and lotus flower paintings may still be noticed. These types of tombs were so easy of access from the outside that most of them have been excavated and property buried with the dead unlawfully taken away. Further down to the south, there are many-mounded Paekche tombs in Pannammyon, Naju, whose unique characteristic is the jar coffin. These coffins are made of two hard, unglazed jars, one big and the other small, with mouths sealed after the remains of the dead were laid inside. The coffins were kept in a stone chamber or pit built underground, the entrance to it cemented later with stone and clay. This method of burial prevailed widely in the Orient just before and after the beginning of the Christian era, but it is still unknown whether they were connected in any way with earlier types or else were influenced by what had prevailed in South China. Pannammyon is the only place where jar coffins have been uncovered. In this sense, the Pannammyon tombs are considered to be of great importance.

East of Naju and west of Naktong River is a region once called the Region of the Kaya* states in the days of the Tripartite Powers. Here, one may notice huge mounded tombs scattered over a wide area quite different from those of Paekche and Silla with elongated rectangular pits serving as grave chambers. The ceilings are made of several board-shaped stones. Their easy accessibility made these tombs the prey of subsequent Japanese confiscations.

Huge mounded tombs are also centered around Kyongju, Silla capital for over a

*Derived from the suffixes of the several states existing then—Taegaya, Kumgwangaya, etc., Kaya fell, state by state, before Silla and Paekche.

thousand years. The are mostly huge, some containing earth ounds as high as seventy feet. The tombs at Nosori, especially, seem to have belonged either to royalty or nobility, judging from their size. The Gold Crown Tomb, thus called by the accidental discovery of a gold crown, is the most famous. Its diameter is said to have been one hundred and fifty feet. Remains of the dead in this region were usually put in a wooden box to be placed in the grave chamber, three meters by four meters, along with the other belongings of the dead, and the lid of the chamber was then cemented with clay and gravel. These tombs of the Silla dynasty have been kept comparatively intact owing to the huge mound, excluding those excavated accidentally by the farmer's plow. It is likely that there may be many grave chambers still hidden under homes in the Kyongju area.

In the suburbs of Kyongju, there are several royal tombs with stone figures of military officers and civil officials lined up in front. The military statues, at least, are not of Korean features. Judging from their wavy hair, heavy beards and high noses, they must have represented professional soldiers of Persia who are known to have served Silla. They are believed to have been founded some time between the latter half of the 7th and 9th century A.D. There were also other tombs, e.g., the Kwae Nung tombs and the tomb of Kim Yusin. Kwae Nung tombs are thought to have been the graves of unidentified monarchs. There are some stones placed upon the lower slabs of the earth mound. These have zodiacs engraved in relief. Another group of ancient tombs behind the town of Yangsan in Kyongsang Namdo are believed to have been erected in the days of the Silla dynasty. One of them, excavated in 1920, had a square grave chamber built of stone under the mound. There was a high platform in the chamber on which remains of the master and mistress were placed. Bone and other evidences make it apparent that the master had been buried earlier than his lady and that two separate funerals had taken place.

Many earth mounds of the ancient tombs have been levelled during the war, and the National Museum has been conducting emergency excavations as the need arose. It is, however, a fundamental policy of government to preserve these tombs as they are rather than excavate them for archaeological studies.

Sites of Buddhist Temples

It would be no exaggeration to say that virtually all of the numerous temples, erected over a thousand year period between the latter half of the 4th century when Buddhism was first introduced into this land in the days of the Three Kingdoms, and the beginning of the Yi dynastic era in the 15th century, have almost all been ruined. Certainly, there is not a single structure still intact. It may be noted that very few stone relics have been found, beside pieces of roof tiles and base stones, at the sites of old temples located all about the former capital cities and elsewhere.

Temple remains, however, have been neglected because of the undue emphasis that has been placed on tomb excavations by archaeologists. In spite of the urgent need to preserve these temple sites as objects of academic study and historical remains, nothing has been done so far to explore these branches of ancient history and collect data for academic research on the structures of ancient buildings. It is desirable that more attention be paid to the preservation of these sites and other remains. Research work on temple sites will not only explain clearly the flow of Buddhist culture into Korea but may also throw light on the cultural exchanges that were going on among China, Korea and Japan in the olden days.

The temples were erected at first mainly around the municipalities as a natural result of the initial dissemination of Buddhism among the populations of big cities. With the gradual penetration of Buddhism into local communities and mountainous areas, many other temples were also erected. During the period of Silla unity, after the introduction and dissemination of the *Zen* creed, construction of temples in many famous mountain regions began to prevail, making it inevitable to change the disposition of unit buildings. When Buddhism became the official state religion, first of Koguryo and later of Silla, largescale temples displaying royal power came into existence. These great projects were mostly completed between the latter half of the 5th century and the 6th. It would be appropriate to assume that construction began in Koguryo days after the removal of the seat of government to Pyongyang. The most typical of all the temple sites existing today is probably the one that has been discovered and excavated at Chongamni in the outskirts of Pyongyang, with the site of the octagonal temple in the center. Others are Paekche's Taetongsa in Kongju erected in the days of King Song some time between 523—553 A.D., Silla's Hungyunsa in Kyongju erected in the days of King Chinhung some time between 540—575, and the Hwangnyongsa which is famous for its nine-storeyed wooden pagoda. Their common characteristics are wooden pagodas and great halls erected along a north-south demarcation line after the Chinese fashion. Buddha remains and images were worshipped. It was a type of Buddhist architecture that continued until the end of the Three Kingdoms period. Needless to say, there were changes in the disposition of unit buildings and other features as time went by. In the case of the Kunsusa and Chongnimsa, it was found, upon excavation, that all these forms had been fully consolidated. The central structure, pagoda, golden hall and auditorium were erected facing north along the meridian, the building being connected by corridors. This disposition has also been found in Japan, a fact which may be taken as proof that the Japanese had learned their architectural techniques from Paekche architects. According to the latest excavation research findings at the site of the Asukadera in the Yamato region of Japan, some difference has been found in the case of this temple, the golden halls being erected on the eastern and western sides of the pagoda. For all that, the new data furnishes enough evidences to confirm the fact that Paekche artists were wholly responsible for the temple, thus ending all controversies on the matter. Renewed consideration should also be given the disposition of pagoda and golden hall on both the eastern and western sides of the main building as may be noticed in the Japanese temples of Horyuji. Judging from the fact that similar dispositions were discovered at the site of a Koguryo temple at Chongamni, it has been established that extensive cultural exchange took place between the Korean peninsula and Japan. It follows that research work on ancient temple sites in Japan will bring no definite conclusions unless their origins in Korea are fully explored and analyzed.

After the unification of the three states by Silla, many others were erected in and around Kyongju. At this stage, a new type of structural feature, namely twin pagodas, built in front of the golden hall, made their first appearance at Sachonwangsa and Kamunsa. According to latest reports, however, this type of architecture was started early in the 7th century at the close of the Three Kingdoms era. This was later confirmed at the Miruksa in Iksan where there still exist huge twin stone statues, the oldest and the largest in Korea. Therefore, an argument that the twin pagoda temple was first erected immediately after the Silla unity should now be reassessed.

Stone towers, one of the many characteristics of the Korean temple, were originated during the Paekche dynasty and later conveyed to Silla where they were perfected. This reverses past contentions that Korean culture merely imitated foreign countries. It has, therefore, become necessary to recognize Korea's own characteristic features and traditions in discussing the growth of Korean culture.

This method, established after the Silla unity, influenced the latter-day temples. The most typical of these are: the Pulguksa in Kyongju and the sites of a temple at Changhangni, Wonwonsa and a temple at Chongunni. The following temples may also be added to the list: Silsangsa in Namwon, Cholla Namdo and the sites of the Tonghwasa in Taegu, Kyongsang Pukdo and Tansoksa in Sanchong, Kyongsang Namdo. At the same time, single pagoda temples were also built in many places and numerous stone towers have been discovered at their sites. In the case of mountain temples, some deviation may be noticed in the architectural techniques and disposition of unit buildings but two main principles have been firmly retained in building the parts of the main temples ever since. After Koryo came to power and the seat of its government was moved to Kaesong, a number of temples were built around the city. These innumerable temples clearly explain the flourishing days of Buddhism during the era. It should be noted, however, that the greater emphasis has been placed on the geographical positions of each unit in erecting these temples. Of them all, the Hungwangsa, built in the 11th century in Kaesong, as King Munjong's royal temple, was the biggest and most famous. The monument has long been destroyed but, according to the research conducted by the National Museum, the technique of a twin-temple structure was applied in constructing the buildings, judging from the two huge, octagonal, many-storeyed, wooden towers erected in front of the golden hall, one on the eastern, and the other on the western side, of the hall.

With the advent of the Yi dynasty when Confucianism replaced Buddhism as the state religion, symbols of Buddhist faith faded, although a limited number of temples continued to be erected. In some cases, temples were either destroyed or removed in order to build local educational institutes or to choose sites for graves. Though Buddhism returned to power for a short period of time in the reign of King Munjong, resulting in new temples, such as the Wongaksa in Seoul and the Hoeamsa in Yangju, it declined again soon afterwards. Furthermore, innumerable temples were destroyed during the Hideyoshi invasion of three hundred years ago. Damages suffered at the time were far greater than those inflicted during the previous Mongol conquest at the close of the Koryo era. It should also be added that great damage was inflicted upon the remaining old temples during the Korean conflict, completely destroying the Songgwangsa in Cholla Namdo and the Woljongsa in Kangwon-do.

Castle and Mountain Fortresses

In discussing castles, it should be pointed out, first of all, that the majority of them are mountain fortresses. The mountain fortress began to appear in Korea in the closing days of the Neolithic Age. Fortresses at this stage were a simple defensive set-up consisting of forts or enclosures surrounded by fences, including residences, remains of which were reported to have been discovered. The primitive forts probably developed into larger fortresses in the days of the Three Han, but this has yet to be confirmed. It is thought that during the Three Han period, each tribal community comprising a few villages set up what appeared to be forts or strongholds on nearby mountains or hills for purely defensive purposes. The forts grew in size and increased in number because they were used by the states as strategic strongholds. As such, they have survived destruction, some being officially registered as historical remains. There are no significant differences in structure. Most of them were usually erected on comparatively flat mountain-tops or on the hills and were surrounded by stone or clay walls. But either around the capital city or at strategic places where large fortresses were needed, big castles of a comprehensive type were built up. They prevailed, particularly, during the Koguryo dynasty.

On the other hand, quite apart from the days of the Three Han, all throughout the Koryo and Yi eras during which this country suffered numerous invasions from without, almost all cities and towns were surrounded by ramparts as a safeguard against sudden attacks. As the prime objective of these ramparts was defense, they were built to surround the main part of the communities along mountain edges. This is one of the unique characteristics of the mountain fortress of Korea, one not to be found either in the castles of the Three Han era or in China. However, some big cities had rectangular ramparts with a gate on each side built around them in a manner that prevailed in contemporary China. These were established in imitation of the Chinese.

Beside these, there are large mountain fortresses made of ramparts, built along steep mountain edges to encircle a vast valley in order to make it more impregnable. For instance, there are the Namhansansong, which has been officially registered, and the Pukhan mountain fortress which has served as a rearguard for Seoul for more than 500 years. Though established during the Yi dynasty, they are also to be counted among the unique characteristics of the Korean fortress.

In addition, there are remains of border garrison forts, long fortresses set up at bottlenecks of the main roads, but these are of little significance. Of all the typical fortresses and castles, very few have thus far been officially registered, and basic research and measures for their preservation have yet to be established, All in all, there are about 1,000 fortresses in this country. Although such insignificant forts and strongholds as earth ramparts of the Four Chinese colonial provinces period and the coastal erections of the invading Japanese forces of the 16th century have been officially registered as historical relics to be preserved, they are foreign in style, and, as such, quite different from our own unique kind.

Sites of Kilns

Korea has had a long history of a fine earthenware industry that stands comparison in the Orient only with China. During the 4th and 5th centuries, mass production of grey, black ceramics of fine quality was carried out in the southern area of the peninsula, while the 6th and 7th centuries witnessed the production of soft, glazed china belonging to the grey, glazed family.

Since the beginning of Koryo in the 10th century, the ceramics industry began to turn out blue, glazed earthenware, developing so rapidly that the 11th and 12th centuries saw celadon, more delicate and finer in quality than those of Sung China, produced in large quantities. In parallel with this fullswing production, other ceramics, including white porcelain, were also refined. On the other hand, since the end of the 14th century, white porcelain replaced celadon. The white porcelains of the Yi dynasty were produced continuously until the end of the 19th century. The industry, in fact, hit its stride from the beginning of Yi when there were already 136 porcelain and 185 ceramic producing points throughout the country. Any reference to porcelain meant white earthenware while ceramics implied the light greenish blue pottery that then prevailed.

This prosperous ceramic industry was badly crippled both in manpower and installations during the Hideyoshi invasion. Japan, undeveloped in the field of ceramic technology, envied the porcelain and other earthenware arts of Korea. They either destroyed or carried off the tools and technicians of the Korean ceramic industry. Japanese ceramics, which is now one of the largest industry of the kind in the world, began with these Korean booties.

With such a long tradition, numerous kilns should have been preserved to this day. To the contrary, structural weaknesses and rapid decline of the industry in modern days led to neglect. There are only seven ancient kiln sites, officially registered as historical remains to be preserved: one (1) apparently of the Paekche era for earthenware, three (3) for the celadon and white porcelain of Koryo, two (2) for the celadon of Latter Koryo and light greenish blue and-white of Early Yi respectively, and one (1) for the light greenish blue pottery of Early Yi.

It is considered essential to preserve these

sites if any headway is to be made in future study of Korean ceramic history.

Besides the seven officially registered, there are many other kiln sites, notably the one at Punwonni in Kwangju, Kyonggido- which turned out white porcelain for royal use.

Conclusion

The historic remains of any country with an ancient culture are an invaluable national asset. Such is the case with Korea. Her monuments, together with her strikingly beautiful landscape and natural surroundings, make tourism an attractive modern proposition. Tourism is considered an ideal source for earning dollar income. One of the three basic objectives recently announced by government for self-sufficiency to anticipate reduced aid funds from the United States was the promotion of tourism for just this reason.

The state divides our cultural assets into two categories: "National Treasure" and "National Remains." Items relegated to one or the other of these two categories during the Japanese Government-General of Chosun are automatically included. Beyond that, other items are included depending on four criteria: age and dynastic symbolism, exellent or rare techinique, relation to outstanding figures in history, and reference value for the research scholar. It is by no means easy to appraise just what constitutes a "national treasure" nor is the distinction between "National Treasure" and "National Remains" always apparent.

"National remains" constitute not only standing monuments like the Pulguksa, but also the sites where they once stood as indicated in this chapter. Historical records have served as guides to these sites and the uncovering of relics from the earth, such as a slab of stone, pins down the location. Roads, bridges and river embankments are among the other items included in the category. On the other hand, such tourist appeals as the Changdok, Kyongbok and Toksu Palaces in Seoul, are not included for they belong to the recent historical past.

National treasures and remains of Korea have a long tradition of an intensively developed culture crippled all too often by wars and depravations of foreign armies. What the Koreans have is but part of a far greater whole even of relics down to recent times, a fact that lends pungency to the efforts undertaken by the state to preserve the Korean people's extant reminders of a brilliant past. Economic considerations, however, are a severe handicap. The Ministry of Education, entrusted with the task of these preservations, is allotted a very limited budget for this purpose.

The economic stringency makes it very difficult to promote the desired objective of tourism which requires, as its premise, lavish expenditures to provide for every tourist comfort. Added to this disadvantage, is the nature of the tourist appeal to be considered. The modern tourist is invariably a Westerner and it is hardly likely that he can be attracted by undue emphasis on Koreas' historical past. The interest a historical relic can evoke in the tourist depends upon his own cultural background. The American tourist, for example, may be emotionally moved by the spot where Marie Antoinette laid her head but the sight of the supposed blood of a famous Koryo scholar named Chong something-or-other upon the Kaesong bridge where he was assassinated six hundred years ago leaves him cold.

Due to modern worldwide trends, however, it is by no means impractical for Korea to promote tourism. The modern tourist is an average middle-class citizen taking time-out from a job rather than the scion of a millionnaire family and the world is his oyster, thanks to the great strides in technological advances that make for swift transportation. There is no reason why enough tourists should not make it a habit of including Korea in their itinerary, especially since the war has made her so prominent. Some progress has been made in developing a tourist industry; more could be made by ascertaining the tourist's own interest and being guided by that rather than by what Koreans expect him to be interested in.

Tourism is dealt as a separate chapter in this book.

XXII MANNERS AND CUSTOMS

Outline

Traditional manners and customs on the wane. The manners and customs considered typically Korean are rapidly dying out and many of them which appeared to be unique have now become phenomena of the past. True, traditions do not disappear overnight and so the old manners and customs are still exerting certain influences over the daily lives of the people. But the new forces of Western civilization and culture have been so overwhelming that what had been built up during the 500 years of the Yi dynasty has crumbled during the past 60 years or so since the influx of things Western. The trend is toward Westernization at an unprecedented rate, and what has been unique and traditional is rapidly passing from view.

Another important point to bear in mind is the vast gap existing between the urban and rural areas. More susceptible to the Western influences, the urban population has cast away many of the things traditional to replace them with what they consider Western. The rural farming population, on the other hand, is still holding on to old manners and customs. Thus Shamanism still offers a potent protection to the farmers from the ubiquitous, supernatural evil spirits through Shaman incantations. The farmers still believe that the Shaman medicine-men can cure diseases. The colorful pageantry of spectacular Shaman rites lasting over a week or more through day and night have disappeared even in the rural districts.

Old gentlemen on the farms pay visits to Seoul attired in the traditional costumes of white with the inevitable bamboo pipes in their mouth and horse hair hats on their heads, to be jostled by their fellow countrymen in the city wearing Western-style suits and hats and smoking filter-tip cigarettes.

The women, however, seem to feel more attached than the men to traditional costumes, for even the urban women still wear the *chogori* and *chima*, the traditional coat and skirt respectively. Urban males, in contrast, have almost completely cast away their traditional attire for Western clothing.

Wedding on the farms and in cities. A wedding in the rural areas is still primarily a family affair over which the parents have the last word. But the "beat generation" and *avant garde* moderns living in cities fall "romantically in love" in defiance of the Confucian ethical code that "a man and woman must not sit together after the age of seven." Thus they marry the one dear to their hearts with or without the consent of parents.

The traditional wedding is a colorful event. The groom rides on a palanquin to the house of the bride, where the couple vow eternal devotion to the family with the ceremonial sipping of wine. After the wedding, the groom has to stay exactly three days with his bride at her house before he can take her to his house in the palanquin. The urban wedding, on the other hand, takes place in a Chrstian church or the commercial wedding "parlor", where the nuptial vows take place, then the couple marches down the aisle arm-in-arm to the strains of Wagner's "Wedding March" from the opera Lohengrin. A waiting car then takes them on a honeymoon trip.

The dining table of the city dwellers includes dishes of Western, Chinese and Japanese recipes together with traditional foods, but the farmers' wives in the country still know nothing more than the traditional *kimchi* and rice with some inexpensive fish cooked with home-made soybean sauce. Even the urbanites have retained most of the traditional dishes in contrast to their almost complete abandonment of what had once been the spiritual food—Shamanism. The unique Korean foods—the *kimchi* (pickled Chinese cabbages and radishes with peppers and other vegetables), soybean sauce and soybean mash are still the most important diets of both the rural and urban people, and they are still prepared at each home by the housewives despite possibility of more efficient factory mass production.

The caste system of the Yi dynasty placed *yangban* above commoners as the privileged minority. The descendents of the *yangban* are still held in respect in the rural areas regardless of their present financial position.

Funeral services that retain tradition. During the Yi dynasty, Korea was referred to by the Chinese as "the Eastern Country of Courtesy" because of the people's rigid adherence to the Confucian ethical codes, especially in the field of ancestor and filial worship. But such strict observances of various Confucian rituals are presently scoffed at more often than not. Nevertheless, the rigid rule of ceremony perfected during the Yi dynasty has survived in the funeral services in sharp contrast to the wedding ceremony, which has undergone drastic changes during the last 50 years or so. The customs of funeral services have remained substantially the same since the Yi dynasty.

Visiting graves of one's parents only once or twice a year on the national Thanksgiving holiday in the fall as observed today both by the urban and rural dwellers is a far cry from the ethical requirements of the past, when hardly a month went by without a rite of ancestor-worship of one kind or another.

But even the present practice of visiting graves of one's parents on one or two national holidays in unique in Korea, indicating the powerful influence of the Confucian ethics on ancestor-worship.

In the old days, family burial grounds had to be located on an ideal site, following faithfully the principles of "geomancy", preferably under the expert guidance of learned scholars of divinity or a professional "geomancer." It was firmly believed that burying one's parents at an "evil site" would invoke wrath of the ancestral spirits, whereas a "lucky site" would bring good fortune to offsprings. Also, sites of community dwellings and private houses had to be chosen with the utmost care, for fortunes of the people were believed to be dependent largely upon the influence of the "fever" of the earth on which the people lived. Modern science, however, has nullified "geomancy," leaving the arduous task of selecting geomancially ideal sites to old generations living in rural districts.

Fortune-tellers of the past. Fortune-telling by scholars of Eastern divinity by means of the theory of "five elements"—a sort of astrology—or by the "spirits" of supernatural gods through mediums in the person of Shamans or blind persons is still a matter of serious concern to the native farmers, but it presents no more than an amusing conversational pastime to most of the rural population. True, the urban gentlemen of elderly age feel more at ease if they are assured of their future by fortune-tellers. But when they talk about fortune-tellers, their cronies as well as young listeners are likely to break into amused smiles rather than take them seriously.

Omens are interpreted quite seriously on

the farms by the old generations, but practicalities of city life have rendered the once mighty power of various omens helpless before urban ridicules.

Farmers build their homes in traditional style, topping the roof with either straw if they are poor or with black tiles if they are well off. But Western-style homes are appealing more and more to the city dwellers, who are more at ease sitting on a chair than cross-legged on the floor.

Nevertheless, the people have held on to their traditional, radiant floor heating system, the *ondol*. Therefore, virtually all homes in Korea have the *ondol*—one of the most efficient heating systems in use since the middle of the Yi dynasty.

Two New Year's Days. The lunar calendar has been serving farmers since the Three Kingdoms' period, but the solar almanac has been the official calendar since the 1900's. Despite the government's efforts to the contrary, the people have steadily refused to abandon their century-old lunar calendar. It has not been without good reason: for one thing, in order to observe all the traditional holidays, they had no other choice but to retain the lunar calendar, because the solar calendar by its very nature cannot designate the traditional holidays.

One of the results of using two kinds of calendars has been the observing of two New Years. But nobody seems to be in a holiday mood on the official New Year of the solar calendar.

The traditional lunar New Year season, on the other hand, finds many people dressed up in their holiday costumes, paying visits to relatives and elders for the traditional *Sebae* (New Year's greeting bow).

Most of the traditional holidays, which used to make each and every month eventful, are now just remembered rather than observed. But the "three great" holidays have survived: the New Year, Tano in the spring and *Chusok* in the fall. Since the end of World War II, Christmas has come to be celebrated as much as or in some respects more than the three major holidays, but to most of the farmers, Christmas means nothing.

Rudimentary folk-lore. Thus, many of the traditional manners and customs have been preserved among the farmers who live far and away from Western influences. But modern transportation, communication as well as popular education are likely to bridge the gap between the urban and rural areas in a short time.

The old traditions are about to be submerged under the tide of the Western influences, but so far the Korean folk-lore has been a subject of rudimentary studies. Anthropological studies of Korean manners and customs will have to go back to the pre-historic days of ancient Korea three to five thousand years back. But most of the studies date back not much beyond the Yi dynasty, which covered slightly over 500 years of the 5,000-year history of Korea.

Gloomy prospect. It has been only 60 years or so since the Western culture and civilization were first introduced to Korea. During this brief span of time, Korean society has gone through so many violent and rapid changes that its manners and customs have undergone nothing less than a social revolution. Furthermore, Westernization has become much more pronounced since the Liberation from Japan in 1945. While the old generations are cherishing many of the old, the young people are casting away the traditional manners and customs as "worn-out straw-shoes."

Certainly the requirements of the time leave no choice to the people but to adopt as much of Western civilization as possible within the shortest possible span of time, but the Eastern culture, much of which is manifested in the traditional manners and customs, may be worthy of further development. If the younger generations are convinced of the merits of the Eastern culture, many of the traditions will certainly survive, and even regain the former glory. The prospect, however, looks rather gloomy.

Food and Dwelling

The Main and Side Dishes

The Korean meal is as a rule made up of one main dish—steamed rice, and side dishes—soup, meat, fish, or vegetables. The main dish may be rice mixed with other grains, such as beans, barley and red beans. The most popular meats are beef and pork, but chicken and pheasant are regarded as greater delicacies. Of the various seafoods, the most widely used for soup is tangle (a seafood), whose dietary value has been so highly appreciated since the old days that a mother is always fed with tangle soup following delivery.

The most important vegetables, without which the Korean meal can never be complete, are radishes and Chinese cabbage, which are prepared into *kimchi*, the Korean equivalent to both the pickles and vegetable salad of the West. Other essential foods are bean paste and soybean sauce, both of which are used to make soup and to flavor other side dishes of all kinds. The bean paste and the soybean sauce are as a rule prepared at each home. The beans are first cooked, then mashed and rolled into balls about five inches in diameter. The balls are then fermented for several days, finally to be immersed into salt water, to turn the salt water into soybean sauce. The residue balls of the fermented beans, on the other hand, become the soybean paste. Being, for the most part, prepared at each home rather than mass produced at factories on a commercial basis, the soybean sauce and the bean paste of each house taste different. Since the two home-made foods find their ways into virtually all kinds of side-dishes, to be mixed with meat, seafoods, and vegetables, the soybean sauce and the bean paste have a decisive say in the taste of all the foods prepared at each particular home.

The other essential home-made food is *kimchi*. Radishes and Chinese cabbages seasoned with liberal amounts of red and black peppers, onions, garlic and a bit of pickled shell-fish are fermented in a pot filled with salt water. When the weather is warm, the fermentation takes place rapidly, making the *kimchi* ready for serving in a few days.

In early winter or late fall, a large quantity of *kimchi* is prepared at each home to ensure a full supply throughout the winter until the next spring when fresh vegetable will again be available. Thus tons of radishes and Chinese cabbages are piled up high in the market places in the fall during the winter *kimchi* preparation season. Each house buys the vegetables by the cart-load, and all the womenfolk are kept busy for several days to prepare the food. The winter *kimchi*, which is specifically referred to as *kimjang*, is stored in a few giant pots buried in the earth, to be taken out bit by bit at each mealtime.

There are many varieties of *kimchi* according to the way it is prepared, the amount of seasoning being the decisive factor: one kind contains so much red pepper that the vegetables look as red as the red pepper itself, another is almost devoid of red pepper.

In recent years, *kimchi* has received a scientific blessing for its rich dietary value from the Central Chemical Laboratory in Seoul. Analyzing several samples, the Laboratory found that *kimchi* contained a surprisingly large amount of vitamin C and caroting together with substantial amounts of protein, fats, carbohydrates, calcium, Vitamin B, etc.

Since the major foods of the Korean people are grains and vegetables with nominal animal foods, *kimchi* is considered an extremely important part of the diet. This is particularly so for the people of the rural areas, where meat is at most times beyond the means of the average farmer. In the urban districts, a larger quantity of meat adorns the table, and the amount of meat consumption has long been regarded as a yardstick to measure a family's economic well-being.

The Feasts

A tremendous variety of foods are prepared for feasts, on such occasions as holidays, birthdays, memorial services, weddings, etc. Besides the main dish of rice or noodles, many meats, fishes, fruits, confections and beverages are served. The table prepared for different feasts is referred to by different names, which more or less determines the kind of foods to be served.

The Table, Food Containers, and Table-Manners

The Table

The regular meal is prepared in the kitchen and brought to the room on a small table. The typical, traditional Korean house does not have a dining room as such, a central room being used for the purpose. For a regular meal, two persons sit on the floor face to face across a small dining table, on which cooked rice is placed to the left and the soup to the right, a spoon and a pair of chopsticks laying along and over the right edge of the table. Other side dishes, which are usually shared by the two persons, are placed in the middle of the table. When a meal is taken by more than two persons, each pair is served at a separate table.

The most common table for regular meals is a square one of about two feet by one and about ten inches high. It is finished in black lacquer. The more elaborate but rarer kind is hexagonal, finished in red with mother-of-pearl inlays of flowers, birds, or scenery.

The tables used for special feasts, such as birthdays, holidays, memorial services, weddings, etc, are referred to by different names.

The "noodle table" derives its name from the noodle soup which is served as the "main dish" in place of rice. Together with rice-cake, vegetables, and some meats, as well as sweetmeats, noodle soup is served on the small table used for regular meals. Noodle soup has been a favorite food to the northern people, who prefer the cold noodle soup even during mid-winter. Noodle soup, either warm or cold, is usually served to guests at large gatherings.

The "wine table" is, as the name indicates, to entertain with wine rather than food. But since the Korean people eat while drinking, a considerably large quantity of "side-dishes" are furnished, such foods as cooked meat, raw meat, broiled meat, *kimchi*, and soup.

The "long table" is used to serve guests at a party. As the "main dish", rice, noodle soup or "bun soup" are placed for each person. Served on the occasion are various rice-cakes, *kimchi*, raw fish and meat, cooked meat, such as beef, pork, and chicken, dried fish, *yakkwa* (fried-cake), honey-water with nuts and persimmons, sweetened water with rice, various fruits, such as apple, pears, chestnuts, tangerene, persimmons, grapes, nuts, dates, plums, melons, etc. The "first birthday table" is prepared to celebrate a child's first birthday — a day of significance in the old days when the infant mortality rate was high. The baby assumes the role of the "host" to invite relatives and neighbors and entertain them with various delicacies. Besides the usual foods, the "first birthday table" contains a bundle of thread, a book, a writing brush and ink, and money. Whatever the baby-host grabs first in his fist is supposed to symbolize the future of the baby: the thread symbolizes longevity, the money wealth, the book or writing brush and ink, scholarship.

The "large table" is used for a very big occasion, such as a wedding and the 6 lst birthday celebration, and is dedicated to the central figures of the celebration. All kinds of delicacies are arranged to present a beautiful sight, for the foods are not to be eaten at the time of the celebration, but to be "presented", after their exhibition, to the guests.

The "memorial service table" is set to offer service to one's ancestors or to the Shaman gods on various holidays or on the day of a parent's death. It is similar to the "large table", except for the "divine tablet" placed at the center, to which the foods are dedicated.

The Food Containers

Traditional food containers are, with few exceptions, shaped in the form of the bowl rather than the dish, and are made of wood, brass or china. Woodware is rare, preserved by some old families to be used on the occasion of memorial services. Typical food containers are made of shiny brass, but inexpensive chinaware is now more widely used. In recent years, alloys of metals and plastics have won increasing popularity.

The spoon is made of brass, silver, or alloys, and the chopsticks are carved of such metals, or of wood, plastic and ivory. But tradition places silver above others as the material for fine spoons and chopsticks.

Besides, the bowls, dishes and cups of Western style have been used more widely in recent years.

Table-Manners

Etiquette requires one to sit erect at the table and to wait until the elder takes up his spoon or chopsticks. First, one is required to pick up the spoon with his right hand and take soup as "appetizer", then eat rice and other side-dishes alternatively. Soup and other liquid foods are to be taken with the spoon, chopsticks being used to pick up solid foods. While not in use, the spoon and chopsticks have to be laid on one's right beside the soup bowl. On no account should they be left in the dish or bowl. Leaving the silver stuck into the rice is a grave offense, for it is a symbol that the food is offered to a deceased soul—the practice of an offering at a memorial service.

Throughout the meal, the left hand is to lie under the table, but may be brought up on the table to hold or tilt a dish or bowl towards oneself, never towards another. Conversation during the course of the meal is positively discouraged, in contrast to the Western practice. As a matter of fact, children are often admonished to stop talking while eating. When a meal is taken with a guest, the host towards the end of the meal urges the guest to eat more, as a measure of politeness, which the guest declines regardless of his state of appetite. The process is repeated several times, the host urging him to take more and the guest politely but, to all outward appearances, firmly declining.

It is considered decorous to leave a slight quantity of rice, but at the persistence of the host, the rice bowl may by emptied clean by pouring warm water into the bowl to eat the rice mixed with the water towards the end of the meal.

When eating out in a restaurant, the Korean people never "go Dutch," even among the most intimate friends, each person insisting on "picking up the check." Tipping at the ordinary restaurant is an exception rather than the rule, except at the high-class places, particularly such places as are patronized by foreigners.

Confections

Aside from the Western-style cakes and candies, which have become popular in recent years, the traditional Korean confections stilll in use include *honggwa, yot, tasig, ttog, tanja,* etc.

Honggwa is prepared by coating molasses on fruits or such vegetables as lotus rhizome, Korean ginseng, ginger, or plum: *yot* is a candy, obtained by fermenting flour of various kinds—most commonly flour of rice, wheat, corn, beans and potatoes: *tasig* is "roasted" rice, beans, or seasame mixed with molasses and cut into pieces. *Tanja* is prepared by cooking the flour of various grains rolled into the size of marbles, to be coated with molasses or the "red bean jelly," the mixture of mashed red bean with molasses.

The most popular confections associated with holidays, festivities, and the frequent memorial services is *ttog* or rice-cake. Not only rice but any kind of grain may be transformed into such cakes but rice is most widely used. Several different processes are required to prepare different kinds of rice cake. To make it pure and simple, ordinary rice is first cooked and then mashed or ground, finally to be rolled into cylinders of about half an inch in diameter. Instead of ordinary rice, the "sticky" glutious rice or other grains such as wheat or barley may be used, but in such cases, the cake is cut into square or circular forms and is usually coated with the red bean jelly or bean powder. Instead of the usual process of cooking the flour first, to be followed by grinding, the sequence may be reversed to make a different kind of cake. The rice or flour may be mixed with each other or small amounts of vegetables or fruits to give a flavor to the final product. The cake may be coated with red bean jelly, bean powder, or molasses, or wrapped with fragrant grass or leaves. In short, almost infinite varieties of the cake may be prepared, the limit being the materials available, financial resources, and the ingenuity of the housewife.

The cake thus prepared usually lasts several days, during the course of which the cake is bound to harden. Then, it is either toasted over a fire or steam-cooked to soften it again. The rice cake has established itself so firmly on holiday and other festival tables of the Korean people that it has become indispensable. On the eve of a national holiday, such as New Year's Day, *Tano* in the spring, and *Chusok* in the fall, every house prepares the cake, sending out the merry sounds of the grinding or beating of cooked rice by the menfolk with giant wooden hammers on a boulder. Thus, the larger and busier the sound of the beating of the cooked rice on the eve of a holiday, the more prosperous the house is judged. In recent years, however, electric mills have stifled all such noices of merriment, at least in cities and towns. Furthermore, many commercial confectioners now mass-produce the traditionally home-made cakes. But preparation of rice-cake is still a responsibility of each housewife.

Beverages

The traditional "soft drinks" are the tea of the Korean ginseng, of ginger, and of cinnamon. Korean ginseng tea has been treasured as a tonic, and cinnamon tea has been endeared for its flavor while ginger tea is appreciated for its refreshing effect. Of late, *ssanghwatang* tea has become quite popular. Originally a beverage of the royal household, it is a pseudo-medicinal drink of herbs, also containing such fruits as nuts, chestnuts, and dates. It is believed to be a potent tonic.

Honey-water, bee-honey diluted with cold water, has been one of the most popular drinks. Adorning practically every wedding party table is *sikhye*, which is also called "sweet wine," despite its non-alcoholic content. It is sweetened rice water made by fermentation. *Sujonggwa*, or liquid fruit cake, is softened persimmons in cinnamon-flavored water served with other fruits, such as nuts and dates. Another traditional beverage served at festivities is *hwachae*, or the flower drink. The water is sweetened with molasses, and flavored with magnolia. Edible small flower petals float in it.

Aside from such beverages, prepared for the occasions of festivities or memorial services, the drink most frequently used today day in and day out after each meal is *sungnyung*, the warm water poured into the cooking pot of rice after the cooked rice is taken out. The residue of the cooked rice is diluted with the water to give the resulting beverage a unique flavor of tightly scorched rice. This *sungnyung* is served after each meal in place of tea or coffee, even though the urban host may serve guests with tea or coffee after the Western-style.

Beverages, such as tea, coffee, and milk, are available at coffee shops and restaurants.

The traditional alcoholic beverages are

takju, yakju and *soju*. Foreign drinks, such as whisky and Japanese "sake," are as popular as the traditional liquors.

Takju is made from inexpensive stock, such as corn, barley, potatoes. Yellowish in color, its alcoholic content ranges from five to ten percent. The drink is filling and becomes sour in a few days when the weather is warm. It is usually favored by farmers and laborers for its inexpensive cost.

Slightly, but not much higher in alcoholic content, *yakju* brewed from rice, is accordingly a little more expensive. This liquor may be drunk as medicine by immersing in it some medical herbs.

The strongest native wine, *soju*, is made from grains or potatoes, and, looks to all outward appearances, as pure as water. Unlike *takju* and *yakju*, it does not turn sour in warm weather, and is therefore drunk more widely during the summer.

Besides the universal wines, some localities produce unique drinks. For instance, Pyongyang is famous for *kamhongnoju* (The Sweet Pink Dew Wine), whose ingredients include honey, cinnamon, and ginger; while *kwahaju* is the unique liquor of Seoul. Cholla-do province produces *chuksunju* (Bamboo Sprout Wine), whereas *tugyolju* is the product of Kimchon City. Various fruits and fragrant vegetables are added to what is basically *soju* to brew wines of many names, such as *igangju* (Plum-ginger Wine), *omiju* (Magnolia Wine), *paekhwaju* (Hundred-flower Wine), *kukhwaju* (Chrysanthemun Wine)—all indicative of the fruits or vegetables mixed in the *soju*.

Cookery

Vegetables predominate in the diet of the Korean people in contrast to the pork of the Chinese and the fish of the Japanese. Unique products of localities, therefore, are mostly vegetable dishes, as in the case of the *kongnamul* (bean sprouts) of Chongju; *pibimbap* (rice mixed with various vegetables and meats) of Chonju and *sinsollo* (mixtures of vegetables, meats and fruits cooked in a brass pot over a charcoal burner and placed on the table to be cooked while eating) of Seoul. *Yot* is rice or other grain fermented into glutin.

The vegetables used most abundantly are radish and Chinese cabbage, while "bean sprouts", spinach, "green bean sprouts", lettuce, etc. are often cooked as separate dishes. Seasoning calls for liberal amounts of red pepper, black pepper, green onion, garlic, ginger and sesame.

The most important meat is beef, other meats used being pork, chicken, rabbit, mutton, pheasant, and dog. The meat is roasted or cooked with water to make soup, frying not being a traditional method, popular as it has now become. Most of the dishes are mixtures of meat and vegetables.

Being a peninsula, Korea produces many kinds of fish. The most widely used are Alaska pollack and cod, both of which furnish indispensable protein to the people, whose diets are otherwise mostly vegetable. Another important seafood is what is popularly called "paper food"-the artificially cultivated seaweed dried and pressed like green paper, which is coated with vegetable oil, preferably with sesame oil, to be broiled.

In addition to the traditional dishes, foods of foreign origin—Western, Chinese, and Japanese—have become increasingly popular. Along with the traditional Korean restaurants, therefore, cities and towns abound with eating houses specializing in Western, Chinese, or Japanese foods. Furthermore, such dishes of foreign origin have made considerable inroads into the daily meals prepared at home.

Three Dominant Types of Houses and the Ondol

Contemporary houses in Korea are of three types: traditional, Japanese or Western. But many houses are hybrids in the sense that they are mixtures of the three basic types. The majority are of the traditional type: Japanese-style houses, vintages of the Japaneses domination period, are disappearing rapidly, while the Western-style has caught increasing fancy.

Whatever the outward appearances, virtually all Korean houses share one thing in common: the underfloor radiant heating systems commonly referred to as the *ondol*. This idea of heating the floor was perhaps introduced from China more than 1,300 years ago. The system was gradually developed and modified to suit the conditions and requirements of the Korean people. By the middle of the Yi dynasty about 350 years ago, it was established firmly. A Korean house without *ondol* is rare. This holds true even for those houses which, in all outward appearances, are of Western or Japanese types.

The floor of a room equipped with the *ondol* is made of slabs of granite stone, rough cut, about 12 by 18 inches and about 2 inches thick, supported on rows of stone or brick forming the smoke flues. They are all laid in mud or clay mortar. Over the rough stone slabs is a layer of beaten clay, or cement worked to a smooth flat surface. Two or three layers of newspapers are pasted over it, and then a layer or two of Korean paper. Finally a layer of heavy oiled paper is pasted over the foundation, and vegetable oil or varnish is applied on the oil paper. The finished floor is tight, smooth and hard, through which flue gases will not escape unless the clay or cement underneath is shrunk, cracked or warped by overheating.

The fireplace is usually located in the kitchen, where wood is fed into the fire, which sends out flues to the *ondol* and, at the same time, heats the food or water in a few pots placed over the fire. Thus *ondol* is the most efficient method of utilizing fuels. The traditional *ondol* rquires firewood for fuels with the result that most of the country's forests have been denuded. In recent years, firewood has become expensive, besides which the government has banned the cutting of trees for *ondol* firewood. As a result, the traditional structure of the *ondol* was slightly modified to use inexpensive coal in place of firewood. Presently most of the urban houses are equipped with the improved version of *ondol* to use coal.

Ingenious as it is, the *ondol* is not without defects. Denudation of fields and forests for fuel with all its consequences is one, and insufficient heating of the air in the room is another. The heat from the floor usually is not sufficient to warm the room temperature to a comfortable degree during the winter when the outdoor mercury drops below zero. Since one can be comfortably warm only when the body is in contact with the heated floor, persons in an *ondol* room are likely to be "floor-bound," becoming inactive. Nor does the radiant heating system warm the floor evenly, the choicest spot in the room being close to the fireplace. Furthermore, the clay or cement structure under the floor becomes shrunk, cracked or warped after a year or two, and accumulated soot impedes flow through flues from the fireplace through the underneath floor to the chimney. Therefore, the *ondol* has to be constructed all over again from its foundation every two or three years. There have been several attempts to use electricity for the *ondol* to solve all defects of the traditional heating system, but its practical application has to wait until the present shortage of electric power is overcome.

Traditional House

The top-heavy outward appearance marks the typical, traditional style house. The black tiled roof looks disproportionately large and heavy for its understructure. Introduced originally from China during the Three Kingdoms period, the elaborate roof style has survived until today with slight modification. The intricate arrangement of tiles together with other decorations on the roof serve no utilitarian purpose, but is considered to add grace and dignity to the house. Sometime during the Yi dynasty, the size and intricate adornment of the roof was a kind of measurement of the financial well-being of the family living in the house, giving rise to the expression "to live in a tiled-house (large) as a whale."

The house with a grass roof is therefore always associated with poverty and tenant-farmers. About 8 to 10 inches thick, the grass roof is not so disproportionately large in relation to its understructure. Practically all Korean farming villages are composed of several such grass roof huts, among which may stand a tile-roof house of the landlord. The Korean pastoral scene cannot be complete without a small grass roof hut or two.

The windows of the typical Korean-style house are invariably small, with a few wooden frames covered with semi-transparent "Korean paper" or glass. Some houses are equipped with inner windows for insulation during the winter. In addition to the door, the Korean house has a gate which leads usually to the yard and then to the door of the house. Walls are of stucco or clay beaten over wood frame construction, joined together with mortice and tenion joints, secured with wooden pins or wedges. The paneling within the framework is usually of wattle construction, consisting of a network of bamboo, twigs and grasses, upon which is placed a mud plaster, with a hard lime or cement stucco finish.

The average house has two to four rooms, a kitchen and a hall of wooden flooring opening on the yard. The rooms with the *ondol* heating system are used both for dining, living, and sleeping. Interior walls of the rooms are covered with wallpaper, and shoes have to be removed when entering the rooms.

Houses of the Yi Dynasty

Many houses of the Yi dynasty were modelled after palace buildings of the period. Several buildings in the Kyongbok palace in Seoul, for example, are characteristic of such models. The building has a hall of wood floorings in the center located between *ondol* rooms to its left and right. A kitchen is absent, and the rooms and the hall are hemmed in by a long strip of wooden floor. A small room may be attached at both ends of the *ondol* rooms: some urban houses in Seoul, Pyongyang and other large cities adopted this basic arrangement, which was presumably a modification of some of the Chinese palace buildings, by substituting clay flooring in the central hall for wood floorings.

Another representative arrangement of the house follows. one *ondol* room is connected with a larger hall of wood floorings. Variations of the basic arrangement were realized by adding another *ondol* room and a passage connecting the two rooms with the kitchen. More elaborate arrangements consist of two or more *ondol* rooms being connected with the hall of wood flooring placed at the center and the kitchen located to one side.

From the Cave to the Ondol

How the primitive race on the Korean peninsula lived during the prehistoric days is mostly a subject of conjecture due to lack of authentic literature on the subject. An ancient record states however that "the people were attired in grass, ate vegetables, and lived in caves." The "cave" dwelling evolved into the "log cabin" type of house, a crude structure of logs tied with cords horizontally on the ground capped with grass roofs, as are erected nowadays in the forests by woodcutters for temporary quarters.

Along the sea coast, meanwhile, the "shell mound" was built. It was so named later because of sea-shells which covered the roof of the abode. When such log cabins and the shell mounds were used as dwellings is not clear, but it is presumed to be as long ago as 10,000 years ago.

How and when the primitive dwellings began to assume the forms of present-day Korean houses is again subject to mere assumptions. One thing, however, is certain. Chinese architecture exerted considerable influence since the introduction of the continental culture and civilization during the Three

↑ The Kuandung Festival
    To celebrate Buddha's birth on April 8th by the lunar calender, various kinds of colored lamps hanging up on many ropes are lighted at night, a spectacle to enjoy from the vantage point of a hill.

↑ Mask Dance
   Different from the Japanese No-Dance, it is neither a sophisticated dance nor a spectacular drama, but only a rustic entertainment with full of old jokes and primitive interest.

← Top Spinning
For children, of course.

Washing at the Stream
You can't imagine a Korean housewife away from her washing. It is a daily chore and streams are ideal for gathering to chat away the hour.
↓

↑ Pounding a Mortar
In villages, such a wooden hand mill is still used to make rice-cake and other foods.

Seesaw →
Girls' most favorite pastime, especially on holidays.

↑ Seesaw In Korean, it is called "Nol-Ttwigi," meaning jumping on the board.

↑ Rural Band
   Time-out for farmers of a summer's day under the shade of trees.

↑ Rural Band
   The band entertains farmers who, as usual, are busy in the field.

↑ "Get Set!"
  While one contestant is ready, another is busy preparing his kite to win the contestant. Both wear quite traditional Korean clothes.

↑ Kite-Flying
  Not for children alone any more but for adults as well. A nation wide contest in kite-flying is held in Seoul every spring.

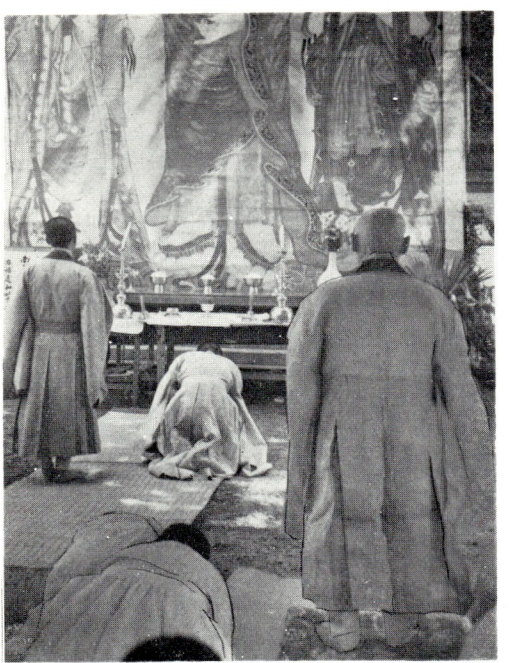

↑ Prayers for Rain
Buddhist priests praying for rain during a period of drought.

A Common Well →
A village scene of Cheju Island.

An Acrobat
A very conventional performer, but still fairly popular among his countrymen.
↓

↑ Stone Mill
This mill is worked mostly by a donkey. But sometimes oxen or horses are used.

↓ Fences on Cheju Island are often of stone like this one.

↑ Flower-Viewing
  When cherry-blossoms bloom in April, the every Korean heart also lightens. Changkyongwon Park where cherry-blossoms are densely planted is then crowded with flower-viewers.

↑ Most of the Changsung resemble generals or other human beings.

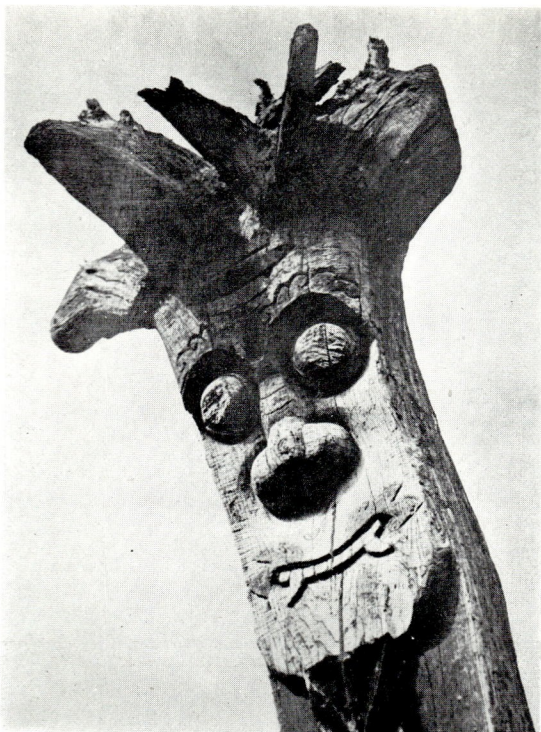

↑ Sometimes there are very queer features as shown in this picture.

Changsung is a mile-post statue that
↓ also serves as a palladium.

Changsungs are not always made
↓ of wood. There are stone ones, too.

A Quern →
This stone hand mill is so simple that a woman can operate it with one hand.

↑ **Worshipper**
Worship for nature is deeply rooted in the Korean people. This woman is reverentially making an obeisance before Yonchudae Arbor on Mount Kwanak.

↑ **Buddhist Worshippers**
Buddhism is one of the influential religions in Korea. Three women are shown here praying before stone Buddhas.

← **Hwangap (Sixtieth Birthday) Party**
When a man or woman reaches 60 years of age, he is blessed with a grand banquet by his offsprings for further longevity.

Folk Dance →
Dressed in boys' garb, girls are shown dancing, each beating a tabor.

↑ Children in Traditional Clothes
The boy is wearing a cap called "Pokkon," with a purse dangling in front of him.

↑ A Witch
A shaman-priestess exorcizing a Korean home of evil spirits.

A Parlor →
A westernized room of a modern Korean house.

↑ Swing and Girls
 Swing has become entirely for girls nowadays. A Korean ballad says, "…up, up, my swing, as high as where I can see my lover over the fence…"

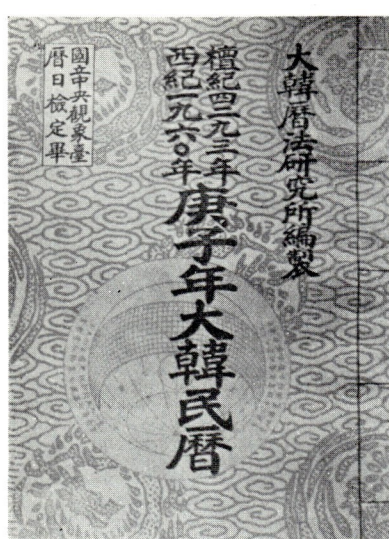

← **Minryok, or People's Calendar**
A few kinds of such calendars are annually publishedin book form to inform farmers of the meteorological changes in every season that are necessary to farming.

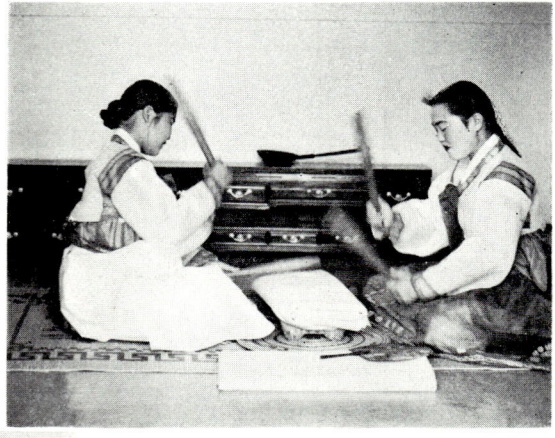

↑ **Fulling Cloth**
Very familiar scene in Korean houses. Putting cloth on a stone-slab, they pound it with fulling blocks just like a cop's billy.

The Cradle Basket in Cheju Island
Since most women of Cheju have to work in the sea, they use baskets as shown in this picture for their children. ↓

↑ **Fighting Bulls**
Two strong bulls are figting desperately.

← **Some Customs of Cheju Island**
The stone fence and tied-up roof are made against a strong wind. Women carry water-jars on their back unlike the mainland's women who carry them on their heads.

↑   A Rrual Scene
   Cosmos is a very common flower in Korea. Wherever you go, the flowers smile and welcome you.

↑ "Yut" Game
 A traditional dice-like game, played with four sticks.

↑ Archery
 On archery days many archers gather all over the country to vie for supremacy.

Double Swinging →
　Korean girls are so skilled in swinging that often two girls sit on a swing and sail up high in the blue sky.

↑
Woman Divers
　Most of them are the women of Cheju Island. Diving under the water for a surprisingly long time, they seek seaweed and shellfish.
↓

Nol-Ttuigi (seesaw)
　A game that may be enjoyed even in a small
↓　garden.

Archery　→
　Not a few woman archers have figured in Korean history.

← Water Wheel
Not many water mills are left working now even in the country.

→ Grain Shop

Home Spinning
After this spinning, they also weave cloths they need with their
↓ own hands at home.

Pottery
Jars for water, kimchi, soybean
↓ sauce, etc.

↑ Kang-Gang-Suwolle Dancing
 Surrounding a girl (singing leader) sitting in the center, girls hand in hand circle singing the song, Gang-Kang-Suwolle. It is the southern Korea's unique folk dance.

Kang-Gang-Suwolle →
A dance for girls in April as in this picture under April flowers.

←
Sailing-ship
Still available for fishing villages of Korea.

Fireworks
A brilliant fireworks display for Seoul on
↓ a national holiday.

Tablet-House for a Filial Son
To commend a model boy's filial duty,
↓ such a monument is often erected.

Traditional Wedding
　Bridegroom boiwng to his bride.

← Wedding Dress
　Some old style dresses in traditional wedding.

↑ Bride
　The bride is ready to bow with the help of her maids of honor.

← Wedding New and Old
　An eclectic wedding of the traditional and Western ways. They bow at the same time.

↑ Western Kind of Wedding
But not quite with a western flavor.

↑ Another New Style in Wedding
Traditional weddings are gradually disappearing today except in rural areas.

↑ Favorite Korean Dolls
  A boy and girl in classic Korean clothes.

↑ Woman in a Korean Dress

↑ Woman in a Korean Dress

← Girl with a Basket on Her Head

↓ Other Various Dolls

"Under the Moon" →

↓ "Old Man on a Tiger"

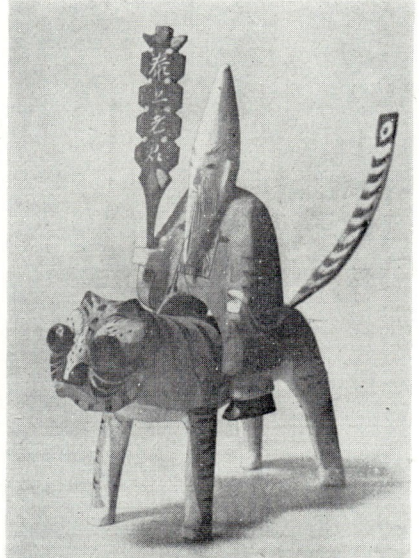

"Lolang Princess's Dragger of Unification" →

↓ A Woman in a Dress

↓ Display of Dolls

↑ Refined Furnitures of Yi Dynasty
A bed used in Changdok Palace.

→ A chair and table as well.

↓ King's furniture in a room of Changdok Palace.

↑ A Sitting Posture in the Native Costume

↑ A Rural Scene

↑ Western-Styles ↑

← Buddhist Priest's Robe
   The color is light grey.

Typical Working Clothes for the Farmer
   Note long smoking pipes and an A-frame behind one of the
↓ farmers.

← Korean Socks (Boson)
   A pair of socks, warmly stuffed with cotton.

One of Mourning Clothes
   Such a large bamboo hat
↓ is also worn.

↓ Ancient-style clothing for a folk dance.

← Wedding Costumes

A Woman Playing Kayagum
Note her hair-do. It is a traditional hair style of Korea's own. The long bodkin is called pinyo.

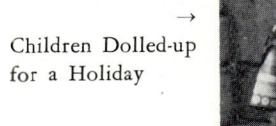

← Mother and Daughter

→ Children Dolled-up for a Holiday

← A Fashion Show in Seoul

↑ Summer Dress

Conventional Dressing for Men
↓ Black hat and white clothes were an invariable pattern of old Korea.

Bathing Suits
↓ For the woman divers of Cheju Island.

↑ Turumagi
A kind of coat that men must wear when they go out.

↑ Ancient Official Uniforms and Formal Dresses

↑ Wonsam
   A formal dress of the queen.

↑ Hwalot
   Princess's ceremonial dress.

↑ Topo
  The most widely worn, man's formal dress coat

↑ Hwangyongpo
  One of king's formal court robes.

↑ Dobok
  A coat worn by taoist priest.

↑ Huktanryong
  Black official's dress.

↑ **Wonsam**
Civilian's formal dress worn in court.

↑ **Taejaot**
The prince's full costume.

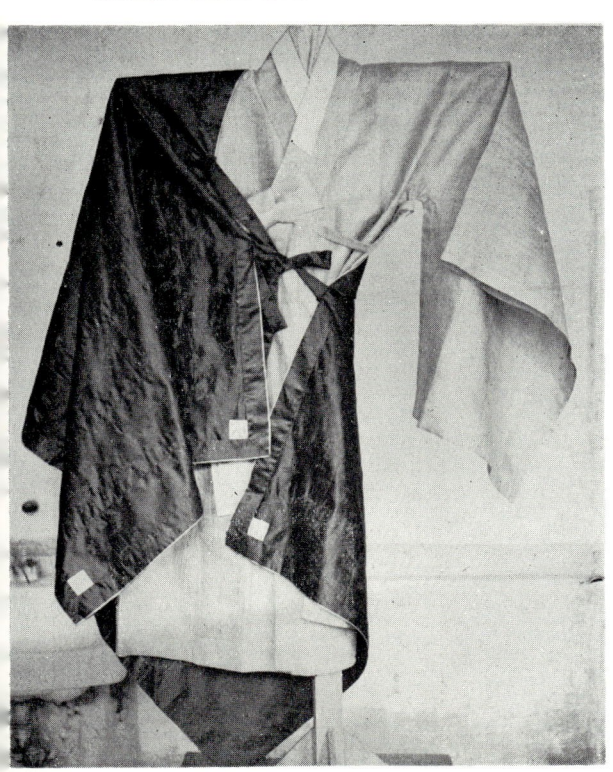

↑ **Kasa**
The Buddhist priest's robe.

↑ **Kunbok (Army Uniform)**
A policeman's uniform in the Yi dynasty.

↑ Tangui
One of women's formal dresses.

↑ Suranchima and Hoechang jokori
A lady's normal clothing.

↑ Wonsam
Woman's formal dress worn in court.

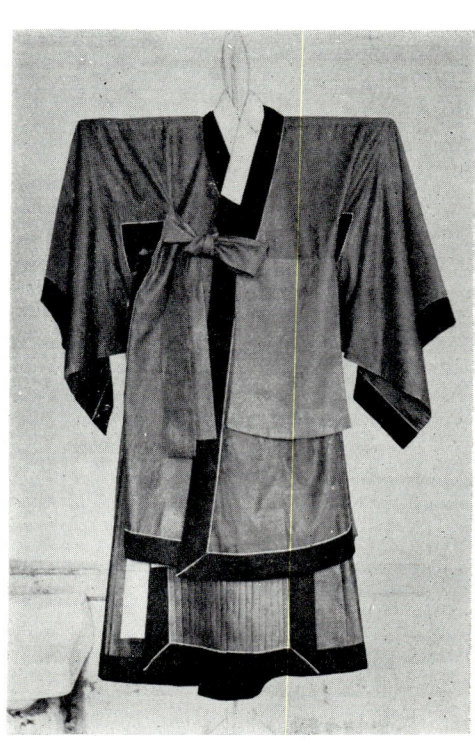

↑ Chobok
A "morning" for the court.

Seal made of silver

Seal with lion-shaped handle made of copper

Seal with lion-shaped handle made of copper

Seal made of celadon

Seal with phoenix-shaped handle made of copper

Seal made of copper

Red stamping pad made of precious stone

Seal with seahorse-shaped handle made of copper

Seal made of copper

Seal box made of copper

Seal made of copper

Seal box made of copper

1

2

3

4

5

6

7

8

9

10

11

Seals   Part   I

1

2

3

4

5

6

7

8

9

10

11

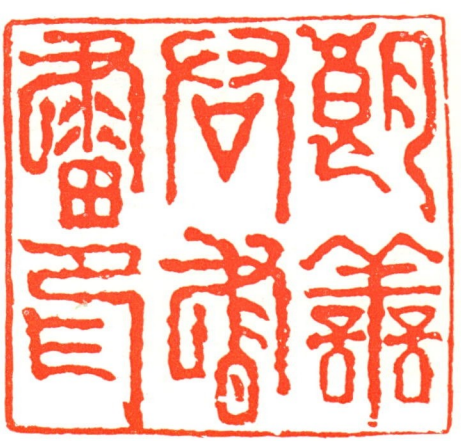
12

Seals Part II

For explanation, see next page.

Seals Part I

1. Seal of the President, Republic of Korea.
2. Seal used by Min Yongik (1860~1911), artist of the Yi dynasty.
3. Seal used by Kim Chonghui (1786~1856), a skilled calligrapher.
4. Seal meaning the three ancient countries of Mahan. Chinhan and Pyonhan.
5. Seal used by Chong Yakyong (1712~1836), a famous scholar of the Yi dynasty.
6. Seal used by O Sechang (1864~1953), a great calligraphist in seal character writing.
7. Seal used by Yi Ham (1633~?), artist of the Yi dynasty.
8. Seal used by Sim Sachong (1707~1768), artist of the Yi dynasty.
9. Seal used by Kim Yunsik (1835~1920), scholar of the Yi dynasty.
10. Seal of Yi Chosun Emperor.
11. Seal of the Republic of Korea.

Seals Part II

1. Seal used by Min Hyongsik (1875~1947), a modern calligrapher.
2. Seal used by Yi Toyong (1884~1933), a modern artist.
3. Seal used by Chong Haun (1702~1769), a calligrapher of the Yi dynasty.
4. Seal used by Ma Songin, a calligrapher of the Yi dynasty.
5. Seal used by Kim Chonghui (1786~1856), a skilled calligrapher.
6. Seal used by Yi Haung (1820~1898), a famous statesman of the Yi dynasty.
7. Seal meaning treasure to be handed down to posterity for one's own family.
8. Seal used by Om Hanmyong (1685~1759), a calligrapher of the Yi dynasty.
9. Seal used by Kim Sangyong (1561~1636), a statesman of the Yi dynasty.
10. Seal used by Hong Sokku (1621~1679), a literary man of the Yi dynasty.
11. Seal used by Cho Yongnok.
12. Seal used by Yi U (1637~1693), an artist of the Yi dynasty.

Kingdoms period.

Since the Korean peninsula extends southwards from the Manchurian border, differences of climate between the north and south are considerable. Therefore somewhat different constructions and arrangements of rooms prevailed between the houses in the south and the north.

In the extreme north, where the climate is semi-frigid, many multi-family houses have been built, whereas most homes in the south are independent, single-family dwellings. Some of the northern houses had no kitchen as such, cooking being done at one corner of the room, while the southern houses are invariably equipped with a kitchen. Another difference is the centrally-located hall of wood floorings, the size of which tends to be larger than totally enclosed rooms in the south. It is usually small or absent in the northern dwellings.

Prior to the reign of King Injo during the middle of the Yi dynasty, private houses were not allowed to install the radiant floor heating system. It remained a privilege of the royal families and few highest court officials. After the royal permission to the people in Seoul to install *ondol* in their homes, the heating system spread so rapidly that within five years virtually all houses in the land had *ondol* floors.

Interior Decoration and Gardens

There has been nothing remarkable in interior decoration and gardening of average Korean homes. The traditional interior decorations call for scrolls of paintings or calligraphy to be hung over the walls; paper or silk screens erected in the room; and the long, large pillow with embroidery decorations placed on the floor to serve as a kind of "arm-rest." Such articles bearing paintings and calligraphic works of sophisticated tastes have been considered as adding dignity to the living or drawing room.

Gardening was developed in the royal palaces and residences of a few high-ranking officials of the court. It attempted to recreate the effect of "deep mountains and steep valleys" as nature had created them. The Secret Garden of the royal palace in Seoul is the outstanding example.

Contemporary and Future Dwellings

Much criticism has been directed against traditional type houses in recent years, as being unfit to offer satisfactory abode for modern, Westernized living. For one thing, the traditional-style house fails to utilize space effectively and is loaded with elaborate and therefore costly decorations, especially on the eaves and roof. Relatively high cost of construction and maintenance is another accusation directed against the traditional-style house because of the materials used and failure to adopt mass-production methods for building homes and parts.

There have been serious attempts to improve the dwellings since 1945 after the Liberation, and many architects have published plans of "model housing" for the middle-class families. Practically all such model homes were blends of traditional types with Western-style improvements, but none has so far been accepted as the "standard" despite overwhelming desires of the people to have a "dream house."

Since the Korean armistice, many "welfare housing" projects have been built by the government. Invariably all of the government housing projects were aimed at maximum efficiency and economy with the result that almost all of the "welfare housing" were simplified "bungalow" types, retaining, however, the *ondol* floor heating system.

Modern apartment housing, on the other hand, has never been popular among the people, even though several large buildings were constructed by the government in recent years. The unpopularity of apartment housing is apparently due to the people's way of life which seems to be somewhat incompatible with multi-storey dwelling units.

Furniture

The few ancient records now available do not furnish us with descriptions in detail of ancient Korean furniture, except some ground for the assumption that wooden chests were the oldest furniture of any sort in Korea.

According to mythological descriptions o prehistoric Korea, Kim Alchi, one fof the founders of the Silla kingdom, emerged out of a "golden chest". The oldest pieces of furniture now remaining are the wooden chests with lacquer finish which were excavated from the ancient tombs of the Lolang period (29—247 A.D.) in northern Korea.

As furniture of the Koryo period, *The Illustrated Book of Koryo* lists the following:

The Sitting Table: Used in government offices, the simple, low-legged table, with no decorations, was apparently used as a bed after covering the top with a grass mattress.

Yondae (The Sparrow Table): A kind of desk, the *yondae* is square with rounded angles. Embroidered silk covered the top and the four corners of the "table" were decorated with pieces of silk.

Kwangmyongdae (The Illumination Stand): A tripod candle stick, the Illumination Stand is about 140 centimeters high and a 45-centimeter diameter of the copperwork was placed on the stand. Oil was poured into the copper work for illumination; when not in use, the apparatus was covered with a silk cloth.

Wadap (The Bed): Of the two kinds, one is of wood and the other of clay. The clay bed was so constructed as to be heated with fire—a predecessor to the *ondol*. The wooden bed has bannisters which bear decorative designs of various kinds. When a person is to lie down, the wooden bed is first covered with a silk cloth, over which a grass mattress is laid.

Suro (The Incense Burner): The 120-centimeter high and 66-centimeter wide silver work bears very elaborate sculptural portrayals of a large lion surrounded by its cubs. The incense burner was used for ceremonial rites.

During the Yi dynasty, most of the furnishings used in the palace were vintages of the preceeding Koryo period. Furniture as merchandise did not develop during the period, and it has been only in recent times that such furniture as chests and bureaus have come to be used by the general public. The only piece of furniture which has a relatively long history among the people is the small wedding chest.

The traditional chest of the most popular kind is a large wooden chest with solid brass decorations dotting the front. The interior of the chest, covered with decorative paper, is bare, and the chest has one door in the front on hinges. The finish is black or brown, either in lacquer or varnish.

More elaborate chests and bureaus have mother-of-pearl inlays, and recent furniture has incorporated Western-style conveniences, such as a mirror, hanging rod, glass, etc. Traditional-style pieces of furniture, however, have become mostly museum pieces, the Western-style becoming more and more popular.

Clothing and Costumes

Foreigners visiting Korea for the first time may be puzzled by the contrast of the old and new, existing side by side everywhere. Rustic grass-thatched huts, tile-roofed houses, and modern "skyscrapers" all apparently enjoying a "peaceful coexistence," may lead foreigners to the erronous impression that the people occupying such different abodes must be leading radically different lives. But the fact is entirely contrary to such an assumption.

The same is true of the costumes of the

Korean people. They wear both traditional Korean clothes and Western suits, as circumstances dictate. While at home, they wear traditional Korean clothes, but don Western attire for street clothes and for work. The *dopo* of Yi dynasty vintage is called for on the occasion of the traditional rites in memory of their ancestors. Such "dualism" of East and West characterizes the present-day Korean society. One may witness the up-to-date vogues of Paris on the streets of Seoul, but at the same time, he will also notice the century-old costume worn proudly by an old man.

Traditional Korean Costumes

Traditional Korean costumes have a history of about 2,000 years, during the course of which many changes have occurred. We can trace the gradual evolution of the traditional Korean costumes in six stages. Throughout these stages, Korean costumes have adhered to the principle of the "two pieces" —a jacket to cover the upper part of the body and trousers to wear on the lower half of the body, as in the case of a "suit" of the West. The stages are:

1) The primitive period
2) The ancient period
3) The period of Chinese influence
4) The period of Mongolian influence
5) The terminal period (of Korean traditional costumes)
6) The period of Western influence

Such foreign influences, however, have not altered the basic features of the Korean costumes itself.

The Primitive Period

The costumes of the primitive period, more than 2000 years ago, are uncertain because no relics of the period are available. According to some ancient records, however, the people of the mystic, ancient kingdom of Euplu wrapped pigskins around their bodies which were greased with fat of pigs during the winter to protect them from cold weather, and in summer the people covered some portion of their bodies with a piece of hemp.

It is presumed that the pigskin and other animal skins were predecessors of the *po* (coat) and the hemp-cloth of the *paji* (trousers) of the ancient period. Shortly after the people moved from the legendary country of Euplu to where Korea is located today, such primitive costumes are presumed to have disappeared. Until recently, however, the latter-day versions of such primitive costumes of animal skins could be seen on the island of Cheju.

The Ancient Period

Somewhere around the first century A.D., the people wore the *chogori* (coat), *paji* (trousers), and *turumagi* (top coat); women adopted the *chima* (skirt), replacing "trousers." They also wore the *koggal* (a headdress with feathers on both sides decorated with gold and silver), a leather band, and leather shoes. This costume of the ancient period resembled the ancient apparel of the Manchus in the north.

The "coat," worn by both sexes, was somewhat longer than its equivalent of the West: a jacket and a leather belt was worn over it. The sleeves of the "coat" were tight, and a wide band of dark color adorned the cuffs and lower edge of the "coat" to give a contrast in colors.

The *paji* (trousers) were similar to those of the present-day, under which the underwear *chambangi*, a pajama-pants like garment, was worn. The "trousers" of the ancient period were tighter than the present-day *paji* and therefore allowed free bodily movement. It is interesting in this connection to note that the noblemen of the period preferred loose-fiting "trousers", in contrast to the tight-fit chosen by the common people.

The women occasionally decked themselves in the *chima* (skirt), but wore "trousers" most of the time.

The Period of Chinese Influence

As the cultural exchanges with China increased around the fifth century, the kingdom of Silla, after unifying the Korean peninsula, adapted the Tang (China) court attire as its official court costume. Also, the colors of the women's dresses followed the Chinese "fashion." The Chinese costume became so popular that finally the king replaced his headwear with the "jewel crown" of China, while the court officials wore a Chinese-style coat and a hood. The women wore their skirts long in the Chinese style, almost to sweep the floor, and their belts were discarded for long strips to bind the clothes.

The Buddhist priest's costumes of Tang were also introduced, and along with them, the custom of shaving the head among the priests.

The Period of Mongol Influence

The Mongol influence on women's costumes became decisive during the middle of the Koryo period when a set of royal intermarriages were effected between Koryo and the Mongol Empire. The *chogori*, the current name for the women's coat, derives its pronunciation from a Mongolian word. The Mongol influence raised the length of the women's "coat" and "skirt".

The mode of the Koryo court was later spread among women during the Yi dynasty. It may be said, therefore, that the present-day costumes of Korean women were formulated in most part during this period of Mongol influence.

The *chollik*, the uniform of the court's military officials, presumably became popular after the middle of the Koryo period under the influence of China.

The Terminal Period of the Korean Costume

The costumes of the Yi dynasty period, which became the basis of our present clothes, appear to have evolved from the ancient costumes after numerous adaptations of Chinese and Mongolian styles.

The court officials' costumes of the Yi dynasty were divided into ritual clothes, public costumes, morning clothes, "plain clothes," military uniforms and private clothes.

The ritual costumes were worn by officials who conducted the court's rites, while the morning clothes had to be worn on the occasion of important national events and auditions of the king on certain holidays. The official clothes were worn during the performances of official functions, and the plain clothes were ordinary day-to-day dress. The military uniform had to be put on when the officials were travelling with the king, and later became a military uniform in every sense of the word.

The court officials were privileged to wear such court costumes even after their retirement.

The coat looked similar, but each official's "accessories" differed and varied decorations on the costumes indicated the wearer's rank. For instance, the highest rank had five vertical gold stripes on the front of the "golden crown", which was a part of the morning clothes. As the rank diminished, the number of the gold stripes on the crown was reduced. Also, a set of two rings attached at the "seal cord" (similar to the key-chain) worn over the "coat," was made either of gold, silver, or copper according to the rank. Furthermore, the belt worn over the "coat" was made of either "rhinoceros horn," gold, black horn or others, indicating the wearer's rank, while the mace of ivory was held by an official of higher rank, and the wooden mace meant lower rank.

Not so elaborate as the "morning clothes" were the "plain clothes," which bore a picture of cranes on the chest and tigers on the back.

Present Costumes

The costumes of Korean women have undergone many changes during the past 50 years or so since the introduction of Western culture. The traditional women's costumes are worn in the following manner. Trousers (*paji*) go first, followed by an inner skirt and the "*chima*". The upper part of the body is first covered with the "inner coat", then the *chogori* (coat). The coat has a set of two long strips to fasten it, used in the place of buttons. The hem of the coat may he decorated with a stripe of contrasting color. Over the coat may be worn the sleeveless *paeja* or the loose-fitting *magoja*, which are used mostly by old women, showing the influence of a Chinese costume during the late Yi dynasty period. The practice of wearing precious stones tied at the end of the coat strip has almost died out.

The picture changes considerably when one observes a Korean urban girl dressed in Korean costume. She wears Western-style underclothing over which are worn a blouse, coat and skirt of varying lengths according to her taste. For the long skirt, the *poson* (sock-boots) and rubber shoes of various colors ranging from the traditional white to pink, blue, and flowered varieties go well. The short skirt, on the other hand, calls for nylon stockings and Western-style shoes with high or low heels. The Western-style brooch has also become a vogue, replacing the former coat strips, and a handbag has become a 'must.' The brassiere is superfluous for the Korean costume, for the skirt waist is at the breasts. One of the most serious disadvantages of the women's dress is the compression of the breasts—a practice which has remained since the ancient days.

Wearing a Western-style overcoat or topcoat over the traditional women's dress has actually become very fashionable in recent years. "Traditional" dress is also subject to changes in fashions, even though the changes are not so marked in tempo or style as in the case of the Western woman's clothes.

Under the ever-increasing influences of Western civilization, however, the traditional Korean women's clothes are losing popularity, and more Korean women, especially in urban districts, appear more often in Western outfits than in the traditional *chogori* and *chima*. Nevertheless, the traditional women's costumes are still favored for "dress-up" wear, and, therefore, it will be some time before they disappear from the Korean scene, even if the present tendency continues.

Entirely different is the case with Korean men's traditional clothes, which are rapidly disappearing.

Professional Costumes

Professional costumes indicating the occupational status of the wearers were used until about 50 year ago: different garments were worn by military officers, soldiers, servants laborers, and merchants.

No such distinction, however, was made during the ancient period, when a sword or two attached to the belt was sufficient to turn the day-to-day wear into a war costume. Armor was not used even during the Koryo period, when the military officer wore *chollik* (heavenly wings) which were not, however, covered with metal plates. It was presumably after the period of the Mongolian influence that armor was worn by military officers. Thereafter, military officers wore the ordinary court costume during peace time, but put on an armor in war. A long sword around the waist, arrow holder or quirer on his back, a bow in his hand, and bird skin shoes on his feet completed his costume when he went out for combat. The bow, which had formerly been long, was reduced in size after the Koryo period, but the sword became longer.

The military officer's uniform during the Yi dynasty was similar to the garments of civil officers, with the exception of a couple of tigers embroidered on the back, thus giving rise to the name, "the tiger units", referring to military officers. As the combat uniform, the military officers detached the loose sleeves of the *chollik*, donned a war cap, wore a sword and bow, and carried a lance. The low-ranking officials of the court put on either the *parimori* (flat-top hoop) or *panggat* (sedge hat), and the purple colored *chongsam*, which was fastened with a narrow belt.

The *saryong* (the servant for various court functions) wore sleeveless "combat clothes", a tan hat on the head, holding a *chido* (security) stick in hand, and wearing a bell at his waist. The court musicians wore the *poktu* hat, pink clothes, and a *kkachi* belt, whereas the students of the state institution of the higher learning, Songgyungwan, wore Confucian costumes and hats.

The Shamans wore unique costumes and carried a Shaman's paper fan. But the designs of these costumes varied according to the localities in which they resided. Some wore the *hwal* clothes of the court, others put on the Buddhist priest's garments, and still others attired themselves in the "combat wear" with the pheasant-feather hat.

The farmers wore coarse but durable "hemp" clothes. The merchants of the Yi dynasty did not distinguish themselves from the farmers with any unique color or design in clothing.

Western Clothes

Western-style clothes were first introduced to Korea in the 1900's together with other products of Western civilization. High government officials began to appear more often in Western attire in place of the traditional court costumes. After the Japanese annexation of Korea in 1910, all officials of the colonial government were required to wear Western-style clothes, in a move not so much designed for modernization as for suppression of Korean culture.

Western clothes spread among the urban population as the people began to appreciate its convenience. The gradual conversion from the traditional to the new has been slower in case of women, who have stuck to convention more doggedly. After the Liberation in 1945, however, Western dresses for women became a vogue, especially among the young generation. All young people have become fashion-conscious in recent years.

Hair-dressing

Practically all Korean men and women use the same hair styles as Westerners, but this has been a quite recent practice. Until about 30 years ago, many people wore their hair in the traditional Korean styles, which showed a clear-cut distinction between the married and the unmarried. Both unmarried males and females had "pig-tails", which were knotted on the head when matrimony was effected. But this tradition has almost become extinct.

During the Three Kingdoms period, the women of Koguryo wore their hair long over the right shoulder, while the women of the kingdom of Paekche parted their hair in the middle to hang down in two streams. In the kingdom of Silla, women swung their hair around the neck, and it slid down the front of the body in a long cascade.

By the end of the Koryo period, the Mongol influence raised the long, hanging hair upon the head, where it was bound up in a coil, known as the *choktori*. The Mongol hair-do became so popular that the women of Koryo paid high prices for bundles of other women's hair to add to their own, for the larger the "coil" on the head, the more ardor was she able to arouse among the male folks of the age. This mode of hair dressing has survived until the present, especially in the northern part of Korea.

Another style, known as *nangja* (young girl style) has been preserved until today. This style is presently worn by most of the older women, who consider the permanent wave "too girlish." The origin of this style goes back to the kingdom of Silla, where women of the court officials around the capital city of Kyongju knotted the hair into a ball just above the nape of the neck. This style was later spread among the population and finally received royal encouragement. By that time, a pin of four to five inches in length made of gold, silver, or other precious stones, known as the *pinyo*, was thrust between the hair-knot above the nape to serve as a fastener as well as a decoration.

Unmarried women, on the other hand, always wore a long pig-tail to indicate their virginity. The end of the "pig-tail" was decorated with a ribbon, known as the *tanggi*, preferably in dark red, over which were drawn flower designs in gold.

Such traditional hair-styles, however, are rapidly disappearing under Western influence. Most women below the age of 40 have their hair permanent-waved at the beauty parlor, and their hair-styles are remarkably sensitive to the fashions of the West. Women of over 40 years of age, however, still cherish the traditional *nangja* (young girl) style.

Headwear

Headwear has always been a male "accessory" in Korea. But even after the introduction of the Western mode of dressing, Korean women have resisted the desire to add hats to their wardrobes.

During the Koguryo period, Korean men wore a hat called the *cholpung* (wind-breaker), the front of which was decorated with bird feathers. The noblemen of the kingdom of Silla liked to don a gold crown, which was decorated with numerous, fine, gold lines studded with innumerable tiny gold pieces, a device to reflect lights in dazzling halos. Under the top-heavy gold crown, a cloth hoop was sometimes worn which evolved into the Han (Chinese) style *mokto* hood. Also, more and more court officials wore the *syamo* hat during the late Silla period. By the Koryo period, the *syamo* and *mokto* hat had established themselves firmly on the heads of the traditional Korean gentleman whenever foreigners depict the Korean scene.

The original version of the horse hair hat did not have a flat top as it has today, but a dome. The height of the crown and the width of the brim also have undergone several changes, as the fashion dictated. At one time the brim extended 70 to 80 centimeters making close conversation between two wearers of the hat a physical impossibility.

During the winter both men and women put on a fur-lined hood which cover the head, ears, and down to the nape of the neck. The winter hood for women is called *chobaui*, and is decorated with a pair of cranes, roosters, and the Chinese character for happiness in front, and a design of bats at the back, all in gold and silver. A pair of cords in red, yellow, or green is attached at the end of the *chobaui*. A similar hood without such elaborate decorations is worn by men and is called *nambaui*. The once-popular winter hood is now seldom seen, but some old women still wear them.

Ornaments on the Head

The traditional Korean head ornaments have almost disappeared except in far away places deep in the country, but large numbers of people, especially women, displayed the traditional head ornaments until the end of World War II.

The traditional hair dressing for the Korean virgin calls for the *tanggi*, which is attached at the end of the "pig-tail". Made of cloth, the *tanggi* is usually about three feet long and one to two inches wide. The strip of cloth, usually of a dark color, is decorated with various designs, including such letters written in gold as "wealth," "nobility," "longevity" and happiness" in Chinese characters.

The *tanggi* worn by married women is shorter and narrower, less than a foot long and half an inch wide. The married women do not let the *tanggi* hang, but entwine it within the hair knot above the nape.

Tho *pinyo*, the ornamental hairpin used by married women, is about ten centimeters long, and is made of gold, silver, jade or other metals with decorative designs engraved on it. The origin of the *pinyo* dates back to the Three Kingdoms. The earliest *pinyo*, however, was not a short metal pin but a bifurcated pin called *chae*. The *pinyo* shrunk as the years went by, and even during the Yi dynasty it was much longer and larger than the present-day version. On the occasion of festivals, women used to stick into their hair a long, heavy *pinyo*, which adorns even the present-day bride on the day of her traditional Korean-style wedding.

Make-Up

Hair-dressing used to be the most important part of make-up for the Korean man. He had to wash his hair thoroughly, pour hair oil, bind the hair into the *sangtu* knot in which to wear a comb made of jade or coral. Another male attraction was a well-tended, long, naturally grown beard. Such asethetic views of the male, however, have completely disappeared. Instead, the Korean male of today has his hair cut in the Western style, and a close shave is considered essential. Gone also is the old taboo of wearing eye-glasses in front of elder persons, which was considered a breach of etiquette.

For Korean women, too, hair-dressing was considered the most important part of her make-up since the Three Kingdoms. The longer, more lustrous, and darker her hair was, the fairer she looked. The length of her hair was such a dominant factor in her appearance that she had to add *tarae* (hair commodity) to her own hair, should she feel that her own was not long enough.

Hair on the high part of her forehead spoiled her looks to so devastating an extent that she had to endure the pain of plucking each and every "surplus" hair, so that her hairline formed a square. She had to suffer further pain to pluck the hair of her eyebrow so they might from graceful arches. This though is not strange for women everywhere are known to pluck their eyebrows.

For a beautiful complexion, she resorted to various devices. As the "base" of her make-up, a green bean extract diluted in water was used to wash her face. Face powder was used sparingly. Heavy make-up with liberal application of face powder and rouge was never considered appropriate for "respectable ladies," except at weddings. Lipstick was unknown until the introduction of Western civilization.

The "lady" had to have beautiful hands: they had to be free from any marks of hard work, with long fingers and lustrous skin. The traditional Korean bow called attention to her show of hands, and, therefore, whoever accepted her bow could judge her upbringing on the spot by looking at these.

Such traditional views on the beauty of the women, however, have been discarded in favor of the Western "look", and Korean "modern" girls are struggling desperately to transform themselves into their favorite stars on the screen.

Footwear

Historical records contain references to "leather shoes" and straw-shoes worn during the pre-historic kingdom of Mahan. Later, during the Three Kingdoms period, the people of Koguryo and Silla wore "bird-skin shoes" and "red leather shoes." Shoes made of brass have also been recovered from the ancient tombs of Silla. During the subsequent Koryo period, straw-shoes were worn by people in all walks of life, and the *kat* shoes, a kind of leather boots, were also used during the time.

After the country entered into the Yi dynasty, wooden boots were worn by court officials as a part of their "morning costumes". The *yangban*, the leading caste of the Yi dynasty, distinguished themselves with leather shoes, in contrast to the straw-shoes worn by the rest of their countrymen.

The leather shoes of the Yi dynasty had flat heels with sharply raised toes and the narrow upper leather exposed most of the upper part of the feet. No distinction was made between the right and left foot, but different decorations were used for men's wear and women's shoes. The men's shoes had white lines at the edges or inside the shoes, while the women's were covered with silk or cotton.

On rainy days people wore clogs carved out of wood. There were also *mituri*, hemp shoes.

These traditional shoes of the Yi dynasty have becoms almost extinct. Presently both men and women wear either Western-style shoes or rubber shoes which look similar to the leather shoes of the Yi dynasty.

Bedding

The *ondol*, an underfloor heating system, which spread to all residences throughout the country during the late Yi dynasty period, had a decisive influence on bedding. Until that time people slept on the unheated floor, and put up a paper screen as a shield from drafts.

The effective heating of the radiant *ondol* floor reduced the importance of bedding to such an extent that some less well-to-do people could entirely dispense with bedding of any kind. The most common bedding is a set of cotton quilts—the *ibul* (comforter) and *yo* (mattress)—as well as a pillow, all of which are laid over the heated floor. The *yangban* always kept a servant to make the bed. The most widely used Korean pillow is cone-shaped, its edges decorated with embroidery and the inside filled with grain husks, which are covered with cotton or silk cloth. A square wood block also serves as a pillow, while bamboo splinters are also woven into an elastic pillow.

A mosquito net may be used during the summer, and heavy drapery in winter.

Marriage and Funerals

Roles of Parents in Marriage

The traditional Korean marriage was basically an affair between the heads of the two families concerned, who arranged the matrimony. Romantic love between the man and woman never entered into the parents' consideration. Man and woman were not allowed any candid exhibition of affection for each other, nor was such a thing possible in most cases because of the system of early marriage which used to prevail.

In many cases, the husband was a young child, whereas the bride was a "woman." By the time the husband came of age, the wife was too old to be physically attractive to the husband. This dilemma was solved by the institution of concubinage, which allowed a "second wife" to live under the same roof with the "main wife."

Matrimony was considered an extremely serious affair upon which hinged the decline or fall of the husband's family. Therefore, an inter-marriage between different social castes was exceptional. Uppermost in the minds of the parents for arranging a matrimony was the "family name" of the other party; the economic status was relegated to secondary place, certain as it was that higher social status usually meant correspondingly higher income.

In addition to the consideration of social caste, virginity on the part of both parties was regarded as essential. Especially for the woman, remarriage was considered shameful debauchery against the soul of her deceased husband. The Confucian civil code never admitted such a thing as a divorce.

Another characteristic custom, which is still in effect, is that a married woman retains her maiden name intact, because the wife is regarded as belonging to the family of her parents rather than her husband's.

Endogamy has been strictly taboo save for the royal families of the ancient days. As a matter of fact, endogamy has been looked upon with so much distaste that marriage between persons with the same surnames came to be forbidden during the Yi dynasty.

Under the influence of Western culture in the past 50 years or so, much has changed. Marriage for "love" in the Western sense of the word has become increasingly popular, especially in urban districts. The young generation has openly defied tradition by "falling in love," a practice which had been not only frowned upon, but strictly forbidden in the bygone days.

Nevertheless Korean social life is still without a general institution comparable to dating, or the social debut of the West. Presently marriage in Korea follows either one or a combination of the following three processes: parental arrangement through an intermediary, "falling in love" between boy and girl, or introduction of the eligible young man and woman by friends.

In contrast to the traditional system of prohibiting social intercourse between the prospective bride and groom, the modern practice allows a certain period of pre-marital acquaintance prior to engagement, and opinions of the parties concerned carry more weight than the desires of the parents.

Still prevailing in connection with marriage is the age-old custom of having the fortune of the prospective match "told". Two sets of formulae have been observed to predict success or failure of a proposed marriage since the introduction of Chinese studies on divination.

Fortune-Telling on Proposed Matrimony

Prediction on the fortune of a proposed match based on the "theory of the five elements" had been one of the decisive factors in an engagement. Born of the ancient Chinese astrology, the "theory of five elements" is applied to matrimony along with every other phenomenon in the universe. In order to have one's fortune on a proposed marriage told, the service of professional fortune-tellers or a scholar versed in the art of Eastern divinity is solicited.

To tell a fortune, the birth years of both parties concerned are ascertained to assign one of the five elements — gold, fire, wood, earth, water—to each person. One of the five elements assigned to the male and female is then paired, and a source book is referred to in order to get an interpretation of the combination. Thus if the man's year of birth is earth and the woman's fire, the source book explains in effect that the pairing symbolizes a fish transforming itself into a dragon indicating longevity and prosperity of the proposed marriage. If the male and female are both earth, it symbolizes that every branch of a tree will blossom out with flowers, predicting prosperity of the offsprings. If the male is earth and the female wood, a withered tree being confronted with autumn, it predicts a short life and half of the proposed matrimony evil. If the man fire and the woman gold, the dragon loses his jade, and therefore the marriage will be sterile and half of it evil. If the man and woman fire, the dragon will be transformed into a fish, and therefore it means death and extreme evil.

There are altogether 25 combinations of the "elements" paired to predict the fortune of a proposed wedding. Fantastic as it certainly is from our present-day knowledge, this divination wielded, and in many cases still wields, a decisive influence, so much so that a proposed marriage would be broken off when the prediction turned out unfavorable, however ideal all other considerations might have been. This practice of matrimonial fortune-telling still exerts considerable influence.

Engagement

Approval of the parents and the fortune-teller is followed by an engagement. The prospective bridegroom has to send the prospective bride materials for at least two sets of green coats and red skirts, the color green symbolizing youth and growth and the red, passion. The contemporary practice, however, is to slip an engagement ring on the girl's finger at a ceremony performed usually at the prospective bride's house.

Subsequently, the family of the prospective groom secures approval of the wedding day from the prospective bride's family. Often a fortune-teller is consulted to select a "lucky day" for the wedding. Social intercourse during the engagement period is not allowed by traditional custom, but modern practice points the other way.

Once the engagement is effected with acceptance of the gifts on the part of the prospective bride, it is considered binding. It is immediately reported to the souls of the ancestors, and therefore the engagement used to be regarded the same thing as the wedding itself. In the old days it was indeed an exceptional case when an engagement could be broken, however justifiable the reason might appear. This was especially so for the woman, for the Confucian ethics had the last word that "a woman should not serve two husbands." There are many cases of women who chose to stay single after a broken engagement.

Wedding Ceremony

The wedding ceremony may take any one of the ritual forms provided for by the various religions—the traditional Confucianism, Buddhism, *Chondoism* and Christianity, or the modern urban style in the commercial "wedding parlor."

The traditional Confucian style, originally stemming from the "Six Etiquettes" by Chu Hsi, a neo-Confucianist, is still popular in the rural districts. The Confucian ritual commands the groom on the wedding day to wait outside the bride's house until he is invited in by one of the bride's family members. Wearing the wedding hat, the "official belt," and the wedding coat, the groom accompanied by parents and relations, starts out on the trip to the bride's house in a brightly decorated palanquin. As he leaves his house, mischievous youths and children send a volley of ashes as a charm against the gods of the plague for the "benefit" of the groom.

After some waiting outside the bride's house, the groom is finally admitted, following the "wedding chest carrier" who has been accompanying him together with the groom's relatives. The "wedding chest carrier" usually has his face painted black, to play the role of a clown, and elicits laughter from the people, thus making the confrontation of families a merry occasion.

The waiting bride, with heavy make-up of face powder and rouge, a tremendous silver hair pin sticking out of her hair, dressed in the traditional wedding costume of yellow and blue coat with a red or pink skirt, greets the groom and his family with deep bows.

Hemmed in by the best men and bridesmaids, the couple is seated at the central position at a long table, which is loaded with various rice cakes, fruits, meats and other delicacies. The nuptial bow takes the form of drinking ceremonial wine by the couple. Then the wedding feast begins. Mischievous friends tease the couple throughout the ceremony and the climax is reached when the friends bind the two legs of the resisting groom together and hang him upside down from the beam of the house. A make-believe torture is administered to the groom by the friends who beat the soles of the groom with a stick, demanding him to "stand" another big feast for all his friends.

The spree over, the bride and groom retire to the bridal chamber to consumate the marriage. The mischievous friends and neighbors still keep hovering at the door of the chamber to peek at the couple on their "first night."

After spending three nights at the bride's home, the groom takes the birde to his own home, where the entire process of the wedding ceremony may or may not be repeated.

In recent years the urban people tend to choose a less elaborate ceremony provided for by the "modern" style. Christians usually observe the ceremony at a church while numerous commercial "wedding parlors" are available for couples with no religious affiliations. Such a wedding is conducted by a prominent citizen who, acting as the master of ceremony, declares the couple duly married to friends and relatives assembled at the "wedding parlor." The costumes of the modern style wedding are similar with Western wedding costumes. A reception party may follow an urban, Western-style wedding, or a small cake encased in a box, may be presented to each guest after the wedding ceremony in place of a party. The honeymoon trip, which had never been known previously, has almost become a rule for Westernized couples. Thus the traditional wedding with its pomp and circumstances are withering rapidly to be replaced with a more expedient and certainly less expensive Western-style wedding.

Funeral Service

Funeral services have been dictated by Confucianism, which places the rite under rigid step-by-step procedures. Ancestoral worship being one of the basic teachings of Confucianism, the greatest possible care is taken in connection with everything related with the funeral service. According to the Confucian code of conduct, one has to be in mourning for three years following the death of one's parent—a system which was forced upon the people by a royal command during the middle of the Yi dynasty. The idea of staying in mourning for such a long time is based on the teaching of Confucius who wrote to the effect that since one stayed for three years within the "bosom" of one's parents after birth, one is obliged to be in mourning for that length of time after a parent's death. The customs of a long mourning period dated back to the Three Kingdoms period, but the time had to be shortened to one hundred days during the Koryo period. The Yi dynasty, however, revived the ancient system of staying in mourning for three years.

We shall now view the rigid procedures governing the Confucian-style funeral service from one's death bed to his final sleeping ground.

The will is usually made by the person himself during old age or one of the family members may write down the remarks of the dying person.

When the last moment comes, a male member of the family straightens the tongue of the dying person with his hand, while all female members of the family are required to leave the scene. As soon as the death is confirmed, the corpse is covered with a comforter and the "formal wail" anounces the death of a "superior person." The long, drawn-out wail is joined in chorus by all other members of the family.

The wailing over, the face of the corpse is covered with a piece of white paper and clean raw cotton, the position of the head is straightened out, both thumbs are bound together, legs are straightened out and both of the legs are also bound together. The corpse is then covered again with a comforter and a wail is begun.

Subsequently the "soul of the deceased person is invited back" by a member of the house or relatives who have never seen the corpse up to that moment. The person assigned to the work climbs up on the roof of the house, holding the white coat of the deceased, and facing south repeats three times in a loud voice, "Scholar so and so (the deceased person's name, come back," in order to invite the deceased person's soul back to the corpse. Coming down from the roof, the person places the deceased person's coat over the corpse and lets out long wails which are repeated many times for several minutes. The departed soul having returned to the corpse, the body is then placed on the "corpse bed" facing south. A paper fence is erected near the "corpse bed" to shield drafts.

Members of the bereaved family then undo their hair to make formal announcement of the death. The official role of the "master of mourning" is assumed by the eldest son or grandson, and straw mattresses are laid on the floor, on which all members of the bereaved family stay up until the funeral is over.

In the meantime, the corpse is washed with perfumed water and then clothed with the garments specially prepared for the occasion. The hair of the corpse is combed and the nails cut. Both the hair and the nails which come out in the process are put into two small cloth bags to be placed on the left and right side of the corpse. Traditional costumes for the corpse are made up of a complete outfit including a band, a hat, a hood. Costumes for the women are considerably different from the man's.

A meal is served to the corpse by the "master of mourning" and his servant. The ritual calls for a spoon made of willow wood, one small bowl full of cooked rice and three "holeless" beads. The master of mourning carrying three beads in a bowl approaches the corpse followed by a male servant, who holds the bowl containing cooked rice with a willow spoon in the rice. The "master of mourning" sits in front of the corpse facing east, while the servant takes a position opposite the master. Then the servant forces the corpse's mouth open slightly to thrust a small quantity of cooked rice into the mouth, and then the master slips one bead into the corpse's mouth. The process is repeated three times and then the master leaves. The servant remains at the place to stuff raw cotton pieces below the jar, cover the face with a cloth, and then stuff the ears with clean cotton balls.

The members of the house, who undid their hair immediately following the death, now comb their hair again. From this time, a meal is served to the corpse on a small table set in front of the corpse with burning incense at every meal time.

The placing of the corpse into a coffin follows. First, all gaps of the coffin are filled with either honey or pine resin, the bottom and inside walls of the coffin are covered with white sheets, and a mattress is laid prior to placing the corpse into the coffin. The corpse is then covered with a loose half-length garment and the coffin is examined from outside to fill any gaps showing. While all members of the house are wailing, the Chinese character for heaven is inscribed on the inside of the coffin top, and then the Chinese word for sea is added at each of the four corners. The top then is nailed down with pegs carved of bamboo or other wood. All traditional coffins are made of wood. Metal of any kind is not used to keep the coffin free from metallic rust.

Placing the coffin in the place of honor, the members of the house put on the formal morning clothes made of coarse, hand woven hemp. The master of mourning receives all guests, at the sight of whom the master is required to let out the long wail, the number of wails depending upon the relationship between the deceased person and each guest. The mourning guests are entertained with wine and food. A wake is observed usually for two nights because the "three-day funeral" is observed most often. Sometimes the funeral is a five-day or seven-day affair.

At sunrise, the master of mourning burns the "morning incense" after a formal wail. A breakfast is dedicated to the corpse as if the person were still living. In the evening, dinner is served and the "evening incense" is burned prior to making a bed for the deceased.

On the third, fifth or seventh day after the formal announcement of the death, the funeral procession starts out for the ancestral burial ground. Leading the procession are funeral flags and incense burners. Decorated with white artificial flowers, the coffin is carried on the shoulders of four servants. It is followed by the "master of mourning" and other mourners, including relatives and friends.

Arriving at the burial ground, the coffin is first placed, at the direction of the "master of ceremony," on the "funeral bed." Incense is burned, and the formal wails are said by the mourners; the women face east. The grave dug by laborers are cleansed of various gods of plague and then sons of the deceased person lower the coffin into the pit. The grave is filled by the sons with the help of the "master of ceremony." Final farewell bows are made to the grave, and a caretaker of the grave is appointed. The funeral is over. After the funeral, however, the offsprings are supposed to stay in mourning for three years, offering a meal to the soul of the deceased at every meal time, morning noon and evening. Some persons noted for filial piety are said to have stayed near the grave for three years, taking care of the grave and subjecting themselves to all kinds of hardships in strict obedience to the Confucian idea that the son is guilty of his parent's death whatever the actual reason.

All members of the house pay a visit to the burial ground on holidays, especially on *Tano* in the spring and "Thanksgiving" in the fall.

In recent years, commercial undertakers have come to assume increasingly more important roles in the funeral service. Christian families, on the other hand, follow more or less similar procedures as performed in the West except for the traditional Korean mourning clothes worn by the family. Cremation, which has been introduced lately, has never been popular.

The funeral of a child is completely free of the elaborate forms which dominate the funeral services of parents. Without much ado, the corpse of a child is placed in a coffin to be buried in the burial ground by a servant.

The decline of Confucianism after the introduction of Western culture is slowly but steadily modifying the age-old customs.

Home and Social Life

Home Life

The home life of the Korean people has been governed by centuries old tradition. One of the most influential codes of ethics has been the "five ethical principles" stemming from Confucianism. The "five ethical principles" teach that there must be affection between father and son, justice between king and subject, discretion between husband and wife, order between old and young, and finally, trust between friends. Somewhat outmoded as the principles may be, they still contain elements applicable to present-day Korean home life.

In the Korean home, courtesy has been accorded the utmost importance. Courteous good manners were so highly regarded that the Yi dynasty had a Minister of Etiquette as one of the court's highest-ranking officials.

The grandparents or parents are the "superiors" of the home, to whom one has to pay absolute obedience and reverence. The "superiors" have to be seated at the place of "honor" at all time; one has to dress neatly to appear before the "superiors," in whose presence smoking, drinking or singing is not allowed. As soon as one gets up in the morning, he or she pays respect to the "superiors" with the morning bow. At the table the superiors have to pick up the silvers first before others can start eating. The highly honorific expression has to be employed whenever speaking with "superiors," whom one must always treat with the deepest reverence both in word and deed.

The superiors, in turn, lavish affection on their offsprings. Unlike in the West, the babies sleep in the same bed with the mother covered with a large quilted comforter.

The boys and girls stay at home with the superiors, receiving instruction on good behavior until they reach the age of seven, when they go to elementary school. Throughout the juvenile and adolescence periods, the mother is tolerant, while the father remains a strict disciplinarian, in whose presence smoking and drinking are not allowed. The eldest son is treated with respect even during his adolescence.

In the old days, the boys went to the Confucian private school to learn the Chinese classics from a strict teacher who never spared the rod. Nowadays they go to the Western-style school to receive group education, which lays emphasis on sincerity and diligence.

During adolescence, the boys enjoy freedom, but numerous restrictions are imposed upon the girls. One of the Confucian ethical codes of conduct used to dictate social intercourse between young men and women of Korea with the iron rule that "male and female should not sit close after the age of seven." The rule has long ceased to apply, but its lingering influences still demand restrictions on young women. In the urban districts, adolescent girls may be engaged in social activities such as visiting the "tea room" and theaters, but the rural virgins are still forced to spend the day at home. After graduating from school, the girls learn the art of house-keeping from the mother in preparation for matrimony if she does not get an outside job.

When the boy and girl reach the age of 20 to 30, the wedding takes place after a period of engagement. The marriage is of two kinds: through an arrangement of the parents, or a Western-style marriage born out of "romance." The traditional marriage through parental arrangement, still popular in the rural areas, is decided between the parents of the parties concerned, and the opinions of the parents usually play the strongest hand. The Western-style "marriage of love" is popular in the urban districts, and is expected to increase. Presently about half of the marriages in the country are presumed to take place from "romance."

After the wedding, the newly-wed couple usually stays in the same house with the husband's parents, even though a separate home may be allowed. Therefore, many homes contain three generations under the same roof. The bride starts working three days after moving to her husband's house.

As a wife, the Korean woman is expected to lead a life of modesty and absolute virtue. This idea has been so deeply rooted that an unfaithful wife is a rare exception, and so is a wife who suggests divorce to her husband on any grounds whatsoever. The traditional ethics for the wife tells her to be, first of all, obedient, then faithful, and finally, cooperative.

The Korean housewives rely almost completely on their husbands for the economic well-being of the home, because career openings are extremely limited for them. With the exception of midwives, beauty parlor operators and school teachers, few occupations are available to Korean women. In recent years, however, an increasingly large number of housewives, many of whom are graduates of colleges, are endeavoring to make both housekeeping and an outside career compatible.

The birth of a son is likely to be greeted with more rejoicing than a daughter, for it is a son who will inherit the "name of the family." In fact, the Korean woman has to suffer the status of "inferiority" which the century-old conventions force upon her. The idea of "superior man and inferior woman" is still harbored by some people.

When the spouse dies, the widower may remarry without any qualms on his conscience, but not the widow. Instead, esteem is accorded the widow who remains single to raise her children.

The grandparents, who usually live under the same roof with their sons' families, are the best playmates of the grand sons and daughters. They spend their declining years giving advice to their sons and daughters-in-law, who must lend respectful ears.

Inheritance

The eldest son is the heir to whom falls all the privileges and responsibilities of the head of a family. Since the eldest son is required to support his aged parents until death, and also to observe various memorial services to ancestors, he acquires most of the family property.

Other sons, on the other hand, set up separate families or may be adopted by other families. Female offsprings are given little if any properties after the parents' deaths, because of the belief that they are destined to become member of other families by marriage.

A recent legislative amendment, however, revolutionized the traditional system by enabling a female offspring to become the head of a family when no male offspring exists. Until the amendment was put into effect, adopting a son, frequently through marriage with a female offspring, was the only way to keep a family name when a son was lacking.

The son who is to inherit the family name, however, was invariably born of the legally married wife. The illegitimate son born of a concubine or a mistress had to suffer public contempt. This was especially so during the Yi dynasty, which ended only about 60 years ago.

So underprivileged were the illegitimate sons that both at home and in society, they had to suffer humiliation. At home, for instance, they were not allowed to call their father and legitimate brothers as such but had to refer to them by some other honorary titles, confirming the belief that the illegitimate sons could not be members of the family even by inference. Neither were they entitled to participate in the memorial services for the ancestors, nor share in the inheritance of property.

Once born illegitimate, they had no choice but to endure all handicaps and humiliations society imposed upon them. An illegitimate son could not marry a legitimate daughter, and the court blocked the way to the advancement of an illegitimate son to a high government post however outstanding his talent.

Living under this shadow, some of the illegitimate sons born of *yangban* made a few scattered attempts to overthrow the existing social system as in the case of the author of the famed classic novel, "Hong Kildong"—a work of a suppressed genius who vent his grudge in his literary work during the late Yi dynasty period.

Since the introduction of Western thoughts, however, the traditional prejudice against illegitimate sons has lost much of its power. Presently no discrimination is directed against them, at least, at all official functions.

Social Life

Caste System

The contemporary Korean society has been without a caste system of any kind since the beginning of the 20th century. But the old feudal society of the Yi dynasty kept alive the system of three distinct castes: the *yangban*, commoner, and the lowly.

Standing at the crest of society, the *yangban* were the leading minority of a leisure class, respected for their birthrights. Originally, the word, *yangban*, was used as a revered form of reference to officials of high rank in the early Yi dynasty court, but gradually descendants of such high-ranking officials came to be called *yangban*. They held the commoners and the lowly in contempt and enjoyed considerable privileges that were denied the other lower classes.

To the class of commoners belonged low officials of the court, farmers, merchants and artisians, forming the majority of the population. Among the commoners, the farmers were placed above others due to the prevailing conception that agriculture had been the backbone of the nation's economy since ancient times.

The lowly, on the other hand, was a much despised minority group engaged hereditarily in occupations regarded as "unclean." To this underprivileged minority group belonged butchers, Shamans, public entertainers, the *kisaeng* (sing-song girls), Buddhist priests and domestic serfs.

All three of the social classes led mutually exclusive social lives, and a marriage between members of different castes was strictly forbidden. Nor could one advance from a low caste to a higher one because of the hereditary requirements.

Such a rigid caste system, however, came to an end with the fall of the Yi dynasty, and equality for all has been the case since the 1900's. But among the older generations, the idea of *yangban* and commoner still exerts a lingering influence.

Occupations

The Yi dynasty accorded the highest prestige to court officials of civic affairs, who were also Confucian scholars. slighting military officials, undoubtedly under the influence of Confucianism. Buddhist priests, who had stood at the crest of the social class during the Koryo period, were degraded deliberately to the lowest class in Yi society because of the dynasty's official policy to discourage Buddhism. Also held in the lowest esteem were the itinerant musicians, acrobats and clowns of the period as well as the Shamans. The professional woman entertainers also had to suffer social contempt, while the butchers were considered the "uncleanest" of them all.

Between the two extremes were the farmers, merchants, and artisans.

With the disappearance of the caste system, such concepts have been replaced with the Western idea of equality of all occupations. But there still lingers an inclination to attach prestige to government officials and scholars. The recent development of material civilization, however, has advanced business careers to the head of the list of desirable occupations, for many people seem to prefer material well-being to prestigious positions.

Social Intercourse

By-gone Days

The Confucianism-bound society of Korea in the by-gone days felt so little need for social intercourse as such that there were no *ad hoc* gatherings for the purpose. Social intercourse, therefore, was an informal affair born out of other meetings. Another frustrating factor was the Confucian teaching that "male and female should not sit close after reaching the age of seven" — a code of conduct which was observed to the letter during the days of "old Korea."

One of the popular gatherings was the "poetry composition meeting" of the Confucian scholars. Congregating at the house of an eminent scholar or strolling in a group to enjoy nature, the "stags" enjoyed themselves in informal chats after the poetry composition. A less sophisticated gathering was the "picnic" of a group of friends.

To the farmers, the best opportunities for social intercourse were offered by the village festivals and periodic market-places. The Korean farmers' market usually opened every fifth day in a small town, where the farmers from nearby villages gathered to exchange greetings and "wine cups" after the business was attended to. Social meetings were also possible on the farm, when the farmers were engaged in "cooperative work," a practice of all members of a village working on a single farm during the busiest season.

The village festivals were Shaman rituals offered to the spirits of the village, observed mostly during the slack farm season in the first month of the first moon. Practically all members of the village gather on the "festival ground" either to witness or to take part in the rite. After the formal ritual is over, the villagers enjoy drinking and dancing. This practice, once almost universal throughout the country, has lost much of its popularity in recent years, but it is still practised in some villages.

Another social gathering which still exists is the "family tree" meeting—an occasional gathering of the members who belong to the same clan. This is more or less a financial aid society to help needy members of the "same large family."

Occasionally, a business or public institution sponsers a meeting to pay homage to old persons residing nearby. Sometimes more than one hundred elderly persons gather to enjoy themselves with feasts prepared for them.

The private mutual finance system, commonly referred to as the *kye*, was as popular during the old day as in recent years, offering an excellent opportunity for social intercourse among the members. The mutual finance system, which requires each member to pay a certain amount of money in installments to receive a lump sum in return at expiration date, was adopted sometimes to help needy friends. It frequently happened that the person who received the lump sum sponsored drinks and food for other members of the *kye*.

Throughout "old Korea," social gatherings were conspicuous for the absence of mingling between the sexes.

Contemporary

The idea—and the "mechanics"—of social intercourse have become much Westernized for contemporary Koreans. The traditional virtue of reserve is not considered socially attractive any longer; instead vivacity, candidness and joviality are held in high esteem. There are many places for social gatherings in cities. The Confucian ethics on social intercourse have lost much ground, especially among the young generation, which is more likely than not to look upon what they consider the "outmoded" with amused contempt.

Nevertheless, social relations between boys and girls such as "dating" have not yet been established as an unquestionably accepted convention, although the trend is moving towards Western customs.

Considerable opportunities for social relations between the sexes exist during college days, for most of the institutions of higher learning are co-educational. But the idea of a "girl friend" or a "boy friend" among high school students is frowned upon, and occasionally regarded as intolerable.

Cities offer many opportunities as well as places for social gathering. Many "tea rooms" are available for meeting friends, and other public places of amusement and entertainment such as theaters, the miniature golf course, the "chess house", and billiard halls provide occasion for informal social get-togethers. The dance hall, which was once a subject of heated controversies, has now become one of the indispensable institutions for one segment of the Korean urban population. Another favorite for gatherings are the innumerable bistros and "high class restaurants," where the "hostesses" entertain the guests.

Offering a glass of wine and tobacco has long been a prelude to a congenial social relationship among men. Even the miser is considered above sparing liquor and tobacco to a new friend.

Housewives are still without public places for social meetings unless accompanied by their husbands. But various gatherings of women's groups, including alumini association meetings, are now available for them.

Another important function for female social life is the private mutual finance system, *kye*. Meeting usually once a month, members of a *kye* take advantage of the opportunity for conversation and recreation.

In the rural districts, opportunities for social intercourse are not so abundant as in the urban areas. In addition to the institutions for social activities provided for by "old Korea," many meetings have come to be sponsored for the farmers by public organizations and youth groups.

Celebrations

Relatives and friends gather on such celebrations as the birthday and wedding. A big birthday celebration takes place on the 100th day after the birth of a child, on the baby's first birthday, and on the 61st. birthday. The last, called *hangap*, is often a large festival, where a large crowd is welcome.

A large crowd is also invited to the wedding, which takes place in the Christian church or commercial "wedding parlor" in the urban area. In the rural districts, the bride's house becomes the ground for marriage. The wedding offers excellent opportunities for social acquaintances, for a dinner is served in most cases immediately following the ceremony, and much drinking as well as singing takes place.

Friends and relatives are also invited to the mourning services, which offers opportunities for subdued social meetings.

Gifts

The most expensive gifts are exchanged usually for the wedding between bride and groom. The traditional custom calls for the groom to send to his bride materials for blue and red skirts, together with a bundle of red and blue thread. The gifts, however, differ according to the locality.

For the modern wedding, the prospective groom usually presents the prospective bride with an engagement ring, preferably with a diamond set in platinum prior to slipping a wedding ring on her finger at the wedding ceremony. The bride, in turn, gives the groom a wrist watch, fountain-pen or similar gift. Friends and relatives invited to the wedding bring gifts of various kinds ranging from money to wine.

Certain specific gifts, however, are considered appropriate for different occasions. For the baby's 100th day and the first birthday, the items are: a bundle of thread wishing the baby a long life, rice overflowing in a large bowl to wish the baby wealth, a set of spoon and chopsticks preferably of silver, a bowl with a top made of shiny brass, clothes, and money.

For other birthday gifts, small personal items or Western cakes are popular, whereas the 61st. birthday celebration welcomes anything, from outright cash to wine, which may be used for the feast.

Holiday gifts are exchanged on the occasions of the New Year, the *Tano* in spring, the *Chusok* (Thanksgiving), and Christmas. Traditionally popular gift items on such holidays are food such as meat, fish, fruits, and wine, but the urban populations seem to appreciate such goods less than the farmers. In the "old" days, the custom prevailed that for the New Year, the provincial government officials sent unique products of their provinces to the court and other high-ranking officials in the capital, who, in turn, distributed the gifts to their subordinates.

Many of the traditional customs on gifts have survived on the farms, but the city dwellers, sepecially the younger generations, have become increasingly Westernized in the matter.

Name and the Calendar

Names of Persons

Surname

The surname which precedes the given name, stems from the Chinese family names which were first used sometime during the early stages of the Three Kingdoms period. Originally without surnames, the people took Chinese family names for their own under the influence of the Chinese culture. Ancient records indicate that the third king of Silla, Yuri, conferred such surnames on the officials of the six ministries of his court. The throne of the kingdom was shared by the three families of Kim, Pak and Sok, each taking turns alternatively.

Surnames have been regarded as being extremely important by the bearers, for the social position of each person was dependent upon the surname one has inherited together with other hereditary titles. Thus, the offsprings of high-ranking officials of the court cherished their family names, because the surnames alone entitled them to membership in the leading *yangban* class in the society. The bearers of the family names whose ancestors had failed to secure prominent positions in the royal court, on the other hand, had to bear up with a feeling of inferiority as commoners. Much has been changed with regard to the social valuation of the family names during the past 50 years or so, but its influence still lingers, particularly in the rural areas.

The surnames, Kim, Yi and Pak, being "the three greatest names" are most numerous in that order. The total number of surnames once stood at 298 according to literature published during the reign of King Sonjo (1568-1608) of the Yi dynasty. The number, however, was reduced to 256 by 1930, when a nationwide survey was made on the subject of names. The decrease in the number of the surnames was caused not by population decrease but by a process of "mergers"— the families of rare surnames being merged into the families of more common and therefore better-known surnames, apparently for practical purposes. By assuming more socially powerful surnames, families with obscure names could be socially accepted.

So much importance has been attached to one's surname since the old days that each family inherits and preserves the "family tree document" to prove the authencity of their surnames.

The 1930 survey showed that Kim 金, the most common surname, was borne by 858,239 families, followed by Yi 李 for 587,271 families, and Pak 朴 for 304,248 families. Other common surnames were Choe 崔 (190,237 families), Chong 鄭 (147,475), Cho 趙(85,994), Kang 姜 (81,841), Chang 張(80,272), Han 韓 (77,224), Yun 尹(74,294), O 吳(60,995), Im 林 (60,140), Sin 申(56,080), An 安(54,165). The surnames of moderate frequency born by 30,000 to 49,000 families were Song 宋, So 徐, Hwang 黃, Hong 洪, Chon 全, Kwon 權, Yu 柳, Ko 高, Mun 文, Paek 白, Yang 梁, Son 孫.

The surnames born by 10,000 to 29,000 families were, in the order of frequency, Yu 劉, Ho 許, Pae 裵, Cho 曺, No 盧, Chu 朱, Sim 沈, Cha 車, Nam 南, Kang 康, Chon 田, Im 任, Ha 河, Kwak 郭, U 禹, Chong 丁, Na 羅, Chi 池, Won 元, Min 閔, Ku 具, Om 嚴, Pang 方, Song 成, Sin 辛, Yu 兪, Chae 蔡, Hyon 玄, Chin 陳.

At the opposite end of the scale, the survey listed rare names; for example, the surnames, Han 漢, Son 先, Sun 淳, So 西, Yom 濂; were shared by no more than two families while 24 families shared theirs with none, such as Chae 采, Chae 菜, Yom 閻, Ung 應, Tan 單, Pyon 扁, Kang 剛, Kun 斤, Chun 俊, Song 星, etc.

Whereas practically all surnames bore a single Chinese character, few exceptions bore two Chinese characters: Namgung 南宮(1,365 families), Sonu 鮮于 (1,226), Hwangbo 皇甫 (927), Tokko 獨孤 (481), Sagong 司空 (232), Chegal 諸葛(153), Tongbang 東方(60).

Given Names

Given names are of two kinds: the legal and the by-name. The legal name is given to the child about 100 days after birth and is registered with the government office. Determining the legal name is a complicated affair. The given name should be not only meaningful, easily articulate and aesthetic but also "lucky." Two Chinese characters are most commonly used for the legal names, but one of the two characters is usually predetermined by the "theory of the five elements." The father and grandfather who usually choose the given name of an offspring, therefore, can select only one character, the other having been predetermined by the "five elements." Thus the predetermined word in combination with the chosen character constitute a person's legal name. The same Chinese character is predetermined for all family members of the same generation; therefore brothers and relatives of a family usually bear names similar to one other. The practice of applying the predetermined character to the legal name, therefore, furnishes outsiders a clue to the person's family lineage.

In the exceptional case of having only one word for a legal name as is often the case with the Ho family, the rule of the predetermined word does not apply. In recent years, women have also been freed from the predetermined dictation of one of the characters for their names.

The names of women have to connote feminine virtue as well as beauty, and therefore favorite words chosen for such an effect include Suk 淑, Ok 玉, Hye 惠, Un 恩, Sun 順, and Hi 姬, implying respectivelly virtue, jade, benevolence, favor, obedience and princess. Occasionally a masculine name is given to a girl for some reason, one being as a charm to fulfill the parents' wish to beget a male offspring when their next child is born.

In the rural districts, pet names used during infancy are occasionally accorded the status of legal names, due either to ignorance of the parents or to some superstitious beliefs. In such case, old women are called by such names as Kannani (the newly-born) and Onnyon (mother's baby-girl).

The God-Father

The legal names are usually chosen by father, grandfather or both. Scholars in the neighborhood are sometimes consulted and assume the role of godfather when the paternal scholarship is judged insufficient. Services of a "professional" godfather may be used, so that the given name may be in complete harmony with the divination of one's name, because it is believed that one's name exerts a decisive influence upon the person's fortune. Professional fortune-tellers of names are seen occasionally sitting at street corners soliciting business from passers-by.

Being devoid of such services of the professional godfathers or learned men, the rural villages used to accord any handy names to babies, who later become identified with absurd names.

Occasionally ridiculous names are given to children as a charm against evil demons. If a child is supposedly threatened by an evil god, an absurd name connoting stupidity or insignificance is given. It is believed that the evil god will not molest a worthless child who is called "the stupid one" or "the straw bag," thereby assuring the child a life of longevity and unhampered good fortune. Some children are given the name "Rock" so that they may be as strong as their names.

Men of letters and artists as a rule use other names appropriate to the pen, stage or the painting brush. The scholars of the old days also enjoyed having one or more added names. In recent years, self-assumed men of intelligence have come to use added names, apparently after the practice of the scholars of old days.

Some people go through the trouble of changing their names officially in an attempt to change the course of their fortunes as a result of the conclusion that their misfortunes have been caused by unlucky names they have been bearing innocently. Women, on the other hand, retain both given name and surname even after marriage.

Addressing a Person by Name

It is considered rude to call a person by name without due distinction. An honorary title has to follow the name of an elder person. Within a family circle, the young people are not supposed to address or call the elders by their names, but have to refer to them as "father," "mother," "elder brother," "uncle," etc.

Addressing socially prominent persons by their legal names from a man of lower standing is also considered rude, aliases being proper for the purpose.

The Korean language is devoid of an acceptable honorary title which is equivalent to "Mr." in English. The most widely used, however, is the word "sonsaeng" (teacher) for one's superiors, and "ssi" for persons of equal or slightly superior social standing. The official position of the person may safely be used after the name for addressing the person—a practice most widely observed if such an official title is available. All such honorary titles follow the name without exception, but the added names of scholars or artists usually precede the surname and legal name.

Calling a person by the last name, that is, the given name, is tolerated only among intimate friends or from an elder to a younger person.

Seal

A seal bearing the name of a person or an organization is affixed in place of a signature on all legal documents. Requirement of a seal on the legal document is so absolute that a personal signature, however authentic it may be, usually does not "seal" a legal contract unless accompanied by a proper seal. Therefore, every organization and virtually all individual persons have a seal ready on hand whenever the need arises.

Engraved by professional artisans, the seal may be easily forged. To prevent this, important seals are registered with the government to establish authenticity. Thus to effect a transaction involving real estates, for example, a seal affixed on the legal papers has to be the one registered with the government.

Seals may be of any size or shape, but the most popular are square, opaque or circular. Garved of various materials such as hardwood, metal, stone, "ivory," the seal may be as small as a quarter of an inch in diameter or larger than a square inch.

Imported originally from China, the seal was first status symbol and the prerogative of royalty. "The History of the Three Kingdoms" contains a reference to seals in mentioning that during the ancient days, a transfer of the throne had to be symbolized by the dethroned king handing over the imperial seal himself to his successor. "The History of Koryo" also mentions that the kingdom had a court function charged exclusively with custody of the government seals. During the Koryo period, however, seals seem to have become popular among individual persons as well, for some such personal seals have survived until the present. Preserved in the National Museum, the personal seals of the Koryo period are engraved in ceramics and copper with intricate designs of a dragon, a fish or a mythological bird carved in the stem.

Engraving seals seem to have been developed as an art during the Koryo period, for a book bearing impressions of many seals published in 1101 has been preserved to date.

By the Yi dynasty period, a set of elaborate rules was established, governing usages of the seals as a status symbol. Thus a king had a certain number of imperial seals to affix, one appropriate for each occasion. Several seals of the kings and queens of the Yi dynasty made in gold or silver are presently preserved in the National Museum. All of the Yi dynasty government offices also had official seals, which had to be handed over to a successor personally by retiring officials whenever a transfer of personnel was effected.

Presently a seal of an individual person or an organization may be of any size, but during the Yi dynasty, the size of a seal had to be proportionate to status as dictated by rule. Thus the highest-ranking court official's seal was about two-inch square, the second highest-ranking official's seal about 0.12 inch square smaller, and the third-ranking official's seal about 0.35 inch square smaller than his superior's. The wives of the highest-ranking officials had seals of slightly smaller size than their husbands'.

Like stamp collecting in the West, many Eastern people collect impressions of seals. The hobby was most highly developed in China. Many kings and scholars of the Yi dynasty became famous connoisseurs in Korea. Some recent names: O Kyongsok, who published the "*Wangjukchae* Seal Collections"; O Sechang who issued the three-volume "*Oue-no-in-ko*", Yi Yongmun who published the four-volume "*Chong-hwang-dang* Seal Book", and Chon Hyongpil who is credited with publication of the four-volume "*Chui-sol-zae* Seal Book."

Of the materials used for engraving seals, crystal has traditionally been considered the best guarantee against forgery, while hard wood has been most popular apparently for reasons of economy.

The impression is made with "ink" in scarlet, a sticky vegetable dye which is inerasable.

Name of Places
Legendary Origins

Names of places in Korea have been derived originally from various factors such as topography, "geomancy," certain legends, or historical events which marked a particular place. Of the various factors, legends have contributed more than any others to these names.

A bear in a legend, for example, gave the name Komjin (Bear's Shore) to the city presently called Kongju, and the name Kom (Bear) River to what is presently known as the Kum River. The legend goes: a young man, who had lost his way deep in a mountain, found a hut, where he was entertained royally by a beautiful woman who lived alone. Enchanted by her beauty, the youth stayed in the place for several days to be honored by the hostess with all the delicacies of the world. Becoming curious as to how the woman could manage to secure so many varieties of food deep inside the mountains, the young man followed the hostess to witness transformation of the beautiful woman into a bear in order to catch a deer. Knowing the identity of the hostess, the youth ran for his life with the bear in hot pursuit. Reaching the end of a precipice, the youth plunged into the river flowing under, followed by the bear. The youth swam ashore, but the bear, being unable to swim, was drowned. Thus the village near which the young man swam came to be called the Komjin (Bear's Shore), and the River the Komgang (Bear's River).

Certain historical events or episodes also gave names to many places. The once-suburban town of Wangsimni (Go-ten-more-miles-town) near the capital city of Seoul is such an example. The name of that place also involves the idea of "geomancy". According to the story, the scholar-geomancer Muhak, having been commissioned by the founder-king of the Yi dynasty to locate the best site for a new capital, was passing through the village which later came to be called the "Go-ten-more-miles-town," when a mysterious old man was heard to mutter, "The man is, alas, as ignorant as Muhak (No learning)." The geomancer immediately paid profound respect to the old man and asked for his advice. "Go ten more miles to the west," was the reply. Following the advice, the geomancer found the most ideal site for a new capital from every geomantic point of view. The new seat of the Yi dynasty, thus located, became Seoul, and the place where the advice was given Wangsimni.

Another suburban town of Seoul, Manguri, was also named 500 years ago after a similar anecdote. The story goes that the founder-king of the Yi dynasty, on his way back to the capital city after locating an ideal site for his royal family burial grounds, cried out in relief: "Now that I have chosen even the burial ground, I may allow myself to forget all worries." Thus the village where the royal remark was uttered acquired the name Manguri, meaning "Forgotten-worries-town."

Some streets were named after famous personalities of the past. Many downtown streets of Seoul, for instance, were renamed after the Liberation from Japan in 1945 after such historical figures as General Ulchi of the Koguryo kingdom, who repulsed the Chinese invasion; Yi Toegye of the Yi dynasty, who was one of the most renowned Confucian soholars throughout the East; Admiral Chungmu Yi Sunsin, who routed the Japanese armadas in 1592 and 1598.

Seoul as a Descriptive Name

The name of the capital is a common noun as well as a proper one, for the word Seoul is also referred to as Hanyang or Hansong, both of which are Chinese equivalents to Seoul, originally devised by the scholars during the early period of the Yi dynasty. The world Keijo for Seoul appearing on some maps was the name given to the city by the Japanese during the occupation period. The Japanese name was promptly dropped after the Liberation, reviving the old name Seoul— a practice followed throughout the country.

The early name for the Silla kingdom, Sorabol, was also descriptive, meaning a newly cultivated town. The word Seoul as a capital city is known to have stemmed from the original Sorabol.

Provincial Traits

Each of the original eight provinces of Korea has been associated with certain traits during the past 500 years since the early Yi dynasty. Concise descriptions were given to each of the original province by a sort of by-name. Thus Kyonggi-do province was described as "the fair maid in a mirror;" Chung-Chong-do as "the clear moon in a cool breeze;" Cholla-do as "the slender willow tree before the wind;" Kyongsang-do as "the high peak in rugged mountains;" Kangwon-do as "the old Buddha under the rocks;" Hwanghae-do as "the cow cultivating a stony field;" Pyongan-do as "the tiger of the blue mountains;" Hamgyong-do as "the fighting dog in a muddy field."

Direction as Names of Places

Some places derived names from directions that are located from a central point of reference. Such references still in use were originally named during the Yi dynasty from the central point of Seoul. Thus the Honam (South of the Lake) area refers to the southern part of Chungchong Namdo and Cholla Namdo and Cholla Pukto provinces; the Yongnam (South of the Mountains) area to Kyongsang Namdo and Kyongsang Pukto provinces; the Kwandong (The East of the Barrier) to Kangwon-do province; the Kwanbuk (The North of the Barrier) to Hamgyong Namdo and Hamgyong Pukto; the Sobuk (The Northwest) to Pyongan Namdo and Pyongan Pukto, while the central area in and around the capital is referred to as the Kino.

In many cases, north is referred to as the back and the south as the front. Thus a village located in the north from a central point of reference may be called the "back village" and the one in the south the "front village." The practice has stemmed from the prehistoric migration of the Korean race from the north, probably somewhere in Manchuria, to the south where the Korean peninsula lies.

Kinds of Calendars in Use

The solar calendar is the official almanac in Korea but the lunar calendar is more widely used in the rural districts. Furthermore, the traditional holidays are set by the lunar calendar. The solar calendar first appeared in the nineteenth century, whereas the adoption of the lunar calendar goes back to the ancient days of the Three Kingdoms period.

The lunar calendar is based on the revolution of the moon around the earth, one revolution taking about 29.53059 days to form a month. Twelve lunar months constitute a year, a month being 29 or 30 days alternatively. The surplus 0.03059 day of each month add up to one month after 33 months, and therefore one 30-day leap month is added every third year. Since the lunar calendar has 354 days against the 365 days of the solar calendar, producing an 11-day difference each year, it would not conform well with the seasons if the leap month is not added every third year.

Originally devised and developed in China, the lunar calendar has gone through numerous revisions. The version currently used in Korea is based on a work of Hsia Yu of the ancient Chinese kingdom of Hsia.

24 Days of the Season

The lunar calendar, being independent of the solar positions on the earth, does not furnish accurate information on seasonal changes. To remedy the defect, the 24 days in "seasonal turning-points" are established by dividing the celestial latitude of the sun. Thus an element of the solar calendar is incorporated into the lunar calendar, designating two specific days each month to indicate changes of the seasons.

The 24 days of seasons compared with the solar days follow:

The 24 days marking "turning-points" of the seasons are important not only for agriculture but also for observation of various annual events, the days of which are decided by the 24 days of the seasons. This is due to the fact that agriculture has been considered as the backbone of the national economy, and, accordingly, all kinds of traditional holidays and other events center around farming.

Measuring and Telling Time

Prior to the introduction of the Western

XXII MANNERS AND CUSTOMS

The Seasonal Days of the Lunar Calendar

Season	Month	Days of Season		Celestial Latitude of the Sun	Approximate Day by Solar Calendar	Meaning of the Day of Season
Spring	1st	Ipchun	立春	315°	Feb. 3	First day of spring
		Usu	雨水	330°	Feb. 18	Rain begins
	2nd	Kyongchip	驚蟄	345°	Mar. 5	Hibernation ends
		Chunbun	春分	0°	Mar. 20	Mid-spring
	3rd	Chongmyong	青明	15°	Apr. 4	Sky clears
		Kogu	穀雨	30°	Apr. 20	Rains fall, grains grow
Summer	4th	Ipha	立夏	45°	May 5	First day of summer
		Soman	小滿	60°	May 20	Summer grains begin to ripen
	5th	Mangjong	芒種	75°	June 5	Barley harvested, rice seedlings planted
		Haji	夏至	90°	June 21	Mid-summer
	6th	Soso	小暑	105°	July 6	Weather becomes hotter
		Taeso	大暑	120°	July 22	Hottest weather
Autumn	7th	Ipchu	立秋	135°	Aug. 7	First day of autumn
		Choso	處暑	150°	Aug. 22	Hot weather ends
	8th	Paengno	白露	165°	Sep. 7	Dew falls
		Chubun	秋分	180°	Sep. 22	Mid-autumn
	9th	Hanno	寒露	195°	Oct. 7	Cold dew falls
		Sanggang	霜降	210°	Oct. 23	Frost begins to fall
Winter	10th	Iptong	立冬	225°	Nov. 7	First day of winter
		Sosol	小雪	240°	Nov. 22	Snow begins to fall
	11th	Taesol	大雪	255°	Dec. 6	Heavy snow
		Tongji	多至	270°	Dec. 21	Mid-winter
	12th	Sohan	小寒	285°	Jan. 5	Colder weather begins
		Taehan	大寒	300°	Jan. 20	Coldest weather

timepiece and its subsequent diffusion, time was measured by the sundial and the hydroscope For example, in or around 1442, Sejong devised several different versions of an ingenious water clock with automatic mechanism to strike a bell.

In order to inform the public of certain times nowadays, electrically operated sirens installed on high structures are turned on. Presently the sirens wail twice a day at noon and midnight. In the old days, different noises told the time to the public. During the late Yi dynasty and the early 20's a cannon blast atop the Namsan Hill and the giant bell-ringings in the Bell Pavillion in downtown Seoul used to inform the morning, noon evening and midnight hours.

In the rural area, however, accurate time was of little concern to the farmers. The first cuckoo announced the dawn, the sun in clear days and hungry stomach on cloudy days informed the farmers of noon-time, and the setting sun was the mark of the day's end.

Besides the noon siren, the radio announces the time at certain intervals nowadays, and many clocks installed in large public buildings provide accurate time for the public.

Standard Time and Daylight Saving Time

Korean standard time follows the international system, being based on 127°30' east latitude. Korean standard time is, therefore, nine hours and 30 minutes earlier than Greenwich.

Daylight saving time is observed each summer from about July 21st to September 22nd by promulgation of the government to advance the Korean standard time by one hour.

The year

Together with the Christian year, the Tangun year is more extensively used for all official functions. All government records are entered in the Tangun year rather than the Christian. Based on the foundation of prehistoric Korea by the legendary son of heaven, Tangun, the official year, calld the Tangi, precedes the Christian year by 2,333 years. 1960, therefore, is Tangi 4293.

Another way of counting the year is based on the ancient Chinese system, which designates ten Chinese characters or symbols to one generation, in the following order:

Kap 甲, Ul 乙, Pyong 丙, Chong 丁, Mu 戊, Ki 己, Kyong 庚, Sin 辛, Im 壬, Kye 癸,

The twelve months are represented by the following characters:

Cha 子, Chuk 丑, In 寅, Myo 卯, Chin 辰, Sa 巳, O 午, Mi 未, Sin 申, Yu 酉, Sul 戌, Hae 亥.

Each single character or symbol of the above two sets is combined with another to form a cycle of 60:

The above combinations are used not only for counting the years, a person's age, and grades, but also for numerals and pronouns.

1	2	3	4	5	6	7	8	9	10	11	12	13	14	15
甲子	乙丑	丙寅	丁卯	戊辰	己巳	庚午	辛未	壬申	癸酉	甲戌	乙亥	丙子	丁丑	戊寅
16	17	18	19	20	21	22	23	24	25	26	27	28	29	30
己卯	庚辰	辛巳	壬午	癸未	甲申	乙酉	丙戌	丁亥	戊子	己丑	庚寅	辛卯	壬辰	癸巳
31	32	33	34	35	36	37	38	39	40	41	42	43	44	45
甲午	乙未	丙申	丁酉	戊戌	己亥	庚子	辛丑	壬寅	癸卯	甲辰	乙巳	丙午	丁未	戊申
46	47	48	49	50	51	52	53	54	55	56	57	58	59	60
己酉	庚戌	辛亥	壬子	癸丑	甲寅	乙卯	丙辰	丁巳	戊午	己未	庚申	辛酉	壬戌	癸亥

Annual Observances and Holidays

Numerous holidays and events are observed or remembered in Korea throughout the year. Some are centuries-old and others are relatively new. One of the striking differences which separate the old from the new is the calendar used to designate the holidays: it is lunar calendar that decides the traditional holidays, while the holidays of recent origin are based on the solar almanac. We shall take a glimpse at the annual observances in two separate parts—first, the traditional and then, the "modern." True, that most of the centuries old holidays are now only remembered and are rapidly being buried in oblivion, but they are nevertheless a part of Korean heritage.

Traditional Holidays
The First Month

New Year's Day. The first day of the first moon is celebrated at home with rendering of the new year's greeting to "superior" members of the family, while in the court, a service used to be observed to worship "heaven, earth, sun and moon" for good harvests in the new year.

Each member of the family gets up early in the morning, dressing himself in new clothes to observe a memorial service to the souls of the ancestors. After the ceremony, formal greetings are said with deep bows to the "superior" members of the family in the order of the grandparents, parents, uncles and aunts. After the new year's morning meal, young boys of the family make a round of relatives and neighbors for further formal greetings, while elders of the house, in turn, receive the same from boys of other houses. The new year bows to "superior" persons are considered essential. The womenfolk, whom the Confucian ethics had forbidden to leave the house unless unavoidable, sent servants in their places. The bow exchanged between adults is followed with a "virtuous talk" in which hopes are exchanged for begetting a son, securing a promotion, making a fortune, enjoying health and other advancements during the new year. The guests are also entertained with wine, food and fruits.

Considered an essential part of manners, the new year's formal greeting has to be rendered to all "superior" persons by the tenth day of the new year at the latest.

On the night of the New Year's day, peddlers hawk "bamboo ladles," because buying all the ladles a family will need during the year on this night is believed to be lucky. On that night, too, the ghost of "night light" is thought to descend on earth from heaven to try out the shoes of human beings and carry away the pair that fits him. Losing one's shoes to the ghost is such an evil omen that the people hide their shoes inside the house, and bar the approach of the ghost either by putting a golden cord across the gate or by hanging a meshwork in a tree.

Other tablets of exorcism with a picture of a couple of fierce-looking armored generals are pasted on the gate to bar entrance into the house of other gods of plague. In the old days, the Painting Office of the court dedicated such tablets to the king. The gate of the house may be further crowded with another picture of three falcons, which is believed to be effective against possible misfortune in the year of the person facing an unlucky new year: one is believed to be in such fix if the "animal" symbolizing his birth year is in hopeless conflict with the "animal" of the new year.

The 13th day of the first month. Men of small stature are forbidden to visit others on this day. Should the unwritten law be violated, farm products for the year will not grow any larger than the height of the unwelcome guest.

The 14th day of the first month. A long pole is erected in the yard, in the hope that the fall crops may be piled up there as high as the pole. This "wishing pole" is later removed on the first day of the second month by the farmer shouting make-believe counting of a bumper crop like ten thousand *sok* of rice, thousand *sok* of barley, another thousand *sok* of wheat, etc. It is believed his counting will be repeated word for word in the fall when the actual harvest is piled up at the place.

Another charm exercised on this "wishing day" is to steal a handful of clay from the site of a well-to-do family or on a highway and then scatter the clay about the four corners of one's own house. This magic formula will lure good luck into the house from the wealthy house and the persons walking along the highway.

On this day, each house cooks a large quantity of "sticky rice" to share with others. One who manages to get the cooked rice from three houses of different surnames on this day will be lucky throughout the year.

Willingly given as the cooked rice is on this particular day, not a drop of drinking water is available for a thirsty stranger, because doing so brings rain on the "wedding day," thus crumbling the foot-path of the rice-paddy.

The 15th day of the month. As one of the important holidays marking the end of the new year, various programs are observed.

Early in the morning, every member of the family, including the womenfolk and children, is treated with "ear-opening wine" which is supposed to improve the drinker's auditory preception. Also "medicine rice" is prepared mixing rice with various fruits and sweets. At breakfast, one puts in his mouth as many pieces of raw rice and hard nuts as the number of years to his age, so that he may be free from tumor during the rest of the year. One may prevent a sunstroke in the coming summer if he succeeds in "selling the heat" to somebody on this day. One's share of the sunstroke may be "sold" by calling someone by his name and then shouting "you get the heat first" to the unsuspecting victim who responds to the name-calling. This preventive measure against sunstroke, however, is not without possible danger, because if the person whose name was called is alert enough to detect what's in store for him, he immediately retaliates with "you get the heat first", thereby making the name-caller "buy" instead of "sell" the sunstroke.

After supper, the people go up a nearby hill to "greet" the first full moon of the year. Whoever sees the moon first is considered the most lucky, but others may also say their wishes to the moon. The prayer to the first full moon is rewarded with an excellent fall harvest to the farmer, a healthy son to childless parents, a handsome youth to the lonely virgin, and a beautiful bride to the bachelor boy. Predication of the year's crops is also told by the color of the moon.

Young men of the village set the field ablaze on the nights of the 14 and 15th days. Occasionally a gang fight develops between youth groups of two villages, hurling rocks and stones against each other. The outcome of the fight decides the year's harvest for the villages.

Many people cross a bridge in the evening in the belief that stepping on a bridge on this night exorcises evil gods and invigorates one's legs. (The words for bridge and leg are identical in Korean).

The First Day of Spring. One day in the month of the first moon falls on the First Day of Spring. On this day, some phrases of good fortune written on a few strips of paper are pasted on the gate to effect the words. In the farmhouse, fortune-telling is practiced with barley stalks.

Folk religious rites observed in the first month. A Shaman rite is performed on certain select "lucky" days during the month of the first moon. The guardian gods of the village are worshipped by Shamans on behalf of all members of the village and gods' powers are invoked for prosperity as well as protection from various gods of plagues.

During the new year's season, a group of cheerful youths of the village organize themselves into a "farm dance" unit to go around each house, chanting exorcisms against evil spirits.

Shaman gods are worshipped and prayers said by individuals some time during the month, so that one may be rewarded with good fortune during the year.

Entertainment and fortune-telling in the first month. A popular "parlor game" enjoyed during new year's season is *yut*. The *yut* game played indoors by the womenfolks uses a set of several split red beans, the number of red and white sides of the bean serving as the dots on the dice. The contestants are divided into two or more groups and advance their "piece" to the goal, according to the "number" appearing at each "throw" of the sticks or the split red beans.

Young boys fly kites and girls play sea-saw, while adults enjoy a tug-of-war. Some localities have unique entertainment programs of their own, such as the lion's dance in the north and northwest.

Most homes have their fortunes of the year told during the new year's season.

The Second Month

The first day of the second month. The day is designated for a thorough house-cleaning, and then the Chinese characters, meaning "the hairy caterpillars hurry 1,000 miles away" is written on a long strip of paper to be posted on a pillar of the house as a charm to keep off the pests. Another magic formula to clear the house of pests is to place a green pine bough on the roof or in the yard.

In the southern district, the goddess of wind is worshipped with a simple rite and offering. Coming down to earth on this day, the goddess of Yongdung Matron, it is believed, stays 20 days until she returns to heaven. A reverent association with the goddess of wind is supposed to be rewarded with protection of one's crops and sea-voyages from storms.

This day is also kind of a "labor day holiday" for the hired farmhands, who are entertained with as many rice cakes as each peasant's age at a feast prepared by the landlord.

In Cholla Namdo province, a "circumcision ceremony" takes place in the form of sharing wine with neighbors.

The 9th day of the second month. Being Arbor Day for the farmers, any tree planted on this day is expected to grow tall.

The Kyonchip day. Falling on about March 5th, the "fever" of spring awakens all animals from their hibernation on this day. Fences and walls of the house are repaired, and doing the wallpaper over on this day is regarded the best charm against bedbugs in the house.

The Lantern Festival. Some evening during the month of the second moon, a service to a god is observed by the people, each holding a lantern.

Divinations during the second month. Simple astrology is practised on the sixth night of the month with the "three stars" in the Orion constellation to predict the year's harvest. If the three stars overtake the moon, it is judged the sign of a lean crop, and vice versa, a fair harvest is predicted if the race between the moon and three stars ends in a "draw."

On the day of the Kyongchip (awakening from hibernation), the year's harvest is predicted with the growth of malt. The fall crop of the year is subjected to a further divination on the 20th day—rain means a bumper crop, fine weather ruins the crop, and a cloudy sky brings a fair harvest in the fall.

The Third Month

The third day of the third month. Being a day of hopeful spring, the sparrows return to their old nests from "south of the river" on this day. Each house prepares the "azalea flower cake" and the "flower noodle." Students of the Confucian school go hiking over the hills while the womenfolk wash their hair with "pure water." Being also a day of prayer for begetting a child, many people worship the god by erecting an altar in front of a "sacred" old tree, giant rock or mountain. If one sees a white butterfly, he must wear mourning clothes sometimes in that year, but a yellow or multicolored butterfly on this day is considered a good omen.

The Day of Cold Feast. Falling on the 105th day after the "central day of winter," everybody eats cold food and rooms remain unheated throughout the day. A memorial service is observed for the ancestors' souls, and then all the offsprings clean the ancestors' burial ground. The practice of eating cold food on this day is based originally on an ancient Chinese legend.

If the day of Cold Feast follows thunder, it is considered an extremely evil omen, foretelling lean crops for the five principal grains or some impending national disaster in the year.

The day of "Rain on Grains." This last day of spring is called the "rain on grain" because the rain is supposed to fall on "the hundred" grains on this day. The work on the rice-bed starts, and chewing a walnut bough on this day is supposed to cure diseases of the skin and stomach.

Entertainment in the third month. The

month of spring is greeted with hiking over the fields and mountains by a group of villagers. Young boys go out into the hills to pick azalea flowers, which are made into a "flower hammer," while maidens of the village make a doll with green grass and dress it up in a red skirt. Young boys also like to make "flutes" from willow boughs. The meeting for paying reverence to the aged is also often held in this month.

The Fourth Month

The eighth day of the fourth month. Being the birthday of Buddha, the old customs call for a "lantern festival". The believer is required to hang out as many lanterns as the number of members in his family, the shapes of the lanterns assuming such various forms as the lotus flower, the Dipper Stars, "ball boat," drum, etc. In the old days, the curfew was lifted for the night, allowing many people to go out into the street to enjoy the millions of lanterns illuminating the city. Later, however, the "lantern festival" was confined to Buddhist circles.

The Fifth Month

The Tano on the fifth day of the fifth month. Being one of the four biggest holidays together with the New Year's day, the Day of Cold Feast, and the "Thanksgiving," the Tano holiday is celebrated with various programs. At home, a feast is prepared, and the family visits the ancestors' burial ground to observe a memorial service. Origin of this holiday is presumed to be the rites observed to the "heavenly gods" by the ancient people after the spring seed-planting.

Both the men and women like to wash their hair with iris water on this day as good luck charm. Plucking the *pinyo* (a hair stick) made of iris stalk on this day is also considered a good luck charm for women. Even at present, peddlers of iris stalks crowd the street on the eve of this holiday.

Wild camomile has to be gathered on this day if the wild plant is to be used for medicinal purposes. Red tablets are posted on the entrance gate of each house on this day to exorcise the gods of plague—a practice originally introduced from China.

The jujube trees are "married off" on this day by placing a pebble between two branches of the tree, so that the tree will be more fruitful. An effective charm to overload other trees with fruits is trimming the tree on this particular day. It also used to be the day when fans were prepared for the warm summer season soon to come. In the old days, the Ministry of Industry would dedicate fans to the king and high officials of the court. Decorated with pictures of flowers, birds or scenery, the shape and type of the official's fan indicated the bearer's rank.

Entertainments in the fifth month. The most spectacular scene adorning the Tano holiday has been the maiden swinging high and low against the clear, blue sky. Be it in a town or in a village, the swing has been one of the most picturesque holiday scenes of Korea. Originally an entertainment for the womenfolk, the swing has come to be enjoyed by men also. A swing contest is held more often than not on the Tano holiday, offering prizes of chests, bureaus, mirrors and other household goods to the women who can swing the highest and kick the suspended bell.

While the womenfolks are exhibiting their skills at swinging, the men demonstrate their physical prowess in wrestling matches, in which a giant cow is traditionally offered the winner as first prize. The wrestling bouts, dating back to the ancient days, are still popular on and around the Tano holiday.

The Rain of Taejong. The rainfall on the 10th day of the fifth month is called the "Rain of Taejong" after the third king of the Yi dynasty whose fervent prayer for rain regardless of his own illness alleviated one of the worst droughts. It was later said that rain fell on every 10th day of the fifth month since the incident. The rain on this particular day, therefore, was considered a good omen for an excellent harvest in the fall.

The Sixth Month

The 15th day of the sixth month. Everybody takes a bath on this day of *yudu* (flowing head) as a prevention against sunstroke during the summer. This custom dates back to the Silla period, and the "Collected Works of Kim Kukchi" contains a reference to such a practice observed in the ancient kingdom during the early period.

In the farm house, services are performed to the god of agriculture and the souls of ancestors with an offering of fresh fruits of the season. A noodle dinner is served, and the noodle cake dyed in five colors are hung at the gate as a charm against gods of plague.

The Three Mid-Summer Days. The peak of the warmest season of the year falls on the Three Mid-Summer Days: the Early Mid-Summer Day, the Central Mid-Summer Day, and the Late Mid-Summer Day, ten days apart. The days are chosen for hiking and a favorite feast on the hottest days is the dog's meat soup, which is regarded as a specially effective tonic against physical weakness during the hottest season of the year.

Collective Work on the Farm. During the busiest season on the farm, collective work by all hands of a village is performed, each taking his turn. A group of farmers flying the "farm colors" and playing "farm dance music" accompany the workers who are treated with wine. Profit earned through the collective work is usually used for community welfare, such as purchasing musical instruments for the "farm dance," building a bridge, observing a Shaman rite, assisting the village high school and other projects.

The Seventh Month

The seventh evening of the seventh month. An ancient legend has it that the prince in the star Altain and the princess in the star Vega are allowed by destiny to meet only once a year on this night. To build a bridge over the Milky Way which separates the two lovers confined in the two stars, all crows and magpies are said to disappear into the sky in the evening. The evening is supposed to be wet with rainfall, which is interpreted as the two imaginary young lovers' tears of rejoicing and sorrow for the brief meeting after the year's separation. The virgins say their wishes to the two stars on the evening before dark so that a princely husband may descend upon her. She may also excel in the art of weaving as a result of the prayer.

Chungwon Day. The 15th day of the seventh month was originally a Buddhist holiday to observe a Buddhist service. Later during the Yi dynasty, the Chungwon Day was evolved into a servants' holiday. Masters of the house treat the servants with a feast and the servants sing and otherwise enjoy themselves. A memorial service with offerings to the ancestors is also observed in the evening.

The Eighth Month

The first Chong Day of the eighth month. Students of the Confucian school render a Confucian memorial service at each school.

The Chusok on the 15th day of the eighth month. Called Chusok, the day of "Thanksgiving" is celebrated as one of the four biggest holidays. At each home, rice cakes, wine and a general feast is prepared from the newly harvested crops, and all members of the family visit the ancestor's graves to offer "Thanksgiving". As entertainment for the holiday, the young girls dress up in bright clothes to play see-saw, while the boys take part in wrestling matches. Other games of the day are the "cow game" in Hwanghae-do province, the "tortoise game" in Kyonggi-do province, the tug-of-war on Cheju-do island, and the *kankkang suwollae*, a maidens' dance, in the southern district. Textile weaving contests used to be featured also during the Silla and Koryo periods.

The day of Meeting "in the Half Way". One day in the "Thanksgiving" holiday season, the womenfolk are allowed to pay a visit to their loved ones—not at home but on the road: both parties concerned meet on the road somewhere between the two houses, and share a feast each has brought to entertain the other party. Called the "half meeting," the custom was devised to relieve the rigid Confucian code of conduct which placed severe restriction on the womenfolk.

The Ninth Month

The ninth day of the ninth month. "Flower cakes" are prepared at each home, while the farmhouse which could not offer to the ancestors' souls new fall crops on "Thanksgiving" on the 15th day of the eighth month because of belated harvest observes the service.

The day used to be chosen by the Confucian scholars for hiking far into the fields and mountains to enjoy the deepening autumn. The sparrows are said to fly back on this day "south of the river."

The Tenth Month

A Thanksgiving Service to Heaven. The work on the farm practically over after the harvest, the farmers of the old days used to set aside one day in the tenth month to observe a "Thanksgiving" service to "heaven".

The 20th day of the tenth month. All boats stay at harbor for fear of the possible storm of Sondol, the sailor. According to a legend, the sailor was killed on this day by command of a king who suspected him of treason while royalty was aboard. The malignant soul of the innocent victim is said to cause a storm on the day.

"HORSE DAY". One day in the tenth month is set aside for service to the god of horse at the stable with an offering of redbean cake.

The Shaman Sungju (Master of the Castle or House) Festival. A Shaman rite is observed in the tenth month for the "Master God of the Castle or House," which is believed to be the ruler of all household gods.

Village Thanksgiving Festival. Some "lucky" day in the tenth month is selected to perform a community service to various gods by all members of the village. Feasts are prepared with new harvests and grateful prayers are said to all gods who helped with the farming.

Service to Early Ancestors. On or around the 14th and 15th day of the tenth month, all offsprings gather together to perform a memorial service to ancestors more than four generations distant. Since the services to the ancestors on other holidays are dedicated to the ancestors of the recent four generations, this is a worship of early ancestors attended by all members of a clan.

Preparation of Winter Vegetables. All womenfolk of the house busy themselves with the *kimjang* for several days in the tenth month to prepare the important winter food. A wagon load of Chinese cabbages and radishes are soaked in salt water with seasoning of red and black pepper, pickles and fruits to be stored in giant jars so that the supplies of vegetables may last through the winter. Preparation of the *kimjang* is one of the most important duties of all Korean housewives.

The Eleventh Month

The Mid-Winter Day. Falling on or about December 22, the Mid-Winter Day traditionally calls for preparation of the "green bean gruel." The gruel is first placed in such a place as the house, yard, barn or the "house shrine," and then shared by all members of the house. Some of the gruel is pasted on the gate or wall as a charm against the gods of plague.

In the old days, the Office of Meteorological Observation in the court would dedicate the forthcoming new year's almanac to the king and other high-ranking officials of the court, while the Royal Household Hospital used to submit to the king a medical cake—a concoction of several herbs with molasses and a cow's leg.

The Twelfth Month

The "Naphyang". The third "sheep's day" after the Mid-Winter Day is called the "Naphyang," and the traditional "rice jelly" is made on the day. Bird-catching is very popular also, because birds eaten on this particular day are supposed to have special tonic effects to prevent small-pox. Snow falling on this day is also believed to turn itself into "medicinal water," which is often preserved in a bottle later to be used for making various pills.

The Last Day of the Year. The womenfolk of each house hurry down to the well at dawn for the "lucky water" because the first to scoop up water on this day is considered to have the best luck. Being the last day of the year, custom dictates settlement of all outstanding accounts of debts and credits by midnight. Failture to clear one's debts by the deadline was considered a grave loss of "face."

In the old days, the people used to pay a visit to their "superiors" to express appreciation for favors rendered during the year, and graves of the ancestors were also visited for the same purpose.

The last night of the year has to be spent with eyes wide open in the house which is illuminated all night long. The children are often teased to the effect that if they fall asleep on this night, their eyebrows will turn white.

Blasts of a cannon or gongs announce the last moment of the year, while the womenfolk are busy in the kitchen preparing the new year's feast which calls for white ricecake and pheasant soup. In recent years, chicken has replaced pheasant.

In the court, on the other hand, a mask dance was performed by about 100 court musicians and dancers as a ritual to exorcise evil gods—a practice originally imported from China.

Leap Month

The extra leap month of the lunar calendar is considered free from any "unlucky day" and therefore various events which are likely to be vexed by gods of plagues are performed during the "safe" leap month. Preparation of wedding costumes and mourning clothes for old persons are often made during the month. Prayer services to Buddha performed in the month are also considered effective.

National Holidays of Recent Origin

Many national holidays have been added to the traditional holidays since the Liberation from Japan in 1945. All the holidays of such recent origin are observed by the solar calendar in contrast to the lunar calendar which designates the traditional celebrations.

The New Year. The New Year of the solar calendar is the official new year, although most people still prefer to observe the lunar version. There has been a movement by the government to change the people's customs of celebrating the lunar new year for the solar new year in order to eliminate the observance of "double new years."

The Samil Day of March the First. Various patriotic programs are observed on March 1, in memory of the nationwide independence movement carried out on this day in 1919 against Japanese domination. In response to U.S. President Woodrow Wilson's suggestion for the "priniple of self-determination by small nations" in the wake of World War I, the entire Korean people under the leadership of 33 representatives demanded immediate independence for Korea. Demonstrations in all cities and towns throughout the country followed, and many patriots were arrested by the Japanese police. The uprising lasting more than a week was quelled with bullets and bayonets of the Japanese police, but its repercussions were considerable. After the Liberation in 1945, the day has been observed with a ceremony at schools and government offices usually to be followed by a parade along the street.

Arbor Day on April 4th. The Government has established Arbor Day as a measure to restore the country's denuded forests. Students and government workers usually go out to a nearby hill or field to plant seedlings.

Anniversary of the Korean War on June 25th. The outbreak of the Korean War on this day in 1950 is remembered with various patriotic programs such as military parades, public lectures, and anti-Communist exhibitions.

Constitution Day on July 17th. This day has been declared an official holiday to celebrate the declaration on the day in 1948 of the Republic of Korea Constitution. The Constitution was prepared by 198 representatives of the people who had been elected at the first general elections held under U.N. observation on May 1, 1948. The event is celebrated with a ceremony performed at schools and government offices.

Liberation Day on August 15th. This anniversary celebrates both the Liberation from Japan in 1945 and also the establishment of the Republic of Korea government in 1948. Various nationalistic programs including a military parade are usual features of the day.

National Foundation Day on October 3rd. Birth of the founder of ancient Korea, Tangun, in 2333 B.C. is remembered on this official holiday.

Hangul Day on October 9th. Various events to commemorate founding of the Korean alphabet, *Hangul*, are observed on the day when the Fourth King Sejong of the Yi dynasty published in 1446 the book, "Correct Pronunciation Manual for the People," thereby making a practical Korean alphabet available to the general public.

U.N. Day on October 4th. The day when the U.N. Charter was declared in 1945 is observed as an official holiday with ceremonies at schools and government offices.

Students' Day on November 3rd. The students' resistance movement against Japanese domination which erupted on this day in 1929 is celebrated with a parade of students to recreate the intense patriotism of the Korean students during the Japanese domination period. Known as the Kwangju City Students' Incident, Korean high school students of that city staged a demonstration in open defiance of Japanese rule after a gang fight with a group of Japanese high school students. The resistance movement soon spread to all other students throughout the country and many Korean students were imprisoned by the Japanese police.

Even though it is not an official holiday, the incident is recalled by present-day students who participate in various programs of commemoration.

Christmas. Christmas has come to assume increasing importance since the end of World War II, and has established itself as one the most important holidays, at least in the urban districts. So popular has Christmas become that most city dwellers now celebrate it regardless of their religious affiliation. Shopping centers are crowded with the Christmas rush and Christmas decorations have become an inevitable part of street scenes during the Yuletide season.

Myths, Legends and Folktales

Introduction

Korean mythology concerns itself primarily with creations of prehistoric kingdoms as well as founders of the earliest kingdoms. Recorded mostly in two early books of history, *Samguk Saki* (Annals of the Three Kingdoms) and *Samguk Yusa* (Reminiscences of the Three Kingdoms), the myths have survived until today, furnishing many clues to symbolic interpretations of prehistoric days.

Korean mythology touches but lightly on the creation of the universe and other phenomena of nature, Instead, elaborate explanations are given for the births of founder kings of prehistoric kingdoms in the land. Oviparous origins are most predominant, but some of the divine births are attributed to marriages between man and animal.

Whereas mythology is an attempt to present historical explanations for prehistoric events, legends are intended to supplement authentic history. The majority of the legends concern landmarks of certain places, such as a giant rock, tree or a famous well or spring, which are interwoven with "human interest" stories.

Folktales differ from myths and legends in that they are mostly "tall tales" with no attempt to ally themselves with history. Unlike the other two, folktales usually do not specify the time and place of events described. The usual beginning, therefore, is "long, long ago...", or "once upon a time when tigers smoked... there lived somewhere..." In contrast to such vague presentation of a story, myths and legends name specific places, years and names of persons involved in attempts to make the story authentic.

Invariably closing with a happy ending, the folktales are a didactic literature, eventually rewarding good and punishing evil.

Here are some myths, legends and folktales which we believe are representative.

Myths

The Sun, Moon and Stars

Once upon a time, there lived a mother with four children. One day, when the mother was coming back from the market, she came across a tiger on a mountain road. The hungry tiger wanted to have her for dinner. She pleaded that she would gladly die after she saw her children for the last time. Her appeal was in vain. The tiger was not satisfied with the mother, but wanted to devour her four children as well. The tiger came down to her house in the dress of the murdered mother. The tiger knocked on the door, calling, "Haesun, Talsun and Pyolsun, mother has come back. Open the door."

Recognizing that the voice was different from that of their mother, they said, "Your voice is not our mother's. If you are really our mother, please show us your hands."

When the tiger pushed a hand through a hole of the door, the children cried, "Why is your hand so yellow?" The tiger replied, "I painted the walls of elder sister's house with yellow mud." The children wanted to see the tiger's feet. When the tiger pushed in a foot, the children cried, "Why is it that your foot in so black?" The tiger answered that he had been beaten in the feet at elder sister's house.

The disguised mother then asked the children to put out the youngest baby so that "she" might feed him with her breast milk. The tiger took the baby to the kitchen. Then the children heard something, and when they peeped through a hole in the door, they found that it was the tiger eating the baby. Frightened, they went out through the back door and climbed up a pine tree.

Having finished eating, the tiger looked for the rest of the children. When the tiger looked in the well, he saw a reflection of the children on the pine tree. He went up to the wall and asked, "How did you climb the tree?" The eldest child said, "We fetched some sesame oil from the neighbor's and painted in on the trunk. That's how."

The tiger fetched some sesame oil and painted it on the tree but it was so slippery that he could not climb. Then the tiger asked again, "Children, how did you get up there?" The youngest one said, "We borrowed a hatchet from the neighboring house and cut steps on the trunk. That's how." The tiger did the same thing and climbed up almost next to the children.

The children were so frightened that they prayed to God for their lives. "If You wish to save us three children," they pleaded, "please send down an iron rope, or a rotten straw rope if you want to get us killed." God heard them and sent an iron rope by which they climbed up to heaven.

The tiger asked the children how they got to heaven. The children replied that they had done so by asking for a rotten straw rope. The tiger made the request. When he was high up in the sky, the rope broke off and he fell down on a field of Indian millet.

The red color on the stalk of the Indian millet is said to be the mark of the tiger's blood when he had bled to death. In the sky, Haesun became the sun, Talsun the moon, and Pyolsun the stars.

The Solar and Lunar Eclipses

The universe was supposed to be composed of three worlds: the earth where man lives, the world of heaven and the world within the earth. If one went down into the earth several hundred feet, one could hear dogs bark and cocks crow.

In heaven, it was believed, there are many countries. One is the dark country where there are many fierce dogs fed on fire. Therefore, they are called fire dogs. The king of the dark country hates darkness and longs for brightness. Therefore, from time to time, he sends his fire dogs to steal the sun or the moon.

One day, the king sent one of his fire dogs to steal the sun. Although the dog clutched the sun in his mouth, it proved so hot that the dog vomited it out. He tried many times all in vain. Although the king rebuked the dog, it could not be helped.

Thereupon, the king sent his dog to steal the moon, which was supposed to be less hot. The dog clutched the moon in his mouth, but it proved too cold to hold. He tried many times but all in vain.

Even after that, the king did not stop trying to steal the sun and the moon, and yet every time the dogs failed. However, the parts of the sun or the moon bitten by the dogs did not shine. That was believed to be the cause of the solar and lunar eclipses.

Creation of the Earth

Once upon a time, there was a girl whom the king of one of the heaven countries loved very tenderly. One day she lost her ring which she valued very highly. The king had his people hunt for it all over the kingdom. It was not found anywhere in the realm. Thinking that it may have fallen down to earth, he sent a giant down. At that time the earth had not yet been formed into mountains, rivers, seas and fields but was all mud. The giant searched for the ring in the mud. The parts of the mud which he raised dried up into mountains, the parts excavated became seas, the parts which he scratched with his fingers became rivers and the parts he smoothed became plains.

How Earthquakes Began to Visit the Earth

Once, in the early days of the universe, the sky was sloping downward at one end. A pillar was made of bronze to prop it up. The sky was so heavy that the pillar sank into the earth. God ordered one of his strongest giants to hold the pillar on his shoulder. Even for this giant, the burden was too much. Therefore, he changed his position from time to time, first holding the pillar on one shoulder, then on the other. This, they believed, was the cause of earthquakes.

What Caused the Tide

A dragon once lived deep in the sea. There was a big cave at the bottom. When the dragon went into the cave, he caused the ebb and when it came out to the sea he caused the tide. The waves of the sea were also caused by the movement of the dragon.

The Origin of Humans

In the early days of the world, there were no human beings save for a brother and sister. Since they were related by blood, they thought they could not sleep together. They knew, however, that other people had to succeed them.

One day, the brother and his sister each took a grinding stone up a hill. The brother rolled the grinding stone east and the sister west. Coming down the hill, they saw that the stones ended up together, one upon the other. They believed that this was the will of heaven and married to give birth to many children who thereafter multiplied generation after generation.

Tangun

Tangun is the first king of this land, founder of Korea.

In the early days of Korea, there lived a bear and a tiger in the same cave. They prayed to God to transform them into human beings. God gave a handful of mugwort and twenty garlics, telling them to eat them and offer prayer for one hundred days. The bear performed God's order faithfully and became a woman in thirty-seven days but the tiger remained what he was for failing to observe God's command.

Since the woman had no man to marry, she prayed under a mahogany tree to get conceived. God took pity on her and conceived her a son. The son was Tangun. Tangun made Pyongyang his capital and called his land Chosun. He is said to have lived 1,408 years.

Haemosu

In the early years of the world, God came down to the earth in a chariot drawn by five dragons and founded a kingdom. He gave the kingdom an earthly name, Haemosu. His son was named Puru and named his kingdom Puk-Puyo.

Kumwa Wang
(King Golden Frog)

King Puru had no offspring. He prayed to God for a male child. One day he was riding on horseback to a place called Konyun. On the way, he found a stone weeping. Surprised, he ordered his retinue to move the stone. Under it, he found a gold-colored frog which looked like a baby. Believing that it had been sent from heaven, he took the frog home and raised it. The creature turned out to be a boy and was named Golden Frog. In due time, he was made Golden Frog prince-heir. After the departure of the king, the heir succeeded to the throne as Kumwa Wang (King Golden Frog).

Chumong

One day, King Golden Frog found a daughter of Habaek named Yuhwa. While playing outdoors with other children, she was abducted by a man, who called himself King Haemosu, to Mount Ungsin on the bank of the Yalu River. There she was confined to a room. Hearing about this, King Golden Frog brought her back and imprisoned her in a room. She shunned the sunshine but a sunbeam reached her and she became pregnant. In due course of time, she gave birth not to a child but a big egg. The king considered the egg a bad omen. He gave it to a pig but the pig would not eat it nor would a dog. When it was thrown away at the roadside, horses and cows did not step upon it. When it was thrown away among mountains and fields, wild birds and beasts did not harm it; instead they offered protection.

The king tried to break the egg but it would not break. At last, the king returned it to Yuhwa. A male baby then emerged. The baby was very strong and beautiful. At the age of seven, he was a fully grown-up boy. He made bows and arrows for himself and became a good archer. According to the custom of that land, one who was good at archery was called Chumong, so the boy came to bear that name.

King Kumwa had seven sons and none could match Chumong in any game. Jealous, the oldest son asked his father to kill Chumong but the king refused. When Yuhwa learned about this, she advised Chumong to flee the land. With three followers he fled to a riverside. When some of the king's men ran after to arrest him, Chumong appealed to Heaven, thus, "I am a descendent of the God, Paekha. They are following to kill me. God save my life." Fishes and turtle came up to the surface of the water and made themselves a bridge across the river. This enabled him to cross the river and leave his pursuers behind, for as soon as he had made the crossing, the fishes and turtles disappeared into the water. Chumong and his followers reached a land called Cholbonju and founded a country called Koguryo.

Pak Hyokkose

In ancient days, there was a small country named Chinhan in the southern tip of the peninsula, which was made up of six villages. On March 1 each year, the chiefs of of the six villages gathered on the bank of the river Alchon along with their children. On one such occasion, they discussed the selection of a king from among the men of virtue in their ranks, for without one, the country was apt to be unruly and discordant. When they climbed up a comparatively high hill, they saw a curious light shining by the well of Kwachung at the foot of Mount Yang and a white horse bowing to something.

When they reached the spot, the horse flew up to the sky, neighing aloud. The people found a red egg there. When they broke the egg a beautiful boy emerged. Surprised, they took the boy to the River Tongchon and washed him. He was shiny; birds and beasts came and danced around him, the earth shook and the sun and moon became brighter. So they named him Hyokkose which meant brightness in the country. Hyokkose became the first king of Silla. His queen was called Alyong for she came out of the cock-dragon which appeared near the well by that name. In her mouth was the dragon's cock beak, but when they washed her in the River Pak, the beak disappeared. Alyong was as beautiful as she was virtuous.

Yunorang and Seonyo

Once upon a time, there lived a couple on an island east of the Silla kingdom. One day, the husband went out to the sea when there suddenly appeared a rock which carried him away to Japan. Since he looked like a great man, they made him king there.

His wife, Seonyo, waited for her husband to return. At last, she went to the seashore and there found the shoes left by her husband. When she went up to a rock, this rock began to move and carried her to Japan. Thinking this strange, those who saw it there reported the matter to the king. Thus man and wife met again. On the other hand, the sun and the moon began to lose brightness in the Silla kingdom. The courtiers told the Silla king that it was because of the fact that Yunorang and Seonyo had gone over to Japan. They, therefore, decided to send some people to bring back the couple. Yunorang refused to come back, saying, "That I have come to Japan was the will of God." Instead, he told the messenger that if they offered a prayer to God with the silk woven by Seonyo, God would be appeased.

When the Silla people did as they were told by Yunorang, the moon and the sun began to shine as before. In fact, Yunorang and Seonyo were incarnations of the sun and the moon.

Kyerim Woods

In the early days of the Silla dynasty, the king was passing by a thick forest. He saw a light shining among the trees. When they reached the spot, they saw golden clouds overhead and a golden box hanging from the branches of a big tree. Beneath the box, a golden cock was crowing. When the king opened the box, he found a male baby within. When the king took the baby to the palace, birds and beasts followed him. The king made the baby prince-heir. He was named Kim Alchi, Kim meaning gold and Alchi child. After this event, they began to call the woods Kyerim, literally meaning cock's forest. Sometimes Korea is called Kyerimguk, the Land of Cock's Woods.

Samsong Cave

In the early days of Korea there lived no men, birds or beasts on Cheju. The whole island was covered with forests only. One day, three men suddenly emerged from a big cave. Their first concern was to find food for themselves. They named themselves Ko Ulna, Pu Ulna and Yang Ulna respectively. The cave was their home.

One day, when they were fishing in the

sea, they saw something strange come floating by. When they approached it, they found that it was a chest. Opening the chest, they saw a venerable old man sitting within. The old man, in turn, opened a stone chest out of which emerged all sorts of animals. Out of a second stone chest came five sorts of grains, and still out of a third, three beautiful girls. The old man said, "I am from Japan. Since you have no wives, I have brought three girls. They are princesses. Make them your wives and rule this land well." So saying, he disappeared among the clouds.

The three Ulna made happy homes with plenty of grains and birds and beasts. The inhabitants of Cheju are said to be their descendents.

Legends

The Pink Plum Children

Once upon a time, there lived in the city of Taegu an 18-year-old virgin by the name of Pink Plum together with her only brother. One moonlit night, the brother heard what sounded like a man snoring in his sister's bed chamber. When he went closer to the room, he saw a glimpse of a fleeing man's shadow reflected on the window. Next day, the outraged brother accused his sister of depravity so severely that the virgin proved her innocence by hanging herself. When night came, the brother again heard a man snoring in his deceased sister's room. Upon his approach, what looked like a man's shadow again flashed past him over the window. Closer examination, however, revealed that it was a willow tree in the yard blown by the wind which emitted the sound and reflected itself on the window. The brother was plagued by his conscience for his hasty accusation of his innocent sister so much that he too committed suicide. Taking pity on the unfortunate sister and brother, the neighbors chanted a song of lament. The nursery rhyme-like song spread, and is sung in chorus nowadays by girls of the Kyongsang-do provinces on moonlit nights.

Choe, the Matron

Near the village of Kupo in Kyongsang Namdo, the guardian spirit of the Matron Choe has been worshipped by villagers. During her life-time the Matron Choe was the most renowned Shaman for her supernatural powers. Once she came across a band of robbers on a lonely mountain road, but her spell transfixed the robbers, who could not lift their feet from the ground, try as they might. Nothing but heartfelt entreaties for forgiveness could break the spell. She had exercised her magic charm not only for her own safety but also for the benefit of others. After the Shaman's death, the grateful villagers erected a shrine in her honor. The guardian god has ever since been worshipped with a rite observed once a year.

The Bridge of Filial Piety and Impiety

Remains of a stone bridge are seen along a brook which flows by a village near the ancient capital city of the Silla kingdom, Kyongju. The name of the stone bridge, "Filial Piety and Impiety," involves a widow who lived in a nearby village with seven sons.

Realizing their mother's lonely heart, the sons of the widow asked their teacher of the village school for a solution. Through the teacher's arrangement the widow married a widower who lived in the village across a brook. Seeing their mother wade across the brook every evening to go to her second husband's home, the sons built a stone bridge over the brook to relieve her of inconvenience. It dawned on them, however, that the bridge was not only a symbol of their filial piety to their mother but of impiety to their deceased father as well, so they began referring to the bridge as the "Bridge of Filial Piety and Impiety." Hearing this, the mother finally decided to remain a widow to dedicate herself to the memory of her deceased husband.

Scholar Pak's Waterfall

A large waterfall near the city of Kaesong is said to be named after a scholar by the name of Pak. One day, the scholar went on an excursion to the waterfall and was so much impressed by its beauty that he chanted a song. The beautiful singing soon charmed the dragon who lived in the waterfall. Transforming itself into a beautiful woman, the dragon presented herself to the scholar Pak, and lured him into her abode at the bottom of the waterfall.

The mother of Scholar Pak, heartbroken with longing for her only son, plunged into the waterfall. Thus the waterfall came to be known as "Scholar Pak's Waterfall."

The Tomb of a Faithful Dog

A tomb of a dog standing in Sonsan County of Kyongsang Pukto province is a reminder of the story of a dog which saved its master's life.

About 100 years ago, a farmer in the village was so intoxicated with wine at the market place that on his way back he fell asleep in a field. A forest fire happened to engulf the place where he lay. The dog which accompanied the farmer tried to awaken his master from slumber by barking and tugging but all in vain. When the fire approached, the dog ran to a nearby brook to wet himself with water and sprinkle it near the place where his master slept. The process was repeated innumerable times until the fire was put out, but the dog himself was so exhausted and so badly burned that he died. Awakening from his slumber, the farmer realized what had happened during his sleep. On the spot where the dog fell, the farmer erected a tomb after a grand funeral service for the faithful animal.

The Buddha's Statue at Unjin

The Buddha's statue at the village of Unjin, Nonsan County, Chungchong Namdo province, is famous for its giant size—the largest in the Orient—74 feet high, 30 feet wide, with a crown seven feet tall. A legend has it that about 1,000 years ago during the reign of the fourth king, Kwangjong, of the Koryo kingdom, a woman went to a nearby hill to gather firewood. Attracted by a strange sound, she went to a place where a giant rock sprang out of the earth. The incident was reported to the court, and the king himself heard the news. Interpreting the strange event as a message from Buddha to make the best use of the rock, the king commanded that a statue of Buddha be erected on the rock which had lifted itself from the earth.

All masons were immediately summoned from every corner of the kingdom and put to work under the supervision of the priest Hemyong. As the Buddha's image began to take shape, the priest could not think of a way to set the giant head and crown upon the body. The key to the puzzle was furnished by a child who was seen in the street by the priest playing with clay. After making an image of Buddha with clay, the child built a mound around the body of the Buddha's image to drag up the head and crown before setting them on the body.

The child who provided the hint was none other than Manjusri, the god of wisdom and intellect, disguised in that form.

Rock of the Virtuous Wife

A lonely shrine stands near a rock by the sea in Hangyong County, Cheju Island off the southern coast. The rock is called "the Rock of the Virtuous Wife" in honor of a woman.

About 100 years ago, a 16-year-old girl named Ko married a man who lived near the place. Her husband was a bamboo basket weaver, who was drowned one day while out on an island to gather bamboo. The woman went to the seashore every day, praying to the dragon of the ocean to return the missing corpse of her husband. Her repeated entreaties unanswered, the woman hanged herself on a tree over a rock at the seashore. The dragon of the sea was finally moved to send the corpse of her husband to the place where the wife had committed suicide. Equally impressed were the villagers, among whom a scholar named Sin Chuk vowed that he would honor the virtuous wife immediately after fulfilling his uppermost ambition of securing a high court position by passing the civil examination.

Some time later the scholar went up to Seoul to take the government examination only to meet with dismal failure. Consultation with a fortune teller disclosed that the spirit of the virtuous wife had taken possession of the scholar, preventing him from succeeding. Rendering appropriate honor and prayer, the scholar was freed of the spirit, and passed the court examination in his next attempt. Arriving at his native island as the provincial governor, the scholar fufilled his earlier vow by erecting a temple near the rock where the wife of virtue had hanged herself.

The Towers of Brother and Sister

A couple of towers stand on a peak in the Kyeryong Mountains in Chungchong Namdo province, one of the towers representing a brother and the other a sister.

In the old days, a Buddhist temple used to stand on the moutnain, where a devout priest was one day visited by a tiger. The tiger's gesture indicated plight, and the priest found that the tiger was suffering from a woman's ring caught in the animal's throat. Thrusting his hand into the tiger's mouth, the priest scooped out the ring, relieving the animal of its suffering.

On the following night, the tiger made an appearance again, this time inviting the priest to ride on his back. The tiger carried the priest to a place where a young woman lay senseless. He brought the woman to his temple and cared for her. Regaining her senses she said that a tiger had carried her away when she was out in a yard at night to go to the toilet. The woman then refused to go back to her house preferring to serve her savior, and finally became a priestess. They became sworn brother and sister, for Buddhism forbade marriage. A pair of towers was later erected on the site of the temple where they devoted themselves to Buddhism.

The Guardian God of Unjin

The village of Unjin near Puyo City in Chungchong Namdo province has a guardian god, for whom a service rite is offered every fourth year by the villagers, attracting thousands of spectators from neighboring villages.

The following legend is told of the origin of the guardian god. The village was once menaced by a dreadful plague and was about to be exterminated. An old man of the village in a dream saw a warrior riding on horseback accompanied by many soldiers and was told that he would dispel the plague from the village if his body abandoned in a nearby mountain was given a decent burial. Awakening from the sleep, the old man led the villager to the place which the warrior in the dream had specified to find many human bones littering the ground of an ancient battlefield. A funeral service soon dispelled the threatening plague, and the warrior in the dream was enshrined in a temple as the guardian god of the village.

The Wall Mountains

An ancient wall encircles the mountains between the cities of Onyang and Chonan. Once upon a time a hut stood at the foot of the mountain where a widow lived with a son and daughter. Both became famous for their almost equal physical prowess. Their fame spread so far and wide, giving rise to so much heated dispute over the superior physical strength of one over the other that a contest was finally arranged. The son was to make a round trip to Seoul wearing iron boots weighing 1,000 pounds and the sister to build a wall on the mountain. Whoever completed the assignment first was to be the winner. The contest started and as the evening approached the daughter completed building the wall except for a gate, while the son was still far away from the goal. By mutual agreement the loser of the contest had to die. The mother, who loved her son more dearly than the daughter, tried to hamper the progress of the daughter's work.

She prepared a hot soup and forced her daughter to eat it, stopping the work. Being extremely hot, it took the daughter quite a while to finish eating the soup. By that time the son caught up and won the race. The daughter, having lost the contest, was beheaded. The son, after being informed of the price of his victory, was so ashamed of himself that he killed himself by smashing his chest with his own fists. The tragic ancient wall is still standing on the mountain.

The Well of Samyongdang, the Living Buddha

About 400 years ago, there lived a virtuous Buddhist priest known as the living Buddha. He left many anecdotes about his magical powers, including this story of a well. While he was passing by the Village of Togok, Sangju County, Kyongsang-do, he was so thirsty that he asked for a bowl of water from a woman in a house by the road. The woman went away and took quite a while to get water from a well. Asked the reason for the delay, the woman told the priest that she had to take a long trip over to the next village for water, because her own village did not have a good well for drinking water.

Appreciating the woman's trouble, the priest struck the ground three times with his wand to draw out pure water. The well has been serving the villagers ever since.

A Woodcutter and an Angel

Once upon a time, there lived in the Diamond Mountains an old bachelor who was a woodcutter. One day when he was gathering firewood deep inside the mountain, a deer ran up to him and asked to hide him. As soon as he had hidden the animal behind a bush, a hunter hurried up to him and asked the whereabouts of the deer. He deliberately misled the hunter.

Coming out of the bush, the deer told the woodcutter that he was no other than the guardian god of the mountain disguised as a deer, and then promised the man who had saved his life to grant his wish. Being an old bachelor, the woodcutter asked for a fair maid for his wife. Thereupon the deer directed him to a pond deep inside the mountain where angels came down from the heaven to take a bath. The deer instructed him to hide the clothes of an angel while they were taking a bath, so that she could not fly up to heaven. The deer also told him never to give back the angel her celestial costumes until she had borne him four offsprings.

Following the deer's instruction, the woodcutter took the most beautiful angel as his wife, and subsequently had three children. By this time, the woodcutter felt his matrimony with the angel secure enough to give back his wife the angelic costume, forgetting the deer's advice to the contrary. But she immediately flew up to heaven, carrying the three offsprings under her wings.

A few days later the grief-stricken woodcutter came upon the deer once again and was told that he could join his wife in heaven by riding on the water scoop drawn down from heaven into the pond where he had abducted the angel, because the angels did not come down to the pond after the abduction but scooped the water up to take their baths in heaven.

Riding on the water scoop, the woodcutter was able to join his wife in heaven, but after a while he missed his mother so much that he decided to take a trip to the earth. A dragon horse was arranged for the trip to the earth, and the angel instructed him at no time to dismount the dragon horse throughout his journey.

His mother on earth welcomed him with squash soup, which was so hot to his hand that he dropped the boiling soup bowl on the back of the dragon horse. Surprised, the celestial animal jumped high up, throwing the rider off his back to the ground. The dragon horse flew up to heaven without the woodcutter, who was left helpless. He died a lonely death and become a cock. Thus it is that the cock looks up to heaven and wails, perched upon an elevated place, yearning after his angel in the sky above.

The Giant Matron of Cheju Island

The matron Samagopa of Cheju Island was so large in stature that when she lay placing her neck on Halla Mountain as a pillow her feet reached the sea, rippling the water.

She would wash clothes with sea water, standing astride Cheju Island and the southern coast of the mainland. Dirt falling out of her shoes formed hills on the island. The three giant rocks standing at the village of Songsang were once used by the matron to cook her meals, placing a pot over the rocks.

She had a never-relenting passion for fine dresses, so much so that once she promised the islanders to span a bridge between the island and the mainland in return for a gift of fine underwear. All villagers contributed to the project but the silk collected proved insufficient to make a dress to fit the giant woman, thereby leaving the island without a connecting link with the mainland.

The frustrated giant grabbed a peak of Mount Halla and hauled it into the sky. Landing on the coast, it became what is presently known as the Sanbang Mountain, while the site of the peak turned into the White Deer Lake atop Halla. But even such a powerful giant woman was not immortal: she was drowned in the bottomless pit atop Halla.

Folktales
The Ungrateful Tiger

A scholar was once travelling along a mountain lane, when he saw a tiger fallen into a pit. Looking up at the scholar, the tiger entreated him to save "a poor animal from doom." So tragic did the tiger look that the scholar set it free from the trap. Thereupon, the ungrateful tiger indicated it intended to make a dinner of its savior.

The indignant scholar admonished the beast in no mild terms, but this did not diminish the tiger's appetite. After a great deal of wrangling, they agreed to settle the issue with a verdict of the wise mouse.

Hearing both sides of the story, the wise mouse said: "Your testimony is contradictory. So I myself have to see what really happened. To begin with, Mr. Tiger, how were you caught in the snare?" "Just like this," so saying the tiger jumped down into the pit. "Hum! If that's the way the ungrateful one was, let him remain as he was," declared the mouse. The scholar and the wise mouse left the place without a glance at the pleading tiger.

The Louse, Bed-bug, Flea, and Mosquito

A louse, bed-bug, flea, and mosquito were once heaving a drinking orgy in the course of which a fight developed among them. After a great deal of hitting, kicking, and inevitable biting, the exhausted pests stopped fighting. The fight, however, had been such a fierce, bloody affair that they found themselves not what they had previously been: the louse had bled so much that it turned white; the mosquito's limbs had been pulled into thin threads; the flea had been hit on the mouth hard enough to make it pointed; the bed-bug had been flattened because he had fallen trying to stop the fight and lay flat on his back under the weight of the other fighting pests. They have never regained their former shapes ever since.

The Mouse, Pheasant, Pigeon and Crow

Once upon a time there lived a mouse, pheasant, pigeon, and a crow. When a lean year befell, all of them were starving, except the mouse, who had hoarded much food deep inside his hole. So the hungry friends decided to beg food from the mouse. The first to visit the mouse was the pheasant who said: "Do you, by any chance, happen to have some left-over of the cat's food? If you do, give me some."

So angry was the mouse with the rude pheasant that he hit the bird with a cane on the hip. That's why the pheasant has red dots on the hip.

Next to come was the pigeon, who said: "Look here, you rice-robber! If you have something to eat, get me some." So mad was the mouse that he hit the pigeon with a cane on the head. That's why the pigeon has a blue scar on its head.

The third to visit the mouse was the crow, who said after a deep bow, "Mr. Mouse, please help me, sir, because I am very hungry."

So impressed was the mouse with the crow's courtesy that he was willing to share his food with the bird. So it is always best to be courteous.

The Deer, Rabbit, and Toad

Once upon a time, there lived together a deer, a rabbit, and a toad, who one day had a party. But they could not agree who should occupy the seat of honor. Finally they agreed to seat the oldest one of three at the top place. Each, then, tried to prove that he had seen more suns and moons than the other.

First to speak was the deer: "I am the oldest, because I helped the angel stud the sky with stars when the universe was being created."

The rabbit said: "When they were studding the sky with stars, they had to climb up on a ladder. The ladder was made from the tree which I had planted. So I am older."

The toad, with tears in his eyes, said between sobs: "Your stories sadden me, for they remind me of my three sons who have long been dead. The eldest son would say that a ladder which he used to stud the sky with stars had been made with a tree a friend of his had planted; and the second son would tell me that when he was plowing the Milky Way he made a plow handle with the tree which he had planted; and my last son helped them to stud the sky with stars and plow the Milky Way. Alas! All of my sons have long been dead."

It soon dawned on the other animals that the toad was indeed the oldest of them all.

The Laziest Man on Earth

Once upon a time, there lived the laziest man on earth. He was so lazy that at every meal time his wife had to feed him by scooping rice with a spoon and thrusting it into his mouth. When his wife had to be away for a few days to her mother's house, she prepared rice cakes for her husband to eat during her absence. She tied many pieces of rice cake with a cord and hung them around her husband's neck so that he could eat the cake without much stir. But the laziest man would not even lift his hand to eat the cake, and so finally starved to death.

The Wise Judge

Once upon a time there was a very wise judge who could settle all disputes to the satisfaction of everybody concerned. One day an old man came upon the judge and said:

"I am a peddler of earthenware pots. On my way back from the market place, a strong gale blew my pots off my back and smashed them into pieces. Please see to it that I get compensated for the loss."

The judge asked a servant to bring a sailor bound for the north and another sailor bound for the south. When the boatmen arrived, the judge asked each of them which wind they preferred. The sailor bound for the north replied that he liked nothing better than the south wind, and the boatman bound for the south answered that the north wind was much preferable.

Then the judge thundered: "You two asked for the south wind and north wind at the same time, thereby causing a gale. I, therefore, command both of you to share the loss which the old man suffered."

The Mirror and the Villagers

Once upon a time a scholar bought a mirror in Seoul and returned to his native village where the mirror was not known. A mirror was very precious at that time, and so the scholar would hide and occasionally take it out to gaze at himself. Seeing her husband looking discreetly at something, the wife's curiosity was aroused. One day while the husband was away, she dug out the mirror from the hiding place, looked at it and saw a young woman.

"Ha! So my husband has brought a concubine from Seoul." Jealous wife immediately reported the case to her mother-in-law, who said after looking at the mirror: "Do not worry, my daughter, she is only an ugly, old woman who lives across the brook. She cannot possibly be your husband's concubine."

The father-in-law exclaimed after looking in the mirror: "Oh Father! How well have you been since your funeral?" When the wife looked at the mirror again, she again saw a young woman looking sullenly at at her. She looked angrier, and finally when she pulled a face, the mirror was shattered into pieces.

The Carp Mermaid

Once upon a time, there lived a fisherman who one day caught a large carp and kept it in a pot in his kitchen. He was hungry but could not eat the carp to which he took a fancy. When he returned home from work, however, he found his kitchen filled with delicious foods. The miracle was repeated several days until the fisherman became so curious that he hid himself in the house instead of going out to sea. Peeping into the kitchen he saw the carp transform itself into the fairest maid and prepare a dinner.

He came out of his hiding and asked her hand in marriage. The maid replied that she was a daughter of the sea-dragon and could marry him after three days. They eventually became man and wife, and lived lavishly in a magnificient mansion, produced by the magic power of the mermaid.

The wife liked to take a bath, and whenever she entered the bathroom, she advised her husband not to look at her while bathing. But he could hardly suppress his curiosity and finally peeped into the bathroom, to see a giant carp swimming in the tub. Realizing that her husband was peeking, she told him that they could have formed a perfectly solid nuptial tie after two more years, had he but heeded her advice. As it were, she would have to depart.

On her departure, the mermaid left word that they would be joined in heaven after three years. After she left, the stately house and pleasures which the magic of the mermaid had produced disappeared, and the fisherman was reduced to his former misery. But three years later he went up to heaven to live happily ever after with the mermaid.

The Secret of Longevity

Once upon a time there lived a youth who was the only son of a family which had but a single male offspring in each of the previous seven generations. One day, an itinerant Buddhist priest came to the house, and looking at the boy's face, shook his head, apparently in disapproval. The priest refused to tell his parents what he had read in the youth's features, but pressed hard, he said that the boy was destined to live only until the age of 19.

The parents besought the priest to avert the calamity, for the premature death of the only son would terminate the family. The priest suggested the boy to pay a visit to two saints playing a chess game atop the South Mountain and beseech their advice.

Next morning, the boy climbed up the mountain, and fell on his knees begging for life in front of the two saints. One saint with a pleasant look consulted the other, who was fierce-looking, suggesting they prolong the boy's life, but the latter shook his head. An argument ensued between them, and finally the suggestion of the mild-looking saint prevailed. He took a tablet out of his sleeve-pocket and finding the name of the boy, revised the figure 19 to 91.

Thus the boy could live until he reached the age of 91 by virtue of the god of the seven stars in the south, who was playing chess with the god of seven stars in the north.

The Whale and the Gamblers

Once upon a time, a man was taking a sea voyage, when a whale swallowed him together with his boat. Entering into the belly of the whale, he saw many people who had previously been swallowed gambling there. One peddler of earthenware pots was watching the game, calmly smoking a pipe beside his wares. Soon a fight broke out among the gamblers, and in the course of the fierce combat, one of the fighters fell upon the earthenware pots, shattering them into pieces. Thereupon the person picked up a sharp fragment of the broken pot and cut the belly of the whale wide open, so that all of them could get out of the confinement. Thus they saved their own lives.

Monster of the Underworld

Once upon a time a warrior was taking a trip to the capital in order to take the government examination for high positions in the court. Passing by a village, he noticed many people gathered before a public notice which read that the prime minister, whose only daughter had been abducted by a monster of the underworld, was offering the maid and heirdom as prizes to whoever rescued her.

The warrior decided to try his luck on the monster hunt, and changed the course of his trip. While roaming around the deep mountains he met three powerful men who were also hunting the monster. They became sworn brothers, the warrior assuming the leadership. Roving the countryside, they eventually came across an old woman who directed them to the entrance of the underworld.

Following the directions of the old woman, the warriors found a giant rock. Dislodging it they found an entrance to a cave. Stricken by awe and dread, everybody hesitated to enter the cave except the leading warrior, who lowered himself into the underworld in a basket hung by a cord from the entrance. Deep down he went into the cave, finally reaching the bottom. He then proceeded along in the underworld until he came to a well.

He climbed up on a pine tree by the well and waited for someone to come. Some time later, a very beautiful young woman approached the well to draw water and fill her pot. When she was about to lift the water-filled pot on her head to carry it away, the warrior on the tree plucked a handful of pine needles and threw them into the pot. Finding her water polluted with pine needles, she emptied her pot and filled it with clear water. The warrior again threw pine needles into the pot, and she again emptied the pot. The process was repeated three times, when she discovered the source of her trouble and shouted to the warrior to come down from the tree if he was a human being or disappear if a ghost. Sliding down the tree, the warrior told her the reason for his being there. The young woman then identified herself as none other than the daughter of the prime minister, abducted by the monster of the underworld. She hid the warrior and instructed him in various magics to deal with the monster, who happened to be away on earth. To test the warrior's power, she requested him to lift a giant rock. The rock did not budge an inch, so she concocted a magical tonic with medicinal wine and a 1000-year-old *ginseng* root. It boosted his power so much that he could lift enormous rocks as so many pebbles. Then she asked him to practice fencing with a mammoth sword weighing 1,000 pounds, but he could scarcely lift the sword. She prepared another tonic, which enabled him to brandish the giant sword like a pocket-knife. Finally he was able to handle a sword weighing 3,000 pounds.

As he was waiting for the return of the monster, sounds like cannon blasts were heard from the distance. The woman informed him that this was the sound of the monster's footsteps, treading 100 miles away.

The sounds became larger and larger as the monster neared his den. Hidden behind a paper screen, the warrior peeped out to behold the hideous monster, with two horns on his head and the mouth on a bloody face split close to the ears.

He grumbled to the woman that he smelt a human, and she promptly assured him that it was her own smell. She then coaxed it to take strong wine and put the intoxicated monster to sleep. He slept with his eyes wide open, snoring so violently that the door opened and closed each time he breathed through his nose.

When midnight came and the monster was in deep slumber, the warrior came out of hiding and struck the neck of the sleeping monster with the mammoth sword. As soon as the head left the body, it sprang back towards the neck from which it had been severed. At that instant the woman, who had ashes ready in the fold of her skirt, poured them onto the stem of the neck, thereby preventing the head from joining back to the monster's body.

After killing the monster, the warrior and the woman searched the den to find many a treasure and prisoners who had been kidnapped to the underworld. The couple returned to the earth, joined in a grand wedding, and lived happily ever after.

The Tiger and the Sweetened Persimmon

Once upon a time an aged, hungry tiger came down from the mountains to a village in search of prey. Sneaking close to the window of a house, the tiger listened to people talking inside. The mother was telling her baby to stop crying, for the tiger would come to eat up a crying child. But the baby only kept crying more loudly. Then the mother said to the baby, "Stop crying. I will bring a sweetened persimmon." The baby's wail stopped abruptly. The tiger, listening from outside, thought that the persimmon must be more dreadful than he, for the baby had stopped crying the moment his mother told him of the persimmon, whereas the menace of the tiger had failed to stop the baby's wailing.

Frightened by the discovery of such a hitherto unknown menace to himself as a persimmon, the tiger gave up his attempt to eat a man. Instead he went to the stable, trying to prey on a cow. A cattle thief happened to be in the stable, and assuming the tiger to be a cow in the darkness, the thief mounted on the animal. The tiger, on the other hand, assumed that it was the dreadful persimmon which dared mount his back. So frightened was the tiger that he ran for his life, trying desperately to shake the dreadful rider off his back. The harder he shook, the tighter the hold of the cattle thief. The tiger kept running madly over the mountains and across the rivers until the dawn broke. The cattle thief then saw that what he had been riding was a fierce tiger and so immediately jumped off its back. The tiger, thinking he had finally shaken himself free of the dreadful persimmon, did not turn, but ran ever the faster.

The Lying Match

Once upon a time there lived in the capital a prime minister who liked lies so much that he would request every guest to tell a good lie. Eventually he made it known throughout the country that any man who could defeat him in a lying match would be awarded his only daughter as his wife. As she was the fairest maid in the country, the prize-offer attracted many an ambitious young man who considered himself a better liar than the prime minister. But none could defeat him.

One day, the prime minister was visited by an unemployed scholar, who told a lie: "Since spring is near, it would be a good idea to dig a large hole in front of the Bell Pavillion on the busiest thoroughfare of the capital city in order to catch the winter gale in the hole. The winter wind could then be sold in the summer and a fortune made."

The prime minister nodded his head in approval and commented that it was a fairly good lie. The guest then produced a piece of dirty, aged paper from his pocket and told the prime minister: "This document was given me by the honorable deceased father of the prime minister as evidence of his debt to me of one million pieces of gold. Now that he has gone to heaven, I have to request that you redeem the debt."

Hearing the claim, the prime minister realized that he had to either pay for the false claim or acknowledge his defeat in the lying match. He choose the latter course.

The Man Holding a Tiger by the Tail

A scholar was once travelling along a lonely mountain road. He sat by large rocks for a rest, and presently saw a mammoth tiger taking a nap between the rocks, its long tail extended towards the scholar. His cry of astonishment awoke the fierce beast from sleep. The instant the tiger was about to jump, the scholar took hold of the tail and pulled it with all his might. A tug-of-war ensued and each of them was pulling desperately for quite a while when a Buddhist priest happened to pass by.

The scholar was overjoyed and asked the priest to kill the tiger with the staff which the priest was carrying. But the priest refused to comply, saying that Buddha's commandments forbade the killing of any living being, however harmful it might appear. Repeated entreaties of the scholar were of no avail. Finally the scholar besought the priest to hold the tiger by the tail in his place so that he might kill the beast with the staff. The priest agreed with reluctance. When the priest did so, however, the scholar started on his way without even touching the tiger with the staff.

This time it was the priest who shouted at the scholar to hit the tiger with the staff. Replied the scholar, "Neither do I like to kill a living being" and went away. Probably the priest is still holding the tiger by the tail.

The Centipede and the Hen

Once upon a time, a scholar hanged himself atop the South Mountain in Seoul for his repeated failures in the court examinations for high positions. After a while the scholar felt a queer sensation and opened his eyes to find that he was being nursed by a beautiful woman.

Receiving no answer but a smile to his question as to what had happened to the hanging, the scholar was led to a magnificiant mansion, where he was royally entertained. Eventually they became man and wife and lived happily for some years, until the scholar began to miss his family in the country. On his departure the woman told him never to listen nor to answer anyone while he was traveling.

Arriving at his native village, the scholar found a large house standing on the site where a tiny, thatched hut had been. All of his family welcomed him back, saying that the fortune he had sent from Seoul enabled the family to live in luxury. After staying in his old house for some time, the scholar missed his wife in Seoul so much that he decided to go back.

On his hurried way back to Seoul, he heard someone calling him by name, but he recalled his mistress' advice on his departure and paid no heed. Then a voice just like his deceased father's called him by name. Surprised, he looked back to be confronted with his deceased father, face to face. The father told him that the woman in Seoul was a centipede in disguise and he should therefore kill her by spitting on her face with tobacco tar while feigning to smoke a pipe.

Returning to the embrace of his beautiful mistress, the scholar thought of following his deceased father's advice, but every time he tried to spit tobacco tar on her face, she looked so fair that he had to spit on the ground in spite of himself.

Looking at her man spitting on the ground, the woman gave a radiant smile and said, "Now I am saved. I, who am a 1,000-

year-old centipede, have finally become a human being this very day. What you met on the way back to Seoul from your native village was not your deceased father but a 1,000-year-old hen in disguise attempting to murder me for she has had a feud of long standing with me. Since you did not kill but saved me, let me devote my entire life to you."

The couple had many children and the scholar even passed the court examination, to secure one of the highest positions in the court.

The Bridegroom Toad

Once upon a time a prime minister lived with his three daughters. His next-door neighbor was a poor widow who had no son, but a toad lived in a hole in the yard of her house. One day the widow was lamenting her fate, which had bequeathed her no son, when the toad emerged from the hole and asked her to adopt him as her son. She did so and raised the toad for ten years. Becoming of age, the toad asked his foster mother to arrange matrimony with one of the daughters of the prime minister living next to their house. With a great deal of hesitation, the widow paid a visit to the prime minister and proposed a marriage between her toad-son and one of his daughters.

The prime minister asked the opinions of his daughters. The two elder daughters were indignant, but the youngest daughter responded that she would marry as her father bade her. Thus the matrimony was arranged. On the night of the wedding, the newly-wed couple went into the bridal chamber, where the groom asked the bride to put out the light, and a little later to light the candles again. The light revealed not a grotesque toad but a handsome lad, who told his bride that he had been a saint in heaven whom destiny had sent down to earth in the guise of a toad so that he could eventually marry her as a human being, by peeling off the toad's skin, which, he emphasized to her, should be well hidden away so that nobody else could lay an eye on it.

Several days later the bridegroom left for the capital, where he passed the court examination with flying colors and was appointed to one of the highest positions in the court. The two elder daughters of the prime minister, in the meantime, felt so much jealousy at their sister's unexpected fortune that they kept asking her questions on the happenings in the bridal chamber on the night of the wedding, until they extracted the complete story, including the hiding place of the toad's skin.

While the youngest sister was away, the two elder sisters took out the toad's skin and burnt it in the kitchen. As a consequence, the bride received a letter from her husband in the capital informing her that the disappearance of his toad's skin had brought him a curse, depriving him of the highest court position and ruining his health with an ailment, thereby forcing him to set out on a journey without a destination. The grief-stricken bride then began a journey in search of her husband.

Roaming around the countryside, she met a group of farmers, who informed her that a virgin chasing sparrows away on the hill would tell her the whereabouts of her husband. The virgin informed her that a saint over the hill fishing at a brook would tell her of the whereabouts of the lost husband. The saint directed her to an ancient temple where she finally found her husband. The couple ascended to heaven riding on a cloud, to live happily ever after.

The Virgin Who Married an Earthworm

Once upon a time there lived a very rich couple in a magnificent house which was so large that it had as many as 12 gates. They had an only daughter born after prayer-rites offered to the mountain god. When she became of age, a handsome lad visited her bed chamber every night and left at dawn when the first cuckoo crew. Becoming pregnant, she confessed her nocternal affairs to her parents, who suggested that she pin a needle with a long thread to her lover's clothes when he visited at night.

Next day she followed the thread, tracing the abode of her lover to a hole in the ground. Digging into the hole, she found a large earthworm in whose side a pin was stuck. Later she gave birth to a son, who grew up to become a fine man, begetting many offspring and enjoying good fortune.

Miss Red-Bean and Miss Yellow-Bean

Once upon a time there lived a couple who had a daughter. After the death of his wife, the man married an ill-tempered woman who gave birth to a daughter. The mother abused her stepdaughter, feeding her nothing better than yellow beans, while coddling her own daughter, feeding her nothing worse than red beans. By the feeding habit, the daughter born of the former wife became known as Miss Yellow-Bean and the girl born of the second wife as Miss Red-Bean. As the two girls grew, Miss Yellow-Bean became fairer, while Miss Red-Bean looked uglier and uglier. The mother's abuses of Miss Yellow-Bean also became harsher and harsher.

One day a grand festival party was held in the village. Much as she wanted to go, the stepmother told Miss Yellow-Bean to finish three back-breaking jobs before coming to the party, and left the house with Miss Red-Bean. Left alone, Miss Yellow-Bean tried to finish her work as fast as she could so that she could join the others at the party. She had to fill a giant pot with water and grind five bags full of rice and then boil ten bales of hemp. It would take all day long to do all this.

Scurrying back and forth between the well and the pot, she tried to fill the pot with water, but the pot did not fill, because the pot had a hole at the bottom. While she was weeping, a crow flew in to tell her to look at the bottom of the cupboard. Finding a piece of resin there, she plugged the hole in the pot, and soon water reached full to the brim.

Sparrows in the meantime had flown into the yard to take the husks off the rice, while the cow in the stable had eaten all the hemp and produced it from between her hips just as if the hemp had been boiled. Thus finishing all her work as her stepmother had bidden her, she hurried to the party. On the way she met a being from heaven who gave her a pair of beautiful flower-shoes which fitted her perfectly. But the step-mother took the flower-shoes away to give it to her own daughter even though the shoes did not fit her.

When the man from heaven was looking for a bride, he thought of the pretty girl to whom he had given the flower-shoes. In answer to his request to wed the maid with the flower-shoes, the stepmother presented her own daughter to the man from heaven, who immediately saw that the flower-shoes did not fit her and so knew that she was not the girl he had in mind. Eventually Miss Yellow-Bean was united with the man from heaven in a grand wedding, and later the stepmother was accused of harsh treatment of her stepdaughter and exiled to a far-away lonely place.

The Old Man with a Wen and Devils

Once upon a time there lived in a village an old man with a large wen on one of his cheeks who was a famous master-singer. Once he went deep into the mountains to gather firewood and lost his way. When the evening darkness gathered, he found a deserted hut, where he decided to spend the night. At midnight a group of playful devils came to the hut to hold a drinking and dancing party, making a great deal of noise. The old man climbed up on the roof to hide himself, and peeping down he saw the devils playing with a magic wand, which produced gold, jade, and all kinds of treasures at the command of the devils. The merry-making in the hut grew so exhilarating that the old man burst out into a song in his beautiful voice. Enchanted by the beautiful singing, the devils invited the old man into the hut and requested him to sing more and more.

The envious devils asked the old man how he could sing so well. The old man answered that it was the wen on his cheek that produced such a fine voice. The devils then wanted to have the wen, and the old man would not part with it until the magic wand was given in exchange for it.

Returning to his village without the wen but with the magic wand, the old man became the richest of all. Another old man with a wen who happened to live in the same village was so envious of the fortunate old man that, when he found out about the devils, he went up into the mountains in search of the same good fortune.

The same thing happened to this old man, except that he was given another wen on his other cheek from the devils, who complained that the wen they had bought from the other old man emitted no beautiful song but a horrible squeak. Thus he had to live with wens on both his cheeks and was always ashamed of his greed. A Korean proverbial expression runs: "He who goes out to have his wen removed comes back with two wens," meaning "Those who go out for more wool come back shorn."

Proverbs

Being the small mirror of a nation, proverbs present us with the characteristics of its people in condensed form — of their wit, taste, manners and customs, religion, social institutions, human nature, both past and present. Let us then consider some features of Korean proverbs.

As pointed out by several Chinese scholars of the past, the national traits of the Korean people are conciliatory and peaceful, resignation being regarded as one of the virtues. Such basic traits of the people are incorporated into many proverbial expressions. For example, let's "Laugh it away" is a familiar expression for optimistic resignation. The proverb, "Can one spit on a smiling face?" is suited to counter a hostile adversary, and if the well-meaning smile does not work, one can fall back on somebody else to step in and mediate on the strength of the proverb, "A fight is to be stopped, and a deal is to be closed (by intervention)." An apter but freer translation of the above proverb may be: "Intervene to stop a fight but also to close a deal." "Three years of patience will divert even a murder," is another preaching for peace, while optimistic resignation is well expressed in "A cobweb doesn't stretch itself inside the mouth of a living man," meaning that as long as a person is alive, he is bound to get his share of food.

Vengeance or cruelty to one's enemy is hard to find in Korean proverbial expressions, and certainly no parable may be found which corresponds to "He who cannot avenge himself is weak, he who will not is vile." Instead, many leave it to fate, preaching slow reaction. The English expression, "sleeping on an idea," is described more specifically as "No vengeance can last a night's sleep, nor a debt of gratitude survive a day." "No flower can stay red for ten days," because everything is destined to decline and fall in a short time.

"Many people mend the stable after the cow has been stolen," even though "Ten guards can't stop one thief."

Impetuosity is frowned upon and so is wishful-thinking. A man who "lies under a persimmon-tree with his mouth wide open," shares the Western belief that the "Lark does (not) fall ready-roasted into his mouth." One who draws an optimistic conclusion of unwarranted nature is further mocked as he who "looks for the *Kimchi*-soup upon hearing the rice cake mill grinding"—the rice cake may be in the process of being prepared at the mill, but it does not necessarily assure one of the delicious food, and so looking for the vegetable soup to drink with the rice cake is certainly ridiculous.

Hasty actions are further ridiculed in the saying, "The traveller with ten days to go makes haste on one day's trip." He has as much as ten days to travel, so what's the use of hurrying the one day?—the proverb says in effect.

Instead, "Hewn ten times, no tree will not fall," and "Dust will gather itself into a mountain." Therefore, it is always best to be slow but steady. "Cross a shallow water as if it were deep," and "Even on a familiar way, ask directions." Discretion should be used in one's action, for "Even the bird chooses a bough to perch on," and in case of a stone fight, "The angular stone hits really hard."

Few Korean proverbs teach adventurous, positive actions, and neither is the spirit of pioneering given much place in proverbial expressions. Instead, reservation is more frequently encouraged, and especially volubility is strictly warned against as in the saying: "Talkative families turn their sweet soybean sauce into bitters." "The rat hears the nighttime whisper, and the bird listens to the daytime talk," and "Go to the home of sweet soybean sauce, but not to the home of sweet words," "A footless (heedless) talk walks 1,000 miles," and a step further, "Can the chimney emit smoke if nothing has been burnt?"

Wry humor is resorted to in many proverbial expressions as "using the telephone pole for a toothpick," and "riding on a bicycle with a horsehair hat on" (they don't match). When something auxiliary or supplementary turns out to be more substantial or expensive than the main thing, it is said that "The navel is bigger than the baby," alluding to the unproportionally large size of the navel of a new-born child.

"The fellow who gets the beatings first is better-off" than the others who wait for their turns to receive the rod if the beatings are unavoidable. "The guest who has too many hosts goes hungry," or "Too many boatmen drive the boat up a hill," as "Too many cooks spoil the meal" in the West.

One who refuses to share his surplus blessings is offten referred to as one who "hates to eat himself but grudges to give to the dog." In Korea, "money is a powerful warrior" instead of being "everything"; "Even sight-seeing in the Diamond Mountains comes after the meal," for a hungry belly will not appreciate the best in life.

"The sin goes where it is committed and the virtue goes where it is developed," meaning we are awarded with the consequnces of our own deeds. "The devil is blocked by the charm, the man is blocked by sympathy."

The institutions of family life are given ample expression in Korean proverbs. The mother-in-law, for instance, is referred to in as many parables as in the case of the wife who "kicks the dog in the belly in malice towards her mother-in-law"; also "the look of the mother-in-law who has missed supper" is supposed to be ghastly and fierce; "Left unbeaten for three days the woman turns into a fox" is a commentary on the role of the husband. The traditional institution of concubinage is also adapted in the expression "as much as the tears for the death of a concubine," the tears being shed not by a crocodile but by the main wife at the news of her rival's death. To the main wife, however, her sister-in-law occasionally looks the worst, giving rise to the saying: "Ten concubines are not as spiteful as one sister-in-law."

Traditional customs are utilized in some of the proverbs, as "Unlucky death as it may be, shall not a lucky day be chosen for the funeral?" Also "Thanks to the memorial service, this rice is mine," is an expression to indicate some unexpected benefit one has received without effort, as a man receives rice for his mere presence at a memorial service for ancestors or Shaman gods. "The widely-talked-about festival dinner offers nothing much to eat," is a mockery of exaggerated publicity, while "Even a beggar will see the day of his grandson's birth" is an allusion to the importance attached by the people to offspring, warning at the same time against contempt of men in lower positions. "Even an earthworm stirs when stepped on," and "Even a rat-hole has a day when the sun shines upon it" are expressions of the extremes man will tolerate, custom or no custom.

Religions, both pseudo and real, are utilized extensively in the proverbial expression, and the Shamans seem to be a favorite target for ridicule: "The Shaman next-door won't do the incantation." "The Shaman cannot perform her own exorcism, and neither can the blind fortune-teller tell the day of his own death." "An immature Shaman murders a man."

Mockery of Buddhist priests found expression in such sayings as: "The priest never minds the incantation but does mind the food offerings," "When the priest appreciates the taste of meat, he will climb up on a higher temple," "When the priest appreciates the taste of meat, the temple will be clean of bed-bugs," because his carnal desire will eventually wipe out the pests, devouring them for meat. The preceeding two proverbs refer also to a case of an arrogant upstart who is likely to forget his better sense once good fortune smiles upon him. So also is the saying: "The calf at the prime minister's house does not know how dreadful the butcher is."

Importance of cultivating good habits during one's early years is emphasized in the saying: "Habits formed at (the age of) three continue until 80." On the bad side, "A needle thief becomes a cattle thief."

Many proverbs use short phrases of four to five words. For instance, anyone who is easy to deal with is referred to as "the drum of the village," which everybody can enjoy hitting without incurring serious consequences. "The rice cakes in a picture" look delicious but do not serve any utilitarian purpose, while "Rice cakes in both hands" is good fortune probably as a result of "gaining a pheasant and its eggs as well."

Many short proverbial expressions use Chinese characters such as: "The eastern wind in the horse's ears" (to fall on deaf ears), "Starting out as a dragon's head but ending as a snake's tail," "Throwing a stone on the Han River,"— it hardly causes a ripple.

Riddles

The traditional riddles of Korea, in the form of questions and answers, reflect much of the forklore and character of the Korean people. They were originally intended to cultivate "thinking power" through the medium of the guessing game. Some of the puzzles are universally applicable, without necessarily involving folk customs. Following are some examples.

* * *

What is the white dress worn by all the mountains, rivers and trees? (Snow)

What is it that is white when young, green when full-sized and red when old? (Red pepper)

What are the ten things which remain ten even if another ten are added or subtracted? (A pair of gloves)

What is it that has eyes and a mouth but no head? (A crab)

What is it that cannot walk around even though it has as many as four legs? (A table)

* * *

The majority of the puzzles, however, have to do with traditional manners and customs, such as:

What is it that becomes fatter and fatter as it becomes older? (The wall of a Korean house, because the inside wall is pasted with new paper, usually once a year.)

What is it that has two wings and spends all day swallowing and vomiting men? (The gate of the Korean house, which has a two-piece door.)

What is it that has its head in a bamboo

field, its body in a hemp field, and its feet in a rice field? (The man in mourning, whose costume is a hat made of bamboo, clothes of hemp cloth, and straw-shoes.)

What is it that sits at the center when guests come? (The charcoal burner, around which guests and host sit in winter, warming their hands)

What is it that is loaded at night and unloaded in the day? (The rack on which clothes are hung before people retire to bed)

What is it whose head and tail are of metal and whose body is of bamboo? (The long traditional Korean smoking pipe, whose bowl and mouthpiece are made of brass attached to each end of a bamboo stem.)

* * *

Many puzzles involve puns, such as:

What is the *pae* (plum) that can't be eaten? (A boat or belly, both, like plum, being *pae*)

What is the *pae* on which one cannot ride? (Plum or belly)

What is the *chang* (window) through which one cannot see? (A lance which is also *chang*.)

What is the *chang* with which one cannot strike? (A window)

* * *

Some of the puzzles involve the structure of Chinese characters: What is the character whose son and daughter stand side by side? (The Chinese character for "like" 好 which is composed of two symbols, the left being woman and the right man or son.)

What is the character of a woman with a hat on? (The character for "safety," 安, a combination of a hat above and a woman below.)

What is the character for jail? (The character for "prisoner" 囚 because the man is surrounded in the square frame □.)

What is the character with one hole that is solid but eight holes that are leaky? (The character for well 井 because of its shape.)

What is the character of a king with horns and a tail? (The character for ship 羊, the king being 王.)

Folksongs

Korean folksongs are especially different from similar songs of other countries in several ways. First of all, it is the women who are credited with compositions of many folksongs, and accordingly they have been endeared more to women than to men. Aside from the popularly believed inborn talent for music of the female, the predominance of women over men in the realm of folksongs is attributed to the traditonal restrictions forced upon women. In other words, Korean women are supposed to have cried their hearts out in such songs.

Another characteristic of the Korean folksong is humor which is resorted to when desperation is about to possess the people. Thus wailful occasions are turned into funny events, and malicious adversaries are chanted about with laughter.

The virtue of obedience colors the folksong lavishly. The obedience of, for example, a wife to her husband, subjects to the king, the young to the old, is much sung about. It was undoubtedly the influence of Confucian teachings, which dominated individual ethics.

The form of the folksong follows the 4—4 pattern, the 4 being the number of words. This pattern has been set as the favorite form for all kinds of verse-forms. Rhymes are effected in most songs with a liberal usage of refrains.

The folksongs are generally devoid of local characteristics, partly due to the smallness of the land and partly due to the relatively frequent interchanges of personnel under the strongly centralized government administration. The only exception are the folksongs of Cheju island, which lies too far off the mainland to be fully subject to such influences.

Unlike the folksongs of practically all other countries, Korean folksongs are usually not accompanied by dancing. Originally, dancing had been an inevitable partner, but the Confucian ethical codes and the prevailing economic hardship of the people since the Yi dynasty are presumed to have driven dancing away from the folksong.

The earliest anthology of folksongs was the *Samdaemok*, compiled in A. D. 882. Ever since, folksongs have been transmitted down to posterity, and presently more than 200 original versions of various folksongs are known to have been sung at one time or another.

Since the influx of Western culture at the dawn of the 20th century, the folksongs have lost much of their popularity, especially among the younger generation, who prefer Western-style songs after the fashion of the time. Thus, folksongs have been declining rather rapidly.

Of all Korean folksongs, the best known is *Arirang*, which is considered representative of the melancholy air predominating in the Korean folksong.

Arirang
Arirang Arirang Ara-ri-yo
    Arirang kogye-rul nomo kanda.
    (He (or she) walks over Arirang Hill)
Narul porigo kasinun nimun
(My love who in deserting me,)
    Simnido motkaso palbyong nanda.
    (Shall have hurt feet ere he (or she) goes even 10-ri)*
Arirang Arirang Arairyo
    Arirang kogye-rul nomo kanda.

Nearly as popular today as Arirang is *Toraji*, or the Bellflower Song. It is about village virgins gathering the edible roots of the bellflower in the hills.

The Song of *Toraji* (Bellflower)
Toraji Toraji Paektoraji
(Bellflower, white bellflower)
    Simsim sanchone Paektoraji
    (Deep in the mountains, far away by the river)
Handu ppuriman kaeyo-do

*10 ri equal about 2.44 miles.

(Picking the roots just one or two)
Taebaguni-e chol-chol nomnun-guna.
(Fills the basket over the brim.)
E-he-yo e-he-ou e-he-yo
    E-yora-nanda chihwa-ja-ja chota
Nega Nae-ganjang-ul Suri-sal-sal Ta-noginda.
(Oh, you melt my whole heart.)

Being a predominantly agricultural country, Korea has produced many folksongs of the farmer. Among them, the Song of Good Harvest may be cited as an example.

The Song of Good Harvest
The year of good harvest has come,
  The year of good harvest has come,
To our beautiful land of rivers and mountains as embroidered on silk.
Chihwaja chota,
  Olsigu choko chota.
(Let us be merry and happy.)
Let us go out next spring in March
  To an excursion among the flowery trees.
What else but farming
  Can be the base of a universe?
Let us work hard on the farm
  Instead of idling away.
Chihwaja chota, olsigu choko chota.
Let us go out next summer in May and June To an excursion by the brook.
Look at Kim Pongsil over yonder
  How he behaves himself.
Looking up at his harvest piles,
  He is just dancing round and round.
Chihwaja chota, olsigu choko chota.
Let us go out next fall in September and October
To the mountains among the tints of fall.

    *   *   *

The traditional funeral procession calls for a dirge to be sung by coffin bearers, the words, first sung by a leader being repeated by the others.

The Dirge
When he (or she) was born in this world,
  100 years of life was hoped for.
(refrain) Nowajung, nowahung, nowahung
  nowanumja nowahung.
Sparing even the food

for the love of young offspring
He (or she) tried hard indeed
   To see 1,000 autumns and 10,000 generations.
The days being numbered,
   The heartless years flew by
Rendering one aged.
   Do not sorrow our way,
For even the kings and saints
   May some day become old.
Even the greatest hero King Chinsi was reduced to a lonely soul at Yesan.

Human life being but a dream in a spring doze,
   Fame and glory are only a dream.
The northern hills and rivers, (where the dead go)
   Which we heard were far and away
Lie just outside the door.
   The yellow spring and well, (of which the dead drink)
Which we heard are far and away
   Are but the brook in front of the house.

Fortune-Telling

Theory of the Five Elements

Fortune-telling in Korea may be considered in two separate parts: professional prophecy based on an elaborate, systematic groundwork, and the prediction of the "seer," interpreting certain symbols in the light of commonly-held beliefs.

Professional fortune-tellers are mostly Shamans, blind persons, or devotees of the Chinese Classics. Their systematic methods are based on ancient Chinese astrology, which was later developed into the theory of the "five elements"—gold, earth, water, fire, and wood. According to this theory, the universe is subject to ever-changing mutual relations among the five elements, each representing certain symbols basic to the composition of the universe.

One of the basic applications of the theory is in pairing one of the five elements with another to see whether the combination is in harmony or in conflict:

In harmony are: gold with water, water with wood, wood with fire, fire with earth, earth with gold;

In conflict are: gold against wood, wood against earth, earth against water, water against fire, fire against gold.

To have one's fourtune told on the basis of the theory of the "five elements," one has to solicit the services of a professional. Instruments used for fortune-telling are either a set of five old coins or short sticks of about 2 to 3 centimeters in length made of a jujube branch extended toward the east. On each of the five pieces is inscribed an appropriate mark to indicate one of the "five elements."

The fortune-teller, holding the magic set in his hands, recites reverently: "As there are words to be said under the sky, so under the earth. May divine response, therefore, lead the way. Now that Mr. so and so residing at such a place is having his fortune of the year told by so and so (the name of the fortune-teller) on such a day of such a month in such a year, may the indication be as directed by divine wisdom."

At the close of the incantation, the fortune-teller throws the sticks or coins on the floor. The "tossing" may take place once, twice, or three times, according to the practice of each individual fortune-teller, and the words of the incantation may also differ. The pattern set by the magic coins or sticks on the floor is then interpreted by referring to a "source book." If the pattern is in the order: gold, wood, water, fire, and earth, for example, the source book interprets the effect this

XXII MANNERS AND CUSTOMS

way:

"Since the sacred griffe and phoenix are embracing gold, and the dragon and tortoise are celebrating a festive event, misfortunes will disappear with the advent of good fortune. The five stars will be shining brilantly in the sky, offsprings will prosper, glory and prosperity will reside for a long time."

If the pattern is gold, wood, and earth, it is explained that: "The mind will become wasted, and so will properties be scattered. Failing in harmony with relatives, noble persons will be repulsed and men of trifling status will become associates."

If the pattern reads wood, fire, and earth, the interpretation would be: "The three stars of wood, earth, and fire being in harmony, everything will comform with expectations, repulsing misfortunes regardless of unexpected events occurring in the sky. The "fever" of harmony will be fostered among them, dissipating worries in routine matters, and the flying-dragon will ascend to the sky to become a great man."

If the pattern shows only the earth, the interpretation is that: "The first half is evil and the last half good. Even Confucius himself was once driven to the wall, but eventually emerged safe. The earth, being located at the center, will first suffer, but from the middle (of the year), in the third, sixth, ninth and 12th months, many things of good fortune will come."

Besides divinity by the "five elements," a similar basis for fortune-telling are the "six elements," "pine needles," "four pillars," "divine tubes" and "pregnancy." To interpret properly symbols derived from such magical formulae, the fortune-teller has to be versed in the knowledge of, not only the "five elements," but also the theories of "male and female" and the *taeguk*." Therefore, fortune-telling by such profound mystics in the East commands the highest respect.

Physiognomy

Physiognomy calls for professional knowledge if it is to be practised properly, for it involves every physical feature of a person, including his face, limbs, bones, and bodily movements. Originally a Chinese contrivance, it became most popular during the Koryo period. It deals with characteristics of the head, bones, hands, shoulders, chests, belly, and feet, each of which is studied separately. Furthermore, bodily movements of the person concerned are analyzed by close observation of the person's walking, sitting, lying, eating and speaking, and the coloring of the skin is inspected. Finally, conclusion is reached by integrating all such information acquired about a person.

Some of the widespread bases for telling one's fortune and personal traits by facial characteristics are as follows:

A high nose indicates bankruptcy and eventual death in a foreign land, but a low nose is a sign of greed. A man with a large mouth will became either a general or a government minister, while a person with thick ears will amass a fortune. A black mole in the ear indicates a devoted son.

A wide forehead is a fortunate sign, but wrinkles on the forehead mean many a hardship. A person with wide eyes is timid, and the narrow-eyed are bold and fearless. Slow-moving irises connote a malicious character.

Abundant hair on the head is an indication of sensual lust, but lack of hair means poverty. A person with long eyebrows will have many brothers, and short eyebrows denote solitude.

Small and chubby hands infer a blessing, while long, slender fingers bespeak laziness. One with a clear, vibrating voice is fortunate and a person who squeaks with metallic sound can never accomplish any task of importance.

Palmistry

Palmistry is a branch of physiognomy, its predictions being based on various lines on the palms and the thickness or moles on the hands. It is more popular than other forms of physiognomy, presumably because of the simplicity of the observation.

Being an ancient Chinese contrivance transmitted to Korea, palmistry as presently practised is based on substantially the same principles and methods throughout the East. The most important are the three dominant lines on the palm—the lines of emotion, intelligence, and life. Some of the other indices of one's fortune as predicted through palmistry are as follows:

A large number of fine lines on the palm is a good omen, and vice versa.

The woman whose palm lines form deep furrow begets male offspring.

Shallow palm lines denote squandering of one's fortune during his youth, and a hard life during his declining years.

One who has a black mole on his palm will amass a fortune.

Thick hands connote good fortune and happiness in life.

Clear, precise palm lines indicate clear, wise personal traits, whereas blurred palm lines bespeak a muddled, stupid personality.

Straight palm lines connote diligence and crooked lines dishonesty.

The person whose palm lines are gathered in one place, forming a cross is prejudiced, and is likely to become the butt of complaints from others, hard as he may try to achieve the contrary.

Scattered palm lines indicate that the person will roam around alien lands away from his native place.

One with short last fingers will become a member of the nobility, and become extremely rich all of a sudden.

One who has wide gaps between the fingers will see his fortune slip away and become poor.

Divination through Mediums

Shamans and blind persons who are said to be possessed by certain spirits act as mediums to tell fortunes through the "voice of a spirit," or interpret patterns formed by rice, money, sticks, and other things thrown on the floor. Being mediums, they are supposed to be able to invoke the supernatural power of the spirit. Many of the professional Shamans and blind fortune-tellers incorporate the theories of the "five elements" in their work.

Besides conducting Shaman rites, fortune-telling is one of the most important functions of Shamans, so much so that Shamans are always associated with fortune-tellers. The blind fortune-tellers, on the other hand, are accredited with mysterious insight compensating for their physical handicaps, and therefore are considered superior to men with eyesight because of the blind's alleged ability of looking into the future by their power of concentration. Therefore, Korea has had many blind fortune-tellers of reputedly outstanding caliber. To this present day, blindness is an asset in establishing onself as a fortune-teller.

The busiest season for such professional fortune-tellers is the lunar New Year's season, when many people knock at their doors, eager to have their fortunes for the year told. The younger generations which have received Western-style education, however, scoff at such fortune-telling by professional "experts" as a matter for serious concern.

Prophets and Books of Prophecy

Prophets of the past proclaimed things to come through writings, chantings, or drawings. The most widely believed book of prophecy in Korea was "*The Secret of Chonggamnok*," a book written by an unidentified prophet during the Yi dynasty. Expressed in words utterly unintelligible to "laymen," the mystic book of prophesy tells forthcoming events of the nation, and has nothing to do with individual fortunes.

More popular among the people is "*The Secret of Tojong*," written by Yi Tojong during the middle of the Yi dynasty. Written in readily comprehensible words and presenting the gist of all books of prophecy concerning personal fortunes, the book is still used widely at home, as well as by fortune-tellers in the street. During the New Year season, "*The Secert of Tojong*" is consulted to tell the fortune for the new year. Familiarity with the book, which is easily accessible and comprehensible, has bred contempt, and nobody seems to take the prophecy of the book as seriously as other forms of fortune-telling.

Among many source books for telling fortunes by professionals is the "*Mai Physiognomy*" transmitted originally from China.

Interpretation of Omens

Besides professional fortune-telling based on the Eastern philosophy of the "five elements," "the male and female," and the "*Taeguk*" or by supernatural spirits through mediums, folklore has established certain interpretations of omens as clues to predict future events. They involve various things observed in daily life, from the stars to animals, plants, and insects. Most of the interpretations concern agriculture, probably because of the predominance of farmers in the population since ancient days.

Natural Phenomena

Certain phenomena of nature are interpreted as good or evil omens.

The eclipse of the sun or the moon, or the appearance of a comet, is an evil omen, foretelling impending nationwide disaster or the outbreak of war. So also is a ring around the sun.

On the 14th and 15th day of the First Moon, the farmers look up to the moon to predict the harvest of the new year: a red moon is an evil omen, warning of a forthcoming drought during the year, whereas a white moon means bumper crops in the fall. If a shooting star falls into the sea, fish will be hard to catch, and a lean year is prophesized by a shooting star falling on land.

Astrology is widely practiced to tell the fortune of an individual.

Rainfall on special days is interpreted generally as an evil omen, except on the eighth day of the Fourth Moon. For instance, rain on a wedding day indicates unhappy matrimony, and an epidemic is likely to break out in the summer if rain falls on the first day of spring (on or around February 3). Rain on the day of the "cold feast" (the 105th day after the central day of winter) foretells a long drought, and the farmers expect a lean barley crop if it rains on the 15th day of the Eighth Moon. If one hears rain on his deathbed, it is supposed to rain on all days when memorial services are rendered for his soul.

Yellow clouds on New Year's Day foretell excellent harvests for the year. The south wind on New Year's Day also indicates bumper crops, whereas the east wind predicts a lean year. If a rainbow rises out of a well, the well is considered sacred.

Animals

Among the many animals which can tell fortunes, the most popular are the cow, horse, dog, fox, cat, chicken, magpie, and crow.

If a cow gives birth to twin calves or straw sticks to a dog's tail, or a magpie crows either at dawn or while perching on a tree in the south, the family will prosper, the master will rise in the world to bring honor to the family, or some other happy event is imminent.

Evil omens are a cow mooing at night, a dog which has climbed up on the roof, and a fox barking at night—all of which will bring bad luck to the house. A death is predicted if a cat goes into a chimney, a dog barks on the roof, or a fox sneaks into the village to bark.

While the magpie is considered a lucky bird, the crow is regarded as of evil omen. The funna of evil luck include the snake, "rock" spinder, and frog, but the sparrow, snowy heron, and white pheasant are lucky birds.

Plants

If flowers blossom during an off-season, it is a good omen, whereas the death of a tree means bad luck. The azalea blossoming twice a year, however, is likely to be followed by a disaster, while the sunflower growing taller than the fence is of evil omen.

Human

If one is visited by a woman early in the morning, or a woman crosses the street in front of a man in the morning, he will suffer bad luck during the day. If the first customer of a shop happens to be a woman, the proprietor will not make much profit during the day. The woman, in turn, regards it of evil omen to see a person in mourning after her childbirth. Confronting a blind person on the street is also of evil omen, and a newly-wed couple will find themselves fighting often if the guests invited to their wedding party set an example by fighting at the feast.

Itching foretells that someone will soon bring a gift of "rice cake"; if one feels itchy inside the ears or sneezes, he is being talked about by somebody else. The person who receives the last glass of wine at a drinking party will beget a son; if one sees a corpse while fishing, he will be rewarded with an excellent catch (which has a grim basis of fact).

Interpretation of Dreams

Flying in a dream is an excellent omen; being bound with a rope means longevity; seeing stars brings material gain.

Evil dreams, on the other hand, are slashing another with a knife; or hair falling out. If a tooth comes out in a dream, one of the parents will soon pass away, and cutting hair will cause a family dispute, while cutting the fingernails in a dream is likely to be followed by a dreadful incident the next day.

A resurrection in a dream indicates good news coming to the dreamer, and it is also of good omen to dream of being seated together with a deceased person.

Eating in a dream catches cold, and drinking wine will also cause illness, but drinking water in a dream is a good luck sign.

Meeting a fair maid in a dream is evil, but meeting your father is of good omen. Meeting a Buddha in a dream will bring enormous wealth, and a fight between a husband and wife is a lucky dream.

Taking a boat ride in a dream is likely to be followed by moving to a new house, and crossing a bridge will secure a position in government. The same thing will happen if one acquires apparel in a dream.

Picking up clothes in the street in a dream will be followed by gaining another's favor.

A pregnant woman will give birth to a son if she sees the sun, but a daughter if flowers appear in her dream. The woman who sees a Buddhist priest in a dream will soon become pregnant, and having a fight with a devil assures a long life and sometimes great wealth through some totally unexpected means.

Fortunes of Games and Sports

Fortunes may be told of a harvest, a village, or individuals from the outcome of games and sports, such as the group stone fight, tug-of-war, kite-flying, swing contest, the "card game" and the *"yut."* Fortune-telling of this nature is mostly related to the annual observances of holidays for games taking place on special occasions.

Geomancy

Geomancy in Korea, which is referred to as the "Secret of Wind and Water," is a divination for locating sites of cities, residences, and burial grounds. According to the theories of Eastern geomancy, originating in ancient China, happiness and prosperity will prevail over the house which is located on an ideal site, and the site for the burial grounds of ancestors has to be selected with the utmost care so that the offspring may prosper, because the location is believed to exert a lasting and decisive influence over the destinies of all persons concerned.

The basic theory of geomancy stemmed from the belief that the earth, being the "mother," is the producer of all and the "fever" of the earth residing in each site exercises a decisive influence over that which utilizes each piece of land.

Origin and Theory

The origin of the geographical determinism of the East dates back to the ancient Chinese kingdom of Chin, where Kuo Po wrote in his *"Chim Nang Chin"* to the effect that one had to have, first of all, water on his land, and secondly, prevent wind from blowing into his place, for it was wind that scattered the "fever" of the earth.

Supbsequently, during the Han period, the book *"Ching Wu Ching"* was published to advocate the "theory of male and female." The theory asserts that where the "male and female" are in concord and heaven and earth communicate with one another, the "inner fever" will spring out and the "outer fever" will ferment, thereby entailing "wind and water."

Topography is the essential factor of geomancy, for a high mountain shields wind and at the same time harbors rivers along the valleys. Therefore, a mountain foot is an ideal location. Besides a mountain and river, directions are also an important consideration.

It is presumed that the primitive mode of living during the early ages gave rise to such a theory so that the people would select their abodes where game was plentiful for hunting, and firewood and water were readily available. Later, when the people of China settled along the Hwangho River for an agricultural economy, the plain was harassed by perpetual gales from Mongolia. It seemed to have obliged the people to seek shelter under a high mountain. The field along the Yangtze River, on the other hand, was frequently struck by recurring floods, thus giving rise to the Oriental expression "governing the water," which means administration of the government.

Such a state of affairs led the people to use discretion in choosing locations for burial grounds as well as sites of abodes to insure that the family would prosper. Thus a house built on an ideally located plot would receive the "fever of the earth," and the spirits of ancestors buried in a suitable location will transmit the blessings of the "fever" by association. If the house or ancestors' graves are located on "evil" ground, the persons concerned will be subject to one misfortune after another.

The essence of the location, therefore, lies in searching after the ground where the "fever" resides.

The most ideal site is located on ground surrounded by mountains—a high, rugged mountain in the north referred to as the *hyonmu,* flanked by hills folded in many ranges both to the left (as the "blue dragon") and to the right (as the "white tiger"). Also, the building or tomb must face a low hill in the south. Furthermore, the center of the site, known as the "bureau," must command a relatively wide expense of plain in the front, which is called the *myongdang* meaning an excellent site. Also, a river must flow through the *myongdang* to make it the perfect site.

Such requirements for the "perfect site" are met to the letter by the location of Seoul, the capital city selected by the founder of the Yi dynasty about 550 years ago. The city proper of Seoul is surrounded by mountains—the high, rugged North Mountain in the north, the Nak "mountain" to the left, the Mo Hill to the right, and Namsan Hill sloping gently in the front. Through the basin flows the Chonggye river, making the site a perfect seat for government.

Applications of the Theory

The "secret of wind and water" seems to

have come to Korea during the Three Kingdoms period. The earliest historical reference on the subject appears in the book "*Reminiscences of the Three Kingdoms.*" According to one of the oldest volumes of recorded history, the fourth king of the Silla kingdom, Talhae, prior to being crowned, climbed atop Toham Mountains and found a crescent-shaped site at the foot of the mountain. He interpreted the basin as an ideal place for his future domain, because the shape of the ground resembled the contours of the moon on the third night of a lunar month, insinuating that lean as it might look, the site was destined to prosper as the new moon would gradually expand to full. He coveted the site so much that he finally tricked the original owner of the land into surrendering the place to him. His selection of the site was amply justified later, it was said, when he ascended to the throne of the kingdom due in large measure to the "fever of the earth" he had been able to draw from the site.

The kingdom of Silla placed so high an esteem on the "secret of wind and water" that in later years they designated four sacred places in the realm—the Blue Pine Mountain in the east, the "Skin Field" in the west, the Chi Mountain in the south, and the Diamond Mountain in the north. Important national affairs were deliberated at one of such "sacred" sites to ensure successful settlement.

In the kingdom of Paekche, the founder, King Onjo, selected his capital on South Han Mountain Castle after due geomantic consideration together with military, economic, and communications problems. Also, Puyo city was selected as the last capital of the Paekche kingdom because of the new, moon-like shape of the site.

Similar practices were observed in the kingdom of Koguryo in selecting sites for its capital cities, as evidenced by the locations and relics uncovered from the tombs of the kingdom.

The practices of geomancy gained firmer ground as the country entered the Koryo period. The founder-king, Taejo, extended the application of the "secret" still further to judge traits of each locality under his domain. Thus he ruled that the people of certain areas were unfit to serve the court because of their possibly treacherous character stemming from the treacherous topography of the localities in which they had been born and raised.

Geomancy dictated the administtration of the Koryo kingdom to such an extent that for some time the kingdom had at least three capitals within its territory — the central capital of Kaesong, the southern capital of Hanyang, and the western capital of Pyongyang. The court functioned in the central capital from the 11th month to the second month of the following year, in the southern capital from the third to the tenth month.

Geomancy, which had been a monopoly of the court, spread to the people during the Yi dynasty. The founder-king of the Yi dynasty selected Seoul as the site of his new capital in fulfillment of the prophecy of Tosun, who had written that "the Yi family will transform themselves into a dragon when Hanyang (Seoul) shall have become the capital."

For some time during the Yi dynasty, the court had a section exclusively devoted to divination itself with the theory and practice of the "male and female," "wind and water," "medical divination," and "Shaman divination." As authentic references, the court section used classic works written in China and Koguryo.

Such a prevailing atmosphere produced numerous authorities on geomancy during the dynasty. Among them, Chong Tasan has left probably the strongest influences among the people. As a brilliant, erudite scholar of the "utilitarian school" during the middle of the Yi dynasty, Chong Tasan wrote the book "Forestry Economy." Included in the book is a chapter on divination, which is divided into sections on topography, residence location, theories on "the water," and theories on the "the wind." Intended as an introductory book on descriptive geography, the "Forestry Economy" was insrtumental in spreading the "secret of wind and water" among the population.

Geomancy still exerts a lingering influence. If a person is visited by one misfortune after another, he tends to attribute it to the possibly disadvantagous location of his house, or the graves of his ancestors, from the viewpoint of "the wind and water" theory. The modern institution of the public cemetery has frustrated attempts to seek the "ideal" site for the burial ground by urban dwellers, but a considerably large number of the rural people are still preoccupied with the principles of geomancy in selecting sites for their parents' graves. They usually employ the services of professional "experts" to select the location, and in some cases, the selection takes place even before the parents have died. When the original selection of the burial ground has proved wrong, the grave is moved from one place to another until the offsprings are contented. The burial ground for the ancestors was supposedly so decisive in the matter of an offspring's fortune that a Korean proverb runs: "It was the ancestor's grave that wronged."

Classification of Sites

Geomancy classifies land into two kinds: the earth of the "male" where one resides during his lifetime, and the earth of the "female" in which one's soul stays after death.

The earth of the "male" is further divided into the place of community dwelling, such as city, town and village, and individual abode. A city, town, or village, therefore, has to be so located as to extend blessings to all the people residing in the place. This is particularly important in selecting the seat of the government, because, hinged on its location is the fortune of the entire nation as well as of the government itself. The site of individual residences influences the "loins" of the master of the house, determining superior or inferior offsprings as the particular "wind and water" of the site dictates. The prosperity or doom of the master of the house also depends upon the same force, working on the site of his residence.

The earth of the "female," or the abode of one's soul, does not have to be wide. A plot of land, occupied by the coffin, in the core of the burial ground, and, therefore, the selection of the spot to lay the coffin is most important. It is extremely difficult to locate, because a slight deviation from the most ideal spot in the earth is believed to lose much of its advantages.

The idea of choosing the best site for burial has gained stronger ground than the selection of house-sites among the people, because of the belief that one can cultivate his own fortune to some extent while he is living, but one is left to follow his destiny after death as the "wind and water" of his grave dictates to his soul. Another reason may presumably be the influence of Confucian ethics, which placed filial piety above all other virtues.

Shamanism

Shamanism is still practiced among large segments of the population under the shadow of modern civilization and culture. The professional services of the Shamans, who are mostly female, are sought by the rural people and a limited number of urban citizens.

Acting as a medium, the Shaman serves the believers by invoking gods for good fortune and exorcising evil spirits. The rite to invoke the gods' blessing is observed in order to pray for rain, render appreciation to the gods, console the guardian goddess, *Sonang*, appeal for the birth of a son, or pray for the well-being of the family. The gods' powers are also invoked to recover from sickness and to get rid of other various evil spirits which lurk in a particular place.

Each particular of the rite differs according to the locality and each individual Shaman. Some families have a particular "house Shaman" who is invited to the house whenever the need for her arises—a practice prevailing mostly in rural districts where the steady service of a medium is considered essential. In urban areas, however, most of the believers go to the professional Shaman's abode to use the facilities available there.

Modern science and popular education have expelled Shamanism from the lives of the people to a great extent, but the centuries old tradition of the medium and the medicine men still cast a magic spell over the older generation, certain as it is that the superstition is withering at a rapid rate.

Origin of Shamanism

The origin of Korea's Shamanism, as elsewhere, is closely related to the instinctive religion of all primitive people, who hold in awe the various changes of nature, such as sunrise and sunset; birth and death; day and night; storm, wind, and rain. The feeling of awe led primitive people everywhere to believe in supernatural beings, to whom they prayed for personal protection and expulsion of evil spirits.

Historical references to Shamanism appear in several ancient records of the Three Kingdoms. According to one of the records, the second king of Koguryo, Yuri (1 B.C.), consulted a Shaman when he become ill, indicating the function of the Shaman as a medicine man. In the kingdom of Silla, the second king, who held the throne from A.D. 4 to 24, was a Shaman, for his last name, Chajaung, which follows the first name, Namhae, is an old dialectical word meaning Shaman. The historical record insinuates that a kind of theocracy was practised in the kingdom of Silla about 2,000 years ago.

Such scattered, fragmentary references, however, fail to give us a clue to the origin of "professional" Shamanism in Korea. We can, nevertheless, get an inkling — indeed several "theories"— on the origin of Shamanism through the folk legends and some of the words chanted by the present-day Shamans as incantations.

One such "theory" involves a Buddhist priest and a giant woman. A legend has it that an eminent Buddhist priest named Pobu, who lived in the ancient days, one day saw a brook overflowing with water even though no rain had fallen. Becoming curious, he climbed up a mountain to investigate the source of the water and was greeted by a giant woman, who told the priest that she was none other than the Heavenly Queen, and had cast the spell of "hydro-magic" to induce the priest to marry her. Their wedlock yielded altogether eight daughters, to whom the parents taught the secrets of incantation, which included ringing bells, dancing with a fan in hand, and chanting a spell. The eight daughters eventually became professional Shamans, each going to one of the eight provinces of Korea to establish herself as the founder of Shamanism there.

Another "theory" concerning the origin of Shamanism involves a queen and two cranes. The princess Kongju of ancient times became possessed by a god when she came of age. Her worried parents confined her in a hut built atop the South Mountain, and later moved her to the Diamond Mountain, where one day she dreamed of a couple of blue and green cranes flying towards her and finally entering into her own body through her mouth. She kept her mouth closed, which made her pregnant later, to give birth to twin sons. The twin brothers grew up to become known as men of the highest virtue and wisdom, rising to high positions in the court. Each of the twins begat four daughters, to whom the secret of incantation was taught and they were dispatched to each of the eight provinces to serve as the first Shaman there. This "theory" is the most popular one of all, and is referred to in many legends and incantations.

The princess Awang is another notable who is credited with originating the female magic. The princess Awang of King Yo in the ancient kingdom of China was so benevolent to her subjects that she frequently visited the huts of the people to pray for their happiness. So effective was her invocation to cure deseases and invite fortune that the people erected a temple for the princess, thereby making her magical incantation that much more potent. Later some people imitated the princess' manner of invocation to become professional Shamans. The contemporary invocation contains a line chanted by the Shaman which goes "Whose *gut* (the Shaman rite) is this? The honorable Awang's *gut* it certainly is."

Another Awang who shares the credit with the princess of the same name is a king of an unidentified ancient kingdom. During King Awang's reign, a certain Shaman was reputed to wield magical power after declaring that she had been ordained by a god to administer the people's fortune. Suspicious of her, the king decided to test her magic power and commanded her to make a wen on his cheek disappear—a trick played on the female magician because the wen had been caused by a chestnut in his mouth. The Shaman invoked a god with her chanting and dancing, which lasted for exactly 100 days, when the "wen" dissolved itself. The delighted king approved the Shaman's practice of the magic, thereby encouraging many other persons to train themselves as professional Shamans.

Another legend concerning the origin of Shamanism involves the seventh daughter of Prince Ubi (Fish's Nose). The prince married at the age of 15 against the advice of a fortune-teller who had warned that the marriage would produce a string of seven daughters but not a single son. The prediction came true, and the enraged prince abandoned the last daughter on a far hill, where she was nursed by birds. What's more, her mouth, ears, and eyes were filled with golden ants. Then the king put her in a box and left it on the seashore, where she was led to the Pari Kongdok Matron by a tortoise and a bird. Living with the Matron, the girl perceived by observing the weather that the king was critically sick, and hastened to the palace. At that time the king was in desperate need for medicinal water to recover from his sickness, but none of his six daughters had the stamina to go to the abode of the Majang god who was known as the sole dispenser of the miracle drug. It was the abandoned seventh daughter who finally acquired the "sacred water" from the god Majong after slaving nine years for him — three years carrying water, three years making fire, and three years gathering firewood. The grateful king recovered completely thanks to the "sacred water" and offered her the choice of a large portion of his territory or innumerable jewels, but the princess declined them all to become the goddess Mansin Sinju (master of ten thousand gods' body,) the guardian of all Shamans.

All such legends and the lines of the Shaman incantations concerning the origin of the Shaman hold in common that the founders are females and that they had supernatural power by being possessed of gods. Shamanism in Korea also has many things in common with similar practices prevailing in Siberia, Manchuria, Japan and the South Sea islands.

Motives and Processes for Becoming a Shaman

Many Shamans have chosen the career as a professional medium to earn a living, and some pursue the "art of black magic" by heredity, while others attribute their path to certain divine inspirations. A survey conducted in 1930 concerning the motives for becoming professional Shamans revealed that of the 527 Shamans covered in the survey, 202 persons indicated that they had chosen it as an occupation for a living, 139 attributed it to hereditary, 127 to some "divine inspiration or urge," 30 to the unrestricted freedom the Shaman enjoys, and 34 to various other reasons, persuasion by others, a hope to expel bad spirits from oneself, a desire to become fertile, a desire to cure oneself of a disease, etc.

The survey shows that "divine inspiration," which had formerly been the prime motive for becoming a Shaman, had fallen out of favor. Instead, more and more of the women have chosen to become Shamans by vocation rather than avocation. True, the Shaman has never inspired the respect of the people, who tend to look down on the *mudang* (Shaman), but the profession has always been rewarded with ample monetary renumeration for relatively easy work. Furthermore, the rare privilege of unrestricted freedom has been accorded to Shamans especially in the field of sexual behavior. Most of the Shamans, therefore, have taken full advantage of the freedom, and the village Shaman's rites occasionally turned into a sexual orgy, the presiding Shaman calling the tune and reaping the most from the extravaganza.

Most of the Shamans who have chosen "black magic" as a means to a living have either been reared in extreme economic poverty or are physically handicapped. Some are blind. The blind are considered especially adapted to the work of the Shaman, because their sensitive ears render them readily able to perceive communications from the gods, and also blindness is believed to allow effective mental concentration required for the work.

Prior to launching herself in the field of Shamanism as a full-fledged professional medium, woman has to undergo several years of training as an apprentice under an established Shaman. In the old days, the art of Shamanism was also taught by a professional association of Shamans. Some enterprising Shamans even set up training schools.

Shamans "by heredity," as one might expect, are trained at home, and the secret magical formulae inherited from ancestors are taught, besides commonly known procedures. Some of the Shamans who have become mediums due allegedly to" divine inspiration," perceived in a dream, mental shock, or through possession by a god, are apparently psychic cases. Upon receiving what they consider to be "divine inspiration," the god is said to have possessed their mentality. Originally, all Shamans were believed to have been inspired by certain divinities.

The Shaman Rites

The scales of the Shaman rites vary. Some last one to two hours, while others require one week to complete, but the rites follow an established procedure:

First, an altar is set up and offerings are piled up on it to invoke the god; then a prayer is chanted, and due appreciation for the god's favor is murmured for having invited fortune and expelled evil. Lastly, a farewell is sung to the god and the altar is removed. Step-by-step procedures of the rite, however, may vary according to each individual Shaman and locality.

The most frequently observed rite is the exorcism against the god of plague when one is taken ill. Many farmers in the rural districts still believe in exorcism as a better cure than the medical doctor. Therefore, they send for the "medicine man" when sick. Arriving at the house of the patient, the Shaman sets up an altar at an appropriate place, on the floor, in the yard, garden, or fields, as the case may be. Offerings of cooked rice, wine, vegetables, and fruits are arranged on the altar, and the Shaman mumbles the incantation to a music-and-dance accompaniment. In the course of the incantation, the sacrifice of a chicken is offered in the place of the patient, and the god of plague is driven into a bottle, which is then sealed, effectively barring its escape.

Of the innumerable gods of plague, the god of small-pox is regarded as the most dreadful and is accorded an honorable title of *mama sonnim* (the honorable guest of small-pox). Whenever the "honorable guest of small-pox" pays a visit after a long journey from "south of the river," the god is treated with extreme reverence: an altar is built hastily; wine, rice cake, and fruits are offered; a doll is made of straw to which prayers and incantations are repeated. At the close of the rite, the straw doll, which impersonates the dreadful god of small-pox, is presented with an outfit for a trip—clothes, money, a pair of straw-shoes—and then is carried to a road, so that the god may go back to the place from where it came without playing havoc among the people.

A rite is observed to console the soul of the person who died a premature death in an accident. Having met with death without enjoying the pleasures of life, the soul of such a person is believed to turn itself into a god of plague, cherishing a grudge against the living. Unless an appropriate rite is observed by erecting an altar with offerings and chanting incantations to pacify the soul at the waterfront or on a boat, the soul of the drowned person may transform itself into a harrassing god of water. In the course of the rite, a doll made of white paper and a bowl of cooked rice are cast into the water where the accident occurred. If the papar doll swings to and fro, it is believed to be a certain sign that the incantation has proved effective. Thus assuring that the soul has ascended to heaven, the Shaman and other persons involved dedicate a prayer of congratulations with upraised hands.

A preventive measure is taken through a rite to exorcise an evil god lying dormant within one's person or in the house. After assuring that such a god of plague is lurking by the process of divination, the Shaman erects an altar within the house to offer a feast and chant incantation with music and dance. When the rite is over, the feast is shared among the people involved, including many spectators.

The rite to lure a god of good fortune into the house is performed in the yard of the house so that the house may prosper, amassing a fortune, begetting many offspring, and rising up in the world. Many farm houses make a rule of observing this rite after a harvest in the fall, but the scale is rather small. Businessmen in the towns resort to the same rite for their success, but of late they tend to economize on the expenses by following the "do-it-yourself" rule; that is without inviting a Shaman. After the rite, offerings are usually shared by the people, and a small feast takes place among friends, neighbors and relatives.

In the new year a rite is performed to exorcise a god of plague, which, if left to stay, may block the fortune of the year. The procedure is similar to the rites for other purposes: offerings on the altar, chanting, and invocation with dance-and-music accompaniment, followed by a farewell to the god.

Another rite to exorcise a god of plague takes place prior to a wedding, when the prospective bride and bridegroom are believed to be possessed by an evil god. Left unexorcised, the god may eventually wreck the otherwise happy marriage.

The most potent god, *Taedol*, which resides in the largest beam of the house, is worshipped in a rite. Of all the gods lurking in and around the house, this *Taedol* god (the god of the largest beam) occupies the place of the highest honor, for the fortune of the family and the master's length of life are at the command of this powerful god. The rite to revere this god is observed often after a harvest.

A rite is dedicated often on the "lucky day" in the month of the first moon to the guardian goddess *Sonang*. The belevolent goddess for travellers is enshrined in a small patch of ground under an old tree at the foot of a hill. The place of her abode is marked with a pile of pebbles, to which grateful travellers passing by have contributed one by one. The rite is performed in front of the pile of pebbles, sponsored by an individual or as a community program. A great deal of dancing and singing usually characterize the rite, which also serves as entertainment for the villagers.

Another guardian god is the mountain god, which is usually enshrined in a small temple at the foot of a hill. A rite to console the mountain god, which looks after the well-being of the villagers, is observed usually on a select "lucky day" in the month of the first moon as a community-wide project. Professional Shamans may be invited, but the "amateurs" may perform the rite also.

When a house or a bridge is complete, a rite is performed under the direction of a Shaman so that the "virtue of the site" may exert a lasting influence over the structure as well as the people using it. An essential offering for this rite is a hog, which is shared among the people concerned in a feast after the ceremony.

The water god or the dragon god is honored and consoled with a rite, which is performed usually at the waterfront or near the water where shipwrecks have been recurring. A largescale rite of this nature is observed under the direction of a professional Shaman, but the fishermen may perform an "abbreviated version" without a Shaman prior to a fishing trip for safe voyage and abundant catch.

The Dipper Stars are worshipped in a rite because they are believed to exert an influence on one's fortune. The rite may be an informal affair at home with an offering of a glass of water accompanied by a deep bow to the stars. It may also be performed by several Shamans, and a large number of people may participate with much music and dancing. The idea of revering the Dipper Stars stemmed from Taoism.

The most spectacular rite often takes place as a "thanksgiving" after the fall harvest, dedicated to the souls of ancestors as well as "all the enlightened gods in heaven and earth." After the harvest, the offerings of the crop have to precede the farmers' own consumption. The offering is always accompanied by a prayer for further fortune. The rite may be observed informally in a house, but a large-scale ceremony calls for several Shamans and may last several days.

The spectacular "thanksgiving" rite is conducted by three professional Shamans with a group of three musicians, who go through the entire repertoire of 12 scenes. Starting out from the first scene of "uncleanliness," the ritual moves in the order of the scenes of god's descent, the mountain matron, the *pyolsang*, the lord, the *Cheguk* (Sakradevanam India), the heavenly king, the *O* devil, the military hero, the chanting man, the *manmyong* god, the *hujon* god. Each of the scenes calls for different costumes, music and dance as well as incantation. The ceremony goes on day and night for several days, during the course of which all kinds of gods have descended upon the scene of the ceremony, have been entertained appropriately, and have departed, receiving a reverent farewell from the Shamans.

Books of Incantations and Articles for Rites

The basic book of incantations, *ponhyang* (Book of the Central Place), is supplemented with various incantations to answer the needs of each occasion. The words are in verses of primitive theogony, which is unintelligible to those who are not versed in it.

The articles used with the altar are the "god's seat," the divine paper screen, straw, yellow clay, pine, a straw cord of leftward twist, the ritual table, and the divine colors (flag). The articles for the incantation include a peach bough, the divine sword, a long knife, a fork lance, the incantation book, devil-imprisonment bottle, a doll, the "soul" divine general stick, a mirror, a paper fan.

The offerings are such foods and drinks as rice, cooked rice, rice cake, wine, sweetwine, fish, meat, vegetables, fruits, cakes, dried fish, and also textile foods, including thread, money, artificial flowers, and incense.

The musical instruments used for the rite include drums of various shapes and sizes, a gong, bells, a flute, and other brass and wind instruments of the traditional Korean style.

It is the scope and magnitude of each particular rite which determines the number of articles employed for the occasion.

Shaman Incantations

As a representative example of Shaman incantations, we can cite the one chanted on the occasion of the rite for the god of

XXII MANNERS AND CUSTOMS

songju, the presiding god of all lesser spirits of a house. The incantation is most often chanted by a Shaman for the benevoloent god of all gods residing in each house, because the god is the object of the most frequent worship.

In verse form, it runs in part as follows:
"*Era* 10,000 blessings, *Era* the great god,
Where is the native land of Songju?
The native place is Chebiwon (the house of sparrows) in the land of Andong in Kyongsang-do province.
A pine seed of Chebiwon had been received to cast it in the Yongmun Mountains (Mountains of Dragon Gate,)
Where it grew
Receiving dew at night and the sunshine at day,
Rains and snows under the moon in autumn and breeze in spring,
Finally to become a long, giant tree.
Era 10,000 blessings, *Era* the great god.
In order to build this Songju (god)
33 members of the work force,
ascended on the blue mountains of 10,000 folds,
With precious axes slung over their shoulders,
There to observe the rite of the divine pot,
Placing the divine earthenware,
Burning three sheets of white paper,
Praying with palms of both hands held together,
Be new timbers brought into the new house,
May the god of the Yellow Emperor,
Who is to stroll the outside,
descend with readiness.
Searching for a tree to be cut
for the beam of the house,
The ones standing on the shadows
Were found unfit for being a tree of shadows,
The ones standing on the sunny sites,
Were found unfit for being a tree of sunny sites.
Looking over the mountain in the front,
An ideal tree for the beams was found standing
Quietly adorned with a belt of gold and jade.
The tree was cut down with zest with axes,
See how splendid it was!
Era 10,000 blessings, *Era* the great god.

The incantation goes on in the same vein, describing how the beams, the most important part of the house, were laid by carpenters with the utmost reverence, how all and every charm and other magic formulae have been meticulously observed for the house to the perfect credit of the family.

The incantations recited by the blind mediums differ from the ones used by the Shamans. They are in the form of Buddhist *sutras*, one of their representative sample being "The Sutra of Virtuous Talks by the Blind," which reads in part as follows:

"...In the east is the god of the Blue Emperor,
In the south is the god of the Red Emperor
In the west is the god of the White Emperor
In the north is the god of the Black Emperor
In the center is the god of the Yellow Emperor.
All the gods of every rank and class
Are serving witness to fulfillments of prayer being offered.
When this year's great fortune prevails upon this family,
As the doors are closed in the winter time,
As the doors are open in the months of the fifth and sixth,
As new costumes are acquired,
May the body be as nimble.
...May the precious baby of this house,
Be as tall as a big mountain,
As deep as rivers and oceans,
To be a royal child to the country,
A filial child to the parents,
A loving child to the brothers,
A friendly child to the relatives,
A virtuous child to friends, and
A superior child to the world."

The invocation continues with prayers to evoke blessings of longevity and all other known forms of good fortune and concludes with the following:

"...May 10,000 blessings visit each time the gate is opened hour after hour,

May gold emerge whenever the land is swept day after day.
Throughout the village, throughout our home,
May he become a flower to the eyes of others,
Leaves blossom out of his person,
To emit fragrance at every step.
May the evil fortune of talk by evil men,
The evil fortunes of ears, the moon, fire, government, tongue,
The three calamities and the eight misfortunes
Be all expelled 1,000 *ri* (miles), 10,000 *ri* away.
May beauty, kindness, fragrance, attractiveness
Together with paper money and silver money
Be all loaded into the residence of this housemaster,
In haste as the laws and ordinances are abided by."

Shamans, Gods, and Evil Spirits

The Basic Ideas of the Shaman Divinity

The Shamanists of Korea believe in two kinds of gods: the benevolent gods which bring good fortune and the malignant spirits which harass the people. It is, therefore, the function of the Shaman to invoke the supernatural power of the gods and to exorcise the evil spirits.

The belief in such gods, both good and evil, was held by the Korean people from the ancient ages, prior to the Three Kingdoms period. According to ancient records, the people of ancient Korea worshipped gods in a community program following seed planting in the spring and the harvest in the fall. The divinities they believed in were the god of heaven as the supreme ruler of the universe as well as various other gods under the heavenly god.

More recently, during the Yi dynasty, certain scholars, such as Kim Sisup (1434-1493) and Yi Ik (1682-1764), applied the basic Oriental philosophy of the "male and female" to their theories on the Shaman gods. According to their theories, a living being is composed of the elements of male and female. The male being usually ascends to heaven after death, but when a person dies an unnatural death, by accident, murder, or suicide, for example, the male being keeps hovering on the earth, eventually to transform itself into a female being—an evil spirit which harasses the people.

Other Confucian scholars advocated a kind of animism to explain the existence of various gods. They held the view that the basic cause of gods is the "fever" or soul which is lodged not only in human beings but also in everything in the universe, including all the stars, animals, and even plants and minerals.

Such ideas spread among the people, who believed that illness and other unfortunate occurances were caused by the malice of evil spirits, while good luck was a certain indication of the benevolent god's help. Being supernatural, the gods' powers were also invoked to tell the fortune of the people through such mediums as the Shaman and the blind person.

The tradition of ancestor-worship is another evidence that the Korean people have been convinced of the existence of the soul after death. Memorial services were offered to the souls of ancestors as frequently as possible throughout the year in the belief that ancestor-worship was not only a gesture of filial duty but also the way to invoke supernatural help for the ancestors' souls. Korean folklore and legends are full of such stories as the soul of an ancestor appearing in a dream to request memorial service. Should the person continue to be negligent in performing his filial duty, it was believed that the wrath of his ancestor's soul would not fail to ruin the family by such means as making the master of the house ill or sterile.

The evil gods of Korean vintage, like ghosts, demons, or goblins of other countries in the world, prefer to haunt such places as abandoned temples, ancient wells, caves, the underside of old trees, and lonely valleys. Their working hours are limited, from sunset to dawn, the cuckoo signalling the time when night is over. There has never been a case where the evil spirits worked overtime by staying after sunrise or appearing in broad daylight.

The Nature of Various Gods

The god of the heaven is the Zeus of Korean mythology, presiding over the growth and changes of the universe. The outcome of the agriculture of the village, therefore, was believed to be dictated by the slightest whim of the god of heaven. So omnipotent was he that each village used to observe a ritual to worship the heavenly god since ancient days.

Less potent but nevertheless worthy of respect are the gods of other heavenly bodies and nature such as the god of the sun, the moon, the stars, the rains, the clouds, the thunder and lightning. Among the innumerable number of stars, the Dipper Stars have endeared themselves to the people above all others.

The guardian god of the mountain is worshipped in a rite performed by all members of a village on a select "lucky day" in the month of the first moon. Enshrined in a temple or on an altar built at the foot of a mountain behind a village, the god of the mountain is believed to guard the village against gods of plague and to provide bumper crops for the village.

In the old days, the state sponsored the ritual for each god of a "sacred" mountain to pray against flood and other disasters.

The water gods lurk in the sea, rivers and even in ponds and swamps. Most of the water gods are the souls of drowned persons, which harass the people. Old fishes in the pond and swamp also may transform themselves into water gods, while the sea god occasionally appears in the guise of a dragon. To console and pacify the water gods, services were performed either by the state, fishermen, or ferrymen at harbors, riversides, and ferries. One of the most popular fictions of ancient Korea concerns a devoted daughter who became a willing virgin sacrifice to a sea god for merchant sailors in exchange for 300 *sok* of rice in the hope of curing her father of his blindness.

Magnificent rocks may also be objects of worship, for such rocks were believed to have souls. The gods of rocks were believed to guard women without a son. Occasionally a mother "sold" her weak son to the god of a rock for protection of the child. Korean legends are full of stories in which a giant rock is depicted as a living being moving, growing, and exhibiting all kinds of emotion.

Each direction of a place is believed to be a domain of five guardian gods: the blue imperial god in the east, the white imperial god in the west, the red imperial god in the south, the black imperial god in the north, and the yellow imperial god in the center. When a site is selected, therefore, an appropriate mark is inscribed in each of the five directions. Similar marks are also pasted on the entrance gates of a house facing each direction to exorcise the gods of plague.

Various gods of farming are believed to look after agriculture. The god of the rice paddy is specially potent against pests in the rice field if worshipped in a rite on the 15th day of the first moon. The god is also revered with an offering of rice cake made of new crops on the 15th day of the eighth moon.

The god of grains, which presides over the "five principal grains" is believed to descend upon the earth from the heaven on the dawn of the seventh day of the seventh moon to investigate the year's farming. Since agriculture was regarded as the backbone of the country's economy in the old days, the king himself used to pray for excellent harvests of the "five principal grains" to the god of grains on certain days each year.

After a harvest, the grains come under the protection of the god of the storehouse, while silkworm raising is under the domain of another god, which rewards women with an excellent silk crop if wine and rice cake are offered on the fifth day of the fifth moon by the matron of the house. A bumper crop is also a result of worship rendered to farm implements on the first "canine" day of the second moon.

Souls of deceased persons become gods. They may be gods of ancestors, kings, generals, or malignant spirits. The gods of ancestors have been so firmly believed that tradition calls for offering of breakfast and dinner every day to the soul of deceased parents for three years after death. During the three-year period, a special place of honor in the house is reserved to keep an altar for the soul, where either a portrait or an inscription is enshrined. After three years of this daily worship, the altar is removed, and the worship is rendered once a year. The memorial services to the souls of one's ancestors are rendered by the male members of the family. Participation of womenfolk is barred as they are considered "unclean." Negligence in observing the service is believed to bring down the wrath of the ancestors' souls, which would ruin the family by sterilizing the offspring or making him beget a deformed child. Faithful obervances of ancestoral worship, on the other hand, are believed to be rewarded with prosperity for the offspring.

Souls of national heros, kings, saints, wise men and other eminent persons are worshipped as guardian gods. The most popular of all the god-saints was the soul of Confucius, for whom a temple was erected in each provincial capital city during the Yi dynasty, when the ritual ceremony of Confucianism was one of the most important of national events.

Memorial services are also offered regularly for the souls of such national figures of bygone days as the founder of ancient Korea, Kija, the founder of the kingdom of Silla, Pak Hyokkose, the founder of the Paekche kingdom, Onjo, and the founder of Koryo, Wanggon. The soul of the legendary Chinese general Kwangu is worshipped at the temples of military generals erected in many parts of the country, because the guardian god of arms is believed to have averted a national disaster by defeating the Japanese invasion forces in the war of 1592-1598.

In contrast to such guardian gods of famous kings, saints, and military generals, the gods of various malignant souls pester the people. Among such gods of malice, the most numerous are the evil spirits of women who met premature, unnatural deaths. They seem to lurk as a special menace to second wives. Another god of plague which is infamous for its omnipresence is the evil spirit of *yongdong*, which lurks on the largest beam of the house during the month of the second moon, effectively blocking any act of "uncleanliness" and dealings in grains with a threat of setting the house on fire. According to one legend, the evil spirit was the soul of a fisherman who had been charmed to death by beautiful women of a virgin island whence he had drifted after a shipwreck.

The virgin goddess of malice, *Songaksi*, on the other hand, molests maidens to work off her jealous grudge, because it is believed that she is the evil spirit of a girl who had to die without experiencing her share of carnal pleasure. When a virgin dies, therefore, various charms are resorted to so that her spirit may not be claimed by *Songaksi*: the body is placed in the coffin in an upside down position, clothed in men's garments, thorny boughs are placed around the coffin, or the body is buried together with a male body.

Not only human beings, but also some animals become gods after death. For instance, it is believed to be evil to keep a cow of over a certain age because old animals may transform themselves into human beings or spirits. Examples of the maximum "safe" ages for cattles or pet animals are ten years for the dog and three for chickens. Other animals which may turn into spirits include the tiger, fox, snake, and certain worms. The spirits of animals are also believed to "even the score" after death with human beings.

Giant old trees are divinated as guardian gods by adorning them with a "sacred straw cord" around the trunk, or scattering yellow clay on the ground around so that people may be warned off against any act of "uncleanliness" toward the "sacred" tree. Since many gods choose to reside in such a tree, the burning of even the dead boughs is regarded as likely to invoke the god's wrath.

The mysterious tonic effect of *ginseng* for prolonging the prime of life is attributed to a divine being within the unique Korean root herb. Shaped like the figure of a human being, *ginseng* which grows deep in the mountain is believed to wield supernatural power, and, therefore, accorded the utmost reverence.

The house is filled with gods of various natures, of whom the god of creation or the god of the largest beam is the ruler of all other lesser household gods. Within the room is the god of birth, whose presence is indicated with white paper or several pieces of straw cord, while the fortunes of the house-site are administered by the god of earth. The kitchen is under the domain of a god of its own, and the gate is guarded by another god occupying that place. The fortunes of the master of house are dependent upon the god of the "imperial seat," which is located in the closet, where rice, beans, and a piece of cotton cloth are enshrined to symbolize the god. The guardian god of the barn and warehouse is enshrined within one animal living in each particular barn or warehouse such as a snake, a "yellow mouse," or a toad. Disappearance or killing of such an animal designated to be the "divine" pet is believed to ruin the fortunes of the house.

Illness of all kinds is attributed to each specific god of plague, of whom the god of small-pox is regarded as the most dreadful. Various charms are used to exorcise the gods of plague.

The mischievous but harmless god, *Tok-kaebi*, often plays tricks on the people. Household articles abandoned after a long use, such as broom, "kitchen stick," and any goods stained with human blood, are believed to transform themselves into the playful god. It appears most like a will-o'-the-wisp, assuming the form of a man with one or no legs. Demonstrating his supernatural power, the mischievous god fools the people, but rarely causes death. Contact with this will-o'-the-wisp is thought occasionally to bring excellent fortune.

Exorcism of Evil Gods

Various means are used to effect the exorcism of evil gods. One is administering a severe beating to the afflicted person as in the case of the attempt to cure a person of insanity. Since a lunatic person is believed to be possessed by an evil spirit, the Shaman incantation has to be supplemented by beating the patient with the bough of a beech tree which stretches to the east, so that the physical pain will drive the evil spirit out of the person. A legend has it that during the period of the Silla kingdom, the nobleman Sunjong rescued his wife from the hands of a devil by having the earth beaten with sticks by many hired hands.

Another device to exorcise an evil spiririt is to scare or shock the devil away: a horrible mask is worn; an image of a tiger, dragon or powerful military general is posted; terrifying sounds are made by discharging a gun at midnight. In the course of the Shaman rite of exorcism, the dancing Shaman occasionally brandishes a glittering knife or places a skeleton of a cow-head for the same purpose — scaring the devil away.

Sometimes threatening an evil god with fire or burning the thing possessed by a devil is judged the best way. The old custom of setting fire to a hut built in a field on the 15th day of the first moon was intended to serve the same purpose.

XXIII SPORTS

Outline

Virtual Necessity

The concept of sports was well-nigh born out of virtual necessity in the daily lives of the ancient Korean people. Stemming from the hunting and fishing experiences of their primitive ancestors, Koreans before the ninth century found in sports the means to develop their physiques, thus improving their chance to acquire food, clothing and dwellings. There was running, jumping, throwing of rocks and hanging from ropes. After the ninth century through the Koryo period to the middle of the Yi dynasty, military skills were tied in to sporting events as the art of warfare assumed paramount importance in the fate of man and state in those sensitive centuries of foreign invasions and internal dissensions. From the thirteenth and fourteenth centuries, however, the military arts began to be regarded lightly as the kingdom adopted a strict policy of seclusion and the non-military officials replaced the military in positions of power. The adoption of Confucianism as the state religion contributed to the "peaceful and civilized" state of affairs in which military arts were neglected. Sports lost their flavor and barely held their own when the great *Kabo* Reform of 1894 brought Korea into her first real contact with the world.

Among the sweeping modern changes that streamed in with the *Kabo* was a variety of Western sports. They came with the rise of modern private schools, initiated by the missionaries and included in the school curricula under the Educational Acts, more specifically, under the Primary School Act of 1895 and the Secondary School Act of 1900. The first interschool athletic meeting took place in Seoul 1896. It was the biggest sports event ever held in Korea. Sports interest was revived overnight and, from 1907 on, there were annual interschool events. Throughout the long period of Japanese domination, sports was the one outlet in which the youth of Korea could preserve their integrity. The Japanese authorities recognized in sports the encouragement of nationalistic sentiments and, accordingly, applied pressure in this as much as in cultural and other fields. In 1938, they dissolved the Korean Athletic Association which had been formed in 1920 and, with the worsening Pacific War situation, imposed tight clamps on all fields of sports on the ground that all physical outlets should be devoted to the war effort. Athletes had to wait until Liberation Day to resume playing.

Ancient Sports

Sports in pre-modern Korea may be classified into three categories: military, recreational and entertainment. Following are the sports in the three different categories:

Military—judo, archery, archery on horseback, throwing the stone, horsemanship and game-hunting;

Recreational—kicking the ball, hitting the ball, wrestling, sledge-riding and rope-pulling (tug-o'-war);

Entertainment—throwing the vase, splashing in water, jumping on wooden board, swinging, kite-flying, sword-dancing, hawking and a dice-like game called *yut* in which four sticks are tossed in the air.

The military sports have been mentioned. They received great state encouragement until the latter Yi days when they were equally neglected. Recreational and entertainment pastimes were enjoyed not only by the upper classes but also among the commoners. They were, in fact, an integral part of Korean life and no holiday passed without fanfare and competitive skills in the sporting events above-listed. Much have gone but a few like swinging, board-jumping and *yut* are still very much in evidence.

Modern Sports

The single largest factor in the growth of Western sports interest was the Young Men's Christian Association. It was the Y.M.C.A. which introduced Koreans to baseball, basketball, volleyball and skating around the turn of the century. The Japanese, however, frowned on these Western sports for Korea and the history of their development became increasingly a history of resisting discouragements. The sole center of encouragement throughout the long years was the Y.M.C.A.

The Samil Movement of 1919 was not without its effects on athletic circles. The Korean Athletic Society was formed in July of the following year and, with considerable support from a people reminded of their national birthright by the Samil, began vigorously to promote sports interest. The authorities made difficulties for the Society and, in the end, ordered it dissolved (1938) but by that time the organization had imprinted its mark so deeply that nothing the Japanese did could erase it. In its place, a Chosun Athletic Association was formed with the task of coordinating all athletic activities in the peninsula. In practice, this meant that Koreans had to labor under severe handicaps to promote athletic standards. The Association was an instrument of an Empire which increasingly stressed war efforts. What occasional record was set by a Korean at athletic meetings sponsored by the Japanese was considered no less than miracle. The fields in which the Korean excelled were soccer, basketball and softball tennis among the team events, weightlifting and boxing in the individual. Especially noteworthy was their prowess on the tennis court. An invention of the Japanese, softball tennis was played for the first time outside Japan in Korea and, from 1935, the Koreans held ten consecutive annual championships. In the individual events, the Korean could boast his weightlifting in all Asia.

After the Liberation, Korea was able to come to her own by participating in international athletic meetings or competing with foreign countries under her own national flag. She has participated in all the three post-W W II International Olympic Games at London (1948), Helsinki (1952) and Melbourne (1956) as well as in the Third and Fourth Asian Olympics held in Manila and Tokyo in 1954 and 1958 respectively. She has also sent more than one hundred athletes abroad to compete in basketball, volleyball, table tennis and track-and-field.

Traditional Sports

Judo

Judo in Korea has been called by various names, *subak, tangsu, teakkwon, yusul* and so forth. It was first introduced in the year 1150 during the reign of Koryo King Uijong and improved upon scientific lines during the reign of the 14th Yi monarch, Sonjo. It was so popular among military officers of both the Koryo and Yi kingdoms that annual *judo* bouts were held. The skills developed from *judo* trials are said to have boosted the fighting capacity of the nation during the Hideyoshi invasion of 1592. For all that, *judo* began to decline gradually and, by the middle of the nineteenth century, completely died off.

Archery

Archery can only be presumed to have had its origin in primitive days. There are no written records about its start. Until fire-arms were introduced, archery was without question a major weapon of war and, before the 14th century at least, considered to be a prerequisite to qualify as a military leader. Both Tongmyong and Yi Songye, founders of the Koguryo and Yi kingdoms respectively, were known to have been supreme archers. With fire-power, archery was relegated to a recreational sport. Today, only elderly people who can afford the leisure participate in archery competitions.

Archery on Horseback

The origin of archery competitions on horseback likewise cannot be traced. Written history only confirms that such competitions were popular among the military officers of both the Koguryo and Yi kingdoms. Undoubtedly, it was even more important than archery on foot in times of war. In turn, the introduction of firearms made the horseback bowman even more superfluous than the footman. At any rate, horseback archery was not merely relegated to a back-seat; it has been pushed off the stage completely.

Stone-Throwing

Stone-throwing, in which rival teams, lined up at a certain distance apart, throw stones at one another, was considered one of the most necessary of military pastimes. Successive kingdoms promoted stone-throwing competitions for whole groups of people and villages. Piles of rocks were mounted on tops of hils and in corners of mountain-lanes as arsenal and the story was that the passer-by who failed to add his lot would fare ill on his journey. One Koguryo king called for annual stone-throwing events by the River Taedong and himself participated as "commander" of one side or the other. The Yi founder is said to have organized an army of stone-throwers in 1440. Indeed, stone-throwing was no mere pastime but a tactical instrument of war. Volume 35 of the Historical Records of Sonjo relates how a General Kwonyul, commander of the Haengju garrison, repelled invading Hideyoshi forces with a powerful company of stone-throwers. It was certainly a favorite throughout history. In 1910, the Japanese colonial authority ordered it banned.

Kicking the Ball

From various unofficial records, it is presumed that "kicking the ball" originated before the Three-Kingdom period. There were two varieties. In one, the ball used consisted of dried grasses and other dry materials shaped into a round form and covered with thin leather. Rival teams kicked it into one another's territory in a contest roughly comparable to soccer. In the other, the ball is really a circular disc, consisting of copper coins wrapped up in cloth or paper. Individual players took turns, kicking it up in the air and keeping it there. Of course, the competitor who kicked it up the greatest number of times without allowing it to drop on ground was the winner. "Kicking the ball" in any variety was enjoyed hugely by people of all classes up to the middle of the Yi dynasty.

Hitting the Ball

Similar to modern field hockey, there are no written records of how the game originated. According to volume 1 of the *Koryosa* (History of Koryo), when the former subjects of defeated Silla came to Wanggon, founder of the new Koryo kingdom, to express their wishes to be naturalized as Koryo subjects, the monarch ordered his protocol officers to led them out to the "hitting the ball" ground for the welcome ceremony. This passage, at the very least, confirms that the game was known in the preceding Three-Kingdom or Unified Silla stages. A noted Japanese historian, Ise, gives us every reason to believe that Koguryo had known the game. In his "Interflow of Eastern and Western Cultures," Ise describes the game as the precursor of polo and, as such, the invention of Persia. From Persia, he adds, it went to India and China, and thence to Koguryo and Japan.

History books yield quite a lot of information about "hitting the ball" compared to other ancient sports. We know that there were two kinds of game, one played on the field, the other on horseback. The players of rival teams used wooden sticks with which they drove a wooden ball approximately the size of a fist toward the goal of the opposite side. The fifth day of the fifth month by the lunar calendar was the big hockey and polo day during the Koryo era. There were also contests for women and the court ladies took this opportunity to trot out on horseback in their colorful best. The 11th Koryo king, Yejong, banned the sports in 1116 lest it lead to wastefulness and immoral sexual intercourse. But the game had penetrated too deeply among the commoners to be forgotten. They kept it alive until it was restored to royal favor under the Yi dynasty. It was not until the early part of the 19th century that "hitting the ball" completely disappeared.

Wrestling

The only difference in Korean wrestling from modern styles is in the formal preliminary. The contestants hold each other from the back and wrap a cloth ring around the opponent's thigh. The fighting itself is similar to modern wrestling in all essential respects; i.e. the opponents try to throw one another by legwork, handwork and bodywork. Originated during the reign of King Chunghye of the Koryo dynasty, it is comparatively recent. Wrestling is still enjoyed by the masses on such feast days as the fifth day of the fifth moon or on the August Harvest. The winner is awarded a bull or a bundle of cloth. As a most popular pastime, it is included in the big athletic event that is held in October every year.

Sledge-Riding

The wooden sledge used for this sport in snowy winter is comparable to the Western version. Ancient Koreans went sledge-riding to hunt bears.

Rope-Pulling, or Tug-o'-War

The rope is made of interwined rice stalks and is about 100 meters long. In olden days, the rival teams were composed of adjoining villages. Defeat meant a bad harvest so everybody in the village, old and young, men or women, came out to pull. Only schoolboys are to be found for the tug-o'-war today and then only rarely.

Vase-Throwing

An object, shaped like a vase, is hurled against a target placed a certain distance away, the most accurate thrower being the winner. Vase-throwing came from Sung China.

Shooting the Ball

A form of recreation, devised from "hitting the ball" during the Three-Kingdom period and the fashion of the Yi dynastic reigns of Kings Taejong and Sejong in the 15th century. From the description of the sport in Volume 14 of Sejong's Historical Records, we learn that it was exactly like golf. The players drove an egg-sized wooden ball for a hole with a wooden stick shaped like a golf-club. The only difference was that it was team play instead of individual and the target hole was located under the goal gate of the opposite team.

Horsemanship

Korea boasted highly advanced standards in horsemanship from the days of the Three Kingdoms. Her skills and techniques were displayed abroad during the 18th century, especially in Japan, where the Korean horseman was regarded with awe.

Other Sports

Other sports listed among the traditonal categories, such as swinging, kite-flying or the *yut* dice, can hardly qualify as sports in the understood term of the word. They are described in the chapter: "Games and Recreation." Hawking or game-hunting were just that and need hardly be described here.

Modern Sports

Track-and-Field.

Track-and-field as an indispensable part of modern sports was first introduced into Korea in or about 1895 when drastic social and political changes took place under the *Kabo* Reform and the nation was brought into contact with the outside world for the first real time. Two foreign instructors of the Foreign Language School, Hutchison and Hallifax, were largely instrumental. Under their aegis, students of this school, consisting mainly of Christians, participated in Korea's first modern track-and-field events in 1896 and 1898. Similar events were held subsequently by the Hansong (Seoul) Y.M. C.A. in 1905 and the Taehan Athletic Club in 1906. Interschool meetings were next sponsored by the Ministry of Education for three consecutive years. Track-and-field became an exciting new challenge overnight and prominent names sprang to the public limelight, such as Kim Tonghyong, who leaped 12 feet in the pole vault in 1916, Kim Tongchol and Ma Chunsik, sensational short-distance sprinters.

In 1919, the Chosen Athletic Association was organized under Japanese sponsorship and, in July of 1920, our own "Chosun Athletic Society" followed suit. These two bodies did much to modernize Korean sports and encouraged the rapid growth of track-and-field interest. Noteworthy athletes during this period were Yi Iljun, Kwak Sokkun and Hwang Taeson in running, Chu Hunggun and Yu Yakhan in the shot put.

In January of 1929, an inter-secondary school long distance meeting was held in Japan under the sponsorship of the Kansai University. The distance to be covered was 36 miles from Osaka and Kobe. The Yangjong middle school represented Korea to win the event in the record time of 3 hours 29 minutes and retained the Japanese Empire championship in the ensuing two years.

In October of 1931, a Yangjong schoolboy, Kim Unbae, surprised the marathon world by winning the Chosen Shrine Marathon Event at a startling though unofficial new world record of 2 hours 26 minutes and 12 seconds. The following year, he went to Los Angeles to participate in the marathon event of the 10th World Olympic Games but only placed sixth at 2 hours 37 minutes 28 seconds. However, he won both the 1,500 and 10,000 meter races at the Far Eastern Athletic meeting held in Manila 1934. Korea's greatest hour came in 1936 when another Yangjong schoolboy, Son Kijong, won the Berlin Olympic marathon in 2 hours 29 minutes 19 seconds, a record unbroken for sixteen years. Nam Sungyong, the other Korean marathoner, added to the triumph by coming in third. The Paejae middle school won the all-Japan Inter-Middle School athletic meets in both 1937 and 1938 and, in indivi-

XXIII SPORTS

All-time Korean records:

Event	Record-Holder	Record	Year	Place
100 meters	Kim Yutaek	10″5	1939	Koshiyen
200 ″	Om Palyong	21″5	1952	Seoul
800 ″	Sim Sangok	1′53″8	1957	″
1500 ″	Choe Yunchil	3′56″2	1954	Manila
5000 ″	Choe Yunchil	15′ flat	1949	Seoul
10,000 ″	Yu Changchun	31′20″2	1934	Tokyo
Marathon	Son Kijong	2 hrs. 24′ 51″2	1934	Seoul
Broad Jump	Kim Wongwon	7.66m	1940	Kashihara
High Jump	Yi Kwangho	1.90m	1957	Pusan
Hop, Step and Jump	Kim Wongwon	15.82m	1941	Japan
Pole Vault	Cho Unghi	3.70m	1940	Seoul
Discus Throw	Yu Yakhan	44.61m	1948	Seoul
Javelin Throw	An Yonghan	58.80m	1933	Seoul
Hammer-Throw	Song Kyosik	56.48m	1956	Seoul
1600-m Relay	Yi Ijae, Yi Tonghyon, Om Palyong, Son Kyongsu	3′23″4	1957	Seoul
Women's Events				
100 ms.	Kim Yonsil	12″5	1952	Seoul
″	Hyon Kumnyo	13″3	1930	Seoul
200 ms.	Chong Imsun	27″ flat	1941	Seoul
200 ms.	Kang Poksin	29″9	1933	Seoul
Discus Throw	Pak Pongsik	39.65m	1949	Seoul
80-m Hurdles	Pak Hijun	13″ flat	1948	Seoul

dual events, there was Kim Yutaek who ran the 100 meters in 10.5 seconds in 1938, and Kim Wongwon who placed first in the hop, step and jump at the 1941 Budapest World Students' event with a 15.76 meter leap.

Little or no meetings were held during the entire course of the Second World War when athletics were discouraged under the total war efforts. The typical reaction with the coming of Liberation was a spurt of revived interest in which various athletic organizations sprang up all over the country and numerous meetings were held. American athletes of the U. S. armed forces of occupation were brought together with Korean stars in goodwill meetings and the first real break for Korea came at the 51st Boston marathon event in 1946. In all former Korean participations in foreign competitions, the Korean athletes had to compete under the Japanese flag. Now, for the first time, the *Taegukki* was entered in its own right in an international gathering and the young schoolboy, So Yunbok, coached and trained by the redoubtable Son Kijong, fulfilled our highest expectations by winning in the record time of 2 hrs 25 mins.

In 1948, Korea entered a 72-man delegation in the World Olympic Games, resumed after a 12-year interruption in London. The expectations of an entire nation were gravely disappointed when the same So Yunbok who had won at Boston came in 27th while the other even more promising runner, Choe Yunchil, dropped out after leading most of the way. Koreans placed nowhere either in the hop, step and jump, hammer-throw and long and medium distance races. All this was attributed to the long slump for track-and-field athletes during the war years. Only in other fields, basketball, boxing and weight-lifting, were Koreans able to draw mild comfort.

A marathon comeback was made at the

1950 Boston race when Ham Kiyong, Song Kilyun and Choe Yunchil came in one-to-three in that order. Choe represented Korea again at the 15th Olympic games at Helsinki where he came in fourth in an arduously-fought race that saw all first six runners topple Son's Berlin record and the amazing Zatopek break the record by six solid minutes. Choe went on to break the 1500-meter record at the Second Asian Olympics in Manila 1954 in 33 mins 3.8 secs. Subsequently, Choe's star was replaced by Yi Changhun who came in fourth at the 1956 Melbourne World Olympics and first at the 1958 Asian Olympics in Tokyo. The best all-round performances were made at the International Armed Forces athletic meet in Athens 1955 where Koreans placed first in the broad jump event, second in hammer-throw and sixth in the 400-meter hurdles.

Soccer

Soccer is the most popular sport in Korea. It was first introduced in 1906 by a Frenchman, Charles Martel, whose Foreign Language School students were the first to play the game. Various organizations were subsequently formed and regular tournaments held among the Paejae middle school, Foreign Language School and the Y.M.C.A. Foreign missionaries and customs officials also organized their own teams in the port city of Inchon, opening the doors to inter-city matches — between Seoul and Inchon. With the organization in 1920 of the Chosun Athletic Association, modern rules began to be observed and soccer became an organized game, with such teams as the Chosun Soccer Club, the Seoul Buddhists and the Pyongyang Muo Club spreading wide public interest.

The foremost Korean eleven was the Chosun Soccer Club. In 1926, they defeated a visiting Osaka team 3-1 and two years later, went abroad to Shanghai for the first to win four out of six matches against Chinese and other teams there. The following year, they were less successful, winning only one out of four games. Win or lose, the Shanghai expeditions gave new impetus to both inter-city and inter-school tournaments at home. Selected teams began to be drawn for annual all-Japan matches and standards were considerably improved. The Pacific War efforts, however, sank all these activities and only the Liberation enabled Koreans to put teams together again. In 1947, an all-Korean eleven went to Shanghai again where they beat such outstanding Chinese teams as the Tonghwa and Chingbae football clubs. The London Olympics of 1948 was the first opportunity for Korean soccerites to meet foreign players other than Chinese or Japanese. The Koreans beat Mexico 3-1 in the first game only to be white-washed 11-0 in the second by Sweden which went ahead to cop the title.

Korea sent no soccer teams to the two subsequent World Olympic Games at Helsinki and Melbourne. Instead, she sent yearly goodwill teams to Hong Kong, Saigon or Singapore. In 1954, she was runner-up at the Second Asian Olympics in Manila and, in March of the same year, she qualified for the 10-nation World Soccer Championship Tournament in Sweden by defeating Japan in the Far Eastern eliminations. At Sweden, however, Korea dropped two straight defeats to Hungary and Turkey. In September 1956, the First Asian Soccer Championship Tournament was held in Hong Kong from which Korea emerged the victor. In foreign goodwill visitations to Korea, the United States Olympic team enroute to Melbourne in 1956, lost 1-0 to an all-Korea eleven. A touring Israeli team fared no better in 1957.

Baseball

A certain Gillet, American missionary, brought baseball to Korea in 1905. He taught the game to members of the Hansong Y.M.C.A. which organized a baseball team in no time with a view to popularizing the game as a modern sport. Overseas Korean students returned home on holidays to help the Y.M.C.A. By 1920, several middle schools had baseball clubs and yearly interschool

↑ Korea's Olympic Delegation
 The Olympic team from Korea marches past the royal box during the 16th Olympiad opening ceremony held in Melbourne, November 22, 1958.

↑ So Yunbok
 Crosses the tape to win the Boston of 1947.

← An American-Korean Goodwill Sprint Race

→ Long Jump
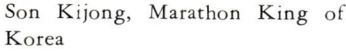

Son Kijong, Marathon King of Korea
↓ Is shown here winning the 1936 Berlin Olympic marathon with a record unbroken for 16 years.

A Cross-Country Race
↓ A relay race is held every autumn from Pusan to Seoul.

↑ Diving
At the swimming pool of Seoul Stadium.

↑ Speedskating
    At the skating rink of Konguk University, Seoul.

→ Students' Skating Race

↓ Skating Rink on the Frozen Han River

↑ Ski Ground of Taekwannyong Mountain
　Inns and ski trails available. The only ski area that is in south Korea.

← An American-Korean Good-Will Soccer Match

→ Rugby

← Volleyball

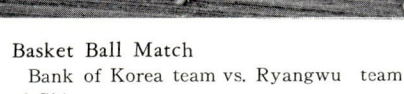

↑ **Basket Ball Match**
   Bank of Korea team vs. Ryangwu team of China.

↑ **Table Tennis**
   Miss Wi Ssangsuk, winner of international contests.

→ Baseball

↓ Field Hockey

↑　Race Horses Running at Full Speed

→　Horse-Race

↓　Hurdle Race

Mass Game
↓ At a middle school.

↑ Weightlifting

↓ Korean Traditional Wrestling

↑ Heavy Gymnastics—College Students

↑ Co-ed's Indian Club Gymnastics

→ School Girls' Gymnastics

A welcome meet for the Korean Team returning from the 3rd
↓ Asian Olympic games.

Taegwondo →
One of Korea's traditional sport. Similar to boxing, but feet are also used.

← Boxing

↓ Judo or Yudo in Korean

↑ Up a Rocky Mountain

↑ Conquering a Peak

← Camping

↑ Mountain Climbing

← Bicycle Race (Sprint)

→ Bicycle Trip

↓ Bicycle Race (Long-Distance)

↑ Mass Game
Combined with Korean folk dance, Kang-gang-suwolle, by high school girls.

→ School Girls' Gymnastics

→ College Students' Mass Game

↑ Mass Games
   For primary school children.

↑ A Mass Game
   On the President's birthday.

games were played thereafter. In 1921, the Huimun high school defeated all other school teams to qualify as Korea's representative at an all-Japan tournament in Tokyo. The Huimun boys made the semi-finals. A rare treat was afforded Korean baseball fans with the arrival of an American Major League team in 1922. Not until 1958 when the St. Louis Cardinals came for a game was Korea to witness baseball at its best. The following year, a team of Korean immigrants to Hawaii came for a series of friendly games, losing all. Perhaps, because of Japan's undoubted superiority, baseball, though popular, was never able to make headway like soccer or basketball.

In March 1946, the year immediately following the Liberation, a group of baseball-lovers organized the Taehan Baseball Association. This Association has been vigorous in promoting baseball interest in the post-Liberation era as never before. It has sponsored numerous goodwill matches between Korean teams and U.S. armed forces, and, more recently, has invited a Nationalist Chinese nine as well as a team from the University of Southern California. In the four-nation Asian Baseball Championships, Korea placed third at Manila in 1955, and was the runner-up at Tokyo in 1958.

All in all, Korea has not shone much on the baseball diamond.

Basketball

Gillet was also the importer of basketball. He brought this game in one year before baseball, in 1904 when he was secretary-general of the Y.M.C.A. For 10 years, the Y.M.C.A. was the center of the basketball world. In the year 1920, a Waseda University team came to Korea as the first foreign players to challenge Korea in basketball. Subsequently, Korean school teams paid frequent visits to Japan as well. It was, however, only after 1930 that Koreans began to demonstrate their undoubted worth on the basketball court. The two most outstanding college teams were Yonhi and Posong; the Sungin commercial and the Kwangsong middle schools in Pyongyang provided the best teams in secondary school competitions. These four teams paid annual visits to Japan from 1932 onwards and distinguished themselves year in and year out. The Sungin Commercial won two successive titles to the all-Japan Inter-Middle School Basketball Championship in 1935 and 1936. The Kwangsong boys were the champions in 1942. In 1936, again, the Yonhi College won the all-Japan college event and three players on its line-up were included in the Japanese basketball team to the Berlin Olympics. The Posong squad, on the other hand, kept the same title for three years—1938-41.

Basketball suffered the same plight as other modern sports during the Pacific War. Interest was revived after the Liberation and a gallant Korean basketball team managed to squeeze into the final tournament in the London Olympics basketball. The Korean team, composed of eight players, scrambled to the top of the heap in a close and hectic six-nation eliminations tournament. With Iran as the general whipping-boy, the other five nations, Korea, China, the Philippines, Chile and Belgium each finished up with a 3-2 win-and-loss column. Korea won on the basis of points. In the six-nation finals, the Koreans ended up at the bottom of the rung.

The war prevented Korea from dispatching a basketball team to the Helsinki Olympics. In 1954, we participated in the Second Asian Olymics basketball in Manila but placed only fourth. Clearly, the standards had dropped considerably and the Taehan Basketball Association began to do something about it. Foreign teams were invited one after another, the Victory Team from America, Nationalist China's crack Kehnan squad, a USAF Far Eastern squad, the Philippines' Seven-up's and Oregon College. A noted American basketball coach, John N. Burn, came under the sponsorship of the Asia Foundation to deliver a four-month course of lectures. More and more teams went abroad to Formosa, Hong Kong and Manila for friendly matches as well as to the Melbourne World Olympics in 1956 and the Tokyo Asian Games in 1958. Improvements have been noted but considering our past standards, the performances have been far from satisfactory. The most outstanding success, in fact, has been achieved by girls although women's basketball is something new. Korea has won two consecutive titles in the Asian Women's Basketball Championship.

Volleyball

Volleyball was introduced in the comparatively late year of 1916. Once again, an American missionary was responsible and the Y.M.C.A. was the venue. The public, however, remained unenthusiastic for a long time. Over a period of 25 years, volleyball was played only among high school and college students. Only as late as 1942 was sufficient interest generated to permit an inter-school tournament at the secondary school level. Volleyball, in fact, was at the pioneering stage up to the eve of the Liberation. With the Liberation, enthusiasm for volleyball was no less than in other fields of sport. A Taehan Volleyball Association, organized in November 1945, proved so vigorous in promoting interest that no other sport today can rival volleyball in general popularity.

In 1954, with the organization of the Asian Volleyball Federation, volleyball was included in the Asian Games for the first time. This occasioned renewed interest in Korea. In October 1954, Korean volleyball players played overseas for the first time at the invitation of the Hong Kong Volleyball Association. The second opportunity was offered with the opening in Tokyo of the Asian Volleyball Championship Tournament in May 1955. Korea was runner-up in this event and took second place again in the Third Asian Games volleyball tournament, Tokyo 1958.

Tennis

In Korea, tennis has always been played with a soft rubberball. "Softball tennis," as the game may well be termed, was the invention of the Japanese. In 1908, officials of the Ministry of Finance of the Yi dynasty government learned about the game from their Japanese advisors. It became so popular among Koreans that Korean players improved to the point where they held all Japan championships for 10 consecutive years since 1930. The outstanding player of this monopolistic decade was Om Inbok. In contrast to other games, "soft ball tennis" faded with the Liberation but not altogether.

Real tennis was first played in Korea in September 1927 on the occasion of the First Tennis Tournament sponsored by the Osaka Asahi Newspaper. In the same year, a Korean graduate-student of Boston University, Kim Taesul, won an all-U.S. collegiate tennis tourney in Boston City Apart from Kim's personal glory, however, tennis was played by a limited number of Koreans. It still is at a very primitive stage. President Rhee himself took account of this fact when, in July of 1955, he invited the chairmen of the Korean Athletic Association and the Korean Tennis Association, presented them with 12 rackets and 12 dozen tennis balls, and urged them to foster tennis interest. The main development has been the goodwill series of matches, sponsored by the Korean Tennis Association between local players and members of the U.N. Armed Forces. In October of the same year that the head of state expressed his personal interest, a galaxy of world tennis aces, including Jack Kramer of the U.S., Pancho Gonzales of Mexico, and Australia's Sedgeman, were invited to Korea by the Association for a series of exhibition games.

Table Tennis

Introduced by the Y.M.C.A. about 50 years ago, table tennis was first played among the 30-age brackets and over the years has become a most popular pastime. Today, it is hardly possible to find a school or major firm or social club that is not without table tennis sets and players of their own.

In October 1945, the Korean Table Tennis

Association was organized to coordinate all ping-pong playing in the country. This body became a member of the International Table Tennis Federation in 1950 and of the Asian Table Tennis Federation two years later. In 1950, Choe Kunhang represented Korea at a U.S. Table Tennis Championship Tournament, thus opening the way for Korea's participation in subsequent international table tennis events. In the 1st Asian Table Tennis Championship held 1952 in Singapore, three Korean players vied with top aces from other Asian countries. The Koreans, as expected, came off poorly. However, considerable progress was evident on the part of the six Korean players at the Third Asian Table Tennis competition in 1954, where Yi Kyongho and Wi Ssangsuk won the mixed doubles' title. In March 1956, another eight-man delegation was dispatched to the 23rd World Table Tennis Tournament at Stockholm where Korea did not win any titles but drew enough attention to be rated highly in press speculations about the future. At the Fourth Asian Table Tennis Tournament in Manila January 1951, Korea was runner-up in the women's team competition, while, in the individual women's play-offs, Misses Choe Kyongja and Wi Ssangsuk placed first and second respectively.

Rugby

Rugby came late. It was first played in Korea by Japanese middle school boys in inter-school matches in 1923. In 1930, the first Korean teams were organized by the Paejae and Yangjong middle schools, and, in 1932, Posong College sent the nation's first team abroad to Japan. For three consecutive years from 1930, the Kyongsong Normal school held the all-Japan middle school title. For all that, rugby was far from being a popular sport in Korea. So it remains today. There are some 100 rugby teams in the country but the criterion for popularity is to be found in the schools and only a few schools carry rugby teams. The most active rugby is played among cadet schools of the Army, Navy and Air Force in annual league affairs started in 1954.

Handball

Introduced about 20 years ago, handball, from the start, was included in various school athletic courses. However, it was not strictly governed by the rules and regulations that governs modern handball. Orthodox play was first noted on the occasion of a lecture on the rules, regulations and techniques of handball given by Yi Pyonghak, a professor of Posong College, in 1938. The first all-Korean handball team was organized in 1942 and, in 1945, immediately after the Liberation, a Korean Handball Association was organized to coordinate the playing of all handball teams, in or out of school.

Gymnastics

Two branches of gymnastics, the horizontal bar and the vaulting horse, were included in compulsory school athletics courses as early as 1895 under the new Educational Act proclaimed with the *Kabo* Reform. With the inclusion of gymnastics in recent Olympic programs, Koreans have begun to show gradually rising interest. A Korean Gymnastic Union was organized in March 1946 and, thanks to its efforts, the horizontal bar, the parallel bars and the vaulting horse are now available for recreation everywhere, in rural no less than in urban districts. Korean gymnastics standards are regarded as among the highest in Asia. In 1956, ten Korean gymnasts visited Taiwan and Hong Kong and, in 1958 and 1959, girl gymnasts of the Muhak and Sudo high schools went to Viet Nam. Everywhere, the Koreans bowled them over.

Weightlifting

Weightlifting took its place among the ranks of modern Korean sports in 1924. The occasion was a gymnasium built by two sports enthusiasts, So Sangchon and Yi Pyonghak, within the compounds of the Chungang Athletic Center, the only athletic organization then existing. Over a hundred youths made it their daily routine to gather at the gymnasium to lift the weights. The result was that ever since 1930, every top spot in every weightlifting class in the annual all-Japan championship meet was occupied by a Korean.

In 1947, Korean weightlifters heaved their way to second, third, or fourth places in a number of classes in the World Weightlifting Championship meet held in Philadelphia, the Koreans winding up second only to the U.S. in the total tabulations. At Korea's first participation in World Olympic Games at London in 1948, her weightlifters were the redeeming feature of the 72-men delegation, winning 1 third place, 2 fourth places and 2 sixth places in all. Their steady levels were maintained at Helsinki as well with 1 third place, 2 fourth places and one sixth. In the Asian Olympics of 1954, Koreans copped top prizes in all five categories and kept all these titles at the Third Asian Games four years later. Finally, at the World Weightlifting meet in Munich 1955, Koreans won 2 fourth places and one fifth.

Swimming

Modern swimming techniques came to Korea about forty years ago. In 1922, a student group of the Kyongbok middle school went to Wonsan beach for their summer holidays and held a research course on swimming there. That was the first time swimming was approached as a modern sport. In the ensuing years, similar research courses were held in various beaches of Korea. In August 1929, the Korean Athletic Association and the Tonga Ilbo daily co-sponsored the first seminar on swimming with over one hundred interested individuals participating. As a direct result of this seminar, a Korean Swimming Association was formed. This Association has sponsored annual interschool swimming meets for over twenty years now. For all that, Korea's standards are still far below international levels.

Other fields of sports, such as horsemanship, boxing, cycling, skiing, field hockey, ice hockey and golf have only a short history behind them. The boxers have done quite well at the World Olympics. Korean cyclists swept the Asian Olympic Games in Tokyo and Korean residents in Japan proved surprisingly strong in field hockey at the same games. Overall, however, they are not considered matured enough to meet international levels.

XXIV GAMES AND RECREATION

Preface

It was only in recent years that the general public in Korea began to consider recreation as a necessary part of daily life and to try to devote as many leisure hours as possible to recreational activity and heal the mental and physical fatigue incidental in modern living.

However, it was impossible in the past for most Koreans, excluding a limited number of well-to-do people, to enjoy their leisure hours in terms of recreation. They just could not afford to organize public recreational organizations or to install public facilities for such purposes. They enjoyed very simple indoor and outdoor games mostly in the winter, when most of them were relatively free from farming and other labor, and also on traditional holidays, such as New Year's day and *Chusok* (harvest festival).

In 1895, King Kojong proclaimed an imperial instruction leading to a social revolution, an effort to put an end to the semi-feudalistic social system that had existed for too long. Under the new proclamation, the traditional class system, that had divided the people into the *yangban* (peerage) and *sangmin* (commoner), was abolished, slaves liberated, and the slave trade prohibited, among many other social changes. As the nation was thus open to Western countries for free trade and diplomatic relations, modern recreational means were introduced with other Western institutions through those countries which came to deal with this country.

During the Japanese rule of Korea, between 1910 and 1945, Koreans were given little chance to develop their own traditional culture and alien customs were forced upon the Koreans. Despite the Japanese effort to assimilate Koreans, however, the Korean people deliberately resisted this and endeavored to maintain their own language, customs and ways of living. This nationalism successfully protected Korea's culture from Japanization, but failed to devleop it further. In other words, Korean culture was saved from retrogression, but at the same time it did not make any progress either.

It was in 1945, when the country was liberated from Japanese rule, that the Korean people again started to enjoy publicly Western sports and other modern recreational activities without fear of political persecution. It must be remembered that during World War II, all Western sports, such as baseball, basketball, and football, were discouraged, and even card games played by several persons in a group were not allowed for Koreans. It was also after 1945 that more people became interested in managing recreational facilities as enterprises. The significant fact, however, is that the general public has come to realize that an adequate amount of recreation today is necessary for proper work tomorrow.

Traditional Games in Korea

Jumping-Seesaw

The jumping-seesaw was first originated in the Koryo dynasty days and became popular during the Yi dynasty. It is a pastime chiefly for young girls and ladies during the New Year holidays, and is still popular today.

In Korean see-saw, each of the two participants stand at each end of a wooden board, usually two meters long and 40-50 centimeters wide. The board is so set to balance upon a pillow made of rice straw at the center and the two girls jump up and down in turn at either end. Well-balanced upon this see-saw, skilled jumpers can bounce high up, in beautiful form. Some say the see-saw was originally designed to enable Korean women in ancient days to peep over the walls of their courtyards. In the older days in Korea, women were generally confined within their houses and very seldom allowed to go outside. But very few people today believe this was the real origin of the leaping see-saw that, so far as we know, is unique to Korea.

Nowadays, the see-saw is to be seen more in the rural areas than in urban areas.

Swinging

Like the jumping see-saw, swinging was also originated in the Koryo dynasty era, and is still a great sport among girls today. It also is a representative game for Korean women, particularly enjoyed on the *Tano* Festival, May 5 by the lunar calendar.

It is a beautiful, traditional scene to see young ladies in colorful Korean costumes on swings hung from high branches of the trees in the woody, green mountains of May around the *Tano* Festival.

A history book of the Yi dynasty records that in the 17th century nationwide swinging contests were held in Seoul, and attracted hundreds of thousands of spectators. Even today, many such contests are held in towns and rural areas, while some girls' high schools have swings in their schoolgrounds for the students.

Kite-Flying

An old legend says kite-flying was originated in 1380 when a general of the Koryo dynasty, Choe Yong, used it for tactical purposes in his conquest of Cheju Island off the southwestern coast.

It is a pastime usually for children during the winter months. It is a traditional custom that children let loose their kites on the fifteenth of January of the lunar calendar, with evil things and names of diseases written on the kites. It was generally believed that they could get rid of these evil things and diseases in this way.

A Korean kite is made of a bamboo skeleton and paper. Sometimes the kite is colored red and blue, and the picture of a tiger, dragon or tortoise is drawn upon the kite. A long string is attached to the kite and it is manipulated to do many tricks, like a plane piloted by an expert flyer. The string is sometimes strengthened with ceramic filings glued to it to make it sharp enough to cut others. In kite-flying contests, each contestant tries to cut the string of his opponent by manipulating his. Kite-flying is traditionally for children, but in recent years, kite-flying contests have been regularly held, sponsored by newspapers and other organizations throughout the country, which are generally participated in by adults.

Yut

Originating in the ninth century during

the Paekche dynasty, this is one of the oldest games played in Korea. Essentially, *yut* is a kind of backgammon, and is played generally among two to four players, or among two to four teams, provided each team comprises two or three members. It is usually played during the New Year holidays.

A *yut* is made from the branch of a hardwood tree. It has a diameter of two to three centimeters. The branch is cut into a piece 20 to 25 centimeters in length, and is vertically cut into two pieces. Four of these *yut* are used to play the game.

A player moves his pawn according to the figure represented by the *yut*, which he throws out of a small bowl. The *yut* board is round with three short-cuts to the goal. A player makes five moves if the four wooden pieces all show their backs, and four moves if they all show faces, three moves if three of them show faces, two moves if two of them show faces, and one move if only one of them shows its face. The player who moves all four of his pawns through to the goal wins the game. *Yut* is a very simple game, but very interesting, too, as one can eliminate any pawn of his opponent when his pawn catches it. Also, there are various ways and choices in moving one's pawns.

Hawking

Although hawking was a sport even before the tenth century in Korea, it became popular after the tenth century during the Koryo dynasty, and was one of the most representative outdoor sports at that time. Hawking involves hunting pheasants, rabbits, and other small birds with hawks which are tamed and trained for the purpose.

First it was encouraged among military personnel to foster a warrior-like spirit and also to help build up their bodies, but gradually it became an exclusive recreation for upper-class people, producing many evil practices.

When hawking was very popular among the nobles, the government established an office to train hawks and take care of various matters concerning hawking. Hawk-trainers and other officials who worked with the office came to be a source of great irritation to outsiders, particularly to farmers living nearby, whose domestic fowl often became prey to the hawks. Furthermore, the general trend, to make a hawking trip as colorful and fancy as possible, accelerated the tendency of officials and military personnel to become corrupt, as against the main original purpose of the game.

The Yi dynasty in the mid-15th century prohibited this pastime for the general public, and allowed only a limited number of high officials and scholars to enjoy hawking as a purely recreational activity. Nowadays, hawking is almost non-existent, even in rural areas, where the rifle and shotgun are the hunter's tools.

Tuho

Tuho was a competitive sport in which competitors threw arrows into a narrow necked vase-like vessel from a distance of about ten steps. About 50 to 60 centimeter-long arrows were used in this game which originated in the Sung dynasty of China.

The game was introduced to this country around the tenth century, and played on and off, but became popular again in the early part of the 12th century, according to a history book of the Koryo dynasty. It was also played among high government officials and royal members of the Yi dynasty. Ladies sometimes enjoyed the game, too.

Sunggyongdo

A kind of backgammon, *sunggyongdo* has long been played by the younger members of the upper class during the New Year holidays.

It can be played among any number of players. *Sunggyongdo* contains, in order, a list of govenment positions from the lowest up to the premiership, and starting from the lowest position, the one who reaches the premier's position first wins. Wooden, usually about 15 centimeters long, pentagonal dice is used to play the game.

In older days, this game was played only among youngsters of the *yangban* (peerage class), because they were the ones who were qualified for government service through civil service examinations. *Sunggyongdo* is still played at some very traditional homes during winter, or during the New Year holidays. *Yut* can be used instead of the pentagonal dice.

Ssangyuk

This is a kind of backgammon introduced from mainland China during the Chinese dynasty of Wei. The dice used in this game originally indicated only one and two on the faces, but later came to have figures from one to six, used universally. A pair of dice was used.

Nowadays, *ssangyuk* is played only in some areas of southwestern Korea among farmers.

Kolpae

A mahjong-like game set, *kolpae* is said to have originated in China. It involves 32 small rectangular objects made of ivory or a combination of anumal bone and bamboo or wood. The *kolpae* set is used for a variety of games, gambling, and fortune-telling. It is particularly popular among older people in farming areas.

Flower-cards
(Korean Playing Cards)

Flower-cards consist of 48 cards, representing the twelve months of the year. January is represented by a pine-tree, February by a plum-tree, March by cherry, April by bush-clover, May by orchids, June by the peony, July by colored bush-clover, August by the moon, September by the chrysanthemum, October by the maple, November by the paulownia, and December by rainfall.

Like Western playing cards, flower-cards are used for a number of card games, fortune-telling, and gambling. Two to five players are best for ordinary games using flower-cards.

Tonchigi
(Coin Game)

Tonchigi used to be very popular among children in the older days, but it is seldom played nowadays. Contestants in this game throw their coins hard against a stone wall, and the one whose coin flies farthest from the wall tries to hit the other scattered coins with his coin from the point where his coin dropped. Sometimes, a foul line is drawn and those whose coins drop outside the line are given another chance and, if they still fail, are eliminated from the game.

This game was played particularly during the first two weeks of the year. Very few play this game with coins today but many children enjoy similar games with marbles and other objects both in big cities and rural areas.

Chegi

Chegi is a coin wrapped in thin but strong paper. A coin with a big hole in the center is used, and about ten centimeter-long tails are attached to help it fly smooth.

Players kick the *chegi* straight up. The one who can kick it without dropping it on the ground wins the game. There are a few different ways of playing. One is to use only one foot in kicking the *chegi*, another is to use both feet in turn, and still another is to use only one foot but keep the other foot steady, the idea being not to move a step while kicking. The one who loses becomes a "servant" and throws the *chegi* towards the winner to be kicked by him. The loser does so until the winner fails to kick the *chegi* properly. The loser tries various bad throws to baffle the kicker, but the winner can wait until the loser serves a good throw.

This is a game particularly popular among children, and is still played both in urban and rural areas.

↑ Zoo-aeroplane for Children
In Changgyongwon Park, Seoul.

↑ Caged Birds

↑ Fishing

↓ Casting a Net

A Riding-club

↑ Goldfishes

↓ Watering in Green House

↑ Trimmed Tropical Plant in the Garden

← Chrysanthemum Growth

↑   A Well Kept Garden

↓   Gardening with Family

Rope Skipping

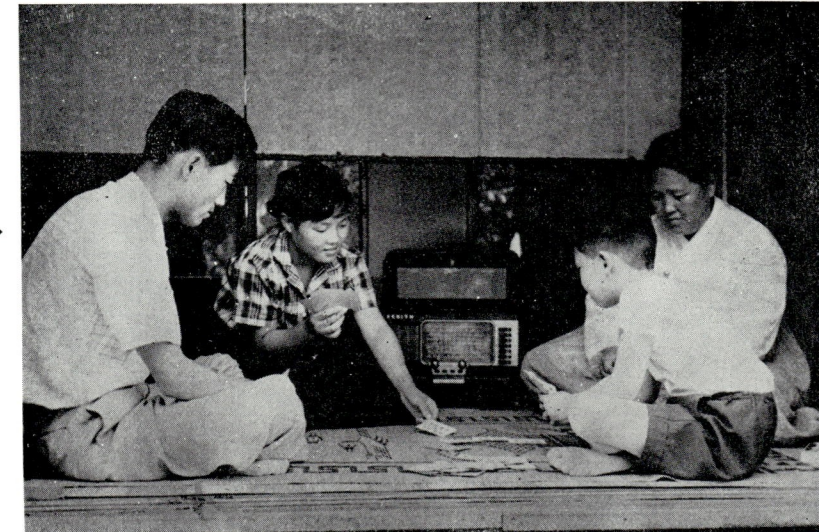
Playing Cards

Playing "Flower Cards"

→ Chess

↓ Dominos

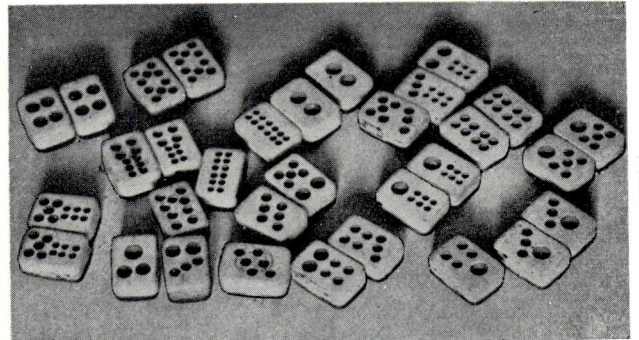

Paduk, an Elaborate Game of
↓ "Checkers"

 ← Billiards

Shuffleboard →

↓ Golf Links

Korean Games in Modern Days

Paduk

Paduk is the Korean name for the chess-like game better known as "go," the Japanese name. It is not known exactly how long ago *paduk* was introduced to this country, but there are historical records showing that it was played in the Koguryo and Paekche days, and also was popular among high-ranking officials of the Silla dynasty. Therefore, it can be assumed the *paduk* came to this country over 2,000 years ago.

In those days, it was played among high officials as both a recreational and politicking sport—in the same manner as golf for wealthy people and politicians today. Commoners did not play *paduk* at all. It was only during the latter days of the Yi dynasty that the game became popular among the general public. But during Japanese rule, it was again limited to well-to-do people in their inner drawing rooms, as the public just could not afford to enjoy the game, not because of the money involved, but because of the time consumed.

Since 1945, the game has become very popular among the public as it is so simple and inexpensive. Many *paduk* houses have been built in almost every town to provide recreation-hungry people with one of the most inexpensive recreational activities in Korea. One of the reasons for the popularization of *paduk* is probably that newspapers and popular magazines, through their recreation pages, are fast spreading fundamental knowledge of the game. Many newspapers sponsor *paduk* contests with various prizes for the winners.

In the past when the need for recreation was not so recognized as it is now, it was frowned upon if young men were caught playing the game. The picture has completely changed now, and you can find many young men, even teen-agers, playing the game against older people in *paduk* halls or at private homes.

In addition, there is a professional *paduk* association in Seoul embracing scores of professional players. The championship holder in this professional world is Cho Namchul, who holds seventh grade, highest in Korea. The association holds semi-annual nationwide tournaments in spring and autumn for advancement of grades held by these professional players. Beside, there are half a dozen other nationwide *paduk* contests sponsored by major newspapers for professional players. There also have been goodwill *paduk* matches between Korea and Nationalist China.

As a rule only two players vie in this traditional Oriental game. The *paduk* or *go* version of chess is a competition between two players to occupy more territory, or houses, over a board divided by 19 vertical and horizontal lines. The rules are very simple and can be mastered within a short period, but the techniques involved are very complex and varied to make each more tenuous and interesting. Extensive study over a long period is needed to acquire techniques for advance play. The one who is senior holds a more advanced grade and uses the white *paduk* while the other uses the black pieces.

In addition to extensive study, *paduk* also calls for mental concentration, judgment, the ability to envision an overall situation, decisiveness, and so on; it is said to be very good for sharpening one's intelligence.

Changgi
(Korean Chess)

The original version of the present *changgi* was invented some 4,500 year ago in Mesopotamia, says an old legend. It is said that a warlike king invented the game to keep his beloved queen inside the palace so she would not follow him along the dangerous frontlines.

This original game was exported to both Europe and China, and there developed different forms of chess. The one now played in Korea is patterned after the one developed in China, and is different from the one played in Japan. The Korean chess board is divided by ten horizontal and nine vertical lines, and has two "palaces", one for each contestant. There are, for each player, one general, two chariots, two cannons, two horses, two elephants, two palace guards, and five soldiers.

The movements are:

a) General: cannot move out of the palace, but can move one step in any direction within the palace. When the general is checked and cannot counter the checking move of the opponent, the match is lost.

b) Chariot: can move in any direction as far as there is no obstacle. It is the most powerful weapon for both defense and offense.

c) Cannon: can also move in any direction, but it must necessarily move by jumping over any other piece except another cannon itself. It is generally used for defense of the palace.

d) Horse: moves one step straight and one diagonally in any direction. It is an important offensive weapon and serves as a vanguard of the force.

c) Elephant: moves one step straight and two diagonally. An offensive weapon, but it can be more useful during the latter half of the game when there are less pawns moving.

f) Soldier (or pawn in Western chess): can move only one step forward or horizontally, but cannot move backward. It generally works as a team with other soldiers.

g) Palace guard: can move one step in any direction only within the palace square.

The weaker player starts the match first. When one player is too strong for the other, he starts the game with certain handicaps. The handicaps may be elimination of one or more soldiers or other powerful weapons. When the players repeat the same moves a number of times and fail to make different moves, the game is declared a draw.

Changgi is played everywhere throughout the country by people in all walks of life. It is particularly popular in rural areas during winter when there is not much to do on the farm. In recent days, many *changgi* halls have been opened in cities not only for renting, but to teach advanced techniques.

Mahjongg

This game was originated in mainland China during the Ching dynasty (17th-18th century) and was mainly played in the court, but gradually spread throughout the world. It is not known when *mahjongg* was first introduced to this country.

The game, popular before the war, was discouraged by the Japanese colonial government during World War II, but with the liberation from Japanese rule it became popular again. *Mahjongg* is played more for gambling purposes than for recreation.

Angling

In Korea, the people enjoy angling in man-made reservoirs or ponds or along main rivers. For economic reasons, very few go out to the sea to fish aboard boats for recreational purposes.

Angling, which used to be a sport among older and well-to-do people in Korea, became suddenly popular and spread like an epidemic among the general public after the Korean armistice agreement was signed in 1953. On Sundays, we can see many urban dwellers go out of town to enjoy their holidays by fishing, and see many people with fishing gear in buses and streetcars. Most of these people belong to angling clubs, which provide transportation for them to fishing places and also sponsor from time to time angling contests for members. A few newspapers also sponsor nationwide fishing contests attracting many participants and stimulating more interest in angling.

Crucian is the fish most frequently caught in Korea by anglers, but occasionally carp is caught too. Crucian caught in Korea ranges in length from three inches to one foot.

One interesting way of angling in Korea is that done during winter on frozen rivers through small holes in the ice. This is practiced except in the warmer southern area, where rivers do not freeze during the winter. The anglers cut holes through the thick ice over rivers, and sit on low stools with their gear dropped through the holes. Experienced anglers catch five to six large carps a day. Most engage in this winter fishing not as a sport, but as a source of income, since carp caught during winter is very expensive in Korea. The Han River, which runs through the capital city of Seoul, is famous for this kind of fishing during winter.

Billiards

It is said that billiards was first introduced to this country around 1915, but there is no way to ascertain the exact time.

First, it was played by Korean students who studied in Japan. They learned the Western game in Japan, where it had already been introduced, and spread it in Korea after returning home. Thus, the game gradually became popular among relatively well-to-do people and pool houses were opened for the first time in Korea around 1925, generally in larger cities.

The Japanese discouraged the game during the Second World War, as they did other Western sports and games. Like other forms of recreation, billiards became especially popular after the truce, and today we can find pool houses in small towns throughout the country. Pool houses are always crowded by students, salaried men, army officers, and most others. Like coffee shops, pool houses serve as places for social intercourse. In recent days Korean women, particularly coeds, have begun to shoot pool among male players.

In Korea the four-ball ordinary game is the most popular. The three-ball game, three-cushion game and other versions are seldom found.

Hunting

As Korea lacks dangerous wild beasts such as lions and tigers, the major game is the wild boar, with deer, rabbits, pheasants, and ducks as follow-ups. In some areas, non-sporting ways of hunting, such as the use of traps, are still practiced, but more and more people are using rifles. Once Korea was famous for its tigers, and during the latter days of the Yi dynasty, hunters came from England and other foreign countries to hunt them. They are now very rare and what few tigers survived deep in the mountains became almost extinct during the recent bitter war.

Koreans generally employ three methods of hunting. One is hawking, another is shooting, and the third is the use of traps and snares. In rural areas, farmers still dig big holes in paths where wild animals frequently pass. They are skillfully camouflaged with branches and grasses to deceive the animals. Once people used poison to hunt pheasants and ducks. They stuffed peas with such poisons as cyankali and left them where pheasants frequently hunted for food. This method, of course, is not a proper way for hunting, and it soon disappeared.

In Korea, a government license is required for possession of a hunting rifle. Rifles can be obtained in government-licensed rifle shops in major cities. There are 14 such shops in Seoul. They are also in such cities as Inchon, Suwon, Chunchon, Wonju, Kangnung, Taejon, Taechon, Kangkyong, Chongju, Masan, Chonju, Sunchon, Taegu, Pusan, and Kwangju.

Korean hunters have been renowned over the centuries for their good manners and sense of courtesy. Korean hunters shared their games with those who were on the spot. After returning to their villages, they usually held big parties for the villagers with their game. They particularly shared the blood of boars and deer, as it is believed in Korea to be very nourishing and good for health.

The 155-mile long Korean Demilitarized Zone may be considered the best hunting place in Korea. Almost every kind of animal and bird abounds along this two-and-half mile-wide truce zone, without any fear of being caught. It is a natural sanctuary because no shooting within the area is allowed under the Korean Armistice Agreement, and this has been so in the past six years.

Pheasant hunting is most popular in Korea. Famous pheasant hunting areas are Yoju, Ichon, Susaek, Nunggok, Kimpo, Kunja, Ilri, Pibong, Kwachon, Songpa, Manguri, and Singoktungni, all not far from Seoul. In addition, Kumchon, Munsan, Taekwangni, Yonchon, Chongok near the frontline, the Hamyol area in Cholla Pukto, Chinan, Imsil, Yosu, and Andong are also renowned for pheasant hunting.

For duck hunting near Seoul, there are Susaek, Ilsan, Hunggok, Ilri, Yamok and Songpa. Namyang, Choam, Anchung, Pyongtaek, Tunpo, Sapkyo, Tangjin, Yohung Island, Taebu Island, Kangwa Island at Kimpo, the Naktong River mouth, and the southwestern coast area are also renowned. Rabbits used to be found in great numbers in almost every mountain area in the past, but the number has greatly decreased in recent years. Boars are usually found in shaded places in spring and fall, and in sunny places where they can find a lot of arrowroot during winter days. Deer usually hide in shady places during winter days, but in spring they came down to the barley fields to eat the barley. For deer-hunting, Yonchon, Koesan, Sangju, Tanyang, Andong, Imsil, Namwon, Chinan, Sunchon, Yosu and Naro Island are renowned. For boar hunting, Hwabok and Hwaryong in Sangju, Mount Paekun in Chinan, Kangjin in Imsil, Kurimyon in Sunchang, Sangdong in Kimhae, Choksong and Emil in Kangwon-do, Kurye, Koksong, Chongsan Island, and Mount Chiri in Cholla Namdo are famous.

Dancing

The Western social dance rapidly spread among Koreans after 1945 together with other Western customs and institutions, becoming especially popular after the war. However, the traditional Confucian ethics on separation of the sexes which underlies Korean society is preventing further popularization of the Western dance. Most Korean houses are not fit for dancing, and therefore, one must go to dance-teaching institutes to learn how to dance. One can enjoy dancing at night clubs, cabarets or dancing halls, and it is becoming customary for dancing to be included in the fare of big parties.

In some high schools and colleges, fundamental steps of the Western dance are taught to students in their gym hours, but most of them do not have the chance to practice their dancing lessons, except at Christmas parties or other special occasions. Dances popular in this country include almost every form of dance popular in other countries, that is, waltz, tango, fox trot, blues, jitterberg, rock'n'roll, calypso, and so on.

Golf

Golf was introduced to Korea for the first time in May, 1919, when a nine-hole course was opened in Hyochang Park in Seoul by an American named H. E. Dannt.

Five years later, a 16-hole course was constructed in Chongnyangni, in the northeastern outskirts of Seoul, and finally in 1931 the present Country Club site was opened to golfers with an 18-hole, 6,500-yard course. The course was closed by the Japanese in 1944 during the Pacific War, and considerable damage was done to the course by the Japanese, who converted it into a glider training center. The course was rehabilitated soon after 1945 when the country was liberated from Japanese rule, but it again suffered damage during the Korean War.

After the armistice, the Seoul Country Club reconstructed the course. It is now 6,800-yards long, and is one of the best golf courses in the Orient. There is a golf course in Pusan, the second largest city in Korea.

Golf is almost exclusively monopolized by high government leaders, foreign diplomats, military leaders and rich businessmen, but has not yet been popularized as a general sport or recreational means in Korea. There are about 300 regular members of the Seoul Country Club, and there has been some discussion among civic leaders about constructing another course on the southern outskirt of the capital near Sihung. Exclusively for personnel of the United Nations Command and American forces stationed in Korea, a nine-hole course was opened in 1959 at the UNC military reservation in Yongsan, Seoul.

Once miniature golf was very popular among the general public throughout Korea, and many courses were built in and around Seoul, too, but the miniature golf frenzy soon passed away, and very few courses now remain.

Flower Arrangement

The art of floral arrangement in this country has been developed under the influence of Buddhist culture. This art is said to have first originated in India, where the Buddhists had the custom of presenting flowers every morning before the images of Buddha.

The custom was introduced to this country through China during the Three Kingdoms period, and then to Japan some 200 years later. The details of the ancient Korean art of flower arrangement, however, are not precisely known at present. We can see some through ancient art works that depict floral arrangement.

There are some vases still preserved that were made more than 2,000 years ago. These vases and some of the ancient drawings indicate that the floral art in ancient Korea must have been very realistic. Although it has such a long tradition in this country, the art of floral arrangement became so popular and developed to such an extent in Japan that many Koreans thought, during the Japanese rule of Korea and even after the Liberation, that the art was exclusively Japanese in nature. Therefore, not many Koreans, except a few housewives and girl students, have developed proficiency in this traditional Korean art and hobby.

Birds and Fish

Bird-keeping became suddenly popular after the Korean War, and now almost every Korean home keeps one or two cagebirds as part of the family. Some Koreans first started keeping birds as a side occupation to help boost their income, but now it has become one of the most popular of home hobbies in Korea.

After the bloody, ruthless fighting of the war, the people seemed to be looking for something inexpensive but effective which would give them comfort and a sense of stabilization, and keeping cage-birds was a hobby which satisfied such a demand. Because of the ideal weather and abundant feed, available bird-keeping will not easily lose its popularity among the Korean people. Except for native Korean larks, most of the cage-birds are those imported from foreign countries. Popular cage-birds include the canary, parrot, bengalee, Java sparrow, and finch.

Meanwhile, keeping goldfish and tropical fishes is also very popular among Koreans. And one can easily find aquaria with goldfish or tropical fishes sold on streets or kept at homes, restaurants, and coffee shops. There are some 20 kinds of goldfish kept by the Korean people. Tropical fishes are not as popular as the cheaper goldfish.

XXV TOURISM

Preface

Tourism a 'Natural'

Since the beginning of 1957, Korea has been concentrating her efforts on the development and promotion of her tourist industry, attaching great importance to the economic benefits of tourism and its influence on foreign relations. The Ministry of Transportation of the Government of the Republic of Korea is in charge of the tourist industry.

Korea, as one of the most beautiful and traditional countries, is undoubtedly rich in tourist potentials. Extending north to south, she has rugged mountains, hot springs, countless gulfs, bights and inlets, with varied topographical and climatic features making for mild and clear weather throughout the year. Korea is proud of her conservative traditions that have gracefully merged into the framework of modern civilization, yielding picturesque landscapes and well-preserved antiquities. Koreans live in a treasure land of ancient culture with exotic music and colorful customs dating back centuries.

For all that, Korea lacks the facilities and publicity necessary to attract the tourist and provide for his comforts and conveniences. To overcome such handicaps, the government has undertaken vast projects, the renovation and construction of hotels, improvement in the means of trapsportation, development of major tourist areas, etc. The results are apparent. The number of foreign visitors to Korea has been increasing year by year. In 1958, it showed a 20% increase over the previous year and in 1959 yet more tourists have come in groups or individually.

Conveniences Provided

Thanks to the accomplishments already made, some thirteen first-class hotels are now catering to the foreigner, most of them naturally concentrated in Seoul but a few also in local resort areas. Lack of hotel accommodations is to be relieved considerably under the "Five-Year Plan for Hotel Construction," drawn up by the Ministry of Transportation in 1959.

At the same time, the government has simplified visa procedures for tourists, one of the major discouragements in former days. To get a visa now, all that is required is to fill in two applications with two pictures attached and a smallpox vaccination certificate.

Transport facilities on trains, buses, airports, docks, highways, and so forth, are also steadily being improved. A general renovation of the Kimpo International Airport has been undertaken, and passenger vessels for coastal cruises will also be built soon. Roads are being beautified by the Ministry of Home

Affairs. On the other hand, the Ministry of Education is caring for historic remains and national treasures.

On the publicity front, the Ministry of Transportation has produced many publications in English, such as general information booklets, district folders, posters, hotel folders, etc, totalling 180,000 copies.

In order to carry out overseas tourist promotion activities, the government of the Republic of Korea has participated in meetings of the International Union of Official Travel Organizations (IUOTO), obtaining full membership in 1957. Also, the Korea Tourist Bureau is participating in similar activities as an active member of the Pacific Area Travel Association (PATA). Furthermore, the Ministry of Transportation has been cooperating with more than 500 travel agents in the United States and countries of the Pacific area. Thanks to all these efforts to foster a 'natural', the tourist trade is expected to flourish within a matter of years.

Tourist Areas

Temples

Pulguk-sa
Location: Chinhyonni, Kyongju, Kyongsang Pukto.

Transportation: Route 1. Seoul to Pulguk Station—397.3 kms—12 hrs 18 mins by train. Station to Temple—3.6 kms—15 mins by bus. Route 2. Seoul to Taegu—323.9 kms—6 hrs 50 mins by train. Taegu to Pulguk Station—90.5 kms—1 hr 50 mins by train. Station to Temple—3.6 kms—15 mins by bus.

History: Built in the 27th year of King Pophung of Silla some 1440 years ago. Rebuilt by Minister Kim Taesong on enlarged scale, underwent repeated restoration during Koryo. Destroyed by Hideyoshi invaders of 1592. Present building dates back 230 years.

Cultural resources: Tabo Pagoda, Three-storey Stone Pagoda, Sari Pagoda, Yonhwa and Chilbo Bridges, Chongun and Paegun Bridges, Sokgul Grotto Cave and Punhwangsa Stone Pagoda.

Facilities: Pulguksa Tourist Hotel (modern). Some private hotels, souvenir shops.

Haein-sa
Location: Kayamyon, Hapchongun, Kyongsang Namdo.

Transportation : Seoul to Taegu—323.9 kms—6 hrs 50 mins by train. Taegu to Temple 116 kms—3 hrs 30 mins by bus.

History: Built by High Priests Sunhung and Yijong in 3rd year of King Aejang some 1000 years ago.

Cultural Resources: Temple houses, 86,000 woodblock plates of engraved Buddhist scriptures and several others such as Buddha image, pavilions, waterfall, hermitages.

Facilities: Inns, recreation facilities, souvenir shops.

Pobju-sa
Location: Songnimyon, Poungun, Chungchong Pukto.

Transportation: Seoul to Okchon—183.2 kms—4 hrs 6 mins by train. Okchon to Temple—46 kms—2 hrs by bus.

History: Built by Priest Uisinchosa in 14th year of King Chinhung 1400 years ago. Repeatedly restored. Completely destroyed by Hideyoshi invaders and rebuilt by Priest Pyogam, in second year of King Injo.

Cultural resources: Ssangsa Stone Lantern, Sachonwang Stone Lantern, Pyolsang Hall, Maaeyuraegi Statue, Suknyon Pond.

Facilities: Hotels, souvenir shops.

Tongdo-sa
Location: Habukmyon, Yangsangun, Kyongsang Namdo.

Transportation: Seoul to Pusan—44 5.6 kms —9 hrs 20 mins by train. Pusan to Temple—52 kms—1 hr 30 mins by bus.

History: Built by Chajangyulsa, a high priest, in 15th year of King Sondok 1312 years ago.

Cultural Resources: Taeungjon Hall and Kukjangsaeng Stone Monument.

Facilities: Two inns within temple grounds.

Taehung-sa

Location: Samsanmyon, Haenamgun, Cholla Namdo.

Transportation: Seoul to Mokpo—427.1 kms—11 hrs 32 mins by train. Mokpo to Temple—65.9 kms—2 hrs 30 mins by bus.

History: Surrounded by Turyun Mountains, built during reign of King Chinhung some 1370 years ago. Features cherry blossoms in spring, colorful maple leaves in autumn.

Cultural resources: Buddhist image, called the Pukmirukam Mayeyuraesang.

Facilities: Nil.

Sudok-sa

Location: Toksanmyon, Yesangun, Chungchong Namdo.

Transportation: Seoul to Sapkyo—146.6 kms—3 hrs by train. Sapkyo to Temple—12 kms—30 mins by bus.

History: The Indian priest, Marananta, propagated Buddhism here for the first time 1450 years ago. Designed and built by Abiji, expert-artisan of Paekche. Enlarged by high priest Wonhyo in fifth year of Silla Queen Songdok 1300 years ago.

Cultural Resources: Taeungjon Hall.

Facilities: Nil.

Magok-sa

Location: Kongjugun, Chungchong Namdo.

Transportation: Seoul to Taejon—166.7 kms—3 hrs 30 mins by train. Taejon to Kongju—36 kms—2 hrs by bus. Kongju to Temple—28 kms—1 hr 40 mins by bus.

History: Originally built by Chajang, a famous priest, in the 10th year of Paekche King Mu. Repeatedly destroyed by war or fire, rebuilt six times.

Cultural resources: 21 Buddha statues, two Buddhist bells and 716 volumes of Buddhist scriptures. Seven temples in vicinity.

Facilities: Nil.

Kumsan-sa

Location: Kumsanmyon, Kimjaegun, Cholla Pukto.

Tranportation: Seoul to Sintaein—285 kms —6 hrs 32 mins by train. Sintaein to Temple —18 kms—15 mins by bus.

History: Built in the first year of King Pob 1360 years ago. Sari and Chongsok pagodas subsequently built in second year of Queen Sondok. Miruk and Taejang Halls destroyed by war, rebuilt in Middle Yi.

Cultural resources: Yoju pillar, Five-storey Stone Pagoda, Stone Bell, Hexagonal Stone Pagoda, Tanggan Pillar, Three-storey Stone Pagoda, Miryuk Hall.

Facilities: Nil.

Chondung-sa

Location: Kanghwagun, Kyonggi-do.

Transportation: Seoul to Temple—91 kms —3 hrs by bus.

History: Date of building uncertain; chronicles only reporting that third restoration work was undertaken in 7th year of Koryo King Wonjong. Most scholars assume the temple was built during the reign of Koguryo King Sosurim 1555 years ago. Repeatedly restored in Yi dynasty.

Cultural resources: Halls of Taeungjon and Taksajon.

Facilities: Nil.

Songgwang-sa

Location: Songgwangmyon, Sungjugun, Cholla Namdo.

Transportation: Seoul to Sunchon—413.8 kms—11 1/2 hrs by train. Sunchon to Temple —48 kms—2 hrs by bus.

History: Biggest temple in South Cholla; built by Su Wu, disciple of high priest Pojo by latter's command.

Cultural resources: Kuksajon Hall and Kyongbi Monument.

Facilities: Nil.

Sunam-sa

Location: Ssangammyon, Sungjugun, Cholla Namdo.

Transportation: Seoul to Sunchon—413.8 kms—11 hrs 25 mins by train. Sunchon to Temple—30 kms—1 hr by bus.

History: Founded by Adohwasang in 15th year of Silla King Pophung (528 A.D.). Burnt down by Hideyoshi invaders in 1597, rebuilt

↑ Changgyongwon Seoul
Once a palace of the Yi kings now serves as the most favored park for Seoul citizens; contains the largest zoo and botanical garden in Korea.

← Altar in the background of Changdok Palace, the spacious grounds of the Yi kings.

Puyong-Chong
In the Changdok is the Secret Garden with beautiful spots such as this lotus-bedecked pond.

The court here is typical of the quiet atmosphere that pervades the Changdok Palace grounds.
↓

→ Songnyu Gate, one of the inner gates of Toksu Palace in downtown Seoul.

← Peonies in full bloom before the king's pleasure-house.

→ The Toksu entrance within a stone's throw from Hotel Bando.

← The East Gate of Namhansan Fortress

Was erected in Kwangju, Kyonggi-do in 1621 on the site of an ancient Silla fortress. When the Manchus invaded Korea, King Injo was besieged here. The scenic beuaty lasts all the year round.

The South Grate of Namhansan Fortress
↓

Mount Pukhan →
Snow-covered site of a fortress erected by the Yi kingdom to defend the capital city of Seoul to the south.

East Gate of Samnang Castle
Located in Kanghwa, Kyonggi-do, legend says that the castle which once stood here was erected by the three sons of Tangun, the national founder.
↓

Kwangnung, Kyonggi-do
These two young ladies are strolling through the dense forest of Kwangnung
↓ on their way to King Sejo's mausoleum.

Kongsimdon
A watchtower of the fortress of Su-
↓ won Castle.

Hwahong-mun
The sluice is part of the Suwon Castle behind the Hwahong-mun gate in the background.

Panghwa-Suryu-Chong
A pavillion within Suwon Castle east of the Hwahong-mun.

Yonju-dae
Name of the cottage at the peak of this precipice of Mount Kwanak in Kyonggi-do. The cottage is a Buddhist temple built more than a thousand years ago.

↑ Nakhwaam, or the Rock of Falling Flowers, at the Bank of the Paengma River

When the Paekche Kingdom fell, three thousand court maids, refusing to submit to the enemy, threw themselves into the water from this cliff.

↑ Subukchong
 Located near Puyo, Chungchong Namdo, the ancient Paekche capital, on the bank of Paengma River.

↑ The Stone Statue of Maitreya in Kwanchok-sa Temple, Nonsan, Chungchong Namdo
 Erected by the Buddhist priest, Hyemyong, in A.D. 967. One of the biggest Buddhist statues in the Far East; height 24.5 ms, girth of the chest 11.2 ms.

↑ The Towers of Pulguksa Temple
　　The Tabo at the extreme left and the Sokka, right-foreground, are noted for their structural beauty as well as for their historical value. The Pulguksa, of course, is the outstanding monument to the glory that was Silla.

← Yonhwagyo Bridge and Chilbogyo Bridge
　The stone staircases in Pulguk-sa Temple are called bridges because an arch was built under the steps. On the top of the steps is a gate called Anyang-mun.

→ Chongungyo (Blue Cloud Bridge) and Paekungyo (White Cloud Bridge)
　Other famous staircases of the Pulguk-sa. The building on the top of the stone steps is a gate named Chaha-mun.

Chomsongdae, Kyongju, Kyongsang Pukto
　The first astronomical observatory in the Far East—probably in the world—was built by the Silla dynasty.
↓

Site of Imhaejon Palace, Kyongju, Kyongsang Pukto
　Although only the base works remain now, Imhaejon built in A. D. 674 was a part of the gorgeuos Wolsong
↓　Palace of Silla Kingdom.

↑ The Buddhist Image in Sokkuram, Kyongju
   The greatest masterpiece of Silla art, and the principal image of Sokkuram Temple.

An Exterior View of Sokkuram Temple
   A magnificent granite cave temple on Mount Toham, Wolsong, Kyongsang Pukto, containing various Buddhist images that are
↓ great works of Silla art.

↑
A Part of the Images of Four Deities
   Carved in relief on the wall of the entrance to Sokkuram Temple.

Najong Well, Kyongju
A spring in which, legend says, the egg of Pak Hyokkose, founder of Silla Kingdom, was found.

Site of Posokchong, Kyongju
A winding stream was made here to float a wine-cup on the water so that when the cup stops in front of any one sitting along the stream, the man has to compose an ode.

Tabo Tower of Pulguk-sa Temple
The granite tower in the Pulguk-sa is one of the masterpieces of Silla art.

Sokka Tower, of Pulguk-sa Temple
Together with the Tabo Tower, this is another of Silla's finest work of art.

← Sokpinggo in Kyongju, Kyongsang Pukto
Granite ice storage built in Silla period.

↑ Kyerim (literally, Poultry Wood) near Kyongju, Kyongsang Pukto
The legendary birthplace of the Kim clan.

Site of Hwangyong-sa Temple, Kyongju
→ Once one of the largest temples in Silla dynasty, only the base stones now remain.

↑ Kwanghanlu, Namwon, Cholla Namdo
An octagon with stone pillars built in 1635, and used for entertainment. Well known for it was the high-stage in the popular love story, Chunhyangjon.

↑ Ojakkyo Bridge, Namwon, Cholla Namdo
The Ojakkyo, meaning literally the bridge of crows and magpies, was named after a legend that crows and magpies fly side by side across the Milky Way on July 7th every year in order to keep a rendezvous with the man-star, Altair, and the woman-star, Vega.

↑ Chonbuldong Valley, Kangwon-do
  Soaring rocky peaks. dense wood and clear water make this valley one of the most beautiful places on Mount Sorak.

↑ Myonggyongdae
Clear water of the abyss in the Inner Kumgang in Kangwon-do.

Manpoktong →
A beautiful valley in the Inner Kumgang.

↑ Kwanumbong, or the Peaks of Avajokitesvara
Lofty peaks on the Outer Kumgang. In winter, the peaks are covered with snow as thick as 1.5 to 6 meters.

←
Obongsan
A grand spectacle of a rocky mountain in the Outer Kumgang. 1,264 meters in height.

↑ Chipsonbong Peaks
   Of Mount Kumgang (Diamond Mountains).

Sainam Rock, Tanyang-gun, Chungchong Pukto
One of the "Eight Best Scenes of Tanyang."

Segomjong House
One of the "Eight Best Scenes of Pyongando." Located in Kanggye-gun, Pyongan Pukto, the northern border of Korea.

↑ **Chongsokchong, Tongchon-gun, Kangwon-do**
These rocky pillars rise from the waters of the Eastern Sea (Japan Sea).

↑ **Chongnyubyok (Clear Stream Cliff)**
As its name shows, this cliff stands along the river bank of the Taedong, making a part of the beautiful Moranbong Mountains.

↑ Hwajinpo
A lake in Kosong, Kangwon-do. The circumference is 11 kms and 2.3 square kms in area. One of the most beautiful spots to visit on the east coast.

↑ Todam-Sambong, Tanyang, Chungchong Pukto
One of the "Eight Best Scenes of Tanyang".

← Angyong (Spectacles) Bridge
One of the best scenes of Outer Kumgang.

↑ Pyokpadam of Inner Kumgang
The clear water of this rivulet flows to make for small falls here and there.

↑ Sokmun, or Stone Gate, Chungchong Pukto
This rock, comprising a huge gate in itself, is also one of the "Eight Best Scenes of Tanyang."

Ipsokni →
A picturesque scene of Sea of Kumgang.

↑ Lake Kyongpo
   One of "Eight Best Scenes of Kangwon-do" northeast of Kangnung city. The beautiful lake (8 kms, in circumference), along with the green forest of pine-trees around and swans on the water, is one of the best sceneries not only in Kangwon-do but in the whole country.

↑ Uisangdae, Yangyang, Kangwon-do
   Also, one of the "Eight Best Scenes of Kangwon do" together with nearby Naksan-sa Temple.

↑ Podokkul
  A hermitage in a mountain of the Inner Kumgang.

← Samsonghyol (Holes of Three Surnames)
  Located in Cheju city on Cheju Island. According to legend, the three gods of the island, Ko, Pu and Ryang, were born here.

↑ Hodo, or the Tiger Island
  An island, apparently made of lava, off the port of Soguipo, Cheju Island. In the left is a cave opening.

  Kumgangmun (Diamond Gate)
↓ The most beautiful place in the Sea of Kumgang, with a magnificent view of the sunrise.

↑ Kugam Rocks
One of the most beautiful sights in the Sea of Kumgang on the east coast of Mount Kumgang.

↑ Yondam Bridge
A viaduct over a valley in Outer Kumgang.

← Tongyonggul, Yongbyon-gun, Pyongan Pukto
One of the largest stalactitic caverns in the world, very strange and mysterious, 2 kms long.

Chonsondae of Outer Kumgang
The pillar-like rocks soaring up on the top of the mountain, when seen from the foot, may appear to be angels that the rocks were named after. ↓ Chonson means angel.

↑ Sochongbong
A peak on Mount Sorak, Kangwon-do.

↑ Buddha Image of Pobju-sa Temple, Poun-gun, Chungchong Pukto
The largest standing statue of Maitreya in the East, 94.4 feet in height, was started to be built 20 years ago and is still uncompleted.

↑ Songmojong on Mount Mani, Kanghwa Island
　　The mythical remains of Tangun, the Founder of Korea.

↑ Chamsongdan on Mount Mani, Kanghwa Island
　　A mythical site of Tangun, the Founder of Korea.

← **Lower Reaches of the Tumen River**
Starting from Mount Paektu, the river flows southeast as the boundary between Korea and Manchuria, on one hand, Korea and Soviet Russia, on the other.

Rafts on the Yalu River
Starting from Mount Paektu, the Yalu flows west along the boundary between Korea and Manchuria to empty itself into the Yellow Sea. ↓

↑ **Palmido Island off Inchon, Kyonggi-do**
It has a good bathing beach where many Seoul citizens come to enjoy their week-ends in summer.

Songdo Watering-Place, Pusan →
One of well-equipped bathing-place in Korea is used summering resort by natives and foreign visitors, and crowded about 20,000~30,000 summering colony in every year.

→ Naksansa Temple, in Mount Obong, Yang-yang-gun, Kangwon-do
One of the "Eight Best Scenes of Kang-won-do," built during the Silla dynasty and extended in Yi period.

← Taehung-sa Temple, Haenam-gun, Cholla Namdo
One of the thirty-one headquarters temples in Korea. Built during the Paeckche period (A. D. 426). When Hideyoshi invaded Korea, Sosan, the most prominent Buddhist priest of the period, gathered monk-soldiers, engaged the enemy here (1520∼1604). His remains still extant in the temple.

Mount Moranbong
The famous historical and beautiful spot in Pyongyang, Pyongan Namdo. Every building here, down to a piece of stone, tells the history as well as plays in which the Moranbong has figured.

Ulsanam Cell on Mount Sorak
A hermitage deeply located in Mount Sorak, the main peak of the Taebaek Ranges. The outstanding beauty attracts many tourists around the year.

← Unsophisticated Beauty on Mount Kumgang
Contributes to make the Diamonds, one of the rarest beauties in the world.

↑ Chonjiyon Falls, Soguipo, Cheju Island
  One of the largest waterfalls in Korea, 33 meters in height and 6 meters in width. Especially, the beautiful scenery of the ravine along the stream which flows from the linn, is noted together with the landscape of volcanic features around Soguipo.

↑ Chinjudam
    A cascade in Inner Kumgang. One of the most beautiful ravines of the Diamond Mountains.

Pakyon Falls, Kaepung-gun, Kyonggi-do
One of the "Best Three Sceneries in Kaesong Vicinity" and the most famous waterfall in
↓ Korea, the inspiration for a popular folksong.

↑ Towangsong Downward Falls
    A linn deep in the Sorak Mountains.
A cool summer resort.

Chonjeyon Falls, Soguipo, Cheju Island
↓ A little Niagara.

Honggyo Bridge →
Stone bridge with an arch in Sonam-sa Temple, Sunchon, Cholla Namdo. Noted for beautiful scenery around bridge and stream.

← **Chongbang Falls**
From the high cliff at the coast of Cheju Island, east of Soguipo port, waters fall directly into the sea.

→
Yongyon(Dragon Abyss) Cheju City, Cheju Island
Named after the shape of the lake. Surrounded by rocky cliffs.

Kuryong Falls in Inner Kumgang
 The waters, falling from 50 meters high, have bored a 10-meters deep linn at the bottom of the rocks.

Piryong Falls
 A waterfall on Sorak Mountains.

↑ A Rivulet in Kwang-nung, Yangju, Kyonggi-do
 A good scenic spot consisting of beautiful ravines and dense woods.

↑ Pulil Falls on Mount Chiri, Cholla Namdo
 Waters fall step by step.

↑ 12 Tangol
   There are various waterfalls in the Sorak Mountains with many precipitous valleys. The best known is the "12 Tangol"

← Tomb of a Paekche King
Kongju, Chungchong Namdo.

Entrance to the tomb chamber
↓ of an unknown Paekche King.

Interior of the Paekche tomb is
↓ shown (right above).

↑ Tomb of King Muyol-Taejong (602〜661)
Kyongju, Kyongsang Pukto.

↑ **Ancient Tombs around Kyongju, Kyongsang Pukto.**
  Mountainous tombs of Silla period still remain here and there.

←

Hui-nung
Yangju-gun, Kyonggi-do.
Tomb of the queen consort of King Injo (1595~1649) of Yi dynasty.

Mok-nung
Yangju-gun, Kyonggi-do.
Tomb of King Sonjo (1552~1608) of Yi dynasty.
↓

Kija-nung
Pyongyang, Pyongan Namdo.
Tomb of Kija, the ruler of the ancient northern Kingdom of Kija Chosun.

← **Koe-nung**
Kyongju, Kyongsang Pukto.
Tomb of King Munmu (661~681) of Silla dynasty.

Interior view of the tomb of King Uija (641~660), the last monarch of Paekche. Located Puyo, Chungchong Namdo. ↓

↑ **Kwang-nung**
Yangju-gun, Kyonggi-do.
Tomb of king Sejo (1417~1468) and his queen consort, Queen Chonghui of Yi dynasty.

→
O-nung (Five Mausoleums)
Kyongju, Kyongsang Pukto.
Tombs of Silla King Sijo, his queen consort, King Namhae, King Yuri, and King Pasa.

Tomb of Kim Yusin
Kyongju, Kyongsang Pukto.

Tomb of King Suro
 Founder of the ancient Kaya state in Kimhae-gun, Kyongsang Namdo.

Stone-Men and Stone-Animals
 In front of the Kumgok-nung, Yangju-gun Kyonggi-do. Kumkok-nung is a popular name of two tombs of Yi kings, Hongnung (for King Kojong) and Yunung (for King Sunjong).

← **Kyong-nung**
Yangju-gun, Kyonggi-do.
Tomb of King Honjong
(1817~1849) of Yi dynasty.

Yu-nung →
Yangju-gun, Kyonggi-do.
Tomb of King Munjo of Yi dynasty.

Hyon-nung
Yangju-gun, Kyonggi-do.
Tomb of King Munjong
(1414~1452) of Yi dynasty.
↓

Chang-nung
Yongwol-gun, Kangwon-do.
↓ Tomb of King Tanjong (1441~1458) of Yi dynasty.

↑ The Pine Tree of Chong Ⅱ Pum
Poun-gun, Chungchong Pukto
Natural Monument No. 103. 30 meters in height; 5.8 meters around the trunk
  This tree is said to have been titled a court rank. The 2nd Grade of Chong (Chong Ⅱ Pum), by King Sejong (1397~1450), for it lifted up the branches when kings vehicle passed by.

White Pine Tree (400 years old)
Chae-dong, Seoul
Natural Monument No. 8

↑ Winter Plum Blossoms
of Paengma River
Puyo-gun, Chungchong Namdo.
Natural Monument No. 105

Willow (Wangbodul)
Wolsong-gun, Kyongsang Pukto.
Natural Monument No. 116

← Wisteria
Wolsong-gun, Kyongsang Pukto.
Natural Monument No. 89

Ginkgo (about 1,200 years old)
Yangpyong-gun, Kyonggi-do   Natural Monument No 30

↑ White Pine Tree
Koyang-gun, Kyonggi-do
Natural Monument No. 60

↑ White Pine Tree (400 years old)
Tongui-dong, Seoul
Natural Monument No. 4

A Pavilion Tree
↓ Such a large tree is often seen beside a country road.

↑ Bando Hotel
   The leading hotel foreigners in Seoul and, as such the crossroads of Korea's international life.

   Chosun Hotel
   Behind the Bando stands Chosun as the finest and oldest hotel in the
↓ country.

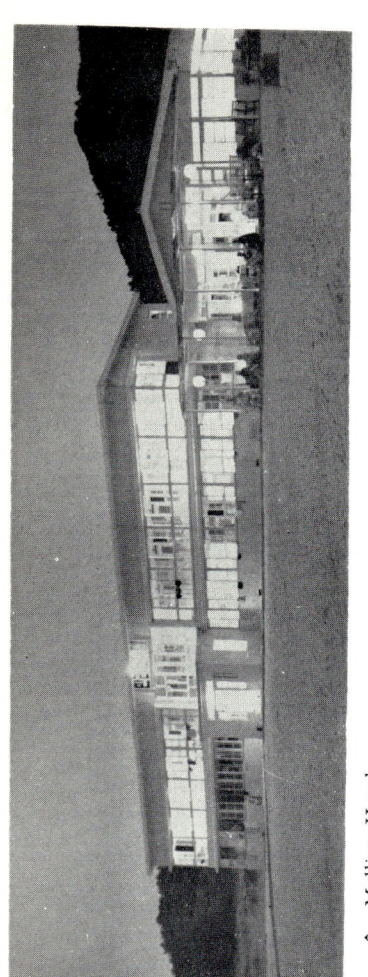

↑ Mallipo Hotel
  For bathers at one of Korea's finest beaches

Onyang Hotel
↓ Famous hot springs resort

↑ Pulguksa Hotel
  For the convenience of tourists sightseeing at Kyongju, capital of the ancient and brilliant Kingdom of Silla.

Korea House
Which welcomes every foreigner into traditional settings with frequent performances in native classical dance, music or drama

← Garden of Korea House

← Guide for foreign travellers at the Korean Tourist Bureau's.

↑ Lobby of a Hotel in Seoul

↓ Smoking Room

↑ **Pagoda Hotel**
  Is one of the newer of modern hotels in Seoul.

Pagoda Park
↓ In the center of Seoul, familiar to every Seoulite.

← Tongnae Hot Springs near Pusan, Kyongsang Namdo

The temperature is 55°~60°C. Many good hotels and bath houses are available.

→ Haeundae Hot Springs, Tongnae-gun, Kyongsang Namdo

Located at the southeastern coast of Korea, there is also a good bathing beach. One of the ideal resorts in Korea.

← Yusong Hot Springs near Taejon, Chungchong Namdo

The temperature is 50°C. Includes a radium spring with rich contents of glucose. Good hotels available.

by three old priests from 1660 to about 1670. Underwent several renovations.

Cultural resources: Taeungjon Hall, Solsondang Hall, Unghyanggak Pavilion.

Facilities: Nil.

Pusok-sa

Location: Pusokmyon, Yongjugun, Kyongsang Pukto.

Transportation: Seoul to Punggi—205.7 kms—7 hrs by train. Punggi to Pusoksa—20 kms—1 hr by bus.

History: Built by Uisang-Pobsa, a high priest, during King Munmu's reign (679), restored repeatedly during the later part of Koryo and early Yi dynasty.

Cultural resources: Muryangsujon and Chosa Halls, oldest wooden buildings extant. Stone Lantern with sculptures in front of the Taeungjon.

Facilities: Nil.

Palaces and Gardens

Toksu Palace. Built more than 450 years ago for Prince Wolsan, first son of King Tokchong. In 1592, after the palaces of Changdok and Kyongbok were destroyed by the Japanese invaders, King Sonjo used the Toksu as his only palace. Save for Sonjo's successor, Kwanghaegun, who moved to Changdok, the Toksu was the royal home for 280 years. The last king, Sunjong moved back to the Changdok early in the 20th century. In 1919, the Toksu was in ruins.

In 1933, the authorities of the Former Royal Household repaired this palace and opened it to the public. Three years later, the Household established the new Art Museum in the palace.

This Museum contains some ten thousand works of sculptures, paintings, and potteries, dating as far back as two thousand years. Recognized as among the world's masterpieces, the treasures were moved during the Communist invasion for safe-keeping.

Major buildings of the palace are the Sokchojon, the first foreign-style building in this country now used as the National Museum, the Chunghwajon, main audience hall, and an Art Gallery built in 1936.

Kyongbok Palace. Most important of the five palaces of Seoul. Oldest and largest, was originally built by Taejo, founder of the Yi dynasty, in 1395. Partly destroyed by fire in 1533, it was restored in 1554. During the Imjin (Korean-Japanese) War of 1592, it was completely destroyed. Two hundred and fifty years of succeeding monarchs did not attempt to undertake the expensive job of restoration.

In the second year of King Kojong (1865), Taewongun, father-regent of the boy monarch and the actual ruler, rebuilt the palace on its former scale and grandeur. The work took about four years. It was in this palace that Queen Min, wife of Kojong and mother of the last King of Korea, Sunjong, was assassinated by Japanese soldiers in 1895.

Kunjongjon, the main audience hall, and the Kyonghwoeru, the most beautifully designed of existing pavilions, are the noteworthy features of the Kyongbok.

Changdok Palace. Built as an auxiliary royal residence in the fourth year of King Taejong, third Yi ruler (1404). Generally called, the Tonggwan Taegwol or East Palace.

The palace grounds comprise 56 buildings, most noteworthy being the Tonhwamun, main gate; the Injongjon Hall which was used for coronation and other similar formal ceremonies; the Sonjongjon Hall which has the only blue-tiled roof in Korea and which is used for state council meetings; the Hijongdang Hall in which the Dowager Taejobi, acted as regent for young King, Kojong (1864-1867); and the Taejojon Hall which contains the private chambers of the King and Queen.

Sacred Garden. The tourist here spends the whole day in complete wonderment. Strolling through the gardens along the sloping paths and trails, one is astonished by the quaint pavilions and ponds, all enlivened with tales hundreds of years old.

The Gardens, landscaped in 1623 for royal recreation, are famed for their magnificent natural beauty. One of the most fascinating features of the gardens is a square lotus pond with curious pavilions around it. One will notice here, for example, the Puyongjong pavilion with its two pillars submerged in the water. The twenty-sided pavilion is known today as one of the world's finest examples of pure geometrical design.

Scattered in the 78-acre gardens are many other sites of interest. Altogether there are 44 buildings of curious shapes. Visitors usually choose the Oknyuchon stream or the Pandoji (Peninsula) Pond as favorite spots.

Changgyongwon Playgrounds. Formerly the Suganggung Palace, built in the 18th year (1418) of King Taejong's reign, 3rd King of Yi dynasty, when he abdicated his throne to Sejong. The name of this palace was changed to Changgyong in 1485, 15th year of King Sunjong's reign.

Burnt down in the 25th year (1692) of King Sonjos, reign, by the Hideyoshi invaders, but the main gate, Hunghwamun, the audience chamber, the Myongjongjon, and the Myongjong Gate were untouched. Rebuilt in the first year of King Kwanghaegun (1609).

In the 2nd year of Sunjong, the 27th and last Yi King, (1908), the Zoological and Botanical Gardens were established in the palace grounds and opened to the public. Once a main palace of the early Yi dynasty, the Changgyongwon became a pleasure ground for Seoul citizens.

Beaches

Taechon Beach. Located on the west coast, some 192 kilometers southwest of Seoul in Chungchong Namdo. Hotels, restaurants, bars and other swimming facilities are available.

Mallipo Beach. Located some 234 kilometers west of Seoul. There are two ways of getting to the beach. Seoul to Hongsong via Chonan, 159 kilometers, by train and Hongsong to the beach, 38 kilometers, by bus; Seoul to Inchon, 38 kilometers, by train and Inchon to the beach by boat. Hotels and restaurants available.

Haeundae Beach. Located near Pusan, 461 kilometers from Seoul; two other good beaches, Songjong and Kijang, in vicinity. The Haeundae Tourist Hotel on the beach offers fine accommodation.

Hwajinpo Beach. Located on east coast, 273 kilometers east of Seoul. The way of getting to the beach is Seoul to Sokcho, 236 kilometers, by bus and Sokcho to the beach, 37 kilometers, by bus. A motel to be constructed some time during 1960.

Pyonsan Beach: Located on east coast, 432 kilometers southeast of Seoul.

Pyonsan Beach. Located on west coast, 321 kilometers southwest of Seoul. It is reached by train from Seoul to Kimjae, 273 kilometers, and by bus from Kimjae to Pyonsan, 48 kilometers.

Kangnung Beach: Located some 273 kilometers from Seoul. It is reached either by air or bus.

Pukpyong Beach. Located on east coast, 375 kilometers from Seoul. It is reached by train from Seoul to Pukpyong via Yongju.

Tokchok Island Beach. Located near Inchon, 38 kilometers from Seoul. It is reached by train or bus from Seoul to Inchon, 35 kilometers, and by boat from Inchon to the beach.

Hot Springs

Scattered about the country, good for nervous diseases, gastric ailments and rheumatism. Four important spots are: Onyang, Tongnae, Haeundae and Yusong.

Onyang. 2 1/2 hours train ride from Seoul in either direction; cars may be changed at Chonan. Hot springs located in center of town within walking distance of station.

Tongnae. In suburbs of Pusan, 12 kilometers from center of town. Can be reached by train or automobile.

Haeundae. On seaside 22 kilometers from downtown Pusan. Can be reached by train or automobile.

Yusong. 8 kilometers northwest of Taejon. Reached by automobile from Taejon station.

Suanbo. 21 kilometers from Chungju by automobile; Chungju reached by train.

Recommended Tourist Areas

Seoul and its suburbs. Established as capital by the first Yi king in 1392, has been capital ever since. Seoul is not only the center of education, administration, business and culture, but also, a paradise for tourists, with beautiful palaces, museums, art galleries, botanical gardens, zoos, theaters, athletic stadia, etc. Suburbs are dotted with numerous historical remains and scenic spots such as royal tombs, castle ruins, Buddhist temples and beautiful playgrounds.

Kyongju area. Capital of Silla kingdom for one thousand years. Buddhist antiquities abound and are easily accessible. Royal tombs, the historical forest of Kyerim, observatories, ice-houses and other evidences of the brilliant Silla culture are the main attractions. Home of the Pulguk-sa, best known of all Buddhist temples in Korea. The broad stairway of the main entrance, the Sokkuram, stone grotto on the hillside behind where Buddha reposes, the Museum which exhibits earthenware, chinaware, tiles, tablets, a bronze Buddha, a stone sundial carved in animal image, and various stone age relics, all make Kyongju and the Pulguk-sa a 'must' on any tourist fare. The attraction is reinforced by the comfortable modern hotel that is available.

Onyang area. A favorite resort, two and an half hour's ride by train from Seoul, temples on route, particularly attractive in cherry blossom time. A modern hotel operated by the Ministry of Transportation.

Puyo: Capital of old kingdom of Paekche, noted for a lofty cliff overlooking Paengma river. Koreans know it as "Rock of Falling Flowers," because more than 3,000 court ladies are said to have leaped to their deaths from the top of this cliff to avoid capture by the armies of a neighboring kingdom. Puyo has an old Paekche pagoda, several Buddhist temples, and a modest but most charming museum.

Pobju-sa. This temple, in the midst of the dense forest of Songni Mountain, is noted for its gracious five-story wooden pagoda, the only one of its type in Korea, in addition to several stone sculptural remains from Silla. This temple is completely off the beaten track.

South Coast. From Pusan one can enjoy a leisurely sightseeing trip by boat for a two-day tour among many colorful islands, including Hansan Island, where Korea won a great victory over the Japanese invaders of the 16th century, and Heuksan Islands, noted for their rugged natural beauty and peculiar plants. Seasides are literally paradises for summer swimmers.

Haein-sa. This temple is situated on Mt. Kaya where boulders and grotesque rocks protrude from a dense forest of pines and maples. Famous for one of the world's most complete sets of wooden type-blocks, made in the 13th century and used to print Buddhist scriptures.

Haeundae. Only a few miles from Pusan, Korea's main international seaport, is Haeundae, whose sandy beaches and salubrious hot-springs are well known. Here the scenery is delightful, and tourists may enjoy it from the comfort of a new modern hotel right on the beach which is also operated by the Ministry of Transportation.

Mt. Surak and East Coast. This area, south of the Demarcation Line on the east coast, provides by far the best of all the scenic spots in this "Land of the Morning Calm." The area is embroidered with rocky peaks, spectacular waterfalls, myth-laden lakes, a bubbling hot springs, and crisp sand beaches. Silla temples and pavilions are here placed along the coast with a fine view of the ocean. Easily accessible, there are fine tourist hotels amidst beautiful woods and beaches.

Cheju Island. Many well-preserved features in customs, tradition, language and legends as distinct from those of mainland. Home of women divers, who earn their living by gathering edibles from the bottom of the sea. Deep within the crater of Mt. Halla, an extinct volcano shrouded in misty clouds and the lore of romantic yesterday, lies a clear blue lake. On the slopes of Halla are majestic waterfalls, sparkling ribbons against backgrounds of green.

Taegwallyong Skiing Slope. Taegwallyong, east of Seoul, is the most favorable area for skiing in Korea. A nationwide tournament is held here each year. The season usually continues from the latter part of December until February. To get to Taegwallyong you take a KNA flight to Kangnung, roughly an hour from Seoul, and from there, frequent bus services run to the ski resort.

Tourists' Guide

Cultural Resources

Korea is an old country with a culture typically and traditionally Korean. Throughout her long history, Korea has been influenced by the introduction of foreign cultures, Chinese, Indian, European and the visitors may find any number of evidences of the assimilating processes that have been going on. Yet basic Korean things remain. Characteristics of the culture traditional to old Korea:

Fine Arts. a) Paintings: water color painting, especially in black-and-white, flourished vigorously in old Korea. Examples are found in city museums and in temples preserving famous mural works. b) Sculpture: old Korea's sculpture was greatly influenced by Buddhism. Accordingly most of the works are keenly related to Buddhism, such as the images of Buddha which can be found in the temples throughout the country. c) Handicraft: as the Korean people are very ingenious with their hands, they produce a lot of exquisite works partly by handiwork and partly with tools and machines, such as lacquerwares, brasswares, bamboo wares, potteries, silk textiles, ambers, gold and silver jewelries, celadon wares, etc.

Literature. Old Korea had many literary classics including novels, poetries, essays and short stories. Among the many works, "Chunhyangjon" and "Simchongjon," beautiful tales of Confucian virtues and fidelity, are outstanding. Vigorous literary activities, both classic and modern, are going on in Korea today.

Play. One of the most important types of the classical plays is the "Kugak." Consisted of acting, singing and dancing with a colorful background, the "Kugak" is usually performed by talented singers as in the modern opera.

Music. A music-loving people, Korean folk songs have been passed down by memory alone, and even today, farmers and fisherman keep the melodies alive. Korean folk music requires string, wind, and percussion instruments. Ideal places for the foreign visitor to sample native musical performances: the Yi Palace orchestra and the Korea House.

Dance. Korean dancing feature the slow, meaningful arm rhythms which are characteristic of many Oriental dances. Many of Korea's dances illustrate folkways. Some of the modern dancers have partially Westernized their style, but traditional patterns of ancient movements enrich their new choreography. Many classic dances are performed by dance troupes outdoors in temple settings.

Recreation

Korea House. "Korea House" is a large building modelled in classic Korean style. It offers foreign visitors Korean food and entertainment every afternoon. Charming Korean hostesses—students from Ewha and other universities—are on hand to greet the guests. A troupe of artists is in attendance to present Korean folk dances and traditional music. In addition, souvenirs are available, along with refreshments, both Korean and Western. These refreshments are offered by voluntary hostesses from such groups as the Bamboo Circle, the Y.M.C.A., and

Capital Women's Club. A snack bar is also available.

Wongaksa Theater. This theater, traditionally designed, was built by the government for introduction of Korean folk dances, music and drama as well as modern theatrical and musical productions.

Korea Information Center. Equipped with an art gallery, a photographic exhibit hall, an extensive library, special facilities for recorded music listening, a television room, and such recreational equipment as shuffleboard and billiards. A competent staff at the Center is ready to furnish visitors with information on everything from sightseeing trips to historic data.

Movie Houses. More than a dozen theaters in Seoul are equipped with hi-fi music systems, air conditioning and central heating. Both Korean and Western films are shown. Opera and dramas are performed at the Municipal Theater. Typical performances are slated throughout the year.

Golf Courses. The Seoul Country Club, located about 7 miles east of downtown Seoul, has an excellent 18-hole golf course, the largest and finest in Korea. A good restaurant and other recreational facilities are available for its members. The Club has some 250 active members.

"Tea-rooms." There are many tea houses, known as "tea-rooms," all over the country. They serve milk, tea, coffee, iced drinks and fruit juice. Quite a number are furnished with hi-fi or stereo music systems and comfortable seats.

Shopping. Shopping in Korea offers the tourists fine, varied and reasonably priced goods, distinctively Korean, for souvenirs. Americans find particularly attractive the variety of fine handicrafts. The best Korean lacquerware inlaid with mother-of-pearl, brassware, bambooware and furniture, good amber, ceramics, gold and silver jewelry, leather products, silks and dolls are for sale, free of tax and at fair prices. Many souvenir shops and department stores in major cities make a specialty of handling souvenirs. For the tourist who enjoys hunting in market places, large markets are found in Seoul, Pusan, Taegu and all other cities.

Calendar of Events

Korea's calendar of events combines the modern holidays and observances with those handed down through a history of more than 4,000 years. Many spectacles—thousands of silk-clad dancers in Seoul Stadium, traditional farmer's festivals in the villages, the precision and color of the Armed Forces parades, special performances of the Royal Court Institute Orchestra, a quiet wait with friends on a hilltop to watch for the first moon of the year—all these and more are the holiday manifestations of the free people of the Republic of Korea. Below is a selected listing of the days and seasons celebrated in the "Land of the Morning Calm."

January 1. New Year's Day, celebrated as in the West.

January 1 in the Lunar Calendar: (Late January or early February by the Solar Calendar). On this day, Koreans pay homage to their ancestors. Sons and daughters bow to their parents and visit relatives and friends to express best wishes for the year. Such a greeting is called "*saebae*." Young visitors receive as a token of their visit a small sum of money or dishes of fruit and a confection made of rice called "*ttok*."

The *yut* game, played with four marked sticks, is especially popular on this holiday. But more colorful features of the day are kite-flying among the boys, and an ancient sea-saw pastime among girls.

Lunar Calendar January 15: Day of the first full moon by the lunar calendar. Families enjoy viewing the full moon on this day—the last day of the New Year season.

March 1: Independence Movement Day: Koreans through the country observe the anniversary of the *Samil Chol*. On March 1, 1919, thirty-three patiots signed a Declaration of Independence and launched a nationwide campaign against Japanese domination. The families of the patriots receive special gifts during official ceremonies. On March

1, services are usually held at Seoul Pagoda Pavilion, where the Declaration was first proclaimed. The largest and most colorful celebration takes place at Seoul Stadium.

March 15: Birthday of King Sejong, inventor of the phonetic alphabet, *Hangul.*

April 5: Arbor Day. Trees are planted on the hills throughout the country as a feature of a nationwide reforestation program.

Lunar Calendar April 8: Birthday of Buddha. Solemn rituals are held at Chogye Temple in Seoul, a fascinating spectacle for visitors. At night, lanterns are lit along the streets leading to the temple. Special rites are conducted at Buddhist temples throughout Korea.

June 6: Memorial Day. On Memorial Day, the Korean people pause to pay tribute to the war dead. The president of the Republic and other government officials join bereaved families in laying wreaths and burning incense at Military Cemetery above the Han River.

June 15: Farmer's Day. Ranking government officials and members of the foreign diplomatic corps join in the transplanting of rice seedlings as a token of oneness with the farm families. Throughout the land ancient colorful mass dances to the tunes of traditional instruments are featured.

Lunar Calendar May 5: Tano Festival. The Tano Festival is observed on the fifth day of the fifth month of the lunar calendar. The month is the most energetic month of the year and, accordingly, young boys everywhere compete in wrestling while girls and housewives enjoy swing contests in a tradition perhaps as old as Korea.

July 17: Constitution Day. Members of the three branches of government celebrate the anniversary of the promulgation of the Constitution. The ceremonies usually take place at Capitol Plaza.

August 15: Liberation Day. The nation celebrates this most significant national holiday with vivid memories of the 36-year period of resistance to Japanese suppression. In Seoul, a military parade highlights the day's activities following Seoul Stadium ceremonies.

Flower-bedecked buses and colorfully decorated streetcars appear on the main streets of Seoul throughout the day. Other events include mass entertainment programs, oratorial contests, sports meets and feasts.

Lunar Calendar August 15: Moon Festival or *Chusok.* Viewing the full moon is a feature of the evening. During the day, Koreans visit their ancestors' graves and mow the weeds growing wild on the burial sites. This custom is followed by offering of food and wine, made from newly cropped rice, and by prayers for the deceased. In older days, archery contests were held, and the winners were awarded prizes. This is thanksgiving time; feasts and harvest celebrations color the period.

October 1: Armed Forces Day. Armed Forces day is one of the most colorful events observed by members of the Republic of Korea Army, Navy, Air Force, and Marine Corps. In the morning, a ceremony of crack honor guards of all branches and their representatives and Academy cadets assemble at Seoul Stadium. Usually the gathering is followed by a review greeting the president along the Capitol Avenue. One of the day's highlights is an air demonstration along the Han River banks to observe the pageant, which was also participated in by combat units of the United States Army.

October 3: National Foundation Day. The government officially marks the nation's birthday in a ceremony at the Capitol Plaza. This day marks the founding of Korea by Tangun in 2333 B.C.

October 9: *Hangul* (Korean Alphabet) Day. The nation observes the holiday with ceremonies and student contests marking the anniversary of the adoption of *Hangul,* the Korean alphabet, invented by King Sejong of the Yi Dynasty. Calligraphy contests are held during the day.

October 24: U. N. Day. United Nations Day is formally observed by the government and members of the United Nations Commission to Korea. Anniversary ceremonies are held at the Capitol plaza in Seoul and the United Nations Cemetery in Pusan. At the Cemetery in Pusan, a memorial service is held in honor of the fighting men of the U.N. who took part in the Korean war.

December 25 : Christmas Day. Koreans and foreigners in this country observe Christmas as in the Western world. Highlighting the holidays are the scenes of mass gift donations and parties for orphans and other needy folks—a prime activity of U.N. troops here as well as Koreans. Francis Cardinal Spellman, American Catholic archbishop, usually spends the Christmas holiday here with American troops along the front lines.

Means of Communication

Air Transportation

International Air Service. Korean National Airlines: Seoul - Seattle. Northwest Airlines: a) Seoul - Tokyo - Seattle. b) Seoul - Tokyo - Honolulu - San Francisco. Civil Air Transport: Seoul - Tokyo - Okinawa - Taipei - Hong Kong.

Domestic Air Service. Korean National Airlines: a) Seoul-Kangnung. b) Seoul-Pusan. c) Seoul - Kwangju. d) Seoul - Cheju.

Land Transportation

Railways. The railway system in Korea is maintained by the Korean National Railroads. KNR has 1,829 miles of railway network throughout south Korea. Satisfactory Pullman accommodations are available if tourists wish to save time by travelling at night; if they prefer day-time train rides, they will have a fine view of Korea's picturesque countryside and its typical villages. Dining cars are also available on most of the express trains. When a tour group of not less than 50 persons wish to travel by train, the Ministry of Transportation arranges a special tour train composed of diesel engine, sleepers, dining car, bar car, observation car, etc.

Taxis. An adequate supply of taxicabs is available in major cities and towns. They cost 200 *hwan* up per trip. The longest drive in a city area might cost 1,500 *hwan*. Cabs are also rented at four to six thousand *hwan* per hour, with or without driver.

Street cars and buses. Street cars run in Seoul and Pusan and the fare is 25 *hwan* per trip. Bus routes are maintained in every city and town in Korea, the fares differing to the number of zones covered, but generally costs 30 *hwan* per trip.

Sea Transportation

Domestic Sea Service. There are 9,523 vessels amounting to 319,200 in total tonnage, connecting islands with the main land or coastal towns with the others.

International Sea Service. For a leisurely ocean voyage, west coast passengers have a choice of six steamship lines: American Pioneer, Pacific Orient Express, State Marine, United States, Pacific Far East, and Waterman Lines. Tramp steamships, sailing two to four times a month, offer interesting and economic passage costs from about $400 up, one-way.

Tourist Accommodations

Hotels

Good comfortable hotels, both Western and Korean style, are available in large cities and leading tourist areas throughout Korea. These hotels are modern, convenient, clean and reasonable, and most rooms have private baths and many have air-conditioning. The hot floor system called *"ondol,"* typical and peculiar to Korean houses and Korean style hotels, is very popular among foreigners. The Ministry of Transportation is operating some tourist hotels in major resorts of Onyang, Pulguk-sa, Haeundae, Suraksan, Mudungsan, and Cheju Island. Those tourist hotels offer a 20% discount of room charge to foreign tourists. Waiters and roomboys in hotels speak English and are ready to help guests in every way. The information desks can be relied on to give them detailed information about city sightseeing and local tours.

Some information on the leading hotels:

Seoul. Bando Hotel; Rooms: 111 guest rooms all with private bath and 100 offices for rent. Facilities: Special dining rooms, coffee shop, barber shop, laundry, sky lounge, pharmacy, souvenir shop, money exchange, cocktail lounge, Dynasty Room, art gallery, photo service, information desk, etc. Operated by the Ministry of Transportation.

International Hotel; Rooms: 27 rooms all with bath. Facilities: Dining rooms, banquet rooms, air conditioning, cocktail lounge and bar.

Pagoda Hotel; Rooms: 42 rooms with or without bath. Facilities: Dining room, bar, sightseeing agency, and sports facilities. Air-conditioning.

Savoy Hotel; Rooms: 60 rooms with bath or shower. Facilities: Dining room, laundry and dry cleaning service. Air-conditioning.

Hotel U. N. Center; Rooms: 38 rooms with or without bath. Facilities: Dining room, cocktail lounge, and ballroom.

Pusan. Haeundae Tourist Hotel; Rooms: 40 rooms with or without bath. Facilities: Dining room, money exchange, billiards, cocktail lounge and bar. Swimming facilities are also available.

Mijin Hotel; Rooms: 11 rooms with bath. Facilities: Dining room.

Onyang. Onyang Tourist Hotel; Rooms: 53 rooms with bath. Facilities: Dining room, cocktail lounge, souvenir shop, laundry and dry cleaning service.

Kyongju. Pulguk-sa Tourist Hotel; Rooms: 22 rooms with bath. Facilities: Dining room, souvenir shop, sightseeing agency, laundry service.

Mt. Surak, East coast. Suraksan Tourist Hotel; Rooms: 10 bungalow-type rooms with bath. Facilities: Dining room.

Cheju Island. Sogwipo Tourist Hotel; Rooms: 7 bungalow-style rooms with bath. Facilities: Dining room.

Mt. Mudung, Kwangju. Mudungsan Tourist Hotel; Rooms: 10 bungalow-style rooms with bath. Facilities: Dining room.

Restaurants

In Seoul, Bando Hotel, International Hotel, Pagoda Hotel, Hosu Grill, Seoul Railway Station Restaurant, Mijang Grill, Diplomatic Club, all serve good and reasonably spiced Western-style foods. Korean dishes are available at the Paegunjang, Chongungak, Kugilgwan and some other restaurants.

Each of these Korean and Western restaurants has a ballroom and several private party rooms for banquet or convention.

Korean food specialties are most delicious. At the top of the list with foreigners is *pulgogi*—charcoal broiled beef marinated Korean sytle. The most famous Korean dish is *kimchi*, usually a highly spiced pickled combination of turnips, onions, celery and other vegetables, and a dish about which few people are neutral. *Sinsollo*, another distinctively Korean dish and a favorite since olden times, consists of meat, fish, eggs and vegetables served in a brazier in the form of a large egg cup with glowing charcoal in the lower segment for keeping the food warm during eating. Chinese cuisines are also available in Seoul at the Asuwon, Taeryodo, Taehwagwan, etc.

Tourist Organizations

Governmental. In the government of the Republic of Korea the Tourist Section of the Ministry of Transportation functions as the central administrative agency relating to the tourist industry in the Republic.

Functions of the Tourism Section are: —

a) General planning relating to tourist industry;

b) Liaison and cooperation with foreign tourist administrative organizations;

c) Publicity;

d) Development and preservation of tourist attractions;

e) Training of guide-interpreters and employees;

f) Guidance and support of travel agencies and hotels;

g) Arrangement and operation of package tours;
h) Management and operation of government-run hotels and restaurants;
i) Investigation and statistics relating to tourist industry.

Private. Korea Tourist Bureau was established in 1954 and is the only experienced travel agency in Korea. It is an active member of the Pacific Area Travel Association (PATA). The Korea Tourist Bureau, with 10 ticket and information offices throughout the country, offers the following services:

a) Information on transportation facilities, tourist resorts, hotel accommodations, etc.
b) Making reservations and furnishing tickets for railways, airplanes, hotels, and sightseeing facilities.
c) Promoting all-expense tours.
d) Publishing guide service for travellers (English and Chinese).

Passport and Visa. Like other countries, the Republic of Korea requires that a visitor be in good health, that he has adequate funds and that his passport be in good order. The nearest embassies, legations, or consulates offer assistance in making applications for visas. Tourists need only a visa application and a certificate of smallpox vaccination to obtain a visa. A "transit" visa allows a visitor to stay in Korea for 15 days from the date of arrival and can be extended another 15 days. A visitor who wishes to stay in Korea more than 30 days is required to apply for a "Residence Permit" to the Ministry of Foreign Affairs of the Republic of Korea.

Currency. The *hwan* is the unit of currency in Korea. The official rate of exchange is 650 *hwan* for one U.S. dollar. The Bank of Korea is authorized to handle foreign exchange and it has branches at various places for the convenience of easy exchange of money for foreign visitors.

Customs. Custom laws are liberal and permit a visitor to bring in practically anything which is for his own use and necessary for his purpose of visit. Clothing and other personal effects and sporting equipment can all be brought in if a visitor plans to take them out with him. There are no restrictions upon the amount of declared currency.

Public Health. The only currently immunization effective required of a visitor is a small-pox vaccination. All others are waived. It should be noted that no plants or animals may be brought into the country without special authorization.

APPENDIX

Conversion Table of Weights and Measures

Length:

Unit	Ja	Chong	Ri	Meter	Inch	Foot	Yard	Mile
Ja	1	0.0028	—	0.303	1.930	0.994	0.331	0.0002
Chong	360.000	1	0.0288	109.091	4293	367.917	110.308	0.068
Ri	12.900	36.000	1	3927.730	1146.7	12.880	12.885	2.440
Meter	3.300	0.009	0.00025	1	39.370	3.281	1.094	0.0006
Inch	0.084	0.000	—	0.025	1	0.083	0.028	—
Foot	1.006	0.0008	—	0.305	1.000	1	0.333	0.0002
Yard	8.107	0.0084	0.0002	0.910	36.000	3.000	1	0.0006
Mile	5311	14.784	0.4093	1809.344	63360	5.280	1760.0	1

Area:

Unit	Pyong	Tan	Chongbo	Square Foot	Square Yard	Square Meter	Acre
Pyong	1	0.003	0.0003	35.586	3.945	3.306	0.003
Tan	300.000	1	0.100	10674.98	1186.107	901.737	0.245
Chongbo	3000.000	10.000	1	106.49	1861.070	9917.309	2.451
Foot²	0.028	0.009	0.0001	1	0.186	0.098	0.00023
Yard²	0.253	0.0008	0.0008	9.000	1	0.836	0.000206
Meter²	0.303	0.001	0.0001	10.764	1.186	1	0.000247
Acre	1244.172	4.080	0.4081	43500	4848.000	4046.84	1

Capacity:

Unit	Hop	Sok	Litter	Gallon	Cubic Inch	Cubic Foot	Cubic Meter
Hop	1	0.001	0.180	0.047	11.004	0.006	—
Sok	1000	1	180.391	47.600	11004.000	6.371	0.1804
Litter	5.544	0.0055	1	0.2942	61.027	0.0353	0.001
Gallon	20.984	0.021	3.785	1	231.000	0.1337	0.0083
Inch³	0.001	—	8.016	0.0043	1	0.0006	—
Foot³	1569.74	0.157	28.316	1.4805	1728.000	1	0.0383
Meter³	5543.5	5.544	1000.000	264.146	61.230	35.310	1

Weight:

Unit	Ton Chung	Kun	Kwan	Gram	Ounce	Pound	Metric Ton
Ton Chung	1	0.00625	0.001	4.850	0.132	0.00326	—
Kun	180.000	1	0.160	600.000	21.164	1.323	0.006
Kwan	1000.000	6.250	1	3750.000	132.175	8.269	0.00375
Gram	0.267	0.00167	0.00027	1	0.035	0.0022	—
Ounce	7.580	0.047	0.00756	28.350	1	0.062	—
Pound	20.960	0.456	0.121	453.000	16.000	1	0.00045
M/T	266667	1866.667	266.667	1000000	35273	2205	1

APPENDIX

Chronology Chart of Korean History Compared with World History

Tangi* Year	Christian Year	Period	Korean History	World History
	B.C.			
1	2333	Age of Mythology, Ancient Chosun	Tangun founds Chosun	
1212	1122		Kija succeeds Tangun	
1779	555			Buddha born
1783	551			Confucius born
2139	194	Uiman Chosun	Uiman founds a new state; Ancient Chosun falls	
2225	108		Four Han Chinese colonial counties including Lolang established	
2277	57	Three Kingdoms	Silla kingdom founded	
2297	37		Koguryo	
2316	18		Paekche	
	A.D.			
2330	4			Christ born
2577	244		Invasion of Koguryo by Sui	
2646	313		Fall of Lolang	
2705	372		Buddhism introduced to Koguryo from China	
2729	396		Koguryo invades Paekche	Roman Empire divided into Western and Eastern halves
2809	476			West Roman Empire falls
2827	494		Koguryo occupies Puyo	
2860	527	T H R E E	Buddhism sanctioned in Silla kingdom	
2885	552		Buddhism transmitted to Japan from Paekche	
2901	568		Silla builds Hwangnyong-sa Temple	
2904	571			Mohammed born
2922	589	K I N G D O M S		Sui Dynasty unifies China
2945	612		Chinese forces invade Koguryo to be repulsed by Gen. Ulchimundok	
2951	618			Tang succeeds Sui in China
2993	660		Paeche kingdom falls; Tang establishes colony there	
3001	668		Koguryo falls	
3003	670		Silla kingdom resists Tang, unifies Korea	
3084	751		Silla builds Sokkuram Temple	
3133	800			Charlemagne crowned Emperor of the Romans

* The official calendar of the Republic of Korea government follows the Tangi Year after Tangun.

APPENDIX

Tangi Year	Christian Year	Period	Korean History	World History
3225	892		Hu-Paekche founded	
3234	901		Hu-Koguryo founded	
3240	907			Tang falls in China
3251	918	Koryo	Koryo kingdom founded by Wanggun	
3268	935		Silla falls, Koryo succeeds to Silla's mantle	
3269	936		Hu-Paekche falls	
3290	957		Civil examination system instituted	
3293	960			Sung dynasty founded in China
3295	962			Holy Roman Empire founded
3344	1011		Work started on the Tripitaka Koreana	
3419	1086		The Supplementary Pitaka edited by Uichon	
3429	1096			The first Crusade
3488	1145		The Annals of the Three Kingdoms published	
3548	1215			Magna Carta
3564	1231		The First Mongol invasion	
3567	1234		Metal type for printing used for first time	
3592	1259		Koryo surrenders to Mongol power	
3605	1272			End of the Crusades
3607	1274		Royal inter-racial marriage with Mongol Empire; the first expedition to Japan	
3608	1275			Marco Polo visits China
3612	1279	K		Sung Dynasty falls in China
3614	1281	O	The second expedition to Japan	
3646	1313	R		Renaissance in Europe
3686	1353	Y	Japanese pirates harass coasts	
3692	1359	O	First invasion by "Red Cloth" tribe.	
3694	1361		Second invasion by "Red Cloth" tribe	
3701	1368			Ming dynasty founded in China
3709	1376		Japanese pirates routed by Choe Yong	
3721	1388		Gen. Yi Sunggye defeats Japanese pirates	
3723	1390		Farmland reform	
3725	1392	Yi Dynasty	Koryo falls, Yi dynasty takes over	
3729	1396		Capital moved to Seoul	
3756	1423		The History of Koryo edited	
3779	1446		Korean Alphabet promulgated	
3786	1453			Eastern Roman Empire falls
3825	1492			Columbus discovers America

APPENDIX

Tangi Year	Christian Year	Period	Korean History	World History
3831	1498		*Muo* Incident	Vasco da Gama discovers Cape route to India
3837	1504		*Kapcha* Incident	
3852	1519		*Kimyo* Incident	
3867	1534			Society of Jesus established by Ignatius Loyola in Paris
3908	1575		Court factional strife intensified between "Easterners" and "Westerners"	
3921	1588			Spanish Armada defeated
3925	1592		Japanese forces invade Korea	
3933	1600			Britain establishes East India Company
3936	1603			Military Government established in Edo (Tokyo), Japan
3960	1627	Y I	The first invasion by Ching China	
3961	1628		The first Westerner, a Dutchman, visits Korea	National isolation policy effected in Japan
3969	1636	D Y	The second invasion by Ching China	
3977	1644	N		Ming Dynasty falls in China
3991	1658	A S T	One of the court factions, the "Easterners," further split into two	
4098	1765	Y		Watts invents steam engine; the Industrial Revolution
4109	1776			U.S. Independence
4112	1779			French Revolution
4134	1801		Persecution of Roman Catholics	
4144	1811		The Revolt of Hong Kyongnae	
4163	1830			The French July Revolution
4172	1839		Persecution of Roman Catholics	
4173	1840			The Opium War
4187	1854			Japan concludes trade treaty with U.S.
4193	1860		"Eastern Learning" advocated by Choe Cheu	
4197	1864		Taewongun assumes regency	
4199	1866		S.S. Gen. Sherman Incident	
4200	1867			Meiji Revolution in Japan
4206	1873		Taewongun yields regency	
4209	1876		"Protective" treaty concluded with Japan, ending national isolation policy	
4215	1882		Trade treaty with U.S.	
4216	1883		First newspaper published	
4217	1884		*Kapsin* Revolution	
4218	1885		A British naval unit occupies Komundo	Tientsin treaty signed between China and Japan

APPENDIX

Tangi Year	Christian Year	Period	Korean History	World History
4227	1894		*Tonghak* Revolt; *Kabo* Incident	Sino-Japanese War
4228	1895		Postal system inaugurated	
4229	1896		Independence Association founded	
4230	1897		Taehan Empire proclaimed; "The Independence News" published	
4232	1899		Train, tram, telephone installed for first time	
4233	1900		Electricity in Seoul	
4235	1902			Alliance between England and Japan
4237	1904		Negotiation with Japan	Russo-Japanese War
4238	1905		"Protective" Treaty with Japan	
4239	1906		Japan establishes *Tonggambu* in Korea	
4240	1907		Army disbanded; renewed negotiation with Japan	
4243	1910	Modern	Japanese annexation of Korea; Japanese Governor-General replaces Resident-General	
4247	1914			World War I breaks out
4250	1917			Russian Revolution
4251	1918		"Land survey" project ends	World War I ends
4252	1919		The March 1 Independence Movement	
4262	1929		Kwangju Students' Revolt	Wall Street Depression
4264	1931			Japanese invasion of Manchuria
4270	1937	M		Japanese invasion of the Chinese mainland
4273	1940	O		World War II begins
4275	1942	D E	Korean youths conscripted into Japanese Army	
4278	1945	R N	Liberation from Japan; division of the land by U.S. and Soviet occupation forces	World War II ends; U.N. established
4279	1946		U.S-Soviet Joint Commission for unification of Korea	
4281	1948		General elections; establishment of Republic of Korea government	
4283	1950		North Korean Communist forces invade south	U.N. forces dispatched to Korea
4286	1953		Korean armistice	

Date Due